Fundamentals of
HUMAN NEUROPSYCHOLOGY

SIXTH EDITION

BRYAN KOLB and **IAN Q. WHISHAW**
University of Lethbridge

Worth Publishers

On the front cover:

The Skeptic, Kim Frohsin's 1991 painting on masonite, portrays the human brain's fascinating ability to interpret the delicate details that constitute the faces of friends, family members, lovers, neighbors, and strangers. A face gives form and color to the languages, emotions, and thoughts originating in the brain operating behind it—all while serving as the focal point of human interaction. *The Skeptic* seems almost devoid of emotion yet profoundly pensive and mysteriously androgynous, shirting and lacking definition. The different shading of the two sides of the skeptic's face corresponds to the intrinsic duality of the human brain, whereby each hemisphere specializes in different higher-order processes including the perception of faces.

Senior Publisher: Catherine Woods

Acquisitions Editor: Charles Linsmeier

Executive Marketing Manager: Katherine Nurre

Development Editor: Barbara Brooks

Assistant Editor: Justin Kruger

Senior Project Editor: Georgia Lee Hadler

Manuscript Editor: Patricia Zimmerman

Art Director: Barbara Reingold

Text and Cover Design: Kevin Kall

Production Manager: Sarah Segal

Illustration Coordinator: Susan Timmins

Illustrations: Dragonfly Media

Photo Research Manager: Ted Szczepanski

Photo Editor: Julie Tesser

Supplements and Media Editor: Graig Donini

Composition: Northeastern Graphic, Inc.

Printing and Binding: RR Donnelley

Library of Congress Control Number: 2007924870

ISBN-13: 978-0-7167-9586-5

ISBN-10: 0-7167-9586-8

Printed in the United States of America

Second printing

Worth Publishers

41 Madison Avenue

New York, NY 10010

www.worthpublishers.com

To Karen Nicholson (1971–2007)

Karen Nicholson exemplified everything that we admire in our students. She began her research career when, as a sophomore, she studied the spatial abilities of marsupials with Ian Whishaw and Dan Kimble, reserving enough time to be on the varsity soccer team. In graduate school, she specialized in the study of human neuropsychology at the University of Western Ontario, in London, Ontario—first with Doreen Kimura and then with Keith Humphrey. Her postdoctoral work with Kevin Munhall focused on brain-imaging studies of the interrelation between language and gesture. While a member of the Department of Psychology at Mount Allison University in Sackville, New Brunswick, she played an important role in this revision of *Fundamentals*, providing many suggestions for improvements. Thank you, Karen, for being a student, colleague, and friend.

BRIEF CONTENTS

Preface xv

PART I Background

The sixth edition of *Fundamentals of Human Neuropsychology* brings all of the color of neuroscience to human neuropsychology. Looking back over the past five editions reveals an amazing evolution of both this exciting field and the textbook itself. The sixth edition continues the trip with many changes, the most obvious being the move to full color.

The color illustrations are a further development of the illustration program that we began in the fifth edition. We believe that the new illustrations are exceptional and will aid students in their understanding of the words of the text. But *Fundamentals* has undergone more change than just the use of color in illustrations. Neuroimaging has continued to develop in the 5 years since the fifth edition was published, and imaging studies are now leading to major changes in the way that we think about human cognition. We have thus included more imaging and added more Snapshots to highlight the role of imaging in our emerging understanding of human brain function.

We have expanded our inclusion of cognitive theory where appropriate because cognitive science is becoming more and more integrated with neuropsychology. A perusal of two leading review journals, *Trends in Neuroscience* and *Trends in Cognitive Science*, shows this emerging integration of neuroscience and cognition: virtually every issue of each journal includes articles that could just as easily be found in the other. This development is certain to continue, and we have tried to reflect this change especially in Chapters 13 through 22, which are the core neuropsychology chapters.

We have continued to resist the temptation to move toward being a cognitive neuroscience text, however. As behavioral neuroscientists, our perspective remains on the neural mechanisms underlying behavior rather than on detailed discussions of cognitive theories that more naturally belong in cognitive neuroscience textbooks.

We have included coverage of the new field of social cognitive neuroscience, an emerging field that has led to a major shift within the psychological and neurological community. Until the past few years, social psychology had not embraced the brain, but that is changing rapidly and promises to lead to exciting changes in the way that we think about the social brain (presented, for example, in Chapter 20).

An additional new feature of each chapter is an expanded summary that encapsulates the content of each major chapter segment. For the beginning student, identifying what the major points of new material might be is often a challenge. We suggest that students begin each chapter by reading the summary and to then keep returning to the summary, which will help them focus their reading on the key points.

Finally, we have updated all chapters to correspond to the changing face of neuropsychology. References to recent reviews will point the way for interested students to do further reading beyond the textbook.

Fundamentals continues to be different from other textbooks of psychology or neuroscience. We still provide basic background information about history, evolution, anatomy, physiology, pharmacology, and methodology in the first seven chapters (Part I). The five chapters of Part II outline the general organization of the cerebral cortex, and the five chapters of Part III focus on the organization of the anatomically defined cortical regions.

Part IV follows with five chapters that shift emphasis from anatomy to psychological constructs (language, memory, emotion, space, and attention/consciousness). This shift naturally means that material from earlier parts is revisited but this time in the context of psychological theory rather than anatomy. In our experience, students find it a helpful way to tackle complex information.

Part V considers brain plasticity and includes a more detailed discussion of brain disorders than is found earlier in the book. Part V also includes chapters on psychiatry, neurology, and neuropsychological assessment. In keeping up with the evolving methodology of neuropsychology, psychological assessment has been extensively updated.

As in the past, we must sincerely thank many people who have contributed to the development of this edition. We are particularly indebted to Michael Peters and Karen Nicholsen, who have provided extensive feedback as they used the text in their classes. Jeanette McGlone provided valuable advice on neuropsychological assessment that led to a restructuring of Chapter 28. We also thank the anonymous reviewers solicited by our editors. Their comments provided us with perspectives that we would not normally encounter. Once again, however, errors remain solely attributable to us.

The staff at Worth Publishers and W. H. Freeman and Company are amazing and have made this task far more enjoyable than it would be without them. These folks include our sponsoring editor, Chuck Linsmeier, our long-time project editor, Georgia Lee Hadler, and our production manager, Sarah Segal. Our manuscript editor, Patricia Zimmerman, has again made many contributions to the book's clarity and consistency. Our gratitude to Barbara Brooks, our development editor, knows no bounds. She has provided a strong guiding hand to our thinking and organization and has done so with humor and a commitment to excellence that shows its stamp all over the book. Thank you, Barbara, for always having a compliment.

We are indebted to the illustrators at Dragonfly Media for their excellent work developing the color illustration program. We also thank the various specialists who found photographs and other illustrative work that we would not have been able to find on our own.

Finally, we thank our students of the past 30 years, who have motivated us to continue the journey of *Fundamentals of Human Neuropsychology*. Seeing the faces of students light up when they begin to understand how the marvelous brain can produce cognition and behavior continues to be rewarding and is what this endeavor is all about.

CHAPTER 1

The Development of Neuropsychology

PORTRAIT: Traumatic Brain Injury

When L.D. was 21 years old, he was invited to participate in a sports promotion at a pub. After a period of drinking and socializing, he became ill and was helped onto a balcony by a pub employee. On the balcony, he slipped out of the employee's grasp and fell down five flights of stairs, striking his head against the stairs and wall as he fell. He was taken, unconscious, to the emergency ward of the local hospital where he was given a Glasgow Coma Scale rating of 3, the lowest score on a scale from 3 to 15.

A computerized tomography (CT) scan revealed bleeding and swelling on the right side of L.D.'s brain, and, to relieve pressure and remove blood, a neurosurgeon performed a craniotomy (skull removal) over his right frontal cortex. A subsequent CT scan revealed further bleeding on the left side of his brain, and a second craniotomy was performed. L.D.'s subsequent recovery was uneventful. When he was discharged from the hospital a month and a half later, his recall of the events consisted only of remembering that he had entered the pub and then becoming aware that he was in a hospital 3 weeks later.

Before discharge, L.D. was given his first neuropsychological evaluation,

CNRI/Phototake

consisting of a number of tests of language and memory. A neuropsychologist noted in his report that L.D. was well dressed, had a positive attitude toward testing, and felt that he had made a good recovery. L.D.'s mother and his girlfriend also reported that he had fully recovered. The neuropsychologist noted that he was impaired on tests of verbal memory and attention, but otherwise his test scores were normal for a young person who had completed high school. He recommended that L.D. receive more comprehensive testing when he had recovered enough to consider returning to work as a cook.

In the next 4 years, L.D. took neuropsychological tests a number of times.

He was unable to return to work because he found the multitasking in preparing meals too difficult. He was seeking compensation from the company that had hosted the sports promotion and from the pub where he had been injured. He also found that he could become frustrated and annoyed quite easily, that he had lost his sense of smell and taste, and that he had lost interest in socializing. He and his girlfriend had ended their 4-year relation.

Neuropsychological examinations repeatedly showed that L.D.'s scores on most tests were normal except for tests of verbal memory and attention. Magnetic resonance imaging (MRI), a brain-scanning method that can reveal the brain's structure in detail, showed some diffuse damage to both sides of his brain. L.D. was able to live on his own, he held a job packing boxes in a grocery store, and he successfully returned to playing golf.

He continued to play golf with a handicap of one and had won a couple of golf tournaments. The company that had held the promotion was willing to make a financial settlement, but its lawyers expressed difficulty in understanding how L.D. could excel at golf but, at the same time, was unable to return to his former work as a cook.

A ccording to National Institute of Neurological Disorders and Stroke estimates, L.D. is one of 1.4 million U.S. residents who receive medical attention each year after suffering a **traumatic brain injury** (TBI), a wound to the brain that results from a blow to the head. Of these patients, 235,000 are hospitalized and 50,000 die. The number of people who endure TBI each year but do not report an injury is not known.

L.D. is not unusual in that, in his own view and in the view of acquaintances, he has mainly recovered but has lingering problems that prevent him from resuming his former level of employment. L.D. is also not unusual in that he puzzles both friends and experts with his ability to do some things well, although he is unable to do other things that appear to be less difficult. Finally, L.D. is not unusual in that the diffuse injury to his brain revealed by brain-scanning methods is not a good predictor of his abilities and disabilities.

Neuropsychological testing is required to confirm that he has enduring cognitive deficits and to identify those deficits. In L.D.'s case, the deficits include poor scores on tests of memory and attention. Memory and attention are abilities that are required for effectively dealing with everyday problem solving, a mental skill referred to as *executive function*. Thus, L.D. can play golf at a high level, because it requires that he deal with only one act at a time, but he cannot prepare a meal, because doing so requires that he keep track of a number of things at the same time.

The objective of this book is to describe the scientific field of **neuropsychology**, the study of the relation between behavior and brain function. Neuropsychology draws information from many disciplines—anatomy, biology, biophysics, ethology, pharmacology, physiology, physiological psychology, and philosophy among them. Its central focus is to develop a science of human behavior based on the function of the human brain. Information obtained from neuropsychological investigations into the relation between the brain and behavior can be employed to identify impairments in behavior that result from brain trauma, such as that experienced by L.D., and from diseases that affect the brain.

Neuropsychology is strongly influenced by two traditional foci of experimental and theoretical investigations into brain function: the **brain hypothesis**, the idea that the brain is the source of behavior; and the **neuron hypothesis**, the idea that the unit of brain structure and function is the **neuron**, or nerve cell. This chapter traces the development of these two ideas and introduces some major ideas obtained from investigating brain function, ideas that we will peruse in subsequent chapters.

The Brain Hypothesis

People knew what the brain looked like long before they had any idea of what it did. Very early in human history, hunters must have noticed that all animals have a brain and that the brains of different animals, including humans, although varying greatly in size, look quite similar. Within the past 2000 years, anatomists began producing drawings of the brain and naming some of its distinctive parts without knowing what functions the brain or its parts perform. We begin this chapter with a description of the brain and some of its major parts and then consider some major insights into brain functions.

What Is the Brain?

Brain is an Old English word for the tissue found within the skull. **Figure 1.1**A shows a typical human brain as oriented in the skull of an upright human. The brain has two almost symmetrical halves called **hemispheres**, one on the left side

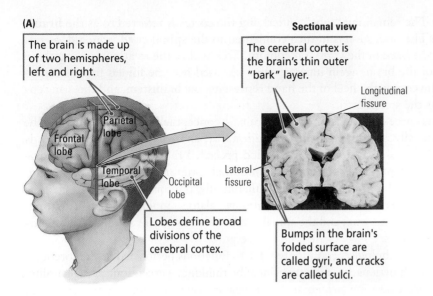

(A)

The brain is made up of two hemispheres, left and right.

Parietal lobe

Frontal lobe

Temporal lobe

Occipital lobe

Lobes define broad divisions of the cerebral cortex.

Sectional view

The cerebral cortex is the brain's thin outer "bark" layer.

Longitudinal fissure

Lateral fissure

Bumps in the brain's folded surface are called gyri, and cracks are called sulci.

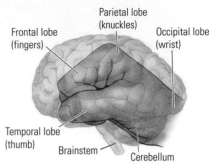

(B)

Your right hand, if made into a fist, represents the positions of the lobes of the left hemisphere of your brain.

Parietal lobe (knuckles)

Frontal lobe (fingers)

Occipital lobe (wrist)

Temporal lobe (thumb)

Brainstem

Cerebellum

Figure 1.1

The Human Brain (A) This representation of the human brain shows its orientation in the head. The visible part of the intact brain is the cerebral cortex, a thin sheet of tissue folded many times and fitting snugly inside the skull. (B) Your right fist can serve as a guide to the orientation of the brain and its lobes. (Glauberman/Photo Researchers.)

of the body and the other on the right. Just as your body is symmetrical, having two arms and two legs, so is your brain. If you make your right hand into a fist and hold it up with the thumb pointing toward the front, the fist can represent the position of the brain's left hemisphere within the skull (Figure 1.1B).

Taken as a whole, the basic plan of the brain is that of a tube filled with salty fluid called **cerebrospinal fluid** (CSF) that cushions the brain and may play a role in removing metabolic waste. Parts of the covering of the tube have bulged outward and folded, forming the more complicated looking surface structures that initially catch the eye. The most conspicuous outer feature of the brain is the crinkled tissue that has expanded from the front of the tube to such an extent that it folds over and covers much of the rest of the brain. This outer layer is the **cerebral cortex** (usually referred to as just the cortex). The word *cortex*, which means "bark" in Latin, is aptly chosen both because the cortex's folded appearance resembles the bark of a tree and because its tissue covers most of the rest of the brain (see Figure 1.1A), just as bark covers a tree.

The folds of the cortex are called **gyri**, and the creases between them are called **sulci** (*gyrus* is Greek for "circle" and *sulcus* is Greek for "trench"). Some large sulci are called fissures, such as the **longitudinal fissure** that divides the two hemispheres and the **lateral fissure** that divides each hemisphere into halves (in our fist analogy, the lateral fissure is the crease separating the thumb from the other fingers).

The cortex of each hemisphere is divided into four lobes, named after the skull bones beneath which they lie. The **temporal lobe** is located at approximately the same place as the thumb on your upraised fist. Lying immediately above the temporal lobe is the **frontal lobe**, so called because it is located at the front of the brain. The **parietal lobe** is located behind the frontal lobe, and the **occipital lobe** constitutes the area at the back of each hemisphere. The brain's hemispheres are connected by pathways called *commissures*, the largest of which is the **corpus callosum**.

The cerebral cortex constitutes most of the **forebrain**, so named because it develops from the front part of the tube that makes up an embryo's primitive brain. The remaining "tube" underlying the cortex is referred to as the **brainstem**. The brainstem is in turn connected to the **spinal cord**, which descends down the back in the vertebral column. To visualize the relations among these parts of the brain, again imagine your upraised fist: the folded fingers represent the cortex, the heel of the hand represents the brainstem, and the arm represents the spinal cord.

This three-part division of the brain is conceptually useful evolutionarily, anatomically, and functionally. Evolutionarily, animals with only spinal cords preceded those with brainstems, which preceded those with forebrains. Anatomically, in prenatal development, the spinal cord forms before the brainstem, which forms before the forebrain. Functionally, the forebrain mediates cognitive functions; the brainstem mediates regulatory functions such as eating, drinking, and moving; and the spinal cord is responsible for sending commands to the muscles.

Neuropsychologists commonly refer to functions performed in the forebrain as higher functions because they include thinking, perception, and planning. Therefore, L.D.'s impairment in executive function is an impairment in forebrain function. The regulatory and movement-producing functions of the brainstem and spinal cord are thus sometimes referred to as lower-level functions.

How Is the Brain Related to the Rest of the Nervous System?

The brain and spinal cord in mammals such as ourselves are protected by bones: the skull protects the brain, and the vertebrae protect the spinal cord. Because both are enclosed within this protective covering, the brain and spinal cord together are called the **central nervous system** or CNS. The central nervous system is connected to the rest of the body through nerve fibers.

Some nerve fibers carry information away from the CNS, and others bring information to it. These fibers constitute the **peripheral nervous system**, or PNS. One of the many distinguishing features of the CNS is that, after damage, it does not regenerate lost tissue—the long-term prospect for L.D. is that he will show little further recovery—whereas PNS tissue will regrow after damage.

Nerve fibers that bring information to the CNS are extensively connected to sensory receptors on the body's surface, to internal body organs, and to muscles, enabling the brain to sense what goes on in the world around us and within our bodies. Organized into **sensory pathways**, collections of fibers carry messages for specific sensory systems, such as hearing, vision, and touch. Sensory pathways carry information collected on one side of the body mainly to the cortex in the *opposite* hemisphere by means of a subdivision of the PNS called the **somatic nervous system** (SNS). The brain uses this information to construct its current images of the world, its memories of past events, and its expectations about the future.

Motor pathways are the groups of nerve fibers that connect the brain and spinal cord to the body's muscles through the SNS. The movements produced by motor pathways include the eye movements that you are using to read this book, the hand movements that you make while turning the pages, and the posture of your body as you read. The parts of the cortex that produce movement mainly use motor pathways to muscles on the opposite side of the body. Thus, one hemisphere uses muscles on the opposite side of the body to produce movement.

Sensory and motor pathways also influence the muscles of your internal organs, such as the beating of your heart, the contractions of your stomach, and the raising and lowering of your diaphragm, which inflates and deflates your lungs. The pathways that control these organs are a subdivision of the PNS called the **autonomic nervous system** (ANS). **Figure 1.2** charts the anatomical organization of the human nervous system.

Figure 1.2

Anatomical Divisions of the Human Nervous System

The Brain Versus the Heart

Since earliest times, people have puzzled over how behavior is produced. Their conclusions are preserved in the historical records of many different cultures. Among the oldest surviving recorded hypotheses are those of two Greeks, Alcmaeon of Croton (ca. 500 B.C.) and Empedocles of Acragas (ca. 490–430 B.C.). Alcmaeon located mental processes in the brain and so subscribed to the brain hypothesis; Empedocles located them in the heart and so subscribed to what could be called the *cardiac hypothesis.*

The relative merits of those two hypotheses were debated for the next 2000 years. Early Greek and Roman physicians, such as Hippocrates (ca. 460–377 B.C.) and Galen (A.D. 129–ca. 199), influenced by their clinical experience, described aspects of the brain's anatomy and argued strongly for the brain hypothesis.

Before becoming the leading physician in Rome, Galen spent 5 years as a surgeon to gladiators and witnessed some of the behavioral consequences of TBI not unlike those suffered by L.D. Galen went to great pains to refute the cardiac hypothesis, pointing out not only that brain damage impairs function but also that the nerves from the sense organs go to the brain and not to the heart. He also reported on his experiences in attempting to treat wounds to the brain or heart. He noted that pressure on the brain causes the cessation of movement and even death, whereas pressure on the heart causes pain but does not arrest voluntary behavior.

Although we now accept the brain hypothesis, the cardiac hypothesis has left its mark on our language. In literature, as in everyday speech, emotion is frequently ascribed to the heart: love is symbolized by an arrow piercing the heart; a person distressed by unrequited love is said to be heartbroken; an unenthusiastic person is described as not putting his or her heart into it; an angry person says, "It makes my blood boil."

Aristotle: The Mind

The Greek philosopher Aristotle (348–322 B.C.) was the first person to develop a formal theory of behavior. He proposed that a nonmaterial *psyche* was responsible for human thoughts, perceptions, and emotions and for such processes as imagination, opinion, desire, pleasure, pain, memory, and reason. The psyche was independent of the body but, in Aristotle's view, worked through the heart

Figure 1.3

Descartes's Concept of Reflex Action In this mechanistic depiction of how Descartes thought physical reflexes might work, heat from the flame causes a thread in the nerve to be pulled, releasing ventricular fluid through an opened pore. The fluid flows through the nerve, causing not only the foot to withdraw but the eyes and head to turn to look at it, the hands to advance, and the whole body to bend to protect it. Descartes applied the reflex concept to behaviors that today are considered too complex to be reflexive, whereas he did not conceive of behavior described as reflexive today. (From Descartes, 1664.)

to produce action. Aristotle's view that this nonmaterial psyche governs behavior was adopted by Christianity in its concept of the soul and has been widely disseminated throughout the world. *Mind* is an Anglo-Saxon word for memory, and, when "psyche" was translated into English, it became mind.

The philosophical position that a person's mind is responsible for behavior is called *mentalism*, meaning "of the mind." Mentalism has wielded great influence on modern neuropsychology: many terms—sensation, perception, attention, imagination, emotion, memory, and volition among them—are still employed as labels for patterns of behavior (see some of the chapter titles in this book). Mentalism also influenced people's ideas about how the brain might work because, inasmuch as the mind was proposed to be nonmaterial and so have no parts, the brain was thought to work as a whole. This idea was used as an argument against subsequent proposals that different parts of the brain might have different functions.

Descartes: The Mind–Body Problem

Simply knowing that the brain controls behavior is not enough: formulating a complete hypothesis of brain function requires knowing how the brain controls behavior. Modern thinking about this idea began with René Descartes (1596–1650), a French anatomist and philosopher who described a relation between the mind and the brain.

Descartes was impressed by machines made in his time, such as those of certain statues that were on display for public amusement in the water gardens of Paris. When a passerby stopped in front of one particular statue, for example, his or her weight depressed a lever under the sidewalk, causing the statue to move and spray water at the person's face. Descartes proposed that the body is like these machines. It is material and thus clearly has spatial extent, and it responds mechanically and reflexively to events that impinge on it (**Figure 1.3**).

Described as nonmaterial and without spatial extent, the mind, as Descartes saw it, was different from the body. The body operated on principles similar to those of a machine, but the mind decided what movements the machine should make. Descartes located the site of action of the mind in the pineal body, a small structure high in the brainstem. His choice of this structure was based on the logic that the pineal body is the only structure in the nervous system not composed of two bilaterally symmetrical halves and moreover that it is located close to the ventricles. His idea was that the mind, working through the pineal body, controlled valves that allowed CSF to flow from the ventricles through nerves to muscles, filling them and making them move.

For Descartes, the cortex was not functioning neural tissue but merely a covering for the pineal body. People later argued against Descartes's hypothesis by pointing out that, when the pineal is damaged, there are no obvious changes in behavior. Today, the pineal body, now known as the **pineal gland**, is thought to take part in controlling biorhythms. Furthermore, the cortex became much more central to understanding behavior as scientists began to discover that it did the things that Descartes attributed to a nonmaterial mind.

Pineal body

Ventricles

The position that mind and body are separate but can interact is called **dualism**, to indicate that behavior is caused by two things. Descartes's dualism originated what came to be known as the **mind–body problem**: for Descartes, a person is capable of being conscious and rational only because of having a mind, but how can a nonmaterial mind produce movements in a material body?

To understand the problem, consider that, in order for the mind to affect the body, it would have to expend energy, adding new energy to the material world. The spontaneous creation of new energy violates a fundamental law of physics, the law of conservation of matter and energy. Thus, dualists who argue that mind and body interact causally cannot explain how.

Other dualists avoid this problem by reasoning either that the mind and body function in parallel without interacting or that the body can affect the mind but the mind cannot affect the body. These dualist positions allow for both a body and a mind by sidestepping the problem of violating the laws of physics. Other philosophers called **monists** avoid the mind–body problem by postulating that the mind and body are simply a unitary whole.

In proposing his dualistic theory of brain function, Descartes also proposed that animals do not have minds and so are only machinelike. The inhumane treatment of animals, children, and the mentally ill was justified by some followers of Descartes on the grounds that they did not have minds. For them, an animal did not have a mind, a child developed a mind only when about 7 years of age when able to talk and reason, and the mentally ill had "lost their minds." Likewise misunderstanding Descartes's position, some people still argue that the study of animals cannot be a source of useful insight into human neuropsychology.

Descartes himself, however, was not so dogmatic. He was kind to his dog, Monsieur Grat. He also suggested that whether animals had minds could be tested experimentally. He proposed that the key indications of the presence of a mind are the use of language and reason. He suggested that, if it could be demonstrated that animals could speak or reason, then such demonstration would indicate that they have minds. As we will demonstrate, some exciting lines of research in modern experimental neuropsychology are directed toward the comparative study of animals and humans with respect to language and reason.

Darwin and Materialism

By the middle of the nineteenth century, another theory of the brain and behavior was taking shape: the modern perspective of **materialism**, the idea that rational behavior can be fully explained by the working of the nervous system without any need to refer to a nonmaterial mind. This perspective had its roots in the evolutionary theories of two English naturalists, Alfred Russell Wallace (1823–1913) and Charles Darwin (1809–1892).

Both Darwin and Wallace looked carefully at the structures of plants and animals and at animal behavior. Despite the diversity of living organisms, they were struck by the number of similarities and common characteristics. For example, the skeleton, muscles, internal organs, and nervous systems of humans, monkeys, and other mammals are remarkably similar. These observations support the idea that living things must be related, an idea widely held even before Wallace and Darwin. But more importantly, these same observations led to the idea that the similarities could be explained if all animals evolved from a common ancestor.

Darwin elaborated further on the topic in *On the Origin of Species by Means of Natural Selection*, published in 1859. He argued that all organisms, both living and extinct, are descended from some unknown ancestor that lived in the remote past. In Darwin's terms, all living things are said to have **common descent**. As the descendants of that original organism spread into various habitats through millions of years, they developed structural and behavioral adaptations that suited them for new ways of life. At the same time, they retained many similar characteristics that reveal their relatedness to one another.

The nervous system is one such common characteristic. It is an adaptation that emerged only once in animal evolution. Consequently, the nervous systems of living animals are similar because they are descendents of that first nervous system. For those animals with brains, the brains are related because all animals with brains are descendents from the first animal to evolve a brain.

Some people reject the idea that the brain is responsible for behavior, because they think it denies the teaching of their religion that the nonmaterial soul will continue to exist after their bodies die. Others regard the biological explanation of brain and behavior as being neutral with respect to religion. Many behavioral scientists with strong religious beliefs see no contradiction between those beliefs and using the scientific method to examine the relations between the brain and behavior. Today, when neuroscientists use the term mind, most are not referring to a nonmaterial entity but are using the term as shorthand for the collective functions of the brain.

Experimental Approaches to Brain Function

Beginning in the early 1800s, scientists began to test their ideas about brain function by examining and measuring the brain and by developing methods to describe behavior quantitatively. Quantitative methods allow researchers to check one another's conclusions. In this section, we describe a number of influential experimental approaches to the study of brain function and some important neuropsychological ideas that resulted from them.

Localization of Function

You may have heard statements such as, "Most people use only 10% of their brains" or "He put his entire mind to the problem." Both statements suggest that the brain or mind does its work as a unified whole. Nevertheless, most victims of brain damage find that some behavior is lost and some survives, as did L.D. at the beginning of this chapter, suggesting that different parts of the nervous system have different functions. In the nineteenth century, physiologists perplexed by such observations often puzzled over the symptoms of brain damage and then speculated about how the observations could be consistent with a holistic notion of the mind.

The first general theory to present the idea that different parts of the brain have different functions was developed by German anatomist Franz Josef Gall

(1758–1828) and his partner Johann Casper Spurzheim (1776–1832). Gall and Spurzheim proposed that the cortex and its gyri were functioning parts of the brain and not just coverings for the pineal body. They supported their position by showing through dissection that the brain's most distinctive motor pathway, the corticospinal (cortex to spinal cord) tract, leads from the cortex of each hemisphere to the spinal cord on the opposite side of the body. Thus, they suggested, the cortex sends instructions to the spinal cord to command movement of the muscles.

Not only did Gall and Spurzheim propose that the cortex is a functioning part of the brain, they also proposed that it produces behavior through the control of other parts of the brain and spinal cord through the corticospinal tract. They also recognized that the two symmetrical hemispheres of the brain are connected by the corpus callosum and can thus interact.

Gall's behavioral ideas began with an observation made in his youth. Reportedly, he was annoyed by students with good memories who achieved excellent marks but did not have an equivalent ability for original thinking. According to his recollection of those days, the students with the best memories had large, protruding eyes. Using this crude observation as a starting point, Gall developed a general theory of how the brain might produce differences in individual abilities into a theory called **localization of function**. For example, Gall proposed that a well-developed memory area of the cortex located behind the eyes would cause the eyes to protrude. You might note that aliens featured in science fiction movies are often portrayed as having bulging foreheads, reminiscent of Gall's idea that the frontal lobes are the seat of intelligence.

Gall and Spurzheim collected instances of individual differences that they related to other prominent features of the head and skull. They proposed that a bump on the skull indicated a well-developed underlying cortical gyrus and therefore a greater capacity for a particular behavior; a depression in the same area indicated an underdeveloped gyrus and a concomitantly reduced faculty.

Thus, just as a person with a good memory had protruding eyes, a person with a high degree of musical ability, artistic talent, sense of color, combativeness, or mathematical skill would have large bumps in other areas of the skull. **Figure 1.4** shows where Gall and Spurzheim located the trait of amativeness (sexiness). A person with a bump there would be predicted to have a strong sex drive, whereas a person low in this trait would have a depression in the same region.

Gall and Spurzheim identified a long list of behavioral traits borrowed from English or Scottish psychology of the time. They assigned each trait to a particular part of the skull and, by inference, to the

(A)

(B)

Gall correlated bumps in the region of the cerebellum with the brain's "amativeness" center.

Figure 1.4

Gall's Theory Depressions (A) and bumps (B) on the skull indicate the size of the underlying area of brain and thus, when correlated with personality traits, indicate the part of the brain controlling the trait. While examining a patient (who because of her behavior became known as "Gall's Passionate Widow"), Gall found a bump at the back of her neck that he thought located the center for "amativeness" in the cerebellum. (After Olin, 1910.)

Figure **1.5**

Phrenology Bust Originally, Gall's system identified putative locations for 27 faculties. As the study of phrenology expanded, the number of faculties increased. Language, indicated at the front of the brain, below the eye, actually derived from one of Gall's case studies. A soldier had received a knife wound that penetrated the frontal lobe of his left hemisphere through the eye. The soldier lost the ability to speak. (Mary Evans Picture Library/Image Works.)

underlying part of the brain. **Figure 1.5** shows the resulting map that they devised. Spurzheim called the study of the relation between the skull's surface features and a person's faculties **phrenology** (*phren* is a Greek word for "mind"). The map of the relation between brain functions and the skull surface is called a phrenological map.

Gall and Spurzheim went to considerable effort to gather evidence for their theory. In developing his idea of the carnivorous instinct, Gall compared the skulls of meat- and plant-eating animals, collecting evidence from more than 50 species, including a description of his own lapdog. His studies of human behavior included accounts of a patricide and a murder, as well as descriptions of people who delighted in witnessing death or torturing animals or who historically had been noted for acts of cruelty and sadism. He also examined the skulls of 25 murderers and even considered evidence from paintings and busts.

Interestingly, Gall placed no emphasis on evidence from cases of brain damage, even though he is credited with giving the first complete account of a case in which left-frontal-lobe brain damage was followed by loss of the ability to speak. The patient was a soldier whose brain was pierced by a sword driven through his eye. Note that, on the phrenological map in Figure 1.5, language is located below the eye. Yet Gall felt that this type of finding was not evidence per se but rather confirmation of a finding that was already established by the phrenological evidence.

Phrenology was seized on by some people as a means of making personality assessments. They developed a method called *cranioscopy*, in which a device was placed around the skull to measure the bumps and depressions there. These measures were then correlated with the phrenological map to determine the person's likely behavioral traits.

Cranioscopy invited quackery and thus, indirectly, ridicule by association. Because most of its practitioners produced extremely superficial personality analyses, the entire phrenological endeavor was eventually brought into disrepute. There were other problems intrinsic to the theory. For example, the faculties described in phrenology—characteristics such as faith, self-love, and veneration—are impossible to define and to quantify objectively. The phrenologists also failed to recognize that the superficial features of the skull reveal little about the underlying brain. The outer skull does not mirror even the inner skull, much less the surface features of the cortex.

A historical remnant from the phrenology era is the naming of the cortical lobes after the overlying bones of the skull (see Figure 1.1). Additionally, Gall's notion of localization of function, although inaccurate scientifically, conceptually laid the foundation for modern views of localization of function, beginning with language, and his phrenological map was the precursor of many subsequent maps of the brain.

Localization and Lateralization of Language

A now legendary chain of observations and speculations led to the discovery that really launched the science of neuropsychology, the localization of language. On February 21, 1825, a French physician named Jean Baptiste Bouillaud (1796–1881) read a paper before the Royal Academy of Medicine in France. Bouillaud argued from clinical studies that certain functions are localized in the cortex and, specifically, that speech is localized in the frontal lobes, in accordance with Gall's theory.

Observing that acts such as writing, drawing, painting, and fencing are carried out with the right hand, Bouillaud also suggested that the part of the brain that controls them might be the left hemisphere. Physicians had long recognized that damage to a hemisphere of the brain impaired movement of the opposite side of the body. A few years later, in 1836, Marc Dax read a paper in Montpellier, France, about a series of clinical cases demonstrating that disorders of speech were constantly associated with lesions of the left hemisphere. Dax's manuscript received little attention, however, and was not published until 1865, by his son.

Ernest Auburtin, Bouillaud's son-in-law, supported Bouillaud's cause. At a meeting of the Anthropological Society of Paris in 1861, he reported the case of a patient who lost the ability to speak when pressure was applied to his exposed frontal lobe. Auburtin also gave the following description of another patient, ending with a promise that other scientists interpreted as a challenge:

> For a long time during my service with M. Bouillaud I studied a patient, named Bache, who had lost his speech but understood everything said to him and replied with signs in a very intelligent manner to all questions put to him. This man, who spent several years at the Bicetre [a Parisian mental asylum], is now at the Hospital for Incurables. I saw him again recently and his disease has progressed; slight paralysis has appeared but his intelligence is still unimpaired, and speech is wholly abolished. Without a doubt this man will soon die. Based on the symptoms that he presents we have diagnosed softening of the anterior lobes. If, at autopsy, these lobes are found to be intact, I shall renounce the ideas that I have just expounded to you. (Stookey, 1954)

Paul Broca (1824–1880), founder of the Society, heard Auburtin's challenge. Five days later he received a patient, a Monsieur Leborgne, who had lost his speech and was able to say only "tan" and utter an oath. He had paralysis on the right side of his body but in other respects seemed intelligent and normal. Broca recalled Auburtin's challenge and invited Auburtin to examine Tan, as the patient came to be called.

Together they agreed that, if Auburtin was right, Tan should have a frontal lesion. Tan died on April 17, 1861, and the next day Broca submitted his findings to the Anthropological Society (this submission is claimed to be the fastest publication ever made in science). Auburtin was correct: the left frontal lobe was the focus of Tan's lesion. By 1863, Broca had collected eight more cases similar to Tan's and stated:

> Here are eight instances in which the lesion was in the posterior third of the third frontal convolution. This number seems to me to be sufficient to give strong presumptions. And the most remarkable thing is that in all the patients the lesion was on the left side. (Joynt, 1964)

As a result of his studies, Broca located speech in the third convolution (gyrus) of the frontal lobe on the left side of the brain (**Figure 1.6**A). Thus, he

Figure **1.6**

Lateralization of Language
(A) Broca's area is located in the posterior third of the inferior, or third, convolution (gyrus) of the frontal lobe in the left hemisphere. (B) Photograph of the left hemisphere of the brain of Leborgne ("Tan"), Broca's first aphasic patient. (Part B, Musee Dupuytren/courtesy of Assistance Publique, Hospitaux de Paris.)

(A)

Superior convolution (1st)
Middle convolution (2nd)
Inferior convolution (3rd)

Broca's area

Broca located speech in this area of the frontal lobe.

(B)

accomplished two feats. He demonstrated that language was localized; thus different regions of the cortex could have specialized functions. He also discovered something new: functions could be localized to a side of the brain, a property that is referred to as **lateralization**.

Because speech is thought to be central to human consciousness, the left hemisphere is frequently referred to as the dominant hemisphere, to recognize its special role in language. In recognition of Broca's contribution, the anterior speech region of the brain is called **Broca's area**, and the syndrome that results from its damage is called **Broca's aphasia** (from the Greek *a*, for "not," and *phasia*, for "speech").

An interesting footnote to this story is that Broca did not do a very careful examination of Tan's brain (Figure 1.6B). Broca's anatomical analysis was criticized by French anatomist Pierre Marie, who reexamined the preserved brains of Broca's first two patients, Tan and Monsieur Lelong, 25 years after Broca's death. Marie pointed out in his article titled "The Third Left Frontal Convolution Plays No Particular Role in the Function of Language" that Lelong's brain showed general nonspecific atrophy, common in senility, and that Tan had additional extensive damage in his posterior cortex that may have accounted for his aphasia.

Broca had been aware of Tan's posterior damage but concluded that, whereas it contributed to his death, the anterior damage had occurred earlier, producing his aphasia. Pierre Marie's criticism aside, Broca's demonstration of localization and lateralization of function became the dogma of neuropsychology for the next hundred years.

Sequential Programming and Disconnection

People who interpreted Broca's findings as evidence that language resides totally in one part of the brain are called strict localizationists. Many other scientists began to argue against such a strict interpretation of Broca's findings. The first notable scientist to dissent was German anatomist Carl Wernicke (1848–1904).

Wernicke was aware that the part of the cortex that receives the sensory pathway, or projection, from the ear—and is thus called the auditory cortex—is located in the temporal lobe, behind Broca's area (see Figure 1.6A). He therefore suspected a relation between the functioning of hearing and that of speech, and he described cases in which aphasic patients had lesions in this auditory projection area that differed from those described by Broca in four ways:

1. Damage was evident in the first temporal gyrus.

2. No opposite-side paralysis was observed (Broca's aphasia is frequently associated with paralysis of the right arm and leg, as described for Tan).

3. Patients could speak fluently, but what they said was confused and made little sense (Broca's patients could not articulate, but they seemed to understand the meaning of words).

4. Although the patients were able to hear, they could neither understand nor repeat what was said to them.

Wernicke's finding that the temporal lobe also is implicated in language disproved the strict localizationists' view. Wernicke's syndrome is sometimes called temporal-lobe aphasia or *fluent aphasia*, to emphasize that the person can say words, but is more frequently called **Wernicke's aphasia**. The region of the temporal lobe associated with this form of aphasia is called **Wernicke's area**.

Wernicke also provided the first model for how language is organized in the left hemisphere and thus the first modern model of brain function (**Figure 1.7**A). Wernicke proposed that auditory information travels to the temporal lobes from the ears. In Wernicke's area, sounds are processed into auditory images or ideas of objects and stored. From Wernicke's area, auditory ideas can be sent through a pathway called the *arcuate fasciculus* (from the Latin *arc*, for "bow," and *fasciculus*, for "band of tissue," because the pathway arcs around the lateral fissure, as shown in Figure 1.7B). The pathway leads to Broca's area, where the representations of speech movements are stored. From Broca's area, neural instructions are sent to muscles that control movements of the mouth to produce the appropriate sounds.

If the temporal lobe were damaged, speech movements could still be mediated by Broca's area but the speech would make no sense, because the person would be unable to monitor words. Because damage to Broca's area produces a loss of speech movements without the loss of sound images, Broca's aphasia is not accompanied by a loss of understanding.

Wernicke also predicted a new language disorder, although he never saw such a case. He suggested that, if the arcuate fibers connecting the two speech areas were cut, disconnecting the areas but without inflicting damage on either one, a speech deficit that Wernicke described as **conduction aphasia** would result. In this condition, speech sounds and movements are retained, as is comprehension, but speech is still impaired because the person cannot judge the sense of the words that he or she heard.

Wernicke's prediction was subsequently confirmed. Wernicke's speech model was updated by American neurologist Norman Geschwind in the 1960s and is now sometimes referred to as the Wernicke–Geschwind model, shown in Figure 1.7B.

Wernicke's idea of disconnection offered a completely new way of viewing symptoms of brain damage. It proposed that, although different regions of the brain have different functions, they are interdependent in that, to work, they must interact. Thus, just as a washed-out bridge prevents traffic from moving from one side of a river to the other and so prevents people from performing complex activities such as commercial transactions or emergency response services, cutting connecting pathways prevents two brain regions from communicating and performing complex functions.

Using this same reasoning, in 1892 French neurologist Joseph Dejerine (1849–1917) described a case in which the loss of the ability to read (**alexia**, meaning "word blindness," from the Greek *lexia*, for "word") resulted from a disconnection between the visual area of the brain and Wernicke's area. Similarly, Wernicke's student Hugo Liepmann (1863–1925) was able to show that

(A) Wernicke's original model

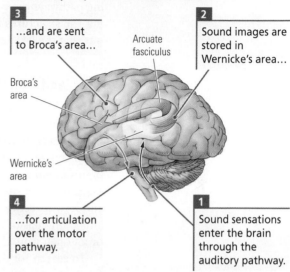

(B) Contemporary version of Wernicke's model

3
...and are sent to Broca's area...

Arcuate fasciculus

Broca's area

Wernicke's area

2
Sound images are stored in Wernicke's area...

4
...for articulation over the motor pathway.

1
Sound sensations enter the brain through the auditory pathway.

Figure 1.7

Organization of Language
(A) Wernicke's 1874 model shows how language functions are organized in the brain. Sounds enter the brain through the auditory pathway (*a*). Sound images are stored in Wernicke's auditory area (*a′*) and sent to Broca's word area (*b*) for articulation through the motor pathway (*b′*). Lesions along this route (*a–a′–b–b′*) could produce different types of aphasia, depending on their location. Curiously, Wernicke drew all his language models on the right hemisphere even though he believed that the left hemisphere is the dominant hemisphere for language. Also curious is that he drew the brain of an ape, which cannot speak, as Wernicke knew. (B) A twentieth-century rendition of Wernicke's model. (Part A after Wernicke, 1874.)

an inability to make sequences of movements (**apraxia**, from the Greek *praxis*, for "movement") resulted from the disconnection of motor areas from sensory areas.

Disconnection is an important idea because it predicts that complex behaviors are built up in assembly-line fashion as information collected by sensory systems enters the brain and travels through different structures before resulting in an overt response. Furthermore, disconnecting brain structures by cutting connecting pathways can result in impairments that resemble those produced by damaging the structures themselves. Nevertheless, for all these functions, agreement was that the left hemisphere is dominant in its contribution.

Loss and Recovery of Function

Although the idea that functions could be localized in the brain gained acceptance, the study of how animals and people recovered function began to challenge localization. The work of French physiologist Pierre Flourens (1794–1867) is illustrative. Flourens's experimental method consisted of removing parts of the brains of animals to study any changes in behavior produced by these surgeries. He removed a small piece of cortex and then observed how the animal behaved and how it recovered from the loss of brain tissue. In essence, Flourens created animal models of humans who had experienced closed-head injury, as L.D. did, or an open wound that pierced the skull.

To search for different functions in the cortex, Flourens varied the location from which he removed brain tissue. He found that, after the removal of pieces of cortex, animals at first moved very little and neglected to eat and drink, but with the passage of time they recovered to the point that they seemed normal. This pattern of loss and recovery of function held for all his cortex experiments, seeming to refute the idea that different cortical areas have specialized functions.

Flourens did find that parts of the brainstem have specialized functions. For example, he found that the brainstem is important for breathing, because animals suffocated if the brainstem had been damaged. He also found that the cerebellum, a part of the brainstem, coordinates locomotion. Recall that Gall had proposed that the cerebellum was the location of "amativeness" (see Figure 1.4).

The experiments performed by Friedrich L. Goltz (1834–1902) in 1892 confirmed Flourens's findings. Goltz argued that, if a part of the cortex had a function, then its removal should lead to a loss of that function. He made large lesions in three dogs, removing almost all of the cortex and a good deal of underlying brain tissue, and then studied the dogs for 57 days, 92 days, and 18 months, respectively, until the dogs died.

The dog that survived for 18 months was studied in the greatest detail. After the surgery, it was more active than a normal dog. Its periods of sleep and waking were shorter than normal, but it still panted when warm and shivered when cold. It walked well on uneven ground and was able to catch its balance when it slipped. If placed in an abnormal posture, it corrected its position.

After hurting a hind limb on one occasion, this dog trotted on three legs, holding up the injured limb. It was able to orient to touches or pinches on its body and to snap at the object that touched it, although its orientations were not very accurate. If offered meat soaked in milk or meat soaked in bitter quinine, it accepted the first and rejected the second. It responded to light and sounds, although its response thresholds were elevated; that is, its senses were not as acute as those of a normal dog.

In sum, removal of the cortex did not appear to eliminate any function completely, though it seemed to reduce all functions to some extent. This demonstration appeared to be a strong argument against localization of function and even to cast doubt on the role of the cortex in behavior.

Hierarchical Organization and Distributed Systems in the Brain

The fundamental disagreement between experiments that appeared to support localization of function and those that did not was resolved by the **hierarchical organization** concept of brain function proposed by English neurologist John Hughlings-Jackson (1835–1911). Hughlings-Jackson had observed recovery of function in humans who, like L.D., had suffered brain injury. He proposed that the nervous system was organized as a functional hierarchy. Each successively higher level controlled more-complex aspects of behavior and did so by means of the lower levels.

Often, Hughlings-Jackson described the nervous system as having three levels: the spinal cord, the brainstem, and the forebrain, which had developed successively in evolution. But, equally often, he assigned no particular anatomical area to a given level. Hughlings-Jackson suggested that diseases or damage that affect the highest levels of the brain hierarchy would produce *dissolution*, the reverse of evolution. That is, the animals would still have a repertoire of behaviors, but the behaviors would be simpler, more typical of an animal that had not yet evolved the missing brain structure.

Thus, for Hughlings-Jackson, Goltz's dogs were "low level" dogs. They appeared normal when they walked and ate but, had food not been presented to them (had they been required to walk to find food), they might have failed to take the necessary action and starved. Under some conditions, their walking did not serve a useful executive function.

Hughlings-Jackson applied novel concepts to many other areas of behavior by proposing that every part of the brain could contribute to a behavior. For example, it was his view that every part of the brain functions in language, with each part making some special contribution. The relevant question was not where language is localized, but what unique contribution each part of the cortex makes. (Apply Hughlings-Jackson's concept to our Portrait case at the beginning of this chapter and note that L.D. had impaired executive function but retained the skill of golf playing.)

An expression used today to encompass Hughlings-Jackson's idea is that behaviors are organized in a **distributed hierarchy**. As is illustrated in the Snapshot on the next page, understanding the concept of hierarchical function still presents a dilemma to people today.

The Binding Problem

On August 23, 1953, neurosurgeon William B. Scoville (1906–1984) bilaterally removed the medial parts of the temporal lobes from patient H.M. for the treatment of epilepsy—abnormal electrical discharges in the brain that produce

SNAPSHOT

The Dilemma in Relating Behavior and Consciousness

In his paper titled "Consciousness Without a Cerebral Cortex: A Challenge for Neuroscience and Medicine," Bjorn Merker reviewed the difficulty in determining what is unconscious and what is conscious behavior. Our understanding of this dilemma dates to Hughlings-Jackson's idea that similar-appearing behaviors have vastly different implications, depending on how they are hierarchically represented in the brain.

The difficulty in relating brain injury to behavior is illustrated by Theresa Marie "Terri" Schiavo, a 26-year-old woman from St. Petersburg, Florida, who collapsed in her home in 1990 and experienced respiratory and cardiac arrest.

Although Terri was completely unresponsive and in a coma for 3 weeks, as she did become more responsive, her normal conscious behavior did not return. Terri was diagnosed as being in a **persistent vegetative state** (PVS): she was alive but unable to communicate or to function independently at even the most basic level. In 1998, Terri's husband and guardian, Michael Schiavo, petitioned the courts to remove her gastric feeding tube, maintaining that she would not wish to live under such severe impairment. Terri's parents, Robert and Mary Schindler, were opposed, citing their belief that Terri's behavior signaled that she was consciously aware and fighting to recover. The battle lines were drawn.

By March 2005, the legal history concerning the Schiavo case included 14 appeals, numerous motions, petitions, and hearings in the Florida courts, and 5 suits in Federal District Court. Florida legislation favorable to the Schindlers was struck down by the Supreme Court of Florida; a subpoena by a U.S. Congressional committee in an attempt to qualify Schiavo for witness protection resulted in federal legislation

A CT scan of a normal adult brain (left) and Terri Schiavo's brain (right). (Michael Schiavo.)

(Palm Sunday Compromise); and the Supreme Court of the United States refused to review the case four times.

Judges, legislators, and the viewing public were presented with videos of Terri glancing around her room, looking at people in the room and smiling. Her parents and the physicians who supported them interpreted these actions as evidence that Terri was conscious and that she would eventually recover normal brain function. Her husband and the physicians who supported him argued that Terri's behaviors were not conscious but rather were reflexive actions.

Amid a storm of national controversy, Michael Schiavo prevailed. Terri's feeding tube was removed, and she died 13 days later at a Pinellas Park, Florida, hospice on March 31, 2005, at the age of 41.

Merker, B. Consciousness without a cerebral cortex: A challenge for neuroscience and medicine. *Behavioural and Brain Sciences* 30:63–134, 2007.

convulsions. The treatment stopped the epilepsy but left H.M. with a severe memory problem: amnesia. He initially appeared to have retained memories from before the surgery but was unable to form new memories that endured for more than a few seconds to minutes.

H.M. has been studied for decades, and more scientific papers have been written about his case than that of any other neuropsychological patient. As described by Canadian neuropsychologist Brenda Milner and her students, his case reveals that there is not just one memory structure in the brain but rather that a number of neural structures encode memories separately and in parallel. For example, H.M. could acquire motor skills but could not remember having done so. Thus, the neural structures for learning motor skills and those for re-membering that one has those skills are separate.

H.M. could remember faces but could not recall emotional experiences. He might state that he had not learned certain events but, if asked to choose among a number of possibilities, he could often choose correctly.

The study of H.M. and others with amnesia suggests that, when people have a memorable experience, they encode different parts of the experience in different parts of the brain concurrently. The location of the experience is stored in one brain region, the emotional content in another brain region, the events comprising the experience in still another region, and so on. In fact, there does not appear to be a place in the brain where all the aspects of the experience come together to form "the memory."

The term **binding problem** expresses the puzzle that, although the brain analyzes sensory events through multiple, parallel channels that do not con-verge on a single brain region, we perceive a unified representation of our ex-periences. For example, we recall a single memory of an event when in fact we have many separate memories, each stored in a different region of the brain. The binding problem extends from perceptive to motor to cognitive processes, the different parts of which are mediated by different neural structures.

The Split Brain

Paul Broca's demonstration that language is lateralized to the left hemisphere dominated theories of how the brain worked for a century. The left hemisphere was proposed to be the dominant hemisphere not only for language but also for all higher cognitive function. Brain researchers and others assumed that the left hemisphere was highly evolved, whereas the right hemisphere was rela-tively retarded, being not only mute, word-deaf, and unable to write but also unable to read or make skilled movements and lacking generally in higher cog-nitive function.

Then, in the early 1960s, to prevent the spread of epileptic seizures from one hemisphere to the other in a number of patients, two neurosurgeons, Joseph Bogen (1926–2005) and Phillip Vogel, cut the corpus callosum and the smaller commissures that connect the two cortical hemispheres. The surgery was effective in reducing the seizures and in improving the lives of these "split brain" patients. Roger W. Sperry (1913–1994) conducted a series of studies on them that overthrew the classical view of the role of the two hemispheres and revolutionized approaches to the study of mental functions.

By taking advantage of the anatomy of the sensory pathways that project preferentially to the opposite hemisphere, the scientists were able to explore the language and other cognitive abilities of the right hemisphere. Although mute, the right hemisphere was nevertheless found to comprehend words spo-ken aloud, read printed words, point to corresponding objects or pictures in an array, and match presented objects or pictures correctly from spoken to printed words and vice versa. Despite these experimental results, so strong was the con-temporary dogma that language is restricted to the left hemisphere that the findings challenged, Bogen withheld his name from the papers that Sperry and colleagues published on language.

In additional split-brain studies, the scientists demonstrated that each dis-connected hemisphere has its own higher gnostic (knowing) functions. Each uses its own percepts, mental images, associations, and ideas. Each has its own learning processes and separate chain of memories, and all are essentially inaccessible to the conscious experience of the other hemisphere.

Further, the idea emerged that each hemisphere has built-in, qualitatively different, and mutually antagonistic modes of cognitive processing. The left hemisphere is dominant for spoken language and for analytic and sequential actions. The right hemisphere is the superior cerebral member when it comes to performing certain kinds of mental tasks entailing spatial and synthetic acts. They include reading faces, fitting designs into matrices, judging circle size from an arc, discriminating and recalling shapes, making spatial transformations, discriminating musical chords, sorting block sizes and shapes into categories, perceiving wholes from a collection of parts, and perceiving and apprehending geometric principles. In the right hemisphere, a picture is worth a thousand words.

In his Nobel lecture in 1981, Sperry concluded that each hemisphere possesses complementary self-awareness and social consciousness and that much of internal mental life, especially that of the right hemisphere, is not accessible to analysis using language. Sperry proposed that a neuropsychology that does not accept the existence of a private mental life and relies solely on quantitative, objective measurement of behavior cannot fully understand a brain in which inner experience itself is causal in the expression of overt behavior.

Conscious and Unconscious Neural Streams

On a tragic day in February 1988 near Milan, Italy, D.F. was poisoned by carbon monoxide (CO) emitted by a faulty space heater. As the CO replaced the oxygen in her blood, her brain was deprived of oxygen and she sank into a coma. When she later recovered consciousness in the hospital, she was alert, could speak and understand, but could see nothing. D.F. was diagnosed as having cortical blindness due to damage to the visual area at the back of the brain rather than to any problem with her eyes.

D.F. eventually regained some vision and could see color and could even identify what objects were made of by their color, but she could not see the shapes of objects and she could not recognize objects visually by their shape. This deficit is **visual form agnosia**. D.F.'s visual acuity was normal, but she could not distinguish vertical lines from horizontal lines. She could not recognize objects or drawings of objects. She could draw objects from memory, but she could not recognize the objects that she had drawn.

One day in a clinical setting in St. Andrews, Scotland, Scottish neuropsychologist David Milner and Canadian neuropsychologist Melvyn Goodale observed that D.F. accurately reached for a pencil that they offered her and grasped it. Nevertheless, she could not see the pencil or tell whether its orientation was horizontal or vertical. D.F.'s ability to perform this act presented a paradox. How could she reach out to grasp the pencil when, at the same time, she could not tell the neuropsychologists what she saw?

In further tests, D.F. demonstrated that she could shape her hand correctly to grasp many objects that she could not recognize and she could even step over objects that she could not see. In sum, D.F. appears to be able to see if she is required to perform an action but, otherwise, she is blind to the form of objects.

D.F.'s visual agnosia stands in contrast to the deficits displayed by patients who display visual **ataxia** (*taxis*, meaning "to move toward"). These patients can describe objects accurately, but they make errors in reaching for them. The brain lesions in agnosia patients such as D.F. occur in neural structures that constitute a pathway from the visual cortex to the temporal lobe, called the **ventral stream**. Brain lesions in patients with optic ataxia are in neural structures that form a pathway from the visual cortex to the parietal cortex called the **dorsal stream** (**Figure 1.8**).

Goodale and Milner propose that the ventral stream mediates actions controlled by conscious visual perception, whereas the dorsal stream mediates actions controlled by unconscious visual processes. The importance of these findings is that, although we believe that we are consciously guiding our visual actions, vision is not unitary. Much of what vision does for us lies outside our conscious visual experience and essentially uses computations that are robotic in nature.

It follows that other sensory systems are not unitary either and consist both of pathways that mediate unconscious actions and of pathways that mediate conscious actions. These results are revolutionary. The historical view was that the cortex mediates conscious actions, but findings such as those obtained from D.F. show that many behaviors controlled by the cortex fall outside the realm of consciousness. Nevertheless, we experience a seamless, binding interaction between conscious and unconscious actions.

In sum, the evolving findings of neuroscience become richer with each generation of study. Brain functions are localized, distributed, and organized hierarchally and in parallel. Even the most complex actions are both conscious and unconscious. Yet we see the world, and ourselves, as whole, so much so that, subsequent to brain damage, such as that described for L.D., people may not be aware of their behavioral deficits.

Figure 1.8

Neural Streams The dorsal and ventral streams mediate vision for action and vision consciousness, respectively.

The Neuron Hypothesis

Following the development of the brain hypothesis, the idea that the brain is responsible for all behavior, the second major influence on modern neuropsychology was the development of the neuron hypothesis, the idea that the unit of brain structure and function is the nerve cell. In this section, we provide a description of the three aspects of the neuron hypothesis: that neurons are discrete, autonomous cells that interact but are not physically connected, that they send electrical signals that have a chemical basis, and that they communicate with one another by using chemical signals.

Nervous System Cells

The nervous system is composed of two basic kinds of cells, neurons and **glia** (from the Greek word for "glue"). Neurons enable us to acquire information, process it, and act on it. Glial cells help the neurons out, holding them together (some *do* act as glue) and providing other supporting functions, such as waste

Figure 1.9

Major Parts of a Neuron

Dendrites

Cell body

Axon

removal. In the human nervous system, there are about 100 billion neurons and perhaps 10 times as many glial cells. (No, no one has counted them all. Scientists have estimated the total number by counting the cells in a small sample of brain tissue and then multiplying by the brain's volume.)

Figure 1.9 shows the three basic parts of a neuron. The core region is called the **cell body**. Most of a neuron's branching extensions are called **dendrites** (Latin for "branch"), but the main "root" is called the **axon** (Greek for "axle"). A neuron has only one axon, but most neurons have many dendrites. Some small neurons have so many dendrites that they look like garden hedges.

The neuron's dendrites and axon are extensions of its cell body, and their main purpose is to extend the cell's surface area. The dendrites of a cell can be a number of millimeters long, but the axon can extend as long as a meter, as do those in the motor pathway that extends from the cortex to the spinal cord. In the giraffe, these same axons are a number of meters long.

Understanding how billions of cells, many with long, complex extensions, produce behavior is a formidable task. Just imagine what the first anatomists with their crude microscopes thought when they first began to make out some of the brain's structural details. Through the development of new, more powerful microscopes and techniques for selectively staining tissue, good descriptions of neurons emerged in the nineteenth century. By applying more-recent electronic inventions to the study of neurons, researchers began to understand how axons conduct information. By studying how neurons interact and by applying a growing body of knowledge from chemistry, they discovered how neurons communicate and, eventually, how learning takes place.

Identifying the Neuron

The earliest anatomists who tried to examine the substructure of the nervous system found a gelatinous white substance, almost a goo. Eventually, they discovered that, if brain tissue were placed in alcohol or formaldehyde, water would be drawn out of the tissue, making it firm. Then, if the tissue were cut into thin sections, many different structures could be seen.

Early theorists, such as Descartes, described nerves as hollow, fluid-containing tubes; however, when the first cellular anatomist, Anton van Leeuwenhoek (1632–1723), examined nerves with a primitive microscope, he found no such thing. As microscopes improved, the various parts of the nerve came into ever sharper focus, eventually leading Theodor Schwann (1810–1882) to enunciate the theory that cells are the basic structural units of the nervous system, just as they are for the rest of the body.

An exciting development in visualizing cells was the introduction of staining, which allows different parts of the nervous system to be distinguished. Various dyes used for staining cloth in the German textile industry were applied to thinly cut brain tissue with various results: some selectively stained the cell body, some stained the nucleus, and some stained the axons. The most amazing cell stain came from the application of photographic chemicals to nervous system tissue.

Italian anatomist Camillo Golgi (1843–1926) in 1875 impregnated tissue with silver nitrate (one of the substances responsible for forming the images in black-

and-white photographs) and found that a few cells in their entirety—cell body, dendrites, and axons— became encrusted with silver. This technique allowed the entire neuron and all its processes to be visualized for the first time. Golgi never described what led him to his remarkable discovery.

Spanish anatomist Santiago Ramón y Cajal (1852– 1934) used Golgi's silver-staining technique to examine the brains of chicks at various ages and produced beautiful drawings of neurons at different stages of growth. He was able to see a neuron develop from a simple cell body with few extensions to a highly complex cell with many extensions (**Figure 1.10**). But he never saw connections from cell to cell.

Golgi and Cajal interpreted their observations in different ways. Golgi proposed that neurons were interconnected and formed a net, thus providing the basis for a holistic mind. Cajal proposed that neurons were autonomous, providing the basis for functional specialization. Their acrimonious debate is manifest in their Nobel speeches in 1906, Golgi supporting his nerve net and Cajal supporting his neuron hypothesis. Images produced by electron microscopes in the twentieth century fully support Cajal's hypothesis.

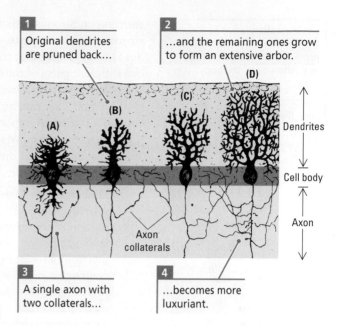

1 Original dendrites are pruned back...

2 ...and the remaining ones grow to form an extensive arbor.

Dendrites

Cell body

Axon

Axon collaterals

3 A single axon with two collaterals...

4 ...becomes more luxuriant.

Figure **1.10**

Neuron Growth Successive phases (A–D) in the development of a type of neuron called a Purkinje cell as drawn by Ramón y Cajal (1937).

Relating Electrical Activity in Neurons to Behavior

Insights into how neurons worked began with Italian physicist Luigi Galvani's (1737–1798) finding that electrical stimulation delivered by wires to a frog's nerve causes muscle contractions. The idea for this experiment came from Galvani's observation that frogs' legs hanging on a metal wire in a market twitched during an electrical storm. Subsequently, many studies considered how electrical conduction through the body might relate to information flow in neurons.

A most interesting experiment demonstrating that information flow in the brain has an electrical basis comes from studies in 1870 by Gustav Theodor Fritsch (1838–1929) and Eduard Hitzig (1838–1907). The technique consisted of placing a thin, insulated wire, an *electrode*, onto or into the cortex and passing a small electrical current through the uninsulated tip of the wire, thus exciting the tissue near the electrode's tip. Hitzig may have derived the idea of electrically stimulating the cortex from an observation that he made while dressing the head wound of a soldier in the Prussian war: mechanical irritation of the soldier's brain on one side caused twitching in the limbs on the opposite side.

The two colleagues performed successful experiments with a rabbit and then a dog in which they showed that stimulating the cortex electrically could produce movements. Furthermore, not only was the cortex excitable, it was selectively excitable. Stimulation of the frontal lobe produced movements on the opposite side of the body, whereas stimulation of the parietal lobe produced no

Electrical stimulation of the frontal lobe at various points produced movements on the opposite side of the body:

Neck
Forelimb
Hind limb

Cerebellum   Cortex

Spinal cord

Figure 1.11

Localizing Function In this drawing from Fritsch and Hitzig (1870), showing the dorsal view of a dog's brain, note that the dog's cortex does not completely cover the brainstem, and so the cerebellum is visible.

movement. Stimulation of restricted parts of the frontal lobe elicited movement of particular body parts—for example, neck, forelimb, and hind limb (**Figure 1.11**)—suggesting that the cortex forms topographic neural representations of the different parts of the body. The study of the **topographic organization** in many brain functions has subsequently remained a central focus of research.

The first experiment describing the electrical (faradic) stimulation of a human cortex was reported in 1874 by Roberts Bartholow (1831–1904), a Cincinnati physician. Mary Rafferty, a patient in his care, had a cranial defect that exposed a part of the cortex in each hemisphere. The following extract is from Bartholow's report:

> Observation 3. *To test faradic reaction of the posterior lobes.* Passed an insulated needle into the left posterior lobe so that the non-insulated portion rested entirely in the substance of the brain. The other insulated needle was placed in contact with the dura mater, within one-fourth of an inch of the first. When the circuit was closed, muscular contraction in the right upper and lower extremities ensued, as in the preceding observations. Faint but visible contraction of the left orbicularis palpebrarum [eyelid], and dilation of the pupils, also ensued. Mary complained of a very strong and unpleasant feeling of tingling in both right extremities, especially in the right arm, which she seized with the opposite hand and rubbed vigorously. Notwithstanding the very evident pain from which she suffered, she smiled as if much amused. (Bartholow, 1874)

Bartholow's publication caused a public outcry, and he was forced to leave Cincinnati. Nevertheless, he had demonstrated that the electrical-stimulation technique can be used with a conscious person, who can then report the subjective sensations produced by the stimulation. (The pain that Rafferty reported that she suffered was not caused by stimulation of pain receptors in the brain—because there are none—but was probably evoked by a part of the brain that normally receives pain messages from other parts of the body.)

Similar experiments can now be conducted without resorting to practices such as placing electrodes into the brains of conscious human subjects. By using transcranial magnetic stimulation (TMS), researchers induce electrical activation in the brain by passing a magnetized coil across the skull. This noninvasive technique allows investigators to study how the normal brain produces behavior and which parts of the brain take part in particular actions.

Connections Between Neurons As the Basis of Learning

In his book titled *The War of the Soups and the Sparks* published in 2005, neuropsychologist Elliott Valenstein recounts the remarkable events and debates about how neurons influence one another. In the early twentieth century, Alan Hodgkin (1914–1988) and Andrew Huxley (b. 1917), at Cambridge University in England, investigated how neurons conduct information. They were awarded the Nobel Prize in physiology in 1963 for their work, which explained that neurons generate brief electrical changes that are conveyed along the neuron's axon.

A puzzle remained: How does one neuron influence the next one? The "Soups" proposed that neurons release chemicals to influence the activity of other neurons and muscles. The "Sparks" proposed that electrical impulses simply travel from one neuron to the next.

Charles Scott Sherrington (1857–1952), an English physiologist, examined how nerves connect to muscles and first suggested that there is no continuous connection. He applied an unpleasant stimulation to a dog's paw, measured how long it took the dog to withdraw its foot, and compared that rate with the speed at which messages were known to travel along axons. According to Sherrington's calculations, the dog took 5 milliseconds too long to respond. Sherrington theorized that neurons are connected by junctions and that additional time is required for the message to get across the junction. He called these junctions **synapses** (from the Greek word for "clasp").

Otto Loewi (1873–1961) eventually demonstrated that chemicals carry the message across the synapse. His decisive and simple experiment consisted of electrically stimulating a nerve to the heart of a frog while washing fluid over the heart and collecting it. When he poured the fluid on the same heart or a second heart, its beating changed in the same way that the electrical stimulation had changed the first heart's beating rate.

The general assumption that developed in response to Loewi's discovery was that a synapse releases chemicals to influence the adjacent cell. In 1949, on the basis of this principle, Canadian neuropsychologist Donald Hebb (1904–1985) proposed a learning theory stating that, when individual cells are activated at the same time, they establish connecting synapses or strengthen existing ones and thus become a functional unit.

Hebb proposed that new or strengthened connections, sometimes called *Hebb* or *plastic synapses*, are the structural bases of memory. Just how synapses form and change is a vibrant area of research today, and this research has found that chemicals actually flow in both directions in a synapse. In doing so, they can change synapses. These changes in turn can be correlated with learning.

Acceptance of the idea that the brain is plastic and is constantly changing at each of its billions of synapses revolutionizes our view of the brain from one that represents "self" by a static structure to one that represents self by dynamic, ongoing reorganization. Consider that each day, as you muse, daydream, remember, and interact with others, you are both reinforcing the activity of millions of existing synapses and creating new synapses that collectively define your identity and allow you to interact with your world in a consistent way. This view has the brain not only representing who we are, but also representing who we are as a work in progress.

Contributions to Neuropsychology from Allied Fields

A number of developments from allied fields have contributed to the emergence of neuropsychology as a distinct scientific discipline: neurosurgery; **psychometrics** (the science of measuring human mental abilities) and statistical analysis; and technological advances that allow us to see a living brain.

(A)

Figure **1.12**

The Original Neurosurgery (A) A trephinated human skull. (B) Today, in the Zulu Nation of southern Africa, shamans carry a model skull indicating locations where holes should be made to relieve pressure on the brains of warriors who have suffered brain trauma in battle. (Part A, Keith and Betty Collins/ Visuals Unlimited; part B, Obed Zilwa/AP.)

Figure **1.13**

Contemporary Neurosurgery A human patient held in a stereotaxic device for brain surgery. The device allows the precise positioning of electrodes. (Michael English, M.D./Custom Medical Stock.)

Neurosurgery

Wilder Penfield (1891–1976) and Herbert Jasper (1906–1999) noted that anthropologists have found evidence of brain surgery dating to prehistoric times: neolithic skulls that show postsurgical healing have been found in Europe. The early Incas of Peru left similar skulls behind (**Figure 1.12**A). These ancient peoples likely found surgery to have a beneficial effect, perhaps by reducing pressure within the skull when an injured brain began to swell up.

(B)

Hippocrates gave written directions for **trephining** (cutting a circular hole in the skull) on the side of the head opposite the site of an injury as a means of therapeutic intervention to relieve pressure from a swelling brain. Between the thirteenth and nineteenth centuries, a number of attempts, some quite successful, to relieve various symptoms with surgery were documented. TBI and its treatment have a long history, and the trephination procedure continues to this day (Figure 1.12B).

The modern era in neurosurgery began with the introduction of antisepsis, anesthesia, and the principle of localization of function. In the 1880s, a number of surgeons reported success with operations for the treatment of brain abscesses, tumors, and epilepsy-producing scars. Later, the "stereotaxic device" was developed for holding the head in a fixed position (**Figure 1.13**). This device immobilizes the head by means of bars placed in the ear canals and under the front teeth. A brain atlas is then used to localize areas in the brain for surgery. Local anesthetic procedures were developed so that the patient could remain awake during surgery and contribute to the success of the operation by providing information about the effects of localized brain stimulation.

The development of neurosurgery as a practical solution to some types of brain abnormality in humans had an enormous influence on neuropsychology. The surgeon would draw a map of the lesion, sometimes after stimulating the surrounding tissue electrically to discover the exact extent of damage. As a result, good correlations were obtained between focal lesions in the brain and the changes in behavior that resulted from the lesions.

Information about behavior obtained from patients who have undergone neurosurgery is very useful for diagnosing the causes of problems in other patients. For example, if tissue removal in the temporal lobes is found to be related to subsequent memory problems (recall H.M.'s case), then people who develop memory problems also might have injury or disease of the temporal lobes.

Psychometrics and Statistical Evaluation

On superficial examination, the brains of different people look very similar, but they must be functionally very different to account for the vast differences in the abilities displayed by different people. The first systematic study into the cause of individual differences was made by Charles Darwin's cousin, Francis Galton (1822–1911). He maintained a laboratory in London in the 1880s, where he gave subjects three pennies to allow him to measure their physical features, perceptions, and reaction times with the goal of finding individual differences that could explain why some people were superior in ability to others. To Galton's surprise, the perceptual and reaction time differences that he measured did not distinguish between the people who he was predisposed to think were average and those he thought were intellectually gifted.

Galton's elegant innovation was to apply the statistical methods of Adolphe Quetelet (1796–1874), a Belgian statistician, to his results. Galton ranked his subjects on a frequency distribution, the so-called bell-shaped curve, a graphic representation showing that, on almost every factor measured, some people perform exceptionally well, some perform exceptionally poorly, and most fall somewhere in between. This innovation was essential for the development of modern psychological tests.

French biologist Alfred Binet (1857–1911) came up with a solution to Galton's problem of identifying who would perform poorly on a test. In 1904, the minister of public instruction commissioned Binet to develop tests to identify retarded children so that they could receive special instruction. The tests that he developed in collaboration with Theodore Simon were derived empirically by administering questions to 50 normal 3-to-11-year-old children and to some mentally retarded children and adults.

The Binet–Simon scale was revised in 1908; unsatisfactory tests were deleted, new tests were added, and the student population was increased to 300 children aged 3 to 13 years. From the tests, a mental level was calculated, a score attained by 80% to 90% of normal children of a particular age. In 1916, Lewis Terman (1877–1956) in the United States produced a version of the Stanford-Binet test in which the **intelligence quotient** (IQ)—mental age divided by chronological age times 100—was first used. He set the average intelligence level to equal an IQ score of 100.

Hebb first gave IQ tests to brain-damaged people in Montreal, Canada, in 1940, with the resultant surprising discovery that lesions in the frontal lobes—since Gall's time considered the center of highest intelligence—did not decrease IQ scores. Recall that L.D.'s frontal-lobe injuries produced impairments in executive function but not in intelligence. Lesions to other main areas not formerly thought to be implicated in "intelligence" did reduce IQ scores. This counterintuitive finding revealed the utility of such tests for assessing the location of brain damage and effectively created a bond of common interest between neurology and psychology.

Many clever innovations used for assessing brain function in various patient populations are strongly influenced by intelligence-testing methodology. The tests are brief, easily and objectively scored, and standardized with the use of statistical procedures. In addition, neuropsychologists use the IQ test to assess patients' general level of competence; many other tests that they administer are IQ-like in that they are rapidly administered paper-and-pencil tests. Although certain applications of "mental testing" are liable to criticism, even harsh critics concede that such tests have appropriate uses in neuropsychology. In turn, mental tests are continually being modified in light of new advances in neuropsychology.

Brain Imaging

In the early history of neuropsychology, relations between the brain and behavior could be made only at autopsy. This restriction often necessitated lags of many years before the effects of brain injury on behavior could be documented.

(A)

(B)

(C)

Figure 1.14

Brain-imaging Techniques

(A) CT scan showing the effects of stroke on the right side of the brain. (B) PET scan of blood flow in a normal brain. Areas of strongest flow appear in red; those of weakest flow appear in blue. (C) MRI showing a brain after removal of the left hemisphere. (Part A, Canadian Stroke Network; part B, Hank Morgan/Photo Researchers; part C, Dr. George Jallo/Johns Hopkins Hospital.)

Nevertheless, investigators such as French physician Jean-Martin Charcot (1825–1893), the director of a mental institution housing thousands of women patients, developed a method of collecting symptoms and relating them to brain pathology after death. One of his many discoveries was that **multiple sclerosis** (MS), a degenerative disease characterized by a loss of sensory and motor function, results from hardening (sclerosis means hardening) of nerve-fiber pathways in the spinal cord.

Today, brain imaging not only allows rapid correlation between symptoms and brain pathology but is as well an essential tool for diagnosis. A variety of brain-imaging methods take advantage of the ability of computers to reconstruct two- and three-dimensional images of the brain. The images describe regional differences in structure or function, electrical activity, cell density, or chemical activity (such as the amount of glucose that a cell is using or the amount of oxygen that it is consuming). The principal imaging methods illustrated in **Figure 1.14** are:

- **Computerized tomography** (CT) scanning entails the passage of X-rays through the head. The X-rays are absorbed less by fluid than by brain cells and less by brain cells than by bone. When the X-rays expose a photographic negative, brain injury can be visualized, because dead cells in the injured area contain more water than do healthy living brain cells and thus produce a darker image on the scan. A computer can generate a three-dimensional image of the brain and thus a three-dimensional image of the region of brain injury.

- **Positron emission tomography** (PET) entails the injection of radioactive substances that decay in minutes into the bloodstream so that they reach the brain. As the radioactivity decays, it gives off photons that are detected by Geiger counters placed around the head. A computer calculates the location from which the photons originate and draws the location on a two- or three-dimensional reconstruction of the brain. For example, if a radioactive form of oxygen is administered, parts of the brain that are more active (use more oxygen) can be identified and correlated with the behavior in which a test subject is engaging. Damaged brain areas will use less oxygen. PET is also useful for studying areas of the brain that are engaged in normal behaviors such as speaking, reading, and writing.

- **Magnetic resonance imaging** (MRI) calculates the location of moving molecules by detecting the electrical charge generated by their movement.

Because brain tissue varies in the concentration of molecules (for example, nerve fibers versus cell bodies), MRI can use regional differences to reveal excellent images of the brain. MRI can also determine the relative concentrations of oxygen and carbon dioxide and so can be used to determine regional differences in brain activity. Thus, brain function (functional MRI, or fMRI) can be imaged and superimposed on brain anatomy (MRI).

The strengths of the varying imaging procedures are different. CT scans can be obtained quickly and cheaply. PET can image many chemicals; thus, diseases in which there are chemical changes can be easily imaged. MRI has very high resolution and can create lifelike images of the brain and provide excellent detail of brain areas active during behavior. In sum, not only can imaging techniques reveal dead tissue formerly accessible only at autopsy, but they can also identify brain regions that are active with a moment-to-moment resolution. Imaging has greatly expanded the kinds of studies that neuropsychologists can conduct to study function, both in normal and in injured brains. From MRI images of many hundreds of subjects, scientists are producing a functional atlas of the human brain, something that phrenology attempted but failed.

Summary

This chapter has sketched the history of two formative ideas in neuropsychology: (1) the brain is the source of behavior and (2) the neuron is its functional unit. In summarizing this history, the chapter has also examined the origin of some major ideas about how the brain functions. The history that led to the current science of neuropsychology is long, and the advances presented here are selective. What we describe as major advances were, taken in context, the small discoveries that tend to cap a long period of investigation by many people.

The Brain Hypothesis

The brain's nearly symmetrical left and right cerebral hemispheres feature a folded outer layer called the cortex, which is divided into four lobes: temporal, frontal, parietal, and occipital. The brain and spinal cord together make up the central nervous system. All the nerve fibers radiating out beyond the CNS as well as all the neurons outside the brain and spinal cord form the peripheral nervous system. Sensory pathways in the PNS carry information to the CNS; motor pathways carry instructions from the CNS to muscles and tissues of the body.

Mentalism is the view that behavior is a product of an intangible entity called the mind. Dualism is the notion that the mind acts through the brain to produce higher functions such as language and rational behavior, whereas the brain alone is responsible for lower functions that we have in common with other animals. Materialism, the view that all behavior—language and reasoning included—can be fully accounted for by brain function, guides contemporary research in neuroscience.

Experimental Approaches to Brain Function

Early scientists argued about whether each specific brain function—language, for example—is localized in a particular part of the brain or whether many different brain areas participate to produce the function. The conclusion is that brain functions are localized and require the participation of a number of different brain areas as well. In addition to producing behavior that appears to be accessible to conscious examination, the brain produces a surprising array of complex behavior that is not so accessible. As described in the Portrait of L.D., who suffered from traumatic brain injury, damage in the cortex often leaves some complex functions intact but damages others. The theories of hierarchical organization, distributed function, and parallel processing all appear to correspond to the step-by-step evolution of the brain, with each step adding a new level of complexity to behavior.

The Neuron Hypothesis

The brain is composed of nerve cells, and these neurons are its functional units. Neurons send electrical signals along their dendrites and axons by chemical means. Neurons exchange information by using chemical messages that they secrete at their synapses. Neurons are plastic and can change many aspects of their function, thus mediating learning.

Contributions to Neuropsychology from Allied Fields

Studies of human surgical patients with well-localized brain lesions, improvements in the use of statistics to develop and interpret behavioral tests, and the continuing development of brain imaging have all provided new ways of evaluating favored neuropsychological theories.

References

Bartholow, R. Experimental investigation into the functions of the human brain. *American Journal of Medical Sciences* 67:305–313, 1874.

Benton, A. L. Contributions to aphasia before Broca. *Cortex* 1:314–327, 1964.

Brazier, M. A. B. The historical development of neurophysiology. In J. Field, H. W. Magoun, and V. E. Hall, Eds. *Handbook of Physiology*, vol. 1. Washington, D.C.: American Physiological Society, 1959.

Broca, P. Sur le siege de la faculte du langage articule. *Bulletin of the Society of Anthropology* 6:377–396, 1865.

Broca, P. Remarks on the seat of the faculty of articulate language, followed by an observation of aphemia. In G. von Bonin, Ed. *The Cerebral Cortex*. Springfield, Ill.: Charles C. Thomas, 1960.

Clark, E., and C. D. O'Malley. *The Human Brain and Spinal Cord*. Berkeley and Los Angeles: University of California Press, 1968.

Corkin S. What's new with the amnesic patient H.M.? *Nature Reviews Neuroscience* 3(2):153–160, 2000.

Descartes, R. *Traite de l'homme*. Paris: Angot, 1664.

Finger, S. *Origins of Neuroscience*. New York: Oxford University Press, 1994.

Flourens, P. Investigations of the properties and the functions of the various parts which compose the cerebral mass. In G. von Bonin, Ed. *The Cerebral Cortex*. Springfield, Ill.: Charles C. Thomas, 1960.

Fritsch, G., and E. Hitzig. On the electrical excitability of the cerebrum. In G. von Bonin, Ed., *The Cerebral Cortex*. Springfield, Ill.: Charles C. Thomas, 1960.

Gazzaniga, M., J. E. Bogen, and R. W. Sperry. Some functional effects of sectioning of the cerebral commissures in man. *Proceedings of the National Academy of Sciences* 48:1765–1769, 1962.

Geschwind, N. *Selected Papers on Language and Brain*. Dordrecht, Holland, and Boston: D. Reidel, 1974.

Goltz, F. On the functions of the hemispheres. In G. von Bonin, Ed. *The Cerebral Cortex*. Springfield, Ill.: Charles C. Thomas, 1960.

Goodale, M. A., and D. A. Milner. *Sight Unseen: An Exploration of Conscious and Unconscious Vision*. Oxford, U.K.: Oxford University Press, 2004.

Gould, S. J. *The Mismeasure of Man*. New York: Norton, 1981.

Head, H. *Aphasia and Kindred Disorders of Speech*. London: Cambridge University Press, 1926.

Hebb, D. O. *The Organization of Behavior: A Neuropsychological Theory*. New York: Wiley, 1949.

Hebb, D. O., and W. Penfield. Human behavior after extensive bilateral removals from the frontal lobes. *Archives of Neurology and Psychiatry* 44:421–438, 1940.

Hughlings-Jackson, J. *Selected Writings of John Hughlings-Jackson*, J. Taylor, Ed., vols. 1 and 2. London: Hodder, 1931.

Joynt, R. Paul Pierre Broca: His contribution to the knowledge of aphasia. *Cortex* 1:206–213, 1964.

Krech, D. Cortical localization of function. In L. Postman, Ed. *Psychology in the Making*. New York: Knopf, 1962.

Marie, P. The third left frontal convolution plays no special role in the function of language. *Semaine Medicale* 26:241–247. Reprinted in *Pierre Marie's Papers on Speech Disorders*, M. F. Cole and M. Cole, Eds. New York: Hafner, 1906, 1971.

Olin, C. H. *Phrenology*. Philadelphia: Penn Publishing, 1910.

Penfield, W., and H. Jasper. *Epilepsy and the Functional Anatomy of the Human Brain*. Boston: Little, Brown, 1954.

Ramón y Cajal, S. *Recollections of My Life*, E. Horne Craigie, Trans., with assistance from J. Cano. Cambridge, Mass.: MIT Press, 1937, 1989.

Scoville, W. B., and B. Milner. Loss of recent memory after bilateral hippocampal lesions. *Journal of Neuropsychiatry and Clinical Neuroscience* 20(1):11–21, 1957.

Stookey, B. A note on the early history of cerebral localization. *Bulletin of the New York Academy of Medicine* 30:559–578, 1954.

Sperry, R. W. Some Effects of Disconnecting the Cerebral Hemispheres. Nobel Lecture, December 8, 1981.

Valenstein, E. S. *The War of the Soups and the Sparks*. New York: Columbia University Press, 2005.

Wernicke, C. *Der aphasische Symptomenkomplex*. Breslau, Poland: M. Cohn and Weigert, 1874.

Young, R. M. *Mind, Brain and Adaption in the Nineteenth Century*. Oxford: Clarendon Press, 1970.

Origins of the Human Brain and Behavior

P O R T R A I T : Evolving a Capacity for Language

Language is such a striking human characteristic that Descartes proposed it as a defining attribute of the presence of a mind. Language, among other traits, was once thought to be unique to humans. Yet evolutionary theory predicts a step-by-step progression, each step adding a new level of complexity to behaviors, including language. Like tool-making, language hardly appeared suddenly and full-blown in modern humans. These cognitive skills have antecedents in other species, especially the species most closely related to us.

The first attempt to teach human vocal language to chimpanzees was an abject failure. Not until 1971, when Allen and Beatrice Gardner taught a version of American Sign Language to a chimp called Washoe, did researchers realize that nonverbal communication might have preceded verbal language. To test this hypothesis, Sue Savage-Rumbaugh and her coworkers began teaching a pygmy chimpanzee called Malatta

Great Ape Trust of Iowa

a symbolic language called Yerkish. (The pygmy chimpanzee, or bonobo, is a species thought to be an even closer relative of humans than the common chimp.)

Malatta and her son Kanzi were caught in the wild, and Kanzi accompanied his mother to class. Even though he was not specifically trained, Kanzi learned more Yerkish than his mother did. Remarkably, Kanzi also displayed clear evidence of understanding complex human speech.

Realizing that chimps in the wild have a rich vocal repetoire and are especially vocal in producing peeps in association with food, Jared Taglialatela (pictured above with Kanzi) and

his coworkers recorded Kanzi's vocalizations when he was interacting with people and eating different kinds of foods. From video records of many interactions with humans, the scientists selected vocalizations associated with "banana," "grape," "juice," and "yes." Spectral analysis of the sounds associated with the semantic context or meaning of each condition were analyzed to determine whether the peeps uttered by Kanzi were similar in similar situations and distinct in different situations.

The analyses confirmed that Kanzi's peeps were indeed similar for vocalizations made within a specific semantic context and structurally different between the different contexts. Although Kanzi is a language-competent chimp, the finding that he uses "chimpanzeeish" in specific situations in his interactions with humans provides further support for the idea that human language may derive from more-primitive forms of communication used by human ancestors.

K anzi, like all of us humans, belongs to the primate order, a group of animal families that includes lemurs, tarsiers, monkeys, and apes, all having diverged from a common ancestor. The primate order is shown in **Figure 2.1** in the form of a **cladogram**, a graph that shows the relative time of origin of various closely related groups. Each branch point in a cladogram distinguishes animals positioned before that time point from animals positioned after it by one or more physical or behavioral traits. All apes, for example, can raise their arms to brachiate (swing through the trees). No primate preceding the ape can do so.

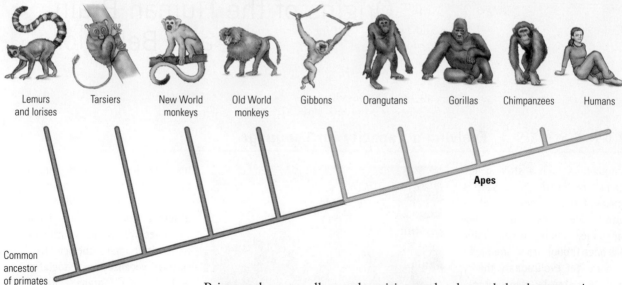

| Lemurs and lorises | Tarsiers | New World monkeys | Old World monkeys | Gibbons | Orangutans | Gorillas | Chimpanzees | Humans |

Apes

Common ancestor of primates

Figure 2.1

The Primates This cladogram illustrates relationships among families of the primate order. Humans are members of the ape family. In general, brain size increases from left to right across the groupings, with humans having the largest brains in the family.

Primates have excellent color vision and enhanced depth perception, and they use this excellent vision to deftly guide their hand movements. Female primates usually produce only one infant per pregnancy, and they spend a great deal more time caring for their young than most other animals do.

In the past 5 million to 8 million years, **hominids**, our humanlike ancestors, diverged from this ancestral ape lineage by acquiring characteristics that distinguished them from other apes. Hominids were taller, and there was less difference in height between males and females. They were bipedal, had long legs, and were such great travelers that their descendants have populated every habitable continent.

Changes in hominid hand structure allowed the skilled use of tools. Changes in tooth structure and a massive reduction in jaw size facilitated the consumption of a more varied diet. The hominid brain underwent an unmatched evolution in size, increasing to more than three times its original volume. Important clues to understanding the brain of the modern human come from considering the brain's origins, the evolutionary forces that sculpted it, and how investigators describe its function by studying the nervous systems of other animals.

Species Comparison

Recall from Chapter 1 that dualists reason for a sharp distinction between studying the human brain and behavior and studying nonhuman animal brains. Like Descartes, they believe that the human mind is special and separate from the body and brain. Dualists also rely on the observation that human behavior is more complex than that of other animals. After all, humans talk, read, write, and do all sorts of things that monkeys and rats do not and cannot do. Consequently, dualists may assume that both human neuroanatomy and human cognitive processes differ fundamentally from those of other animals.

Why Study Nonhuman Animals?

Comparative studies of the brain and behavior of different animal species do not dispute that the human brain and human behavior are different from those of other animals. But, as demonstrated by Kanzi, they also reveal many similarities between humans and other animals that can shed light on human evolution. Consider the anatomical and behavioral similarities between humans and their closest relatives, chimpanzees—the many similarities in physical stature and facial features and expressions, for example. The brains of both species are very similar in appearance and in structure, although the chimpanzee brain is smaller. Both humans and chimpanzees have behavioral traits in common, including social living, tool use, and omnivorous foraging.

Psychologists who work with chimps and other apes assume that the things that they learn about our closest animal cousin apply to the human brain and to human behavior. Researchers also find comparisons with more distantly related species, such as rats or cats and even slugs and fruit flies, informative.

The behavior of the rat, for example, is extremely complex. Most structures of the rat brain are much like those of the human brain, and cortical function in laboratory rats is remarkably similar to that of humans. Slugs are useful for studying how neurons interconnect to produce behavior because their nervous system is relatively simple. Fruit flies are useful for studying the genetic basis of behavior because many generations of flies with nervous system alterations can be bred quickly in the laboratory. (**Genes** are the functional units that control the transmission and expression of traits from one generation to the next.)

In emphasizing the utility of interspecies comparisons, we are not saying that other animals are merely little people in fur suits, but without socks and shoes. We are emphasizing, rather, that the similarities between humans, monkeys, rats, and other animals show that studying them makes an important contribution toward understanding human behavior–brain relations. Behavior–brain comparisons across species provide information that is difficult to obtain from studying a single species, even one as interesting as humans. Additionally, the behavior–brain relations of other animals are interesting in themselves, as bird watchers, pet owners, and animal husbandry confirm.

The differences between the brains and behaviors of different animal species are as informative as their similarities (**Figure 2.2**). The brains of birds are clearly similar to those of mammals, but the arrangement of component structures is different. Birds have no cerebral cortex as such, which is externally the most imposing feature of the mammalian brain.

Figure **2.2**

Brain Evolution The brains of fish, frogs, birds, and people have many structures in common, illustrating a single basic brain plan across species having central nervous systems.

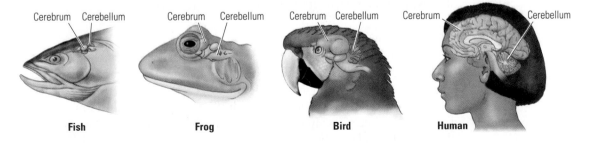

Fish   Frog   Bird   Human

Cerebrum   Cerebellum

The rodents are evolutionarily the most closely related order to the primates. Yet the rodent brain is distinguished by having large olfactory bulbs and a small cerebral cortex, whereas primates have small olfactory bulbs and a large cerebral cortex. More striking still are differences between the brains of dolphins and other species of whales and those of terrestrial mammals. Many whale species have neither olfactory bulbs nor some cortical structures associated with olfactory bulbs.

In terrestrial mammals, the cortical structures associated with the olfactory bulbs are the hippocampus in the temporal lobe, thought to take part in memory, and some parts of the frontal cortex, thought to take part in social behavior. Yet dolphins and whales have good memories and engage in complex social behavior. Clearly, many discoveries are yet to be made before we understand how the brain has adapted to produce typical behavior in different species of animals.

Questions Addressed by Studying Nonhuman Animals

Three primary lines of research drive neuropsychological investigations with animals: (1) understanding basic brain mechanisms, (2) designing animal models of human neurological disorders, and (3) describing the phylogenetic (evolutionary) development of the brain. We shall consider each line separately.

Understanding Brain Mechanisms

Cross-species comparisons in neuropsychology are designed to arrive at an understanding of the basic mechanisms of brain function—for example, vision. The eye takes vastly different forms in different species. Fruit flies and mammals have eyes that apparently have little in common, and their differences were taken as evidence that the eye evolved a number of times. But results from studies of the genes responsible for encoding information about how the eye will develop in various species show that the same genes are implicated in all species.

According to Claudia Hetzer-Egger and coworkers, a gene called *Pax* is responsible for eye development in all seeing animals, demonstrating a much closer relationship among very diverse kinds of animals than had been suspected previously. Similar genes, called *homeobox genes*, dictate body segmentation in both fruit flies and humans. Thus, segmentation of the human nervous system into the spinal cord, brainstem, and forebrain is produced by genes first discovered in fruit flies. The differences in the structure of the eye and the nervous system in different animal species are the products of slight alterations, called **mutations**, in genes such as *Pax* and in the way in which the products of those genes interact with the products of other genes.

Designing Animal Models

The second goal of comparative research is to design animal models of human neurological disorders. Research animals substitute for humans because similar principles are assumed to underlie the emergence and treatment of a disorder in humans and nonhumans alike. Ideally, researchers want to produce the disorder in animals, manipulate multiple variables to understand its cause, and ultimately formulate a treatment.

For example, **Parkinson's disease** is associated with aging in humans and can affect as many as 1% of the population older than 65 years of age. The symptoms include rigidity that impedes voluntary movement, balance problems, and tremors of the head, hands, and limbs. The cause of Parkinson's disease is unknown, however, and there is no cure. Thus, scientists have three goals in finding treatments: to prevent the disease, to slow its progression once it has developed, and to treat symptoms as the disease progresses.

Parkinson models have been developed in the mouse, rat, and monkey. A major symptomatic treatment for human Parkinson's disease, the drug L-dopa, was developed by studying rats that had a similar form of the disease.

Describing Evolutionary Adaptations

The study of the evolutionary development of the human brain is as important to understanding what humans are as the study of infants is to understanding what adults are. Comparative research on how the mammalian brain and behavior evolved progresses in three ways:

1. Experiments with rats, cats, rhesus monkeys, and other mammals permit inferences about how the environment in which each species lived shaped its evolution, brain, and behavior. All mammalian species evolved independently from some common ancestor, as shown in **Figure 2.3**.

2. Because mammalian species are related, commonalities tell us what humans inherited in common with other mammals and, especially, with the species in our own primate lineage.

3. Differences in the brains and behaviors of different species are sources of insight into how species and individual differences arose.

A salient attribute of modern humans is tool use. Evidence for tool use is found both in living humans and in their extinct predecessors. But tool use is also found among other species, including many species of birds. In research described in the Snapshot on the next page, the surface area of the cerebellums of tool-using birds is larger than that of birds that do not use tools. From this discovery, we can generalize that the evolution and elaboration of the human cerebellum is associated with the development of tool use.

Figure **2.3**

Mammals Phylogenetic tree showing the times of origin and affinities of the orders of mammals most commonly studied in comparative psychology and neuropsychology. Note that all contemporary species are the same evolutionary age. (After Young, 1962.)

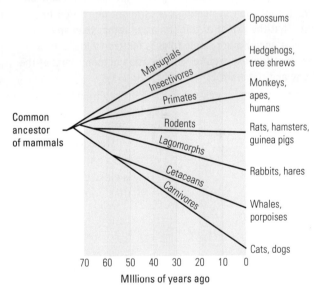

Use of a Quasi-evolutionary Sequence

To conduct comparative investigations from a phylogenetic perspective, researchers choose species that constitute what William Hodos and C. B. G. Campbell term a **quasi-evolutionary sequence**, a hypothetical sequence of animals that represent consecutive stages in evolutionary history. In some cases, an animal can be chosen because it is the living descendant of an extinct ancestor. The lineage of humans includes ancestors of hedgehogs, tree shrews, bush babies, monkeys, and apes, including earlier humans (**Figure 2.4**).

Tool use was once considered the exclusive domain of humans but is now recognized in all the great apes, other primates, and in birds, including parrots, corvids, herons, and raptors. Comparative research on nonhuman species allows for contrast among the behaviors and brains of many living species occupying widely different habitats.

The evolution of tool use in both taxa is correlated with significant increases in the relative size of the brain. Andrew Iwaniuk and his colleagues examined whether the size of the cerebellum and the extent of its foliation (Figure A)—that is, its folding—are related to tool use. Taking advantage of the many species of birds that do and do not use tools, they compared the volume and the extent of foliation (degree of folding) in the cerebellums of birds that use tools with those that do not. The investigators found that, although the volume of the brain in tool users was, if anything, smaller than that in those not using tools, the extent of foliation was positively correlated with tool use.

A similar trend toward a relatively smaller cerebellum but greater foliation in hominids thus might be related to tool use. That the extent of total foliation rather than an expansion of one or more single folds is related to tool use signifies that tool use requires coordination of many parts of the body and the brain.

(A) Cresyl violet stained section of the cerebellum of the Australian magpie, a tool user. (B) MRI representation of the brain of a living bird showing the forebrain and cerebellum. The blurry image is an artifact of the size of the brain and the limits of the technology. (Part A, Iwaniuk et al., 2006; part B, Van Meir et al., 2006.)

The development of magnetic resonance imaging procedures for animals, especially small animals, allows the study and measurement of brains of living animals of many species, as shown in an MRI image of the starling brain (Figure B).

Iwaniuk, A. N., L. Lefebvre, and D. R. Wong-Wylie. The role of the cerebellum in the evolution of tool using behavior in birds. *Brain, Behavior and Evolution* 68:113, 2006.

Researchers assume that the evolutionarily older present-day animals resemble a common ancestor closely enough to stand for it. A present-day chimpanzee is close enough to the common ancestor of chimpanzees and humans to stand for that common ancestor, and a present-day hedgehog is similar enough to the

Figure 2.4

Quasi-evolutionary Lineage Neuropsychologists regard such living animals as hedgehogs, tree shrews, bush babies, monkeys, and apes as close approximations of the ancestors of humans. Phylogenetic relationships thus represent brain changes that occurred at the branches in this quasi-evolutionary sequence. (After Masterton and Skeen, 1972.)

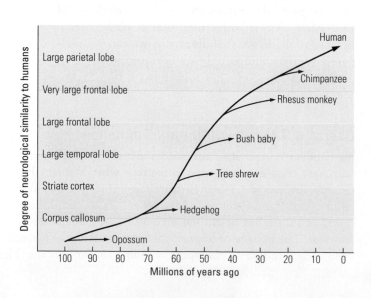

common ancestor of the primate lineage to stand for the common ancestor of all primates.

When a quasi-evolutionary sequence is constructed for the primate lineage, a comparison of the brains and behaviors of the animals in the sequence reveals a correspondence between new structural developments and new behaviors. For example, in tree shrews, the presence of *striate cortex* (primary visual cortex with a striped appearance) confers on shrews an ability to see branches, heights, and insects. This ability is not important to (and striate cortex is not present in) the ground-dwelling hedgehog, which represents an earlier stage in the sequence shown in Figure 2.4. It is from the tree shrew that we inherit our massive striate cortex.

By the same token, the large temporal lobe in the bush baby is related to this animal's ability to select for itself a highly varied diet of insects, fruits, leaves, and more, and, correspondingly, for the excellent human memory. The large frontal lobes of the rhesus monkey are related to its very complex group social life and to the complex social life of humans. The large parietal lobe of humans is probably a correlate of our ability to perform the skilled movements required in tool making.

Thus, the evolution of new brain features in living primates explains the evolution of the brain and behavior of humans. The same quasi-evolutionary sequence is used to analyze the genetic basis of neural and behavioral evolution in primates. For example, Michael Oldham and Daniel Geschwind are now using comparative genetic analysis of this quasi-evolutionary sequence of primates to investigate the neural basis for the origins of language and other behaviors.

Human Origins

Our knowledge about human origins began in 1859 with Darwin's publication of *On the Origin of Species by Means of Natural Selection*. Later, in 1871, Darwin concluded in his book titled *The Descent of Man* that humans descended from an ancestral "hairy, tailed quadruped, probably arboreal in its habits."

Speciation occurred very rapidly in the hominid lineage. Multicellular animals have existed on Earth for 650 million years, mammals have existed for 150 million years, and monkeylike mammals, or primates, for about 25 million. Yet dozens of hominid species have appeared and disappeared in only the past 8 million years.

Hominid Evolution

The evolution of humans from an ape ancestor to *Homo sapiens* is not linear. The hominid family tree is a bush: for most of its history, many family members were alive at the same time. As recently as 20,000 to 40,000 years ago, a number of human species coexisted, including modern humans, Neanderthals in Europe, a newly discovered species, *Homo floresiensis*, on the island of Flores in Indonesia, and perhaps other species yet to be discovered. Today, however, our species is the only surviving member, sitting alone on the last living hominid branch. The three general lines of research through which scientists attempt to reconstruct the story of human evolution are archeological, biochemical and genetic, and behavioral.

Archeological Research

Using the ages of the sediments within which the bones of different hominids are found, archeologists have created a lineage of hominid species that includes their approximate time of origin. Skull casts are sources of insight into brain structure. Examination of the habitat in which these hominid species lived and the tools that they used can be sources of insight into their behavior. With the use of similar archeological methods, the features and behavior of other modern human ancestors can be reconstructed.

By using morphological reconstruction, for example, investigators can approximate the appearance of a hominid body, often from only skeletal remains, to reveal similarities and differences between hominids and us. **Figure 2.5** shows a morphological reconstruction of Neanderthal, a hominid species related to modern humans who lived in Europe but disappeared about 40,000 years ago. Contrary to the original assumption that the Neanderthal people were brutish, stooped characters, reconstructions demonstrate how similar to us they really were.

Archeologists generally agree that Neanderthal people used tools very similar to the tools used by *Homo sapiens* living at that time. They also lived in similar family groups, made music, and buried their dead. From these insights, we can infer that Neanderthals probably communicated by using language and held religious beliefs.

Biochemical and Genetic Research

Evidence for rapid hominid speciation is supported by biochemical research. The amino acid sequence of a cellular protein in one species can be compared with the amino acid sequence of the same protein in another species. A change in one amino acid may occur on average about once every million years, and so the differences between proteins provide a molecular clock that can be used to compare the ages of different species.

For example, geological evidence says Old World and New World monkeys diverged from each other 30 million years ago. Their 24 differences in albumin amino acids suggest a rate of one amino acid change every 1.25 million years. If we apply this rate of change to apes, we can conclude that chimpanzees and humans diverged from each other between 5 million and 8 million years ago.

Figure 2.5

Neanderthal Man The reconstructed facial features of a Neanderthal contrast markedly with previous depictions that represented them as dull witted and stooped. To create this morphological reconstruction, from the bare bones shown at the left, temporal muscles and an outline of the skin are added. Arrows mark points where thickness is based on needle probes of humans or orangutans. Nose shape is based on projections from bony landmarks. (Reconstruction by Jay Matternes. From B. Rensberger. Facing the past. *Science* 41–81, October 1981. Copyright © 1981. Reprinted with permission.)

The relatedness of different species can also be determined by comparing their **deoxyribonucleic acid** (DNA), the genetic material in the nucleus of the cell. Genes are segments of DNA that specify what proteins a cell should make. Each gene is a long chain of four kinds of nucleotide bases. Through mutations, the sequence of bases can change to some extent and still leave a functional gene.

Researchers can identify the sequence of nucleotide bases in different genes and compare the genes of different species. They can even recapture the DNA from the fossils of long-extinct animals. Signatures of modern humans and chimpanzees suggest that they have 99% of their genes in common and are each other's closest living relatives. So chimps and humans have a common ancestor. Obviously, the difference of 1% produces a huge difference between the two species. As progress in describing the **genome**, the full set of genes of a species, improves, an ideal description of human evolution would include information on what genetic modifications led to the evolution of modern humans.

Behavioral Research

Comparative behavioral research yields evidence for theories about human evolution. Ethologist Jane Goodall's behavioral studies of chimpanzees paint a picture of a species so similar to humans that one has the impression of looking into a mirror. These animals occupy large territories that the males defend as a group. The males wage war and kill neighbors to expand their territories.

Chimps are great travelers, ambulating along the ground at a rate that humans have difficulty matching for distances of 8 kilometers or more a day. They are omnivores, eating vegetation, fruit, and insects, but they can also hunt cooperatively to catch monkeys, pigs, and other mammals. They live in complex social groups within which family relations are important both for the individual chimpanzee and for the group structure. They have rich manual, facial, and vocal communication capabilities, and they construct and use tools for defense and to obtain food and water.

After experience with a mirror, a chimpanzee points to a dot that has been placed on its forehead. Gallup's mirror test demonstrates that self-recognition is a cognitive ability displayed by higher primates. (Courtesy of Cognitive Evolution Group, University of Louisiana at Lafayette, New Iberia Research.)

Stages of Human Evolution

Recall that our family tree is bushy, and so, in **Figure 2.6**A, representative species are shown disconnected rather than in a connected evolutionary sequence. The behavioral changes in this sequence, including tool making, were associated with the increases in brain size illustrated in Figure 2.6B. Investigators agree that four general steps led from a chimpanzee-like common ancestor to modern humans. These steps were the evolution in hominids of

1. an upright posture in which the hands were free;

2. extensive tool use;

3. a traveling life style; and

4. an elaborate culture.

We now trace these four stages in the evolution of modern humans.

(A)

(B)

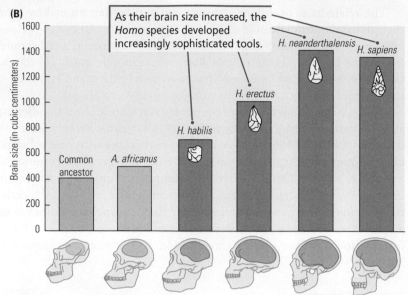

As their brain size increased, the *Homo* species developed increasingly sophisticated tools.

Figure **2.6**

Origins of Humans (A) Relation in time of some recognized species of the human family. Because the exact relationships among hominid species are not known, they constitute a discontinuous sequence. (B) Increases in brain volume. Notice the development of tools by the *Homo* species. (After Stanley, 1981, and Johanson and Edey, 1981.)

Australopithecus: Upright Posture

The ancestor of all hominids was an animal somewhat like *Australopithecus* (*Australo*, meaning "southern" and *pithecus*, meaning "ape"). The name was coined by an Australian anthropologist, Raymond Dart, for a find that he made in South Africa (he was probably feeling homesick). These animals lived in eastern Africa and possessed a distinctly human characteristic: they walked upright.

The conclusion that they walked upright is based on the description of numerous bones and on the discovery of fossilized footprints dated from 3.6 million to 3.8 million years ago. The footprints feature a well-developed arch and big toe and point straight ahead, a pattern much more like that of humans than that of apes. Fossilized remains show that many distinct species of *Australopithecus* lived in East Africa and Ethiopia.

Why did the hominid lineage diverge from its ape ancestor? Climate change was an important evolutionary determinant. For example, Yves Coppens advanced what he calls the "east side theory." Geological deposits on the eastern side of the Great Rift Valley, which runs from north to south and divides Africa in two, have yielded many fossils of hominids deposited through millions of years, but no fossils of apes at all. On the western side of the Rift Valley, the fossil record indicates that chimpanzees and gorillas currently live pretty much unchanged from their ancestors of more than 15 million years ago.

Coppens proposed that, about 8 million years ago, a tectonic crisis (a deformation of Earth's crust) produced the Great Rift Valley, leaving a wet jungle climate to the west and a much drier climate to the east. To the west, the apes continued unchanged, whereas, to the east, the apes had to evolve rapidly to survive in the mixture of trees and grass that formed their new brushwood habitat.

A distinctive feature of the new hominids was a change in dentition that included a reduction in the size of the incisors and a flattening of the molars. These animals were able to consume a much more varied diet than that consumed by ancestral apes. Their legs were longer, too, and thus better suited to over-ground locomotion.

Two versions of how the evolution of hominids took place vie for prominence. The *down-from-trees hypothesis* proposes that the trees being farther apart required apes to adopt bipedal locomotion. The accompanying change in posture reduced the area of the body exposed to the sun and permitted the loss of body hair. The *water-baby hypothesis*, proposed by Alister Hardy, suggests a different order of events, beginning with a hypothetical naked ape swimming and foraging on ocean beaches and later forced to abandon its semiaquatic habitat when the ocean receded. In this scenario, the animal is described as finding bipedalism and lack of body hair advantageous in swimming; it then retains these features when it adapts to the land.

Whichever story is correct, the ape continued to climb trees but changed to an upright posture and adopted a much more varied diet. As shown in Figure 2.6B, brain size did not change much, an indication that changes in brain size could not have been due simply to adopting an upright posture and thus having the hands free.

Homo habilis: Tool Use

The oldest fossils designated as *Homo* (the genus to which modern humans belong) were found by English anthropologist Louis Leakey in the Olduvai Gorge in Tanzania in 1964, dated at about 1.75 million years old. The specimens bear a strong resemblance to *Australopithecus*, but Leakey argued that the dental pattern is more similar to that of modern humans. The characteristic of these animals was that they made stone tools, which also were found in the Olduvai Gorge, and so Leakey named the species *Homo habilis* (that is, "handy people").

Coppens argued that the appearance of *Homo habilis* was also related to climatic change. He studied a geological site on the Omo River that contains a continuous stratigraphic record starting 4 million years ago and ending 1 million years ago. The record indicates that, 4 million years ago, the climate was more humid and the vegetation was brushwood, whereas, 1 million years ago, the area was less humid and the vegetation was savanna or grassland with only sporadic trees. It was in the latter period that *Homo habilis* appeared, having a distinctively larger brain and using tools (see Figure 2.6).

Robert Blumenschine and John Cavallo (1992), propose that the most likely ecological niche for a savanna hominid to occupy was that of a scavenger. Many animals died from age, hunger during droughts, or predation. Carcasses could be found on the open savanna around water holes or in trees where they had been stored by predators such as leopards. The meat would be fresh for a day or two after death.

A scavenger that could locate and butcher animal carcasses quickly by daylight could compete with nocturnal scavengers such as jackals and large cats and so would have an ample supply of food. Such a scavenger would have to learn to read the environment and watch the activities of vultures, predators, and animal herds. It would also have to be a good carrier to retreat quickly to the safety of trees or rocks without abandoning the meat and bones. Lacking the sharp teeth (for tearing skin) and strong jaws (for crushing bones to get the marrow) that other scavengers possessed, the new scavenger would need tools and to learn to fashion them from sharp flakes of rock by using stone hammers.

Importantly, scavenging, toolmaking, and butchering would have been a family affair. Children, with their keen eyesight, would have made an important contribution by locating carcasses, and the entire community would have participated in toolmaking, butchering, and carrying.

Homo erectus: The Traveler

Homo habilis gave rise to another species, *Homo erectus* ("upright people"), so named because of a mistaken notion that its predecessors were stooped. It first shows up in the fossil record about 1.9 million years ago and survived until quite recently. *Homo erectus* has a pivotal position in hominid history.

Its brain was significantly larger than that of any preceding animal (see Figure 2.6). Unlike *Australopithecus* and *Homo habilis*, this creature was a globetrotter: its remains are found in East Africa as well as in Java (Java man) and China (Peking man). *Homo erectus* first left Africa about 1.9 million years ago, making a number of new incursions into Europe and Asia in the next million years.

Homo sapiens: Elaborating Culture

A distinguishing behavioral feature of modern humans is their various cultures, including language, art, and science; and political organization, agriculture, and other complex economic relations. In their explanation of the origins of *Homo sapiens*, Alan Thorne and Mildred Wolpoff (1992) argue that modern humans evolved in many places from *Homo erectus*, at about the same rate. New adaptive genes, such as those that might have increased brain size and behavioral abilities, were disseminated throughout these diverse populations by migration, trade, and other social interactions. Nevertheless, regional differences in people persisted, just as they do today.

Another explanation is that modern humans had a distinct origin. Rebecca Cann and her coworkers suggest that all modern people descended from an ancestral "Eve" who lived in Africa about 200,000 years ago and whose ancestors migrated out of Africa to populate the rest of the world. They base their conclusion on the analysis of changes in *mitochondria*, DNA-containing structures found in every cell that help produce energy for the cell's use. Mitochondrial DNA is passed from females to their offspring in the cytoplasm (inner fluid) of the ovum. In other words, whereas humans receive nuclear DNA from both parents, they receive mitochondrial DNA from their mothers only.

Cann's "out of Africa" hypothesis is supported in an analysis by Jin and Su (2000) of DNA from the Y chromosome (the male sex chromosome). This technique permits the tracking of relationships through substances inherited only from and by males. Asiatic males have mutations on the Y chromosome that are similar to the mutations on the Y chromosome of African males. The logic of parsimony says that these mutations are unlikely to have occurred twice. Instead, the ancestors of all males originated in Africa.

The out-of-Africa hypothesis faces competitors, however, including suggestions that modern humans may have originated in Asia, in Indonesia, or even in Australia (Adcock et al., 2001). Part of the argument for these various origin theories is that various biochemical markers can each have their own unique evolutionary history. For example, although all modern human mitochondria might have their common origin in one woman 200,000 years ago, other biochemical markers might have a different evolutionary history.

The Origin of Larger Brains

The relation between brain size and behavior presents a fascinating problem. Large brains, relative to body size, have evolved independently in many groups of animals, including parrots and other birds, dolphins and other whales, and hominids. Because they use more energy than any other body part, large brains are expensive to maintain in regard to energy needs. To be worth their upkeep, big brains must accord their owners advantages in adapting to energy-rich biological niches.

Dean Falk, impressed by the observation that a car engine can be bigger only if its cooling system is improved, suggests that a change in the hominid brain's blood flow removed a constraint that had to that point placed an upper limit on the growth of the ape's brain. Falk noted a difference in pattern between the skull holes of australopithecines and those of *Homo erectus*. She suggests that the blood-flow change had the fortuitous effect of allowing the brain to grow larger in response to other kinds of pressure and that this change may have allowed the "runaway" increase in brain size in subsequent hominids. Subsequent increases in brain size were likely driven by changes in life style, including improved tool use, developing culture, and intergroup cooperation and competition.

The Encephalization Quotient

Estimating nervous system size is no simple problem, and anything but absolute. First, consider the small roundworm, *Caenorhabditis elegans*, a favorite research species for many neuroscientists. *C. elegans* has 959 cells, 302 of which are neurons. In contrast, the blue whale—the largest animal that has ever lived, weighing as much as 200 tons—has a brain weighing 15,000 grams. As a percentage of cell number, 30% of *C. elegans* is nervous system, whereas in terms of body weight, less than 0.01% of the blue whale is nervous system. Thus, clearly, in an evaluation of brain contributions to behavior, actual nervous system size has to be considered in addition to relative nervous system size.

A consideration of relative brain size requires a metric. Harry Jerison developed what he termed the **encephalization quotient** (EQ) for mammals—the ratio of actual brain size to expected brain size. Expected brain size is based on an average for living mammals that takes body size into account. Thus, the average typical mammal, which incidentally is the cat, has an EQ of 1.0.

As animals increase in body size, the size of the brain increases somewhat less, about two-thirds the extent of the increase in body size. With the use of Jerison's formula, an EQ can be calculated for an animal of any size by knowing only its body size and brain size. **Figure 2.7** graphs the body and brain sizes of some common mammals.

Animals that deviate from 1.0, the diagonal line marked by the cat, have brains larger or smaller than would be expected for a mammal of that particular body

Figure 2.7

Brain and Body Sizes of Some Common Mammals The measurements along the axes increase logarithmically to represent the wide range of body and brain sizes. The shaded polygon contains the brain and body sizes of all mammals. The line through the polygon illustrates the expected increase in brain size as body weight increases. Animals that lie above the diagonal line have brain sizes that are larger than would be expected for an animal of that size. (After Jerison, 1973.)

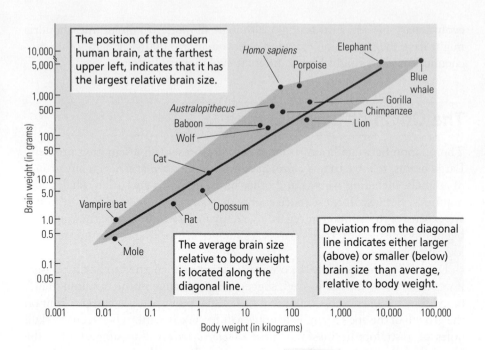

The position of the modern human brain, at the farthest upper left, indicates that it has the largest relative brain size.

The average brain size relative to body weight is located along the diagonal line.

Deviation from the diagonal line indicates either larger (above) or smaller (below) brain size than average, relative to body weight.

size. Relatively larger brains fall above the line and relatively smaller brains fall below the line. Note that the modern human brain is the farthest above the diagonal line, indicating that it has the relatively largest size.

Table 2.1 summarizes the EQs for common laboratory animals and for humans. Notice that the rat's EQ is 0.4, whereas the human's EQ is 7.3. The rat's brain, then, has about half the mass expected for a mammal of the rat's body size, and the brain of a modern human is 7.3 times as large as that expected for a mammal of our body size. Note that the chimpanzee brain is about 2.5 times as large as that predicted for a mammal of a chimpanzee's body size (EQ = 2.48), but its EQ is only one-third that of humans.

These measurements make it clear that the human brain is exceptionally large. An EQ of this magnitude is not unique to humans, however; the EQ of the dolphin (porpoise) has a value of about 6.0. The EQ of an elephant, 1.3, on the other hand, is only a little bigger than expected for an animal of its size.

As is illustrated in **Figure 2.8**, early hominids had brains the size of other apes, about 440 cubic centimeters (cm³), and then quite rapidly brain size increased to the 1350 cm³ characteristic of modern humans. This increase in brain size was due to two changes: (1) member species in the hominid lineage were becoming larger and (2) their brains were becoming larger. But not at the same rate: recall that, as animals increase in body size, their brain size increases only about two-thirds the extent of the increase in body size.

Note in Figure 2.8 that the first increase in brain size between *Australopithecus* and *Homo* was quite sudden in relation to the time scale, but thereafter increases in size were more gradual. A comparison of brain size in the hominid lineage clearly shows that a change in relative brain size was important to the evolution of modern humans

Table 2.1 Comparison of brain sizes of species most commonly studied in neuropsychology

Species	Brain Volume (ml)	Encephalization Quotient
Rat	2.3	0.40
Cat	25.3	1.01
Rhesus monkey	106.4	2.09
Chimpanzee	440.0	2.48
Human	1350.0	7.30

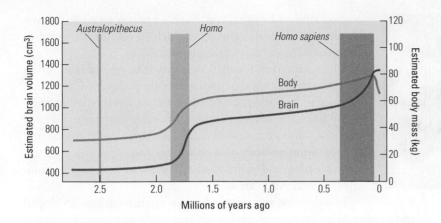

Figure **2.8**

Hominid Absolute Brain Size Note the sudden increase in brain size between *Australopithecus* and *Homo,* and the more gradual increase in *Homo* species thereafter. Increase in brain size is due to increases in both body size and relative brain size. (After Striedter, 2005, p. 316.)

(**Figure 2.9**). The sudden appearance of large-brained *Homo erectus* implies not a gradual selection of individuals with larger brains but rather that having a larger brain must have conferred a decisive and immediate advantage.

Changes in the Cortex

Stephan and his colleagues (1970), in comparing the brains of more than 60 species of mammals, found that, although nearly all brain structures increase in size as the EQ increases, the cortex shows the most dramatic size increase. Thus, the increase in human brain size is largely in the cortex.

This idea has been explored by comparing the human brain with the brains of other primates by using a variety of measures of cortical structure, including cell density and the volume and distribution of the cortex. Stephan and his co-workers calculated that the volume of the human cortex is 3.2 times as great as the predicted volume for nonhuman primates in general and nearly 3 times as great as what would be predicted for a chimpanzee of the same body weight. Comparatively speaking, the human cortex is very large.

What accounts for this disproportionate growth? Georg Striedter proposes the "late equals largest" hypothesis. Because the cortex is the last brain region to mature, slowing its rate of development would allow a longer period for

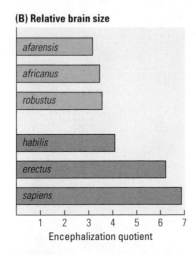

Figure **2.9**

Brain Phylogeny Endocranial volume (A) and encephalization quotients (B) for fossil hominids and *Homo sapiens*. Notice the sudden increase in brain size in *H. erectus*. (Data from McHenry, 1975.)

Figure 2.10

Neoteny A juvenile (left) and adult (right) chimpanzee show the greater resemblance of the baby chimp to humans, illustrating the principle of neoteny in human evolution. (Left: C. A. Schmidecker/FPG; right: R. Stacks/Index Stock.)

cortical cells to be produced. Such a process requires an evolutionary mechanism through which development slows to accommodate increases in brain size.

This adaptation is called **neoteny**: the rate of maturation slows down enough that some juvenile features of predecessor species become the adult features of descendant species. Many features of the human anatomy resemble juvenile stages of other primates—a small face, a vaulted cranium, and a large brain-to-body-size ratio; an unrotated big toe, upright posture, and primary distribution of hair on the head, armpits, and pubic areas.

It is the case as well that human infants are less developed at birth and mature at a slower rate after birth than do other apes. Because a human infant's head is large relative to its body size, neoteny is postulated as having led to "adult babies" with large brains. Humans also retain behavior from their forebears' infants, including exploration, play, and adaptability. The human who walks upright on two legs "is" an infant chimpanzee (**Figure 2.10**).

Variation in Cortical Structure

The human cortex, as well as the cortices of other animals with disproportionately big brains, is distinctive in its many variations. The typical mammalian cortex can be divided into areas that are specialized for movement, body senses, audition, vision, and olfaction. In general, the frontal (movement), parietal (body senses), temporal (audition), and occipital (vision) lobes subserve these functions in humans (**Figure 2.11**A). Olfactory functions are located on the ventral surface of the frontal lobe and beneath the cortex in the limbic system (Figure 2.11B).

Figure 2.11

Cortical Functions (A) Lateral views of the human brain, identifying its general functional correlates. The visible sensory and motor regions connect to many subregions, each representing a subfunction within that modality. (B) Ventral views of the human brain, where the olfactory bulbs and connections are visible. (Photographs courtesy of Yakolev Collection/AFIP.)

(A) Lateral view

(B) Ventral view

In simple animals such as the hedgehog, each of these regions is relatively homogeneous compared with those of more complex animals, in which each lobe can be divided into a number of subregions. For example, although the visual cortex occupies the occipital lobe of all animals, the squirrel has 4 separate visual areas, the cat has at least 12, and the owl monkey has as many as 14. The number in humans is not known but is probably about 30 or more. Because each area has a special function, the growth of the human cortex is characterized not only by a larger size but by many more functional areas as well.

The addition of new cortical regions contributes to behavior, as illustrated by hypothetical cortical maps. **Figure 2.12**A maps the brain of a hedgehog and indicates the various regions that participate in movement and sensation. Iwaniuk and Whishaw propose that, if the forepaw area expands in size by means of mutation, then more-complex, skilled forepaw movements for food handling become possible, allowing the animal to exploit a new habitat.

Accordingly, the mammal's motor cortex in Figure 2.12B has acquired a new subregion, becoming comparatively larger and enabling the animal to use its forepaws more dexterously. Rodents, such as the laboratory rat, are representative of animals that have undergone such an increase in motor-cortex size: they have a large topographic forepaw representation in the motor cortex and correspondingly good food-handling skills.

Primates are characterized by their ability to find and handle food and to get around in an arboreal habitat. Good color vision makes it easier to find food, and good depth perception is useful in gauging jumps from one small branch to another. Primates acquired depth perception because some cells in each eye became specialized for seeing the same object from different views, a development made possible by the association of these cells with a new region of the visual cortex. This new cortical area, as well as another that evolved for color vision, added mass to the primate brain, as is shown in Figure 2.12C.

Animals antecedent to primates have relatively large olfactory systems, and most of their motor behavior, such as locating food, is guided by sniffing. Primates use vision to locate food. Thus, another characteristic of the primate brain is that the amount of cortex accorded to olfaction has decreased (compare Figure

Figure **2.12**

Variation in Cortical Structure (Dorsal View) (A) The cortical map of a hedgehog, illustrating the extent and number of sensory and motor areas. (B) In a hypothetical rodent that develops forelimbs for skilled food handling, the sensory and motor cortex areas representing the paw increase to accommodate new receptors in the hands and the increased complexity of muscle arrangement. (C) In a hypothetical primate that develops color and depth vision, two new visual areas have evolved in the cortex. Note the increase in brain size associated with the expansion of visual areas and the addition of areas that will contribute to this animal's improved locomotion and feeding in the trees.

(A)

Motor   Visual

Smell

Sensory I

Sensory II   Auditory

1 The cortex of a primitive mammal has regions for various functions.

(B)

Hand motor area   Hand sensory area

Smell

2 As new behaviors evolve, cortical size enlarges and new areas are added, allowing increased skill in food handling.

(C)

Color vision

Smell

Stereoscopic vision

3 A still larger brain allows for new visual abilities, which, in turn, supplant the need for keen smell. That area is reduced.

2.12A and B with Figure 2.12C). This change makes room for the other sensory systems, such as vision, to expand their extent of cortex. Thus, at least three factors determine cortical size: absolute increases in size, the addition of new skills, and the relative changes in sensory and motor abilities.

Brain Size and Intelligence

In *The Descent of Man*, Charles Darwin admonished:

> No one, I presume, doubts the large proportion which the size of man's brain bears to his body, compared to the same proportion in the gorilla or orang, is closely connected with his higher mental powers. . . . On the other hand, no one supposes that the intellect of any two animals or of any two men can be accurately gauged by the cubic contents of their skulls. (Darwin, 1871, p.37)

Ignoring Darwin, many have tried to tie individuals' intelligence to their brain size. Nineteenth-century investigators attempted to correlate gross human brain size and behavior with three questions in mind. They asked whether brain size was related to

1. a person's intelligence.

2. intelligence differences between sexes.

3. intelligence differences among nationalities and races.

Among the evidence they considered was that brain size did vary in different racial groups and that the male brain is about 10% larger than the female brain. Stephen Jay Gould reviewed these investigations in his book titled *The Mismeasure of Man* and invalidated them for their inadequate procedures for measuring brain size, for the absence of any method for measuring intelligence, or both.

Some examples cited by Gould: the brain-size investigators made little attempt to control for body size and were insensitive to the fact that head size and brain size are not closely correlated. They were as well unaware that the brain loses mass with age (most of the brains measured came from people who had died in old age). In the end, French investigators concluded that the French had the largest brains and German investigators concluded that Germans had the largest brains.

This line of brain-size investigation was no more successful in the twentieth century, even though the investigators had by that time solved two of the problems faced by their predecessors. First, magnetic resonance imaging (MRI) was available to create a virtual representation of the brain of a young, healthy adult. **Figure 2.13** shows a functional MRI image juxtaposed with a photograph of a human brain. Second, IQ tests allowed these later investigators to estimate and compare people's intelligence by using a single number, the IQ score, calculated by averaging a subject's scores on a number of intelligence tests, including tests of information, arithmetic, memory, and so on.

The twentieth-century investigators found wide variation in gross brain size among individual persons, among members of the same national and racial groups, and among people of the same sex, as well as a statistical difference between the sexes, together with wide variation in intelligence. The correlation between gross brain size and intelligence between people, nations, races, or

Figure 2.13

Imaging Brain Size Comparison of (A) an actual human brain and (B) a virtual brain produced by functional MRI. (Part A, Dr. Fred Hossler/Visuals Unlimited; part B, Collection CNRI/Phototake.)

(A)

(B)

sexes is poor. As Darwin pointed out first, two good scientific reasons reveal this line of inquiry into gross brain size and intelligence as superficial:

1. Even though between-species differences in brain size may be correlated with between-species differences in behavior, to apply the correlation within a species is faulty, because within-species behavior is much more uniform. For example, no chimpanzee can read and all normal-functioning modern humans can read.

2. IQ tests are a biased measure of intelligence. IQ tests largely measure the function of the left-hemisphere cortex and ignore the rest of the brain. Howard Gardner has proposed that an adequate measure of human intellectual abilities would have to consider seven different kinds of intelligence: verbal, mathematical, musical, spatial, motoric, interpersonal, and extrapersonal.

IQ test scores are also sensitive to many outside variables, including time. When IQ tests that were given to young adults 50 years ago are given to young adults today, today's subjects score as much as 25 points higher (a phenomenon called the *Flynn effect*). Taken at face value (though it shouldn't be), the increase suggests that human intelligence has risen to such a degree in two generations that most young adults fall in the superior IQ category relative to their grand-parents. (Obviously, the score change has not been accompanied by a similar increase in brain size.)

Attempts to correlate overall brain size and intelligence also overlook more interesting matters. For one thing, the brain is organized in functional units, each of which mediates a different kind of behavior. Variation in the size of specific functional units may be related to specific skills. For example, Fernando Nottebohm and his colleagues show that, in songbirds, the size of the auditory and vocal regions of the brain are related to the complexity of song. Accordingly, people gifted in music likely have large auditory cortices. Thus, Gardner and colleagues argue that each of the different kinds of human intelligence may be related to a different functional region of the brain.

Further, an adult animal's brain size can be markedly affected by injury, especially if the injury occurs early in life. One of us (Bryan Kolb) and his colleagues reported that slight injury to the rat cortex within the first 10 days of life can result in disproportionate brain-size reductions of more than 25% at maturity. Rat pups at 10 days are equivalent in age to late-stage human embryos. Consequently, a host of prenatal injuries likely can and do affect human brain size.

A final observation is that, beginning with findings obtained by Mark Rosensweig and his colleagues more than 50 years ago, we now know that environmental experiences can affect cortical size. The Rosensweig team found that rats raised in a visually enriched environment undergo an increase in cortical size and a disproportionate increase in the size of visual regions of the cortex. Miles Storfer suggests that similar enrichment of human experience, such as learning to read and write, enlarges the size of the human cortex.

The Acquisition of Culture

The evolution of humans, from the first hominid to the appearance of morphologically modern men and women, took less than 6 million years, an extremely short span of time in evolutionary terms. Thus, the modern human brain evolved very rapidly. Even so, most of the changes in behavior that differentiate us from our primate ancestors took place more rapidly still, long after the modern brain had evolved.

Only 25,000 years ago, modern humans left the first artistic relics: elaborate paintings on cave walls and carved ivory and stone figurines. The tempo of change has quickened further in the past 10,000 years. Agriculture and animal husbandry were established in the Middle East by 9000 years ago, followed by ideographic writing in the same region by about 5000 years ago.

Saint Ambrose, who lived in the fourth century A.D., is reportedly the first person who could read silently. Today, most readers have more difficulty reading aloud than silently. The modern technological age began in Europe about A.D. 1500: it was after this time that most of what we see around us today was invented or discovered. How interesting that most of what we associate with modern humans is of such very recent origin, considering that the basic tools (a big brain, free hands, and bipedal locomotion) had been with us long before.

Some investigators suggest that the acquisition of culture is not entirely independent of the brain's evolution. Alex Mesoudi and his colleagues suggest that the elements of culture, called *memes* (after genes, the elements of physical evolution), can also be studied within an evolutionary framework. They propose, for example, that individual differences in brain structure may favor the development of certain memes. Once developed, memes would in turn exert selective pressure on further brain development.

For example, chance variations in individuals' brain structure may have favored the development of tool use in those individuals. The use of tools could then have been so beneficial that tool making itself exerted selective pressure on a population to favor more-skilled tool fabrication. Similar arguments can be made with respect to other memes, including language, music, mathematics, and art. According to Mesoudi's line of reasoning, the field of neuropsychology can expand to include other seemingly separate disciplines including linguistics, the arts, and economics.

Summary

Species Comparison

Three primary lines of research drive comparative investigations with animals: (1) understanding the basic biological mechanisms of the brain, (2) designing animal models of human neurological disorders, and (3) describing the evolutionary development (phylogeny) of the brain.

Human Origins

The divergence of the human brain from that of other living species has a history of at least 5 million years. In the past 2 million years, this history has been characterized by a major expansion of the brain that apparently took place in a number of quick steps. A number of different humanlike animals have coexisted until quite recently. Climate changes seem closely correlated with the appearance of new hominid species. Today's humans have been here for only about 200,000 years, and they have replaced all their predecessors.

The Origin of Larger Brains

The general structure of the human brain is quite similar to that of other animals, even to relatively simple animals such as rats. The human brain is larger than that of other apes both because humans are larger and because the size of the brain relative to the body has increased. Most of the increase in size has been in the cortex.

The increase in brain size in mammals generally and in the primate lineage in particular is also associated with the appearance of new cortical areas for mediating new behavior. The enlargement and new subregions probably allowed for the development of many advantageous new skills rather than a single decisive skill or ability. Culture is a hallmark of modern human behavior and has allowed for remarkable increases in behavioral complexity from a seemingly similar brain.

References

Adcock, G. J., E. S. Dennis, S. Easteal, G. A., Huttley, S. Lars, L. S., Jermiin, W. James, W. J. Peacock, and A. Thorne. Mitochondrial DNA sequences in ancient Australians: Implications for modern human origins. *Proceedings of the National Academy of Sciences* 98:537–542, 2001.

Beals, K. L., C. L. Smith, and S. M. Dodd. Brain size, cranial morphology, climate, and time machines. *Current Anthropology* 25:301–330, 1984.

Blinkov, S. M., and J. I. Glesner. *The Human Brain in Figures and Tables.* New York: Basic Books, 1968.

Blumenschine, R. J., and J. Q. Cavallo. Scavenging and human evolution. *Scientific American*, 90–96, October 1992.

Campbell, C. B. G., and W. Hodos. The concept of homology and the evolution of the nervous system. *Brain, Behavior and Evolution* 3:353–367, 1970.

Cann, R. L. Genetic clues to dispersal in human populations: Retracing the past from the present. *Science* 291:1742–1748, 2001.

Coppens, Y. The east side story: The origin of humankind. *Scientific American*, 88–95, May 1994.

Darwin, C. *On the Origin of Species by Means of Natural Selection.* London: J. Murray, 1859.

Darwin, C. *The Descent of Man, and Selection in Relation to Sex.* London: J. Murray, 1871.

Diamond, I. T., and K. L. Chow. Biological psychology. In S. Koch, Ed. *Psychology: A Study of a Science*, vol. 4. New York: McGraw-Hill, 1962.

Falk, D. A reanalysis of the South African australopithecine natural endocasts. *American Journal of Physical Anthropology* 53:525–539, 1980.

Falk, D. Brain evolution in *Homo:* The "radiator" theory. *Behavioral and Brain Sciences* 13:344–368, 1990.

Gallup, G. G., Jr. Chimpanzees: Self-recognition. *Science* 167:86–87, 1970.

Gardner, H. E., M. L. Kornhaber, and W. E. Wake. *Intelligence: Multiple Perspectives.* Fort Worth, Tex., and Toronto: Harcourt Brace College, 1997.

Goodall, J. *The Chimpanzees of Gombe.* Cambridge, Mass.: The Belknap Press of Harvard University Press, 1986.

Gould, S. J. *The Mismeasure of Man.* New York: Norton, 1981.

Hardy, A. Was man more aquatic in the past? *New Scientist* 7:642–645, 1960.

Hetzer-Egger, C., M. Schorpp, and T. Boehm. Evolutionary conservation of gene structures of the *Pax*1/9 gene family. *Biochemistry and Biophysics Acta* 1492:517–521, 2000.

Hodos, W., and C. B. G. Campbell. Scale naturae: Why there is no theory in comparative psychology. *Psychological Review* 76:337–350, 1969.

Holloway, R. L. Revisiting the South African Tuang australopithecine endocast: The position of the lunate sulcus as determined by the stereoplotting technique. *American Journal of Physical Anthropology* 56:43–58, 1981.

Iwaniuk, A. N., L. Lefebvre, and D. R. Wong-Wylie. The role of the cerebellum in the evolution of tool using behavior in birds. *Brain, Behavior and Evolution* 68:113, 2006.

Iwaniuk, A. N., and I. Q. Whishaw. On the origin of skilled forelimb movements. *Trends in Neurosciences* 23:372–376, 2000.

Jerison, H. J. *Evolution of the Brain and Intelligence.* New York: Academic Press, 1973.

Jin, L., and B. Su. Natives or immigrants: Modern human origin in east Asia. *National Review of Genetics* 1:126–133, 2000.

Johanson, D., and M. Edey. *Lucy: The Beginnings of Humankind.* New York: Warner Books, 1981.

Jorde, L. B. Human genetic distance studies: Present status and future prospects. *Annual Review of Anthropology* 14:343–373, 1987.

Kolb, B. *Brain Plasticity and Behavior.* Mahwah, N.J.: Erlbaum, 1997.

Lockhart, R. B. The albino rat: A defensible choice or bad habit. *American Psychologist* 23:734–742, 1968.

Masterton, B., and L. C. Skeen. Origins of anthropoid intelligence: Prefrontal system and delayed alternation in hedgehog, tree shrew, and bush baby. *Journal of Comparative and Physiological Psychology* 81:423–433, 1972.

McHenry, H. M. Fossils and the mosaic nature of human evolution. *Science* 190:425–431, 1975.

Mesoudi, A., A. Whiten, and K. N. Laland. Towards a unified science of cultural evolution. *Behavioural and Brain Sciences* 29:329–347, 2006.

Nottebohm F. The King Solomon Lectures in Neuroethology: A white canary on Mount Acropolis. *Journal of Comparative Physiology* 179:149–156, 1996.

Oldham, M. C., and D. H. Geschwind. Deconstructing language by comparative gene expression: From neurobiology to microarray. *Genes, Brain and Behavior* 5(Suppl 1):54–63, 2006.

Passingham, R. E. *The Human Primate.* San Francisco: W. H. Freeman and Company, 1982.

Pickford, M. Discovery of earliest hominid remains. *Science* 291:986, 2001.

Rosensweig, M. R., D. Krech, E. L. Bennett, and M. C. Diamond. Effects of environmental complexity and training on brain chemistry and anatomy: A replication and extension. *Journal of Comparative and Physiological Psychology* 55:427–29, 1962.

Sarnat, H. B., and M. G. Netsky. *Evolution of the Nervous System*. New York: Oxford University Press, 1974.

Semaw, S. The world's oldest stone artifacts from Gona, Ethiopia: Their implications for understanding stone technology and patterns of human evolution between 2.6–1.5 million years ago. *Journal of Archaeological Science* 27:1197–1214, 2000.

Stanley, S. M. *The New Evolutionary Timetable*. New York: Basic Books, 1981.

Stephan, H., R. Bauchot, and O. J. Andy. Data on the size of the brain and of various parts in insectivores and primates. In C. R. Noback and W. Montagna, Eds. *The Primate Brain*. New York: Appleton, 1970, pp. 289–297.

Storfer, M. Myopia, intelligence, and the expanding human neocortex: Behavioral influences and evolutionary implications. *International Journal of Neuroscience* 98:153–276, 1999.

Striedter, G. F. *Principles of Brain Evolution*. Sunderland, Mass.:Sinauer, 2005.

Taglialatela, J. P., S. Savage-Rumbaugh, and L. A. Baker. Vocal production by a language-competent *Pan paniscus*. *International Journal of Primatology* 24:1–17, 2003.

Teaford, M. F., and P. S. Ungar. Diet and the evolution of the earliest human ancestors. *Proceedings of the National Academy of Sciences of the United States of America* 97:13506–13511, 2000.

Thorne, A., and M. H. Wolpoff. The multiregional evolution of humans. *Scientific American*, 76–83, April 1992.

Van Meir, V., D. Pavlova, M. Verhoye, R. Pinxten, J. Balthazart, M. Eens, and A. Van der Linden. In vivo MR imaging of the seasonal volumetric and functional plasticity of song control nuclei in relation to song output in a female songbird. *Neuroimage* 31:981–992, 2006.

White, T. H. *The Once and Future King*. London: Collins, 1958.

Young, J. Z. *The Life of Vertebrates*. New York: Oxford University Press, 1962.

Organization of the Nervous System

PORTRAIT: Stroke

R.S.'s first job in high school was as an usher in a movie theater. After graduation, he became the manager of the theater and eventually its owner. Not only did he enjoy his business, he also loved movies and had a remarkable knowledge of all aspects of cinema, including movie plots and actors. He enjoyed discussing movies and took pride in being able to answer questions about how they are produced, directed, and marketed.

One day while repairing the roof of his garage, R.S. felt numbness in his left hand and then he collapsed, unable to stand, and fell to the ground. He had suffered a **stroke**, an interruption of blood to the brain that kills brain cells and causes the sudden appearance of neurological symptoms. His condition resulted from an **ischemia**, a deficiency of blood flow to the brain due to functional constriction or to the actual obstruction of a blood vessel, such as by a clot.

R.S. was quickly taken to a nearby hospital, where a CT scan showed that the stroke had damaged his right frontal cortex. In the adjoining CT image showing the effects of stroke on the brain, the dark area on the right side is the area that has been damaged by the loss of blood flow. R.S. was given no treatment and was eventually taken to a rehabilitation ward to receive physical therapy.

In the United States, someone suffers a stroke approximately every minute, producing more than a half

Canadian Stroke Network

million new stroke victims every year. Worldwide, stroke is the second leading cause of death. For every 10 people who have a stroke, 2 die, 6 are disabled to varying degrees, and 2 recover to various degrees but still endure a diminished quality of life. With rehabilitation, R.S. recovered the ability to walk, although his left leg was stiff, but his left arm was somewhat rigid and flexed and he made no attempt to use it.

Although to his friends and family R.S. appeared to be able to do most of the things that he had done before his stroke, he was apathetic and appeared to have lost interest in everything. He no longer enjoyed his hobby of gardening, he had no interest in his business, he no longer talked about the movies, and he no longer watched television, as he had done before his stroke. Although formerly talkative, he no longer initiated conversation;

when he did speak, it was without affect. Ten years after his stroke, despite neuropsychological assessment and a number of attempts at behavioral and physical therapy, R.S. is unchanged.

Unlike the more severe hemorrhagic stroke that results from a burst vessel bleeding into the brain, ischemic stroke can be treated with a drug called **tissue plasminogen activator** (t-PA) that breaks up clots and allows the return of normal blood flow to the affected region. R.S. was not given the drug within the required 3 hours of suffering his stroke, however, because the attending physician was unsure whether the fall from the garage roof had caused a hemorrhagic stroke as a result of a concussion and burst blood vessel. An anticlotting drug decreases tissue death in ischemic stroke but aggravates cell death in hemorrhagic stroke.

Scientists are interested in developing new treatments for the postacute stroke period because most patients do not make it to an emergency unit within 3 hours. They are also searching for ways to stimulate the brain to initiate reparative processes for both ischemic and hemorrhagic stroke, because the poststroke survival period for many patients is long. Neuropsychologists also are interested in developing rehabilitative procedures that help patients cope with and overcome not only motor symptoms but also the apathy that so diminished R.S.'s quality of life.

The complexity of the brain and the complexity of behavior present a major challenge to anyone trying to explain how the one produces the other. The human brain is composed of more than 100 billion neurons that engage in information processing. Each neuron receives as many as 15,000 connections from other cells.

The neurons in the brain are organized in layers as well as in groups called **nuclei** (from the Latin *nux*, meaning "nut"), groups of cells forming clusters that can be visualized with special stains to identify a functional grouping. Some brain nuclei are folded, and others have distinctive shapes and colors. Within nuclei, cells that are close together make most of their connections with one another.

Thus, the anatomical pattern of the brain is like that of human communities, whose inhabitants share most of their work and engage in social interactions with others who live nearby. Each community of cells also makes connections with more-distant neural communities through pathways made by their axons. These connections are analogous to the thoroughfares linking human communities.

The brain can undergo enormous changes during the life span of a person; but, after many kinds of damage, its ability to compensate is limited, as R.S.'s case illustrates. What aids neuropsychologists' efforts to understand brain function is knowledge about the order in the arrangement of neurons and their connections, a topic that we now address in our description of the brain's anatomy.

Neuroanatomy: Finding Your Way Around the Brain

Although the sizes and shapes of the brains of different people vary, just as their facial features do, the component structures—the communities and main roads of the brain—are common to all human beings. In fact, most of these structures seem to be common to all mammals.

About 100 years ago, anatomist Lorente de Nó, making one of the first detailed descriptions of a mouse brain through a microscope, discovered to his surprise that its fine structure is similar to that of the human brain. Because brain cells are similar in all animals and because the structures of animal brains are so similar, a great deal of what we know of the function of parts of the human brain is derived from comparative studies of those same parts in other animals.

Describing Locations in the Brain

The locations of the layers, nuclei, and pathways of the brain can be described by their placement with respect to other body parts of the animal, with respect to their relative locations, and with respect to a viewer's perspective. The most frequently used sets of terms are illustrated in **Figure 3.1**:

- Figure 3.1A describes brain structures in relation to other body parts. In Latin, *rostum* is "beak," *caudum* is "tail," *dosum* is "back," and *ventrum* is "stomach." Accordingly, *rostral*, *caudal*, *dorsal*, and *ventral* parts of the brain are located toward those body parts. Occasionally, the terms *superior*

(A)

Dorsal (superior)

Rostral — Caudal

Ventral (inferior)

(B)

Dorsal

Medial — Anterior — Posterior — Lateral

Ventral

(C)

Plane of section | **View of brain**

Coronal section — Frontal view

Horizontal section — Dorsal view

Sagittal section — Medial view

Figure 3.1

Anatomical Orientation (A) Terms that describe the brain in relation to parts of the body. (B) Terms that describe the brain in relation to orientation of the body. (C) Terms that describe the brain in relation to cuts through it that allow visualization of its internal structures: here, a coronal section revealing a frontal view of the brain, a horizontal section revealing a dorsal view, and a sagittal section revealing a medial view. (Photographs courtesy of Dr. D. Armstrong, University of Toronto/Lifeart.)

and *inferior* are used to refer to structures that are located dorsally or ventrally.

- Figure 3.1B illustrates how brain parts are described in relation to one another from the frame of reference of the face. *Anterior* or *frontal* is in front, *posterior* structures are located behind, *lateral* structures are at the side, and *medial* structures are located at the center or between.

- Figure 3.1C illustrates terms that describe the direction of a cut, or section, through the brain from the perspective of a viewer. A *coronal* section is cut in a vertical plane, from the crown of the head down. A *horizontal* section (because the view or cut is along the horizon) is usually viewed looking down on the brain from above. A *sagittal* section is cut lengthways, front to back, and viewed from the side (imagine the brain oriented as an arrow—in Latin, *sagitta*).

The nervous system, like the body, is symmetrical, with a left side and a right side. Structures that lie on the same side are **ipsilateral**; if they lie on opposite sides, they are **contralateral** to each other. If one of them lies in each hemisphere, the structures are **bilateral**.

Sensory pathways are afferent.

Motor pathways are efferent.

Sensory endings

Structures that are close to one another are **proximal**; those far from one another are **distal**. And any movement toward a brain structure is **afferent**, whereas movement away from it is **efferent**. Thus, the body's sensory pathways that carry messages toward the brain and spinal cord are afferent, and motor pathways leading to the body from the brain and spinal cord are efferent.

You know that humans are distinguished in that they stand upright, and nonhuman animals typically have a quadruped posture. The spatial orientations of human and nonhuman animal brains are similar, but the spatial orientations of their spinal cords are different. Dorsal and ventral in quadrupeds are anterior and posterior in upright humans, but, if humans stand on "all fours," the orientation of the spinal cord is then similar to that of other animals.

A Wonderland of Nomenclature

To the beginning student, the naming of brain parts might seem chaotic. And it is, because neuroscientists have been at it for a long time, and names accumulate as knowledge of brain parts and their functions grows. Consequently, structures may have several names, often used interchangeably, that describe their appearance, their location, or one or more of their functions.

The **precentral gyrus**, a part of the brain damaged by stroke in R.S. and responsible for his diminished motor ability, has many other names. It is called *gyrus precentralis* in Latin and "the motor strip" in colloquial English. It is also called "Jackson's strip," after Hughlings-Jackson, who noted that, in epileptic attacks, the limbs of the body convulse in an orderly arrangement, suggesting to him that the representation of the body in the brain also is orderly.

Electrophysiologists refer to the precentral gyrus as the *primary motor cortex* or *M1*, to distinguish it from other motor regions of the cortex. Because they can obtain movements of different body parts after stimulating this area, as was first found by Fritsch and Hitzig (see Chapter 1), they have also called it the "somatomotor strip" or "the motor homunculus" (motor human). Additionally, because anatomists such as Gall found that the pyramidal tract that extends from the cortex into the spinal cord comes mainly from this cortical region, they called it "area pyramidalis."

For a lot of brain regions, Greek, Latin, French, and English terminology alternate with slang. Additionally, neuroscientists' imaginations have compared brain structures to body anatomy (mammillary bodies), flora (amygdala, or "almond"), fauna (hippocampus, or "sea horse"), and mythology (Ammon's horn). Other terms make use of color—substantia nigra ("black substance"), locus coeruleus ("blue area"), and red nucleus—or of consistency, such as substantia gelatinosa ("gelatinous substance").

Some names are puzzling: substantia innominata ("unnamable substance"), zone incerta ("uncertain area"), nucleus ambiguus ("ambiguous nucleus"); others are based entirely on expediency: cell groups A-1 to A-15 or B1 to B9. The longest name for a brain structure is nucleus reticularis tegmenti pontis Bechterewi, affectionately known as NRTP because, as you will observe, neuroscientists have a special fondness for abbreviations. We attempt to use consistent and simple terms in this book; but, in many cases, because neuroscientists in different fields use different terms in presenting their findings, we must do so as well.

An Overview of Nervous System Structure and Function

From an anatomical viewpoint, the central nervous system (CNS) consists of the brain and the spinal cord, and the peripheral nervous system (PNS) encompasses everything else (see Figure 1.2). In a functional scheme, the focus shifts from anatomy to how the parts of the nervous system work together. Here, both major divisions of the PNS step up to constitute, along with the CNS, the three-part functional scheme illustrated in **Figure 3.2**:

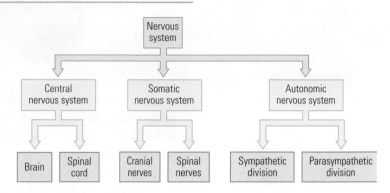

Figure 3.2

Functional Divisions of the Human Nervous System

- The (CNS) consists of the brain and spinal cord.

- The somatic nervous system (SNS) consists of all the spinal and cranial nerves to and from the sensory organs and the muscles, joints, and skin. The SNS produces movement and transmits incoming sensory information to the CNS, including vision, hearing, pain, temperature, touch, and the position and movement of body parts.

- The autonomic nervous system (ANS) balances the body's internal organs to "rest and digest" through the **parasympathetic** (calming) **nerves** or to "fight and flee" or engage in vigorous activity through the **sympathetic** (arousing) **nerves**.

Support and Protection

The brain and spinal cord are supported and protected from injury and infection in four ways:

1. The brain is enclosed in a thick bone, the skull, and the spinal cord is encased in a series of interlocking bony vertebrae. Thus, the CNS lies within bony encasements, whereas the PNS, although connected to the CNS, lies outside them. The PNS, although more vulnerable to injury because it lacks bony protection, can renew itself after injury by growing new axons and dendrites, whereas self-repair is much more limited within the CNS.

2. Within the bony case enclosing the CNS is a triple-layered set of membranes, the **meninges**, shown in **Figure 3.3**. The outer *dura mater* (from the Latin, meaning "hard mother") is a tough double layer of tissue enclosing the brain in a kind of loose sack. The middle *arachnoid membrane* (from the Greek, meaning "resembling a spider's web") is a very thin sheet of delicate tissue that follows the contours of the brain. The inner *pia mater* (from the Latin, meaning "soft mother") is a moderately tough tissue that clings to the surface of the brain.

3. The brain and spinal cord are cushioned from shock and sudden changes of pressure by the cerebrospinal fluid that circulates in the four ventricles inside the brain, in the spinal column, and within the subarachnoid space

Figure 3.3

Cerebral Security A triple-layered covering, the meninges, encases the brain and spinal cord, and the cerebrospinal fluid (CSF) cushions them.

Skull
Dura mater
Arachnoid membrane } Meninges
Pia mater
Subarachnoid space (filled with CSF)
Brain

in the brain's enclosing membranes. Cerebral spinal fluid is continually being made and drained off into the circulatory system. If the outflow is blocked, as occurs in a congenital condition called **hydrocephalus** (literally, water brain), severe mental retardation and even death can result.

4. The brain and spinal cord are protected from many chemical substances circulating in the rest of the body by the **blood–brain barrier**. To form this barrier, the cells of the capillaries—the very small blood vessels—form tight junctions with one another, thus preventing many blood-borne substances from crossing from the capillaries into the CNS tissues.

Blood Supply

The brain receives its blood supply from two internal carotid arteries and two vertebral arteries that course up each side of the neck. The four arteries connect at the base of the brain, where they enter the skull. From there, the cerebral arteries branch off into several smaller arteries that irrigate the brainstem and cerebellum and give rise to three arteries that irrigate the forebrain.

The distribution zones of the cerebral arteries in the cortex are shown in **Figure 3.4**. If you place your hand so that the wrist represents the artery trunk at the base of the brain, the extended digits offer an approximate representation of the area of the cortex that is irrigated in each zone. Thus, the **anterior**

Anterior cerebral artery   **Middle cerebral artery**   **Posterior cerebral artery**

Dorsal view   Lateral view   Ventral view

Lateral view   Medial view   Medial view

Figure 3.4

Distribution of the Major Cerebral Arteries If you align your hand so that your wrist represents the base of an artery, the extended digits will spread over the area of cortex to which blood is distributed by that artery.

cerebral artery (ACA) irrigates the medial and dorsal part of the cortex, the **middle cerebral artery** (MCA) irrigates the lateral surface of the cortex, and the **posterior cerebral artery** (PCA) irrigates the ventral and posterior surfaces of the cortex.

For most people, if an artery becomes blocked by the formation of a blood clot, as described for R.S., who suffered an MCA ischemic stroke, stroke symptoms will vary according to the location of the loss of blood supply. Note in Figure 3.4 that a large clot in an initial portion of a blood vessel will deprive a great deal of the cortex of its blood supply, whereas a smaller clot in the more distal branches of the artery will result in more-restricted damage. For some people, there are connections between the different arteries; so, subsequent to a clot, other arteries can supply blood.

The veins of the brain, through which spent blood returns to the heart, are classified as external and internal cerebral and cerebellar veins. The venous flow does not follow the course of the major arteries but instead follows a pattern of its own.

Neurons and Glia

The brain has its origin in a single undifferentiated cell called a **neural stem cell** (also called a *germinal cell*). Not only does this stem cell and its progeny produce the various specialized cells that make up the adult brain, they also produce additional stem cells that persist into adulthood.

A stem cell has extensive capacity for self-renewal. To initially form a brain, it divides and produces two stem cells, both of which can divide again (**Figure 3.5**). In the adult, one stem cell dies after each division; so the mature brain contains a constant number of dividing stem cells. Adult stem cells serve as a source of new neurons for certain parts of the adult brain. Thus, for those regions, they may play a role in brain repair after injuries such as stroke or other trauma.

In the developing embryo, stem cells give rise to **progenitor cells** that migrate and act as precursor cells, giving rise to nondividing, primitive types of nervous system cells called **blasts**. Some blasts differentiate into neurons; others differentiate into the glia. These two basic brain-cell types—neurons and glia—take many forms and make up the entire adult brain.

Neuroscientists once thought that the newborn child had all the neurons that it would ever possess. Among the most remarkable discoveries of the past decade is that, in fact, new neurons are produced after birth and, in some regions of the brain, continue to be produced through adulthood.

Neurons differ chiefly in overall size, in the length and branching of their axons, and in the complexity of their dendritic

Figure **3.5**

Origin of Brain Cells Cells in the brain begin as multipotential stem cells, which become progenitor cells, the precursors of blasts that finally develop into specialized neurons and glia. Adult stem cells are located in the brain's ventricular zone, which surrounds the ventricles, and in the spinal cord and the retina of the eye as well.

Cell type	Process		
Stem	Self-renewal		
Progenitor	Progenitor produced		
Blast	Neuroblasts and glioblasts produced	Neural	Glial
Specialized	Neuro and glia differentiatens	Interneuron Projecting neuron	Oligodendroglia Astrocyte

(A) Sensory neurons

Bring information to the central nervous system

Bipolar neuron (retina) — Dendrite — Axon — Somatosensory neuron (skin, muscle)

(B) Interneurons

Associate sensory and motor activity in the central nervous system

Dendrites

Dendrites — Axon — Axon

Stellate cell (thalamus) — Pyramidal cell (cortex) — Purkinje cell (cerebellum)

(C) Motor neurons

Send signals from the brain and spinal cord to muscles

Dendrites — Axon — Motor neuron (spinal cord)

Figure 3.6

Neuron Types Neurons are specialized in regard to function. These schematic representations show the relative sizes and configurations, not drawn to scale, of (A) sensory neurons, (B) interneurons in the brain, and (C) motor neurons in the spinal cord.

processes. **Figure 3.6** shows examples of the differences in size and shape that characterize neurons from different parts of the nervous system. The simplest **sensory neuron**, a **bipolar neuron** shown on the left in Figure 3.6A, consists of a cell body with a dendrite on one side and an axon on the other.

Somatosensory neurons, which project from the body's sensory receptors into the spinal cord, are modified so that the dendrite and axon are connected, which speeds information conduction because messages do not have to pass through the cell body (Figure 3.6A right). **Interneurons** within the brain and spinal cord link up sensory- and motor-neuron activity in the CNS. There are many kinds of interneurons and all have many dendrites that branch extensively but, like all neurons, a brain or spinal-cord interneuron has only one axon, although it can branch as well (Figure 3.6B). **Motor neurons** located in the brainstem project to facial muscles, and motor neurons in the spinal cord project to other muscles of the body (Figure 3.6C). Together, motor neurons are called the final common path because all behavior produced by the brain is produced through them.

Thus, the architecture of neurons differs from region to region in the nervous system. These differences provide the basis for dividing the brain into different anatomical regions. The various types of glial cells have different functions as well. Some are described in **Table 3.1**.

Table **3.1** Types of glial cells

Type	Appearance	Features and Function
Ependymal cell		Small, ovoid; secretes cerebrospinal fluid (CSF)
Astrocyte		Star shaped, symmetrical; nutritive and support function
Microglial cell		Small, mesodermally derived; defensive function
Oligodendroglial cell		Asymmetrical; forms insulating myelin around axons in brain and spinal cord
Schwann cell		Asymmetrical; wraps around peripheral nerves to form insulating myelin

Gray, White, and Reticular Matter

When a human brain is sectioned to reveal its internal structures, some parts appear gray, some white, and some mottled. In general, these visually contrasting parts are described as gray matter, white matter, and reticular matter (**Figure 3.7**).

Gray matter acquires its characteristic gray-brown color from the capillary blood vessels and neuronal cell bodies that predominate there. **White matter** consists largely of axons that extend from these cell bodies to form connections with neurons in other brain areas. These axons are covered with an insulating layer of glial cells that are composed of the same fatty substance (lipid) that gives milk its white ap-

Figure 3.7

Coronal Section Through the Brain The brain is (A) cut from the top down and (B) frontally viewed at a slight angle. The regions that are relatively white are largely composed of nerve fibers, whereas the relatively gray brown areas are composed of cell bodies. The large bundle of fibers joining the two hemispheres, visible above the ventricles, is the corpus callosum. Each ventricle is a fluid-filled cavity. (Photograph: Glauberman/Photo Researchers.)

pearance. As a result, an area of the nervous system rich in axons covered with glial cells looks white.

Many prominent cell groupings and pathways in the brain can be seen by eye in fresh tissue. They can be seen in much more detail after being highlighted with various kinds of stains and viewed through a microscope. This detail provides information for many drawings and maps presented in this chapter and throughout this book.

Reticular matter (from the Latin *rete*, meaning "net") contains a mixture of cell bodies and axons from which it acquires its mottled gray and white, or netlike, appearance. Thus, with respect to our analogy equating brain regions with communities and roads, communities are gray, roads are white, and reticular matter is suburbia.

Microscopic views of (left) Nissl-stained gray-matter section of a monkey brain and (right) selective fiber stain of a white-matter section from a different cortical region.

Layers, Nuclei, Nerves, and Tracts

As already mentioned, a large, well-defined group of cell bodies can form layers or nuclei. The architecture of these groupings suggests that each nucleus or layer has a particular function, and such is indeed the case. A large collection of axons projecting to or away from a nucleus or layer in the CNS is called a **tract** (from Old French, meaning "path") or, sometimes, a *fiber pathway*.

Tracts carry information from one place to another within the CNS; for example, the corticospinal (pyramidal) tract carries information from the cortex to the spinal cord. The optic tract carries information from the retina of the eye (the retina, strictly speaking, is part of the brain) to other visual centers in the brain. Fibers and fiber pathways that enter and leave the CNS are called **nerves**, such as the auditory nerve or the vagus nerve; but, after they have entered the central nervous system, they, too, are called tracts.

The Origin and Development of the Central Nervous System

The developing brain is less complex than the adult brain and provides a clearer picture of the vertebrate brain's basic three-part structure (**Figure 3.8**A). Later in mammals, two of the three regions, the front and back components, expand

(A) Vertebrate	(B) Mammalian embryo	(C) Fully developed human brain	
Prosencephalon (forebrain)	Telencephalon (endbrain)	Neocortex, basal ganglia, limbic system olfactory bulb, lateral ventricles	Forebrain
	Diencephalon (between brain)	Thalamus, hypothalamus, pineal body, third ventricle	Brainstem
Mesencephalon (midbrain)	Mesencephalon	Tectum, tegmentum, cerebral aqueduct	
Rhombencephalon (hindbrain)	Metencephalon (across brain)	Cerebellum, pons, fourth ventricle	
	Myelencephalon (spinal brain)	Medulla oblongata, fourth ventricle	
Spinal cord	Spinal cord	Spinal cord	Spinal cord

Figure 3.8

Steps in the Development of the Brain (A) A three-chambered brain. (B) A five-chambered brain. (C) Medial view through the center of the human brain.

greatly and subdivide further, yielding five regions in all (Figure 3.8B). Embryologists use rather cumbersome names for these regions; because some names are also used to describe parts of the adult brain (Figure 3.8C), they are included in the illustration.

The three regions of the primitive, developing brain are recognizable in Figure 3.8A as a series of three enlargements at the end of the embryonic spinal cord. The adult brain of a fish, amphibian, or reptile is roughly equivalent to this three-part brain: the **prosencephalon** ("front brain") is responsible for olfaction, the **mesencephalon** ("middle brain") is the seat of vision and hearing, and the **rhombencephalon** (hindbrain) controls movement and balance. Here, the spinal cord is considered part of the hindbrain.

In mammals (Figure 3.8B), the prosencephalon develops further to form the cerebral hemispheres (the cortex and related structures), which are known collectively as the **telencephalon** ("endbrain"). The remaining part of the old prosencephalon is referred to as the **diencephalon** ("between brain") and includes the thalamus. The back part of the brain also develops further. It is subdivided into the **metencephalon** ("across brain," which includes the enlarged cerebellum) and the **myelencephalon** ("spinal brain"), the lower region of the brainstem.

The human brain is a more complex mammalian brain, retaining most of the features of other mammalian brains and possessing especially large cerebral hemispheres. As we describe the major structures of the CNS in the sections that follow, we group them according to the three-part scheme of forebrain, brainstem, and spinal cord (Figure 3.8C). These three subdivisions reinforce the concept of *levels of function*, with newer levels partly replicating the work of older ones. Nevertheless, most behaviors are thus not the product of a single locus in the brain but rather of many brain areas and levels that do not simply replicate function; instead, each region adds a different dimension to the behavior. This hierarchical organization affects virtually every behavior in which humans engage.

The brain begins as a tube, and, even after it folds and matures, its interior remains "hollow." The four prominent pockets created by the folding of this hollow interior in the brain are called **ventricles** ("bladders") and are numbered 1 through 4. The "lateral ventricles" (first and second) form C-shaped lakes underlying the cerebral cortex, whereas the third and fourth ventricles extend into the brainstem and spinal cord (**Figure 3.9**). All are filled with cerebrospinal fluid, which is produced by ependymal glial cells located adjacent to the ventricles (see Table 3.1). Cerebral spinal fluid flows from the lateral ventricles out through the fourth ventricle and eventually drains into the circulatory system.

Figure 3.9

Cerebral Ventricles The four ventricles are interconnected. There are two lateral cerebral ventricles, one in each hemisphere, and a third and fourth ventricle, each of which lies in the midline of the brain.

The Spinal Cord

We begin our description of neuroanatomy with the spinal cord. It is structurally the simplest part of the CNS, and the basic plan of the spinal cord is also seen in the plan of the brainstem. Along with the spinal cord, we also detail the functions of the somatic and the autonomic nervous systems.

Spinal-Cord Structure and the Spinal Nerves

In a simple animal, such as the earthworm, the body is a tube divided into segments. Within the body is a tube of nerve cells that also is divided into segments. Each segment receives nerve fibers from afferent sensory receptors in the part of the body adjacent to it and sends efferent fibers to control the muscles of that part of the body. Each segment functions relatively independently in the earthworm, although fibers interconnect the segments and coordinate their activity. This basic plan also holds for the human body.

Let us take a look at our "tube of nerves." The spinal cord lies inside the bony spinal-column vertebrae, which are categorized into five regions from top to tail. **Figure 3.10**A details our 30 spinal-cord segments: 8 cervical (C), 12 thoracic (T), 5 lumbar (L), and 5 sacral (S). Figure 3.10B shows the segmental

Figure 3.10

Spinal-cord Structure (A) The five groups of spinal-cord segments making up the spinal column (cervical, C; thoracic, T; lumbar, L; sacral, S; and coccygeal vertebrae) are shown in this sagittal view. (B) Each spinal segment corresponds to a region of body surface (a dermatome) that is identified by the segment number, for example, C5 or L2.

organization of the human body. The segments, called **dermatomes** ("skin cuts"), encircle the spinal column as a stack of rings.

Mammalian limbs evolved perpendicularly to the spinal cord, but humans have an upright posture; so the dermatomes in our bodies are distorted into the pattern shown in Figure 3.10B. As many as six segments (C4 through T2) can be represented on the arm. If you imagine the person in the drawing standing on all fours, you can see how this pattern makes sense.

Each spinal segment is connected by SNS spinal nerve fibers to the body dermatome of the same number, including the organs and musculature that lie within the dermatome. In the main, the cervical segments control the forelimbs, the thoracic segments control the trunk, and the lumbar segments control the hind limbs.

Figure 3.11 shows a cross section of the spinal cord. Afferent fibers entering the dorsal part of the spinal cord (posterior in humans) bring information from the sensory receptors of the body. These spinal nerve fibers converge as they enter the spinal cord, forming a strand of fibers referred to as a **dorsal root**. Efferent fibers leaving the ventral (anterior in humans) part of the spinal cord, carrying information from the spinal cord to the muscles, form a similar strand of spinal nerves known as a **ventral root**.

You can see in Figure 3.11A that the outer part of the spinal cord itself consists of white matter, or tracts, arranged so that, with a few exceptions, the dorsally located tracts are sensory and the ventrally located tracts are motor. The spinal tracts carry information to and from the brain. The inner part of the cord consists of gray matter; that is, it is composed largely of neural cell bodies, which, in this case, organize movements and give rise to the ventral roots. In cross section, this gray-matter region has the shape of a butterfly (Figure 3.11B).

Spinal-Cord Function and the Spinal Nerves

François Magendie, a French experimental physiologist, reported in a three-page paper in 1822 that he had succeeded in cutting the dorsal roots of one group of puppies and the ventral roots of another group (the youth of the dogs allowed the different surgeries; in adult dogs, the roots are fused). He found

Figure 3.11

Spinal Nerve Connections (A) A cross section of the spinal cord, viewed ventrally, illustrating a sensory neuron in the dorsal root and a motor neuron in the ventral root. Collateral branches of the sensory fiber may cross to the far side of the spinal cord to influence motor neurons on that side and may extend to adjacent segments to influence adjacent body parts. The inner regions of the spinal cord consist of neural cell bodies (gray matter), and the outer regions consist of tracts (white matter) traveling to and from the brain. (B) Dorsal view with the spinal cord exposed. (Bassett/Visuals Unlimited.)

(A)

1 Fibers entering the dorsal root bring sensory information from sensory receptors.

Dorsal root (sensory)

Sensory neuron

Motor neuron

Ventral root (motor)

2 Fibers leaving the ventral root carry motor information to the muscles.

3 Collateral branches of sensory neurons may cross to the other side and influence motor neurons there.

Gray matter White matter

4 White-matter fiber tracts carry information to and from the brain.

(B)

that cutting the dorsal roots caused loss of sensation and cutting the ventral roots caused loss of movement.

Eleven years earlier, in 1811, Charles Bell, a Scot, had suggested the opposite functions for each of the roots, basing his conclusions on anatomical information and the results from somewhat inconclusive experiments on rabbits. When Magendie's paper appeared, Bell hotly disputed priority for the discovery, with some success. Today, the principle that the dorsal part of the spinal cord is sensory and the ventral part is motor is called the **Bell–Magendie law**.

Magendie's experiment has been called the most important ever conducted on the nervous system. It enabled neurologists for the first time to distinguish sensory from motor impairments, as well as to draw general conclusions about the location of neural damage, on the basis of the symptoms displayed by patients. Because of the segmental structure of the spinal cord and the body, rather good inferences can also be made about the location of spinal-cord damage or disease on the basis of changes in sensation or movement in particular body parts.

Further major advances toward understanding spinal-cord function came from the work of Charles Sherrington and his students, who showed that the spinal cord retains many functions even after it has been separated from the brain. Sherrington published a summary of this research in 1906, and it had an important influence in the treatment of people with spinal-cord injury.

Persons whose spinal cords are cut so that they no longer have control over their legs are **paraplegic**; if the cut is higher on the cord, making them unable to use their arms either, they are **quadriplegic**. Once thought untreatable, growing understanding of spinal-cord function has led to such huge improvements in treatment that spinal-cord patients today can lead long and active lives. A Canadian paraplegic, Rick Hansen, the "man in motion," propelled his wheelchair around the world to campaign for the funding of research and treatment of spinal-cord injuries. The late actor Christopher Reeve, famed for his cinematic role as Superman, became quadriplegic after a horse-riding accident yet continued for the rest of his life to make movies and to campaign for medical treatment and research for spinal-cord injuries.

Despite the fact that the spinal cord controls both simple and complex behavior, it does depend on the brain, as evidenced by the severe behavioral impairments that follow spinal-cord injury. Because the main effect of such injury is to sever connections between the cord and the brain, scientists believe that simply reestablishing these connections can restore function to spinal-cord-injured people. Unfortunately, although the fibers in the spinal tracts do regrow in some vertebrates, such as fish, and in the early stages of development in other animals, they do not regrow in adult mammals.

Researchers continue to experiment with various approaches to induce spinal-cord regrowth. These approaches include the idea that new growth is prevented by the presence of certain inhibitory molecules on the tracts of the cord below the cut. If these inhibitory molecules can in turn be inhibited, investigators reason, fibers will begin to grow across the injured zone.

Another line of research is focused on the scarring that accompanies most spinal-cord damage and the possibility that scarring inhibits new growth. Some scientists are conducting experiments in which they attempt to remove the scar, whereas other scientists are attempting to build bridges across the scar over which fibers can grow. All these approaches have been partly successful in nonhuman animal studies, but they have not approached the level of success to be considered a cure for spinal-cord injury.

In addition to the local connections that pain and tactile receptors in the SNS make within the segments of the spinal cord corresponding to their dermatomes, these receptors communicate with fibers in many other segments of the spinal cord and can thus produce appropriate adjustments in many body parts. For example, when one leg is withdrawn in response to a painful stimulus, the other leg must simultaneously extend to support the body's weight.

The spinal cord is capable of producing actions that are more complex than just adjustments of a limb. If the body of an animal that has had its spinal cord sectioned from the brain is held in a sling with its feet touching a conveyor belt, the animal is capable of walking. Thus, the spinal cord contains all the SNS connections required for allowing an animal to walk.

Recall from Figure 3.2 that the SNS consists of all the spinal and cranial nerves that produce movement and transmit incoming sensory information to the CNS. Sensory information plays a central role in eliciting different kinds

Table 3.2 The cranial nerves

Number	Name	Function*	Method of Examination	Typical Symptoms of Dysfunction
1	Olfactory	Smell (s)	Various odors applied to each nostril	Loss of sense of smell (anosmia)
2	Optic	Vision (s)	Visual acuity, map field of vision	Loss of vision (anopsia)
3	Oculomotor	Eye movement (m)	Reaction to light, lateral movements of eyes, eyelid movement (ptosis), deviation of eye outward	Double vision (diplopia), large pupil, uneven dilation of pupils, drooping eyelid
4	Trochlear	Eye movement (m)	Upward and downward eye movements	Double vision, defect of downward gaze
5	Trigeminal	Masticatory movements (s, m)	Light touch by cotton baton; pain by pinprick; thermal by hot and cold tubes, corneal reflex by touching cornea; jaw reflex by tapping chin, jaw movements	Decreased sensitivity or numbness of face, brief attacks of severe pain (trigeminal neuralgia); weakness and wasting of facial muscles, asymmetrical chewing
6	Abducens	Eye movement (m)	Lateral movements	Double vision, inward deviation of the eye
7	Facial	Facial movement (s, m)	Facial movements, facial expression, testing for taste	Facial paralysis, loss of taste over anterior two-thirds of tongue
8	Auditory vestibular	Hearing (s)	Audiogram for testing hearing; stimulating by rotating patient or by irrigating the ear with hot or cold water (caloric test)	Deafness, sensation of noise in ear (tinnitus); disequilibrium feeling of disorientation in space
9	Glossopharyngeal	Tongue and pharynx (s, m)	Testing for sweet, salt, bitter, and sour tastes on tongue; touching walls of pharynx for pharyngeal or gag reflex	Partial dry mouth, loss of taste (ageusia) over posterior third of tongue, anesthesia and paralysis of upper pharynx
10	Vagus	Heart, blood vessels, viscera, movement of larynx and pharynx (s, m)	Observing palate in phonation, touching palate for palatal reflex	Hoarseness, lower pharyngeal anesthesia and paralysis, indefinite visceral disturbance
11	Spinal accessory	Neck muscles and viscera (m)	Movement, strength, and bulk of neck and shoulder muscles	Wasting of neck with weakened rotation, inability to shrug
12	Hypoglossal	(m) Tongue muscles	Tongue movements, tremor, wasting or wrinkling of tongue	Wasting of tongue with deviation to side of lesion on protrusion

*The letters "s" and "m" refer to sensory and motor function, respectively, of the nerve.

of movements organized by the spinal cord. Movements dependent only on spinal-cord function are referred to as **reflexes**, specific movements elicited by specific forms of sensory stimulation. There are many kinds of sensory receptors in the body, including receptors for pain, temperature, touch and pressure, and the sensations of muscle and joint movement. The size of the spinal nerve fiber coming from each kind of receptor is distinctive; generally, pain and temperature fibers are smaller, and those for touch and muscle sense are larger.

The stimulation of pain and temperature receptors in a limb usually produces **flexion** movements that bring the limb inward, toward the body and away from injury. If the stimulus is mild, only the distal part of the limb flexes in response to it but, with successively stronger stimuli, the size of the movement increases until the whole limb is drawn back.

The stimulation of fine touch and muscle receptors in a limb usually produces **extension** movements, which extend the limb outward, away from the body. The extensor reflex causes the touched part of the limb to maintain contact with the stimulus; for example, the foot or hand touching a surface will maintain contact with the surface through this reflex. Because each of the senses has its own receptors, fibers, connections, and reflex movements, each sense can be thought of as an independent sensory system.

Connections Between Central and Somatic Nervous Systems

The somatic nervous system is monitored and controlled by the CNS. The spinal cord oversees the spinal nerves, and the brain oversees the 12 pairs of **cranial nerves**. The linkages provided by the cranial nerves between the brain and various parts of the head and neck as well as various internal organs are tabulated in **Table 3.2** and illustrated in **Figure 3.12**. Cranial nerves can have afferent functions, such as for sensory inputs to the brain from the eyes, ears, mouth, and nose, or they can have efferent functions, such as for motor control of the facial muscles, tongue, and eyes.

Some cranial nerves have both sensory and motor functions, such as the modulation of both sensation and movement in the face, and the vagus nerve makes connections with many body organs, including the heart. Knowledge of the organization and function of the cranial nerves is important for making neurological diagnoses.

Autonomic Nervous System Connections

The internal autonomic nervous system (see Figure 3.2) is a hidden partner in controlling behavior. Even without our conscious awareness, it stays on the job to keep the heart beating, the liver releasing glucose, the pupils of the eyes adjusting to light, and so forth. Without the ANS, which regulates the internal organs and glands by connections through the SNS to the CNS, life would quickly cease.

Although the exertion of some conscious control over some of these vegetative activities can be learned, such conscious interference is unnecessary. One important reason is that the ANS must keep working during sleep when

Figure **3.12**

Cranial Nerves Each of the 12 pairs of cranial nerves has a different function, as detailed in Table 3.2. Some cranial nerves are sensory; others are motor; and still others are both. A common mnemonic device for learning the order of the cranial nerves is, On old Olympus's towering top, a Finn and German view some hops. The first letter of each word is, in order, the first letter of the name of each nerve.

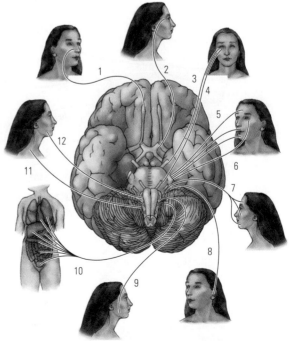

conscious awareness is off-duty. Recall that the functions retained by Terri Schiavo were vegetative (see Chapter 1).

The two divisions of the ANS—sympathetic and parasympathetic—work in opposition. The sympathetic system arouses the body for action, for example, by stimulating the heart to beat faster and inhibiting digestion when we exert ourselves during exercise or times of stress, referred to as the "fight or flight" response. The parasympathetic system calms the body down, for example, by slowing the heartbeat and stimulating digestion to allow us to "rest and digest" after exertion and during quiet times.

Like the SNS, the ANS interacts with the rest of the nervous system. Activation of the sympathetic system starts in the thoracic and lumbar spinal-cord regions, as illustrated on the left in **Figure 3.13**. But note that the spinal nerves

Figure 3.13

Autonomic Nervous System The pathways of the two ANS divisions exert opposing effects on the organs that they innervate. All autonomic fibers connect at "stops" en route from the CNS to their target organs. (Left) Arousing sympathetic fibers connect to a chain of ganglia near the spinal cord. (Right) Calming parasympathetic fibers connect to individual parasympathetic ganglia near the target organs.

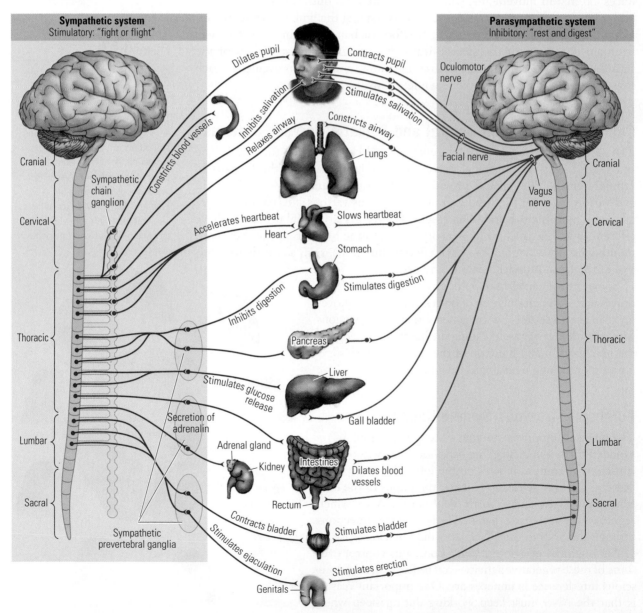

do not directly control the target organs. Rather, the spinal cord is connected to a chain of autonomic control centers, collections of neural cells called *sympathetic ganglia*. These **ganglia**, collections of nerve cells that function somewhat like a primitive brain, control the internal organs.

A part of the parasympathetic system also is connected to the spinal cord—specifically, to the sacral region as diagrammed in the middle and on the right in Figure 3.13. As the illustration reveals, however, the greater part of the parasympathetic system derives from three cranial nerves: the vagus nerve, which calms most of the internal organs; the facial nerve, which controls salivation; and the oculomotor nerve, which controls pupil dilation and eye movements. In contrast with the arousing sympathetic system, which forms a chain running parallel to the spinal cord, the calming parasympathetic system connects with parasympathetic ganglia near the target organs, as shown in the middle and on the right in Figure 3.13.

The internal organs, although arranged segmentally in relation to the spinal cord, appear not to have their own sensory representation within it. Pain in these organs is perceived as coming from the outer parts of the dermatome and so is called **referred pain**. For example, pain in the heart is felt in the shoulder and arm, and kidney pain is felt in the back. Physicians use what is known about the location of referred pains to diagnose problems within the body.

The Brainstem

The brainstem begins where the spinal cord enters the skull and extends upward to the lower areas of the forebrain. **Figure 3.14** shows its three main regions: the diencephalon, the midbrain, and the hindbrain. In general, the brainstem produces more-complex movements than does the spinal cord, but its overall plan is similar, with the region dorsal to the fourth ventricle responsible for sensory functions and that ventral to the ventricle (posterior and anterior for the upright human brain) responsible for motor functions.

A distinctive part of the brainstem comprises the many cranial-nerve nuclei that converge there and send their axons to the muscles of the head. The core of the brainstem consists of those cranial-nerve nuclei as well as many bundles of fibers from the spinal cord that pass through the brainstem on their way to the forebrain. Conversely, fibers from the forebrain connect with the brainstem or pass through it on their way to the spinal cord. The brainstem also regulates many complex functions, with the diencephalon, midbrain, and hindbrain regulating somewhat different functions as described next.

The Hindbrain

The most distinctive part of the hindbrain is the **cerebellum**. It protrudes above the core of the brainstem, and its surface is gathered into narrow folds, or **folia**, like the gyri and sulci of the cortex but smaller (**Figure 3.15**). At

Figure **3.14**

Brainstem Structures Medial view of the brain (left) shows the relation of the brainstem to the cerebral hemispheres. In accord with the plan of the spinal cord, brainstem structures perform both sensory (posterior regions) and motor (anterior regions) functions.

Diencephalon

Midbrain

Hindbrain

Cerebellum

Figure **3.15**

The Cerebellum Necessary for fine, coordinated movements, the cerebellum, like the cerebrum, has a cortex containing gray and white matter and subcortical nuclei, shown in the detailed horizontal section.

White matter (cerebellar cortex)

Subcortical nuclei

Gray matter (cerebellar cortex)

Figure 3.16

Hindbrain Structures The principal structures of the hindbrain integrate both voluntary and involuntary body movement and contribute to cycles of sleeping and waking.

Pons
Reticular formation
Medulla
Cerebellum

the base of the cerebellum are several nuclei that send connections to other parts of the brain.

The cerebellum plays a role in coordinating and learning skilled movements. Thus, damage to the cerebellum results in equilibrium problems, postural defects, and impairments of skilled motor activity. The parts that receive most of their impulses from the vestibular system (sensory receptors for balance and movement located in the middle ear) help to maintain the body's equilibrium. Cerebellar parts receiving impulses mainly from the receptors in the body's trunk and limbs control postural reflexes and coordinate functionally related groups of muscles.

Within the core of the hindbrain's mixture of nuclei and fibers lies a network referred to as the **reticular formation**, diagrammed in **Figure 3.16**. In 1949, Giuseppe Moruzzi and Horace Magoun stimulated this area electrically in anesthetized cats and found that the stimulation produced a waking pattern of electrical activity in the cats' cortices. They concluded that the function of the reticular formation is to control sleeping and waking—that is, to maintain "general arousal" or "consciousness." As a result, the reticular formation came to be known as the *reticular activating system*.

Neuroscientists now recognize that the various nuclei within the upper part of the brainstem (the pons) and the lower part (the medulla) serve many functions; some take part in waking and sleeping and others take part in locomotion.

The Midbrain

The midbrain, diagrammed in **Figure 3.17**, has two main subdivisions: located dorsally is the **tectum**, or "roof," which is the roof of the third ventricle, and located ventrally is the **tegmentum**, or "floor" of the third ventricle. The tectum receives a massive amount of sensory information from the eyes and ears. Located on the brainstem's posterior, the tectum consists primarily of two sets of bilaterally symmetrical nuclei. The **superior colliculi** ("upper hills") receive projections from the retina of the eye, and they mediate many visually related behaviors. The **inferior colliculi** ("lower hills") receive projections from the ear, and they mediate many auditory-related behaviors. Another class of behaviors mediated by the colliculi is the orientation of movements related to sensory input, such as turning your head to look at the source of a sound.

Lying ventral to the tectum, as shown in Figure 3.17, the tegmentum is composed of nuclei related to motor functions, diagrammed at the upper right in the illustration. The *red nucleus* controls limb movements, and the **substantia nigra** (black substance) is

Figure 3.17

Midbrain Structures in the midbrain mediate a range of visual- and auditory-related behaviors and are critical in producing orienting movements, in species-specific behaviors, and in the perception of pain.

Substantia nigra
Periaqueductal gray matter
Ventral
Cerebral aqueduct
Dorsal
Red nucleus
Reticular formation
Superior colliculus

Tegmentum
Superior colliculus (receives visual input)
Inferior colliculus (receives auditory input)
Tectum
Cerebellum

connected to the forebrain, a connection important for reward and for initiating movements. The *periacqueductal gray matter*, made up of cell bodies that surround the aqueduct joining the third and fourth ventricles, contains circuits for controlling species-typical behaviors (for example, sexual behavior) and for modulating responses to pain.

The Diencephalon

The diencephalon borders the older and newer parts of the brain (see Figure 3.14). Its "between brain" status is reinforced in a neuroanatomical inconsistency: some anatomists place it in the brainstem, as we do; others place it in the forebrain (see Figure 3.8). The diencephalon consists mainly of the three thalamic structures: hypothalamus ("lower room"); epithalamus ("upper room"); and thalamus ("inner room" or "chamber").

The **hypothalamus**, comprising about 22 small nuclei and the fiber systems that pass through it, interacts with the pituitary gland. Although only about 0.3% of the brain's weight, the hypothalamus takes part in nearly all aspects of motivated behavior, including feeding, sexual behavior, sleeping, temperature regulation, emotional behavior, movement, and, through its interactions with the pituitary gland, endocrine function.

The **thalamus**, the largest structure in the diencephalon, is composed of 20-odd large nuclei, each of which projects to a specific area of the cerebral cortex, as shown in **Figure 3.18**. These nuclei route information from three sources to the cortex:

1. One group of thalamic nuclei relays information from sensory systems to their appropriate targets. For example, the *lateral geniculate body* (LGB) receives visual projections; the *medial geniculate body* (MGB) receives auditory projections; and the *ventrolateral posterior nuclei* (VLP) receive touch, pressure, pain, and temperature projections from the body. In turn, these areas project to the visual, auditory, and somatosensory regions of the cortex.

2. Some thalamic nuclei relay information between cortical areas. For example, a large area of the posterior cortex sends projections to the *pulvinar nucleus* (P) at the tip of the thalamus and receives projections back from that nucleus.

3. Some thalamic nuclei relay information from other forebrain and brainstem regions.

Figure 3.18

Thalamus (A) The arrows indicate the sources of input and output from major nuclei of the thalamus: anterior nucleus, A; dorsomedial nucleus, DM; ventral anterior nucleus, VA; ventrolateral nucleus, VL; lateral posterior nucleus, LP; ventrolateral posterior nucleus, VLP; pulvinar, P; lateral geniculate body, LGB; and medial geniculate body, MGB. (B) The relations between major thalamic nuclei and the various areas of the cortex to which they project.

(A) Thalamus

(B) Cortex

In short, almost all the information received by the cortex is first relayed through the thalamus.

The **epithalamus** is a collection of nuclei at the posterior of the diencephalon. Its overall function is poorly understood, but one of its structures, the pineal gland, secretes the hormone melatonin, which influences daily and seasonal body rhythms. Another structure, the habenula, regulates hunger and thirst.

The Forebrain

Of the three main forebrain structures, two are subcortical: the basal ganglia and the limbic system. Enveloping all is the cerebral cortex. These regions share many connections, forming functional circuits. Nevertheless, each is sufficiently anatomically and functionally distinct to describe separately.

The Basal Ganglia

The **basal ganglia** ("lower knots," referring to "knots below the cortex") are a collection of nuclei lying mainly beneath the anterior regions of the cortex (**Figure 3.19**). They include the **putamen** ("shell"), the **globus pallidus** ("pale globe"), and the **caudate nucleus** ("tailed nucleus"). The basal ganglia form a circuit with the cerebral cortex.

The caudate nucleus receives projections from all areas of the cortex and sends its own projections through the putamen and globus pallidus to the thalamus and, from there, to the frontal cortical areas. The basal ganglia also have reciprocal connections with the midbrain, especially with the substantia nigra in the midbrain tegmentum (see Figure 3.17). The ganglia have functions related to movement and to simple forms of learning.

Figure 3.19

Basal Ganglia This frontal section of the cerebral hemispheres shows the basal ganglia relative to the surrounding structures. Two associated brainstem structures that are instrumental in controlling and coordinating movement, the substantia nigra and subthalamic nucleus, also are illustrated.

The Basal Ganglia and Movement

Damage to different parts of the basal ganglia can produce changes in posture, increases or decreases in muscle tone, and abnormal movements such as twitches, jerks, and tremors. So the ganglia are thought to take part in such motor functions as the sequencing of movements into a smoothly executed response. Three diseases of the basal ganglia illustrate its motor functions:

1. In **Huntington's chorea**, a genetic disorder, cells of the basal ganglia die progressively, and, associated with this cell death, many involuntary movements of the body occur almost continuously. These abnormal movements have a "dancelike" quality, which is what *chorea* means in Latin.

2. In **Parkinson's disease**, the projections from the substantia nigra to the basal ganglia die. Associated with this cell death, the patient becomes rigid

and has difficulty moving and maintaining balance. The patient may also display rhythmical tremors of the hands and legs.

3. In **Tourette's syndrome**, another disorder of the basal ganglia, the most frequent symptoms are involuntary motor tics, especially of the face and head, and complex movements, such as hitting, lunging, or jumping. Tourette's is also characterized by involuntary vocalizations, including curse words and animal sounds.

These disorders of the basal ganglia are not disorders of *producing* movements, as in paralysis. Rather they are disorders of *controlling* movements. The basal ganglia, therefore, must play a role in the control and coordination of movement patterns, not in activating the muscles.

The Basal Ganglia and Learning

The second function of the basal ganglia is to support stimulus-response, or habit, learning. For example, a bird learns, after a number of experiences, that brightly colored butterflies have a bitter taste. Its basal ganglia are critical in learning the association between taste and color and in refraining from eating the insects. Similarly, many of our actions are responses to sensory cues—for example, flicking a light switch to turn on a light or turning the handle on a door to open it. People with basal ganglia disorders can have difficulty performing such stimulus-response actions.

The Limbic System

In the course of evolution in amphibians and reptiles, a number of three-layered cortical structures that sheath the periphery of the brainstem developed. With the subsequent growth of the **neocortex** ("new bark"), these older cortical structures became sandwiched at the border between the new brain and the old. Because of their evolutionary origin, some anatomists have referred to them as the *reptilian brain*, but the term **limbic lobe** (from the Latin *limbus*, meaning "border" or "hem"), coined by Broca in 1878, is more widely recognized among neuroscientists.

The limbic lobe is also referred to as the **limbic system**, which has proved to be a misnomer. The first theory of limbic function stemmed from the observation that connections exist between the olfactory system and the limbic lobe. On this evidence, anatomists hypothesized that the limbic structures processed olfactory information, and so collectively the structures became known as the **rhinencephalon**, or "smell-brain." A number of subsequent experiments have been unable to precisely demonstrate what olfactory function the limbic lobe has, but it is not required for simply identifying odors.

The limbic lobe consists of a number of interrelated structures, including the **amygdala** ("almond"), **hippocampus** ("sea horse"), and the **septum** ("partition"). The cingulate ("girdle") gyrus, or **cingulate cortex**, is a strip of limbic cortex that lies just above the corpus callosum along the medial walls of the cerebral hemispheres as shown in **Figure 3.20**A. The nuclei that form the amygdala and the septum play roles in emotional and species-typical behaviors. The hippocampus is proposed to mediate memory and spatial navigation and is particularly vulnerable to the effects of stress. The history of how the limbic

Figure **3.20**

Limbic Lobe (A) This medial view of the right hemisphere illustrates the principal structures of the limbic lobe that play roles in emotional and sexual behaviors, in memory, and in spatial navigation. (B) This model of the human limbic system and its major structures reveals a circuit proposed by Papez, in which the hypothalamic mammillary bodies connect to the hippocampus through the cingulate cortex, and the hippocampus connects to the hypothalamus through the fornix. (After Hamilton, 1976.)

(A) The limbic lobe, medial view

Cingulate cortex (limbic cortex)

Temporal lobe

Amygdala

Hippocampus

1 The limbic-lobe structures are in the midline,...

2 ...the hippocampus curves away into the temporal lobe,...

3 ...and the limbic lobe terminates in the amygdala.

(B) The limbic lobe (dissected out)

Cingulate cortex

Fornix

Septum

Olfactory bulb

Amygdala

Hypothalamus (mammillary bodies)

Hippocampus

"lobe" became the limbic "system" is one of the most interesting chapters in neuroscience.

In 1937, James Papez, in what at the time amounted to a scientific *tour de force*, asked, "Is emotion a magic product, or is it a physiologic process which depends on an anatomic mechanism?" He suggested that emotion, which had no known anatomic substrate, is a product of the limbic lobe, which had no recognized function at the time. Papez proposed that the emotional brain consists of a circuit in which information flows from the mammillary bodies in the hypothalamus to the anterior thalamic nucleus to the cingulate cortex to the hippocampus and back to the mammillary bodies (Figure 3.20B).

Input could enter this circuit from other structures to be elaborated as emotion. For example, an idea ("It is dangerous to walk in the dark") from the neocortex could enter the circuit to be elaborated as a fear ("I feel frightened in the dark") and ultimately influence the hypothalamus to release a hormone to prompt the appropriate physical response to the idea and its emotional corollary. The hippocampus contains many receptors for the stress hormone corticosterone, which is seen as support for Papez's idea.

In Chapter 1, we described Scoville and Milner's now-famous patient H.M., whose medial temporal lobe, including his hippocampus, was removed bilaterally as a treatment for epilepsy. His primary deficits were not emotional; rather, he displayed little ability to learn new information. Thereafter, the limbic system was proposed to be the memory system of the brain. In the years since H.M. was first described, many other regions of the brain also have become recognized as playing a part in memory, diminishing the apparent role of the limbic system in that function.

Today, neuroscientists have concluded that the limbic lobe is not a unitary "system" at all. Although some limbic structures play roles in emotional and sexual behaviors, limbic structures also serve other functions in memory, motivation and reward, and navigation.

The Neocortex

Anatomists use the term *cortex* to refer to any outer layer of cells. In neuroscience, the terms *cortex* and *neocortex* (new cortex) are often used interchangeably to refer to the outer part of the forebrain, and so, by convention, "cortex" refers to "neocortex" unless otherwise indicated, for example, as the older limbic cortex (see Figure 3.20A). The neocortex is the part of the brain that has expanded the most in the course of evolution: it comprises 80% by volume of the human brain and is unique to mammals. Its primary function is to create and respond to perceptions of the world.

The human neocortex has an area as large as 2500 square centimeters but a thickness of only 1.5 to 3.0 millimeters. It consists of six layers of cells (gray matter) and is heavily wrinkled. This wrinkling is nature's solution to the problem of confining the huge neocortical surface area within a skull that is still small enough to pass through the birth canal. Just as crumpling a sheet of paper enables it to fit into a smaller box than it could when flat, the folding of the neocortex permits the human brain to fit comfortably within the relatively fixed volume of the skull.

To review some of the main features of the cortex introduced in Chapter 1, **Figure 3.21** shows the two nearly symmetrical cerebral hemispheres, the left and the right, separated by the longitudinal fissure and subdivided into four lobes: frontal, parietal, temporal, and occipital. The frontal lobes have fixed boundaries: they are bounded posteriorly by the **central sulcus**, inferiorly by the lateral fissure, and medially by the **cingulate sulcus**.

The anterior boundary of the parietal lobes is the central sulcus, and their inferior boundary is the lateral fissure. The temporal lobes are bounded dorsally by the lateral fissure. On the lateral surface of the brain, there are no definite boundaries between the occipital lobes and the parietal and temporal lobes.

Fissures, Sulci, and Gyri

The most conspicuous surface feature of the neocortex is its crinkled tissue, consisting of clefts and ridges. Recall from Chapter 1 that a cleft is called a *fissure* if it extends deeply enough into the brain to indent the ventricles; it is called a *sulcus* (plural, sulci) if it is shallower. A ridge is called a *gyrus* (plural, gyri).

Figure 3.21

Views of the Human Brain
Locations of the lobes of the cerebral hemispheres are shown in these top, bottom, side, and midline views, as are the cerebellum, the central sulcus, and the longitudinal and lateral fissures. (Photographs courtesy of Yakolev Collection/AFIP.)

Dorsal view

Central sulcus
Frontal lobe
Parietal lobe
Longitudinal fissure
Occipital lobe

Lateral view

Central sulcus
Frontal lobe
Parietal lobe
Lateral fissure
Temporal lobe
Occipital lobe

Ventral view

Frontal lobe
Temporal lobe
Cerebellum
Cranial nerves
Occipital lobe
Brainstem

Medial view

Frontal lobe
Central sulcus
Parietal lobe
Occipital lobe
Temporal lobe
Brainstem
Cerebellum

Figure 3.22

Major Gyri and Sulci Lateral (A) and medial (B) views of the cortical gyri; lateral (C) and medial (D) views of the cortical sulci.

Figure 3.22 shows the location of the more important fissures, sulci, and gyri of the brain. The location and shape of these features vary somewhat on the two sides of a person's brain, and the location, size, and shape of the gyri and sulci vary substantially in the brains of different persons. Adjacent gyri differ in the that cells are organized within them, and the shift from one kind of arrangement to another is usually at the sulcus. There is evidence that gyri can be associated with specific functions.

The major gyri on the outer surface of the neocortex are shown in Figure 3.22A, and those on the inner surface of the neocortex are shown in Figure 3.22B. Note that the cingulate gyrus, located just above the corpus callosum, spans the inner surface of the four neocortical lobes. Figure 3.22C illustrates the main sulci and fissures on the lateral surface of the cortex, and Figure 3.22D locates some of the main sulci and fissures on the medial surface of the cortex.

Organization of the Cortex in Relation to Its Inputs and Outputs

The locations of the various inputs and outputs to the cortex can be represented by a **projection map**, which is constructed by tracing axons from the sensory systems into the brain and by tracing axons from the neocortex to the motor systems of the brainstem and spinal cord (**Figure 3.23**). Different regions of the neocortex have different functions. Some regions receive information from sensory systems, others command movements, and still others are the sites of connections between the sensory and the motor areas, enabling them to work in concert.

Recall that inputs to the cortex are relayed through the thalamic nuclei (see Figure 3.18). Overall, the neocortex can be conceptualized as consisting of a number of fields: visual, auditory, body senses, and motor (see Figure 2.11A). Because vision, audition, and body senses are functions of the posterior cortex, this region of the brain (parietal, temporal, and occipital lobes) is considered largely sensory; because the motor function is located in the frontal neocortex, that lobe is considered largely motor. Finally, because each lobe contains one of the primary projection areas, it can be associated roughly with a general function:

Frontal lobes: motor functions

Parietal lobes: body senses

Temporal lobes: auditory functions

Occipital lobes: visual functions

1 Primary projection areas receive sensory input or project to spinal motor systems.

2 Secondary areas interpret inputs or organize movements.

3 Association areas (uncolored) modulate information between secondary areas.

Primary Areas

As Figure 3.23 shows, sensory projections from the eye can be traced to the occipital lobe, projections from the ear to the temporal lobe, and projections from the somatosensory system to the parietal lobe. The olfactory system sends projections to the ventral frontal lobe (see Figure 3.21 ventral view). The major motor projection to the spinal cord originates in the frontal lobe.

The areas that receive projections from structures outside the neocortex or send projections to it are called **primary areas**. Note that the lateral view of the brain presented in Figure 3.23 does not represent the entire extent of these primary projection areas, because they also extend down into the cortical gyri and fissures. Much of the auditory zone, for example, is located within the lateral fissure. Nevertheless, the primary projection areas of the neocortex are small relative to its total size.

Secondary Areas

The primary sensory areas send projections into the areas adjacent to them, and the motor areas receive fibers from areas adjacent to them. These adjacent **secondary areas** are less directly connected with the sensory receptors and motor neurons. The secondary areas are thought to be more engaged in interpreting sensory input or organizing movements than are the primary areas.

Tertiary Areas

The cortical areas between the various secondary areas may receive projections from them or send projections to them. These patches of cortex are referred to as **tertiary areas** and often as **association cortex** because early views of neocortical function proposed that tertiary areas serve to connect and coordinate the functions of the secondary areas. Tertiary areas encompass all cortex that is not specialized for sensory or motor function but rather mediates complex activities such as language, planning, memory, and attention. The accompanying Snapshot describes a newly found connection between such neural activity and heretofore unexplained physical symptoms.

Figure 3.23

Projection Map Primary projection areas receive input from the sensory systems or project to spinal motor systems. Secondary areas interpret sensory input or organize movement. White and black arrows indicate that information flows from primary to secondary sensory areas and from secondary motor areas to primary motor areas. Information also flows from secondary to higher-order association, or tertiary, areas and between association areas of the four cortical lobes.

○SNAPSHOT
Imaging the Conversion Reaction

Understanding brain function requires knowledge not only of neuroanatomy but also of what specific brain regions do. New insights into an old disorder illustrate the understanding obtained by combining anatomical and functional views of the brain.

Conversion reaction was once called *hysteria* (the Greek term for "uterus"). Coined by the Egyptian physician Hippocrates, hysteria has been assigned to the present day to a variety of disorders, mainly in women, including paralysis, changes in sensory ability such as loss of vision, and a variety of other illnesses that seemingly could not be explained as physical ailments. According to Hippocrates, if the uterus wandered in the body and became lodged in a particular body part, the functional blockage of the part resulted in a patient's symptoms.

Hysteria was popularized by Sigmund Freud's account of his patient Anna O. and his theory that unconscious conflict manifests as physical symptoms. The term *conversion reaction* has now replaced *hysteria* in the *Diagnostic and Statistical Manual of Mental Disorders* (DSM).

In contrast with the general finding of an absence of a physical cause for conversion reactions, brain imaging of patients with its symptoms reveals changes in the function of certain brain regions (Black et al., 2004). The brain-imaging studies do not explain the cause of conversion reaction, but they do, for the first time, reveal a physical basis for the condition. For example, Sean Spence (2000) used positron emission tomography to reveal the extent of brain blood flow,

In response to attempted movement, PET scanning (frontal view) reveals that regional blood flow decreased in the left dorsolateral prefrontal cortex in the paralyzed patients (red) and in the right anterior prefrontal cortex in the feigners (green). (After Spence et al., 2000.)

hence revealing brain regions that are hypoactive or hyperactive, to examine brain function in three patients who suffered from forelimb paralysis. To obtain a comparison group, control subjects were asked to feign comparable paralysis.

As participants attempted limb movements, regional cerebral blood flow was decreased in the paralyzed patients' left dorsolateral prefrontal cortices (red areas) but in the right anterior prefrontal cortices of the feigners (green areas). Because the dorsolateral prefrontal cortex is associated with movement planning, the investigators suggested that the patients' paralysis is associated with the brain's executive control of movement.

Black, D. N., A. L. Seritan, K. H. Taber, and R. A. Hurley. Conversion hysteria: Lessons from functional imaging. *Journal of Neuropsychiatry and Clinical Neuroscience* 16:245–251, 2004.

Spence, S. A., H. L. Crimlisk, H. Cope, M. A. Ron, and P. M. Grasby. Discrete neurophysiological correlates in prefrontal cortex during hysterical and feigned disorder of movement. *Lancet* 355:1243–1244, 2000.

Cellular Organization of the Cortex

The neurons of the neocortex are arranged in six layers, as shown in **Figure 3.24**. There are regional differences in the shape, size, and connections of the cells among the six layers:

- Layers V and VI send axons to other brain areas. Both the layers and the cells of which they are composed are particularly large and distinctive in the motor cortex, which sends projections to the spinal cord. (Large size is typical of cells that send information long distances.)

- Layer IV receives axons from sensory systems and other cortical areas. This layer features large numbers of small, densely packed cells in the primary areas of vision, somatosensation, audition, and taste–olfaction, which receive large projections from their respective sensory organs.

- Layers I, II, and III, receive input mainly from layer IV and are quite well developed in the secondary and tertiary areas of the cortex.

A map based on the organization, structure, and distribution of cortical cells is called a **cytoarchitectonic map**. One in wide use, known as **Brodmann's map**, is shown in lateral and medial views in **Figure 3.25**A. In Brodmann's map, the different areas are numbered, but the numbers themselves have no special meaning.

To perform his analysis, Brodmann divided the brain at the central sulcus and then examined the front and back halves separately, numbering new conformations of cells as he found them but without following a methodical path over the surface or through the layers. Thus, he named areas 1 and 2 in the posterior section, then switched to the anterior section and named areas 3 and 4, then switched back again, and then looked somewhere else.

The regions of Brodmann's map correspond quite closely with regions discovered with the use of noncytoarchitectonic techniques, including electrical stimulation, tract tracing, and analysis of brain injury. Figure 3.25B summarizes some of the relations between areas on Brodmann's map and areas that have been identified according to their known functions. For example, area 17 corresponds to the primary visual projection area, whereas areas 18 and 19 correspond to the secondary visual projection areas. Area 4 is the primary motor cortex. Broca's area, related to the articulation of words, is area 44. Similar relations exist for other areas and functions.

One problem with Brodmann's map is that new, more powerful analytical techniques have shown that many Brodmann areas can be further subdivided. For this reason, the map has been updated and now consists of a mixture of numbers, letters, and names.

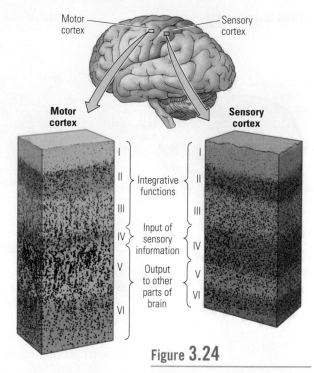

Figure **3.24**

Layering in the Neocortex As this comparison of cortical layers in the sensory and motor cortices shows, layer IV is relatively thick in the sensory cortex and relatively thin in the motor cortex, whereas layers V and VI are relatively thick in the motor cortex and thin in the sensory cortex.

(A) Lateral view

Medial view

(B) Function	Map code	Brodmann area
Vision		
primary		17
secondary		18, 19, 20, 21, 37
Auditory		
primary		41
secondary		22, 42
Body senses		
primary		1, 2, 3
secondary		5, 7
Sensory, tertiary		7, 22, 37, 39, 40
Motor		
primary		4
secondary		6
eye movement		8
speech		44
Motor, tertiary		9, 10, 11, 45, 46, 47

Figure **3.25**

Mapping the Cortex

(A) Brodmann's areas of the cortex. A few numbers are missing from the original sources of this drawing, including 12 through 16 and 48 through 51. (B) This table coordinates known functional areas and Brodmann cytoarchitectonic areas. (Part A after Elliott, 1969.)

(A) Lateral view

1 Axon fibers connect one lobe of the brain to another,...

Inferior occipital frontal tract

Superior occipital frontal tract

Superior longitudinal tract

Uncinate tract

Inferior longitudinal tract

(B) Medial view

2 ...one part of a lobe to another part,...

Cingulum   Arcuate fibers

Corpus callosum

Inferior longitudinal tract

(C) Frontal view

Corpus callosum

Anterior commissure

3 ...and one hemisphere of the brain to the other.

Figure 3.26

Connections Between Various Regions of the Cortex

Connections Between Cortical Areas

The various connections between regions of the cortex are of functional interest because, as you know, damage to a pathway can have consequences as severe as damage to the functional areas connected by the pathway. A glance at **Figure 3.26** shows that it is difficult indeed to damage any area of the cortex without damaging one or more of its interconnecting pathways. The various neocortical regions are interconnected by four types of axon projections:

1. Long connections between one lobe and another (Figure 3.26A)

2. Relatively short connections between one part of a lobe and another (Figure 3.26B)

3. Interhemispheric connections (commissures) between one hemisphere and the other (Figure 3.26C)

4. Connections through the thalamus

Most interhemispheric connections link **homotopic** points in the two hemispheres—that is, contralateral points that correspond to each other in the brain's mirror-image structure. Thus, the commissures act as a zipper to link together the two sides of the brain's representation of the world and of the body in it. The two main interhemispheric commissures are the corpus callosum and the anterior commissure (see Figure 3.26C).

The Crossed Brain

One of the most peculiar features of the brain's organization is that each of its symmetrical halves responds mainly to sensory stimulation from the contralateral side of the body or sensory world and controls the musculature on the contralateral side of the body. The visual system, diagrammed in **Figure 3.27**, is illustrative.

For animals, such as the rat, with eyes located on the side of the head, about 95% of the optic fibers from one eye project to the opposite hemisphere. For primates, such as humans, having their eyes on the front of the head, about 50% of the optic fibers from each eye project to the opposite hemisphere. Thus, for both kinds of animals, visual pathways are arranged to ensure that each hemisphere gets visual information from the opposite visual field.

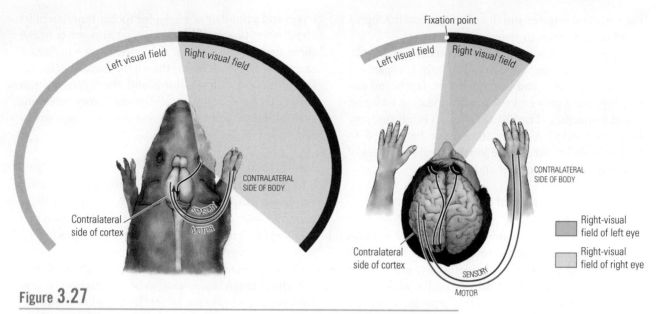

Figure 3.27

Crossed Neural Circuits (Left) The projection of visual and somatosensory input to contralateral areas of the cortex and the projection of the motor cortex to the contralateral side of a rat's body. The rat's eyes are laterally positioned, and so most of the input from each eye travels to the opposite hemisphere. (Right) In the human head, the two eyes are frontally placed. As a result, visual input is split in two, and input from the right side of the world as seen by both eyes goes to the left hemisphere, whereas input from the left side of the world as seen by both eyes goes to the right hemisphere. Somatosensory input of both rats and humans is completely crossed: information coming from the right paw or hand goes to the left hemisphere

In a similar arrangement, about 90% of the fibers of the motor and the somatosensory systems cross over in the spinal cord. Projections from the auditory system go to both hemispheres, but there is substantial evidence that auditory excitation from each ear sends a stronger signal to the contralateral hemisphere.

As a result of this arrangement, numerous crossings, or **decussations**, of the sensory and motor fibers are found along the center of the nervous system. Functionally, the existence of these crossings means that damage to a hemisphere produces symptoms related to perception and movement related to the opposite side of the body. Recall that, for R.S., who suffered a stroke to the right cerebral hemisphere, impairments in movement were in his left leg and arm. Later chapters contain detailed descriptions of some of the decussations, when they are relevant to the discussion of how a given system works.

Summary

Neuroanatomy: Finding Your Way Around the Brain

The brain's anatomy is organized but complex, and the names of its many structures provide a wonderland of nomenclature related to the rich history behind its description and determination of the functions of its parts.

Overview of Nervous System Structure and Function

The brain is protected by the skull and by the meninges that cushion it. It is also protected by a blood–brain barrier that excludes many substances from entry into neural tissue. The brain receives its blood supply from the internal carotid arteries and the vertebral arteries and distributes blood through a number of arteries to specific brain regions.

The brain is composed of neurons and glial cells, each present in many forms. The brain is organized into layers, nuclei, and tracts, with the layers and nuclei appearing gray and the tracts appearing white on visual inspection. The visualization of brain anatomy in greater detail requires that tissue be stained to highlight differences in the biochemical structures of different groups of nuclei and tracts.

Origin and Development of the Central Nervous System

The developing central nervous system first consists of three divisions surrounding a canal filled with cerebrospinal fluid. In adult mammals, increases in the size and complexity of the first and third divisions produce a brain consisting of five separate divisions.

The Spinal Cord

The spinal cord communicates with the body through dorsal roots, which are sensory, and ventral roots, which are motor. The spinal cord is also divided into segments, each representing a dermatome, or segment, of the body. This segmentation and the dorsal-is-sensory and ventral-is-motor organization continue into the brainstem.

The cranial and spinal nerves of the somatic nervous system carry afferent sensory input to the central nervous system and transmit efferent motor output from the brain to the body. The autonomic nervous system acts either to activate (sympathetic nerves) or to inhibit (parasympathetic nerves) the body's internal organs.

The Brainstem

Hindbrain structures include the cerebellum, and its core contains the nuclei giving rise to the cranial nerves The midbrain contains the superior and inferior colliculi (for vision and hearing) in its tectum

(roof) and a number of nuclei for motor function in its tegmentum (floor). The diencephalon consists of the three thalamic structures: the epithalamus (including the pineal gland for biorhythms); the thalamus (for relaying sensory information); and the hypothalamus (which contains many nuclei for regulatory functions such as temperature, eating and drinking, and sexual activity).

The Forebrain

The forebrain consists of three functional regions: the basal ganglia, associated with motor coordination; the limbic system, associated with emotion and memory; and the neocortex, associated with sensory, motor, and cognitive functions.

The neocortex, or cortex, comprising about 80% of the adult human brain, consists of a large sheet of neurons organized into six layers. In the adult brain, the sheet is crinkled to form gyri and sulci. The cortex can be divided into functional regions and continues the spinal-cord organization, with motor functions in the front and sensory functions in the rear.

Individual lobes also can be associated with general functions: vision in the occipital lobe, audition in the temporal lobe, somatosensation in the parietal lobe, and movement in the frontal lobe. The lobes can be further subdivided into primary, secondary, and tertiary regions, each of which deals with more-complex and associative functions.

The cortex does not function in isolation from its subcortical structures but receives sensory information through the thalamus and works through the basal ganglia to produce movement and through the limbic system to organize emotion and memory.

The Crossed Brain

In the main, each hemisphere of the cortex responds to sensory stimulation to the side opposite that hemisphere and produces movements of the opposite side of the body.

References

Brodmann, K. *Vergleichende Lokalisationlehr der Grosshirnrinde in ihren Prinzipien dargestellt auf Grund des Zellenbaues.* Leipzig: J. A. Barth, 1909.

Damasio, H. *Human Brain Anatomy in Computerized Images.* New York: Oxford University Press, 2005.

DiSalle, F., H. Duvernoy, P. Babischong, T. Scarabino, and U. Salvolini. *Atlas of Morphology and Functional Anatomy of the Human Brain.* New York: Springer, 2005.

Duvernay, H. M. *The Human Brain: Surface, Blood Supply, and the Three-Dimensional Sectional Anatomy,* 2nd ed. New York: Springer, 1999.

Elliott, H. *Functional Neuroanatomy.* Philadelphia: Lea & Febiger, 1965.

Hamilton, L. W. *Basic Limbic System Anatomy of the Rat.* New York and London: Plenum, 1976.

Herrick, C. J. *Brains of Rats and Men.* Chicago: University of Chicago Press, 1926.

MacLean, P. D. Psychosomatic disease and the "visceral brain": Recent developments bearing on the Papez theory of emotion. *Psychosomatic Medicine* 11:338–353, 1949.

Moruzzi, G., and W. H. Magoun. Brain stem reticular formation and activation of the EEG. *Electroencephalography and Clinical Neurophysiology* 1:455–473, 1949.

Papez, J. W. A proposed mechanism of emotion. *Archives of Neurology and Psychiatry* 38:724–744, 1937.

Penfield, W., and E. Boldrey. Somatic motor and sensory representation in the cerebral cortex as studied by electrical stimulation. *Brain* 60:389–443, 1958.

Penfield, W., and H. H. Jasper. *Epilepsy and the Functional Anatomy of the Human Brain.* Boston: Little, Brown, 1954.

Sarnat, H. B., and M. G. Netsky. *Evolution of the Nervous System.* New York: Oxford University Press, 1974.

Scoville, W. G., and B. Milner. Loss of recent memory after bilateral hippocampal lesions. *Journal of Neurology, Neurosurgery, and Psychiatry* 20:11–21, 1957.

4 The Structure and Electrical Activity of Neurons

PORTRAIT: Single-Cell Recording

The subject lay in bed facing a laptop computer. Images of famous people, ordinary people, buildings, or strings of letters from words were briefly presented. The subject was one of a few patients who volunteered for the experiment and who suffer from **epilepsy**, a disease in which discharges of abnormal electrical activity in the brain interfere with normal movements, thought, and consciousness.

Noninvasive recordings from the surface of the skull had failed to indicate the location of the epileptic discharges, and so ultrathin wires had been inserted into the subject's temporal lobes to achieve that end (see the accompanying photograph) by recording the electrical activity of neurons through the wire's uninsulated tip. Once the source of the epilepsy was established, surgeons would remove the abnormal brain tissue that produced the epileptic discharges. Each wire contained eight smaller insulated wires with uninsulated tips from which electrical recordings could be obtained.

Fritz Goro

In addition to revealing the source of the epileptic discharges, each wire could record the activity of nearby neurons. This *single-cell-recording* technique enabled the subjects to participate in an experiment at the University of California at Los Angles (UCLA). The experiment would reveal how single neurons code information and so contribute to conscious behavior.

One electrode in the subject revealed that a nearby cell produced electrical discharges when the subject saw pictures of the actress Halle Berry. This cell responded to pictures of Halle Berry in different postures, dressed as Catwoman, a role that she once played in a movie, to a drawing of Halle Berry, and to letter strings of her name. The cell did not respond when pictures of other actresses or people were displayed, and it did not respond to pictures of Catwoman played by other actresses.

Quian Quiroga and his coworkers at UCLA identified other neurons, in the patient described herein and in other patients who participated in the study, that respond to pictures of individual persons or of well-known buildings. They called neurons with these response properties *grandmother cells* to convey the simplistic notion that we have separate neurons for detecting and representing every object, including our grandmothers. The selective response of such neurons to visual images allows us to recognize individual persons in a fraction of a second, even when we see them in strikingly different conditions.

S cientists believe that many thousands of neurons acting in concert are required to form a representation of our "grandmother" (see the preceding Portrait), but the remarkable responses of individual neurons contribute much to our understanding of how neurons allow us to create our representations of reality. To discover how single neurons code information, as well as how they can produce the abnormal discharges of epilepsy, this chapter gives a brief description of the physical features of neurons, the techniques used to study their electrical activity, and how activated neurons send messages throughout the nervous system.

The Neuron's Structure

Neurons are the information-conducting units of the nervous system. A neuron has many characteristics in common with other cells in the body, but it also has special characteristics that allow it to send electrical impulses by using changes in chemical charges on its cell membrane. The word "information" is used loosely here to mean that neuroscientists believe the activity of the neuron to be meaningful with respect to the behavior of the animal.

Overview of a Neuron

Figure 4.1 displays the external and internal features of a neuron. Perhaps the most prominent distinguishing features are the dendrites, whose presence greatly increases the cell's surface area (Figure 4.1A and B). The dendrites' surface area is further increased by many branches and by many small protrusions called **dendritic spines** that cover each branch (Figure 4.1C).

A neuron may have from 1 to 20 dendrites, each of which may have one or many branches, and the spines on the branches may number in the many thousands. Because dendrites collect information from other cells, their surface areas determine how much information a neuron can gather. Because the dendritic spines are the points of communication between neurons, the many thousands of spines provide some indication of how much information a neuron may receive.

Each neuron has a single axon, extending out of an expansion of the cell body known as the **axon hillock** (hillock means "little hill"; Figure 4.1D). The axon may have branches called **axon collaterals**, which usually emerge from it at right angles. Toward its end, the axon may divide into a number of smaller branches called **teleodendria** ("end branches"). At the end of each teleodendrion is a knob called an *end foot* or **terminal button** (see Figure 4.1B).

The terminal button sits very close to a dendritic spine on another neuron, although it does not touch that spine (see Figure 4.1C). This "almost connection," consisting of the surface of the axon's end foot, the corresponding surface of the neighboring dendritic spine, and the space between the two, is the **synapse**. In contrast with the extensive information-gathering capacity of the dendrites and spines, the single axon limits the neuron to only one output channel for communication.

Figure 4.1

Major Parts of a Neuron (A) A typical neuron has been stained by using the Golgi technique to reveal some of its major physical features, including the dendrites and cell body. (B) A drawing of the neuron highlights its dendrites, cell body, and axon. (C) An electron micrographic image captures the synapse formed where the teminal button of one neuron meets a dendritic spine on a dendrite of another neuron. (D) High-power light microscopic view inside the cell body.

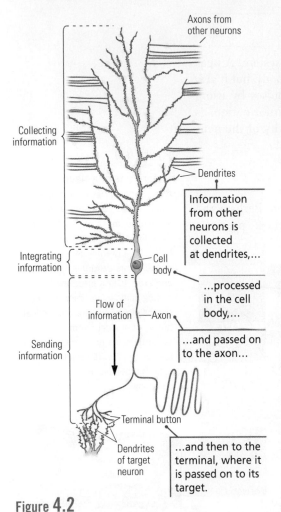

Axons from other neurons

Collecting information

Dendrites

Information from other neurons is collected at dendrites,...

Integrating information

Cell body

...processed in the cell body,...

Flow of information

Axon

...and passed on to the axon...

Sending information

Terminal button

Dendrites of target neuron

...and then to the terminal, where it is passed on to its target.

Figure 4.2

Information Flow in a Neuron

The flow of information through a neuron from dendritic tree to the terminal button is illustrated in **Figure 4.2**. The neuron's cell wall encloses its contents, much as the banks of a river enclose its water. The dendrites and the axon are simply fluid-filled extensions of the cell body. Information flows from the dendrites to the cell body and axon, just as tributaries feed a river. The axon's dividing into teleodendria is analogous to the main river channel's breaking up into a number of smaller channels at the river delta before discharging its contents into the sea. At each terminal button, information in the form of a chemical message is released onto a target.

Although information does flow from the dendrites to the cell body and then along the axon, a neuron does not function simply like an unregulated river system, carrying all the input that it receives to the delta that disgorges it into the sea. Rather, a neuron is both an information-collecting and an information-processing device. It receives a great deal of information on its hundreds to thousands of dendritic spines, but it has only one axon; so the message that it sends must be an averaged or summarized version of all the incoming signals. Thus, the neuron can also be compared to a river system regulated by a dam located at the axon hillock. A dam can be opened or closed to allow more water flow at some times and less at others.

Information that travels through a neuron does not consist of a flow of liquid. Instead, it travels on a flow of electrical current that begins on the dendrites and travels along the axon to the terminals. In the axon, the summarized flow consists of discrete electrical impulses. As each impulse reaches the terminal buttons, they release one or more chemicals. The released chemical, a **neurotransmitter**, carries the message across the synapse to influence the electrical activity of the receiving cell, or target—to excite it or inhibit it—and pass the message along.

The next sections of this chapter describe how neurons gain or lose electrical charge and how changes in charge enable them to transmit information throughout the nervous system. Neurotransmission is explained in Chapter 5.

The Cell As a Factory

The cell is a miniature factory, with departments that cooperate to make, ship, and export **proteins**, the cell's products. Proteins are complex organic compounds, including enzymes, hormones, and antibodies, and they form the principal components of all cells as well. **Figure 4.3** illustrates the structure and function of many parts of a cell. As we describe these parts and their functions, you will see that the factory analogy is apt indeed.

A factory has outer walls that separate it from the rest of the world and discourage unwanted intruders; a cell's outer *cell membrane* separates it from its surroundings and allows it to regulate the materials that enter and leave its domain. The cell membrane envelops the cell body, the dendrites and their

Dendrite: Cell extension that collects information from other cells

Dendritic spine: Small protrusion on a dendrite that increases surface area

Nucleus: Structure containing the chromosomes and genes

Nuclear membrane: Membrane surrounding the nucleus

Mitochondrion: Structure that gathers, stores, and releases energy

Endoplasmic reticulum: Folded layers of membrane where proteins are assembled

Golgi body: Membranous structure that packages protein molecules for transport

Intracellular fluid: Fluid in which the cell's internal structures are suspended

Lysosomes: Sacs containing enzymes that break down wastes

Tubule: Tiny tube that transports molecules and helps give the cell its shape

Microfilaments: Threadlike fibers making up much of the cell's "skeleton"

Axon: Extension that transmits information from cell body to other cells

Cell membrane: Membrane surrounding the cell

Figure **4.3**

Internal Structure of a Neuron
This view inside a typical cell reveals its organelles and other internal components.

spines, and the axon and its terminals and so forms a boundary around a continuous intracellular compartment.

Unassisted, very few substances can enter or leave a cell, because the cell membrane presents an almost impenetrable barrier. Proteins embedded in the cell membrane serve as the factory's gates, allowing some substances to leave or enter and denying passage to the rest. Within the cell, as shown in Figure 4.3, are other membranes that divide its interior into compartments, similar to the work areas created by a factory's inner partitions. This setup allows the cell to concentrate chemicals where they are needed and otherwise keep them out of the way. Prominent among the cell's internal membranes is the *nuclear membrane* that surrounds the cell's nucleus.

The **nucleus**, like the executive office of a factory, houses the blueprints—genes and chromosomes—where the cell's proteins are stored and copied. When needed, copies are sent to the factory floor, the part of the cell called the **endoplasmic reticulum** (ER). The ER, an extension of the nuclear membrane, is where the cell's protein products are assembled in accordance with the genes' instructions.

The finished products are packed in a membrane and addressed in the **Golgi bodies**, which then pass them along to the cell's transportation network, a system of **tubules** that carries the packaged proteins to their final destinations (much like the factory's interior system of conveyor belts and forklifts). **Microfilaments** constitute the cell's structural framework; **microtubules** contract and aid in the cell's movements.

Two other components of the cellular factory are important for our consideration: **mitochondria** are the cell's power plants that supply its energy needs, whereas **lysosomes** are saclike vesicles that not only transport incoming supplies but also move and store wastes. Interestingly, more lysosomes are found in old cells than in young ones. Cells apparently have trouble disposing of their garbage just as we do.

With this overview of the cell's internal structure in mind, let's look at some of its components in more detail, beginning with the cell membrane.

The Cell Membrane: Barrier and Gatekeeper

Neurons and glia are tightly packed together in the brain, but, like all cells, they are separated and cushioned by **extracellular fluid**. This fluid is composed mainly of water in which salts and many other chemical substances are dissolved. Fluid is found inside a cell as well. This **intracellular fluid**, or *cytoplasm*, also is made up mainly of water with dissolved salts and other chemicals, but the concentrations of dissolved substances inside and outside the cell are very different. This difference helps explain the information-conducting ability of neurons.

Membrane Structure

The cell membrane encases a cell and separates the intracellular from the extracellular fluid, allowing the cell to function as an independent unit. The special, double-layer structure of the membrane makes this separation possible (**Figure 4.4**A). The membrane bilayer also regulates the movement of substances into and out of the cell. For example, if too much water enters a cell, the cell can burst, and, if too much water leaves, the cell can shrivel. The cell membrane helps ensure that neither happens. The cell membrane also regulates the con-

Figure 4.4

Basic Structure of a Cell Membrane (A) The cell membrane bilayer, with the tails of each layer facing inward. (B) Conventional symbol for the phospholipid molecule, distinguishing its head and tail regions. (C) Space-filling model of a phospholipid molecule detailing the head's hydrophilic polar regions and the hydrophobic tails, which do not have polar regions for attracting polar water molecules.

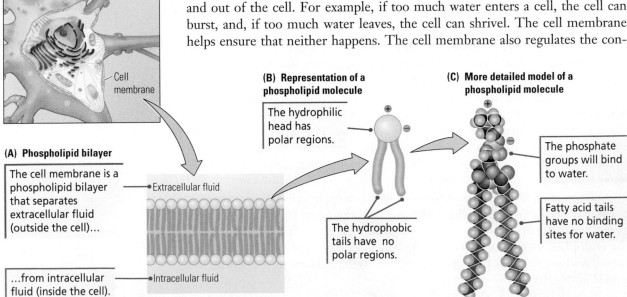

Cell membrane

(B) Representation of a phospholipid molecule

The hydrophilic head has polar regions.

The hydrophobic tails have no polar regions.

(C) More detailed model of a phospholipid molecule

The phosphate groups will bind to water.

Fatty acid tails have no binding sites for water.

(A) Phospholipid bilayer

The cell membrane is a phospholipid bilayer that separates extracellular fluid (outside the cell)...

Extracellular fluid

...from intracellular fluid (inside the cell).

Intracellular fluid

centrations of salts and other chemicals on either side, because precise concentrations of chemicals within a cell are essential to its normal function.

The membrane bilayer is composed of a special kind of molecule called a **phospholipid**, shown in detail in Figure 4.4B. The name comes from the molecule's structure, which features a "head" that contains the element phosphorus (P) and two "tails" that are lipid, or fat, molecules. The head has a slight positive charge in one location and a slight negative charge in another. The tails consist of hydrogen and carbon atoms bound tightly to one another, making them electrically neutral. Figure 4.4C shows a more detailed model of the phospholipid molecule.

A glance back at Figure 4.4A shows how the phospholipid molecules align to form a *phospholipid bilayer*, the double-layered cell membrane. The differences in the electrical polarity of the head and tails of a phospholipid molecule are the underlying reason why it can form membranes. The head, being polar, is hydrophilic (from the Greek *hydro*, meaning "water," and *philic* meaning "love": literally, "water loving"): it is attracted to water molecules because they, too, are polar. The charges on the molecules attract each other. The nonpolar tails have no such attraction for water. In fact, they are hydrophobic, or "water hating" (from the Greek *phobos*, meaning "fear").

Quite literally, then, the head of a phospholipid molecule loves water and the tails hate it. These phospholipid molecules form a bilayer arranged so that the heads of one layer are in contact with the intracellular fluid and the heads of the other layer are in contact with the extracellular fluid. The tails of both layers point toward the inside of the bilayer, where they are hidden from water.

How the Cell Membrane Functions

The cell membrane is pliant and yet impermeable to a wide variety of substances. It is impenetrable to intracellular and extracellular water, because polar water molecules cannot pass through the hydrophobic tails of the membrane. Phospholipid heads repel the charges carried by other polar molecules in the extracellular and intracellular fluid and so prevent them from crossing the membrane. In fact, only a few, small, nonpolar molecules, such as oxygen (O_2), can pass freely through a phospholipid bilayer.

Because the heads of the phospholipid molecules are polar, the cell membrane can also regulate salt concentrations within the cell. *Salts* are molecules that separate into two parts when dissolved in water, with one part carrying a positive charge and the other part a negative charge. These charged particles are collectively called **ions**. Ordinarily, the tightly packed polar surface of the phospholipid membrane prevents ions from passing through the membrane, either by repelling them, binding to them, or blocking their passage if they are large.

If the cell membrane is such an effective barrier, how do substances necessary to the function of the cell pass in and out? After all, the cell factory must have doors to facilitate the delivery of supplies, disposal of wastes, and shipment of products. Proteins embedded in the cell membrane provide one way for substances such as ions to cross the membrane.

In water, common table salt—sodium chloride (NaCl)—dissolves into sodium ions (Na^+) and chloride ions (Cl^-), both quite small. Other ions are much more complicated. Protein molecules can ionize in water but consist of hundreds of atoms, and so negatively charged protein ions (A^-) are hundreds of times as large as the ions of dissolved table salt. The sizes and the charges of these ions are factors influencing how they cross the cell membrane.

Proteins embedded in the cell membrane act as gates and transportation systems that allow selected substances to pass through the membrane. Proteins are manufactured by the cell on instructions from the nucleus and different proteins enable the transport of different ions.

The Nucleus: Blueprints for Proteins

We have called the nucleus the cell's executive office where the blueprints for making proteins are stored and copied; the copies are then sent out to the cell's factory floor for synthesis. The blueprints for proteins are embedded in the chemical structure of giant molecular complexes in the nucleus called **chromosomes**. The name means "colored body," referring to the fact that chromosomes can be readily stained with certain dyes.

As shown in **Figure 4.5**, chromosomes consist chiefly of DNA, which in turn consists of two strands of four *nucleotide bases* that are the constituent molecules of the genetic code, *adenine* (A), *thymine* (T), *guanine* (G) and *cytosine* (C). A **gene** is a segment of a DNA strand that encodes the synthesis of a particular type of protein molecule. The code for protein synthesis is in fact the sequence of the nucleotide bases.

Much as a sequence of letters spells out a word, the sequence of bases "spells out" the order in which **amino acids**, the building blocks of proteins, should be assembled to construct a certain kind of protein. Genes are thus the functional units that control the transmission and expression of traits from one generation to the next.

Each chromosome has a double-helical (spiral) structure in which its two strands of nucletide bases wrap around each other and each chromosome contains hundreds of genes. Collectively, the chromosomes are like a set of books containing a list of all of the parts necessary for making a complex build-

Chromosome

Each chromosome is a double-stranded molecule of DNA.

DNA

Adenine (A) binds with thymine (T). Guanine (G) binds with cytosine (C).

Figure **4.5**

A Chromosome The cell nucleus houses chromosomes, each containing many genes. A chromosome is made up of two strands of DNA twisted in a helix and bound to each other by their nucleotide bases adenine (A), thymine (T), guanine (G) and cytosine (C).

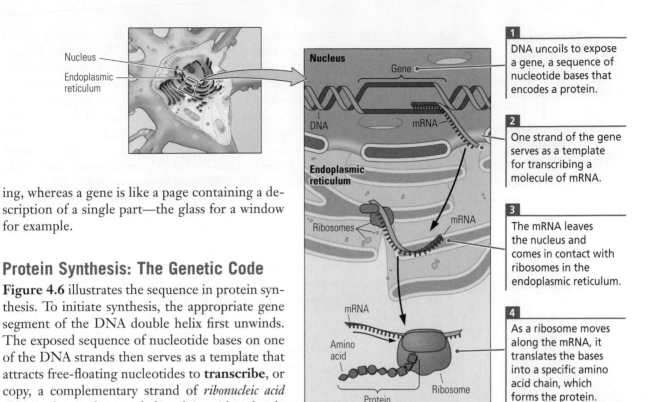

1. DNA uncoils to expose a gene, a sequence of nucleotide bases that encodes a protein.

2. One strand of the gene serves as a template for transcribing a molecule of mRNA.

3. The mRNA leaves the nucleus and comes in contact with ribosomes in the endoplasmic reticulum.

4. As a ribosome moves along the mRNA, it translates the bases into a specific amino acid chain, which forms the protein.

ing, whereas a gene is like a page containing a description of a single part—the glass for a window for example.

Protein Synthesis: The Genetic Code

Figure 4.6 illustrates the sequence in protein synthesis. To initiate synthesis, the appropriate gene segment of the DNA double helix first unwinds. The exposed sequence of nucleotide bases on one of the DNA strands then serves as a template that attracts free-floating nucleotides to **transcribe**, or copy, a complementary strand of *ribonucleic acid* (RNA), the single-stranded nucleic acid molecule required for protein synthesis.

The RNA leaves the nucleus and passes through a ribosome in the endoplasmic reticulum, the cell's protein-manufacturing center, which consists of a series of membranous sheets folded to form numerous channels. The ER is studded with **ribosomes**, complexes of enzymes and RNA that play a critical role in protein building. When the RNA molecule reaches the ER, it passes through a ribosome, where its genetic code is **translated**; that is, as the ribosome moves along the RNA, it "reads" the sequence of bases along the RNA strand, translating them into a specific amino acid chain, which is the protein.

Protein synthesis can be considered a two-step process as illustrated in **Figure 4.7**. First, a strand of DNA is transcribed into RNA—copied as you would copy a passage from a book in writing. The sequence of nucleotide bases in the DNA is reproduced as a complementary set of nucleotide bases composing a strand of **messenger RNA** (mRNA), so called because it carries the genetic code out of the nucleus to the cellular "factory floor" where proteins are manufactured (see Figure 4.6).

After some modification, the mRNA is then translated into a **polypeptide chain** (many peptides), a chain of amino acids. Translation,

Figure **4.6**

Protein Synthesis The flow of information in a cell is from DNA to mRNA to protein (peptide chain of amino acids).

Figure **4.7**

Transcription and Translation In protein synthesis (see Figure 4.6), a strand of DNA is transcribed into mRNA. Each sequence of three bases in the mRNA strand (a codon) encodes one amino acid. Directed by the codons, the amino acids link together to form a polypeptide chain. The amino acids illustrated are tryptophan (Trp), phenylalanine (Phe), glycine (Gly), and serine (Ser).

(A) Primary structure

Amino acid chains...

(B) Secondary structures

Pleated sheet

Helix

...form pleated sheets or helices.

(C) Tertiary structure

Sheets and helices fold to form a protein.

(D) Quaternary structure

A number of proteins combine to form a more complex protein.

Figure 4.8

Levels of Protein Structure

Whether a polypeptide chain (A) forms a pleated sheet or a helix (B) and its ultimate three-dimensional shape (C and D) are determined by the sequence of amino acids in the primary structure.

converting one language into another, is distinguished from transcription, a copying process in which one chain of nucleotide bases produces a complementary chain of nucleotide bases. Each group of three consecutive nucleotide bases along an mRNA molecule selects one amino acid from the surrounding fluid.

These three-base sequences are called *codons*. For example, in Figure 4.7, the nucleotide sequence cytosine, guanine, guanine (abbreviated CGG) encodes the amino acid arginine (Arg), whereas the nucleotide sequence uracil, uracil, uracil (UUU; mRNA contains uracil instead of thymine) encodes the amino acid phenylalanine (Phe). Essentially, each of the different nucleotide codons encodes 1 of the 20 different amino acids found in protein molecules.

The amino acids link to one another by a chemical bond between carbon and nitrogen, a *peptide bond*, into a polypeptide chain. Just as a remarkable number of words can be made from the 26 letters of the English alphabet, a remarkable number of different peptide chains can be made from the 20 different kinds of amino acids that form proteins. These amino acids can form 400 (20 × 20) different dipeptides (two-peptide combinations), 8000 (20 × 20 × 20) different tripeptides (three-peptide combinations), and an almost endless number of polypeptides.

A polypeptide chain and a protein are related in a way similar to a ribbon and a bow of a particular size and shape that can be made from that ribbon. **Figure 4.8** shows how a protein is formed when polypeptide chains assume a particular, functional shape.

Long polypeptide chains (Figure 4.8A) have a strong tendency to curl into helixes or to form pleated sheets (Figure 4.8B), and these secondary structures, in turn, have a strong tendency to fold together to form more-complex shapes. The folded-up polypeptide chains constitute a protein (Figure 4.8C). In addition, two or more polypeptide chains may combine, and the result also is a protein (Figure 4.8D). Many proteins are globular in shape (roundish), whereas others are fibrous (threadlike), but, within these broad categories, countless variations are possible.

Humans have about 25,000 genes (scientists are still debating the number but the winner of a Gene Pool, Lee Rowen, set the number at 25,947) , which can therefore make about 25,000 polypeptide chains or proteins. These chains can be cleaved into pieces or combined with others, leading to recombinations that, in principle, could result in millions of proteins. What makes a protein functional are its shape, its ability to change shape in the presence of other molecules, and its ability to combine with other molecules to make more-complex structures, as we will soon describe. Thus, in principle, the nature of the genetic code is quite simple:

$$DNA \rightarrow mRNA \rightarrow protein$$

Golgi Bodies and Microtubules: Protein Packaging and Shipment

As many as 10,000 protein molecules may coexist within any one neuron, all manufactured in the cell. Some proteins are destined to be incorporated into the structure of the cell, becoming part of the cell membrane, the nucleus, the ER, and so forth. Other proteins remain in the intracellular fluid where they act as enzymes, facilitating many of the cell's chemical reactions. Still other

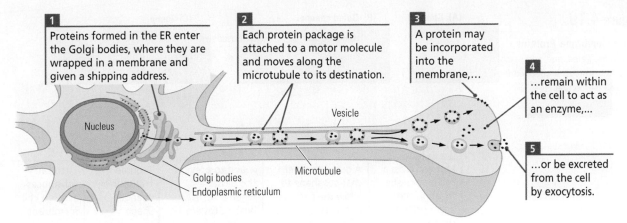

1 Proteins formed in the ER enter the Golgi bodies, where they are wrapped in a membrane and given a shipping address.

2 Each protein package is attached to a motor molecule and moves along the microtubule to its destination.

3 A protein may be incorporated into the membrane,...

4 ...remain within the cell to act as an enzyme,...

5 ...or be excreted from the cell by exocytosis.

Nucleus

Vesicle

Golgi bodies

Endoplasmic reticulum

Microtubule

Figure 4.9

Protein Transport Exporting a protein entails packaging, transport, and its function at the destination.

proteins are excreted out of the cell as hormones or neurotransmitters. To deliver all these different proteins to the right destinations, the cell contains a set of components, the Golgi bodies (see Figure 4.3), that operate much like a postal service, dedicated to packaging, labeling, and shipping.

The Golgi bodies wrap newly formed protein molecules coming from the ER within membranes and label them to indicate where in the cell they are to go (**Figure 4.9**). The packaged proteins are then loaded onto motor molecules that "walk" along the tubules radiating throughout the cell and carrying each protein to its destination.

If a protein is destined to remain within the cell, it is unloaded into the intracellular fluid. If it is intended to be incorporated into the cell membrane, it is carried to the membrane and inserts itself there, shedding its covering membrane (see Figure 4.9). Recall that protein molecules are too large to diffuse through the cell membrane. Proteins destined to be excreted, a process called **exocytosis**, remain within their membranes, which fuse with the cell membrane, allowing the protein to be expelled into the extracellular fluid, perhaps as a neurotransmitter carrying a message to another neuron.

What Do Membrane Proteins Do?

Proteins embedded in the cell membrane transport substances across it. Knowing something about how membrane proteins work is useful for understanding many functions of neurons. We describe three categories of membrane proteins that assist in transporting substances across the membrane. In each case, the protein's function is an emergent property of its shape or its ability to change shape. The categories are:

1. **Channels.** Some membrane proteins are shaped in such a way that they create channels, or holes, through which substances can pass. Different proteins with different-sized holes allow different substances to enter or leave the cell. **Figure 4.10**A illustrates a protein whose shape forms a channel large enough for potassium ions (K^+) to travel through it. Other protein molecules serve as channels for other ions.

2. **Gates.** An important feature of some protein molecules is their ability to change shape. Figure 4.10B illustrates a **gated channel** that opens and closes to allow Na^+ ions to enter at some times but not at others. Some

Figure 4.10

Transmembrane Proteins
Channels, gates, and pumps are
different proteins embedded in
the cell membrane.

(A) Channel

K$^+$

Ions can cross a
cell membrane
through the
appropriately
shaped
channel.

(B) Gated channel

Gates open

Na$^+$

Gate closed

A gated channel
changes shape to
allow the passage
of substances
when gates are
open...

...and to prevent
the passage
when one or
both gates are
closed.

(C) Pump

Na$^+$ K$^+$

K$^+$ Na$^+$

A pump
transporter
changes
shape...

...to carry
substances
across a cell
membrane.

gates work by changing shape when another chemical binds to them. In
these cases, the embedded protein molecule acts as a door lock. When a
key of the appropriate size and shape is inserted into it and turned, the
locking device changes shape and becomes activated. Other gates change
shape when certain conditions in their environment, such as electrical
charge or temperature, change.

3. **Pumps.** In some cases, a membrane protein acts as a **pump**, a transporter
molecule that requires energy to move substances across the membrane.
The protein shown in Figure 4.10C changes its shape to pump Na$^+$ ions
in one direction and K$^+$ ions in the other direction. Many substances are
transported by protein pumps.

Channels, gates, and pumps play an important role in a neuron's ability to convey information, a process whose underlying electrical mechanism are described
in the next sections.

The Neuron's Electrical Activity

Water
forced out
for propulsion

Stellate
ganglion

Mantle
axons

Giant
axon

Figure 4.11

Laboratory Specimen *Loligo*'s
giant axons, projecting from the
stellate ganglion to the mantle,
form by the fusion of many smaller
axons. Their size allows them to
convey messages with extreme
rapidity, instructing the mantle to
contract and propel the squid
through the water.

The neurons of most animals, including humans, are very tiny, on the order of
1 to 20 **micrometers** (μm) in diameter (1 μm = one-millionth of a meter or
one-thousandth of a millimeter). The small size of the neuron made it difficult
to study at first. Pioneering work with much larger neurons led to the technology that made it possible to record from single neurons in the human brain.

British zoologist J. Z. Young, dissecting the North Atlantic squid *Loligo*, noticed that it has truly giant axons, as much as a millimeter (1000 μm) in diameter. These axons lead to the squid's body wall, or mantle, which contracts to
propel the squid through the water. The squid itself, portrayed in **Figure 4.11**,
is not giant. It is only about a foot long. But these particular axons are giant as
axons go. Each is formed by the fusion of many smaller axons into a single large
one. Because larger axons send messages faster than smaller axons, these giant
axons allow the squid to jet propel away from predators.

In 1936, Young suggested to Alan Hodgkin and Andrew Huxley, two neuroscientists at Cambridge University in England, that *Loligo*'s axons were large

enough to study. A giant axon could be removed from a live squid and kept functional in a bath of liquid designed to approximate the squid's body fluids. In this way, Hodgkin and Huxley determined how neurons send information and laid the foundation for what we now know about the electrical activity of neurons. They discovered that differences in the concentration of ions on the two sides of a cell membrane create an electrical charge across the membrane. They also discovered that the charge can travel along the surface of the membrane.

Recording from an Axon

Hodgkin and Huxley's experiments with the giant squid axon were made possible by the invention of the **oscilloscope**, an instrument that turns electrical fluctuations into visible signals. You are familiar with one form of oscilloscope, an old-fashioned television set. An oscilloscope can also be used as a sensitive voltmeter to measure the very small and rapid changes in electrical currents that come from an axon.

As shown in **Figure 4.12**A, the oscilloscope is connected by wires to the squid nerve axon to record its electrical charge. As shown in Figure 4.12B, the charge and any change in the charge can be graphed. Sensitivity is important because the duration and size of electrical charges are very small, on the order of **milliseconds** (ms; 1 ms = one-thousandth of a second) and **millivolts** (mV; 1 mV = one-thousandth of a volt). Oscilloscopes are still used today for recording the activities of neurons, although the job can also be—and frequently is—performed with the use of computers.

Recordings from the axon are made with microelectrodes—insulated wires with very tiny, uninsulated tips. Microelectrodes were inserted into to the subject's temporal lobes in the single-cell recording described in the Portrait at the beginning of this chapter. Here, placing the tip of a microelectrode on a squid axon provides an extracellular measure of the electrical current from a very small part of the axon. If a second microelectrode is used as a reference, one

(A)

The vacuum tube contains an electron gun that shoots a beam of electrons toward a screen.

Vertical plates are connected to a sweep generator that controls the charge on the plates, moving the beam of electrons in the horizontal plane.

Sweep generator
Electron gun
Beam of electrons
Vertical plates
Horizontal plates

Horizontal plates are connected to an axon from which recordings are made.

Recording electrode
Reference electrode
Vacuum tube
Screen

Changes in electrical current across the axon's membrane deflect the electron beam in the vertical plane.

Squid axon

(B)

Figure 4.12

Oscilloscope Recording (A) Changes in electrical current across the cell membrane deflect the electron beam in the oscilloscope's vertical plane. (B) The graph of a trace, where S stands for stimulation. Before and after stimulation, the voltage of the axon shown in part A is represented as −70 mV.

tip can be placed on the surface of the axon and the other inserted into the axon, as shown in Figure 4.12A.

This technique measures the **voltage**, or strength of the charged electrical current, across the cell membrane (Figure 4.12B). Using the giant axon of the squid, an oscilloscope, and microelectrodes, Hodgkin and Huxley recorded the voltage across the axon's membrane and proposed a model for explaining a nerve impulse. The basis of the membrane's electrical activity is the movement of intracellular and extracellular ions, which carry positive and negative charges.

How the Movement of Ions Creates Electrical Charges

Three factors influence the movement of ions into and out of cells: (1) a concentration gradient, (2) a voltage gradient, and (3) the structure of the membrane.

Concentration Gradient

All molecules have an intrinsic kinetic energy called thermal motion, or heat: they move constantly. Because of thermal motion, they spontaneously spread out from where they are more concentrated to where they are less concentrated. This spreading out is called **diffusion**.

Requiring no work, diffusion results from the random motion of molecules as they jostle and bounce about, gradually dispersing throughout the solution. Ink poured into water diffuses from its initial point of contact to every part of the liquid. When salts are placed in water, they dissolve into ions surrounded by water molecules. Carried by the random motion of the water molecules, the ions diffuse throughout the solution until every part of it has very nearly the same concentration. When diffusion is complete, the system is in equilibrium, with each component—ions and water molecules—distributed evenly throughout the system.

When the substance is not evenly dispersed, the term **concentration gradient** describes the relative difference in the amount of a substance at different locations in a container. As illustrated in **Figure 4.13**A, a little ink placed in water will start out concentrated at the site of first contact, but, even in the absence of mechanical stirring, the ink will quickly spread away from that site.

(A) Concentration gradient

1 Ink dropped into water flows away from the initial point of contact...

2 ...until it is equally distributed throughout the water.

Ink

Time

(B) Electrostatic gradient

3 If a salty solution is poured into water,...

4 ...the positive and negative ions will flow down their electrostatic gradients until positive and negative charges are everywhere equal.

Salt water

Time

Figure 4.13

Moving to Equilibrium (A) A concentration gradient. (B) An electrostatic gradient.

The ink spontaneously diffuses down a gradient from a high concentration into places of low concentration until it is diffused, distributed equally throughout the water. At that point, all the water in the container is equally inky. The process is similar when a salt solution is poured into water. The dissolved salt's concentration is initially high in the location where it enters the water, but the ions soon diffuse until their concentrations are uniform throughout.

Voltage Gradient

Because ions carry an electrical charge, we can describe their diffusion pattern not only by a concentration gradient but also by a **voltage gradient**—the difference in charge between two regions that allows a flow of current if the two regions are connected. The voltage gradient allows for measuring the relative concentrations of positive and negative electrical charges in the current across the cell membrane.

The intracellular and extracellular fluids of a neuron are filled with positively charged ions (**cations**) of both sodium, Na^+ and potassium, K^+, as well as negatively charged **anions** (A^-) of chlorine, Cl^-, or chloride ions. Recall that the neural fluids also contain protein anions—large, negatively charged molecules.

In Figure 4.13B, Na^+ and Cl^- ions move down a voltage gradient from a highly charged area to an area of lower charge, just as they move down a concentration gradient from an area of high density to an area of lower density. When salt is dissolved in water, then, it diffuses either by movement down a concentration gradient as shown in Figure 4.13A or by movement down a voltage gradient as shown in Figure 4.13B.

Cell-Membrane Structure

The third factor that influences the movement of ions in the nervous system is the cell membrane. The container in Figure 4.13B allows the unimpeded movement of ions throughout the water. Fully dispersed, their positive and negative charges balance one another, and so there is no concentration gradient or voltage gradient.

Such is not the case with intracellular and extracellular fluid, because the cell membrane acts as a partial barrier to the movement of ions between the cell's interior and its exterior. As stated earlier, a cell membrane is composed of a phospholipid bilayer with its hydrophobic tails pointing inward, toward one another, and its hydrophobic heads pointing outward (see Figure 4.4). This membrane is impermeable to salty solutions because the salt ions, which are encased in water molecules, will not pass through the membrane's hydrophobic tails.

An imaginary experiment will help illustrate how a cell membrane influences the movement of ions. **Figure 4.14**A shows a container of water that is divided in half by a partition representing the cell membrane. If we place a few grains of NaCl in one half of the container, the salt dissolves. Sodium and chloride ions diffuse down their concentration and voltage gradients until the water in that side of the container is in equilibrium.

At this point, within the salty side of the container, there are no longer concentration or voltage gradients for either Na^+ or Cl^- ions, because the water everywhere in that side is equally salty. There are no concentration or voltage gradients for these ions within the other side of the container either, because there are no Na^+ and Cl^- ions there. But notice how there are concentration

(A) Impermeable membrane

1 Salt placed in one side of a glass of water that is divided by a barrier dissolves.

2 Positive and negative ions distribute themselves evenly through half of the container but cannot cross the barrier.

Salt (NaCl)

Cell membrane

Time

(B) Semipermeable membrane

3 If the barrier has a hole through which Cl⁻ can pass but Na⁺ cannot, Cl⁻ will diffuse from the side of high concentration through the hole in the barrier.

4 Cl⁻ will not be equally distributed on the two sides, because of the voltage gradient pulling them back toward the positve sodium ions.

5 At equilibrium, one half of the container will be positively charged,...

6 ...the other half will be negatively charged, and the voltage difference will be greatest close to the membrane.

Time   Time

Figure 4.14

Modeling the Cell Membrane
(A) An impermeable membrane.
(B) A semipermeable membrane.

and voltage gradients for both Na^+ and Cl^- ions *across* the membrane—that is, from one side of it to the other.

Recall that various protein molecules embedded in the cell membrane act as pores to allow certain kinds of ions to pass through the membrane. In our imaginary experiment, we'll place a chloride channel in the membrane and envision how the channel will affect the activity of the dissolved particles.

Chloride ions are now permitted to cross the membrane, as shown at the left in Figure 4.14B. The ions will move down their concentration gradient from the side of the container where they are abundant to the side of the container from which they were formerly excluded, as shown in the middle of Figure 4.14B. The Na^+ ions, in contrast, are still unable to cross the membrane. (Although Cl^- ions are larger than Na^+ ions, Na^+ ions have a greater tendency to hold on to water molecules; as a result, the Na^+ ions are bulkier and unable to enter the chloride channels).

If the only factor influencing the movement of Cl^- ions were the chloride concentration gradient, the efflux (outward flow) of Cl^- ions from the salty to the unsalty side of the container would continue until Cl^- ions were in equilibrium on both sides. But this equilibrium is not achieved. Because the Cl^- ions carry a negative charge, they are attracted back toward the positively charged Na^+ ions (opposite charges attract). Consequently, the concentration of Cl^- ions remains higher in the left half of the container than in the right half, as illustrated on the right in Figure 4.14B.

The efflux of Cl^- ions from the left side of the container to the right side, down the chloride *concentration* gradient, is counteracted by the influx (inward flow) of Cl^- ions down the chloride *voltage* gradient. At some point, an equilibrium is reached in which the concentration gradient of Cl^- ions is balanced by the voltage gradient of their negative charge. At that point,

Concentration gradient = voltage gradient

At this equilibrium, different ratios of positive and negative ions exist on each side of the membrane, and so a voltage gradient exists across the membrane. The left side of the container is positively charged because some Cl^- ions have migrated to the other side, leaving a preponderance of positive (Na^+)

charges behind them. The right side of the container is negatively be-cause some Cl^- ions have entered that chamber, where no ions (of any charge) were before. The charges are highest on the surfaces of the membrane, where positive and negative ions accumulate in an attempt to balance each other.

The results obtained in this imaginary experiment are similar to what happens in a real cell. Keep them in mind as we describe and explain the role that ion channels, gates, and pumps play in five aspects of the cell membrane's electrical activity: (1) the resting potential, (2) graded potentials, (3) the action potential, (4) the nerve impulse, and (5) saltatory conduction.

The Resting Potential

As in our diffusion experiment, a neuron at rest maintains an unequal distribution of ions that leaves a neuron's intracellular fluid negatively charged (as in the right side of the container) relative to the fluid outside the cell (as in the left side of the container). In **Figure 4.15**A, when one microelectrode tip is placed on the outer surface of an axon's membrane and another is placed on the

(A) Resting potential

...while another records the inner surface.

One electrode records the outer surface of an axon...

Axon

By convention, the extracellular side of the membrane is given a charge of 0 mV;...

...therefore the intracellular side of the membrane is –70 mV relative to the extracellular side. This measurement is the membrane's resting potential.

(B) Ion distribution

A^- ions and K^+ ions have higher concentration inside the axon relative to the outside,...

...whereas Cl^- ions and Na^+ ions are more concentrated outside the axon.

Axon

Intracellular

Extracellular

(C) Channels and pumps

Intracellular fluid

Extracellular fluid

K^+ is free to enter and leave the cell.

Na^+ channels are ordinarily closed to prevent entry of Na^+.

Na^+–K^+ pumps out three Na^+ for two K^+.

(D) Charge

Unequal distribution of different ions causes the inside of the axon to be relatively negatively charged.

Figure 4.15

Resting Potential The electrical charge across a cell membrane is maintained by differences in ion concentration. Protein ions are represented by A^-.

cell membrane's inner surface, the difference in charge, due to the unequal distribution of ions, is about 70 mV.

Although the charge on the outside of the membrane is actually positive, scientists follow the convention of assigning it a charge of 0 mV. The summed charges of the unequally distributed ions give the inside of the membrane a charge of −70 mV relative to the outside. This charge is the membrane's **resting potential**.

If we were to continue recording for a long period of time, the resting charge across the membrane would remain much the same. This charge has the potential to change, however, given certain changes in the membrane, because charge is a store of potential energy (thus the expression "resting potential"). You might use the idea of potential in the same way when you think about the financial potential of the money that you have stored in a bank. Just as you have the potential to spend the money at some future time, the cell membrane's resting potential stores energy that can be used at a later time.

The resting potential is not identical on every axon. It can vary from −40 mV to −90 mV on axons of different animal species. Four kinds of charged particles interact to produce the resting potential: sodium ions (Na^+), chloride ions (Cl^-), potassium ions (K^+), and large protein anions (A^-). As Figure 4.15B shows, these charged particles are distributed unequally across the axon's membrane, with more protein anions and K^+ ions in the intracellular fluid and more Cl^- and Na^+ ions in the extracellular fluid. Let's consider how each contributes to the membrane's resting potential.

Large protein anions manufactured inside cells remain there because there are no membrane channels through which they can leave the cell. Their charge contributes to the negative charge on the inside of the cell membrane. The negative charge of protein anions alone is sufficient to produce a transmembrane voltage gradient. Because most cells in the body manufacture these large, negatively charged protein molecules, most cells have a charge across their membranes.

To balance the negative charge of the large protein anions in the intracellular fluid, cells accumulate positively charged K^+ ions inside their membranes. Potassium ions pass through the cell membrane through open potassium channels, as shown in Figure 4.15C, to the extent that about 20 times as much K^+ resides inside the cell as outside it. With this very high concentration of K^+ ions inside the cell, however, an efflux of K^+ ions also is produced, owing to the potassium concentration gradient across the membrane. In other words, some K^+ ions leave the cell because the internal concentration of K^+ ions is much higher than the external K^+ ion concentration.

The efflux of even a very small number of K^+ ions is enough to contribute to the charge across the membrane, with the inside of the membrane being negatively charged relative to the outside. You may be wondering whether you read that last sentence correctly. If there are 20 times as many positively charged K^+ ions on the inside of the cell as on the outside, why should the inside of the membrane have a negative charge? Shouldn't all of those K^+ ions in the intracellular fluid give the inside of the cell a positive charge instead? No, because not quite enough K^+ ions are able to enter the cell to balance the negative charge of the protein anions.

Think of it this way: If there were no restriction on the number of K^+ ions that could accumulate on the inside of the membrane, the positive charges on the intracellular K^+ ions would exactly match the negative charges on the intracellular protein anions, and there would be no charge across the membrane at all. But there is a limit on the number of K^+ ions that accumulate inside the cell because, when the intracellular potassium concentration becomes higher than the extracellular concentration, K^+ ions start moving out of the cell, down its concentration gradient.

The equilibrium of the potassium voltage gradient and the potassium concentration gradient results in some K^+ ions remaining outside the membrane. Only a few K^+ ions are needed outside the membrane to produce a relative negative charge on the inside of the membrane. As a result, K^+ ions contribute to the charge across the membrane.

What about the other two ions that contribute to the production of the resting potential—Na^+ and Cl^-? If positively charged Na^+ ions were free to move across the membrane, they could diffuse into the cell and reduce the transmembrane charge produced by the unequal distribution of K^+ ions. In fact, a cell membrane does have sodium channels, but they are ordinarily closed, blocking the entry of most Na^+ ions (see Figure 4.15C). Still, given enough time, sufficient Na^+ could leak into the cell to reduce its membrane potential to zero. What prevents this leakage from occurring?

The high concentration of Na^+ ions outside relative to inside the cell membrane is caused by the action of a **sodium–potassium pump** (Na^+–K^+ pump), a protein molecule embedded in the membrane that shunts Na^+ ions out of the cell and K^+ ions into it. A neuron membrane's many thousands of Na^+–K^+ pumps work continuously, each one exchanging three intracellular Na^+ ions for two K^+ ions with each pumping action (see Figure 4.15C). The K^+ ions are free to leave the cell through open potassium channels, but closed sodium channels prevent reentry of the Na^+. Consequently, at equilibrium, there are about 10 times as many Na^+ ions on the outside of the axon membrane as there are on the inside.

Sodium–potassium pump

Chloride ions ordinarily contribute little to the resting potential of the membrane. They move in and out of the cell through open chloride channels in the membrane, just as the K^+ ions move through open potassium channels. At equilibrium, the chloride concentration gradient equals the chloride voltage gradient at approximately the membrane's resting potential.

As summarized in Figure 4.15D, the unequal distribution of anions and cations leaves a neuron's intracellular fluid negatively charged at about -70mV relative to the fluid outside the cell. Three aspects of the semipermeable cell membrane contribute to this resting potential:

1. Large, negatively charged protein molecules remain inside the cell.

2. Gates keep out positively charged Na^+ ions, and channels allow K^+ and Cl^- ions to pass more freely.

3. Na^+–K^+ pumps extrude Na^+ from the intracellular fluid.

Graded Potentials

The resting potential is an energy store that the cell can expend if the membrane's barrier to ion movement is suddenly removed. This energy store can also be restored by the flow of ions. Moreover, if the barrier to the flow of ions is changed, the voltage across the membrane will change.

Slight, sudden changes in the voltage of an axon's membrane are **graded potentials**, highly localized and restricted to the vicinity on the axon where they are produced. Just as a small wave produced in the middle of a large, smooth pond disappears before traveling much of a distance, graded potentials produced on a membrane decay before traveling very far. For a graded potential to occur, an axon must receive some kind of stimulation that changes the ion flow. Stimulating the axon electrically through a microelectrode is one way to increase or decrease the membrane voltage (to polarize it) and produce a graded potential. Such changes are brief, lasting no more than the duration of the applied current.

If negative current is applied to the membrane, the membrane potential becomes more negative by a few millivolts, increasing its polarity. As illustrated in **Figure 4.16**A, it may change from the resting potential of -70 mV to a new, slightly higher potential of, say, -73 mV, a **hyperpolarization**. Conversely, if the current applied to the membrane is positive, the membrane potential becomes more positive by a few millivolts, decreasing its polarity. As illustrated in Figure 4.16B, it may change from a resting potential of -70 mV to a new, slightly lower potential of, say, -65 mV, a **depolarization**.

What are the specific causes of these changes in the membrane's polarity? In each case, electrical stimulation influences ion flow through the gates and channels in the membrane:

- For the membrane to become hyperpolarized, the inside must become more negative, which can be accomplished with an efflux of K^+ ions or an influx of Cl^- ions.

- For the membrane to become depolarized, the inside must become less negative, which can be accomplished by an influx of Na^+ ions.

Figure 4.16

Graded Potentials (A) Stimulation (S) that increases relative membrane voltage produces a hyperpolarizing graded potential. (B) Stimulation that decreases relative membrane voltage produces a depolarizing graded potential.

Figure 4.17

Measuring Action Potentials The time scale on the horizontal axis is compressed to chart (A) the phases of a single action potential, (B) each action potential as a discrete event, and (C) the ability of a membrane to produce many action potentials in a short time.

The Action Potential

Electrical stimulation of the cell membrane at resting potential produces localized graded potentials on the axon. An **action potential**, in contrast, is a brief but extremely large flip in the polarity of an axon's membrane, lasting about 1 ms (**Figure 4.17**). In an action potential, the voltage across the membrane suddenly reverses, making the inside positive relative to the outside, and then abruptly reverses again, after which the resting potential is restored. This rapid change in the polarity of the membrane takes place when electrical stimulation produces a large graded potential that causes the membrane's potential to depolarize to **threshold potential** at about −50 mV. At this voltage level, the membrane undergoes a remarkable change with no further stimulation.

When threshold potential is reached, the resting voltage of the membrane suddenly drops to 0 mV and then continues to become more positive until the charge on the inside of the membrane is as great as +30 mV—a total voltage change of 100 mV. Then, almost as quickly, the membrane potential reverses again, returning to its resting potential and then bypassing it and becoming slightly hyperpolarized. This change is a reversal of a little more than 100 mV. After this second reversal, the membrane gradually returns to its resting potential.

The Role of Voltage-Sensitive Ion Channels

What cellular mechanisms underlie the movement of Na$^+$ and K$^+$ ions to produce an action potential? The answer lies in the behavior of a class of gated sodium and potassium channels that are sensitive to the membrane's voltage. These **voltage-sensitive channels** are closed when an axon's membrane is at its resting potential, and so ions cannot pass through them.

But, when the membrane reaches the threshold voltage, the configuration of the voltage-sensitive channels changes, causing them to open and let ions pass through (**Figure 4.18**). In other words, these channels are sensitive to the threshold voltage of −50 mV. The voltage-sensitive sodium channels open more quickly than the potassium channels, and so the depolarizing phase of the action potential is due to Na$^+$ influx, and the hyperpolarization phase of the action potential is due to K$^+$ efflux. In short, Na$^+$ rushes in and then K$^+$ rushes out.

Phases of the Action Potential and Refractory Periods

Although a neuron can exhibit hundreds of action potentials in a second, their frequency has an upper limit. If the axon membrane is stimulated during the depolarizing or repolarizing phases of the action potential, it does not respond

Figure **4.18**

Triggering an Action Potential

The *combined* influx of Na⁺ and efflux of K⁺...

...results in an action potential that consists of the *summed* voltage changes due to Na⁺ and K⁺.

Neuron axon

−50 mV

Na⁺

Na⁺

K⁺

K⁺

Na in

Na⁺ + K⁺

Threshold

K out

Voltage (mV)

Time (ms)

with a new action potential. The axon in this phase is described as **absolutely refractory**.

If, on the other hand, the axon membrane is stimulated during the hyperpolarization phase, a new action potential can be induced, but only if the intensity of stimulation is higher than that which initiated the first action potential. During this phase, the membrane is described as **relatively refractory**. The refractory periods place a limit on the frequency with which action potentials can occur. An axon can produce action potentials at a maximum rate of about 200 per second, but neurons typically fire at a much lower rate of about 30 action potentials per second.

Refractory periods are caused by the way in which the gates of the voltage-sensitive sodium and potassium channels open and close. The sodium channels have two gates and the potassium channels have one. **Figure 4.19** illustrates the position of these gates before, during, and after the various phases of the action potential.

During the resting potential, gate 1 of the sodium channel is closed and only gate 2 is open. At the threshold level of stimulation, gate 1 also opens. Gate 2, however, closes very quickly after gate 1 opens. This sequence produces a brief period during which both gates are open. When gate 2 is closed, the membrane cannot be changed by further stimulation, at which time the axon membrane is absolutely refractory.

Both sodium gates are eventually restored to their resting-potential positions, with gate 1 closed and gate 2 open. But, because the potassium channels close more slowly than the sodium channels, the hyperpolarization produced by a continuing efflux of potassium ions makes the membrane relatively refractory for a period of time after the action potential has occurred. The refractory periods have very practical uses in conducting information, as you will see when we consider the nerve impulse in the next section.

Figure **4.19**

Phases of an Action Potential

Initiated by changes in voltage-sensitive sodium and potassium channels, an action potential begins with a depolarization (gate 1 of the sodium channel opens and then gate 2 closes). The slower-opening potassium channel contributes to repolarization and hyperpolarization until the resting membrane potential is restored.

0

Absolutely refractory

Absolutely refractory

Threshold

Relatively refractory

Gate 1 (voltage sensitive)

Gate 2 (not voltage sensitive)

Na⁺

K⁺

K⁺

Na⁺   K⁺   Na⁺   K⁺   K⁺

Resting   Depolarize   Repolarize   Hyperpolarize   Resting

A lever-activated toilet provides an analogy for some of the stages of an action potential. Pushing the lever slightly produces a slight flow of water, which stops when the lever is released. This response is analogous to a graded potential. A harder press of the lever brings the toilet to threshold and initiates flushing, a response that is out of all proportion to the pressure on the lever. This response is analogous to the action potential. During the flush, the toilet is absolutely refractory, meaning that another flush cannot be induced at that time. During the refilling of the bowl, in contrast, the toilet is relatively refractory, meaning that reflushing is possible, but harder to bring about. Only after the cycle is completed and the toilet is once again "resting" can the usual flush be produced again.

Poisoning the Action Potential

One piece of evidence that voltage-sensitive K^+ and Na^+ channels underlie the action potential is that, when they are blocked, as illustrated in **Figure 4.20**, a normal action potential is prevented. A chemical called *tetraethylammonium* (TEA), which blocks potassium channels, also blocks hyperpolarization. The participation of sodium channels in depolarization is indicated by the fact that the chemical *tetrodotoxin*, which blocks sodium channels, blocks depolarization. Puffer fish, which are considered a delicacy in certain countries, especially Japan, secrete tetrodotoxin; so skill is required to prepare this fish for dinner. The fish is lethal to the guests of careless cooks because tetrodotoxin impedes the electrical activity of neurons.

Tetrodotoxin and TEA are but two examples of the many chemicals that can act as poisons or that can modify behavior through their effects on the electrical and chemical activity of neurons. Genetic abnormalities in sodium and potassium channels also can modify behavior through their effects on the the electrical and chemical activity of neurons. Finally, the activity and the number

The opening of Na^+ channels produces a Na^+ influx.

An action potential is produced by changes in voltage-sensitive K^+ and Na^+ channels, which can be blocked by TEA and tetrodotoxin, respectively.

Extracellular fluid

Intracellular fluid

The opening of K^+ channels produces a K^+ efflux.

Figure 4.20

Blocking an Action Potential An action potential, produced by changes in voltage-sensitive K^+ and Na^+ channels, can be blocked by an array of chemicals such as tetraethylammonium (TEA) and tetrodotoxin, respectively.

of channels can be influenced by behavior and contribute to how we learn and remember. We will give more examples of the relation between channels and behavior in the chapters that follow.

Sending a Message along an Axon

The ability of the axon membrane to produce an action potential does not in itself explain how a neuron sends messages. A message has to travel along the length of the axon. In some cases, the trip is a long one along the axons of corticospinal tract neurons, which extend from the cortex to the spinal cord. Recall the squid, where the message must travel from the ganglia to the mantle muscles (see Figure 4.11).

In this section, we describe how the action potential travels and carries information long distances. An important feature of the action potential is that, because each part of the membrane takes part in its generation, the same potential that leaves the cell body arrives at the other end of the axon: there is no decay in the signal.

The Nerve Impulse

Suppose you place two recording electrodes at a distance from each other on an axon's membrane and then electrically stimulate an area adjacent to one of these electrodes with a current sufficient to bring the membrane to threshold (**Figure 4.21**). That electrode immediately records an action potential, followed very quickly by a similar recording at the second electrode. Apparently, an action potential has arisen near the second electrode also, even though the electrode is some distance from the original point of stimulation.

Is this second action potential simply an echo of the first, being felt along the axon? No, that cannot be the case, because the size and shape of the action potential is exactly the same at the two electrodes. The second is not just a faint, degraded version of the first but instead equal to it in magnitude. Somehow the full action potential has moved along the axon to induce a **nerve impulse**, the propagation of an action potential on the axon membrane.

Why does an action potential move? Remember that the voltage change during an action potential is 100 mV, which is far beyond the 20-mV change needed to bring the membrane to the threshold level of −50 mV. A 100-mV voltage change at the point of the original action potential is large enough to bring adjacent parts of the membrane to a threshold of −50 mV.

When the membrane of an adjacent part of the axon reaches −50 mV, the voltage-sensitive channels at that location pop open to produce an action potential there as well. This action potential, in turn, induces a change in the volt-

Figure 4.21

Propagating an Action Potential Voltage sufficient to open sodium channels and potassium channels (top) spreads to adjacent sites of the membrane, inducing voltage-sensitive gates to open there (middle) and spreading the voltage change farther along (bottom). Because the gates are briefly inactivated after closing, the impulse cannot travel back in the direction from which it has come. Here, the voltage changes are shown on one side of the membrane only.

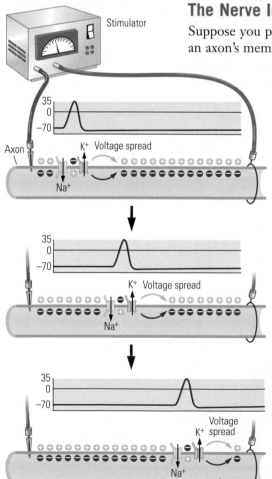

age of the membrane still farther along the axon, and so on, and so on, down the axon's length.

Figure 4.21 illustrates this process by which a nerve impulse travels along an axon. The nerve impulse is produced because each action potential propagates another action potential on an adjacent part of the axon membrane. The word *propagate* means to give birth, which is exactly what happens. Each successive action potential gives birth to another down the length of the axon. Because a membrane is refractory for a brief period of time during an action potential, the action potential cannot reverse direction and move back to where it came from. Thus, the creation of a single, discrete neural impulse that travels in one direction is ensured.

To summarize the action of a nerve impulse, another analogy may help. Think of the voltage-sensitive ion channels along an axon as a series of dominoes. When one domino falls, it knocks over its neighbor, and so on down the line. The wave cannot return to its starting position until the dominoes are set back up again.

There is also no decrement in the size of the propagated event: the last domino falls exactly the same distance and just as heavily as did the first one. Essentially the same can be said about voltage-sensitive ion channels: the opening of one channel triggers the opening of the next, just as one domino knocks over its neighbor. When gate 2 on a voltage-sensitive sodium channel closes, that channel is inactivated, much as a domino is temporarily inactivated after it has fallen over. Both channel and domino must be restored to their original condition before they can work again, and this restoration requires the same expenditure of energy for each domino.

Furthermore, the channel-opening response does not grow any weaker as it moves along the axon. The last channel opens exactly like the first, just as the domino action stays constant until the end of the line. Because of this behavior of voltage-sensitive ion channels, a single nerve impulse of constant size moves in one direction along an axon.

Saltatory Conduction and Myelin Sheaths

Large axons convey nerve impulses quickly; smaller axons convey impulses slowly. Because the giant axons of squids are so large—as much as a millimeter wide—they can send nerve impulses very quickly. But large axons take up a substantial amount of space; so a squid cannot accommodate many of them, because its body would become too bulky.

For us mammals, with our repertoires of complex behaviors, giant axons are out of the question. Our axons must be extremely slender because our complex behaviors require a great many of them. Our largest axons are only about 30 μm wide, and so the speed with which they convey information should not be especially fast. And yet most mammals are far from sluggish creatures. We process information and generate responses with impressive speed. How do we manage to do so if our axons are so thin? The mammalian nervous system has evolved a solution that has nothing to do with axon size.

Among their other functions, glial cells play a role in enhancing the speed of nerve impulses in the mammalian nervous system. Schwann cells in the peripheral nervous system and oligodendroglia in the central nervous system

(A)

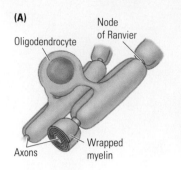

Oligodendrocyte

Node of Ranvier

Axons

Wrapped myelin

Figure 4.22

Myelination An axon is myelinated by (A) oligodendroglia in the CNS and (B) Schwann cells in the PNS. Glial cells are separated from one another by a gap, or node of Ranvier.

(B)

Nodes of Ranvier

Wrapped myelin

Axon

Schwann cell

Figure 4.23

Saltatory Conduction Myelinated stretches of axon are interrupted by nodes of Ranvier, rich in voltage-sensitive channels. The action potential jumps from node to node, carrying the action potential rapidly along.

wrap around each axon, insulating it except for a small region separating the glial cells from one another (**Figure 4.22**). This insulation is referred to as **myelin** or a **myelin sheath**, and insulated axons are said to be *myelinated*. The uninsulated regions between the myelinated segments of the axon are called **nodes of Ranvier**. Larger mammalian axons tend to be more heavily myelinated than smaller axons, and, on larger axons, the nodes are farther apart.

Action potentials cannot be produced where myelin surrounds an axon. For one thing, the myelin creates a barrier to the flow of electrical current. For another, regions of an axon that lie under myelin have few channels through which ions can flow and, as you know, such channels are essential to generating an action potential.

But, as we have just seen, the axons are not totally encased in myelin. The nodes of Ranvier are richly endowed with voltage-sensitive ion channels. These tiny gaps in the myelin sheath are sufficiently close to one another that an action potential at one node can trigger voltage-sensitive gates to open at an adjacent node. In this way, an action potential jumps from node to node, as shown in **Figure 4.23**. This flow of energy is called **saltatory conduction** (from the Latin verb *saltare*, meaning "to leap").

Jumping from node to node greatly increases the rate at which an action potential can travel along an axon. On the largest myelinated mammalian axons, the nerve impulse can travel at a rate as high as 120 meters per second, compared with only about 30 meters per second on smaller, less-myelinated axons.

Think of how a wave made by spectators consecutively rising to their feet travels around a sports stadium. As one person rises, the person's immediate neighbor begins to rise also, producing the wave effect. This wave is like conduction along an uninsulated axon.

Now think of how much faster the wave would complete its circuit around the field if only spectators in the corners rose to produce it. This wave effect is

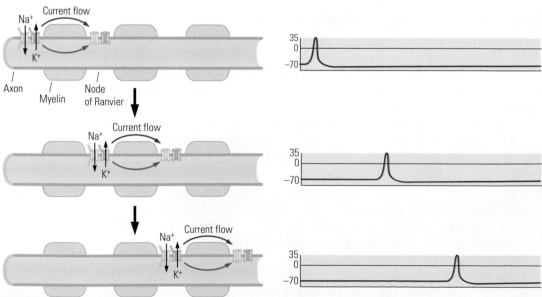

analogous to a nerve impulse that travels by jumping from one node of Ranvier to another. That humans and other mammals are capable of quick reactions is owed in part to saltatory conduction in their nervous systems. When myelin breaks down, nerve impulses are disrupted, as detailed in the accompanying Snapshot.

The Neuronal Code

The single-cell technique of recording action potentials from the giant axon of the squid was quickly adapted to record the electrical activity of mammalian neurons, including those of humans. Let's return to the "Halle Berry cell" referred to in the Portrait at the beginning of this chapter. Recall that the subject

SNAPSHOT
Diagnosing MS

The degenerative disease multiple sclerosis attacks the protective myelin covering of axons, causing inflammation and often destroying the myelin in patches. Eventually, a hard scar, or *plaque*, may form in the affected areas, which is why the disease is called *sclerosis* (from the Greek word meaning "hardness"). When plaque forms, the usual flow of nerve impulses along axons is distorted.

Multiple sclerosis is an unpredictable and often disabling disease of the brain and spinal cord. Its cause remains unknown, but researchers believe that it is an autoimmune disease; that is, in MS, the body's immune system malfunctions and starts attacking myelin. Some evidence points to a common virus or bacteria as the disease trigger, and certain people may be more susceptible to developing MS because of genetic factors.

Remissions and relapses are striking features of MS. To counter its unpredictability, magnetic resonance imaging (MRI) is an important diagnostic tool. Note in the adjoining MRI scan that plaques or lesions appear as white patches in fiber-rich, myelinated areas of the brain.

Multiple sclerosis is usually diagnosed between the ages of 15 and 40, in the career and family-building years, but can make its first appearance in young children and in older adults. The disease is more than twice as likely to develop in women than in men and is seen most commonly in people of northern European background. Prevalence rates range from one MS case per 500 people to one in 1,000.

Symptoms of MS not only are unpredictable, but also vary greatly from person to person and may include vision disturbances such as double or blurred vision. Extreme fatigue,

Imaged by MRI, discrete multiple sclerosis lesions appear around the lateral ventricles and in the white matter of the brain. (After Ciccarelli et al., 2000.)

loss of balance, problems with coordination, muscle stiffness, speech problems, bladder and bowel problems, short-term memory problems, and even partial or complete paralysis are common. Among a number of types of MS, symptoms are intermittent in the most common form, and progressive in a less common form.

Ciccarelli, P. A., A. J. Brex, A. J. Thompson, and D. H. Miller. Disability and lesion load in MS: A reassessment with MS functional composite score and 3D fast flair. *Journal of Neurology* 249:18–24, 2000.

Pyhtinen, J., A. Karttunen, and T. Tikkakoski. Increasing benefit of magnetic resonance imaging in multiple sclerosis. *Acta Radiology* 47:960–971, 2006.

in the Portrait suffered from epilepsy, a condition in which neurons discharge abnormally.

Recording electrodes were inserted into the subject's temporal lobes to locate the source of the epileptic discharges. The recording procedure developed for locating neurons that display epileptic discharges is essentially the same as that developed for measuring voltage changes on the giant squid axon (see Figure 4.12). The main difference in measuring humans is that very thin electrodes are used to minimize damage to the brain tissue through which they are inserted.

Epilepsy appears to occur when scar tissue or some other irritant causes many thousands of neurons to begin to discharge abnormally in a synchronized pattern. Between epileptic attacks, these neurons behave normally and respond with action potentials to complex stimuli such as pictures of Halle Berry. Thus, the same neurons can, when behaving abnormally, produce epileptic seizures and, when behaving normally, contribute to conscious behavior.

We must point out the "grandmother cells" that are responsible for the perception of Halle Berry are many neurons distant from the neurons that first bring visual information into the cortex. Thus, a message in the form of an action potential has been passed through a number of neurons to those that play the role of grandmother cells.

One of the great puzzles in understanding consciousness is how our perceptions from different senses are so different when all the neurons in the nervous system communicate only with action potentials. We address how neurons pass information from one to the other in Chapter 5.

Summary

This chapter has described the various parts of a neuron and illustrated how understanding the parts leads to an overall understanding of neuron function.

The Neuron's Structure

Neurons serve as factories for making protein molecules. The chromosomes of the nucleus contain genes, and each gene contains the code for one protein's polypeptide chain. The DNA of a gene is transcribed into mRNA, which then carries the code for the polypeptide to a ribosome. The code contained in the mRNA is translated on the ribosome into a series of amino acids connected by peptide bonds.

The resulting long chains of amino acids fold in different ways and combine to form proteins, which are packaged and shipped by Golgi bodies and then travel on microtubules to various destinations within the cell. Some proteins are embedded in the neuron's membrane, forming channels, gates, and pumps that regulate the flow of ions across the cell membrane.

The Neuron's Electrical Activity

Neurons carry an electrical charge, the resting potential, across their membranes. The charge is produced by unequal concentrations of ions across the membrane, an inequality maintained and regulated by the membrane's ion channels, gates, and pumps. If the gates on the membrane open briefly, ion efflux or influx can occur briefly, changing the membrane's charge. Such a change is called a graded potential. If a graded potential is sufficient to change the membrane's charge to the threshold, voltage-sensitive sodium and potassium channels open and an action potential commences.

All neurons communicate by inducing action potentials in other neurons. Abnormal electrical activity in neurons produces epilepsy. Thus, an understanding of the electrical activity of neurons leads to an understanding of both behavioral disorders and an understanding of how normal consciousness is produced. The channels that underlie ionic flow across the cell membrane are sensitive to different toxins, which explains certain kinds of poisoning; can be altered by genetic mutations, which explains some inherited disorders; and can be influenced by behavior, which explains some kinds of learning.

Sending a Message along an Axon

The voltage change induced on the axon membrane by an action potential is sufficiently large to open adjacent voltage-sensitive channels, thus propagating the action potential along the membrane as a nerve impulse. On myelinated axons, the action potential can be propagated only at the nodes between glial cells, and this form of propagation, called saltatory conduction, is especially rapid.

References

Eccles, J. The synapse. *Scientific American* 212:56–66, January 1965.

Hodgkin, A. L., and A. F. Huxley. Action potentials recorded from inside nerve fiber. *Nature* 144:710–711, 1939.

Kandel, E. R., J. H. Schwartz, and T. M. Jessell. *Principles of Neural Science.* New York: McGraw-Hill, 2000.

Katz, B. How cells communicate. In J. L. McGaugh, N. M. Weinberger, and R. H. Whalen, Eds. *Psychobiology: Readings from Scientific American.* San Francisco: W. H. Freeman and Company, 1972.

Penfield, W., and H. H. Jasper. *Epilepsy and the Functional Anatomy of the Human Brain.* Boston: Little, Brown, 1954.

Posner, M. I., and M. E. Raichle. *Images of Mind.* New York: W. H. Freeman and Company, 1994.

Quiroga, R. Q., L. Reddy, G. Dreiman, C. Koch, and I. Fried. Invariant visual representation by single neurons in the human brain. *Nature* 3687:1102–1107, 2005.

Shepherd, G. M. *Neurobiology.* New York: Oxford University Press, 1997.

CHAPTER 5

Communication Between Neurons

PORTRAIT: Otto Loewi

In 1921, Otto Loewi conducted a now well known experiment on the control of heart rate. The design came to him in a dream. Loewi enjoyed storytelling, and he recounted that, after having fallen asleep while reading a short novel, he awoke suddenly and completely, with the experiment fully formed. He scribbled the plan on a scrap of paper and went back to sleep. The next morning, he could not decipher what he had written, yet he felt it was important.

All day, Loewi went about distracted, looking occasionally at his notes but wholly mystified about their meaning. That night he again awoke, vividly recalling the ideas in his previous night's dream. This time he still remembered them the next morning and immediately set up and successfully performed the experiment.

Loewi's experiment consisted of electrically stimulating a frog's vagus nerve, which leads from the brain to the heart (see Table 3.2, Figure 3.12), while the heart was immersed in a fluid-filled container. Meanwhile, he channeled the fluid in the container to a second container holding a second frog heart that Loewi did not stimulate electrically, as is illustrated in part A of the adjoining drawing.

Loewi recorded the beating rates of both hearts. The electrical stimulation decreased the rate of the first heart, but what was much more important was that the fluid transferred from the first to the second container slowed the rate of beating of the second heart

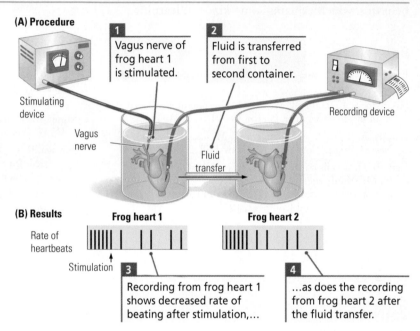

(A) Procedure

1 Vagus nerve of frog heart 1 is stimulated.

2 Fluid is transferred from first to second container.

Stimulating device

Vagus nerve

Fluid transfer

Recording device

(B) Results

Rate of heartbeats

Stimulation

Frog heart 1

Frog heart 2

3 Recording from frog heart 1 shows decreased rate of beating after stimulation,…

4 …as does the recording from frog heart 2 after the fluid transfer.

too (part B of the drawing). Clearly, the fluid was somehow carrying a message about the speed at which to beat.

But where did the message originally come from? The only way that it could have gotten into the fluid was through a chemical released from the vagus nerve. This chemical must have dissolved into the fluid in sufficient quantity to influence the second heart. The experiment therefore demonstrated that the vagus nerve contains a chemical that tells the heart to slow its rate of beating.

In further experiments, Loewi stimulated another nerve, called the accelerator nerve, and observed a speeding-up of heart rate. The fluid that bathed the accelerated heart increased the rate of beating of a second heart that was not

electrically stimulated. Together, these complementary experiments showed that chemicals from the vagus nerve and the accelerator nerve modulate heart rate, one inhibiting heartbeat and the other exciting it.

At the time at which Loewi performed his experiments, most scientists doubted that the chemical reactions required of the cell for making a chemical, releasing it, inactivating it, and then removing it could take place quickly enough to carry a message from one electrically activated neuron to the next. Nevertheless, in the 40 years that followed, as Otto Loewi's methods were developed for the study of neurons in the brain, they proved that virtually all communication between neurons in the central nervous system is chemical.

In this chapter, we will pursue the story of chemical neurotransmission and the role of the synapse in neurotransmission. Spurred by action potentials, the presynaptic membrane releases chemicals from within the cell to communicate with a target cell. We will examine the general function of neural communication first and then consider the general structure of synapses and their variety in the nervous system.

You will discover links between groups of neurochemicals and aspects of behavior. When a chemical transmitter system is damaged, neurological disorders in brain and behavior can result. Drugs, hormones, and toxins can interfere with neurochemicals, replace them or block them, and relieve or cause disorders of brain and behavior.

Neurotransmitter Discovery

Otto Loewi identified the chemical that communicates a message to inhibit, or slow, a frog's heart rate as **acetylcholine** (ACh) and the chemical that carries an excitatory message to speed up frog heart rate as **epinephrine** (EP, or *adrenaline*; the term *adrenaline* is seldom used in the United States because of its similarity to Adrenalin, a name taken as a trademark by Park, Davis and Company). In doing so, he discovered a new class of chemicals, the neurotransmitters that carry messages from one neuron to the next. And, rather than just two complementary chemicals taking part in this communication, neuroscientists now know that more than a hundred may act as neurotransmitters.

Groups of neurons that release a chemical neurotransmitter of a certain type are named after that neurotransmitter. For example, neurons that release ACh are called acetylcholine neurons or **cholinergic neurons**, and neurons that release EP are called epinephrine neurons. In mammals, a closely related neurotransmitter, **norepinephrine** (NE)—also called *noradrenaline* (NA)—replaces EP as the excitatory neurotransmitter in **noradrenergic neurons**.

At about the time that Otto Loewi was conducting his heart-rate expeiments, physiologist Walter Cannon demonstrated that cholinergic neurons and noradrenergic neurons play complementary roles in controlling many bodily functions in the autonomic nervous system. They thus constitute chemical systems that produce widespread and coordinated influences on behavior. Cannon coined the phrases "rest and digest" to summarize the collective inhibitory actions of acetylcholine neurons in the parasympathetic autonomic nervous system and "fight or flight" to summarize the collective excitatory actions of norepinephrine neurons in the sympathetic ANS (**Figure 5.1**).

In fact, each neurotransmitter can be either excitatory or inhibitory: its action is determined by the receptor with which it interacts. One class of receptors for most neurotransmitters is excitatory and another class is inhibitory. Acetylcholine, for example, is inhibitory by means of a receptor on organs of the ANS, mediating rest-and-digest behavior, but excitatory on body muscles connected to the somatic nervous system. Receptor subtypes in each class further expand the dimension of excitatory or inhibitory influence of a neurotransmitter—for example, allowing it to exert a short-lasting action at one site and a long-lasting action at another site.

Acetylcholine (ACh)

Epinephrine (EP)   Norepinephrine (NE)

Figure 5.1

Controlling Biological Functions in the ANS (Left) In the sympathetic (arousing) division, cholinergic neurons from the spinal cord activate autonomic noradrenergic neurons that stimulate organs required for fight or flight and suppress those that activate organs used to rest and digest. (Right) In the parasympathetic (calming) division, cholinergic neurons from the spinal cord activate cholinergic neurons in the autonomic nervous system to inhibit activity in organs used for fight or flight and excite organs used to rest and digest.

Sympathetic division "fight or flight"

KEY
- ● — Acetylcholine
- ● — Norepinephrine

Parasympathetic division "rest and digest"

The Structure of Synapses

The first usable electron micrographs made in the 1950s revealed many structures of a typical synapse, as are shown in the contemporary micrograph in **Figure 5.2**A. The axon and its terminal are visible in the upper part of this photomicrograph; the dendrite is seen in the lower part. The round granular substances in the terminal are filled with neurotransmitter. The dark band of material just inside the dendrite contains the receptors for the neurotransmitter. The terminal and the dendrite do not touch but are separated by a small space.

The three main parts of a synapse, as diagrammed in Figure 5.2B, are an axon terminal, the membrane encasing the tip of an adjacent dendritic spine, and the very small space separating these two structures. That tiny space is the **synaptic cleft**. The membrane on the tip of the dendritic spine is the **postsynaptic membrane**. The patch of dark material in the postsynaptic membrane shown in Figure 5.2A consists largely of protein molecules specialized for receiving chemical messages. The dark patches in the **presynaptic membrane**—the membrane of the axon terminal—consist largely of protein molecules, most of them serving as channels and pumps and as receptor sites.

Within the axon terminal are many other specialized structures, including mitochondria (the organelles that supply the cell's energy needs); round granules called **synaptic vesicles** that contain the chemical neurotransmitter; and

(A)

Axon
Presynaptic terminal
Presynaptic membrane
Synaptic vesicles
Synaptic cleft
Postsynaptic membrane
Dendritic spine
Glial cell

(B)

Presynaptic neuron

Dendrite of postsynaptic neuron

Microtubule: Transport structure that carries substances to the axon terminal.

Mitochondrion: Organelle that provides the cell with energy.

Synaptic vesicle: Round granule that contains neurotransmitter.

Storage granule: Large compartment that holds synaptic vesicles.

Presynaptic membrane: Encloses molecules that transmit chemical messages.

Synaptic cleft: Small space separating presynaptic terminal and postsynaptic dendritic spine.

Postsynaptic membrane: Contains receptor molecules that receive chemical messages.

Presynaptic terminal

Neurotransmitter

Channel

Dendritic spine

Postsynaptic receptor: Site to which a neurotransmitter molecule binds.

tubules that give the terminal button its shape. In some axon terminals, larger **storage granules** hold a number of synaptic vesicles. In the micrograph in Figure 5.2A, you can also see that the synapse (located at the center) is closely surrounded by many other structures, including glial cells, other axons and dendritic processes, and other synapses.

Steps in Neurotransmission

Information is transmitted across a synapse in four basic steps, as illustrated in **Figure 5.3**. Each step requires a different chemical reaction:

1. During *synthesis,* either the transmitter is created by the cell's DNA or its building blocks are imported and stored in the axon terminal.

2. During *release,* the transmitter is transported to the presynaptic membrane and released in response to an action potential.

3. During *receptor action,* the transmitter traverses the synaptic cleft and interacts with receptors on the membrane of the target cell.

4. During *inactivation,* the transmitter either is drawn back into the axon of the presynaptic cell or breaks down in the synaptic cleft. Otherwise, it would continue to work indefinitely.

Figure 5.2

Chemical Synapse (A) Electron photomicrograph of a synapse. Surrounding the centrally located synapse are glial cells, axons, dendrites, and other synapses. (B) Characteristic parts of a synapse. Neurotransmitter, contained in vesicles, is released from storage granules and travels to the presynaptic membrane where it is expelled into the synaptic cleft through the process of exocytosis. The neurotransmitter then crosses the cleft and binds to receptor proteins on the postsynaptic membrane. (Photomicrograph courtesy of Jeffrey Kleim.)

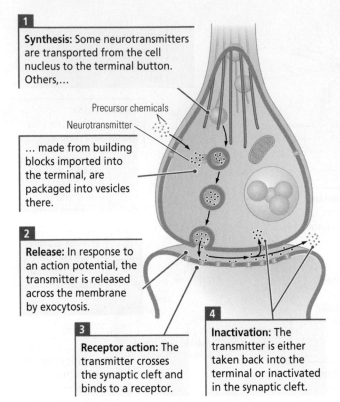

1

Synthesis: Some neurotransmitters are transported from the cell nucleus to the terminal button. Others,...

Precursor chemicals

Neurotransmitter

... made from building blocks imported into the terminal, are packaged into vesicles there.

2

Release: In response to an action potential, the transmitter is released across the membrane by exocytosis.

3

Receptor action: The transmitter crosses the synaptic cleft and binds to a receptor.

4

Inactivation: The transmitter is either taken back into the terminal or inactivated in the synaptic cleft.

Figure **5.3**

Steps in Synaptic Transmission in a Generalized Synapse

Step 1: Transmitter Synthesis and Storage

Neurotransmitters are derived in two basic ways. Some are synthesized as proteins in the cell body according to instructions contained in the neuron's DNA. These neurotransmitters are then packaged in membranes on the Golgi bodies and transported on microtubules to the axon terminal. Messenger RNA also may be transported to the synapse, where it directs the synthesis of a transmitter within the axon terminal rather than within the ribosomes surrounding the nucleus.

Other neurotransmitters are synthesized in the axon terminal from building blocks derived from food. Transporter proteins in the cell membrane absorb these precursor chemicals from the blood supply, as shown in Figure 5.3. (Sometimes, the transporters absorb entire, readymade neurotransmitters from the blood.) Mitochondria in the axon terminal provide the energy for synthesizing neurotransmitters from their precursor chemicals.

These two basic modes of synthesis divide most neurotransmitter substances into two large classes, a quicker-acting class derived from nutrient building blocks and a slower-acting class of proteins derived from DNA. Regardless of their origin, neurotransmitters in the axon terminal are gathered inside membranes that form synaptic vesicles. Depending on the type of neurotransmitter they house, synaptic vesicles are stored in three ways:

1. Some are collected in storage granules, as mentioned earlier.

2. Others are attached to the microfilaments in the terminal button.

3. Still others are attached to the presynaptic membrane, ready to release a neurotransmitter into the synaptic cleft. When a vesicle is emptied from the presynaptic membrane, other vesicles move to take its place so that they, too, are ready to release their contents when needed.

Step 2: Neurotransmitter Release

The action potential triggers the release of a neurotransmitter from a presynaptic membrane rich in voltage-sensitive calcium channels. The surrounding extracellular fluid is rich in calcium ions (Ca^{2+}). As illustrated in **Figure 5.4**, the arrival of the action potential opens these voltage-sensitive calcium channels, allowing an influx of calcium into the axon terminal.

The incoming calcium ions bind to a chemical called **calmodulin**, forming a molecular complex that participates in two chemical reactions: one of them releases vesicles bound to the presynaptic membrane, and the other releases vesicles bound to filaments in the axon terminal. The vesicles released from the presynaptic membrane empty their contents into the synaptic cleft through the process of exocytosis described in Chapter 4. The membrane surrounding the transmitter substances fuses with the cell membrane. The vesicles that were formerly bound to the filaments are then transported to the membrane to replace the vesicles that were just released there.

Step 3: Activation of Receptor Sites

A neurotransmitter released from the presynaptic membrane diffuses across the synaptic cleft and binds to specialized protein molecules in the postsynaptic membrane, as shown in Figure 5.4. These transmitter-activated protein molecules are called **receptors**, because the sites that they occupy on the membrane receive the transmitter substance. The type of neurotransmitter and the kind of receptors on the postsynaptic membrane determine whether the neurotransmitter

- depolarizes the postsynaptic membrane and so has an excitatory action;

- hyperpolarizes the postsynaptic membrane and so has an inhibitory action;

- initiates other chemical reaction sequences that can modulate either the excitatory or the inhibitory effect or influence other functions of the postsynaptic neuron;

- creates new synapses; or

- brings about other changes in the cell.

In addition to acting on the postsynaptic membrane's receptors, a neurotransmitter may interact with **autoreceptors** on its own presynaptic membrane; that is, it may influence the cell that just released it. Autoreceptors receive messages from their own axon terminal.

The amount of neurotransmitter released from the presynaptic membrane in response to a single action potential depends on (1) the amount of Ca^{2+} that enters the axon terminal in response to the action potential and (2) the number of vesicles docked at the cell membrane and waiting to be released. Synapses that are put to frequent use, such as those that contract an exercised muscle, develop more calcium channels and synaptic vesicles than do synapses that receive little use. This development is one way in which a synapse corresponds to behavioral experience.

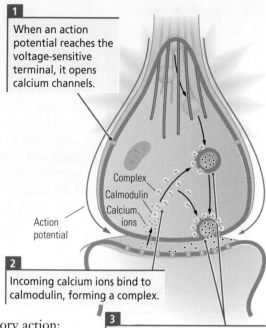

1 When an action potential reaches the voltage-sensitive terminal, it opens calcium channels.

Complex
Calmodulin
Calcium ions

Action potential

2 Incoming calcium ions bind to calmodulin, forming a complex.

3 This complex binds to vesicles, releasing some from filaments and inducing others to bind to the presynaptic membrane and to empty their contents.

Figure 5.4

Release of a Neurotransmitter

Step 4: Neurotransmitter Deactivation

After a neurotransmitter has done its work, it is removed quickly from receptor sites and from the synaptic cleft to make way for other messages sent by the presynaptic neuron. Deactivation of a neurotransmitter takes place in at least four ways: it may (1) diffuse away from the synapse, (2) be degraded by enzymes in the synaptic cleft, (3) be brought back up into the axon terminal in a process called **reuptake**, or (4) be taken up by neighboring glial cells. A glial cell may contain enzymes that further degrade the transmitter into its constituent parts, and it may export the transmitter or its parts back to the axon terminal for reuse.

Axon terminal

Muscle cell

Muscle membrane

| 0.1 μm |

Figure 5.5

Acetylcholine Synapse on a Muscle Cell (From J. F. Heuser and T. Reese, 1977 in E. R. Kandel, Ed., *The Nervous System,* vol. 1, *Handbook of Physiology,* Oxford University Press, p. 266.)

Chemical mechanisms enable the axon to regulate the amount of neurotransmitter in its terminal. If the terminal is not put to frequent use, enzymes there may break down excess transmitter. The by-products of this breakdown are then put to other uses or excreted from the cell.

On the other hand, if the terminal is very active, synapsing on a muscle cell such as the heart muscle tested by Otto Loewi, the amount of neurotransmitter made and stored there increases. All the synapses with muscles of the somatic nervous system are cholinergic, using ACh as their neurotransmitter (**Figure 5.5**). Changes in the structure and function of the ACh synapse contributes to "getting in shape" as a result of intense physical exercise. Exercise that creates a high demand for ACh at nerve–muscle junctions leads to an increase in the amount of ACh being produced in the terminals, thus preparing them to respond to future high demand. In the CNS, similar changes in the synapse contribute to learning and memory and to "keeping the brain in shape."

Types of Synapses

So far, for the most part we have been describing a generic synapse, with features possessed by most synapses. But the nervous system actually features many different kinds of synapses, specialized in regard to location, structure, and function.

Synaptic Variations

Synapses are an extremely versatile chemical delivery system. In one kind, the axon terminal of a neuron meets a dendrite or dendritic spine of another neuron. Called an **axodendritic synapse**, it is the kind shown in Figure 5.2. Another kind of synapse with which you are already familiar is an **axomuscular synapse**, such as that studied by Otto Loewi, shown in Figure 5.5.

Figure 5.6 shows these and many other types of synapses, including an **axosomatic synapse**, in which an axon terminal ends on a cell body; an **axoaxonic synapse**, in which an axon terminal ends on another axon; and an **axosynaptic synapse**, in which an axon terminal ends at another terminal. Axon terminals that have no specific target but instead secrete their transmitter chemicals nonspecifically into the extracellular fluid are called **axoextracellular synapses**.

In an **axosecretory synapse**, an axon terminal synapses with a tiny blood vessel called a capillary and secretes its transmitter directly into the blood. Synapses need not include even a single axon terminal. Instead, dendrites may send messages to other dendrites through **dendrodendritic synapses**. Thus, a synapse can produce an extremely local effect on another synapse or a very general effect by releasing chemicals into the bloodstream.

Excitatory and Inhibitory Messages

As you know, despite the versatility of synapses, in the end they convey only two types of messages: excitatory or inhibitory. That is to say, a neurotransmitter either increases or decreases the probability that the cell with which it comes in contact will produce an action potential. In keeping with this dual message system, synapses can be divided into excitatory and inhibitory cate-

Figure **5.6**

The Versatile Synapse

Dendrodendritic: Dendrites send messages to other dendrites.

Axodendritic: Axon terminal of one neuron synapses on dendritic spine of another.

Axoextracellular: Terminal with no specific target. Secretes transmitter into extracellular fluid.

Axosomatic: Axon terminal ends on cell body.

Axosynaptic: Axon terminal ends on another terminal.

Axoaxonic: Axon terminal ends on another axon.

Axosecretory: Axon terminal ends on tiny blood vessel and secretes transmitter directly into blood.

Dendrites

Cell body

Axon

Capillary

gories—also known as Type I and Type II synapses, respectively—that differ in location and appearance.

As shown in **Figure 5.7**, excitatory synapses are typically located on the shafts or the spines of dendrites, whereas inhibitory synapses are typically located on a cell body. Additionally, excitatory synapses have round synaptic vesicles, whereas the vesicles of inhibitory synapses are flattened. Furthermore, the material making up the presynaptic and postsynaptic membranes is denser at an excitatory synapse than it is at an inhibitory synapse, and the excitatory synaptic cleft is wider. Finally, the active zone on an excitatory synapse is larger than that on an inhibitory synapse.

The different locations of Type I and Type II synapses divide a neuron into two zones: an excitatory dendritic tree and an inhibitory cell body. This arrangement suggests that excitation comes in over the dendrites and

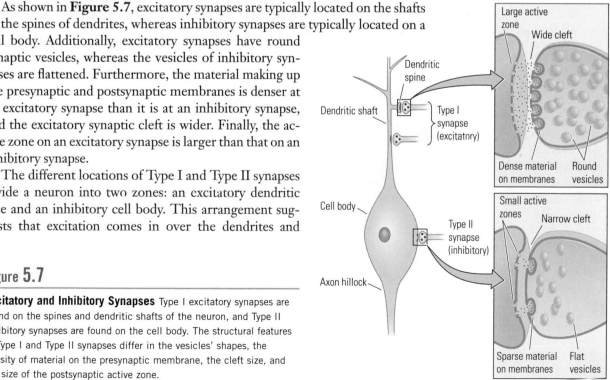

Figure **5.7**

Excitatory and Inhibitory Synapses Type I excitatory synapses are found on the spines and dendritic shafts of the neuron, and Type II inhibitory synapses are found on the cell body. The structural features of Type I and Type II synapses differ in the vesicles' shapes, the density of material on the presynaptic membrane, the cleft size, and the size of the postsynaptic active zone.

spreads to the axon hillock, where it may trigger an action potential that travels down the length of the axon. If the message is to be inhibited, the most efficient place to inhibit it is close to the axon hillock, the origin of the action potential.

Varieties of Neurotransmitters

We are in the midst of a research revolution in the study of neurotransmitters. Few scientists are willing to put an upper limit on the eventual number of transmitters that will be found, but, as already noted, there may be a hundred or more. In this section, we describe how neurotransmitters are identified and examine how they are categorized on the basis of their chemical structures. The functional aspects of neurotransmitters interrelate and are intricate, with no simple one-to-one relation between a single transmitter and a single behavior.

Identifying Neurotransmitters

The four experimental criteria used to identify neurotransmitters, and shown in **Figure 5.8**, follow from the four-step process of chemical neurotransmission charted in Figure 5.3:

1. The chemical must be *synthesized* in the neuron or otherwise be present in it.

2. When the neuron is active, the chemical must be *released* and produce a *response* in some target cell.

3. The same response *(receptor action)* must be obtained when the chemical is experimentally placed on the target.

4. A mechanism must exist for *deactivating* or removing the chemical from its site of action after its work is done.

By systematically applying these criteria, researchers can determine which of the many thousands of chemical molecules that exist in every neuron are neurotransmitters. They can also synthesize transmitters and use them as drugs.

Identifying chemical transmitters in the central nervous system is not easy. In the brain and spinal cord, thousands of synapses are packed around every neuron, preventing easy access to a single synapse and its activities. Consequently, for many of the substances thought to be CNS neurotransmitters, the four criteria needed as proof have been only partly met. A chemical that is suspected of being a neurotransmitter but has not yet met all the criteria for proof is called a *putative* (supposed) *transmitter.*

Acetylcholine was the first substance identified as a neurotransmitter in the CNS, a discovery greatly facilitated by a logical argument predicting its presence there even before experimental proof had been obtained. All motor-neuron axons leaving the spinal cord are cholin-

Figure 5.8

Criteria for Identifying a Neurotransmitter

1
Chemical must be *synthesized* or present in neuron.

2
When *released*, chemical must produce *response* in target cell.

Chemical

3
Same *receptor action* must be obtained when chemical is experimentally placed on target.

4
There must be a mechanism for *removal* after chemical's work is done.

ergic, and each has an axon collateral within the spinal cord that synapses on a nearby CNS interneuron. The interneuron, in turn, synapses back on the motor neuron's cell body. This circular set of connections, termed a **Renshaw loop** after the researcher who first described it, is shown in **Figure 5.9**.

Because the main axon to the muscle releases ACh, investigators suspected that its axon collateral also might release it. Knowing what chemical to look for greatly simplified the task of finding it and then proving that it was in fact a neurotransmitter in this location, too. The Renshaw loop acts as a feedback circuit that enables the motor neuron to inhibit itself and not become overexcited if it receives a great many excitatory inputs from other parts of the CNS. The inhibitory neurotransmitter in the Renshaw cell, the amino acid **glycine**, can be blocked by the chemical strychnine, which acts as a poison by causing muscles to contract synchronously, producing convulsions that interfere with breathing and thus cause death.

Classifying Neurotransmitters

Today, the term "neurotransmitter" is used quite broadly. A neurotransmitter may carry a message from one neuron to another by influencing the voltage on the postsynaptic membrane; it may also induce effects such as changing the structure of a synapse. Furthermore, researchers have discovered that neurotransmitters communicate not only in the orthodox fashion, by delivering a message from the presynaptic side of a synapse to the postsynaptic side, but also, in some cases, in the opposite direction, in which case the message is sent from the postsynaptic membrane to the presynaptic membrane.

The original idea that each neuron had only one transmitter at all its synapses has now also been modified to recognize that different neurotransmitters can coexist within the same synapse, and different synapses on the same cell can house different neurotransmitters. Yet another layer of complexity is the fact that some transmitters are gases and act so differently from a classic neurotransmitter such as acetylcholine that it is hard to compare the two. Because neurotransmitters are so diverse and work in such a variety of ways, their definition and the criteria used to identify each one have become increasingly flexible.

We can impose some order on this complex situation by classifying neurotransmitters into three groups on the basis of their chemical composition as (1) small-molecule transmitters, (2) neuropeptides, and (3) transmitter gases. Here, we briefly describe the major characteristics and interactions of each group and list some representative transmitters.

Small-Molecule Transmitters

All small-molecule transmitters are small organic molecules, as their name suggests. In most cases, **small-molecule transmitters** are synthesized and packaged for use in axon terminals, and they act relatively quickly at the

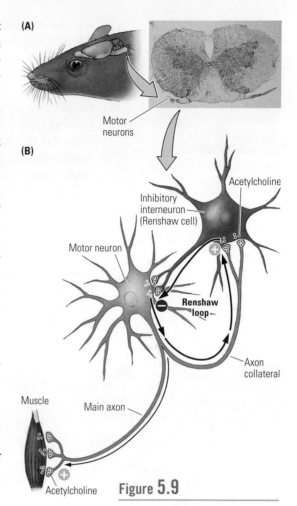

(A)

Motor neurons

(B)

Acetylcholine

Inhibitory interneuron (Renshaw cell)

Motor neuron

Renshaw loop

Axon collateral

Muscle   Main axon

Acetylcholine

Figure **5.9**

Renshaw Loop (A) Location of spinal-cord motor neurons that project to the muscles of the rat's forelimb. (B) In a Renshaw loop, the motor neuron's main axon synapses on a muscle, and its axon collateral remains in the spinal cord to synapse with an inhibitory Renshaw interneuron there. Both the main axon and the collateral terminals contain acetylcholine; the interneuron contains glycine. When the motor neuron is highly excited (plus signs), it modulates its activity level (minus sign) through the Renshaw loop.

synapse compared with other classes. When a small-molecule transmitter is released from an axon terminal, it can quickly be replaced at the presynaptic membrane.

Small-molecule transmitters or their main components are derived from the foods that we eat. Therefore, their levels and activities in the body can be influenced by diet. This fact is important in the design of drugs that affect the nervous system. Many neuroactive drugs are designed to reach the brain in the same way that small-molecule transmitters or their precursor chemicals do, by ingesting them. **Table 5.1** lists some of the best known and most extensively studied small-molecule transmitters, including acetylcholine.

Figure 5.10 illustrates how ACh is synthesized and broken down. The molecule is made up of two substances: choline and acetate. Choline is among the breakdown products of fats, such as that in fish and egg yolk, and acetate is a compound found in acidic foods, such as vinegar and apples.

As depicted in Figure 5.10, inside the cell, acetyl coenzyme A (Acetyl CoA) carries acetate to the synthesis site, and the transmitter is synthesized as a second enzyme, choline acetyltransferase (ChAT), transfers the acetate to choline to form ACh. After Ach has been released into the synaptic cleft and diffuses to receptor sites on the postsynaptic membrane, a third enzyme, acetylcholinesterase (AChE), reverses the process by detaching acetate from choline. These breakdown products can then be taken back into the presynaptic terminal for reuse.

In addition to acetylcholine, the small-molecule transmitter list includes four amines, (chemicals that contain an amine group, NH, in their chemical structure), and four amino acids, such as glycine, that contain a carboxyl group (COOH) in addition to an amine. A few other substances are sometimes classified as small-molecule transmitters. In the future, researchers are likely to find additional ones as well.

Some amine transmitters are synthesized by the same biochemical pathway and so are related to one another. One such grouping consists of the amines **dopamine** (it plays a role in coordinating movement, in attention and learning, and in behaviors that are reinforcing), norepinephrine (noradrenaline), and epinephrine (adrenaline). The last two are the excitatory transmitters in the reptilian heart, as we know from Otto Loewi's experiment, and the mammalian heart, respectively.

Figure 5.11 shows that epinephrine is the third transmitter produced by a single biochemical sequence. The precursor chemical is tyrosine, an amino acid abundant in

Table 5.1 Small-molecule neurotransmitters

Acetylcholine (ACh)

Amines
Dopamine (DA)
Norepinephrine (NE, or noradrenaline, NA)
Epinephrine (EP, or adrenaline)
Serotonin (5-HT)

Amino Acids
Glutamate (Glu)
Gamma-aminobutyric acid (GABA)
Glycine (Gly)
Histamine (H)

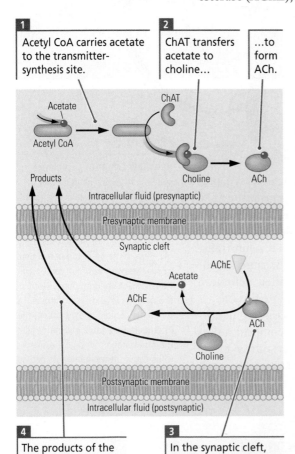

1 Acetyl CoA carries acetate to the transmitter-synthesis site.

2 ChAT transfers acetate to choline… …to form ACh.

4 The products of the breakdown can be taken up and reused.

3 In the synaptic cleft, AChE detaches acetate from choline.

Figure 5.10

Chemistry of Acetylcholine Two enzymes—acetyl coenzyme A (acetyl CoA) and choline acetyltransferase (ChAT)—combine the dietary precursors of ACh within the cell, and a third—acetylcholinesterase (AChE)—breaks them down in the synaptic cleft for reuptake.

food. The enzyme tyrosine hydroxylase (enzyme 1 in Figure 5.11) changes tyrosine into L-dopa, which is sequentially converted by other enzymes into dopamine, norepinephrine, and finally epinephrine.

An interesting fact about this biochemical sequence is that the amount of the enzyme tyrosine hydroxylase in the body is limited and, consequently, so is the rate at which dopamine, norepinephrine, and epinephrine can be synthesized, regardless of how much tyrosine is present or ingested. This **rate-limiting factor** can be bypassed by orally ingesting L-dopa, which is why L-dopa is a medication used in the treatment of Parkinson's disease, a condition produced by an insufficiency of dopamine.

The amine transmitter **serotonin** (5-HT, for 5-hydroxytryptamine) is synthesized differently. Serotonin plays a role in regulating mood and aggression, appetite and arousal, the perception of pain, and respiration. Serotonin is derived from the amino acid tryptophan, which is abundant in turkey, milk, and bananas, among other foods.

Two amino acid transmitters, **glutamate** and **gamma-aminobutyric acid** (GABA), also are closely related: GABA is formed by a simple modification of glutamate (**Figure 5.12**). These two transmitters are called "the workhorses of the nervous system," because so many synapses use them. In the forebrain and cerebellum, glutamate is the main excitatory transmitter and GABA is the main inhibitory transmitter. Interestingly, glutamate is widely distributed in neurons, but it becomes a neurotransmitter only if it is appropriately packaged in vesicles in the axon terminal. The amino acid transmitter glycine is a much more common inhibitory transmitter in the brainstem and spinal cord, where it acts within the Renshaw loop, for example.

Among its many functions, which include the control of arousal and of waking, the amino acid transmitter **histamine** can cause the constriction of smooth muscles and so, when activated in allergic reactions, contributes to asthma, a constriction of the airways. You are probably familiar with antihistamine drugs used to treat allergies.

Peptide Transmitters

More than 50 known peptide transmitters—short chains of amino acids—form the families listed in **Table 5.2**. As explained in Chapter 4, amino acids link together by peptide bonds to form chains, which accounts for the name. Thus, **neuropeptides**, multifunctional chains of amino acids that act as neurotransmitters, are made through the translation of mRNA from instructions contained in the neuron's DNA (see Figure 4.7).

Although these transmitters are produced in the axon terminal in some neurons, most are assembled on the cell's ribosomes, packaged inside a membrane by Golgi bodies, and

Figure **5.11**

Sequential Synthesis of Three Amines A different enzyme is responsible for each step in this biochemical sequence.

Figure **5.12**

Amino Acid Transmitters Removal of the carboxyl (COOH) group from the bottom of the glutamate molecule produces gamma-aminobutyric acid (GABA). Their different shapes allow these amino acid transmitters to bind to different receptors.

Glutamate

GABA

Table **5.2** Peptide neurotransmitters	
Family	**Example**
Opioids	Enkephaline, dynorphin
Neurohypophyseals	Vasopressin, oxytocin
Secretins	Gastric inhibitory peptide, growth-hormone-releasing peptide
Insulins	Insulin, insulin growth factors
Gastrins	Gastrin, cholecystokinin
Somatostatins	Pancreatic polypeptides

Met-enkephalin

(Tyr)(Gly)(Gly)(Phe)(Met)

Leu-enkephalin

(Tyr)(Gly)(Gly)(Phe)(Leu)

Figure 5.13

Opioid Peptides Parts of the amino acid chains of some neuropeptides that act on the brain centers for pleasure and pain are similar in structure and are similar to narcotic drugs, such as opium and morphine, that mimic their functions.

transported on the microtubule highway to the axon terminals. The entire process of synthesis and transport is relatively slow compared with that of small-molecule transmitters. Consequently, neuropeptides that have been used are not replaced quickly.

Peptides have an enormous range of functions in the nervous system, as might be expected from the large number found there. They serve as hormones (growth hormone), are active in responses to stress (corticotropin), encourage a mother to bond to her infant (oxytocin), facilitate learning (glucogen-like peptide), and help to regulate eating (cholecystokinin) and drinking (vasopressin) and pleasure and pain (beta-endorphin).

With regard to pleasure and pain, opium, obtained from seeds of the poppy flower, has long been known to both produce euphoria and reduce pain. Opium and a group of related synthetic chemicals, such as morphine, appear to mimic the actions of three peptide transmitters: **met-enkephalin**, **leu-enkephalin**, and **beta-endorphin**. (The term *enkephalin* derives from the phrase "in the cephalon," meaning "in the brain or head," whereas the term *endorphin* is a shortened form of "endogenous morphine," or morphine made within us.)

A part of the amino acid chain is structurally similar in all three of these peptide transmitters (**Figure 5.13**). Presumably, opium mimics this part of the chain. The discovery of these naturally occurring opium-like peptides suggested that one or more of them might have a role in the management of pain. Opioid peptides, however, have a number of functions in the brain and so are not just pain-specific transmitters.

Peptides' amino acid chains are degraded by digestive processes, and so, unlike the small-molecule transmitters, they generally cannot be taken orally as drugs. Their large size may also prevent them from crossing the blood–brain barrier to reach the brain.

Transmitter Gases

The water-soluble gases **nitric oxide** (NO) and **carbon monoxide** (CO) are the most unusual neurotransmitters yet identified. They are neither stored in synaptic vesicles nor released from them; instead, they are synthesized as needed. Unlike classical neurotransmitters, nitric oxide is produced in many regions of a neuron, including the dendrites. On synthesis, each gas diffuses away from the site where it was made, easily crossing the cell membrane and immediately becoming active. Both NO and CO activate metabolic (energy-expending) processes in cells, including those modulating the production of other neurotransmitters.

Nitric oxide is a particularly important neurotransmitter because it serves as a messenger in many parts of the body. It controls the muscles in intestinal walls, and it dilates blood vessels in brain regions that are in active use, allowing these regions to receive more blood. It also dilates blood vessels in the genital organs and is therefore active in producing penile erections in males. The drug sildenafil citrate (trade name Viagra) was the first widely used treatment for male erectile dysfunction and acts by enhancing the action of NO.

Receptors for Direct and Indirect Effects

When a neurotransmitter is released from a synapse, it crosses the synaptic cleft and binds to a receptor on the postsynaptic cell. What happens next depends on how the receptor works. One class works directly on the postsynaptic membrane, the other changes it indirectly.

Ionotropic Receptors for Direct Effects

Ionotropic receptors allow the movement of charged atoms across a cell membrane when the membrane's charge fluctuates (the suffix *tropic* means "to move toward"). As **Figure 5.14** illustrates, an ionotropic receptor has two parts: a binding site for a neurotransmitter and a pore or channel through the membrane. When the neurotransmitter attaches to the binding site, the receptor changes its shape, either opening the pore and allowing ions to flow through it or closing it and blocking the ion flow. Because the binding of the transmitter to the receptor is quickly followed by a one-step response—either opening or closing the pore—that directly affects the flow of ions, ionotropic receptors bring about very rapid changes in membrane voltage.

Structurally, ionotropic receptors are similar to voltage-sensitive channels. They are composed of a number of membrane-spanning subunits that form "petals" around the channel's central pore. Within the pore is a shape-changing segment that causes the pore to open or close, regulating the flow of ions through it.

Transmitter binds to the binding site. | The pore opens, allowing the influx or efflux of ions.

Extracellular fluid — Ion — Transmitter — Binding site

Intracellular fluid — Pore closed — Pore open

Figure 5.14

Ionotropic Receptor When activated, these embedded proteins bring about direct, rapid changes in membrane voltage.

Metabotropic Receptors for Indirect Effects

In contrast with an ionotropic receptor, a **metabotropic receptor**, a single protein that spans the cell membrane, does not possess a pore of its own through which ions can flow, and so it must act indirectly. As diagrammed at the top of **Figure 5.15**, the outer part of the receptor has a site for transmitter binding. The internal part of the receptor is associated with one of a family of proteins called **guanyl-nucleotide-binding proteins** (**G proteins** for short) that translates the transmitter's message into biochemical activity within the cell.

A G protein consists of three subunits, one of which is the α (alpha) subunit. When a neurotransmitter binds to the G protein's associated metabotropic receptor, the α subunit detaches from the other two units and can then bind to other proteins within the cell membrane or within its cytoplasm. When a neurotransmitter binds to a metabotropic receptor, it either opens nearby ion channels or sends a message to change the cell's metabolic activity.

Figure 5.15A shows the first effect: opening an ion channel. If the α subunit binds to a nearby ion channel in the membrane, the structure of the channel changes, modifying the flow of ions through it. If the channel is already open, the α subunit may close it or, if already closed, the α subunit may open it. This change in the channel and the flow of ions across the membrane influences the membrane's electrical potential.

(A) Metabotropic receptor coupled to an ion channel

Transmitter

Binding site — Ion

Receptor

G protein — β γ α

Closed ion channel

Transmitter binds to receptor in both reactions.

Receptor-bound transmitter

The binding of the transmitter triggers the activation of a G protein in both reactions.

Alpha subunit — β γ α — Open ion channel

The α subunit of the G protein binds to a channel, causing a structural change in the channel that allows ions to pass through it.

The α subunit binds to an enzyme, which activates a second messenger.

The second messenger can activate other cell processes.

(B) Metabotropic receptor coupled to an enzyme

Transmitter

Binding site

Receptor

G protein — β γ α

Enzyme

Receptor-bound transmitter

Alpha subunit — β γ α

Second messenger

Activates DNA — Forms new ion channel

Figure 5.15

Metabotropic Receptor When activated, these embedded membrane proteins trigger associated G proteins, thereby exerting indirect effects (A) on nearby ion channels or (B) in the cell's metabolic activity.

The second effect of binding a neurotransmitter to a metabotropic receptor, sending a message to change the cell's metabolic activity, triggers cellular reactions that are more complicated. Summarized in Figure 5.15B, the process begins when the detached α subunit binds to an enzyme, which in turn activates another chemical called a **second messenger** (the neurotransmitter is the "first messenger"). A second messenger, as the name implies, carries a message to other structures within the cell. A second messenger acts in the following ways:

- It binds to a membrane channel, causing the channel to change its structure and thus alter ion flow through the membrane.

- It initiates a reaction that causes protein molecules within the cell to become incorporated into the cell membrane, as a result forming new ion channels.

- It sends a message to the cell's DNA instructing it to initiate the production of a new protein.

Researchers now use imaging methods both to observe and to manipulate the normal brain and its activity, for example, to study cognitive function. Imaging is also helpful for locating brain injury. Mosso's results (described in the Portrait) foreshadowed these modern brain-imaging methods, of which there are the following varieties:

- **Electrical recording** methods detect changes in the electrical activity of neurons.

- **Brain stimulation** methods induce changes in the electrical activity of the brain.

- **X-ray imaging** methods are sensitive to the density of different parts of the brain, the ventricles, nuclei, and pathways.

- **Dynamic imaging** methods record and manipulate ongoing changes in brain activity, including the electrical activity of cells, biochemical events, differences in glucose consumption, and the flow of blood to various regions.

We begin our survey of brain imaging by examining techniques that make use of the brain's electrical activity. In later sections, we examine techniques that make use of differences in the physical and chemical properties of brain substances or of differences in brain metabolic activity.

Recording the Brain's Electrical Activity

As you know, the activity of nerve cells has an electrochemical basis; it can be recorded with instruments sensitive to small changes in electrical activity. Researchers have developed electrical recording techniques not only for answering basic questions about brain function but also for ready use in clinical diagnosis. These techniques for recording the brain's electrical activity include (1) single-cell recording; (2) electroencephalographic recording; and (3) event-related potential recording.

Single-Cell Recording

What is each of the brain's 10 billion neurons doing at any given moment? If you are watching television, are your visual and auditory neurons active while the neurons responsible for olfaction, taste, and movement remain at rest? When you are watching an actor jump from the roof of one building to the roof of another, do the motor regions of your brain become active, even though your arms and legs remain still? Why does the actor's distance above the ground give you a feeling of vertigo, even though you feel no sensation of contact or pain as he lands on the roof of the second building? How does each neuron decode the sensory signals you receive from the world, create what you experience as reality, and allow you to interact with that reality?

Such questions can be addressed with single-cell-recording techniques—refinements of the historical experiments that detected the electrical activity of individual squid axons (see Chapter 4). An electrode is inserted directly into an animal's brain, adjacent to a single neuron, and the neuron's electrical activity is recorded on a computer, thus supplying information about the activity of that neuron.

Various behaviors in mammals and other animals can be sources of remarkable insight into what single neurons are up to during these behaviors. Most experiments must be done with nonhuman animals, however, because single-cell recording calls for placing the electrodes directly on the brain tissue. Although the nerves of the peripheral nervous system are accessible for recording, only a few occasions (such as brain surgery) permit researchers such access to a living human brain.

Some animal species are preferable to others for studying given behaviors. For example, investigators favor nonhuman primates and cats for recording the single-cell activity of visual functions because these species have excellent vision. The barn owl is frequently used for studying auditory function because of its excellent hearing and because it automatically orients its head to locate the sound of its prey. Rats are used for recording single-cell activity associated with spatial behavior because they are small enough to be physically active in a limited space. For studies of reaching, in which recordings are made as the animal uses a single hand to grasp objects, nonhuman primates are again preferred. Their reaching movements are under visual control and therefore resemble human reaching movements.

In early studies, only a single recording electrode was used, and a great deal of electronic equipment was required to record from only one cell at a time. Today, however, miniaturization, computerization, and arrays of as many as 50 thin wires forming an electrode allow the recording of many individual neurons simultaneously. Furthermore, techniques have been developed to identify specific neurons so that their activity can be followed for long periods of time. For example, an electrode that is quite close to a neuron will provide a large-amplitude signal of that neuron's activity, whereas an electrode a little farther away will provide a smaller-amplitude signal produced by the same activity. The ratio of the amplitude of the two signals will provide a unique "signature," allowing researchers to monitor the ongoing activity of that specific neuron.

The visual recordings produced in single-cell studies differ somewhat from the graphs of action potentials that we have looked at in earlier chapters. Graphs of single action potentials, such as those examined in Chapter 4, are usually drawn with the x-axis (indicating the passage of time) scaled in milliseconds. In contrast, graphs for single-cell studies are usually drawn with the x-axis scaled on the order of seconds. This practice allows researchers to correlate the serial action potentials produced by a given neuron with the ongoing behavior (measured in seconds) of the animal under observation.

Figure 6.1 illustrates the different graphic representations that can be obtained by changing the time base. In graph A, which represents the passage of a single millisecond, only a single action potential can be graphed. In graph B, which represents 3 ms, a couple of action potentials can be graphed. Graph C represents a longer period, during which many action potentials are graphed, but, because they must be packed together so tightly, each is seen as only a single vertical stroke. There are many additional ways of graphing these action potentials so as to correlate them with behavior.

(A) A single action potential occurs in 1 ms.

(B) Two action potentials occur in 3 ms.

(C) The occurence of many action potentials in a 40-ms period reveals a changing pattern of brain activity.

Figure 6.1

Correlating Cell Activity with Behavior In these representations of an action potential, the scale of the horizontal, *x,* axis is changed to illustrate (A) the phases of a single action potential; (B) each action potential as a discrete event; and (C) the many action potentials that a membrane can produce with varying patterns of occurrence within a fraction of a second.

Action potentials are the currency with which the brain operates. The sensation of a mosquito landing on your arm is conveyed from one neuron to the next in the form of action potentials: somatosensory neurons convey action potentials to the spinal cord, and spinal neurons convey them to the cortex. In the cortex, action potentials record the perception that a mosquito is on your arm. When the cortex instructs the hand to swat at the mosquito, it sends the message in the form of action potentials.

Action potentials in the brain represent sights, sounds, smells, tastes, sensations of pain and temperature, and even our desires and emotions. A longstanding puzzle in the study of perception is how an action potential in one neuron represents a visual signal, whereas a similar action potential in another, similar neuron represents an auditory signal, and an action potential in still another neuron records the face of a relative. This puzzle has not been satisfactorily solved.

The Neuronal Code

Neurons exhibit many firing patterns in different animal species. Some discharge at a steady rate that appears unrelated to behavior. Others fire in bursts in association with an observable behavior. Still others hardly ever discharge at all. Some neurons discharge in the morning and in the evening, in rhythm with the cycle of the day. Other neurons discharge once a year, in association with some important annual event. Many neurons exhibit a rhythmical discharge that is in some way related to breathing or heart rate.

Some neurons behave differently in different circumstances. While recording the activity of single neurons in the limbic region of a rat's brain, James Ranck noticed that the action potentials of a single neuron had a remarkable relation to the rat's behavior. Whenever the rat faced in a particular direction, this neuron vigorously fired. When the rat turned somewhat away from this direction, the neuron fired more slowly. When the rat faced opposite the neuron's favored direction, the neuron did not fire at all. We humans may have such cells that help us locate where we are in relation to some reference point, such as home. We can keep track of both our active and our passive movements to maintain a "sense of direction" when we turn or are turned.

More than a hundred years ago, theorists speculated that neurons in the visual system might provide a representation of our visual world in very much the way that bits of silver produce the image on photographic film or bits of cardboard assemble to produce a picture in a jigsaw puzzle. In a photograph, bits of silver or spots of dye are packed close together to produce the image. Likewise it seemed reasonable that, in the visual areas of the brain, action potentials in different neurons might be the units of the perceived image. Bright areas of the visual image might be represented by neurons firing more rapidly, whereas dark areas might be represented by reduced or absent firing. The pattern of brightness and darkness across the visual cortex would create a picture of the scene being picked up by the eyes.

It is now clear, however, that this theory is incorrect. Single-cell-recording techniques have been an important source of insight into this aspect and other aspects of the neural code. Remember the description of the "Halle Berry cell" given in the Portrait in Chapter 4: the impression is that a single neuron has a more complex and dynamic role in creating images.

Neurons encode information in several ways. A simple way of representing sensory events is with a time code, in which the presence of an event is signaled by neural firing. For example, as long as a light is present, a neuron discharges; the discharging stops when the light is turned off. Alternatively, this same information could be represented as an event code: a neuron might discharge when the light comes on and then discharge again when the light goes off. In this case, a given neuron's firing might signal change.

The intensity of an event might be represented by a frequency code. For example, the brightness of a light or the intensity of a pain stimulus is represented by the rapidity of a cell's firing. Pain fibers in the PNS appear to encode pain in this way, with a few action potentials signaling mild pain and more-frequent action potentials signaling more-severe pain.

The frequency with which a neuron fires could also represent much more complicated information. For example, when a neuron in the visual system is very active, it represents the color red; when it is less active, it represents the color green. Neurons that encode bimodal information in this way have a "resting" state characterized by moderate activity; then, an increase in activity serves as one signal, and a decrease in activity serves as the other signal.

Levels of Neural Processing

The anatomy of the brain suggested to researchers that it must use codes to represent information. Consider the numbers of neurons at various levels of the visual system, from the receptors in the retina of the eye to the cortical areas that presumably take part in perception. As diagrammed in **Figure 6.2**A and B, relative to the large number of rods and cones, which are the receptor cells for light in the retina, the numbers of retinal ganglion cells and lateral geniculate body (LGB) cells carrying visual information from the thalamus to area 17, the first visual area of the neocortex, are very low. In higher visual association areas, the numbers of cells again increase. The changing numbers of cells argues that visual information must be transmitted as a code rather than as an image. Single-cell recordings confirm this hypothesis.

Single-cell recordings at these different levels (Figure 6.2C) show that ganglion cells and LGB cells respond only to dots of light, whereas the cells in the primary visual cortex respond to bars of light of specific orientation. Cells in higher visual areas respond to more-complex stimuli, including the position

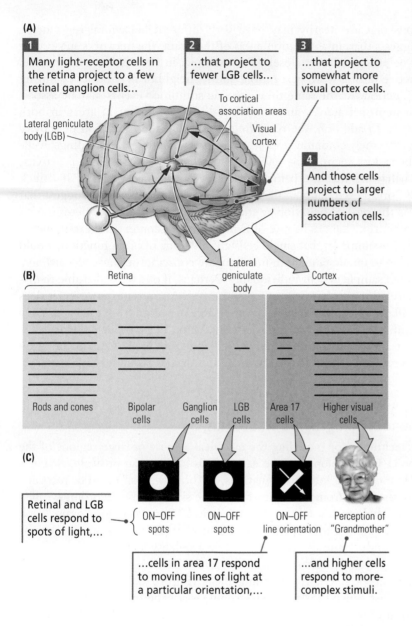

(A)

1 Many light-receptor cells in the retina project to a few retinal ganglion cells...

2 ...that project to fewer LGB cells...

3 ...that project to somewhat more visual cortex cells.

4 And those cells project to larger numbers of association cells.

Lateral geniculate body (LGB)

To cortical association areas

Visual cortex

(B)

Retina

Lateral geniculate body

Cortex

Rods and cones | Bipolar cells | Ganglion cells | LGB cells | Area 17 cells | Higher visual cells

(C)

Retinal and LGB cells respond to spots of light,...

ON–OFF spots

ON–OFF spots

ON–OFF line orientation

Perception of "Grandmother"

...cells in area 17 respond to moving lines of light at a particular orientation,...

...and higher cells respond to more-complex stimuli.

Figure 6.2

Levels of Processing (A) Schematic representation of projections from the eye to the visual cortex and from the visual cortex to cortical association areas. (B) Schematic representation of the relative numbers of cells at each level of the visual projection, indicated both by the number of lines and by their length. Relatively few neurons carry information from the retina to the visual cortex, but cell numbers increase again in the primary visual cortex and higher areas. (C) Coding of information in the visual pathways.

and movement of objects, and perhaps even to the specific features of the face such as "Halle Berry" or "Grandmother." In some way, the visual cortex takes information encoded as dots by numerous cells and bars in fewer cells and translates it into the complex, ongoing visual experience that tells us the "look" of our world.

The single-cell recordings made from the human neocortex (usually during neurosurgery) illustrate a number of interesting features of single-cell activity in the human brain. Generally, cortical neurons fire at a relatively low rate of fewer than 3 discharges per minute, which may increase to about 10 discharges per minute when the neurons become more active. Furthermore, most neurons have a narrow behavioral repertoire, responding to only one kind of sensory event or behavior.

Figure **6.3**

Polygraph Recording EEG The first polygraphs used this simple method for recording electrical activity in the human brain. (Photograph from Michael Rosenfeld/Stone Images; chart from SIU/Photo Researchers.)

1

Electrodes are attached to the skull, corresponding to specific areas of the brain.

Polygraph pen recorder

2

Polygraph electrodes are connected to magnets, which are connected to pens...

3

...that produce a paper record of electrical activity in the brain. This record indicates a relaxed person.

Neurons that are nearby may have very different behavioral repertoires, which suggests that, in association areas of the brain, the networks subserving different behaviors interact closely. For example, in Broca's area, one neuron may be active during word perception, and its neighbor may be active during word production. At the same time, specific stimuli or events may be associated with neuronal activity in a surprisingly large number of areas in both hemispheres. In addition, the recordings show that the inhibition of activity also is an extremely common response. Finally, in single-cell recordings, well-learned behaviors seem to be encoded by relatively sparse cortical activity, whereas behaviors that are being newly learned are accompanied by much more widespread excitability in the cortex. These general findings suggest that not only is the type of behavior or stimulus event important for determining whether a neuron changes its rate of firing, but so is context and experience.

With the assumption that single cells are the units of brain function, would it be possible to understand brain function and consciousness after recording a large enough sample of cells individually? Perhaps, if one were also able to discover the relation of each neuron to all the rest. At present, however, it does not seem likely that researchers will ever be able to record from each and every neuron and fully chart the relations among them. Thus, other imaging techniques that allow investigators to view the activity of large areas of the brain concurrently provide important alternate approaches to understanding brain function.

Electroencephalographic Recording

A simple technique for recording the electrical activity of large regions of the human brain was developed in the early 1930s by German physiologist Hans Berger. He found that voltage fluctuations, or "brain waves," could be recorded by placing the leads from a voltmeter onto the skull. These recordings, called **electroencephalograms** (*electro*, for "electrical," *encephala*, for "brain," and *grams*, for "graphs") or **EEGs**, are a valuable tool for (1) studying sleep, (2) monitoring the depth of anesthesia, (3) diagnosing epilepsy and brain damage, and (4) studying normal brain function.

In a typical EEG recording arrangement (**Figure 6.3**), one electrode (a small metal disc called the "active electrode") is attached to the scalp to detect the electrical activity in the underlying brain area. A second electrode (the "indifferent electrode") is attached to the ear lobe, where there is no electrical activity to detect. The two electrodes detect the difference in the electrical potentials.

The electrodes are fixed in place with a paste that is a good electrical conductor. The electrical fluctuations in the brain are rather small, usually much less than a millivolt, but, when amplified, they can be displayed on a **polygraph** (meaning "many graphs"). In the original polygraph, the electrical signals powered magnets, which were connected to pens. A motor pulled a long sheet of paper at a constant rate beneath the pens, allowing the patterns of electrical activity to be traced on the paper. Today, computers store the patterns and replay the electrical signals on a screen.

What does the EEG record? You know that individual neurons produce graded potentials—small depolarizations and hyperpolarizations of membrane voltage (see Figure 4.16). If a large number of neurons undergo graded potential changes of the same charge and at the same time, the signal is large enough to be recorded from as far away as the skull. The neurons of the neocortex are arranged in horizontal layers, and a substantial part of the EEG signal comes from the large pyramidal neurons of layers V and VI (see Figure 3.24). *Pacemaker cells* ensure that these neurons undergo graded potentials at the same time, presumably so that they can synchronize their action potentials. The signal recorded by the EEG consists of the rhythmical graded potentials on many thousands of neurons.

The rhythms of the pyramidal cells are produced in a number of ways. Cells in the thalamus or brainstem act as pacemakers, driving the graded potentials rhythmically. Interneurons within the cortex that are connected to many dozens of pyramidal cells also discharge rhythmically, thus driving the rhythm of the pyramidal cells. Additionally, the pyramidal cells have intrinsic rhythms, and the connections between adjacent neurons can serve to synchronize those patterns. Finally, the rhythm of the cells can fluctuate with heart rate or respiration, events that provide oxygen and glucose to the cells and thus influence their activity.

No matter how a given signal is produced, the neurons that produce it are referred to as the signal's **generator**. The many different waves recorded at a single location correspond to the changing inputs onto the cells that are producing the EEG signal.

That the electrical activity detected through the skull actually comes from generators in the brain has been demonstrated in a number of ways. During surgery, neurologists have taken EEG recordings both from the skull and directly from the underlying brain and have found that the rhythms from the two locations are similar, although the waves are larger in amplitude when recorded from the brain tissue. In research with animals, microelectrodes placed within neurons have demonstrated that these neurons do generate the waves.

The waves recorded from the skull are **volume conducted** through the brain and through the skull—conducted in the manner in which waves travel through water. As the electrodes are moved farther away from the source, the amplitude of the waves from a given generator grows smaller. Thus, if a number of electrodes are placed on the skull, amplitude differences can be used to estimate the approximate location of the generator that is producing a given set of waves.

Subsequent to Berger's discovery, EEG recordings were soon found to be useful in a number of ways. **Figure 6.4** shows that certain patterns of waves are associated with particular behavioral states. When a person is aroused, excited, or even just alert, the EEG pattern has a low amplitude (the height of the brain waves) and a high frequency (the number of brain waves per second), as seen in Figure 6.4A. This pattern, called the **beta (β) rhythm**, is typical of an EEG taken from anywhere on the skull of an alert subject—not only a human subject but other animals, too.

In contrast, when a person is calm and resting quietly, especially with eyes closed, the rhythmical brain waves shown in Figure 6.4B

Figure **6.4**

Characteristic EEG Recordings
Brain-wave patterns correspond to different states of consciousness in humans. (After *Epilepsy and the Functional Anatomy of the Human Brain* by W. Penfield and H. H. Jasper. Boston: Little, Brown, 1954, p. 12.)

(A) Awake or excited—beta rhythm

(B) Relaxed, eyes closed—alpha waves

(C) Drowsy—slowed frequency, increased-amplitude waves

(D) Asleep—slower, higher-amplitude delta waves

(E) Deep sleep—even slower and higher-amplitude waves

(F) Coma—further slowing

Time (sec)

often emerge. These so-called *alpha* (α) waves are extremely rhythmical but with waxing and waning amplitude and a frequency of approximately 11 cycles per second. In humans, the largest alpha rhythms are detected coming from the region of the visual cortex at the back of the head. If a relaxed person is disturbed or opens his or her eyes, the alpha rhythm abruptly stops.

Not everyone displays alpha rhythms, and some people display them much more consistently than others. You can buy a small voltmeter for monitoring your own alpha rhythms if you're interested. The voltmeter transforms EEG waves into "beeps" so that the brain-wave rhythm can be heard. After attaching a lead from one pole of the voltmeter to your skull and attaching the reference wire to your ear lobe, you relax with eyes closed and try to make the voltmeter "beep" in an alpha rhythm. Many people quickly learn to turn alpha waves on and off in this way. Beeping voltmeters were once promoted as a tool for learning transcendental meditation.

An EEG is a sensitive indicator of conscious states other than arousal and relaxation. Figure 6.4C through E illustrates the electroencephalographic changes that take place as a person goes from drowsiness to sleep and finally enters deep sleep. As the EEG rhythms become slower in frequency and larger in amplitude, 4- to 7-cycle-per-second *theta* (θ) waves and finally 1- to 3-cycle-per-second **delta** (δ) **waves** are produced. These distinctive brain-wave patterns make the EEG a reliable tool for monitoring waking and consciousness, estimating the depth of anesthesia, evaluating the severity of head injury, and searching for other brain abnormalities. If the brain ceases to function (the condition called brain death), the EEG becomes a flat line.

The EEG finds a useful clinical application in the diagnosis of epilepsy, a condition characterized by changes in consciousness or by convulsions of the body. The cause of epileptic seizures was unknown until the results of EEG experiments demonstrated that different varieties of epilepsy are associated with different abnormal electrical rhythms in the brain (**Figure 6.5**). Some forms of epilepsy, called **petit mal** (from the French words meaning "little bad") **epilepsy**, are generally associated with brief losses of consciousness, perhaps lasting only a few seconds. Other forms of epilepsy may be associated with a loss of memory lasting for many minutes. Still other forms, called **grand mal** (meaning "big bad") **epilepsy**, are characterized by convulsions of the body, falling down, and loss of consciousness.

Electroencephalographic recordings can provide information both about the cause of epilepsy and about the location of the problem. First, the duration of an epileptic attack correlates closely with the duration of abnormalities in the EEG, which may consist of a loss of recording, a slowing of recording, or large distinctive spikes. This correspondence indicates that epilepsy is associated with the abnormal activity of neurons. Second, the EEG can identify the region of the brain in which the abnormal rhythm is produced. The focus of the abnormality is usually located in the brain region that first generates the abnormal electrical activity. For example, although abnormal waves

Figure **6.5**

Patterns of Seizure Examples of electroencephalographic patterns recorded during a grand mal seizure. Abbreviations: LT and RT, left and right temporal; LF and RF, left and right frontal; LO and RO, left and right occipital. Dots on the hemispheres indicate the approximate recording sites. Column numbers refer to the stages of the seizure: (1) normal record before the attack; (2) onset of the attack; (3) clonic phase, in which the person makes rhythmic movements in time with the large abnormal discharges; and (4) period of coma after the seizure ends.

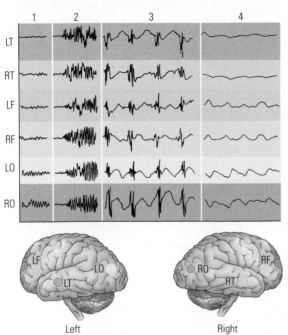

might be recorded from a number of regions of the brain, all of them may be produced in one location and volume conducted across the brain to be detected by electrodes at other locations.

Alternatively, the waves may originate in a particular location, then recruit adjacent regions, and in that way spread across the brain. Note that the largest abnormal spikes in Figure 6.5 appear to be coming from the right occipital (RO) cortex recording site, suggesting that the abnormality producing the epileptic attack is located in this region of the brain. Computerized techniques are used to make comparisons of the onset times and amplitude of EEG waves and thus reliably indicate the region of the brain in which the abnormal waves originate.

Electroencephalographic imaging is also used to study cognitive functions. With the use of computer processing, many channels of EEG information are recorded simultaneously to generate averages of amplitudes and frequencies of the EEG as it changes from one moment to the next. The miniaturization of the equipment allows recordings to be taken from as many as 125 sites on the skull. The computer then makes a two-dimensional map of the brain surface, with different colors indicating the relative activity of different brain regions. This technique produces an ongoing "online" representation of the "working" brain.

Event-Related Potentials

Event-related potentials, or ERPs, are brief changes in a slow-wave EEG signal in response to a discrete sensory stimulus. An ERP is not easy to detect, because the signal is "hidden" in the EEG. The ERP, which consists of a graded potential generated by the sensory stimulus of interest, is mixed with many other electrical signals and so is impossible to spot just by visually inspecting an EEG. One way to detect an ERP is to produce the stimulus repeatedly and average the recorded responses. Averaging tends to cancel out any irregular and unrelated electrical activity, leaving only the graded potentials generated by the stimulus event.

Event-related potentials have another distinctive feature. The neural response evoked by a sensory stimulus travels through the brainstem and then through processing regions of the cortex. At each synapse, a new graded potential is generated. Event-related potentials represent the location and the time of processing at each generator, yielding a picture of information flow through the brain.

An analogy will in part clarify the procedure. Imagine throwing a small stone into a lake of choppy water. Although the stone produces a splash, that splash is hard to see among all the lake's ripples and waves. The splash made by the stone is analogous to an event-related potential caused by a sensory stimulus.

If a number of stones exactly the same size are thrown, hit exactly the same spot in the water, and produce exactly the same splash, then the splash becomes easier to detect. If your stone skipped along the surface of the water, the successive splashes would provide a record of its movement. Using a computer to average the water's random wave movements would make the regular splashes produced by the stones stand out as clearly as if a single stone had been thrown across a pool of calm water.

Figure 6.6 shows how averaging reveals an ERP in response to an auditory stimulus—in this case, a tone. Notice that the EEG made when the tone is first

Figure **6.6**

Detecting ERPs In the averaging process for obtaining an ERP, a stimulus is presented at time 0, as indicated by the vertical shaded bar, and the electroencephalographic activity that occurs in response to the tone is recorded (First response). The second, third, and fourth graphs then show the results of averaging the electroencephalographic responses after 10, 50, and 100 presentations, respectively. The averaged wave sequence develops a more and more distinctive shape until, after 100 presentations, the ERP pattern is sharp and clear. Positive (P) and negative (N) waves produced at every repetition of the stimulus are used for analysis.

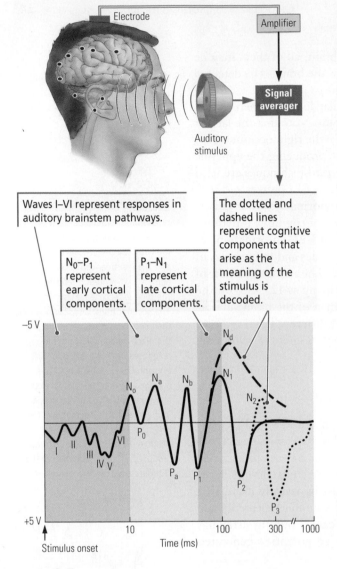

Waves I–VI represent responses in auditory brainstem pathways.

N_0–P_1 represent early cortical components.

P_1–N_1 represent late cortical components.

The dotted and dashed lines represent cognitive components that arise as the meaning of the stimulus is decoded.

Figure 6.7

Brain Mapping with ERP Event-related potential from the parietal cortex of a subject in response to the presentation of an auditory stimulus. (After Neville, 1980.)

presented is very irregular. But, when the recordings of more than 100 stimulus presentations are averaged, a distinctive wave pattern appears. This ERP consists of a number of negative (N) and positive (P) waves produced in a period of a few hundred milliseconds after the stimulus is presented.

By convention, the waves depicted as going downward on the ERP graph are called positive, and the waves depicted as going upward are called negative. Positive and negative waves are numbered according to the time at which they are produced. For instance, P_1 in Figure 6.6 is a positive wave produced about 100 ms after the presentation of the stimulus.

Not all waves in the ERP are unique to this particular stimulus. Some are common to any auditory stimulus perceived by the brain. The waves produced at longer latencies, from 100 to 300 ms after a stimulus is presented, are likely to be related to the meaning of a stimulus. For example, the long latency ERPs produced in response to the spoken words "cat" and "rat" contain distinctive peaks and patterns that allow researchers to differentiate one response from the other.

Maps of cortical function can be produced using ERPs. **Figure 6.7** shows an ERP produced by the parietal cortex in response to the presentation of an auditory stimulus. Note that the ERP is made up of many positive and negative waves. Each wave is produced by a different neural generator—that is, by a different group of neurons responding successively to the signal with a change in their electrical activity. The signals shown in Figure 6.7 correspond to the successive activation of regions of the auditory pathway from the brainstem to the cortex. The signals identified as I though VI are from brainstem generators, those designated N_0 through P_1 are from primary auditory cortex regions, and those designated N_1 though P_3 are from secondary and tertiary regions of the cortex. The dotted lines indicate waves that are associated with thought processes in response to the signal. For example, P_3, produced 300 ms after stimulus presentation, represents the process of decoding the meaning of the sounds.

Figure 6.8 shows a multiple-recording method that uses 64 electrodes simultaneously to detect ERPs at many cortical sites. Computerized averaging techniques reduce the masses of information obtained to simpler comparisons between electrode sites. For example, if the focus of interest is P_3, a computer record displays an image of the skull in which only the amplitude of P_3 is shown. The record is then converted into a color code, creating a graphic representation showing which brain regions are most responsive to the signal.

At the top of Figure 6.8, a subject is being monitored while viewing a picture of a rat that flashes repeatedly in the same place on a computer screen.

The P₃ wave recorded on the posterior right side of the subject's head is larger than the same P₃ wave recorded anywhere else, showing that this region is a "hot spot" for processing the visual stimulus. Presumably, for this particular subject, the right posterior part of the brain performs an important operation in the decoding of the picture of the rat 300 ms after it was presented.

Because an ERP produced in response to a stimulus represents the activity of the entire pathway and all the nuclei engaged in processing the signal evoked by that stimulus, the ERP has many experimental uses. It is used to study the normal function of the pathway through which the signal passes, the normal function of the nuclei taking part in processing the signal, and the cognitive processes in the neocortex that are employed in discriminating or learning about the signal.

Because measures are taken from both hemispheres, studies of ERPs recorded during cognitive tasks compare the different responses of the hemispheres with the stimulus signal. Finally, ERPs also reveal electrical changes associated with the planning and execution of movement. For example, researchers have identified certain potentials produced in the motor cortex later than 300 ms after the presentation of a given stimulus. They call it a **readiness potential** because it signals an impending movement.

Magnetoencephalography

When a magnetic field passes across a wire, it induces a current in the wire. When a current flows along a wire, it induces a magnetic field around the wire. This reciprocal relation between electricity and magnetism is also seen in neurons.

Neural activity, by generating an electrical field, also produces a magnetic field. Although the magnetic field produced by a single neuron is extremely small, the field produced by many neurons is sufficiently strong to be recorded on the surface of the skull. Such a record is called a **magnetoencephalogram** (MEG), and it is the magnetic counterpart of the EEG or ERP.

Calculations based on MEG measurements not only provide a description of the electrical activity of neurons but also permit a three-dimensional localization of the cell groups generating the measured field. Magnetic waves being conducted through living tissue undergo less distortion than electrical signals do, and so an MEG can have a higher resolution than an ERP. Thus, a major advantage of the MEG over the EEG and ERP is its ability to more precisely identify the source of the activity being recorded. For example, the MEG has proved useful in locating the source of epileptic discharges. The disadvantage of the MEG is its cost. The equipment for producing it is expensive in comparison with the apparatus used to produce EEGs and ERPs.

The heart of a magnetoencephalogram probe is a sensing device containing the special superconducting coils needed to detect the brain's very weak magnetic fields. This so-called **SQUID** (superconducting quantum interference device) is immersed in liquid helium to keep it at the low temperature necessary for superconductivity. One or more probes are moved across the surface of the skull, sending signals to the SQUID.

Electrodes attached to the scalp of a research subject are connected to...

Electrodes in geodesic sensor net

...a computer display of electrical activity, showing a large positive (P₃) wave at the posterior right side of the head.

This electrical activity can be converted into a color representation showing the hot spot for the visual stimulus.

Resting   300 ms after viewing

Figure **6.8**

Using ERPs to Image Brain Activity

Each probe produces an "isocontour map," a chart with concentric circles representing different intensities of the magnetic field. Such gradient maps allow the calculation of the three-dimensional location of the neurons generating the field. They are also converted into a graph of electrical events very similar to the electrical potentials recorded by electroencephalographic instruments.

Brain Stimulation

You know that placing an electrode near a neuron and passing an electrical current through it produces action potential in that neuron. Neuroscientists discovered long ago that they could learn about the functions of different brain areas by electrically stimulating the tissue. The results of the earliest studies of brain stimulation indicated that movements are elicited by stimulating the motor cortex, sensations are elicited by stimulating the sensory cortex, and complex cognitive functions such as speech are disrupted by stimulating speech areas of the cortex. Electrical stimulation of the brainstem can also activate many complex actions, such as mating, aggression, nest building, or food carrying in experimental animals.

Intracranial Brain Stimulation

Electrical stimulation of the brain is used for applications other than just mapping its functional regions. For example, stimulation of certain regions of the brainstem produce pleasurable sensations, and some early studies experimented with this form of brain stimulation to treat depression. Electrical brain stimulation, because it can arrest neural activity, has also been used to treat the abnormal discharges of the brain in epilepsy. Electrical stimulation of the brain can potentially aid in movement production after brain injury or in conditions where brain disease has produced a movement abnormality. For example, stimulation of cortex adjacent to tissue damaged by stroke can aid in recovery.

One widely used application of electrical brain stimulation is in the treatment of Parkinson's disease and some other disorders of movement. Parkinson's disease is characterized both by tremors and by **akinesia**, an absence or poverty of movement. When electrodes are implanted in the brain so that **deep brain stimulation** (DBS) can be applied to a number of brainstem regions, both tremors and akinesia are lessened.

This neurosurgery facilitates normal movements by fixing an electrode in place in the globus pallidus or subthalamic nucleus and connecting it to an external electrical stimulator controlled by the patient. When a patient turns the switch on, appropriate current is delivered to the electrode, both lessening abnormal movement and improving desired movement.

Although DBS treatment can give a Parkinson patient from months to years of relief from disease symptoms, the treatment can have adverse effects. In a review of more than a thousand cases of deep brain stimulation for Parkinson's disease, Yasin Temel and colleagues document that, although the treatment helps many patients, cognitive changes including changes in mood and anxiety also ensue. Additionally, electrode implants can produce infection and irritation, and frequently DBS is ineffective.

What limits both experimentation with intracranial electrical stimulation and its use in treating brain disorders is its invasiveness: the skull must be opened to introduce the electrode. This procedure of itself can damage the brain or introduce infection. Thus, the application of intracranial stimulation techniques is limited to conditions in which the brain is undergoing surgery for other reasons or to severe conditions for which other treatment options are limited. Additionally, when brain stimulation does produce therapeutic effects, their basis is not fully understood.

Transcranial Magnetic Stimulation

The relation between magnetism and electricity forms the basis of **transcranial magnetic stimulation** (TMS), a noninvasive method that allows the brain to be stimulated through the skull. In the TMS technique, a small wire coil is placed adjacent to the skull. A high voltage current is passed through the coil in pulses as rapid as 50 times per second. Each pulse of electricity produces a rapid increase and then decrease in the magnetic field around the coil. The magnetic field easily penetrates the skull and changes the electrical activity of adjacent neurons.

By using a coil in a figure-8 shape, the magnetic field can be quite high in a focused area below the coil, and so the change in neural activity can be focused. **Figure 6.9** shows a typical experimental setup, including a possible placement of the coil on the skull (top) and the area of the brain that the coil, so placed, would stimulate (bottom).

Transcranial magnetic stimulation was originally used by neurosurgeons to stimulate brain tissue to monitor its functional condition during brain surgery and to identify the function of the tissue. From this initial use, it became clear that TMS did not harm tissue, even after thousands of pulses of stimulation, and so could be used to stimulate the normal brain through the skull. One use of TMS was to map the brain in regard to functional areas. By moving the TMS stimulation and noting the results, researchers can identify and map the functions of the cortex in just the same way as with intracranial electrical stimulation.

These initial experiments suggested that TMS might be used therapeutically for many of the same purposes for which electrical stimulation by intracranial electrodes is used. That is, can TMS be used as a therapy for patients with movement disorders? Can it be used as a treatment to reduce the akinesia and tremors of Parkinson's disease? Can it lessen chronic pain? And can it

Figure **6.9**

Transcranial Magnetic Stimulation (Composite MRI and PET scan from Tomas Paul, Montreal Neurological Institute.)

A transcranial magnetic stimulator is placed on the skull over this region of the cortex.

TMS COIL

L   R

The TMS coil, shown here in a composite MRI and PET-scan photograph, interferes with brain function in the adjacent area.

be used as a treatment for depression? Additionally, in what ways can TMS be used to study normal brain function? By now, more than 4,000 scientific papers have been written on the effects of TMS, and it has become a mature and useful experimental and clinical tool.

X-Ray Imaging Techniques

Aside from surgery, the first methods for peering into the living brain to see what was "in there" required taking X-rays. X-ray methods were and continue to be important for medical diagnosis, especially to the neurologist looking for evidence of a brain tumor, stroke, or abnormality in brain vasculature. The most obvious limitation of X-ray techniques, however, is that they produce a static, two-dimensional image of what, in contrast, is a dynamic, three-dimensional structure.

Today, with the assistance of powerful computing techniques, dynamic three-dimensional images of the living brain can be produced, not only to locate abnormalities more precisely but also to detect changes in normal brain activity that are associated with ongoing behavior. These new methods allow brain structure and function to be imaged together. We first consider some of the early static techniques and then look at new, dynamic methods of imaging the living brain.

Conventional Radiography

The first method for producing a visual image of the brain, **conventional radiography**, consists of passing X-rays through the skull onto an X-ray-sensitive film. As the X-rays travel through the head, they are absorbed to different degrees by different tissues: to a great degree by dense tissue such as bone, to a lesser degree by neural tissue, and less still by fluid such as that in the blood vessels and ventricles.

Thus some parts of the film receive a greater dose of X-rays emerging from the far side of the skull than do others. When the film is developed, a shadowy negative image is revealed, showing the locations of different kinds of tissue. Radiography is still used for examining the skull for fractures and the brain for gross abnormalities.

Pneumoencephalography

Pneumoencephalography (literally, air–brain graph) is a method for enhancing conventional X-ray radiography by taking advantage of the fact that X-rays are not absorbed by air. First, a small amount of cerebrospinal fluid is removed from the subarachnoid space in a subject's spinal cord and replaced by air. Then, with the subject sitting upright, X-rays are taken as the air moves up the spinal cord and enters the ventricular system. Because of the air inside them, the ventricles stand out clearly in the resulting image. Although it has diagnostic value (because expanded ventricles can mean loss of brain tissue and because constricted ventricles can indicate the presence of tumors), pneumoencephalography is painful and has been supplanted by newer imaging methods.

Angiography

Angiography is similar to pneumoencephalography except that a substance that absorbs X-rays is injected into the bloodstream (**Figure 6.10**). The presence of this "radioopaque" material in the blood produces an excellent image of the blood vessels, thus revealing circulatory abnormalities that might affect blood flow. Injecting a substance into the bloodstream is dangerous, however, and can be painful, and newer imaging methods are supplanting angiography.

Computerized Tomography

The modern era of brain imaging began in the early 1970s, when Allan Cormack and Godfrey Hounsfield independently developed an X-ray approach now called **computerized tomography** (*tomo*, meaning "cut," thus producing a picture through one section): the **CT scan**. Cormack and Hounsfield both recognized that one could pass a narrow X-ray beam through the same object at many different angles, creating many different images of it, and then combine the images with the use of computing and mathematical techniques to create a three-dimensional image of the brain.

The method has some resemblance to the way in which our two eyes (and our brains) work in concert to perceive depth and distance so as to locate an object in space. The CT scan, however, coordinates many more than two images, analogous perhaps to our walking to several new vantage points to obtain other views.

As described earlier, the absorption of X-ray radiation varies with tissue density. High-density tissue, such as bone, will absorb a lot of radiation. Low-density material, such as ventricular fluid or blood, will absorb little radiation. Neural-tissue absorption lies between these two extremes. The software of CT scanning translates these differences in absorption into an image of the brain in which dark colors indicate low-density regions and light colors indicate high-density regions.

Figure 6.11A shows a typical example. The skull is seen as a white border. The density of the brain's gray matter does not differ sufficiently from that of white matter for a CT scan to clearly distinguish between the two, and so the cortex and its underlying white matter show up as a more or less homogeneous gray. Ventricles can be visualized, however, because the fluid in them is far less dense; they, as well as some of the major fissures, are rendered darker in the CT scan.

Figure 6.10

X-Ray Technique A normal carotid angiogram showing the brain's large blood vessels. The face is pointing down toward the left. (From S. J. DeArmond et al., 1976. Copyright 1976 by Oxford University Press, Inc. Reprinted with permission.)

Figure 6.11

X-Ray Computerized Tomography (A) A horizontal CT scan of a subject who presented with Broca's aphasia. The dark region at the left anterior is the location of the lesion. (B) A schematic representation of the horizontal section, with the area of the lesion shown in black. (C) A reconstruction of the brain, showing a lateral view of the left hemisphere with the lesion shown in black. (After Damasio and Damasio, 1989, p. 56.)

(A) CT scan
Lesion

(B) Horizontal section
Anterior

Lesion

Posterior

(C) Reconstruction, lateral view

Lesion

Plane of section in parts A and B

Each point on this image represents about a 1-mm-diameter circle of tissue, a resolution sufficient to distinguish two objects about 5 mm apart and appropriate for localizing brain tumors and lesions. The lesion revealed in Figure 6.11A is a damaged region where the presence of fewer neurons and more fluid produces a contrast that appears as a darker area in the CT scan. This subject presented with symptoms of Broca's aphasia, a diagnosis confirmed by the location of the lesion in the left frontal cortex (adjacent to the butterfly-shaped lateral ventricles).

Figure 6.11B, a drawing of the same horizontal section, uses shading to portray the lesion. Figure 6.11C is a lateral drawing of the left hemisphere showing the extent of the lesion, reconstructed from a series of horizontal CT scans.

Dynamic Brain Imaging

The development of the CT scan was momentous in two respects. First, it changed the practice of neurology by providing a way to look inside the head without using unpleasant or dangerous procedures. Second, it inspired other scientists to use clever mathematics and computer strategies to develop even more sophisticated image-reconstruction methods, such as positron emission tomography (PET), magnetic resonance imaging (MRI), and functional magnetic resonance imaging (fMRI).

Figure 6.12 displays images obtained by the CT, PET, and MRI methods, along with a photograph of a dissected brain for comparison. The clarity of the photograph, in which the gray matter of the cortical surface and the white matter of the underlying fibers are easily distinguishable, provides a useful frame of reference for evaluating the resolution of the various techniques.

Figure **6.12**

Imaging Contrast The CT, PET, and MRI scans shown here were created by three different techniques for imaging a slice of the brain (A, anterior; P, posterior). The fourth image is a photograph of a brain section removed from a cadaver. (After Posner and Raichle, 1994.)

Positron Emission Tomography

Positron emission tomography, or PET, was the first post-CT development in imaging. A PET camera, like the one shown in **Figure 6.13**, is a doughnut-shaped array of radiation detectors positioned to encircle a subject's head. Either a small amount of water, containing radioactive molecules to label it, is injected into the bloodstream or a gas containing the radioactive molecule is inhaled. The radioactive molecules pose little danger to the subject because they are very unstable and break down in just a few minutes. In the process, they release particles that are detected by the PET camera.

A small amount of radioactively labeled water is injected into a subject. Active areas of the brain use more blood and thus have more radioactive labels.

Annihilation photon detectors

Annihilation photons

Positrons from the radioactivity are released; they collide with electrons in the brain, and photons (a form of energy) are produced, exit the head, and are detected.

A computer reconstructs variations in the density of the flow of particles from different locations to produce an image of a section of the brain (see Figure 6.13, right). Because the radioactive molecules are carried in the bloodstream, the variations in the image represent areas of higher and lower blood flow. A color gradient proceeding from white through reds, greens, and then blues represents maximum to minimum levels of blood flow. Color images made during different kinds of mental activity indicate which areas of the brain are active during the execution of particular cognitive functions.

The particles detected by the PET camera are produced as illustrated in **Figure 6.14**. Briefly, positron emission tomography is based on the unique behavior of positrons, atomic particles having the size and mass of electrons but positively charged. When a radioactive substance is injected into the blood or enters the bloodstream through the lungs, it is carried by the blood to the brain and, as it travels, it decays by releasing positrons.

Positrons emerge from the nucleus of a radioactive atom because the nucleus has a deficiency of neutrons and so is unstable (see Figure 6.14A). The nucleus of a radioactive form of oxygen, ^{15}O, for example, has eight protons and seven neutrons, whereas the stable, nonradioactive form of oxygen that we breathe, ^{16}O, has eight of each. In the unstable nucleus, the extra proton breaks down into a positron and a neutron. The positron is expelled from the nucleus and the neutron stays.

Positrons released from the nucleus lose their kinetic energy after traveling just a few millimeters in brain tissue and, when they come to rest, are attracted to the negative charge of electrons. A positron and an electron are annihilated when they come together, and the resulting energy creates two very powerful annihilation gamma rays (a gamma ray is a photon, or light particle, of a certain frequency) that leave the area of the annihilation event in exactly opposite directions. Because of their energy (511 kiloelectron volts, abbreviated keV), the annihilation photons exit the head at the speed of light.

In the PET scanner, pairs of radiation detectors, each member of a pair placed opposite the other in a ring, are placed around the head to record these

Figure **6.13**

PET Scanner and Image A subject lying in a PET scanner, the design of which is illustrated in the drawing. In the scan, the bright red and yellow areas are regions of high blood flow. (PET scanner from Hank Morgan/Science Source/Photo Researchers; PET scan from Alan Carruthers/Photo Researchers.)

(A)

A positron released by an unstable nucleus of ^{15}O meets an electron and their mass is converted into two annihilation photons traveling in opposite directions.

Annihilation photon

Positron

^{15}O nucleus

Electron

180°

Coincidence circuit

Opposing radiation detectors record the event when struck simultaneously by annihilation photons.

(B)

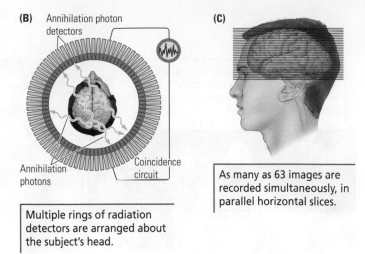

Annihilation photon detectors

Coincidence circuit

Annihilation photons

Multiple rings of radiation detectors are arranged about the subject's head.

(C)

As many as 63 images are recorded simultaneously, in parallel horizontal slices.

Figure 6.14

The Technique of PET Imaging

(After Posner and Raichle, 1994, p. 19.)

events (see Figure 6.14B). The paired detectors record an event only when both are struck by annihilation photons simultaneously. The simultaneous collisions are counted, and the counts are converted into an image of the blood flow in the brain during the first minute after injection. Because the radioactive substance has been injected into the blood, areas of the brain with more blood flow will emit more photons.

Each detector in the PET camera ring is coupled to a detector 180° opposite so that annihilation events in any region through the horizontal plane of the ring can be detected. Through the use of multiple detector rings, each of which can sample a slice of brain, annihilation events in many brain slices can be recorded.

Modern PET cameras can obtain multiple parallel slices simultaneously, as shown in Figure 6.14C. Each image consists of **voxels**, three-dimensional imaging regions, that are 2 mm³ in size. The shades indicate the density of annihilation events, as shown in **Figure 6.15**. Note that PET does not measure local

Figure 6.15

Resting State PET Images of blood flow obtained from a single subject resting quietly with eyes closed. Each scan represents a horizontal plane, or section, from the top surface (1) to the bottom slice (31) of the brain. (From M. E. Raichle, Mallinckrodt Institute of Radiology, Washington University School of Medicine.)

neural activity directly; rather, it infers neural activity on the assumption that blood flow increases in areas where neuron activity increases.

We can conclude from Figure 6.15 that the distribution of blood flow in the brain is not uniform. To arrive at conclusions about the link between blood flow and mental activity, however, PET researchers must resort to a statistical manipulation. They subtract the blood-flow pattern imaged when the brain is in a carefully selected control state—resting, for example, as depicted in the sections in Figure 6.15—from that imaged when the subject is engaged in an experimental task from the blood-flow pattern. This subtractive process, illustrated in the top row of **Figure 6.16**.

This subtraction process images the change in blood flow from state to state, revealing which areas of the brain are selectively active under different circumstances. The change can be averaged across subjects (see Figure 6.16, middle row) to yield an average, or mean, difference image (bottom).

The radioactive materials used in PET have a half-life ranging from minutes to hours—from 2.2 minutes for radioactive oxygen, for example, to a little more than an hour for radioactive fluorine. Consequently, the radioactive materials must be prepared close to the PET apparatus just before use, requiring the presence of a cyclotron in the vicinity of the experimental room. In spite of the expense incurred by this requirement, PET has important advantages over other imaging methods:

- PET can detect the decay of a wide range of radiochemicals. Literally hundreds of radiochemicals are used with PET to map a wide range of brain changes and conditions, including changes in pH, glucose, oxygen, amino acids, and proteins.

- PET can detect relative amounts of a given neural transmitter, the density of neurotransmitter receptors, or metabolic activities associated with learning, brain poisoning, or degenerative processes that might be related to aging.

- PET is widely used for the study of cognitive function, and here it has also had great success. For example, PET confirms that various regions of the brain have different functions.

An early study of PET relating blood flow to language use confirmed that Broca's area and Wernicke's area are centers of language, and further, that a number of other areas, such as the supplementary motor cortex, take part as well, in both the left and the right hemispheres (**Figure 6.17**). This finding resolved a longstanding debate in neuroscience. When Paul Broca proposed that language was highly localized and lateralized in the brain, John Hughlings-Jackson dissented on theoretical grounds, claiming that all areas of the brain contribute to language but in different ways. Positron emission tomography reveals that both

Figure **6.16**

The Procedure of Subtraction
In the upper row of scans, the control condition of resting while looking at a static fixation point is subtracted from the experimental condition of stimulation by looking at a flickering checkerboard. The subtraction produces a somewhat different image for each of the five experimental subjects shown in the middle row, but all show increased blood flow in the occipital region. The images are averaged to produce the averaged image at the bottom. (From M. E. Raichle, Mallinckrodt Institute of Radiology, Washington University School of Medicine.)

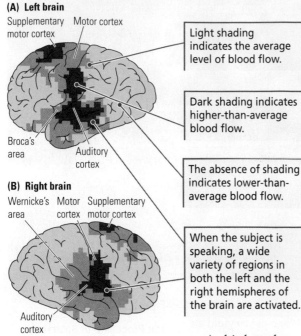

(A) Left brain

Supplementary motor cortex

Motor cortex

Broca's area

Auditory cortex

(B) Right brain

Wernicke's area

Motor cortex

Supplementary motor cortex

Auditory cortex

Light shading indicates the average level of blood flow.

Dark shading indicates higher-than-average blood flow.

The absence of shading indicates lower-than-average blood flow.

When the subject is speaking, a wide variety of regions in both the left and the right hemispheres of the brain are activated.

Figure 6.17

Relating Brain Function to Regional Blood Flow Because the pattern of blood flow varies with the behavioral task, the relative importance of different areas in different functions can be inferred from PET scans showing blood flow under different experimental conditions.

positions are correct: speech is localized to Broca's area, but many areas of the brain contribute to language.

In spite of their value, PET studies of cognitive function also have limitations. Recall that PET imaging is indirect; it measures regional blood flow rather than neuronal activity.

A second limitation is that PET imaging requires a subtraction process. A neutral condition is used as a baseline and subtracted from an active condition of cognitive function. The subtraction process provides researchers not with a specific list of what areas of the brain are taking part in a task but with an indication of what areas become relatively more or less active as a task is performed. In some experiments, a number of subtractions are made. For example, a state imaged when a subject is resting may be subtracted from a state imaged when the subject is reading a book, and this result may be subtracted from a state in which a subject is reading only nouns. Each subtraction provides a more refined view of brain function but a view that is more artificial.

A third weakness of PET is that, in interpreting the data, researchers are making certain assumptions that might not be equally valid in every circumstance. For example, when a subject is given a visual task, researchers might be assuming that lower visual areas are active during all forms of visual activity, whereas higher visual areas are much more specific in function. Even if this assumption turns out to be correct when applied to vision, it may be incorrect when applied elsewhere.

Magnetic Resonance Imaging

Magnetic resonance imaging, or MRI, is a technology for noninvasively creating pictures of the soft tissues of the human body. It is named for its use of a large magnet (M) and a specific radiofrequency pulse (R) to generate a brain signal that produces an image (I). Magnetic resonance imaging can be used to study both brain anatomy and neural function; and, because it does not make use of ionizing radiation, it is safe enough to use repeatedly on volunteers and patients, adult and child alike.

A standard clinical MRI scanner typically has a three-dimensional resolution, or voxel size, better than 1 mm³, meaning that it can discriminate the activity in a piece of tissue of that size. Our description of MRI is simplified in several ways, because the phenomenon would have to be described by using quantum mechanics to be completely accurate.

Magnetic resonance imaging is based on the principle that a hydrogen atom's nucleus, which consists of a single proton, behaves like a spinning bar magnet. In other words, each proton has a dipole, and so, as the proton spins around hydrogen's lone electron, one end of its axis acts like the north pole of a bar magnet and the other end acts like the south pole.

Ordinarily, protons are oriented at random, and so a given piece of tissue (all soft tissue contains water, which contains hydrogen) has no net dipole

(A)

Each proton of a hydrogen atom rotates about its axis, acting as a small magnet with its own dipole. Normally, the protons of hydrogen atoms are randomly positioned and so the tissue has no net charge.

(B)

Vertical external magnetic field

When placed in a magnetic field, the protons become aligned in parallel.

(C)

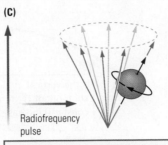

Radiofrequency pulse

A radiofrequency pulse applied to the tissue pushes the protons to their sides, causing them to wobble about their axes and about their north–south orientation. This motion,...

(D)

Vertical component

Horizontal component

...called precession, produces measurable vertical and horizontal magnetic fields.

Figure 6.18

The Physics of MRI The movements of hydrogen protons under normal conditions (A) and wobbling under the influences of a vertical magnetic field (B) and a horizontal radiofrequency pulse (C), provide the basis for magnetic resonance imaging. (D) The wobbling (precession) of the protons under these influences produces two measurable magnetic fields.

(**Figure 6.18**A). When placed in a magnetic field, however, the spinning protons orient themselves with respect to the field's lines of force and thus all line up in parallel (Figure 6.18B). In other words, the protons behave like the needle of a compass that aligns itself north and south with Earth's magnetic field.

Because of their spin, protons generate an electrical current, and, because proton density varies in different brain tissue (cerebral spinal fluid, myelin, neurons), a recorder sensitive to such a current can be used to produce proton-density images of the brain when all the protons are aligned. Most such imaging is done with a magnetic field measuring 1.5 teslas in strength. Considering that 1 tesla is 10,000 gauss and Earth's magnetic field is only about 0.5 gauss, it is a big magnet.

Another way to make an image is to perturb the protons when they are aligned and record the changes in the electrical field that take place as a result of the perturbation. A brief radiofrequency pulse that resonates with the target molecule is applied to a brain in which the atoms have been aligned vertically in a magnetic field, and the horizontal radiofrequency pulses form a second magnetic field. The pulses generated by the second magnetic field push the protons over onto their sides (Figure 6.18C).

Such "tipped" protons will now have two motions: they spin about their own axes and they spin about their longitudinal (north–south) orientation (Figure 6.18D). The protons wobble like a spinning top, a motion called **precession**.

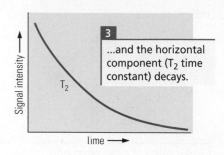

Figure 6.19

MRI Time Constants When the horizontal radiofrequency pulse is turned off, relaxation in the vertical and horizontal components of the magnetic field provides two time constants: T_1 measures the recovery of the vertical component of the magnetic field, and T_2 measures the decay of the horizontal component (synchronous spinning) of the magnetic field.

Imagine a dancer doing a never-ending pirouette while falling onto the floor to do a break-dance spin, all the time continuing to pirouette. This behavior in protons forms the basis for two other ways of making a magnetic resonance image.

When the horizontal magnetic field is turned off, the protons that are spinning about their horizontal axes in synchrony begin to relax; that is, they begin to "stand up" again and to fall out of synchrony with one another. These relaxation processes are described by two time constants, T_1 and T_2 (**Figure 6.19**):

- For T_1, a current detector having an orientation that is horizontal to the vertical axis of the protons' initial alignment measures the time that it takes the protons to "right" themselves from their tipped position and realign with the original magnetic field.

- For T_2, a second detector having an orientation that is perpendicular to that of the first detector, measures the rate at which the protons lose synchrony about the horizontal axis after the magnetic pulse is turned off.

Protons have different relaxation rates and corresponding T_1 and T_2 time constants, depending on whether they are in fat, cerebrospinal fluid, neurons, bone, or other tissue (**Figure 6.20**). Therefore, differences in electrical current at a set time—for example, at the midpoint of relaxation—related to the composition of surrounding tissue can be measured. The relaxation rates for cerebral spinal fluid are slower than those for white matter.

Figure 6.20

Translating Relaxation Rates into a Brain Image (A) Protons have different relaxation rates in different types of tissue (CSF, cerebral spinal fluid). (B) The differences can be translated into an image of the brain. (Magnetic resonance image from Gregory G. Dimijian/Photo Researchers.)

Figure 6.21

Magnetic Resonance Imaging The subject is placed in a long metal cylinder that has two sets of magnetic coils arranged at right angles, as detailed in the drawing. An additional coil (not shown) surrounds the head. This radiofrequency coil perturbs the static magnetic fields to produce a magnetic resonance image of a horizontal section through the head. (Scanner from Bob Schatz/Liasion International; scan from Gregory G. Dimijian/Photo Researchers.)

These differences in time constants can be translated into images of the brain made up of gradients that correspond to its different tissues, with dark color indicating low-density tissue and light color indicating high-density tissue. Either T_1 or T_2 constants are used, though one may be more suitable than the other in a given situation. For example, T_2 imaging is more sensitive than T_1 to differences between damaged tissue and intact tissue and so is useful for detecting lesions.

The MRI procedure is illustrated in **Figure 6.21**. The subject, lying prone on a bed with his or her head inserted into the center of the magnetic coils, must remain as still as possible. (Corrections are made for the slight head and brain movement produced by pulsations of blood flow through the brain.) Density differences in the imaged slice through the head are portrayed as colors, producing a horizontal cross section of the head and of the brain.

The resolution of MRI is derived from two- or three-dimensional readings acquired from the magnetic fields placed around the head. The gradients effectively divide the tissue into slices. The intersection of the slices provides 1-mm³ voxels, each having a unique signal. A computer performs a mathematical transformation on the voxels to produce an image of the brain (see Figure 6.21, bottom). Thus, the resolution of the image is measured in voxels, with each voxel containing thousands of cells. The Snapshot on the next page shows the significance of MRI in revealing individual differences in brain anatomy.

Functional Magnetic Resonance Imaging

A century after Angelo Mosso's experiments suggested that increased blood flow in the brain accompanies increased brain activity, Peter Fox and his colleagues discovered that, during increases in functional activity within the human brain, the increase in oxygen produced by increased blood flow actually

○SNAPSHOT
Describing Individual Differences in Cortical Anatomy

A major advantage of magnetic resonance imaging is the clarity with which it can distinguish between different regions of the brain and even different regions of the cortex. Consequently, fissures and gyri can be visualized, and individual differences in brain anatomy can be examined.

The accompanying illustration shows some of the variations found by Francesco Tomaiuolo and his colleagues with the use of T_1 imaging of a part of the frontal cortex called the **pars opercularis**, a region that constitutes part of Broca's area. Electrical stimulation of this area in human surgical patients reliably interferes with speech production, confirming that the area has a role in speech. The MRI analysis shows individual differences there, with some people having one convolution, some having two small convo-

lutions, and others having convolutions hidden within the surrounding gyri.

The researchers also looked for hemispheric differences and sex differences (by comparing the left and the right hemispheres in male and female subjects) and found the size of the pars opercularis to be similar in the two hemispheres and uncorrelated with the subject's sex. These results suggest that, if there are sex and hemispheric differences in this part of Broca's area, they must reside in the function of the region rather than in its gross structure.

Tomaiuolo, F., J. D. MacDonald, S. Caramanos, G. Posner, M. Chivaras, A. C. Evans, and M. Petrides. Morphology, morphometry and probability mapping of the pars opercularis of the inferior frontal gyrus: An in vivo MRI analysis. *European Journal of Neuroscience* 11:3033–3064, 1999

Subject A

Subject B

Subject C

Pars opecularis with one gyrus   Pars opecularis with two gyri   Pars opecularis hidden in sulcus between gyri

Magnetic resonance images of the human brain can be used for anatomical comparisons. A study of Broca's area in different people shows that the pars opercularis can consist of one gyrus (left), two gyri (middle), or a gyrus that is hidden beneath adjacent gyri (right). (After Tomaiuolo et al., 1999.)

exceeds the tissue's need for oxygen. As a result, the amount of oxygen in an activated brain area increases.

More specifically, as neurons become active, they increase their use of oxygen, resulting in a temporary dip in the amount of oxygen in the blood. At the same time, they signal the blood vessels to dilate to increase blood flow. The resulting increase in blood flow brings more oxygen to the area than the neurons can actually use, thus producing a relative increase in local oxygen.

Thus, before neuronal activation, the amounts of *deoxyhemoglobin* (hemoglobin without oxygen) and *oxyhemoglobin* (hemoglobin with oxygen) are about equal; but, after neuronal activation, the amount of oxyhemoglobin is higher (**Figure 6.22**). Changes in the oxygen content of the blood alter the magnetic properties of the blood's water: the T_2 signal changes more rapidly in the unoxygenated state than in the oxygenated state.

S. L. Ogawa and his colleagues showed that MRI can accurately match these changes in magnetic properties to specific locations in the brain. The resulting images are known as **functional MRIs** (fMRIs). As shown at the bottom of Figure 6.22, the fMRI signals which areas of the brain are active relative to other areas.

Functional MRI also signals which areas are displaying change in activity. **Figure 6.23** shows changes in the fMRI signal in the visual cortex of a person who is being stimulated visually with light. When the light is turned on, the visual cortex (bottom of the brain images) becomes more active than it was during baseline (no light). In other words, from increases and decreases in the MRI signal produced by changes in oxygen levels, functional changes in the brain are inferred.

When superimposed on MRI-produced brain images, fMRI changes in activity can be attributed to particular structures. The dense blood-vessel supply to the cerebral cortex allows for a spatial resolution of fMRI on the order of 1 mm. Thus, fMRI has better spatial resolution than does PET. Moreover, because fMRI can be used to accurately estimate metabolic changes in the brain of a single subject, no averaging across subjects is required.

On the other hand, because changes in blood flow take as long as a third of a second, the temporal resolution of fMRI is not as precise as that obtained with EEG recordings and ERPs. Another drawback to fMRI is that the resolution required for brain research is expensive. The standard hospital MRI is not adequate for specialized neuroscience research; even more expensive equipment is required.

In addition, fMRI can be difficult for subjects to endure. They must lie motionless in a long, noisy tube, an experience that can be claustrophobic. The confined space and lack of mobility also restrict the types of behavioral experiments that can be performed. A typical solution to the lack of space and mobility is to have subjects look at images presented on mirrors and signal their responses with finger movements. Despite these drawbacks, MRI and fMRI provide wonderful information concerning brain structure and function.

KEY
- Deoxyhemoglobin
- Oxyhemoglobin

When neurons are active, the amount of oxyhemoglobin in the blood increases.

Inactive neuron

Capillary blood flow

Neuron

Active neuron

The T$_2$ relaxation curve of oxyhemoglobin is not as steep as that of deoxyhemoglobin.

Blood oxygen level

Time

fMRI of a subject viewing a visual stimulus detects higher blood-oxygen levels in the visual cortex.

Figure **6.22**

Blood Oxygen and Brain Activity
The different relaxation curves of protons in unoxygenated (blue) and oxygenated (red) blood provide a means for obtaining functional magnetic resonance images of brain activity. (After Kwong et al., 1992, p. 5678.)

Magnetic Resonance Spectroscopy

The images produced by MRI are actually depictions of differences in water density in the various tissues of the brain. The hydrogen nuclei affected by MRI's magnetic fields belong to water molecules, and water makes up 80% of the brain's soft-tissue composition. Thus, MRI does not image the remaining 20% of brain material, including all macromolecules (DNA, RNA, most proteins, and phospholipids), cell membranes, organelles (such as mitochondria), and glial cells.

Baseline

Figure 6.23

Imaging Changes in Brain Activity Functional MRI sequence of a horizontal section at mid-occipital lobe (bottom of each image) in a normal human brain during visual stimulation. A baseline acquired in darkness (far left) was subtracted from the subsequent images. The subject wore tightly fitting goggles containing light-emitting diodes that were turned on and off as a rapid sequence of scans was obtained in a period of 270 seconds. Note the prominent activity in the visual cortex when the light is on and the rapid cessation of activity when the light is off, all measured in the graph of signal intensity below the images. (After Kwong et al., 1992, p. 5678.)

This remaining 20% of the brain is imaged by using a magnetic technique called **magnetic resonance spectroscopy** (MRS). In MRS, the frequency of the radio waves determines what tissue can be imaged. Varying the frequency of the radio waves allows different components of the remaining 20% of brain tissue to be imaged.

One example of MRS's utility is provided by *N*-acetylaspartate, a substance that is found in both neurons and glial cells and thus serves as a marker for brain cells. Magnetic resonance spectroscopic imaging of this substance distinguishes brain cells from other substances. Analyses of *N*-acetylaspartate can be used to detect the loss of brain cells in degenerative diseases such as Alzheimer's or the loss of myelin in demyelinating disease such as multiple sclerosis.

Creatin is used in a further refinement of MRS analysis. It is present in much higher concentrations in neurons than in glia and so can be used as a neuronal marker, for example, to detect the loss of brain neurons in certain degenerative diseases.

Magnetic resonance spectroscopy can also image some of the molecules that you'll recognize as participants in transmitting information between neurons. One such molecule is choline, the precursor molecule for acetylcholine; another is glutamate, the major excitatory neurotransmitter molecule in the brain. In the future, MRS will likely be able to image many other brain molecules and so provide new avenues for investigating brain development, brain function, and brain disease.

Diffusion Tensor Imaging

As proposed by Dominic ffytche and Marco Catani, Alfred W. Campbell's 1905 paper on the relation between fiber pathways of the neocortex and behavior was a landmark in the study of *hodology* (from the Greek *hodo*, for "way," and *ology*, for "study"), or *tractology*. Not until 1985, with Denis LeBihan and Ernest Breton's description of diffusion tensor imaging, could fiber pathways be visualized in the living human brain. **Diffusion tensor imaging** (DTI) is a magnetic resonance imaging method that, by detecting the directional movements of water molecules, can image fiber pathways in the brain. (*Diffusion* refers to the movement of water molecules, *tensor* is a linear quality, and *imaging* detects the direction of diffusion.)

Water molecules in the ventricles and even in cell bodies move relatively unimpeded in random directions. In nerve fibers, however, the movement of water molecules is restricted by the orientation of the fiber and its contents. Movement tends to follow the direction of the longitudinal axis of the fiber, a property referred to as *anisotropy* (for unequal movement).

Because MRI is sensitive to the directional movement of water molecules, it can image nerve fibers. The images are virtual, however, inasmuch as short sections of the fibers are pieced together from computer-based estimates of fiber orientation. They do not reveal individual fibers, whether fibers are afferent or efferent, or the location of synapses.

Diffusion tensor imaging has a number of uses in revealing short- and long-fiber pathways in the brain (**Figure 6.24**). It can detect the degeneration of axons as might occur in multiple sclerosis, the distortion of fibers that might occur as a result of tumors, and the damage to fibers that results from traumatic brain injury or stroke. Diffusion tensor imaging can be combined with MRI to superimpose nerve pathways on a magnetic resonance image of the brain, allowing fiber-pathway mapping in individual brains. It can also be combined with MRI, fMRI, and ERP to locate the connections between functional areas of the brain.

Broca's area

Wernicke's area

Figure **6.24**

Diffusion Tensor Images of the Language Pathways Connecting Broca's and Wernicke's Regions of the Brain Colors represent different language pathways. (After Marco Catani.)

Brain-Imaging Techniques Compared

Historically, brain researchers studied brain function by examining the effects of brain injuries on behavior. The many imaging methods that we have described complement that approach. But, is there a one-best-way of imaging the brain and its activity?

The strength of brain-injury studies is that they allow investigators to reduce behavior to its component parts. For instance, the examples of language impairments after brain injury described in Chapter 1 revealed that patients suffering from Broca's aphasia are unable to articulate words and yet are able to understand them. Those who have Wernicke's aphasia are impaired in comprehension and yet are able to articulate words. The process of articulation, then, is partly independent of other aspects of language.

In addition to areas controlling articulation, the brain has a region that selectively controls comprehension. With the examination of more patients with language disorders, a "taxonomy" of brain processes controlling language has been created. Now, with the new imaging techniques, researchers can literally "watch" these language areas in action, as well as identify other brain regions that contribute to the control of language.

The main advantage of single-cell recording is that it provides the highest resolution of all the functional imaging techniques: it provides a lot of information about what a few neurons are doing. Its weakness is that it has the lowest generalizability. Even when a large number of electrodes are used concurrently, recordings can be obtained from only a hundred or so neurons. Additionally, because single-cell recording requires that an electrode be put into the brain, the technique can be used with humans only when they are undergoing surgery for clinical reasons.

Electroencephalographic recording provides information about the function of the brain as a whole but has little to offer about the activity of single neurons. Event-related potential recording has lower resolution than that of single-unit recordings but greater resolution than that of EEGs. The EEG and ERP imaging techniques—uncomplicated, inexpensive, and noninvasive—are easy to use with any kind of experimental subject and are widely used for clinical diagnosis and treatment.

X-ray methods provide a quick, static snapshot of the brain and are useful for locating injury to the skull, intracranial bleeding, tumors, and malformations in blood vessels. Thus, CT scans remain the first imaging procedure used to assess possible brain injury or tumors.

The advantage of MRI is the higher resolution that it provides for examining brain structures and fiber pathways of both normal and injured brains. PET imaging is useful because it can image the biochemical status of the brain, whereas fMRI can image function with reasonably high resolution. Magnetic resonance spectroscopy can detect the degeneration of myelin that occurs in multiple sclerosis or the degeneration of neurons that occurs in Alzheimer's disease.

In answer to the question posed at the beginning of this section, it is important to note that none of these techniques is the "best." In fact, many techniques find complementary uses, and each has its place in basic research and in clinical diagnosis.

Toward Multimodal Atlases of the Brain

Brain atlases have been used for centuries to locate structures of the brain, to represent the circuits that they form one with another, and to represent possible functions. Early maps were derived from one or a few specimens. Now, brain-imaging methods can sample large populations representing both sexes, subjects of different ages, and subjects with varying natural and learned abilities. Brain-imaging atlases can represent neural structures and their pathways, neurochemistry, and even active genes. Brain-imaging methods can be used to document the progress of brain diseases and the effects of treatments of those diseases.

Computing methods allow atlases to represent more than static images of the brain: they can represent changes related to age, function, and disease conditions. Arthur Toga and his colleagues propose that a transition from a static atlas representation to a computational one allows an atlas to become a database for representing function and for testing hypotheses. Such a database can combine information from different imaging methods—for example, electro-

Figure **6.25**

Brain-imaging Atlas MRI scans of the maturation of gray matter in normal development, showing the length and pattern of maturation. (Courtesy of Paul Thompson, Kiralee Hayashi, and Arthur Toga, UCLA; Nitin Gogtay, Jay Gledd, and Judy Rapoport, NIMH.)

5 yrs

Age

20 yrs

>0.5
0.4
0.3
0.2
0.1
0.0
Gray-matter volume

physiological, chemical, and functional—to enable students and investigator to search the literature on brain function as well as to add to that literature by posting updates on the atlas. As an example of the dynamic representation provided by a brain-imaging atlas, **Figure 6.25** shows the changes in gray matter in a normal brain from the age of 5 years to maturity at 20 years.

Summary

In this chapter, we described a number of brain-imaging methods. Some provide a static image of brain structure, and others provide a dynamic image of brain function.

Recording the Brain's Electrical Activity

From single-cell recordings, we know that neurons employ a code and that cortical neurons are organized into functional groups. Electroencephalographic recordings tell us that, when a person is awake and engaged in some behavior, the whole brain is in an active state: the entire neocortex is displaying the beta-wave pattern. Similarly, when a person is resting or sleeping, the entire brain rests or sleeps, as indicated by the slower alpha- and delta-wave patterns. On the other hand, event-related potentials tell us that, even though the entire brain is active during waking, certain parts are momentarily much more active than others. The location of increased activity changes as information moves from one brain area to another.

Brain Stimulation

Brain stimulation methods induce changes in the electrical activity of the brain. Electrodes can be implanted into the brain to directly stimulate tissue, as is done for deep brain stimulation, or stimulation can be produced through the skull with transcranial magnetic stimulation.

X-Ray Imaging Techniques

X-ray imaging methods are sensitive to the density of different parts of the brain, the ventricles, nuclei, and pathways. Thus, X-rays can be used to assess skull damage, and CT scans can be used to assess brain damage from traumatic brain injury or tumors.

Dynamic Brain Imaging

Metabolic imaging methods show that any behavior requires the collaboration of widespread circuits within the brain. Positron emission tomography records blood flow and other metabolic changes in periods of time measured in minutes and requires complex subtraction procedures and the averaging of responses across a number of subjects.

Magnetic resonance imaging provides an exceptionally clear image both of nuclei and of fiber pathways of the brain and indicates that different people's brains can be structurally quite different.

Records of blood flow obtained by using fMRI can be combined with MRI to identify the location of changes in the individual brain. Magnetic resonance spectroscopy can distinguish gray and white matter to detect the degeneration of myelin or of neurons.

Brain-Imaging Techniques Compared

Imaging techniques are useful not only for understanding how the brain produces normal behavior but also in diagnosing disease. In the past, neurologists and neuropsychologists depended on laborious and imprecise behavioral testing to localize a tumor or diagnose a disease. Today, imaging procedures can quickly localize tumors and lesions. Because all these imaging methods are central to many ongoing lines of research into brain function and dysfunction, subsequent chapters present further examples of their use.

References

Catani, M., R. J. Howard, S. Pajevic, and D. K. Jones. Virtual in vivo interactive dissection of white matter fasciculi in the human brain. *NeuroImage* 17:77–94, 2002.

Cormack, A. M. Reconstructions of densities from their projections, with applications in radiological physics. *Physics, Medicine, and Biology* 18:195–207, 1973.

Damasio, H., and A. R. Damasio. *Lesion Analysis in Neuropsychology.* New York: Oxford University Press, 1989.

DeArmond, S. J., M. M. Fusco, and M. Dewey. *Structure of the Human Brain: A Photographic Atlas,* 2nd ed. New York: Oxford University Press, 1976.

ffytche, D. H., and M. Catani. Beyond localization: From hodology to function. *Philosophical Transactions of the Royal Society B* 360:767–779, 2005.

Fox, P. T., and M. E. Raichle. Focal physiological uncoupling of cerebral blood flow and oxidative metabolism during somatosensory stimulation in human subjects. *Proceedings of the National Academy of Sciences of the United States of America* 83:1140–1144, 1986.

Housfield, G. N. Computerized transverse axial scanning (tomography) I: Description of system. *British Journal of Radiology* 46:1016–1022, 1973.

Kwong, K. K., et al. Dynamic magnetic resonance imaging of human brain activity during primary sensory stimulation. *Proceedings of the National Academy of Sciences of the United States of America* 89:5675–5679, 1992.

LeBihad, D., and E. Breton. Imagerie de diffusion in-vivo par resonance magnétique nucléaire. *CR Academie of Science (Paris)* 301:1109–1112, 1985.

Neville, H. Event-related potentials in neuropsychological studies of language. *Brain and Language* 11:300–318, 1980.

Ogawa, S. L., L. M. Lee, A. R. Kay, and D. W. Tank. Brain magnetic resonance imaging with contrast dependent on blood oxygenation. *Proceedings of the National Academy of Sciences of the United States of America* 87:9868–9872, 1990.

Ojemann, G. A., S. G. Ojemann, and I. Fried. Lessons from human brain: Neuronal activity related to cognition. *The Neuroscientist* 4:285–300, 1998.

Posner, M. I., and M. E. Raichle. *Images of Mind.* New York: Scientific American Library, 1994.

Temel, Y., A. Kessels, S. Tan, A. Topdag, P. Boon, and V. Visser-Vandewalle. Behavioural changes after bilateral subthalamic stimulation in advanced Parkinson disease: A systematic review. Parkinsonism & Related Disorders 12(5):265–272. Epub April 18, 2006.

Toga, A. W., and J. C. Mazziotta. *Brain Mapping: The Methods.* New York: Academic Press, 1996.

Toga, A. W., P. W. Thompson, S. Mori, K. Amunts, and K. Zilles. Towards multimodal atlases of the human brain. *Neuroimaging* 7:952–966, 2006.

Tomaiuolo, F., J. D. MacDonald, S. Caramanos, G. Posner, M. Chivaras, A. C. Evans, and M. Petrides. Morphology, morphometry and probability mapping of the pars opercularis of the inferior frontal gyrus: An in vivo MRI analysis. *European Journal of Neuroscience* 11:3033–3064, 1999.

Windhorst, U., and H. Johansson. *Modern Techniques in Neuroscience Research.* New York: Springer, 1999.

The Influence of Drugs and Hormones on Behavior

PORTRAIT: The Case of the Frozen Addict

During the first 4 days of July 1982, a 42-year-old man used 4.4 grams of a synthetic heroin manufactured in an illegal laboratory. The substance was injected intravenously three or four times daily and caused a burning sensation at the site of injection. The immediate effects were different from heroin, producing an unusual "spacey" high as well as transient visual distortions and hallucination. Two days after the final injection, he awoke to find that he was "frozen" and could move only in "slow motion." He had to "think through each movement" to carry it out. He was described as stiff, slow, nearly mute, and catatonic during repeated emergency room visits from July 9 to July 11. He was admitted to a psychiatric service on July 15, 1982, with a diagnosis of "catatonic schizophrenia" and was transferred to our neurobehavioral unit the next day. (Ballard, Tetrud, and Langston, 1985, p. 949)

The story does not end here. This patient, George Carillo, was one of

Dr. Hakan Widner, M.D., PhD., Lund University, Sweden

seven adults who were hospitalized at about the same time in California. They were eventually correctly diagnosed with Parkinson's disease, a condition usually associated with aging and unusual in its sudden onset in people of their age. Their accidental encounter with a new form of heroin provided scientists with one explanation of the cause of Parkinson's disease.

Heroin is a derivative of opium, which has been used as a therapeutic and recreational drug for centuries. Although highly addictive, heroin is an effective treatment for pain and is not known to produce any kind of brain injury. But, in the case just cited, an error in heroin synthesis produced a contaminant called MPTP. This compound acts as a selective neurotoxin, killing the cells of the substantia nigra in the midbrain, thereby reducing the amount of the neurotransmitter dopamine in the brain and producing a condition of Parkinson's disease in the users.

In 1988, George Carillo was taken to Lund, Sweden, where human fetal dopamine cells were inserted into the caudate and putamen regions of his basal ganglia. Haken Widner and his colleagues have reported some success with the fetal dopamine transplants. In the adjoining PET images of Carillo's brain before the implantation of fetal dopamine neurons (left) and 12 months after the operation (right), the increased areas of red and gold show that the transplanted neurons are producing dopamine. Eight years after the surgery, his brain showed evidence of increased dopamine function and his motor symptoms improved to the point that he could function more independently.

Psychopharmacology is the study of how drugs affect the nervous system and behavior. In this chapter, we group various drugs by their behavioral effects. You will learn that the effects of drugs depend on how they are taken, in what quantities, and under what circumstances.

We begin by looking at the major ways in which drugs are administered, what routes they take to reach the central nervous system, and how they are eliminated from the body. We consider how drugs act at the synapse, and why different people may respond differently to the same dose of a drug. Many principles related to drugs also apply to the action of hormones, the chapter's closing topic.

Before considering how drugs produce their effects on the brain for good or for ill, we must raise a caution: the sheer number of neurotransmitters, receptors, and possible sites of drug action is astounding. Psychopharmacology research has made important advances on some principles of drug action, but neuroscientists do not know everything there is to know about any drug.

Principles of Psychopharmacology

A *drug* is a chemical compound that is administered to bring about some desired change in the body. Usually drugs are used to diagnose, treat, or prevent illness, to relieve pain and suffering, or to improve an adverse physiological condition. On the other hand, throughout human history, drugs have also been used as food substances, for recreation, and even as poisons. Today, they are also used as research tools.

In this chapter, we focus on **psychoactive drugs**—substances that act to alter mood, thought, or behavior and are used to manage neuropsychological illness. Many psychoactive drugs are also *substances of abuse*. That is, people take them for nonmedical reasons or recreationally to the point that their functioning becomes impaired. Many psychoactive drugs promote craving and can produce addiction. Some can also act as toxins, producing sickness, brain damage, or death.

Routes of Drug Administration

To be effective, a psychoactive drug has to reach its target in the nervous system. The way in which a drug enters and passes through the body to reach that target is called its *route of administration*. Many drugs are taken orally—the most natural and generally the safest way to consume a substance. Drugs can also be inhaled, administered through rectal suppositories, absorbed from patches applied to the skin, or injected into the bloodstream, into a muscle, or even into the brain (**Figure 7.1**).

Taking a drug by mouth is convenient, but not all drugs can withstand the acidity of gastric secretions or are able to penetrate the digestive-tract walls. Generally, there are fewer barriers between a drug and its target if the drug is inhaled rather than swallowed, and fewer still if it is injected into the blood. The fewest obstacles are encountered if a drug is injected directly into the brain.

To reach the bloodstream, an ingested drug must first be absorbed through the lining of the stomach or small intestine. If the drug is liquid, it is absorbed more readily than if it is a solid. Drugs taken in solid form are not absorbed unless they can be dissolved by the stomach's gastric juices.

Absorption is also affected by other chemical properties of the drug. If a drug is a weak acid, such as alcohol, it is readily absorbed across the stomach lining. If it is a weak base, it cannot be absorbed until it passes through the stomach and into the intestine, by which time the digestive juices may have destroyed it.

The drug must next enter the bloodstream. This part of the journey presents a different set of barriers. Blood has a high water concentration, and so a

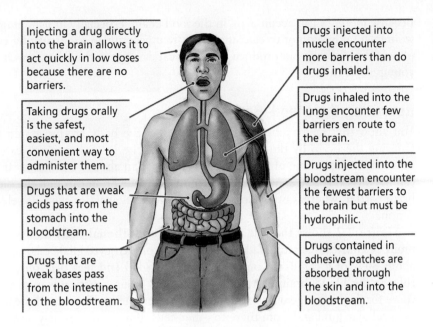

Injecting a drug directly into the brain allows it to act quickly in low doses because there are no barriers.

Taking drugs orally is the safest, easiest, and most convenient way to administer them.

Drugs that are weak acids pass from the stomach into the bloodstream.

Drugs that are weak bases pass from the intestines to the bloodstream.

Drugs injected into muscle encounter more barriers than do drugs inhaled.

Drugs inhaled into the lungs encounter few barriers en route to the brain.

Drugs injected into the bloodstream encounter the fewest barriers to the brain but must be hydrophilic.

Drugs contained in adhesive patches are absorbed through the skin and into the bloodstream.

Figure 7.1

Routes of Drug Administration

drug must be hydrophilic to mix with it. A hydrophobic substance will be blocked from entering the bloodstream. If a drug does make its way into the circulatory system, it becomes diluted by the blood's 6-liter volume.

To reach a neurological target, a drug must also travel from the blood into the extracellular fluid. This part of the journey requires that molecules of the drug be small enough to pass through the pores of capillaries, the tiny vessels that carry blood to the body's cells. Even if the drug makes this passage, it encounters other obstacles. The extracellular fluid's volume of roughly 35 liters of water dilutes the drug even further, and, if it passes through cell membranes, the drug is at risk of being modified or destroyed by various metabolic processes taking place in the cells.

Routes of Drug Removal

Soon after a drug is taken, the body begins to remove it. Drugs are metabolized throughout the body, but particularly in the kidneys, liver, and bile. They are excreted in urine, feces, sweat, breast milk, and exhaled air. Drugs manufactured for therapeutic purposes are usually designed to optimize their chances of reaching their targets and to prolong their survival in the body.

The body has trouble removing some substances, however, and these substances are potentially dangerous because, with repeated exposure, they can build up in the body and become poisonous. Many metals, such as mercury, are not easily eliminated from the body and, when they accumulate there, they can cause severe neurological problems. The saying, "mad as a hatter," derives from nineteenth-century hat makers in England, who as a consequence of using mercury in hat making, suffered neurological damage.

In 1956 in Minamata, Japan, many people suffered physical and psychiatric effects from eating fish caught near a factory that released mercury into the sea. This case gave rise to improved rights for Japanese citizens affected by industrial by-products and to a new term for mercury poisoning—Minamata disease.

Because mercury can accumulate in the food chain, especially in fish, pregnant women are advised not to eat tuna, a fish that accumulates mercury by eating other fish. Mercury can produce neurological damage in the fetus as well as in young children.

Revisiting the Blood–Brain Barrier

You know that many substances that can affect the body are prevented from entering the brain by the blood–brain barrier. The brain has a rich capillary network. In fact, none of its neurons is farther than about 50 μm away from a capillary. Nevertheless, many drugs cannot enter the brain through the blood–brain barrier, whereas other drugs can. How does the barrier exert its selective action?

Figure 7.2 shows that the single layer of **endothelial cells** that compose brain capillaries is surrounded by the end feet of astrocyte glial cells, covering about 80% of a capillary's outer surface. The glial end feet play only minor roles in the blood–brain barrier. The glial cells' main function is to provide a route for the exchange of food and waste between the capillaries and the brain's extracellular fluid and from there to other cells. But astrocytes may also play a role in maintaining the **tight junctions** between endothelial cells and in making capillaries dilate to increase blood flow to areas of the brain in which neurons are very active. Thus, substances that can pass through the endothelial cells' junctions in the body cannot do so in the brain.

Many substances—for instance, oxygen, glucose, and amino acids (the building blocks of proteins)—must routinely travel from the blood to brain cells, just as carbon dioxide and other waste products must routinely be excreted from brain cells into the blood. Figure 7.2 shows how molecules of these substances cross the blood–brain barrier in two ways:

1. Small molecules such as oxygen and carbon dioxide, which are not ionized and so are fat soluble, can pass through the capillary wall.

2. Molecules of glucose, amino acids, and other nutrients can be carried across the capillary by **active-transport systems**, which are pumps, such

Figure **7.2**

Blood–Brain Barrier
Capillaries in most of the body allow for the passage of substances across capillary cell membranes, but those in the brain, stimulated by the actions of astrocytes, form the tight junctions of the blood–brain barrier.

Capillaries in the brain have tight junctions and are covered with astrocyte feet. These properties prevent materials from moving in and out easily.

Astrocyte feet

Capillaries in the body have few tight junctions. Materials can move in and out quite easily.

Endothelial cells

Small, uncharged molecules are able to pass through the endothelial membrane.

Certain other molecules are carried across the membrane by active transport.

CO_2 O_2 Amino acids Glucose Fats
Transporter
CO_2 O_2
Capillary
Astrocyte feet
Tight junction

Large and electrically charged molecules are unable to pass out of the capillary.

as the sodium–potassium pump described in Chapter 4, that are specialized for the transport of a particular substance.

A few brain regions lack tight junctions between the cells of capillary walls and so lack a blood–brain barrier. These regions are shown in **Figure 7.3**. The **pituitary gland** of the hypothalamus is a source of many hormones that are secreted into the blood, and their release is triggered in part by other hormones carried to the pituitary gland by the blood. The absence of a blood–brain barrier at the **area postrema** of the lower brainstem allows toxic substances in the blood to trigger a vomiting response. The **pineal gland** also lacks a blood–brain barrier and is therefore open to the hormones that modulate the day–night cycles controlled by this structure.

Drug Routes and Dosage

To review, drugs that can make the entire trip from the mouth to the brain have certain chemical properties. The most effective consist of molecules that are small in size, weakly acidic, water or fat soluble, potent in small amounts, and not easily degraded.

Given the many obstacles that psychoactive drugs encounter on their journey from mouth to brain, it is clear why inhaling a drug or injecting it into the bloodstream has advantages: these routes of administration bypass the obstacle of the stomach. In fact, with each obstacle eliminated on the route to the brain, the dosage of a drug can be reduced by a factor of 10 and the drug will still have the same effects.

For example, 1 milligram (1000 µg) of amphetamine, a psychomotor stimulant, produces a noticeable behavioral change when ingested orally. If inhaled into the lungs or injected into the blood, thereby circumventing the stomach, 100 µg of the drug (1000 µg ÷ 10) produces the same results. Similarly, if amphetamine is injected into the cerebrospinal fluid, thereby bypassing both the stomach and the blood, 10 µg is enough to produce an identical outcome, as is 1 µg if dilution in the CSF also is skirted and the drug is injected directly onto target neurons.

This math is well known to users of illicit drugs. Drugs that can be inhaled or injected intravenously are much cheaper to use because the doses required are a fraction of those needed for drugs taken by mouth.

Pineal gland: Entry of chemicals that affect day–night cycles.

Pituitary gland: Entry of chemicals that influence pituitary hormones.

Area postrema: Entry of toxic substances that induce vomiting.

Figure 7.3

Barrier-Free Brain Sites

Drug Actions in Synapses

You may be surprised to learn that almost all potent psychoactive drugs have been discovered accidentally, many thousands of years ago. In a critical history, Elliott Valenstein recounts how therapeutic actions of the major drugs used to treat neuropsychological illness were likewise discovered accidentally. These drugs are listed by use in **Table 7.1**, along with their dates of discovery and the names of their discoverers.

One of the great triumphs of neuroscience research has been the uncovering of the mechanisms of drug action. Most psychoactive drugs work by influencing the chemical reactions at synapses. Scientists and pharmaceutical companies

Table **7.1** Drugs used for the treatment of mental illness

Illness	Drug Class	Representative Drug	Common Trade Name	Discoverer
Schizophrenia	Phenothiazines	Chlorpromazine	Largactile, Thorazine	Jean Delay and Pierre Deniker (France), 1952
	Butyrophenone	Haloperidol	Haldol	Paul Janssen (Belgium), 1957
Depression	Monoamine oxidase (MAO inhibitors)	Iproniazid	Marsilid	Nathan S. Kline and J. C. Saunders (United States), 1956
	Tricyclic antidepressants	Imipramine	Tofranil	Roland Kuhn (Switzerland), 1957
	Selective serotonin reuptake inhibitors	Fluoxetine	Prozac	Eli Lilly Company, 1986
Bipolar disorder	Lithium (metallic element)			John Cade (Australia), 1949
Anxiety disorders	Benzodiazepines	Chlordiazepoxide	Valium, Miltown	Leo Sternbach (Poland), 1940
		Meprobamate	Equanil	Frank Berger and William Bradley (Czechoslovakia), 1946

continue to develop many forms of each drug in attempts to increase penetration to the brain, increase effectiveness, and reduce side effects.

As an understanding of synaptic activity in the brain advances, drugs that have a more selective action in their therapeutic effects can be designed. At the same time, this research helps explain the psychoactive effects of drugs and their potential benefits and harm. Thus, to understand the psychoactive effects of drugs, we must explore the ways in which they modify synaptic activity.

Steps in Synaptic Transmission

Figure 7.4 summarizes seven major events that contribute to synaptic neurotransmission. Synthesis of the neurotransmitter (1) can take place in the cell body, axon, or terminal. The neurotransmitter may then be (2) stored in storage granules or in vesicles until it is (3) released from the terminal's presynaptic membrane to (4) act on a receptor embedded in the postsynaptic membrane. Excess neurotransmitter in the synapse is either (5) deactivated or (6) taken back into the presynaptic terminal for (7) reuse. The synapse also has mechanisms for degrading excess neurotransmitter and removing unneeded by-products from the synapse.

Each component of neurotransmission entails one or more chemical reactions that drugs can potentially influence. Drugs that increase the effectiveness of neurotransmission are called **agonists**, whereas those that decrease its effectiveness are called **antagonists**. Agonists and antagonists can work in a variety of ways, but their end results are always the same.

For example, all drugs that stimulate the release of the neurotransmitter dopamine or block the reuptake

Figure **7.4**

Points of Influence In principle, a drug can modify seven major chemical processes, any of which results in reduced or enhanced synaptic transmission.

1 Synthesis

Precursor chemicals
Neurotransmitter

2 Storage

3 Release

4 Receptor interaction

7 Degradation

6 Reuptake

5 Inactivation

of dopamine or block dopamine's inactivation are considered dopamine agonists, because they increase the amount of dopamine available in the synapse. Conversely, all drugs that block the synthesis of dopamine or its release from the presynaptic membrane or that block dopamine receptors or speed up dopamine's inactivation are considered dopamine antagonists, because they decrease the biochemical effect of this transmitter in the synapse.

Examples of Drug Action: An Acetylcholine Synapse

Figure 7.5 uses the acetylcholine synapse between motor neurons and muscles to show how several representative drugs and toxins act as agonists or antagonists to ACh. Some of these drugs will be new to you, but you have probably heard of others. Knowing their effects at the synapse will enable you to understand their behavioral effects as well as illustrate the actions of drugs at a synapse.

Two substances named in Figure 7.5 are toxins that influence the release of acetylcholine from the axon terminal:

1. **Black widow spider venom** is an agonist because it promotes the release of acetylcholine. In the insects on which black widow spiders prey, the excitation caused by excess acetylcholine is sufficient to cause paralysis and death. A black widow spider bite does not contain enough toxin to similarly affect a human.

2. **Botulinum toxin** is a poisonous agent produced by a bacterium that sometimes grows in improperly processed canned foods. The toxin acts as an antagonist because it blocks the release of acetylcholine. The effects of botulinum poisoning can last from weeks to months. A severe case can result in paralysis of movement and breathing, leading to death. Botulinum toxin also has medical uses. If injected into a muscle, it paralyzes that muscle, blocking unwanted muscular twitches or contractions in conditions such as cerebral palsy. It is also sold under the trade name Botox for use in cosmetic surgery to reduce wrinkles by relaxing muscles, and, because it can also inactivate pain fibers, it is injected into muscles and joints to reduce pain.

Figure 7.5 also includes two drugs that act on acetylcholine receptors:

1. **Nicotine**, one of the chemicals in cigarette smoke, acts as an agonist to stimulate cholinergic receptors. The cholinergic receptor at the neuromuscular junction (see Figure 5.5) is called a **nicotinic receptor** because of this action of nicotine. Nicotine's structure is enough like that of acetylcholine to fit into the ACh receptors' binding sites.

2. **Curare**, a poison extracted from the seeds of a South American plant, acts as an antagonist at cholinergic receptors, blocking them and

Figure **7.5**

Acetylcholine Agonists and Antagonists Drugs can affect ACh transmission by affecting its release, its binding to the postsynaptic receptor, and its breakdown or inactivation.

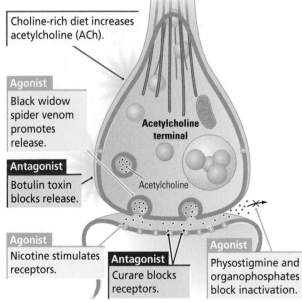

Choline-rich diet increases acetylcholine (ACh).

Agonist
Black widow spider venom promotes release.

Antagonist
Botulin toxin blocks release.

Acetylcholine terminal

Acetylcholine

Agonist
Nicotine stimulates receptors.

Antagonist
Curare blocks receptors.

Agonist
Physostigmine and organophosphates block inactivation.

preventing acetylcholine from acting. Curare acts quickly and is cleared from the body in minutes. Large doses, however, arrest movement and breathing long enough to result in death. Early European explorers encountered Indians along the Amazon River who killed small animals by using arrows coated with curare. The hunters themselves were not poisoned when eating the animals, because ingested curare cannot pass from the gut into the body. Many curare-like drugs have been synthesized. Some are used to briefly paralyze large animals for identification tagging or examination. Skeletal muscles are more sensitive to curare-like drugs than respiratory muscles are; so an appropriate dose will paralyze an animal but still allow it to breathe.

The final drug action shown in Figure 7.5 is that of **physostigmine**, which inhibits acetylcholinesterase, the enzyme that breaks down ACh. It therefore acts as an agonist to increase the amount of ACh available in the synapse. Physostigmine, obtained from a species of African bean, was used as a poison by tribes in Africa. Large doses can be toxic because, like black widow spider venom, they produce excessive excitation of the neuromuscular synapse and so disrupt movement and breathing.

Small doses of physostigmine, however, are used to treat a condition called **myasthenia gravis** (the name means "muscular weakness") in which muscle receptors are less than normally responsive to acetylcholine. Myasthenia gravis, once called "tired housewife's syndrome" because of its symptoms of fatigue and its tendency to affect women, was formerly viewed as a psychological condition until an understanding of the ACh synapse provided the correct explanation and treatment.

The action of physostigmine is short-lived, lasting from only a few minutes to at most half an hour, but another class of compounds, called **organophosphates**, bind irreversibly to acetylcholinesterase and consequently are extremely toxic. Many insecticides are organophosphates, and they are also used in chemical warfare.

In summary, understanding the nicotinic ACh synapse provides a relatively simple explanation for the physical actions of many diverse drugs. Does this understanding also explain their psychological effects? That depends on whether the substance can cross the blood–brain barrier, which depends in turn on the size and structure of the substance's molecules. Some drugs that act on ACh synapses at muscles—physostigmine and nicotine, for example—do cross the blood–brain barrier and act on ACh synapses in the brain. Curare, on the other hand, cannot cross the barrier and therefore has no psychoactive effects.

Classification of Psychoactive Drugs

Devising a classification system for the many thousands of psychoactive drugs has proved difficult. Classification based on a drug's chemical structure is not successful, because drugs with similar structures can have different effects, whereas drugs with different structures can have effects that are similar. Classification schemes based on receptors in the brain also are problematic, because a single drug can act on many different receptors. The same problem exists for classification systems based on the neurotransmitter affected by a drug, because a drug can act on more than one transmitter.

The classification system summarized in **Table 7.2** divides drugs into seven classes according to the most pronounced psychoactive effect of a drug. The classes are further divided into subcategories containing from a few to thousands of chemicals. Because many drugs within a classification affect a similar neurotransmitter, we include, in the following sections, summaries of their action on neurotransmitters where possible.

Class I. Sedative-Hypnotics and Antianxiety Agents

The effects of sedative-hypnotics ("sedative," to calm or moderate nervousness or excitement, and "hypnotic," sleep inducing) and antianxiety agents depend on the dose, as shown in **Figure 7.6**. At low doses, they reduce anxiety; at medium doses, they have a tranquilizing effect; and, at successively higher doses, they anesthetize, induce coma, and kill. The most common members of this diverse class of drugs are alcohol, barbiturates, and benzodiazepines.

- **Alcohol** is well known to most people as a beverage and an intoxicant. It is potentially devastating to fetuses because it harms brain development, producing a syndrome of retardation called **fetal alcohol syndrome** (FAS).

- **Barbiturates** are sometimes prescribed as a sleeping medication, but they are mainly used to induce anesthesia before surgery.

- **Benzodiazepines**, also known as **minor tranquilizers** or **antianxiety agents**, are used to treat stress. An example is the widely prescribed drug Valium.

Whereas both alcohol and barbiturates can produce sleep, anesthesia, and coma at doses only slightly higher than those that produce sedation, the dose of benzodiazepines that produces sleep and anesthesia is substantially higher than that needed to relieve anxiety.

All sedative-hypnotic drugs may act by influencing a receptor of the neurotransmitter gamma-aminobutyric acid, the **GABA$_A$** receptor. As illustrated on the left in **Figure 7.7**, this receptor controls a chloride channel, and excitation of the receptor produces an influx of Cl$^-$ ions. Remember that an influx of Cl$^-$ ions increases the concentration of negative charges inside the cell

Table **7.2** Classification of psychoactive drugs

I. Sedative hypnotics and antianxiety agents
   Barbiturates (anesthetic agents), alcohol
   Benzodiazepines: diazepam (Valium)
   Dissociative anesthetics: GHB, ketamine

II. Antipsychotic agents
   Phenothiazines: chlorpromazine
   Butyrophenones: haloperidol

III. Antidepressants
   Monoamine oxidase (MAO) inhibitors
   Tricyclic antidepressants: imipramine (Tofranil)
   Atypical antidepressants: fluoxetine (Prozac)

IV. Mood stabilizers
   Lithium

V. Narcotic analgesics
   Morphine, codeine, heroin

VI. Psychomotor stimulants
   Cocaine, amphetamine, caffeine, nicotine

VII. Psychedelics and hallucinogens
   Anticholinergics: atropine
   Noradrenergics: mescaline
   Serotonergics: LSD (lysergic acid diethylamide), psilocybin
   Tetrahydrocannabinol: marijuana

Figure **7.6**

Continuum of Behavioral Sedation Increasing doses of sedative-hypnotic and antianxiety drugs affect behavior: low doses reduce anxiety and very high doses result in death.

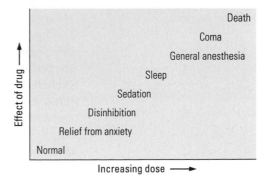

Effect of drug → / Increasing dose →

Death
Coma
General anesthesia
Sleep
Sedation
Disinhibition
Relief from anxiety
Normal

Figure 7.7

Drug Effects at the GABA_A Receptor Sedative hypnotics, antianxiety agents, and GABA each work at different binding sites.

Sedative-hypnotic drugs (alcohol or barbiturates) act like GABA, causing increased chloride conductance.

Antianxiety drugs (benzodiazepines) enhance the binding of GABA.

Because of their different actions, these drugs should not be taken together.

membrane, hyperpolarizing the membrane and thus making it less likely to propagate an action potential. GABA, therefore, produces its inhibitory effect by decreasing a neuron's rate of firing. GABA is the inhibitory workhorse of the nervous system with widely distributed receptors, thus allowing drugs that affect the receptor to have widespread effects.

The GABA_A receptor possesses not only a binding site for GABA but two other binding sites, all shown in Figure 7.7. The binding site where alcohol and barbiturates work, the **sedative-hypnotic site**, increases the influx of chloride ions and so produces the same effect as that of GABA. Consequently, the higher the dose of these drugs, the greater their inhibitory effect on neurons.

The **antianxiety site** accepts benzodiazepines and enhances the binding of GABA to its receptors, which means that the availability of GABA determines the potency of an antianxiety drug. Because GABA is very quickly reabsorbed by the neurons that secrete it and by surrounding glial cells, GABA concentrations are never excessive; as a result, people are generally unlikely to overdose on antianxiety drugs.

Because of their different actions on the GABA_A receptor, sedative-hypnotic and antianxiety drugs should not be taken together. A sedative-hypnotic acts like GABA but, unlike GABA, is not quickly absorbed by surrounding cells. Instead, it remains on the site, allowing its effects to be enhanced by an antianxiety drug. The cumulative action of the two drugs will therefore exceed the individual action of either one. Even small combined doses of antianxiety and sedative-hypnotic drugs can produce coma or death.

One group of sedative-hypnotics, called **dissociative anesthetics**, was developed as anesthetic agents but receive restricted use as such because they also produce altered states of consciousness and hallucinations. They include GHB (gamma-hydroxybutyric acid), flunitrazepam, and ketamine. They have gained notoriety as "date rape" drugs or, more properly, "drug-assisted sexual assault" drugs. They are soluble in alcohol, act quickly, and, like other sedative-hypnotics, impair memory for recent events. Because a dissociative anesthetic drug can be placed in a drink, party goers are advised not to accept drinks from strangers, drink out of punch bowls, or leave drinks unattended.

Figure 7.8

Trends in Resident Care The dramatic decrease in the number of resident patients in state and municipal hospitals in the United States began after 1955, when antipsychotic drugs were introduced into widespread therapeutic use. (After Julien, 2004.)

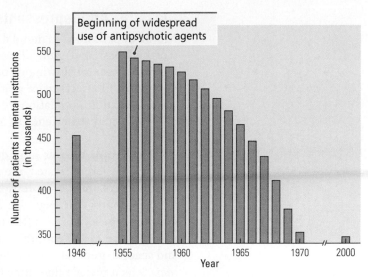

Class II. Antipsychotic Agents

The term **psychosis** refers to various neuropsychological conditions, such as schizophrenia, that are characterized by hallucinations (false sensory perceptions) or delusions (false beliefs). Drugs used to treat psychosis are the antipsychotic agents also known as **major tranquilizers** and **neuroleptics**. They include the phenothiazines (for example, chlorpromazine) and butyrophenones (for example, haloperidol). The use of antipsychotic agents has greatly reduced the number of patients held in mental institutions, as **Figure 7.8** shows. Improving the functioning of people who develop schizophrenia has been a particularly important achievement, because its incidence in the population is high—about 1 in every 100 people.

Although major tranquilizers have been widely used for half a century, their therapeutic actions are still not understood. One effect that all have in common is an immediate reduction of motor activity, which helps to alleviate the excessive agitation of some patients. Unfortunately, one negative side effect of their prolonged use can be to produce symptoms reminiscent of Parkinson's disease and dyskinesia (involuntary movements), including rhythmical movements of the mouth, hands, and other body parts that are reversible if the person stops taking the drug.

At least part of the action of antipsychotic drugs is to block one kind of dopamine receptor, the **D_2 receptor**. This action of antipsychotic drugs led to the **dopamine hypothesis of schizophrenia**. It holds that some forms of schizophrenia may be related to excessive dopamine activity.

Other support for the dopamine hypothesis comes from the schizophrenia-like symptoms of chronic users of amphetamine, a stimulant drug described in a subsequent section. As **Figure 7.9** shows, amphetamine is a dopamine agonist that fosters the release of dopamine from the presynaptic membrane of dopamine synapses and blocks its reuptake from the synaptic cleft. If amphetamine causes schizophrenia-like symptoms by increasing dopamine activity, perhaps naturally occurring schizophrenia is related to excessive dopamine action, too.

Figure 7.9

Drug Effects at D_2 Receptors That the antipsychotic agent chlorpromazine can lessen schizophrenia symptoms, whereas the abuse of amphetamine and cocaine can produce them, suggests that excessive activity at the D_2 receptor is related to schizophrenia.

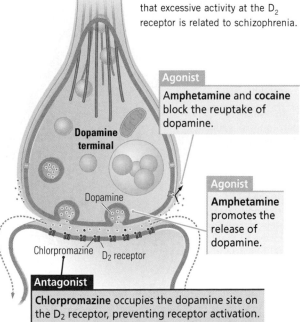

Agonist
Amphetamine and **cocaine** block the reuptake of dopamine.

Agonist
Amphetamine promotes the release of dopamine.

Antagonist
Chlorpromazine occupies the dopamine site on the D_2 receptor, preventing receptor activation.

Class III. Antidepressants

Major depression—a mood disorder characterized by prolonged feelings of worthlessness and guilt, disruption of normal eating habits, sleep disturbances, a general slowing of behavior, and frequent thoughts of suicide—is common and affects twice as many women as men. At any given time, about 6% of the adult population worldwide suffer from it, and as many as 30% of all people may experience at least one episode of major depression in their lives.

Most people recover from depression within a year of its onset; but, if the condition is left untreated, the incidence of suicide is high. Of all psychological disorders, major depression is one of the most treatable, and Ronald Comer reports that cognitive and interpersonal therapies are as effective as drug therapies. Three different types of drugs have antidepressant effects: **monoamine oxidase inhibitors** (MAO inhibitors), **tricyclic antidepressants**, and **second-generation antidepressants**, sometimes called *atypical antidepressants*, which include fluoxetine (Prozac) and are similar to the tricyclics.

Antidepressants are thought to act by improving chemical transmission in serotonin, noradrenaline, histamine, and acetylcholine synapses and perhaps in dopamine synapses, too. **Figure 7.10** shows their action at a serotonin synapse, where most antidepressant research is focused. As you can see, the mechanisms of MAO inhibitors differ from those of the tricyclic and second-generation antidepressants for increasing the availability of serotonin.

Monoamine oxidase is an enzyme that breaks down serotonin within the axon terminal. The inhibition of MAO by an MAO inhibitor therefore provides more serotonin for release with each action potential. The tricyclic antidepressants block the transporter that takes serotonin back into the axon terminal. The second-generation antidepressants are thought to be especially selective in blocking serotonin reuptake, and consequently some are also called **selective serotonin reuptake inhibitors** (SSRIs). Because the transporter is blocked, serotonin remains in the synaptic cleft for a longer period, thus prolonging its action on postsynaptic receptors.

There are significant questions concerning how antidepressants work. The drugs begin to affect synapses very quickly, and yet their antidepressant effects take weeks to develop. No one is sure why. In addition, about 20% of patients with depression fail to respond to antidepressant drugs. There is also controversy over whether some or all tricyclic antidepressants increase the risk of suicide. The difficulty here is that major depression can lead to suicide, creating a question whether any given suicide is related to major depression or to a drug treatment. Furthermore, the issue of why people commit suicide is aggravated by a report by Emel Serap Monkul and her colleagues that the brains of suicide victims featured

Figure **7.10**

Drug Effects at the Serotonin Synapse Different antidepressant drugs act on serotonin synapses in different ways to increase the availability of serotonin.

Agonist

MAO inhibitor inhibits the breakdown of serotonin...

...so that more serotonin is available for release.

Agonist

Selective serotonin reuptake inhibitors block transporter protein for serotonin reuptake so that serotonin stays in synaptic cleft longer.

MAO inhibitor

Serotonin terminal

Serotonin

smaller orbital frontal cortex and amygdala. They suggest that these brain regions contribute to executive decisions, which, when impaired, could lead to impulsivity and suicide.

Antidepressant side effects include increased anxiety, sexual dysfunction, sedation, dry mouth, blurred vision, and memory impairments. Many people hoped that the second-generation antidepressants would produce fewer side effects than the tricyclic antidepressants, but that hope has not been realized. In fact, most antidepressants do not appear to be particularly selective in their action on the brain. Even Prozac, one of the more selective antidepressant compounds, is advertised as a treatment not only for depression but also for obsessive–compulsive disorder, bulimia, and panic disorder.

The major symptoms of **obsessive–compulsive disorder** (OCD) are obsessive thoughts and compulsive behaviors—ideas that people cannot get out of their heads and ritual-like actions that they perform endlessly. Although OCD, like depression, is associated with guilt and anxiety, most experts consider it a separate disorder.

Class IV. Mood Stabilizers

Bipolar disorder, once referred to as manic–depressive illness, is a disorder of mood in which a person might undergo periods of depression alternating with normal periods and periods of intense excitation. According to the National Institute of Mental Health, bipolar disorder can affect as much as 2.6% of the adult population.

Bipolar disorder is frequently treated with drugs called **mood stabilizers**, which include the salt lithium and a variety of other drugs including valproate, which is also used to treat epilepsy. The mechanism of action of mood stabilizers is not well understood, but lithium may increase the synaptic release of serotonin, and valproate may stimulate GABA activity. Typically, mood stabilizers mute the intensity of one pole of the disorder, thus making the other pole less likely to reoccur.

Class V. Narcotic Analgesics

The **narcotic analgesic** drugs have both sleep-inducing (narcotic) and pain-relieving (analgesic) properties. Many are derived from opium, an extract of the seeds of the opium poppy, *Papaver somniferum*. Opium has been used for thousands of years to produce euphoria, analgesia, sleep, and relief from diarrhea and coughing.

In 1805, German chemist Friedrich Sertürner synthesized two pure substances from the poppy plant—**codeine** and **morphine**—that demonstrate narcotic properties. Codeine is included in cough medicine and in pain relievers such as aspirin, although not in the United States. Morphine, which was named after Morpheus, the Greek god of dreams, is a very powerful pain reliever.

Despite decades of research, no other drug has been found that exceeds morphine's effectiveness as an analgesic. **Heroin**, another opiate drug, is synthesized from morphine. It is more fat soluble than is morphine and so penetrates the blood–brain barrier more quickly, thus producing very rapid relief from pain. The Portrait at the beginning of this chapter describes one synthetic

Opium is obtained from the seeds of the opium poppy (top). Morphine (middle) is extracted from opium, and heroin (bottom) is a powder synthesized from morphine. (Top: Eye Ubiquitous/Corbis. Middle: National Archives. Bottom: Bonnie Kamin/PhotoEdit.)

form of heroin. Another is methadone, a drug widely used to treat addiction by acting as a substitute for heroin or other abused opiod drugs.

Endorphin-containing neurons exist in many brain regions, and morphine is similar enough to these endogenous substances to mimic their action in the brain. Opium antagonists such as nalorphine and naloxone block the action of morphine by blocking endorphin receptors and so are useful in quickly reversing opioid overdoses. Endorphins are peptides and can be ingested to relieve pain, but they do not easily cross the blood–brain barrier. Consequently, morphine, which obviously does, remains a preferred pain treatment.

Class VI. Psychomotor Stimulants

Stimulants, a diverse class of drugs, increase the activity of neurons in several ways. They are divided into two groups: behavioral stimulants and general stimulants.

Behavioral Stimulants

Behavioral stimulants such as cocaine and amphetamine increase motor behavior as well as elevating a person's mood and level of alertness. **Cocaine** is extracted from the Peruvian coca shrub. Indigenous Peruvians originally discovered it in coca leaves, which they chewed to increase their stamina in the harsh environment of the high elevations at which they live.

Purified cocaine can be taken either by sniffing (snorting) or by injection. Many cocaine users do not like to inject cocaine intravenously, and so they sniff a highly concentrated form of it called *crack*. Crack is chemically altered so that it vaporizes at low temperatures, and the vapors are inhaled. **Amphetamine** is a synthetic compound that was discovered in attempts to synthesize the neurotransmitter epinephrine.

As shown in Figure 7.9, both amphetamine and cocaine are dopamine agonists that act by blocking dopamine transport back into the presynaptic terminal, leaving more dopamine available in the synaptic cleft. Amphetamine also stimulates the release of dopamine from presynaptic membranes. Both mechanisms increase the amount of dopamine available in synapses to stimulate dopamine receptors.

Cocaine was popularized as an antidepressant by Viennese psychoanalyst Sigmund Freud. In an 1884 paper titled "Über Coca," Freud concluded:

> The main use of coca will undoubtedly remain that which the Indians have made of it for centuries: it is of value in all cases where the primary aim is to increase the physical capacity of the body for a given short period of time and to hold strength in reserve to meet further demands—especially when outward circumstances exclude the possibility of obtaining the rest and nourishment normally necessary for great exertion.

Later, as Freud became aware of its addictive properties, he withdrew his endorsement of cocaine. There is also evidence that cocaine can produce circulatory disturbances, some of which can result in sudden death. Freud also recommended that cocaine be used as a local anesthetic and many of its derivatives, such as Novocaine, are used for this purpose. Cocaine was once used in soft drinks and wine mixtures, which were promoted as invigorating tonics. It

Cocaine (top) is obtained from the leaves of the coca plant (middle). Crack cocaine (bottom) is chemically altered to form "rocks" that vaporize when heated. (Top: Timothy Ross/The Image Works. Middle: Gregory G.Dimijian/Photo Researchers. Bottom: Tek Image/ Science Photo Library/Photo Researchers.)

is responsible for the origin of the trade name Coca-Cola, as suggested by the advertisement in **Figure 7.11**.

Amphetamine was first used as a treatment for asthma. A form of amphetamine, Benzedrine, was sold in inhalers as a nonprescription drug through the 1940s. Soon people discovered that they could open the container and swallow its contents to obtain a sudden energizing effect. In 1937, an article in the *Journal of the American Medical Association* reported that Benzedrine tablets improved performance on mental-efficiency tests. This information was quickly disseminated among students, who began to use "bennies" when studying for exams.

Amphetamine has been widely used since World War II to keep tired troops and pilots alert and to improve the productivity of wartime workers. It has also been used as a diet aid. In the 1960s, drug users discovered that they could obtain an immediate pleasurable "rush," often described as a whole-body orgasm, by intravenous injection of amphetamine. People who took amphetamine in this way, called "speed freaks," would inject the drug every few hours for days, remaining in a wide-awake, excited state without eating. They would then crash in exhaustion and hunger and, after a few days of recovery, would begin the cycle again. One explanation for repeated injections was to prevent the depressive crash that occurred when the drug wore off.

In addition to amphetamine, two other forms, dextroamphetamine and methamphetamine, all vary in their potency but are very similar in their behavioral and addictive effects. They have many street names. Crystal meth, one street form of methamphetamine, comes in clear, chunky crystals that are inhaled or smoked. It is also called "ice," "crystal," "glass," and "tina." Crystal meth is easy to produce in small, clandestine laboratories, sometimes in a kitchen or bathroom, by mixing a cocktail of about 15 substances.

The recipe consists mostly of pseudoephedrine (a cold remedy), red phosphorous, and iodine, along with ammonia, paint thinner, ether, Drano, and the lithium from batteries. An investment of about $150 can yield as much as $10,000 worth of the drug, but the homemade product is often impure. Crystal meth has become the most widespread and popular form of amphetamine, largely because it is so easy to make. Anyone can set up a laboratory: instructions are widespread on the World Wide Web, and motorcycle gangs, which are becoming dominant in organized drug trafficking, effectively distribute the drug.

General Stimulants

General stimulants increase the metabolic activity of cells. A widely used general stimulant is caffeine. **Caffeine** inhibits an enzyme that ordinarily breaks down the important regulatory biochemical cyclic adenosine monophosphate (cyclic AMP). The resulting increase in cyclic AMP leads to an increase in glucose production within cells, thus making available more energy and allowing higher rates of cellular activity throughout the body and brain.

Caffeine is a widely used drug, and users have little idea of what dose they receive either in home-brewed or purchased coffee. Nor do most people realize that many soft drinks and energy drinks contain significant amounts of caffeine. And, when you choose decaffinated coffee, be aware that it, too, contains some caffeine.

Figure **7.11**

Warning Label Cocaine was once an ingredient in a number of invigorating beverages, including Coca-Cola. (Granger Collection.)

Class VII. Psychedelics and Hallucinogens

Psychedelic drugs alter sensory perception and cognitive processes and can produce hallucinations. The four major groups of psychedelics are categorized by their actions on specific neurotransmitters:

1. *Acetylcholine psychedelics* either block or facilitate transmission at ACh synapses in the brain. They act on an acetylcholine receptor called the **muscarine receptor** (muscarine is a chemical obtained from *Amanita muscaria*, a mushroom that affects the parasympathetic system but does not cross the blood–brain barrier). Atropine, from the plant *Atropa belladonna* (Italian for "pretty woman"), is a muscarinic blocker that does cross the blood–brain barrier. It dilates the pupils and reddens the cheeks, and it produces a dreamy state that was once perceived as sexy. In higher doses, atropine has been used as a poison. Other acetylcholine psychedelics are obtained from plants including the deadly nightshade, jimsonweed, stinkweed, thorn apple, and mandrake.

2. *Norepinephrine psychedelics* include the hallucinogen **mescaline**, obtained from the flowering heads (buttons) of the peyote cactus, which produces an intoxication with delusions of color and sound. Mescaline is legal for use by Native Americans for religious practices.

3. **Tetrahydrocannabinol**, or THC, the active ingredient in marijuana, is obtained from the female hemp plant *Cannabis sativa*. *Cannabis* acts on the CB1 and CB2 receptors for a neurotransmitter called **anandamide**. Surprisingly, anandamide plays a role in forgetting, a mechanism that prevents memory systems of the brain from being overwhelmed by the information to which the brain is exposed each day. Thus, THC may have a detrimental effect on memory.

4. *Serotonin psychedelics* include both **LSD** (lysergic acid diethylamide), a synthetic compound, and **psilocybin**, obtained from the mushroom *Psilocybe cubensis*, otherwise known as magic mushroom. Both drugs produce altered states of consciousness associated with visual hallucinations. **MDMA** (3,4 methylenedioxymethamphetamine) is a synthetic, psychoactive drug chemically similar to the stimulant methamphetamine and the hallucinogen mescaline.

Cannabis sativa is an annual herb that reaches a height of 3 to 15 feet. Hemp grows in a wide range of altitudes, climates, and soils and has myriad practical uses. (Phil Schermeister/Stone.)

Street names for MDMA include Ecstasy, Adam, XTC, hug, beans, and love drug. It produces a sense of openness, empathy, energy, euphoria, and well-being. Tactile sensations are enhanced for some users, making general physical contact with others more pleasurable; but, contrary to popular mythology, MDMA does not have aphrodisiac effects. Its reported ability to facilitate self-examination with reduced fear may prove useful in some therapeutic settings, leading, in 2001, to permission from the U.S. Food and Drug Administration for testing in patients with posttraumatic stress disorder in conjunction with psychotherapy.

MDMA appeared sporadically as a street drug in the early 1970s, but it came into prominence in the early 1980s in certain trendy yuppie bars in the Dallas, Texas, area and then in gay dance clubs. From there, use spread to rave clubs and then to mainstream society. During the 1990s, along with the growing popularity of the rave subculture, MDMA use became increasingly widespread among young adults in universities and later in high schools. It rapidly became one of the four most widely used illegal drugs in the United States, along with cocaine, heroin, and marijuana. MDMA exerts its primary effects in the brain on neurons that use serotonin, but it also affects many other neurotransmitters including dopamine and norepinephrine.

The Effects of Experience, Context, and Genes

Among the striking features of psychoactive drugs are that their effects change from one administration to another, depend on context, vary from one person to another, and depend on previous experience. In the following sections, we describe a number of ways that repeated use of drugs changes the brain and behavior. Such variable effects have implications for recreational drug use and for their use in treating disorders.

Tolerance

A dramatic example of **tolerance**—the decline in response to the repeated administration of a drug—was described by H. Isbell and coworkers for a group of prisoners who had volunteered for the study. These researchers gave subjects enough alcohol daily in a 13-week period to keep them in a constant state of intoxication (**Figure 7.12**A). Yet they found that the subjects did not stay drunk for 3 months straight.

In the first days of the experiment, all the subjects showed rapidly rising levels of blood alcohol and behavioral signs of intoxication after consuming alcohol, as shown in the top graph in Figure 7.12B. Between the 12th and 20th days, however, blood-alcohol concentrations and the signs of intoxication fell to very low levels (middle graph), even though the subjects maintained a constant alcohol intake. Interestingly, too, although blood-alcohol levels and signs of intoxication fluctuated in subsequent days of the study, the one did not always correlate with the other. A relatively high blood-alcohol level was sometimes associated with a low outward appearance of being drunk (bottom graph). Why?

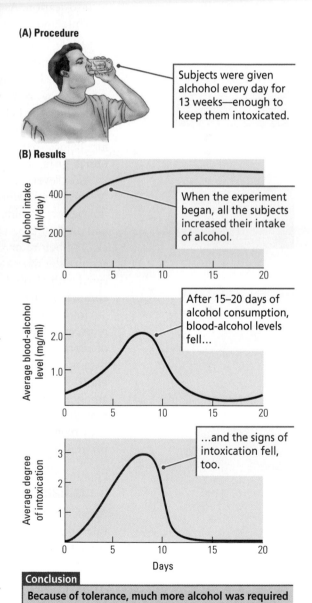

(A) Procedure

Subjects were given alchohol every day for 13 weeks—enough to keep them intoxicated.

(B) Results

When the experiment began, all the subjects increased their intake of alcohol.

After 15–20 days of alcohol consumption, blood-alcohol levels fell...

...and the signs of intoxication fell, too.

Days

Conclusion

Because of tolerance, much more alcohol was required by the end of the study to obtain the same level of intoxication that was produced at the beginning.

Figure 7.12

Alcohol Intake, Blood-Alcohol Level, and Behavior Over the first 20 days of steady drinking, the relation between blood-alcohol level and behavioral intoxication changed owing to tolerance. (After Isbell et al., 1955.)

These results were the products of three different kinds of tolerance:

1. **Metabolic tolerance** consists of an increase in the enzymes needed to break down alcohol in the liver, blood, and brain. As a result, the body metabolizes alcohol more quickly, and so blood-alcohol levels are reduced.

2. **Cellular tolerance** consists of adjustments in the activities of neurons so as to minimize the effects of alcohol in the blood. Cellular tolerance helps explain why the behavioral signs of intoxication may be very low despite a relatively high blood-alcohol level.

3. **Learned tolerance** also contributes to the drop in outward signs of intoxication. As people learn to cope with the daily demands of living while under the influence of alcohol, they may no longer appear to be drunk.

The results of many studies confirm that learning plays a role in tolerance to alcohol. For instance, J. R. Wenger and his coworkers trained rats to walk on a narrow conveyor belt to prevent electric shock to their feet from a grid over which the belt was traveling. One group of rats received alcohol after having been trained to walk on the belt, whereas another group received alcohol just before their training sessions. A third group received training only, and a fourth group received alcohol only.

After several days of exposure to their respective conditions, all groups were given alcohol before a walking test. The rats that had previously received alcohol before training performed well, whereas those that had received training and alcohol separately performed just as poorly as those that had never had alcohol before or those that had never been trained. Apparently, animals can acquire the motor skills needed to balance on a narrow belt even when intoxicated with alcohol. With the passage of time, in other words, they can learn to compensate for being drunk.

Tolerance can develop to many other drugs besides alcohol, such as barbiturates, amphetamines, and narcotics. In humans, for instance, a dose of 100 mg of morphine is sufficient to cause profound sedation and even death in some first-time users, but those who have developed tolerance to this drug have been known to take 4000 mg without adverse effects. Similarly, long-time users of amphetamine may need to take doses 100 or more times as great as the doses that they initially took to produce the same behavioral effect. In other words, with repeated administration of a drug, the effect produced by the drug may progressively diminish owing to tolerance.

Sensitization

An increasing response to the effects of a drug is called **sensitization**. Whereas tolerance generally develops with constantly repeated use of a given drug, sensitization is much more likely to develop with occasional use.

For example, Terry Robinson and Jill Becker isolated rats in observation boxes and recorded their reactions to an injection of amphetamine, paying particular attention to increases in sniffing, rearing, and walking, which are typical rat responses to this drug. Every 3 or 4 days, the investigators repeated the procedure. The results, shown in **Figure 7.13**A, reveal that the rats' level of activity increased with each periodic trial.

(A) Procedure 1

In the Robinson and Becker study, animals were given periodic injections of the same dose of amphetamine. Then the researchers measured the number of times each rat reared in its cage.

(B) Procedure 2

In the Whishaw study, animals were given different numbers of swims after being injected with Flupentixol. Then the researchers measured their speed to escape to a platform in a swimming pool.

Figure 7.13

Sensitization from Agonists and Antagonists (A) Amphetamine stimulates dopamine release and blocks reuptake. Each injection of the same dose of the drug in rats produces a greater effect as measured by an increase in locomotion. (B) The major tranquilizer Flupentixol blocks dopamine receptors. After each injection, a swimming trial is slower until the rat can no longer escape from the swimming pool. (After Robinson and Becker, 1986, and Whishaw et al., 1989.)

Agonist
Amphetamine

Antagonist
Flupentixol

Results 1

Results 2

Conclusion 1

Sensitization, as indicated by increased rearing, develops with periodic repeated injections.

Conclusion 2

Sensitization depends on the occurrence of the behavior. The number of swims, not the spacing of swims or the treatment, causes an increase in the time taken for a rat to reach the platform.

This increased response on successive tests was not due to the animals becoming "comfortable" with the test situation. Control animals that received no drug did not display a similar escalation in sniffing, rearing, and walking. Moreover, the sensitization to amphetamine was enduring. Even when two injections of amphetamine were separated by months, the animals still showed an increased response to the drug.

Sensitization also develops to drugs with depressive effects, such as the major tranquilizer Flupentixol, a dopamine antagonist that blocks dopamine receptors. Figure 7.13B shows the changing effects of Flupentixol on the swimming behavior of rats in a study conducted by Whishaw and his colleagues.

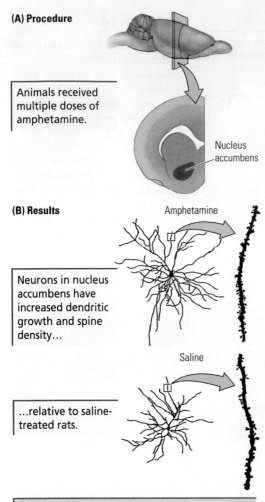

(A) Procedure

Animals received multiple doses of amphetamine.

Nucleus accumbens

(B) Results

Amphetamine

Neurons in nucleus accumbens have increased dendritic growth and spine density...

Saline

...relative to saline-treated rats.

Sensitization induced by repeated exposure to amphetamine changes the structure of neurons.

Figure 7.14

Structural Changes Accompany Sensitization Rats that show sensitization to amphetamine (or to cocaine) undergo increased dendritic growth and increased spine density in comparison with saline-treated rats. (After Robinson and Kolb, 1997, p. 8495.)

The researchers trained the rats to swim a short distance to a platform in a swimming pool. When the rats were reaching the platform within 1 to 2 seconds of immersion, they were given an injection of Flupentixol. On the first few swims after the injections, the rats swam normally; but, in subsequent trials, they began to slow down. After about 12 trials separated by a few minutes, they simply sank when placed in the water and had to be removed to prevent them from drowning.

This effect was not simply due to fatigue from 12 successive trials given on the same day. If the rats were injected and placed in water only once each day for 12 days, the same pattern of results was obtained. On the first few days, the rats swam normally, but thereafter they began to slow down until, by the 12th day, they simply sank after being injected and placed in the water. Sensitization to the drug depended on the number of trials regardless of the time that elapsed between them or the number of times that the drug was given. Presumably, Flupentixol changes dopamine neurons that mediate the behavior only if the rats engage in the behavior.

Sensitization is difficult to demonstrate in an animal that is tested in its home cage. Animals are accustomed to performing a certain repertoire of behaviors in their home environments and are unlikely to change that behavior even under the influence of a drug. When animals are placed in a novel environment, however, and given widely spaced injections of a drug, their responses to the drug can be seen to increase. Presumably, humans, too, will show sensitization to a drug when they take it periodically and in novel circumstances.

Sensitization is long-lasting because it is accompanied by structural changes in the brain that are long-lasting. Robinson and his colleagues found a dramatic increase in dendritic growth and spine density in rats that were sensitized to amphetamine or cocaine relative to rats that received injections of a saline solution. **Figure 7.14** compares the effects of amphetamine and saline treatments on cells in the nucleus accumbens, a part of the subcortical basal ganglia. Neurons in the amphetamine-treated brains have more dendritic branches and an increased number of spines compared with those treated with saline. These plastic changes were not found throughout the brain but were limited to regions that receive a large dopamine projection.

Addiction and Dependence

Substance abuse is a pattern of drug use in which people rely on a drug chronically and excessively, allowing it to occupy a central place in their lives. A more advanced state of drug abuse is **substance dependence**, popularly known as **addiction**. People who are substance dependent have developed a **physical dependence** on a drug in addition to abusing it. They need to take the drug to feel "normal." This physical dependence is usually accompanied by tolerance to the drug, and so a user requires increased doses to obtain the desired effect.

The person may also experience unpleasant, sometimes dangerous **withdrawal symptoms** if he or she suddenly stops taking the drug. These symptoms can include muscle aches and cramps, anxiety attacks, sweating, nausea, and, for some drugs, even convulsions and death. Withdrawal symptoms can begin within hours of the last dose of a drug and intensify for several days before they subside.

Many different kinds of drugs are abused or cause addiction, including sedative-hypnotics, antianxiety agents, narcotics, and stimulants. Drugs that are abused have a property in common: they produce psychomotor activation over some part of their dose range. That is, at certain levels of consumption, these drugs make the user feel energetic and in control. This common effect has led to the hypothesis that abused drugs may all act on the same target in the brain.

One proposed target is the dopamine system, because stimulation of dopamine neurons is associated with psychomotor activity. Brain imaging of subjects who have taken nicotine shows that many brain regions display increased activity under the drug, including the nucleus accumbens, amygdala, thalamus, and prefrontal cortex (see the Snapshot below, on nicotine). All these structures receive projections from dopamine neurons.

ꝱNAPƧHOT
Imaging the Effects of Nicotine

Cigarette smoking is the most common substance-abuse disorder and the leading preventable cause of death. Approximately 26% of North Americans are regular smokers. Smokers display compulsive use, difficulty in quitting, and withdrawal symptoms on cessation of chronic use. Only about 3% of smokers who quit remain abstinent for 1 year.

Although cigarette smoke contains thousands of compounds, nicotine is generally considered the addictive and reinforcing agent responsible for continued smoking behavior. One study used fMRI to identify active regions in the brains of 16 cigarette smokers soon after they were injected with nicotine (Stein et al., 1998). The nicotine induced a dose-dependent increase in feelings of "rush" and "high" and in drug liking.

As the accompanying fMRIs show, nicotine also induced a dose-dependent increase in neuronal activity in the nucleus accumbens (A), amygdala (B), and cingulate gyrus and frontal lobes (C). All these structures are the targets of dopamine projections. Their activation is consistent with the idea that the activation of dopamine systems is related to addiction.

Using brain imaging of the electrical activity of these regions in smokers and former smokers (abstinence of more than 10 years), Neuhaus et al. (2006) report that these same areas are hypoactive in the absence of nicotine administration when subjects are given a task entailing the processing of complex stimuli. Thus, the effects of nicotine on the dopamine-activating system are both immediate and enduring.

Neuhaus, A., M. Bajbouj, T. Kienast, P. Kalus, D. von Haebler, G. Winterer, and J. Gallinat. Persistent dysfunctional frontal lobe activation in former smokers. *Psychopharmacology* 186:191–200, 2006.

Stein, F. A., J. Pankiewicz, H. H. Harsch, J. K. Cho, S. A. Fuller, R. G. Hoffmann, M. Hawkins, S. M. Rao, P. A. Bandettini, and A. S. Bloom. Nicotine-induced limbic cortical activation in the human brain: A functional MRI study. *American Journal of Psychiatry* 155:1009–1015, 1998.

(A) Nucleus accumbens

(B) Amygdala

(C) Cingulate–orbitofrontal

Functional magnetic resonance imaging of brain regions activated by nicotine, indicated by arrows. (From Stein et al., 1998.)

Three lines of evidence support a central role for dopamine in drug abuse:

1. Animals are easily trained to press a bar to receive electrical stimulation of the dopamine system in the brain, but they quickly discontinue that behavior if the dopamine system is blocked or damaged. This evidence suggests that the release of dopamine is somehow rewarding.

2. Abused drugs cause the release of dopamine or prolong its availability in synaptic clefts. Even drugs that have no primary action on dopamine synapses have been found to increase dopamine's effects. When activated, many brain regions that contain no dopamine neurons themselves may stimulate dopamine neurons elsewhere in the brain.

3. Drugs that block dopamine receptors or decrease the availability of dopamine at dopamine receptors are not substances that people abuse. For example, the major tranquilizers that block dopamine receptors and are widely available for treating psychosis are not abused drugs.

Explaining Drug Abuse

Why do people become addicted to drugs? An early idea, the **dependence hypothesis**, suggests that habitual users of a drug experience psychological or physiological withdrawal symptoms when the effects of the drug wear off. They feel anxious, insecure, or just plain sick in the absence of the drug, and so they take the drug again to alleviate those symptoms.

Although this hypothesis accounts for part of drug-taking behavior, it has shortcomings. An addict may abstain from a drug for months, long after any withdrawal symptoms have abated, yet still be drawn back to using the drug. Moreover, the dependence hypothesis fails to explain why certain drugs that produce withdrawal symptoms when discontinued, such as the tricyclic antidepressants, are not abused.

The **hedonic hypothesis** proposes that people take drugs because they produce pleasure. Its weakness is that addicted people frequently say that the drugs that they take give them little pleasure.

Incentive-sensitization theory proposes that addiction is acquired unconsciously and is the result of conditioned learning. Proposed by Terry Robinson and Kent Berridge, incentive-sensitization theory sees addiction as developing in stages:

- Stage 1 is the activation of pleasure as a consequence of drug taking. In other words, the user likes the experience.

- In stage 2, pleasure becomes linked through associative learning to mental representations of objects, acts, places, and events connected to taking the drug. This associative learning occurs through **classical** (also called **Pavlovian**) **conditioning**. That is, the drug-taking context, the sight of drug paraphenalia, or the sight of the drug are repeatedly paired with the use of the drug, which produces a pleasurable reaction.

- Stage 3 is the attribution of **incentive salience** to the cues associated with drug use. In other words, those cues become highly desired and sought-after incentives in themselves. Stimuli that signal the availability of these incentives also become attractive. For instance, acts that have led to the

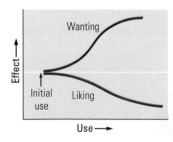

Figure 7.15

Incentive-Sensitization Theory
Wanting and liking a drug change in opposite directions with repeated drug use.

drug-taking situation become attractive, as do new acts that the drug taker predicts will lead again to the drug.

In this sequence of events, then, a number of repetitions of the drug-taking behavior lead from the act being liked to its being sought out or wanted. The incentive-sensitization perspective is also called the **wanting-and-liking theory** because, in it, wanting and liking a drug are affected differently, as is illustrated in **Figure 7.15**. Wanting is equivalent to craving a drug, which increases in addiction, whereas liking is defined as the pleasure produced by drug taking, which decreases in addiction.

The neural bases for liking and wanting may reside with two different transmitter systems. Liking may be due to the activity of opioid neurons (endorphins), which are associated with the pleasure of early drug use. Wanting may be due to activity in the **mesolimbic dopamine system** shown in **Figure 7.16**. This dopamine pathway consists of dopamine neurons in the midbrain that have axons projecting to the nucleus accumbens, the frontal cortex, and the limbic system.

Cues previously associated with drug taking activate the mesolimbic dopamine system, producing the subjective experience of wanting. The process that awakens the desire for the drug would not be conscious but would derive from unconsciously acquired associations between drug taking and various cues related to it. Importantly, even long after drug use has ended, cues previously associated with drug taking can elicit craving through their effect in activating the mesolimbic dopamine system.

Drug-Induced Behavior

Drugs can cause behavioral and mood changes as unpredictable as they are extreme. People who drink alcohol, for example, may feel happy at one moment, sad the next, and perhaps belligerent or reckless the next. What accounts for such wide variability? We will use alcohol as an example to present a range of theories that attempt to account for the variability in the behavioral effects of drugs.

An early and still popular explanation of the effects of alcohol is the **disinhibition theory**, which holds that alcohol has a selective depressant effect on the neocortex, the region of the brain dealing with judgment, while sparing subcortical structures, the sites of more-primitive instincts. Stated differently, alcohol presumably depresses learned inhibitions based on reasoning and judgment, thus releasing the "beast" within. Disinhibition theory is the basis for such often-heard excuses for alcohol-related behavior as "She was too drunk to know better" or "The boys had a few too many and got carried away."

Craig MacAndrew and Robert Edgerton challenged disinhibition theory with their **learned-behavior theory**. They cite many instances in which behavior under the influence of alcohol changes from one context to another in ways that contradict the idea that alcohol lowers inhibitions. They also cite examples of cultures in which people are disinhibited when sober only to become inhibited after consuming alcohol and cultures in which people are inhibited when sober and become more inhibited when drinking.

How can all these differences in alcohol's effects be explained? MacAndrew and Edgerton conclude that behavior under the effects of alcohol is learned

Frontal cortex

Nucleus accumbens of basal ganglia

Hippocampus (part of limbic system)

Ventral tegmental area of midbrain

Figure 7.16

Mesolimbic Dopamine Pathways and Drug Craving Dopamine cells in the ventral tegmental area of the midbrain project axons to the nucleus accumbens of the basal ganglia, to the limbic system (including the hippocampus), and to the frontal cortex, suggesting that these areas may play a role in addiction.

behavior that is specific to the drug, culture, group, and setting. Often, it simply represents a time-out from the rules of daily life that would normally apply.

Tara MacDonald and her coworkers suggest that alcohol-related behavior can be explained by what they call **alcohol myopia** (nearsightedness). They coined this expression to describe what they see as a tendency for people under the influence of alcohol to respond to a restricted set of prominent cues that are at hand while ignoring more remote cues and potential consequences.

For example, if there is a fight, a person with alcohol myopia will be quicker than normal to take a swing because the cue of the fight is so strong; if someone is complaining, they will be quick to complain; and if others are happy, they will be the happiest. Alcohol myopia can be applied to other lapses in judgment that lead to risky behavior while a person is on drugs, including aggression, date rape, and reckless driving—or driving at all.

Individual Differences and Drugs

Vast individual differences exist in people's responses to drugs, as do differences that correlate with age, sex, body size, and other factors that affect sensitivity to a given substance. Larger people are less sensitive to a given dose of a drug than smaller people are, because the drug is more diluted in a large person's body fluids. Females are about twice as sensitive to drugs as males are. This difference is due in part to a female's relatively smaller body size, but it is also due to hormonal differences between females and males. Old people also may be twice as sensitive to drugs as young people are. The elderly often have less-effective barriers to drug absorption as well as less-effective processes for metabolizing and eliminating drugs from their bodies. Similarly, there are differences in the susceptibility of individual persons and of different groups to become addicted to drugs.

Observing that some people are more prone to drug abuse and dependence than other people are, scientists have wondered if this difference might be genetically based. Three lines of evidence suggest a genetic contribution:

1. The results of studies show that, if one of a pair of twins abuses alcohol, there is a greater likelihood for the other twin to abuse it, too, if the twins are identical (have the same genetic makeup) rather than fraternal (have only some of their genes in common).

2. The results of studies of people adopted shortly after birth reveal that they are more likely to abuse alcohol if their biological parents were alcoholic, even though they have had almost no contact with those parents.

3. Although most animals do not care for alcohol, the selective breeding of mice, rats, and monkeys can produce strains that consume large quantities of it.

David Moore suggests, however, that attempts to explain behavior by one or a few genes is problematic. Perhaps identical twins show greater concordance for alcohol abuse because they are exposed to more-similar environments than fraternal twins are. And perhaps the link between alcoholism in adoptees and their biological parents has to do with nervous system changes due to prebirth exposure to the drug. Finally, just because animals can be selectively bred for alcohol consumption does not mean that humans who become alcoholic have similar genetic makeups.

Primary among the compelling arguments against the idea that addictions generally have a genetic basis is this one: the single strongest predictor of drug use is whether others in a peer group use drugs. In societies where smoking tobacco is accepted, for example, the rate of smoking is much greater than in societies that hold negative attitudes toward smoking. Thus, as many as 60% of people in some groups may smoke, whereas fewer that 10% in other groups do.

Learning and experience also account for much of the "fashionable" abuse of drugs, where drug use is influenced by age and social group. Addictions are generally so widespread that almost everyone is afflicted, whether it be to "wine, or poetry, or love" in the words of the playwright Eugene O'Neill. According to this notion, the reward systems of the brain are designed to addict us to life's necessities, but it is the prevalence of opportunity that leads us to abuse.

Drugs Acting As Neurotoxins

Table 7.3 shows that many substances can act as neurotoxins, causing damage to neurons. We present evidence for two ways in which drugs can kill neurons.

In the late 1960s, there were many reports that monosodium glutamate (MSG), a salty-tasting, flavor-enhancing food additive, produced headaches in some people. In the process of investigating why this happened, scientists placed large doses of MSG on cultured neurons. The neurons died. Subsequently, they injected monosodium glutamate into the brains of experimental animals, where it also produced neuron death.

These findings raised the question whether large doses of the neurotransmitter glutamate, which MSG resembles structurally, also might be toxic to neurons. It turns out that they are. This finding suggests that a large dose of any substance that acts like glutamate or activates glutamate might be toxic.

In 1987, in Canada, an outbreak of food poisoning occurred after people had eaten mussels. In all, nine people died and a number suffered confusion and

Table **7.3** Some neurotoxins, their sources, and their actions

Substance	Origin	Action
Tetrodotoxin	Puffer fish	Blocks membrane permeability to Na^+ ions
Magnesium	Natural element	Blocks Ca^{2+} channels
Reserpine	*Rauwulfia* shrubs	Destroys storage granules
Colchicine	Crocus plant	Blocks microtubules
Caffeine	Coffee bean	Blocks adenosine receptors and Ca^{2+} channels
Spider venom	Black widow spider	Stimulates ACh release
Botulinum toxin	Food poisoning (*Clostridium botulinum* bacteria)	Blocks ACh release
Curare	Berry of *Strychnos* vine	Blocks ACh receptors
Rabies virus	Animal bite	Blocks ACh receptors
Ibotenic acid	*Amanita muscaria* and *Amanita pantherina* mushrooms	Similar to that of domoic acid
Strychnine	Plants of genus *Strychnos*	Blocks glycine
Apamin	Bees and wasps	Blocks Ca^{2+} channels

Monosodium glutamate
(MSG)

Glutamate

Domoic acid

memory loss that proved permanent. Autopsies revealed extensive cell loss in the hippocampus, amygdala, and surrounding cortex and in the thalamus. An examination of the mussels showed that they contained a chemical called domoic acid, a substance that, like glutamate, is an agonist on glutamate receptors. Domoic acid in large quantities excessively stimulates the glutamate receptors of certain brain cells and kills them.

Researchers have since discovered that many brain insults—including traumatic blows to the head, strokes in which blood supply is temporarily stopped, and epilepsy or abnormal electrical discharges—can result in excessive glutamate release and subsequent brain injury from its action. Glutamate is thought to cause an increase in intracellular calcium that poisons the cell. Knowing this mechanism of cell death, many researchers are investigating ways to block glutamate or calcium influx or both in neurons as a way of helping them survive insults.

Substantial evidence indicates that, when neurons are stressed, they can commit suicide. Cell suicide, or **apoptosis** (from the Greek words *apo*, meaning "from," and *ptosis*, meaning "falling," commonly pronounced ap-a-**tow**-sis), can take place weeks or months after the initial stress. Stress activates genes within a cell that then shut down the cell's metabolic activity and send signals to glial cells to remove the cell.

Apoptosis is a natural process that takes place in development to remove surplus neurons, and it is harnessed to remove diseased and damaged cells. Rabi Simantov and coworkers suggest that at least one psychoactive drug, MDMA (Ecstasy), activates genes in neurons that induce apoptosis. In principal, it is also possible that general neuronal stress induced by certain psychoactive drugs or excessive drug use can induce apoptosis. Additionally, investigators are searching for ways in which the genes that induce apoptosis can be blocked to prevent cell death.

The Potential Harmfulness of Recreational Drugs

An oft-asked question concerning the use of recreational drugs is, Do they directly harm the brain? The answer is not easy to determine.

First, there is the problem of sorting out the effects of the drug itself from the effects of other factors related to taking the drug. For instance, although chronic alcohol use can be associated with damage to the thalamus and limbic system, producing severe memory disorders, related complications of alcohol abuse, including vitamin deficiencies resulting from poor diet, rather than the alcohol itself, seem to cause this damage. Alcoholics typically consume insufficient amounts of thiamine (vitamin B_1), and the alcohol in their systems compounds that problem by interfering with the absorption of thiamine by the liver. Thiamine plays a vital role in maintaining cell-membrane structure.

Second, there are many reports of people who suffer some severe psychiatric disorder subsequent to the abuse of other recreational drugs. Yet determining, in most of these cases, whether the drug initiated the condition or just aggravated a previously existing problem is difficult.

Third, determining whether the drug itself or some contaminant in it might be producing a harmful outcome also is difficult. For example, in the case of Parkinson's disease described in the Portrait at the beginning of this chapter, the onset of the disease followed the use of synthetic heroin, but the disease was actually caused by a contaminant (MPTP) and not by the heroin itself.

Fourth, the use of one drug is often associated with the ingestion of other compounds. For example, there are cases of chronic use of marijuana *(Cannabis sativa)* being associated with psychotic attacks. But the marijuana plant contains at least 400 chemicals, 60 or more of which are structurally related to its active ingredient tetrahydrocannabinol. Clearly, determining whether the psychotic attacks are related to THC or to some other ingredient in marijuana is almost impossible.

Fifth, the conditions under which drugs are taken can influence their effects. For example, the strongest evidence that a recreational drug can cause brain damage comes from the study of amphetamine, methamphetamine, and the synthetic amphetamine-like drug MDMA (Ecstasy). The results of animal studies show that doses of MDMA approximating those taken by human users result in the degeneration of very fine serotonergic neuron terminals. In rodents, these terminals regrow within a few months after drug use is stopped; but, in monkeys, the terminal loss may be permanent, as shown in **Figure 7.17**.

Cognitive declines in MDMA users have been reported by J. Morton, but researchers still want to know if human use of MDMA is associated with the same loss of serotonergic terminals as that in rodents and monkeys. The results of studies with rodents show that MDMA, amphetamine, and methamphetamine also produce increases in brain temperature, which contributes to brain injury.

MDMA is likely to be taken in party-like conditions in which the setting is hot and noisy. Thus, the extent to which the drug or temperature or both produce damage is unclear. Some party goers attempt to lessen the effects of MDMA on body temperature by drinking large amounts of water, which has resulted in some deaths due to "water intoxication."

Sixth, the methods used to detect brain damage in animals are difficult to apply to humans. Phencyclidine (PCP), or "angel dust," originally developed as an anesthetic, blocks one of the glutamate receptors called the NMDA receptor. Its use as an anesthetic was discontinued after studies found that about half of treated patients displayed psychotic symptoms for as long as a week after coming out of anesthesia.

Users of PCP report perceptual changes and the slurring of speech after small doses, with high doses producing perceptual disorders and hallucinations. Some of the symptoms can last for weeks. T. Hajszan and colleagues, using the electron microscope, report decreased numbers of synapses in the rat due to PCP toxicity and propose that the method could be used as an animal model of schizophrenia.

Taken together, this evidence should not be interpreted as showing that psychoactive drugs do not directly produce brain damage in humans. Rather, it shows that any potential damaging effects of drugs are difficult to demonstrate.

Figure 7.17

Drug Damage Treatment with MDMA changes the density of serotonin axons in the neocortex of a squirrel monkey: (left) normal monkey; (right) monkey 18 months after MDMA treatment. (After McCann et al., 1997, p. 401.)

Hormones

In 1849, European scientist A. A. Berthold performed the first experiment to demonstrate the existence and function of *hormones*, chemicals released by an endocrine gland. *Endocrine glands* are cell groups in the body that secrete hormones into the bloodstream to circulate to a body target and affect it.

Berthold removed the testes of a rooster and found that the rooster no longer crowed; nor did it engage in sexual or aggressive behavior. Berthold then reimplanted one testis in the rooster's body cavity. The rooster began crowing and displaying normal sexual and aggressive behavior again. The reimplanted testis did not establish any nerve connections, and so Berthold concluded that it must release a chemical into the rooster's circulatory system to influence the animal's behavior.

That chemical, we now know, is *testosterone*, the sex hormone secreted by the testes and responsible for the distinguishing characteristics of the male. The effect that Berthold produced by reimplanting the testis can be mimicked by administering testosterone to a castrated rooster, or capon. The hormone is sufficient to make the capon look and behave like a rooster.

Hormones, like other drugs, are used to treat or prevent disease. People take synthetic hormones as a replacement therapy because of the removal of glands that produce those hormones or because of their malfunction. People also take hormones, especially sex hormones, to counteract the effects of aging, and they take them to increase physical strength and endurance and to gain an advantage in sports.

As many as 100 hormones in the human body are classified as either steroids or peptides. **Steroid hormones** are synthesized from cholesterol and are lipid (fat) soluble. Steroids diffuse away from their site of synthesis in glands, including the gonads, adrenal cortex, and thyroid, easily crossing the cell membrane. They enter target cells in the same way and act on the cells' DNA to increase or decrease the production of proteins. **Peptide hormones**, such as insulin and growth hormone, are made by cellular DNA in the same way that other proteins are made. A peptide hormone influences its target cell's activity by binding to metabotropic receptors on the cell membrane, generating a second messenger that affects the cell's physiology.

Hormones fall into one of three main groups with respect to their behavioral functions, and they may function in more than one of these groups:

1. Hormones that maintain **homeostasis**, a state of internal metabolic balance and regulation of physiological systems in an organism, form one group. (The term comes from the Greek words *homeo*, meaning "the same place," and *stasis*, meaning "standing.") Homeostatic mineralocorticoids (for example, aldosterone) control the concentration of water in blood and cells; control the levels of sodium, potassium, and calcium in the body; and promote digestive functions.

2. **Gonadal (sex) hormones** control reproductive functions. They instruct the body to develop as male (for example, testosterone) or female (for example, estrogen), influence sexual behavior and the conception of children, and, in women, control the menstrual cycle (for example, estrogen and progesterone), the birthing of babies, and the release of breast milk (for example, prolactin and oxytocin).

3. Hormones activated in physiologically or psychologically challenging events or emergencies prepare the body to cope by fighting or fleeing. **Glucocorticoids** (cortisol and corticosterone are examples), a group of steroid hormones secreted in times of stress, are important in protein and carbohydrate metabolism, controlling sugar levels in the blood and the absorption of sugars by cells.

Hierarchical Control of Hormones

Figure 7.18 shows that the control and action of hormones are organized into a hierarchy consisting of the brain, the pituitary and remaining endocrine glands, and the target cells affected by the hormones. The brain, mainly the hypothalamus, releases neurohormones that stimulate the pituitary to pump hormones into the circulatory system. The pituitary hormones, in turn, influence the endocrine glands to release appropriate hormones into the bloodstream. These hormones then act on various targets in the body, also providing feedback to the brain about the need for more or less hormone release.

Although many questions remain about how they produce complex behavior, hormones not only affect body organs but also target the brain and neurotransmitter-activating systems there. Almost every neuron in the brain contains receptors on which various hormones can act. In addition to influencing sex organs and physical appearance in a rooster, for example, testosterone may have neurotransmitter-like effects on the brain cells that it targets, especially neurons that control crowing, male sexual behavior, and aggression.

In these neurons, testosterone is transported into the cell nucleus, where it activates genes. The genes, in turn, trigger the synthesis of proteins needed for cellular processes that produce the rooster's male behaviors. Thus, the rooster receives not only a male body but a male brain as well. The diversity of testosterone's functions clarifies why the body uses hormones as messengers: their targets are so widespread that the best possible way of reaching all of them is to travel in the bloodstream, which goes everywhere in the body.

Homeostatic Hormones

The body's internal environment must remain within constant parameters in order for us to function. An appropriate balance of sugars, proteins, carbohydrates, salts, and water is required in the bloodstream, in the extracellular compartments of muscles, in the brain and other body structures, and within all cells. Homeostasis of the internal environment must be maintained regardless of a person's age, activities, or conscious state. As

1 In response to sensory stimuli and cognitive activity, the hypothalamus produces neurohormones that enter the anterior pituitary through veins and the posterior pituitary through axons.

Hypothalamus

Sensory stimuli

Pituitary gland

3 Endocrine glands release their own hormones that stimulate target organs, including the brain.

Target organs and tissues

Endocrine hormones

Target endocrine gland

2 On instructions from these releasing hormones, the pituitary sends hormones into the bloodstream to target endocrine glands.

Figure 7.18

Hormonal Hierarchy

children or adults, when we rest or engage in strenuous work or when we overeat or are hungry, to survive we need a constant internal environment.

Insulin is a homeostatic hormone. The normal concentration of glucose in the bloodstream varies between 80 and 130 milligrams per 100 milliliters of blood. One group of cells in the pancreas releases insulin, which causes blood sugar to fall by instructing the liver to start storing glucose rather than releasing it and by instructing cells to increase glucose uptake. The resulting decrease in glucose then decreases the stimulation of pancreatic cells so that they stop producing insulin.

Diabetes mellitus is caused by a failure of these pancreatic cells to secrete enough insulin. As a result, blood-sugar levels can fall (hypoglycemia) or rise (hyperglycemia). In hyperglycemia, blood-glucose levels rise because insulin does not instruct cells of the body to take up that glucose. Consequently, cell function, including neural function, can fail through glucose starvation, even in the presence of high levels of glucose in the blood. In addition, chronic high blood-glucose levels cause damage to the eyes, kidneys, nerves, heart, and blood vessels. In hypoglycemia, inappropriate diet can lead to low blood sugar, which can be so severe as to cause fainting.

Gonadal Hormones

We are prepared for our adult reproductive roles by the gonadal hormones that give us our sexual appearance, mold our identity as male or female, and allow us to engage in sex-related behaviors. Sex hormones begin to act on us even before we are born and continue their actions throughout our lives.

For males, sex hormones produce the male body and male behaviors. The Y chromosome of males contains a gene called the sex-determining region or *SRY* gene. If cells in the undifferentiated gonads of the early embryo contain an *SRY* gene, they will develop into testes and, if they do not, they will develop into ovaries.

The **organizational hypothesis** proposes that actions of hormones in the course of development alter tissue differentiation. Thus, testosterone masculinizes the brain early in life by being taken up in brain cells where it is converted into estrogen by the enzyme aromatase. Estrogen then acts on estrogen receptors to initiate a chain of events that include the activation of certain genes in the cell nucleus. These genes then contribute to the masculinization of brain cells and their interactions with other brain cells.

Hormones play a somewhat lesser role in producing the female body; but, in women, they control menstrual cycles, regulate many facets of pregnancy and birth, and stimulate milk production for breast-feeding babies. That estrogen, a hormone usually associated with the female, masculinizes the male brain might seem surprising. Estrogen does not have the same effect on the female brain, because females have a blood enzyme that binds to estrogen and prevents its entry into the brain.

Stress Hormones

Stress is a term borrowed from engineering to describe a process in which an agent exerts a force on an object. Applied to humans and other animals, a *stressor* is a stimulus that challenges the body's homeostasis and triggers arousal.

Stress responses are not only physiological but also behavioral, and they include both arousal and attempts to reduce stress. A stress response can outlast a stress-inducing incident and may even occur in the absence an obvious stressor. Living with constant stress can be debilitating.

Surprisingly, the body's response is the same whether the stressor is exciting, sad, or frightening. Robert Sapolsky (1994) uses the vivid image of a hungry lion chasing down a zebra to illustrate the stress response. The chase elicits very different reactions in the two animals, but their physiological stress responses are exactly the same.

The stress response begins when the body is subjected to a stressor, especially when the brain perceives a stressor and responds with arousal. The autonomic response consists of two sequences, one fast and the other slow.

The left side of **Figure 7.19** shows the fast response. The sympathetic division of the autonomic nervous system is activated to prepare the body and its organs for "fight or flight," and the parasympathetic division for "rest and digest" is turned off. In addition, the sympathetic division stimulates the interior medulla of the adrenal gland to release epinephrine. The epinephrine surge (often called the adrenaline surge after epinephrine's original name) prepares the body for a sudden burst of activity. Among its many functions, epinephrine stimulates cell metabolism so that the body is ready for action.

The hormone controlling the slow stress response is the steroid cortisol, a glucocorticoid released from the outer layer (cortex) of the adrenal gland, as shown on the right side of Figure 7.19. The cortisol pathway is activated more slowly, taking from minutes to hours. Cortisol has a wide range of functions, which include turning off all bodily systems not immediately required to deal with a stressor. For example, cortisol turns off insulin so that the liver starts releasing glucose, thus temporarily producing an increase in energy supply. It

Figure 7.19

Activating a Stress Response
Abbreviations: ANS, autonomic nervous system; CRF, corticotropin releasing factor; ACTH, adrenocorticotropic hormone.

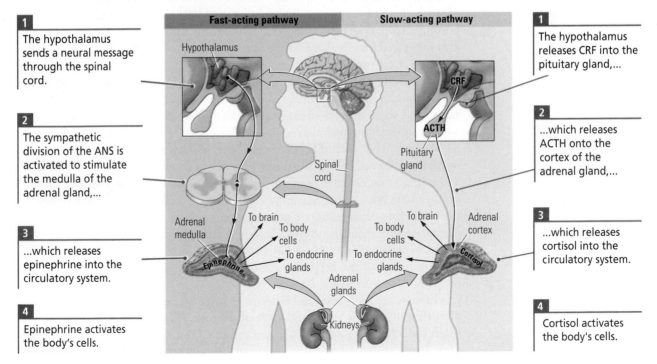

1 The hypothalamus sends a neural message through the spinal cord.

2 The sympathetic division of the ANS is activated to stimulate the medulla of the adrenal gland,...

3 ...which releases epinephrine into the circulatory system.

4 Epinephrine activates the body's cells.

1 The hypothalamus releases CRF into the pituitary gland,...

2 ...which releases ACTH onto the cortex of the adrenal gland,...

3 ...which releases cortisol into the circulatory system.

4 Cortisol activates the body's cells.

also shuts down reproductive functions and inhibits the production of growth hormone. In this way, the body's energy supplies can be concentrated on dealing with the stress.

Ending a Stress Response

Normally, stress responses are brief. The body mobilizes its resources, deals with the challenge physiologically and behaviorally, and then shuts down the stress response. Just as the brain is responsible for turning on the stress reaction, it is also responsible for turning it off. Consider what can happen if the stress response is not shut down:

- The body continues to mobilize energy at the cost of energy storage.

- Proteins are used up, resulting in muscle wasting and fatigue.

- Growth hormone is inhibited, and so the body cannot grow.

- The gastrointestinal system remains shut down, reducing the intake and processing of food to replace used resources.

- Reproductive functions are inhibited.

- The immune system is suppressed, contributing to the possibility of infection or disease.

Posttraumatic stress disorder (PTSD) is characterized by physiological arousal symptoms related to recurring memories and dreams concerning a traumatic event—for months or years after the event. People with PTSD feel as if they are reexperiencing the traumatic events, and the accompanying physiological arousal enhances their belief of impending danger.

Research has not led to a clear-cut answer to whether the cumulative effects of stress damage the human brain. Sapolsky (2003) has proposed that the hippocampus is part of a feedback system that turns off the stress response. He has also suggested that excessive stress may damage the hippocampus, leading to a runaway stress response.

To examine this idea, investigators have studied women who were sexually abused in childhood and were diagnosed as suffering from PTSD. Their results yield some reports of no changes in hippocampal volume, as measured with brain-imaging techniques, and some reports of reductions in hippocampal volume. That such different results can be obtained in what appear to be similar studies can be explained in a number of ways.

First, how much damage to the hippocampus must occur to produce a stress syndrome is not certain. Second, brain-imaging techniques may not be sensitive to subtle changes in hippocampal cell function or moderate cell loss. Third, large individual and environmental differences influence how people respond to stress. Finally, Mark Gilbertson and his colleagues propose that preexisting injury to the hippocampus or other brain regions could increase the probability of developing PTSD.

Humans are long-lived and have many life experiences that complicate simple extrapolations from a single stressful event. Nevertheless, changes to the brain induced by prolonged stress complicate the treatment of stress-related disorders and suggest that it is important to treat stress so that brain and bodily injury do not occur.

Summary

Principles of Psychopharmacology

The target of psychoactive drugs is the brain, and the dose required and the route to the brain are successively smaller if the drug is administered orally, to the lungs, into the blood stream, or directly into the brain. Major barriers to drug action include the stomach lining, dilution by the blood volume, absorption by other body cells, and the blood–brain barrier. The many routes of drug elimination include general metabolism, respiration, and elimination in feces, urine, and sweat.

Drug Actions in Synapses

Synapses play a central role in the way that drugs produce their effects on behavior. Drugs can influence any of the biochemical events pertaining to neurotransmission—synthesis of a transmitter, its release from the axon terminal, its interaction at the postsynaptic receptor, and its inactivation, reuptake, or degradation. Any modification of synaptic communication results in increased or decreased action by the transmitter. In this way, drugs can act as agonists to increase synaptic transmission or as antagonists to decrease it.

Classification of Psychoactive Drugs

Although there are an extraordinary number of psychoactive drugs, they can be classified according to the behavioral effects that they produce. Thus, drugs can act as sedative-hypnotics and antianxiety agents; as antipsychotic agents, antidepressants, and mood stabilizers; and as narcotic analgesics, stimulants, and psychedelics.

The Effects of Experience, Context, and Genes

Drugs are extremely variable in producing their effects, both with respect to different persons and with respect to the same person on different occasions. A decrease in the response to a drug with use is called tolerance, whereas an increase in response is called sensitization. Responses to drugs may be affected by a person's genetic makeup and by environmental factors including the availability of a drug and learning.

In addition to their therapeutic effects, drugs can cause addiction. The incentive-sensitization theory suggests that a liking for the effects produced by a drug develops in the initial stage of drug use, but, with repeated use, the user becomes conditioned to the cues associated with drug use; subsequent exposure to these cues then elicits a craving for the drug. Drugs can also act as neurotoxins, and some drugs that are used for recreational purposes have been implicated in producing brain injury.

Hormones

Steroid and peptide hormones are produced by endocrine glands and circulate in the bloodstream to affect a wide variety of targets. Hormones are under the hierarchical control of the brain, the pituitary gland, and the endocrine glands, which all interact to regulate hormone levels.

Homeostatic hormones regulate the balance of sugars, proteins, carbohydrates, salts, and other substances in the body. Sex hormones regulate the physical features and behaviors associated with reproduction and the care of offspring. Stress hormones regulate the body's ability to cope with arousing and challenging situations. Failures to turn stress responses off after a stressor has passed can contribute to susceptibility to posttraumatic stress disorder and other psychological and physical diseases.

References

Ballard, P. A., J. W. Tetrud, and J. W. Langston. Permanent human Parkinsonism due to 1-methyl-4-phenyl-1,2,3, 6-tetrahydropyridine (MPTP). *Neurology* 35:949–956, 1985.

Comer, R. J. *Abnormal Psychology.* New York: W. H. Freeman and Company, 2004.

Cooper, J. R., F. E. Bloom, and R. H. Roth. *The Biochemical Basis of Neuropharmacology.* New York: Oxford University Press, 2007.

Efron, D. H., Ed. *Psychopharmacology: A Review of Progress.* Washington, D. C.: U.S. Department of Health, Education, and Welfare, 1988.

Eto, K. Minamata disease: A neuropathological viewpoint. *Seishin Shinkeigaku Zasshi* 108:10–23, 2006.

Fraioli, S., H. S. Crombag, A. Badiani, and T. E. Robinson. Susceptibility to amphetamine-induced locomotor sensitization is modulated by environmental stimuli. *Neuropsychopharmacology* 20:533–541, 1999.

Gilbertson, M. W., M. E. Shenton, A. Ciszewski, K. Kasai, N. B. Lasko, S. P. Orr, and R. K. Pitman. Smaller hippocampal volume predicts pathologic vulnerability to psychological trauma. *Nature Neuroscience* 5:1242–1247, 2002.

Guindalini, C., et al. A dopamine transporter gene functional variant associated with cocaine abuse in a Brazilian sample. *Proceedings of the National Academy of Sciences* 103:4552–4557, 2006.

Hajszan, T., C. Leranth, and R. H. Roth. Subchronic phencyclidine treatment decreases the number of dendritic spine synapses in the rat prefrontal cortex. *Biological Psychiatry* 60:639–644, 2006.

Hynie, I., and E. C. D. Todd. Domoic acid toxicity. *Canada Diseases Weekly Report* 16:1–77, 1990.

Isbell, H., H. F. Fraser, R. E. Wikler, R. E. Belleville, and A. J. Eisenman. An experimental study of the etiology of "rum fits" and delirium tremens. *Quarterly Journal for Studies of Alcohol* 16:1–35, 1955.

Julien, R. M. *A Primer of Drug Action.* New York: W. H. Freeman and Company, 2004.

Kestler, L. P., E. Walker, and E. M. Vega. Dopamine receptors in the brains of schizophrenia patients: A meta-analysis of the findings. *Behavioural Pharmacology* 12:355–371, 2001.

Langston, W. J. *Case of the Frozen Addicts.* New York: Pantheon, 1995.

Liberzon, I., and K. L. Phan. Brain-imaging studies of posttraumatic stress disorder. *CNS Spectroscopy* 8:641–650, 2003.

MacAndrew, C., and R. B. Edgerton. *Drunken Comportment: A Social Explanation.* Chicago: Aldine, 1969.

MacDonald, T. K., M. P. Zanna, and G. T. Fong. Alcohol and intentions to engage in risky health-related behaviours: Experimental evidence for a casual relationship. In J. Adair and F. Craik, Eds. *Advances in Psychological Science*, vol. 2, *Developmental, Personal, and Social Aspects.* East Sussex, U. K.: Psychology Press, 1998.

McCann, U. D., K. A. Lowe, and G. A. Ricaurte. Long-lasting effects of recreational drugs of abuse on the central nervous system. *Neurologist* 3:399–411, 1997.

Monkul, E. S., J. P. Hatch, M. A. Nicoletti, S. Spence, P. Brambilla, A. L. T. Lacerda, R. B. Sassi, A. G. Mallinger, M. S. Keshavan, and J. C. Soares. Fronto-limbic brain structures in suicidal and non-suicidal female patients with major depressive disorder. *Molecular Psychiatry* 12:360–366, 2007.

Moore, D. S. *The Dependent Gene: The Fallacy of Nurture vs. Nature.* New York: Henry Holt, 2003.

Morton, J. Ecstasy: Pharmacology and neurotoxicity. *Current Opinion in Pharmacology* 5:79–86, 2005.

Olney, J. W., O. L. Ho, and V. Rhee. Cytotoxic effects of acidic and sulphur-containing amino acids on the infant mouse central nervous system. *Experimental Brain Research* 14:61–67, 1971.

Pert, C. B., M. J. Kuhar, and S. H. Snyder. Opiate receptor: Autoradiographic localization in rat brain. *Proceedings of the National Academy of Sciences of the United States of America* 73:3729–3733, 1976.

Pogarell, O., W. Koch, F. J. Gildehaus, A. Kupsch, O. Lindvall, W. H. Oertel, and K. Tatsch. Long-term assessment of striatal dopamine transporters in Parkinsonian patients with intrastriatal embryonic mesencephalic grafts. *European Journal of Nuclear Medicine and Molecular Imaging* 33:407–411, 2006.

Robinson, T. E., and J. B. Becker. Enduring changes in brain and behavior produced by chronic amphetamine administration: A review and evaluation of animal models of amphetamine psychosis. *Brain Research Reviews* 11:157–198, 1986.

Robinson, T. E., and K. C. Berridge. The neural basis of drug craving: An incentive-sensitization theory of addiction. *Brain Research Reviews* 18:247–291, 1993.

Robinson, T. E., and B. Kolb. Persistent structural adaptations in nucleus accumbens and prefrontal cortex neurons produced by prior experience with amphetamine. *Journal of Neuroscience* 17:8491–8498, 1997.

Sapolsky, R. M. *Why Zebras Don't Get Ulcers.* New York: W.H. Freeman and Company, 1994.

Sapolsky, R. M. Stress and plasticity in the limbic system. *Neurochemical Research* 28:1735–1742, 2003.

Simantov, R., and W. Peng. MDMA (Ecstasy) controls in concert a group of genes involved in GABA neurotransmission. *FEBS (Federation of European Biochemical Societies) Letters* 9:1–3, 2004.

Teitelbaum, J. S., R. J. Zatorre, S. Carpenter, D. Gendron, A. C. Evans, A. Gjedde, and N. R. Cashman. Neurologic sequelae of domoic acid intoxication due to the ingestion of contaminated mussels. *New England Journal of Medicine* 322:1781–1787, 1990.

Valenstein, E. *Blaming the Brain: The Truth about Drugs and Mental Health.* New York: New York Free Press, 1998.

Wenger, J. R., T. M. Tiffany, C. Bombardier, K. Nicholls, and S. C. Woods. Ethanol tolerance in the rat is learned. *Science* 213:575–577, 1981.

Widner, H., J. Tetrud, S. Rehngrona, B. Snow, P. Brundin, B. Gustavii, A. Bjorklund, O. Lindvall, and W. J. Langston. Bilateral fetal mesencephalic grafting in two patients with Parkinsonism induced by 1-methyl-4-phenyl-1,2,3,6 tetrahydropyradine (MPTP). *New England Journal of Medicine* 327:1551, 1992.

Whishaw, I. Q., G. Mittleman, and J. L. Evenden. Training-dependent decay in performance produced by the neuroleptic cis(Z)-Flupentixol on spatial navigation by rats in a swimming pool. *Pharmacology, Biochemistry, and Behavior* 32:211–220, 1989.

Organization of the Sensory Systems

PORTRAIT: Effects of a Sensory Loss on Movement

One day in May 1971, when he was 19, Ian Waterman cut his finger. Because he was a butcher, the event was hardly unusual. The cut became infected, however, and, over the next day or so, the redness and inflammation spread a little way up his arm. Nevertheless, Ian ignored it, and eventually the problem seemed to disappear.

Shortly afterward, Ian began to suffer alternating hot and cold spells and was very tired, to such an extent that he was forced to take time off work. One day, although tired, he attempted to mow the lawn but lost control of the mower and stood helplessly as it careened away. About a week later, after falling as he tried to get out of bed, Ian was taken to the hospital.

By this time, Ian could not move, had no sense of touch or pressure in his hands and feet (although he felt a tingling sensation in both areas), and was having trouble talking. The physicians in the hospital, who had never seen a case like Ian's, diagnosed him as having a *neuropathy* (a disorder of the peripheral nerves) and suggested that he would soon recover. Seven months later, he still had difficulty moving, and he still could not feel touch or pressure, although he was sensitive to temperature and pain.

IBM Research

Ian's mother tried to look after him at home, but he could do little for himself. Any attempt at activity exhausted him. He eventually was sent to a rehabilitation hospital where he began to learn some alternative ways of accomplishing everyday tasks.

His physicians finally concluded that Ian had lost all the fine touch and pressure fibers from the sensory nerves that provided his nervous system with information about the position of his limbs and their movements. His body was no longer aware of itself. Without this vital aspect of somatosensation, what some have called our "sixth sense," his motor system was helpless and he was unable to engage in the "melody of movement." Sensation stimulates movement, beginning in the frontal cortex with the activity of motor neurons (simulated in gold in the accompanying image).

Ian Waterman never recovered from his sensory loss, although with enormous effort he did learn to walk, to care for himself, and to drive a car. He did so by learning to replace body awareness with vision: by watching his hands as he made them perform and by watching his feet as he made them step. He was able to drive by using vision to estimate his movement speed and direction. But, if the lights went out or if his eyes were covered, he lost all ability to control the voluntary movements of his body.

Ian was eventually able to hold a job, to marry, and to enjoy life, but movement always required an enormous conscious effort of him. He describes the effects of his loss in this way:

I am trying not to sound melodramatic and I'm sorry if it does, but sometimes I wake up in the morning and the knowledge of how much mental effort I'll have to put in to get by makes me feel down. It is like having to do a marathon everyday, a daily marathon. (Cole, 1991)

W e may believe that we see, hear, touch, smell, and taste real things in a real world. In fact, the only input that our brains receive from the "real" world is a series of action potentials passed along the neurons of our various sensory pathways. Although we experience visual and body sensations as being fundamentally different from one another, the nerve impulses in the

(© Gerry Lemmo.)

neurons of these two sensory systems are very similar, as are the neurons themselves.

Neuroscientists understand how nerves can turn energy, such as light waves, into nerve impulses. They also know the pathways taken by those nerve impulses to reach the brain. But they do not know how we end up perceiving one set of nerve impulses as what the world looks like and another set as what moves us.

Ask yourself this question, "How much of what I know comes through my senses?" Taken at face value, this question seems reasonable. At the same time, we realize that our senses can deceive us—that two people can look at the same optical illusion (such as the adjoining photograph of two cheetahs) and see very different images, that a person dreaming does not normally think that the dream images are real, that you often do not think that a picture of you looks like you. Many scientists think that much of what we know comes to us through our senses, but they also think that our brains actively transform sensory information into forms that help us to adapt and are thus behaviorally useful.

This chapter presents an overview of how sensory information reaches the cortex, placing special emphasis on two features of sensory organization: (1) the presence of many submodalities in each sensory system and (2) the design of each submodality for a specific function.

General Principles of Sensory-System Function

Our sensory systems are extremely diverse, and, at first blush, vision, audition, body senses, taste, and olfaction appear to have little in common. But, although our perceptions and behavior in relation to these senses are very different, each sensory system is organized on a similar, hierarchical plan. In this section, we consider the features common to the sensory systems, including their receptors, neural relays between the receptor and the neocortex, and central representations within the neocortex.

Sensory Receptors

Sensory receptors are specialized cells that *transduce*, or convert, sensory energy (for example, light photons) into neural activity. The next six subsections deal with properties that our wide range of sensory receptors have in common, properties that allow them to provide us with a rich array of information about our world.

Receptors are Energy Filters

If we put flour into a sieve and shake it, the more finely ground particles will fall through the holes, whereas the coarser particles and lumps will not. Similarly, sensory receptors are designed to respond only to a narrow band of energy—analogous to particles of certain sizes—within each modality's energy spectrum.

Figure **8.1**

Visible Light The slice of the electromagnetic spectrum that is visible to the human eye lies within a narrow range from about 400 nanometers (violet) to 700 nanometers (red). A nanometer (nm) is one-billionth of a meter.

Figure 8.1 illustrates the entire electromagnetic spectrum, for example, and indicates the small part of it that our visual system can detect. Were our visual receptors somewhat different, we would be able to see in the ultraviolet or infrared parts of the electromagnetic spectrum, as some other animals can.

We refer to people who lack receptors for parts of the usual visual spectrum as being *color deficient* or *color-blind*. There are also differences in the visual receptors of individual people who see the usual range of color. Joris Winderickx and his colleagues report that about 60% of men have one form of the red receptor and 40% have another form. Many females may have both forms. Hence, different people may see different "reds."

For audition, the receptors of the human ear respond to sound waves between 20 and 20,000 hertz (Hz, cycles per second), but elephants can hear and produce sounds below 20 Hz, and bats can hear and produce sounds as high as 120,000 Hz. In fact, in comparison with those of other animals, human sensory abilities are rather average. Even our pet dogs have "superhuman" powers: they can detect odors that we cannot detect, they can hear the ultrasounds emitted by rodents and bats, they can hear the low-range sounds of elephants, and they can see in the dark. We can hold up only our superior color vision. Thus, for each species and individual, sensory systems filter the possible sensory world to produce an idiosyncratic representation of reality.

Receptors Transduce Energy

Each sensory system's receptors are specialized to filter a different form of energy:

- For vision, light energy is converted into chemical energy in the photoreceptors of the retina, and this chemical energy is in turn converted into action potentials.

- In the auditory system, air-pressure waves are converted into a number of forms of mechanical energy, the last of which eventually activates the auditory receptors, which then produce action potentials.

- In the somatosensory system, mechanical energy activates mechanoreceptors, cells that are sensitive, say, to touch or pain. Somatosensory receptors in turn generate action potentials.

Unlike the pyramidal motor neurons simulated on page 197, the dendrites and axons of somatosensory neurons are continuous.

Somatosensory neuron

Figure 8.2

Tactile Stimulation

- For taste and olfaction, various chemical molecules carried by the air or contained in food fit themselves into receptors of various shapes to activate action potentials.

- For pain sensation, tissue damage releases a chemical that acts like a neurotransmitter to activate pain fibers and thus produce action potentials.

Thus, each type of sensory receptor transduces the physical or chemical energy that it receives into action potentials. **Figure 8.2** illustrates how the displacement of a single hair on the arm results in an action potential that we interpret as touch. The dendrite of a somatosensory neuron is wrapped around the base of the hair. When the hair is displaced, the dendrite is stretched by the displacement.

The dendrite has Na^+ channels that are "stretch sensitive" and open in response to the stretching of the dendrite's membrane. If the influx of sodium ions in the stretch-sensitive Na^+ channels is sufficient to depolarize the dendrite to its threshold for an action potential, the voltage-sensitive K^+ and Na^+ channels will open, resulting in a nerve impulse heading to the brain.

Receptive Fields Locate Sensory Events

Every receptor organ and cell has a **receptive field**, a specific part of the world to which it responds. For example, if you fix your eyes on a point directly in front of you, what you see of the world is the scope of your eyes' receptive field. If you close one eye, the visual world shrinks, and what the remaining eye sees is the receptive field for that eye.

Within the eye is a cup-shaped retina that contains thousands of receptor cells called rods and cones. Each photoreceptor points in a slightly different direction and so has a unique receptive field. You can appreciate the conceptual utility of the receptive field by considering that the brain uses information from the receptive field of each sensory receptor not only to identify sensory information but also to contrast the information that each receptor field is providing.

For each of the sensory systems, its receptors' unique "view" of the world is its receptive field. Receptive fields not only sample sensory information but also help locate sensory events in space. Because the receptive fields of adjacent sensory receptors may overlap, their relatively different responses to events help in localizing sensations. The spatial dimensions of sensory information produce cortical patterns and maps of the sensory world that form, for each of us, our sensory reality.

Receptors Identify Change and Constancy

Each sensory system answers questions such as, Is something there? And is it still there? Sensory receptors differ in sensitivity. They may adapt rapidly or slowly to stimulation or react only to a specific type of energy.

Rapidly adapting receptors detect whether something is there. They are easy to activate but stop responding after a very short time. If you touch your arm very lightly with a finger, for example, you will immediately detect the touch, but, if you then keep your finger still, the sensation will fade as the receptors adapt. It fades because the rapidly adapting hair receptors on the skin are designed to detect the *movement* of objects on the skin.

If you push a little harder when you first touch your arm, you will feel the touch much longer because many of the body's pressure-sensitive receptors are **slowly adapting receptors** that adapt more slowly to stimulation. In the visual system, the rapidly adapting rod-shaped receptors in the eye respond to visible light of any wavelength and have lower response thresholds than do the slowly adapting cone-shaped receptors, which are sensitive to color and position. A dog, having mainly black–white vision, is thus very sensitive to moving objects but has more difficulty detecting objects when they are still.

Receptors Distinguish Self from Other

Our sensory systems are organized to tell us both what is happening in the world around us and what we ourselves are doing. Receptors that respond to external stimuli are called **exteroceptive**; receptors that respond to our own activity are called **interoceptive**. For example, objects in the world that we see, that touch us, or that are touched by us and objects that we smell or taste act on exteroceptive receptors, and we know that they are produced by an external agent.

When we move, however, we ourselves change the perceived properties of objects in the world, and we experience sensations that have little to do with the external world. When we run, visual stimuli appear to stream by us, a stimulus configuration called **optic flow**. When we move past a sound source, we hear **auditory flow**, changes in the intensity of the sound that take place because of our changing location.

Some of the information about these changes comes to us through our exteroceptive receptors, but we also learn about them from interoceptive receptors in our muscles and joints and in the vestibular organs of the inner ear. These interoceptive receptors tell us about the position and movement of our bodies, the awareness that Ian Waterman lost (see the Portrait at the beginning of this chapter).

Not only do interoceptive receptors play an important role in helping to distinguish what we ourselves do from what is done to us, they also help us to interpret the meaning of external stimuli. For example, optic or auditory flow is useful in telling us how fast we are going, whether we are going in a straight line or up or down, and whether it is we who are moving or an object in the world that is moving.

Try this experiment. Slowly move your hand back and forth before your eyes and gradually increase the speed of the movement. Your hand will eventually get a little blurry because your eye movements are not quick enough to follow its movement. Now keep your hand still and move your head back and forth. The image of the hand remains clear. When the interoceptive receptors in the inner ear inform your visual system that your head is moving, the visual system responds by compensating for the head movements, and you observe the hand as a stationary image.

Some psychological conditions appear to be characterized by difficulty in distinguishing between self and other. People who experience hallucinations perceive events that are being generated internally as coming from outside themselves. In the "checking" abnormality displayed by persons with obsessive–compulsive disorder, they seem unable to believe that an action that they have completed is actually done.

Receptor Density Determines Sensitivity

Receptor density is particularly important in determining the sensitivity of a sensory system. For example, consider the difference in sensitivity on your digit tips and on your arm. The tactile receptors on the fingers are numerous compared with those on the arm. This difference explains why the fingers can discriminate remarkably well and the arm not so well.

Two-point sensitivity

You can prove it by moving the tips of two pencils apart to different degrees as you touch different parts of your body. The ability to recognize the presence of two pencil points close together, a measure called **two-point sensitivity** or discrimination, is highest on the parts of the body having the most touch receptors.

Our sensory systems use different receptors to enhance sensitivity under different conditions. For example, the visual system uses different sets of receptors to respond to light and color. In the **fovea** (a small area of the retina where color photoreceptors are concentrated), the receptors—all cone cells—are small and densely packed to make sensitive color discriminations in bright light. In the periphery of the retina, the rod cells that are the receptors for black–white vision are larger and more scattered, but their sensitivity to light (say, a lighted match at a distance of 2 miles on a dark night) is truly remarkable.

Differences in the density of sensory receptors determine the special abilities of many animals, such as excellent olfactory ability in dogs and excellent tactile ability in the digits of raccoons. Variations in receptor density in the human auditory receptor organ may explain such abilities as perfect pitch displayed by some musicians.

Neural Relays

Inasmuch as receptors are common to each sensory system, all receptors connect to the cortex through a sequence of three or four intervening neurons. The visual and somatosensory systems have three, for example, and the auditory system has four. Information can be modified at different stages in the relay, allowing the sensory system to mediate different responses.

Neural relays also allow sensory systems to interact. There is no straight-through, point-to-point correspondence between one neural relay and the next; rather, there is a recoding of activity in each successive relay. Sensory neural relays are central to the hierarchy of motor responses in the brain.

Relays Determine the Hierarchy of Motor Responses

Some of the three to four relays in each sensory system are in the spinal cord, others are in the brainstem, and still others are in the neocortex. At each level, the relay allows a sensory system to produce relevant actions that define the hierarchy of our motor behavior. For example, the first relay for pain receptors in the spinal cord is related to reflexes that produce withdrawal movements of a body part from a painful stimulus. Thus, even after section of the spinal cord from the brain, a limb will still withdraw from a painful stimulus.

The pain pathway also has relays in the brainstem, especially in the midbrain **periaqueductal gray matter** (PAG) that surrounds the cerebral aqueduct (see Figure 3.17). This region is responsible for a number of complex responses to pain stimuli, including behavioral activation and emotional responses. Pain relays in the neocortex not only localize pain in a part of the body, but also identify the kind of pain that is felt, the external cause of the pain, and potential remedies.

Recall that the superior colliculus is a major visual center of the brainstem and the inferior colliculus is a major auditory center. In animals without a neocortex, these brainstem regions are the main perceptual systems. For animals with visual and auditory areas in the neocortex, these subcortical regions still perform their original functions of

- detecting stimuli and

- locating them in space

Message Modification Takes Place at Relays

The messages carried by sensory systems can be modified at relays. For example, descending impulses from the cortex can block or amplify pain signals at the level of the brainstem and at the level of the spinal cord. Many of us have had the experience when we are excited by an activity, as occurs when we are playing a sport, that we may not notice an injury only to find later that it is quite severe. This inhibition, or **gating**, of sensory information can be produced by descending signals from the cortex, through the periaqueductal gray matter, and on to lower sensory relays.

Descending messages from the brain gate the transmission of a pain stimulus from the spinal cord to the brain. Later, when we think about the injury, it might be much more painful because a modified descending signal from the brain now amplifies the pain signal from the spinal cord. Inhibition gates many senses when we are otherwise occupied. All of us have not "heard" something said to us or not "noticed" something that we have seen.

Relays Allow Sensory Interactions

Where relays take place in sensory pathways, systems can interact with one another. For example, we often rub the area around an injury to reduce the pain or shake a limb to reduce the sensation of pain after an injury. These actions increase the activity in fine touch and pressure pathways, and this activation can block the transmission of information in spinal-cord relays of the pain pathways. There are other examples of the modification of sensory information by competing signals from other senses that are due to similar interactions taking place at sensory relays.

A dramatic effect of sensory interaction is the visual modification of sound known as the *McGurke effect*. If a speech syllable such as "ba" is played by a recorder to a listener who at the same time is observing someone whose lips are articulating the syllable "da," the listener hears not the actual sound *ba*, but the articulated sound *da*. The viewed lip movements modify the auditory perception of the listener.

The potency of the *McGurke* effect highlights the fact that our perception of speech sounds is influenced by the facial gestures of a speaker. As described by Roy Hamilton and his coworkers, the synchrony of gestures and sounds is an important aspect of our acquisition of language. A difficulty for people learning a foreign language can be related to the difficulty that they have in blending a speaker's movements of articulation with the sounds produced by the speaker.

Central Organization of Sensory Systems

The code sent from sensory receptors through neural relays is interpreted and eventually translated into perception, memory, and action in the brain, especially in the neocortex. Much of the richness of behavior is determined by the varieties of information produced within each major sensory system. These sensory subsystems, or information channels, are preserved by multiple representations within the neocortex.

Sensory Information Is Coded

After it has been transduced, all sensory information from all sensory systems is encoded by action potentials that travel along peripheral-system nerves until they enter the brain or spinal cord and then on tracts within the central nervous system. Every bundle carries the same kind of signal. How do action potentials encode the different kinds of sensations (how does vision differ from touch), and how do they encode the features of particular sensations (how does purple differ from blue)?

Parts of these questions seem easy to answer and other parts are a fundamental challenge to neuroscience. The presence of a stimulus can be encoded by an increase or decrease in the discharge rate of a neuron, and the amount of increase or decrease can encode the stimulus intensity. Qualitative visual changes, such as from red to green, can be encoded by activity in different neurons or even by different levels of discharge in the same neuron (for example, more activity might signify redder and less activity greener).

What is less clear, however, is how we perceive such sensations as touch, sound, and smell as being different from one another. Part of the explanation is that these different sensations are processed in distinct regions of the cortex. Another part is that we learn through experience to distinguish them. A third part is that each sensory system has a preferential link with certain kinds of reflex movements, constituting a distinct wiring that helps keep each system distinct at all levels of neural organization. For example, pain stimuli produce withdrawal responses, and fine touch and pressure stimuli produce approach responses.

The distinctions between the sensory systems, however, are not always clear: some people hear in color or identify smells by how the smells sound to them. This mixing of the senses is called **synesthesia**. Anyone who has shivered when hearing certain notes of a piece of music or at the noise that chalk or fingernails can make on a blackboard has "felt" sound.

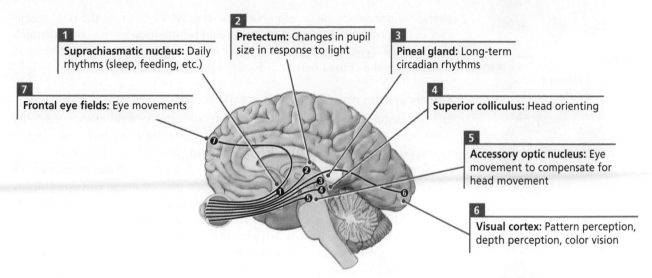

1 Suprachiasmatic nucleus: Daily rhythms (sleep, feeding, etc.)

2 Pretectum: Changes in pupil size in response to light

3 Pineal gland: Long-term circadian rhythms

7 Frontal eye fields: Eye movements

4 Superior colliculus: Head orienting

5 Accessory optic nucleus: Eye movement to compensate for head movement

6 Visual cortex: Pattern perception, depth perception, color vision

Figure **8.3**

Visual Subsystems Each pathway from eye to brain traces a visual subsystem that culminates in a visual center, numbered 1 through 7, in the brain.

Each Sensory System Is Composed of Subsystems

Within each of our five sensory systems are many subsystems, which are surprisingly independent in their functions. Neuroscientists are aware of the operation of some of these subsystems but will not know of the operation of others until the subsystems are discovered through further study of the brain. The known visual subsystems each consists of a discrete visual center in the brain, numbered 1 through 7 in **Figure 8.3**, and the pathway that connects the retina to the visual center.

The pathway from the eye to the suprachiasmatic nucleus (number 1) of the hypothalamus controls the daily rhythms of such behaviors as feeding and sleeping in response to light changes. The pathway to the pretectum (2) in the midbrain controls pupillary responses to light. The pathway to the pineal gland (3) controls long-term circadian rhythms. The pathway to the superior colliculus (4) in the midbrain controls head orientation to objects. The pathway to the accessory optic nucleus (5) moves the eyes to compensate for head movements. The pathway to the visual cortex (6) controls pattern perception, depth perception, color vision, and the tracking of moving objects. The pathway to the frontal cortex (7) controls voluntary eye movements. Many of these pathways are less direct than the illustration implies, and they may connect with other brain centers as well.

Many visual subsystems projecting into different brain regions also have submodalities of their own. In the projection to the visual cortex (number 6), for example, the systems for pattern perception, color vision, depth perception, and visual tracking are as independent from one another as the systems that encode hearing are independent from those that encode taste. The fact that they are in close anatomical proximity cannot be taken to mean that they are functionally identical or interchangeable.

Like vision, all the other sensory modalities contain subsystems that perform distinct and specific roles. One indication that taste, for example, consists of more than one modality is the existence of separate pathways for taste. The taste receptors located in the front two-thirds of the tongue send information

(A) Squirrel

(B) Cat

Arrows indicate areas hidden in sulci.

(C) Owl monkey

(D) Rhesus monkey

This drawing represents sulci pulled open to reveal visual areas.

KEY

■ Somatic cortex

■ Auditory cortex

■ Visual cortex

Figure 8.4

Multiple Representations Maps of the sensory cortex of several mammals reveal that (A) the squirrel has 5 somatic areas, 2 or 3 auditory areas, and from 2 to 4 visual areas and (B) the cat has 12 visual areas, 4 somatic areas, and 5 auditory areas. (C) The owl monkey has 14 visual areas, 4 auditory areas, and 5 somatic areas, and (D) the rhesus monkey has 12 visual areas, 4 auditory areas, and 8 somatic areas. (After Kaas, 1987.)

to the brain through the facial nerve (cranial nerve 7), whereas the taste receptors in the posterior third of the tongue send information to the brain through the glossopharyngeal nerve (cranial nerve 9). (You can review the locations and functions of the cranial nerves in Figure 3.12 and Table 3.2.)

Sensory Systems Have Multiple Representations

In most mammals, the neocortex represents the sensory field of each modality (that is, of vision, hearing, touch, smell, or taste) not once but a number of times. How many times a representation occurs depends on the species.

Note that the squirrel depicted in **Figure 8.4**A has 3 visual areas, each of which topographically represents the receptive field of the eye. **Topographic organization** is a neural–spatial representation of the body or areas of the sensory world perceived by a sensory organ. The owl monkey has 14 representations of the visual world (Figure 8.4C). If each of these visual areas responds to one feature of the environment—assuming that the visual areas of these species have been mapped adequately—then owl monkeys can "see" 11 kinds of things that squirrels cannot see. Considering that both species live in trees, have color vision, good depth perception, and so on, what those 11 things might be is not immediately obvious.

Monkeys, however, make better use of their fingers, make use of facial expressions, and have a more varied diet than squirrels do, and these differences might account for some of the monkey's additional visual areas. We humans, in turn, have many more representations than do rhesus monkeys, perhaps as many as 30, and so, we presumably perceive the visual world in ways that rhesus monkeys cannot. (Perhaps some of the additional visual areas are necessary for such cognitive tasks as reading and writing.)

All mammals have at least one primary cortical area for each sensory system. Additional areas are usually referred to as *secondary areas* because most of the information that reaches them is relayed through the primary area (see Figure 3.26). Each additional representation is probably dedicated to encoding one specific aspect of the sensory modality. Thus, for vision, different areas may take part in the perception of color, of movement, and of form.

Vision

> For I dipped into the future, far as human eye could see,
> Saw the vision of the world, and all the wonder that would be

These lines from Alfred, Lord Tennyson's poem, "Locksley Hall" illustrate that our vision is much richer than the sensory code relayed from the visual receptors in the eye to the visual regions of the brainstem and neocortex. Nevertheless, the following sections are limited to a description of the sensory receptors and pathways of the visual system. Subsequent chapters detail the perceptual and neuropsychological aspects of vision that Tennyson evokes.

Photoreceptors

A schematic representation of the eye and its visual-receptor surface, the retina, is presented in **Figure 8.5**. In Figure 8.5A, rays of light enter the eye through the cornea, which bends them slightly, and then through the lens, which bends them to a much greater degree so that the visual image is focused on the receptors at the back of the eye. The light then passes through the photoreceptors to the **sclera**, which reflects the light back into the photoreceptors.

The light's having to pass through the layer of retinal cells (to be bounced back at them by the sclera) poses little obstacle to our visual acuity for two reasons. First, the cells are quite transparent and the photoreceptors are extremely sensitive; they can be excited by the absorption of a single photon. Second, as detailed in Figure 8.5B, many of the fibers forming the optic nerve bend away from the retina's central part, or fovea, so as not to interfere with the passage of light through the retina. Because of this bending, the fovea is seen in the micrograph in Figure 8.5C as a depression on the retinal surface.

The retina contains two types of photoreceptive cells that transduce light energy into action potentials. **Rods**, which are sensitive to dim light, are used mainly for night vision. **Cones** are better able to transduce bright light and are used for daytime vision. Three types of cones, each type maximally responsive to a different set of wavelengths—either red or blue or yellow—mediate color vision.

Rods and cones differ in their distribution across the retina: cones are packed together densely in the foveal region, whereas rods are absent from the fovea entirely and more sparsely distributed in the rest of the retina. Thus, to see in bright light, acuity is best when looking directly at things and, to see in dim light, acuity is best when looking slightly away.

The photoreceptive cells synapse with a simple type of neuron called a bipolar cell and induce graded potentials in such cells. **Bipolar cells**, in turn, induce action potentials in ganglion cells. Retinal **ganglion cells** send axons into the brain proper (remember that the retina is a part of the brain).

In addition to the photoreceptive cells that relay information to the cortex, other cells in the retina—including horizontal and amacrine cells—play a role in the retina's encoding of information. One type of specialized ganglion receptor in the retina relays into the retinohypothalamic tract that connects to the suprachiasmatic nucleus—pathway 1 in Figure 8.3—which plays a role in regulating circadian rhythms.

Visual Pathways

Note in Figure 8.5B that the axons of ganglion cells leave the retina to form the optic nerve. Just before entering the brain, the two optic nerves (one from each eye) meet and form the **optic chiasm** (from the Greek letter X, or chi). At this point, about half the fibers from each eye cross as illustrated in **Figure 8.6**. So the right half of each eye's visual field is represented in the left hemisphere of the brain, and the left half of each eye's visual field is represented in the right hemisphere of the brain. In an animal with eyes on the sides of its head (the rat, for

(A) Eye

(B) Retina

(C) SEM of fovea

Figure **8.5**

Anatomy of the Eye

(Photomicrograph from Professor P. Motta, University La Sapienza, Rome/Science Photo Library/Photo Researchers.)

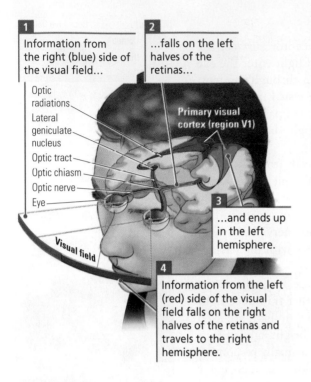

1 Information from the right (blue) side of the visual field...

Optic radiations
Lateral geniculate nucleus
Optic tract
Optic chiasm
Optic nerve
Eye

Visual field

2 ...falls on the left halves of the retinas...

Primary visual cortex (region V1)

3 ...and ends up in the left hemisphere.

4 Information from the left (red) side of the visual field falls on the right halves of the retinas and travels to the right hemisphere.

Figure 8.6

Crossing the Optic Chiasm
Horizontal view of the visual pathways from each eye to region V1 in each occipital hemisphere.

example), as many as 95% of its optic fibers cross to ensure this crossed representation of the visual fields.

Having entered the brain proper, the optic tract, still consisting of the axons of retinal ganglion cells, diverges to form two main pathways to the visual cortex. Both pathways relay through the thalamus. The larger projection synapses in the lateral geniculate nucleus (LGN) of the thalamus, on neurons that then project to the primary visual cortex, V1, as shown in Figure 8.6.

The LGN has six well-defined layers: layers 2, 3, and 5 receive fibers from the ipsilateral eye, and layers 1, 4, and 6 receive fibers from the contralateral eye. The topography of the visual field is reproduced in the LGN: the central parts of each layer represent the central visual field, and the peripheral parts represent the peripheral visual field.

The LGN cells project mainly to layer IV of the primary visual cortex. This layer is very large in primates and has the appearance of a stripe across the visual cortex; hence the name **striate** (striped) **cortex**. The striate cortex defines region V1 (Brodmann's area 17). The visual field is again topographically represented in V1, although, as illustrated in **Figure 8.7**, the cortical representation of the retinoptic map is upside down, inverted, and reversed.

The central part of the visual field is represented at the back of the visual cortex, and the peripheral part is represented toward the front of the visual cortex. The upper part of the visual field is represented below the calcarine fissure at the middle of the occipital lobe, and the lower part of the visual world is represented above the calcarine fissure. Figure 8.7 also shows that the visual input striking the left side of each retina, and therefore originating from the right side of the world, eventually travels to the left hemisphere.

The major visual pathway from the retina to the LGN to the striate cortex is the **geniculostriate pathway**, bridging the thalamus (geniculate) and the

Figure 8.7

Retinoptic Map Projection of the right visual field map (left) from a medial view of the left hemisphere (right). Note the relation between the topography of the visual field and the topography of the cortex. (After Poggio, 1968.)

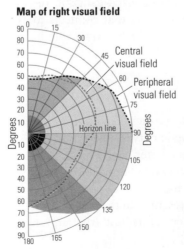

Map of right visual field

Central visual field
Peripheral visual field
Horizon line
Degrees
Degrees

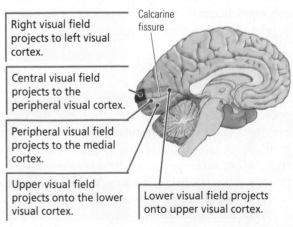

Left hemisphere, medial view

Right visual field projects to left visual cortex.

Central visual field projects to the peripheral visual cortex.

Peripheral visual field projects to the medial cortex.

Upper visual field projects onto the lower visual cortex.

Calcarine fissure

Lower visual field projects onto upper visual cortex.

Figure **8.8**

The Major Visual Pathways

striate cortex, as diagrammed at the top of **Figure 8.8**. The geniculostriate pathway takes part in pattern recognition and conscious visual functions. The second main visual pathway takes part in detecting and orienting to visual stimulation. This **tectopulvinar pathway** relays from the eye to the superior colliculus in the midbrain tectum and reaches the visual areas in the temporal and parietal lobes through relays in the lateral posterior-pulvinar complex of the thalamus, as charted at the bottom of Figure 8.8.

In fact, the tectopulvinar pathway constitutes the entire visual system in fish, amphibians, and reptiles and so is capable of sophisticated vision. Although there is likely much redundancy of function in the tectopulvinar and the geniculostriate systems, having two main visual pathways to the human neocortex lessens the chance that complete destruction of the geniculostriate pathway will render a subject completely blind.

Hearing

Hearing is the ability to construct perceptual representations from pressure waves in the air. Hearing abilities include *sound localization*—identifying the source of pressure waves—and *echo localization*—detecting pressure waves reflected from objects—as well as the ability to detect the complexity of pressure waves, through which we hear speech and music.

The auditory system is complex both because many transformations of pressure waves take place within the ear before action potentials are generated in the auditory nerve and because the auditory nerve projects to many targets in the brainstem and cortex. In this section, we describe only the major features of the auditory system.

Auditory Receptors

Sounds are changes in air-pressure waves. The frequency, amplitude, and complexity of these changes determine what we hear. We hear the frequency, or speed, of pressure changes as changes in pitch; we hear the amplitude, or intensity, of pressure changes as loudness; and we hear the complexity of pressure changes as timbre, the perceived uniqueness of a sound (**Figure 8.9**). These differences in air pressure are detected by receptor cells in the inner ear and are conveyed from there to the brain as action potentials. Areas of the cortex in the temporal lobe interpret the action potentials as sounds, language, and music.

Figure **8.9**

Breaking Down Sound Sound
waves have three physical
dimensions—frequency, amplitude,
and complexity—that correspond to
the perceptual dimensions of pitch,
loudness, and timbre.

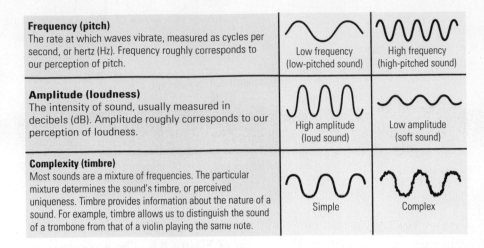

Frequency (pitch) The rate at which waves vibrate, measured as cycles per second, or hertz (Hz). Frequency roughly corresponds to our perception of pitch.	Low frequency (low-pitched sound)	High frequency (high-pitched sound)
Amplitude (loudness) The intensity of sound, usually measured in decibels (dB). Amplitude roughly corresponds to our perception of loudness.	High amplitude (loud sound)	Low amplitude (soft sound)
Complexity (timbre) Most sounds are a mixture of frequencies. The particular mixture determines the sound's timbre, or perceived uniqueness. Timbre provides information about the nature of a sound. For example, timbre allows us to distinguish the sound of a trombone from that of a violin playing the same note.	Simple	Complex

The human ear has three major anatomical divisions: outer ear, middle ear, and inner ear (**Figure 8.10**). The outer ear consists of the **pinna** and the external ear canal. The pinna catches waves of air pressure and directs them into the external ear canal, which amplifies them somewhat and directs them to the eardrum. The middle ear consists of the eardrum and, connected to it, the **hammer, anvil,** and **stirrup,** a series of three little bones (the ossicles). The ossicles in turn connect to the **oval window** of the inner ear.

When sound waves strike the eardrum, it vibrates. The vibrations are transferred to the bones, producing an action like that of a piston; this action not

Figure **8.10**

**Anatomy of the
Human Ear**

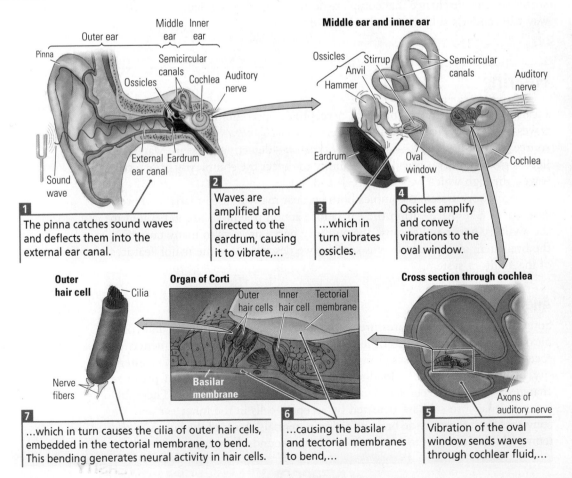

1 The pinna catches sound waves and deflects them into the external ear canal.

2 Waves are amplified and directed to the eardrum, causing it to vibrate,...

3 ...which in turn vibrates ossicles.

4 Ossicles amplify and convey vibrations to the oval window.

5 Vibration of the oval window sends waves through cochlear fluid,...

6 ...causing the basilar and tectorial membranes to bend,...

7 ...which in turn causes the cilia of outer hair cells, embedded in the tectorial membrane, to bend. This bending generates neural activity in hair cells.

only conveys the vibrations to the oval window but also amplifies them, much as a drumstick amplifies the movement of the drummer striking a drumhead. In short, pressure waves in the air are amplified and transformed a number of times in the ear: by deflection in the pinna, by oscillation as they travel through the external ear canal, and by the movement of the bones of the middle ear.

In the inner ear is the **cochlea**, which contains auditory sensory receptors called **hair cells**. The cochlea is rolled up into the shape of a snail (see Figure 8.10). It is filled with fluid, and floating in the middle of this fluid is the **basilar membrane**. The hair cells are embedded in a part of the basilar membrane called the **organ of Corti**.

When the oval window vibrates, a second membrane within the cochlea, the *round window*, bulges, sending waves through the cochlear fluid that cause the basilar membrane to bend and thus to stimulate the hair cells to produce action potentials. The larger the air-pressure changes, the more the basilar membrane bends, causing larger numbers of hair cells to generate action potentials.

The frequency of a sound is transduced by the longitudinal structure of the basilar membrane, which proves to be a sheet of tissue when the cochlea is unrolled (**Figure 8.11**A). The basilar membrane is not uniform from end to end; rather, it is narrow and thick at its base near the round window and thinner and wider at its apex. In 1960, George von Békésy found a way to observe the actual movement of a sound wave along the membrane. He placed particles of silver on the membrane and filmed them jumping to different heights in different places, depending on the sound frequency.

Higher sound frequencies cause maximum peaks near the cochlear base (that is, near the oval window), and lower sound frequencies cause maximum peaks near the apex (farthest from the oval window). These patterns are roughly analogous to what happens when you shake a towel. If you shake it very quickly, the waves are very small and remain close to the part of the towel that you are holding. But, if you shake the towel slowly with a large movement of your arms, the waves reach their peak farther away from you.

(A) Structure of basilar membrane

Basilar membrane

20,000   4,000   1,000   100
Uncoiling of cochlea (Hz)

Cochlear base

Basilar membrane

A narrow, thick base is tuned for high frequencies.

A wide, thin apex is tuned for low frequencies.

Sound waves at medium frequencies cause peak bending of the basilar membrane at this point.

(B) Tonotopic organization

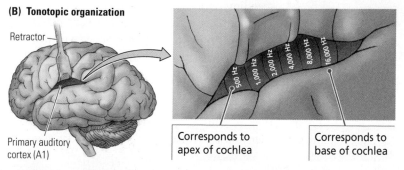

Retractor

Primary auditory cortex (A1)

500 Hz
1,000 Hz
2,000 Hz
4,000 Hz
8,000 Hz
16,000 Hz

Corresponds to apex of cochlea

Corresponds to base of cochlea

Figure 8.11

Auditory Mapping (A) Unwound cochlea shows the locations of sound-wave frequencies along the basilar membrane, measured from high to low in pitch in cycles per second, or hertz. (B) A tonotopic representation of sound-frequency transfers from the basilar membrane to the primary auditory cortex. A retractor reveals the primary auditory cortex buried within the lateral (Sylvian) fissure.

The hair cells in the organ of Corti are maximally disturbed at the point where the wave peaks, producing their maximal neural discharge at that place. A signal composed of many frequencies causes several different points along the basilar membrane to vibrate and excites hair cells at all those points.

Single-cell recordings from the primary auditory cortex in the temporal lobes show that different points in the cortex respond maximally to different frequencies, just as occurs in the basilar membrane (Figure 8.11B). Thus, the **tonotopic theory**, which states that different points on the basilar membrane represent different sound frequencies, also applies to the auditory cortex: there, too, different locations represent different sound frequencies. Presumably, projections from hair cells of the organ of Corti create a representation of the basilar membrane in the neocortex.

As in the visual system, each auditory receptor cell has a receptive field, and so does each cell in the higher auditory centers. The receptive field of a hair cell is not a point in space, as it is in the visual system, but rather a particular frequency of sound. Thus, in contrast with the retinotopic maps in the visual system, the auditory system is composed of tonotopic maps. Employing sound and echo location and comparing the time of a sound's arrival at each ear, the auditory system maps sound in space and localizes the sources of sound within the space around the body.

Auditory Pathways

The axons of hair cells leave the cochlea to form the major part of the auditory nerve, the eighth cranial nerve (**Figure 8.12**). This nerve first projects to the level of the medulla in the hindbrain, synapsing either in the dorsal or ventral cochlear nuclei or in the superior olivary nucleus. The axons of neurons in these areas form the lateral lemniscus, which terminates in discrete zones of the inferior colliculus in the midbrain. (Recall that the superior colliculus functions to orient the head toward the direction of sounds.)

Two distinct pathways emerge from the colliculus, coursing to the ventral and the dorsal medial geniculate nuclei in the thalamus. The ventral region projects to the core auditory cortex (A1 or Brodmann's area 41), and the dorsal region projects to the secondary auditory regions, thus adhering to the sensory systems' general pattern of having multiple, independent ascending pathways to the cortex.

In contrast with the visual-system pathways, the projections of the auditory system provide both ipsilateral and contralateral inputs to the cortex; so there is bilateral representation of each cochlear nucleus in both hemispheres. As described for the visual system, A1 projects to many other regions of the neocortex, forming many other tonotopic maps of the auditory system.

Figure **8.12**

Auditory Pathways Multiple nuclei process inputs en route from the cochlear nucleus to the auditory cortex. Auditory inputs cross to the hemisphere opposite the ear in the hindbrain and midbrain, then recross in the thalamus so that information from each ear reaches both hemispheres. The pathway from the ventral cochlear nucleus through the thalamus projects to auditory cortex A1 in the temporal lobes, and the dorsal projection links to A2.

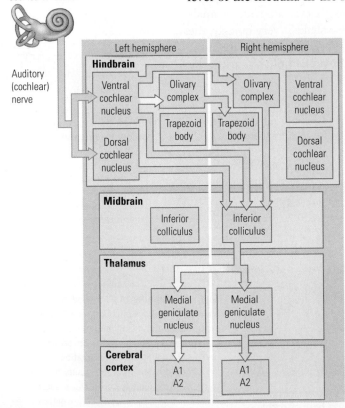

Body Senses

Both the visual and the auditory senses are exteroceptive systems because they are sensitive to stimuli from the external environment. The somatosensory system—literally, the "body awareness" system—also has an exteroceptive function: it feels the world around us. But it is also interoceptive, monitoring internal bodily events and informing the brain of the positions of body segments relative to one another and of the position of the body in space. Thus the somatosensory system, like the others, is not a single sense but rather is composed of several submodalities, even with respect to its extereoceptive and interoceptive functions.

Four major somatosensory submodalities are:

1. **nocioception**, the perception of unpleasant stimuli, particularly pain and temperature;

2. **hapsis**, the perception of objects with the use of fine touch and pressure receptors;

3. **proprioception**, or body sense, the sense that Ian Waterman lost, as described in the Portrait at the beginning of this chapter; and

4. **balance**, which is mediated by a specialized receptor system in the inner ear.

The various receptors that mediate sensation in submodalities 1 through 3 are detailed in **Figure 8.13**.

Figure 8.13

Somatosensory Receptors The perceptions derived from the body-sense submodalities attuned to unpleasant stimuli, to touch, and to body awareness depend on different receptors located variously in skin, muscles, joints, and tendons.

Hair

Nocioception (pain and temperature)	Response	Stimulus
Free nerve endings for pain (sharp pain and dull pain)	Slow	Damage to the dendrite or to surrounding cells
Free nerve endings for temperature (heat or coldness)	Slow	

Hapsis (fine touch and pressure)	Response	Stimulus
Meissner's corpuscle (touch)	Rapid	
Pacinian corpuscle (flutter)	Rapid	
Ruffini corpuscle (vibration)	Rapid	Pressure
Merkel's receptor (steady skin indentation)	Slow	
Hair receptors (flutter or steady skin indentation)	Slow	

Proprioception (body awareness)	Response	Stimulus
Muscle spindles (muscle stretch)	Rapid	Movement stretching the receptors
Golgi tendon organs (tendon stretch)	Rapid	
Joint receptors (joint movement)	Rapid	

Somatosensory Pathways

Two major somatosensory pathways extend from the spinal cord to the brain: a dorsal tract for hapsis and proprioception and a ventral tract for nocioception (**Figure 8.14**). The fibers of the somatosensory neurons that make up the hapsis and proprioception system are relatively large and heavily myelinated. Their cell bodies are located in the dorsal-root ganglia, their dendrites project to the sensory receptors in the body, and their axons project into the spinal cord (recall Figure 3.11).

Recall that the dendrite and axon of each somatosensory neuron are joined into one continuous nerve fiber. In the spinal cord, the axons of this system ascend through the dorsal column to synapse in the dorsal-column nuclei in the base of the brainstem. The cell bodies of these nuclei send their axons across the spinal cord to form the medial lemniscus, which ascends to synapse in the ventrolateral thalamus. This thalamic nucleus then projects to the primary somatosensory cortex (SI, or Brodmann's area 3-1-2), as well as to area 4, the primary motor cortex.

The fibers of the pathway for pain and temperature sensations are somewhat smaller and less myelinated than those of the hapsis and proprioception pathway. They follow the same course to enter the spinal cord but, once there, project to neurons in the more central region of the spinal cord, the substantia gelatinosa. The second-relay cells then send their axons across to the other side of the cord, where they form the ventral spinothalamic tract.

These ventral fibers eventually join the dorsal touch and proprioception fibers in the medial lemniscus. They, too, terminate primarily in the ventrolateral thal-

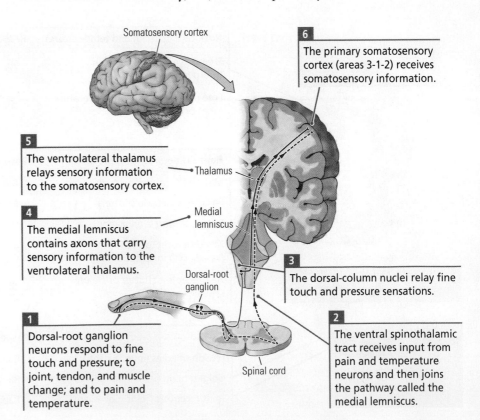

Somatosensory cortex

6 The primary somatosensory cortex (areas 3-1-2) receives somatosensory information.

5 The ventrolateral thalamus relays sensory information to the somatosensory cortex.

Thalamus

4 The medial lemniscus contains axons that carry sensory information to the ventrolateral thalamus.

Medial lemniscus

Dorsal-root ganglion

3 The dorsal-column nuclei relay fine touch and pressure sensations.

1 Dorsal-root ganglion neurons respond to fine touch and pressure; to joint, tendon, and muscle change; and to pain and temperature.

Spinal cord

2 The ventral spinothalamic tract receives input from pain and temperature neurons and then joins the pathway called the medial lemniscus.

Figure 8.14

Somatosensory Pathways As neurons from the dorsal-root ganglia enter the spinal cord, the somatosensory pathways to the brain diverge.

Figure 8.15

Two Models of Somatosensory Homunculi

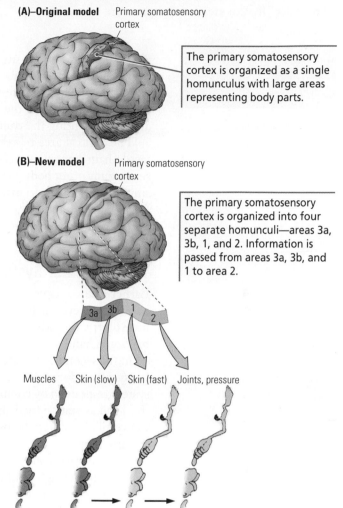

(A)–Original model

Primary somatosensory cortex

The primary somatosensory cortex is organized as a single homunculus with large areas representing body parts.

(B)–New model

Primary somatosensory cortex

The primary somatosensory cortex is organized into four separate homunculi—areas 3a, 3b, 1, and 2. Information is passed from areas 3a, 3b, and 1 to area 2.

| 3a | 3b | 1 | 2 |

Muscles   Skin (slow)   Skin (fast)   Joints, pressure

amus, as well as in the posterior thalamus; and these messages, too, are relayed in turn to area 3-1-2 of the cortex. As for vision and hearing, we see two somatosensory pathways, each taking a somewhat different route to the brain and somatosensory cortex of the opposite hemisphere.

Somatosensory Cortex

When Wilder Penfield first stimulated the sensory cortex in conscious epilepsy patients and had them report the sensations that they felt, he created a map that topographically represented the body surface on the primary somatosensory cortex, SI. The regions representing feeling in the mouth and eyes were in the ventral part of SI, the regions representing hand and finger sensation were in the middle, and the regions corresponding to feet were in the dorsal area (**Figure 8.15**A). The map is called a **homunculus**, meaning "little human," on which the relative sensitivity of body parts are represented by size. The homunculus is represented in three dimensions in **Figure 8.16**.

Like other sensory systems in the cortex, the somatosensory cortex is composed of a primary area and a number of secondary areas. As illustrated in Figure 8.15B, SI (Brodmann's area 3-1-2) is the primary area, and it sends projections into SII and Broadmann's areas 5 and 7. Area SI also sends projections into the adjacent primary motor cortex, Broadman's area 4.

Studies subsequent to those of Penfield mainly used monkeys and took advantage of smaller recording electrodes. The results suggest that the primary somatosensory cortex contains a number of homunculi, one for each of its four known subregions, 3a, 3b, 1, and 2, as elaborated in the lower part of Figure 8.15B. The results of recording experiments show that each of these areas is dominated by responses to one type of body receptor, although there is overlap. Area 3a represents muscle sense (position and movement of muscles), area 3b represents both slowly and rapidly adapting skin receptors, area 1 represents rapidly adapting skin receptors, and area 2 represents deep pressure and joint sensation.

Thus, the body is represented at least four times in SI. Additionally, a number of other receptor types are represented in each area; so it is possible that there are still more body-representation areas.

Although Penfield underestimated the number of homunculi, he was correct about the disproportionate sizes of some parts of the homunculi relative

Figure 8.16

Homuncular Man The sculpture represents the relative sensitivity of body parts by size. (The British Museum, Natural History.)

to other parts. The density of somatosensory receptors varies greatly from one place to another on the body surface (and varies from species to species), and somatotopic maps manifest this variability. Thus, in the human homunculus, the areas representing the hands and tongue are extremely large, whereas the areas representing the trunk and legs are small.

The coritcal area representing the face of the rat, including input from the tactile hairs known as vibrissae on its face, is very large relative to that representing any other body part. The face and vibrissae of the rat are extremely sensitive, enabling rats to make tactile discriminations with only a single vibrissa. In contrast, an anteater, which uses its tongue to explore for ants, should have a truly impressive tongue representation on its sensory cortex.

The Vestibular System: Motion and Balance

Earlier in the chapter, you observed your hand moving slowly back and forth before your eyes at first and eventually shaking quickly. Your hand became a little blurry. But, when you held your hand still and moved your head back and forth, the hand remained clear.

In the second observation, interoceptive receptors in the inner-ear **vestibular system** informed your visual system that your head was moving. The visual system responded by compensating for the head movements, and you observed the hand as stationary. Like other submodalites of the somatosensory system, the vestibular system helps us to distinguish among our own behavior and the actions of others.

The inner ear contains the organs that allow us to perceive our own motion and to stand upright without losing our balance. Named for an entranceway, the vestibular organs contain hair cells that bend when the body moves forward or when the head changes position relative to the body. Shown in **Figure 8.17**, the three *semicircular canals* are oriented in the three planes that correspond to the three dimensions in which we move and so can respond to any movement of the head. The *otolith organs* detect linear acceleration of the head and are responsive to changes in the position of the head with respect to gravity as well. In addition, the otoliths are sensitive to the static position of the head in space, in contrast with the semicircular canals' sensitivity to head movement.

Fibers from the balance receptors project over the eighth cranial nerve to a number of nuclei in the brainstem. These nuclei interact in the hindbrain to help keep us balanced while we move; they also aid in controlling eye move-

Figure 8.17

Vestibular System The vestibular organs in each inner ear contain hair cells sensitive to the movement of the head and to gravity.

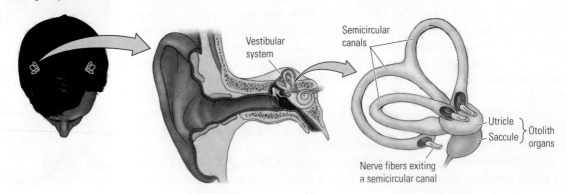

ments at the midbrain level. Ultimately, information from the vestibular system allows us to record and replay the movements that we have made through connections in the cerebellum.

Taste and Smell

Unlike carnivores and rodents, primates have a reputation for relatively vestigal gustatory and olfactory systems compared with their well-developed visual system. Dolphins and other whales also are mammals in which the olfactory system has become reduced in size or even absent. Nevertheless, taste and smell are sophisticated senses in humans and do have a representation in the neocortex, as imaged in the Snapshot on page 218.

The Chemical Receptors

All the senses described so far use various forms of physical energy, such as light and air pressure, as stimuli. The stimuli for taste and smell sensations are chemical. Specialized receptors have evolved for each system, as for all the others.

Taste Receptors

For taste, the receptors are the taste buds, which most people mistakenly believe to be the bumps on the tongue. In fact, the bumps, called *papillae*, are probably there to help the tongue grasp food; the taste buds lie buried around them (**Figure 8.18**). Chemicals in food dissolve in the saliva that coats the tongue and disperse through the saliva to reach the taste receptors. Thus, if the tongue is dry, the taste buds receive few chemical signals, and food is difficult to taste.

Each of the four main taste-receptor types responds to a different chemical component of food. The four most familiar are sweet, sour, salty, and bitter. The specificity of any given taste receptor is not absolute, however; single fibers can respond to a variety of chemical stimuli. The perceived taste of any stimulus therefore seems likely to result from a pattern of firing of the entire population of taste receptors.

Curiously, significant differences in taste preferences exist both within and between species. Humans and rats like sucrose and saccharin solutions, but dogs reject saccharin and cats are indifferent to both. Similarly, within the human species, there are clear individual differences in taste thresholds. Older people generally have higher thresholds, largely because there is a dramatic reduction in the number of taste buds as we age. Children tolerate spicy foods poorly because their sense of taste is stronger. And, as Linda Bartoshuk has shown, some people perceive certain tastes as being strong and offensive, whereas other people are indifferent to them.

Smell Receptors

The receptor surface for olfaction is the olfactory epithelium, which is located in the nasal cavity and composed of three cell types: receptor hair cells and supporting cells on an underlying

Figure **8.18**

Anatomy of a Taste Bud
(Adapted from Smith and Shepherd, 2003, p. 720.)

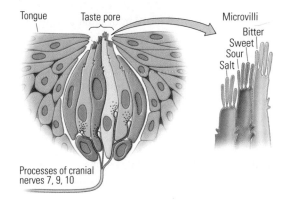

SNAPSHOT
Watching the Brain Make Flavor

After falling from a horse while riding in the mountains of Iran, J.H. required surgery to remove a blood clot from her right frontal cortex. She recovered quickly from her accident and the surgery but experienced a lingering disability from the accident: she no longer enjoyed food. Although she had always enjoyed cooking and took pride in her expertise in preparing food from many regions of the world, hardly a meal now went by when she did not complain that she wished she could taste what she was eating.

Flavor, our sense of the taste of food, is a marriage of stimuli from the tongue and the nose. Where in the brain does this union of senses take place? Imaging methods are helping researchers to answer this question.

To image the effects of odors and tastes, researchers must first eliminate from the imaging record the effects of the movement of air through the nostrils and the movements of the tongue and mouth. The separation of "sniffing" from "smelling" can be accomplished in part by having subjects sample air on control trials or by anesthetizing the nostrils so that the movement of air is not perceived. The usual "sip and spit" method employed in laboratory taste tests cannot be used, because the movements of the mouth produce movement artifacts that interfere with recording the brain image. Special delivery techniques that use droppers or even the electrical stimulation of taste buds can partly circumvent the problem.

A review of various imaging studies suggests that the orbitofrontal cortex, especially the right orbitofrontal cortex, plays a special role in the perception of odors and taste (Zatorre and Jones-Gotman, 2000). The adjoining illustration, for example, presents the results of a number of independent studies (including studies on odor recognition, odor intensity, and the connection between odor and affect, or mood) in which PET or MRI was used to record responses to olfactory stimuli. The location of brain activity recorded in each study is represented by plus signs.

These summaries of olfactory and taste research suggest that the union of olfaction and taste to produce flavor is likely to take place in the orbitofrontal cortex. Interestingly, perceptions of odors are affected by body posture, and so a prone posture during imaging may distort smell perception somewhat (Lundstrom et al., 2006).

Although no PET or MRI studies have been directed specifically at the perception of flavor, the results of single-cell

(A) Olfactory stimuli   **(B) Taste stimuli**

Left hemisphere   Right hemisphere   Left hemisphere   Right hemisphere

Activity relating to taste and smell is concentrated in the orbitofrontal cortex.

Horizontal sections of the brain, shown in ventral view, illustrate the locations of responses to (A) olfactory stimuli in six different studies and (B) taste stimuli in four different studies. (From Zatorre and Jones-Gotman, 2000.)

recording studies have been helpful in determining where flavor perception takes place. Edmund Rolls (1998), recording the activity of neurons in the orbitofrontal cortex of the rhesus monkey, found that some neurons respond to taste stimuli, others to olfactory stimuli, and still others to both olfaction and taste. Rolls suggested that the third group are flavor neurons that participate in learning to discriminate among flavors, to associate flavor with the visual images of foods that might have a flavor, and in learning that some flavors are pleasant and reinforcing, whereas others are not.

Rolls, E. T. The orbitofrontal cortex. In A. C. Roberts, T. W. Robbins, and L. Weiskrantz, Eds. *The Prefrontal Cortex.* Oxford: Oxford University Press, 1998, pp. 67–86.

Zatorre, R. J., and M. Jones-Gotman. Functional imaging in the chemical senses. In A. W. Toga and J. C. Mazziota, Eds. *Brain Mapping: The Applications.* San Diego: Academic Press, 2000, pp. 403–424.

Lundstrom, J. N., J.A. Boyle, and M. Jones-Gotman. Sit up and smell the roses better: Olfactory sensitivity to phenyl ethyl alcohol is dependent on body position. *Chemical Senses* 31:249–252, 2006.

Figure **8.19**

Olfactory Epithelium

layer of basal cells (**Figure 8.19**). The axons projecting from the olfactory receptors relay onto the ball-like tufted dendrites of glomeruli in the olfactory bulb. From the glomeruli, mitral cells form the olfactory tract (cranial nerve 1). The mitral-cell projection reaches the pyriform cortex and, from there, reaches the hypothalamus, the amygdala, the entorhinal cortex of the temporal lobe, and the orbitofrontal region of the neocortex.

The epithelium's outer surface is covered by a layer of mucus in which the receptor cell's cilia are embedded. Thus, odors must pass through the mucus to reach the receptors, which means that changes in the properties of the mucus (such as occur when we have a cold) may influence how easily an odor can be detected.

It is interesting to note the extent to which the area of the olfactory epithelium varies across species. In humans, the area is estimated to range from 2 to 4 cm^2; in dogs, the area is about 18 cm^2; and, in cats, it is about 21 cm^2. Such differences support the observation that some species are more sensitive to odors than others.

Linda Buck and Richard Axel have described the very large family of about 1,000 genes that give rise to an equivalent number of odorant receptor types. Each receptor type is located on one receptor cell and is sensitive to only a few odors. Receptors of like types project to one of the 2,000 glomeruli, and the pattern of activation produced to the glomeruli cells allows us to distinguish as many as 10,000 odors. It is the summed action of many chemical receptors, leading to a particular mosaic of neural activity, that the olfactory system identifies as a particular odor.

Taste and Smell Pathways

The chemical senses, like all the other senses, employ dual pathways to primary and secondary areas in the cortex.

Figure 8.20

Gustatory Pathways

Gustatory Pathways

Three cranial nerves carry information from the tongue: the glossopharyngeal nerve (9), the vagus nerve (10), and the chorda tympani branch of the facial nerve (7). All three nerves enter the solitary tract, the main gustatory tract. At that point, as illustrated in **Figure 8.20**, the pathway divides into two routes. One route, shown in red in Figure 8.20, goes to the ventroposterior medial nucleus of the thalamus, which in turn sends out two pathways, one to SI and the other to a region just rostral to SII, in the insular cortex. The latter region is probably dedicated entirely to taste, because it is not responsive to tactile stimulation.

In contrast, the SI projection is sensitive to tactile stimuli and is probably responsible for the localization of tastes on the tongue. (Those who enjoy wine are familiar with this distinction because wines are described not only by their gustatory qualities but also by the way that they taste on different parts of the tongue.) These areas project in turn to the orbitofrontal cortex, in a region near the input of the olfactory cortex, which may be the secondary taste area.

The other route (shown in blue in Figure 8.20) from the solitary tract leads to the pontine taste area, which in turn projects to the lateral hypothalamus and amygdala. Both areas have roles in feeding, although the gustatory input's precise contribution to this behavior is uncertain.

Olfactory Pathways

The axons of the olfactory-receptor relays synapse in the olfactory bulb, which is made up of several layers and may be conceptualized as an analogue to the retina. The major output of the bulb is the lateral olfactory tract, which passes ipsilaterally to the pyriform cortex, the amygdala, and the entorhinal cortex (**Figure 8.21**). The primary projection of the pyriform cortex goes to the central part of the dorsomedial nucleus of the thalamus, which in turn projects to the orbitofrontal cortex. Thus, the orbitofrontal cortex can be considered the primary olfactory neocortex.

Figure 8.21

Olfactory Pathways

Perception

We have reviewed the basic organization of the sensory systems, traced their neural pathways from the receptors to the cortex, and identified some principles governing their operation and integration. But there is far more to sensation than the simple transduction of physical or chemical energy into nervous activity. When compared with the richness of actual sensation, this chapter's description of sensory neuroanatomy and function is bound to seem rather sterile.

Part of the reason for the disparity is that our sensory impressions are affected by the contexts in which they take place, by our emotional states, and by our past experiences. All these factors contribute to **perception**, the subjective experience of the transduction events outlined in this chapter. Perception, rather than sensation, is of most interest to neuropsychologists.

(A) Ambiguous reversible figure

(B) Müller–Lyer illusion

Figure 8.22

Perceptual Illusions (A) Edgar Rubin's ambiguous or reversible image can be perceived as a vase or as two faces. (B) In the Müller–Lyer illusion, the top line appears longer than the bottom line because of the contextual cues provided by the arrowheads.

As clear proof that perception is more than sensation, consider that different people transform the same sensory stimulation into totally different perceptions. The classic demonstration is an ambiguous image such as the well-known Rubin's vase shown in **Figure 8.22**A. This image may be perceived either as a vase or as two faces. If you fix your eyes on the center of the picture, the two perceptions will alternate, even though the sensory stimulation remains constant.

Perceptions are affected by the context of the sensory input. The Müller–Lyer illusion in Figure 8.22B demonstrates the influence of context. The top line is perceived as longer than the bottom line, although both are exactly the same length. The contextual cues (the arrowheads) alter the perception of each line's length.

Such ambiguous images and illusions demonstrate the workings of complex perceptual phenomena that are mediated by the neocortex. Perception is an enlightening source of insight into cognitive processes.

Summary

Each of the five major senses has different receptors, pathways, and brain targets and comprises many submodalities within it.

General Principles of Sensory-System Function

Receptors are energy filters that transduce incoming physical energy and identify change and constancy in the energy. Neural receptive fields locate sensory events, and receptor density determines sensitivity to sensory stimulation. Neural relays between sensory receptors and the brain modify messages and allow the senses to interact. Any sensory information that converges does so in higher cortical areas.

At the same time, the primary brain targets for different modalities and submodalities are discrete. Some sensory systems have both exteroceptive and interoceptive receptors, which respond to stimuli outside and within the body, respectively. This division no doubt helps us to distinguish "self" from "other," as well as to interpret the stimuli themselves.

The Sensory Code

The sensory systems all use a common code, sending information to the brain in the currency of action potentials. We distinguish one sensory modality from another by the source of the stimulation, its target in the brain, and by reflexes and movements made in relation to the stimulation.

Sensory Receptors and Pathways
The anatomical organization is similar for each sense in that each has many receptors, sends information to the cortex through a sequence of three or four neuron relays, and diverges into more than one pathway through the brain. In addition, although each sensory modality has a primary cortical target, such as area 17 (V1) for vision, each modality also has a number of other brain targets. For all sensory systems, the primary cortical area projects to a number of secondary areas, and, in these areas, sensory information is recoded in more-complex ways.

Perception
The function of the sensory systems is to allow animals, including ourselves, to engage in adaptive behavior, and so it is not surprising that animals adapted to different environments vary widely in their sensory abilities. Primates and humans in particular are considered to have well-developed visual systems. What is perhaps more distinctive about humans is the extent to which sensory information is transformed into perceptual information to mediate many aspects of language, music, and culture.

References

Bartoshuk, L. M. Gustatory system. In R. B. Masterton, Ed. *Handbook of Behavioral Neurobiology*, vol. 1. New York: Plenum, 1978.

Bloom, F. E., and A. Lazerson. *Brain, Mind, and Behavior*. New York: W. H. Freeman and Company, 1988.

Buck, L., and R. Axel. A novel multigene family may encode odorant receptors: A molecular basis for odor recognition. *Cell* 65:175–187, 1991.

Cole, J. *Pride and a Daily Marathon*. London: MIT Press, 1991.

Galaburda, A., and F. Sanides. Cytoarchitectonic organization of the human auditory cortex. *Journal of Comparative Neurology* 190:597–610, 1980.

Hamilton, R. H., J. T. Shenton, and H. B. Coslett. An acquired deficit of audiovisual speech processing. *Brain and Language* 98:66–73, 2006.

Imig, T. J., M. A. Ruggero, L. M. Kitzes, E. Javel, and J. F. Brugge. Organization of auditory cortex in the owl monkey *(Aotus trivirgatus)*. *Journal of Comparative Neurology* 171:111–128, 1977.

Kaas, J. H. The organization and evolution of neocortex. In S. P. Wise, Ed. *Higher Brain Functions*. New York: Wiley, 1987.

Kandel, E. R., J. H. Schwartz, and T. M. Jessell. *Principles of Neural Science*. New York: Elsevier, 2000.

Lashley, K. S. The mechanisms of vision XVI: The functioning of small remnants of the visual cortex. *Journal of Comparative Neurology* 70:45–67, 1939.

Livingston, M., and D. Hubel. Segregation of form, color, movement and depth: Anatomy, physiology, and perception. *Science* 240:740–749, 1988.

Masterton, R. B., Ed. *Handbook of Behavioral Neurobiology*, vol. 1. New York: Plenum, 1978.

Merzenich, M. M., and J. F. Brugge. Representation of the cochlear partition on the superior temporal plane of the macaque monkey. *Brain Research* 50:276–296, 1973.

Poggio, G. F. Central neural mechanisms in vision. In V. B. Mountcastle, Ed. *Medical Physiology*. St Louis: Mosby, 1968.

von Békésy, G. *Experiments in Hearing*. Toronto: McGraw-Hill, 1960.

Winderickx, J., D. T. Lindsey, E. Sanocki, D. Y. Teller, B. G. Motulsky, and S. S. Deeb. Polymorphism in red photopigment underlies variation in color matching. *Nature* 356:431–433, 1992.

Wolfe, J. M., K. R. Kluender, D. M. Levi, L. M. Bartoshuk, R. S. Herz, R. L. Klatzky, and S. J. Lederman. *Sensation and Perception*. New York: Sinauer, 2006.

Organization of the Motor System

PORTRAIT: Spinal-Cord Injury

In 1995, Christopher Reeve, a well-known actor who portrayed Superman in film, was thrown from his horse at the third jump of a riding competition. Reeve's spinal cord was severed at the C1–C2 level, near the upper end of the vertebral column (see Figure 3.10). The injury left his brain and the remainder of his spinal cord intact and functioning, but his brain and spinal cord were no longer connected. Reeve's body below the neck was paralyzed.

A few decades ago, such a severe injury would have been fatal. Modern and timely medical treatment allowed Christopher Reeve to survive until he succumbed to an infection on October 10, 2004. Even though paralyzed, Reeve campaigned energetically on behalf of the disabled, fighting to prevent the imposition of lifetime caps on compensation for spinal-cord injuries and raising money for spinal-cord research through the Christopher Reeve Paralysis Foundation.

He was optimistic about research, knowing that, if even just a few fibers

Photofest

Peter Morgan/Reuters/Corbis

between the brain and the spinal cord can be reestablished after the spinal cord has been severed, the result will be enormously beneficial. As he documents in *Nothing Is Impossible*, written just before his death, Reeve continued to make a remarkable recovery, facilitated by an intense exercise program and some remaining fibers, confirmed by MRI, that bypassed the injury. The photographs show Reeve in the 1980 film *Superman II* and, in 2002, with his wife Dana.

Reeve learned to wiggle his toes on both feet, move the fingers of his left hand, raise his right hand, and distinguish between hot and cold and sharp and dull sensations over his body. With the assistance of aquatherapy, he regained the ability to kick his legs and make his way across the pool. His success in developing intense physical therapy regimens made Reeve an advocate of activity-dependent training for people with nervous system injury.

From one point of view, we can consider the entire nervous system to be the motor system: it functions to move the body. **Figure 9.1**A shows the steps by which the human nervous system directs a hand to pick up a coffee cup. The visual system must first inspect the cup to determine what part of it should be grasped. This information is then relayed from the visual cortex to corticomotor regions, which plan and initiate the movement, sending instructions to the part of the spinal cord that controls the muscles of the arm and hand.

As the handle of the cup is grasped, information from sensory receptors in the fingers travels to the spinal cord; and, from the spinal cord, messages are

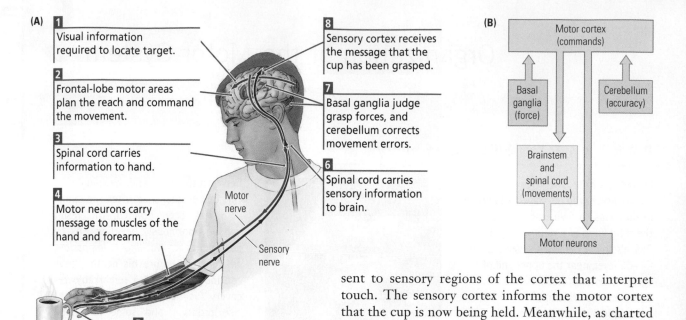

(A)

1 Visual information required to locate target.

2 Frontal-lobe motor areas plan the reach and command the movement.

3 Spinal cord carries information to hand.

4 Motor neurons carry message to muscles of the hand and forearm.

8 Sensory cortex receives the message that the cup has been grasped.

7 Basal ganglia judge grasp forces, and cerebellum corrects movement errors.

6 Spinal cord carries sensory information to brain.

Motor nerve

Sensory nerve

5 Sensory receptors on the fingers send message to sensory cortex saying that the cup has been grasped.

(B)

Motor cortex (commands)

Basal ganglia (force)

Cerebellum (accuracy)

Brainstem and spinal cord (movements)

Motor neurons

Figure 9.1

The Motor System (A) Movements such as reaching for a cup require the participation of many nervous system components. (B) Major regions of the motor system that participate in all movements.

sent to sensory regions of the cortex that interpret touch. The sensory cortex informs the motor cortex that the cup is now being held. Meanwhile, as charted in Figure 9.1B, other regions of the central nervous system have been modulating and adjusting the movement. The basal ganglia (the collection of nuclei and tracts that lie beneath the frontal cortex) help to produce the appropriate amount of force, and the cerebellum at the base of the brain helps to regulate timing and corrects any errors as the movement takes place.

Thus, most of the nervous system participates in motor control of what is a fairly simple motor act. Nevertheless, the term *motor system* is usually reserved for those parts of the nervous system charted in Figure 9.1B that most directly take part in producing movement and for the neural circuits of the spinal cord that issue commands to muscles through the peripheral nerves. In this chapter, we consider how the brain and spinal cord work together to produce movement, and we explore the contributions of the neocortex, brainstem, basal ganglia, and cerebellum.

The Neocortex and the Initiation of Movement

Four general regions of the neocortex produce our skilled movements. As diagrammed in **Figure 9.2**, these regions are the **posterior cortex**; the **prefrontal cortex**; the **premotor cortex** (Brodmann's area 6, which includes a ventral region and a dorsal region called the *supplementary motor cortex*); and the **primary motor cortex** (M1, or Brodmann's area 4). The function of each region and their interactions are as follows:

1. The posterior sensory regions of the cortex specify movement goals and send information to the prefrontal cortex by a number of routes. More-direct routes are used to prompt M1 to execute relatively automatic movements. Indirect routes through the temporal cortex are used for movements requiring conscious control.

2. Instructions travel from the prefrontal cortex, which generates plans for movements, to the premotor cortex to the primary motor cortex.

3. The premotor cortex contain a repertoire of movements—a lexicon—that allows it to recognize the movement of others and select similar or different actions.

4. The lexicon of the primary motor cortex consists of movements that are somewhat more elementary than those of the premotor cortex.

Thus, in general, the goal for movement arises in the posterior cortex, the planning of movement takes place in the prefrontal cortex, and the motor cortex executes the appropriate movements. In an exemplar experiment, Per E. Roland's use of cerebral blood flow (which, as we have seen, serves as an indicator of neural activity) illustrates this theory of neocortical motor control. **Figure 9.3** shows the regions of the brain that were active when subjects in one such study were performing different tasks.

When a subject is tapping a finger, increases in blood flow are limited to the primary somatosensory and motor cortex (Figure 9.3A). When the subject is executing a sequence of finger movements, the blood flow increases in the premotor motor cortex as well (Figure 9.3B). And, when the subject is using a finger to navigate a drawing of a maze—a task that requires coordinated movements in pursuit of a goal as well as specific movements corresponding to the shape of the maze—blood flow increases in the prefrontal cortex and regions of the parietal and temporal cortex, too (Figure 9.3C).

Notice that blood flow does not increase throughout the entire neocortex during the performance of these motor tasks. Relative increases in blood flow occur only in the regions contributing to the particular movements.

3 Premotor cortex organizes movement sequences.

4 Motor cortex produces specific movements.

2 Prefrontal cortex plans movements.

1 Posterior cortex provides sensory information to the frontal cortex.

Posterior sensory cortex sends goals. → Prefrontal cortex plans. → Premotor cortex sequences. → Motor cortex executes actions.

Figure 9.2

Initiating a Motor Sequence

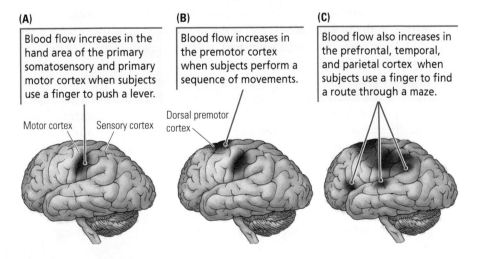

(A) Blood flow increases in the hand area of the primary somatosensory and primary motor cortex when subjects use a finger to push a lever.

Motor cortex   Sensory cortex

(B) Blood flow increases in the premotor cortex when subjects perform a sequence of movements.

Dorsal premotor cortex

(C) Blood flow also increases in the prefrontal, temporal, and parietal cortex when subjects use a finger to find a route through a maze.

Figure 9.3

Movement Hierarchy Blood flow in the cerebral cortex in subjects performing three different tasks supports the idea that (A) simple motor movements are mainly controlled by the motor cortex, (B) movements requiring sequencing are additionally controlled by the premotor cortex, and (C) movements requiring planning are additionally controlled by regions of the prefrontal, parietal, and temporal cortices. (After Roland, 1993, p. 63.)

Identifying the Motor Cortex with the Use of Electrical Stimulation

The specialization of body parts for performing skilled movements is widespread among animals. Elephants use their trunks to manipulate objects; dolphins and seals deftly do the same with their noses; and many other animals, including domestic dogs, accomplish the same ends by using their mouths. Different bird species have beaks designed for obtaining particular foods, for building nests, and even for making and using tools.

Tails can be handy, too. Some marsupials and some New World primates can grasp and carry objects with them. Horses' lips are dexterous enough to manipulate items as small as a blade of grass. Humans tend to rely primarily on their hands for manipulating objects, but they can do manual tasks with other body parts, such as the mouth or a foot, if they have to. (Some people without arms have become extremely proficient at writing with a foot, for example.) What properties of the motor system explain these differences in carrying out skilled movements?

In the 1950s, Wilder Penfield used brief pulses of electrical stimulation to map the cortices of conscious human patients who were about to undergo neurosurgery. He and his colleagues found that most of the movements induced by their experiments were triggered by stimulation of the precentral gyrus (Brodmann's area 4), the region that, because of its role in movement, is called the primary motor cortex or M1. Penfield also obtained evidence that movement can be produced by stimulating the dorsal part of the premotor cortex, and, for this reason, this region was designated the supplementary motor cortex.

Just as he had summarized the results of his work on sensation with epilepsy patients, described in Chapter 8, Penfield summarized the results of his motor studies by drawing cartoons of body parts to represent the areas of the primary motor cortex and the premotor cortex where stimulation caused those parts to move. The result was one homunculus ("little person") spread out across the motor cortex, as illustrated for the primary motor cortex in **Figure 9.4**.

Because the body is symmetrical, each hemisphere contains an almost mirror-image representation of this homunculus. Penfield located a secondary homunculus in the supplementary motor cortex.

As we observed in the somatosensory homunculus, the most striking feature of the motor homunculus is the disproportion in the relative sizes of its body parts compared with their relative sizes in the body itself (see Figure 8.16). The homunculus has very large hands with an especially large thumb. It also has very large lips and a large tongue. In contrast, the trunk, arms, and legs, which constitute most of the area of a real body, occupy much less space, relatively speaking, in the motor cortex. These size distortions are due to the fact that large parts of the motor cortex regulate hand, finger, lip, and tongue movements, giving us precise motor control over those body parts. Parts of the body over which we have much less motor control have a much smaller representation in the motor cortex.

Another distinctive feature of the homunculus when it is sketched according to its representation in the motor cortex is that the arrangement

Figure **9.4**

Penfield's Motor Homunculus
Movements are topographically organized in the motor cortex. Electrical stimulation of the dorsomedial regions of M1 produces movements in the lower limbs; stimulation in ventral regions produces movements in the upper body, hands, and face.

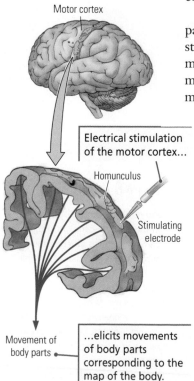

Motor cortex

Electrical stimulation of the motor cortex...

Homunculus

Stimulating electrode

Movement of body parts

...elicits movements of body parts corresponding to the map of the body.

of body parts is somewhat different from that of the body itself. For instance, the area of the cortex that produces eye movements is located in front of the area that produces movement in the head, as is the area that produces movement of the lips. In addition, the head of the homunculus in Figure 9.4 is oriented with the chin up and the forehead down, rather than the other way around as Penfield originally drew it.

Nevertheless, these details do not prevent his homunculus from being a useful concept for understanding the topographic organization, or functional layout, of the motor cortex. It shows at a glance that relatively larger areas of the brain control the parts of the body that make the most-complex and finely tuned movements.

Multiple Representations in the Motor Cortex

Penfield's original maps of the motor cortex were constructed from a few points of electrical stimulation with large electrodes placed on or near the surface of the neocortex. Subsequent studies in primates, using microelectrodes and many sites of electrical stimulation, indicate that there are many more homunculi than were recognized by Penfield. There may be as many as 10 different homunculi within the motor cortex and premotor cortex. In addition, parts of the homunculi are not arranged as simply as Penfield sketched them.

For example, the loci from which electrical stimulation can elicit the movement of a finger are not located in a discrete area representing that finger, adjacent to areas representing the other fingers, as Penfield's original homunculus suggests. Finger movements can be obtained from many points. Furthermore, many of the locations from which finger movements are obtained also elicit movements of other body parts.

Movement Sequences

To explain these findings, researchers now propose that the motor cortex is organized not for the control of individual muscles but rather for the control of movements, any of which might require the coordinated action of many muscles in different combinations. Different homunculi represent different classes of movement. Using half-second long trains of electrical stimulation in conscious monkeys rather than brief pulses of electrical stimulation, Michael Graziano finds that stimulation elicits actions that he calls "ethological categories of movement" because these movements are useful to the monkey. (*Ethology* is the scientific study of animal behavior under natural conditions.)

The drawings in **Figure 9.5** illustrate the end points of a number of these categories: defensive postures of the face (A), movement of the hand to the

Figure **9.5**

Ethological-Movement Categories Five categories of movements evoked by electrical stimulation of the motor cortex in the monkey. (After Graziano, 2006.)

(A) (B) (C) (D) (E)

mouth (B), manipulation and shaping of the hand and digits in central body space (C), outward reach with the hand (D), and climbing and leaping postures (E).

Thus, in Figure 9.5B, for example, stimulation that causes the hand to move to the mouth also causes the digits to close with the forefinger positioned against the thumb, the forearm supinated (turned upward), and the wrist flexed such that the grip is aimed at the mouth. Not only is the hand moved precisely to the mouth, but the mouth is opened as if to receive a carried object. The movement is smooth and coordinated, resembling a spontaneous movement that the monkey might make.

The movement categories observed by Graziano have the same end irrespective of the location of a monkey's limb or its other ongoing behavior. Electrical stimulation that results in the hand coming to the mouth always recruits that movement, but in a variety of ways, depending on the starting point of the hand. If a weight is attached to the monkey's arm, the evoked movement compensates for added load. Nevertheless, the movement lacks the flexibility of a normal movement because, when an obstacle is placed between the hand and the mouth, the hand hits the obstacle. Additionally, if stimulation continues after the hand has reached the mouth, the hand remains there for the duration of the stimulation.

Graziano proposes that the motor cortex represents three types of organization: the part of the body that is to be moved, the spatial location to which the movement is directed, and the function. The motor representation of this organization implies that there are many maps of the body, each representing somewhat different movements, the part of space in which an action is to take place, and the function that the action is intended to perform.

Nevertheless, movements of a certain type—for example, reaching—cluster together with respect to the part of motor cortex from which they are elicited, but reaching to different parts of space will be elicited from slightly different points in the reaching map. The cortical map representing reaching also is proposed to be quite flexible, depending on the past experience of the monkey, its recent experience, the objects that are available to reach for, and even just-completed actions. At least part of Grazinio's conception of cortical control of movement is that the function of arm or body actions is to take the hands to different parts of working space—for example, to spatial locations to grasp objects or to the mouth for eating them.

(A) Pincer grip

(B) Whole-hand grip

Figure 9.6

Getting a Grip (The Photo Works.)

The Movement Lexicon

Grazinio's results support the view that humans have a lexicon, or repertoire, of movement categories in the motor cortex. An observation that supports this idea is the similarity in the ways that different people perform skilled movements. Most people who reach for a small object use a variation of the pincer grip; that is, the thumb and another finger, usually the index finger, are used to grasp the object (**Figure 9.6**A). The pincer grip entails moving the thumb, the second digit, and the arm. By 3 months of age, most healthy babies begin to spontaneously make a pincer grip when making spontaneous hand and finger movement and, by 12 months of age, they use it to pick up tiny objects such as breadcrumbs.

Other evidence includes the following two facts. First, most primate species use this same grip pattern. Second, people who have incurred small lesions of the motor cortex in the area of the thumb region of the homunculus have a weakness not only in the thumb but in the other fingers of the hand and in the arm as well. The latter finding suggests to Mark Schieber that the lesions impair not the muscles of the hand or individual digits but rather the overall action of reaching for an object and grasping it. After incurring such a lesion, in which the pincer grip is lost, a person is likely to substitute a new movement but one in which a whole-hand grip (Figure 9.6B) is substituted for the pincer grip.

Apparently, then, the pincer grip and other skilled movements are not entirely learned but are part of a prewired movement lexicon in the motor cortex. They are encoded in the neural connections as basic patterns of movement that are common to the particular species, to be called on and modified as situations demand. The human movement lexicon will presumably be more complex than that of the monkey, and the lexicon of primate movements will be different, again, from that of animals in other mammalian orders such as rodents, carnivores, or pachyderms.

Findings from lesion studies suggest that the premotor cortex and the primary motor cortex have a movement lexicon in common and that the repertoire available to the premotor cortex is more complex than that of the primary motor cortex. C. Brinkman shows that damage to the premotor cortex does not produce muscle weakness, but it does disrupt more-complex movements. For example, the monkey depicted in **Figure 9.7** is given the task of extracting a piece of food wedged in a hole in a table.

If the monkey merely pushes the food through the hole with a finger, the food will drop to the floor and be lost. The monkey has to catch the food by holding one palm beneath the hole while using the other hand to push the food out. Five months after the premotor cortex has been ablated, the monkey is unable to make the two complementary movements together. It can push the food with a finger and it can extend an open palm, but it cannot coordinate these actions of its two hands. Thus, the premotor cortex plays a greater role in organizing whole-body movements than the motor cortex, which controls specific acts.

Movements encoded by the neocortex are not limited to movements of the hand and arm but include movements in which many parts of the body are used. For example, a person pitching a ball, as illustrated in **Figure 9.8**, must coordinate the entire body to deliver the ball to the target. The action requires stepping movements of the leg, constant adjustments of the trunk to maintain balance, and the throwing movement of the arm.

Note, by the way, that some of these movements are also used in walking, particularly the coordinated movements of the diagonal limb couplets: the pitcher has the left arm forward and the right leg back, just as you would if you

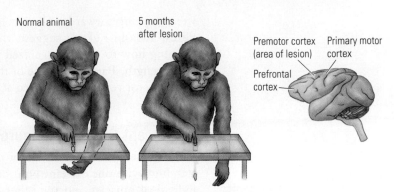

Normal animal   5 months after lesion

Premotor cortex (area of lesion)   Primary motor cortex

Prefrontal cortex

Figure **9.7**

Premotor Control On a task requiring both hands, a normal monkey can push a peanut out of a hole with one hand and catch it in the other; but, 5 months after the premotor cortex has undergone lesioning, the monkey cannot coordinate this movement. (After Brinkman, 1984, p. 925.)

Figure **9.8**

Baseball Pitcher Winding Up Movement patterns used in sports are similar to the movements used in everyday activities. Apparently, the nervous system has a set of basic plans for movement.

were stepping forward with your left leg. In an extensive analysis of body reflexes, Tadashi Fukuda suggests that a large part of learning to move entails learning how to use preorganized patterns of movement to acheive both skill and strength. Part of the role of the neocortex in movement must thus be to blend motor reflexes and skilled actions together.

Movement Coding by Neurons in the Neocortex

The debate over how the motor cortex contributes to movement is of long standing, with one extreme position suggesting that the motor cortex controls individual muscles and the other extreme suggesting that the motor cortex controls coordinated actions. The results of certain single-cell studies of the motor regions of the neocortex suggest that the cells play a direct role in instructing particular muscles to contract, whereas findings from other studies suggest that the cells specify the target of the movement. We can also imagine movements, as described in the Snapshot on page 231, and so other cells must take part in visualizing movements. In the following sections, we consider evidence describing how the neocortex specifies movements.

Motor-Cortex Cells Specify Movements and Their Force and Direction

To investigate how the cells of the motor cortex produce movement, Edward Evarts used the simple procedure illustrated in **Figure 9.9**A. He trained a monkey to flex its wrist to move a bar to which weights of different heaviness could be attached. An electrode implanted in the wrist region of the motor cortex recorded the activity of neurons there.

The recordings in Figure 9.9B show that these neurons begin to discharge even before the monkey flexes its wrist, which means that they participate in planning the movement as well as initiating it. The neurons then continue to discharge during the wrist movement, confirming that they also play a role in executing the movement. The neurons also discharge at a higher rate when the bar is loaded with a weight, an indication that motor-cortex neurons increase the force of a movement by increasing their rate of firing.

The results of Evarts's experiment also reveal that the motor cortex specifies the direction of a movement. The neurons of the motor-cortex wrist area discharge when the monkey flexes its wrist to bring the hand inward but not when the monkey extends its wrist to move the hand back to its starting position. These on–off responses of the neurons, depending on whether the wrist is flexed toward the body or is extended away, are a simple way of encoding the direction in which the wrist is moving.

Apostolos Georgopoulos (1982) and his coworkers used a method similar to that of Evarts to further examine the encoding of movement direction. They trained

Figure **9.9**

Corticomotor-Neuron Activity in Planning and Executing Movements (After Evarts, 1968, p. 15.)

(A) Procedure

Electrode from motor-cortex neurons to recording device

Monkey flexes wrist to rotate lever.

Pulley

Lever

Restraint

Wrist movement

Weight

Attached weight can be changed to vary force of movement.

(B) Results   Response of motor-cortex neurons to wrist movement

No weight

Neural activity increases before movement, suggesting motor-cortex participation in planning.

Neural activity continues throughout movement, suggesting motor-cortex participation in execution.

Weight added

Movement begins

Neural activity increases over no-weight condition, suggesting that motor-cortex neurons code force of movement.

SNAPSHOT

Observing, Remembering, and Imagining Movements

Before ascending the diving tower, a diver mentally rehearses the movements of the perfect dive that she hopes to make. After the diver is on the tower, she may again imagine and rehearse the movement sequence that she is about to execute. Does this mental preparation help? Is she activating the circuits of the motor system that she is about to use in performing the dive?

Scientists have used various imaging techniques to study the role of the motor regions of the neocortex in observing, remembering, and imagining movements. Alex Martin and colleagues used PET imaging to identify brain regions that are active when subjects silently rehearse various words. The scans reveal increases in blood flow in the hand regions of the motor cortex when subjects name tools. This finding suggests a connection between the hand region of the motor cortex and knowledge about the tool and its use.

Haueisen and Knosche, intrigued by reports that pianists involuntarily move their fingers as if playing when in fact they are only listening to a piece of music, used magnetoencephalography to compare the motor activation in pianists and nonpianists while the subjects listened to piano pieces. Only the pianists exhibit increased activity above the region of the motor cortex. Furthermore, when the piece that they listened to requires more thumb than little-finger activity, the pianists' brain scans show more activity in the thumb region of the motor cortex than in the digit region, and vice versa. Thus, for piano players, the motor cortex is active during listening, suggesting that it contributes to music appreciation.

Nyberg and colleagues make a more direct comparison of the brain activity evoked by performing a movement and the activity evoked by imagining a movement. They made PET scans of subjects performing certain movements with the right hand (such as rolling a ball) and compared these scans with PET scans of subjects who were verbally encoding the same movement by silently describing the movement to themselves in their minds. The results are presented in the accompanying illustration and reveal similarities in brain activation with overt movements and rehearsed movements.

The results of these studies are consistent with the notion that practice, rather than dreaming, makes perfect, but that dreaming helps. They also indicate that, after we have become proficient at a skill that requires movement, such as playing the piano, the brain's representations of the imagined performance and the real performance of those movements become more alike. Jean Decety and Julie Grezes

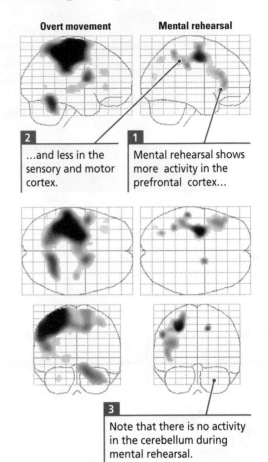

Overt movement   **Mental rehearsal**

2 ...and less in the sensory and motor cortex.

1 Mental rehearsal shows more activity in the prefrontal cortex...

3 Note that there is no activity in the cerebellum during mental rehearsal.

Comparisons of brain activation measured with PET for movements that are overtly performed (left) and only mentally rehearsed (right). Although some similarities in neocortical activation appear, the differences, especially with respect to the absence of cerebellar activation during covert movement, are obvious. (After Nyberg et al., 2001.)

suggest the close relation between brain mechanisms controlling imagination and doing also provide the neural basis for social cognition, the ability of groups to have a shared view of the world.

Haueisen, J., and T. R. Knosche. Involuntary motor activity in pianists evoked by music perception. *Journal of Cognitive Neuroscience* 13:786–792, 2001.

Martin, A., C. L. Wiggs, L. G. Ungerleider, and J. V. Haxby. Neural correlates of category-specific knowledge. *Nature* 379:649–652, 1996.

Nyberg, L., K. M. Petersson, L.-G. Nilsson, J. Sandblom, C. Aberg, and M. Ingvar. Reactivation of motor brain areas during explicit memory for actions. *Neuroimage* 14:521–528, 2001.

Decety, J., and J. Grezes. The power of simulation: Imagining one's own and other's behavior. *Brain Research* 1079:4–14, 2006.

(A) Procedure

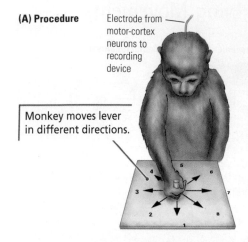

Electrode from motor-cortex neurons to recording device

Monkey moves lever in different directions.

(B) Results Activity of a single motor-cortex neuron

Minimal discharge as lever is moved backward (0°)

Maximal discharge as lever is moved forward (180°)

Figure 9.10

Individual Motor-Cortex Neurons Tune in to Preferred Directions (After Georgopoulos et al., 1982, p. 1530.)

monkeys to move a lever in different directions across the surface of a table (**Figure 9.10**A). Recording from single cells in the arm region of the motor cortex, they found that each neuron is maximally active when the monkey moves its arm in a particular direction (Figure 9.10B).

As a monkey's arm moves in directions other than the one to which a particular cell maximally responds, the cell decreases its activity in proportion to the displacement from the "preferred" direction. For example, if a neuron discharges maximally as the arm moves directly forward, its discharge is attenuated if the arm moves to one side and ceases altogether if the arm moves backward. According to Georgopoulos and his coworkers, the motor cortex seems to calculate both the direction and the distance of movements. Each neuron in a large population of motor-cortex neurons participates in producing a particular movement, but the discharge rate of a particular neuron depends on that movement's direction.

To compare how the premotor cortex and the primary motor cortex contribute to movement, Shinji Kakei (1999) and his colleagues made a slight modification to Georgopoulos's task. The monkey still moved its arm in different directions, but it did so with the palm facing downward, sideways, or upward. They found that about half of the neurons from which they recorded in the primary motor cortex were active in relation to the orientation of the hand, suggesting that these neurons activate muscles to produce the appropriate hand orientation. The remaining neurons were sensitive to the direction of the hand's movement, suggesting that they encode the target of the movement.

When Kakei (2001) and his colleagues recorded premotor cortex cells, they found that the neurons responded exclusively to a target and did not take part in orienting the hand. Thus, the primary motor cortex appears to specify the movement to be made by the hand as well as the target to which the hand is directed, whereas premotor-cortex neurons appear to make a more abstract contribution and are especially concerned with the objective of the movement.

Mirroring Movement

Carlo Umilta and his colleagues further extend our understanding of the contribution of cells in the premotor cortex to movement. In the course of their studies in monkeys, they made a remarkable finding. Many premotor-area neurons not only discharge when a monkey itself makes a movement but also discharge—and in the same way—when the monkey sees other monkeys make the same movement and even when the monkey sees people make the same movement.

These neurons, now called **mirror neurons**, do not respond to objects or to isolated hand movements, and they do not respond very well to pictures or video of movements. Mirror neurons encode a complete action. Some of them have very exacting requirements, responding only to a particular hand movement and only if it is used to pick up a small object rather than a large object, for example.

Other mirror neurons are more broadly tuned and continue to respond when the grip pattern changes or the size of the target varies somewhat. The researchers propose that all mirror neurons represent actions, whether one's own or those of others, and that the representations can be used both for imitating and for understanding the meaning of others' actions, thus permitting the selection of appropriate responses.

Umilta and his colleagues also report that mirror neurons can "fill in the blanks" by recognizing a given movement made by a demonstrator even when the monkey is unable to see part of the movement. **Figure 9.11** shows an instance in which such a neuron responds when the human demonstrator reaches for a block but not when the demonstrator reaches for an object that is not there. The same neuron, however, does respond when the demonstrator reaches for an object that is hidden behind a screen.

We can summarize part of the role of mirror neurons by recognizing that they enable communication between a sender and a receiver. Humans also have mirror neurons, but a major difference between humans and monkeys is that, in humans, the mirror neurons are found largely in the left hemisphere. The ability of mirror neurons to have a role in self-action as well as in the perception of action of others, suggests that they provide the substrate for self-awareness, social awareness, and awareness of the intention and actions of others and that they are likely important for gestural and verbal language.

Roles of the Prefrontal and Posterior Cortex

Movements are usually made in response to sensory stimuli—information from touch, vision, audition, and so forth—although they can also be made in the absence of such information. Sensory information may instruct movements in two ways:

1. Direct connections from the parietal cortex to the primary motor cortex suggest that movements can be made in direct response to sensory stimulation. Such movements are likely to be simple and reflexive.

2. The various sensory systems also send information to the prefrontal cortex and motor cortex, which can use the information to produce or modify movements that are more complex in action and intention.

The importance of sensory information for movement is illustrated by the severe motor disabilities that arise after **deafferentation**, the loss of somatosensory

Premotor cortex (area of mirror cells)   Primary motor cortex

Prefrontal cortex

Monkey premotor cell   No response

Human demonstrator

No target

1 A mirror neuron in the premotor cortex of a monkey does not respond when a target is absent...

Response

Target

2 ...but does respond when the target is present...

Response

Hidden target

3 ...or when it is hidden.

Figure 9.11

Activity of a Mirror Neuron The same neuron would perform in the same way were the monkey to perform the movement. (After Umilta et al., 2001.)

input that results from damage to the fibers that would otherwise convey sensory information from the body to the brain. The importance of sensory information for normal walking in humans is demonstrated by people who suffer from a genetic disorder called *Friedreich's ataxia*, a degeneration of the dorsal columns of the spinal cord. Through this pathway, fine touch and pressure information is conveyed from the body to the cortex.

Like Ian Waterman, who suffered a loss of sensory control as a result of the degeneration of sensory pathways, as described in the Portrait in Chapter 8, people who have Friedreich's ataxia have little or no position sense and a poor sense of passive movement and vibration. When they walk, they support the body on a broad base, legs apart, and tend to shuffle, reel, and stagger. **Ataxia**, from Greek for "disorderly," is a failure of muscular coordination.

For humans, walking is a balancing act: we shift our weight forward from one leg to the other while balancing on one leg at a time. This balancing requires ongoing afferent input, because ataxia does not lessen with time or practice. Locomotion is more severely impaired in people with ataxia than in monkeys with the same condition, because of our more complex bipedal mode of locomotion (monkeys walk with four feet on the ground).

John Rothwell and coworkers described the motor abilities of G.O., who was deafferented by a severe peripheral-nervous-system sensory disease. His motor power was unaffected, and he could produce a range of finger movements with accuracy, including simple, isolated finger movements; outlining figures in the air with his eyes closed; and moving his thumb accurately through different distances and at different speeds. He could judge weights and match forces with his thumb. (He could also drive his old car but was unable to learn to drive a new car.)

Yet, in spite of all that he could still do, G.O.'s hands were relatively useless to him in daily life. He was unable to write, to fasten shirt buttons, or to hold a cup. His difficulties lay in maintaining force for any length of time. He could begin movements quite normally, but the patterns would gradually fall apart and become unrecognizable.

When he tried to carry a suitcase, for example, he would soon drop it unless he continually looked down at it to confirm that it was there. G.O.'s symptoms support the findings with monkeys by suggesting that sensory feedback is not required to *generate* a movement. Instead, his symptoms suggest that sensory feedback is necessary to *sustain* a single movement or series of movements.

Control and modification of movement are not simply produced by the motor regions of the frontal cortex. Cosimo Urgesi and his colleagues show that even visual information influences movement. Using transcranial magnetic stimulation (TMS) of the hand region of the motor cortex of human volunteers, they evoked a response in the muscles of the hand that produces the pincer grip.

They quantified the size of the muscle activation by recording muscle activity with the use of electromyography (EMG). They then showed the subjects a variety of pictures—of airplanes parked on a runway or taking off, of a waterfall, of a hand in a static open position on a table or making a pincer reaching movement, and of a hand that had completed a pincer grasping movement. Viewing the picture of the hand in the act of making a pincer grasping movement resulted in increased TMS-induced EMG activity in muscles of the hand that controls the pincer grasp.

The other pictures of moving or static objects did not produce an increase in EMG activity, and EMG activity did not increase in other muscles unrelated to the pincer grip. The experiment demonstrates that, just as the visual system can extract information about implied motion from static images, the motor system itself extracts visual information from the visual cortex. In fact, the perception of implied motion may be the specific neuronal activity in the pathway from the visual cortex to the spinal cord.

The Brainstem and Motor Control

In addition to the major pathways that carry messages from the cortex to the spinal cord, about 26 pathways to the spinal cord originate in various locations in the brainstem. These pathways are important for sending information from the brainstem to the spinal cord pertaining to posture and balance and for controlling the autonomic nervous system. For all motor functions, the motor neurons are the final common path, but, unlike the skilled movements of the limbs and digits organized by the neocortex, movements produced by the brainstem tend to be whole-body movements.

The general idea that the brainstem is responsible for many movements performed by animals was most dramatically revealed in a series of studies done by Swiss neuroscientist Walter R. Hess. Hess developed the technique of implanting and cementing electrodes into the brains of cats and other animals. These electrodes could subsequently be attached to stimulating leads, causing little discomfort to the animal and allowing it to move freely.

When Hess stimulated the brainstem of a freely moving animal, he was able to elicit almost every innate movement that an animal of that species might be expected to make. For example, a resting cat could be induced to suddenly leap up with an arched back and erect hair, as though frightened by an approaching dog. The movements would begin abruptly when the stimulating current was turned on and end equally abruptly when the stimulating current was turned off.

The behaviors were performed without vigor when the stimulating current was low but increased in vigor as the stimulating current was turned up. Some stimulation sites produced turning of the head, others produced walking or running, still others produced aggressive or fear movements, and so forth. The emotional behavior of the animal also could be modulated. When shown a stuffed toy, a cat might respond to electrical stimulation of some sites by stalking the toy, whereas it would respond to stimulation of other sites with fear and withdrawal.

Other functions of the brainstem pertain to the control of the movements used in eating and drinking and in sexual behavior. The brainstem is also important for posture, for the ability to stand upright and make coordinated movements of the limbs, for swimming and walking, and for movements used in grooming and making nests. Grooming is in fact a particularly complex example of a movement pattern coordinated mainly by the brainstem.

When grooming, a rat sits back on its haunches, licks its paws, wipes its nose with its paws, wipes its paws across its face, and finally turns to lick the fur on its body. These movements are always performed in the same order. The next time you dry off after a shower or a swim, note the "grooming sequence" that you use. Your grooming sequence is very similar to the sequence used by the rat.

The Basal Ganglia and Movement Force

The basal ganglia, a collection of subcortical nuclei in the forebrain, connect the motor cortex with the midbrain. As shown in **Figure 9.12**, a prominent structure of the basal ganglia is the **caudate putamen**, itself a large cluster of nuclei located beneath the frontal cortex. Part of the caudate extends as a "tail" (*caudate* means "tailed") into the temporal lobe, ending in the amygdala.

The basal ganglia receive inputs from two main sources. First, all areas of the neocortex and limbic cortex, including the motor cortex, project to the basal ganglia. Second, the nigrostriatal dopamine pathway extends into the basal ganglia from the substantia nigra, a cluster of darkly pigmented cells in the midbrain (see Figure 5.17). Conversely, the basal ganglia send projections back to both the motor cortex and the substantia nigra.

Two different, and in many ways opposite, kinds of movement disorders result from basal ganglia damage, depending on the injury that it sustains. If cells of the caudate putamen are damaged, unwanted choreiform (writhing and twitching) movements result. For example, the genetic disorder **Huntington's chorea** destroys caudate putamen cells and is characterized by involuntary and exaggerated movements. Another example of involuntary movements related to caudate putamen damage consists of the unwanted tics and vocalizations peculiar to **Tourette's syndrome**. People with Tourette's syndrome make involuntary movements such as head twists or sudden movements of a hand or arm or will often utter a cry.

In addition to causing *involuntary* movements, called **hyperkinetic symptoms**, if the cells of the basal ganglia are left intact but its inputs are damaged, the injury results in difficulty in *making* movements—that is, in **hypokinetic symptoms**. **Parkinson's disease**, for example, caused by the loss of dopamine cells in the substantia nigra and their input into the basal ganglia, is characterized by muscular rigidity and difficulty in initiating and performing movements. These two opposing sets of symptoms—hyperkinetic and hypokinetic—after basal ganglia damage suggest that a major function of the basal ganglia is to modulate movement.

Steven Keele and Richard Ivry tried to connect the two different kinds of basal ganglia symptoms by hypothesizing that the underlying function of the basal ganglia is to generate the force required for each movement. According to this idea, some types of basal ganglia damage cause errors of too much force and so result in excessive movement, whereas other types of damage cause errors of too little force and so result in insufficient movement. Keele and Ivry tested their hypothesis by giving healthy subjects as well as patients with various kinds of basal ganglia disorders a task that tested their ability to exert appropriate amounts of force.

Figure **9.12**

Basal Ganglia Connections The caudate putamen makes reciprocal connections with the forebrain and with the substantia nigra in the midbrain (After Alexander and Crutcher, 1990.)

Caudate putamen

Tail of caudate nucleus

Amygdala

Substantia nigra

Substantia nigra → Caudate → Thalamus → Cortex → Movement

While looking at a line projected on a television screen, the experimental and control subjects attempted to produce a second line of the same length by pressing a button with the appropriate amount of force. After a number of practice trials, the subjects were then asked to press the button with appropriate force even when the first line was no longer visible as a guide. Patients with basal ganglia disorders were unable to do this task reliably. The force that they exerted was usually too little or too much, resulting in a line too short or too long.

What neural pathways enable the basal ganglia to modulate the force of movements? Basal ganglia circuits are complex, but Peter Redgrave reviews evidence that they affect the activity of the motor cortex through two pathways: an inhibitory pathway and an excitatory pathway. Both pathways converge on an area of the basal ganglia called the internal part of the **globus pallidus** (GPi), as charted in **Figure 9.13**.

The GPi in turn projects to the thalamus (more specifically, to the anterior thalamic nucleus), and the thalamus projects to the motor cortex. The thalamic projection modulates the size or force of a movement produced by the cortex, but the GPi influences the thalamic projection. The GPi is thought of as acting like the volume dial on a radio, because its output determines whether a movement will be weak or strong.

The inputs to the GPi are shown in red and green in Figure 9.13 to illustrate how they affect movement. If activity in the inhibitory pathway (red) is high relative to that in the excitatory pathway (green), inhibition of the GPi will predominate and the thalamus will be free to excite the cortex, thus amplifying movement. If, on the other hand, activity in the excitatory pathway is high relative to that in the inhibitory pathway, excitation of the GPi will predominate and the thalamus will be inhibited, thus reducing input to the cortex and decreasing the force of movements.

The idea that the GPi acts like a volume control over movement has been instrumental in devising treatments for Parkinson's disease, in which movements are difficult to perform. Recordings made from cells of the globus pallidus show excessive activity in people with Parkinson's disease, and, according to the volume-control theory, movements become more difficult to make. If the GPi is surgically destroyed in Parkinson patients or if it is electrically stimulated to interfere with its output, muscular rigidity is reduced and the ability of Parkinson patients to make normal movements is improved. The technique of stimulating the GPi or other structures in the basal ganglia circuitry, deep brain stimulation (DBS, discussed in Chapter 6), is a widely used therapy for treating the symptoms of rigidity in Parkinson patients.

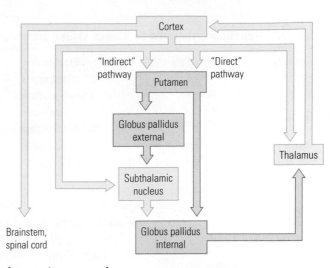

Figure 9.13

Regulation of Movement Force

Two pathways in the basal ganglia modulate cortically produced movements. Green indicates parts of the pathways that are excitatory; red indicates parts of the pathways that are inhibitory. The indirect pathway has an excitatory effect on the internal part of the globus pallidus (GPi), whereas the direct pathway has an inhibitory influence on the GPi. If inhibition dominates, the thalamus is shut down and the cortex is unable to produce movement. If excitation predominates, the thalamus can become overactive, thus amplifying movement. (After Alexander and Crutcher, 1990.)

The Cerebellum and Motor Learning

Musicians have a saying: "Miss a day of practice and you're okay, miss two days and you notice, miss three days and the world notices." Evidence of the enormous amount of practice required to maintain motor skills is summarized in

Table 9.1 Repetitions required to master skilled movements

Activity	Subjects	Repetitions
Cigar making	Women	3.0 million cigars
Knitting	Women	1.5 million stitches
Rug making	Women	1.5 million knots
Violin playing	Children	2.5 million notes
Basketball	Professional athletes	1.0 million shots
Baseball pitching	Professional athletes	1.6 million pitches

Table 9.1. The cerebellum seems to be the part of the motor system that participates in acquiring and maintaining motor skills, from playing a musical instrument to pitching a baseball to keyboarding on a computer.

Large and conspicuous, the cerebellum sits atop the brainstem and is clearly visible just behind and beneath the cerebral cortex (**Figure 9.14**). Like the cerebral cortex, it is divided into two hemispheres. A small lobe called the **flocculus** projects from its ventral surface. Despite its small size relative to the neocortex, the cerebellum contains about half of all the neurons in the entire nervous system.

The cerebellum is divided into several regions, each specializing in a different aspect of motor control. The flocculus receives projections from the vestibular system and so takes part in the control of balance. Many of its projections go to the spinal cord and to the motor nuclei that control eye movements.

Different parts of the hemispheres of the cerebellum subserve different movements, as diagrammed by the areas in Figure 9.14 bordered in white in the bottom drawing. The most medial parts control the face and the midline of the body. The more lateral parts are associated with movements of the limbs, hands, feet, and digits. The pathways from the hemispheres project to cerebellar nuclei in the base of the cerebellum, which in turn project to other brain regions, including the motor cortex.

To summarize the cerebellum's topographic organization, the midline of the homunculus is represented in the central part of the cerebellum, whereas the limbs and digits are represented in the cerebellum's lateral parts. Tumors or damage in midline areas of the cerebellum disrupt balance, eye movements, upright posture, and walking but do not substantially disrupt other movements, such as reaching, grasping, and using the fingers. When lying down, a person with medial damage to the cerebellum may show few symptoms. In contrast, damage to lateral parts of the cerebellum disrupts arm, hand, and finger movements much more than movements of the body's trunk.

Attempts to understand how the cerebellum controls movements have centered on two major ideas: the cerebellum (1) has a role in the timing of movements and (2) helps maintain movement accuracy. Keele and Ivry support the first hypothesis. According to them, the cerebellum acts like a clock or pacemaker to ensure that both movements and perceptions are appropriately timed.

In a motor test of timing, subjects are asked to tap a finger in rhythm with a metronome. After a number of taps, the metronome is turned off, and the subjects attempt to go on tapping with the same beat. Those with damage to the cerebellum, especially to the lateral cerebellum, perform poorly.

Figure 9.14

Cerebellar Homunculus The cerebellar hemispheres encode body movements, and the flocculus, visible at the bottom center of the photograph, encodes eye movements and balance. The cerebellum's topographic organization has more-medial parts representing the midline of the body and more-lateral parts representing the limbs and digits. (Photograph of cerebellum reproduced from *The Human Brain: Dissections of the Real Brain,* by T. H. Williams, N. Gluhbegovic, and J. Jew, on CD-ROM. Published by Brain University, brain-university.com, 2000.)

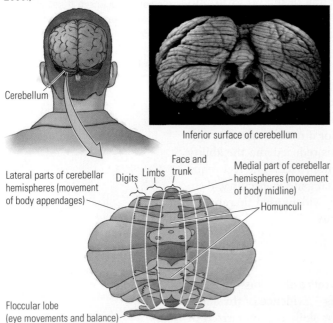

Cerebellum

Inferior surface of cerebellum

Lateral parts of cerebellar hemispheres (movement of body appendages)

Digits   Limbs   Face and trunk

Medial part of cerebellar hemispheres (movement of body midline)

Homunculi

Floccular lobe (eye movements and balance)

In a perceptual test of timing, subjects are presented with two pairs of tones. The silent period between the first two tones is always the same length, whereas the silent period between the second two tones changes from trial to trial. The subjects are required to tell whether the second silent period is longer or shorter than the first. Those with damage to the cerebellum perform poorly on this task, too. The results demonstrate that the underlying impairment in disorders of the cerebellum is a loss of timing, both in movement and in perception.

The cerebellum also plays a role in maintaining movement accuracy. Tom Thatch and coworkers gathered evidence in support of this hypothesis by having subjects throw darts at a target, as shown in **Figure 9.15**. After a number of throws, the subjects put on glasses containing wedge-shaped prisms that displace the apparent location of the target to the left. When a subject wearing the glasses throws a dart, it now lands to the left of the intended target. All subjects showed this initial distortion in aim. But then came an important difference.

When normal subjects see the dart miss the mark, they adjust each successive throw until reasonable accuracy is restored. In contrast, subjects with damage to the cerebellum do not correct for this error. They keep missing the target far to the left time after time.

Next, the subjects remove the prism glasses and throw a few more darts. Again, another significant difference emerges. Normal subjects throw their first darts much too far to the right (corresponding to the previous adjustment that they had learned to make), but soon they adjust once again until they regain their former accuracy.

In contrast, subjects with damage to the cerebellum show no aftereffects from having worn the prisms, seeming to confirm the impression that they had never compensated for the glasses to begin with. This experiment suggests that many movements that we make—throwing a dart, hitting a ball with a bat, writing neatly, painting a work of art—depend on moment-to-moment motor learning and adjustments that are made by the cerebellum.

To better understand how the cerebellum improves motor skills by making required adjustments to movements, imagine throwing a dart yourself. Suppose you aim at the bull's eye, throw the dart, and find that it misses the board completely. On your next throw, you aim to correct for the original error. Notice that there are actually two versions of each throw: (1) the movement that you intended to make and (2) the

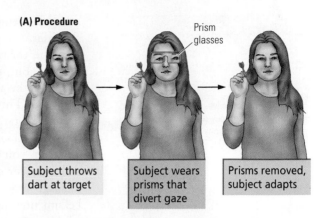

(A) Procedure

Subject throws dart at target → Subject wears prisms that divert gaze → Prisms removed, subject adapts

(B) Results—Normal subject

Initial throws | With prisms | Prisms removed

(C) Results—Patient with damage to cerebellum

Initial throws | With prisms | Prisms removed

Figure **9.15**

The Cerebellum and Movement Accuracy (A) A subject throws darts at a target before, during, and after wearing prisms that divert her gaze to the left. (B) A normal subject throws the dart accurately without prisms, initially throws to the left and then corrects the throws when wearing prisms, and finally throws to the right and then corrects the throws when the prisms are removed. (C) A patient with damage to the cerebellum fails to correct throws when wearing prisms and shows no aftereffect when the prisms are removed. (After Thatch et al., p. 429.)

Figure **9.16**

Intention, Action, Feedback A feedback circuit allows the cerebellum to correct movements to match intentions. By comparing the message for the intended movement with the movement that was actually performed, the cerebellum can send an error message to the cortex to improve the accuracy of a subsequent movement.

actual movement as recorded by sensory receptors in your arm and shoulder.

If the throw is successful, you need make no correction on your next try. But, if you miss, an adjustment is called for. One way to accomplish the adjustment is through the feedback circuit shown in **Figure 9.16**. The cortex sends instructions to the spinal cord to throw a dart at the target. A copy of the same instructions is sent to the cerebellum through the inferior olivary nucleus.

When you first throw the dart, the sensory receptors in your arm and shoulder encode the actual movement that you make and send a message about it through the spinal cord to the cerebellum. The cerebellum now has information about both versions of the movement: what you intended to do and what you actually did. The cerebellum can now calculate the error and tell the cortex how it should correct the movement. When you next throw the dart, you incorporate that correction into your throw.

Communicating with the Spinal Cord

The neocortex sends major projections to the brainstem, as the **corticobulbar tracts**, and to the spinal cord, as the **corticospinal tracts**. (The term *cortico* indicates that these tracts begin in the neocortex, and the terms *bulbar* and *spinal* indicate where the tracts end.) The corticobulbar tracts terminate in nuclei that control facial muscles and thus take part in controlling facial movements. The corticospinal tracts terminate in the vicinity of the motor neurons in the spinal cord and control movements of the limbs and body.

The axons that form the corticobulbar and corticospinal tracts do not come only from the primary motor cortex. Some parts come from the somatosensory cortex (area 3-1-2), others come from the primary motor cortex (area 4), and still others come from the premotor cortex (area 6). The part of the corticospinal tract that comes from the somatosensory cortex terminates in dorsal-column nuclei of the ascending sensory tracts and modulates sensory signals that are sent to the neocortex. The parts of the tract that originate in the primary motor cortex and premotor cortex descend to the interneurons and motor neurons of the brainstem and spinal cord and more directly control movement. Thus, the neocortex not only controls movement but also modulates sensory information coming from the body.

The axons of the corticobulbar and corticospinal tracts originate in layer-V pyramidal cells of the neocortex. These neurons have especially large cell bodies, in keeping with the fact that they support axons that travel a long way. The axons of the corticospinal tract descend into the brainstem, sending collaterals to a few brainstem nuclei and eventually emerging on the brainstem's ventral surface, where they form a large bump on each side of that surface. These bumps, known as *pyramids*, give the corticospinal tracts their alternate name, the **pyramidal tracts**.

From this location, about 95% of the axons descending from the left hemisphere cross over to the right side of the brainstem, whereas a comparable

Figure 9.17

Corticospinal-Tract Pathway

The corticospinal, or pyramidal, tracts descend from the motor cortex to the brainstem, producing protrusions called pyramids on the ventral surface of the brainstem where each tract branches into the spinal cord. A lateral corticospinal tract (representing the limbs) crosses the midline, and a ventral corticospinal tract (representing the body) remains on the same side. (Photograph of spinal cord reproduced from *The Human Brain: Dissections of the Real Brain,* by T. H. Williams, N. Gluhbegovic, and J. Jew, on CD-ROM. Published by Brain University, brain-university.com, 2000.)

Left-hemisphere motor cortex

Dorsal

Brainstem

Spinal cord

Left-hemisphere corticospinal tract

Pyramidal protrusion

Ventral

Lateral corticospinal tract moves limbs and digits.

Ventral corticospinal tract moves muscles of midline of the body.

proportion of the axons descending from the right hemisphere cross over to the left side of the brainstem. The rest of the axons stay on their original sides. The division produces two corticospinal tracts descending on each side of the spinal cord. **Figure 9.17** illustrates the division of axons for the tract originating in the left-hemisphere cortex.

The corticospinal-tract fibers that cross to descend into the spinal cord originate mainly in the hand-and-arm and leg-and-foot regions of the cortical homunculi. The fibers that do not cross originate in the trunk regions of the homunculi. Therefore, each motor cortex controls the limbs on the opposite side of the body, whereas it controls the trunk on the same side of the body.

Looking at the cross section of the spinal cord in Figure 9.17, you can see the location of the two tracts—the one that crosses and the one that remains uncrossed—on each side. Those fibers that cross to the opposite side of the brainstem descend the spinal cord in a lateral location, giving them the name **lateral corticospinal tract**. Those fibers that remain on their original side of the brainstem continue down the spinal cord in a ventral location, giving them the name **ventral corticospinal tract**. The lateral corticospinal tract sends messages to the limbs, whereas the ventral corticospinal tract sends messages to the trunk.

The Motor Neurons

The spinal-cord motor neurons that connect to muscles are located in the ventrolateral spinal cord and jut out to form the spinal column's ventral horns. Interneurons lie just medially to the motor neurons and project onto them. The fibers of the corticospinal tracts make synaptic connections with both the interneurons and the motor neurons, but all nervous system commands to the muscles are carried by the motor neurons.

Figure 9.18 shows that motor neurons are arranged as a homounculus, with more

Ventral horn of spinal cord

Fingers

Arms

Shoulders

Trunk

Lateral corticospinal tract synapses with interneurons and motor neurons that innervate muscles of the limbs and digits.

Interneurons project to motor neurons.

Motor neurons project to muscles of the body.

Ventral corticospinal tract synapses with interneurons and motor neurons that innervate the trunk (midline of the body).

The interneurons and motor neurons of the spinal cord are envisioned as a homunculus representing the muscles that they innervate.

Figure 9.18

Relations among Interneurons, Motor Neurons, and Muscles

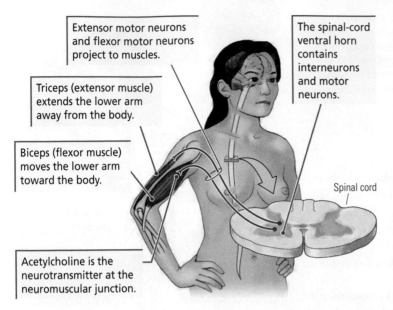

Extensor motor neurons and flexor motor neurons project to muscles.

Triceps (extensor muscle) extends the lower arm away from the body.

Biceps (flexor muscle) moves the lower arm toward the body.

Acetylcholine is the neurotransmitter at the neuromuscular junction.

The spinal-cord ventral horn contains interneurons and motor neurons.

Spinal cord

Figure 9.19

Muscular Coordination

laterally located motor neurons projecting to muscles that control the fingers and hands, intermediately located motor neurons projecting to muscles that control the arms and shoulders, and the most medially located motor neurons projecting to muscles that control the trunk. Axons of the lateral corticospinal tract connect mainly with the lateral motor neurons, whereas axons of the ventral corticospinal tract connect mainly to the medial motor neurons.

Limb muscles are arranged in pairs as shown in **Figure 9.19**. One member of a pair, the **extensor**, moves the limb away from the trunk. The other member of the pair, the **flexor**, moves the limb toward the trunk. Connections between the interneurons and the motor neurons of the spinal cord cause the muscles to work in concert: when one muscle of the pair contracts, the other relaxes. Thus, the interneurons and motor neurons of the spinal cord not only relay instructions from the brain but also, through their connections, cooperatively organize the movement of many muscles.

Overview of Corticospinal Function

The limb regions of the motor homunculus contribute most of their fibers to the lateral corticospinal tract. Because these fibers have crossed over to the opposite side of the brainstem, they activate motor neurons that move the arm, hand, leg, and foot on the *opposite side of the body*.

In contrast, the trunk regions of the motor homunculus contribute their fibers to the ventral corticospinal tract and, because these fibers do not cross over at the brainstem, they activate motor neurons that move the trunk on the *same side of the body*. In short, the neurons of the motor homunculus in the left-hemisphere cortex control the trunk on the left side of the body but the limbs on the body's right side. Similarly, neurons of the motor homunculus in the right-hemisphere cortex control the trunk on the right side of the body but the limbs on the body's left side.

A simple one-to-one relation between an "upper" motor neuron in the neocortex and a "lower" motor neuron in the spinal cord is unlikely. Upper motor neurons, through their corticospinal connections, each synapse with many spinal-cord interneurons and with motor neurons in many segments of the spinal cord. Just as the motor cortex represents ethologically relevant movements, the spinal cord likely does so, too. The spinal cord likely represents movements as more "reflexive," whereas the motor cortex represents movements as more "voluntary." In mediating voluntary movement, the neocortex allows all the sensory systems a say in the final outcome of action.

Summary

Movement of the body's muscles is represented in the motor regions of the brain. Skilled movements of the mouth and limbs are controlled by the motor cortex, whole-body movements requiring a certain level of coordination are controlled by the brainstem, and the neural circuits for executing these actions are represented in the spinal cord.

The Neocortex and the Initiation of Movement

Within the neocortex, more-elementary movements are controlled by the primary motor cortex, whereas coordinated movements are controlled by the premotor cortex. The prefrontal cortex organizes movement plans and instructs the premotor cortex on how the plans should be executed. The sensory regions of the posterior cortex can initiate rapid responses to sensory events through projections made to the primary motor cortex and can influence plans for movements through projections to the prefrontal cortex.

Single-cell recordings in the neocortex suggest that cells in the primary motor cortex specify the movement that is to be made, as well as its force and direction. Cells in the premotor cortex are active during more-complex movements in which not only the movement itself but also the movement's target must be considered. One class of premotor cells, mirror neurons, are active when we make a particular goal-oriented movement, when we observe someone else make the same movement, and even when we see only a picture of the movement. Mirror neurons provide a substrate for self- awareness and for social awareness.

The Brainstem and Motor Control

The basal ganglia's reciprocal connections with the cortex and brainstem contribute to motor control by adjusting the force associated with each movement. Consequently, damage to the basal ganglia can result either in unwanted involuntary movements (too much force being exerted) or in such rigidity that movements are difficult to perform (too little force being exerted).

The cerebellum contributes to the accuracy and control of movement and to motor learning by improving movement skill. It does so by coordinating the timing of movements and by comparing intended movement with actual movement to calculate any necessary correction.

Communicating with the Spinal Cord

The descending corticospinal pathways from the brain to the spinal cord partly cross, and so the right and left motor cortex each controls the limbs on the opposite side of the body and the trunk on the same side of the body. The motor neurons of the spinal cord have a homuncular organization, with lateral neurons controlling the distal parts of the body and medial neurons controlling the trunk. Thus, all major parts of the motor system have a topograpic organization, with different regions controlling different body parts.

References

Alexander, R. E., and M. D. Crutcher. Functional architecture of basal ganglia circuits: Neural substrates of parallel processing. *Trends in Neuroscience* 13:266–271, 1990.

Brinkman, C. Supplementary motor area of the monkey's cerebral cortex: Short- and long-term deficits after unilateral ablation and the effects of subsequent callosal section. *Journal of Neuroscience* 4:918–992, 1984.

Evarts, E. V. Relation of pyramidal tract activity to force exerted during voluntary movement. *Journal of Neurophysiology* 31:14–27, 1968.

Friedhoff, A. J., and T. N. Chase, Eds. *Advances in Neurology*, vol. 35, *Gilles de la Tourette Syndrome*. New York: Raven Press, 1982.

Fukuda, T. *Statokinetic Reflexes in Equilibrium and Movement.* Tokyo: University of Tokyo Press, 1981.

Galea, M. P., and I. Darian-Smith. Multiple corticospinal neuron populations in the macaque monkey are specified by their unique cortical origins, spinal terminations, and connections. *Cerebral Cortex* 4:166–194, 1994.

Georgopoulos, A. P., J. F. Kalaska, R. Caminiti, and J. T. Massey. On the relations between the direction of two-dimensional arm movements and cell discharge in primate motor cortex. *Journal of Neuroscience* 2:1527–1537, 1982.

Georgopoulos, A. P., G. Pellizzer, A. V. Poliakov, and M. H. Schieber. Neural coding of finger and wrist movements. *Journal of Computational Neuroscience* 6:279–288, 1999.

Graziano, M. The organization of behavioral repertoire in motor cortex. *Annual Reviews of Neuroscience* 29:105–134, 2006.

Hess, W. R. *The Functional Organization of the Diencephalon.* London: Grune & Stratton, 1957.

Kaas, J. H. The organization and evolution of neocortex. In S. P. Wise, Ed. *Higher Brain Functions.* New York: Wiley, 1987, pp. 237–298.

Kakei, S., D. Hoffman, and P. L. Strick. Direction of action is represented in the ventral premotor cortex. *Nature Neuroscience* 4:1020–1025, 2001.

Kakei, S., D. Hoffman, and P. L. Strick. Muscle and movement representations in the primary motor cortex. *Science* 285:2136–2139, 1999.

Kandel, E. R., J. H. Schwartz, and T. M. Jessell. *Principles of Neural Science,* vol. 4. New York, Elsevier, 2000.

Keele, S. W., and R. Ivry. Does the cerebellum provide a common computation for diverse tasks? A timing hypothesis. In A. Diamond, Ed. The Development and Neural Bases of Higher Cognitive Functions. *Annals of the New York Academy of Sciences* 608:197–211, 1991.

Kuypers, H. G. J. M. Anatomy of descending pathways. In V. B. Brooks, Ed. *The Nervous System,* vol. 7, *Handbook of Physiology.* Bethesda, Md.: American Physiological Society, 1981.

Leonard, C. M., D. S. Glendinning, T. Wilfong, B. Y. Cooper, and C. J. Vierck, Jr. Alterations of natural hand movements after interruption of fasciculus cuneatus in the macaque. *Somatosensory and Motor Research* 9:61–75, 1991.

Mountcastle, V. B. An organizing principle for cerebral function: The unit module and the distributed system. In G. M. Edelman and V. B. Mountcastle, Eds. *The Mindful Brain.* Cambridge, Mass.: MIT Press, 1978, pp. 7–50.

Penfield, W., and E. Boldrey. Somatic motor and sensory representation in the cerebral cortex as studied by electrical stimulation. *Brain* 60:389–443, 1958.

Redgrave, P. Basal ganglia. *Scholarpedia* 2205, 2007.

Reeve, C. *Nothing Is Impossible.* New York: Random House, 2002.

Roland, P. E. *Brain Activation.* New York: Wiley-Liss, 1993.

Rothwell, J. C., M. M. Taube, B. L. Day, J. A. Obeso, P. K. Thomas, and C. D. Marsden. Manual motor performance in a deafferented man. *Brain* 105:515–542, 1982.

Schieber, M. H. Constraints on somatotopic organization in the primary motor cortex. *Journal of Neurophysiology* 86:2125–2143, 2001.

Schieber, M. H. Somatotopic gradients in the distributed organization of the human primary motor cortex hand area: Evidence from small infarcts. *Experimental Brain Research* 128:139–148, 1999.

Thatch, W. T., H. P. Goodkin, and J. G. Keating. The cerebellum and the adaptive coordination of movement. *Annual Review of Neuroscience* 15:403–442, 1992.

Umilta, M. A., K. Kohler, V. Gallese, L. Fogassi, L. Fadiga, C. Keysers, and G. Rizzolatti. I know what you are doing: A neurophysiological study. *Neuron* 31:155–165, 2001.

Urgesi, C., V. Moro, M. Candidi, and S. M. Aglioti. Mapping implied body actions in the human motor system. *Journal of Neuroscience* 26:7942–7949, 2006.

Principles of Neocortical Function

10

PORTRAIT: Hemispherectomy

A.R. was a strictly average boy until the age of 11, when he developed seizures, but only on the right side of his body. In time, he developed a persistent right-side weakness and increasing difficulty in talking, or **dysphasia**, impairment of speech caused by damage to the central nervous system.

In the next 6 years, A.R. was admitted to the hospital many times, but the cause of the seizures and his language and motor problems remained undetermined. Although he had initially been right-handed, he was unable to use his right hand and began to write and draw with his left hand. (Recall that the motor and sensory nerves cross over, for example, from the right side of the body to the left cerebral hemisphere.)

By age 15, A.R.'s IQ score had dropped 30 points and, by age 17, his

Courtesy of George Jallo/Johns Hopkins Hospital

language and emotional problems made psychological testing impossible. At 17, his condition was diagnosed as Rasmussen's encephalitis, a chronic brain infection that slowly leads to a virtual loss of function in one cerebral hemisphere. Because the only successful treatment is removal of the diseased tissue, most of A.R.'s left cerebral

hemisphere was surgically removed, a procedure called **hemispherectomy**. (The adjoining postoperative MRI scan is of a patient's skull after a right-hemisphere hemispherectomy.)

When A.R. was reassessed 10 years later, at age 27, he showed remarkable improvement. His oral language skills appeared to be average. He communicated freely and could both initiate and respond to conversation. He was, however, functionally illiterate and unable to read or write except at a very simple level.

His motor skills also had improved. He could move about on his own, although he still had a significant limp, and he could lift his right arm to shoulder level. He could also open and close his hands to grasp objects with his right hand.

People can lose an enormous amount of cerebral tissue and still show remarkable cognitive and motor abilities. The achievements of patients such as A.R. described in the Portrait, even those with severe neuron loss in both cerebral hemispheres, prompt the question, What roles do the cerebral hemispheres and the subcortical regions play in controlling behavior? To search for answers, in this chapter we focus on the hierarchical organization of the central nervous system from spinal cord to cortex, on the structure of the cortex, and on theories of functional brain organization. We conclude by asking another question: Does the human brain possess unique properties?

A Hierarchy of Function from Spinal Cord to Cortex

The brain is organized in a functional hierarchy, the higher levels providing an animal with more precision and flexibility in behavior. A.R.'s intelligence test score was 70 (borderline retarded) after his surgery, which is much below his childhood IQ score of about 100 (normal range). Although severely impaired, A.R. nonetheless functioned rather well with so much of his brain gone. He did so for two reasons:

1. **Levels of function.** Subcortical structures are capable of mediating complex behaviors. The relation of the cortex to subcortical structures is analogous to that of a piano player to a piano. The cortex represents the piano player, producing behavior by playing on subcortical keys. This idea dates to Herbert Spencer's mid-nineteenth-century speculation that each step in evolution has added a new level of brain and of behavioral complexity. John Hughlings-Jackson adopted Spencer's idea, and it became a central focus of neurological theories of the twentieth century (see Chapter 1).

2. **Brain plasticity.** The brain's considerable capacity to change its structure in response to experience, drugs, hormones, or injury is due to its **plasticity**, as is its ability to compensate for loss of function caused by damage. At the time of his surgery, A.R. had no language ability at all, but that was partly because the dysfunctioning left hemisphere, where language functions are concentrated in most of us, was interfering with the right hemisphere's ability to engage in language functions. Shortly after the left hemisphere was removed, at least some of A.R.'s language functions reemerged, as though the left hemisphere had been surpressing functioning in the right.

Indeed, we can trace the focus on functional levels of nervous system organization in part to early findings that the brain has remarkable plasticity. The brain's resiliency to damage gained popular exposure in 1700, when Joseph Du Verney, in a public demonstration, showed that, when a nerve and muscle were dissected away from a frog, the nerve continued to function, because it produced muscle contractions when touched.

In the 300 or so years since then, it has become clear that both laboratory animals and humans can function surprisingly well with rather large amounts of the brain removed. We hasten to point out that the mere fact that people can live fairly normally with large amounts of brain tissue missing does not imply that those parts of the brain are not needed. People can compensate for lost brain tissue just as they can compensate for lost limbs. But this ability to compensate does not mean that such people would not be better off with all their limbs—or brains—intact.

Throughout the twentieth century, the capacities of animals with extensive regions of the nervous system removed were recorded in many neurologic studies. One study was conducted by Kent Berridge on grooming in the rat. Recall from Chapter 9 that rats (as well as other animals, including ourselves) begin by grooming the head and then work their way down the body. As illustrated in **Figure 10.1**, a rat begins to groom by using its paws, rubbing its nose with symmetrical circular movements. Then it sweeps its paws across its face and behind its ears before turning to lick its body. This series of actions can be divided into as many as 50 linked movements.

In examining this movement complex, Berridge found that many levels of the nervous system take part in producing the elements and the syntax (the organization) of the behavior. That is, grooming behavior is produced not by one locus in the brain but rather by many brain areas and levels, including the spinal cord, hindbrain, midbrain, diencephalon, basal ganglia, and cortex. These dif-

Rats have a fixed grooming sequence, which starts with ellipical strokes to the head,...

...followed by grooming of each side of the face.

They move to the ears, using bilateral strokes,...

...and then continue moving toward the rear of the body.

Figure 10.1

Grooming Sequences in the Rat
(After Berridge and Whishaw, 1992.)

Highest remaining functional area	Behaviors
Spinal cord (spinal)	**Reflexes:** Responds by stretching, withdrawal, support, scratching, paw shaking, etc. to appropriate sensory stimulation.
Hindbrain (low decerebrate)	**Postural support:** Performs units of movement (hissing, biting, growling, chewing, lapping, licking, etc.) when stimulated; shows exaggerated standing, postural reflexes, and elements of sleepwalking behavior.
Midbrain (high decerebrate)	**Spontaneous movement:** Responds to simple features of visual and auditory stimulation; performs automatic behaviors such as grooming; performs subsets of voluntary movements (standing, walking, turning, jumping, climbing, etc.) when stimulated.
Hypothalamus, thalamus (diencephalic)	**Affect and motivation:** Voluntary movements occur spontaneously and excessively but are aimless; shows well-integrated but poorly directed affective behavior; thermoregulates effectively.
Basal ganglia (decorticate)	**Self-maintenance:** Links voluntary movements and automatic movements sufficiently well for self-maintenance (eating, drinking) in a simple environment.
Cortex (normal)	**Control and intention:** Performs sequences of voluntary movements in organized patterns; responds to patterns of sensory stimulation. Contains circuits for forming cognitive maps and for responding to the relationships between objects, events, and things. Adds emotional value.

Figure 10.2

Central Nervous System Hierarchy Anatomical and behavioral levels in the central nervous system, shown here in an inverted hierarchy from spinal cord at the top to cortex at the bottom, highlighting the highest remaining functional area at each level.

ferent nervous system layers do not simply replicate function; rather, each region adds a different dimension to the behavior.

This hierarchical organization is true not only of grooming but also of virtually every behavior in which we (as well as rats) engage. Understanding this general principle is critical to understanding what role the cortex plays in controlling behavior. The following sections summarize some of the functions mediated at different anatomical levels of the nervous system (**Figure 10.2**). We note parallel functions that may exist in humans as appropriate. As in Figure 10.2, we begin with the "lowest" level of the central nervous system, the spinal cord, and add structures to see how the corresponding behaviors increase in complexity.

The Spinal Cord and Reflexes

In Chapter 9, we met the actor Christopher Reeve, whose spinal cord was severed just below the brain in a tragic equestrian accident. This spinal-cord injury left the Superman of the movies unable to move or even to breathe without

Figure 10.3

Spinal Animal Walking on Treadmill

the aid of a respirator. The question we wish to ask is, What behaviors could his spinal cord initiate without any descending influence from the brain?

Like Christopher Reeve, an animal whose spinal cord is disconnected from the brain is unable to move voluntarily, because the brain has no way to communicate with the spinal neurons. Nonetheless, the spinal cord is intact and can mediate many reflexes, such as limb approach to a tactile stimulus and limb withdrawal from a noxious stimulus.

The spinal cord also contains the circuitry to produce stepping responses and walking, provided that body weight is supported. For example, if **spinal** animals are suspended in a hammock and placed such that their limbs are in light contact with a moving treadmill, their legs will begin to make stepping movements automatically, as illustrated in **Figure 10.3**. This behavior tells us that circuitry in the spinal cord, not the brain, produces the stepping movements. The role of the brain is control—to make those movements at the right time and place.

The Hindbrain and Postural Support

If the brain is injured such that the hindbrain and spinal cord are still connected but both are disconnected from the rest of the brain, the subject is called a **low decerebrate** (see Figure 10.2). This type of injury produces a very different syndrome from that produced in an animal with a spinal-cord transection. A spinal animal is alert; a person who has sustained such an injury can still talk, express emotion, and so on. However, a low-decerebrate animal no longer shows any alertness, because many essential inputs to the brain regions above the injury are now disconnected, presumably leaving the forebrain "in the dark," with difficulty maintaining consciousness.

Sensory input into the hindbrain comes predominantly from the head and is carried over cranial nerves 4 to 12 (see Figure 3.12). Most of these nerves also have motor nuclei in the hindbrain, whose efferent (outgoing) fibers control muscles in the head and neck. Sensory input to the hindbrain is not limited to the cranial nerves: the spinal somatosensory system has access to hindbrain motor systems, just as the hindbrain has access to spinal motor systems. But sensory input into the hindbrain of the low decerebrate can no longer reach the upper parts of the brain, resulting in a serious disturbance of consciousness.

A classic example of the effects of low-decerebrate injury is revealed in the results of extensive studies on cats done in the early part of the twentieth century by researchers such as H. C. Bazett, Wilder Penfield, and Philip Bard. The researchers kept low-decerebrate cats alive for periods of weeks or months. The cats were generally inactive when undisturbed and showed no effective ability to thermoregulate (maintain normal body temperature), but they swallowed food placed on their tongues and so could be fed.

If the animals were stimulated lightly in any of a variety of sensory modalities (such as touch, pain, or sounds), they moved from their normal reclining position into a crouch. If the stimulation was stronger, they walked, somewhat unsteadily. These stimuli also elicited such normal affective (emotional) behaviors as biting, hissing, growling, and lashing of the tail.

A characteristic aspect of behavior accorded by the hindbrain is a peculiar kind of stiffness called **decerebrate rigidity**. This stiffness is due to excessive muscle tone, particularly in the antigravity muscles that hold the body up to maintain posture and are the body's strongest. When a low-decerebrate animal is placed in an upright position, its limbs extend and its head flexes upward in a posture that is often referred to as "exaggerated standing."

Against the background of decerebrate rigidity, a number of postural reflexes can be elicited by changes in head position. If the head of a standing animal is pushed down toward the floor, the front limbs flex and the hind limbs extend; if the head is pushed upward, the hind legs flex and the front legs extend. The first posture would be used by a normal cat looking under a couch, the second by a normal cat looking upward onto a shelf. Turning the head to the side elicits extension of the limbs on the same side and flexion of the limbs on the opposite side of the body. This response occurs in a normal cat that has turned its head to look at some object and is prepared to pursue it.

Normal animals exhibit two types of sleep: *quiet sleep*, characterized by muscle tone and commonly referred to as slow-wave sleep, and *active sleep*, characterized by an absence of muscle tone and commonly referred to as *dream sleep* or *REM* (rapid eye movement) *sleep* (**Figure 10.4**). Low-decerebrate animals display both types of sleep at different times. Those left undisturbed gradually lose their rigidity and subside or droop into a prone posture. Any mild stimulus such as a noise or a touch reinstates rigidity. This behavioral change seems analogous to quiet sleep.

Low-decerebrate animals also show a sudden collapse, accompanied by the loss of all body tone, which lasts from 15 seconds to 12 minutes, analogous to active, or REM, sleep. People with an illness called **narcolepsy** similarly collapse uncontrollably into active sleep. The results of research with low-decerebrate animals thus demonstrate that the neural centers that produce sleep are located in the hindbrain.

The behavioral changes seen in low-decerebrate animals are paralleled in people who enter a persistent vegetative state (PVS) after brainstem damage of the type that essentially separates the lower brainstem from the rest of the brain. R. Barrett and his colleagues documented numerous cases. Like Terri Schiavo (see the Snapshot on page 16), these people may alternate between states of consciousness resembling sleeping and waking, make eye movements to follow moving stimuli, cough, smile, swallow food, and display decerebrate rigidity and postural adjustments when moved. When cared for, PVS patients may live for months or years with little change in their condition.

Awake

Quiet sleep
(slow-wave sleep)

Active sleep

Figure 10.4

Postures of a Normal Cat

The Midbrain and Spontaneous Movement

The next level of brain organization can be seen in an animal that has an intact midbrain (mesencephalon) but lacks higher-center functioning. Damage that separates the diencephalon from the midbrain regions containing, in the tectum, the coordinating centers for vision (superior colliculus) and hearing (inferior colliculus) and, in the tegmentum, a number of motor nuclei, produces this condition, called **high decerebration** (see Figure 10.2). Visual and auditory inputs allow the animal to perceive events at a distance, and so the high-decerebrate animal can respond to distant objects by moving toward them.

Bard and Macht report that high-decerebrate cats can walk, stand, resume upright posture when turned on their backs, and even run and climb when stimulated. Bignall and Schramm found that kittens decerebrated in infancy could orient themselves toward visual and auditory stimuli. The animals could even execute an attack response and pounce on objects at the source of a sound.

In fact, Bignall and Schramm fed the cats by exploiting this behavior: they placed food near the source of the sound. Attacking the sound source, the cats then consumed the food. Although the cats attacked moving objects, they gave no evidence of being able to see, because they bumped into things when they walked.

These experiments demonstrate that all the subsets of **voluntary movements**—movements that take an animal from one place to another, such as turning, walking, climbing, swimming, and flying—are present at the subcortical level of the midbrain. Normal animals use voluntary movements to satisfy a variety of needs—for example, to find food, water, or a new home territory, or to escape a predator. Voluntary movements have also been variously called *appetitive, instrumental, purposive,* or *operant.*

Because they are executed through lower-level postural support and reflex systems, voluntary movements can also be elicited by lower-level sensory input; that is, a pinch or postural displacement can elicit turning, walking, or climbing. Thus, function at the midbrain level is integrated with lower levels by both ascending and descending connections, exactly as the hindbrain and spinal levels are interconnected.

High-decerebrate animals can also effectively perform **automatic movements**, units of stereotyped behavior linked in a sequence. Grooming, chewing food, lapping water, and rejecting food are representative automatic behaviors of the rat. Generally, automatic behaviors (also variously called *reflexive, consummatory,* or *respondent*) are directed toward completing an act and are not specifically directed toward moving an animal from one place to another.

Grooming is an excellent example of an automatic behavior, because it consists of a large number of movements executed sequentially in an organized and stereotyped fashion. Food rejection comprises a similarly complex series of behaviors. If high-decerebrate rats are given food when they are not hungry, they perform a series of movements consisting of tongue flicks, chin rubbing, and paw shaking to reject the food. These behaviors are similar to the rejection behaviors of normal rats—as well as people, as illustrated in **Figure 10.5**—in response to food that they find noxious. If the animals are not sated, they will lap water and chew food brought to their mouths.

Among the accounts of infants born with large parts of the forebrain missing, one child studied by E. Gamper had no brain present above the diencephalon and only a few traces of the diencephalon intact. This child was,

Figure 10.5

Human Reactions to Taste
Positive (hedonic) reactions, such as licking the fingers or lips, are elicited by sweet and other palatable tastes. Negative (aversive) reactions, elicited by bitter tastes (such as quinine) and by other unpalatable flavors, include spitting, making a face of distaste, and wiping the mouth with the back of the hand. (After K. C. Berridge, Food reward: Brain substrates of wanting and liking. *Neuroscience and Biobehavioral Reviews* 20, p. 6, 1996.)

Positive reactions

Negative reactions

therefore, anatomically and behaviorally equivalent to a high-decerebrate animal. As shown in **Figure 10.6**, the child could sit up and showed many behaviors of newborn infants, periodically asleep and wakeful, sucking, yawning, stretching, crying, and following visual stimuli with the eyes. However, the child showed little spontaneous activity and, if left alone, remained mostly in a drowsy state.

Yvonne Brackbill studied a similar child and found that, in response to moderately loud sounds (60–90 decibels), this infant oriented to stimuli in much the same way as normal infants do. Unlike normal babies, however, this child's responses did not change in magnitude and did not habituate (gradually decrease in intensity) to repeated presentations. Brackbill concluded that the forebrain is not important in producing movements but is important in attenuating and inhibiting them. Generally, babies born with such extensive brain abnormalities do not live long, and, among those who live for several months, the complex behaviors seen in normal infants do not develop.

The Diencephalon and Affect and Motivation

A **diencephalic** animal, although lacking the basal ganglia and cerebral hemispheres, has an intact olfactory system, enabling it to smell odors at a distance (see Figure 10.2). The hypothalamus and pituitary also are intact, and their control over hormonal systems and homeostasis no doubt integrates the body's physiology with the brain's activity. Diencephalic animals thermoregulate, for example, but they do not eat or drink well enough to sustain themselves.

The diencephalon adds a dimension of affect and motivation to behavior in the sense that behavior becomes "energized" and sustained. As already mentioned, high-decerebrate animals show many of the component behaviors of rage, but their behaviors are not energetic, well integrated, or sustained. Walter Cannon and S. W. Britton studied diencephalic cats and described what they called "quasi-emotional phenomena," or sham rage, such as that usually seen in an infuriated animal. This affective behavior is inappropriately displayed and is thus called sham rage to distinguish it from the directed rage of a normal cat.

Sham rage consists of lashing the tail, arching the trunk, making limb movements, displaying claws, snarling, and biting. A diencephalic animal displays sympathetic nervous system signs of rage, including erection of the tail hair, sweating of the toe pads, dilation of the pupils, urination, high blood pressure, high heart rate, and increases in epinephrine and blood sugar. These emotional attacks sometimes last for hours.

Bard removed varying amounts of forebrain and brainstem and found that, for sham rage to occur, at least the posterior part of the hypothalamus must be left intact. Clinical reports indicate that similar sham emotional attacks can

(A) Yawning, spreading arms

(B) Sucking after lips are touched, with deviation of eyes

(C) Coordinated gaze and mouth snapping after finger is removed from view

(D) Spontaneous sucking of own hand

(E) Turning left to suck, with deviation of head and eyes and tonic neck reflexes in arms

Figure **10.6**

Mesencephalic Human Infant
Among the instinctive behaviors and oral automatisms studied by Gamper are the five shown here. (From E. Gamper, *Z. ges. Neurol. Psychiat.* 104, p. 49, 1926.)

occur in people who have suffered hypothalamic lesions. These people show unchecked rage or literally laugh until they die. In addition to sham rage, another pronounced feature of a diencephalic animal's behavior is its constant activity. For example, when placed in an open field, it wanders aimlessly.

These two behaviors suggest that the diencephalon energizes an animal's behavior, which may have led some researchers to consider the behavior affective or motivated. Perhaps the hyperactivity of a diencephalic animal should be called *sham motivation* to distinguish it from a normal animal's goal-oriented behavior. In this sense, the sham affect and sham motivation of a diencephalic animal are like the exaggerated standing observed in low-decerebrate animals. Under appropriate forebrain control, the behavior can be released for functional purposes but, in the absence of that control, the behavior of a diencephalic animal is excessive and seems inappropriate.

The Basal Ganglia and Self-Maintenance

Decortication is the removal of the neocortex, leaving the basal ganglia and brainstem intact (see Figure 10.2). Decorticate animals have been studied more closely than any other neurologically impaired class, because they are able to maintain themselves without special care in laboratory conditions.

The first careful experiments were done by Friedrich Goltz with decorticate dogs (see Chapter 1), but the most thorough studies have used rats as subjects. Within a day after surgery, rats eat and maintain body weight on a wet mash diet and eat dry food and drink water brought in contact with the mouth. With a little training in drinking (holding the water spout to the mouth), they find water and become able to maintain themselves on water and laboratory chow. They have normal sleeping–waking cycles; run, climb, and swim; and even negotiate simple mazes.

They can also sequence series of movements. For example, copulation consists of a number of movements that take place sequentially and last for hours, yet decorticate animals can perform these acts almost normally. As described early in this chapter, grooming also requires the sequential use of about 50 discrete movements, and decorticate rats also perform it normally.

In sum, to a casual observer, a decorticate rat appears indistinguishable from normal animals. In fact, in laboratory exercises in which students are tasked to distinguish between normal and decorticate animals, they not only find the job difficult, but often fail. A decorticate rat does indeed have a lot of behavioral difficulties, but seeing these problems requires a trained eye. All the elementary movements that animals might make seem to be part of their behavioral repertory after decortication. They can walk, eat, drink, mate, and raise litters of pups in a seemingly adequate fashion.

What is observed in a decorticate rat, and what is presumably conferred by functions in the basal ganglia, is the ability to link automatic movements to voluntary movements so that the behaviors are biologically adaptive. A major part of this linking probably includes the inhibition or facilitation of voluntary movements. For example, the animal walks until it finds food or water and then inhibits walking to consume the food or water. Thus, the basal ganglia probably provide the circuitry required for the stimulus to inhibit movement so that ingestion can occur.

The Cortex and Intention

What the cortex does can also be ascertained by studying what decorticate animals (with the neocortex alone removed or with the limbic system also removed) do not do. They do not build nests, although they engage in some nest-building behaviors. They do not hoard food, although they might carry food around. They also have difficulty making skilled movements with the tongue and limbs, because they are unable to reach for food by protruding the tongue or by reaching with one forelimb.

They can perform pattern discriminations in different sensory modalities but only if these tasks are relatively simple. For example, a decorticate could discriminate two pure tones but would be unable to distinguish complex sounds such as the noises from a lawn mower and an automobile. The results of a series of experiments by David Oakley show that decorticate animals can perform well in tests of classical conditioning, operant conditioning, approach learning, cue learning, and pattern discrimination. These experiments confirm that the cortex is not essential for learning itself. However, decorticate animals fail at learning, for example, complex pattern discriminations and how to find their way around in space.

The results of studies of decortication tell us that the cortex does not add much to an animal's behavioral repertory in the way of new movements. Rather, the cortex appears to extend the usefulness of all behaviors or to make them adaptive in new situations. An animal without a cortex can see and hear and can use its limbs for many purposes, but an animal with a cortex can make plans and combine movement sequences together to generate more-complex behavioral patterns.

The Structure of the Cortex

As our summary of the behaviors of animals with only subcortical brain function makes clear, the cortex adds new dimensions to the analysis of sensory events and new levels of control to movements. What structural features of the cortex permit these enhancements?

Recall from Chapter 3 that the cortex can be divided by topographic maps, which are based on various anatomical and functional criteria. The first complete cortical map of the human brain was published in 1905 by Alfred Campbell, and it was based on both cell structure and myelin distribution. Soon after, several alternative versions emerged, the most notable by Korbinian Brodmann, reproduced in **Figure 10.7**.

The various maps do not correspond exactly, and they use different criteria and nomenclature. Furthermore, as new staining techniques are devised, it is possible to subdivide and redefine cortical areas in a truly bewildering manner, with estimates of the number of cortical areas in the human brain ranging from the approximately 50 of Brodmann to more than 200. (One neuroanatomical wag was quoted as concluding that "in cortical anatomy the gain is in the stain!") Most recently, MRI technology has been employed to map the human brain, as illustrated in the Snapshot on page 254.

Figure **10.7**

Brodmann's Map Lateral and medial views highlighted with primary, secondary, and tertiary (association) areas, as described by Paul Flechsig. The primary cortex is brightest (areas 4, 3-1-2, 41, 17); the secondary cortex is medium bright, and the tertiary is lightest.

Lateral view

Medial view

⌐SNAPSHOT

Mapping the Human Cortex

About 70% of the human cerebral cortex is buried in sulci, which complicates our ability to visualize its extent from a surface view or a topographic map. Surface views of the brain thus hide the source of the majority of activation recorded in imaging studies. One display format that solves this problem is the flat map, which allows imagers to visualize the entire surface area of a hemisphere in a single view and to identify the location of activated areas.

David van Essen and H. A. Drury used the MRI analysis of the Visible Man, a digital atlas of the human body, to generate flat maps of the human cortex. Part A of the adjoin-

Cortical surface-area measurements

Region	Left Hemisphere in cm² (%)	Right Hemisphere in cm² (%)
Frontal	278 (36)	297 (37)
Temporal	161 (21)	161 (21)
Parietal	139 (18)	161 (20)
Occipital	144 (19)	145 (18)
Paralimbic	46 (6)	40 (5)
Total	766 (100)	803 (100)

ing illustration shows lateral and medial surface views of the Visible Man's two hemispheres, with the lobes identified by different colors. Flat maps (part B) display the areas of cortex buried within sulci and gyri, which are shown in darker shades around each sulcus. The accompanying table contrasts the relative surface-area measurements of the cortical lobes and the paralimbic cortex.

The location of brain areas in a whole brain can be calculated by using a three-dimensional atlas. Sections are taken at regular intervals (typically 4 millimeters in the human brain), much as if an atlas of the Earth were made by taking sequential cuts through the globe at regular intervals and then displaying the map obtained of each cut on a single page.

As you flip through the pages of the atlas, you can visualize how the Earth appears going from one side to the other in space. By linking the data from the Visible Man to this so-called Talairach space, van Essen and Drury identified the coordinates for the cortical regions in their flat map, making it possible to identify the location of activations in three-dimensional imaging studies.

(A) Left hemisphere — Central sulcus — Lateral view — Medial view; Right hemisphere — Central sulcus — Lateral view — Medial view

(B) Anterior — Olfactory bulb — Corpus callosum and paralimbic cortex — Central sulcus — Frontal lobe — Parietal lobe — Temporal lobe — Hippocampus — Occipital lobe — Posterior — Temporal lobe — Hippocampus

Cortical maps. (A) Digital surface maps. (B) Flat maps provide a perspective on the relative size of various cortical regions and on the amount of tissue dedicated to different functions, as detailed in the table.

van Essen, D. C., and H. A. Drury. Structural and functional analyses of human cerebral cortex using a surface-based atlas. *Journal of Neuroscience* 17:7082–7102, 1997.

A consistent theme in neuroanatomy throughout the past century is that cortical regions can be categorized as primary sensory cortex, primary motor cortex, and association cortex. Association areas are usually also categorized as secondary cortex, which elaborates information coming from primary areas, and as **higher-order areas** (sometimes called tertiary areas), which may combine information from more than one system. This idea can be traced to Paul Flechsig and his studies of the development of myelin in the cortex.

Flechsig divided cortical regions into (1) an early-myelinating primordial zone including the motor cortex and a region of visual, auditory, and somatosensory cortex; (2) a (secondary) field bordering the primordial zone that myelinates next; and (3) a late-myelinating (tertiary) zone that he called "association." The three zones are color-coded in Figure 10.7. Flechsig hypothesized psychological functions for his hierarchy, with the general idea being that the primary zones perform simple sensorimotor functions, whereas the secondary and tertiary zones conduct the highest mental analyses. Flechsig's ideas greatly influenced neurological thinking throughout the twentieth century.

Cortical Cells

Nerve cells are easily distinguished in the cortex as **spiny neurons** or **aspiny neurons** by the presence or absence, respectively, of dendritic spines. Essentially, much as rose thorns extend the surface area of rosebush branches, dendritic spines extend of the surface area of dendrites (see Figure 4.1). Dendritic spines serve as functional compartments for chemicals as well as locations for synaptic connections with other cells.

Spiny neurons are excitatory and are likely to use glutamate or aspartate as neurotransmitters. About 95% of all excitatory synapses on spiny neurons are found on the spines. (For an extensive series of books on the structure of the cortex, see Peters and Jones, 1984–1999.)

Spiny neurons include **pyramidal cells**, whose pyramid-shaped cell bodies generally send information from a region of the cortex to another area of the central nervous system, and spiny **stellate cells**, smaller, star-shaped interneurons whose processes remain within the region of the brain in which the cell body is located. Pyramidal cells, which constitute the largest population of cortical neurons (70%–85%), are the efferent projection neurons of the cortex. They are found in layers II, III, V, and VI.

In general, the largest cells send their axons the farthest. The pyramidal cells of layer V are the largest, projecting from the cortex to the brainstem and spinal cord. Those in layers II and III are smaller and project to other cortical regions, as diagrammed in **Figure 10.8**.

Aspiny neurons are interneurons with short axons and no dendritic spines. They are diverse in appearance, with different types named largely on the basis of the configurations of their axons and dendrites. One type of aspiny stellate cell is called a *basket cell* because its axon projects horizontally, forming synapses that envelop the postsynaptic cell like a basket. Another, the *double-bouquet* type, has a proliferation of dendrites on either side of the cell body, much as if two bouquets of flowers were aligned stem to stem (see Figure 10.8).

Despite differences in shape, all aspiny neurons are inhibitory and are likely to use gamma-aminobutyric acid (GABA) as a neurotransmitter. Aspiny neurons also use many other transmitters; virtually every classical transmitter and neuropeptide has been colocalized with GABA in aspiny cells. Thus, aspiny cells not only are morphologically diverse, but also show a remarkable chemical diversity.

Figure 10.8

Neocortical Cell Types The most important neuron types, pyramidal cells and stellate cells, are elaborated here. The direction of the arrows indicates afferent (up) or efferent (down) projections. (After Szentagothai, 1969.)

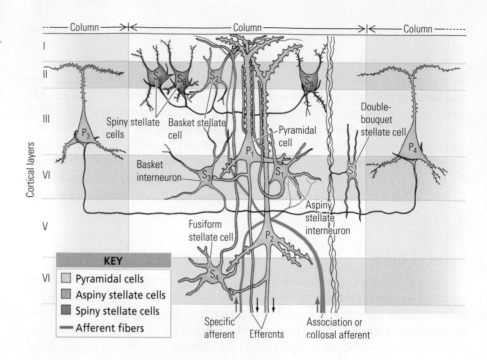

Cortical Layers, Efferents, and Afferents

Each of the four to six layers of the cortex has different functions, different afferents, and different efferents. The cells of the middle cortical layers, especially in and around layer IV, constitute a zone of sensory analysis in that they receive projections from other areas of the cortex and other areas of the brain. The cells of layers V and VI constitute a zone of output in that they send axons to other cortical areas or other brain areas.

It is hardly surprising, then, that the somatosensory cortex has a relatively large layer IV and a small layer V, whereas the motor cortex has a relatively large layer V and a small layer IV. **Figure 10.9** illustrates this difference and shows that the various cortical layers can be distinguished by the neuronal elements that each contains and that the thickness of the layers corresponds to their function. The superficial layers (II and III) receive inputs from other cortical areas and can thus integrate information coming to layer IV as well as that from other cortical regions.

Figure 10.9 illustrates another feature of cortical organization: afferents to the cortex are of two general types, specific and nonspecific:

1. **Specific afferents** bring information (sensory information, for example) to an area of the cortex and terminate in relatively discrete cortical regions, usually in only one or two layers. Specific afferents include projections from the thalamus as well as from the amygdala. Most of these projections terminate in layer IV, although projections from the amygdala and certain thalamic nuclei may terminate in the more superficial layers.

2. **Nonspecific afferents** presumably serve general functions, such as maintaining a level of activity or arousal so that the cortex can process information. They terminate diffusely over large regions of the cortex—in some cases, over all of it. Nonspecific afferents even release their transmitter substances into the extracellular space. The noradrenergic projections from

KEY TO CONNECTIONS

S, specific afferents
NS, nonspecific afferents
C–C, cortical–cortical efferents arise from
    layers II and III
Ca, callosal efferents arise from layer III
C–S, cortical–subcortical efferents arise
    from layer V
C–Sp, cortical–spinal efferents arise from
    layer V
C–T, cortical–thalamic efferents arise from
    layer VI

Figure **10.9**

Cortical Layers A comparison of cortical layers in the somatosensory and motor cortices shows that the somatosensory cortex is much thinner than the motor cortex and that the size of each layer is markedly different in the two. Note especially that layer IV is far thicker in the somatosensory cortex than in the motor cortex. The specific and nonspecific inputs to the cortex illustrate the distribution of these afferents to the different layers. The outputs (efferents) from the cortex arise from different layers, depending on their destination. (After Shepherd, 1979.)

the brainstem, the cholinergic projections from the basal forebrain, and the projections from certain thalamic nuclei are examples of nonspecific afferents (see Figure 5.17 to review the neurotransmitter systems).

Cortical Columns, Spots, and Stripes

Most interactions between the layers of the cortex take place within the neurons directly above or below adjacent layers. Less interaction takes place with cells more than a couple of millimeters on either side. This vertical bias in cortical organization forms the basis for a second type of neocortical organization.

Among the many terms for the vertical organization of the cortex, the two most common are **column** and **module** (see Figure 10.8). Although these terms are not always interchangeable, the underlying idea is that groups of 150 to 300 neurons form little circuits ranging from about 0.5 millimeter to 2.0 millimeters wide, depending on the cortical region. Evidence for some kind of modular unit comes from two principal sources: staining and probing.

When the brain is cut horizontally and stained in special ways, patterns of spots or stripes in the cortex are visible (**Figure 10.10**). Some examples will illustrate:

- If a radioactive amino acid is injected into one eye of a monkey, the radioactivity is transported across synapses to the primary visual cortex (region V1, or area 17). The radioactivity is not evenly distributed across

Figure **10.10**

Cortical Spots and Stripes Modular patterns are revealed by staining. (After Purves et al., 1992.)

(A) Ocular dominance columns in area 17

(C) Stripes in area 18

(B) Blobs in area 17

(D) Barrels in area SI

the cortex, however, in that it travels only to places that connect with the affected eye called *ocular dominance columns* (Figure 10.10A). The pattern of radioactivity seen in region V1 is a series of stripes, much like those on a zebra's coat.

- When a different technique is used, however, a different pattern emerges. If area 17 is stained with cytochrome oxidase, which shows areas of high metabolic activity by staining mitochondria, the primary visual cortex appears spotted. These spots, known as "blobs," have a role in color perception (Figure 10.10B).

- Curiously, if the same stain is applied to area 18, an adjacent, secondary visual region, the pattern of staining is more like stripes (Figure 10.10C) than like spots.

- Finally, if the primary somatosensory cortex (area SI) of a rat is stained with succinic dehydrogenase, the cortex shows a pattern of spots that are known as "barrels" (Figure 10.10D). Each barrel corresponds to one of the vibrissae on the face of the rat.

As these examples illustrate, many types of cortical modules appear to exist, and even the same stain shows a different modular organization in different regions.

A second way to demonstrate modular organization is physiological. If a microelectrode is placed in the somatosensory cortex and lowered vertically from layer I to layer VI, for example, all the neurons encountered appear to be functionally similar. Neurons in each layer are excited, say, by a particular tactile stimulus (for example, a light touch) in a particular part of the body (for example, the left thumb).

The cells of layer IV are activated earliest by an afferent input, not surprising considering the direct afferent connections to this layer. Cells of the other layers must have longer latencies: they would have at least one more synapse on an interneuron in layer IV before receiving the sensory input. The pyramidal neurons of layer V are the last to be activated, again as we would expect, because the efferents are there (see Figure 10.8).

The functional similarity of cells across all six layers at any point in the cortex suggests that its simplest functional unit is a vertically oriented column of cells that composes a minicircuit. Groups of these columns may be organized in somewhat larger units as well. If an electrode samples the cells of area 17, all the cells in a column will respond to a line of a given orientation (for example, 45°). If the electrode is moved laterally across the cortex, adjacent columns will respond to successively different orientations (for example, 60°, 90°, and so on) until all orientations covering 360° are sampled. The pattern will then repeat itself. Thus, in the visual cortex, columns are arranged in larger modules.

As interesting as cortical spots, stripes, and columns are, considerable controversy continues over what the definition of a module is and what the presence of a module means functionally. One problem is that, although modules are apparent in primary sensory regions, they are less apparent in the association or motor areas of the cortex. Another problem is that, if we are looking for a common definition of the dimensions of a module, then the stripes and spots are a problem because they differ greatly in size.

Furthermore, closely related species often have very different patterns of spots and stripes, which seems strange if they are fundamental units of cortical function. For example, although Old World monkeys have beautiful ocular dominance columns, these columns are not found in New World monkeys, even though the visual abilities of the two monkey groups are similar.

Semir Zeki suggested that the search for the basic module of cortical organization is like the physicist's search for the basic unit of all matter. The underlying assumption is that the cortical module might be performing the same basic function throughout the cortex. In this view, the evolutionary expansion of the cortex corresponds to an increase in the number of basic units, much as one would add chips to a computer to expand its memory or processing speed. This notion has some appeal, but we are left wondering what the basic function and operation of the cortical module might be.

Dale Purves and his colleagues have offered a provocative answer. They noted that the spots and stripes on the cortex resemble markings on the fur of many animals. They suggest that, though these arresting patterns may provide camouflage or broadcast sexual signals, these functions are secondary to the fur's fundamental purpose of maintaining body temperature.

Pursuing this analogy, the researchers propose that some modular patterns in the cortex may well correspond to secondary functions of cortical organization. One suggested possibility is that cortical modules may be an incidental consequence of the nature of synaptic processing in the cortex. In other words, as the cortex forms its intrinsic connections to process information, one efficient pattern of connectivity is the vertical module.

The module certainly conforms to an important aspect of cortical connectivity, but it does not cause cortical connectivity. There must be an alternative way (or ways) of organizing complex neural activity that does not require a constant module. In fact, the bird brain provides an example.

Birds clearly exhibit complex behavior, and some birds, such as crows, are extremely intelligent, likely more intelligent than many mammals (such as mice). In spite of their complex behavior, birds do not have a cortex but rather a neural organization in which different

Lateral view of the canary brain shows several nuclei that control vocal learning and their connections.

Canary brain

12th cranial nerve

To syrinx (vocal organ)

KEY
■ Nuclei specialized for vocal learning
■ Nuclei specialized for vocal learning and adult song

nuclei function rather like cortical layers. We can see therefore that, although a cortical organization with columns is a useful arrangement, it is not the only way to organize a brain.

Clearly, a vertical component to cortical organization exists, but the structure and function of a basic module is difficult to define at present. Further, a single way of organizing cortical connectivity across all mammalian species and cortical regions seems unlikely.

Multiple Representations: Mapping Reality

Early ideas about visual, auditory, and somatic function held that one or two representations of the external environment in the cortex are responsible for our basic sensations. When Wilder Penfield and his colleagues stimulated the motor and somatosensory strips of their patients at the Montreal Neurological Hospital in the 1950s, they identified two regions of the parietal cortex that appeared to represent localized body parts such as the leg, hand, and face (see Figure 9.4). These regions, called homunculi, were seen as the areas of the cortex responsible for basic tactile sensations such as touch, pressure, and temperature.

Subsequent investigations of nonhuman subjects led to the identification of analogous maps of the visual and auditory worlds as well. Thus, half a century ago, most neuroscientists believed that the vast majority of the human cortex generally took part in complex mental analyses that we might loosely call **cognition** (knowledge and thought).

Doubt about this simple view of cortical organization arose in the late 1970s and the 1980s, however, as more-refined physiological and anatomical research techniques began to reveal literally dozens of maps in each sensory modality rather than just one or two. For example, between 25 and 32 regions in the monkey cortex have roles in visual functioning, depending on the definition used.

Although the somatosensory and auditory maps are less numerous in the monkey, from about 10 to 15 cortical maps in each of these modalities do not duplicate the original maps but rather process different aspects of sensory experience. For example, visual areas are specialized for analyzing basic features such as form, color, and movement. Furthermore, many psychological processes, such as visual object memory and visually guided movements, require visual information.

In addition to the demonstration of multiple maps, areas were identified that function in more than one modality (for example, vision and touch). These areas, known as **multimodal**, or **polymodal**, cortex, presumably function to combine characteristics of stimuli across different sensory modalities. For example, we can visually identify objects that we have only touched, which implies some common perceptual system linking the visual and somatic systems.

Until recently, neuroscientists believed that several distinct regions of multimodal cortex exist, but it is becoming increasingly clear that multimodal processing is surprisingly pervasive (for a review see Ghazanfar and Schroeder). **Figure 10.11** summarizes the multimodal areas in the monkey brain and shows that multimodal cortex is found in both primary and secondary cortex. The integration of information from different sensory systems thus appears to be a basic characteristic of cortical functioning. The convergence of qualitatively different sensory information clearly alters our perception of the world.

Asif Ghazanfar and his colleagues nicely illustrated this point in a study of neurons in the monkey auditory cortex. When monkeys listened to a recording of another monkey's voice (a "coo" vocalization), the firing rate of the auditory neurons increased by about 25% if the voice was accompanied by a visual image of a monkey making the coo vocalization, but only if the voice and facial movements were in synchrony. The Ghazanfar study is consistent with our own perception that speech is easier to hear and understand if we can see the speaker's face moving synchronously with the sound.

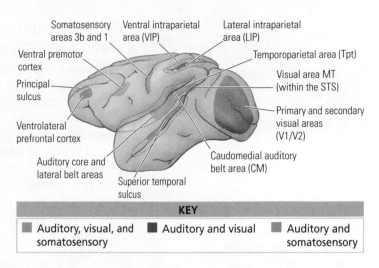

Figure 10.11

Multisensory Areas in the Monkey Cortex Colored areas represent regions where anatomical or electrophysiological data or both types demonstrate multisensory itneractions. Dashed lines represent open sulci. (After Ghazanfar and Schroeder, 2006.)

Multimodal cortex appears to be of two general types, one related to the recognition and related processing of information and the other controlling movement related to the information in some manner. This important concept suggests that we have parallel cortical systems: one system functions to understand the world and the other to move us around in the world and allow us to manipulate our world. This distinction is counterintuitive, because our impression is that our sensory and motor worlds are the same. We shall see that they are not.

The emerging view is that the cortex is fundamentally an organ of sensory perception and related motor processes. This idea has an interesting implication: animals with more cortex must engage in more sensory processing than do animals with less or no cortex and must experience a different perception of the world as well. Harry Jerison pursued this idea by suggesting that our knowledge of reality is related directly to the structure and number of our cortical maps.

As the number of maps possessed by an animal brain increases, more of the external world is known to the animal and more behavioral options are available to it. For instance, animals such as rats and dogs, whose brains lack a cortical region analyzing color, perceive the world in black and white. It must limit their behavioral options, at least with respect to color. Similarly, although difficult for us to imagine, species such as dogs that are not "smell blind" as we are may know their world through object-specific olfactory images that are as useful to them as our visual images are to us.

Jerison suggested that cortical maps determine reality for a given species. Furthermore, he noted that the more maps a species has, the more complex the internal representation of the external world must be. Thus, if humans have more maps than dogs, then our representation of reality must be more complex than that of a dog. Similarly, if dogs have more maps than mice, then a dog's understanding of the world is more complex than that of a mouse.

This viewpoint suggests an interesting implication: the relative intelligence of different mammalian species may be related to the number of maps used by the cortex to represent the world. Dogs would have more olfactory maps than people have and would thus be more intelligent about smells, but the total number of maps in all sensory regions taken together is far greater in humans than in dogs.

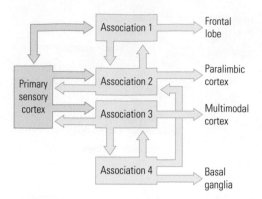

Figure 10.12

Levels of Organization in the Cortex The primary sensory cortex projects to sensory association regions that are interconnected. These regions project to several cortical targets—including the frontal lobe, paralimbic cortex, and multimodal cortex—and to a subcortical target, the basal ganglia. Several levels of association cortex exist but, for simplicity, only a single level is illustrated here.

Cortical Systems: Frontal Lobe, Paralimbic Cortex, and Subcortical Loops

The connections among cortical areas in a sensory system constitute only a part of all cortical connections. The four other principal connections in the cortical hierarchy are with the frontal lobe, paralimbic cortex, multimodal cortex, and subcortical connections and loops (**Figure 10.12**).

The frontal lobe can be subdivided into (1) primary motor cortex, forming the motor homunculus; (2) premotor cortex lying just in front of the motor cortex; and (3) prefrontal cortex, which occupies the remainder of the frontal lobe (see Figure 9.2). Sensory regions do not connect directly with the motor cortex but may project to either the premotor or the prefrontal cortex. Connections to the premotor cortex participate in ordering movements in time and controlling hand, limb, or eye movements with respect to specific sensory stimuli. Projections to the prefrontal cortex take part in the control of movements in time and in forming short-term memories of sensory information (detailed in Chapter 18).

The **paralimbic cortex**—phylogenetically older than the neocortex—plays a role in the formation of long-term memories. It is adjacent and directly connected to the limbic structures and comprises roughly three layers (**Figure 10.13**). Paralimbic cortex can be seen in two places: (1) on the medial surface of the temporal lobe, where it is known as *perirhinal cortex*, *entorhinal cortex*, and *parahippocampal cortex*; and (2) just above the corpus callosum, where it is referred to as *cingulate cortex*.

The neocortex receives all its sensory input from subcortical structures, either directly from the thalamus or indirectly through midbrain structures, such as the tectum. These cortical–subcortical connections are reciprocal feedback loops, or **subcortical loops** (**Figure 10.14**). Each level interacts and is integrated with higher and lower levels by ascending and descending connections. Subcortical loops connect the cortex, thalamus, amygdala, and hippocampus; an indirect loop with the striatum connects with the thalamus.

Subcortical loops presumably play some role in amplifying or modulating cortical activity. Consider, for example, how the amygdala adds affective tone to visual input. A ferocious dog may generate a strong affective response in us as it charges, in part because the amygdala adds affective tone to the visual threat of the dog. Indeed, in the absence of the amygdala, laboratory animals display absolutely no fear of threatening objects. Cats whose amygdalas have been removed take leisurely strolls through rooms housing large monkeys, whereas no normal cat would even contemplate doing such a thing.

Figure 10.13

Paralimbic Cortex In these views of the cerebral cortex of the rhesus monkey, the rusty color indicates the paralimbic areas in the frontal and temporal lobes and in the cingulate gyrus.

(A) Medial view
Cingulate sulcus
Corpus callosum
Cingulate
Entorhinal
Parahippocampal Perirhinal Temporal polar

(B) Lateral view
Central sulcus
Temporal polar

(C) Ventral view
Rhinal sulcus
Orbital
Calcarine sulcus

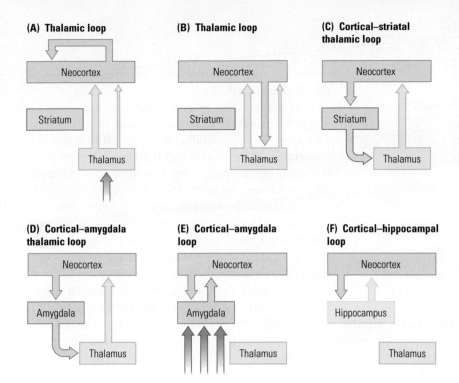

(A) Thalamic loop

Neocortex

Striatum

Thalamus

(B) Thalamic loop

Neocortex

Striatum

Thalamus

(C) Cortical–striatal thalamic loop

Neocortex

Striatum

Thalamus

(D) Cortical–amygdala thalamic loop

Neocortex

Amygdala

Thalamus

(E) Cortical–amygdala loop

Neocortex

Amygdala

Thalamus

(F) Cortical–hippocampal loop

Neocortex

Hippocampus

Thalamus

Figure **10.14**

Subcortical Loops Note that parts A and B show two different thalamic loops. Each feedback loop through the midbrain presumably functions to modify ongoing cortical activity. Thickness of the arrows represents the relative size of the connections. The arrows into the amygdala in part E indicate various subcortical inputs to it.

Cortical Connections, Reentry, and the Binding Problem

We have seen that the cortex has multiple anatomically segregated and functionally specialized areas. How does brain organization translate into our perception of the world as a **gestalt**—a unified and coherent whole? When you look at a person's face, for example, why do shape, color, and size combine into a coherent, unchanging image? This question identifies the **binding problem**, which asks how sensations in specific channels (touch, vision, hearing, and so forth) combine into perceptions that translate as a unified experience that we call reality (see Chapter 1).

There seem to be three possible solutions to the binding problem. One is a high-order cortical center that receives input from all the different cortical areas and integrates (binds) them into a single perception. Although this hierarchical idea makes sense, unfortunately no such area exists.

A second solution is to interconnect all the different cortical areas so that information is somehow shared. The problem is that not all cortical areas are connected with one another, not even within a sensory modality. Various researchers have tried to determine the rules of connectivity, but they are not simple and are beyond the scope of the discussion here (for details, see Felleman and van Essen, 1991; Pandya and Yeterian, 1985; and Zeki, 1993).

Suffice it to say that only about 40% of the possible intercortical connections within a sensory modality are actually found, which leads us to the third solution: intracortical networks of connections among subsets of cortical regions. This idea has considerable appeal.

First, all cortical areas have internal connections among units with similar properties. These connections link neurons that are neighbors and synchronize their activity. Second, through a mechanism called **reentry**, any cortical area can influence the area from which it receives input. This remarkable interactive aspect of cortical connectivity means that, when area A sends information

(A) Flow of information

(B) Principles of reentry

Pyramidal cells

1 Cortical area A sends information from layers II and III, terminating in layer IV area B.

2 In reentry, area B modifies the input from area A by sending a return connection from layers V and VI to layers I and VI in area A.

Figure 10.15

Interareal and Intraareal Connections (A) Flow of information to and from the cortex. Information from the thalamus goes to the primary cortex, which then projects to the association cortex. The reciprocal connections at each level represent feedback loops. (B) Principles of reentry. A receiving cortical area can modify the inputs that it gets from another area. Reentry holds for all levels of cortical–cortical connectivity.

to area B, area B reciprocates and returns a message to area A (**Figure 10.15**).

Zeki suggests that an area could actually modify its inputs from another area before it even receives them. An important point detailed in Figure 10.15 is that the connections from areas A and B do not originate from the same layers, suggesting that they play different roles in influencing each other's activity.

How can the flow of information through intraareal and interareal connections and interaction through reentry solve the binding problem? Computer modeling suggests that the primary function of the neural connections is to coordinate activity within and between areas to produce a globally coherent pattern, known as integration, over all areas of the perceptual system.

Integration requires a way of binding the areas together briefly to form a unified percept. The computer models show that perceptual integration can be almost immediate, on a time scale of 50 to 500 ms. (This concept of cortical organization is likely to be foreign to many readers. We recommend Zeki's readable book for a longer discussion.)

Jerison related the binding problem to his analogy of multiple cortical maps. The evolutionary expansion of the cortex in area has implications for a brain with multiple neurosensory channels that are trying to integrate information into a single reality. Because so many different kinds of sensory information reach the cortex, it is necessary somehow to discriminate equivalent features in the external world. It would be useful to the brain to label these equivalencies and organize them.

Suppose that the brain creates labels to designate objects and a coordinate system to locate objects in the external world—that is, in space and time. Suppose also that some sensory information must be tagged to persist through time and must be categorized to be retrieved (remembered) when needed.

Labels, coordinates, and categories are products of cognition. Viewed in this way, Jerison's analogy of multiple cortical maps provides a basis for thinking about how the information that is arriving to the cortex is integrated into perception and organized as knowledge and thought. It should not be a surprise that injuries to discrete cortical areas alter the way that people perceive the world and the way that they think about it. In Chapter 13, we shall see that one form of sensory deficit, **agnosia** (literally, not knowing), renders a partial or complete inability to recognize sensory stimuli. Agnosias are unexplainable by subcortical deficits in elementary sensation or alertness.

Functional Organization of the Cortex

Knowledge of the world is constructed by the brain. To Jerison, this knowledge is mind. As cortical maps develop, the brain must also develop the mind to organize the maps in a way that produces knowledge of the external world. It is a small jump to the idea that the next step in mental development is language. After all, language is a way of representing knowledge.

A Hierarchical Model of Cortical Function

Flechsig was the first to suggest that anatomical criteria could be used to delineate a hierarchy of cortical areas, but Alexander Luria fully developed the idea in the 1960s. Luria divided the cortex into two functional units:

- The posterior part of the cortex is the sensory unit (**Figure 10.16**A). It receives sensations, processes them, and stores them as information.

- The anterior cortex (the frontal lobe) is the motor unit (Figure 10.16B). It formulates intentions, organizes them into programs of action, and executes the programs.

Both of Luria's cortical units have a hierarchical structure with three cortical zones arranged functionally one above the other. The first zone corresponds to Flechsig's primary cortex; the second corresponds to the slower-developing cortex bordering the primary cortex, which Luria labeled *secondary cortex*; and the third is the slowest-developing cortex, which Luria labeled *tertiary cortex*.

Luria conceived of the cortical units as working in concert along zonal pathways. Sensory input enters the primary sensory zones, is elaborated in the secondary zones, and is integrated in the tertiary zones of the posterior unit. To execute an action, activation is sent from the posterior tertiary sensory zones to the tertiary frontal motor zone for formulation, to the secondary motor zone for elaboration, and then to the primary frontal zone for execution.

Consider a simplified example of Luria's model. Say you are walking along and come upon a soccer game. The actual perception of the movements of players and the ball is in the primary visual area. The secondary visual sensory zone recognizes that those activities constitute a soccer game. In the tertiary zone, the sounds and movements of the game are synthesized into the realization that one team has scored and is ahead and that the game has a certain significance for league standings. By the time the information is integrated in the tertiary sensory zone, there is considerably more to it than what we would think of as "sensory." Rather, there is knowledge.

Information in the tertiary sensory zone activates the paralimbic cortex for memory processing and the amygdala for emotional assessment. These cortical events can then activate, in the tertiary zone of the frontal (motor) cortex, the intention to find a viewing spot and root for your team. The execution of this plan is formulated in the secondary frontal zones. The actual movements required to join the crowd are initiated in the primary motor zone of the frontal cortex.

Using the soccer game example, we can also describe the effects of brain lesions on levels of processing. A lesion in the primary visual zone produces a blind spot in some part of the visual field, requiring the spectator to move his or her head backward and forward to see the entire game. A lesion in the

Figure **10.16**

Functional Units of the Cortex
(A) Sensory unit. In traveling from primary to secondary to tertiary zones, sensation is elaborated and integrated into information. (B) Motor unit. Information from the sensory unit travels forward to tertiary motor zones where it is translated into intention and then into patterns of action in the secondary and primary motor zones. (After A. R. Luria. © 1973. The Copyright Agency of the USSR. Reprinted with permission.)

(A) Sensory unit

1 Sensory input travels from primary to secondary...

2 ...to tertiary and is elaborated from sensation into symbolic processes.

(B) Motor unit

3 Symbolic processes from the sensory unit are translated into intentions in the tertiary motor zones...

4 ...and then into patterns of action in the secondary and primary motor zones.

secondary visual zone might produce a perceptual deficit, making the person unable to recognize the activity as a soccer game. A lesion in the tertiary sensory zone might make it impossible to recognize the significance of the game in its abstract form—that one team wins.

Damage to the paralimbic cortex leaves no memory of the event, and damage to the amygdala renders the person unresponsive to the event's emotional significance. A lesion in the tertiary motor area might prevent forming the intention to become a soccer player and join a club, buy a uniform, or get to practice on time. A lesion in the secondary motor zone might make it difficult to execute the sequences of movements required in play. A lesion in the primary zone might make it difficult to execute a discrete movement required in the game—for example, kicking the ball.

Evaluating the Hierarchical Model

Luria based his theory on three assumptions:

1. The brain processes information serially, one step at a time. Thus, information from sensory receptors goes to the thalamus, then to the primary cortex, then to the secondary cortex, and finally to the tertiary sensory cortex. Similarly, the output goes from tertiary sensory to tertiary motor, then to secondary motor, and finally to primary motor.

2. Serial processing is hierarchical: each level of processing adds complexity that is qualitatively different from the processing in the preceding levels. The tertiary cortex could be considered a "terminal station" insofar as it receives input from the sensorimotor and perceptual areas and performs higher cognitive processes on that input.

3. Our perceptions of the world are unified and coherent entities. Luria's formulation was in accord with the commonsense view that some active process creates each percept, and, naturally, the simplest way to do so is to form it in the tertiary cortex.

The beauty of Luria's theory is that it used the then known anatomical organization of the cortex to provide a simple explanation for observations that Luria made daily in his clinic and published in 1973. The difficulty is that its basic assumptions have been questioned by newer anatomical and physiological findings. Consider the following problems.

First, a strictly hierarchical processing model requires that all cortical areas be linked serially, but this serial linkage is not the case. We have seen that all cortical areas have reentrant (reciprocal) connections with the regions to which they connect: there is no simple "feed forward" system. Furthermore, as noted earlier, only about 40% of the possible connections among different areas in a sensory modality are actually found. Thus no single area receives input from all other areas, which presents a difficulty in actively forming a single percept in one area.

Second, Zeki made the interesting point that, because a zone of cortex has connections with many cortical areas, it follows that each cortical zone is probably undertaking more than one operation that is subsequently relayed to different cortical areas. In addition, the results of the same operation are likely to be of interest to more than one cortical area, which would account for multiple connections.

These principles can be seen in the primary visual cortex, which appears to make calculations related to color, motion, and form. These calculations are relayed to specific cortical regions for these processes. And the same calculation may be sent to cortical as well as to subcortical regions.

The fact that cortical operations are relayed directly to subcortical areas is important because it implies that cortical processing can bypass Luria's motor hierarchy and go directly to subcortical motor structures. Further, the fact that given cortical areas can perform multiple calculations that are sent to multiple areas raises a question about what is hierarchical in the processing. Can we assume that areas that are serially connected are actually undertaking more complicated operations? It would seem that an area such as the primary visual cortex, which is processing color, form, and movement, might be considered more complex than an area that processes only color.

Finally, Luria assumed that his introspection about perception being a unitary phenomenon was correct. It appears, however, that it is not. Thus, we can experience a single percept despite the fact that no single terminal area is producing it. Indeed, this ability is the essence of the binding problem.

How can we put this knowledge together in a meaningful way to see organization in the cortex? Two logical possibilities exist. One is that there is no hierarchical organization but rather some sort of nonordered neural network. As individual organisms gain experiences, this network becomes ordered in some way and so produces perceptions, cognitions, and memories. Many neural-network models of brain function propose that this possibility is exactly what happens. However, the results of a wealth of perceptual research suggest that the brain filters and orders sensory information in a species-typical fashion.

The other organizational possibility, suggested by Daniel Felleman and David van Essen, is that cortical areas are hierarchically organized in some well-defined sense, with each area occupying a specific position relative to other areas but with more than one area allowed to occupy a given hierarchical level. Felleman and van Essen propose that the pattern of forward and backward connections could be used to determine hierarchical position.

Thus, ascending (or forward) connections terminate in layer IV, whereas descending (or feedback) connections do not enter layer IV, usually terminating in the superficial and deep layers (see Figure 10.15). Felleman and van Essen also recognize a third type of connection, which is columnar in its distribution, terminating in all layers. This type of connection is uncommon but provides a basis for placing areas in the same location in the hierarchy.

By analyzing the patterns of connectivity among the visual, auditory, and somatosensory areas, Felleman and van Essen found evidence of what they call a *distributed hierarchical system*. **Figure 10.17** contrasts this model with Luria's model. Notice in Figure 10.17B the several levels of processing and, across the levels, interconnected processing streams that presumably represent different elements of the sensory experience. Note, too, that some connections skip levels and that the number of areas expands as the hierarchy unfolds.

A Contemporary Model of Cortical Function

The Felleman and van Essen distributed hierarchy proposes a simple organization for sensory processing in the cortex. With the addition of the idea that the backward or lateral connections provide a basis for solving the binding

Figure **10.17**

Hierarchical Models (A) Luria's simple serial hierarchical model of cortical processing. (B) Felleman and van Essen's distributed hierarchical model, which features several levels of association areas. Areas at each level are interconnected with one another.

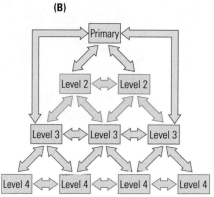

Figure 10.18

Flat Map of Cortical Areas in the Macaque The locations of 32 visual areas are indicated in purple (see the Snapshot on page 254). The abbreviations are summarized in Table 10.1 on page 270. (After Felleman and van Essen, 1991.)

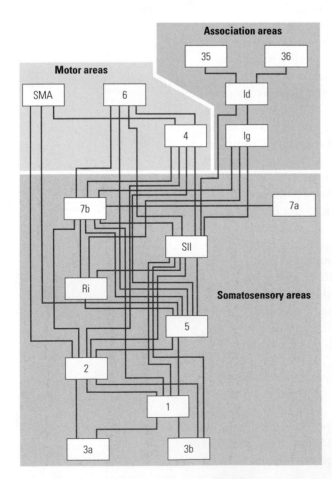

problem, their model offers an explanation of our experience of a single, coherent perception of the world.

To illustrate this **distributed hierarchy model**, we will not use the soccer example used to illustrate Luria's model, but we certainly invite the reader to attempt the exercise. Rather, we begin with some simpler examples, and, because this information was obtained from studies of rhesus monkeys, we use some examples relevant to monkeys.

Imagine that we set a monkey the task of reaching into a box in which, among other things, there are some jellybeans. If the monkey finds a jellybean, it is allowed to keep it; if it takes something else, it loses that object and, as punishment, has to wait before getting another trial. Thus, the monkey has to feel the

Figure 10.19

Cortical Wiring Diagram A proposed hierarchy for somatosensory and motor areas, based on 62 linkages among 9 somatosensory and 3 motor areas. Hierarchical assignments are based on the information contained in Table 10.1. Also included in the hierarchy are connections with visual area 7a and with higher associational areas 35 and 36. With the highest level included, the hierarchy consists of 10 levels, and possibly an 11th, depending on uncertainties with regard to interconnections among motor areas. (After Felleman and van Essen, 1991.)

Figure **10.20**

Hierarchy of Visual Areas This hierarchy shows 32 visual cortical areas, plus several nonvisual areas [area 7b of somatosensory cortex, perirhinal area 36, the entorhinal (ER) cortex, and the hippocampal (HC) complex]. These areas are connected by 187 linkages, most of which are reciprocal pathways. (After Felleman and van Essen, 1991.)

objects until it finds a jellybean, and then it has to grasp the jellybean by using a pincer grasp (see Figure 9.6A).

Using the model to speculate about how information flows through and gets organized by the monkey's cortex, we follow Felleman and van Essen's cortical map (**Figure 10.18**) and their wiring diagrams of how to get from one area of the somatosensory system to the next and from one area of the visual system to the next (**Figures 10.19** and **10.20**). **Table 10.1** charts the functions of each mapped area.

From Table 10.1, we see that tactile information is first analyzed in area 3b of the somatosensory cortex and that the motor output to grasp comes from area 4 of the motor cortex. Although areas 3a and 4 are side by side on the cortical

Table **10.1** Summary of cortical areas in the monkey

Lobe	Structure	Name	Putative Function
Occipital	V1	Visual area 1 (17)	Visual sorting
	V2	Visual area 2 (18)	Visual sorting
	V3	Visual area 3	Vision—dynamic form
	V3A	Visual area 3A	Vision—?
	V4	Visual area 4	Vision—color
	V4t	V4 transitional	Vision—?
	MT (V5)	Visual area 5	Motion
	VP	Ventral posterior visual	Vision—?
	VOT	Ventral occipital-temporal	Vision—?
Temporal	FST	Floor of superior temporal	Vision
	PITd	Posterior inferotemporal, dorsal	Vision
	PITv	Posterior inferotemporal, ventral	Vision
	CITd	Central inferotemporal, dorsal	Vision
	CITv	Central inferotemporal, ventral	Vision
	AITd	Anterior inferotemporal, dorsal	Vision
	AITv	Anterior inferotemporal, ventral	Vision
	STPp	Superior temporal polysensory, posterior	Polymodal
	STPa	Superior temporal polysensory, anterior	Polymodal
	FT	FT (hippocampal formation)	Memory
	TH	TH (hippocampal formation)	Memory
	AI	Primary auditory	Audition
	RL	Rostrolateral auditory	Audition
	CM	Caudomedial auditory	Audition
	L	Lateral auditory	Audition
	PA	Postauditory	Somato or auditory?
Hippocampus	ER	Entorhinal cortex	Memory or space or both
	35	Brodmann's 35	Memory or space or both
	36	Brodmann's 36	Memory or space or both
	Subicular	(Pre, post, sub)	Memory or space or both
	CAl	Ammon's horn, area 1	Memory or space or both
	CA3	Ammon's horn, area 3	Memory or space or both

map in Figure 10.18, the wiring diagram in Figure 10.19 shows that these somatosensory areas are not connected.

Figure 10.19 also shows that three visual streams go to area 4. One goes through areas 1, 5, and SII (SII is important for pattern discriminations); another goes through areas 2 and 7b (possibly important for shape discrimination); and the third goes through areas 2 and SMA (supplementary motor cortex, which may be important for producing a series of movements). It is possible that the monkey's problem could be solved by only one of the three streams, but it could also be solved by all of them working together.

Lobe	Structure	Name	Putative Function
Parietal	3a	Primary somatosensory	Cutaneous?
	3b	Primary somatosensory	Tactile; muscle, joint
	1	Somatosensory	Tactile—?
	2	Somatosensory	Vestibular
	SII	Secondary somatosensory map	Tactile patterns
	5	Secondary somatosensory (area PE)	Tactile patterns
	7a	Secondary visual (area PG)	Visuomotor guidance
	7b	Secondary somatosensory (area PF)	Visuomotor guidance
	MSTd	Medial superior temporal, dorsal	Visuomotor guidance
	MSTl	Medial superior temporal, lateral	Visuomotor guidance
	PO	Parietal-occipital	Visuomotor guidance
	PIP	Posterior intraparietal	Visuomotor guidance
	LIP	Lateral intraparietal	Visuomotor
	VIP	Ventral intraparietal	Visuomotor
	MIP	Medial intraparietal	Visuomotor
	MDP	Medial dorsal parietal	Visuomotor
	DP	Dorsal prelunate	Visuomotor
Frontal	4	Primary motor	Fine movements
	6	Secondary motor	Sequences
	SMA	Supplementary motor cortex	Bimanual movements
	MEF	Supplementary eye fields	Eye movements
	FEF	Frontal eye fields	Eye movements
	46	Dorsolateral prefrontal	Memory, movement, planning
	9, 10, 14	Dorsal prefrontal	Memory, movement, planning
	11, 12, 13	Orbital prefrontal	Emotion, memory
	25–32	Medial prefrontal	Memory, movement, planning
	G	Gustatory	Taste
	PRO	Prosiocortex	?
	PAL	Periallocortex	?
	PIR	Olfactory	Olfaction
	PAC	Olfactory	Olfaction
	ER	Olfactory	Olfaction
Cingulate	23, 24, 29, 30		Motivation, emotion, space, memory

Here is a second problem for the monkey, who is presented with a television screen that displays some jellybeans of various colors. If the monkey touches a red jellybean on the screen, it receives a reward, but there is no reward for touching other jellybeans. Using the list of functions in Table 10.1, we can hypothesize that the monkey uses the color vision system, beginning in V1 (area 17), to identify the correct jellybean, and uses area 4 of the motor system to point.

Turning to the wiring diagram in Figure 10.20, we can imagine that the monkey must use the geniculostriate system for color vision (see Figure 8.8). The geniculostriate pathway passes into V1 and then V2 and, from there, information must go to V4 (the color module of the visual system). We already know that area 7b will reach area 4. This route is at least one of those possible.

The second jellybean problem is still very simple. Consider what would happen if the correct jellybean not only were red but also had to be large and moving. The monkey would now have to use area V4 (color), area V3 (dynamic form), and MT, or area V5 (motion) and have all this information converge on area 7b. But even this trial is a simple problem for a monkey (although the wiring diagram may be becoming a little complex for some of us).

Let us give the monkey a problem that poses a challenge: if, on the last trial, a large, moving, red jellybean was correct, then, on the present trial, a small, stationary, green jellybean is correct. Now the monkey has to remember what it did on the last trial, and Table 10.1 tells us that the temporal cortex and perhaps even the hippocampus is required for memory.

It is no longer sufficient to take a route to area 7a; the temporocortical areas also must take part. Now the solution to the problem requires activity in the occipital, parietal, temporal, and motor cortex almost simultaneously. It is a simple matter to select a set of connections that could do the job, but now the question is whether that is how the monkey is doing it.

When we think of all the areas and connections that are required, the question is not so easily answered. As experimenters, we can always simplify the problem a little by creating a computer program that is regularly updated with areas, functions, and connections and that generates solutions to problems such as the ones that we have posed here. When we have done so, we can begin to work on different problems, such as why monkeys are inordinately fond of red jellybeans.

An obvious feature of the wiring diagrams is that there are a lot of wires (connections). As the brain evolved, there would obviously have been a premium on efficient connections, because connections between cortical regions take up space. In the primate brain, they occupy about 40% of the entire cortical volume.

Vitaly Klyachko and Charles Stevens showed how efficiently the primate brain is wired. They examined all possible connections in 11 areas in the frontal lobe of the rhesus monkey and calculated 39.9 million possible arrangements of connections. They found that the actual pattern of connections is indeed optimal, inasmuch as any deviation increases axonal volume.

Do Human Brains Possess Unique Properties?

A long tradition of scholars have looked for unique mental abilities in humans. Three allegedly unique abilities are grammatical langauge; **theory of mind**, or social cognition—the capacity to understand another's mental state and to take it into account; and certain forms of intelligence, such as intuition. Although the presence and nature of such supposedly unmatched capacities remain debatable, we can ask whether the human brain has unique properties.

As discussed in Chapter 2, the human brain is relatively larger than those of other species, but all mammalian species have a common plan of cortical organization that evolution has modified to suit specific ecological niches (see review by Krubitzer and Kaas). Two characteristics of the human brain may be special, however.

Figure **10.21**

Location of von Economo Neurons The frontal insula at the border of the temporal lobe (left) and the anterior cingulate (right) are the brain regions that contain von Economo neurons, which bear the name of anatomist Constantin von Economo, who first described them in the 1920s. (After Allman et al., 2005.)

The first is that humans have a higher density of cortical neurons combined with a higher conduction velocity. Gerhard Roth and Ursula Dicke propose that this combination leads to increased processing capacity in the human brain. The second is a class of cortical neurons found only in humans and the great apes but is far more abundant in humans. These *von Economo neurons* are large bipolar neurons located in the deep layers of the anterior cingulate cortex and in the insula, a lateral cortical region (**Figure 10.21**).

The von Economo neurons develop late in ontogeny and only reach adult levels by about 4 years of age, possibly through the differentiation of some preexisting cell type or even through neurogenesis. John Allman and his colleagues propose that von Economo neurons are associated with the emergence of theory of mind and, even more provocatively, that these cells fail to develop normally in people with **autism**, thus leading to the faulty social intuition that is characteristic of this disorder.

In sum, although humans do not evince any obvious, gross difference in brain organization from other mammals, the intrinsic organization of the human neocortex, including the presence of specialized von Economo neurons, may allow the emergence of qualitatively different mental capacities from those found in other mammals.

Summary

A Hierarchy of Function from Spinal Cord to Cortex

The primary interest in neuropsychology is the function of the human neocortex. This chapter has described the levels of function in the central nervous system hierarchically and then focused on the structure and functional organization of the cortex. The levels of function begin in the spinal cord and end in the cortex. The functional hierarchy can be demonstrated by studying animals that have undergone surgical removals of successively more brain tissue.

The Structure of the Cortex

The neocortex comprises two basic types of neurons—spiny and aspiny—organized into about six layers. The cortical layers can be considered sensory, motor, and associational. The vertical organization of the cortical layers in columns, or modules, can be seen in the spots and stripes visible in specific histological preparations and with the use of neuroimaging technologies.

Multiple representations of sensory and motor functions exist in the cortex, and an evolutionary change in mammals has been an increase in the number of these representations. A characteristic of cortical connectivity is reentry: each cortical area is reciprocally connected with many other regions in a given sensory modality, but not all.

The cortex processes information about the world in multiple representations and these representations are not formally connected, yet we perceive the world as a unified whole. This conundrum is the binding problem.

Functional Organization of the Cortex

Cortical activity is influenced by feedback loops not only from other cortical regions but also from subcortical forebrain regions such as the amygdala and hippocampus. Thus the cortex is functionally organized as a distributed hierarchical network.

Do Human Brains Possess Unique Properties?

Although all mammals have a remarkably similar general brain organization, there appear to be unique forms of human cognition. One unique cell type comprising von Economo cells may provide the clue to the neural basis of qualitatively different cognitions such as social intuition.

References

Allman, J. M., K. K. Watson, N. A. Tetreault, and A. Y. Hakeem. Intuition and autism: A possible role for von Economo neurons. *Trends in Cognitive Science* 9:367–373, 2005.

Bard, P., and M. B. Macht. The behavior of chronically decerebrate cats. In G. E. W. Wolstenholm and C. M. O'Connor, Eds. *Ciba Foundation Symposium on Neurological Basis of Behavior.* London: Churchill, 1958.

Barrett, R., H. H. Merritt, and A. Wolf. Depression of consciousness as a result of cerebral lesions. *Research Publications of the Association for Research in Nervous and Mental Disease* 45:241–276, 1967.

Bazett, H. C., and W. G. Penfield. A study of the Sherrington decerebrate animal in the chronic as well as the acute condition. *Brain* 45:185–265, 1922.

Berridge, K. C. Measuring hedonic impact in animals and infants: Microstructure of affective taste reactivity patterns. *Neuroscience and Biobehavioral Reviews* 24:173–198, 2000.

Berridge, K. C., and I. Q. Whishaw. Cortex, striatum, and cerebellum: Control of serial order in a grooming sequence. *Experimental Brain Research* 90:275–290, 1992.

Bignall, K. E., and L. Schramm. Behavior of chronically decerebrate kittens. *Experimental Neurology* 42:519–531, 1974.

Brackbill, Y. The role of the cortex in orienting: Orienting reflex in an encephalic human infant. *Developmental Psychology* 5:195–201, 1971.

Cannon, W. B., and S. W. Britton. Pseudoaffective medulliadrenal secretion. *American Journal of Physiology* 72:283–294, 1924.

Felleman, D. J., and D. C. van Essen. Distributed hierarchical processing in the primate cerebral cortex. *Cerebral Cortex* 1:1–47, 1991.

Flechsig, P. *Anatomie des menschlichen Gehirns und Rückenmarks.* Leipzig: Georg Thieme, 1920.

Gamper, E. As cited in R. Jung and R. Hassler. The extrapyramidal system. In J. Field, H. W. Magoun, and V. E. Hall, Eds. *Handbook of Physiology*, vol. 2. Washington, D.C.: American Physiological Society, 1960, pp. 863–927.

Ghazanfar, A. A., and C. E. Schroeder. Is neocortex essentially multisensory? *Trends in Cognitive Science* 10:278–285, 2006.

Ghazanfar, A. A., J. X. Maier, K. L. Hoffman, and N. K. Logothetis. Multisensory integration of dynamic faces and voices in rhesus monkey auditiory cortex. *Journal of Neuroscience* 25:5004–5012, 2005.

Goltz, F. On the functions of the hemispheres. In G. von Bonin, Ed. *The Cerebral Cortex.* Springfield, Ill.: Charles C. Thomas, 1960.

Grill, H. J., and R. Norgren. Neurological tests and behavioral deficits in chronic thalamic and chronic decerebrate rats. *Brain Research* 143:299–312, 1978.

Grillner, S. Locomotion in the spinal cat. In R. B. Stein, Ed. *Control of Posture and Locomotion.* New York: Plenum, 1973.

Jerison, H. J. *Brain Size and the Evolution of Mind.* New York: American Museum of Natural History, 1991.

Klyachko, V. A., and C. F. Stevens. Connectivity optimization and the positioning of cortical areas. *Proceedings of the National Academy of Sciences of the United States of America* 100: 7937–7941, 2003.

Krubitzer, L., and J. Kaas. The evolution of the neocortex in mammals: How is phenotypic diversity generated? *Current Opinion in Neurobiology* 15:444–453, 2005.

Kuhn, R. A. Functional capacity of the isolated human spinal cord. *Brain* 73:1–51, 1950.

Luria, A. R. *The Working Brain.* Harmondsworth, England: Penguin, 1973.

Oakley, D. A. Cerebral cortex and adaptive behavior. In D. A. Oakley and H. C. Plotkin, Eds. *Brain, Evolution and Behavior.* London: Methuen, 1979.

Pandya, D. N., and E. H. Yeterian. Architecture and connections of cortical association areas. In A. Peters and E. G. Jones, Eds. *Cerebral Cortex*, vol. 4. New York: Plenum Press, 1985.

Penfield, W., and E. Boldrey. Somatic and motor sensory representation in the cerebral cortex of man as studied by electrical stimulation. *Brain* 60:389–443, 1937.

Peters, A., and E. G. Jones. *Cerebral Cortex*, vols. 1–14. New York: Plenum, 1984–1999.

Purves, D., D. R. Riddle, and A.-S. LaMantia. Iterated patterns of brain circuitry (or how the brain gets its spots). *Trends in Neuroscience* 15:362–368, 1992.

Roth, G., and U. Dicke. Evolution of the brain and intelligence. *Trends in Cognitive Science* 9:250–257, 2005.

Shepherd, G. M. *The Synaptic Organization of the Brain*, 2nd ed. New York: Oxford University Press, 1979.

Sherrington, C. S. *The Integrative Action of the Nervous System.* New Haven: Yale University Press, 1906.

Szentagothai, J. Architecture of the cerebral cortex. In H. H. Jasper, A. A. Ward, and A. Pope, Eds. *Basic Mechanisms of the Epilepsies.* Boston: Little, Brown, 1969.

Talairach, J., and P. Tournoux. *Coplanar Stereotaxic Atlas of the Human Brain.* New York: Thieme, 1988.

Tononi, G., O. Sporns, and G. M. Edelman. Reentry and the problem of integrating multiple cortical areas: Simulation of dynamic integration in the visual system. *Cerebral Cortex* 2:336–352, 1991.

van Essen, D. C., and H. A. Drury. Structural and functional analyses of human cerebral cortex using a surface-based atlas. *Journal of Neuroscience* 17:7092–7102, 1997.

Whishaw, I. Q. The decorticate rat. In B. Kolb and R. Tees, Eds. *The Neocortex of the Rat.* Cambridge, Mass.: MIT Press, 1989.

Woods, J. W. Behavior of chronic decerebrate rats. *Journal of Neurophysiology* 27:634–644, 1964.

Zeki, S. *A Vision of the Brain.* London: Blackwell Scientific, 1993.

11 Cerebral Asymmetry

PORTRAIT: Words and Music

M.S., a 25-year-old mother of two, had a lifetime history of epilepsy. Her seizures were well controlled by medication until after her second child was born. From that time, she endured about one uncontrolled seizure a month on average. Neurological examination revealed that the source of her seizures was a long-standing cyst in her left temporal lobe. M.S. agreed to neurosurgery to remove the cyst and the surrounding abnormal brain tissue.

The accompanying photograph, a transparent representation of an intact cerebral cortex, highlights the major left-hemisphere language areas, with Broca's area in green and Wernicke's area in blue. The yellow area is

Courtesy Dr. Arthur Toga, Laboratory of Neuro Imaging at UCLA

the corpus callosum, which connects the hemispheres.

Initially M.S.'s postoperative course was uneventful, and her seizures appeared to be cured. Unexpectedly, she developed an infection that proved resistant to antibiotics. Within a few days, M.S. suffered extensive damage

to her left hemisphere. The illness left her unable either to produce or to understand language, a condition known as *global aphasia*. For weeks, the only words that she was able to say were "I love you," and she said them to everyone she knew well.

In spite of her severe language problems, her ability to enjoy music was unimpaired. M.S. could sing versions of songs that she had known before her surgery. Thus, although she could not use or understand words to talk or read, she could use words in music and could tell immediately if the words in songs were wrong. Learning the words to new songs proved to be very difficult, however, though she was able to learn new tunes and hum along.

The single most curious feature of human brain organization is *cerebral asymmetry:* the left and right cerebral hemispheres have partly separate functions. As described in the preceding Portrait, cerebral asymmetry was especially apparent in M.S.'s loss of language skills but maintenance of musical skills.

This chapter explores cerebral asymmetry in humans. To set the stage, we address the basic anatomical principles. Next, we examine and contrast neurological and behavioral research on damaged brains and on intact persons. In the concluding sections, we compare experimental results with brain scans, contrast sets of theories about cerebral asymmetry, and evaluate the quest to measure behavior. In Chapter 12, we will examine the biological and environmental factors that produce variations in cerebral asymmetry.

Anatomical Asymmetry in the Human Brain

Perhaps no idea about human brain organization has so fascinated neuroscientists as has **laterality**, the idea that the two cerebral hemispheres have separate functions. In Chapter 10 we focused on how an anatomical and functional hierarchy in the cortex leads to unity of experience and the idea of a mind. Laterality leads to the notion that two different minds control our behavior.

After more than 100 years of studying cerebral asymmetry, psychologists now know that the hemispheres do perform separate functions. The left hemisphere plays a special role in producing and understanding language and in controlling movement on the right side of the body, whereas the right hemisphere specializes in perceiving and synthesizing nonverbal information, including music and facial expression. And the right hemisphere controls movement on the left side of the body. Four variables complicate the research on laterality:

1. **Laterality is relative, not absolute.** Both hemispheres play a role in nearly every behavior; thus, although the left hemisphere is especially important for the production of language, the right hemisphere also has some language capabilities.

2. **Cerebral *site* is at least as important in understanding brain function as cerebral *side*.** The frontal lobes are asymmetrical, but their functions are more similar to each other than they are to those of the posterior cortex on the same side. In fact, in the absence of neurological data, it is often very difficult to localize lesions in neurological patients to one hemisphere even though the site (frontal rather than temporal or parietal) may be immediately obvious. Perhaps it is best to think of many of the functions of the cerebral cortex as being localized and of hemispheric side as being only one feature of the localization.

3. **Laterality is affected by environmental and genetic factors.** As discussed in Chapter 12, for example, the cerebral organization of some left-handers and females appears less asymmetrical than that of right-handers and males.

4. **Laterality is exhibited by a range of animals.** A functionally asymmetrical brain was once believed to be a uniquely human characteristic and related to language, but certain songbirds, rats, cats, monkeys, and apes have functionally and anatomically asymmetrical brains as well.

Cerebral Asymmetry

According to John Hughlings-Jackson, Pierre Gratiolet first observed in the 1860s that the cortical convolutions (gyri and sulci) on the left hemisphere mature more rapidly than those on the right. Anatomical asymmetry was described again later in the nineteenth century by a number of researchers, but these observations were largely ignored until the 1960s, when Norman Geschwind and Walter Levitsky described a significant anatomical asymmetry of the planum temporale in the temporal lobes.

Also called Wernicke's area, the **planum temporale** lies just posterior to the primary auditory cortex (Heschl's gyrus) within the Sylvian, or lateral, fissure (**Figure 11.1**, top). On average, in 65 of the 100 brains studied by Geschwind and Levitsky, the planum temporale in the left hemisphere was nearly 1 cm longer than that in the right hemisphere. Geschwind and Levitsky's finding has been replicated by numerous investigators, with the percentage of cases having a larger planum temporale in the left hemisphere varying from 65% to 90% in different samples. In contrast, the neighboring primary auditory cortex of Heschl's

Figure 11.1

Anatomical Asymmetry (Top) Viewed laterally, the slope of the lateral (Sylvian) fissure differs in the two hemispheres. (Bottom) The extent of the auditory areas and planum temporale are visible in this section along the lateral fissures. The planum temporale is often larger in the left hemisphere than in the right hemisphere, whereas two Heschl's gyri appear in the right hemisphere but only one in the left hemisphere.

gyrus is larger in the right hemisphere because there are usually two Heschl's gyri in the right hemisphere and only one in the left (Figure 11.1, bottom).

MRI scans of living brains confirm eight major anatomical differences between the two hemispheres:

1. The right hemisphere is slightly larger and heavier than the left, but the left contains more gray matter relative to white matter.

2. The temporal lobes display a marked structural asymmetry that may provide an anatomical basis for the observed specialization of the left and right temporal lobes in language and in music functions, respectively. (See Geschwind and Levitsky).

3. The asymmetry in the cortex of the temporal lobes is correlated with a corresponding asymmetry in the thalamus. This anatomical asymmetry complements an apparent functional asymmetry in the thalamus, the left thalamus being dominant for language functions. (See Eidelberg and Galaburda.)

4. The slope of the lateral fissure is gentler on the left hemisphere than on the right (see Figure 11.1, top). The region of the temporoparietal cortex lying ventral to the lateral fissure therefore appears larger on the right. (See Toga and Thompson.)

5. The *frontal operculum* (Broca's area) is organized differently on the left and right. The area visible on the surface of the brain is about one-third larger on the right than on the left, whereas the area of cortex buried in the sulci (ridges) of the region is greater on the left than on the right. This

anatomical asymmetry probably corresponds to the lateralization of the regions, the left side affecting the production of grammar in language and the right side possibly influencing tone of voice.

6. The distribution of various neurotransmitters is asymmetrical, in both the cortical and the subcortical regions. The particular asymmetries in the distribution of acetylcholine, gamma-aminobutyric acid (GABA), norepinephrine, and dopamine depend on the structure under consideration. (See Falzi et al., Glick et al., and Oke et al.)

7. The right hemisphere extends farther anteriorly than does the left, the left hemisphere extends farther posteriorly than does the right, and the occipital horns of the lateral ventricles are five times as likely to be longer on the right as on the left. These asymmetries presumably correspond to some gross difference in cerebral organization that has yet to be identified.

8. The details of anatomical asymmetry are affected by both sex and handedness, as we shall see in Chapter 12.

Many more anatomical asymmetries between the two cerebral hemispheres have been reported (**Table 11.1**). Overall, anatomical asymmetries center on the language areas, with most of the frontal and parietal lobes showing little gross asymmetry. It is thus tempting to speculate that the asymmetries evolved to subserve language. Moreover, these asymmetries are

Table 11.1 Summary of studies demonstrating anatomical asymmetry

Measure	Basic Reference
Asymmetries Favoring the Left Hemisphere	
Greater specific gravity	von Bonin, 1962
Longer lateral (Sylvian) fissure	Eberstaller, 1884; LeMay and Culebras, 1972; Heschl, 1878
Larger insula	Kodama, 1934
Doubling of cingulate gyrus	Eberstaller, 1884
Relatively more gray matter	von Bonin, 1962; Gur et al., 1980
Thicker cortex	Luders et al., 2006
Larger planum temporale	Geschwind and Levitsky, 1968; Galaburda et al., 1978; Teszner et al., 1972; Witelson and Pallie, 1973; Wada et al., 1975; Rubens et al., 1976; Kopp et al., 1977
Larger lateral posterior nucleus	Eidelberg and Galaburda, 1982
Larger inferior parietal lobule	Lemay and Culebras, 1972
Larger area Tpt of temporoparietal cortex	Galaburda and Sanides, 1980
Wider occipital lobe	LeMay, 1977
Longer occipital horn of lateral ventricles	McRae et al., 1968; Strauss and Fitz, 1980
Larger total area of frontal operculum	Falzi et al., 1982
Larger medial temporal lobe	Good et al., 2001
Asymmetries Favoring the Right Hemisphere	
Heavier	Broca, 1865; Crichton-Browne, 1880
Longer internal skull size	Hoadley and Pearson, 1929
Doubling of Heschl's gyrus	von Economo and Horn, 1930; Chi et al., 1977
Larger medial geniculate nucleus	Eidelberg and Galaburda, 1982
Larger area of convexity of frontal operculum	Wada et al., 1975
Wider frontal lobe	LeMay, 1977

An MRI averaged from the brain images of 20 normal subjects shows areas of significant anatomical asymmetry. The greatest asymmetry appears in the language zones, and the least asymmetry is in the anterior temporal lobe and the dorsomedial frontal lobe. (Courtesy Dr. Arthur Toga, Laboratory of Neuro Imaging at UCLA.)

0.05
0.01
0.005
0.001
0.0005
0.0001
0.00002

P value

present in preterm infants, which seems to support the proposition that language is innate in humans.

In fact, the brains of australopithecines had many anatomical asymmetries in common with modern humans, but the hominids had no vocal apparatus that allowed language as we conceive of it. In addition, some asymmetries, such as a heavier and larger right hemisphere and a longer lateral fissure, can also be seen in many nonhuman primate species.

With all the emphasis on finding anatomical asymmetries that can be associated with language, research on right-hemisphere function has lagged. If the left hemisphere has asymmetries related to language, then the right hemisphere must be specialized for some other function. After all, the two hemispheres are quite similar in size and other symmetries: it is not as though language areas evolved on the left and nothing happened on the right.

Neuronal Asymmetry

Demonstrating gross morphological asymmetries in the human brain is a natural starting point in comparing the two hemispheres structurally. But remember that the activities of the brain are carried out by neurons. Do the structures of neurons differ on the two sides of the brain?

The identification of structural differences in the neurons in any two areas of the brain is a formidable task in view of the sheer number of neurons. Nonetheless, Arnold Scheibel and his colleagues compared the dendritic fields of pyramidal cells in Broca's area, the left frontal operculum (LOP), with those in the facial area of the motor cortex in the left precentral cortex (LPC) and with homologous regions in the right hemisphere.

Their results show that the neurons in each of these regions have distinct patterns of dendritic branching, as diagrammed in **Figure 11.2**. The degree or pattern of branching is important, because each branch is a potential location for the enhancement or suppression of the graded potentials in the dendritic tree. Thus, more branch points allow more degrees of freedom with respect to the final activity of the cell. Note the abundant branches in neurons in Broca's area (LOP), far more than in the other areas.

We must approach Scheibel's data on neural asymmetry with caution, because the sample of brains was small ($n = 6$). However, five of the six brains were similar to the pattern shown in Figure 11.2. These five brains came from right-handers; the atypical brain came from a left-handed person.

Figure 11.2

Neuronal Asymmetry Differences in the dendritic morphology in neurons in the left and right frontal operculum (LOP, ROP) and in the left and right precentral cortex (LPC, RPC). (After Scheibel et al., 1985.)

Genetic Asymmetry

The Human Genome Project, completed in 2003, allows investigators to address the genetic regulation of cerebral asymmetry. Tao Sun and colleagues compared gene expression levels in the perisylvian regions of the left and right hemispheres of the fetal brain. Although their results are still preliminary, they found genes that are expressed differently in the two hemispheres.

The mechanism whereby differential gene expression affects anatomical and functional asymmetry is still unknown, although the researchers suggest that some of the genes may regulate the production of growth factors that would, in turn, facilitate the development of specific regions in one hemisphere or the other. A provocative idea is that the asymmetrical expression of genes may account for functional properties such as handedness, which to date has no known basis. (We will return to this idea in Chapter 12.)

Asymmetry in Neurological Patients

Cerebral asymmetry was first established by studying patients with neurological disease, such as epilepsy, that is lateralized to one hemisphere. Improved neurosurgical treatment for such disorders has provided researchers with a large source of subsequently healthy subjects who are usually very willing to participate in neuropsychological studies. Current knowledge about both the lateralization and the localization of functions in the cerebral cortex owes a great debt to these patients.

In this section, we consider the evidence that demonstrates the lateralization of function, emphasizing the study of patients with lateralized lesions and those undergoing surgical disconnection of the hemispheres, as well as of those who had one hemisphere anesthetized.

Patients with Lateralized Lesions

The oldest research on hemispheric specialization infers function from behavioral deficits that arise as a result of strokes or surgery. Such circumscribed, unilateral lesions in the left hemisphere of right-handed patients can produce aphasias that do not develop from lesions in the right hemisphere. Recall, for example, the case history of M.S. presented in the Portrait at the beginning of this chapter. The study of such patients demonstrates that the functions of the two hemispheres are lateralized, or *dissociated*.

To conclude that the cortical area has a special or lateralized function, however, it is also necessary to show that lesions in other areas of the brain do not produce a similar deficit. In the strongest experimental method for demonstrating the lateralization of function, called **double dissociation** by Hans-Leukas Teuber, two areas of the neocortex are functionally dissociated by two behavioral tests. Each test is affected by a lesion in one zone but not in the other.

Lesions in the left hemisphere of right-handed patients consistently produce deficits in language functions (speech, writing, and reading) that are not produced by lesions in the right hemisphere. Thus, the functions of the two hemispheres are dissociated. However, performing spatial tasks, singing, playing musical instruments, and discriminating tonal patterns are more disrupted by right-hemisphere than by left-hemisphere lesions. Because right-hemisphere

Table **11.2** Hypothetical double-dissociation behavioral test

Neocortical Lesion Site	Reading	Writing
102	Impaired	Normal
107	Normal	Impaired

lesions disturb tasks not disrupted by left-hemisphere lesions and vice versa, the two hemispheres are doubly dissociated.

A similar logic is used to localize functions within a hemisphere. Behavioral tests that are especially sensitive to damage to a specific locus but not to others can be used. As illustrated in **Table 11.2**, two hypothetical cortical regions, 102 and 107, are doubly dissociated on tests of reading and writing: damage to area 102 disturbs reading, whereas damage to area 107 impairs writing. In principle, this logic can be extended to dissociate the functions of additional areas concurrently by triple dissociation, quadruple dissociation, and so on.

To illustrate the nature of lateralized functions in neurological cases, we contrast two patients, neither of whom was aphasic at the time of assessment. The first patient, P.G., a 31-year-old man, had developed seizures in the 6 years preceding his neurosurgery. At the time at which he was admitted to the hospital, his seizures were poorly controlled by medication, and subsequent neurological investigations revealed a large tumor in the anterior part of the left temporal lobe.

Preoperative psychological tests showed P.G. to be of superior intelligence, with the only significant deficits being on tests of verbal memory. Two weeks after surgery, psychological testing showed a general decrease in intelligence ratings and a further decrease in the verbal memory scores. Performance on other tests, including tests of recall of complex drawings, was normal.

The second patient, S.K., had a tumor removed from the right temporal lobe. In contrast with P.G.'s test results, preoperative testing of S.K. showed a low score on the recall of complex drawings. Two weeks after surgery, repeat testing showed a marked decrease in the performance IQ rating and a decline in the nonverbal memory score, both for simple and for complex designs.

The comparison of these two patients' test results in **Figure 11.3** provides a clear example of double dissociation: subsequent to the removal of the left

Figure **11.3**

Double Dissociation A comparison of psychological test results (A) for patient P.G. after a left temporal lobectomy and (B) for patient S.K. after a right temporal lobectomy. The respective regions removed, shown in red, are as estimated by the surgeon at the time of operation. (After Taylor, 1969.)

(A)

Left temporal lobectomy

Test	Preoperative	Postoperative
Full scale IQ	123	109
Verbal IQ	122	103
Performance IQ	121	114
Memory quotient	96^a	73^a
Verbal recall	7.0^a	2.0^a
Nonverbal recall	10.5	10.5
Card sorting	6 categories	6 categories
Drawings: Copy	34/36	34/36
Recall	22.5/36	23.5/36

^{a} Significantly low score

(B)

Right temporal lobectomy

Test	Preoperative	Postoperative
Full scale IQ	114	103
Verbal IQ	115	115
Performance IQ	110	89^a
Memory quotient	121	101
Verbal recall	16.0	12
Nonverbal recall	7.5	5.5^a
Card sorting	3 categories	3 categories
Drawings: Copy	31/36	28/36^a
Recall	11/36^a	13/36^a

^{a} Significantly low score

temporal lobe, P.G. was impaired only on verbal tests, whereas S.K., subsequent to the removal of the right temporal lobe, was impaired only on nonverbal tests. Furthermore, both patients performed normally on many tests, providing evidence for localization, as well as lateralization, of function.

Patients with Commissurotomy

Epileptic seizures may begin in a restricted region of one hemisphere and then spread through the fibers of the corpus callosum (the commissure) to the homologous location in the opposite hemisphere. To prevent the spread of a seizure when medication has failed to impose control, **commissurotomy**, the surgical procedure of disconnecting the two hemispheres by cutting the 200 million nerve fibers of the corpus callosum, was performed first in the early 1940s by William Van Wagnen, an American neurosurgeon. The therapeutic outcome of the procedure initially appeared too variable and was subsequently abandoned until the 1960s, when research with monkeys and cats by Ron Myers and by Roger Sperry led neurologists to reconsider it.

At the time, two California surgeons, Joseph Bogen and Philip Vogel, performed complete sections of the corpus callosum and of the smaller anterior commissure in a new series of about two dozen patients suffering from intractable epilepsy. The procedure was medically beneficial, leaving some patients virtually seizure free afterward, with minimal effects on their everyday behavior. More extensive psychological testing by Sperry and his colleagues soon demonstrated, however, a unique behavioral syndrome that has been a source of new insights into the nature of cerebral asymmetry.

Figure 11.4 illustrates the effect of commissurotomy on the normal function of the brain. After sectioning, the two hemispheres are independent: each receives sensory input from all sensory systems, and each can control the muscles of the body, but the two hemispheres can no longer communicate. Because the functions in these separate cortexes, or **split brains**, are thus isolated, sensory information can be presented to one hemisphere, and its function can be studied, without the other hemisphere having access to the information.

Figure 11.5 illustrates how information seen in a particular part of the visual world by both eyes is sent to only one hemisphere. Input from the left side of the world (the left visual field) goes to the right hemisphere, whereas input from the right side of the world (the right visual field) goes to the left hemisphere. The two sides of the world are joined by a connection through the corpus callosum, as illustrated in **Figure 11.6**. With the corpus

Figure **11.4**

Effect of Commissurotomy on Connections Between the Hemispheres

1 Cortical connections between homotopic points of the two hemispheres are severed.

2 Each hemisphere therefore functions independently of the other and without access to the other's sensations, thoughts, or actions.

Auditory stimulus

Visual stimulus

3 Cortical connections with the sensory and motor systems and their bodily receptors and effectors, however, are unaffected.

Corpus callosum

Motor

Somatosenso

Auditory

Visual

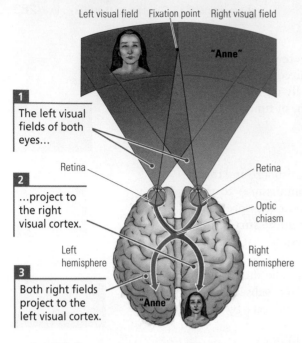

Left visual field   Fixation point   Right visual field

1 The left visual fields of both eyes...

Retina

2 ...project to the right visual cortex.

Left hemisphere

3 Both right fields project to the left visual cortex.

"Anne"

Retina

Optic chiasm

Right hemisphere

"Anne"

Figure 11.5

The Visual Fields Our visual pathways are crossed; thus both visual fields—not both eyes—are represented in each hemisphere. The entire field left of the fixation point (red region) is represented in the right visual cortex, and the entire field right of the fixation point (blue region) is represented in the left visual cortex.

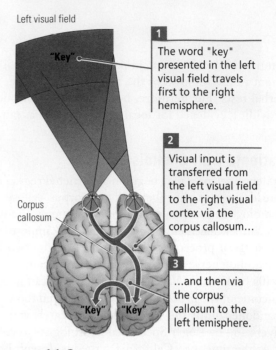

Left visual field

"Key"

Corpus callosum

"Key"   "Key"

1 The word "key" presented in the left visual field travels first to the right hemisphere.

2 Visual input is transferred from the left visual field to the right visual cortex via the corpus callosum...

3 ...and then via the corpus callosum to the left hemisphere.

Figure 11.6

Connecting the Two Sides of the World The word "key" presented in the left visual field travels first to the right hemisphere and then through the corpus callosum to the left hemisphere. Commissurotomy prevents the transfer.

callosum severed, the brain cannot relate the different views of the left and right hemispheres.

When the left hemisphere of a split-brain patient has access to information, it can initiate speech and hence communicate about the information. The right hemisphere apparently has reasonably good recognition abilities but is unable to initiate speech, because it lacks access to the speech mechanisms of the left hemisphere. The following example and **Figure 11.7** illustrate the split-brain phenomenon:

> Patient N.G., a California housewife, sits in front of a screen with a small black dot in the center [a different patient is shown in Figure 11.7]. She is asked to look directly at the dot. When the experimenter is sure she is doing so, a picture of a cup is flashed briefly to the right of the dot. N.G. reports that she has seen a cup. Again she is asked to fix her gaze on the dot. This time, a picture of a spoon is flashed to the left of the dot. She is asked what she saw. She replies, "No, nothing." She is then asked to reach under the screen with her left hand and to select, by touch only, from among several items the one object that is the same as she has just seen. Her left hand manipulates each object and then holds up the spoon. When asked what she is holding, she says "pencil." (Springer and Deutsch, 1998, p. 36).

The behavior of patient N.G. clearly demonstrates the different behaviors of the two hemispheres when they are not interacting. The picture of the cup was presented to the speaking left hemisphere, which could respond. The picture of the spoon was presented to the right hemisphere and, because the right hemisphere does not speak and the speaking left hemisphere was not connected

Procedure

The split-brain subject fixates on the dot in the center of the screen while an image is projected to the left or right visual field. He is asked to identify verbally what he sees.

Figure 11.7

Split-Brain Phenomenon Basic testing arrangement used to lateralize visual and tactile information and allow tactile responses. (Adapted with permission from S. P. Springer and G. Deutsch. *Left Brain, Right Brain: Perspectives from Cognitive Neuroscience*, 5th ed. New York: W. H. Freeman and Company, 1998, p. 37.)

Results

If the spoon is presented to the right visual field, the subject verbally answers, "Spoon."

If the spoon is presented to the left visual field, the subject verbally answers, "I see nothing."

Left visual field   Right visual field   Left visual field   Right visual field

Severed corpus callosum

Conclusion

When the left hemisphere, which can speak, sees the spoon in the right visual field, the subject responds correctly. When the right hemisphere, which cannot speak, sees the spoon in the left visual field, the subject does not respond.

to the right hemisphere, N.G. failed to identify the picture correctly. The abilities of the right hemisphere were demonstrated when the left hand, which is controlled by the right hemisphere, picked up the spoon. Finally, when asked what the still-out-of-sight left hand was holding, the left hemisphere did not know and incorrectly guessed "pencil."

The special capacities of the right hemisphere in facial recognition also can be demonstrated in the split-brain patient. Jere Levy devised the chimeric-figures test, which consists of pictures of faces and other patterns that have been split down the center and recombined in improbable ways (**Figure 11.8**). When the recombined faces were presented selectively to each hemisphere, split-brain patients appeared to be unaware of the gross discordance between the two sides of the pictures. When asked to pick out the picture that they had seen, they chose the face seen in the left visual field (that is, by the right hemisphere), demonstrating that the right hemisphere has a special role in the recognizing faces.

In summary, the results of careful and sometimes ingenious studies of commissurotomy patients provide clear evidence of the complementary specialization of the two cerebral hemispheres. As interesting as these split-brain patients are, however, they represent only a very small population, and their two hemispheres are by no means normal. Most had focal lesions, which caused the initial seizure disorder, and some may have had brain damage early in life, leading to a significant reorganization of cerebral function. Thus, generalizations and inferences must be made cautiously from these fascinating patients. We shall return to them in Chapter 17.

Figure 11.8

Facial Recognition (Left) To produce chimeric stimuli, Levy and coworkers used photographs 1 through 8 to create composite pictures A through D. (Right) When asked to choose the face that they had seen from the array of original pictures 1 through 8, split-brain patients chose the face that had been presented to their left visual fields. (From J. Levy et al., 1972. Reprinted with the permission of Oxford University Press, Oxford.)

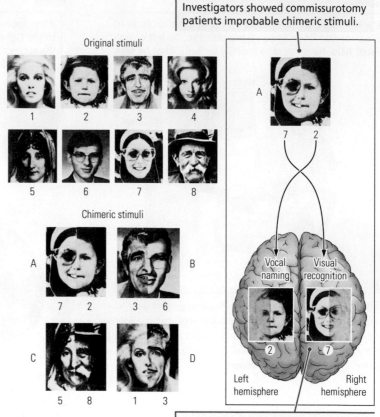

Original stimuli

Chimeric stimuli

Investigators showed commissurotomy patients improbable chimeric stimuli.

Vocal naming

Visual recognition

Left hemisphere

Right hemisphere

Asked to choose the face that they had seen from the array of original pictures, the patients chose the face that was presented to their left visual field.

Brain Stimulation

In the early 1930s, Wilder Penfield and his associates at the Montreal Neurological Institute pioneered the use of surgical treatment for epilepsy in patients whose seizures were poorly controlled by drug therapy. The logic of this procedure is to remove the region of cortex where the abnormal neural discharge originates. Because this therapeutic surgery is elective, it can be planned for, and considerable care is taken to ensure that areas of the cortex critical for the control of speech and movement are not damaged.

To identify speech and movement areas and to localize the extent of the epileptogenic tissue, the surgeon stimulates the exposed cortex and records the responses of the conscious patient, as illustrated in **Figure 11.9**. Careful study of hundreds of patients in Montreal by Penfield and his students and, more recently, by George Ojemann and his colleagues at the University of Washington provides clear evidence of cerebral asymmetry. Stimulation of the left hemisphere can block the ability to speak, whereas stimulation of the right hemisphere seldom does so.

Applying an electrical current to the cortex of a conscious patient has four general effects—three excitatory and one inhibitory:

(A)

(B)

Central sulcus

Lateral fissure

Figure **11.9**

Identifying Speech and Movement Areas of the Brain
(A) Localizing an epileptogenic focus in the brain. The patient is fully conscious, lying on his right side, with the left hemisphere of his brain exposed. He is kept comfortable with local anesthesia. In the background, the neurologist studies the electroencephalographic recording from the patient's cortex. The EEG will help to identify the source of seizures. (B) Identifying critical cortical areas. A drawing of the entire skull overlies a photograph of the patient's exposed brain at surgery. The numbered tags identify the points that the surgeon stimulated. The application of a stimulating electrode at points 26, 27, and 28, for example, interfered with speech. (Part A, Montreal Neurological Institute.)

1. Stimulation can produce localized movements, localized dysthesias (numbness or tingling in the skin), light flashes, or buzzing sensations. These effects are normally evoked from primary motor, somatosensory, visual, and auditory areas and pathways, respectively, and are produced by the stimulation of either hemisphere with about the same frequency, a result that illustrates the often overlooked fact that the brain has symmetrical as well as asymmetrical functions.

2. Stimulation can produce what Penfield called "interpretive" and "experiential" responses. These uncommon but often highly reliable phenomena include alterations in the interpretation of the patient's surroundings, such as deja vu, fear, and dreaming states, and the reproduction of visual or auditory aspects of specific earlier experiences. That is, patients report specific "memories" in response to specific stimulation. These phenomena usually arise from tissue showing epileptogenic discharge, but their occurrence reveals an asymmetry: stimulation of the right temporal lobe produces these phenomena more frequently than does stimulation of the left temporal lobe, suggesting that the right hemisphere has perceptual functions not shared by the left hemisphere.

3. Stimulation of the left frontal or temporal regions may accelerate speech production. Ojemann suggested that this acceleration may result from a type of "alerting response" and may occur in other cognitive processes, especially memory, although this possibility is difficult to demonstrate unequivocally.

4. Stimulation blocks function. This inhibitory effect is most evident in complex functions such as language and memory and is apparent only when current is applied while a patient is actively engaged in these behaviors. Stimulation of the same site in a quiet patient has no discernible effect. Disruption of speech is a well-documented effect of stimulation of the left hemisphere, but only recently has stimulation of the right hemisphere been shown to disrupt behavior. Ojemann and his colleagues report that stimulation of the right hemisphere disrupts

judgments of line orientation, labeling of facial expressions, and short-term memory for faces. These effects come almost exclusively from the right temporoparietal cortex, a result consistent with its presumed role in visuospatial behavior.

In summary, stimulation of the cortex has proved a useful tool in demonstrating both localization and lateralization of function. The effect of disrupting stimulation can be quite localized, often changing as the site of stimulation is moved as little as a few millimeters, and it is often very reliable for individual patients. An additional intriguing aspect of data from cortical stimulation is the great variation from patient to patient in the exact location and extent of sites with particular effects on behavior. One can speculate that this variation forms a basis for individual differences in skills, because people presumably have different amounts of cortex assigned to particular functions.

Carotid Sodium Amobarbital Injection

Language is usually located in the left hemisphere but, in a small percentage of people, most of them left-handed, language is represented in the right hemisphere. In the event of elective surgery, preventing inadvertent damage to the speech zones requires that the surgeon be certain of their location. To achieve certainty in doubtful cases, Jun Wada pioneered the technique of injecting sodium amobarbital into the carotid artery to produce a brief period of anesthesia of the ipsilateral hemisphere, as shown in **Figure 11.10**. (Injections are now normally made through a catheter inserted into the femoral artery.)

The Wada test results in an unequivocal localization of speech, because injection into the speech hemisphere results in an arrest of speech lasting up to several minutes; as speech returns, it is characterized by aphasic errors. Injection into the nonspeaking hemisphere may produce no speech arrest or only brief arrest. The advantage of this procedure is that each hemisphere can be studied separately in the functional absence of the other, anesthetized one. Because the period of anesthesia lasts several minutes, a variety of functions, including memory and movement, can be studied to determine the capabilities of one hemisphere while the other is anesthetized.

In a typical Wada test, a patient is given a "dry run" to become familiar with the tests that will be done during and after the drug injection. This dry run establishes a baseline performance level against which to compare postinjection performance. The patient is then given a series of simple tasks, entailing immediate and delayed memory for both verbal (sentences or words) and nonverbal (photographs of faces or objects) material, for the same purpose.

Moments before the drug is injected, the supine patient raises both arms and wiggles the fingers and toes. The patient is asked to start counting from 1, and, without warning, the neurosurgeon injects the drug through the catheter for 2 to 3 seconds. Within seconds, dramatic changes in behavior are apparent.

Figure **11.10**

The Wada Test To prevent damage to the speech zones of patients about to undergo brain surgery, surgeons inject sodium amobarbital into the carotid artery. The sodium amobarbital anesthetizes the hemisphere on the side where it is injected (in this case, the left hemisphere), allowing the surgeon to determine whether that hemisphere is dominant for speech.

When the left carotid artery is injected, the left hemisphere is briefly anesthetized; so the person cannot speak, move the right arm, or see on the right visual field. Although the right hemisphere is awake, for most people it is nondominant for speech, and the patient can neither speak nor later report on the experience.

Injection into the right side produces sensory and motor symptoms on the left but no speech disturbance, unless the patient's right hemisphere is domininant for speech.

Left carotid artery

Sodium amobarbital

The contralateral arm falls to the bed with a flaccid paralysis, and there is no response whatsoever to a firm pinch of the skin of the affected limbs. If the injected hemisphere is nondominant for speech, the patient may continue to count and carry out the verbal tasks while the temporary hemiparesis is present, although often the patient appears confused and is silent for as long as 20 to 30 seconds but can typically resume speech with urging. When the injected hemisphere is dominant for speech, the patient typically stops talking and remains completely aphasic until recovery from the hemiparesis is well along, usually in 4 to 10 minutes.

Speech is tested by asking the patient to name a number of common objects presented in quick succession, to count and recite the days of the week forward and backward, and to perform simple object naming and spelling. In addition to aphasia and paresis, patients with anesthesia of either hemisphere are totally nonresponsive to visual stimulation in the contralateral visual field. For example, there is no reflexive blinking or orientation toward suddenly looming objects.

The sodium amobarbital test, like direct brain stimulation, has been very useful in determining which hemisphere controls speech. In a series of studies, Brenda Milner and her colleagues demonstrated that about 98% of right-handers and 70% of left-handers show speech disturbance after sodium amobarbital injection into the left hemisphere but not after injection into the right hemisphere. Curiously, roughly 2% of the speech functions of right-handers are lateralized to the right cerebral hemisphere, which is roughly the proportion of right-handed people who show aphasia from right-hemisphere lesions.

This finding reminds us that speech is sometimes found in the right hemisphere of right-handed people. The results for left-handed patients support the view that the pattern of speech representation is less predictable in left-handed and ambidextrous subjects than in right-handers but that the majority of left-handers do have speech represented in the left hemisphere.

Whereas none of the right-handers studied by Milner showed evidence of bilateral speech organization, 15% of the non-right-handers displayed some significant speech disturbance subsequent to the injection of either side. These patients probably did not have a symmetrical duplication of language functions in the two hemispheres. The injection of one hemisphere tended to disrupt naming (for example, naming the days of the week), whereas the injection of the other hemisphere disrupted serial ordering (for example, ordering the days of the week).

Hence, although people may have bilateral representation of speech, it is probably asymmetrical and need not imply that the person has "two left hemispheres." Further study of these patients would probably reveal that visuospatial functions are bilaterally and asymmetrically represented as well, although it is mere conjecture on our part.

Behavioral Asymmetry in the Intact Brain

The study of neurological patients demonstrates a clear difference between the effects of lesions in the two hemispheres, particularly in the control of language. The reason for this difference is not so clear, however, because many problems arise in trying to make inferences about the functioning of the normal brain from the results of clinical studies of the dysfunctioning brain.

Just because a specific behavioral symptom is associated with damage to a particular brain area does not necessarily mean that the region once controlled the disrupted function. For example, the fact that a left-hemisphere stroke in the "language areas" disrupts language function in 98% of right-handers does not mean that the function of the left hemisphere is language. Rather, it means that the left hemisphere executes instructions that are required for normal language functions.

What are these functions? One experimental approach is to study the normal brain noninvasively and to make inferences about the functions of its components from the behavior produced by each component. The most common behavioral approach is the laterality experiment, which takes advantage of the anatomical organization of the sensory and motor systems to "trick" the brain into revealing its mode of operation. Laterality studies, then, are designed to determine which side of the brain controls various functions. Laterality studies are not without problems of their own, however, as we shall see.

Asymmetry in the Visual System

The organization of the visual system provides an opportunity to present each hemisphere selectively with specific visual information. As seen in Figure 11.5, stimuli in the right visual field travel to the left visual cortex, whereas stimuli in the left visual field project to the right visual cortex. With the use of a special instrument called a *tachistoscope*, visual information can be presented to each visual field independently.

Normal subjects fixate on a center point marked by a dot or cross (see Figure 11.7). An image is then flashed in one visual field for about 50 ms—a time short enough to allow the image to be processed before the eyes can shift from the fixation point. By comparing the accuracy with which information from the two visual fields is processed, investigators can infer which hemisphere is best suited to processing different types of information.

The simple conclusion to be drawn from the results of more than 50 years of tachistoscopic studies is that information presented to only one visual field is processed most efficiently by the hemisphere that is specialized to receive it. Words presented to the verbal left hemisphere, therefore, are processed more efficiently than are words presented to the nonverbal right hemisphere. Similarly, a left-visual-field advantage is found for faces and other visuospatial stimuli thought to be processed by the right hemisphere. These results with normal subjects are consistent with those demonstrated anatomically with neurological patients and reinforce the evidence for a fundamental difference in the perceptual processes of the two hemispheres.

Asymmetry in the Auditory System

The auditory system is not as completely crossed as the visual, because both hemispheres receive projections from each ear. The crossed auditory connections are more numerous, however, and more rapidly conducting than the ipsilateral projections.

In the early 1960s, Doreen Kimura studied neurological patients while they performed dichotic-listening tasks, such as the one illustrated in **Figure 11.11**.

(A) Monaural presentation

Ipsilateral pathway

L R

"Ba" "Ba"

"Ba"

Contralateral pathway

(B) Dichotic presentation

Ipsilateral pathway suppressed

Corpus callosum

"Ga" "Ba"

"Ba" "Ga"

Figure 11.11

Kimura's Model of Dichotic Listening (A) If information is played to either ear, it reaches both hemispheres by both ipsilateral and contralateral pathways. (B) In dichotic presentation, the contralateral pathways have preferred access to the hemisphere, possibly because the ipsilateral pathways are suppressed. Thus, the syllable "ba" presented to the left ear can gain access to the left hemisphere only through the corpus callosum. If the callosum is cut, the patient can only report hearing "ga." (Adapted with permission from S. P. Springer and G. Deutsch. *Left Brain, Right Brain: Perspectives from Cognitive Neuroscience*, 5th ed. New York: W. H. Freeman and Company, 1998, p. 99.)

Pairs of spoken digits (say, "two" and "six") were presented simultaneously through headphones, but one digit only was heard in each ear. The subjects heard three pairs of digits and then were asked to recall as many of the six digits as possible, in any order. Kimura noticed that subjects recalled more digits that had been presented to the right ear than had been presented to the left.

This result led Kimura to propose that, when different stimuli are presented simultaneously to each ear, the pathway from the right ear to the speaking hemisphere has preferred access, and the ipsilateral pathway from the left ear is relatively suppressed. Thus, during a dichotic task, the stimulus to the left ear must travel to the right hemisphere and then across the cerebral commissures to the left hemisphere. This longer route puts the left ear at a disadvantage, and words played to the right ear are recalled more accurately.

With a right-ear advantage for perceiving dichotically presented speech stimuli having been found, the next step was to search for tasks that gave a left-ear superiority. In 1964, Kimura reported just such an effect in the perception of melodies. Two excerpts of instrumental chamber music were played simultaneously through headphones, one to each ear. After each pair, four excerpts (including the two that had been played dichotically) were presented binaurally (to both ears), and the subject's task was to identify the two that had been heard previously. Amazingly, Kimura found a left-ear advantage on this task.

Not all normal subjects show the expected ear advantages in dichotic studies, the effects are not large when they are found (seldom exceeding a twofold difference in accuracy in the two ears), and dichotic results are apparently affected by various contextual and practice effects. Nonetheless, the Kimura studies are seminal in laterality research, because Kimura's behavioral methods complement results from the neurological literature (**Table 11.3**). As a result, her research opened up an entire field of experimentation to anyone with imagination and a stereo audio recorder.

More importantly, Kimura's experiments provide a noninvasive technique for identifying the hemisphere dominant for language—a question of special clinical importance, particularly in left-handed patients. In addition, the dichotic test has other clinical uses. It turns out that patients with left-temporal-lobe damage are very poor at this task. Patients with damage to the corpus callosum exhibit an almost complete inhibition of words presented to the left ear, even though they can recall words presented to this ear if there is no competing stimulus to the right ear.

Table 11.3 Ear advantages for various dichotic signals

Test	Basic Reference
Tests Showing a Right-Ear Advantage	
Digits	Kimura, 1961
Words	Kimura, 1967
Nonsense syllables	Kimura, 1967
Formant transitions	Lauter, 1982
Backward speech	Kimura and Folb, 1968
Morse code	Papcun et al., 1974
Difficult rhythms	Natale, 1977
Tone used in linguistic decisions	Zurif, 1974
Tonal sequences with frequency transitions	Halperin et al., 1973
Ordering temporal information	Divenyi and Efron, 1979
Movement-related tonal signals	Sussman, 1979
Tests Showing a Left-Ear Advantage	
Melodies	Kimura, 1964
Musical chords	Gelfand et al., 1980
Environmental sounds	Curry, 1967
Emotional sounds and hummed melodies	King and Kimura, 1972
Tones processed independently of linguistic content	Zurif, 1974
Complex pitch perception	Sidtis, 1982
Tests Showing No Ear Advantage	
Vowels	Blumstein et al., 1977
Isolated fricatives	Darwin, 1974
Rhythms	Gordon, 1970
Nonmelodic hums	Van Lancker and Fromkin, 1973

Source: After Noffsinger (1985).

The Kimura experiments imply that the left hemisphere is specialized for processing language-related sounds, whereas the right hemisphere processes music-related sounds. There is, however, another interpretation: the asymmetry could be related to the temporal or spectral structure of the sounds—their rhythm and frequency—rather than to language and music themselves.

Consider, for example, the finding by George Papcun and colleagues. They showed that Morse-code operators have a right-ear superiority for the perception of the code, even though the sounds are distinguished only by their temporal structures. The results of this study might be taken as evidence that the left hemisphere is not as specialized for language as much as it is for "something else." One possibility is the analysis of signals with a complex temporal microstructure. We will return to this idea later.

Asymmetry in the Somatosensory System

Experiments on laterality in somatosensation are not as numerous as those in vision and audition. The primary somatosensory system is almost completely crossed, as illustrated in **Figure 11.12**, which allows an easy behavioral comparison of the two sides by testing right and left limbs separately. By blindfolding subjects and requiring them to perform various tasks separately with each hand, for example, investigators can identify differences in each hand's efficiency—differences that can be taken to imply functional asymmetry in cerebral organization.

One line of somatosensory research compares the performance of the left and right hands in the recognition of shapes, angles, and patterns. The left hand of right-handed subjects is superior at nearly all tasks of this type. Both blind and sighted subjects read Braille more rapidly with the left hand (Rudel et al.). Some children are fluent readers with the left hand but are totally unable to read with the right. Because Braille patterns are spatial configurations of dots, this observation is congruent with the proposed right-hemisphere role in processing spatial information that is not shared by the left hemisphere.

A second type of somatosensory test employs an analogue of the dichotic-listening procedure, the **dichaptic test**. Subjects feel objects, then look at an array of objects and select those that they previously touched. Using this task, Candace Gibson and Philip Bryden presented subjects with cutouts of irregular shapes or letters made of sandpaper, which were moved slowly across the fingertips. Their subjects showed a right-hand advantage for identifying letters and a left-hand advantage for identifying other shapes.

Motor pathway
Sensory pathway

Somatosensory and motor pathways are almost wholly crossed.

Primary motor cortex

Primary somatosensory cortex

Each limb is served primarily by the cerebral hemisphere on the opposite side.

Figure 11.12

Primary Sensorimotor Cortex

Asymmetry in the Motor System

Neuroscientists have long known that left-hemisphere lesions can produce **apraxia**—severe deficits in copying sequences of movements. The logic of studying asymmetry in intact sensory systems makes it seem reasonable to look for asymmetries in motor control. A difficulty immediately confronts researchers, however: because an asymmetry exists in the processing of sensory input, the study of motor asymmetries is potentially confounded by the fact that the two sides do not start off equally.

For example, if we found that the right hand reacts to verbal stimuli faster than the left hand, we could not conclude that this difference is due to motor asymmetry itself. It could be entirely due to perceptual asymmetry. To overcome such potential pitfalls, two different types of experiments have been devised to assess motor asymmetries: (1) direct observation and (2) interference tasks.

Direct Observation

If asymmetry in the control of movement is inherent, it might be observable as people engage in other behaviors. For example, perhaps the right hand is more active during the performance of verbal tasks that do not require a manual response, whereas the left hand is more active during the performance of nonverbal tasks, such as listening to music, which also do not require a manual response.

To examine this possibility, Kimura and her colleagues videotaped subjects talking or humming. They found that right-handed people tend to gesture with their right hands when talking but are equally likely to scratch themselves, rub their noses, or touch their bodies with either hand. Kimura interpreted the observed gesturing with the limb contralateral to the speaking hemisphere to indicate a relation between speech and certain manual activities.

Differences in gesturing, which favor the right hand in right-handed subjects, could simply be due to a difference in preferred hand rather than to functional asymmetry in motor control. Thus, another series of observational studies compared hand-movement asymmetries during analogous verbal and nonverbal tasks.

The procedure consisted of videotaping right-handed subjects while they assembled blocks in three different tests. The first, a "neutral task," required subjects to combine white blocks to form a five-by-five matrix. The second test, a "verbal task," required subjects to combine blocks with letters on them in a series of crossword-puzzle tasks. In the third test, a "nonverbal task," subjects assembled jigsaw puzzles with the same size blocks as those used in the two preceding tests.

Analysis of the movements showed that, in the neutral task, subjects manipulated blocks with the right hand while supporting them with the left. Other movements seldom occurred. In the verbal test, most task-directed movements showed a right-hand preference. In the nonverbal test, in contrast, task-directed movements showed a leftward shift from the neutral condition, subjects now making far more movements with the left hand. These results suggest that the two hemispheres may have complementary roles in the control of movement—an asymmetry moderated by a native hand preference.

A second observed motor asymmetry was reported in the performance of complex movements of the mouth. Marilyn Wolf and Melvyn Goodale did single-frame analyses of videotaped mouth movements produced when people make verbal or nonverbal sounds. **Figure 11.13** illustrates their principal finding: the right side of the mouth opens wider and more quickly than the left side for both verbal and nonverbal tasks. Goodale's observations support the idea that the left hemisphere has a special role in the selection, programming, and production of verbal and nonverbal oral movements.

Is there an analogous role for the right hemisphere? Indeed there is. Considerable evidence shows that the left side of the face displays emotions more strongly than the right side, and Goodale showed that the onset of facial expressions is sooner on the left side of the face. Thus, it is not the control of movement itself that is asymmetrical but rather the function—movement for a particular purpose.

Interference Tasks

A variety of interference tasks (known in common parlance as *multitasking*) examine a well-known phenomenon manifested by most people: the difficulty of doing two complex tasks at the same time. Perhaps the most interesting interference study known to us is an unpublished experiment by Robert Hicks and Marcel Kinsbourne. They persuaded several unemployed musicians to come to their laboratory daily to play the piano.

The task was to learn a different piece of music with each hand so that the two pieces could be played simultaneously. When the musicians had mastered this very difficult task, the experimenters then asked them to speak or to hum while playing. Speaking disrupted playing with the right hand, and humming disrupted playing with the left hand.

Figure 11.13

Motor Asymmetry Successive video frames illustrate that the right side of the mouth opens more quickly and wider during the production of the syllable "ma" in the sequence "mabopi." (Adapted with permission from *Neuropsychologia* 25, M. E. Wolf and M. A. Goodale, Oral asymmetries during oral and nonoral movements of the mouth, © 1987.)

(A) Start of speaking "ma"

(B) 67 ms later

Interference studies provide a useful way to study the roles of the two hemispheres in controlling movement, but much more work is needed before researchers can identify the hemispheres' complementary roles (see reviews by Murphy and Peters and by Caroselli et al.). The identification of which types of movements that each hemisphere is especially good at controlling will be necessary, because these movements will probably be resilient to interference effects. Furthermore, studies should be conducted on the capacities of the hemispheres to produce simultaneous finger-versus-limb movements. Perhaps finger movements are more sensitive to interference effects when performed by the right hemisphere than by the left hemisphere.

Studies of interference effects are intriguing because they may be sources of fresh insight into the cortical organization of the motor systems, but interference effects are poorly understood and appear capricious. In addition, as we become proficient at motor tasks, we are less prone to interference effects. Consider the difficulty of talking while learning to play tennis, an interference paradigm of little challenge to a tennis professional.

What Do Laterality Studies Tell Us about Brain Function?

Laterality studies provide a behavioral complement to the anatomical study of neurological patients. Much current theorizing about the nature of cerebral asymmetry is based on laterality research. However, these noninvasive studies are indirect measures of brain function and are far less precise than anatomical measures. Consider the following problems.

Behavioral measures of laterality do not correlate perfectly with invasive measures of cerebral asymmetry. For example, the results of dichotic-listening studies show a right-ear bias for words in about 80% of right-handed subjects, but sodium amobarbital testing and brain stimulation show language represented in the left hemisphere in more than 98% of right-handers. What causes this discrepancy? One possibility is that the behavioral test is measuring several things, only one of which is relative cerebral dominance.

A curious paradox is that the behavioral tests may correlate with anatomical asymmetries more closely than data from the invasive tests do. Thus, from anatomical studies, we know that only about 75% to 80% of brains show a left-side advantage in the posterior lateral area of right-handers, yet 98% of these brains show language in the left hemisphere in a sodium amobarbital test.

Esther Strauss and colleagues propose that the results of laterality studies may provide correlations between anatomy and behavior. One way to test this proposal would be to perform a battery of laterality tests with subjects for whom MRIs also are available. Yet the question remains, Why do the results of both the amobarbital test and the brain-stimulation studies show a larger percentage of people with left-hemisphere speech?

In addition, measures of laterality do not correlate very highly with one another. We might expect tachistoscopic and dichotic measures in the same subjects to be highly concordant, but they are not. Perhaps these tests are not really measuring the same things.

Furthermore, the behavioral strategies that subjects adopt in laterality tasks can alter performance significantly. If subjects are instructed to pay particular attention to words entering the left ear in dichotic tasks, they can do so, abolishing the right-ear effect. Subjects can also enter tests with preconceived biases that may affect test performance. Finally, laterality effects may simply be a result of experience rather than biological factors. Suspicion about laterality effects is reinforced by the observation that repeated testing of the same subjects does not always produce the same results.

Skepticism regarding the usefulness of laterality research reaches its peak in an insightful and provocative book by Robert Efron. His thesis is that the apparent right–left difference in laterality studies can be explained entirely by the way in which the brain "scans" sensory input. Imagine the following experiment.

Six numbers are presented for 100 ms, in a line going from left to right. Three appear in each visual field such that 1, 2, and 3 fall in the left visual field and 4, 5, and 6 fall in the right visual field. Subjects are asked to repeat the numbers that they saw in sequence. As it turns out, they tend to respond with the sequence 4, 5, 6, 1, 2, 3. The subjects appear to be scanning, from left to right, the contents of the right visual field followed by the contents of the left visual field.

Note that the apparent scanning has nothing to do with actually moving the eyes to read the numbers, because the numbers are present for only 100 ms, which is not enough time for one eye movement. Thus, the sequencing scan is taking place after the presentation of the stimuli has ended. We might expect that, the longer it takes to scan, the poorer the performance will be at the end of the scan because the information has been decaying.

Subsequent experiments confirm this expectation. Efron's numerous scanning experiments led him to conclude that the brain has a tendency to scan information serially. If so, then the brain must necessarily examine some stimuli before others. If there is a tendency to examine stimuli in one visual half-field earlier than those in the other half-field, the result will be a left–right performance asymmetry without entailing any hemispheric differences in processing capacity.

There is still a bias in what is scanned first, but that is a different question. Efron does not argue that the two hemispheres are functionally and anatomically identical. He does argue that the evidence of laterality does not constitute an explanation and that we should be very skeptical when we read about descriptions of hemispheric "specialization." What, indeed, is actually lateralized?

Neuroimaging and Asymmetry

Neuroimaging studies, described in Chapter 6, allow researchers to map cerebral activity as it takes place in normal subjects. The primary interest in most imaging studies is the localization, rather than the lateralization, of functions. Because both hemispheres are scanned, however, left–right differences in cerebral activation can be assessed during a large range of behavioral measures. Virtually all imaging measures, including those by PET, fMRI, ERP, and MEG, reveal the expected asymmetry in cerebral activation in tasks similar to those used in laterality studies.

As expected, for example, there is asymmetrical cerebral activity when subjects either listen to conversation or engage in it (**Figure 11.14**). Thus, when

(A) Left hemisphere, speaking

Supplementary
motor cortex   Motor cortex   Somatosensory
cortex

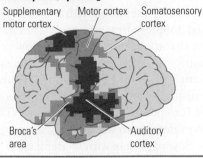

Broca's
area   Auditory
cortex

1

Speaking activates the mouth, tongue, and
larynx representations in the motor and
somatosensory cortex, the supplementary motor
area, the auditory cortex, and the language
zones in the left hemisphere.

(B) Right hemisphere, speaking

Wernicke's   Motor cortex   Supplementary
area   motor cortex

Auditory
cortex

2

In the right hemisphere, the mouth area and
auditory cortex are active but are less active
than in the left hemisphere.

(C) Left hemisphere, listening

Auditory
cortex

3

Sensation changes the pattern of blood flow in
the cortex, revealing the localization of areas
that mediate perception. Here the subjects
listened to spoken words, resulting in increased
activity localized to the auditory cortex.

Figure 11.14

Relating Brain Function to Regional Blood Flow
These images, averaged from nine different subjects,
show differences in the activity of the left and right
hemispheres as the pattern of blood flow varies with
the behavioral task. Light shading indicates the
average level of blood flow; dark shading indicates
higher-than-average blood flow; the absence of shading
indicates lower-than-average blood flow. Note that the
position of the lateral (Sylvian) and central fissures is
approximate; the actual position could be determined
only by opening the skull. The squared-off shapes are
an artifact of the recording-and-averaging procedure
and thus do not accurately indicate the shapes of
areas in the brain. (After Lassen et al., 1978.)

a subject is listening to speech, both hemispheres show regional changes in
cerebral activity, especially within the auditory cortex, but the left hemisphere
also shows increased activity in Broca's and Wernicke's areas. When speaking,
subjects also show activity in the motor areas that represent the face and
mouth, as well as activity in the supplementary motor cortex (the dorsal premotor area described in Chapter 9).

Curiously, repetition of what has been called "automatic" speech, such as
naming the days of the week over and over again, fails to produce increased activity in Broca's area. This result would not be predicted from the idea that this
area takes part in producing movement or from the results of the sodium amobarbital or stimulation studies discussed earlier. In contrast with the increased
activity on the left side during speech perception, right-side activity in the temporal lobe increases when subjects hear music.

The mere demonstration of asymmetry is not going to be the principal advantage of imaging studies in the future. Rather, that advantage will be in examples in which predicted asymmetries are not found, such as the absence of
activity in Broca's area during automatic speech.

The changes in cerebral perfusion during cognitive tasks that underlie fMRI
result in alterations of blood-flow velocities in the feeding basal arteries. The

changes in blood flow in these arteries can be measured with the use of a procedure known as functional transcranial doppler ultrasonography (fTCD). Stefan Knecht and colleagues have shown that the changes in blood-flow velocity in the basal arteries can be used to identify the language-dominant hemisphere.

These researchers tested each patient with both fTCD and the Wada procedure to determine the speaking hemisphere. In every case, both tests found the same hemisphere to be dominant for speech. The advantage of fTCD is that it is noninvasive and may thus be preferable to the Wada procedure. The question at this point is how the blood flow of people with bilateral speech representation would change with fTCD.

Theoretical Arguments: What Is Lateralized?

It is tempting to conclude that the functional asymmetries described thus far indicate a fundamental difference in the basic cognitive processes of the left and right cerebral hemispheres. Before turning to this matter, however, we will summarize the data, because any theoretical statements are best considered in light of available information.

Table 11.4 summarizes the major data on cerebral lateralization and illustrates the range of functions lateralized principally in the left or right hemisphere. In right-handed people, the left hemisphere has a greater role in language and in the control of complex voluntary movements than does the right hemisphere, and the right hemisphere has a greater role in the control of certain visuospatial and nonverbal abilities.

An enormous number of proposals have been made on what is lateralized in the brain (see Allen for a readable summary). At the broadest level, these the-

Table 11.4 Summary of data on cerebral lateralization

Function*	Left Hemisphere	Right Hemisphere
Visual system	Letters, words	Complex geometric patterns Faces
Auditory system	Language-related sound	Nonlanguage environmental sounds Music
Somatosensory	?	Tactile recognition of complex system patterns Braille
Movement	Complex voluntary movement	Movements in spatial patterns
Memory	Verbal memory	Nonverbal memory
Language	Speech Reading Writing Arithmetic	Prosody
Spatial processes		Geometry Sense of direction Mental rotation of shapes

*Functions predominantly mediated by one hemisphere in right-handed people.

ories fall into two groups: specialization theories propose unique functions for each hemisphere, and interaction theories propose cooperation between the two hemispheres.

Specialization Models

At the extreme, a unilateral specialization model states that only one hemisphere facilitates a given psychological process. For example, it has been argued since Broca that the left hemisphere alone performs language functions. Perhaps the most thorough modern version of the "left for language" theory is Eric Lenneberg's modification of the language theory proposed by Hugo Liepmann at the turn of the twentieth century. Liepmann proposed that the left hemisphere is specialized for some form of motor control, which would account for both aphasia and apraxia as the major symptoms of left-hemisphere damage.

Kimura extended this idea by proposing that, although the left hemisphere mediates verbal function, it is specialized not for verbal function itself but rather for certain kinds of motor function, both verbal and nonverbal. Kimura's argument is based on two premises:

1. Lesions of the left hemisphere disturb the production of voluntary movement—an impairment correlated with disturbance in speech.

2. Verbal communication among humans evolved from a stage that was primarily gestural, though with vocal concomitants, to one that is primarily vocal but that retains the capacity for gestural communication. Because the neurological control of speech and language thus evolved out of a manual system of motor control, the left hemisphere is specialized not for language itself but rather for motor control.

Several researchers (for example, Efron) suggest that it is not motor control itself that is located in the left hemisphere but rather the capacity for the fine resolution of stimuli in time. In other words, because the analysis and production of speech require fine discrimination over very short intervals, the left hemisphere might be specialized for temporal sequencing. Elaborations of this idea stress the capacity of the left hemisphere to make fine discriminations in time, whether or not the stimuli are verbal (see, for example, Sergent). Recall the study of Morse-code operators discussed earlier: there is a left-hemisphere advantage even though the code is not verbal; it is a temporal sequence.

Robert Zatorre and his colleagues expanded the Efron timing idea by emphasizing that speech and musical sounds exploit different acoustical cues: speech is highly dependent on rapidly changing broadband sounds, whereas tonal patterns of music tend to be slower, although small and precise changes in frequency are important. Zatorre proposed that the auditory cortices in the two hemispheres are therefore specialized such that temporal resolution is better in the left and spectral resolution is better in the right auditory areas. Zatorre made the point that, because an acoustical system cannot simultaneously analyze both temporal and spectral aspects of sound, the cortical asymmetries related to acoustical processing may have evolved as a solution for optimizing the processing of acoustical stimuli.

Rather than specifying different processing of specified psychological processes, other specialization models focus on the idea that the two hemispheres might process information in distinctly different ways. The first clear proposal of this sort was made by Josephine Semmes in 1968. On the basis of the results of her previous studies of World War II veterans suffering from penetrating brain injuries, Semmes concluded that the left hemisphere functions as a collection of focalized regions, whereas the right hemisphere functions more diffusely.

Her logic was as follows. She had noticed that small lesions in the left hemisphere produced a wide variety of specific deficits (for example, impaired spelling and reading), the precise deficit depending on the locus of the lesion. Similar-sized lesions within the right hemisphere were often without obvious effect. In contrast, large lesions of either hemisphere produced a large number of deficits.

To account for these differences, Semmes argued that a person with a small lesion in the right hemisphere exhibits no deficits, because specific functions are not localized in discrete regions in the right hemisphere, the functions being diffusely represented. A large lesion of the right hemisphere produces many more deficits than would be predicted from the total of smaller lesions because an entire functional field is removed. A large lesion of the left hemisphere produces many deficits simply because many small focal regions have been destroyed; that is, in the left hemisphere, the total is equal to the sum of the parts.

Semmes proposed that this differential organization of the two hemispheres is advantageous for efficient control of their respective functions. The diffuse organization of the right hemisphere is seen as advantageous for spatial abilities, because spatial analysis requires that different sensations (visual, auditory, tactile) be integrated into a single percept. Language functions, in contrast, remain discrete individual units in the left hemisphere.

From these basic ideas about distinct functions of the two hemispheres has arisen the idea that the hemispheres represent two distinct modes of cognitive processing (see Springer and Deutch). The left hemisphere operates in a more logical, analytical, computer-like fashion, analyzing stimuli input sequentially and abstracting the relevant details to which it attaches verbal labels. The right hemisphere is primarily a synthesizer, more concerned with the overall stimulus configuration, and organizes and processes information as gestalts, or wholes.

Specialization models have stimulated interest among philosophers and the general public. However, it is important to remember that they are based entirely on inference and have jumped a long way from the data, such as those summarized in Table 11.4.

Interaction Models

All interaction models have in common the idea that both hemispheres have the capacity to perform all functions, but they do not. The specific reasons "why not" have spawned debates, experiments, and models. Three versions of the interaction model are

1. The two hemispheres function simultaneously but work on different aspects of processing. This version is a direct analogue of the multiple-channel idea of sensory processing but takes it one step further, proposing that the two hemispheres represent a class of sensory channel. Although simultaneous processing is generally appealing as a model, this hypothesis

has yet to offer a satisfactory explanation of how information is combined into a single percept or behavior.

2. An entire group of interaction models proposes that, although the two hemispheres have the capacity to perform a given function, they inhibit or suppress each other's activity (see Kinsbourne, for example, and Moscovitch). Thus, the left hemisphere inhibits language processing in the right hemisphere, and the right hemisphere inhibits music processing in the left hemisphere. Developmentally, this inhibition model has appeal because functions such as language appear to be able to develop in the "wrong" hemisphere if the normally dominant hemisphere is damaged, as illustrated in the Snapshot. Thus, if the language zones are damaged in infancy, language can develop in the right hemisphere. A difficulty with these models is that the physiological mechanisms of hemispheric inhibition have not been clearly specified.

ꝑSNAPSHOT
Imaging the Brain's Plasticity

Recall from Chapter 10 that hemispherectomy is sometimes performed to treat children with severe seizures. These disorders can arise from progressive viral infections, such as Rasmussen's encephalitis, or as congenital or acquired dysfunction of one cerebral hemisphere. Although such children may have severe behavioral difficulties after the surgery, they often compensate remarkably, communicating freely and, in some cases, showing considerable motor control over the limbs opposite the excised hemisphere.

Using both functional magnetic resonance imaging (fMRI) and somatosensory evoked potentials (SEPs), Holloway and colleagues investigated the sensorimotor functions of 17 hemispherectomy patients. Ten patients showed SEPs in the normal hemisphere when the nerves of the limb opposite the excised hemisphere were stimulated.

Similarly, as illustrated in the adjoining micrographs, fMRI shows that, for at least some of the patients, passive movement of the same limb produces activation in a region of somatosensory cortex that normally responds to the opposite hand. The Holloway team concluded that the responses to the hand ipsilateral to the normal hemisphere must occur because direct ipsilateral pathways run from the normal hemisphere to the affected limb.

Curiously, the novel ipsilateral responses were found not only in hemispherectomy patients with congenital disease, but also in those with acquired disease, suggesting that, although age at injury may be important, other factors must be

Damage to right hemisphere

Passive movement of the right hand is seen in the left sensorimotor cortex.

Passive movement of the left (hemiplegic) hand shows an abnormal ipsilateral pathway.

influencing the cerebral reorganization. The injury-induced reorganization is characteristic of the brain's plasticity—the ability of the nervous system to alter its organization to compensate for injury. We will return to plasticity in the context of brain development in Chapter 23.

Holloway, V., D. G. Gadian, F. Vargha-Khadem, D. A. Porter, S. G. Boyd, and A. Connelly. The reorganization of sensorimotor function in children after hemispherectomy. *Brain* 123:2432–2444, 2000.

3. Interaction models based on information processing suggest either that the two hemispheres receive information preferentially and thus perform different analyses simultaneously or that some mechanism enables each hemisphere to "pay attention" to specific types of information, thus leading to different hemispheric analyses (see, for example, Moscovitch). Information-processing models are complex, detailed, and based heavily on theories of cognitive psychology. An interesting proposal of the simultaneous-processing models is analogous to networked, or distributed, processing by computer. That is, if one hemisphere is busy, it ought to be able to allocate functions to the other hemisphere. A problem with attention-based information-processing models is that they are necessarily vague on what physiological mechanisms might be responsible for selective attention.

In summary, the question of what is lateralized does not have a simple or a generally accepted answer. There is no shortage of theory. What is needed is more information about the nature of asymmetry and its origins, both developmentally and phylogenetically.

Preferred Cognitive Mode

From the preceding theoretical arguments, we can speculate that individual differences in the behavior of normal subjects result, at least in part, from individual differences in how the cerebral hemispheres are organized and how functions are lateralized. **Preferred cognitive mode** refers to the use of one thought process in preference to another. At one extreme, people who are logical, analytical, and verbal are assumed to rely more on their left hemispheres to solve problems in everyday life, whereas people who are visual, intuitive, and tend to look at the big picture are assumed to rely more on their right hemispheres.

Consider an example, albeit a tongue-in-cheek one. Two professors, Alpha and Beta, are both excellent scholars, but they work and think in totally different ways.

Alpha is meticulous and leaves no detail to chance; when learning new material, he masters every detail and has total command of the topic. Alpha is verbal and easily wins debates with his quick thinking and elegant arguments. His writing is clear and concise, with flawless grammar and spelling. Alpha is athletic and is a nationally ranked tennis player. Curiously, he is only mediocre at other sports but, with prolonged practice, he masters them. Alpha's office is neat and tidy, with every item carefully placed in its correct location. On his desk is the project on which he is currently working and nothing else.

Beta appears messy and disorganized compared with Alpha and has poor recall for details. He grasps the heart of an idea quickly, however, and can tie diverse concepts into a meaningful picture. Communicating his thinking poses Beta a challenge, however, because he has difficulty expressing his ideas in words. Like Alpha, Beta is athletic, but Beta acquires the general motor skills of new sports rapidly, although he has never been able to become a top participant in any event. In contrast with Alpha, who works on only one project at a time, Beta works on several projects concurrently, leading to piles of papers and books in his work space, unlike Alpha's meticulous desk.

In both the cognitive and the motor skills of Alpha and Beta is a basic difference assumed to correspond to a fundamental difference either in brain organization or in the "dominance" of one hemisphere over the other. Alpha and Beta represent extreme left-hemisphere and right-hemisphere people, respectively. The fundamental difference between them is their preferred cognitive mode. Alpha is analytical, logical, verbal, and meticulous, whereas Beta is a synthesizer more concerned with organizing concepts and visualizing meaningful wholes.

As intriguing as the Alpha–Beta analysis might be, we caution that it is pure speculation, without empirical basis. Factors other than brain organization probably contribute to preferred cognitive mode. For example, the results of a study by William Webster and Ann Thurber demonstrate that **cognitive set**, the tendency to approach a problem with a particular bias in thought, can affect some tests of lateralization.

They repeated the dichaptic test (described earlier) but added an additional variable. One group (the gestalt bias) was encouraged to learn the shapes by imagining their overall appearance. A second group (the analytical bias) was encouraged to identify distinctive features of each shape and list them to themselves.

This manipulation of cognitive set demonstrably influenced the degree of left-hand superiority, because the gestalt group had a significantly larger performance difference between the hands than did the analytical group. Although the basis for this effect is uncertain, it implies that strategies used by subjects can significantly influence tests of lateralization. Thus, differences in preferred cognitive mode can be reasonably assumed to be due to biases in socialization or environmental factors in addition to neuronal, genetic, or constitutional biases. Nevertheless, the idea that individual differences in behavior result in part from individual differences in brain organization is a provocative assumption worthy of serious study.

Measuring Behavior in Neuropsychology

At this point, a brief consideration of the problem of measuring behavior is appropriate. You might think that, of all the procedures used in neuropsychology, the measurement of things or events may be the easiest to perform and replicate. It is not true.

Many measurements are made to obtain inferences about some other processes. For example, in dichotic listening, if more words are recalled from the right ear than from the left ear, the inference is that speech is lateralized to the left hemisphere. The assumptions underlying this inference are simple, yet so many variables affect the result that Phil Bryden wrote an entire book on the problem.

Perhaps, we may ask, if a more objective measure of something like brain size were used, would the results be clearer? This outcome, however, seems unlikely. There appear to be so many different ways to measure objects that almost any result can be obtained. Consider the following example.

Probably everyone has had the feeling that his or her feet are not exactly the same size. Often the difference manifests itself as greater discomfort in one foot when breaking in a new pair of shoes (we have never heard anyone suggest that

Figure 11.15

Growth and the Brain Destruction of the left frontoparietal region at birth produced this growth asymmetry in the right foot. Such cases demonstrate that growth affecting limb size has a cortical component, quite aside from the effect of disuse of the limb. (From W. Penfield and H. Jasper, © 1954. Reprinted with permission.

the shoes might be different sizes). Foot size may be related to differences in brain organization. For example, people in medicine have long known that damage to one hemisphere at an early age leads to smaller limbs on the contralateral side of the body (**Figure 11.15**).

To make inferences about cerebral organization, Jere and Jerome Levy attempted to measure differences in foot size in normal people. They measured foot size in 150 persons and found that significantly more right-handed females had larger left than right feet, whereas significantly more right-handed males had larger right than left feet. Just the opposite result was obtained for left-handed females and males.

The Levys' measures were made by converting foot size into shoe size and then converting differences into a seven-point rating scale. A number of studies attempted to repeat the Levys' work. Nicholas Mascie-Taylor and his coworkers measured foot size by using a "standard anthropometric technique" (described elsewhere as heel to longest toe with the subject seated and with the toenails cut). They found that the left foot was longer than the right in both sexes, confirming the results of seven earlier studies. There were no handedness effects.

Michael Peters and his coworkers measured the actual foot length from the heel to the longest toe in 365 seated subjects. They found no significant differences between the left and the right foot for any sex or handedness group, and they claimed partial support for their results from three other studies. Another study, in which the outlines of 105 subjects' feet were traced on a large sheet of paper, found no differences in foot size with regard to sex or handedness (Yanowitz et al.).

The final score on this series of studies is as follows: one study for sex and handedness effects, eight studies for a left-foot effect, and two studies for no differences, with the results of three additional studies partly supporting no differences. This story—like all good stories—has a sequel, and we refer the interested reader to Peters's review.

Measuring foot size might seem easy. This series of studies shows that it is not. The results obtained depend on the measuring device, the points across which length is measured, whether subjects are seated or standing, the time of day, and perhaps even shoe type worn before measurement. In many of the studies, the importance of these variables was not recognized; in others, the procedure was not described in sufficient detail to permit exact replication. The most objective measure, photography, was not used in any of the studies. A photographic record of the feet would permit a reevaluation of the results at any time by investigators interested in the question of appropriate measurement.

We can derive three lessons from this example (one of them is not that it is impossible to make measurements). The first is that, if measuring something like feet is difficult, then inferring something about the brain from such measurements should be done with caution. The second is that there is nothing wrong with making multiple measurements. If they correlate, then each is measuring the same thing; if they do not, then either multiple factors are at work or some of the measures are not reliable. The third is that, if a measurement is to be made, it should be the most meaningful one that can be made.

Summary

Anatomical Asymmetry in the Human Brain

A striking feature of the organization of the human brain is that its two hemispheres are anatomically and functionally asymmetrical. The asymmetries in structure are visible not only in an overall view but also at the level of the morphology of individual neurons, and asymmetries in function exist not only in neurological patients but also in the normal brain. Although there is little disagreement about the facts of asymmetry in the human brain, there is considerable disagreement about why the two hemispheres are asymmetrical and about what the asymmetry means with regard to how we humans process information.

The observed asymmetries can be assumed to represent functional specializations of the hemispheres. Thus, the increased size of the language areas in certain auditory regions of the temporal lobe presumably corresponds to the special role of this tissue in processing acoustical stimuli related to language. But, given that the total area of the auditory cortex is similar in the two hemispheres, the tissue of the right hemisphere must be specialized for the analysis of some other characteristic of sound, which is likely the characteristic of sound related to music.

Asymmetry in Neurological Patients

Analyses of patients undergoing specialized neurological and surgical procedures provide an opportunity to study functional aspects of the hemispheres' anatomical asymmetries. Converging evidence from patients with lateralized lesions or split brains, as well as those undergoing brain stimulation and sodium amobarbital injection, confirm the left hemisphere's special role in language and motor functions and the right hemisphere's complementary role in musical and spatial functions.

Behavioral Asymmetry in the Intact Brain

The intact brain does not normally reveal its asymmetrical processing in everyday life, but it can be tricked into doing so. The simplest way is to strain processing capacity by the presentation of multiple stimuli simultaneously, such as in dichotic listening, or briefly, such as in tachistoscopic presentation, or by interference, in which the brain is asked to perform two conflicting tasks. With the use of such procedures, the intact brain reveals its processing biases.

Neuroimaging and Asymmetry

Asymmetry in the intact brain can also be studied by using imaging procedures that measure brain activity as it happens (that is, "on-line."). Such procedures include measures of glucose or oxygen utilization, electrical activity, or blood flow. These procedures not only show cerebral asymmetries but also allow relative localization to different regions within each hemisphere.

Theoretical Arguments: What Is Lateralized?

Specialization theories propose unique functions for each hemisphere, although there is no agreement on what the underlying unique functions might be. Likely candidates are related to differences in processing sensory inputs and differences in the role of movement control. Interaction theories propose cooperation between the hemispheres: both have the capacity for all functions but, for some reason, they are relatively specialized. The jury is still out, however, on why the brain is lateralized.

Four cautions must be reiterated before we consider variations in the "textbook pattern" of cerebral asymmetry in Chapter 12.

1. *Many functions of the cerebral hemispheres are symmetrical rather than asymmetrical.* In an examination in our undergraduate course in human neuropsychology, we asked, In what ways is the human brain symmetrical? Thinking it to be a trick question, a majority of the students answered, "It isn't symmetrical, it's asymmetrical." This answer is wrong, because many functions—especially of the primary sensory and motor areas—appear to be identical on the two sides of the brain.

2. *The functional differences between the two hemispheres are not absolute, but relative.* Just because sodium amobarbital renders one hemisphere aphasic does not mean that language functions are carried out only in the aphasic hemisphere.

3. *Cerebral* site *is at least as important in understanding brain function as cerebral* side. Thus the functions of the two frontal lobes, though asymmetrical, are more similar to each other than they are to those of the posterior cortex on the same side. We can

think of the functions of the cerebral cortex as being localized and of hemispheric side as being only one step in localizing them.

4. *The leap from the data available to explanations of what those data mean is a long inferential one.* Although it is tempting to conclude, for example, that the function of the left hemisphere is "language," the appropriate conclusion is that the left hemisphere takes part in processes that are necessary for certain aspects of language. Similarly, the right hemisphere appears to take part in processing required for visuospatial functions. Indeed, at present, we can safely conclude that we do not know what processes the two hemispheres are specialized to perform.

References

Allen, M. Models of hemispheric specialization. *Psychological Bulletin* 93:73–104, 1983.

Blumstein, S., V. Tartter, D. Michel, B. Hirsch, and E. Leiter. The role of distinctive features in the dichotic perception of words. *Brain and Language* 4:508–520, 1977.

Broca, P. Sur la faculté du langage articule. *Bulletins et Memoires de la Societé D'Anthropologie de Paris* 6:377–393, 1865.

Bryden, M. P. *Laterality: Functional Asymmetry in the Intact Brain.* New York: Academic Press, 1982.

Caroselli, J. S., M. Hiscock, and T. Roebuck. Asymmetric interference between concurrent tasks: An evaluation of competing explanatory models. *Neuropsychologia* 35:457–469, 1997.

Chi, J. G., E. C. Dooling, and F. H. Gilles. Left–right asymmetries of the temporal speech areas of the human fetus. *Archives of Neurology* 34:346–348, 1977.

Crichton-Browne, J. On the weight of the brain: Its component parts in the insane. *Brain* 2:42–67, 1880.

Curry, F. A comparison of left-handed subjects on verbal and nonverbal dichotic listening tasks. *Cortex* 3:343–352, 1967.

Darwin, C. Ear differences and hemispheric specialization. In F. O. Schmitt and F. G. Worden, Eds. *The Neurosciences: Third Study Program.* Cambridge, Mass: MIT Press, 1974.

Divenyi, P., and R. Efron. Spectral versus temporal features in dichotic listening. *Brain and Language* 7:375–386, 1979.

Eberstaller, O. Zur Oberflächenanatomie der Grosshirnhemispharen. *Wiener Medizinische Blätter* 7:479–482, 542–582, 644–646, 1884.

Efron, R. *The Decline and Fall of Hemispheric Specialization.* Hillsdale, N.J.: Erlbaum, 1990.

Eidelberg, D., and A. M. Galaburda. Symmetry and asymmetry in the human posterior thalamus. *Archives of Neurology* 39:325–332, 1982.

Falzi, G., P. Perrone, and L. A. Vignolo. Right–left asymmetry in anterior speech region. *Archives of Neurology* 39:239–240, 1982.

Galaburda, A. M., M. LeMay, T. L. Kemper, and N. Geschwind. Right–left asymmetries in the brain. *Science* 199:852–856, 1978.

Galaburda, A. M., and F. Sanides. Cytoarchitectonic organization of the human auditory cortex. *Journal of Comparative Neurology* 190:597–610, 1980.

Gelfand, S., S. Hoffmand, S. Waltzman, and N. Piper. Dichotic CV recognition at various interaural temporal onset asynchronies: Effect of age. *Journal of the Acoustical Society of America* 68:1258–1261, 1980.

Geschwind, N., and W. Levitsky. Left–right asymmetries in temporal speech region. *Science* 161:186–187, 1968.

Gibson, C., and M. P. Bryden. Dichaptic recognition of shapes and letters in children. *Canadian Journal of Psychology* 37:132–143, 1983.

Glick, S. D., D. A. Ross, and L. B. Hough. Lateral asymmetry of neurotransmitters in human brain. *Brain Research* 234:53–63, 1982.

Good, C. D., I. Johnsrude, J. Ashburner, R. N. Henson, K. J. Friston, and R. S. Frackowiak. Cerebral asymmetry and the effects of sex and handedness on brain structure: A voxel-based morphometric analysis of 465 normal adult brains. *Neuroimage* 14:685–700, 2001.

Gordon, H. Hemispheric asymmetries in the perception of musical chords. *Cortex* 6:387–398, 1970.

Gur, R. C., I. K. Packer, J. P. Hungerbuhler, M. Reivich, W. D. Obrist, W. S. Amarnek, and H. Sackheim. Differences in distribution of gray and white matter in human cerebral hemispheres. *Science* 207:1226–1228, 1980.

Halperin, Y., I. Nachson, and A. Carmon. Shift of ear superiority in dichotic listening to temporally patterned nonverbal stimuli. *Journal of the Acoutistical Society of America* 53:46–50, 1973.

Heschl, R. L. *Über die vordere quere Schlafentwindung des Meschlichen Grosshirns.* Wien: Braumüller, 1878.

Hoadley, M. D., and K. Pearson. Measurement of internal diameter of skull in relation to "pre-eminence" of left hemisphere. *Biometrika* 21:94–123, 1929.

Kimura, D. Some effects of temporal-lobe damage on auditory perception. *Canadian Journal of Psychology* 15:156–165, 1961.

Kimura, D. Left–right differences in the perception of melodies. *Quarterly Journal of Experimental Psychology* 16:355–358, 1964.

Kimura, D. Functional asymmetry of the brain in dichotic listening. *Cortex* 3:163–178, 1967.

Kimura D. The asymmetry of the human brain. *Scientific American* 228:70–78, 1973.

Kimura D., and S. Folb. Neural processing of background sounds. *Science* 161:395–396, 1968.

King, F., and D. Kimura. Left-ear superiority in dichotic perception of vocal, non-verbal sounds. *Canadian Journal of Psychology* 26:111–116, 1972.

Kinsbourne, M. Eye and head turning indicates cerebral lateralization. *Science* 176:539–541, 1971.

Knecht, S., M. Deppe, B. DRager, L. Bobe, H. Lohmann, E. Ringelstein, and H. Henningsen. Language lateralization in healthy right-handers. *Brain* 123:74–81, 2000.

Kodama, L. Beitrage zur Anatomie des Zentralnervensystems der Japaner: VIII. Insula Reil ii. *Folia Anatomica Japanica* 12:423–444, 1934.

Kopp, N., F. Michel, H. Carrier, A. Biron, and P. Duvillard. Hemispheric asymmetries of the human brain. *Journal of Neurological Sciences* 34:349–363, 1977.

Lassen, N. A., D. H. Ingvar, and E. Skinhøj. Brain function and blood flow. *Scientific American* 239:62–71, 1978.

Lauter, J. Dichotic identification of complex sounds: Absolute and relative ear advantages. *Journal of the Acoustical Society of America* 71:701–707, 1982.

LeMay, M. Asymmetries of the skull and handedness. *Journal of the Neurological Sciences* 32:243–253, 1977.

LeMay, M. Morphological aspects of human brain asymmetry. *Trends in Neurosciences* 5:273–275, 1982.

LeMay, M., and A. Culebras. Human brain-morphologic differences in the hemispheres demonstrable by carotid arteriography. *New England Journal of Medicine* 287:168–170, 1972.

Levy, J., and J. M. Levy. Human lateralization from head to foot: Sex-related factors. *Science* 200:1291–1292, 1978.

Levy, J., and J. M. Levy. Foot-length asymmetry, sex, and handedness. *Science* 212:1418–1419, 1981.

Levy, J., C. Trevarthen, and R. W. Sperry. Perception of bilateral chimeric figures following hemispheric deconnection. *Brain* 95:61–78, 1972.

Luders, E., K. L. Narr, P. M. Thompson, D. E. Rex, L. Jancke, and A. W. Toga. Hemispheric asymmetries in cortical thickness. *Cerebral Cortex* 16:1232–1238, 2006.

Mascie-Taylor, C. G. N., A. M. MacLarnon, P. M. Lanigan, and I. C. McManus. Foot-length asymmetry, sex, and handedness. *Science* 212:1416–1417, 1981.

McRae, D. L., C. L. Branch, and B. Milner. The occipital horns and cerebral dominance. *Neurology* 18:95–98, 1968.

Moscovitch, M. Information processing and the cerebral hemispheres. In M. Gazzaniga, Ed. *Handbook of Behavioral Neurobiology*, vol. 2. New York: Plenum, 1979.

Murphy, K., and M. Peters. Right-handers and left-handers show differences and important similarities in task integration when performing manual and vocal tasks concurrently. *Neuropsychologia* 32:663–674, 1994.

Natale, M. Perception of nonlinguistic auditory rhythms by the speech hemisphere. *Brain and Language* 4:32–44, 1977.

Noffsinger, D. Dichotic-listening techniques in the study of hemispheric asymmetries. In D. F. Benson and E. Zaidel, Eds. *The Dual Brain.* New York: Guilford Press, 1985.

Ojemann, G. A. Brain organization for language from the perspective of electrical stimulation mapping. *Behavioral and Brain Sciences* 6:189–230, 1983.

Oke, A., R. Keller, I. Mefford, and R. N. Adams. Lateralization of norepinephrine in human thalamus. *Science* 200:1411–1413, 1978.

Papcun, G., S. Krashen, D. Terbeek, R. Remington, and R. Harshman. Is the left hemisphere organized for speech, language and/or something else? *Journal of the Acoustical Society of America* 55:319–327, 1974.

Penfield, W., and H. Jasper. *Epilepsy and the Functional Anatomy of the Human Brain.* Boston: Little, Brown, 1954.

Peters, M. Footedness: Asymmetries in foot preference and skill and neuropsychological assessment of foot movement. *Psychological Bulletin* 103:179–192, 1988.

Peters, M. B., B. Petries, and D. Oddie. Foot-length asymmetry, sex, and handedness. *Science* 212:1417–1418, 1981.

Rubens, A. M., M. W. Mahowald, and J. T. Hutton. Asymmetry of the lateral (Sylvian) fissures in man. *Neurology* 26:620–624, 1976.

Rudel, R. G., M. B. Denckla, and E. Spalten. The functional asymmetry of Braille letter learning in normal sighted children. *Neurology* 24:733–738, 1974.

Scheibel, A. B., I. Fried, L. Paul, A. Forsythe, U. Tomiyasu, A. Wechsler, A. Kao, and J. Slotnick. Differentiating characteristics of the human speech cortex: A quantitative Golgi study. In D. F. Benson and E. Zaidel, Eds. *The Dual Brain.* New York: Guilford Press, 1985.

Semmes, J. Hemispheric specialization: A possible clue to mechanism. *Neuropsychologia* 6:11–26, 1968.

Sergent, J. Role of the input in visual hemispheric asymmetries. *Psychological Bulletin* 93:481–512, 1983.

Sidtis, J. Predicting brain organization from dichotic listening performance: Cortical and subcortical functional asymmetries contribute to perceptual asymmetries. *Brain and Language* 17:287–300, 1982.

Springer, S. P., and G. Deutsch. *Left Brain, Right Brain: Perspectives from Cognitive Neuroscience*, 5th ed. New York: W. H. Freeman and Company, 1998.

Strauss, E., and C. Fitz. Occipital horn asymmetry in children. *Annals of Neurology* 18:437–439, 1980.

Strauss, E., B. Kosaka, and J. Wada. The neurological basis of lateralized cerebral function: A review. *Human Neurobiology* 2:115–127, 1983.

Sun, T., R. V. Collura, M. Ruvolo, and C. A. Walsh. Genomic and evolutionary analyses of asymmetrically expressed genes in human fetal left and right cerebral cortex. *Cerebral Cortex* 16:118–125, 2006.

Sussman, H. M. Evidence for left hemisphere superiority in processing movement-related tonal signals. *Journal of Speech and Hearing Research* 22:224–235, 1979.

Taylor, L. B. Localisation of cerebral lesions by psychological testing. *Clinical Neurology* 16:269–287, 1969.

Teszner, D., A. Tzavaras, and H. Hécaen. L'asymetries droite-gauche du planum temporale: A-propos de l'étude de 100 cerveaux. *Revue Neurologique* 126:444–452, 1972.

Teuber, H.-L. Physiological psychology. *Annual Review of Psychology* 6:267–296, 1955.

Toga, A. W., and P. M. Thompson. Mapping brain asymmetry. *Nature Reviews Neuroscience* 4: 37–48, 2003.

Van Lancker, D., and V. Fromkin. Hemispheric specialization for pitch and "tone": Evidence from Thai. *Journal of Phonetics* 1:101–109, 1973.

von Bonin, B. Anatomical asymmetries of the cerebral hemispheres. In V. B. Mountcastle, Ed. *Interhemispheric Relations and Cerebral Dominance*. Baltimore: Johns Hopkins University Press, 1962.

von Economo, C. V., and L. Horn. Über Windungsrelief, Masse and Rindenarchitektonik der Supratemporalfläche, ihre individuellen und ihre Seitenunterschiede. *Zeitschrift für Neurologie and Psychiatrie* 130:678–757, 1930.

Wada, J. A., R. Clarke, and A. Hamm. Cerebral hemispheric asymmetry in humans: Cortical speech zones in 100 adult and 100 infant brains. *Archives of Neurology* 32:239–246, 1975.

Wada, J., and T. Rasmussen. Intracarotid injection of sodium amytal for the lateralization of cerebral speech dominance. *Journal of Neurosurgery* 17:266–282, 1960.

Webster, W. G., and A. D. Thurber. Problem solving strategies and manifest brain asymmetry. *Cortex* 14:474–484, 1978.

Witelson, S. F., and W. Pallie. Left hemisphere specialization for language in the newborn: Neuroanatomical evidence of asymmetry. *Brain* 96:641–646, 1973.

Wolf, M. E., and M. A. Goodale. Oral asymmetries during verbal and non-verbal movements of the mouth. *Neuropsychologia* 25:375–396, 1987.

Yanowitz, J. S., P. Satz, and K. M. Heilman. Foot-length asymmetry, sex, and handedness. *Science* 212:1418, 1981.

Zatorre, R. J., P. Belin, and V. B. Penhume. Structure and function of auditory cortex: Music and speech. *Trends in Cognitive Sciences* 6:37–46, 2002.

Zurif, E. Auditory lateralization: Prosodic and syntactic factors. *Brain and Language* 1:391–401, 1974.

CHAPTER 12

Variations in Cerebral Asymmetry

PORTRAIT: Individual Responses to Injury

No two brains are alike; indeed, no two hemispheres are even grossly alike, as the accompanying photograph, looking down on the brain from above, clearly illustrates. Brains (and hemispheres) differ in size, gyral patterns, distribution of gray and white matter, cytoarchitectonics, vascular patterns, and neurochemistry, among other things. Do variations in the brain's anatomical asymmetry correlate with functional asymmetries?

Consider A.B. and L.P., two middle-aged college graduates who suffered similar brain injuries but responded very differently. After an injury to the posterior part of the left temporal lobe, A.B. had verbal difficulties, in reading, speaking, and remembering words. In

Ralph Hutchings/Visuals Unlimited

contrast, L.P., whose injury was similar, had no language difficulties. But L.P. had trouble recognizing faces and drawing pictures, symptoms that A.B. did not exhibit.

Given their similar injuries and education (both had been psychology majors in college and presumably above average in intelligence before their injuries), we would expect their symptoms to be quite similar, but they were, in a sense, opposite.

Two significant differences between these people help explain their differing symptoms: A.B. was a right-handed man and L.P. was a left-handed woman. We shall see that these two factors—sex and handedness—influence the organization of the cerebral hemispheres and ultimately the effects of cerebral injury. In this case, L.P. was found to have language in the right hemisphere, which explains why she had no language impairments.

Handedness and sex are easily identified factors influencing cerebral asymmetry, but they are not the only factors that lead to individual differences in brain organization and behavior. This chapter examines a range of biological and environmental factors that produce individual variations in cerebral asymmetry. We examine the effects of the relations between brain organization and hand preference, sex differences, and genes and environment on individual patterns of asymmetry. In the final section, we consider the incidence of asymmetry in nonhuman animals.

Handedness and Functional Asymmetry

People use the word *sinister* as a synonym for wicked or evil. Originally a Latin word meaning "left-hand side," our contemporary English meaning implies that left-handedness has been historically viewed at best as strange or unusual. Today, terms such as southpaw in baseball suggest an evolution of tolerance toward left-handers and, in professional sports, even admiration.

Table **12.1** Summary of handedness in performing various tasks

Task	Left (%)	Either (%)	Right (%)
Dealing cards	17.02	3.32	79.66
Unscrewing jar	6.50	17.49	66.01
Shoveling	13.53	11.89	74.58
Sweeping	13.49	16.89	69.62
Threading needle	13.10	9.74	77.16
Writing	10.60	0.34	89.06
Striking match	9.95	8.74	81.31
Throwing ball	9.44	1.29	89.47
Hammering	9.22	2.54	88.24
Using toothbrush	9.18	8.49	82.33
Using racket	8.10	2.59	89.31
Using scissors	6.20	6.81	86.99

Note: Percentages are based on 2321 respondents.
Source: Annett (1970).

The most commonly cited statistic for left-handedness in the general population is 10%, referring to the percentage of people who write with the left hand. But, when broader criteria are used, estimates range from 10% to 30%. The problem is that handedness is not absolute: some people are nearly totally left- or right-handed, whereas others are ambidextrous (that is, they use either hand with equal facility).

A useful distribution of handedness was constructed by Marion Annett (**Table 12.1**), who asked more than 2000 adults to indicate the hand that they use to perform each of 12 different tasks. The evidence of left-handedness on Annett's tasks varies from a low of about 6% when cutting with scissors to a high of about 17% when dealing cards.

Anatomical Studies

Hand preference is correlated with differential patterns of right–left asymmetry in the parietal operculum, frontal cortex, occipital region, vascular patterns, and cerebral blood flow, as summarized in **Table 12.2**. Thus, in comparison with right-handers, a higher proportion of left-handers show no asymmetry or, like L.P. in the Portrait at the beginning of this chapter, a reversal of left and right anatomical asymmetries.

Are variations in anatomical organization related in any meaningful way to handedness? To answer this question, Graham Ratcliffe and his colleagues correlated the asymmetry in the course of the Sylvian (lateral) fissure, as revealed by carotid angiogram, with the results of carotid sodium amobarbital speech testing (see Chapter 11). They found that left- and right-handers with speech in the left hemisphere had a mean right–left difference of 27° in the angle formed by the vessels leaving the posterior end of the Sylvian fissure. In left- and right-handers with speech in the right hemisphere or with bilaterally represented speech, the mean difference shrank to 0°.

Thus, the anatomical asymmetry in the population studied by Ratcliffe was related to speech representation and not necessarily to handedness. The location of speech proved a better predictor of individual variation in cerebral organization than handedness.

Handedness may appear more closely related to anatomical anomalies because left-handers display more variation in the lateralization of speech. A series of studies by P. Yakovlev and Pasko Rakic are germane. In a study of more than 300 cases, they found that, in 80%, the pyramidal tract descending to the right hand contains more fibers than does the same tract going to the left hand. Apparently, more fibers descend to the right hand both from the contralateral left hemisphere and from the ipsilateral right hemisphere than to the left hand. In addition, the contralateral tract from the left hemisphere crosses at a higher level in the medulla than does the contralateral tract from the right hemisphere.

Even though the sample of left-handers that Ratcliffe studied was small—only 11—the pattern was remarkably similar to that observed in the population at large: 9 of 11 (82%) had the typical right-side bias. Statistically, we expect that two-thirds of these left-handers have speech localized in the left hemisphere; and so there appears to be a closer relation between locus of language and pyramidal tract organization than between handedness and pyramidal tract organization.

A difficulty in accounting for variations in anatomical asymmetries is that some left- and right-handers show a marked dissociation between morphological (structural) and functional asymmetry. Thus, carotid sodium amobarbital testing may show speech to reside in the left hemisphere, but the enlarged temporoparietal speech zone is inferred from other neurological studies to be in the right hemisphere. Consider also that a large percentage of the right-handed cases summarized in Table 12.2 do not show the expected asymmetries but have reversed

Table 12.2 Variations in anatomical asymmetry related to handedness

| Measure | Handedness | ANATOMICAL DIFFERENCES | | |
		Left Hand Larger	Right Hand Larger	No Difference
Blood volume	Right	25	62	13
	Left	64	28	8
Parietal operculum	Right	67	8	25
	Left	22	7	71
Frontal width	Right	19	61	20
	Left	27	40	33
Occipital width	Right	66	9	25
	Left	38	27	35
Occipital horns	Right	60	10	30
	Left	38	31	31

Sources: Hochberg and LeMay (1975), LeMay (1977), and Carmon et al. (1972).

asymmetries or no differences at all. These cases do pose a significant interpretation problem, and they suggest that other variables, still unknown, also may account for individual differences in both left- and right-handers.

We considered the possibility in Chapter 11 that there may be differences in gene expression in cortical neurons in left- and right-handers. Although there are no direct data from humans, studies in mice by Tao Sun and colleagues have shown a regionally specific expression of the gene *Lmo4* that is asymmetrically expressed and may be related to paw preference.

Another place to look for anatomical differences related to handedness is in MRI studies of left- and right-handed subjects. Curiously, although many investigators have looked for handedness effects in MRI scans, they find little evidence of gross differences in anatomy. An exception is in the depth of the Sylvian fissure. Katrin Amunts and colleagues found that male right-handers have a significantly deeper fissure on the right than on the left, but there was no difference in left-handers. How this difference between left- and right-handers might relate to handedness remains unknown, however.

Another place to look for handedness-related differences is in the connections between the two hemispheres. To test this idea, Sandra Witelson studied the hand preference of terminally ill subjects on a variety of unimanual tasks. She later conducted postmortem studies of their brains, paying particular attention to the size of the corpus callosum. She found that the cross-sectional area was 11% greater in left-handed and ambidextrous people than in right-handed people.

Whether the larger callosum of non-right-handers contains a greater total number of fibers, thicker axons, or more myelin remains to be determined. If the larger callosum is due to the number of fibers, the difference would consist of some 25 million fibers. Confirmation of Witelson's result by others will imply greater interaction between the hemispheres of left-handers and will suggest that the pattern of cerebral organization may be fundamentally different in left- and right-handers.

Functional Cerebral Organization in Left-Handers

Although the belief that cognitive functions are more bilaterally organized in left-handers than in right-handers is widespread in the neurological literature, little evidence exists for this generalization. In Chapter 11, we considered the sodium amobarbital procedure. Using this procedure, Ted Rasmussen and Brenda Milner found that, in left-handers, language is represented in the left hemisphere in 70%, in the right hemisphere in 15%, and bilaterally in 15%.

Similarly, Doreen Kimura reported the incidence of aphasia and apraxia in a consecutive series of 520 patients selected for unilateral brain damage only. The frequency of left-handedness in her population was within the expected range, and these patients did not have a higher incidence of either aphasia or apraxia than right-handers did. In fact, the incidence of aphasia in left-handed patients was approximately 70% of the incidence in right-handers, exactly what would be predicted from the sodium amobarbital studies. Thus, although a small proportion of left-handers have bilateral speech or right-hemisphere speech, the majority of left-handers do not.

Henri Hécaen and Jean Sauguet suggested that left-handers can be subdivided into two genetic populations differing in cerebral organization: familial left-handers, who have a family history of left-handedness, and nonfamilial left-handers, who have no such family history. According to Hécaen and Sauguet, the performance of nonfamilial left-handed patients with unilateral lesions is like that of right-handed patients on neuropsychological tests. In contrast, familial left-handers perform much differently, suggesting to Hécaen and Sauguet that they have a different pattern of cerebral organization.

In summary, we can find little evidence that the cerebral organization of speech or nonspeech functions in the 70% of left-handers with speech represented in the left hemisphere differs from the cerebral organization of these functions in right-handers. One caveat must be stated, however: there is a larger incidence of left-handedness among mentally defective children and children with various neurological disorders than is found in the general population.

This finding is not surprising, because, if the dominant hemisphere is injured at an early age, handedness and dominance can move under the control of what would normally be the nondominant hemisphere. Because there are so many more right-handed children, it can be expected by probability alone that more right-handed children with left-hemisphere damage would switch to right-hemisphere dominance than would switch in the reverse direction. That such switching can take place, however, cannot be used as grounds for predicting cognitive deficits or differences in cerebral organization in the general population of left-handers.

An additional question concerns the organization of the cerebral hemispheres in left-handers who have right-hemisphere speech. Is there simply a straight reversal of functions from one hemisphere to the other? Unfortunately, little is known about cerebral organization in people who have right-hemisphere speech and otherwise typical asymmetries.

Theories of Hand Preference

The many theories put forward to account for hand preference can be categorized broadly according to their environmental, anatomical, hormonal, or genetic emphasis. Each category shelters widely varied points of view.

Environmental Theories

Three variations on an environmental theory of handedness stress either the utility of the behavior or reinforcement for hand use or a cerebral deficit caused by accident.

Behavioral utility. Sometimes called the theory of the Peloponnesian Wars, or the sword-and-shield hypothesis, the behavioral theory proposes that a soldier who held his shield in his left hand better protected his heart and improved his chances of survival. Because the left hand was holding the shield, the right hand became more skilled at various offensive and defensive movements, and eventually was used for most tasks. A female-oriented variant hypothesizes that it is adaptive for a mother to hold an infant in her left hand, to be soothed by the rhythm of her heart. The mother, like the soldier, uses the free right hand for executing skilled movements. Utility-of-behavior theories have difficulties, the most obvious being their failure to consider the probability that right-handedness preceded the behavior and is thus responsible for it rather than having been caused by it.

Environmental reinforcement. This variation states that handedness is established by a bias in the environment. A child's world is right-handed in many ways, which reinforces the use of that hand; in some cultures, the left hand was considered unclean. In addition, children in many countries, including the United States, were historically forced to write with their right hands. Although reinforcement theory emphasizes the potential importance of environmental factors, it does not account for biological factors such as differences between patterns of familial and nonfamilial handedness or the relation of handedness to cerebral dominance. Reinforcement theory also seems to be contradicted by what happened when children in the United States were given their choice of hand in learning to write: the incidence of left-handed writing rose to only 10%, which is the norm in most societies that have been studied.

Environmental accident. The third variation on environmental theory postulates a genetically determined bias toward being right-handed. Left-handedness develops through a cerebral deficit caused by accident. This idea comes from correlating statistics on the incidence of left-handedness and neurological disorders in twins. About 18% of twins are left-handed, close to twice the occurrence in the population at large. Twins also show a high incidence of neurological disorders, which are suspected to result overwhelmingly from intrauterine crowding during fetal development and stress during delivery. For more on genetic relationship and brain structure, see the Snapshot on page 314.

Genetic Influences on Brain Structure

Unrelated subjects
Average differences in quantity of gray matter are shown as an even color.

Left hemisphere   Right hemisphere

Fraternal twins
Red shading shows about a 30% reduction in differences, especially in Wernicke's area.

Wernicke's area

Identical twins
The differences are even less (10%–30%) and include frontal and sensorimotor areas.

Frontal   Wernicke's area   Sensorimotor areas

100   Unrelated subjects

60   More similar

30

0   No difference

Average gray-matter-difference (as percentage of normal differences)

Average differences in quantity of gray matter in each cortical region for identical and fraternal twins compared with average differences between pairs of randomly selected, unrelated persons. (After Thompson et al., 2001, p. 1254.)

One way to investigate the contributions of genes and experience to cerebral organization is to analyze MRIs from normal brains and to vary the genetic relationships among the subjects. Thompson and colleagues varied genetic relatedness by comparing the MRIs of pairs of unrelated people, dizygotic twins, and monozygotic twins. They took advantage of advances in MRI mapping technology that allows detailed mapping of gray-matter distribution across the cerebral hemispheres.

The results were striking, as you can see in the adjoining illustration. The quantity of gray matter, especially in frontal, sensorimotor, and posterior language cortices was dissimilar in unrelated people but almost identical in monozygotic twins. Because monozygotic twins are genetically identical, we can presume that any differences must be

attributable to environmental effects. Curiously, there was an asymmetry in the degree of similarity, the left-hemisphere language zones being significantly more similar than the right in the monozygotic twins.

The high similarities among monozygotic twins likely accounts for their highly similar cognitive abilities. Similarly, given that various diseases, such as schizophrenia and some dementias, affect the integrity of the cortex, the high correlation between the brain structures of identical twins could account for the strong genetic component of these diseases.

Thompson, P. M., T. D. Cannon, K. L. Narr, T. van Erp, V. P. Poutanen, M. Huttunen, J. Lonnqvist, C. G. Standertskjold-Nordenstam, J. Kaprio, M. Khaledy, R. Dail, C. I. Zoumalan, and A. W. Toga. Genetic influences on brain structure. *Nature Neuroscience* 4:1253–1258, 2001.

The conclusion that stressful gestation and birth result in an elevated incidence of brain damage is logical. Is left-handedness a form of brain damage? Paul Bakan and his colleagues extend this logic to nontwins. They argue for a high probability of stressful births among left-handers, which increases the risk of brain damage to an infant and so maintains the statistical incidence of left-handedness. This theory was tested directly by Murray Schwartz, who tracked children beginning at age 2 and examined hospital records and maternal reports of birth stress. He did not find compelling support for the environmental accident theory.

Anatomical Theories

Among the several anatomical theories of handedness, two explain hand preference on the basis of anatomical asymmetry.

The first theory attributes right-handedness to enhanced maturation and ultimately greater development of the left hemisphere. Generalizing from this assumption, the theory predicts that nonfamilial left-handers will show an asymmetry mirroring that of right-handers, whereas familial left-handers will show no anatomical asymmetry. These predictions are difficult to assess, because no studies have specifically considered anatomical asymmetry with respect to handedness or to familial history and handedness. A major problem with this theory is that it simply pushes the question one step backward, asking not, "Why handedness?" but instead, "Why anatomical asymmetry?"

The second theory addresses this question in part. Many animals have a left-sided developmental advantage that is not genetically encoded. For example, there is a left-side bias for the location of the heart, the size of the ovaries in birds, the control of birdsong, the size of the left temporal cortex in humans, the size of the left side of the skull in the great apes, and so on. This predominance of left-favoring asymmetries puts the more celebrated left-hemisphere speech dominance in the more general, structural perspective of all anatomical asymmetries.

Hormonal Theories

Norman Geschwind and Albert Galaburda proposed that brain plasticity can modify cerebral asymmetry significantly early in life, leading to anomalous patterns of hemispheric organization. A central factor in their theory is the action of the sex-linked male hormone testosterone in altering cerebral organization in the course of development. Testosterone does affect cerebral organization (discussed in detail later), and so the suggestion that differences in testosterone level might influence cerebral asymmetry is reasonable, particularly if the testosterone receptors were asymmetrically distributed.

Geschwind and Galaburda suggested that testosterone's effect is largely inhibitory, meaning that higher-than-normal levels of testosterone will slow development, possibly acting directly on the brain or indirectly through an action on genes. Central to the Geschwind–Galaburda theory is the idea that testosterone's inhibitory action takes place largely in the left hemisphere, thus allowing the right hemisphere to grow more rapidly, which leads to altered cerebral organization and, in some people, to left-handedness. A further feature of the theory is that testosterone also affects the immune system, leading to more diseases related to a malfunctioning immune system. (A parallel theory of the relation between the immune system and male afflictions had been proposed by Gualtieri and Hicks.)

The Geschwind–Galaburda theory is elaborate and has generated considerable research. Unfortunately, the bulk of available evidence does not support the model (for a thorough review, see Bryden et al.). For example, in one study, Gina Grimshaw and her colleagues studied handedness in children whose mothers had undergone amniocentesis and therefore fetal levels of testosterone could be assessed. Increased testosterone levels did not result in increased left-handedness. Nonetheless, the data in the literature do show that left-handers are at greater risk for allergies and asthma, whereas autoimmune disorders such as arthritis are more prevalent in right-handers. These differences still require explanation.

Genetic Theories

Most genetic models for handedness postulate a dominant gene or genes for right-handedness and a recessive gene or genes for left-handedness (see Hardyck and Petrinovich for a review of these models). But the model that best predicts the actual number of left-handers in the population, by Annett, rejects this idea in favor of a dominant gene (rs^+) responsible for the development of speech in the left hemisphere.

Annett hypothesized further that the processes necessary for left-hemisphere speech also confer an advantage on motor control in the right hand. The recessive form of the gene (rs^-) results in no systematic bias either for speech or for handedness. If both alleles occurred equally often statistically, then 50% of the population would be (rs^{+-}) and the rest would be equally divided, 25% (rs^{++}) and 25% (rs^{--}). People in the rs^{+-} and rs^{++} groups, constituting 75% of the population, would show a left-for-speech and right-handedness shift. The remaining 25%, people in the rs^{--} group, would show no bias: half would, by chance, be left-handed.

Thus, Annett's model predicts about 12.5% left-handers, which is pretty close to what we see in the population. Unfortunately, her theory neither predicts the number of left-handers with right-hemisphere speech nor attempts to differentiate between familial and nonfamilial left-handers. Similar problems are found with other genetic models (for example, McManus; Klar).

Clearly, we do not know why handedness develops, and we may never know. On the basis of the various theories just presented, however, there is likely no single cause. Undoubtedly, some genetic basis exsits for the development of left-handedness in some people, but how it relates to cerebral organization remains a mystery. There is little doubt, however, that the major factor in cerebral asymmetry is the asymmetrical representation of language and spatial functions rather than handedness.

Sex Differences in Cerebral Organization

An obvious source of individual variation in human behavior is sex: men and women behave differently. The question is whether any differences in cognitive behavior between men and women can be attributed to biological differences between their brains. Substantial anecdotal and experimental evidence reveals cognitive differences, and several researchers have attempted to relate them to differences in brain organization.

If one neurological principle can be abstracted to distinguish the sexes, it is that, on average, women tend to be more fluent than men in using language, and men tend to perform better than women in spatial analysis. But sex, like handedness, is not absolute. All men and women exhibit both male and female traits to greater and lesser degrees. As always, before considering the theories on differences in the pattern of cerebral organization between the sexes, we shall consider the data.

Sex Differences in Behavior

In her book *Sex and Cognition*, Kimura examines five cognitive behaviors and finds compelling sex differences in all—namely, motor skills, spatial analysis, mathematical aptitude, perception, and verbal abilities. **Table 12.3** summarizes her major conclusions and shows that the verbal–spatial dichotomy just noted is a gross oversimplification. We briefly consider each class of behavior, as well as sex differences in aggression.

Motor Skills

An obvious difference in motor skills is that, on average, men are superior in throwing objects, such as balls or darts at targets, and are superior at intercepting objects thrown toward them. Although we could conclude that the difference is related to practice, this conclusion is unlikely, because these differences are present in children as young as 3 years of age. Furthermore, chimpanzees show a similar sexual dimorphism, although their motor control is far less accurate than that of humans.

Table **12.3** Summary of sex differences in cognitive behavior

Behavior	Sex Difference	Basic Reference
Motor Skills		
Target throwing and catching	M > F	Hall and Kimura, 1995
Fine motor skills	F > M	Nicholson and Kimura, 1996
Spatial Analysis		
Mental rotation	M > F	Collins and Kimura, 1997
Spatial navigation	M > F	Astur et al., 2002
Geographical knowledge	M > F	Beatty and Troster, 1987
Spatial memory	F > M	McBurney et al., 1997
Mathematical Aptitude		
Computation	F > M	Hyde et al., 1990
Mathematical reasoning	M > F	Benbow, 1988
Perception		
Sensitivity to sensory stimuli	F > M	Velle, 1987
Perceptual speed	F > M	Majeres, 1983
Sensitivity to facial and body expression	F > M	Hall, 1984
Visual recognition memory	F > M	McGivern et al., 1998
Verbal Abilities		
Fluency	F > M	Hyde and Linn, 1988
Verbal memory	F > M	McGuinness et al., 1990

In contrast, women have superior fine motor control and surpass men in executing sequential and intricate hand movements. This difference is also unlikely to be related to experience, because young girls are superior to young boys at each of these skills.

Spatial Analysis

Although men are generally believed to be superior to women at spatial analysis, this belief applies only to some types of spatial behaviors. Men are superior at tasks requiring the mental rotation of objects, such as those illustrated in **Figure 12.1**, and they are superior at spatial navigation tasks. An example of the latter difference can be seen in a task illustrated in **Figure 12.2**.

Subjects are given a tabletop map on which they must learn a designated route. On average, men learn such tasks faster and with fewer errors than women do. Although this map test is not a real-world test of spatial navigation, the findings are consistent with those of studies showing that men have better overall map knowledge than women.

Male superiority in spatial-navigation tasks contrasts with female superiority in tests of spatial memory, such as the one illustrated in Figure 12.1. Women are better than men at identifying which objects have been moved, or displaced. In the map test (Figure 12.2), women have better recall for landmarks along the route. Thus, the spatial information itself is not the critical factor in this sex difference; rather, the critical factor is the required behavior—how the spatial information is to be used.

Mathematical Aptitude

The difference in mathematical ability is perhaps the oldest-established sex difference and undoubtedly the most controversial. On average, men get better scores on tests of mathematical reasoning, whereas women do better at tests of computation (see Figure 12.1).

Figure **12.1**

Tasks That Illustrate Sex Differences in Behavior On average, women perform tests of calculation, verbal memory, object memory, fine motor skills, and perception better than men do. In contrast, men, on average, perform tests of mathematical reasoning, geometric form perception, mental rotation, target-directed motor skills, and visual imaging better than women do.

Tasks favoring women

Mathematical calculation	65 73	$13 \times 4 - 21 + 34$ $2(13 + 17) + 18 - \dfrac{20}{4}$
Recall of a story, a paragraph, or unrelated words	Story...	Run, flower, casserole, water, explosion, pencil, horse, newspaper, book, pliers, bath, dancer...
Remembering displaced objects		
Precision, fine motor coordination		
Rapidly matching items in perceptual tests		

Tasks favoring men

Tests of mathematical reasoning	1650	If only 40% of seedlings will survive, how many must be planted to obtain 660 trees?
Mentally finding a geometric form in a complex picture		
Mentally rotating a solid object		
Target-directed motor skills		
Visualizing where holes punched in a folded paper will fall		

Figure **12.2**

Tabletop Map for Route Learning Men learn routes in fewer trials than women do, but women recall more landmarks along the way. (After Kimura, 1999.)

Perhaps the most interesting studies to date on mathematical aptitude were done by Camille Benbow and Julian Stanley. In 1971, Stanley founded the Study of Mathematically Precocious Youth. Within a 15-year period, thousands of 12-year-old children were given the Scholastic Aptitude Test Mathematics exam. Stanley was particularly interested in the children with the highest scores, because they might be assumed to be least affected by extraneous environmental factors such as social pressure.

The curious thing discovered in the Stanley study is that the sex difference increased as the scores increased. That is, although the average score was only marginally higher for boys than for girls, when the researchers looked only at the children with the highest scores, they found an enormous sex difference: 12 times as many mathematically "gifted" boys as girls at the top. Furthermore, this ratio was found worldwide across different cultures, although the absolute scores varied with educational system. Benbow and Stanley have searched for support for a primarily environmental explanation of their data but have not found it.

Perception

Perception refers to the recognition and interpretation of the sensory information that we take in from the external world. There would appear to be no a priori reason to expect a sex difference, but the evidence suggests that women are more sensitive to all forms of sensory stimulation, except for vision. That is not to say that there is no difference in the perception of some types of visual material, however, because women are more sensitive than men to facial expressions and body postures.

Not only do women have lower thresholds for stimulus detection, they also detect sensory stimuli faster. Males may have one perceptual advantage, however,

Figure 12.3

Performance of Boys and Girls of Different Ages on Three Neuropsychological Tests

(Whishaw and Kolb, unpublished.)

in that their drawings of mechanical objects such as bicycles are superior (**Figure 12.3**A). This particular advantage does not mean that they have a general advantage in drawing, as illustrated in Figure 12.3B.

Verbal Ability

Women are superior to men on tests of verbal fluency, on average, and they have superior verbal memory. The sex difference in verbal ability has long been known, in part because girls begin talking before boys and appear to be more fluent throughout life. For example, the Chicago Word-Fluency Test asks subjects to write as many words beginning with "s" as possible in 5 minutes and as many four-letter words beginning with "c" as possible in 4 minutes. As Figure 12.3C illustrates, girls performed better—at some ages by as many as 10 words—in a broad study that we did with children.

Aggression

Although not a cognitive behavior in the sense of verbal or spatial abilities, physical aggression is more prevalent in men than in women. A sex difference is present as early as social play begins, at age 2 to 3 years, and remains through the college years. The results of studies on nonhuman primates and rodents show that the increased aggression in males is probably a result of the male hormone testosterone both pre- and postnatally. The castration of infant male rats or monkeys decreases aggression, and treating females with testosterone increases aggression.

Genes or Experience?

Sex-related differences are often argued to be related to life experience, but Kimura argues compellingly that this relation is unlikely for the cognitive behaviors summarized in Table 12.3. In particular, most if not all of these differences, as well as differences in aggression, are found in both children and adults, and the differences are largely unaffected by training. The effects of training certainly exist for most tests, but the effects tend to be of similar magnitude in both sexes.

Furthermore, some sex differences seem unrelated to life experience. Consider the test illustrated in **Figure 12.4**. The task is to draw in the water line in a series of half-filled, tilted glass jars. Women consistently underperform on this task relative to men, and this difference is seen in both young and old subjects and in university students whether science or non-science majors. The difference in performance is due not to the inability of women to understand the concept that the water line will always be horizontal but rather to the fact that women are more affected by the tilt of the jar than men are. The difference remains even if women are given training on the test.

Figure 12.4

A Water-Level Task The water line must be drawn on each jar.

Sex Differences in Brain Structure

A complicating factor in analyzing sex differences in cerebral organization is that the male brain is larger than the female brain, and differences in body size cannot account for this difference. In one study, C. D. Ankney compared the brains of men and women of the same body size and found that men's brains are about 100 grams heavier than women's throughout the range of body sizes. In another study, Bente Pakkenberg and Hans Gundersen found that the male brains in their sample had about 4 billion more neurons than the female brains, and body size did not account for this difference.

What such a difference might mean is not immediately apparent, in part because it is not the number of cells that is important but rather their connections. Nonetheless, some researchers (Alexopoulis, for example, and Lynn) have concluded that men have a small (4 points) advantage in IQ scores, on average. Needless to say, this idea has proved to be controversial (as indicated by other articles published in the same issue of the journal containing the Lynn article).

Is the sex difference in brain size related to a sex difference in cerebral asymmetry? When different cerebral regions are examined separately, with the results corrected for relative sizes of the cerebra of different brains, the findings of many studies show areal-dependent sex differences, as summarized in **Table 12.4**. Sex-related differences in brain volume are not diffusely spread across the cerebral hemispheres.

In general, female brains appear to have larger volumes in regions associated with language functions, in medial paralimbic regions, and in some frontal-lobe regions. In addition, women have a greater relative amount of gray matter and, at least in the

Table 12.4 Summary of sex differences in gross brain anatomy

Sex Difference	Basic Reference
Differences Favoring Female Brains	
Larger language areas	Harasty et al., 1997
Larger medial paralimbic areas	Filipek et al., 1994
Larger lateral frontal areas	Schlaepfer et al., 1995
Greater relative amount of gray matter	Gur et al., 1999
More densely packed neurons in temporal lobe	Witelson et al., 1995
More gyri	Luders et al., 2004
Thicker cortex	Luders et al., 2006
Differences Favoring Male Brains	
Larger medial frontal areas	Goldstein et al., 2001
Larger cingulate areas	Paus et al., 1996
Larger amygdala and hypothalamus	Swaab et al., 1985
Larger overall white matter volume	Gur et al., 1999
Larger cerebral ventricles	Murphy et al., 1996
Larger right planum parietale	Jancke et al., 1994
More neurons overall	Pakkenberg and Gunderson, 1997
Larger brain	Sowell et al., 2002

planum temporale (Wernicke's area), they have more densely packed neurons. Conversely, men have a larger medial frontal and cingulate region, a larger amygdala, and a larger hypothalamus. They also have a larger overall white-matter volume and larger cerebral ventricles.

A proposed contrasting organizational difference is that male brains tend to have more neurons (gray matter) and female brains more neuropil (that is, dendrites and axons and thus connections) per neuron. This conclusion is likely an overgeneralization and may depend on the particular brain region or cortical layer under investigation.

Indeed, Eileen Luders and her colleagues used MRI scans to identify regions of the gray matter that have a high signal intensity—a measure that they call gray-matter concentration. Whereas males have more-uniform gray-matter concentration, females have a patchwork of concentration differences, as shown in **Figure 12.5**. Although the authors do not show how this sex difference relates to cognitive differences, the conclusion that it must do so is not a difficult stretch. For example, the increased concentration in the peri-Sylvian regions representing the finger areas (see the middle scan) could be related to the female advantage in fine motor skills.

Another measure of cortical structure is the thickness of gray matter, independent of its composition. The Luders group found increased cortical thickness in females throughout much of the cortex, but thickness was greatest in the parietal and posterior temporal regions (see also the study by Sowell et al.). There was no sex difference in the more-anterior temporal cortex, and no areas were thicker in males. The researchers also found that females have a more complex pattern of gyrification in the cortex, which corresponds to differences in the underlying cytoarchitecture and connectivity.

In sum, although male brains are larger than those of females and thus have a larger volume of gray matter, the gray matter of females is organized differently, such that it offsets the difference in volume. Finally, we must emphasize that brain size and cortical volume varies considerably within each sex and that little is known about how size relates to cognitive function within each sex. The increasing use of MRIs to measure individual differences in cerebral measurements

Figure 12.5

Gray-Matter Concentration Compared Women have increased gray-matter concentration in the regions of the cortex shown in color. All gray-shaded regions are not statistically different in males and females. (Courtesy Dr. Arthur Toga, Laboratory of Neuro Imaging at UCLA.)

will likely lead to more correlative studies investigating brain and cognitive measures both within and between the sexes.

Influence of Sex Hormones

The presence of sex differences in brain structure has been related to differences in the distribution of estrogen and androgen receptors during development. Jill Goldstein and her colleagues did a large MRI study of sexual dimorphism in the male and female brain (**Figure 12.6**). Sex differences were largest in regions of the human brain in which the results of studies of nonhumans show sex differences in the developmental expression of estrogen or androgen receptors. Thus, the Goldstein team proposes that a large part of the observed sex differences in cerebral organization is related to differences in the distribution of receptors for gonadal hormones during development.

The investigators note that their conclusions have limitations, because they do not consider differences in cerebral organization that might be related to circulating hormones in adulthood. Furthermore, the findings in many studies suggest that the rate of cell death in the course of aging may be higher in men than in women, especially in the frontal lobe; so we must consider the possibility that some of the sex differences observed in adults may not be present in childhood.

Established Asymmetries

The presence of sex differences in overall size and in relative sizes of different regions does not speak directly to the question of whether there are sex differences in the degree of cerebral asymmetry. Although the cerebral hemispheres of women are often said to be more symmetrical than those of men, this conclusion is based largely on nonsignificant trends or impressions. There are, however, several reliable sex differences in anatomical asymmetry:

1. Asymmetry (left larger than right) in the planum temporale is seen more often in men than in women. In fact, an MRI study by Jennifer Kulynych and her colleagues found a large asymmetry in males (left 38% larger) but no asymmetry in females. This result is not found universally, however (Aboitiz et al. obtained different results); so we must interpret it with caution.

2. Sandra Witelson and Debra Kigar quantified the slope of the Sylvian (lateral) fissure with reference to various cortical landmarks (**Figure 12.7**A). This quantification led to a separate measure of the horizontal and vertical components of the Sylvian fissure. They found that, although the horizontal component was longer in the left hemisphere of both sexes, men had a larger horizontal component in the left hemisphere than did

Lateral view   Medial view

Figure 12.6

Sex Differences in Brain Volume Relative to Cerebral Size Women have significantly higher volumes in the major frontal and medial paralimbic regions (purple) than in those of men, whereas men have larger relative volumes in the medial frontal cortex and the angular gyrus (pink). The purple areas correspond to regions that have high levels of estrogen receptors during development; the pink areas correspond to regions high in androgen receptors during development. (After Goldstein et al., 2001.)

Figure 12.7

Measuring the Brain (A) Lateral view of the left hemisphere illustrating the measuring points on the Sylvian (lateral) fissure. (B) The human corpus callosum shown in midsagittal section. The subdivisions typically measured are indicated: the entire length and cross-sectional area; the anterior and posterior halves; and the splenium.

Table 12.5 Summary of brain measures in four groups classified by handedness and sex

Group	Number in Group	Age (years)	Brain Weight (g)	Callosal Area (mm2)
Males				
RH	7	48	1442	672
MH	5	49	1511	801[a]
Females				
RH	20	51	1269	655
MH	10	49	1237	697[a]

Note: RH, consistently right-handed; MH, left-handed or ambidextrous.
[a]Differs significantly from other same-sex group.
Source: Simplified from Witelson (1985).

women. There was no difference in the right hemisphere. Thus, male brains have a larger asymmetry in the Sylvian fissure than do female brains. Taken together, the results of the studies of the planum temporale and the Sylvian fissure reinforce evidence for a sex difference in the organization of language-related functions.

3. The asymmetry in the planum parietale, which favors the right hemisphere, is about twice as large in men as in women (Jancke et al.).

4. Numerous studies claim that women have more interhemispheric connections, in both the corpus callosum and the anterior commissure, than do men. The callosal studies have proved to be controversial, but the consensus appears to be that the posterior part of the callosum (the splenium) is significantly larger in women than in men (Figure 12.7B and **Table 12.5**). The sex difference found in the anterior commissure, a structure that connects the temporal lobes, appears to be less controversial (see Chapter 17). Laura Allen and Roger Gorski found that women have a larger anterior commissure than do men, even without correcting for brain size. This difference is likely due to a difference in the number of neural fibers in the two sexes, a difference presumably due to some difference in the way in which the two hemispheres interact.

5. The ridges in our fingerprints, which are established early in fetal life, are asymmetrical, with the fingers on the right hand having more ridges than do fingers on the left hand (**Figure 12.8**). Given that this pattern is visible in utero, it could not be influenced by environmental factors such as differences in limb use. Kimura found that most people have the asymmetry, but women are far more likely to show an atypical pattern, much as seen for brain asymmetries. The critical part of the Kimura studies (and later studies by others) is that the pattern of ridges is correlated with performance on certain cognitive tests.

Kimura also followed up on the studies of others, looking at asymmetries in sexually dimorphic body parts—namely, the size of the testes in men and of the breasts in women. She found that, whereas the right testicle tends to be larger

Figure 12.8

Fingerprint Pattern

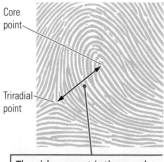

Core point

Triradial point

The ridge count is the number of lines between the triradial and core points.

than the left testicle, breasts tend to be larger on the left than on the right. Importantly, the sex difference in gonad size is found in fetuses.

Once again, we must ask what such a finding might mean. At this time, the meaning is not obvious, but one conclusion is inescapable. If there is an asymmetry in gonad or breast size that is sexually dimorphic, then there is every reason to also expect sex differences in other body regions, especially in those, such as the brain, that are influenced by gonadal hormones.

The Homosexual Brain

Although few studies consider brain asymmetry and sexual orientation, there is evidence that parts of the the hypothalamus of homosexual men differ from those of both herterosexual males and females, who also differ from one another in this regard (see reviews by Gooren and by Swaab). Investigators have looked at the performance of heterosexual and homosexual males and females on tests that reveal sexual dimorphism in heterosexuals. The general finding is that sexual orientation is related to performance. For example, Qazi Rahman and colleagues found that homosexual men outperform all groups on verbal fluency, a test in which heterosexual women outperform heterosexual men, whereas homosexual women had the lowest scores.

Similarly, an examination of throwing ability (Hall and Kimura) showed that heterosexual men outperform heterosexual women, whereas homosexual men threw less accurately and homosexual women tend to throw more accurately than their heterosexual counterparts. Differences in sports history or hand strength did not account for these effects. Although such studies are intriguing, relating them to differences in brain organization is difficult. Perhaps the simplest way to relate sexual orientation to brain and behavior will be the use of noninvasive imaging, although it has not yet been done to our knowledge.

Sex Differences Revealed in Imaging Studies

The results of virtually all types of neuroimaging studies show sex-related differences, as summarized in **Table 12.6**. In general, EEG, MEG, and fMRI studies show more asymmetrical activity in men than in women, particularly in language-related activities. Measures of blood flow, including those obtained with the use of PET, show that women have more rapid overall blood exchange

Table **12.6** Sex differences in imaging studies

Measure	Result	Representative Reference
EEG	Males more asymmetrical	Corsi-Cabrera et al., 1997
MEG	Males more asymmetrical	Reite et al., 1995
Blood flow	Females > males	Gur et al., 1982
	Females > males in frontal-lobe tests	Esposito et al., 1996
PET	Males > females in anterior blood flow	Haverkort et al., 1999
	Females > males in posterior blood flow	
fMRI	More left-hemisphere activity in language-related tasks (but see Frost et al., 1999) in males	Pugh et al., 1996

than do men, possibly owing to the difference in the density of neurons or the distribution of gray matter and white matter.

The main point to take from these results is that not only are there differences in the anatomical organization of the male and female brain, but there are differences in the functional activity of the brains as well, a result that is hardly surprising. Presumably, the anatomical differences correspond to the functional differences that researchers have found.

Research with Neurological Patients

If the brains of females and males differ in anatomical organization as well as in metabolic activity, as the results of blood-flow and fMRI studies indicate, then the effects of injury also might differ. Two types of lesion-related differences are possible:

1. **Degree of asymmetry in the lesion effects.** Such a difference might exist if the two hemispheres were more similar functionally in one sex than in the other sex. Indeed, the greater asymmetry observed in EEG, MEG, and fMRI studies in men suggests that men might show more asymmetrical effects of unilateral lesions than women.

2. **Intrahemispheric organization.** Injury to the frontal lobe might have greater effects in one sex than in the other, a difference that would be consistent with greater relative volume of much of the frontal lobes of women.

In fact, there is evidence of both effects.

One way to assess the asymmetry of left- or right-hemisphere lesions is to look at the effects of the lesions on general tests of verbal and nonverbal abilities. A way of measuring this difference is to examine the pattern of results in the effects of lateralized lesions on the performance and verbal achievement subscales of the Wechsler Adult Intelligence Scale (WAIS; see Chapter 28 for details on this IQ test). By using various statistical procedures with these data, James Inglis and Stuart Lawson showed that, although left- and right-hemisphere lesions in men affected the verbal and performance subscales differently, left-hemisphere lesions in women depressed both IQ scores equally, and right-hemisphere lesions in women failed to depress either IQ score (**Figure 12.9**).

Thus, Inglis and Lawson found an equivalent effect of left-hemisphere lesions on verbal IQ in both sexes, but men with right-hemisphere lesions were more disrupted than women were on the performance IQ. This finding could imply that right-hemisphere organization differs in men and women. This conclusion seems unlikely, however, because there is no evidence of a sex difference in a variety of symptoms commonly associated with right-hemisphere damage. On the other hand, women could be more likely than men to use verbal strategies (that is, a verbal cognitive mode) to solve the tests in the WAIS.

Work by Kimura (1999) shows that the pattern of cerebral organization within each hemisphere also

Figure 12.9

Effects of Injury In this summary of Inglis and Lawson's tabulation of studies reporting verbal and performance IQ scores in neurological patients, a clear sex difference emerged. Males with left-hemisphere lesions exhibited a depression in verbal IQ, whereas males with right-hemisphere lesions exhibited a complementary deficit in performance IQ. In contrast, females with right-hemisphere lesions showed no significant depression in either IQ scale.

differs between the sexes. Men and women are almost equally likely to be aphasic subsequent to left-hemisphere lesions. But men are likely to be aphasic and apraxic after damage to the left posterior cortex, whereas women are far more likely to experience speech disorders and apraxia after anterior lesions (**Figure 12.10**).

Kimura also obtained data from a small sample of patients that suggest an analogous sex-related difference subsequent to right-hemisphere lesions. Anterior, but not posterior, lesions in women impaired their performance of the block-design and object-assembly subtests of the WAIS, whereas men were equally affected on these tests by either anterior or posterior lesions.

Finally, Esther Strauss and her colleagues obtained a surprising result. They gave sodium amobarbital to 94 epileptic patients who were being considered for elective surgery after infant brain damage. Left-hemisphere injury in infancy is known to lead to the shifting of language to the right hemisphere; so Strauss expected this shift to take place in those patients with left-hemisphere injury.

The unexpected result was a sex difference in the likelihood of cerebral reorganization subsequent to left-hemisphere injury after 1 year of age: girls were unlikely to show reorganization, whereas boys appeared likely to shift language, perhaps as late as puberty. This unexpected result suggests that the male brain may be more plastic after cortical injury, a conclusion that has important implications if it proves reliable.

Taken together, the data from neurological patients support the idea that unilateral cortical lesions have different effects on male and female brains. The precise nature of the differences is still being debated, however.

Explanations of Sex Differences

We have considered sex differences in cerebral organization as inferred from studies of behavior, anatomy, imaging, and neurological patients. Why are these differences present? We can identify five explanations commonly advanced to account for sex differences: (1) hormonal effects on cerebral function, (2) genetic sex linkage, (3) maturation rate, (4) environment, and (5) preferred cognitive mode.

Hormonal Effects

Clear sex differences are apparent in the neural control of a wide variety of reproductive and nonreproductive behavioral patterns in most vertebrate species. In birds and mammals, the presence of testosterone at critical times in the course of development has unequivocal effects on the organization of both hypothalamic and forebrain structures, and the observed morphological effects are believed to be responsible for the behavioral dimorphism. The influence of gonadal hormones on brain and behavioral development is often referred to as

Figure 12.10

Patterns of Injury Evidence for intrahemispheric differences in cortical organization of males and females. Apraxia is associated with frontal damage to the left hemisphere in women and with posterior damage in men. Aphasia develops most often when damage is to the front of the brain in women but to the rear of the brain in men. (After Kimura, 1999.)

an *inductive*, or *organizing*, *effect* and, in the brain, this organizing effect is said to lead to *sexual differentiation*.

The actions of gonadal hormones (largely androgens) in the course of development are permanent, but the mechanisms of action are still not well understood. Androgens (typically "male" hormones) appear to be converted into estradiol (normally "female" hormones) in the brain, and the binding of this estradiol to receptors leads to masculinization of the brain. Estradiol receptors have been found in the cortices of developing rodents and nonhuman primates, but they are not found in the adults.

This finding suggests that the hormones may have an organizing effect on the mammalian brain only during development, although they can still influence neuronal function later in life. As mentioned earlier, regions of the human brain that have clear sex-related differences in adulthood are the same ones that have a high density of estrogen receptors in development (see Figure 12.6).

Although the principal organizing action of sex hormones is assumed to take place in development, there might be longer significant functional effects of hormones in adulthood. One way to test this hypothesis would be to see whether a relation exists between behavior and the level of hormones observed at different times in adults of each sex.

The collection of data relating hormone levels to cognitive functions has been made much easier in recent years by the advent of testing hormone levels in saliva. For example, the performance of women on certain tasks changes throughout the menstrual cycle as estrogen levels rise and fall (Hampson and Kimura). High estrogen levels are associated with depressed spatial ability as well as enhanced articulatory and motor capability.

The effect of estrogen fluctuations in the course of the menstrual cycle may be direct or indirect. Catecholamine (for example, epinephrine and dopamine) levels are affected by estrogen, and catecholamine levels fluctuate in the estrous cycle in rats. In view of the importance of catecholamines in movement and other behaviors, estrogen could obviously alter behavior through its stimulation of dopamine receptors in particular. There are dopamine receptors in the prefrontal cortex and medial temporal region; so the possibility that estrogen alters functioning in these regions is reasonable.

Goldstein and her colleagues investigated this possibility, using fMRI to assess cerebral activity in women at low and high estrogen levels in the menstrual cycle when the subjects were shown high arousal (negative valence) pictures versus neutral pictures. Greater blood oxygenation was found in a variety of cerebral regions including the amygdala, hippocampus, and frontal lobe at the low-estrogen time point versus the high-estrogen point with arousing stimuli. These results are important in understanding fluctuating rates of anxiety and mood as well as cognitive function in women.

Estrogen also directly affects the structure of neurons. Catherine Woolley and her colleagues showed that, in the female rat's estrous cycle, there are large changes in the number of dendritic spines on hippocampal neurons (**Figure 12.11**). Thus the number of synapses in the female rat's hippocampus goes up and down in 4-day cycles. There is little reason to believe that similar changes are not also taking place in the human brain, albeit at a slower pace.

Similarly, female rats whose ovaries are removed in middle age show a dramatic increase in dendrites and spines of cortical neurons (see Stewart and

Figure 12.11

Estrogen Effects Dendrites of hippocampal pyramidal neurons at high and low levels of estrogen in the rat's (4-day) estrous cycle. There are many fewer dendritic spines during the low period. (After Woolley et al., 1990.)

Kolb). In this study, such changes were not correlated with cyclic fluctuations in estrogen levels, but the results are consistent with the general idea that estrogen has direct effects on cerebral neurons in the adult animal.

There is also reason to believe that testosterone affects cognition in men. The level of testosterone in men fluctuates both seasonally and daily. Testosterone levels in men are higher in the fall than in the spring, and they are higher in the morning than in the evening. Kimura showed that men's spatial scores fluctuate with testosterone levels: men with lower testosterone levels have the highest scores. So there appears to be an optimal level of testosterone, and increasing the level is actually detrimental to cognitive performance.

Thus, men perform better on spatial tests in the spring and in the evening. Furthermore, men with lower average levels of testosterone do better both on spatial tests and on mathematical reasoning tests than do those with higher average levels. A reasonable question is whether a relation exists between testosterone level and spatial ability in women. It does. Women with higher levels do better, again suggesting that some optimal hormone level benefits at least some cognitive activities.

Finally, we might ask whether administering testerone to men with very low levels might improve spatial or other abilities. Bioavailable testosterone levels decline with age in both men and women, and many studies now show that testosterone can enhance spatial cognition and verbal memory in older men (see Janowksy for a readable review). Prostate cancer is nearly always androgen responsive, and so men are often given a drug to block testosterone production if they are at high risk for prostate-cancer progression. The results of several studies have now shown that testosterone blockade adversely affects verbal memory and attention but not nonverbal memory. These cognitive effects can be reversed by estradiol, which is a metabolite of testosterone.

The results from studies of men lead to the role of hormone replacement therapy in menopausal women. The data have been controversial, but one consistent finding is that estrogen treatment in postmenopausal women improves verbal fluency and verbal and spatial memory. Recent controversy arose from a large Women's Health Initiative study that failed to support the cognitive findings, which led to concern over the value of hormone replacement.

Barbara Sherwin has formulated the critical period hypothesis, which holds that estrogen has maximal beneficial effects on cognition in women when it is initiated closely in time to natural or surgical menopause. She argues that beginning the hormone treatment 20 years after menopause is too late and without benefit. One explanation is that, although estrogen is neuroprotective, neurons become less sensitive to it after a prolonged absence of the hormone. Another explanation is that so many neurons have died or atrophied in the absence of estrogen that it is not possible to reverse the effect of aging.

In summary, gonadal hormones unquestionably have significant effects on brain development and function. Although little direct evidence points to how these effects might relate to the sex differences in cognitive function, there is good reason to suppose that at least some sex differences are related to gonadal hormones.

Perhaps the most interesting possibility is that gonadal hormones alter the brain and make male and female brains more or less responsive in different environments. One way that hormones have such an influence is by altering the susceptibility of cortical neurons to the effects of environmental stimuli. For example, Janice Juraska found that exposure to gonadal hormones perinatally (near birth) determines the later ability of environmental stimulation to alter the synaptic organization of the cerebrum. Furthermore, she showed that environmentally induced changes in the hippocampus and neocortex are affected differently by gonadal hormones. For instance, the female hippocampus is far more plastic in new environments than the male hippocampus, and this plasticity depends on estrogen.

This type of hormonally mediated selective effect of experience on the brain is important because it provides a route through which experiential factors (including social factors) could influence the male and female brain differently, leading to sex-related variations in brain and behavior. The fact that sex hormones are important to cerebral function in adults leads to an interesting possibility: the cognitive functions of the two sexes may diverge functionally at puberty and begin to converge again after menopause. We are unaware of any direct test of this hypothesis.

Genetic Sex Linkage

A number of investigators have proposed that the major factor in determining variation in spatial ability is genetic. A recessive gene on the X (female) chromosome is postulated to be responsible. Every normal person has 46 chromosomes arranged in 23 pairs, one set from the father and one from the mother. The 23rd pair is composed of the sex chromosomes; if both sex chromosomes are X, the child is female (XX) but, if one sex chromosome is X and the other is Y, the child is male (XY).

If a gene for a particular trait, such as spatial analysis, is recessive, the trait will not be expressed in a girl unless the recessive gene is present on both X chromosomes. However, the recessive gene need be present on only one chromosome if the child is a boy. Thus, if a mother carries the gene on both X chromosomes, all her sons will have the trait, but her daughters will possess it only if their father also carries the recessive gene on his X chromosome. This hypothesis has generated a lot of interest and research, but a thorough review by David Boles concludes that it has yet to be proved.

Maturation Rate

The results of developmental studies indicate that a fundamental difference in male and female cerebral maturation may help to account for the sex differences observed in adulthood. As has long been known, girls begin to speak sooner than boys, develop larger vocabularies in childhood, and use more-complex linguistic constructions than boys do. Furthermore, the speech of young girls may be better enunciated than boys' speech, and girls are generally better readers.

Although developmental studies of laterality in children yield conflicting results, findings from dichotic and tachistoscopic studies often indicate an earlier evolution of cerebral asymmetry in girls than in boys. Because girls typically attain physical maturity at an earlier age than do boys, it is reasonable to propose that the male brain matures more slowly than the female brain and that maturation rate is a critical determinant of brain asymmetry. That is, the more slowly a child matures, the greater the observed cerebral asymmetry.

A study by Deborah Waber demonstrates just this finding. She found that, regardless of sex, early-maturing adolescents perform better on tests of verbal abilities than on tests of spatial ones, whereas late-maturing adolescents do the opposite. Her findings, then, imply that maturation rate may affect the organization of cortical function. Because, on average, girls mature faster than boys, superior spatial abilities in boys may be directly related to their relatively slow development.

Environment

Probably the most influential psychological view of sex-related differences is that environmental factors shape the behaviors. For example, boys are expected to exhibit greater independence than girls and thus to engage in activities such as exploring and manipulating the environment—activities that improve spatial skills.

Lauren Harris considered all the research support for this argument and concluded that, although a few studies can be found to support the environmental view, the bulk of the evidence fails to do so. In a study by Hoben Thomas and colleagues on the horizontality of a liquid, for example, women who failed the task were repeatedly shown a bottle half-filled with red water that was tilted at various angles (see Figure 12.4). They were asked to adjust the "pretend water line" by moving a disc, half red, half white, in a second bottle. Even when the subjects simply had to adjust the pretend water line to match the visible real water line, these women failed to show much improvement and were likely to state that "water is level when the bottle is upright but is inclined when the bottle is tilted."

Men and women who perform correctly state that "water is always level." A priori, one would expect that women have as much experience as men with tilting vessels and, even if they do not, that special instruction would be helpful. This expectation, however, does not seem to be the case. In conclusion, although environmental theories may be appealing, there is no evidence that environmental or social factors can solely account for the observed sex differences in verbal and spatial behaviors.

Preferred Cognitive Mode

As already mentioned, the difference in strategies used by men and women to solve problems may be at least partly responsible for the observed sex differences in behavior. Genetic, maturational, and environmental factors may predispose men and women to prefer different modes of cognitive analysis. Women solve problems primarily by using a verbal mode, for example. Because this cognitive mode is less efficient in solving spatial problems, women exhibit an apparent deficit, on average. By the same logic, women should do better than men at primarily verbal tasks, on average. This proposition has yet to be thoroughly investigated.

Conclusions

At least six significant behavioral differences are sex related: verbal ability, visuospatial analysis, mathematical ability, perception, motor skills, and aggression. Although the precise causes of sex-related differences are unknown, biology likely plays a part. Consider the following data.

Richard Harshman and his associates, in a very ambitious study of the interaction of sex and handedness in cognitive abilities, found a significant interaction between sex and handedness; that is, sex-related differences in verbal and visuospatial behavior vary as a function of handedness. (Recall that Witelson found that callosal size also varies by sex and handedness.) It is difficult to imagine how biological or environmental factors alone could account for this result. Thus, the idea that neurological factors that may be modulated by the environment partly account for sex-related differences has plausibility.

Environmental Effects on Asymmetry

Environment produces significant effects on brain growth in laboratory animals. Therefore, the hypothesis that different environments affect the human brain differently and produce variation in the pattern of cerebral asymmetry is a reasonable one. Two broad environmental variables are especially good candidates: culture, especially language, and a range of environmental deficits.

Culture and Language

Most studies of cultural differences center on language. Asian languages such as Japanese and Chinese might promote more right-hemisphere participation than European languages, because the Asian languages appear to have more prosody (or song) and the reading of pictorial Chinese characters requires more spatial processing. Those who speak two or more languages may develop a different pattern of language organization from that of those who speak only one.

The results of laterality studies lend some support to the idea that Asian and Native American languages may be represented more bilaterally in the brain than, for example, Spanish. However, as we have seen, laterality studies can be influenced by many factors, such as cognitive strategy and task requirements. Thus inferring cultural differences in brain organization from the results of these studies should be done with caution. (Good discussions of the difficulties can be found in Uyehara and Cooper, as well as in Obler et al.)

The results of studies of neurological patients provide no evidence for culturally or linguistically based differences in cerebral organization. A good example is a study by Richard Rapport and his coworkers. They evaluated the language functions of seven Chinese–English polyglots whose mother tongues were Malay, Cantonese, or Hokkien. Their methods included the use of carotid sodium amobarbital injection, cortical stimulation, and clinical examination. They found that all these patients were left-hemisphere dominant for both the

Chinese and the English languages; there was no consistent evidence of increased participation by the right hemisphere for oral language functions.

All oral language is probably located in the left hemisphere of bilingual people, but the possibility that their left-hemisphere language zones are enlarged or slightly different in microorganization from those who speak only a single language cannot be ruled out. Experience is known to alter somatosensory organization; so an analogous effect of experience on the language zones is a reasonable expectation. However, the major effects of language and environment on the brain are likely on the development of particular styles of problem solving (that is, preferred cognitive mode) that heavily depend on culture rather than on changes in cerebral asymmetry.

Exposure to multiple languages could be expected to change the normal pattern of brain organization, but, again, this change does not appear to take place. The results of PET studies by Denise Klein (1999) and her colleagues show, for example, that no difference appears in the cerebral activation for various language tasks performed in English and French or in English and Chinese by bilingual subjects. In particular, no activation of the right hemisphere was recorded for any task in either language.

There may, however, be subtle differences in the cerebral representation of different languages within the left hemisphere. Using fMRI, Kyung Kim and coworkers showed that languages acquired later in life may activate different, although adjacent, frontal regions from those activated by first languages or second languages acquired early in life.

The Japanese writing system provides an unusual opportunity for studying cerebral organization because, unlike Indo-European writing, it consists of two types of symbols: phonograms *(kana)* and ideograms *(kanji)*. Phonograms are analogous to English letters; each phonogram represents a spoken sound. In contrast, an ideogram represents a unit of meaning, which may correspond to a word or words.

In reading, the brain may process these two types of characters differently; furthermore, the right hemisphere might process *kanji*, whereas the left hemisphere processes *kana*. There is little support for either idea. For example, in a large series of patients, Morihiro Sugishita and his colleagues found no clear relation between deficits in reading either script and locus of left-hemisphere injury. In fact, most of their cases were impaired equally in both forms of reading Japanese.

Some imaging evidence supports the idea that alphabetic language (for example, English) and *kanji* might be processed differently, however. Yun Dong and colleagues showed that reading pictorial Chinese produces right-hemisphere activation not seen in reading English. The investigators used a phonological task, in which the subjects were to determine whether two pictorial words sound similar, and a semantic task, in which they were to determine if two pictorial words have related meanings. The phonological task activated large regions of the left hemisphere as would be expected (**Figure 12.12**A),

Figure **12.12**

Unique Chinese Language Activation (A) The phonological matching task, in which subjects had to decide whether Chinese words sounded similar, activated Broca's area in the left hemisphere. (B) The semantic matching task, requiring subjects to determine whether the words' meanings were related, activated Broca's area and the inferior frontal cortex on the right. Pictographic language appears to require the activation of the spatial processing networks in the right hemisphere, which is not normally seen in semantic tasks using alphabetical languages. (After Dong et al., 2005.)

(A) Phonological matching

Broca's area

(B) Semantic association

Inferior frontal

whereas the semantic task also activated the right inferior frontal cortex, a result not seen in semantic matching in English (Figure 12.12B).

An interesting question raised by the Dong findings is whether learning pictographic languages alters the way in which the brain processes other types of information. For example, given the visuospatial nature of the Chinese pictographs, we could imagine that visuospatial processing might develop differently as children learn the language. There are studies, for example, suggesting that native Chinese male subjects do not show the male advantage in spatial rotation-type tasks observed in native English-speaking males. The early pictographic language learning may lead to the development of cognitive biases that are more like the typical Western female strategies in visuospatial tasks. This idea will most certainly provide the basis for much research in the next decade.

Sensory or Environmental Deficits

Both education and congenital deafness are alleged to alter hemispheric specialization. As already noted, early pictographic language learning may influence cognitive skills, but the evidence that schooling changes cerebral organization is scanty and inconclusive. Unfortunately, most evidence regarding sensory deficits and asymmetry is based largely on the results of laterality studies, which are difficult to interpret. Furthermore, illiterate aphasics do not appear to differ from those who are educated. On the other hand, there is some evidence that congenital deafness may alter cerebral processing.

Brain Organization in Nonhearing People

As it does for hearing people, left-hemisphere damage produces aphasia in people who converse by using American Sign Language (Ameslan), possibly because of the praxic requirements. But evidence hints that the congenitally deaf may have atypical patterns of cerebral organization.

First, several laboratories report independently that congenitally deaf persons fail to show the usual right-visual-field superiority in tasks of linguistic processing. This failure could be interpreted as evidence that, if experience with auditory language is absent, lateralization of some aspect or aspects of nonauditory language function is abolished. Or these data could result from strategy differences (preferred cognitive mode again) due to the absence of auditory experience.

Second, Helen Neville reported that, during the perception of line drawings, visual evoked potentials are significantly larger on the right in children with normal hearing and significantly larger on the left in deaf children who use Ameslan to communicate. Curiously, no asymmetry at all appears in deaf children who cannot sign but merely use pantomime to communicate. From the signers' left-hemisphere effect for line drawings, Neville inferred that the deaf signers acquire their visual signing symbols much as hearing children acquire auditory verbal symbols: with the left hemisphere.

Thus, visuospatial functions may develop in the left hemisphere of people who sign, producing an unexpected left-hemisphere effect. The lack of asymmetry in nonsigners could mean that the absence of language experience somehow abolishes certain aspects of cerebral asymmetry or, alternatively, that the expression of cerebral asymmetry depends on language experience. If the non-signers learn Ameslan and do so before puberty, they might develop an asymmetrical evoked-potential pattern similar to that of their contemporaries who already sign.

Although congenital deafness may be suspected to affect the development of certain aspects of cerebral lateralization, the results of studies of brain-injured patients show little difference between hearing and nonhearing subjects. Gregory Hickok and his coworkers studied 34 congenitally deaf patients who had unilateral brain injury. Left-hemisphere patients performed poorly on all measures of language use, whereas right-hemisphere patients performed poorly on visuospatial tasks—exactly what would be expected in hearing people. Exposure to spoken language was not necessary for hemispheric specialization.

Environmental Deprivation

Evidence pointing to early environment as a factor in asymmetry is based on a study of Genie, an adolescent girl who endured nearly 12 years of extreme social and experiential deprivation and malnutrition. She was discovered at the age of 13½, after having spent most of her life isolated in a small, closed room. During this time, she was punished for making any noise. After her rescue, Genie's cognitive development was rapid, although her language lagged behind other abilities.

Results of her dichotic listening tests proved to be provocative for a right-handed person: although both ears showed normal hearing, there was a strong left-ear (hence, right-hemisphere) effect for both verbal and nonverbal (environmental) sounds. In fact, the right ear was nearly totally suppressed, a phenomenon characteristic of people with severe left-hemisphere injury. Genie's right hemisphere appeared to be processing both verbal and nonverbal acoustical stimuli, as would be the case in people who had a left hemispherectomy in childhood.

At least three explanations for Genie's abnormal lateralization are plausible. First, disuse of the left hemisphere may simply have resulted in degeneration, which seems unlikely. Second, in the absence of appropriate auditory stimulation, the left hemisphere lost the ability to process linguistic stimuli. This explanation is possible because, without early exposure to foreign languages, adults have difficulty in learning many phoneme discriminations, even though they were able to make these discriminations as infants (see Werker and Tees). Third, either Genie's left hemisphere was being inhibited by the right hemisphere or by some other structure or it was performing other functions.

Not all deprivation experiences are as severe as Genie's, which raises the question of how other early experiences might affect brain development. Abandoned Romanian children, for example, were warehoused by the communist regime during the 1970s and 1980s in dreadful state-run orphanages. The children had little environmental stimulation, and, in many cases, a single caregiver looked after as many as 25 children.

After the fall of the communist government, many children about 2 years of age were adopted into homes in the United Kingdom, the United States, Canada, and Australia. Extensive study of these children shows that, even after placement in excellent conditions, the effect of early experience on their brain development is long lasting. At 12 years of age, their average brain size was reduced by as much as 20%, and the children have significant cognitive and other behavioral problems. Little is known about the nature of cerebral asymmetry in these children, but ongoing studies are beginning to explore this important question.

Epigenetics

Epigenetics refers to changes in gene regulation that take place without a change in the DNA sequence (that is, the genotype). Not all the genes in a genotype are turned on at any particular time. Changes in gene expression may occur spontaneously or in response to environmental factors.

The powerful effect of experience on epigenetics can be seen in an analysis of monozygotic twins. At birth, monzygotic twins have a genotype in common, but, as they age, they are often observed as not being "identical." Mario Fraga and his colleagues examined gene expression in 3-year-old versus 50-year-old identical twins and found a marked shift in gene expression with aging. The difference was greater in twins who had lived apart and had different life styles, including diet and exercise.

Although this study does not speak directly to brain asymmetry, it does show us that genotype, including genes regulating brain function, can be affected by experience. Given that cerebral asymmetry is ultimately controlled by gene expression during development, we can therefore see that alterations in gene expression throughout the lifetime can influence cerebral function. This mechanism could provide a powerful means for culture, sex, or abnormal experiences to influence cerebral activity.

Effects of Hemispherectomy

If life-threatening seizures result from severe infantile cerebral injury, the neocortex of an entire hemisphere may be surgically removed to control the seizures (see the Portrait about A.R. in Chapter 10.). Although most hemispherectomies are performed in a patient's early adolescence, the surgery is sometimes done in the first year of life, before speech has developed. The latter case is particularly germane to the question of how cerebral lateralization develops. If the hemispheres vary functionally at birth, then the left and right hemispherectomies would be expected to produce different effects on cognitive abilities. If they do not vary at birth, then no cognitive differences would result from left or right hemispherectomies.

The general results of studies of linguistic and visuospatial abilities in patients with unilateral hemidecortications support the conclusion that both hemispheres are functionally specialized at birth, although both appear capable of assuming some functions usually performed by the missing hemisphere. **Table 12.7** summarizes these data. Note that the left hemidecortication does not produce severe deficits in visuospatial abilities. Yet the left hemisphere cannot completely compensate for the absent right hemisphere, as evidenced by the patients' difficulty in performing complex visuospatial tasks.

In an analysis of language abilities, Maureen Dennis and Harry Whitaker found that, unlike right-hemisphere removals, left hemispherectomies produce deficits in understanding spoken language when the

Table 12.7 Summary of effects of hemidecortication on verbal and visuospatial abilities

	Left	Right
Intelligence	Low normal	Low normal
Language Tests		
Simple	Normal	Normal
Complex	Poor	Normal
Visuospatial Tests		
Simple	Normal	Normal
Complex	Normal	Poor

meaning is conveyed by complex syntactic structure, particularly if the sentence contains an error (for example, "The tall guard wasn't shot by the armed robber"). Likewise, removal of the left hemisphere leads to difficulty in determining sentence implication, in integrating semantic and syntactic information to replace missing pronouns, and in forming judgments of word interrelations in sentences.

In an analysis of word comprehension, Dennis found that both hemispheres understand the meaning of words and both can spontaneously produce lists of names of things. In a search for words by using different cues, however, the left hemisphere has an advantage over the right. Both hemispheres can name an object from its picture or from its description, but the left hemisphere can identify the object on the basis of "rhymes with," whereas the right hemisphere is oblivious to this type of cue.

In an analysis of reading skills, Dennis and her coworkers found that both hemispheres had almost equal ability in higher-order reading comprehension; however, the left hemisphere is superior to the right hemisphere in reading and spelling unfamiliar words and in using sentence structure to achieve fluent reading. The left hemisphere also reads prose passages with greater decoding accuracy, more fluency, and fewer errors that violate the semantic and syntactic structure of the sentence. The superiority of the left hemisphere seems to be its ability to manipulate and exploit language rules. Yet the right hemisphere is not without its strengths in language. Performance is better with the right hemisphere in a task that requires learning an association between nonsense words and symbols.

In summarizing the results of studies on language, Dennis suggests that, if written language structure is thought of as a combination of meaning cues (morphology), sound cues (phonology), and picture cues (logography), then the isolated left hemisphere will show superior performance with morphology and phonology and inferior performance with logographic cues. The isolated right hemisphere will show superior performance with logographic cues and inferior performance with morphological and phonological cues. In light of the study by Dong and colleagues (see Figure 12.12), it would be interesting to know how the isolated right hemispheres of Chinese subjects might perform with Chinese (or Japanese) pictographs.

An almost analogous pattern of results was found on tests of visuospatial function (Kohn and Dennis). The investigators observed that, although patients with right hemispherectomies performed normally on simple tests of visuospatial functions such as drawing, they were significantly impaired on complex tests such as negotiating a maze and reading a map.

To summarize, each hemisphere can assume some of its opposite's functions if the opposite hemisphere is removed in the course of development, but neither hemisphere is totally capable of mediating all of the missing hemisphere's functions. Thus, although the developing brain gives evidence of considerable plasticity, there is convincing evidence against **equipotentiality**: both hemispheres appear to have a processing capacity that probably has an innate structural basis. Furthermore, there seems to be a price for assuming new responsibilities. With few exceptions, patients undergoing hemispherectomy are of below-average or, at best, average intelligence, and their proficiency on tests of the intact hemisphere's function is often less than normal.

Ontogeny of Asymmetry

The results of anatomical studies generally show that adultlike cerebral asymmetries are present before birth, a result that supports an innate predisposition for cerebral asymmetry in humans. Findings in an MRI study in which Elizabeth Sowell and colleagues examined asymmetries in the sulcal patterns in a large sample of children, adolescents, and young adults confirm this general impression. In addition, the findings show that the extent of asymmetries in the sulcal patterns increases even past adolescence and well into adulthood.

Thus, a basic template for cortical development appears to lay down an asymmetrical organization prenatally, and the pattern progresses after birth. Presumably, this pattern can be influenced by the environment, especially by injury. The results of ERP studies by Dennis and Victoria Molfese confirm a functional asymmetry in which the left hemisphere shows a greater response to speech stimuli as early as 1 week of age. There is apparently little change in this difference during development.

Recall from Chapter 11 that two polar theoretical positions postulate the ontogeny (development in the individual) of cerebral specialization. Unilateral specialization culminates in a left-for-language hypothesis: the left hemisphere is genetically organized to develop language skills; the right hemisphere is dumb. At the opposite pole of cerebral interaction, the parallel-development hypothesis posits that both hemispheres, by virtue of their construction, play special roles, one destined to specialize in language and the other in nonlanguage functions.

Research points to a parallel-development theory that initially permits some flexibility or equipotentiality to most usefully explain the bulk of the available data. The cognitive functions of each hemisphere can be conceived as hierarchical. Simple, lower-level functions are represented at the base of the hierarchy, corresponding to functions in the primary somatosensory, motor, language, or visuospatial areas. More-complex, higher-level functions ascend the hierarchy, with the most complex at the top. These advanced functions are the most lateralized.

At birth, the two hemispheres overlap functionally because each is processing low-level behaviors. By age 5, the newly developing, higher-order cognitive processes have very little overlap, and each hemisphere thus becomes increasingly specialized. By puberty, each hemisphere has developed its own unique functions (**Figure 12.13**). Note that the cerebral hemispheres are not becom-

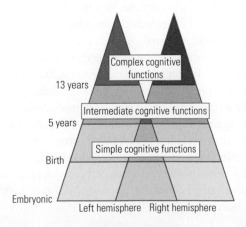

Figure 12.13

Development of Cognitive Function in the Left and Right Hemispheres
At birth, the functions of the two hemispheres overlap considerably, but, by adulthood, their functions do not overlap at all. The hemispheres are not themselves becoming more lateralized with respect to a given function; rather, they are developing more highly specialized functions.

Complex cognitive functions

Intermediate cognitive functions

Simple cognitive functions

13 years

5 years

Birth

Embryonic

Left hemisphere   Right hemisphere

The hemispheres are more highly specialized in older people,...

...whereas there is considerable overlap at birth.

If brain damage occurs early in life, each hemisphere can adopt functions of the other.

ing more lateralized in development; rather, developing cognitive functions are built on the lower functions, which are innately located in one hemisphere or the other.

All models of cerebral development must answer the question of how functions become restricted to one hemisphere rather than becoming bilateral. The interactive parallel-development hypothesis answers that question. In a series of papers, Morris Moscovitch emphasizes the possibility that one hemisphere actively inhibits the other, thus preventing the contralateral hemisphere from developing similar functions. This active inhibition presumably develops at about age 5, as the corpus callosum becomes functional.

Moscovitch proposes that this inhibitory process not only prevents the subsequent development of language processes in the right hemisphere but also inhibits the expression of the language processes already in the right hemisphere. Support for this idea comes from the observation that the right hemispheres of commissurotomy patients appear to have greater language abilities than expected from the study of normal patients, presumably because the right hemisphere is no longer subjected to inhibition by the left. Furthermore, people born with no corpus callosum demonstrate little or no functional asymmetry as inferred from dichotic listening, suggesting that the absence of interhemispheric connection results in attenuated hemispheric asymmetry (see Netley). This phenomenon follows directly from the Moscovitch proposal.

Asymmetry in Nonhumans

Many participants in discussions on the nature of cerebral asymmetry and its role in behavioral diversity in humans implicitly assume that asymmetry is linked with especially human intellectual characteristics such as language. Asymmetry is not a uniquely human characteristic, however. Elements of communicative vocalizations in frogs and salamanders are lateralized to the left side of the brain, for example.

Thus, understanding the origins and evolution of lateral asymmetries in the nonhuman brain is germane to any understanding of the nature of asymmetry in the human brain. Here, we present the most stimulating and robust data so far gathered on birds, rodents, and nonhuman primates. For a complete discussion, we recommend the book by John Bradshaw and Lesley Rogers listed in the References.

Asymmetry in Birds

Fernando Nottebohm made a startling discovery in 1971. He severed the hypoglossal nerve in canaries and found a severe disruption in the birds' song after left-hemisphere lesions but not after right-hemisphere ones. Subsequent work in his laboratory, as well as in many others, show anatomical differences in the structures controlling bird song in the two avian hemispheres and identify many song-related regions as sexually dimorphic.

Curiously, although a left-hemisphere dominance for song has been shown in many species of songbirds (and even in chickens), it is not characteristic of all songbirds. Apparently, the zebra finch has little anatomical or functional asymmetry, even though it sings. The lateralization may not be for singing itself but for some other still-unrecognized feature of bird vocalizations.

Nottebohm's discovery led to interest in the possibility of asymmetry in the visual system of birds, because the optic nerves of most birds cross over almost completely at the optic chiasm. Thus, each hemisphere receives most input from a single eye. The beauty of this arrangement is that lateralization of visual function can be investigated by testing birds monocularly. Furthermore, birds have no corpus callosum and, although other small commissures connect the hemispheres, there is less interhemispheric transfer in birds than in mammals.

Lateralization has now been shown for a range of visually guided functions in birds. According to Bradshaw and Rogers, the right-eye system is specialized for categorizing objects, such as food versus nonfood items, whereas the left-eye system is specialized for responding to the unique properties of each stimulus (color, size, shape, and so forth), including topographic information. Thus, the left hemisphere of birds appears to be specialized for categorizing objects, whereas the right hemisphere is specialized for processing topographic information.

The results of research by Gabriel Horn and his colleagues shows an asymmetry for memory formation in the chicken brain. Different synaptic and neurochemical changes take place in each hemisphere when the animals learn, presumably owing to some difference in information processing by the two hemispheres.

One curious asymmetry is in sleep. Birds spend much of their sleep time with only one hemisphere asleep, which presumably allows them to monitor the environment. On the other hand, it also means that there is a transient asymmetry in sensory processing, which might have significant implications for the animals. We note parenthetically that unilateral sleep is also characteristic of cetaceans (whales, dolphins) and seals, a sensible adaptation in mammals that can drown.

In summary, the results of studies of birds reveal that lateralization takes many forms in the brain and is not a unique property of mammals. Indeed, Bradshaw and Rogers suggest that, in view of the growing list of functional and structural asymmetries in birds, one begins to wonder whether it is not cerebral symmetry that needs to be explained.

Asymmetry in Rodents

Studies in rats and mice focus on two rather different types of asymmetry. The first type comprises postural and motor asymmetries such as paw preference and direction of movement. This form of lateralization is present in individual animals and correlates with individual differences in the distribution of neurotransmitters, especially dopamine. Unlike handedness in humans, most postural asymmetries in rodents are random across the population. Thus, although the neural bases of individual preferences may be relevant for understanding motor or postural asymmetries in humans, the directions of the asymmetries do not relate directly to human brain–behavior relations.

The second type of asymmetry in rodents is more interesting in the current context because it is seen in the population, much as is seen in birds. Like humans, rodents display an asymmetry in the anatomy of the two cerebral hemispheres, with the right hemisphere being larger. In addition, the cortex of the right hemisphere is thicker, especially in the visual and posterior parietal regions, and this difference is modulated by hormones. For example, several groups of researchers have seen a sex difference in the asymmetry: male rodents have a greater difference than females. Furthermore, both prenatal stress and postnatal castration were shown to abolish the anatomical asymmetry in males, presumably owing to alterations in the normal hormonal environment (Stewart and Kolb).

Studies of functional correlates of the anatomical asymmetries have proved to be controversial. Nonetheless, evidence is accumulating to support the conclusion that the left hemisphere is specialized for processing species-specific calls. The auditory asymmetry may represent a left-hemisphere advantage in processing rapidly changing acoustical stimuli, a conclusion that has also been made for the human left temporal lobe (see Chapter 15). Claims that the right hemisphere is specialized for controlling emotional and spatial behavior remain speculative.

An intriguing asymmetry in rodents is an apparent lateralization of the modulation of immune responses. For example, lesions in the left hemisphere of mice, but not in the right, suppress T-cell functions. (T-cells are specialized to respond to immune challenges, such as infections.) The T-cell suppression may be due to lateralized control of the secretion of specific hormones, such as prolactin. Whether similar asymmetries exist in the control of immune functions in humans is not yet known, although such asymmetry has been hypothesized by Duck-hee Kang and colleagues.

As noted earlier, stress may alter anatomical asymmetries in the rat cortex, and many research groups suggest that stress may also alter functional asymmetries. For example, Victor Dennenberg and his coworkers hypothesize that specific experiences might alter the two hemispheres differentially in the course of development. If different experiences differ in stress levels, then Dennenberg's results could be explained by the lateralized responses to various stress-related hormones, such as glucocorticoids.

Asymmetry in Nonhuman Primates

In the past decade, it has become increasingly clear that chimpanzees show humanlike asymmetries in both Broca's area and the planum temporale (see a series of papers by Hopkins and colleagues). Such asymmetries are intriguing because they imply that the neuroanatomical substrates for human language were present at least 5 million years ago and predate the emergence of human language. Michael Petrides and his colleagues have shown that rhesus monkeys also have a region that can be called Broca's area and that this region controls orofacial actions.

The general conclusion is that language evolved from gestural communication using both the face and the limbs. Curiously, although chimpanzees and baboons do not show much preference for the right hand in manipulating objects,

Figure 12.14

Manual Communication Baboons use the right hand to make communicative gestures. A female baboon sends a threat signal to another baboon by rubbing her right hand on the ground rapidly. (© Adrien Meguerditchian.)

both species show a strong preference in using the right hand for communicative actions, as illustrated in **Figure 12.14**.

A recent study by Jared Taglialatela and colleagues looked at the relation between the asymmetry in gestural movements and neuroanatomical asymmetries. Their analysis reveals that chimpanzees that reliably use the right hand for manual gestures have larger left inferior frontal gyri than those of animals that do not use the right limb as reliably. These results are intriguing, in part because we are unaware of any systematic studies looking at differences in inferior frontal anatomy in human left- versus right-handers.

The results of studies of hand preference in nonhuman primates are controversial. Studies in the 1960s by Mike Warren unequivocally failed to find any systematic hand preference in rhesus monkeys, and he concluded that observed preferences are task dependent and are strongly affected by learning.

More recently, Peter MacNeilage and his colleagues argued that, because earlier studies concentrated on particular types of movements, a hand preference in monkeys has been overlooked. Their basic premise is that primates evolved a preference for reaching with one limb (the left) while supporting the body with the other (the right). As the prehensile hand developed and primates began to adopt a more upright posture, the need for a hand used primarily for postural support diminished and, because this hand was free, it became specialized for manipulating objects. They later proposed that the hand specializations were accompanied by hemispheric specializations: a right-hemisphere (left-hand) perceptuomotor specialization for unimanual predation (grasping fast-moving insects or small animals) and a left-hemisphere specialization for whole-body movements.

This hypothesis has been hotly debated. A significant difficulty is that studies of limb use in primates are hampered by poor control of myriad confounding factors including species, age, sex, task difficulty, learning, and sample size. Nonetheless, evidence is accumulating in support of at least some components of the hypothesis. For example, there are left-hand preferences for prey catching and food retrieval in prosimians and some Old World monkeys.

An objection to the hypothesis is that cerebral asymmetry must precede handedness, and whether this asymmetry did indeed precede handedness and why it might have done so are not clear. If anything like cerebral asymmetry in humans is to be demonstrated in nonhuman primates, tests of tactile, visual, and auditory perception would be a good place to start looking. Consider the following examples.

W. Horster and George Ettlinger trained 155 rhesus monkeys to make a tactile response in a task in which the subjects had to discriminate a cylinder from a sphere. The results showed that the 78 monkeys spontaneously using the left hand outperformed the 77 using the right hand. Thus, as in humans, the right hemisphere outperformed the left one, suggesting an asymmetry.

Charles Hamilton and Betty Vermeire took a different approach. They taught 25 split-brain monkeys to discriminate two types of visual stimuli that have shown lateralization in humans. In one task, the animals had to discriminate between pairs of lines differing in slope by 15° (15° versus 30°, for example, or 105° versus 120°). For each pair, the more vertical line was designated as positive, and the monkey received a food reward for choosing it.

Each hemisphere was tested separately, and the results showed that most monkeys learned the line-orientation discriminations faster with the left hemisphere. The other task required the animals to discriminate different monkey faces. The right hemispheres of most animals showed better discrimination and memory of the faces. There was no hemispheric difference in making a simple discrimination of black-and-white patterns.

A curious thing about these results is that, a priori, the line-orientation task appears to be one in which humans would show a right-hemisphere bias, rather than the left-hemisphere bias shown by the monkeys. At any rate, there appears to be evidence in nonhuman primates of hemispheric specialization for the processing of different types of visual information.

There is also evidence from primates that the two hemispheres may differ in their production of facial expressions. Split-brain monkeys viewed videotapes of people, monkeys, other animals, and scenery. The amount of time spent watching the recordings and the number of species-typical facial expressions made were recorded. The number of facial expressions elicited from the right hemisphere was greater than the number from the left hemisphere, which is predictable from studies of humans. In other studies, the left side of the chimpanzee's or monkey's face begins to display facial expression before the right side does and is more expressive. Recall from Chapter 11 that a similar result is reported for humans.

Finally, many studies look for asymmetries in auditory perception. In an early study, John Dewson removed the superior temporal gyri (roughly equivalent to Wernicke's area in humans) from four rhesus monkeys, producing a lasting deficit on an auditory–visual task if the lesion was in the left hemisphere but not if it was in the right hemisphere. The monkeys were required to press a panel that activated one of two acoustical stimuli, either a 1-kHz tone or white noise. They were then presented with two panels, one green and one red. If the tone was heard, the monkeys pressed the red panel to receive a reward; if the white noise was heard, they pressed the green panel to receive it. Lesions on the left impaired performance of this task, but lesions on the analogous area on the right did not.

The possibility of asymmetry in the auditory system was confirmed, however, by the work of Michael Petersen and his colleagues. They compared the ability of Japanese macaques to discriminate between communicatively relevant sounds and irrelevant sounds. The animals could discriminate relevant sounds presented to the right ear better than those presented to the left. The researchers suggest that the Japanese macaques engage in left-hemisphere processing in a way analogous to that in humans.

The results of a further study by Henry Heffner and Rickye Heffner support this conclusion. They trained monkeys to discriminate between two forms of their "coo" vocalization. Then they removed the left or right superior temporal gyrus or the left or right parietal cortex. Removal of the left, but not the right, temporal cortex produced impairment in the performance of this task. Parietal lesions were without effect. Curiously, with training, the animals with left temporal lesions were able to relearn the task. When the remaining side was later removed, the animals had a permanent deficit in the task and were unable to relearn it.

Summary

Considerable individual variation exists among humans in the pattern of left–right hemisphere asymmetry. Neuropsychologists study anatomical and functional variations in individual persons—the ontogeny of asymmetry—to separate the processes that are lateralized. These studies can be sources of insight into the nature of cerebral asymmetry in our species (phylogeny).

Systematic relations exist between normal variations in cerebral organization and individual differences in cognitive abilities. Each of us has unique behavioral capacities as well as shortcomings that are related to cerebral organization. Demonstrations related to handedness and sex imply that some asymmetric variation is biologically based, although environmental variables certainly modify cerebral organization.

Handedness and Functional Asymmetry

The basis for handedness in humans has been the focus of much debate and theorizing, yet no adequate explanation exists for why people are either right- or left-handed. Presumably a neuroanatomical basis of some sort must exist, but the only consistent finding is a deeper left central fissure in right-handers. There is likely some genetic component because left-handedness tends to run in families, but we still must account for nonfamilial left handedness.

The relation between handedness and language lateralization is clear in right-handers, but the presence of language in the left hemisphere of most left-handers casts some doubt on the relation between language and handedness. Rather, the major factor in cerebral asymmetry is the asymmetrical representation of language and spatial functions.

Sex Differences in Cerebral Organization

Progress has been made in understanding the nature of sex differences. The most likely explanation is that gonadal hormones alter brain organization in development and continue to influence brain activity in adulthood. Evidence continues to accumulate showing that the cerebral cortex of the female brain fundamentally differs in organization from the male brain. This altered organization and activity interacts with experience to enhance or diminish the sex-related differences.

Environmental Effects on Asymmetry

Although experience and environment seem likely to alter cerebral organization, the nature of experience-dependent variations in brain organization is not yet understood. Pathological experience in infancy and early childhood appear to severely affect brain development, but less is known about more subtle experiential differences such as those observed in different cultures. Epigenetics provides one route by which environment can influence cerebral function.

Asymmetry in Nonhumans

The results of studies of nonhuman species show that lateral asymmetry is not unique to humans. The demonstration of asymmetry in nonhuman brains implies that asymmetry in the human brain predates the development of human language. There could be a correspondence between the emergence of gestural movements that are primarily with the right hand in both apes and monkeys and the emergence of gestural language and asymmetry with a later emergence of human oral language. But cerebral asymmetry is also found in birds and rodents, and so the general phenomenon of asymmetry is not simply a reflection of gestural language evolution.

References

Aboitiz, F., A. B. Scheibel, and E. Zaidel. Morphometry of the Sylvian fissure and the corpus callosum, with emphasis on sex differences. *Brain* 115:1521–1541, 1992.

Alexopoulos, D. S. Sex differences and IQ. *Personality and Individual Differences* 20:445–450, 1996.

Allen L. S., and R. A. Gorski. Sexual orientation and the size of the anterior commissure in the human brain. *Journal of Comparative Neurology* 312:97–104, 1991.

Amunts, K., L. Jancke, H. Mohlberg, H. Steinmetz, and K. Zilles. Interhemispheric asymmetry of the human motor cortex related to handedness and gender. *Neuropsychologia* 38:304–312, 2000.

Ankney, C. D. Sex differences in relative brain size: The mismeasure of woman too? *Intelligence* 16:329–336, 1992.

Annett, M. A classification of hand preference by association analysis. *British Journal of Psychology* 61:303–321, 1970.

Annett, M. The distribution of manual asymmetry. *British Journal of Psychology* 63:343–358, 1972.

Astur, R. S., M. L. Ortiz, and R. J. Sutherland. A characterization of performance by men and women in a virtual Morris water task: A large and reliable sex difference. *Behavioural Brain Research* 93:185–190, 1998.

Astur, R. S., J. Tropp, S. Sava, R. T. Constable, and E. J. Markus. Sex differences and correlations in a virtual Morris water task, a virtual radial arm maze, and mental rotation. *Behavioural Brain Research* 151:103–115, 2004.

Bakan, P., G. Dibb, and P. Reed. Handedness and birth stress. *Neuropsychologia* 11:363–366, 1973.

Barrera, A., L. Jimenez, G. M. Gonzalez, J. Montiel, and F. Aboitiz. Dendritic structure of single hippocampal neurons according to sex and hemisphere of origin in middle-aged and elderly human subjects. *Brain Research* 906:31–37, 2001.

Beatty, W. W., and A. I. Troster. Gender differences in geographic knowledge. *Sex Roles* 16:202–229, 1987.

Benbow, C. P. Sex differences in mathematical reasoning ability in intellectually talented preadolescents: Their nature, effects, and possible causes. *Behavioral and Brain Sciences* 11:169–232, 1988.

Benbow, C. P., and J. C. Stanley. Sex differences in mathematical ability: Fact or artifact? *Science* 210:1262–1264, 1980.

Bishop, K. M., and D. Wahlsten. Sex differences in the human corpus callosum: Myth or reality? *Neuroscience and Biobehavioral Review* 21:581–601, 1997.

Boles, D. B. X-linkage of spatial ability: A critical review. *Child Development* 51:625–635, 1980.

Bradshaw, J., and L. Rogers. *The Evolution of Lateral Asymmetries, Language, Tool Use, and Intellect*. New York: Academic Press, 1993.

Bryden, M. P., I. C. McManus, and M. B. Bulman-Fleming. Evaluating the empirical support for the Geschwind–Behan–Galaburda model of cerebral lateralization. *Brain and Cognition* 26:103–167, 1994.

Cantalupo, C., and W. D. Hopkins. Asymmetric Broca's area in great apes. *Nature* 414:505, 2001.

Carmon, A., Y. Harishanu, E. Lowinger, and S. Lavy. Asymmetries in hemispheric blood volume and cerebral dominance. *Behavioral Biology* 7:853–859, 1972.

Collins, D. W., and D. Kimura. A large sex difference on a two-dimensional mental rotation task. *Behavioral Neuroscience* 111:845–849, 1997.

Corballis, M. C. Is the handedness gene on the X chromosome? *Psychological Review* 108(4):805–810, 2001.

Corsi-Cabrera, M., C. Arce, J. Ramos, and M. A. Guevara. Effect of spatial ability and sex on inter- and intrahemispheric correlation of EEG activity. *Neurophysiology* 102:5–11, 1997.

Curtiss, S. *Genie: A Psycholinguistic Study of a Modern-Day "Wild Child."* New York: Academic Press, 1978.

de Lacaste-Utamsing, C., and R. L. Holloway. Sexual dimorphism in the human corpus callosum. *Science* 216:1431–1432, 1982.

Dennenberg, V. H. Hemispheric laterality in animals and the effects of early experience. *Behavioral and Brain Sciences* 4:1–50, 1981.

Dennis, M. Capacity and strategy for syntactic comprehension after left or right hemidecortication. *Brain and Language* 10:287–317, 1980.

Dennis, M. Language acquisition in a single hemisphere: Semantic organization. In D. Caplan, Ed. *Biological Studies of Mental Processes*. Cambridge, Mass.: MIT Press, 1980.

Dennis, M., M. Lovett, and C. A. Wiegel-Crump. Written language acquisition after left or right hemidecortication in infancy. *Brain and Language* 12:54–91, 1981.

Dennis, M., and H. A. Whitaker. Language acquisition following hemidecortication: Linguistic superiority of the left over the right hemisphere. *Brain and Language* 3:404–433, 1976.

Dewson, J. H. Preliminary evidence of hemispheric asymmetry of auditory function in monkeys. In S. Harnad, R. W. Doty, L. Goldstein, J. Jaynes, and G. Krauthamer, Eds. *Lateralization in the Nervous System*. New York: Academic Press, 1977.

Dong, Y., K. Nakamura, T. Okada, T. Hanakawa, H. Fukuyama, J. C. Mazziotta, and H. Shibasaki. Neural mechanisms underlying the processing of Chinese words: An fMRI study. *Neuroscience Research* 52:139–145, 2005.

Esposito G., J. D. van Horn, D. R. Weinberger, and K. F. Berman. Gender differences in cerebral blood flow as a function of cognitive state with PET. *Journal of Nuclear Medicine* 37:559–564, 1996.

Fernandez-Carriba, S., A. Loeches, A. Morcillo, and W. D. Hopkins. Asymmetry in facial expression of emotions by chimpanzees. *Neuropsychologia* 40:1523–1533, 2002.

Filipek, P. A, C. Richelme, D. N. Kennedy, and V. S. Caviness, Jr. The young adult human brain: An MRI-based morphometric analysis. *Cerebral Cortex* 4:344–360, 1994.

Fraga, M. F., E. Ballestar, M. F. Paz, S. Ropero, F. Setien, M. L. Ballestar, D. Heine-Suner, J. C. Cigudosa, M. Urioste, J. Benitez, M. Boix-Chornet, A. Sanchez-Aguilera, C. Lin, E. Carlsson, P. Poulsen, A. Vaag, Z. Stephan, T. K. Spector, U.-Z. Wu, C. Ross, and M. Esteller. Epigenetic differences arise during the lifetime of monozygotic twins. *Proceedings of the National Academy of Sciences of the United States of America* 102:10604–10609, 2005.

Frost, J. A., J. R. Binder, J. A. Springer, T. A. Hammeke, P. S. F. Bellgowan, S. M. Rao, and R. W. Cox. Language processing is strongly left lateralized in both sexes: Evidence from functional MRI. *Brain* 122:199–208, 1999.

Geschwind, N., and A. M. Galaburda. *Cerebral Lateralization: Biological Mechanisms, Associations, and Pathology.* Cambridge, MA: MIT Press, 1987.

Goldstein, J. M., L. J. Seidman, N. J. Horton, N. Makris, D. N. Kennedy, V. S. Caviness, Jr., S. V. Faraone, and M. T. Tsuang. Normal sexual dimorphism of the adult human brain assessed by in vivo magnetic resonance imaging. *Cerebral Cortex* 11:490–497, 2001.

Goldstein, J. M., M. Jerram, R. Poldrack, T. Ahern, D. M. Kennedy, L. J. Seidman, and N. Makris. Hormonal cycle modulates arousal circuitry in women using functional magnetic resonance imaging. *Journal of Neuroscience* 25A:9390–9316, 2005.

Gooren, L. The biology of human psychosexual differentiation. *Hormones and Behavior* 50:589–601, 2006.

Grimshaw, G. M., M. P. Bryden, and J. K. Finegan. Relations between prenatal testosterone and cerebral lateralization at age 10. *Journal of Clinical and Experimental Neuropsychology* 15:39–40, 1993.

Gualtieri, T., and R. E. Hicks. An immunoreactive theory of selective male affliction. *Behavioral and Brain Sciences* 8:427–477, 1985.

Gur, R. C., R. E. Gur, W. D. Obrist, J. P. Hungerbuhler, D. Younkin, A. D. Rosen, B. E. Skolnick, and M. Reivich. Sex and handedness differences in cerebral blood flow during test and cognitive activity. *Science* 217:659–660, 1982.

Gur, R. C., B. I. Turetsky, M. Yan, W. Bilker, P. Hughett, and R. E. Gur. Sex differences in brain gray and white matter in healthy young adults: Correlations with cognitive performance. *Journal of Neuroscience* 19:4065–4072, 1999.

Hall, J. *Nonverbal Sex Differences.* Baltimore: Johns Hopkins University Press, 1984.

Hall, J. A. Y., and D. Kimura. Sexual orientation and performance on sexually dimorphic motor tasks. *Archives of Sexual Behavior* 24:395–407, 1995.

Hamilton, C. R., and B. A. Vermeire. Complementary hemispheric superiorities in monkeys. *Science* 242:1691–1694, 1988.

Hamilton, D. *The Monkey Gland Affair.* London: Chatto & Windus, 1986.

Hampson, E. Variations in sex-related cognitive abilities across the menstrual cycle. *Brain and Cognition* 14:26–43, 1990.

Hampson, E., and D. Kimura. Sex differences and hormonal influences on cognitive function in humans. In J. B. Becker, S. M. Breedlove, and D. Crews, Eds. *Behavioral Endocrinology.* Cambridge, Mass.: MIT Press, 1992.

Harasty, J., K. L. Double, G. M. Halliday, J. J. Kril, and A. McRitchie. Language-associated cortical regions are proportionally larger in the female brain. *Archives of Neurology* 54:171–175, 1997.

Hardyck, C., and L. F. Petrinovich. Left-handedness. *Psychological Bulletin* 84:384–404, 1977.

Harris, L. J. Sex differences in spatial ability: Possible environmental, genetic, and neurological factors. In M. Kinsbourne, Ed. *Asymmetrical Function of the Brain.* Cambridge, U.K.: Cambridge University Press, 1978.

Harshman, R. A., E. Hampson, and S. A. Berenbaum. Individual differences in cognitive abilities and brain organization: I. Sex and handedness—Differences in ability. *Canadian Journal of Psychology* 37:144–192, 1983.

Hauser, M. D. Right hemisphere dominance for the production of facial expression in monkeys. *Science* 261:475–477, 1993.

Haverkort, M., L. Stowe, B. Wijers, and A. Paans. Familial handedness and sex in language comprehension. *Neuroimage* 9:12–18, 1999.

Hécaen, H., M. DeAgostini, and A. Monzon-Montes. Cerebral organization in left-handers. *Brain and Language* 12:261–284, 1981.

Hécaen, H., and J. Sauguet. Cerebral dominance in left-handed subjects. *Cortex* 7:19–48, 1971.

Heffner, H. E., and R. S. Heffner. Temporal lobe lesions and perception of species-specific vocalizations by macaques. *Science* 226:75–76, 1984.

Hickok, G., U. Bellugi, and E. S. Klima. Sign language in the brain. *Scientific American* 284(6):58–65, 2001.

Hochberg, F. H., and M. LeMay. Arteriographic correlates of handedness. *Neurology* 25:218–222, 1975.

Hopkins, W. D. Comparative and familial analysis of handedness in great apes. *Psychological Bulletin* 132:538–559, 2006.

Horn, G. Neural basis of recognition memory investigated through an analysis of imprinting. *Philosophical Transactions of the Royal Society London B* 329:133–142, 1990.

Horster, W., and G. Ettlinger. An association between hand preferences and tactile discrimination performance in the rhesus monkey. *Neuropsychologica* 21:411–413, 1985.

Hyde, J. S., E. Fennema, and S. J. Lamon. Gender differences in mathematics performance: A meta-analysis. *Psychological Bulletin* 107:139–155, 1990.

Hyde, J. S., and M. C. Linn. Gender differences in verbal ability: A meta-analysis. *Psychological Bulletin* 104:53–69, 1988.

Ide, A., and F. Aboitiz. A sex difference in the postcentral sulcus of the human brain. *Brain Research* 890:330–332, 2001.

Ifune, C. K., B. A. Vermeire, and C. R. Hamilton. Hemispheric differences in split-brain monkeys viewing and responding to videotape recordings. *Behavioral and Neural Biology* 41:231–235, 1984.

Inglis, J., and J. S. Lawson. A meta-analysis of sex differences in the effects of unilateral brain damage on intelligence test results. *Canadian Journal of Psychology* 36:670–683, 1982.

Inglis, J., M. Rickman, J. S. Lawson, A. W. MacLean, and T. N. Monga. Sex differences in the cognitive effects of unilateral brain damage. *Cortex* 18:257–276, 1982.

Jancke, L., G. Schlaug, Y. Huang, and H. Steinmetz. Asymmetry of the planum parietale. *Neuroreport* 5:1161–1163, 1994.

Janowsky, J. S. Thinking with your gonads. *Trends in Cognitive Sciences* 10:77–82, 2006.

Juraska, J. Sex differences in developmental plasticity of behavior and the brain. In W. T. Greenough and J. M. Juraska, Eds. *Developmental Neuropsychology.* New York: Academic Press, 1986.

Kang, D.-H., R. J. Davidson, C. L. Coe, R. E. Wheeler, A. J. Tomarken, and W. B. Ershler. Frontal brain asymmetry and immune function. *Behavior Neuroscience* 105:860–869, 1991.

Kim, K., N. R. Relkin, K. Lee, and J. Hirsch. Distinct cortical areas associated with native and second languages. *Nature* 388:171–174, 1997.

Kimura, D. *Sex and Cognition.* Cambridge, Mass.: MIT Press, 1999.

Kimura, D. Sex differences in cerebral organization for speech and praxic functions. *Canadian Journal of Psychology* 37:9–35, 1983.

Klar, A. J. A single locus, *RGHT,* specifies preferences for hand utilization in humans. *Cold Spring Harbor Symposia on Quantitative Biology* 61:59–65, 1996.

Klein, D., B. Milner, R. J. Zatorre, E. Meyer, and A. C. Evans. The neural substrates underlying word generation: A bilingual functional-imaging study. *Proceedings of the National Academy of Sciences of the United States of America* 92:2899–2903, 1995.

Klein, D., B. Milner, R. J. Zatorre, V. Zhao, and J. Nikelski. Cerebral organization in bilinguals: A PET study of Chinese–English verb generation. *Neuroreport* 10:2841–2846, 1999.

Kohn, B., and M. Dennis. Selective impairments of visuospatial abilities in infantile hemiplegics after right cerebral hemidecortication. *Neuropsychologia* 12:505–512, 1974.

Kolb, B., and J. Stewart. Sex-related differences in dendritic branching of cells in the prefrontal cortex of rats. *Journal of Neuroendocrinology* 3:95–99, 1991.

Kolb, B., R. J. Sutherland, A. J. Nonneman, and I. Q. Whishaw. Asymmetry in the cerebral hemispheres of the rat, mouse, rabbit, and cat: The right hemisphere is larger. *Experimental Neurology* 78:348–359, 1982.

Kulynych, J. J., K. Vladar, D. W. Jones, and D. R. Weinberger. Gender differences in the normal lateralization of the supratemporal cortex: MRI surface-rendering morphometry of Heschl's gyrus and the planum temporale. *Cerebral Cortex* 4:107–118, 1994.

Lansdell, H. A sex difference in effect of temporal-lobe neurosurgery on design preference. *Nature* 194:852–854, 1962.

LeMay, M. Asymmetries of the skull and handedness: Phrenology revisited. *Journal of Neurological Science* 32:243–253, 1977.

Luders, E., K. L. Narr, P. M. Thompson, D. E. Rex, L. Jancke, H. Steinmatz, and A. W. Toga. Gender differences in cortical complexity. *Nature Neuroscience* 7:799–800, 2004.

Luders, E., K. L. Narr, P. M. Thompson, D. E. Rex, R. P. Woods, H. DeLuca, L. Jancke, and A. W. Toga. Gender effects on cortical thickness and influence of scaling. *Human Brain Mapping* 27:314–324, 2006.

Luders, E., K. L. Narr, P. M. Thompson, R. P. Woods, D. E. Rex, L. Jancke, H. Steinmatz, and A. W. Toga. Mapping cortical gray matter in the young adult brain: Effects of gender. *Neuroimage* 26:493–501, 2005.

Lynn, R. Sex differences in intelligence and brain size: A paradox resolved. *Personality and Individual Differences* 17:257–271, 1993.

MacNeilage, P. F., M. G. Studdert-Kennedy, and B. Lindblom. Primate handedness reconsidered. *Behavioral and Brain Sciences* 10:247–303, 1987.

MacNeilage, P. F., M. G. Studdert-Kennedy, and B. Lindblom. Primate handedness: A foot in the door. *Behavioral and Brain Sciences* 11:737–746, 1988.

Majeres, R. L. Sex differences in symbol–digit substitution and speeded matching. *Intelligence* 7:313–327, 1983.

McBurney, D. H., S. J. C. Gaulin, T. Devineni, and C. Adams. Superior spatial memory of women: Stronger evidence for the gathering hypothesis. *Evolution and Human Behavior* 19:73–87, 1997.

McGivern, R. F., K. L. Mutter, J. Anderson, G. Wideman, M. Bodnar, and P. J. Huston. Gender differences in incidental learning and visual recognition memory:

Support for a sex difference in unconscious environmental awareness. *Personality and Individual Differences* 25:223–232, 1998.

McGlone, J. Sex differences in human brain asymmetry: A critical survey. *Behavioral and Brain Sciences* 3:215–263, 1980.

McGuinness, D., A. Olson, and J. Chapman. Sex differences in incidental recall for words and pictures. *Learning and Individual Differences* 2:263–285, 1990.

McManus, I. C. Handedness, langauge dominance and aphasia: A genetic model. *Psychological Medicine Monograph Supplement* 8: 1–40, 1985.

Meguerditchian, A., and J. Vauclair. Baboons communicate with their right hand. *Behavioural Brain Research* 171:170–174, 2006.

Molfese, D. L., and V. J. Molfese. Right-hemisphere responses from preschool children to temporal cues to speech and nonspeech materials: Electrophysiological correlates. *Brain and Language* 33:245–259, 1988.

Morgan, M. Embryology and inheritance of asymmetry. In S. Harnad, R. W. Doty, L. Goldstein, J. Jaynes, and G. Krauthamer, Eds. *Lateralization in the Nervous System.* New York: Academic Press, 1977.

Moscovitch, M. The development of lateralization of language functions and its relation to cognitive and linguistic development: A review and some theoretical speculations. In S. J. Segalowitz and F. A. Gruber, Eds. *Language Development and Neurological Theory.* New York: Academic Press, 1977.

Murphy, D. G. M., C. DeCarli, A. R., McIntosh, E. Daly, M. J. Mentis, P. Peitrini, J. Szczepanik, M. B. Schapiro, C. L. Grady, B. Horwitz, and S. I. Rapaport. Sex differences in human brain morphometry and metabolism: An in vivo quantitative magnetic resonance imaging and positron emission tomography study on the effect of aging. *Archives of General Psychiatry* 53:585–594, 1996.

Netley, C. Dichotic listening of callosal agenesis and Turner's syndrome patients. In S. J. Segalowitz and F. A. Gruber, Eds. *Language Development and Neurological Theory.* New York: Academic Press, 1977.

Neville, H. Electroencephalographic testing of cerebral specialization in normal and congenitally deaf children: A preliminary report. In S. J. Segalowitz and F. A. Gruber, Eds. *Language Development and Neurological Theory.* New York: Academic Press, 1977.

Nicholson, K. G., and D. Kimura. Sex differences for speech and manual skill. *Perceptual and Motor Skills* 82:3–13, 1996.

Nottebohm, F. Brain pathways for vocal learning in birds: A review of the first 10 years. *Progress in Psychobiology and Physiological Psychology* 9:85–124, 1980.

Obler, L. K., R. J. Zatoree, L. Galloway, Jr., and J. Vaid. Cerebral lateralization in bilinguals: Methodological issues. *Brain and Language* 15:40–54, 1982.

Pakkenberg, B., and H. J. Gundersen. Neocortical neuron number in humans: Effect of sex and age. *Journal of Comparative Neurology* 384:312–320, 1997.

Paus, T., N. Otaky, Z. Caramanos, D. MacDonald, A. Zijdenbos, D. D'Avirro, D. Gutmans, C. Holmes, F. Tomaiuolo, and A. C. Evans. In vivo morphometry of the intrasulcal gray matter in the human cingulate, paracingulate, and superior-rostral sulci: Hemispheric asymmetries, gender differences, and probability maps. *Journal of Comparative Neurology* 376:664–673, 1996.

Peters, M. Corpus callosum. *Canadian Journal of Psychology* 42:313–324, 1988.

Peters, M. Description and validation of a flexible and broadly usable handedness questionnaire. *Laterality* 3:77–96, 1998.

Petersen, M. R., M. D. Beecher, S. R. Zoloth, D. B. Moody, and W. C. Stebbins. Neural lateralization: Evidence from studies of the perception of species-specific vocalizations by Japanese macaques *(Macada puscata). Science* 202:324–326, 1978.

Petrides, M., G. Cadoret, and S. Mackey. Orofacial somatomotor responses in the macaque monkey homologue of Broca's area. *Nature* 435:1235–1238, 2005.

Pugh, K. R., B. A. Shaywitz, S. E. Shaywitz, R. T. Constable, P. Skudlarski, R. K. Fulbright, R. A. Bronen, J. M. Fletcher, D. P. Shankweiler, L. Katz, J. M. Fletcher, and J. C. Gore. Cerebral organization of component process in reading. *Brain* 119:1221–1238, 1996.

Rahman, Q., S. Abrahams, and G.D. Wilson. Sexual-orientation-related differences in verbal fluency. *Neuropsychology* 17:240–246, 2003.

Rapport, R. L., C. T. Tan, and H. A. Whitaker. Language function and dysfunction among Chinese- and English-speaking polyglots: Cortical stimulation, Wada testing, and clinical studies. *Brain and Language* 18:342–366, 1983.

Ratcliffe, G., C. Dila, L. Taylor, and B. Milner. The morphological asymmetry of the hemispheres and cerebral dominance for speech: A possible relationship. *Brain and Language* 11:87–98, 1980.

Reite, M., J. Sheeder, P. Teale, D. Richardson, M. Adams, and J. Simon. MEG based brain laterality: Sex differences in normal adults. *Neuropsychologia* 33:1607–1616, 1995.

Schlaepfer, T. E., G. J. Harris, A. Y. Tien, L. Peng, S. Lee, and G. D. Pearlson. Structural differences in the cerebral cortex of healthy female and male subjects: A magnetic resonance imaging study. *Psychiatry Research* 61:129–135, 1995.

Sherwin, B. B. The critical period hypothesis: Can it explain descrepancies in the oestrogen-cognition literature? *Journal of Neuroendocrinology* 19:77–81, 2007.

Sowell, E. R., P. M. Thompson, D. Rex, D. Kornsand, K. D. Tessner, T. L. Jernigan, and A. W. Toga. Mapping sulcal pattern asymmetry and local cortical surface gray matter distribution in vivo: Maturation in perisylvian cortices. *Cerebral Cortex* 12:17–26, 2002.

Springer, S. P., and G. Deutsch. *Left Brain, Right Brain: Perspectives from Cognitive Neuroscience,* 5th ed. New York: W. H. Freeman and Company, 1998.

Stark, R. E., K. Bleile, J. Brandt, J. Freeman, and E. P. G. Vining. Speech-language outcomes of hemispherectomy in children and young adults. *Brain and Language* 51:406–421, 1995.

Stewart, J., and B. Kolb. The effects of neonatal gonadectomy and prenatal stress on cortical thickness and asymmetry in rats. *Behavioral and Neural Biology* 49:344–360, 1988.

Strauss, E., J. Wada, and M. Hunter. Sex-related differences in the cognitive consequences of early left-hemisphere lesions. *Journal of Clinical and Experimental Neuropsychology* 14:738–748, 1992.

Sugishita, M., K. Otomo, S. Kabe, and K. Yunoki. A critical appraisal of neuropsychological correlates of Japanese ideogram (kanji) and phonogram (kana) reading. *Brain* 115:1563–1585, 1992.

Sun, T., R. V. Collura, M. Ruvolov, and C. A. Walsh. Genomic and evolutionary analyses of asymmetrically expressed genes in human fetal left and right cerebral cortex. *Cerebral Cortex* 16:18–125, 2006.

Sun, T., P. C. Patoine, A. Abu-Khalil, J. Visvander, E. Sum, T. J. Cherry, S. H. Orkin, E. H. Geschwind, and C. A. Walsh. Early asymmetry of gene transcription in embryonic human left and right cerebral cortex. *Science* 308:1794–1798, 2005.

Swaab, D. F. Sexual differentiation of the human brain: Relevance for gender identity, transsexualism and sexual orientation. *Gynecology and Endocrinology* 19:301–312, 2004.

Swaab, D. F., and E. Fliers. A sexually dimorphic nucleus in the human brain. *Science* 228:1112–1115, 1985.

Taglialatela, J. P., C. Cantalupo, and W. D. Hopkins. Gesture handedness predicts asymmetry in the chimpanzee inferior frontal gyrus. *Neuroreport* 17:923–927, 2006.

Thomas, H., W. Jamison, and D. D. Hummel. Observation is insufficient for discovering that the surface of still water is invariantly horizontal. *Science* 191:173–174, 1973.

Uyehara, J. M., and W. C. Cooper, Jr. Hemispheric differences for verbal and nonverbal stimuli in Japanese-and English-speaking subjects assessed by Tsunoda's method. *Brain and Language* 10:405–417, 1980.

Velle, W. Sex differences in sensory functions. *Perspectives in Biology and Medicine* 30:490–522, 1987.

Waber, D. P. Sex differences in cognition: A function of maturation rate. *Science* 192:572–573, 1976.

Warren, J. M. Functional lateralization in the brain. *Annals of the New York Academy of Sciences* 299:273–280, 1977.

Wechsler, A. F. Crossed aphasia in an illiterate dextral. *Brain and Language* 3:164–172, 1976.

Werker, J. F., and R. C. Tees. The organization and reorganization of human speech perception. *Annual Review of Neuroscience* 15:377–402, 1992.

Witelson, S. F. The brain connection: The corpus callosum is larger in left-handers. *Science* 229:665–668, 1985.

Witelson, S. F. Hand and sex differences in the isthmus and genu of the human corpus callosum: A postmortem morphological study. *Brain* 112:799–835, 1989.

Witelson, S. F., and C. H. Goldsmith. The relationship of hand preference to anatomy of the corpus callosum in men. *Brain Research* 545:175–182, 1991.

Witelson, S. F., and D. L. Kigar. Sylvian fissure morphology and asymmetry in men and women: Bilateral differences in relation to handedness in men. *Journal of Comparative Neurology* 323:326–340, 1992.

Witelson, S. F., I. I. Lezner, and D. L. Kigar. Women have greater density of neurons in posterior temporal cortex. *Journal of Neuroscience* 15:3418–3428, 1995.

Woolley, C. S., E. Gould, M. Frankfurt, and B. S. McEwen. Naturally occurring fluctuation in dendritic spine density on adult hippocampal pyramidal neurons. *Journal of Neuroscience* 10:4035–4039, 1990.

Yakovlev, P. I., and P. Rakic. Patterns of decussation of bulbar pyramids and distribution of pyramidal tracts on two sides of the spinal cord. *Transactions of the American Neurological Association* 91:366–367, 1966.

CHAPTER 13

The Occipital Lobes

Portrait: An Injured Soldier's Visual World

P.M., a colonel in the British army who fought in North Africa during the Second World War, was struck by a bullet that went through the back of his brain. Miraculously, P.M. survived, but his vision was severely affected. He completely lost sight in the right visual field, but the central part of his left visual field survived. He reported that he could see "normally" in a region of the left visual world that was about the diameter of your fist held at arm's length directly in front of your face.

P.M.'s symptoms reveal a topographic map of the visual world in the occipital cortex (see adjoining illustration) and the possibility of seeing through only a small part of it. But what did P.M. experience in the rest of

his visual world? Shortly after his injury, he reported that the lost world appeared black, as though the lights were out. Occasionally, however, he was aware that the lost regions were different, "almost gray," although he could never express specifically what exactly was different other than the grayness.

P.M. also experienced a phenomenon that many patients with extensive visual-field defects experience: if asked to guess whether a spot of light had blinked in his blind field, he could "guess" at above-chance levels. He was not consciously aware that the light had appeared and seemed bemused that he could guess, sometimes quite accurately, about the presence or absence of the light.

In spite of his residual central vision, P.M. had two particular (and, for him, aggravating) problems: he found it very difficult to read and he had difficulty recognizing faces. Curiously, however, P.M. could recognize other objects more easily, even though he could not see any more of them than he could of the faces.

Our brains are organized around vision. Our perception of the world is predominantly visual, our movements are guided by visual information, our social and sexual behavior is highly visual, our entertainment is largely visual, and our nights are enriched by visual dreams.

In this chapter, we first consider the anatomical organization of the occipital lobes and then examine the extent of the visual system within the brain. Next, we examine disorders of the visual pathways and of the visual system. Then, we shall see why the ability of humans to visualize presents neuropsychologists a unique opportunity to study cerebral functioning.

Anatomy of the Occipital Lobes

The occipital lobes form the posterior pole of the cerebral hemispheres, lying beneath the occipital bone at the back of the skull. On the medial surface of each hemisphere, the occipital lobe is distinguished from the parietal lobe by the parietal-occipital sulcus, as illustrated in **Figure 13.1**.

No clear landmarks separate the occipital cortex from the temporal or parietal cortex on the lateral surface of the hemisphere, however, because the occipital tissue merges with the other regions. The lack of clear landmarks makes it difficult to define the extent of the occipital areas precisely and has led to much confusion about their exact boundaries—especially on the ventral surface of the brain, where the occipital cortex extends forward to merge with medial and ventral temporal cortices.

Within the visual cortex, however, are three clear landmarks, identified in Figure 13.1. The most prominent is the calcarine sulcus, which contains much of the primary cortex. The calcarine sulcus divides the upper and lower halves of the visual world. On the ventral surface of each hemisphere are two gyri (lingual and fusiform). The lingual gyrus includes part of visual cortical regions V2 and VP, whereas V4 is in the fusiform gyrus.

Figure **13.1**

Medial View of the Occipital Lobe, Illustrating Major Landmarks

Subdivisions of the Occipital Cortex

The monkey cortex was first divided by Brodmann into three regions (areas 17, 18, and 19; refer to Figure 10.7), but studies with the use of imaging, physiological, and newer anatomical techniques have produced much finer subdivisions. Although the map is still not complete, the consensus is that the monkey occipital cortex contains multiple different visual areas, as illustrated in **Figure 13.2**. Note, too, that many visual areas are found in the adjacent parietal and temporal cortices.

Figure 13.2A shows the locations of these areas on the lateral surface of the monkey brain, and Figure 13.2B shows their locations on a two-dimensional flat map that includes both the lateral areas and those located on the medial surface of the hemisphere. The precise locations of the human homologues are still not settled, but **Figure 13.3** includes a flat map constructed by Roger Tootell and his colleagues. A difficulty in comparing the monkey and human maps is that the monkey maps are based on anatomy and connections, whereas the human maps are now heavily based on noninvasive imaging such as fMRI.

The names of the some of the regions in the human map, such as V4, were based on functional information in monkeys that later proved incorrect, but the names have stuck. For example, V4 was believed to be a color region in monkeys, but areas TE and TEO actually process color. Because V4 in humans was named by using the earlier information about the monkey V4 region, V4 in humans, along with V8, are color regions.

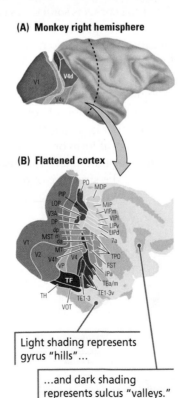

(A) Monkey right hemisphere

(B) Flattened cortex

Light shading represents gyrus "hills"...

...and dark shading represents sulcus "valleys."

Figure **13.2**

Topography of the Visual Cortex of the Macaque Monkey (A) A nearly normal rendition of the lateral surface of the right hemisphere in which the sulci are opened slightly. (B) A flattened cortical surface showing both the lateral and the medial regions. The darker areas around the sulci represent regions that are normally curved up (gyri) or down (sulci). (After Tootell and Hadjikhani, 2001, and Tootell et al., 2003.)

(A) Right hemisphere, lateral view

(B) Right hemisphere, medial view

Figure 13.3

Topography of the Human Visual Cortex (After Tootell and Hadjikhani, 2001, and Tootell et al., 2003.)

Figure 13.4

Visual Cortex (A) The visual cortex is highly laminated, as can be seen in a cell-body stain (left) or a myelin stain (right) in these sections from a monkey brain. (B) This drawing of a flattened section through the monkey's visual cortex illustrates the blobs in V1 and the stripes in V2.

(C) Flattened view of occipital cortex

Some of the areas contain a complete visual field, whereas others have only an upper or lower visual field. This distinction is curious, and Fred Previc suggested that the upper and lower fields may have different functions, with the upper more specialized for visual search and recognition and the lower more specialized for visuomotor guidance.

A remarkable feature of area V1 is its complex laminar organization, which, as illustrated in **Figure 13.4A**, is probably the most distinct of all cortical areas. Although we usually say that the cortex has six layers, it is possible to see many more in area V1, partly because layer IV alone features four distinct layers.

Another surprising feature of area V1 is that, although it appears to be anatomically homogenous, it can be shown to actually be heterogeneous by staining it for the enzyme cytochrome oxidase, which is crucial in making energy available to cells. Regions of cytochrome-rich areas, the blobs, are separated by interblob regions of little cytochrome activity (see Figure 10.10B). Cells in the blobs take part in color perception and the interblobs have a role in form and motion perception.

The discovery that area V1 is functionally heterogeneous—that a given cortical area may have more than one distinct function—was unexpected. Area V2 also is heterogeneous when stained with cytochrome oxidase, but, instead of blobs, stripes are revealed (see Figure 10.10C). Because of the distinct stripes, the visual cortex is sometimes called the **striate cortex**. The "thin stripe," takes part in color perception. "Thick stripes" and "pale stripes" have roles in form and motion perception, respectively. Thus, we see that the heterogeneity of function observed in area V1—representing color, form, and motion—is preserved in area V2, although it is organized in a different way, as diagrammed in Figure 13.4B.

The distribution of color function across much of the occipital cortex and beyond (that is, areas V1, V2, V4, V8) is important because, until recently, the perception of form or movement was believed to be color-blind. It has now become clear that color vision is integral to the analysis of position, depth, motion, and the structure of objects (see a review by Tanaka et al., 2001).

(A)

Because of the distinct stripes, the visual cortex is sometimes called the striate cortex.

(B)

A key point here is that, although the relative amount of color processing certainly varies across occipital regions, with area V4 having color processing as its major function, the processing of color-related information does more than simply allow us to tell red from green. It also enriches our capacity to detect motion, depth, and position. In the absence of significant color analysis, dogs and cats thus not only see an essentially black-and-white world, but have reduced visual capacities more generally as well.

An example of the advantage of color vision can be seen in the type of photoreceptors in primates. The color system of primates is optimized for differentiating edible fruits from a background of leaves (Sumner and Mollon, 2000). This ability to differentiate is an important advantage when having to select edible fruits from a complex scene and is especially important when the fruits are partly occluded by leaves, which is fairly common. In fact, color provides important information for object recognition in such cases. A partly occluded yellow banana is quickly seen, whereas a gray banana would be difficult to detect in a scene viewed in black and white.

Connections of the Visual Cortex

By the late 1960s, the consensus held that the visual cortex is hierarchically organized, with visual information proceeding from area 17 to area 18 to area 19. Each visual area was thought to provide some sort of elaboration on the processing of the preceding area. This strictly hierarchical view is now considered too simple and has been replaced by the notion of a distributed hierarchical process with multiple parallel and interconnecting pathways at each level, much as illustrated in Figure 10.17B.

A hierarchy is still proposed for vision, but with separate functions. As indicated in Chapter 10, the details of all the connections between the occipital areas and from them to the parietal, temporal, and frontal regions are bewildering, but it is possible to extract a few simple principles (**Figure 13.5**):

- V1 (the striate cortex) is the primary vision area: it receives the largest input from the lateral geniculate nucleus of the thalamus, and it projects to all other occipital regions. V1 is the first processing level in the hierarchy.

- V2 also projects to all other occipital regions. V2 is the second level.

- After V2, three distinct, parallel pathways emerge en route to the parietal cortex, superior temporal sulcus (STS), and inferior temporal cortex, for further processing.

As we shall see in more detail shortly, the parietal pathway, or **dorsal stream**, has a role in the visual guidance of movement, and the inferior temporal pathway, or **ventral stream**, is concerned with object perception (including color). The middle pathway along the superior temporal sulcus (the *STS stream*) is probably important in visuospatial functions and in the perception of certain types of movements.

Figure **13.5**

Visual Streaming In both monkey and human brains the occipito-parietal (dorsal) stream takes part in vision for action and flows from area V1 to the posterior parietal visual areas. The occipitotemporal (ventral) stream takes part in object recognition and flows from area V1 to the temporal visual areas. The STS stream, where information to and from the dorsal and ventral streams converges, flows from area V1 into the superior temporal sulcus.

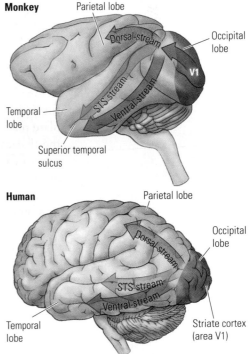

A Theory of Occipital-Lobe Function

As already stated, areas V1 and V2 are functionally heterogeneous and both segregate processing for color, form, and motion. The heterogeneous functions of areas V1 and V2 contrast with the functions of the areas that follow in the hierarchy. In a sense, areas V1 and V2 appear to serve as mailboxes into which different types of information are assembled before being sent on to the more specialized visual areas.

From areas V1 and V2 flow three parallel pathways that convey different attributes of vision. The information derived from the blob areas of V1 goes to area V4, considered to be a color area. Cells in area V4 are not solely responsive to color, however; some cells respond to both form and color.

Other information from area V1 also goes to area V2 and then to area V5 (also known as middle temporal or MT), which is specialized to detect motion. Finally, an input from areas V1 and V2 to area V3 concerns what Semir Zeki calls "dynamic form"—that is, the shape of objects in motion. Thus, we see that vision begins in the primary cortex (V1), which has multiple functions, and then continues in more specialized cortical zones.

It is not surprising to discover that selective lesions up the hierarchy in areas V3, V4, and V5 produce specific deficits in visual processing. People who suffer damage to area V4 are able to see only in shades of gray. Curiously, patients not only fail to perceive colors but also fail to recall colors perceived before their injuries or even to imagine colors. In a real sense, the loss of area V4 results in the loss of color cognition, or the ability to think about color.

Similarly, a lesion in area V5 produces an inability to perceive objects in motion. Objects at rest are perceived but, when the objects begin to move, they vanish. In principle, a lesion in area V3 will affect form perception but, because area V4 also processes form, a rather large lesion of both V3 and V4 would be required to eliminate form perception.

An important constraint on the functions of areas V3, V4, and V5 is that all these areas receive major input from area V1. People such as Colonel P.M. (whose case is presented in the Portrait at the beginning of this chapter), with lesions in area V1, act as though they are blind, but visual input can still get through to higher levels—partly through small projections of the lateral geniculate nucleus to area V2 and partly through projections from the colliculus to the thalamus (the pulvinar) to the cortex. People with V1 lesions seem not to be aware of visual input and can be shown to retain some aspects of vision only by special testing. Thus, when asked what they see, patients with V1 damage often reply that they see nothing. Nonetheless, they can act on visual information, indicating that they do indeed "see."

Area V1 thus appears to be primary for vision in yet another sense: V1 must function for the brain to make sense of what the more specialized visual areas are processing. We must note, however, reports of people with significant V1 damage who are capable of some awareness of visual information, such as motion. John Barbur and his colleagues suggest that the integrity of area V3 may allow this conscious awareness, but this suggestion remains a hypothesis.

Visual Functions Beyond the Occipital Lobe

Neuroscientists have known since the early 1900s that the occipital lobes house vision, but only in the past few decades have they begun to understand the extent of visual processing that takes place beyond the occipital lobes. In fact, it is now clear that more cortex concerns vision than with any other function in the primate brain.

Daniel Felleman and David van Essen's flattened cortical map in Figure 10.18 illustrates that, of the 32 cortical areas (of a total of about 70 in their scheme) that have visual functions in the monkey brain, only 9 are in the occipital lobe. The total surface area of the vision-related regions is about 55% of the whole cortical surface, which compares with 11% and 3% for the somatosensory and auditory regions, respectively. (Of interest is that so little of the monkey cortex represents audition, which is certainly evidence of a major difference between the brains of humans and those of monkeys; we humans have a much larger auditory representation, which is no doubt responsible for our preoccupation with both language and music.)

Visual processing in humans therefore does not culminate in secondary areas such as V3, V4, and V5 but continues within multiple visual regions in the parietal, temporal, and frontal lobes. Functions have not been assigned to all these additional visual regions, but evidence is accumulating that different regions have quite specific functions. **Table 13.1** summarizes the putative functions of regions in both the ventral and dorsal streams. For example, in the ventral stream, several regions appear to be tuned selectively to identify body parts such as hands (EBA, extrastriate body area; FBA, fusiform body area), faces (FFA, fusiform face area), or moving bodies (STSp). Another region, PPA (parahippocampal place area) has a totally different function—namely, the analysis of information about the appearance and layout of scenes.

Table **13.1** Summary of visual regions beyond the occipital lobe

	Region	Proposed Function
Ventral Stream Regions		
LO	Lateral occipital	Object analysis
FFA	Fusiform face area	Face analysis
EBA	Extrastriate body area	Body analysis
FBA	Fusiform body area	Body analysis
STS	Superior temporal sulcus	Analysis of biological motion
STSp	Superior temporal sulcus (posterior)	Moving-body analysis
PPA	Parahippocampal place area	Analysis of landmarks
Dorsal Stream Regions		
LIP	Lateral intraparietal sulcus	Voluntary eye movement
AIP	Anterior intraparietal sulcus	Object-directed grasping
VIP	Ventral intraparietal sulcus	Visuomotor guidance
PRR	Parietal reach region	Visually guided reach
cIPS	Intraparietal sulcus	Object-directed action

Although it is tempting to regard each of the ventral-stream regions as an independent visual processor, all ventral-stream regions are clearly responsive to some degree to all categories of stimuli. The differences among the regions are a matter of *degree* of activity, not the mere *presence* of activity. This is illustrated nicely in an fMRI study by Timothy Andrews and his colleagues. They showed subjects the perceptually ambiguous Rubin's vase (see Figure 8.22A). The fusiform face area responded more strongly when subjects reported seeing the faces rather than the vase, even though exactly the same physical stimulus gave rise to the two percepts. Such changes were not seen in adjacent visual areas such as the parahippocampal place area.

Table 13.1 also identifies several dorsal-stream regions specialized for moving the eyes (LIP) or for object-directed grasping (AIP, PRR). Not all neurons in these regions control movements directly but rather appear to be "purely visual." These neurons are presumed to take part in converting visual information into the necessary coordinates for action.

One conclusion that we can make is that vision is not unitary but is composed of many quite specific forms of processing. These different forms can be organized into five general categories: vision for action, action for vision, visual recognition, visual space, and visual attention.

Vision for Action

This category is visual processing required to direct specific movements. For example, when reaching for a particular object such as a cup, the fingers form a specific pattern that enables a person to grasp the cup. This movement is obviously guided by vision, because people do not need to shape their hands consciously as they reach.

Although you may consciously decide to reach for an object such as a mug, your hand forms the appropriate posture automatically, without your conscious awareness.

In addition to guiding grasping, various visual areas guide all kinds of specific movements, including those of the eyes, head, and whole body. A single system could not easily guide all movements, because the requirements are so different. Reaching to pick up a jellybean requires a very different kind of motor control than that required to duck from a snowball, but both are visually guided.

Finally, vision for action must be sensitive to movement of the target. Catching a moving ball requires specific information about the location, trajectory, speed, and shape of the object. Vision for action is a function of the parietal visual areas in the dorsal stream.

Action for Vision

In a more "top down" process, the viewer actively searches for only part of the target object and attends selectively to it. When we look at a visual stimulus, we do not simply stare at it; rather, we scan the stimulus with numerous eye movements. These movements are not random but tend to focus on important or distinct features of the stimulus.

When we scan a face, we make a lot of eye movements directed toward the eyes and mouth. Curiously, we also make more eye scans directed to the left visual field (the right side of the person's face) than to the right visual field (**Figure 13.6**A). This scanning bias may be important in the way that we process faces, because it is not found in the scanning of other stimuli (Figure 13.6B). People with deficits in action for vision are likely to have significant deficits in visual perception (Figure 13.6C), although such deficits have not been studied systematically.

An interesting aspect of action for vision consists of the eye movements that we often make when we visualize information. For example, when people are asked to rotate objects mentally to answer simple questions about the objects' appearance, they usually make many eye movements, especially to the left. When people are doing things in the dark, such as searching for objects on a counter, they also make many eye movements. Curiously, if the eyes are closed, these movements stop. Indeed, it appears that it is easier to do many tasks in the dark with closed eyes. Because things are done by touch in the dark, the visual system may interfere until the eyes are closed.

Visual Recognition

We enjoy the ability both to recognize objects and to respond to visual information. For example, we can both recognize specific faces and discriminate and interpret different expressions in those faces. Similarly, we can recognize letters or symbols and assign meaning to them.

We can recognize different foods, tools, or body parts, but it is not reasonable to expect that we have different visual regions for each category or object. We do have at least some specialized areas in the temporal regions, however, for biologically significant information, such as faces and hands, as well as regions for objects and places.

Visual Space

Visual information comes from specific locations in space. This information allows us to direct our movements to objects in space and to assign meaning to objects. But spatial location is not a unitary characteristic. Objects have location both relative to an individual (**egocentric space**) and relative to one another (**allocentric space**).

Egocentric visual space is central to the control of your actions toward objects. It therefore seems likely that visual space is coded in neural systems related to vision for action. In contrast, the allocentric properties of objects are necessary for you to construct a memory of spatial location.

A key feature of allocentric spatial coding is that it depends on the identity of particular features of the world. Thus, it is likely to be associated with the regions of visual recognition. In summary, different aspects of spatial processing probably take place in both the parietal and the temporal visual regions, and respective functions are integrated in areas that interact and exchange information.

Visual Attention

We cannot possibly process all the visual information available. This page has shape, color, texture, location, and so on, but the only really important characteristic is that it has words and images. Thus, when we read the page, we select specific aspects of visual input and attend to them selectively.

In fact, neurons in the cortex have various attentional mechanisms. For example, neurons may respond selectively to stimuli in particular places or at

(A) Normal subject

Eye movements of a normal subject concentrate on facial features and are directed more to the left side of the photograph.

(B) Normal subject

Eye movements of a normal subject concentrate on the shapes of the objects examined,...

(C) Agnosic subject

...but those of an agnosic subject are random.

Figure **13.6**

Eye Movements While Examining a Visual Stimulus

(From A. R. Luria, *The Working Brain*, © 1973, The Copyright Agency of the USSR. Reprinted with permission.)

particular times or if a particular movement is to be executed. Independent mechanisms of attention are probably required both for the guidance of movements (in the parietal lobe) and for object recognition (in the temporal lobe).

Visual Pathways Beyond the Occipital Lobe

Vision evolved first for motion, not for recognition. Simple organisms can detect light and move to or from the light. For example, the single-cell organism *Euglena* alters its swimming pattern as a function of the ambient light levels in different parts of the pond in which it lives. Because sunlight helps manufacture food in this aquatic environment, it is an advantage for *Euglena* to move toward the light.

Notice that *Euglena* needs neither to "perceive" the light nor to make an internal map of the outside world. Rather, only some type of link between the amount of ambient light and locomotion is necessary. For *Euglena*, "vision" acts to guide movement—the most primitive form of vision for action.

Even though our vision is far more complicated than that of *Euglena*, much of human vision can be understood without reference to recognition. Consider, for example, a major-league baseball batter who swings at a fastball before it is possible for him to perceive what the object actually is. The visual guidance of his movement is independent of his recognition of the ball.

Nonetheless, as primitive animals interact with their environment, they are adapted to learn more about it. Thus, distinct visual systems evolved to recognize objects in the environment. The system of knowing what an object is includes the flow of visual information from area V1 to the temporal lobe in the ventral stream (see Figure 13.5). The system controlling the visual guidance of movements includes the flow of information from area V1 to the parietal lobe in the dorsal stream.

The distinction between the ventral and the dorsal streams can be seen clearly in a series of patients studied by David Milner and Melvyn Goodale. They first described D.F., a patient with a selective lesion to area LO, illustrated in **Figure 13.7**. D.F. was blind but nevertheless shaped her hand appropriately when asked to reach for objects. Her dorsal stream was intact, as revealed by the fact that she could "unconsciously" see location, size, and shape. On the other hand, Milner and Goodale note that patients with dorsal-stream damage consciously report seeing objects but cannot reach accurately or shape the hand appropriately when reaching.

Milner and Goodale propose that the dorsal stream be thought of as a set of systems for the on-line visual control of action. Their argument is based on three main lines of evidence:

Figure 13.7

Extent of D.F.'s Lesion (Left) On the right-hemisphere lateral view of D.F.'s brain, the area in blue shows that her lesion envelops area LO. (Right) The ventral view of D.F.'s brain reveals bilateral lesions in LO. (Adapted with permission from Milner and Goodale, 2006.)

1. The predominant characteristic of the neurons in posterior parietal regions is that they are active during a combination of visual stimulation and associated behavior. For example, cells may be active only when a monkey reaches out to a particular object. Looking at an object in the absence of movement does not activate the neurons. Thus, these "visual" neurons are unique in that they are active only when the brain acts on visual information.

2. These posterior parietal neurons can therefore be characterized as an interface between analysis of the visual world and motor action taken on it. The demands of action have important implications for what type of information must be sent to the parietal cortex—information such as object shape, movement, and location. Each of these visual features is likely to be coded separately, and at least three distinct pathways within the dorsal stream run from area V1 to the parietal cortex. As illustrated on the right in **Figure 13.8**, one pathway goes from area V1 directly to area V5 to the parietal cortex, a second goes from area V1 to area V3a and then to parietal regions, and a third goes from area V1 to area V2 to the parietal cortex. These three pathways must certainly be functionally dissociable.

3. Most of the visual impairments associated with lesions to the parietal cortex can be characterized as visuomotor or orientational. (We return to this subject in Chapter 14.)

The Milner–Goodale model is an important theoretical advance in understanding how our visual brain is organized. As detailed in Figure 13.8, the two distinct visual streams have evolved to use visual information in two fundamentally different ways: the dorsal stream for guiding movements and the ventral stream for identifying objects. This model can likely be applied to the organization of the auditory and somatosensory systems as well: both systems also function to guide movements and identify stimuli. An important point here is that we are conscious of only a small amount of what the brain actually does; even with effort, we cannot gain awareness of much of our sensory processing.

One wrinkle can be added to the Milner–Goodale model: the third stream of visual processing originates from structures associated with both the parietal and the temporal pathways and flows to a region of the temporal lobe that is buried in the superior temporal sulcus (see Figure 13.5). The STS is part of the multimodal cortex described in Chapter 10 and is characterized by **polysensory neurons**—neurons that are responsive to both visual and auditory or both visual and somatosensory input.

The interaction of the parietal and temporal streams in the STS stream is probably due to interaction between the dorsal and the ventral—the "action" and "recognition"—streams. Milner and Goodale suspect that this "third stream" is largely an elaboration of the ventral stream that provides a perceptual representation of the actions of others as well as the perception of spatial relations among elements in a scene. (See Rizzolatti and Matelli for a different interpretation.)

Figure 13.8

Summary of the Visual Processing Hierarchy The dorsal stream, which takes part in visual action, guides movements such as the hand postures for grasping a mug or pen, as illustrated on the right. The ventral stream, which takes part in object recognition, identifies objects such as mugs and pens in our visual world, as shown on the left. The dorsal and ventral streams exchange information through polysensory neurons in the STS stream, as shown by double-headed arrows. (After Goodale, 1993.)

Imaging Studies of Dorsal and Ventral Streams

Neuroscientists identify brain regions associated with specific visual pathways by measuring regional blood flow as people perform visual tasks. Leslie Ungerleider and James Haxby reviewed such PET studies, as summarized in **Figure 13.9**.

In studies by Haxby and his colleagues, subjects were given two tasks. In the first task, the subjects indicated which of two faces was identical with a

(A)

KEY

● Facial recognition
■ Spatial location

Lateral view

Ventral view

(B)

KEY

■ Color perception
● Motion perception
▲ Shape perception

Figure 13.9

Imaging Visual Pathways A summary of results of PET studies illustrates selective activation of (A) cortical regions by tasks of facial recognition (circles) and spatial location (squares) and (B) areas associated with perception of color (squares), motion (circles), and shape (triangles). (After Ungerleider and Haxby, 1994.)

sample face. In the second task, the subjects were asked to identify which of two stimuli had a dot (or square) in the same location as in a sample. The results showed activation of the temporal regions for the facial stimuli and activation of the posterior parietal region for the location task (see Figure 13.9A). Note, in addition, the activation of frontal areas for the spatial task, supporting the idea that the frontal lobe plays a role in certain aspects of visual processing.

One difficulty in interpreting the spatial-task PET images is that subjects have to move their eyes, which activates regions in the dorsal stream; so whether the spatial or the movement components activate the parietal region is not clear. The important point, however, is that different regions take part in the two tasks.

A similar dissociation was identified among the processes that detect motion, color, and shape (see Figure 13.9B). The detection of motion activates regions in the vicinity of area V5, whereas the detection of shape activates regions along the STS and the ventral region of the temporal lobe. The perception of color is associated with activation of the region of the lingual gyrus, which is the location of area V4. One study also found activation of a lateral occipital region, which is difficult to interpret in light of lesion studies. This study made special visual attention demands of its participants, potentially an important factor in interpreting the observed activation.

In summary, studies of regional blood flow in normal subjects show results consistent with the general notion of two separate visual streams, one to the parietal lobe and the other to the temporal lobe. In addition, separate visual functions clearly reside in different temporal-occipital regions.

Disorders of Visual Pathways

Before we consider the deficits associated with damage to the visual pathways, we must revisit two key elements in the way in which the brain organizes the visual fields:

1. The left half of each retina sends its projections to the right side of the brain, whereas the right half of each retina sends its projections to the left side of the brain (see Figure 11.5). Thus, the representation of each side of the visual world seen by each eye is sent to the same place in area V1. As a result, damage to area V1 affects vision in both eyes. Conversely, if a visual disturbance is restricted to just one eye, then the damage must be outside the brain, either in the retina or in the optic nerve.

2. Different parts of the visual field are topographically represented in different parts of area V1 (**Figure 13.10**). Thus, injury to a specific region of area V1 produces a loss of vision in a specific part of the visual world.

Now let us consider what happens when damage is done to different places in the visual pathways, as keyed on Figure 13.10.

Destruction of the retina or optic nerve of one eye produces *monocular blindness*—the loss of sight in that eye. A lesion of the medial region of the optic chiasm severs the crossing fibers, producing **bitemporal hemianopia**—loss of vision of both temporal fields. This symptom can arise when a tumor develops in the pituitary gland, which sits medially, next to the chiasm. As the tumor grows, it can put pressure on the medial part of the chiasm and produce the loss, or disturbance, of lateral vision.

A lesion of the lateral chiasm results in a loss of vision of one nasal field, or *nasal hemianopia*. Complete cuts of the optic tract, lateral geniculate body, or area V1 result in **homonymous hemianopia**—blindness of one entire visual field (**Figure 13.11**A). Note that, because the disturbance affects information coming from both eyes, the visual defect is present in both eyes (see field 5 in Figure 13.10).

Indeed, the effects of such injuries enable investigators to determine whether a lesion is in the eye or optic tract versus the optic nerve or brain. The former injuries produce visual disturbance in one eye, whereas the latter injuries produce visual disturbance in the visual field and thus in both eyes. Should this lesion be partial, as is often the case, only a part (quadrant) of the visual field is destroyed (Figure 13.11B; see field 6 in Figure 13.10).

Lesions of the occipital lobe often spare the central, or macular, region of the visual field, although the reason is uncertain. The most reasonable explanations are either (1) the macular region receives a double vascular supply, from both the middle and the posterior cerebral arteries, making it more resilient to large hemispheric lesions, or (2) the foveal region of the retina projects to both hemispheres, and so, even if one occipital lobe is destroyed, the other receives projections from the fovea. The first explanation is more likely.

Macular sparing of the central visual field helps to differentiate lesions of the optic tract or thalamus from cortical lesions, because macular sparing occurs only after lesions (usually large) to the visual cortex. Macular sparing does not always occur, however, and many people with visual-cortex lesions have a complete loss of vision in one-quarter (**quadrantanopia**) or one-half (*hemianopia*) of the fovea (see Figures 13.10 and 13.11). A curious aspect of both hemianopia and quadrantanopia is that the border between the impaired visual area and the adjacent, intact visual field, or quadrant, is sharp, much as if a pair of scissors were used to cut away part of the visual field (see Figure 13.10). This sharp demarcation of intact and impaired visual regions is due to the anatomical segregation between the left and the right and the upper and the lower visual fields.

Small lesions of the occipital lobe often produce **scotomas**, small blind spots in the visual field (Figure 13.11C). A curious aspect of scotomas is that people are often totally unaware of them because of *nystagmus* (constant, tiny, involuntary eye movements) and "spontaneous filling in" by the visual system. The eyes are usually in constant motion; so the scotoma moves about the visual field, allowing the brain to perceive all the information in the field. If the eyes are held still, the visual system actually completes objects, faces, and so on, resulting in a normal percept of the stimulus.

The visual system may cover up the scotoma so successfully that its presence can be demonstrated to the patient only by "tricking" the visual system.

Patient's actual visual field

❶ Normal

❷ Monocular blindness

❸ Bitemporal hemianopia

❹ Right nasal hemianopia

❺ Homonymous hemianopia

❻ Quadrant-anopia

❼ Macular sparing

Figure 13.10

Effects of Injury Visual defects subsequent to damage at different levels of the visual system, keyed by number. A blue region in the visual field key denotes a blind area. (After Curtis, 1972.)

Figure 13.11

Consequences of Lesions in Area V1 The shaded areas indicate regions of visual loss. (A) The effect of a complete lesion of area V1 in the left hemisphere is hemianopia affecting the right visual field. (B) A large lesion of the lower lip of the calcarine fissure produces a quadrantanopia that affects most of the upper-right visual quadrant. (C) A smaller lesion of the lower lip of the calcarine fissure results in a smaller injury, a scotoma. (Photographs by Jim Pickerell/Stock Connection/PictureQuest.)

Left visual cortex

(A) Hemianopia

Injury

Left visual field   Right visual field

(B) Quadrantanopia

Injury

(C) Scotoma

Injury

Such tricking can be achieved by placing objects entirely within the scotoma region of the patient's visual field and, without allowing the patient to shift gaze, asking what the object is. If no object is reported, the examiner moves the object out of the scotoma so that it suddenly "appears" in the intact region of the patient's visual field, thus demonstrating the existence of a blind region.

A similar phenomenon can be demonstrated in your own "blind spot," the region in each eye where axons forming the optic nerve leave the eye and there are no photoreceptors. Stand beside a table, close or cover one eye, stare at a spot on the table, and move a pencil along the table laterally, from directly below your nose to between 20 and 30 centimeters toward the periphery. Part of the pencil will vanish when you reach the blind spot. You can move the pencil through the blind spot slowly, and it will suddenly reappear on the other side. Notice that, like a scotoma, the normal blind spot is not noticeable, even when you look around the world with just one eye. Even the normal brain "fills in" missing bits of the visual world.

Disorders of Cortical Function

Research into selective disturbances of human visual functions is limited mainly to case studies, such as that of Colonel P.M., whom you met in the Portrait at the beginning of this chapter, and these natural lesions seldom respect the boundaries of specific visual areas. Several case histories, each with distinctly different symptoms and pathology, will give you an idea of the specific symptoms of injury to the visual cortex. We begin with damage to area V1 and proceed along the hierarchy to higher-order areas and more-complicated visual disturbances.

Case B.K.: V1 Damage and a Scotoma

One morning B.K. awoke to discover that he was hemianopic in the left visual field. Given a history of classic migraine, in which the aura was nearly always in the left visual field, he likely had a migraine stroke. (For a thorough discussion of migraine, see Chapter 26.) Within a few hours, the left lower field began to return, but the left upper quadrant was slow to show any change.

The MRI in **Figure 13.12**A shows a clear **infarct** (dead tissue) in the right occipital area. The size of a visual-field defect is routinely measured with *perimetry*, a standardized method in which the subject fixates on a black dot in the center of a large, white hemisphere. A small light is moved around the field, and the task is to indicate when the light can be seen. The brightness and size of the light can be varied, thus manipulating the difficulty of the task.

Performance is mapped by indicating the area of "blindness" on a schematic map of the visual fields (Figure 13.12B). Size in the visual field is measured by visual angle, in degrees. (A degree is roughly the size of your thumb viewed at arm's length.) Thus, for B.K., the area of complete inability to perceive even a very large bright light is measured from the center, 6° upward along the vertical midline and about 15° laterally along the horizontal midline. The area

Figure **13.12**

Scan of B.K.'s Brain and Map of Visual Fields (A) B.K.'s MRI scan, showing the infarct (the black area) in the right occipital area. (B) Map of B.K.'s visual fields 6 months after the stroke. Subnormal vision persists in the upper-left quadrant. (Part A, Keith Humphrey.)

(A) MRI scan of B.K.'s brain

(B) B.K.'s left and right visual fields

Left eye

Right eye

KEY	
■	Area of scotoma
■	Area of reduced acuity
■	Normal blind spot

beyond this zone in the left upper quadrant does not have normal vision, however, because B.K. is still unable to perceive less-bright lights in this area.

The nature of B.K.'s visual defects can be illustrated best in the context of their poststroke evolution. For the first 2 to 3 days, his visual field appeared dark, much as though a piece of smoked glass were blocking his view of the world beyond. On the fourth day, this darkness had disappeared and was replaced by "visual noise" (a *scintillating scotoma*) throughout much of the field, especially in the area of the scotoma.

Visual noise is best described as being like colored "snow" on a television screen. At about the same time that it appeared, B.K. first perceived movement in the field as a traveling "wave," much like ripples on a pond. There was no perception of form or pattern.

A curious phenomenon was first observed during perimetry testing 4 days after the stroke. If the stimulus light was moved into the blind field, B.K. did not perceive it until it moved into another quadrant. Curiously, however, B.K. immediately became aware (in hindsight) that the light had been present in the blind field and could accurately state where it entered the blind field. In other words, B.K. perceived location without being able to perceive content. Recall that Colonel P.M also experienced this phenomenon, known as **blindsight**.

In the ensuing 4 to 6 months, the area of blindness decreased somewhat and acuity in the periphery improved significantly for B.K. Nonetheless, roughly 20 years later, form vision remains poor in the left upper quadrant, outside the scotoma. The scintillating scotoma is still present, showing little change from the first few days after the stroke.

The visual phenomena observed by B.K. indicate that area V1 (and perhaps area V2) probably has an area of total cell death (the dense scotoma). The presence of poor form vision in the rest of the quadrant may be due to a loss of some but not all neurons in area V1, possibly only those neurons that are especially sensitive to a period of reduced blood flow, or **ischemia**. The poor form vision might also be attributed to the fact that other visual areas, especially area V2, remain intact.

B.K.'s symptoms show that other occipital areas are functional, because he perceives color and motion even without form perception. Thus, B.K. can accurately perceive the color or motion of objects that he cannot identify. Those who are myopic (nearsighted) experience a similar phenomenon: the colors of objects or lights can be perceived, whereas the form is not recognizable. B.K.'s stroke thus indicates the presence of at least four independent visual functions: form (which is absent), as well as color, movement, and location (which are spared).

The loss of one-quarter of the fovea leads B.K. to make a variety of visual errors. Immediately after the stroke, he was able to read only with great difficulty. When we look at a word, the fixation point is in the center of the word; so, for B.K., half of the word is absent. Indeed, he had difficulty finding the edge of the page because it was in the blind field. Normal reading returned as B.K. learned to direct his gaze slightly to the left and upward (probably about 2° in each direction), which allowed words to fall into the normal visual field.

This "recovery" took about 6 weeks. Returning to playing squash and tennis was equally challenging because, when a ball entered the scotoma, it was lost to B.K. Similarly, facial recognition was slower than it had been before the stroke, because the information in the left visual field appears to be particularly important for face recognition.

Case D.B.: V1 Damage and Blindsight

D.B. is one of the most extensively studied people with visual disturbance from an occipital lesion (see the detailed monograph by Weiskrantz). D.B.'s right calcarine fissure was removed surgically to excise an **angioma**, a collection of abnormal blood vessels that results in abnormal blood flow (**Figure 13.13**). D.B. therefore has a hemianopia based on standard perimetry but nevertheless has surprising visual capacities.

When questioned about his vision in the left field, D.B. usually reports that he sees nothing, as did P.M. and B.K. Occasionally, D.B. indicates that he had a "feeling" that a stimulus was "approaching" or was "smooth" or "jagged." But, according to Lawrence Weiskrantz, D.B. always stresses that he "saw" nothing, that typically he is guessing, and that he is at a loss for words to describe any conscious perception.

In contrast, when D.B. was asked to point to locations in the impaired field in which spots of light were turned on briefly, he was surprisingly accurate. His blindsight contrasts with his subjective impression that he saw nothing at all. Furthermore, he appears to be able to discriminate the orientation of lines, which he could not report "seeing." Thus, he can discriminate a 10° difference in orientation (the width of your fist held at arm's length) between two successively presented gratings in his impaired field.

Finally, D.B. can detect some forms of movement. When a vigorously moving stimulus was used, he reported "seeing" something. In this case, he did not report actually seeing a visual stimulus but rather spoke of complex patterns of lines and grids. These patterns may have been something like B.K.'s moving lines. In summary, D.B. has "cortical blindness," or blindsight, in which he reports no conscious awareness of "seeing" but still is able to report the movement and location of objects that he cannot recognize.

Case J.I.: V4 Damage and Loss of Color Vision

Oliver Sacks and Robert Wasserman report the touching story of J.I., an artist who suddenly became color-blind. In 1986, he was in a car accident in which he sustained a concussion. His principal symptoms after the injury were an inability to distinguish any colors whatsoever, but his visual acuity had actually improved. "Within days . . . my vision was that of an eagle—I can see a worm wiggling a block away. The sharpness of focus is incredible."

The effect of losing his color vision, however, was far greater than one would have expected. J.I. could barely stand the pain of living in a world that appeared in shades of gray. He found the changed appearance of people unbearable, because their flesh was an abhorrent gray ("rat colored") to him. He found foods disgusting in their grayish, dead appearance, and he had to close his eyes to eat. He could not even imagine colors any longer. The mental image of a tomato looked as black as its actual appearance to him. Even his dreams, which had once been in vivid colors, were now in black and gray.

Figure 13.13

MRI Scan of Brain Showing an Angioma This scan looks down on the surface of the brain of an 18-year-old woman with an angioma. The abnormal cerebral blood vessels (in white) form a balloonlike structure (the blue area at lower right) that caused an infarct around it in the right occipital cortex. (Simon Fraser/Royal Victoria Infirmary/Newcastle Upon Tyne/Science Photo Library/Photo Researchers.)

Detailed visual testing by Sacks and Wasserman, and later by Zeki, revealed that J.I. was color-blind by the usual definitions, but this color blindness was attributed to specific damage to the occipital cortex. In addition, his acuity did appear to have improved, especially at twilight or at night. Two years after his injury, J.I.'s despair had declined, and he appeared to no longer be able to remember color well.

This failure to remember color is curious, because people who become blind through injury to the eyes or optic nerves do not lose their imagery or memory of color. There is little doubt from J.I.'s case that imagery and memory rely on the operation of at least some cortical structures necessary for the original perception.

Case P.B.: Conscious Color Perception in a Blind Patient

Zeki and his colleagues describe the case of a man who was electrocuted, resulting in cardiac and respiratory arrest. P.B. was resuscitated but had suffered brain ischemia that produced a large area of posterior cortical damage. P.B. was left virtually blind, although he can detect the presence or absence of light. The remarkable visual feature, however, is that P.B.'s capacity to identify and name colors remains intact, as does his ability to name the typical color of imagined objects.

P.B.'s vision is in many ways opposite that of J.I.; the results of fMRI studies show that P.B. has activation in areas V1 and V2 in response to colored stimuli. As we reflect on the visual capacity of P.B., it is hard to imagine a world that is filled with color but no form, almost like an out-of-focus kaleidoscope that changes as we gaze around the world.

Case L.M.: V5 (MT) Damage and the Perception of Movement

Josef Zihl and his colleagues report the case of a 43-year-old woman who had a bilateral posterior injury resulting from a vascular abnormality. Her primary chronic complaint was a loss of movement vision. For example, she had difficulty pouring tea into a cup because the fluid appeared to be frozen. And she could not stop pouring, because she could not see the fluid level in the cup rise.

L.M. found being in a room with other people disturbing because she could not see them moving: they suddenly appeared "here or there," but she did not see them move in between. The results of other tests of visual function appeared essentially normal. She could discriminate colors, recognize objects, and read and write.

Her condition is especially intriguing because we would not believe intuitively that such a syndrome is likely. The loss of color or form vision fits with our everyday experience that people can be color-blind or myopic; loss of the ability to see moving objects is counterintuitive indeed. Case L.M. is important because she shows that the brain must analyze the movement of form separately from the form itself.

More recently, Thomas Schenk and his colleagues also studied L.M. and showed that not only is she unable to perceive movement, she is also unable to intercept moving objects by using her hand. Schenk's group mimicked the findings in L.M. by delivering transcranial magnetic stimulation (TMS) to V5. TMS interfered not only with motion perception but also with interception. The inescapable conclusion is that V5 must play a role in both visual streams, much like V1, but it is a role in motion processing.

Case D.F.: Occipital Damage and Visual Agnosia

Visual agnosia is the term coined by Sigmund Freud for an inability to combine individual visual impressions into complete patterns—thus, the inability to recognize objects or their pictorial representations or the inability to draw or copy them. Goodale and Milner and their colleagues have extensively studied a visual agnosic who suffered carbon monoxide poisoning at age 35, resulting in bilateral damage to the LO region and in the tissue at the junction of the parietal and occipital cortex (see Figure 13.7).

D.F., whom we met earlier in the chapter in considering Goodale and Milner's distinction between the dorsal and the ventral streams, has essentially normal color vision and can see well enough to get about in the world. Her principal deficit is *visual form agnosia*, a severe inability to recognize line drawings of objects. Thus, although D.F. can recognize many actual objects, she is unable to recognize drawings of them. Furthermore, as illustrated in **Figure 13.14**, although she can draw objects from memory, she has difficulty in drawing objects from life and even more difficulty in copying line drawings. Thus, D.F. appears to have a serious defect in form perception.

Recall that the remarkable thing about D.F. is her apparently nearly intact ability to guide hand and finger movements toward objects that she cannot recognize. For example, although D.F. had a gross deficit in judging lines as horizontal or vertical, she could reach out and "post" a hand-held card into a slot rotated to different orientations, as illustrated in **Figure 13.15**. Indeed, analysis of video recordings of D.F.'s reaching reveal that, like normal control subjects, she began to orient the card correctly even as her hand was being raised from the start position of the task. In other words, D.F. could use visual form information to guide movements to objects (the dorsal stream), but she could not use visual information to recognize the same objects (the ventral stream).

Figure **13.14**

Samples of D.F.'s Drawings
(A) Examples of the original drawings presented to D.F.
(B) D.F.'s drawings of the models.
(C) D.F.'s drawings based on memory of the models. Note that the drawings from memory are superior to the copies of the line drawings of the models.

(A) Line-drawing models **(B) Drawn from the models** **(C) Drawn from memory**

Figure **13.15**

Testing Visuomotor Guidance
(A) The apparatus used to test sensitivity to orientation in patient D.F. The task is to "post" the card into the slot as shown. (B) Plots of the card's orientation in a perceptual matching task and in the visuomotor posting task. For illustration, the correct orientation has been rotated to vertical. D.F. was unable to match the orientation of the card to that of the slot unless she made a movement to post it. (Adapted with permission from Goodale, 2000.)

(A)

The slot can be rotated 360° to any position.

(B)

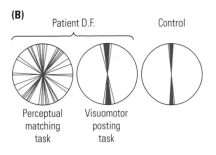

Patient D.F.   Control

Perceptual matching task   Visuomotor posting task

Case V.K.: Parietal Damage and Visuomotor Guidance

Damage to the posterior parietal lobe produces **optic ataxia**, a deficit in visually guided hand movements, such as reaching, that cannot be ascribed to motor, somatosensory, or visual-field or -acuity deficits. V.K. is a woman with bilateral hemorrhages in the occipitoparietal regions, as described by Lorna Jakobson and her colleagues. Although V.K. initially appeared virtually blind, her symptoms dissipated in a month, and she was left with disordered control of her gaze, impairment in visual attention, and optic ataxia. (Collectively, these symptoms are known as *Balint's syndrome*, discussed in Chapter 14.)

V.K. had good form and color vision and could recognize and name objects; however, her ability to reach for objects was grossly impaired. Thus, in contrast with D.F., who was able to reach and orient her hand posture toward different objects that she could not perceive, V.K. was unable to coordinate reaching and grasping for objects that she could perceive.

This difficulty was not merely one of being unable to direct movements in space, because V. K. could point to objects. What she could not do was to form the appropriate hand postures needed to grasp objects of different shapes, as illustrated in **Figure 13.16**. Taken together, cases D.F. and V.K. suggest that the mechanisms underlying the conscious perception of object form are dissociable from the mechanisms controlling visually guided movements to the same objects.

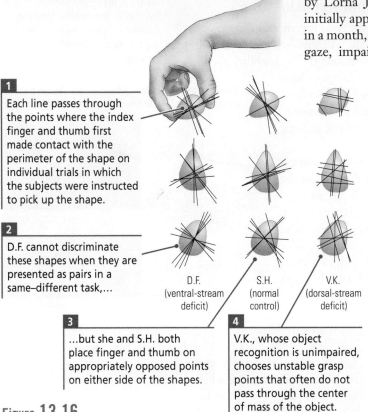

1 Each line passes through the points where the index finger and thumb first made contact with the perimeter of the shape on individual trials in which the subjects were instructed to pick up the shape.

2 D.F. cannot discriminate these shapes when they are presented as pairs in a same–different task,...

D.F.
(ventral-stream deficit)

S.H.
(normal control)

V.K.
(dorsal-stream deficit)

3 ...but she and S.H. both place finger and thumb on appropriately opposed points on either side of the shapes.

4 V.K., whose object recognition is unimpaired, chooses unstable grasp points that often do not pass through the center of mass of the object.

Figure 13.16

Grasp Patterns The brain has different systems for visual object recognition and visual guidance of movement. Representative "grasping" axes for three different shapes by patient D.F. with visual form agnosia (ventral-stream deficit), by control subject S.H. with no brain damage, and by V.K., a patient with bilateral occipitoparietal damage resulting in optic ataxia (dorsal-stream deficit). Even though D.F. does not recognize the object, she perceives enough information about shape to control her grasp as she picks it up. In contrast, V.K. recognizes objects but cannot control her movements in relation to them. (Adapted with permission from Milner and Goodale, 2006.

Cases D. and T.: Higher-Level Visual Processes

Two cases described by Ruth Campbell and her colleagues illustrate an intriguing dissociation of visual functions. D. has a right occipitotemporal lesion associated with a left upper quadrantanopia that extends into the lower quadrant. As would be expected from B.K.'s case, D. had some initial difficulties in reading, but her language abilities were intact. Curiously, she was completely unable to recognize people by their faces and had difficulty in identifying handwriting, including her own.

Recall from the Portrait at the beginning of this chapter that P.M. also had difficulty recognizing faces. His view on his difficulty was that, although he could see the different bits of the face quite clearly, he had trouble putting it all together because, unless a person was a long way off, the entire face was not in his visual field all at once. You can imagine what it would be like to try to recognize people by looking at snapshots of different parts of their faces.

The facial-recognition deficit, **prosopagnosia**, is particularly interesting, because many prosopagnosics cannot recognize even their own faces in a mirror. Although D. could not recognize faces, she could make use of information in faces. For example, when given various tests of lip reading, she appeared completely normal. Furthermore, she could imitate the facial movements and expressions of another person.

Case T. provides an interesting contrast to case D. T. had a left occipitotemporal lesion with a right hemianopia. She had great difficulty reading (**alexia**) and was unable to name colors, even though she could discriminate them. In contrast with D., T. had no difficulty in recognizing familiar faces but was impaired in lip reading.

Taken together, cases D. and T. indicate that identifying faces and extracting speech information from faces do not call on the same cortical systems. In addition, the fact that D. has a lesion on the right and a deficit in face identification and that T. has a lesion on the left and a deficit in lip reading suggests an asymmetry in some aspects of occipital-lobe functions. Exactly what visual processes are impaired in the two cases and what the necessary lesions for deficits in facial recognition and lip reading might be remain to be shown.

Conclusions from Case Studies

Several conclusions can be extracted from the behavior and pathology of the foregoing cases:

- There are clearly distinct syndromes of visual disturbance.

- Some symptoms can be taken as evidence of a fundamental dissociation between vision for guiding movements (the dorsal stream) and visual recognition (the ventral stream).

- The dissociability of the symptoms in the various patients implies that our introspective view of a unified visual experience is false. The fact that objects can be seen when they are still but not when they are moving is particularly disturbing, because it seems to defy the commonsense view that an object is the same object whether it is moving or still. Clearly, the brain does not treat objects in the same way in the two conditions.

- Neuroscientists have at least suggestive evidence of an asymmetry in occipital-lobe functions.

Visual Agnosia

One difficulty in describing the symptomatology and pathology of agnosia is the bewildering variety of patients and symptoms described in the neurological literature. Another, as Martha Farah has pointed out, is that a lack of agreement on a taxonomy of agnosia makes the classification of different patterns of symptoms very difficult. We shall separate visual agnosias into object agnosias and other agnosias.

Object Agnosias

The traditional way to classify visual object agnosia is to distinguish two broad forms: apperceptive agnosia and associative agnosia.

Apperceptive Agnosia

Any failure of object recognition in which basic visual functions (acuity, color, motion) are preserved is **apperceptive**. This agnosia category has been applied to an extremely heterogeneous set of patients, but the fundamental deficit is an inability to develop a percept of the structure of an object or objects. In the simplest case, patients are simply unable to recognize, copy, or match simple shapes, much as in D.F.'s case.

Many patients have another unusual symptom, too, often referred to as **simultagnosia**. In this case, patients can perceive the basic shape of an object, but they are unable to perceive more than one object at a time. Thus, if two objects are presented together, only one is perceived. Such patients often act as though they were blind, possibly because they are simply overwhelmed by the task at hand. Imagine trying to see the world one object at a time.

Apperceptive agnosia does not result from a restricted lesion but usually follows gross bilateral damage to the lateral parts of the occipital lobes, including regions sending outputs to the ventral stream. Such injuries are probably most commonly associated with carbon monoxide poisoning, which appears to produce neuronal death in "watershed" regions—that is, regions lying in the border areas between territories of different arterial systems in the brain (see Figure 3.4).

Associative Agnosia

The inability to recognize an object despite its apparent perception is **associative agnosia**. Thus, the associative agnosic can copy a drawing rather accurately, indicating a coherent percept, but cannot identify it. Associative agnosia is therefore conceived as being at a "higher cognitive" level of processing that is associated with stored information about objects—that is, with memory.

In effect, failure of object recognition is a defect in memory that affects not only past knowledge about the object but also the acquisition of new knowledge. Associative agnosias are more likely with damage to regions in the ventral stream that are farther up the processing hierarchy, such as the anterior temporal lobe.

Other Agnosias

A critical point in understanding the nature of visual agnosia is that the most commonly affected region is the tissue at the occipitotemporal border, which is part of the ventral visual pathway. Visual agnosias do not appear to result from damage to the dorsal stream. Note, however, that agnosias are at least partly dissociable, which means that different streams of visual information processing must flow within the ventral pathway. We now briefly consider three other visual agnosias.

Prosopagnosia

Patients with facial agnosia (recall cases D. and P.M.) cannot recognize any previously known faces, including their own as seen in a mirror or photograph. They can recognize people by face information, however, such as a birthmark, mustache, or characteristic hairdo.

Prosopagnosics may not accept the fact that they cannot recognize their own faces, probably because they know who must be in the mirror and thus see themselves. We saw one young woman who was convinced of the severity of her problem only when she was presented with her identical twin sister. When asked who her twin was, she indicated that she had never seen the woman before. Imagine her amazement to discover that the person was her twin.

According to Antonio Damasio and his colleagues, most facial agnosics can tell human from nonhuman faces and can recognize facial expressions normally. All postmortem studies on facial agnosics have found bilateral damage, and the results of imaging studies in living patients confirm the bilateral nature of the injury in most patients, with the damage centered in the region below the calcarine fissure at the temporal junction. These results imply that the process of facial recognition is probably bilateral, but asymmetrical.

Alexia

An inability to read has often been regarded as a symptom complementary to facial-recognition deficits. Alexia is most likely to result from damage to the left fusiform and lingual areas (see Figure 13.1). Either hemisphere can read letters, but only the left hemisphere appears able to combine the letters to form words. Alexia can be conceived to be a form of object agnosia in which there is an inability to construct perceptual wholes from parts or to be a form of associative agnosia, in which case word memory (the lexical store) is either damaged or inaccessible.

Visuospatial Agnosia

Among this variety of disorders of spatial perception and orientation, one disruptive form is *topographical disorientation*—the inability to find one's way around familiar environments such as one's neighborhood. People with this deficit seem unable to recognize landmarks that would indicate the appropriate direction in which to travel. Most people with topographical disorientation have other visual deficits, especially defects in facial recognition. Thus, it is not surprising to find that the critical area for this disorder lies in the right medial occipitotemporal region, including the fusiform and lingual gyri.

Visual Imagery

Our ability to conjure up mental images of things that cannot be perceived is central to human thought. Visualization is crucial in problem-solving tasks such as mental arithmetic, map reading, and mechanical reasoning. How crucial can be seen in a patient such as D.F., who was unable to copy drawings or to recognize actual objects but who could nonetheless produce drawings of the same objects from memory (see Figure 13.14).

Marlene Behrmann and her colleagues described another such patient, C.K. The curious thing about C.K. is that, although he cannot recognize objects, he can imagine them and can draw them in considerable detail from memory. This ability implies some dissociation between the neural system dealing with object

SNAPSHOT

Generating Mental Images

What is the neural basis for visual imagery? It may result from activity in the same visual areas as those active when an image is actually viewed. Another possibility is that some other region of the brain is selectively active when we use our imagination.

Mark D'Esposito and his colleagues addressed this question in an fMRI study by asking subjects to generate mental images from memory, cued by an aurally presented word such as "tree." These cues were common objects rather than abstract representations ("tree" rather than "love," for example).

The subjects kept their eyes closed throughout the experiment so that any neural activation could be attributed to imagery rather than to direct activation of the visual pathways. In the baseline condition, the subjects heard abstract words that would not easily allow visualization, and they were asked simply to listen to the words.

Left temporal-occipital region
(fusiform gyrus, area 37)

The results, illustrated here, show that visualizing concrete words increases activation in the left posterior temporal-occipital region, corresponding to the fusiform gyrus (area 37). There was no activation in area V1.

The fMRI data are consistent with those of other imaging studies, as well as with a case history of a patient with a left-occipital lobectomy (including area 37) who had a hemianopia in both real and imagined stimuli. The pronounced asymmetry is consistent with Farah's hypothesis that, in most people, the left hemisphere is specialized for image generation.

D'Esposito, M., J. A. Detre, G. K. Aguirre, M. Stallcup, D. C. Alsop, L. J. Tippet, and M. J. Farah. A functional MRI study of mental image generation. *Neuropsychologia* 35:725–730, 1997.

perception and that dealing with the generation of images. We can conclude that neural structures mediating the perception and visualization of objects are unlikely to be completely independent, but a deficit in object perception clearly cannot be due simply to a loss of mental representations (that is, memory) of objects.

Whether the mental rotation of objects might be localized to some region of the right hemisphere is controversial. In her review of the literature on this subject, Farah concludes that the studies have been "distressingly inconsistent." She proposes that mental rotation probably entails both hemispheres, with some degree of right-hemisphere superiority. (For more detail, see both Farah, 2000, and Kosslyn and Thompson.)

Nonetheless, mental rotation likely implicates structures related to the dorsal stream. We can imagine that, before a brain can visualize rotating an object, it first has to have actually rotated it manually. It is a small step to presume that visualizing an object rotating requires the activation of at least part of the motor cortex—the regions needed to actually do it.

In the past two decades, cognitive neuroscientists have conducted a flurry of imaging studies designed to identify the neural events underlying the generation of a mental image. Farah concludes that, although the data are noisy, a reasonably consistent answer is emerging from the results of imaging studies such as the one described in the Snapshot. Mental imagery appears to be a top-down activation of a subset of the brain's visual areas. In other words, at least some cortical areas are used both for perception and for visualization.

These common areas carry the same representational functions for both purposes, carrying information specifically about color, shape, spatial location, and so on. There is evidence for a distinct mechanism for image generation as well, one separate from the processes needed for perception. Farah notes that the evidence, although mixed, points to a region in the left temporal-occipital region as the key location for this mechanism.

Summary

The function of the occipital lobe is vision, but visual functions extend beyond the occipital lobe. We consider further aspects of visual functions in Chapters 14 and 15, which explore the parietal and temporal lobes.

Anatomy of the Occipital Lobes
Separate anatomical regions within the occipital lobe take part in the perception of form, movement, and color. Occipital structures are merely the beginning of visual processing, because multiple visual systems can be divided into at least three major routes, one going ventrally into the temporal lobe, another going dorsally into the parietal lobe, and a middle route going to the superior temporal sulcus.

The ventral stream is most certainly implicated in various aspects of stimulus recognition. The dorsal stream is for the guidance of movement in space. The middle route is likely a part of the ventral stream that processes biological motion.

A Theory of Occipital-Lobe Function
The representation of spatial information relies on recognizing cues within the environment, which would therefore make visuospatial recognition dependent on processing in the ventral stream. An important aspect of the dorsal–ventral distinction in visual processing is that neither route is a single system. Rather, clearly dissociable subsystems take part in various functions. Finally, some occipital regions, especially those adjoining the temporal cortex, may be functionally asymmetrical. In particular, there appears to be some specialization for word recognition on the left and facial recognition and mental rotation on the right.

Disorders of Visual Pathways
Visual dysfunction can result from injury anywhere from the retina to the cortex. Damage to the retina or the axons of the retinal ganglion cells forming the optic nerve produce deficits that are specific to one eye. Once the optic nerves enter the brain and the information from the two eyes merges, disorders of vision affect information from both eyes and are related to a visual field rather than an eye.

Disorders of Cortical Function
Damage to the occipital cortex can produce a variety of deficits ranging from blindness in all or part of a visual field to specific deficits in the perception of color, form, and movement.

Visual Agnosia
Visual agnosia is a loss of knowledge about visual information. Although visual agnosias may result from damage to either the occipital or the temporal lobe, they have different characteristics. The most common form of visual agnosia from damage to the lateral occipital region is object agnosia, which is an inability to develop a percept about the structure of an object.

Visual Imagery
Humans are capable of conjuring up mental images of things that are not physically present. Although there is some dissociation between structures taking part in imagining versus perceiving visual information, there must be some overlap as well. Neuropsychologists still do not have a clear understanding of precisely how the systems interrelate.

References

Andrews, T. J., D. Schluppeck, D. Homfray, P. Matthews, and C. Blakemore. Activity in the fusiform gyrus predicts conscious perception of Rubin's vase–face illusion. *Neuroimage* 17:890–901, 2002.

Barbur, J. L., J. D. G. Watson, R. S. J. Frackowiak, and S. Zeki. Conscious visual perception without V1. *Brain* 116:1293–1302, 1993.

Behrmann, M., G. Winocur, and M. Moscovitch. Dissociation between mental imagery and object recognition in a brain-damaged patient. *Nature* 359:636–637, 1992.

Boussaud, D., L. G. Ungerleider, and R. Desimone. Pathways for motion analysis: Cortical connections of the medial superior temporal and fundus of the superior temporal visual areas in the macaque. *Journal of Comparative Neurology* 296:462–495, 1990.

Campbell, R., T. Landis, and M. Regard. Face recognition and lip reading: A neurological dissociation. *Brain* 109:509–521, 1986.

Clarke, S., and J. Miklossy. Occipital cortex in man: Organization of callosal connections, related myelo- and cytoarchitecture, and putative boundaries of functional visual areas. *Journal of Comparative Neurology* 298:188–214, 1990.

Curtis, B. Visual system. In B. A. Curtis, S. Jacobson, and E. M. Marcus, Eds. *An Introduction to the Neurosciences.* Philadelphia and Toronto: Saunders, 1972.

Damasio, A. R., H. Damasio, and G. W. Van Hoesen. Prosopagnosia: Anatomical basis and behavioral mechanisms. *Neurology* 32:331–341, 1982.

Damasio, A. R., D. Tranel, and H. Damasio. Disorders of visual recognition. In F. Boller and J. Grafman, Eds. *Handbook of Neuropsychology*, vol. 2. Amsterdam: Elsevier, 1989.

Diamond, R., and S. Carey. Why faces are and are not special: An effect of expertise. *Journal of Experimental Psychology: General* 15:107–117, 1986.

Farah, M. J. *Visual Agnosia.* Cambridge, Mass.: MIT Press, 1990.

Farah, M. J. What is "special" about face perception? *Psychological Review* 105:482–498, 1998.

Farah, M. J. The neural basis of mental imagery. In M. S. Gazzaniga, Ed. *The New Cognitive Neurosciences*, 2nd ed. Cambridge, Mass.: MIT Press, 2000, pp. 965–974.

Felleman, D. J., and D. C. van Essen. Distributed hierarchical processing in primate cerebral cortex. *Cerebral Cortex* 1:1–47, 1991.

Goodale, M. A. Visual pathways supporting perception and action in the primate cerebral cortex. *Current Opinion in Neurobiology* 3:578–585, 1993.

Goodale, M. A. Perception and action in the human visual system. In M. Gazzaniga, Ed. *The New Cognitive Neurosciences.* Cambridge, Mass.: MIT Press, 2000, pp. 365–377.

Goodale, M. A., D. A. Milner, L. S. Jakobson, and J. D. P. Carey. A neurological dissociation between perceiving objects and grasping them. *Nature* 349:154–156, 1991.

Hancock, P. J. B., V. Bruce, and A. M. Burton. Recognition of unfamiliar faces. *Trends in Cognitive Sciences* 4:330–337, 2000.

Haxby, J. V., E. A. Hoffman, and M. I. Gobbini. The distributed human neural system for face perception. *Trends in Cognitive Science* 4:223–233, 2000.

Haxby, J. V., L. G. Ungerleider, V. P. Clark, J. L. Schouten, E. A. Hoffman, and A. Martin. The effect of face inversion on activity in human neural systems for face and object perception. *Neuron* 22:189–199, 1999.

Jakobson, L. S., Y. M. Archibald, D. P. Carey, and M. A. Goodale. A kinematic analysis of reaching and grasping movements in a patient recovering from optic ataxia. *Neuropsychologia* 29:803–809, 1991.

Kingdom, F., H.-C. O. Li, and E. J. MacAulay. The role of chromatic contrast and luminance polarity in stereoscopic segmentation. *Vision Research* 41:375–383, 2001.

Kolb, B., B. Milner, and L. Taylor. Perception of faces by patients with localized cortical excisions. *Canadian Journal of Psychology* 37:8–18, 1983.

Kosslyn, S. M., and W. L. Thompson. Shared mechanisms in visual imagery and visual perception: Insights from cognitive neuroscience. In M. Gazzaniga, Ed. *The New Cognitive Neurosciences.* Cambridge, Mass.: MIT Press, 2000, pp. 975–986.

Luria, A. R. *The Working Brain.* New York: Penguin, 1973.

Meadows, J. C. Disturbed perception of colors associated with localized cerebral lesions. *Brain* 97:615–632, 1974.

Milner, A. D., and M. A. Goodale. *The Visual Brain in Action*, 2nd ed. Oxford: Oxford University Press, 2006.

Previc, F. H. Functional specialization in the lower and upper visual fields in humans: Its ecological origins and neurophysiological implications. *Behavioral and Brain Sciences* 13:519–575, 1990.

Rizzolatti, G., and M. Matelli. Two different streams form the dorsal visual system: Anatomy and function. *Experimental Brain Research* 153:146–157.

Sacks, O., and R. Wasserman. The case of the colorblind painter. *New York Review of Books* 34:25–33, 1987.

Schenk, T., A. Ellison, N. J. Rice, and A. D. Milner. The role of V5/MT+ in the control of catching movements: An rTMS study. *Neuropsychologia* 43:189–198, 2005.

Schenk, T., N. Mai, J. Ditterich, and J. Zihl. Can a motion-blind patient reach for moving objects? *European Journal of Neuroscience* 12:3351–3360, 2000.

Servos, P., M. A. Goodale, and G. K. Humphrey. The drawing of objects by a visual form agnosic: Contribution of surface properties and memorial representations. *Neuropsychologia* 31:251–259, 1993.

Sumner, P., and J. D. Mollon. Catarrhine photopigments are optimized for detecting targets against a foliage background. *Journal of Experimental Biology* 203:1963–1986, 2000.

Tanaka, J., D. Weiskopf, and P. Williams. The role of color in high-level vision. *Trends in Cognitive Sciences* 5:211–215, 2001.

Tootell, R. B. H., and N. Hadjikhani. Where is "dorsal V4" in human visual cortex? Retinotopic, topographic and functional evidence. *Cerebral Cortex* 11:298–311, 2001.

Tootell, R. B. H., D. Tsao, and W. Vanduffel. Neuroimaging weights in: Humans meet macaques in "primate" visual cortex. *Journal of Neuroscience* 23:3981–3989, 2003.

Ungerleider, L. G., and J. V. Haxby. "What" and "where" in the human brain. *Current Opinion in Neurobiology* 4:15–165, 1994.

Valentine, T. Upside-down faces: A review of the effect of inversion upon face recognition. *British Journal of Psychology* 79:471–491, 1988.

Weiskrantz, L. *Blindsight: A Case History and Implications.* Oxford: Oxford University Press, 1986.

Zeki, S. *A Vision of the Brain.* Oxford: Blackwell, 1993.

Zeki, S., S. Aglioti, D. McKeefry, and G. Berlucchi. The neurological basis of conscious color perception in a blind patient. *Proceedings of the National Academy of Sciences of the United States of America* 96:14124–14129, 1999.

Zihl, J., D. von Cramon, and N. Mai. Selective disturbance of movement vision after bilateral brain damage. *Brain* 106:313–340, 1983.

14 The Parietal Lobes

Portrait: **Varieties of Spatial Information**

H.P., a 28-year-old account-ant, was planning his wedding with his fiancée when she noticed that he was making addition errors as he calcu-lated the budget for their re-ception. At first, they joked about it, especially given his occupation, but in the follow-ing weeks H.P.'s problem with numbers became serious. In fact, he was no longer able to perform a simple subtraction, such as 30 minus 19, in which the solution requires "bor-rowing" 10 when subtracting 9 from 0.

At first, H.P. simply put it down to working too hard, but soon he began

to have trouble reaching for objects. He was constantly knocking over his water glass, because his reach was clumsy and misdirected. Simple ma-nipulations, such as playing with the Rubic's cube puzzle pictured here,

would have become difficult if not impossible for H.P. He began confusing left and right and having difficulties reading. Some of the words appeared backward or upside down to him, and he could not make sense of them.

Finally, when H.P. visited a neurologist for testing, it was obvious that something was seriously wrong. Indeed, something was: he had a fast-growing tumor in his left parietal lobe. Unfortunately, the tumor was extremely virulent and, within a couple of months, H.P. died.

The parietal cortex processes and integrates somatosensory and visual in-formation, especially with regard to the control of movement. In this chapter, we first describe the anatomy of the parietal lobes and then pres-ent a theoretical model of parietal-lobe organization. Next, we consider the major somatosensory symptoms of parietal injury, survey the most commonly observed disorders of the posterior parietal region, and conclude the chapter with a survey of behavioral tests that reliably predict brain injury.

Anatomy of the Parietal Lobes

H.P.'s symptoms described in the portrait at the beginning of this chapter are typical of left parietal injury and illustrative of the curious pattern of symptoms that have proved a challenge for neuropsychologists to understand. Part of the challenge is that these symptoms are difficult to demonstrate in animals. Common laboratory animals such as rats and cats have very modest parietal "lobes," and, although monkeys with parietal damage show many symptoms similar to those seen in human patients, symptoms related to language or cognition are difficult to study in monkeys. Furthermore, the parietal lobes in the human brain have evolved to a much larger size, which might imply that humans will show some symptoms not seen in monkeys.

Subdivisions of the Parietal Cortex

The parietal region of the cerebral cortex lies between the frontal and the occipital lobes, underlying the parietal bone at the roof of the skull. This area is roughly demarcated anteriorly by the central fissure, ventrally by the lateral (Sylvian) fissure, dorsally by the cingulate gyrus, and posteriorly by the parietal-occipital sulcus. The principal regions of the parietal lobe, mapped in **Figure 14.1**A and B, include the postcentral gyrus (Brodmann's areas 1, 2, and 3), the superior parietal lobule (areas 5 and 7), the parietal operculum (area 43), the supramarginal gyrus (area 40), and the angular gyrus (area 39).

Together, the supramarginal gyrus and angular gyrus are often referred to as the *inferior parietal lobe*. The parietal lobe can be divided into two functional zones: an anterior zone including areas 1, 2, 3, and 43; and a posterior zone, which includes the remaining areas. The anterior zone is the somatosensory cortex; the posterior zone is referred to as the **posterior parietal cortex**.

The parietal lobes have undergone a major expansion in the course of human evolution, largely in the inferior parietal region. This increase in size has made comparisons of various areas in the human brain with those in the monkey brain confusing, especially because Brodmann did not identify areas 39 and 40 in the monkey. Whether monkeys actually have regions homologous to areas 39 and 40 is debatable. One solution to this problem is to consult another anatomist, Constantin von Economo.

On von Economo's maps, in which parietal areas are called PA (parietal area A), PB, and so forth, are three posterior parietal areas (PE, PF, PG) that von Economo described in both humans and monkeys (Figure 14.1C). If we use this system, area PF is equivalent to area 7b and PE to area 5 in Felleman and van Essen's flat map of cortical areas in the macaque (see Figure 10.18). Similarly, area PG in the monkey includes areas 7a, VIP, LIP, IPG, PP, MSTc, and MSTp. These PG areas are primarily visual (see Chapter 15).

An area of significant expansion in the human brain appears to consist of the polymodal parts of area PG and the adjoining polymodal cortex in the superior temporal sulcus (STS). (Recall from Chapters 10 and 13 that polymodal cells receive inputs from more than one sensory modality.) Those in PG respond to both somatosensory and visual inputs, whereas those in the STS (the third visual pathway discussed in Chapter 13) respond to various combinations of auditory, visual, and somatosensory inputs.

The increase in the size of area PG and the superior temporal sulcus is especially interesting because this region is anatomically asymmetrical in the human brain (see Figure 11.1). This asymmetry may be due to a much larger area PG (and possibly STS) on the right than on the left. If PG has a visual function and is larger in humans, especially in the right hemisphere, then we might expect unique visual symptoms after right parietal lesions, which is indeed the case. Note, however, that PG is also larger on the left in the human

(A) Major parietal lobe gyri and sulci

(B) Brodmann's cytoarchitectonic regions

(C) von Economo's cytoarchitectonic regions

Figure 14.1

Gross Anatomy of the Parietal Lobe

Figure 14.2

Parietal Areas of the Dorsal Stream Homologous regions in the monkey (A) and human (B) that contribute to saccadic eye movement (area LIP), visual control of grasping (area AIP), and visually guided grasping (area PRR). (Part A: Reproduced with permission from Y. F. Cohen and R. A. Andersen. A common reference frame for movement plans in the posterior parietal cortex. *Nature Reviews Neuroscience* 3:553–562, 2002; part B: A. D. Milner and M. A. Goodale. *The Visual Brain in Action,* 2nd ed. New York: Oxford University Press, 2006.)

than in the monkey, which would lead us to expect humans to have unique deficits after left-hemisphere lesions. This outcome, too, is the case.

Specific parietal-lobe regions take part in the dorsal stream of visual processing (see Table 13.1). In particular, we have identified the intraparietal sulcus (cIPS) and the parietal reach regions (PRR), illustrated in the monkey and human in **Figure 14.2**. The monkey regions in Figure 14.2A were mapped by using single-neuron recording techniques, whereas the human regions in Figure 14.2B have been defined by fMRI. The regions in the intraparietal sulcus contribute to the control of saccadic eye movements (area LIP) and the visual control of object-directed grasping (AIP), whereas the PRR has a role in visually guided grasping movements. (As discussed in detail later, a **saccade** is a series of involuntary, abrupt, and rapid small movements or jerks made by both eyes simultaneously in changing the point of fixation.)

Connections of the Parietal Cortex

The anterior parietal cortex has rather straightforward connections, which are illustrated in Felleman and van Essen's hierarchy (see Figure 10.19). There are projections from the primary somatosensory cortex (area 3-1-2) to area PE (area 5), which has a tactile recognition function, as well as to motor areas, including the primary motor cortex (area 4) and the supplementary motor and premotor regions (area 6). The motor connections must be important for providing sensory information about limb position in the control of movement (see Chapter 9).

Although more than 100 inputs and outputs of areas 5 and 7 in the monkey (PE, PF, and PG) have been described (see Figure 10.19), a few basic principles will summarize the connections diagrammed in **Figure 14.3**:

1. Area PE (Brodmann's area 5) is basically a somatosensory area, receiving most of its connections from the primary somatosensory cortex (areas 1, 2, and 3). Its cortical outputs are to the primary motor cortex (area 4) and to the supplementary motor (SMA) and premotor (6 and 8) regions, as well as to PF. Area PE therefore plays some role in guiding movement by providing information about limb position.

2. Area PF (area 7b) has a heavy input from the primary somatosensory cortex (areas 1, 2, and 3) through area PE. It also receives inputs from the motor and premotor cortex and a small visual input through area PG. Its efferent connections are similar to those of area PE, and these connections

presumably provide some elaboration of similar information for the motor systems.

3. Area PG (area 7b and visual areas) receives more-complex connections including visual, somesthetic (skin sensations), proprioceptive (internal stimuli), auditory, vestibular (balance), oculomotor (eye movement), and cingulate (motivational?). MacDonald Critchley described area PG as the "parieto-temporo-occipital crossroads," which is apparent from the connectivity. Its function likely corresponds to this intermodal mixing. Area PG, which is part of the dorsal stream, is assumed to have a role in controlling spatially guided behavior with respect to visual and tactile information.

4. There is a close relation between the posterior parietal connections and the prefrontal cortex (especially area 46). Thus, there are connections between the posterior parietal cortex (PG and PF) and the dorsolateral prefrontal region. Additionally, both the prefrontal and the posterior parietal regions project to the same areas of the paralimbic cortex and the temporal cortex as well as to the hippocampus and various subcortical regions. These connections emphasize a close functional relation between the prefrontal cortex and the parietal cortex. This relation probably has an important role in the control of spatially guided behavior.

A Theory of Parietal-Lobe Function

If we consider the anterior (somatosensory) and posterior parietal zones as functionally distinct regions, we can identify two independent contributions of the parietal lobes. The anterior zone processes somatic sensations and perceptions; the posterior zone is specialized primarily for integrating sensory input from the somatic and visual regions and, to a lesser extent, from other sensory regions, mostly for the control of movement. The anterior zone's somatosensory functions were discussed in Chapter 8; we are concerned here mostly with the functions of the posterior parietal zone.

Imagine that you are having dinner with a friend in a restaurant. You are confronted with a set of cutlery, some dishes, a basket of bread, a glass of water, perhaps a glass of wine or a cup of coffee, a napkin, and, of course, your companion. Seemingly without effort, you select various utensils and foods as you chat with your friend.

If we analyze what is required to do all these things, however, we see that your brain is faced with several complex tasks. For example, you must reach and correctly grasp a glass or cup or fork or piece of bread. Each of those movements is directed toward a different place and requires a different hand posture or limb movement or both. Your eyes and head must be directed toward various places in space, and you must coordinate the movements of your limbs and your head to get food to your mouth.

Furthermore, you must attend to certain objects and ignore others. (You do not take your companion's fork or wine, for example.) You also must attend to

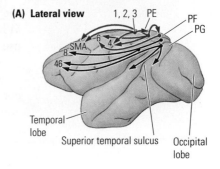

(A) Lateral view

Temporal lobe — Superior temporal sulcus — Occipital lobe

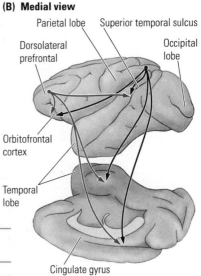

(B) Medial view

Parietal lobe — Superior temporal sulcus

Dorsolateral prefrontal — Occipital lobe

Orbitofrontal cortex

Temporal lobe

Cingulate gyrus

Figure 14.3

Connections of the Monkey's Parietal Lobe (A) Major cortical–cortical projections of the parietal lobe. (B) Posterior parietal and dorsolateral prefrontal projections to cingulate, orbitofrontal, and temporal regions.

the conversation with your friend and ignore other conversations around you. When you eat items from your plate, you must choose which one you want to use and select the correct utensil. It would be inappropriate to try to eat your peas by using a knife.

You must also make movements in the correct order. For example, you must cut your food before picking it up. Similarly, when you choose a bit of bread you must pick up a knife, get some butter, place the butter on the bread, and then eat the bread.

As we think about how the brain can manage these tasks, some sort of internal representation of the location of different objects around us seems obvious— a sort of map in the brain of where things are. Furthermore, we assume that the map must be common to all our senses, because we can move without apparent effort from visual to auditory to tactile information. On the basis of clinical observations of patients with parietal injury, it has been widely believed for more than 60 years that the parietal lobe plays a central role in the creation of this brain map. But what is the map?

The commonly held introspective view is that real space must be mapped topographically because that is how it appears to us. That is, we take it for granted that the world around us is as we perceive it and, thus, that the brain must employ some sort of unified spatial map. (This view is a form of the binding problem discussed in Chapter 10.)

Unfortunately, very little evidence supports the existence of such a map in the brain. Likely, rather than a single map, there are a series of representations of space that vary in two ways. First, different representations are used for different behavioral needs. Second, representations of space vary from simple ones, which are applicable to the control of simple movements, to abstract ones, which may represent information such as topographic knowledge. We consider each of these aspects of brain maps in turn.

Uses of Spatial Information

David Milner and Melvin Goodale emphasize that spatial information about the location of objects in the world is needed both to direct actions at those objects and to assign meaning and significance to them. In this sense, spatial information is simply another property of visual information, much like form, motion, and color. However, just as form is coded in more than one way in visual processing, so is spatial information. The critical factor for both form and space is how the information is to be used.

Recall that form recognition is of two basic types: one is for object recognition and the other is for guiding movements. Spatial information can be thought of in the same way.

Object Recognition

The spatial information needed to determine the relations between objects, independent of what the subject's behavior might be, is very different from the spatial information needed to guide eye, head, or limb movements to objects. In the latter case, the visuomotor control must be viewer-centered; that is, the location of an object and its local orientation and motion must be determined relative to the viewer. Furthermore, because the eyes, head, limbs, and body are constantly moving, computations about orientation, motion, and location must take place every time we wish to undertake an action. Details of object characteristics, such as color, are irrelevant to visuomotor guidance of the viewer-centered movements; that is, a detailed visual representation is not needed to guide hand action.

Milner suggests that the brain operates on a "need to know" basis. Having too much information may be counterproductive for any given system. In contrast with the viewer-centered system, the object-centered system must be concerned with such properties of objects as size, shape, color, and relative location so that the objects can be recognized when they are encountered in different visual contexts or from different vantage points. In this case, the details of the objects themselves (color, shape) are important. Knowing where the red cup is relative to the green one requires identifying each cup.

The temporal lobe codes relational properties of objects. Part of this control is probably in the polymodal region of the superior temporal sulcus, and another part is in the hippocampal formation. We return to the role of the temporal cortex in Chapter 15.

Guidance of Movement

The posterior parietal cortex has a role in the viewer-centered system. To accommodate the many different types of viewer-centered movements (eyes, head, limbs, body, and combinations of them) requires separate control systems. Consider, for example, that the control of the eyes is based on the optical axis of the eye, whereas the control of the limbs is probably based on the positions of the shoulders and hips. These examples are very different types of movements.

We have considered many visual areas in the posterior parietal region and multiple projections from the posterior parietal regions to the motor structures for the eyes (frontal eye fields, area 8) and limbs (premotor and supplementary motor). There also are connections to the prefrontal region (area 46) that have a role in short-term memory of the location of events in space (see Figure 14.3).

The role of the posterior parietal region in visuomotor guidance is confirmed by the results of single-cell studies in the posterior parietal lobes of monkeys. The activity of these neurons depends on the concurrent behavior of an animal with respect to visual stimulation. In fact, most neurons in the posterior parietal region are active both during sensory input and during movement. For example, some cells show only weak responses to stationary visual stimuli but, if the animal makes an active eye or arm movement toward the stimulus or even if it just shifts its attention to the object, the discharge of these cells is strongly enhanced.

Some cells are active when a monkey manipulates an object and respond to the structural features of the object, such as size and orientation, as well. That is, the neurons are sensitive to the features of an object that determine the posture of the hand during manipulation.

A characteristic common to all the posterior parietal neurons is their responsiveness to movements of the eyes and to the location of the eye in its socket. When cells are stimulated at the optimum spot in their receptive fields, they discharge at the highest rate when the eyes are in a particular position. This discharge appears to signal the size of the saccade necessary to move the visual target to the fovea of the retina.

In other words, these cells detect visual information and then move the eye to get the fine vision of the fovea to examine it. A curious aspect of many posterior parietal eye-movement cells is that they are particularly responsive to behaviorally relevant visual stimuli, such as a cue signaling the availability of a reward. This responsiveness has been interpreted to suggest that these cells are affected by the "motivational" characteristics of information.

John Stein summarized the responses of posterior parietal neurons by emphasizing that they all have two important characteristics in common. First, they receive combinations of sensory, motivational, and related motor inputs. Second, their discharge is enhanced when an animal attends to a target or makes a movement toward it. These neurons are therefore well suited to transforming the necessary sensory information into commands for directing attention and guiding motor output.

Although the activity of single cells in the human posterior parietal region cannot be studied, event-related potentials (ERPs) in response to visual stimuli can be recorded (see Figure 6.8). Thus, when a stimulus is presented in one visual field, activation would be expected in the opposite hemisphere, which receives information from the contralateral visual field. Stephen Hillyard showed that, when a visual stimulus is presented, there is a large negative wave from about 100 to 200 ms later in the posterior parietal region. The wave is larger than that seen in the occipital cortex and is largest in the hemisphere contralateral to the stimulus.

Two interesting characteristics of these waves are reminiscent of neurons in monkeys. First, if a subject is asked to pay attention to a particular spot in one visual field, the ERP is largest when the stimulus is presented there rather than elsewhere. Second, there is a large parietal response between 100 and 200 ms before eye movements. Per Roland also showed that, when subjects direct their attention to visual targets, blood flow increases preferentially in the posterior parietal region.

Taken together, the results of electrophysiological and blood-flow studies in monkeys and humans support the general idea that the posterior parietal region plays a significant role in directing movements in space and in detecting stimuli in space. We can predict, therefore, that posterior parietal lesions impair the guidance of movements (much as in H.P.'s case presented in the Portrait at the beginning of this chapter) and, perhaps, the detection of sensory events.

The role of the superior parietal cortex in the control of eye movements has important implications for PET studies of visual processing. Recall from Chapter 13 that James Haxby and his colleagues found an increase in blood flow in the posterior parietal cortex when subjects identified different spatial locations. This finding was taken as evidence that the dorsal stream of processing deals with "spatial processing."

A difficulty with this interpretation, however, is that, when people solve spatial tasks, they move their eyes. The increased PET activation, therefore, could be due to the movement of the eyes rather than to processing the location of the target in space. Indeed, when people solve problems in which they must rotate objects mentally, they move their eyes back and forth. These saccades may indicate the ongoing activity of parietal circuits, but they also present a problem for PET studies: the construction of experimental designs in brain-imaging studies presents a practical difficulty.

Sensorimotor Transformation

When we move toward objects, we must integrate the movements of different body parts (eyes, body, arm, and so forth) with the sensory feedback of what movements are actually being made (the *efference copy*) and the plans to make the movements. As we move, the locations of our body parts change and must constantly be updated so that we can make future movements smoothly. These neural calculations are called **sensorimotor transformation**. Cells in the posterior parietal cortex produce both the movement-related and the sensory-related signals to make these transformations.

Another aspect of sensorimotor transformation is movement planning. Although less is known about the role of the parietal cortex in planning, Richard Andersen and his colleagues have shown that area PRR is active when a subject is preparing and executing a movement (see Figure 14.2). Importantly, PRR is coding not the limb variables required to make the movement but rather the desired goal of the movement. Thus, the goal of grasping a cup, for example, is coded rather than the details of the movements toward the cup.

Andersen's group devised novel experiments with monkeys in which they decoded from neural activity the animals' intentions to reach to position a cursor on a screen, as illustrated in **Figure 14.4**. Monkeys first were trained to make a series of reaches to touch different locations on a computer screen (Figure 14.4A). The cell activity was analyzed to determine which activity was associated with movement to each location. The monkeys then were instructed with a briefly flashed cue to plan to execute a reach to different locations but without making a movement.

The cellular activity was compared with activity associated with actual movements to the requested target, and, if it was the same as in an actual movement, the monkeys were rewarded with a drop of juice in the mouth and a visual feedback showing the correct location (Figure 14.4B). The authors had to use this approach because they could not simply say to the monkeys "think about reaching to the target." Rather, they had to devise a way for the monkeys to show that they were thinking about reaching to target.

This type of study is potentially very important, because it means that paralyzed people can use mental activity to move prosthetics. In principle, an array of electrodes could be implanted over the PRR, and the recorded activity could be used to move the mechanical devices. The implications of such advances go well beyond limb movements. Implants over speech areas might allow a verbal readout of thoughts, thus bypassing cumbersome letter boards and spelling

(A) Reach trial   **(B) Brain-control trial**

Cue

Memory

Decode

Go

Feedback

Reach

Figure **14.4**

Moving with the Mind

(A) Monkeys are trained to touch a small central green cue and to look at a red fixation point. A large green cue is flashed, and the monkeys are rewarded if they reach to the target after a 1500-ms memory period. (B) Monkeys are rewarded if their brain activity indicates that they are preparing to move to the correct target location. (After Andersen et al., 2004, p. 487.)

programs. Similarly, one could ask patients questions and have the them move a cursor to identify the correct answers, thus gaining access to a wide variety of their thoughts and even emotions.

Spatial Navigation

When we travel in the real world, we can take the correct route subconsciously, making the correct turns at choice points until we reach our destination. To do so, we must have some type of "cognitive spatial map" in our brains, as well as a mental list of what we do at each spatial location. The internal list is sometimes referred to as "route knowledge."

This route knowledge is unlikely to be located in a single place in the brain. Findings from both lesion and neuroimaging studies in humans suggest that the medial parietal region (MPR), which includes the parietal region ventral to the PRR in Figure 14.2B as well as the adjacent posterior cingulate cortex (see Figure 21.2), takes part. Neurons in the dorsal visual stream could be expected to participate in route knowledge, insofar as we must make specific visually guided movements at specific locations in our journey. To explore this idea, Nobuya Sato and colleagues trained monkeys to perform a navigation task in a virtual environment.

Three-quarters of the cells in the MPR showed responses associated with a specific movement at a specific location. The same movement in a different location did not activate the cells. Thus, like the cells in PRR that control the planning of limb movements to locations, the cells in MPR contol only body movements to specific locations. When the authors inactivated the MPR pharmacologically, the monkeys became lost and failed to navigate correctly. Thus, the monkeys acted like human patients with medial parietal lesions who often become lost. We return to this problem in Chapter 21.

The Complexity of Spatial Information

The first aspect of our theory of parietal-lobe function considers the uses of spatial information for object recognition and for guiding movement. The second aspect of spatial representation is complexity. The control of limb or eye movements is concrete and relatively simple, but other types of viewer-centered representations are far more complex. For example, the concept of "left" and "right" is viewer-centered but need not require movement. Patients with posterior parietal lesions, such as H.P., are impaired at distinguishing left from right.

Other spatial relations are even more complex. For example, you can visualize objects and manipulate these mental images spatially, as described in the Snapshot. Patients with posterior parietal lesions are impaired at mental manipulations. The ability to manipulate objects mentally is likely an extension of the ability to manipulate objects with the hands. Thus, mental manipulation is really just an elaboration of the neural control of actual manipulation, much as visual imagery is an elaboration of the neural record of actual visual input.

Other Aspects of Parietal Function

Three parietal-lobe symptoms do not fit obviously into a simple view of the parietal lobe as a visuomotor control center. These symptoms include difficulties with arithmetic, certain aspects of language, and movement sequences—deficits encountered by H.P.

⊶SNAPSHOT

White-Matter Organization and Spatial Cognition

The ability to imagine object transformations is a fundamental aspect of spatial cognition. Everyday activities, such as constructional tasks (say, putting a bookshelf together), require an ability to manipulate pieces both mentally and physically. Studies of lesion patients and noninvasive imaging reveal that mental transformations such as object rotation are carried out by the posterior parietal cortex.

Humans vary substantially in their capacity to perform mental object transformations, however, and there is a significant sex difference favoring males in such tasks (see Chapter 12). This intersubject variation could result from differences in cognitive strategy or in the ability to maintain a representation in memory as it is manipulated, but the variation could also be related to differences in the underlying neuroanatomy. Thomas Wolbers and his colleagues hypothesized that the anatomical difference could be in white-matter organization, which would correspond to connectivity of the posterior parietal region.

To determine the role of white-matter differences in mental rotation, the researchers gave male subjects the difficult mental rotation task illustrated in Figure A. As expected,

Figure B Brain organization and mental rotation scores. The structure of the shaded region was positively correlated with mental rotation scores. (T. Wolbers, E. D. Schoell, and C. Buchel. *Neuroimage* 32:1450–1455, 2006.)

they found considerable intersubject variability, despite controlling for spatial short-term memory ability. They used MRI to characterize the white-matter organization in the posterior parietal cortex. As shown in Figure B, there was a tight relation between mental spatial rotation proficiency and white-matter organization near the anterior part of the intraparietal sulcus.

This anatomical measure provides an indirect measure of brain organization because it includes a variety of factors such as myelinization, axon diameter and density, and fiber crossing. Nonetheless, the results support the general idea that the details of neuroanatomical organization are related to individual differences in cognitive abilities.

Whether such differences are purely genetic or are influenced by experience remains to be determined. Similarly, because the investigators studied only males, we do not yet know if sex differences in mental rotation are related to differences in white-matter organization in the posterior parietal cortex.

Figure A Mental rotation task. Subjects had to determine whether the reference cube on the left might be identical with any of the other six cubes. The middle cube in the lower row fits the bill. (After T. Wolbers, E. D. Schoell, and C. Buchel. *Neuroimage* 32:1450–1455, 2006.)

Wolbers, T., E. D. Schoell, and C. Buchel. The predictive value of white matter organization in posterior parietal cortex for spatial visualization ability. *Neuroimage* 32:1450–1455, 2006.

Alexander Luria proposed that mathematics and arithmetic have a quasi-spatial nature analogous to the mental manipulation of concrete shapes but entailing abstract symbols. For example, addition and subtraction have spatial properties that are important to calculating a correct solution. Consider the problem of subtracting 25 from 52. The "2" and "5" occupy different positions and have different meanings in the two numbers. There must be a "borrowing" from the 10's column in 52 in order to subtract, and so on.

From this perspective, the reason that parietal-lobe patients such as H.P. experience **acalculia** (an inability to do arithmetic) stems from the spatial nature of the task. Indeed, if parietal-lobe patients are given simple problems such as 6 minus 4, they usually solve them because the spatial demands are few. Even when the problems are somewhat more difficult, such as 984 minus 23, the patients have little problem. When more-complex manipulations, such as borrowing, must be made, however, as in 983 minus 24, the patients' arithmetic abilities break down. Thus, arithmetic operations may depend on the polysensory tissue at the left temporoparietal junction.

Language has many of the same demands as arithmetic. The words "tap" and "pat" have the same letters, but the spatial organization is different. Similarly, the phrases "my son's wife" and "my wife's son" have identical words but very different meanings. These observations have led Luria and others to suggest that language can be seen as quasi-spatial. Patients such as H.P. may have a clear understanding of individual elements, but they are unable to understand the whole when the syntax becomes important. This ability, too, may depend on the polysensory region at the temporoparietal junction.

The deficit in organizing individual elements of behavior can be seen not only in language but in movement as well. People with parietal-lobe injuries have difficulty in copying sequences of movements, a problem that we shall return to shortly.

In summary, the posterior parietal lobe controls the visuomotor guidance of movements in egocentric (that is, viewer-centered) space. This control is most obvious in regard to reaching and to eye movements needed to grasp or manipulate objects. The eye movements are important, because they allow the visual system to attend to particular sensory cues in the environment. The polymodal region of the posterior parietal cortex is also important in various aspects of "mental space," ranging from arithmetic and reading to the mental rotation and manipulation of visual images to sequencing movements.

Somatosensory Symptoms of Parietal-Lobe Lesions

In this section, we consider the somatosensory symptoms associated with damage to the postcentral gyrus (see Figure 14.1A and areas 1, 2, and 3 in Figure 14.1B) and the adjacent cortex (areas PE and PF in Figure 14.1C).

Somatosensory Thresholds

Damage to the postcentral gyrus is typically associated with marked changes in somatosensory thresholds. The most thorough studies of these changes were done by Josephine Semmes and her colleagues on World War II veterans with missile wounds to the brain and by Suzanne Corkin and her coworkers on patients who had undergone cortical surgery for the relief of epilepsy.

Both research groups found that lesions of the postcentral gyrus produced abnormally high sensory thresholds, impaired position sense, and deficits in **stereognosis** (tactile perception). For example, in the Corkin study, patients performed poorly at detecting a light touch to the skin (pressure sensitivity), at determining if they were touched by one or two sharp points (two-point sensitivity described in Chapter 8), and at localizing points of touch on the skin on the side of the body contralateral to the lesion. If blindfolded, the patients also had difficulty in reporting whether the fingers of the contralateral hand were passively moved.

Lesions of the postcentral gyrus may also produce a symptom that Luria called **afferent paresis**. Movements of the fingers are clumsy because the person has lost the necessary feedback about their exact position.

Somatoperceptual Disorders

The presence of normal somatosensory thresholds does not preclude the possibility of other types of somatosensory abnormalities. First, there is **astereognosis** (from the Greek *stereo*, meaning "solid"), which is the inability to recognize the nature of an object by touch. This disturbance can be demonstrated in tests of tactile perception of object qualities, illustrated in **Figure 14.5**. In these tests, objects are placed on the palms of blindfolded subjects or the subjects are told to handle shapes. The task is to match the original shape or object to one of several alternatives solely on the basis of tactile information.

A second somatoperceptual disorder, **simultaneous extinction**, can be demonstrated only by a special testing procedure. The logic of this test is that a person is ordinarily confronted by an environment in which many sensory stimuli impinge simultaneously, yet the person is able to distinguish and perceive each of these individual sensory impressions. Thus, a task that presents stimuli one at a time represents an unnatural situation that may underestimate sensory disturbances or miss them altogether.

To offer more-complicated sensory stimulation, two tactile stimuli are presented simultaneously to the same or different body parts. The objective of such double simultaneous stimulation is to uncover those situations in which both stimuli would be reported if applied singly, but only one would be reported if both were applied together, as illustrated in **Figure 14.6**. A failure to report one stimulus is usually called **extinction** and is most commonly associated with damage to the somatic secondary cortex (areas PE and PF), especially in the right parietal lobe.

(A)

1 A pattern is placed on a blindfolded subject's palm for 5 seconds and then placed within an array.

2 The task is to identify the original pattern after handling all six patterns.

(B)

1 A duplicate of one of another group of patterns is handled by the subject.

2 The task is to identify the matching pattern in the array.

Figure 14.5

Tests for Tactile Perception of Objects Somatosensory abnormalities such as astereognosis can be identified by such tests. (After Teuber, 1978.)

Figure 14.6

Testing for Extinction in a Stroke Patient The patient responds differently, depending on whether objects in the left and right visual fields are similar or different.

When shown two identical objects

Patient sees only the object in his right visual field.

Patient's right visual field   Patient's left visual field

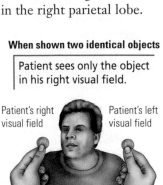

When shown two different objects

Patient sees the object in both visual fields.

When shown two kinds of an object

Patient sees only the object in his right visual field.

Blind Touch

Evidence that patients can identify the location of a visual stimulus even though they deny "seeing" it was presented in Chapter 13. Jacques Paillard and his colleagues reported the case of a woman who appears to have a tactile analogue of blindsight. This woman had a large lesion of areas PE, PF, and some of PG, resulting in a complete anesthesia of the right side of the body so severe that she was likely to cut or burn herself without being aware of it. Nevertheless, she was able to point with her left hand to locations on her right hand where she had been touched, even though she failed to report feeling the touch.

Although reported in a single case, the phenomenon is clearly reminiscent of blindsight. The presence of a tactile analogue of blindsight is important because it suggests the existence of two tactile systems—one specialized for detection and the other for localization. Such specialization may be a general feature of sensory-system organization.

Somatosensory Agnosias

There are two major types of somatosensory agnosias: astereognosis (see the preceding discussion of somatoperceptual disorders) and **asomatognosia**—the loss of knowledge or sense of one's own body and bodily condition. Although astereognosis is essentially a disorder of tactile perception (see Figure 14.5), it is included here because it is often described clinically simply as an agnosia.

Asomatognosia is one of the most curious of all agnosias. It is an almost unbelievable syndrome—until you actually observe it. The varieties of asomatognosias include **anosognosia**, an unawareness or denial of illness; **anosodiaphoria**, indifference to illness; **autopagnosia**, an inability to localize and name body parts; and **asymbolia for pain**, the absence of normal reactions to pain, such as reflexive withdrawal from a painful stimulus.

Asomatognosias may affect one or both sides of the body, although most commonly the left side, as a result of lesions in the right hemisphere. An exception comprises the autopagnosias, which usually result from lesions of the left parietal cortex. The most common autopagnosia is **finger agnosia**, a condition in which a person is unable either to point to the various fingers of either hand or show them to an examiner.

A curious relation exists between finger agnosia and dyscalculia (difficulty in performing arithmetic operations). When children learn arithmetic, they normally use their fingers to count. We might predict that children who are unable to use their fingers to count, such as those with finger agnosia, would have difficulty learning arithmetic. In fact, children with a condition known as spina bifida have finger agnosia and have been found to be terrible at arithmetic.

Symptoms of Posterior Parietal Damage

The clinical literature describes a bewildering array of symptoms of posterior parietal injury. We will restrict our consideration here to the most commonly observed disorders.

Balint's Syndrome

In 1909, Rezsö Bálint described a patient whose bilateral parietal lesion was associated with rather peculiar visual symptoms. The patient had full visual fields and could recognize, use, and name objects, pictures, and colors normally. Nevertheless, he had three unusual symptoms:

1. Although he spontaneously looked straight ahead, when an array of stimuli was placed in front of him, he directed his gaze 35° to 40° to the right and perceived only what was lying in that direction. Thus, he could move his eyes but could not fixate on specific visual stimuli.

2. When his attention was directed toward an object, he did not notice other stimuli. With urging, he could identify other stimuli placed before him, but he quickly relapsed into his former neglect. Bálint concluded that the patient's field of attention was limited to one object at a time, a disorder that made reading very difficult because each letter was perceived separately. (This disorder, described in Chapter 13, is often referred to as *simultagnosia*.)

3. The patient had a severe deficit in reaching under visual guidance. Bálint described this symptom as *optic ataxia* (see Chapter 13). He noted that the patient could still make accurate movements directed toward the body, presumably by using tactile or proprioceptive information, but could not make visually guided movements.

Although Balint's syndrome is quite rare, optic ataxia is a common symptom of posterior parietal lesions and can develop after unilateral lesions. Consider the following description of a patient of Antonio Damasio and Arthur Benton:

> She consistently misreached for targets located in the nearby space, such as pencils, cigarettes, matches, ashtrays and cutlery. Usually she underreached by 2 to 5 inches, and then explored, by tact [touch], the surface path leading to the target. This exploration, performed in one or two groping attempts, was often successful and led straight to the object. Occasionally, however, the hand would again misreach, this time on the side of the target and beyond it. Another quick tactually guided correction would then place the hand in contact with the object. . . . In striking contrast to the above difficulties was the performance of movements which did not require visual guidance, such as buttoning and unbuttoning of garments, bringing a cigarette to the mouth, or pointing to some part of her body. These movements were smooth, quick and on target. (Damasio and Benton, 1979, p. 171)

The deficits in eye gaze and visually guided reaching are most likely to result from lesions in the superior parietal region (area PE). Optic ataxia does not accompany lesions in the inferior parietal region, suggesting a clear functional dissociation of the two posterior parietal regions.

Contralateral Neglect and Other Symptoms of Right Parietal Lesions

McDonald Critchley remarked in his 1953 textbook on the parietal lobes that the symptoms of parietal lesions differ widely—one patient showing only a few abnormal signs that are mild in nature but another showing an intricate clinical picture with elaborate symptoms. What causes this diversity is still not known. We must keep this uncertainty in mind as we consider the symptoms of right parietal lesions, because the range and severity of symptoms varies widely among individual patients.

Contralateral Neglect

A perceptual disorder subsequent to right parietal lesions was described by John Hughlings-Jackson in 1874. Not until the 1940s, however, was the effect of right parietal lesions clearly defined by Alan Paterson and Oliver Zangwill. A classic paper by John McFie and Zangwill, published in 1960, reviewed much of the previous work and described several symptoms of right parietal lesions, which are illustrated in the following patient.

Mr. P., a 67-year-old man, had suffered a right parietal stroke. At the time of our first seeing him (24 hours after admission), he had no visual-field defect or paresis. He did, however, have a variety of other symptoms:

- Mr. P. neglected the left side of his body and of the world. When asked to lift up his arms, he failed to lift his left arm but could do so if one took his arm and asked him to lift it. When asked to draw a clock face, he crowded all the numbers onto the right side of the clock. When asked to read compound words such as "ice cream" and "football," he read "cream" and "ball." When he dressed, he did not attempt to put on the left side of his clothing (a form of dressing apraxia) and, when he shaved, he shaved only the right side of his face. He ignored tactile sensation on the left side of his body. Finally, he appeared unaware that anything was wrong with him and was uncertain about what all the fuss was about (anosagnosia). Collectively, these symptoms are referred to as **contralateral neglect**.

- He was impaired at combining blocks to form designs (constructional apraxia) and was generally impaired at drawing freehand with either hand, at copying drawings, or at cutting out paper figures. When drawing, he often added extra strokes in an effort to make the pictures correct, but the drawings generally lacked accurate spatial relations. In fact, patients showing neglect commonly fail to complete the left side of the drawing, as illustrated in **Figure 14.7**.

- Mr. P. had a topographic disability, being unable to draw maps of well-known regions from memory. He attempted to draw a map of his neighborhood, but it was badly distorted with respect to directions, the spatial arrangement of landmarks, and distances. Despite all these disturbances, Mr. P. knew where he was and what day it was, and he could recognize his family's faces. He also had good language functions: he could talk, read, and write normally.

Contralateral neglect as observed in Mr. P. is one of the most fascinating symptoms of brain dysfunction. Neglect occurs in visual, auditory, and somesthetic stimulation on the side of the body or space or both body and space opposite the lesion. Neglect may be accompanied by denial of the deficit.

Recovery passes through two stages. **Allesthesia** is characterized by a person's beginning to respond to stimuli on the neglected side as if the stimuli

Model   Patient's copy

Figure 14.7

Drawings Copied by a Patient with Contralateral Neglect (From F. E. Bloom and A. Lazerson. *Brain, Mind, and Behavior,* 2nd ed. New York: W. H. Freeman and Company, p. 300. Copyright © 1988.)

were on the unlesioned side. The person responds and orients to visual, tactile, or auditory stimuli on the left side of the body as if they were on the right.

The second stage of recovery, noted earlier, is simultaneous extinction (see Figure 14.6). The person responds to stimuli on the hitherto neglected side unless both sides are stimulated simultaneously, in which case he or she notices only the stimulation on the side ipsilateral to the lesion.

Neglect presents obstacles to understanding. What is the location of the lesion that produces this effect? **Figure 14.8**A is a composite drawing of the region damaged (as inferred from brain scans) in 13 patients with neglect as described by Kenneth Heilman and Robert Watson. A recent review by Argye Hillis concludes that both the right intraparietal sulcus (roughly dividing PE and PF) and the right angular gyrus are necessary for contralateral neglect. Furthermore, Neil Muggleton and his colleagues used transcranial magnetic stimulation over these regions to induce neglect in intact subjects.

Note, however, that contralateral neglect is occasionally observed subsequent to lesions to the frontal lobe and cingulate cortex, as well as to subcortical structures including the superior colliculus and lateral hypothalamus. What is not clear is whether the same phenomenon results from lesions in these various locations.

Why does neglect arise? The two main theories argue that neglect is caused by either (1) defective sensation or perception or (2) defective attention or orientation. The strongest argument favoring the theory of defective sensation or perception is that a lesion to the parietal lobes, which receive input from all the sensory regions, can disturb the integration of sensation into perception. Derek Denny-Brown and Robert Chambers termed this function *morphosynthesis* and its disruption *amorphosynthesis.*

A current elaboration of this theory proposes that neglect follows a right parietal lesion, because the integration of the spatial properties of stimuli becomes disturbed. As a result, although stimuli are perceived, their location is uncertain to the nervous system and they are consequently ignored. The neglect is thought to be unilateral because, in the absence of right-hemisphere function, the left hemisphere is assumed to be capable of some rudimentary spatial synthesis that prevents neglect of the right side of the world. This rudimentary spatial ability cannot compensate, however, for the many other behavioral deficits resulting from right parietal lesions.

Critchley and, later, others suggested that neglect results from defective attention or orientation—that is, an inability to attend to input that has in fact been registered. Heilman and Watson elaborated on this suggestion. They proposed that neglect is manifested by a defect in orienting to stimuli; the defect results from the disruption of a system whose function is to "arouse" the person when new sensory stimulation is present.

Figure **14.8**

The Locus of Right Parietal Symptoms (A) Composite map of the region damaged (inferred from brain scans) in 13 patients with contralateral neglect as described by Heilman and Watson. The area of greatest overlap is the right inferior parietal lobule. (B) Composite outline of the region of overlap among lesions producing deficits in Warrington and Taylor's recognition test for objects seen in unfamiliar views. The lightly shaded region is the area of maximal overlap. Note the locational similarity between parts A and B.

(A) Intraparietal sulcus | Angular gyrus

Right inferior parietal lobe

(B)

(A)

(B)

Figure 14.9

Objects in Strange Views

Drawing of a bucket in (A) familiar and (B) unfamiliar views. Patients with right parietal lesions have difficulty in recognizing objects in unfamiliar views, such as that shown in part B.

Object Recognition

Elizabeth Warrington and her colleagues described another common symptom of right-parietal-lobe lesion: although able to recognize objects shown in familiar views, patients having these lesions are badly impaired at recognizing objects shown in unfamiliar views (**Figure 14.9**). Warrington concluded that the deficit is not in forming a gestalt, or concept—in this case, of "bucket"—but rather in perceptual classification—the mechanism for categorizing information as being part of the idea "bucket."

Such allocation can be seen as a type of a spatial matching in which the common view of an object must be rotated spatially to match the novel view. Warrington and Taylor suggested that the focus for this deficit is roughly the right inferior parietal lobule, the same region proposed as the locus of contralateral neglect (see Figure 14.8B).

The Gerstmann Syndrome and Other Left Parietal Symptoms

In 1924, Josef Gerstmann described a patient with an unusual disorder subsequent to a left parietal stroke: finger agnosia, an asomatognosia described earlier in the chapter. Gerstmann's patient was unable to name or indicate recognition of the fingers on either hand. This symptom aroused considerable interest, and, in the ensuing years, three other symptoms were reported to accompany finger agnosia: right–left confusion, **agraphia** (inability to write), and acalculia. These four symptoms collectively became known as the Gerstmann syndrome.

Gerstmann and others argued that these symptoms accompany a circumscribed lesion in the left parietal lobe, roughly corresponding to the angular gyrus (area PG). If these four symptoms arose as a group, the patient was said to demonstrate the Gerstmann syndrome, and the lesions could be localized in the angular gyrus. The Gerstmann syndrome is a doubtful diagnostic tool in routine investigations, but all the symptoms can be associated with left parietal lesions. Various other symptoms of left parietal lesions are illustrated in the following case history.

On August 24, 1975, S.S., an 11-year-old boy, suddenly had a seizure that was characterized by twitching on the right side of the body, particularly the arm and face. He was given anticonvulsant medication and was free of symptoms until September 16, 1975, when he began to write upside down and backward. S.S. was immediately referred to a neurologist, who diagnosed a left parietal malignant astrocytoma. Careful neuropsychological assessment revealed a number of symptoms characteristic of left parietal lesions:

- **Disturbed language function.** S.S. was unable to write even his name (agraphia), had serious difficulties in reading (dyslexia), and spoke slowly and deliberately, making many errors in grammar (dysphasia).

- **Apraxia.** S.S. was unable to combine blocks to form designs and had difficulty learning a sequence of novel movements of the limbs (see the next subsection).

- **Dyscalculia.** He was very poor at mental arithmetic and could not solve even simple additions and subtractions.

- **Recall.** He had an especially low digit span, being able to master the immediate recall of only three digits, whether they were presented orally or visually.

- **Right–left discrimination.** He was totally unable to distinguish left from right, responding at random on all tests of this ability.

- **Right hemianopia.** Probably because his tumor had damaged the geniculostriate connections, as S.S.'s tumor progressed, movement of the right side of his body became disturbed as the tumor placed pressure on the frontal lobe.

By the end of October 1975, S.S. died; neither surgery nor drug therapy could stop the growth of the tumor. The symptoms exhibited by S.S. resemble those of other patients whom we have seen with left parietal lesions, including H.P., whose story begins this chapter. Curiously, S.S. did not have finger agnosia, one of the Gerstmann symptoms, illustrating the point that even very large lesions do not produce the same effects in every patient.

Apraxia and the Parietal Lobe

Apraxia is a disorder of movement in which the loss of skilled movement is not caused by weakness, an inability to move, abnormal muscle tone or posture, intellectual deterioration, poor comprehension, or other disorders of movement such as tremor. Among the many types of apraxia, we shall focus on two: ideomotor apraxia and constructional apraxia.

In ideomotor apraxia, patients are unable to copy movements or to make gestures (for example, to wave "hello"). Patients with left posterior parietal lesions often present ideomotor apraxia. Doreen Kimura showed that the deficits in such patients can be quantified by asking the patients to copy a series of arm movements such as those illustrated in **Figure 14.10**A. Patients with left-parietal-lobe lesions are grossly impaired at this task, whereas people with right-parietal-lobe lesions perform the task normally. We return to ideomotor apraxia in Chapter 22.

In constructional apraxia, a visuomotor disorder, spatial organization is disordered. Patients with constructional apraxia cannot assemble a puzzle, build a tree house, draw a picture, or copy a series of facial movements (Figure 14.10B). Constructional apraxia can develop after injury to either parietal lobe, although debate over whether the symptoms are the same after left- and right-side lesions is considerable (see the review by Benton). Nonetheless, constructional apraxia often accompanies posterior parietal lesions.

Figure **14.10**

Testing for Apraxia (A) Sample items from a serial arm-movement copying test. To assess ideomotor apraxia, subjects are asked to copy each movement in the series as accurately as they can. (B) Sample items from a serial facial-movement copying test used to assess constructional apraxia.

(A) Serial arm-movement copying test

(B) Serial facial-movement copying test

You can view both ideomotor and constructional apraxia as disturbances of movement that result from a disruption of the parietofrontal connections that control movement. Vernon Mountcastle proposed that the posterior parietal cortex receives afferent signals not only of the tactile and visual representations of the world but also of the position and movement of the body. He proposed that the region uses this information to function as "a command apparatus for operation of the limbs, hands, and eyes within immediate extrapersonal space."

Thus, the parietal lobe not only integrates sensory and spatial information to allow accurate movements in space but also functions to direct or guide movements in the immediate vicinity of the body. Both ideomotor and constructional apraxia can be seen as examples of a dysfunction in this guidance system.

Drawing

Although drawing deficits are known to arise subsequent to lesions in either hemisphere, the deficits in drawing are generally believed to be greater after damage to the right hemisphere than after damage to the left, and the right parietal damage is believed to have the greatest influence on drawing ability. This conclusion is consistent with the general idea that the right hemisphere plays a dominant role in spatial abilities, but it may not be correct. Rather, disturbances in drawing appear to differ, depending on whether the lesion is in the right or the left hemisphere.

For example, Kimura and Faust asked a large sample of patients to draw a house and a man. Apraxic or aphasic left-hemisphere patients did very poorly, producing fewer recognizable drawings and fewer lines than did right-hemisphere patients. In contrast, right-hemisphere patients tended to omit details from the left side of their drawings and to rotate the drawings on the page.

In sum, drawing is a complex behavior that may require verbal as well as nonverbal (for example, spatial) processes. If asked to draw a bicycle, many people will make a mental checklist of items to include (fenders, spokes, chain, and so on). In the absence of language, we would expect such people to draw less-complete bicycles. Further, if patients are apraxic, there is likely to be a deficit in making the required movements. Similarly, the parts of a bicycle have a particular spatial organization. If spatial organization is poor, the drawing is likely to be distorted.

Spatial Attention

As we move about the world, we are confronted with a vast array of sensory information, all of which cannot possibly be treated equally by the nervous system. Thus, the brain must select certain information to process. Consider, for example, the sensory overload to which we are subjected when we stop to chat with an old friend in a department store. Several other people may be nearby, and there will certainly be displays of various items to purchase, competing sounds (others talking, music, cash registers), novel odors, and so on.

Nonetheless, we can orient to a small sample of the incoming information and ignore most of the other input. In fact, we may focus to the exclusion of other, potentially more important information. Cognitive psychologists refer to this orienting of the sensory systems as *selective attention.* Thus, we are said to attend to particular stimuli.

Michael Posner proposed that one function of the parietal cortex is to allow attention to shift from one stimulus to another, a process that he calls **disengagement**. Consider our earlier example of dining with a friend. As we eat, we shift from peas to bread to wine. We are disengaging each time we shift from one food to another.

An aspect of disengagement is that we must reset our visuomotor guidance systems to form the appropriate movements for the next target. We can extend this idea to the mental manipulation of objects and spatial information, too: we must reset the system for the next operation. We return to the problem of selective attention in Chapter 22.

Disorders of Spatial Cognition

We use the term "spatial cognition" to refer to a broad category of abilities that require mentally using or manipulating spatial properties of stimuli, including the ability to mentally manipulate images of objects and maps. The mental-rotation tasks illustrated in Figures 12.1 and 21.11 provide good examples. Another is the ability to follow an upside-down map.

There is little doubt that posterior lesions, most likely including the PG region and the polymodal cortex of the superior temporal sulcus, produce deficits in mental-rotation and map-reading tasks. Although it is widely assumed in the neuropsychological literature that the right hemisphere is "spatial" and that deficits in spatial cognition should thus result from right posterior lesions, the clinical evidence is far from convincing. Indeed, there is little doubt that both left- and right-hemisphere lesions produce deficits in spatial-cognition tasks.

The emerging view, however, is that left- and right-hemisphere lesions have different effects on the performance of spatial cognition. For example, Michael Corballis suggested that mental rotation requires two different operations: (1) the mental imaging of the stimulus and (2) the manipulation of the image. Freda Newcombe and Graham Ratcliff suggested that the left-hemisphere deficit may result from an inability to generate an appropriate mental image. As discussed in Chapter 13, visual-imaging deficits result from left occipital lesions. In contrast, the right-hemisphere deficit may be due to an inability to perform operations on this mental image.

Deficits in the ability to use topographic information are more likely to be associated with damage to the right hemisphere than to the left. Such disorders include the loss of memory of familiar surroundings, the inability to locate items such as countries or cities on a map, and the inability to find one's way in one's environment. Not surprisingly, such deficits are likely to be associated with other visual deficits (such as contralateral neglect or visual agnosia), but specific disorders of topographic orientation have been described for some patients.

Emillio de Renzi concluded that injury to the right posterior hemisphere is a prerequisite for such disorders. Newcombe and Ratcliff noted that such disorders are often associated with injury to the right posterior cerebral artery and are thus likely to include the right occipitotemporal and right hippocampal region. When the parietal cortex is affected, it is most likely to be the inferior part, probably including area PG and the superior temporal sulcus.

Left and Right Parietal Lobes Compared

In their classic paper, McFie and Zangwill compared the symptoms of patients with left or right parietal lesions. Although they found some overlapping symptoms, the asymmetry is clear (**Table 14.1**). In addition, as noted earlier, ideomotor apraxia is more likely to be associated with left parietal lesions.

A puzzling feature of the McFie and Zangwill study noted in Table 14.1 is that lesions to the two hemispheres produce some overlapping symptoms, despite the clear asymmetry. The results of neuropsychological studies tend to emphasize the asymmetry of lesion effects, but the overlapping symptoms are important theoretically. Indeed, as noted earlier, both constructional apraxia and disorders of spatial cognition are poorly lateralized. Many theories of hemispheric asymmetry, discussed in Chapter 11, do not predict such ambiguity in symptom localization and tend to assume far greater dissociation of lesion effects than is actually observed.

One explanation for the overlapping symptoms relates to the concept of preferred cognitive mode, introduced in Chapter 11, where we note that many problems can be solved by using either a verbal cognitive mode or a spatial nonverbal cognitive mode. Genetic, maturational, and environmental factors may predispose people to use different cognitive modes. For example, you might solve a complex spatial problem, such as reading an upside-down map, either directly, by "spatial cognition" (the directions to travel are intuited spatially), or indirectly, by "verbal cognition" (the spatial information is encoded into words and the problem is solved by being "talked" through step by step).

People who are highly verbal prefer the verbal mode even when it is less efficient; we expect lesions of the left parietal lobe in these people to disturb functions that ordinarily are disrupted preferentially by right parietal lesions. Little direct evidence favors this explanation of functional overlap, but it is a provocative idea that accounts in part for individual differences as well as for the apparent functional overlap revealed by the results of lesion studies.

Table **14.1** Effects of left- and right-parietal-lobe lesions compared

	PERCENTAGE OF SUBJECTS WITH DEFICIT*	
	Left (%)	Right (%)
Unilateral neglect	13	67
Dressing disability	13	67
Cube counting	0	86
Paper cutting	0	90
Topographical loss	13	50
Right–left discrimination	63	0
Weigl's Sorting Test	83	6

*Note the small but significant overlap in symptoms of left and right lesions. Source: Based on data presented by McFie and Zangwill, 1960.

Major Symptoms and Their Assessment

Table 14.2 summarizes the major symptoms of parietal-lobe lesions. Damage to the anterior parietal cortex, including area PE, produces deficits in various somatosensory functions. Damage to the posterior parietal regions produces most of the other disorders.

Table 14.2 also lists the regions most likely to be associated with the deficits, but few studies clearly demonstrate anatomical dissociations of such deficits. A major difficulty in dissociating the regions is that natural lesions rarely respect anatomical boundaries and affect only the neocortex. Additionally, in contrast with the frontal and temporal lobes, which are often implicated in epilepsy and thus may be removed surgically, the parietal lobe is rarely epileptogenic, and so surgical removal is rare, as is the opportunity for follow-up research.

Table **14.2** Summary of major symptoms of parietal-lobe damage

Symptom	Most probable lesion site	Basic reference
Disorders of tactile function	Areas 1, 2, 3	Semmes et al., 1960 Corkin et al., 1970
Tactile agnosia	Area PE	Hécaen and Albert, 1978 Brown, 1972
Defects in eye movement	Areas PE, PF	Tyler, 1968
Misreaching	Area PE	Damasio and Benton, 1979
Manipulation of objects	Areas PF, PG	Pause et al., 1989
Apraxia	Areas PF, PG, left	Heilman and Rothi, 1993 Kimura, 1980
Constructional apraxia	Area PG	Benton, 1990
Acalculia	Areas PG, STS*	Levin et al., 1993
Impaired cross-modal matching	Areas PG, STS	Butters and Brody, 1968
Contralateral neglect	Area PG right	Heilman et al., 1993
Impaired object recognition	Area PG right	Warrington and Taylor, 1973
Disorders of body image	Area PE?	Benton and Sivan, 1993
Right–left confusion	Areas PF, PG	Semmes et al., 1960
Disorders of spatial ability	Areas PE, PG	Newcombe and Ratcliff, 1990
Disorders of drawing	Area PG	Warrington et al., 1966 Kimura and Faust, 1987

*STS, superior temporal sulcus.

Clinical Neuropsychological Assessment

As we have seen, restricted lesions of the parietal cortex produce a wide variety of behavioral changes. Behavioral tests used to evaluate brain damage in neurologically verified cases could be logically employed to predict the locus and extent of damage or dysfunction in new cases. (See Chapter 28 for more detail on the rationale of neuropsychological assessment.)

This section briefly summarizes the behavioral tests that have proved sensitive and valid predictors of brain injury. Although these tests, summarized in **Table 14.3**, do not assess all the symptoms of parietal injury, they do evaluate a broad range of parietal-lobe functions. It would be highly unusual for a person to perform normally on all these tests yet show other symptoms of parietal-lobe damage. In addition to these tests, Howard Goodglass and Edith Kaplan describe a good series of tests in their "parietal lobe battery."

Somatosensory Threshold

Recall that subsequent to lesions of the postcentral gyrus, the somatosensory threshold increases on the contralateral side of the body. The two-point discrimination test requires a blindfolded subject to report whether he or she felt one or two points touch the skin (usually on the face or on the palm of the hand). The distance between the points is at first very large (say, 3 centimeters) and is gradually reduced until the subject can no longer perceive two points. In extreme cases, the process is reversed: the distance must be increased to find when the subject first perceives two points.

Table 14.3 Standardized clinical neuropsychological tests for parietal-lobe damage

Function	Test	Basic reference
Somatosensory threshold	Two-point discrimination	Corkin et al., 1970
Tactile form recognition	Seguin–Goddard Form Board (tactile patterns)	Teuber and Weinstein, 1954 Benton et al., 1983
Contralateral neglect	Line bisection	Schenkenberg et al., 1980
Visual perception	Gollin Incomplete Figures Mooney Closure	Warrington and Rabin, 1970 Milner, 1980
Spatial relations	Right–left differentiation	Benton et al., 1983
Language		
Speech comprehension	Token	de Renzi and Faglioni, 1978
Reading comprehension	Token	
Apraxia	Kimura Box	Kimura, 1977

Note: These standardized tests have been validated on large samples of patients with known localized brain damage.

Tactile Form Recognition

In the Seguin–Goddard Form Board test, a blindfolded subject manipulates 10 blocks of different shapes (star, triangle, and so forth) and attempts to place them in similarly shaped holes on a form board. When the test is completed, the form board and blocks are removed and the subject is asked to draw the board from memory.

The precise locus of the lesion producing deficits on this test is controversial, and no claims have been proved. Nevertheless, the results of research on tactile performance in monkeys with parietal lesions indicate that blindfolded tactile recognition is probably sensitive to lesions of areas PE and PF, whereas, in humans, the drawing part—a test of both memory and cross-modal matching—is probably sensitive to lesions in area PG.

Contralateral Neglect

A variety of tests for contralateral neglect have been devised, but we favor the line-bisection test by Thomas Schenkenberg and his colleagues because it is particularly sensitive. In this test, the subject is asked to mark the middle of each of a set of 20 lines. Each line is a different length and is located at a different position on the page—some left of center, some in the middle, and some right of center. Patients showing contralateral neglect typically fail to mark the lines on the left side of the page.

Visual Perception

Visual perceptual capacity is easily assessed by either the Mooney Closure Test or the Gollin Incomplete-Figures Test. In both tests, a series of incomplete representations of faces or objects are presented, and the subject must combine the elements to form a gestalt and identify the picture. These tests are especially sensitive to damage at the right parietotemporal junction, presumably in regions of the ventral visual stream.

Spatial Relations

In the right–left differentiation test, a series of drawings of hands, feet, ears, and so on, are presented in different orientations (upside down, rear view, and so forth), and the subject's task is to indicate whether the drawing is of the left or the right body part. In a verbal variant of this test, subjects are read a series of commands that are to be carried out (for example, "Touch your right ear with your left hand"). Both tests are very sensitive to left-parietal-lobe damage, but caution is advised, because subjects with left-frontal-lobe damage also are often impaired at these tasks.

Language

The Token Test is an easily administered test of language comprehension. Twenty tokens—four shapes (large and small circles, large and small squares) in each of five colors (white, black, yellow, green, red)—are placed in front of a subject. The test begins with simple tasks (for example, touching the white circle) and becomes progressively more difficult (for example, touching the large yellow circle and the large green square).

A Token Test of reading comprehension can also be given by having the subject read the instructions out loud and then carry them out. We have not considered language a function of the parietal lobe, but the posterior speech zone borders on area PG. Thus, injuries affecting PG often include temporal speech-related cortex, and aphasia is observed.

Apraxia

It is unfortunate that there are no standardized tests for apraxia analogous to the Token Test for aphasia. However, the Kimura Box Test (**Figure 14.11**) is probably the best test currently available. Subjects are required to make consecutive movements of pushing a button with the index finger, pulling a handle with four fingers, and pressing a bar with the thumb. Apraxics perform very poorly on this test, and many of them appear unable to perform this very simple series of movements even with extensive practice.

Figure 14.11

Kimura Box Test Subjects are required to learn a three-step movement series. Apraxic subjects are impaired at this task, and they may be unable to learn it at all.

Movement series
1. Pushing with index finger
2. Pulling handle
3. Pressing bar down with thumb

Summary

Anatomy of the Parietal Lobes

The parietal lobe can be divided into three functional zones, for somatosensory processes, movement, and spatial cognition. The most anterior zones primarily take part in somatosensory functions. The superior parietal region primarily controls the visual guidance of movements of the hands and fingers, limbs, head, and eyes. This region has expanded in humans to include areas controlling not only the actual manipulation of objects but also the mental manipulation of objects.

Movements of the body, or in the imagination, necessarily include the space around the body and the object. Thus, the posterior parietal region can be conceived of as having a "spatial" function, although the precise nature of this spatial function is far from clear.

A Theory of Parietal-Lobe Function

The hand can be considered the organ of the parietal lobe; so the parietal lobe has a primary function of guiding limb movements to place the hand in specific spatial locations. The inferior parietal region also has a role in processes related to spatial cognition and in what have been described as quasi-spatial processes, such as are used in arithmetic and reading.

Somatosensory Symptoms of Parietal-Lobe Lesions

Damage to the somatosensory regions of the parietal lobe produces deficits in tactile functions ranging from simple somatosensation to the recognition of objects by touch.

Symptoms of Posterior Parietal Damage

Posterior parietal-lobe injury interferes with the visual guidance of hand and limb movements. Thus, for left parietal injury, there may be limb apraxias, whereas, for right parietal injury, constructional apraxias may result. Left parietal injury also produces a range of cognitive symptoms including deficits in arithmetic and writing; right parietal injury produces a complementary range of symptoms including contralateral neglect and various deficits in spatial cognition.

Major Symptoms and Their Assessment

Neuropsychological analyses of parietal-lobe functions utilize tests that are sensitive to discrete parietal-lobe injuries. Such tests include the assessment of tactile functioning, visual guidance of movement, and cognitive functions such as spatial orientation, including both the copying of complex geometric figures and mental rotation.

References

Andersen, R. A., D. Meeker, B. Pesaran, B. Breznen, C. Buneo, and H. Scherberger. Sensorimotor transformations in the posterior parietal cortex. In M. S. Gazzaniga, Ed., *The Cognitive Neurosciences III*, pp. 463–474, 2004.

Andersen, R. A., J. W. Burdick, S. Musallam, B. Pesaran, and J. G. Cham. Cognitive neural prosthetics. *Trends in Cognitive Sciences* 8:486–493, 2004.

Bálint, R. Seelenlahmung des "Schauens," optische Ataxie, raumliche Störung der Aufmerksamkeit. *Monatsschrift fuer Psychiatrie und Neurologie* 25:51–81, 1909.

Benton, A. L. Constructional apraxia. In F. Boller and J. Grafman, Eds. *Handbook of Neuropsychology*, vol. 2. Amsterdam: Elsevier, 1990.

Benton, A. L., K. de S. Hamsher, N. R. Varney, and O. Spreen. *Contributions to Neuropsychological Assessment*. New York: Oxford University Press, 1983.

Benton, A. L., and A. B. Sivan. Disturbances of body schema. In K. M. Heilman and E. Valenstein, Eds. *Clinical Neuropsychology*, 3rd ed. New York: Oxford University Press, 1993.

Brown, J. *Aphasia, Apraxia, and Agnosia: Clinical and Theoretical Aspects*. Springfield, Ill.: Charles C. Thomas, 1972.

Butters, N., and B. A. Brody. The role of the left parietal lobe in the mediation of intra- and cross-modal associations. *Cortex* 4:328–343, 1968.

Corballis, M. C. Mental rotation: Anatomy of a paradigm. In M. Potegal, Ed. *Spatial Abilities: Development and Physiological Foundations*. New York: Academic Press, 1990.

Corkin, S., B. Milner, and T. Rasmussen. Somatosensory thresholds. *Archives of Neurology* 23:41–58, 1970.

Critchley, M. *The Parietal Lobes*. London: Arnold, 1953.

Damasio, A. R., and A. L. Benton. Impairment of hand movements under visual guidance. *Neurology* 29:170–178, 1979.

Denny-Brown, D., and R. A. Chambers. The parietal lobe and behavior. *Research Publications, Association for Research in Nervous and Mental Disease* 36:35–117, 1958.

de Renzi, E., and P. Faglioni. Normative data and screening power of a shortened version of the Token Test. *Cortex* 14:41–49, 1978.

Eidelberg, D., and A. M. Galaburda. Inferior parietal lobule: Divergent architectonic asymmetries in the human brain. *Archives of Neurology* 41:843–852, 1984.

Gerstmann, J. Some notes on the Gerstmann syndrome. *Neurology* 7:866–869, 1957.

Goodglass, H., and E. Kaplan. *The Assessment of Aphasia*. Philadelphia: Lea & Febiger, 1972.

Hécaen, H., and M. L. Albert. *Human Neuropsychology*. New York: Wiley, 1978.

Heilman, K. M., and L. J. Gonzalez Rothi. Apraxia. In K. M. Heilman and E. Valenstein, Eds. *Clinical Neuropsychology*, 3rd ed. New York: Oxford University Press, 1993.

Heilman, K. M., R. T. Watson, and E. Valenstein. Neglect and related disorders. In K. M. Heilman and E. Valenstein, Eds. *Clinical Neuropsychology*, 3rd ed. New York: Oxford University Press, 1993.

Hillis, A. E. Neurobiology of unilateral spatial neglect. *The Neuroscientist* 12:153–163, 2006.

Hillyard, S. A., and L. Anllo-Vento. Event-related brain potentials in the study of visual selective attention. *Proceedings of the National Academy of Sciences of the United States of America* 95:781–787, 1998.

Hyvarinen, J. *The Parietal Cortex of Monkey and Man*. Berlin: Springer, 1982.

Kimura, D. Acquisition of a motor skill after left hemisphere damage. *Brain* 100:527–542, 1977.

Kimura, D. Neuromotor mechanisms in the evolution of human communication. In H. D. Steklis and

M. J. Raleigh, Eds. *Neurobiology of Social Communication in Primates: An Evolutionary Perspective.* New York: Academic Press, 1980.

Kimura, D., and R. Faust. Spontaneous drawing in an unselected sample of patients with unilateral cerebral damage. In D. Ottoson, Ed. *Duality and Unity of the Brain.* Wenner-Gren Center International Symposium Series, vol. 47. New York: MacMillan, 1987.

Levin, H. S., F. C. Goldstein, and P. A. Spiers. Acalculia. In K. M. Heilman and E. Valenstein, Eds. *Clinical Neuropsychology,* 3rd ed. New York: Oxford University Press, 1993.

McFie, J., and O. L. Zangwill. Visual-constructive disabilities associated with lesions of the left cerebral hemisphere. *Brain* 83:243–260, 1960.

Milner, B. Complementary functional specializations of the human cerebral hemispheres. In R. Levy-Montalcini, Ed. *Neurons, Transmitters, and Behavior.* Vatican City: Pontificiae Academiae Scientiarum Scripta Varia, 1980.

Milner, D. A., D. P. Carey, and M. Harvey. Visually guided action and the "need to know." *Behavioral and Brain Sciences* 17:213–214, 1994.

Milner, D.A., and M. A. Goodale. *The Visual Brain in Action.* Oxford: Oxford University Press, 2006.

Mountcastle, V. B., J. C. Lynch, A. Georgopoulos, H. Sakata, and C. Acuna. Posterior parietal association cortex of the monkey: Command functions for operation within extra-personal space. *Journal of Neurophysiology* 38:871–908, 1975.

Muggleton, N. G., P. Postma, K. Moutsopoulou, I. Nimmo-smith, A. Marcel, and V. Walsh. TMS over right posterior parietal cortex induces neglect in a scent-based frame of reference. *Neuropsychologia* 44:1222–1229, 2006.

Newcombe, F., and G. Ratcliff. Disorders of visuospatial analysis. In F. Boller and J. Grafman, Eds. *Handbook of Neuropsychology,* vol. 2. Amsterdam: Elsevier, 1990.

Paillard, J., F. Michel, and G. Stelmach. Localization without content: A tactile analogue of "blindsight." *Archives of Neurology* 40:548–551, 1983.

Paterson, A., and O. L. Zangwill. Disorders of space perception association with lesions of the right cerebral hemisphere. *Brain* 67:331–358, 1944.

Pause, M., E. Kunesch, F. Binkofski, and H.-J. Freund. Sensorimotor disturbances in patients with lesions of the parietal cortex. *Brain* 112:1599–1625, 1989.

Posner, M. I., A. W. Inhoff, F. J. Friedrich, and A. Cohen. Isolating attentional systems: A cognitive-anatomical analysis. *Psychobiology* 15:107–121, 1987.

Posner, M. I., J. A. Walker, J. J. Friedrich, and R. D. Rafal. Effects of parietal lobe injury on covert orienting of visual attention. *Journal of Neuroscience* 4:1863–1874, 1984.

Roland, P. E. *Brain Activation.* New York: Wiley, 1993.

Sato, N., H. Sakata, Y. L. Tanaka, and M. Taira. Navigation-associated medial parietal neurons in monkeys. *Proceedings of the National Academy of Sciences of the United States of America* 103:17001–17006, 2006.

Schenkenberg, T., D. C. Bradford, and E. T. Ajax. Line bisection and unilateral visual neglect in patients with neurologic impairment. *Neurology* 30:509–517, 1980.

Semmes, J., and B. Turner. Effects of cortical lesions on somatosensory task. *Journal of Investigations in Dermatology* 69:181–189, 1977.

Semmes, J., S. Weinstein, L. Ghent, and H.-L. Teuber. *Somatosensory Changes after Penetrating Brain Wounds in Man.* Cambridge, Mass.: Harvard University Press, 1960.

Semmes, J., S. Weinstein, L. Ghent, and H.-L. Teuber. Correlates of impaired orientation in personal and extra-personal space. *Brain* 86:747–772, 1963.

Stein, J. F. The representation of egocentric space in the posterior parietal cortex. *Behavioral and Brain Sciences* 15:691–700, 1992.

Teuber, H.-L. The brain and human behavior. In R. Held, W. Leibowitz, and H.-L. Teuber, Eds. *Handbook of Sensory Physiology,* vol. 7, *Perception.* Berlin: Springer, 1978.

Teuber, H. L., and S. Weinstein. Performance on a formboard task after penetrating brain injury. *Journal of Psychology* 38:177–190, 1954.

Tyler, H. R. Abnormalities of perception with defective eye movements (Balints syndrome). *Cortex* 4:154–171, 1968.

Warrington, E. K., M. James, and M. Kinsbourne. Drawing disability in relation to laterality of cerebral lesion. *Brain* 89:53–82, 1966.

Warrington, E. K., and P. Rabin. Perceptual matching in patients with cerebral lesions. *Neuropsychologia* 8:475–487, 1970.

Warrington, E. K., and A. M. Taylor. The contribution of the right parietal lobe to object recognition. *Cortex* 9:152–164, 1973.

Warrington, E. K., and L. Weiskrantz. An analysis of short-term and long-term memory defects in man. In J. A. Deutsch, Ed. *The Physiological Basis of Memory.* New York: Academic Press, 1993.

15 The Temporal Lobes

When he was 40 years old, H.H., a successful corporate lawyer with a wife and two school-age children, was finding his job increasingly stressful. His wife was taken off guard when he suddenly announced that he was quitting his law firm.

He complained of being so stressed that he simply could not remember the cases on which he was and felt that he could not continue as a lawyer. He had no plan about how he would support his family but, curiously, he seemed unconcerned about it.

A couple of weeks later, H.H. shaved his hair off, donned a flowing robe, and left his family to join a fringe religious group. His wife of 15 years was

WDCN/University College London/Photo Researchers

stunned by this sudden change in behavior: up to this point, H.H. had been an atheist.

H.H.'s wife was notified 2 weeks later that he had collapsed with a seizure while handing out flowers and peace pamphlets in a large U.S. airport. He was taken to a hospital in a confused

state, and a neurological examination revealed a left-temporal-lobe tumor. Fortunately, the tumor was operable and was removed.

H.H. was aphasic after his surgery, but this condition cleared in a matter of weeks. He was left with enduring word-finding difficulties, problematic only when he was tired. He continued to complain of verbal-memory problems, however.

H.H.'s wife said that his personality remained different from what it had been, largely because he remained religious. Eventually, H.H. successfully returned to his law firm, although with a reduced caseload compared with that of his pretumor days.

Typical symptoms of temporal-lobe disorder include radical changes in affect and personality, memory disturbance, and at least a transient disturbance of language, such as those exhibited by H.H. In this chapter, we survey the anatomy of the temporal lobe, present a theoretical model of its function, describe the basic symptoms that signal temporal-lobe damage, and briefly describe clinical tests of temporal-lobe function.

Anatomy of the Temporal Lobe

The temporal lobe comprises all the tissue that lies below the lateral (Sylvian) fissure and anterior to the occipital cortex (**Figure 15.1**). Subcortical temporal-lobe structures include the limbic cortex, the amygdala, and the hippocampal formation (**Figure 15.2**). Connections to and from the temporal lobe extend throughout the brain.

Subdivisions of the Temporal Cortex

Brodmann identified 10 temporal areas, but many more areas in the monkey were identified in more-recent studies (see Felleman and van Essen's flat map, Figure 10.18). Likely, there are more areas in the human as well. We can di-

(A) Lateral view

Lateral
(Sylvian)
fissure

Superior temporal gyrus
Middle temporal gyrus
Inferior temporal gyrus

(B) Auditory and visual areas

41
42
22
21 37
38
20

Inferotemporal cortex
(Area TE)

(C) Medial view

Corpus
callosum

Uncus

Fusiform
gyrus

Parahippocampal
gyrus

Inferior
temporal
gyrus

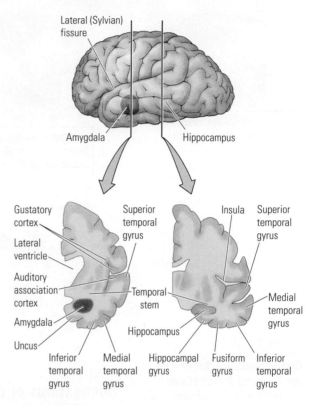

Lateral (Sylvian)
fissure

Amygdala   Hippocampus

Gustatory
cortex

Superior
temporal
gyrus

Insula Superior
temporal
gyrus

Lateral
ventricle

Auditory
association
cortex

Temporal
stem

Medial
temporal
gyrus

Amygdala

Uncus

Hippocampus

Inferior
temporal
gyrus

Medial
temporal
gyrus

Hippocampal
gyrus

Fusiform
gyrus

Inferior
temporal
gyrus

Figure 15.1

Gross Anatomy of the Temporal Lobe (A) The
three major gyri visible on the lateral surface of the
temporal lobe. (B) Brodmann's cytoarchitectonic
zones on the lateral surface. Auditory areas are
shown in yellow and visual areas in purple. Areas
20, 21, 37, and 38 are often referred to by von
Economo's designation, TE. (C) The gyri visible on
a medial view of the temporal lobe. The uncus
refers to the anterior extension of the hippocampal
formation. The parahippocampal gyrus includes
areas TF and TH (see Figure 15.3D).

Figure 15.2

Internal Structure of the Temporal Lobe (Top) Lateral view
of the left hemisphere illustrating the relative positions of the
amygdala and hippocampus buried deeply in the temporal lobe.
The vertical lines indicate the approximate location of the
coronal sections in the bottom illustration. (Bottom) Frontal
views through the left hemisphere illustrating the cortical and
subcortical regions of the temporal lobe.

vide the temporal regions on the lateral surface into those that are auditory
(Brodmann's areas 41, 42, and 22 in Figure 15.1B) and those that form the ventral visual stream on the lateral temporal lobe (areas 20, 21, 37, and 38 in Figure 15.1B). The visual regions are often referred to as **inferotemporal cortex**
or by von Economo's designation, TE.

The sulci of the temporal lobe contain a lot of cortex, as you can see in the
frontal views at the bottom of Figure 15.2. In particular, the lateral (Sylvian)
fissure contains tissue forming the **insula**, which includes the gustatory cortex
as well as the auditory association cortex.

The **superior temporal sulcus** (STS) separates the superior and middle
temporal gyri and contains a significant amount of neocortex as well. **Figure**

(A) Brodmann's areas

Auditory areas are yellow and visual areas are purple.

(B) Von Bonin and Bailey's areas

Superior temporal sulcus

Figure 15.3

Cytoarchitectonic Regions of the Temporal Cortex of the Rhesus Monkey (A) Brodmann's areas. (B) Von Bonin and Bailey's areas. (C and D) Lateral and ventral views of Seltzer and Pandya's parcellation showing the multimodal areas in the superior temporal sulcus. The subareas revealed in part C are normally not visible from the surface.

(C) Lateral view

The banks of the sulcus have been spread to show many subareas on the bank.

(D) Ventral view

15.3 diagrams its many subregions of **multimodal**, or **polymodal**, **cortex** that receive input from auditory, visual, and somatic regions, as well as from the other two polymodal regions (frontal and parietal) and the paralimbic cortex (compare Figure 10.11).

The medial temporal region (limbic cortex) includes the amygdala and adjacent cortex (uncus), the hippocampus and surrounding cortex (subiculum, entorhinal cortex, perirhinal cortex), and the fusiform gyrus (see Figure 15.2). The entorhinal cortex is Brodmann's area 28, and the perirhinal cortex comprises Brodmann's areas 35 and 36.

Cortical areas TH and TF at the posterior end of the temporal lobe (see Figure 15.3D) are often referred to as the parahippocampal cortex. The fusiform gyrus and inferior temporal gyrus are functionally part of the lateral temporal cortex (see Figures 15.1 and 15.2).

Connections of the Temporal Cortex

The temporal lobes are rich in internal connections, afferent projections from the sensory systems, and efferent projections to the parietal and frontal association regions, limbic system, and basal ganglia. The neocortex of the left and right temporal lobes is connected by the corpus callosum, whereas the medial temporal cortex and amygdala are connected by the anterior commissure.

The results of studies on the temporocortical connections of the monkey reveal five distinct types of cortical–cortical connections, which are illustrated in **Figure 15.4**. Here, we list the different functions that each projection pathway presumably subserves:

1. **A hierarchical sensory pathway.** This pathway subserves stimulus recognition. The hierarchical progression of connections emanates from the primary and secondary auditory and visual areas, ending in the temporal pole (see Figure 15.4A). The visual projections form the ventral stream of visual processing, whereas the auditory projections form a parallel ventral stream of auditory processing.

2. **A dorsal auditory pathway.** Projecting from the auditory areas to the posterior parietal cortex (Figure 15.4A), this pathway is analogous to the dorsal visual pathway and thus concerned with directing movements with respect to auditory information. The dorsal auditory pathway likely plays a role in detecting the spatial location of auditory inputs.

3. **A polymodal pathway.** This pathway is a series of parallel projections from the visual and auditory association areas into the polymodal regions

(A)

Lateral (Sylvian) fissure

Visual information

Auditory information

(B)

STS

(C)

(D)

8

46

13

Figure 15.4

Major Intracortical Connections of the Temporal Lobe (A) Auditory and visual information progresses ventrally from the primary regions toward the temporal pole en route to the medial temporal regions. Auditory information also forms a dorsal pathway to the posterior parietal cortex. (B) Auditory, visual, and somatic outputs go to the multimodal regions of the superior temporal sulcus (STS). (C) Auditory and visual information goes to the medial temporal region, including the amygdala and the hippocampal formation. (D) Auditory and visual information goes to two prefrontal regions, one on the dorsolateral surface and the other in the orbital region (area 13).

of the superior temporal sulcus (see Figure 15.4B). The polymodal pathway probably underlies stimulus categorization.

4. **A medial temporal projection.** Crucial to long-term memory, the projection from the auditory and visual association areas into the medial temporal, or limbic, regions goes first to the perirhinal cortex, then to the entorhinal cortex, and finally into the hippocampal formation or the amygdala or both (see Figure 15.4C). The hippocampal projection forms the **perforant pathway**. A disturbance of this projection results in a major dysfunction in hippocampal activity.

5. **A frontal-lobe projection.** This series of parallel projections, necessary for various aspects of movement control, short-term memory, and affect, reaches from the temporal association areas to the frontal lobe (see Figure 15.4D).

As will be seen in the next section, these five projection pathways play unique roles in temporal-lobe functions.

A Theory of Temporal-Lobe Function

The multifunctional temporal lobe houses the primary auditory cortex, the secondary auditory and visual cortex, the limbic cortex, and the amygdala and hippocampus. The hippocampus works in concert with the object-recognition and memory functions of the neocortex and plays a special role in organizing memories of objects in space. The amygdala adds affective tone (that is, emotion) to sensory input and memories. On the basis of the cortical anatomy, we can identify three basic sensory functions of the temporal cortex:

1. Processing auditory input

2. Visual object recognition

3. Long-term storage of sensory input—that is, memory

Temporal-lobe functions are best understood by considering how the brain analyzes sensory stimuli as they enter the nervous system. Imagine that you are hiking in the woods. On your journey, you notice many different birds, and you decide to keep a mental list of the species that you encounter so that you can tell your sister, who is an avid birder.

As you walk along, you suddenly stop and back up—you have encountered a rattlesnake in the middle of the path. You decide to change routes and look for birds elsewhere! What temporal-lobe functions take part in your experience?

Sensory Processes

As you search for different birds, you need to be aware of the specific colors, shapes, and sizes of birds that you might encounter. This process of object recognition is the function of the ventral visual pathway in the temporal lobe.

You also need to categorize the birds quickly, because they often fly away, and you do so by using information that varies in perspective from sighting to sighting (for example, lateral view versus rear view). Developing object categories is crucial to both perception and memory and depends on the inferortemporal cortex. Categorization may require a form of directed attention, because certain characteristics of stimuli likely play a more important role in classification than do others.

For example, classifying two different yellow birds requires directing attention away from color and focusing on shape, size, and other characteristics. Damage to the temporal cortex leads to deficits in identifying and categorizing stimuli. There is no difficulty in locating the stimulus or recognizing that it is present, however, because these activities are functions of the posterior parietal and primary sensory areas, respectively.

As you walk along, you may also hear bird song, and you need to match songs with the visual input. This process of matching visual and auditory information is called **cross-modal matching**. It likely depends on the cortex of the superior temporal sulcus.

As you see more and more birds, you have to form memories that you can access later. Furthermore, as you see different birds, you need to access their names from your memory. These long-term memory processes depend on the entire ventral visual stream as well as the paralimbic cortex of the medial temporal region.

Affective Responses

When you encounter the snake, you first hear the rattle, which alerts you, and you stop. As you scan the ground, you see and identify the snake, and your heart rate and blood pressure rise. Your affective response is a function of the amygdala. Associating sensory input and emotion is crucial for learning, because stimuli become associated with their positive, negative, or neutral consequences, and behavior is modified accordingly.

In the absence of this affective system, all stimuli would be treated equivalently. Consider the consequences of failing to associate the rattlesnake, which is poisonous, with the consequences of being bitten. Or consider being unable to associate good feelings (such as love) with a specific person. Laboratory animals with amygdala lesions become very placid and do not react emotionally to threatening stimuli. For example, monkeys that were formerly terrified of snakes become indifferent to them and may reach to pick them up.

Spatial Navigation

When you change routes and go elsewhere, you use the hippocampus, which contains cells that code places in space. Together, these cells allow you to navigate in space and to remember where you are.

As we consider these general functions of the temporal lobes—sensory, affective, and navigational—we can see that losing them has devastating consequences for behavior: an inability to perceive or to remember events, including language and a loss of affect. But a person lacking temporal-lobe function would be able to use the dorsal visual system to make visually guided movements and, under many circumstances, would appear rather normal.

The Superior Temporal Sulcus and Biological Motion

An additional temporal-lobe function was not included in the hiking example. Animals engage in what we can call *biological motion*, movements that have particular relevance to a species. For example, our eyes, faces, mouths, hands, and bodies make movements that can have social meanings. We shall see that the superior temporal sulcus analyzes biological motion.

As already mentioned, the STS receives multimodal inputs that play a role in categorizing stimuli. A major category is social perception, which includes the analysis of actual or implied bodily movements that provide socially relevant information. This information plays an important role in **social cognition**, or "theory of mind," that allows us to develop hypotheses about other people's intentions. For example, the direction of a person's gaze provides us considerable information about what that person is attending (or not attending) to.

In a nice review, Truett Allison and colleagues proposed that cells in the superior temporal sulcus play a key role in social cognition. For example, cells in the monkey STS respond to various forms of biological motion including the direction of eye gaze, head movement, mouth movement, facial expression, and hand movement. For social animals such as primates, knowledge about biological motion is critical information needed to infer the intentions of others. As illustrated in **Figure 15.5**, imaging studies show activation along the STS during the perception of various forms of biological motion.

An important correlate of mouth movements is vocalization, and so we might predict that regions of the STS are also implicated in perceiving species-typical sounds. In monkeys, cells in the superior temporal gyrus, which is adjacent to the STS and sends connections to it, show a preference for "monkey calls," and imaging studies in humans show that the superior temporal gyrus is activated both by human vocalizations and by melodic sequences.

We could predict activation in some part of the superior temporal sulcus in response to the combination of the visual stimulus (mouth movements) and talking or singing. Presumably, talking and singing can be perceived as complex forms of biological motion. We could predict that, if people have

Figure 15.5

Biological Motion Summary of the activation (indicated by dots) of the STS region in the left (A) and right (B) hemispheres during the perception of biological motion. (After Allison, Puce, and McCarthy, 2000.)

(A) Left hemisphere

Superior temporal sulcus (STS)

(B) Right hemisphere

STS

Body view

Direction of walk

Static

STS neurons in the observing monkey respond more strongly to an approaching body...

...than to the same body moving in other directions or standing still.

Figure 15.6

Neuronal Sensitivity to Direction of Body Movements

(Top) Schematic representation of the front view of a body. (Bottom) The histogram illustrates a greater neuronal response of STS neurons to the front view of a body that approaches the observing monkey compared with the responses to the same view of the body when the body is moving away, to the right and to the left, or is stationary. (After Perrett et al., 1990.)

temporal-lobe injuries that lead to impairments in analyzing biological motion, there is likely to be a correlated deficit in social awareness. Indeed, there is.

The nature of processing in the STS is illustrated by the studies of David Perrett and his colleagues, who showed that neurons in the superior temporal sulcus may be responsive to particular faces seen head-on, faces viewed in profile, posture of the head, or even particular facial expressions. More recently, Perrett also showed that some STS cells are maximally sensitive to primate bodies that are moving in a particular direction, another characteristic biological motion (**Figure 15.6**). This finding is quite remarkable because the basic configuration of the stimulus is identical as the body moves in different directions; only the direction changes.

Visual Processing in the Temporal Lobe

Recall that the ventral stream of visual processing is performed by several discrete visual regions including specialized facial and object-recognition zones (see Table 13.1). The role of these regions in natural vision is beautifully demonstrated in a heroic study by Uri Hasson and his colleagues. These investigators allowed subjects to freely view a 30-minute segment of a feature film, *The Good, The Bad, and The Ugly*, while cortical activity was monitored by fMRI. The investigators reasoned that such a rich and complex visual stimulation would be far more similar to ecological vision than are the highly contrained visual stimuli normally used in the laboratory.

Another aspect of the free-viewing study was to determine how similar brain activity was in different people by correlating the activity of five individual subjects watching the same film segment. To do so, the investigators had to normalize all five brains by using a standard coordinate system and then smooth the data by using sophisticated statistical procedures to allow analysis. There were three principal findings.

First, as shown in **Figure 15.7**A, extensive activity throughout the entire temporal lobe was highly correlated across subjects. Thus, the brains of different individual subjects tended to act in unison during the free viewing, both in the auditory and visual regions of the temporal lobe and in the STS and cingulate regions. This surprising activity coherence implies that a large expanse of the human cortex is stereotypically responsive to naturalistic audiovisual stimuli.

Second, although there was a general activation of the temporal cortex during the film clip, there were selective activations related to the precise moment-to-moment film content. Figure 15.7B reveals that, when the subjects viewed closeups of faces, they showed high activity in the fusiform face area (FFA), whereas, when they viewed broad scenes, they showed enhanced activity in the nearby parahippocampal place area (PPA). When, later, Hassan and his colleagues showed subjects static views of faces or places, they found increased

(A)

Left hemisphere

Faces ◯

Objects ◯

Buildings ◯

Greater correlation

Right hemisphere

(B)

FFA   PPA

Figure 15.7

Brain Activity During Natural Vision (A) The correlation in brain activity among five subjects watching a segment of the movie *The Good, The Bad, and The Ugly*. The ventral stream is coincidently active in all subjects, but there is little coherence in the rest of the brain. (B) Regional selectivity of activity for specific visual stimuli. The fusiform face area (FFA) is active for faces, and the parahippocampal place area (PPA) is active for scenes. (Adapted with permission from Hasson et al., 2004.)

fMRI signals in precisely the same regions, a finding that nicely validates their free-viewing results. The selective activations were not specific to visual processing, however, inasmuch as the investigators also found activations of the postcentral hand region related to hand movements and activations of the auditory cortex related to specific types of auditory information.

Third, regions of the parietal and frontal lobes showed no intersubject coherence. As subjects viewed the film, they may have had quite different thought patterns beyond the sensory processing. Such thoughts were likely about past experiences related to the film content or perhaps even related to planning what to have for supper once the experiment was over. In addition, we can infer that just because the film clip produced remarkable coherence in sensory processing does not mean that there was coherence in the different subjects' subjective film experience.

The selective activation of FFA and PPA related to categories of visual stimulation that include very different exemplars of the specific categories leads us to wonder how such dissimilar objects are treated equivalently by specialized cortical regions. Not only are different views of the same object linked together as being the same, but different objects appear to be linked together as being part of the same category as well. The automatic categorization of sensory information must be at least partly learned, because we categorize unnatural objects such as cars or furniture. The brain is unlikely to be innately designed for such categorizations. So how are they learned?

One way to address this question is to look for changes in neural activity as subjects learn categories. Kenji Tanaka began by attempting to determine the critical features for activating neurons in the monkey inferotemporal cortex. He and his colleagues presented many three-dimensional animal and plant representations to find the effective stimuli for given cells. Then, they tried to determine the necessary and sufficient properties of these cells.

Neurons in the temporal lobe form columns that respond to categories of shapes.

Temporal lobe

Figure 15.8

Columnar Organization in Area TE Cells with similar but slightly different selectivity cluster in elongated vertical columns, perpendicular to the cortical surface.

Tanaka found that most cells in area TE require rather complex features for activation. These features contain a combination of characteristics such as orientation, size, color, and texture. Furthermore, as illustrated in **Figure 15.8**, he found that cells with similar, although slightly different, selectivity tend to cluster vertically in columns.

These cells were not identical in their stimulus selectivity; so an object is likely represented not by the activity of a single cell but rather by the activity of many cells within a columnar module. Tanaka speculated that an object's representation by multiple cells in a columnar module in which the selectivity varies from cell to cell and effective stimuli largely overlap can provide a way for the brain to minimize the effect of small changes in input images and leads to the categorization of similar objects.

Tanaka and others have described two other remarkable features of inferotemporal neurons in monkeys. First, the stimulus specificity of these neurons is altered by experience. In a period of 1 year, monkeys were trained to discriminate 28 complex shapes. The stimulus preferences of inferotemporal neurons were then determined from a larger set of animal and plant models. In the trained monkeys, 39% of the inferotemporal neurons gave a maximum response to some of the stimuli used in training. This percentage compared with only 9% of the neurons in naïve monkeys.

This result confirms that the temporal lobe's role in visual processing is not determined genetically but is subject to experience even in the adult. We can speculate that this experience-dependent characteristic allows the visual system to adapt to different demands in a changing visual environment. This feature is important for human visual recognition abilities that have demands in forests that greatly differ from those on open plains or in urban environments. In addition, experience-dependent visual neurons ensure that we can identify visual stimuli that were never encountered in the evolution of the human brain.

The second interesting feature of inferotemporal neurons is that they may not only process visual input but also provide a mechanism for the internal representation of the images of objects. Joaquin Fuster and John Jervey first demonstrated that, if monkeys are shown specific objects that are to be remembered, neurons in the monkey cortex continue to discharge during the "memory" period. These selective discharges of neurons may provide the basis of working memory for the stimuli. Furthermore, the discharges of these neurons may provide the basis for visual imagery. That is, the discharge of groups of neurons that are selective for characteristics of particular objects may provide a mental image of the object in its absence.

Are Faces Special?

Most of us probably spend more time looking at faces than at any other single stimulus. Infants prefer to look at faces almost from birth, and adults are excellent at identifying familiar faces despite large variations in expression and viewing angles, even when the faces are disguised with beards, spectacles, or hats. Faces also convey a wealth of social information, and we humans are unique among primates in spending a good deal of time looking directly at the faces of other members of our species.

The importance of faces as visual stimuli has led to the idea that a special pathway exists in the visual system for the analysis of faces (see Farah, 1998, for a review). Several lines of evidence support this view. In the first place, the results of studies of monkeys show neurons in the temporal lobe that are specifically tuned to different faces, with some cells attuned to facial identity and others to facial expression. In the second place, inverting a photograph of any object that has a usual right side up makes it harder to recognize, but the effect on faces is disproportionate (see a review by Valentine).

Similarly, we are particularly sensitive to the configuration of upright faces. Consider the classic "Thatcher illusion" shown in **Figure 15.9**, which illustrates this effect. The importance of an upright orientation to facial perception is also seen in imaging studies. For example, James Haxby and his colleagues showed that inverted faces are processed by the same cortical regions as are other visual stimuli, whereas upright faces are processed in a separate face-perception system. This face-perception system is surprisingly extensive and includes regions in the occipital lobe as well as several different regions of the temporal lobe.

Figure 15.10 summarizes a model by Haxby and his colleagues in which different aspects of facial perception (such as facial expression versus identity) are analyzed in core visual areas in the temporal part of the ventral stream. The model also includes other cortical regions as an "extended system" that includes the analysis of other facial characteristics such as emotion and lip reading. The key point here is that the analysis of faces is unlike that of other visual stimuli.

Finally, a clear asymmetry exists in the role of the temporal lobes in the analysis of faces. Right temporal lesions have a greater effect on facial processing than do similar left temporal lesions. Even in normal subjects, researchers can see an asymmetry in face perception.

Figure 15.9

The Thatcher Illusion Look at the face of former British Prime Minister Margaret Thatcher as presented (upside down) and then invert the page and look again. There is a compelling illusion of normalcy in the inverted face but, in the upright view, the reconfigured face appears hideous. Lady Thatcher was the original subject of the illusion that now bears her name.

Figure 15.10

A Model of the Distributed Human Neural System for Face Perception The model is divided into a core system (top), consisting of occipital and temporal regions, and an extended system (bottom), including regions that are part of neural systems for other cognitive functions. (After Haxby, Hoffman, and Gobbini, 2000.)

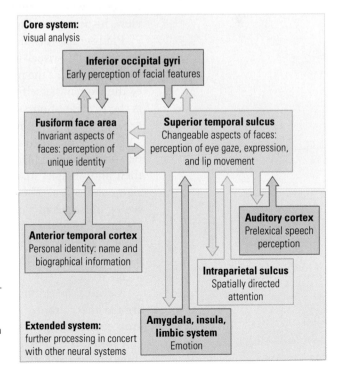

Figure 15.11

The Split-Faces Test Subjects were asked which of the two pictures, B or C, most closely resembles picture A. Control subjects chose picture C significantly more often than picture B. Picture C corresponds to that part of picture A falling in a subject's left visual field. The woman pictured chose B, closer to the view that she is accustomed to seeing in the mirror. (After Kolb, Milner, and Taylor, 1983.)

(A) Original face

(B) Composite of right sides

(C) Composite of left sides

We presented subjects with photographs of faces, as illustrated in **Figure 15.11**. Photographs B and C are composites of the right or the left sides, respectively, of the original face shown in photograph A. Asked to identify which composite most resembled the original face, normal subjects consistently matched the left side of photograph A to its composite in photograph C. They did so whether the photographs were presented upright or inverted. Furthermore, patients with either right temporal or right parietal removals failed to consistently match either side of the face in either the upright or the inverted presentation.

The results of this split-faces test not only show an asymmetry in facial processing but also speak to the nature of our perceptions of our own faces. Self-perception provides a unique example of visual perception, because your own image of your face comes largely from looking in a mirror, where the image is reversed, whereas the image that others have of your face comes from direct view. Inspection of Figure 15.11 illustrates the implications of this difference.

Photograph A is the image that other people see of this woman and, because there is a left-visual-field bias in our perception, most right-handers choose photograph C as the picture most resembling the original. Consider the choice of the woman herself, however. Her common view of her face (in the mirror) is the reverse of ours, and hence she is more likely to choose (and in fact did choose) composite photograph B as most resembling her own face.

An intriguing consequence of our biased self-facial image is our opinion of personal photographs. Many people complain about not being photogenic, that their photographs are never taken at the correct angle, that their hair wasn't just right, and so on. The problem may be rather different: we are accustomed to seeing ourselves in a mirror image and hence, when we view a photograph, we are biased to look at the side of the face that we do not normally perceive selectively in the mirror. Indeed, we appear not to see ourselves as others see us. The more asymmetrical the face, the less flattering the person will see his or her image to be.

A critical question about facial processing remains, however. James Tanaka argued that, although face recognition appears to tap into a specialized face area, the same region could be used for other forms of expertise and is not specific for faces. For example, imaging studies have shown that real-world experts show an overlapping pattern of activation in FFA for faces in control participants, for car stimuli in car experts, and for bird stimuli in bird experts (see, for example, Gauthier et al.). The general idea is that the FFA is rather plastic as a consequence of perceptual experience and training. In this view, the FFA is innately biased to categorize complex objects such as faces but can be recruited for other forms of visual categorization expertise.

Auditory Processing in the Temporal Lobe

As discussed in Chapter 8, a sound reaching the ear stimulates a cascade of mechanical and neural events in the cochlea, the brainstem, and, eventually, the auditory cortex that results in a percept of sound. Like the visual cortex, the auditory cortex has multiple regions, each of which has a tonotopic map. The precise functions of these maps are poorly understood, but the ultimate goal is to perceive sound objects, locate sound, and make movements in relation to sounds.

Many cells in the auditory cortex respond to specific frequencies, often referred to as sound pitches or to multiples of those frequencies. Two of the most interesting sound types for humans are language and music.

Speech Perception

Speech differs from other auditory input in three fundamental ways:

1. Speech sounds come largely from three restricted ranges of frequencies, which are known as *formants*. **Figure 15.12**A illustrates sound spectrograms of different two-formant syllables. The dark bars indicate the frequency bands seen in more detail in Figure 15.12B, which shows that the syllables differ both in the onset frequency of the second (higher) formant and in the onset time of the consonant. Notice that vowel sounds are in a constant frequency band, but consonants show rapid changes in frequency.

2. The same speech sounds vary from one context in which they are heard to another, yet all are perceived as being the same. Thus, the sound spectrogram of the letter "d" in English is different in the words "deep," "deck," and "duke," yet a listener perceives all of them as "d." The auditory system must have a mechanism for categorizing varying sounds as being equivalent, and this mechanism must be affected by

Figure 15.12

Speech Sounds (A) Schematic spectrograms of three different syllables, each made up of two formants. (B) Spectrograms of syllables differing in voice onset time. (After Springer, 1979.)

experience, because a major obstacle to learning foreign languages in adulthood is the difficulty of learning equivalent sound categories. Thus, a word's spectrogram depends on context—the words that precede and follow it. (There may be a parallel mechanism for musical categorization.)

3. Speech sounds change very rapidly in relation to one another, and the sequential order of the sounds is critical to understanding. According to Alvin Liberman, we can perceive speech at rates of as many as 30 segments per second, although normal speech is from about 8 to 10 segments per second. Speech perception at the higher rates is truly amazing, because it far exceeds the auditory system's ability to transmit all the speech as separate pieces of auditory information. For example, nonspeech noise is perceived as a buzz at a rate of only about 5 segments per second.

Clearly, the brain must recognize and analyze language sounds in a special way, much as the echolocation system of the bat is specialized in the bat brain. Likely, that special mechanism for speech perception is in the left temporal lobe. This function may not be unique to humans, because the results of studies in both monkeys and rats show specific deficits in the perception of species-typical vocalizations after left temporal lesions.

Music Perception

Music is fundamentally different from language because music relies on the relations between auditory elements rather than on individual elements. Consider that a tune is not defined by the pitches of its constituent tones but by the arrangement of the pitches' duration and the intervals between them. Musical sounds may differ from one another in three aspects: loudness, timbre, and pitch (see Figure 8.9).

- **Loudness** refers to the magnitude of a sensation as judged by a given person. Loudness, although related to the intensity of a sound as measured in decibels, is in fact a subjective evaluation described by such terms as "very loud," "soft," "very soft," and so forth.

- **Timbre** refers to the distinctive character of a sound, the quality that distinguishes it from all other sounds of similar pitch and loudness. For example, we can distinguish the sound of a violin from that of a trombone even though they may play the same note at the same loudness.

- **Pitch** refers to the position of a sound in a musical scale, as judged by the listener. Pitch is clearly related to frequency, the vibration rate of a sound wave. Consider the note middle C, described as a pattern of sound frequencies depicted in **Figure 15.13**. The amplitude of acoustical energy is conveyed by the darkness of the tracing in the spectrogram. The lowest component of this note is the *fundamental frequency* of the sound pattern, which is 264 Hz, or middle C. Frequencies above the fundamental frequency are known as *overtones* or *partials*. The overtones are generally simple multiples of the fundamental (for example, 2×264, or 528 Hz; 4×264, or 1056 Hz), as shown in Figure 15.13. Overtones that are multiples of the fundamental are known as *harmonics*.

If the fundamental frequency is removed from a note by means of electronic filters, the overtones are sufficient to determine the pitch of the fundamental frequency—a phenomenon known as *periodicity pitch*.

The ability to determine pitch from the overtones alone is probably due to the fact that the difference between the frequencies of the various harmonics is equal to the fundamental frequency (for example, 792 Hz − 528 Hz = 264 Hz = the fundamental). The auditory system can determine this difference, and we perceive the fundamental frequency.

For tones and overtones based on this fundamental frequency, the first five harmonics are dominant in the perception of pitch.

Figure 15.13

Spectrographic Display of the Steady-State Part of Middle C (264 Hz) Played on a Piano
Bands of acoustical energy are present at the fundamental frequency, as well as at integer multiples of the fundamental (harmonics). (After Ritsma, 1967.)

An important aspect of pitch perception is that, although we can generate (and perceive) the fundamental frequency, we still perceive the complex tones of the harmonics. This pitch is referred to as *spectral pitch*. When individual subjects hear complex sounds and are asked to make judgments about the direction of shifts in pitch, some will base their judgments on the fundamental and others on the spectral pitch. This difference is not related to musical training but rather to a basic difference in temporal-lobe organization.

The primary auditory cortex of the right temporal lobe appears to make this periodicity-pitch discrimination. For example, Robert Zatorre (2001) found that patients with right temporal lobectomies that include the primary auditory cortex (area 41 or **Heschl's gyrus**) are impaired at making pitch discriminations when the fundamental is absent but are normal at making such discriminations when the fundamental is present. The patients are also impaired at identifying the direction of a pitch change (see Tramo et al.).

Timing is a critical component of music, and two types of time relations are fundamental to the rhythm of musical sequences: the segmentation of sequences of pitches into groups based on the duration of the sounds and the identification of temporal regularity, or beat, which is also called *meter*. These two components can be dissociated by having subjects tap a rhythm versus keeping time with the beat (such as in spontaneous tapping of the foot with the strong beat).

Isabelle Peretz and Robert Zatorre concluded that studies of patients with temporal-lobe injuries as well as neuroimaging studies support the conclusion that the left temporal lobe plays a major role in temporal grouping for rhythm, whereas the right temporal lobe plays a complementary role in meter. But they also noted that there is a motor component of rhythm that is broadly distributed to include the supplementary motor cortex, premotor cortex, cerebellum, and basal ganglia.

Music is more than the perception of pitch, rhythm, timbre, and loudness, however. Peretz and Zatorre reviewed the many other features of music and the brain, including music memory, emotion, performance (both singing and playing), music reading, and the effect of musical training. The contribution of memory to music processing is crucial because music unfolds over time for us to perceive a tune.

Although injury to either temporal lobe impairs the learning of melodies, the retention of melodies is more affected by right temporal injury. Although both

Figure 15.14

Music and Brain Morphology
(A) At left, a three-dimensional cross section through the head showing the primary auditory cortex (AC) in each hemisphere, with the location of auditory evoked potentials shown at red and blue markers. At right, reconstructed dorsal views of the right auditory cortical surface showing the difference in morphology among three people. Heschl's gyrus is shown in red. (B) Examples from individual brains of musicians (top row) and nonmusicians (bottom row) showing the difference in morphology between people who hear fundamental frequency and those who hear spectral pitch. Hechl's gyrus is bigger on the left in the former group and on the right in the latter group. Note also that Heschl's gyrus is larger overall in the musicians. (Reproduced with permission from P. Schneider, V. Sluming, N. Roberts, M. Scherg, R. Goebel, H. J. Specht, H.G. Dosch, S. Bleeck, C. Stippich, and A. Rupp. Structural and functional asymmetry of lateral Heschl's gyrus reflects pitch perception preference. *Nature Neuroscience* 8:1241–1247, 2005.)

hemispheres take part in the production of music, the role of the right temporal lobe appears to be generally greater in producing melody and that of the left temporal lobe appears to be generally greater in rhythm. Zatorre (2001) suggested that the right temporal lobe has a special function in extracting pitch from sound, regardless of whether the sound is speech or music. In regard to speech, the pitch will contribute to "tone" of voice, which is known as **prosody**.

We learned from Kenji Tanaka's studies of visual learning that cells in the temporal lobe alter their perceptual functions with experience. The same appears to be true of musical experience. Peretz and Zatorre reviewed noninvasive imaging studies and concluded not only that the brains of professional musicians have more-pronounced responses to musical information than do those of nonmusicians, but also that musicians' brains are morphologically different in the area of Heschl's gyrus. Peter Schneider and his colleagues used MRI to estimate the volume of gray and white matter in Heschl's gyrus and found much larger volumes in both temporal lobes in the musicians (**Figure 15.14**).

The gray-matter differences are positively correlated with musical aptitude: the greater the aptitude, the larger the gray-matter volume. These researchers also found that fundamental-pitch listeners exhibit a pronounced leftward asymmetry of gray-matter volume in Hechl's gyrus, whereas spectral-pitch listeners have a rightward asymmetry, independent of musical training (see Figure 15.14B). The Schneider results imply that innate differences in brain morphology are related to the way in which pitch is processed and that some of the innate differences are related to musical ability. Practice and experience with music seem likely to be related to anatomical differences in the temporal cortex

(A)

(B)

as well, but this relation will be difficult to demonstrate without brain measurements before and after intense musical training.

We have emphasized the role of the temporal lobes in music but, like language, which is distributed in the frontal lobe as well, music perception and performance include the inferior frontal cortex in both hemispheres. Vanessa Sluming and her colleagues have shown that professional orchestral musicians have significantly more gray matter in Broca's area on the left. This frontal-lobe effect may be related to similarities in aspects of expressive output in both language and music. The key point, however, is that music likely has widespread effects on the brain's morphology and function that we have only begun to unravel.

Asymmetry of Temporal-Lobe Function

The temporal lobes are sensitive to epileptiform abnormalities, and surgical removal of the abnormal temporal lobe is often of benefit in treating epilepsy. These circumstances also allow neuropsychologists to study the complementary specialization of the left and right temporal lobes.

A comparison of the effects of left and right temporal lobectomy by Brenda Milner and her colleagues reveals that specific memory defects vary according to which side has the lesion. Damage to the left temporal lobe is associated with deficits in verbal memory; damage to the right temporal lobe is associated with deficits in nonverbal memory (for example, for faces). Similarly, left temporal lesions are associated with deficits in processing speech sounds, whereas right temporal lesions are associated with deficits in processing certain aspects of music.

Little is known, however, about the relative roles of the left and right temporal lobes in social and affective behavior. Right-, but not left-, temporal-lobe lesions lead to impairments in the recognition of faces and facial expression; so the two sides likely play different roles in social cognition. In fact, clinical experience dictates that left- and right-temporal-lobe lesions have different effects on personality.

Although the left and right temporal lobes are relatively specialized in their functions, do not be overly impressed by the apparent functional asymmetry. Substantial functional overlap is revealed in the relatively minor effects of unilateral temporal lobectomy, a striking result considering that such a large zone of the cerebral hemispheres is removed. Recall, for example, the striking recovery of function by H.H., whom we met in the Portrait at the beginning of the chapter.

It is incorrect to assume, however, that the removal of both temporal lobes merely doubles the symptoms of damage seen in unilateral temporal lobectomy. Bilateral temporal-lobe removal produces dramatic effects on both memory and affect that are orders of magnitude greater than those observed subsequent to unilateral lesions.

Symptoms of Temporal-Lobe Lesions

Nine principal symptoms are associated with disease of the temporal lobes: (1) disturbance of auditory sensation and perception, (2) disorders of music perception, (3) disorders of visual perception, (4) disturbance in the selection

Table **15.1** Summary of major symptoms of temporal-lobe damage

Symptoms	Most Probable Lesion Site	Basic Reference
Disturbance of auditory sensation	Areas 41, 42, 22	Vignolo, 1969; Hécaen and Albert, 1978
Disturbance of selection of visual and auditory input	Areas TE, STS	Sparks et al., 1970; Dorff et al., 1965
Disorders of visual perception	Areas TE, STS, amygdala	Milner, 1968; Meier and French, 1968
Disorders of auditory perception	Areas 41, 42, 22	Samson and Zatorre, 1988; Swisher and Hirsch, 1972
Disorders of music perception	Superior temporal gyrus	Zatorre et al., 2002
Impaired organization and categorization of material	Areas TE, STS	Wilkins and Moscovitch, 1978; Read, 1981
Poor contextual use	Area TE	Milner, 1958
Disturbance of language comprehension	Area 22 left	Hécaen and Albert, 1978
Poor long-term memory	Areas TE, TF, TH, 28	Milner, 1970
Changes in personality and affect	Area TE, plus amygdala	Blumer and Benson, 1975; Pincus and Tucker, 1974
Changes in sexual activity	Amygdala, plus?	Blumer and Walker, 1975

of visual and auditory input, (5) impaired organization and categorization of sensory input, (6), inability to use contextual information, (7) impaired long-term memory, (8) altered personality and affective behavior, and (9) altered sexual behavior. **Table 15.1** summarizes the major symptoms of temporal-lobe damage, lists the most probable lesion sites, and cites basic references. The sections that follow sample the range of temporal-lobe disorders and their clinical assessment.

Disorders of Auditory and Speech Perception

Damage to the primary visual or somatic cortex leads to a loss of conscious sensation; so it is reasonable to predict that bilateral damage to the auditory cortex will produce *cortical deafness*, an absence of neural activity in the auditory regions. The results of neither clinical nor animal laboratory studies support this prediction, however. As the Snapshot on page 419 illustrates, auditory hallucinations, which result from spontaneous activity in the auditory regions, are essentially the opposite of cortical deafness.

Auditory hallucination is the perception of sounds (hearing voices) that are not actually present. The auditory cortex plays a role in discriminating two forms of auditory processing—namely, rapidly presented stimuli and complex patterns of stimuli. Language is fast and must be analyzed quickly, whereas music generally contains relatively slower changes in frequency, but the ear must be sensitive to the small differences in frequency important in music.

Impaired auditory processing reveals the difficulty that temporal-lobe patients have in discriminating speech sounds. Although related to the common complaint among patients with left-temporal damage that people are talking too quickly, the problem is not so much the quickness of the speech; rather, it is the patient's inability to discriminate sounds presented quickly. This difficulty is commonly encountered by normal people trying to learn a new language.

The problem is not just in discriminating the speech sounds, however, but also in judging the temporal order in sounds heard. If a normal subject is pre-

SNAPSHOT
Imaging Auditory Hallucinations

Auditory hallucinations are the most common symptom of schizophrenia, reported by about 65% of people diagnosed with the disease. Auditory hallucinations are not simply sounds: a patient hears fully formed verbal passages that appear to be coming from an external source. The patient's thoughts are usually hostile or paranoid, as in the following example:

> Days later while in the Metropolis again, I was once more startled by those same pursuers, who had threatened me several days before. It was night-time. As before, I could catch part of their talk, but, in the theatre crowds, I could see them nowhere. I heard one of them a woman, say: "You can't get away from us; we'll lay for you and get after a while!" To add to the mystery, one of these "pursuers" repeated my thoughts aloud verbatim. I tried to elude those pursuers as before, but this time I tried to escape from them by means of subway trains, darting up and down subway exits and entrances, jumping on and off trains, until after midnight. But, at every station where I got off a train, I heard the voices of these pursuers as close as ever. (L. Percy King, from a letter written in the 1940s protesting the writer's imprisonment in a mental hospital and published in Frith, 1999, p. 414)

Dierks and colleagues described an experiment with paranoid schizophrenia patients whose hallucinations could be monitored within one fMRI session. In this study, the verbal

Functional MRI activation of auditory cortex during hallucinations in a schizophrenia subject. (After Dierks et al., 1999.)

hallucinations activated the primary auditory cortex, Broca's area, and the speech zone in the posterior temporal cortex in the left hemisphere, as diagrammed in the adjacent illustration and revealed in the fMRI image. In addition, there was some activation of the limbic areas.

These results suggest that verbal hallucinations have their origin in the patients' own inner language systems. The researchers proposed that activation in the auditory cortex leads to the perception that the voices are coming from an external source. The limbic activity presumably results from the anxiety generated by hearing voices, especially hostile voices.

Dierks, T., D. E. J. Kinden, M. Jandl, E. Formisano, R. Goebel, H. Lanfermann, and W. Singer. Activation of Heschl's gyrus during auditory hallucinations. *Neuron* 22:615–621, 1999.

---

sented with two sounds, a separation of only 50 to 60 ms is sufficient to identify which sound was presented first. Subjects with temporal-lobe lesions may require as much as 500 ms between two sounds (a 10-fold increase) to perform at the same level. Each of these audioperceptual impairments appears more severe after left-temporal-lobe lesions than after right-temporal-lobe lesions—a result suggesting that these auditory skills are especially important in discriminating speech sounds.

The fact that left-temporal-lobe lesions alter the perception of speech sounds ought not to be surprising: since the time of Wernicke, lesions of the left temporal association cortex (primarily area 22) have been known to produce aphasia (see Chapter 1). The classical view of **Wernicke's aphasia** is that it is associated with disturbed recognition of words, the extreme form being "word deafness"—an inability to recognize words as such despite intact hearing of pure tones.

Disorders of Music Perception

As noted earlier, patients with right temporal lesions including the primary auditory cortex are impaired at making pitch discriminations. Catherine Liegeois-Chauval and her colleagues pointed out that distinct musical processes may depend on specific cortical sites in the superior temporal gyrus (see Figure 15.1). In their study of patients with temporal lobectomies, these investigators found that rhythm discrimination was most affected by right posterior superior temporal gyrus damage, whereas meter discrimination (for example, distinguishing a waltz and a march) was more affected by anterior damage to either temporal lobe.

Although it is tempting to compartmentalize music and language on opposite sides of the brain, in fact, only certain characteristics of musical and language input are analyzed selectively by the two hemispheres. Zatorre emphasized the key difference: the left hemisphere is concerned more with speed and the right hemisphere with distinguishing frequency differences, a process called *spectral sensitivity*.

That the brain appears to have neural networks dedicated to processing language and music leads to the conclusion that both language and music have biological roots. Although this conclusion seems obvious for language, it is less obvious for music, which has often been perceived as an artifact of culture. But considerable evidence suggests that humans are born with a predisposition for processing music.

Infants show learning preferences for musical scales and are biased toward perceiving the regularity (such as harmonics) on which music is built. Peretz argued that one of the strongest bits of evidence favoring the biological basis of music is that a surprising number of people have a condition known as *congenital amusia*. They are tone deaf.

Apparently, amusic people have an abnormality in their neural networks for music, and no amount of training makes much difference. In fact, we have a colleague whose parents were both music teachers and, to their chagrin, she is amusic. She likes to note that she knows that the national anthem is being played because people stand up!

Liegeois-Chauvel and colleagues studied musical processing in a large group of patients with temporal lobectomies and found that injury to the right superior temporal gyrus impairs various aspects of processing necessary for discriminating melodies. In addition, a dissociation between the roles of the posterior and anterior regions of the superior temporal gyrus on different aspects of musical processing suggests their relative localization within the superior temporal gyrus.

The alignment of the holes in this piece of bear femur found in a cave in northern Slovenia suggests that Neanderthals made a flute from it and made music with the flute at least 43,000 years ago. Like modern humans, Neanderthals probably had complementary hemispheric specialization for language and music. (Courtesy of Ivan Turk/Institut 2A Archeologijo, ZRC-Sazu, Slovenia. Photograph by Marko Zaplatil.)

Disorders of Visual Perception

Although persons with temporal lobectomies do not normally have large defects in their visual fields, they do have deficits in visual perception. Such deficits were first demonstrated by Milner, who found her patients with right temporal lobectomies impaired in interpreting cartoon drawings in the McGill Picture-Anomalies Test.

For example, one item illustrating a monkey in a cage features an oil painting on the wall of the cage—an obvious oddity or anomaly. But, although patients with right temporal lesions can describe the contents of the cartoon accurately, they are impaired at recognizing the anomalous aspects of this picture and others. Similarly, on a test such as the Mooney Closure Test or tests requiring the discrimination of complex patterns (**Figure 15.15**), patients with temporal-lobe damage perform very poorly.

One of the most interesting visual perceptual deficits is in facial perception and recognition. When Kolb and his associates presented patients with the split-faces test (see Figure 15.11), they found that those with right-temporal-lobe resections fail to show a bias for that part of the face falling in the left visual field, suggesting that these patients perceive faces abnormally. This conclusion is consistent with reports that patients with right-temporal-lobe damage are impaired at the recognition and recall of faces or photographs of faces.

Furthermore, these patients do not appear able to perceive subtle social signals such as discreet but obvious glances at one's watch, a gesture often intended as a cue to break off a conversation. Presumably, the patients fail to perceive the significance of the visual signal. Facial signals are a form of biological motion, the analysis of which we have seen to be a function of the temporal lobe.

The description of deficits in visual perception in people with temporal-lobe injury is consistent with the hypothetical role of the inferotemporal cortex in the ventral visual stream (compare Figures 13.5 and 15.1B). An extensive literature shows that monkeys with inferotemporal lesions have severe and selective deficits in learning tasks that require the visual recognition of objects. Furthermore, inferotemporal cortex neurons in monkeys have long been known to have selective characteristics, such as a preference for faces or hands. Recall that these preferences may be quite specific (see Figure 15.8).

(A)
(B)
(C)

(D)

Figure **15.15**

Tests for Visual Disorders
(A) Meier and French's test, in which the subject must identify the drawing that is different. (B) Sample of the Gottschaldt Hidden-Figures Test. The task is to detect and trace the sample (upper drawing) in each of the figures below it. (C) In the Rey Complex-Figure Test, the subject is asked to copy the drawing as exactly as possible. (D) Sample of the Mooney Closure Test in which the task is to identify the face within the ambiguous shadows.

Disturbance of Selection of Visual and Auditory Input

We must select which inputs to process from the wealth of information in our environment. This selectivity is generally not conscious, because the nervous system automatically scans input and selectively perceives the environment. (Conscious control can be exerted, of course, as when you search for a cash machine to make a withdrawal.)

Selectivity in auditory perception is best illustrated by the problem of listening to two conversations simultaneously. Because it is impossible to process the two competing inputs concurrently, the auditory system adopts one of two strategies: either one conversation is ignored or attention shifts back and forth from one conversation to the other. In either case, there is a selection of input.

Selective perception in the visual system operates similarly. For example, it is not possible to watch all floor events at a gymnastics meet simultaneously. Either we focus our attention entirely on one event or shift it from one event to another.

Let us now consider the person with temporal-lobe damage. Selection of both auditory and visual input is impaired, which is ordinarily demonstrated only by special testing procedures. Selective attention to auditory input can be tested by dichotic listening (see Figure 11.11). Recall that, when subjects are presented with two words simultaneously, one to each ear, normal subjects report more of the words presented to the right ear; if tonal sequences are presented dichotically, there will be a left-ear advantage.

This left-ear advantage is maintained in patients with temporal-lobe lesions, but left-temporal-lobe lesions result in an overall drop in the number of words recalled. One explanation for this effect is that the nervous system has difficulty focusing selectively on the input into one ear and attempts to process all the input concurrently; as a result, performance drops significantly.

Analogous findings are reported for visual input. If two different visual stimuli are presented simultaneously, one to each visual field, damage to the left temporal lobe impairs recall of content of the right visual field, but damage to the right temporal lobe impairs recall of content in both visual fields. Again, the nervous system may now be unable to focus on distinctive features of the stimuli to allow efficient perception and storage of the input.

In regard to visual input, however, it is noteworthy that right temporal lesions produce bilateral deficits, whereas left temporal lesions produce unilateral ones. This difference implies that the right temporal lobe may have a greater role than the left in selective attention to visual input.

Organization and Categorization

Asked to learn a list of words such as "dog, car, bus, apple, rat, lemon, cat, truck, orange," most of us will organize the words into three different categories—animals, vehicles, and fruit. If the list is later recalled, the items are likely to be recalled by category, and recall of the categories is likely to be used as an aid in recall of the items.

The ability to organize material is especially important for language and memory. For example, categorizing makes it possible to comprehend complex, extended sentences, including both the meaning of individual clauses and the information inferred from them. Organization of sensory input appears to be a function of the temporal lobes. Patients with left temporal lobectomies are impaired in their ability to categorize even single words or pictures of familiar objects.

Thus, patients have difficulty placing words or pictures into discrete categories, even when they are requested to do so, and they also have difficulty in using categories that most of us use automatically. For example, Milner has found that, when these patients are given a category name (such as animal) and are asked to recall exemplars of the category (such as dog, cat, rat), they have difficulty, even though they are fluent in other types of tests. Given that these patients have difficulty in simple types of categorization tasks studied in the laboratory, you can imagine that their difficulty in spontaneous organization may represent a significant deficit in cognition, especially in memory for complex material.

Neurolinguists propose that another type of categorization may be undertaken in the left temporal lobe. *Semantic categories* are hierarchies of meaning in which a single word might belong to several categories simultaneously. For example, a duck belongs to the categories animal, bird, and waterfowl. Each of these categories is a refinement of the preceding one. Patients with posterior temporal lesions may show dysphasic symptoms in which they can recognize the broader categorization but have difficulty with the more specific ones.

Using Contextual Information

The meaning of identical stimuli can vary, depending on context. The word "fall," for example, can refer to a season or to a tumble, depending on the context. Similarly, context may be a major cue for facial recognition. Most of us have encountered someone completely out of context (for example, while in Paris you encounter a clerk from your neighborhood store at home) and have been unable to recall who the person is until information about the context is provided.

A more complex example of extracting meaning from context is found in social situations. The interpretation of events, and indeed our role in events, depends on the social context. Thus, stimuli may be interpreted in one way when we are with our parents and in a different way when we are with our peers.

A simple example of the use of contextual information can be found in the McGill Picture-Anomalies Test described earlier in the section on visual perceptual deficits. The only clue to the correct choice in the McGill anomalies is the context.

Memory

Interest in the temporal lobes' function in memory was stimulated in the early 1950s by the discovery that bilateral removal of the medial temporal lobes, including the hippocampus and amygdala, results in amnesia for all events after the surgery (**anterograde amnesia**). It is now clear that both the medial temporal regions and the temporal neocortex are important for memory functions (see Chapter 18).

Damage to the inferotemporal cortex specifically interferes with conscious recall of information, the extent of the memory disturbance increasing in direct proportion to the amount of temporal-lobe damage. Lesions of the left temporal lobe result in impaired recall of verbal material, such as short stories and word lists, whether presented visually or aurally; lesions of the right temporal lobe result in impaired recall of nonverbal material, such as geometric drawings, faces, and tunes. Two case histories demonstrate the roles of the left and right temporal lobes in memory.

Mr. B., age 38, was suffering from an astrocytoma in the left temporal lobe. Before onset, he had been a successful executive in an oil company and was noted for his efficiency. As his tumor developed, he became forgetful and, at the time of hospital admission, his efficiency had dropped drastically: he had begun to forget appointments and other important events. Forgetfulness had become such a problem that he had begun to write notes to himself to cover his memory problem, but he often mislaid the notes, leading to even greater embarrassment.

On formal tests of memory, Mr. B. had special difficulty in recalling short stories read to him a few minutes earlier. In one test, he was read the following story from the Wechsler Memory Scale and was asked to repeat it as exactly as

Stimulus drawing | Ms. C's sketch

Figure 15.16

Impaired Recall In each set shown, the drawing at the left is the original stimulus and the drawing at the right is Ms. C.'s sketch made immediately after viewing each figure for 10 seconds. Note that Ms. C.'s impairment is worse with the more complex figures. Ms. C. was unable to recall even the simplest figure 10 minutes after viewing it.

possible: "Anna Thompson of South Boston, employed as a scrub woman in an office building, was held up on State Street the night before and robbed of $15. She had four little children, the rent was due and they had not eaten for two days. The officers, touched by the woman's story, made up a purse for her."

Mr. B. recalled: "A woman was robbed and went to the police station where they made her a new purse. She had some children too." This performance is very poor for a person of Mr. B.'s intelligence and education. On the other hand, his immediate recall of digits was good; he could repeat strings of seven digits accurately. Similarly, his recall of geometric designs was within normal limits, illustrating the asymmetry of memory functions, because his right temporal lobe was intact.

Ms. C. illustrates the complement of Mr. B.'s syndrome. She was a bright 22-year-old college student who had an indolent tumor of the right temporal lobe. When we first saw her, after surgery, she complained of memory loss.

She was within normal limits on formal tests of verbal memory, such as the story of Anna Thompson, but was seriously impaired on formal tests of visual memory, especially geometric drawings. For example, in one test, she was shown geometric designs for 10 seconds and then asked to draw them from memory. Ten minutes later, she was asked to draw them again. She had difficulty with immediate recall (**Figure 15.16**) and, after 10 minutes, was unable to recall any of the drawings.

Affect and Personality

Although temporal-lobe disorder has been associated with disturbance of affect in humans for nearly 100 years, knowledge about the details of this role is still surprisingly fragmentary. Wilder Penfield and others reported that stimulation of the anterior and medial temporal cortex produces feelings of fear (see Chapter 11), an effect also occasionally obtained from stimulating the amygdala. Recall, too, that H.H.'s wife reported that H.H.'s personality was different after his tumor and surgery from what it had been before.

Temporal-lobe epilepsy has traditionally been associated with personality characteristics that overemphasize trivia and the petty details of daily life. Symptoms of this personality include pedantic speech, egocentricity, perseveration in discussions of personal problems (sometimes referred to as "stickiness," because one is stuck talking to the person), paranoia, preoccupation with religion, and proneness to aggressive outbursts (Pincus and Tucker, 1974). This constellation of behaviors produces what is described as *temporal-lobe personality*, although very few people combine all these traits.

Similar personality traits arise after temporal lobectomy. There appears to be a relative asymmetry in the symptoms, with right temporal lobectomy more likely to be associated with these personality traits than left temporal lobectomy. This observation has not been quantified, however, and warrants further study.

Changes in Sexual Behavior

A classic symptom of bilateral temporal-lobe damage that includes the amygdala is a release of sexual behavior. This symptom is not observed after unilateral injury. We return to the effects of amygdala damage on sexual and social behavior in Chapter 20.

Clinical Neuropsychological Assessment of Temporal-Lobe Damage

A number of standardized assessment tools have proved sensitive and valid predictors of temporal-lobe injury (**Table 15.2**). Like the clinical neuropsychological tests of parietal-lobe function described in Chapter 14, these tests do not assess all possible temporal-lobe symptoms, but it would be highly unusual for a person to perform normally on all these tests if there were damage to either temporal lobe.

- Auditory- and visual-processing capacity can be assessed by using dichotic listening and the *McGill Picture-Anomalies Test*. The picture-anomalies task is not as sensitive an indicator today as it was when first used in the 1950s, perhaps because video-based home entertainment has made the average person more sophisticated visually. Nevertheless, a poor score on this test almost invariably denotes right temporal abnormality.

- The best test of general verbal-memory ability is the revised Wechsler Memory Scale. However, because the Wechsler memory quotient is affected by nonspecific disorders of attention, two subtests—paired associates and logical stories—are often used as a purer measure of verbal-memory capacity. The paired-associates subtest requires a subject to learn a series of word pairs (for example, north–south, cabbage–pen) such that, when one word is read (north, cabbage), its paired-associate word (south, pen) can be recalled. An example of the logical memory test was presented in reference to Mr. B.'s verbal-memory defect.

- The Rey Complex-Figure Test has proved one of the best for evaluating nonverbal memory function of the right temporal lobe (see Figure 15.15C). A printed copy of a complex geometric pattern is placed before the subject with the instructions, "Copy the drawing as accurately as you can." Forty-five minutes later, the subject is asked to reproduce as much of the figure as he or she can remember. Although the scoring criteria provide an objective measure of nonverbal memory, the test has the drawback that depressed or poorly motivated subjects may perform poorly, not because of right-temporal-lobe damage but because they refuse to try to recall the figure. There is no easy solution to this problem, because all tests of nonverbal memory are subject to this complication.

Table **15.2** Standardized clinical neuropsychological tests for temporal-lobe damage

Function	Test	Basic Reference
Auditory processing capacity	Dichotic words and melodies	Sparks et al., 1970
Visual processing capacity	McGill Picture Anomalies	Milner, 1958
Verbal memory	Revised Wechsler Memory Scale; logical stories and paired associates	Milner, 1975
Nonverbal memory	Rey Complex Figure	Taylor, 1969
Language	Token	de Renzi and Faglioni, 1978

- A deficit in language comprehension could be the result of a lesion in any of the language zones of the left hemisphere (that is, in the parietal, temporal, or frontal lobes). No current neuropsychological assessment tool can localize the area of damage within the left hemisphere. For this reason, we once again recommend the Token Test as the test of choice for language comprehension.

Summary

Anatomy of the Temporal Lobe

The temporal lobe can be divided into four functional zones: (1) for auditory processes (superior temporal gyrus), (2) for visual processes (inferotemporal cortex), (3) for emotion (amygdala), and (4) for spatial navigation and spatial and object memory (hippocampus and associated cortex).

A Theory of Temporal-Lobe Function

The temporal lobe adds two features to both auditory and visual information—namely, tone (affect) and categorization. These features are important for understanding sensory input as well as for using it in biologically relevant ways, such as in biological motion. A surprisingly extensive face-perception system includes regions in the occipital lobe as well as several different regions of the temporal lobe.

Whereas the parietal lobe processes spatial location with respect to movement, the temporal lobe uses spatial location as a feature of object recognition and in the development of memories for object location.

The processing of auditory information is specialized for two characteristics: speed and frequency. Language processing requires analysis of rapid changes in sounds; but, because people talk at different pitches ranging from high, squeaky voices to deep, resonant voices, understanding language sounds can tolerate differences in frequencies. In contrast, music is relatively slower than language, but differences in frequency are critical.

Symptoms of Temporal-Lobe Lesions

The left temporal lobe is more concerned with speed, the right with complex frequency patterns. Damage to the auditory regions of the temporal lobe produces deficits in the recognition of language (primarily left) and music (primarily right), as well as in sound localization.

Damage to the visual regions of the temporal lobe disrupts the recognition of complex visual stimuli, such as faces. Damage to medial temporal regions produces deficits in affect, personality, spatial navigation, and object memory.

Clinical Neuropsychological Assessment of Temporal-Lobe Damage

Neuropsychological analyses of temporal-lobe functions utilize tests that are sensitive to discrete temporal-lobe injuries. Such tests include those of auditory processing (dichotic listening), visual processing (object recognition), memory (both verbal and nonverbal), and language.

References

Allison, T., A. Puce, and G. McCarthy. Social perception from visual cues: Role of the STS region. *Trends in Cognitive Sciences* 4:267–278, 2000.

Belin, P., R. J. Zatorre, P. Lafaille, P. Ahad, and B. Pike. Voice-selective areas in human auditory cortex. *Nature* 403:309–312, 2000.

Blumer, D., and D. F. Benson. Personality changes with frontal and temporal lesions. In D. F. Benson and F. Blumer, Eds. *Psychiatric Aspects of Neurologic Disease*. New York: Grune & Stratton, 1975.

Blumer, D., and D. E. Walker. The neural basis of sexual behavior. In D. F. Benson and D. Blumer, Eds. *Psychiatric Aspects of Neurologic Disease*. New York: Grune & Stratton, 1975.

Chedru, F., V. Bastard, and R. Efron. Auditory micropattern discrimination in brain damaged patients. *Neuropsychologia* 16:141–149, 1978.

de Renzi, E., and P. Faglioni. Normative data and screening power of a shortened version of the token test. *Cortex* 14:41–49, 1978.

Dierks, T., D. E. J. Kinden, M. Jandl, E. Formisano, R. Goebel, H. Lanfermann, and W. Singer. Activation of Heschl's gyrus during auditory hallucinations. *Neuron* 22:615–621, 1999.

Dorff, J. E., A. F. Mirsky, and M. Mishkin. Effects of unilateral temporal lobe removals on tachistoscopic recognition in the left and right visual fields. *Neuropsychologia* 3:39–51, 1965.

Farah, M. J. What is "special" about face perception? *Psychological Review* 105:482–498, 1998.

Frith, C. How hallucinations make themselves heard. *Neuron* 22:414–415, 1999.

Fuster, J. M., and J. P. Jervey. Neuronal firing in the inferotemporal cortex of the monkey in a visual memory task. *Journal of Neuroscience* 2:361–375, 1982.

Gauthier, I., M. J. Tarr, A. W. Anderson, P. Skudlarksi, and J. C. Gore. Activation of the middle fusiform "face area" increases with expertise in recognizing novel objects. *Nature Neuroscience* 2:568–573, 1999.

Geschwind, N. Disconnexion syndromes in animals and man. *Brain* 88:237–294, 585–644, 1965.

Hancock, P. J. B., V. Bruce, and A. M. Burton. Recognition of unfamiliar faces. *Trends in Cognitive Sciences* 4:330–337, 2000.

Hasson, U., Y. Nir, I. Levy, G. Fuhrmann, and R. Malach. Intersubject synchronization of cortical activity during natural vision. *Science* 303:1634–1640, 2004.

Haxby, J. V., E. A. Hoffman, and M. I. Gobbini. The distributed human neural system for face perception. *Trends in Cognitive Sciences* 4:223–333, 2000.

Haxby, J. V., L. G. Ungerleider, V. P. Clark, J. L. Schouten, E. A., Hoffman, and A. Martin. The effect of face inversion on activity in human neural systems for face and object peception. *Neuron* 22:189–199, 1999.

Hécaen, H., and M. L. Albert. *Human Neuropsychology.* New York: Wiley, 1978.

Kolb, B., B. Milner, and L. Taylor. Perception of faces by patients with localized cortical excisions. *Canadian Journal of Psychology* 37:8–18, 1983.

Kolb, B., and L. Taylor. Facial expression and the neocortex. *Society for Neuroscience Abstracts* 14:219, 1988.

Lackner, J. R., and H. L. Teuber. Alterations in auditory fusion thresholds after cerebral injury in man. *Neuropsychologia* 11:409–415, 1973.

Liberman, A. On finding that speech is special. *American Psychologist* 37:148–167, 1982.

Liegeois-Chauvel, C., I. Peretz, M. Babai, V. Laguitton, and P. Chauvel. Contribution of different cortical areas in the temporal lobes to music processing. *Brain* 121:1853–1867, 1998.

Meier, M. S., and L. A. French. Lateralized deficits in complex visual discrimination and bilateral transfer of reminiscence following unilateral temporal lobectomy. *Neuropsychologia* 3:261–272, 1968.

Milner, B. Psychological defects produced by temporal lobe excision. *Research Publications of the Association for Research in Nervous and Mental Disease* 38:244–257, 1958.

Milner, B. Visual recognition and recall after right temporal lobe excision in man. *Neuropsychologia* 6:191–209, 1968.

Milner, B. Memory and the medial temporal regions of the brain. In K.H. Pribram and D.E. Broadbent, Eds. *Biological Basis of Memory.* New York: Academic Press, 1970.

Milner, B. Psychological aspects of focal epilepsy and its neurosurgical management. *Advances in Neurology* 8:299–321, 1975.

Peretz, I. Brain specialization for music: New evidence from congenital amusia. *Annals of the New York Academy of Sciences* 930:153–165, 2001.

Peretz, I., and R. J. Zatorre. Brain organization for music processing. *Annual Review of Psychology* 56:89–114, 2005.

Perrett, D. I., M. H. Harries, P. J. Benson, A. J. Chitty, and A. J. Mistlin. Retrieval of structure from rigid and biological motion: An analysis of the visual responses of neurones in the macaque temporal cortex. In A. Blake and T. Troscianko, Eds. *AI and the Eye.* New York: Wiley, 1990.

Pincus, J. H., and G. J. Tucker. *Behavioral Neurology.* New York: Oxford University Press, 1974.

Rauschecker, J. P., and B. Tian. Mechanisms and streams for processing of "what" and "where" in auditory cortex. *Proceedings of the National Academy of Sciences of the United States of America* 97:11800–11806, 2000.

Read, D. E. Solving deductive-reasoning problems after unilateral temporal lobectomy. *Brain and Language* 12:116–127, 1981.

Ritsma, R. Frequencies dominant in the perception of pitch of complex sounds. *Journal of the Acoustical Society of America* 42:191–198, 1967.

Samson, S., and R. J. Zatorre. Discrimination of melodic and harmonic stimuli after unilateral cerebral excisions. *Brain and Cognition* 7:348–360, 1988.

Schneider, P., M. Scherg, H. G. Dosch, H. J. Specht, A. Gutschalk, and A. Rupp. Morphology of Hechl's gyrus reflects enhanced activation in the auditory cortex of musicians. *Nature Neuroscience* 5:688–694, 2002.

Schneider, P., V. Sluming, N. Roberts, M. Scherg, R. Goebel, H. J. Specht, H. G. Dosch, S. Bleeck, C. Stippich, and A. Rupp. Structural and functional asymmetry of lateral Heschl's gyrus reflects pitch perception preference. *Nature Neuroscience* 8:1241–1247, 2005.

Schulhoff, C., and H. Goodglass. Dichotic listening: Side of brain injury and cerebral dominance. *Neuropsychologia* 7:149–160, 1969.

Sidtis, J. J. Music, pitch perception, and the mechanisms of cortical hearing. In M. S. Gazzaniga, Ed. *Handbook of Cognitive Neuroscience.* New York: Plenum, 1984.

Sluming, V., T. Barrick, M. Howard, E. Cezayirli, A. Mayes, and N. Roberts. Voxel-based morphometry reveals increased gray matter density in Broca's area in male symphony orchestra musicians. *Neuroimage* 17:1613–1622, 2002.

Sparks, R., H. Goodglass, and B. Nickel. Ipsilateral versus contralateral extinction in dichotic listening from hemispheric lesions. *Cortex* 6:249–260, 1970.

Springer, S. P. Speech perception and the biology of language. In M. S. Gazzaniga, Ed. *Handbook of Behavioral Neurology: Neuropsychology*. New York: Plenum, 1979.

Swisher, L., and I. J. Hirsch. Brain damage and the ordering of two temporally successive stimuli. *Neuropsychologia* 10:137–152, 1972.

Tanaka, J. W. Object categorization, expertise, and neural plasticity. In M. S. Gazzaniga, Ed. *The Cognitive Neurosciences III*, 3rd ed. Cambridge, Mass.: MIT Press, 2004.

Tanaka, K. Neuronal mechanisms of object recognition. *Science* 262:685–688, 1993.

Taylor, L. B. Localization of cerebral lesions by psychological testing. *Clinical Neurosurgery* 16:269–287, 1969.

Tramo, M. J., G. D. Shah, and L. D. Braida. Functional role of auditory cortex in frequency processing and pitch perception. *Journal of Neurophysiology* 87:122–139, 2002.

Trehub, S., E. G. Schellenberg, and S. B. Kamenetsky. Infants' and adults' perception of scale structure. *Journal of Experimental Psychology: Human Perception and Performance* 25:383–396, 1999.

Valentine, T. Upside-down faces: A review of the effect of inversion upon face recognition. *British Journal of Psychology* 79:4571–4591, 1988.

Vignolo, L. A. Auditory agnosia: A review and report of recent evidence. In A. L. Benton, Ed. *Contributions to Clinical Neuropsychology*. Chicago: Aldine, 1969.

Wilkins, A., and M. Moscovitch. Selective impairment of semantic memory after temporal lobectomy. *Neuropsychologia* 16:73–79, 1978.

Wolberg, Z., and J. D. Newman. Auditory cortex of squirrel monkey: Response patterns of single cells to species-specific vocalizations. *Science* 175:212–214, 1972.

Zatorre, R. J. There's more to auditory cortex than meets the ear. *Hearing Research*, in press.

Zatorre, R. J. Neural specializations for tonal processing. *Annals of the New York Academy of Sciences* 930:193–210, 2001.

Zatorre, R. J., and P. Belin. Spectral and temporal processing in human auditory cortex. *Cerebral Cortex* 11:946–953, 2001.

Zatorre, R. J., P. Belin, and V. Penhume. Structure and function of the auditory cortex: Music and speech. *Trends in Cognitive Sciences* 6:37–46, 2002.

Zatorre, R. J., and A. R. Halpern. Effect of unilateral temporal-lobe excision on perception and imagery of songs. *Neuropsychologia* 31:221–232, 1993.

The Frontal Lobes

Portrait: Losing Frontal-Lobe Functions

E.L. was a professor of botany at a college in upstate New York. Known for his organizational skills, E.L. had developed a large herbarium at the college and truly enjoyed having students work with him on research projects.

Late in the spring semester when he was 60 years old, E.L. began to have headaches and felt as if he had the flu, but, after a few days bed rest, he was not getting any better. He eventually visited his physician, who determined that E.L. had an infection, although the source was difficult to identify.

Meanwhile, E.L. began to develop cognitive symptoms that his wife found very worrisome. He seemed disorganized, showed little emotion, and, although a chapter of his unpublished book was due and he was never late for

G.JLP/Photo Researchers

deadlines, he said that he just could not think of anything to write.

The most striking thing about E.L. when he arrived for his neuropsychological assessment was his flat affect

and the virtual absence of facial expression—symptoms typical of left-frontal-lobe patients. This lack of affect was not associated with a lack of effort on the tests, however, because the assessment ranked his intelligence and general memory scores in the superior range. He did, nevertheless, register significant impairments on tests sensitive to frontal-lobe functions.

Talking with E.L. and his wife of more than 30 years made it clear that he was having difficulty not only with his academic work but also in his social interactions with colleagues, friends, and his family. He found it difficult to interact even with close friends, and his wife was concerned that her husband was "not the man I married."

All neural roads eventually lead to the frontal lobes. As is apparent in E.L.'s case, presented in the Portrait, when some of the roads lead nowhere, people can have major problems generating appropriate behavior. In this chapter, we consider the anatomical organization of the frontal lobes, including the neural roads for information flow to and from them, before looking at a general theory of frontal-lobe function, the various symptoms associated with frontal-lobe injury, and diseases that affect the frontal lobes.

Anatomy of the Frontal Lobes

Children are notorious for their social faux pas because they do not recognize that the rules of behavior change with the social and environmental circumstances. Indeed, controlling our behavior in response to the social or environmental situation that we are in requires considerable skill, and we can all relate examples in which we goofed and behaved inappropriately. Fortunately, most of us do not err often, because our frontal lobes control our behavior with respect to time and place. Yet the frontal lobe can perform such a function only if it is provided with all the relevant sensory and mnemonic (that is, memory) information available.

Subdivisions of the Frontal Cortex

In the human brain, the frontal lobes include all the tissue anterior to the central sulcus. This vast area, constituting 20% of the neocortex, is made up of several functionally distinct regions that we shall group into three general categories—motor, premotor, and prefrontal, as diagrammed in **Figures 16.1** and **16.2**.

The motor cortex is area 4. The premotor cortex includes areas 6 and 8, which can be divided into four regions:

- **lateral area 6**: premotor cortex
- **medial area 6**: supplementary motor cortex
- **area 8**: frontal eye field
- **area 8A**: supplementary eye field

In humans, the lateral premotor area expanded as Broca's area (area 44) developed.

Prefrontal cortex is a peculiar name that derives from Jersey Rose and Clinton Woolsey's observation that the frontal lobes of all the mammalian species that they examined have a region that receives projections from the dorsomedial nucleus of the thalamus. They saw this thalamic projection as being parallel to the projections of the lateral and medial geniculate nuclei to the visual and the auditory cortex, respectively, and concluded that the dorsomedial pro-

(A) Lateral view

(C) Ventral view

(B) Medial view

(D) Functional zones

Premotor and supplementary motor

Frontal eye fields

Motor

Face sensory

Face motor

Dorso-lateral

Orbital

Broca's area

Figure 16.1

Mapping the Human Frontal Lobe (A–C) Petrides and Pandya's cytoarchitectonic maps of the frontal lobe redrawn. (D) Approximate boundaries of frontal-lobe functional zones.

(A) Lateral view

(B) Medial view

(C) Ventral view

Olfactory bulb

(D) Major sulci

Multimodal cortex   Arcuate sulcus   Central sulcus

Principal sulcus

Figure **16.2**

Frontal Areas of the Monkey
(A–C) Petrides and Pandya's cytoarchitectonic maps of the frontal lobe of the rhesus monkey. (D) The two major sulci in the monkey frontal lobe are the principal sulcus and the arcuate sulcus.

jection could be used to define a similar region in different animal species. They termed this region the prefrontal cortex.

In primates, the prefrontal cortex can be divided into three regions (refer to Figures 16.1 and 16.2): (1) dorsolateral prefrontal cortex (areas 9 and 46); (2) inferior (ventral) prefrontal cortex (areas 11, 12, 13, and 14); and (3) medial frontal cortex (areas 25 and 32). The inferior frontal cortex is sometimes referred to as the **orbitofrontal cortex** because of its relation to the orbit (eye socket). The medial frontal area is sometimes considered part of the anterior cingulate region rather than part of the prefrontal cortex, even though it may receive dorsomedial projections.

As in the temporal lobe, many areas in the frontal cortex are multimodal. Cells responsive to combinations of visual, auditory, and somatic stimuli are found in the lateral premotor cortex (area 6) and in area 46. In contrast, cells responsive to taste and olfaction are found in area 13. The latter cells likely produce our perception of flavor in foods.

Connections of the Motor and Premotor Areas

The motor and premotor areas are part of a functional system to control movements directly. Several groups of connections form this system:

- The motor cortex projects to the spinal motor neurons to control limb, hand, foot, and digit movements and to the appropriate cranial-nerve motor neurons to control facial movements. It also projects to subcortical motor structures such as the basal ganglia and the red nucleus.

- The premotor areas can influence movement directly through corticospinal projections or indirectly through projections to the motor cortex. The premotor regions also receive projections from the posterior parietal areas PE and PF. Thus, the premotor regions are connected to areas concerned with the execution of limb movements.

- The frontal eye fields (areas 8 and 8A) receive projections from regions controlling eye movements and send projections to these regions. Thus, these regions receive visual input from posterior parietal region PG and the superior colliculus.

- All premotor areas receive projections from the dorsolateral prefrontal cortex, which implies that this prefrontal area has some role in the control of limb and eye movements.

Connections of the Prefrontal Areas

The prefrontal areas can be viewed as the end points of the dorsal (object recognition) and ventral (spatial behavior) visual streams. In fact, Daniel Felleman and David van Essen include prefrontal regions as part of the visual cortex (see Figure 10.20).

The dorsolateral prefrontal cortex (areas 9 and 46) receives its main inputs from the posterior parietal areas and the superior temporal sulcus. These connections are reciprocal. In addition, the dorsolateral cortex has extensive connections to regions to which the posterior parietal cortex also projects, including the cingulate cortex, basal ganglia, and superior colliculus (see Figure 14.2). The key to understanding the functions of the dorsolateral cortex lies in its relation to the posterior parietal cortex (**Figure 16.3**A).

The orbitofrontal cortex (areas 11 through 14) receives its main afferents from the temporal lobe, including the auditory regions of the superior temporal gyrus, the visual regions of the inferotemporal cortex (area TE), and the superior temporal sulcus, and from the amygdala (Figure 16.3B). In addition, connections from the somatosensory cortex (area 43), gustatory cortex (in the

Figure **16.3**

Corticocortical Connections of the Rhesus Monkey Refer to the frontal-lobe areas diagrammed in Figure 16.2. (A) Connections to the dorsolateral surface include projections from posterior parietal as well as temporal regions. (B) Connections to the inferior frontal region are from the temporal lobe. Connections from the gustatory and olfactory cortices are shown in Figure 16.4.

(A) Spatial behavior

Lateral view

Ventral view

(B) Object recognition

Medial view

insula), and olfactory regions of the pyriform cortex are illustrated in **Figure 16.4**. The orbital cortex therefore gains input from all sensory modalities.

The orbitofrontal area projects subcortically to the amygdala and hypothalamus, providing a route for influencing the autonomic nervous system, which controls changes in blood pressure, respiration, and so on. These physiological changes are important in emotional responses.

The prefrontal regions receive significant input from dopaminergic cells in the tegmentum (see Figure 5.17). This modulatory input plays an important role in regulating how prefrontal neurons react to stimuli, including stressful stimuli, and probably plays some role in our different emotional states. Abnormalities in this projection play a central role in schizophrenia.

A Theory of Frontal-Lobe Function

Imagine the following scenario. On the spur of the moment, you invite friends for dinner. Because you have nothing to serve, you must go shopping after you leave work at 5:00 P.M. Before leaving, you prepare a list of items to buy.

You are working under a time constraint because you must return home before your guests arrive and you need time to prepare. Because the items that you need are not all at the same store, you must make an efficient plan of travel. You also must not be distracted by stores selling items (such as shoes) that you do not need or by extended chats with store clerks or friends whom you might encounter.

The task that you have set yourself is a bit rushed but, for most people, it offers little challenge. People with frontal-lobe injury, however, cannot manage it. The fundamental requirements of the task that challenge frontal-lobe patients are:

- Planning in advance and selecting from many options

- Ignoring extraneous stimuli and persisting in the task at hand

- Keeping track of the stores to which they have gone and the items that they have already purchased

The behavioral requirements of this task can be described as the temporal organization of behavior, and this sort of sequential organization is the general function of the frontal lobe. Thus, the frontal lobe contains control systems that implement different behavioral strategies in response to both internal and external cues. In recent years, it has become fashionable to refer to these temporal systems as *executive functions*, but we do not want to read too much into this label. The premotor and prefrontal regions contribute in different ways to this control function, and so we will consider them separately.

Functions of the Premotor Cortex

Whereas the motor cortex provides a mechanism for executing individual movements, the premotor cortex selects the movements to be executed (see Figure 9.2). Consider the behavior of a resting dog. It may get up and respond to its owner's call or it may get up for no apparent reason and wander about the yard.

Figure **16.4**

Inputs to the Orbitofrontal Cortex This schematic representation of the ventral surface of the monkey orbitofrontal cortex includes inputs from all major sensory regions as well as the amygdala. (After Rolls, 1998.)

The former movements are made in response to a specific environmental cue, whereas the latter behavior can be regarded as a response to an internal event. Richard Passingham suggested that the premotor region functions primarily to choose behavior in response to external cues and the supplementary motor region makes a greater internal contribution when no such cues are available.

Just as we choose limb movements, we must select eye movements, which is the function of the frontal eye fields. Like limb movements, eye movements can be made to specific targets that are visible or they can be made on the basis of internal cues. Thus, we can make eye movements to look at specific objects or we can gaze around, seemingly without purpose. Passingham suggested that area 8 is specialized for stimulus-directed movements, whereas area 8A is responsible for internally driven movements.

The role of the premotor cortex in response selection was first shown in normal subjects by Per Roland and his colleagues. They compared the cerebral blood flow in subjects making either a repetitive movement of one finger or a complex sequence of 16 movements of the fingers of one hand. The increase in blood flow in the supplementary motor cortices in both hemispheres was larger in the sequence task than in the repetitive task. There was, however, no increase in blood flow in the premotor region.

Roland concluded that the supplementary motor region plays a special role in the selection and direction of motor sequences. An important aspect of Roland's experiment is that there was no external cue for the movements. That is, the production of the movement sequence was self-paced, or internally driven. The results of subsequent studies by others have shown that the premotor cortex is activated when movement sequences are paced externally by a cue.

Not only are motor acts paced by cues, but they also can become associated with cues. For example, to drive safely, we must learn that red means stop and green means go. When subjects are trained on such arbitrary associations in an fMRI paradigm, there is an increase in functional activity in the premotor cortex (see, for example, Amiez et al.).

Functions of the Prefrontal Cortex

The motor cortex is responsible for making movements. The premotor cortex selects movements. The prefrontal cortex controls cognitive processes so that appropriate movements are selected at the correct time and place. This selection may be controlled by internalized information or by external cues or it may be made in response to context or self-knowledge. We now consider these four aspects of movement selection separately.

Internal Cues

Part of the development of internalized information entails the development of "rules" that can be used to guide thoughts and actions. The internalized record of what has just taken place is independent of existing sensory information and can be called *temporal memory*, *working memory*, or *short-term memory*. We use **temporal memory** here to refer to a neural record of recent events and their order. These events may be related to things or to movements and thus derive their information from the object-recognition or motor streams of sensory processing.

Recall that both streams project to the prefrontal cortex, although to different places (see Figure 16.3), which suggests temporal memory for both motor and object information, although the memory will be localized in different places in the frontal cortex. The dorsolateral areas are especially engaged in the selection of behavior based on temporal memory.

External Cues

People whose temporal memory is defective become dependent on environmental cues to determine their behavior. That is, behavior is not under the control of internalized knowledge but is controlled directly by external cues. One effect of this condition is that people with frontal-lobe injuries have difficulty inhibiting behavior directed to external stimuli.

In our dinner-party example, frontal-lobe patients would enter a shoe store or chat with friends as they responded to environmental cues that they encountered. We have probably all experienced occasions when the temporal organization of our behavior failed and we were controlled by external cues rather than internalized information. How many times have you started to do something, been distracted by a question or event, and then been unable to recall what you were going to do? (Sadly, this phenomenon increases with age, which is not reassuring information about the state of one's prefrontal cortex.)

One type of environmental cue is feedback about the rewarding properties of stimuli. For example, if you imagine that a certain stimulus, such as a photograph of your grandmother, is always associated with a reward, such as wonderful food, then you learn the association between the visual stimulus (the photograph of grandma) and the reinforcement (food). Learning such associations is central to much of what we do as we learn about the world, and the orbitofrontal cortex is central to learning by association.

Context Cues

We humans live complex lives. We live in social groups in which we have multiple simultaneous roles as children, parents, friends, siblings, lovers, workers, and so on. Each role is governed by rules of behavior that we are expected to follow: our behavior around our grandparents is certainly different from our behavior with our high-school friends. Similarly, our behavior varies with the environment: we are quiet at a movie theater or in a library, but we may be noisy at a football game or at a picnic.

Behavior, then, is context dependent. Hence, behavior that is appropriate at one moment may not be appropriate if there are subtle changes in the context. This point is beautifully illustrated in Jane Goodall's graphic descriptions of the different behavioral patterns exhibited by chimpanzees.

The makeup of the social group at any given time dictates the behavior of each chimpanzee. Given the presence and position of certain animals, a particular chimp may be bold and relaxed, whereas, with a different group of animals, the chimp is quiet and nervous. Further, an error in evaluating the context can have grievous consequences.

It may be no accident that the frontal lobe has grown so large in highly social primates. We can easily see the importance of social context when we reflect on our behavior with our grandparents versus that with our closest friends. It is common experience that our tone of voice, use of slang or swear words, and the content of conversations are vastly different in the two contexts.

The choice of behaviors in context requires detailed sensory information, which is conveyed to the inferior frontal cortex from the temporal lobe. Context also means affective context, and this contribution comes from the amygdala. People with orbitofrontal lesions, which are common in closed-head injury, or traumatic brain injury (TBI), have difficulty with context, especially in social situations, and are notorious for making social gaffes. We consider TBI in detail in Chapter 26.

Autonoetic Awareness

Not only is our behavior under the control of ongoing sensory input, temporal memory, and context, but it is also affected by a lifetime of experiences and goals. Endel Tulving called this autobiographic knowledge **autonoetic awareness** (that is, self-knowing). Tulving's idea is that autonoetic awareness allows one to bind together the awareness of oneself as a continuous entity through time.

Impairment in autonoetic awareness results in a deficit in the self-regulation of behavior. Thus our behavior is under the influence of our personal past experiences and life goals for the future such that we interpret the world in our daily life within our own frames of reference. Patients with medial or ventral frontal injury often lose this self-knowledge and have difficulty in daily living.

Brian Levine and his colleagues described M.L., a salesman whose orbitofrontal injury resulted from TBI. M.L. noted that maintaining a close relation with his wife of 10 years was very difficult. "I have a hard time relating to my wife. I don't know why I married this person. . . . I told myself I must have been happy, and they said I was." This type of symptom would surely be very disruptive to daily living, but it is not easy to capture with a neuropsychological test, in part because such symptoms are so individual.

Asymmetry of Frontal-Lobe Function

In keeping with the general complementary organization of the left and right hemispheres, as a rule, the left frontal lobe has a preferential role in language-related movements, including speech, whereas the right frontal lobe plays a greater role in nonverbal movements such as facial expression. Like the asymmetry of the parietal and temporal lobes, the asymmetry of frontal-lobe function is relative rather than absolute; the results of studies of patients with frontal lesions indicate that both frontal lobes play a role in nearly all behavior. Thus, the laterality of function disturbed by frontal-lobe lesions is far less striking than that observed for lesions in the more-posterior lobes.

Nonetheless, as with the temporal lobe, there is reason to believe that some effects of bifrontal lesions cannot be duplicated by lesions of either hemisphere alone. **Table 16.1** summarizes a study comparing the behavioral effects of unilateral and bilateral frontal lesions. People with bifrontal lesions, for example, are severely impaired in reporting the time of day and in decoding proverbs, effects seldom seen subsequent to unilateral frontal lesions.

Table **16.1** Relative frequency of defective performance on neuropsychological tests

Test	PERCENTAGE OF GROUP SHOWING A DEFICIT		
	Left Hemisphere	Right Hemisphere	Bilateral
Verbal fluency	70	38	71
Verbal learning	30	13	86
Block construction	10	50	43
Design copying	10	38	43
Time orientation	0	0	57
Proverbs	20	25	71

Source: After Benton, 1968.

Tulving and his colleagues proposed that the left and right frontal lobes may play different roles in memory processing: the left prefrontal cortex is proposed to have a greater role in encoding information into memory, whereas the right prefrontal cortex is more engaged than the left in memory retrieval. This proposal remains controversial, in part because squaring such a finding with our notions of what cerebral asymmetry represents is difficult. We shall return to the Tulving proposal in Chapter 18 (for a review, see Lepage et al., 2000, and Tulving, 2002).

Heterogeneity of Frontal-Lobe Function

Tim Shallice and Paul Burgess noted that correlations among performances on tasks sensitive to frontal-lobe injury are relatively low. Among the many explanations offered for low interest correlations, one of them is that the tests require different cognitive operations for their successful solution. These different functions require different bits of the frontal lobe, and, given that the exact site of injury will vary among patients, performance on the different tests is impaired to different degrees.

Thus, as we consider the different symptoms of frontal-lobe injury, we must remember that any individual patient is unlikely to show all the symptoms and the severity of symptoms will vary with lesion location. Few imaging studies have addressed the matter of heterogeneity and, as we shall see, the trend has been for evidence favoring homogeneity of function. The Snapshot on page 439 shows, however, that, at least in the orbitofrontal cortex, there is evidence of discrete localization of functions.

Symptoms of Frontal-Lobe Lesions

Of primary concern here are the effects of unilateral lesions to the frontal cortex. In an effort to organize the symptoms conceptually, we group them into eight major categories (**Table 16.2**). We do not mean to imply that the brain respects these categories but rather that the categories provide a conceptual framework within which to consider the symptoms.

Table **16.2** Summary of major symptoms of frontal-lobe damage

Most Probable Symptom	Lesion Site	Basic Reference
Disturbances of Motor Function		
Loss of fine movements	Area 4	Kuypers, 1981
Loss of strength	Areas 4 and 6; dorsolateral	Leonard et al., 1988
Poor movement programming	Premotor; dorsolateral	Roland et al., 1980 Kolb and Milner, 1981a
Poor voluntary eye gaze	Frontal eye fields	Guitton et al., 1982
Poor corollary discharge	Premotor; dorsolateral	Teuber, 1964
Broca's aphasia	Area 44	Brown, 1972
Loss of Divergent Thinking		
Reduced spontaneity	Orbital	Jones-Gotman and Milner, 1977
Poor strategy formation	Dorsolateral?	Shallice, 1988
Poor frequency estimate	Dorsolateral	Smith and Milner, 1984
Environmental Control of Behavior		
Poor response inhibition	Prefrontal	Milner, 1964
Impaired associative learning	Dorsolateral	Petrides, 1997
Risk taking and rule breaking	Prefrontal	Miller, 1985
Gambling	Orbital	Bechara et al., 2000
Self-regulatory disorder	Orbital	Levine et al., 1998
Poor Temporal Memory		
Poor working memory	Dorsolateral	Petrides, 2000
Poor delayed response	Dorsolateral	Freedman and Oscar-Berman, 1986a
Other Symptoms		
Impaired social behavior	Orbital; dorsolateral	Blumer and Benson, 1975
Altered sexual behavior	Orbital	Walker and Blumer, 1975
Impaired olfactory discrimination	Orbital	Jones-Gotman and Zatorre, 1993
Disorders associated with damage to the facial area	Face	Taylor, 1979

Disturbances of Motor Function

Frontal lesions can impair a person's ability to make a wide variety of movements, to order movement sequences, and even to speak.

Fine Movements, Speed, and Strength

Damage to the primary motor cortex is typically associated with a chronic loss of the ability to make fine, independent finger movements, presumably owing to a loss of direct corticospinal projections onto motor neurons (see Chapter 9). In addition, there is a loss of speed and strength in both hand and limb movements in the contralateral limbs. The loss of strength is not merely a symptom of damage to area 4, because lesions restricted to the prefrontal cortex also lead to a reduction in hand strength.

SNAPSHOT

Heterogeneity of Function in the Orbitofrontal Cortex

The large orbitofrontal region includes at least five subregions—namely, Brodmann's areas 10 through 14, diagrammed below. Different regions have different patterns of connectivity. Area 13, for example, has extensive connections with the amygdala and hypothalamus, whereas area 11 has connections with medial temporal cortical areas taking part in recognition memory.

The orbitofrontal cortex is a challenge to study functionally in the laboratory, because its location makes discrete lesions difficult to produce. Furthermore, although the orbitofrontal cortex is often affected in traumatic brain injury, these injuries are not focal but tend to be diffuse across the orbital region.

Stephen Frey and Michael Petrides examined functional heterogeneity in the orbital region in two parallel PET studies. In one study, subjects heard either the sounds of violent car crashes, which the investigators suspected would be perceived as unpleasant, or familiar abstract sounds generated from an electronic keyboard. In the other study, the subjects were presented with novel abstract visual designs that they had to either commit to memory or just view. Abstract designs were used to prevent subjects from verbalizing the images and thus provoking semantic associations.

As shown in the diagram, area 13 showed increased activation in response to the unpleasant auditory stimuli, whereas area 11 showed increased activation when subjects had to learn new visual information. These results show a clear functional dissociation of the two orbital regions: area 13 (richly connected to the amygdala and hypothalamus) processes unpleasant auditory information; area 11 (medial temporal cortical connections) processes the encoding of new visual information.

We can think of area 13 as a region that can alert an organism to attend to stimuli that have affective qualities. We might predict that people with damage to area 13 would be less responsive to threatening stimuli, and they are. It would be interesting to determine whether both areas would be implicated if unpleasant stimuli were to be encoded.

Area 11 showed increased activation when subjects had to learn new visual information,...

...whereas area 13 showed increased activation in response to unpleasant auditory stimuli.

Activation of the orbitofrontal cortex by sensory stimulation. (After Frey and Petrides, 2000, and Frey et al., 2000.)

Frey, S., and M. Petrides. Orbitofrontal cortex: A key prefrontal region for encoding information. *Proceedings of the National Academy of Sciences of the United States of America* 97:8723–8727, 2000.

Frey, S., P. Kostopoulous, and M. Petrides. Orbitofrontal involvement in the processing of unpleasant auditory information. *European Journal of Neuroscience* 12:3709–3712, 2000.

Movement Programming

In a classic paper in 1950, Karl Lashley asked how movements are put together in a particular order. How is it, he asked, that a violinist can play an arpeggio so quickly and flawlessly? Clearly, each note is not "thought of" separately. And how is it that, in a tennis game, a player can make very rapid movements, seemingly much too fast to have considered each movement by itself?

Lashley presumed that this function—serially ordering complex chains of behavior in relation to varying stimuli—must somehow be a function of the neocortex. Although he believed it to be a function of the entire neocortex, it appears more likely to be a function of the frontal lobes. Removal of the supplementary motor cortex results in a transient disruption of nearly all voluntary movements (including speech, if the removal is on the left). There is rapid recovery, however, and the only permanent disability appears to be in the performance of rapidly alternating movements with the hands or fingers.

The likely reason that relatively minor symptoms result from rather large supplementary motor lesions is that both the left and the right premotor cortices participate in the control of movement. This idea is supported by observations that both left and right premotor areas show an increase in blood flow during unimanual tasks in humans; in monkeys, cells in both the left and the right areas show increased activity regardless of which hand is moving. There is also a bilateral projection from each supplementary motor cortex to the basal ganglia.

Further evidence favoring a role for the frontal cortex in movement programming comes from the results of a study in which patients with localized unilateral frontal lobectomies (most of which did not include the premotor cortex) were asked to copy a series of arm or facial movements (Kolb and Milner, 1981a; see Figure 14.10A). Although the patients showed mild impairment in copying the arm movements, it was small compared with the performance of patients with left-parietal-lobe lesions. In contrast, patients with both left- and right-frontal-lobe damage were very poor at copying a series of facial movements.

An analysis of the facial-movement task showed that the groups with frontal-lobe lesions made more errors of sequence than did normal controls or other groups of patients. In other words, patients with frontal-lobe lesions had difficulty ordering the various components of the sequence into a chain of movements. The components were recalled correctly but in the wrong order. To be sure, these patients made other sorts of errors as well, especially errors of memory in which items were not recalled. The reproduction of movement sequences requires temporal memory, and our impression is that the largest deficits come from dorsolateral lesions.

The observation that frontal injury severely disrupts the copying of facial but not arm movements implies that the frontal lobe may play a special role in the control of the face, perhaps even including the tongue. Recall from E.L.'s case in the Portrait at the beginning of this chapter that patients with frontal-lobe damage exhibit little spontaneous facial expression—a result in accordance with the possible special role of the frontal lobe in the control of the face.

Voluntary Gaze

In a number of studies using quite different procedures, frontal-lobe lesions produced alterations in voluntary eye gaze. For example, Hans-Leukas Teuber presented patients with an array of 48 patterns on a screen. The patterns could be distinguished by shape or color or both (**Figure 16.5**). At a warning signal, a duplicate of 1 of the 48 patterns appeared in the center of the array, and the subject's task was to identify the matching pattern by pointing to it. Patients with frontal-lobe lesions were impaired at finding the duplicate pattern.

Alexander Luria recorded patients' eye movements as they examined a picture of a complex scene. The eye-movement patterns of the patients with large frontal-lobe lesions were quite different from those of normal control subjects or those of patients with more-posterior lesions. For example, if a normal control was asked

Figure **16.5**

Visual Search Task In Teuber's experiment, the subject must locate a duplicate of the shape or color or both inside the central box by pointing to it. (After Teuber, 1964.)

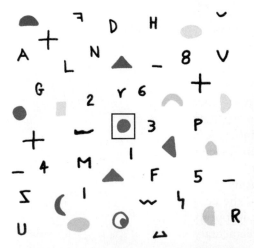

about the ages of the people in a picture, his or her eyes fixed on the heads; if asked how they are dressed, the eyes fixed on the clothing. Patients with large frontal-lobe lesions tended to glance over the picture more or less at random, and a change in the question about the picture failed to alter the direction or the pattern of eye movements. Visual search in Luria's task would require internalized knowledge to direct the eyes.

Dan Guitton and his colleagues examined a different type of oculomotor defect in frontal-lobe patients. They studied the ability of patients to make voluntary eye movements toward or away from briefly appearing targets presented at random to the right or the left of a fixation point. Normally, if a stimulus cue is presented briefly in either visual field, a person will make a quick eye movement (a saccade) toward the stimulus.

Patients with frontal-lobe lesions had no difficulty doing so, and so Guitton and his coworkers added a second feature to the task. Rather than making eye movements toward a target, the patients had to move their eyes to the same place in the opposite visual field. The task therefore required inhibition of the normal saccade and a voluntary saccade toward a similar point in the opposite direction.

Patients with frontal-lobe lesions had two deficits on this variation of the task. First, although normal subjects failed to inhibit a short-latency response toward the cue in about 20% of the trials, patients with frontal-lobe lesions had much more difficulty. Second, after the initial saccade in the incorrect direction, normal subjects had no difficulty making a large corrective saccade toward the opposite field. In contrast, patients with frontal-lobe lesions, which included the frontal eye fields, had difficulty executing the corrective response when the response had to be generated by the damaged hemisphere. In other words, they had difficulty in moving the eyes to the field contralateral to the frontal lesion. Corrective movements could be made normally in the field on the same side as the lesion.

The difficulty encountered by patients with frontal-lobe lesions in the visual-search task and in the saccade task indicates the importance of the frontal cortex for certain aspects of oculomotor control. Only the study by Guitton and associates localized the effect in the frontal eye fields (area 8), but the most severe deficits in performing such tasks are likely associated with damage to those fields (see Figure 16.1).

Corollary Discharge

If you push on your eyeball, the world appears to move. If you move your eyes, the world remains stable. Why? Teuber proposed that, for a movement to take place, a neural signal must produce the movement as well as a signal that the movement is going to take place. If the eyes are moved mechanically, there is no such signal, and the world moves. However, when you move your eyes, there is a neural signal that movement will happen, and the world stays still. This signal has been termed **corollary discharge** or **reafference**.

Teuber argued that voluntary movements require two sets of signals rather than one. A movement command, through the motor system, effects the movements, and a signal (corollary discharge) from the frontal lobe to the parietal and temporal association cortex presets the sensory system to anticipate the motor act. Thus, a person's sensory system can interpret changes in the external world in light of information about his or her movement.

When you are running, for example, the external world remains stable even though your sense organs are in motion, because the corollary discharge from the frontal lobe to the parietotemporal cortex signals that the movements are taking place. A frontal-lobe lesion therefore can not only disturb the production of a movement but also interfere with the message to the rest of the brain that a movement is taking place. By this indirect means, perception of the world by the posterior association cortex is altered.

A source of evidence that the frontal lobe plays a role in corollary discharge comes from the results of studies of cells in the frontal eye fields. Emelio Bizzi and Peter Schiller, among others, found that some cells in the frontal eye fields fire simultaneously with movements of the eyes. These cells cannot be causing the eyes to move, because, to do so, they would have to fire before the eye movements (just as to accelerate an automobile, you must first depress the gas pedal). Rather, these cells must be monitoring the ongoing movement—a process suspiciously similar to what would be expected from a region controlling corollary discharge.

Speech

Speech is an example of movement selection. Passingham suggested that words are responses generated in the context of both internal and external stimuli. If the frontal lobe has a mechanism for selecting responses, then it must select words, too. The frontal lobe contains two speech zones: Broca's area, which can be regarded as an extension of the lateral premotor area, and the supplementary speech area, which may be an extension of the supplementary motor area (see Figure 16.1D).

Viewed in this way, Broca's area plays a critical role when a word must be retrieved on the basis of an object, word, letter, or meaning. That is, like the premotor area's role in other behaviors, Broca's area selects words on the basis of cues. In contrast, the supplementary speech area is required to retrieve words without external cues, which also is consistent with the general function of the supplementary motor area.

People with strokes in Broca's area are impaired in their ability to use verbs and to produce appropriate grammar, a symptom known as **agrammatism**. People with strokes that include the supplementary speech area and extend into the left medial frontal region are often mute. The ability to speak usually returns after a few weeks in people with unilateral lesions but not in those with bilateral lesions.

This outcome again supports the bilateral participation of the supplementary motor areas in movement selection. The role of the supplementary motor region is corroborated by the results of blood-flow studies done by Roland, who showed activation of the medial premotor area when subjects recall the months of the year, which is done without external cues.

Loss of Divergent Thinking

One of the clearest differences between the effects of parietal- and temporal-lobe lesions and the effects of frontal-lobe lesions is in performance on standard intelligence tests. Posterior lesions produce reliable, and often large, decreases in IQ scores, but frontal lesions do not. The puzzle is why patients with frontal-lobe damage appear to do such "stupid" things.

Joy Paul Guilford noted that traditional intelligence tests appear to measure what can be called **convergent thinking**, in the sense that there is just one correct answer to each question. Thus, definitions of words, questions of fact, arithmetic problems, puzzles, and block designs all require correct answers that are easily scored. Another type of intelligence test, in which the number and variety of responses to a single question rather than a single correct answer are emphasized, can measure **divergent thinking**. An example is a question asking for a list of the possible uses of a coat hanger. Frontal-lobe injury interferes with the intelligence required by divergent thinking rather than the convergent type measured by standard IQ tests. Several lines of evidence support Guilford's idea.

Behavioral Spontaneity

Patients with frontal-lobe lesions have long been recognized to exhibit a loss of spontaneous speech. Various investigators have been able to quantify this loss by using tests such as the Thurstone Word-Fluency Test (also referred to as the Chicago Word-Fluency Test). Patients are asked to first write or say as many words starting with a given letter as they can think of in 5 minutes and then say as many four-letter words starting with a given letter in 4 minutes.

Patients with frontal-lobe lesions have a low output of words in this test. For example, when asked to generate as many words as he could think of beginning with a specific letter, E.L., introduced in the Portrait at the beginning of this chapter, sat for about 2 minutes before asking if he could use the Latin names of plants. He was assured that he could do so but, after another couple of minutes, he remarked, "I can't think of any!" He abandoned the plant names but, even with an additional 5 minutes, he could think of only six words.

Although the principal locus of this defect appears to be in the left orbitofrontal region, lesions in the right orbitofrontal region also may produce a marked reduction in verbal fluency. Again, we see less asymmetry in the frontal lobes than we might expect. The following case exemplifies low spontaneous verbal fluency resulting from a lesion of the right frontal lobe.

Mrs. P., a 63-year-old woman with a college degree, was suffering from a large astrocytoma of the right frontal lobe. Her word fluency is reproduced in **Figure 16.6**A. Four features of frontal-lobe damage are illustrated in her test performance:

1. Her total output of words is remarkably low: only 8 words beginning with the letter "s" and 6 words beginning with the letter "c." (Control subjects of similar age and education produce a total of about 60 words in the same time period, as shown in Figure 16.6B.)

2. Rule breaking is a common characteristic of patients on this test. We told Mrs. P. several times that the words starting with "c" could have only four letters. She replied. "Yes, yes, I know, I keep using

Figure 16.6

Word Fluency Subjects were given 5 minutes to write as many English words as possible starting with the letter "s" and 4 minutes to write as many four-letter words as possible starting with the letter "c."

(A) Mrs. P's lists

Note low output, shaky script, and rule breaking in the four-letter "c" words.

(B) Normal control's lists

more each time." Even though she understood the instructions, she could not organize her behavior to follow them successfully.

3. Her writing was not fluid but rather jerky, much like that seen in a child learning to write, implying that her tumor had invaded the motor or premotor cortex.

4. Mrs. P. insisted on talking throughout the test—complaining that she simply could not think of any more words—and kept looking around the room for objects starting with the required letter.

A study by Marilyn Jones-Gotman and Brenda Milner raises the question whether this verbal-fluency deficit might have a nonverbal analogue. The researchers devised an ingenious experiment in which they asked patients to draw as many different designs as they could in 5 minutes. The drawings were not supposed to be representational of anything, but rather much like the doodles that students are prone to put in the margins of their notes or textbooks. The patients were then asked to draw as many different designs as they could, but this time using only four lines (a circle was counted as a single line).

The results show a beautiful analogue to the verbal-fluency results. As you can see in **Figure 16.7**, lesions in the right frontal lobe produced a large decrease in the number of different drawings produced. Normal controls drew about 35 drawings, left-frontal-lobe patients drew about 24 drawings, and right-frontal-lobe patients drew about 15 drawings.

This deficit appears to be related to an impoverished output, high perseveration, and, in some cases, the drawing of nameable things (that is, representational drawings). As with verbal fluency, lesions in the orbital cortex or central facial area in the frontal lobe appear to produce a larger deficit than do the more-dorsal lesions.

Frontal-lobe patients likely show reduced spontaneity not only in speech or doodling but also in their behaviors in general. For example, One of us (Kolb) and Laughlin Taylor recorded the spontaneous behavior of frontal-lobe patients taking a battery of neuropsychological tests. Patients with frontal-lobe removals displayed fewer spontaneous facial movements and expressions than did normal controls or patients with more-posterior lesions. In addition, there were dramatic differences in the number of words spoken by the patients in a neuropsychological interview: patients with left frontal removals rarely spoke, whereas patients with right frontal lesions were excessively talkative.

Although the range of behaviors studied to date is small, there is reason to believe that frontal-lobe patients have a general loss of spontaneous behavior. Frontal-lobe patients characteristically appear lethargic or lazy: they often have difficulty getting out of bed in the morning, getting dressed, or initiating other daily activities such as going to work. One patient offers a particularly dramatic example. He was a prominent lawyer who suffered a midline meningioma in the frontal lobe. The tumor was removed surgically, but he was left with bilateral damage to the superior aspect of both frontal lobes.

Figure 16.7

Design Fluency In an analogue to the word-fluency test, subjects were allowed 5 minutes to draw as many nonrepresentational doodles as they could.

(A) Normal subject

(B) Frontal lobe patient showing perseveration

(C) Frontal lobe patient showing lack of spontaneity

His IQ score was still superior (higher than 140), and his memory for legal matters was unimpaired, in part because much of this skill is related to convergent thinking processes that were intact. Nonetheless, he was unable to function in his profession, because he could not get up in the morning to go to work, preferring to stay in bed and watch television. When his wife forced him to get up and go to work, he was disruptive at the office because he could not concentrate on any law-related work. Rather, he was distracted by anything else going on in the office. Curiously, he remained an excellent resource for his colleagues; however, they found his behavior intolerable and consequently preferred to consult him by telephone.

Strategy Formation

Patients with frontal-lobe lesions are especially impaired at developing novel cognitive plans or strategies for solving problems. For example, when Tim Shallice and Margaret Evans asked subjects questions that require reasoning based on general knowledge for which no immediate obvious strategy is available, they found that frontal-lobe patients did very poorly and often gave bizarre responses.

In a later study, Shallice and Burgess gave patients a task very much like our dinner-party problem. The subjects were given a list of six errands (for example, "Buy a loaf of brown bread") and an instruction to be at a particular place 15 minutes after starting. They were also to get answers to four questions (for instance, the price of a pound of tomatoes). They were not to enter shops except to buy something and were to complete the tasks as quickly as possible without rushing.

The frontal-lobe patients found this simple task very difficult. They were inefficient, they broke rules (for example, entered unnecessary shops), and two of the three patients failed at least four of the tasks. Yet when quizzed, all the patients understood the task and had attempted to comply.

Similar difficulty with everyday problems is seen in a study by Mary-Lou Smith and Brenda Milner. They asked subjects to estimate the average price of a particular object, such as a sewing machine. They suggested that, to perform such a task, one must develop a strategy that might include deciding what a typical sewing machine is, judging the range of possible prices, and selecting a representative price for a machine of average quality.

Patients with frontal-lobe lesions—especially right frontal lesions—were very poor at this task. In contrast, patients with temporal-lobe damage who showed memory deficits on other tasks performed like controls on this task. Thus, a simple explanation of impaired memory seems unlikely to account for the poor performance of the frontal-lobe patients.

Shallice and Burgess argued that, although the frontal lobe may have a general role in planning behavior, it has a critical role in coping with novel situations in contrast with routine ones. They suggested that coping with a novel situation, by which they mean a novel set of external and internal states, entails the activation of a wide variety of processes to solve the problem. In contrast, the solution of a familiar task can rely on strategies that have been well practiced and are therefore more easily accessed.

The extreme case of novel situations is found in development, when most situations are novel. Donald Hebb noted in the 1940s that, relative to frontal-lobe

Figure 16.8

Wisconsin Card-Sorting Test
The subject's task is to place each card from the pile (bottom) with the appropriate card in the top row, sorting by one of three possible categories: color, number of elements, or shape. Subjects are not told the correct sorting category but only whether their responses are correct or incorrect. When a subject selects the correct category, the correct solution changes unexpectedly. (After Milner, 1964.)

Figure 16.9

Stroop Test The task is to name the color of the ink in which each word is printed as quickly as possible. When the ink color and the color name are the same, the task is simple. When they are different, there is a tendency to read the word rather than name the ink color.

BLUE GREEN
RED   YELLOW
YELLOW GREEN
BLUE RED

injuries acquired in adulthood, people whose frontal-lobe injuries were acquired in childhood often show surprisingly severe deficits in behavioral control. He believed that these people are not able to properly develop the behavioral schemas necessary to solve problems. That is, they would find few situations routine.

Environmental Control of Behavior

Perhaps the most commonly observed trait of frontal-lobe patients is their difficulty in using information from environmental cues (feedback) to regulate or change their behavior. This difficulty manifests itself in a number of ways.

Response Inhibition

Patients with frontal-lobe lesions consistently perseverate on responses in a variety of test situations, particularly those in which there are changing demands. The best example of this phenomenon is observed in the Wisconsin Card-Sorting Test, which has become one of the standard clinical tests of frontal-lobe injury. As **Figure 16.8** shows, a subject is presented with four stimulus cards, bearing designs that differ in color, form, and number of elements. The subject's task is to sort the cards into piles in front of one or another of the stimulus cards. The only help given the subject is to be told whether the choice is correct or incorrect.

The test works on the following principle: the correct solution is, first, color; when the subject has figured out this solution, the correct solution then becomes, without warning, form. Thus, the subject must now inhibit classifying the cards on the basis of color and shift to form. When the subject has succeeded at selecting by form, the correct solution again changes unexpectedly, this time to the number of elements. It will later become color again, and so on.

Shifting response strategies is particularly difficult for people with frontal lesions. They may continue responding to the original stimulus (color) for as many as 100 cards until testing is terminated. Throughout this period, they may comment that they know that color is no longer correct. They nevertheless continue to sort on the basis of color. One person stated (correctly): "Form is probably the correct solution now so this [sorting to color] will be wrong, and this will be wrong, and wrong again."

Such perseveration is common on any task in which a frontal-lobe patient is required to shift response strategies, demonstrating that the frontal lobe is necessary for flexibility in behavior. It is important to note that, on card-sorting tasks, the subjects must not be given any hint that they are to expect a change in the correct solution, because many frontal-lobe patients improve dramatically when given this warning. The cue apparently allows enough flexibility in behavior to solve the problem.

From the results of Milner's work, the principal locus of this card-sorting effect appears to be roughly around Brodmann's area 9 in the left hemisphere. Lesions elsewhere in the left frontal lobe, and often in the right frontal lobe, also will produce a deficit on this task, although an attenuated one.

Performance of the Stroop Test (**Figure 16.9**) further demonstrates the loss of response inhibition subsequent to frontal-lobe damage. Subjects are presented with a list of color words (blue, green, red, and so forth), each word being printed in colored ink but never in the color denoted by the word (for example, the word "yellow" is printed in blue, green, or red ink). The subject's task is to name the color in which each word is printed as quickly as possible.

Correct response requires the inhibition of reading the color name, an inhibition that is difficult even for many control subjects. In one study, patients with left frontal lesions were unable to inhibit reading the words and thus were impaired in this task (Perret, 1974).

Risk Taking and Rule Breaking

Frontal-lobe patients are distinguished from other neurological patients in their common failure to comply with task instructions. Milner found this failure to comply especially common on tests of stylus-maze learning in which a buzzer indicates that the patient has made an error and is to stop and start at the beginning of the maze again. Subjects with frontal-lobe lesions tend to disregard the signal, thereby continuing the incorrect path and making more errors. This behavior is reminiscent of their inability to modify their responses in the card-sorting task.

Lori Miller gave subjects a task in which words had to be guessed on the basis of partial information. With each additional clue, a subject was assigned a successively lower point value for a correct answer, but points could be collected only if the answer was correct. An incorrect answer forfeited all the points for an item. Frontal-lobe patients took more risks (and made more mistakes) than did other patients, and the risk taking was greatest in those frontal-lobe patients who also had temporal-lobe damage.

The role of the orbitofrontal cortex in risk taking has been studied extensively by Antoine Bechera, Antonio Damasio, and their colleagues, who designed a gambling task in which subjects gradually learn how to play a unique card game. They are presented with four decks of cards and are asked to turn over the first card in any deck. Some cards are associated with a payoff ($50 or $100), whereas other cards result in a $50 or $100 penalty. Each subject is given $2000 in play money to play the game, and the goal is to make as much money in the game as possible.

The trick is that the reward and penalty contingencies of each deck differ. For example, one deck may have high payoffs but also has high penalties, whereas another may have lower payoffs but also low penalties. The game is set so that playing two of the four decks results in a net loss, whereas playing the other two yields a net gain.

The results from the Bechera studies are clear: normal subjects and patients without frontal damage sample from all the decks for a while but quickly learn which decks have the best payoff. In contrast, patients with orbitofrontal injuries do not learn this strategy and play predominantly from the bad decks, thus losing all their money.

An important aspect of the task is that subjects are not allowed to keep a running tally of how they are doing; rather they must "sense" which decks are risky and which are profitable. This ability is clearly a function of the prefrontal cortex, and its loss makes it difficult for orbitofrontal patients to make wise decisions, especially in social or personal matters—that is, situations in which an exact calculation of future outcomes is not possible.

Figure 16.10

Brain Activation in Ambiguous Circumstances The amygdala and orbitofrontal cortex of control subjects show enhanced activity when the probability of risk in a gambling task is ambiguous. (Photo courtesy of Ming Hsu.)

Amygdala

Orbitofrontal cortex

The brain-injury data are consistent with a recent finding by Ming Hsu and colleagues, who looked at brain activation (fMRI) in subjects who were engaged in a gambling task in which the risk was ambiguous. For example, subjects were asked to bet on whether a card was red or blue without any knowledge of the probability that a card was red or blue. The brain activity was compared to a condition in which they knew that the probability was 50:50.

In contrast with patients with orbitofrontal lesions, who did not find the ambiguous task aversive, control subjects found it much more aversive than the known-risk task. The subjective difference was demonstrated by higher activation in the orbitofrontal cortex and amgydala of control subjects during the ambiguous-risk task (**Figure 16.10**). Taken together, the imaging and lesion studies suggest that the orbitofrontal cortex is part of a neural decision-making circuit that evaluates degrees of uncertainty in the world.

Self-regulation

We noted earlier that people with ventral frontal injuries, such as M.L., have deficits in regulating their own behavior in unstructured situations, in part because of a loss of autonoetic awareness. M.L. had been a salesman, and he knew what his job had been and that he had traveled a great deal. When pressed, however, he was unable to provide a single personal example of this job.

For example, when asked if he traveled to conferences, M.L. said that, yes, he traveled to conferences often; it was a major part of his job. Yet he could not name a single experience that he had had at a conference. His autobiographic knowledge was lost.

You can imagine what this impairment would be like if you think about your high-school experience. We are all aware of having gone to high school and can describe what high school was like, and, presumably, so could patients such as M.L. The difference, however, is that we can describe personal events that happened in high school, whereas M.L. would not be able to do so. We can immediately see why M.L. had difficulty relating to his wife: he simply could not recall instances that would explain why they were married. The loss of biographic knowledge clearly makes it difficult to put ongoing life events in context and leads to difficulties in regulating behavior flexibly.

Associative Learning

Patients with large frontal-lobe lesions are often claimed to be unable to regulate their behavior in response to external stimuli—that is, to learn from experience. Alexander Luria and Evgenia Homskaya described patients with massive frontal-lobe tumors who could not be trained to respond consistently with the right hand to a red light and with the left hand to a green light, even though the patients could indicate which hand was which and could repeat the instructions.

In an extensive series of studies, Michael Petrides examined the ability of both human patients and monkeys with frontal lesions to make arbitrary stimulus-response associations. In one study, Petrides asked frontal-lobe patients to learn arbitrary associations between colors and hand postures, as illustrated in **Figure 16.11**. For example, patients were presented with nine colored stimuli, and their task was to learn which posture was associated with which colored stimulus.

Damage to either the left or the right hemisphere results in poor performance on this task. Again, the behavioral impairments in the frontal-lobe patients could not be attributed to a deficit in memory, because temporal-lobe patients who performed poorly on other tests of memory performed normally at these tasks. Rather, the problem is in learning to select, from a set of competing responses, the appropriate ones for the various stimuli.

Poor Temporal Memory

Perhaps the single most important experimental discovery for understanding the functions of the frontal lobe is Carlyle Jacobsen's finding that chimpanzees with frontal-lobe lesions were impaired in the delayed-response test. In this task, an animal observes a reward being placed under a plaque, in a well. The chimp's view is blocked for a few seconds, and then it is allowed to retrieve the reward.

Animals with prefrontal lesions perform at chance, even with extended practice. Although the behavioral impairment is unlikely to be due to a single deficit, the impairment is difficult to interpret without recourse to some sort of memory difficulty. Four additional experiments are especially germane here.

In the first experiment, Passingham presented monkeys with a task in which the animals were required to open each of 25 doors to obtain a food reward. Food was placed behind each door only once per day; so the animals had to learn not to return to locations where the reward had been obtained already. Passingham found that lesions in area 46 produced marked impairments in this task. Thus, whereas the normal monkeys developed a door-opening strategy that led to few repetitions, the lesioned animals were inefficient, often returning to previously accessed doors (**Figure 16.12**A).

In the second experiment, monkeys were trained to fixate on a central spot of light while target lights were flashed in different parts of the visual field (Funahashi et al., 1986). The monkeys had to wait for the fixation spot to disappear before moving their eyes to the spot where the target light had been flashed. The researchers found that unilateral lesions in the principal sulcus (part of area 46) impaired the monkeys' ability to remember the location of the target in a restricted region of the contralateral visual field, as illustrated in Figure 6.12B. They interpret this result as showing that the principal sulcus contains a mechanism for guiding responses on the basis of stored information, which in this case is spatial.

The third experiment was conducted by Mortimer Mishkin and Frederick Manning. They trained monkeys in a task known as delayed nonmatching to sample. In this test, a monkey is confronted with an unfamiliar object, which it

Figure **16.11**

Testing Associative Learning
The nine hand postures that constitute responses in the Petrides experiments. In this study, subjects had to learn to associate each hand posture with one of nine different colors and to perform the movement in response to the presentation of the appropriate color.

Lesion site

Experimental task

Control   Frontal

(A) Passingham study

Food boxes

1

The task is to retrieve a food reward from each of 25 food boxes. Notice that the control animal seldom returns to a previously visited location, whereas the monkey with a sulcus principalis lesion makes numerous errors.

(B) Funahashi et al. study

2

The task is to fixate at the central point, and then after a 3-second delay move the eye to locate the place where a target light had flashed. Correct performance percentage is indicated by the relative positions of the lines along axes drawn through the central fixation point. Note that the monkey performed poorly in one region of the visual field contralateral to the lesion.

(C) Mishkin and Manning study

3

The monkey is shown an object, which is displaced, and a food reward is obtained. The monkey is then presented with two objects after a short delay; the task is to obtain a reward, which is under the novel object. Monkeys with medial lesions are impaired at this task, which is nonspatial.

Figure 16.12

Testing for Temporal Memory

Schematic representations at the left show the sites of frontal-lobe lesions in monkeys that correspond to the results of the three experiments illustrated on the right. Each result reveals a temporal memory deficit.

displaces to find a reward. After a delay, the animal sees the same object paired with a new one. The monkey must recognize the object that it saw earlier and move the new one instead to get a reward (Figure 6.12C). Monkeys with lesions of areas 10 and 32 are impaired in this task. Mishkin and Manning interpreted this result as showing that this area of the frontal cortex participates in the short-term storage of object information.

The fourth experiment was a 1991 study by Petrides in which monkeys were given two different tasks. In the first task, the animals were presented with three objects and allowed to choose one for reward. The animals were then given an option between the chosen object and one of the other objects, with the correct choice being the one that was not previously selected. In the second task, the animals were again presented with three objects and allowed one choice. On this task, however, they were then presented with the previously selected object and a novel object.

In the first task, a monkey must recall what it did with the objects. In the second task, the monkey must recall only which object was seen before. Monkeys with dorsolateral lesions performed at chance on the first task but performed as well as controls on the second. This result suggests that the dorso-lateral cortex plays a role in monitoring self-generated responses.

Taken together, these five experiments point to an unequivocal role for the frontal cortex in short-term-memory processes and to the fact that different regions of the prefrontal cortex control the storage of different types of information. In view of the anatomical connections, area 46 likely plays a role in providing an internal representation of spatial information, and the medial regions likely play a similar role with object information.

The results of electrophysiological studies lend further support for the role of area 46: cells in this area are active during the intervals in delayed-response tests, and their activity ends abruptly when an animal responds. Some neurons respond selectively to the spatial position of the cues, and we might expect to find similar neurons coding some features of objects as well.

Studying Temporal Memory in Humans

Studies of temporal memory have taken a slightly different slant with human subjects. On the basis of earlier work by others, Brenda Milner, Phil Corsi, and Gabriel Leonard designed an ingenious test of memory for the order in which things have happened, which is often called *recency memory*. Subjects were shown a long series of cards, each card bearing two stimulus items, which were either words or pictures. On some cards, a question mark appeared between the items, and the subjects' task was to indicate which of the two items had been seen more recently. Successful performance required the subjects to recall the order of presentation of the stimuli.

On most test trials, both items had appeared previously, but, on some trials, one item was new. In this case, the task became one of simple recognition memory. Patients with frontal-lobe lesions performed normally on the recognition trials, but they were impaired in judging the relative recency of two previously seen items. Further, there is relative asymmetry in the frontal lobes in this regard: the right frontal lobe appears to be more important for memory for nonverbal, or pictorial, recency; the left frontal lobe appears to be more important for verbal recency.

In contrast, patients with temporal-lobe lesions were impaired in the recognition test but not in the recency test. This latter finding is curious, because it seems analogous to blindsight in that people who fail to recognize items can identify which was observed most recently. Might this suggest a memory location system that is separate from a memory recognition system?

Petrides and Milner designed an experiment that is conceptually similar to Passingham's self-ordering task for monkeys. Subjects were presented with stacks of cards on which were displayed an array of 12 stimuli, including words or drawings in parallel versions of the task. The stimuli in the array remained constant, but the position of each stimulus varied randomly from card to card.

The subjects' task appeared rather simple: go through the stack and point to only one item on each card, taking care not to point to the same item twice. Thus, the subjects themselves initiated the plan to follow and determined the order of responding. Although the task appears easy to us, frontal-lobe patients did not find it so: left-frontal-lobe lesions were associated with impaired performance of both verbal and nonverbal versions of the task, whereas right-frontal-lobe lesions were associated with poor performance only on the nonverbal test.

Petrides and Milner suggested that, in contrast with the recency tests, the self-ordered tasks require subjects to organize and carry out a sequence of responses. From the moment the subjects begin to respond, they must constantly compare the responses that they have made with those that still remain to be carried out. Hence, the self-ordered task demands an accurate memory as well as an organized strategy.

When questioned about their approach to the task at the end of testing, patients with frontal lesions were less likely than other subjects to report that they had used a particular strategy, and, when they had, the strategy often appeared to be ill defined and to have been used inconsistently. The deficit is unlikely one of simple memory, because temporal-lobe patients, who would be expected to have defects of memory, performed normally at this task.

Recent Findings on Temporal Memory

Temporal memory deficits both in laboratory animals and in human patients have caught the imagination of researchers for more than 60 years. Recently, both imaging studies and single-unit studies in monkeys have confirmed what the lesion studies had suggested—namely, that the prefrontal cortex plays a critical role in temporal memory.

A study by Joaquin Fuster and colleagues serves as a nice illustration. In this experiment, monkeys were trained to associate each of two different tones with one of two different colors, as illustrated in **Figure 16.13**A. The trick was that a monkey heard the tone and then had to remember which tone it had heard for 10 seconds before making a response to obtain reward.

A large contingent of dorsolateral frontal cells (in areas 6, 8, 9, and 46) responded selectively to one tone or the other and, later, to its associated color (Figure 16.13B). These cells appear to integrate sound and color across time. Curiously, in trials on which the animals made errors, the cells failed to respond, indicating no temporal correlation of sound and color.

Impaired Social and Sexual Behavior

Social and sexual behaviors require flexible responses that are highly dependent on contextual cues. It is hardly surprising that frontal-lobe lesions interfere with both. Perhaps the most obvious and striking effect of frontal-lobe damage in humans is a marked change in social behavior and personality.

The most publicized example of personality change subsequent to frontal-lobe lesions is that of Phineas Gage, first reported by John Harlow in 1868. Gage was a dynamite worker who survived an explosion that blasted an iron tamping bar

Figure 16.13

Prefrontal Cells That Code Sensory Associations

1 A monkey faces a panel with buttons that can be lit in colors.

2 A high or low tone sounds for 2 seconds...

3 ...followed by a 10-second delay after which both buttons light up.

4 If the tone is low, the monkey must touch the blue button to receive a reward...

(A) Procedure

Low tone trial (240 Hz)

Buttons

Correct

or

Correct

High tone trial (3000 Hz)

Correct

Buttons

or

Correct

5 ...and, if the tone is high, it must choose the white button.

(B) Results

9
46
8 6

Tone–color correlations are recorded in the dorsolateral frontal cortex.

through the front of his head. The bar, shown as part of the reconstruction in **Figure 16.14**, was about a meter long and 3 centimeters wide at its widest point.

After the accident, Gage's behavior changed completely. He had been of average intelligence and was "energetic and persistent in executing all of his plans of operation" according to Harlow, who described Gage's personality after the injury as follows:

> The equilibrium or balance, so to speak, between his intellectual faculties and animal propensities seems to have been destroyed. He is fitful, irreverent, indulging at times in the grossest profanity, manifesting but little deference to his fellows, impatient of restraint or advice when it conflicts with his desires, at times pertinaciously obstinate, yet capricious and vacillating, devising many plans of operation, which are no sooner arranged than they are abandoned in turn for others appearing more feasible. A child in his intellectual capacity and manifestations, he has the animal passions of a strong man. (Blumer and Benson, 1975, p. 153)

Gage's injury affected primarily the left frontal lobe from the medial orbital region upward to the precentral region. Although Gage's skull has been examined carefully, the first person with extensive frontal damage to undergo close scrutiny at autopsy was a furrier who fell 30 meters from a window. He suffered a compound fracture of the frontal bones and severe injury to the right frontal lobe but, remarkably, was never unconscious and was confused only briefly.

Before the fall, the man had been good natured and sociable but, afterward, he became nasty and cantankerous. Autopsy, about a year after the accident, revealed deep scarring of the orbital part of both frontal lobes, although it was more extensive on the right.

From 1900 until about 1950, there were many excellent psychiatric studies of the effect of brain lesions on personality. A consistent finding of this work (especially Kleist's, cited in Zangwill) was that damage to the orbital regions of the frontal lobe is associated with more-dramatic changes in personality than are dorsolateral lesions, although the latter also have significant effects. Clinical descriptions of the effects of frontal-lobe lesions on personality abound, but there are few systematic studies.

At least two types of personality change have been clinically observed in such patients: Dietrich Blumer and Frank Benson have termed them **pseudodepression** and **pseudopsychopathy**. Patients classified as being pseudodepressed exhibit such symptoms as outward apathy and indifference, loss of initiative, reduced sexual interest, little overt emotion, and little or no verbal output. Patients classified as pseudopsychopathic exhibit immature behavior, lack of tact and restraint, coarse language, promiscuous sexual behavior, increased motor activity, and a general lack of social graces. Two case histories illustrate these personalities.

Pseudodepression

At the age of 46, a successful salesman sustained a compound depressed fracture of the left frontal bone in a traffic accident. Treatment included debridement [surgical removal] and amputation of the left frontal pole. Recovery was slow, and 9 months after the injury he was referred for long-term custodial management. By this time, he had recovered motor function with only a minimal limp and slight hyperreflexia on the right

Figure 16.14

Reconstructing a Frontal Injury
No autopsy was performed when Phineas Gage died in 1861, but his skull was later recovered. Skull measurements were combined with imaging techniques to reconstruct the accident and determine the probable location of the lesioning. The image makes it obvious that Gage's frontal cortex in both hemispheres was damaged. (Department of Neurology and Image Analysis Facility, University of Iowa.)

side, had normal sensation, no evidence of aphasia, and normal memory and cognitive ability (IQ 118). Nonetheless, he remained under hospital care because of marked changes in personal habits.

Prior to the accident, the patient had been garrulous, enjoyed people, had many friends and talked freely. He was active in community affairs, including Little League, church activities, men's clubs, and so forth. It was stated by one acquaintance that the patient had a true charisma, "whenever he entered a room there was a change in the atmosphere, everything became more animated, happy and friendly."

Following the head injury, he was quiet and remote. He would speak when spoken to and made sensible replies but would then lapse into silence. He made no friends on the ward, spent most of his time sitting alone smoking. He was frequently incontinent of urine, occasionally of stool. He remained unconcerned about either and was frequently found soaking wet, calmly sitting and smoking. If asked, he would matter-of-factly state that he had not been able to get to the bathroom in time but that this didn't bother him. Because of objectionable eating habits he always ate alone on the ward. His sleep pattern was reversed; he stayed up much of the night and slept during the day. He did not resent being awakened or questioned. He could discuss many subjects intelligently, but was never known to initiate either a conversation or a request. He could give detailed accounts of his life prior to the accident, of the hospitals he had been in, the doctors and treatment he had had, but there was an unreality to his conversation. When asked, he would deny illness, state emphatically that he could return to work at any time, and that the only reason he was not working was that he was being held in the hospital by the doctors. At no time did he request a discharge or weekend pass. He was totally unconcerned about his wife and children. Formerly a warm and loving father, he did not seem to care about his family. Eventually, the family ceased visiting because of his indifference and unconcern. (Blumer and Benson, 1975, pp. 156–157)

Pseudopsychopathy

A 32-year-old white male was admitted for behavioral evaluation. History revealed that he had sustained a gunshot wound in Vietnam 5 years previously. A high-velocity missile had entered the left temple and emerged through the right orbit. Infection necessitated surgical removal of most of the orbital surface of the right frontal lobe. On recovery, he was neither paralyzed nor aphasic but suffered a remarkable change in personality.

Prior to injury he had been quiet, intelligent, proper, and compulsive. He was a West Point graduate and spent the ensuing years as a military officer attaining the rank of captain. Both as a cadet and later as an officer, he was known to be quiet, strict, and rigid. He was considered a good commander, trusted by his men, but never shared camaraderie with his troops or with his peers.

Subsequent to injury, he was outspoken, facetious, brash, and disrespectful. There was no evidence of self-pity, although he frequently made rather morbid jokes about his condition (for example, "dummy's head"). On admission to the hospital, he had just failed at an extremely simple job.

He was not aphasic but misused words in a manner that suggested inability to maintain specific meanings. For instance, when asked whether the injury had affected his thinking his response was, "Yeah—it's affected the way I think—it's affected my senses—the only things I can taste are sugar and salt—I can't detect a pungent odor—ha ha—to tell you the truth it's a blessing this way." When the examiner persisted, "How had it affected the way you think?" his response was "Yes—I'm not as spry on my feet as I was before." He was never incontinent, but did show a messiness in attire. His remarks to the nurses and other female personnel were open and frank but were never blatantly sexual. His premorbid IQ was reported at about 130. Present examination showed a full-scale IQ of 113. (Blumer and Benson, 1975, pp. 155–156)

Blumer and Benson are probably correct in their assertion that all elements of pseudodepression and pseudopsychopathy are observable only after bilateral frontal-lobe damage. Nevertheless, some elements of these two rather different syndromes can be observed in most, if not all, persons with unilateral frontal-lobe lesions. Pseudodepression appears most likely to follow lesions of the left frontal lobe, whereas pseudopsychopathic behavior seems likely to follow lesions of the right frontal lobe.

Deficits in Social and Sexual Behavior

Changes in sexual behavior are among the most difficult symptoms of frontal-lobe damage to document properly, largely because of social taboos against investigating people's sexual lives. To date, there are no such empirical studies, but there is anecdotal evidence that frontal lesions do alter libido and related behavior. Orbitofrontal lesions may introduce abnormal sexual behavior (such as public masturbation) by reducing inhibitions, although the frequency of sexual behavior is not affected. On the other hand, dorsolateral lesions appear to reduce interest in sexual behavior, although patients are still capable of the necessary motor acts and can perform sexually if led through the activity "step by step."

The results of several studies show that frontal-lobe lesions in monkeys significantly alter social behavior. In one interesting study, the dominant (so-called alpha) male was removed from each of several groups of monkeys (Butter and Snyder, 1972). The frontal lobes were removed from half of these alpha monkeys. When the animals were later returned to their groups, all of them resumed the position of dominant male but, within a couple of days, all the monkeys without frontal lobes were deposed and fell to the bottom of the group hierarchy.

Analogous studies of wild monkeys show similar results: monkeys with frontal-lobe lesions fall to the bottom of the group hierarchy and eventually die, because they are helpless alone. Exactly how the social behavior of these animals changed is not known, but there is little doubt that the changes are as dramatic as those in the social behavior of humans.

The social interactions of monkeys are complex and include a significant amount of context-dependent behavior. The behavior of a monkey will change in accord with the configuration of the proximal social group, and monkeys may lose this ability after frontal-lobe lesions. There are likely to be additional components of this behavioral change, however, that relate to the interpretation of species-typical sensory cues, whether they be odors, facial expressions, or sounds.

The deficit in the perception of facial expression by frontal-lobe patients may be related to the loss of cells that code for facial expression. Certain cells in the temporal lobe are especially responsive to facial expression (see Chapter 15), and Edmund Rolls and his colleagues showed that a population of cells in the orbitofrontal cortex also codes for faces. Some of these face-selective neurons are responsive to facial expression or movement.

It is thus not surprising that patients with orbitofrontal lesions might have difficulty in understanding facial expression. We could speculate that there are also likely to be cells in the prefrontal cortex that are responsive to tone of voice, which would be a verbal analogue of facial expression.

Is There a Spatial Deficit?

Recall that a key to understanding the functions of the dorsolateral frontal cortex is found in its relation to the posterior parietal cortex, which plays a central role in the visuomotor guidance of movements in space. Region PG and the superior temporal sulcus play some role in more-complex spatial behavior such as mental rotation (see Chapter 14). These parietotemporal regions provide a major input into the dorsolateral region (see Figure 16.3), which implies some role of this frontal area in spatially guided behavior.

The precise role has been difficult to determine, however. Clearly, dorsolateral lesions impair short-term memory for the location of events, and this deficit could presumably interfere with the selection of behaviors with respect to places in space. Indeed, the delayed-response deficit and the deficit in Passingham's and Goldman-Rakic's tasks (see Figure 16.12A and B) have spatial components.

The role of the dorsolateral cortex in "spatial thinking" can also be seen in a blood-flow study by Per Roland and Lars Friberg. They asked subjects to imagine walking along a familiar route and taking first a left turn, then a right, and so on, alternating turns along the path. A major increase in blood flow in the dorsolateral region suggests a role for the dorsolateral cortex in the selection of spatially guided behaviors.

Taken together, results of the blood-flow and lesion studies suggest that the frontal lobe has a role in selecting among different visual locations. This role may be related to some aspect of attention, an idea to which we return in Chapter 22. Note, however, that little evidence favors the role of the prefrontal cortex in parietal-lobe functions such as topographic orientation or in the ability to mentally manipulate or organize spatial information (see Chapter 14).

Symptoms Associated with Damage to the Frontal Facial Area

Through the years, Taylor and his colleagues have accumulated some remarkable data from a small group of patients with localized surgical removals of the precentral and postcentral gyri, containing, respectively, the motor and sensory representations of the face (see Figure 16.1D). Unlike the removal of cortical areas for the hand, the removal of areas for the face is seldom associated with long-lasting somatosensory deficits on the face, even if both the sensory and the motor representations are removed completely.

There has been no systematic study of the facial motor abilities of patients who have undergone the removal of both precentral and postcentral gyri, but one of us (Kolb) and Milner found such patients able to perform facial-movement sequences normally. Furthermore, although these patients had difficulty in making individual facial movements in the initial postoperative period, especially on the side of the face contralateral to the lesion, they appeared to regain normal voluntary facial control a month after surgery, although closer examination might have revealed subtle defects. In addition, their faces were expressive, and they displayed normal spontaneous facial expressions at frequencies well within normal limits.

In the immediate postoperative period, patients with left-hemisphere facial-area lesions are aphasic, being impaired at both language comprehension and language production, as well as being alexic. However, these symptoms subside rapidly, probably having resulted from swelling and trauma associated with the surgical procedure. Within about 6 months to a year after surgery, only a slight residual expressive dysphasia remains. Yet these same patients are severely impaired at certain other language tests. In particular, they perform very poorly on tests of word fluency and are unable to make effective use of the phonetic elements of language.

In addition, these same patients are very poor spellers, occasionally writing words that are unrecognizable. Their low verbal fluency is complemented by a very low design fluency (see Figure 16.7). Patients with right-facial-area lesions are worse at design fluency than are patients with very large anterior frontal lesions. This lack of spontaneity in verbal and design fluency is remarkable, considering the normal spontaneity of facial expressions.

In summary, unilateral removal of the cortical area representing the face results in no significant chronic loss in sensory or motor control of the face, presumably because of the face's bilateral representation in the cortex. But, surprisingly, it does result in chronic deficits in phonetic discrimination, spelling, verbal fluency, and design fluency. Taylor has preliminary data suggesting that these deficits may result primarily from damage to the precentral motor representation of the face rather than from damage to the postcentral sensory representation. The origin of these deficits, however, is unexplained to date.

Clinical Neuropsychological Assessment of Frontal-Lobe Damage

Considering the number and variety of symptoms associated with frontal-lobe damage, surprisingly few standardized neuropsychological tests are useful for assessing frontal-lobe function. Furthermore, some symptoms of frontal-lobe injury, such as the loss of behavioral self-regulation, are not easily assessed by a neuropsychological test. Nonetheless, a number of very good clinical tests are summarized in **Table 16.3**. As with the parietal- and temporal-lobe tests discussed in Chapters 14 and 15, it would be highly unusual for a person to perform normally on all these tests if there were damage to either frontal lobe.

The Wisconsin Card-Sorting Test (see Figure 16.8) is the best available test of dorsolateral frontal cortex function. As described earlier, a subject is told to sort the cards into piles in front of one or another of the stimulus cards bearing designs that differ in color, form, and number of elements. The correct

Table **16.3** Standardized clinical neuropsychological tests for frontal-lobe damage

Function	Test	Basic Reference
Response inhibition	Wisconsin Card Sorting	Milner, 1964
	Stroop	Perret, 1974
Verbal fluency	Thurstone Word Fluency	Milner, 1964
		Ramier and Hecaen, 1970
Nonverbal fluency	Design Fluency	Jones-Gotman and Milner, 1977
Motor	Hand dynamometry	Taylor, 1979
	Finger tapping	Reitan and Davison, 1974
	Sequencing	Kolb and Milner, 1981a
Language comprehension	Token	de Renzi and Faglioni, 1978
	Spelling	Taylor, 1979
	Phonetic discrimination	Taylor, 1979
Working memory	Self-ordering	Owen et al., 1990
		Pouchon et al., 2001
Planning	Tower of London	Owen et al., 1995

solution shifts without the subject's knowledge when he or she has figured out each solution.

Recall that the Thurstone Word-Fluency Test requires subjects to say or write as many words beginning with a given letter as possible in 5 minutes and then as many four-letter words beginning with a given letter in 4 minutes (see Figure 16.6). Although subjects with lesions anywhere in the prefrontal cortex are apt to do poorly on this test, subjects with facial-area lesions perform the worst, and those with orbital lesions perform only slightly better. Performance is poorest when the lesion is in the left hemisphere.

The Gotman–Milner Design-Fluency Test (see Figure 16.7) also is very useful, although somewhat difficult to score. Subjects are asked to draw as many unnameable, abstract drawings as they can in 5 minutes. Frontal-lobe patients will draw very few items, draw nameable objects, or draw the same figure repeatedly. Like the verbal-fluency tests, the design-fluency task appears most sensitive to orbital injury.

Two tests, the Tower of Hanoi and the Tower of London, have proved sensitive to frontal injury, although the Tower of London appears to be a purer test of planning functions. In both tests, a person is presented with several pegs and several discs of varying size. The discs must be moved from the presented location to another configuration and location according to different rules. For example, only one disc can be moved at a time, and a large disc may never be placed on a smaller one. Damage to either the left or the right prefrontal cortex produces impairments on these tasks.

Tests of motor function include tests of strength (hand dynamometry), finger-tapping speed, and movement sequencing. Strength and finger-tapping speed are significantly reduced contralaterally to a lesion that is in the vicinity of the precentral or postcentral gyri. Motor sequencing can be assessed by using Kolb and Milner's facial-sequence test, although this test requires considerable practice to administer and scoring should be from videotaped records. Simpler tests of movement programming such as the Kimura Box Test (see Figure 14.11) are not suitable, because frontal-lobe patients are unlikely to perform very poorly unless the lesion extends into the basal ganglia.

As in preceding chapters, we recommend the Token Test as a quick screening test for aphasia, to be followed if necessary by more-extensive aphasia testing (see Chapter 19). Although damage to Broca's area is widely believed to result in deficits only in language production and not in comprehension, this outcome is not strictly true. Left frontal lesions in the vicinity of Broca's area produce deficits in comprehension as well as in production.

Spelling is seriously impaired by facial-area lesions and can be assessed by any standardized spelling test. Phonetic differentiation (a test described by Stitt and Huntington and used for neurological patients by Taylor) is another means of assessing facial-area function. A series of nonsense words, such as "agma," is presented and a subject's task is to identify the first consonant sound. This test proves difficult even for controls, but subjects with facial-area damage, especially damage on the left side, perform it most poorly. However, frontal-lobe lesions outside the facial area also may significantly impair performance on this test.

In the absence of language deficits, localizing frontal-lobe damage in either the left or the right hemisphere with neuropsychological tests may prove difficult, presumably because the functions of the two frontal lobes overlap significantly. Clinical evaluation of personality as pseudodepressed or pseudopsychopathic (as discussed earlier) may prove useful in localizing the dysfunction to the left or the right hemisphere, respectively, but caution is advised. Unfortunately, no standardized quantitative measures of these symptoms are available.

Imaging Frontal-Lobe Function

In general, the results of imaging studies, such as those listed in **Table 16.4**, show specific activation for prefrontal functions that were identified historically in lesion studies. Thus, for example, the results of many studies show dorsolateral

Table **16.4** Some functional imaging studies of frontal-lobe function

Presumed Function	Locus of Activation	Basic Reference
Self-ordering	Dorsolateral	Petrides, 2000
Conditioned learning	Dorsolateral	
Spatial working memory	Dorsolateral; ventrolateral	Owen et al., 1996
Visuomotor skill learning	Dorsolateral	Doyon et al., 1996
Verbal memory retrieval	Dorsolateral	Buckner et al., 1995 Tulving et al., 1994
	Ventrolateral	Petrides et al., 1995
Encoding visual information	Orbitofrontal	Frey and Petrides, 2000
Encoding unpleasant auditory information	Orbitofrontal	Frey et al., 2000
Facial expression or recognition or both	Inferior prefrontal	Idaka et al., 2001
Autobiographic memory	Medial; ventrolateral	Svoboda et al., 2006

Left lateral view

Left medial view

Right lateral view

Right medial view

Figure 16.15

Patterns of Activation Prefrontal activations produced by widely different cognitive demands are mapped on lateral and medial views of each hemisphere. Despite the diversity of cognitive demands in these experiments, frontal activations show apparent clustering, with most points within middorsolateral, midventrolateral, and dorsal anterior cingulate regions.

prefrontal participation in tasks tapping verbal and nonverbal working temporal memory.

A review of the patterns of frontal-lobe activation associated with a broad range of different cognitive demands—including aspects of perception, response selection, executive functions, working memory, long-term memory, and problem solving—yielded an especially intriguing finding (Duncan and Owen). Given such a diverse set of presumed cognitive functions, one can reasonably imagine that different regions of the frontal lobe are active during the performance of cognitive tasks that require different cognitive functions. The surprising finding, however, is that a striking regularity in activation emerged: for most cognitive demands, there was a similar recruitment of the dorsolateral, ventrolateral, and anterior cingulate regions, as summarized in **Figure 16.15**.

The reviewers concluded that, although regional specialization exists within the frontal lobe, a frontal-lobe network is consistently recruited for the solution of a diverse set of cognitive problems. How these three regions work in concert to produce behavior is not immediately obvious, but the overlap of activation in such diverse cognitive processes makes it easy to see how the frontal lobe is central to the control of such a diversity of behavior.

Diseases Affecting the Frontal Lobe

Many symptoms of frontal-lobe injury are characteristic of people with psychiatric or neurological disorders, including, especially, schizophrenia (see Chapter 27); Parkinson's disease (see Chapter 27); **Korsakoff's syndrome**, a metabolic disorder of the central nervous system often associated with chronic alcoholism detailed in Chapter 18; and drug addiction. In each of these disorders, a disturbance of frontal-lobe function likely contributes significantly to the behavioral symptoms of the disease.

In schizophrenia, there are believed to be an abnormality in the mesocortical dopamine projection that terminates largely in the frontal lobes, a decrease in blood flow to the frontal lobes, and possible frontal-lobe atrophy. Schizophrenia patients perform poorly on all tests of frontal-lobe function and exhibit abnormalities in the control of eye movements, but they perform normally on tests of parietal-lobe function.

Parkinson's disease results from a loss of the dopamine cells in the substantia nigra. Although the primary projection of these cells is to the caudate nucleus, they project directly to the prefrontal cortex, too, and indirectly through the dorsomedial nucleus of the thalamus. Parkinson patients are characterized by a lack of facial expression similar to that seen in frontal-lobe patients, and they are impaired in the Wisconsin Card-Sorting Test and at delayed-response tasks.

Korsakoff patients suffer from alcohol-induced damage to the dorsomedial thalamus and may have a deficiency in catecholamines in the frontal cortex. They perform poorly on the Wisconsin Card-Sorting Test, as well as on tests of spatial memory such as delayed response.

Drug addicts are characterized by their inability to control drug-seeking behavior, despite aversive consequences. Drug addicts can often be described as showing impulsive or compulsive behavior or perseveration of their behaviors, all of which are symptoms of frontal-lobe dysfunction. Studies of addicts in decision-making tasks, such as the gambling tasks described earlier, show impairments reminiscent of orbitofrontal patients, and imaging studies show impairments in orbitofrontal blood flow during acute withdrawal and even after long periods of abstinence (for reviews, see Gom et al. and Schoenbaum et al.).

Furthermore, addictive drugs lead to changes in the structure of neurons in both the orbitofrontal and the medial prefrontal regions in rats (for a review, see Robinson and Kolb). Drug addiction is likely related to abnormalities in prefrontal structure and function, which are associated with the maladaptive decision-making characteristic of drug addiction.

Summary

The frontal lobe can be conceived to be the end point for the visuomotor and object-recognition functions that are initiated in the occipital lobe. The frontal lobe's function in these processes is to select behaviors with respect to context and internalized knowledge.

Anatomy of the Frontal Lobes
The frontal lobe can be subdivided into three distinct functional zones: motor cortex, premotor cortex, and prefrontal cortex. The motor cortex is responsible for making movements. The premotor cortex selects movements. The prefrontal cortex controls cognitive processes so that appropriate movements are selected at the correct time and place.

A Theory of Frontal-Lobe Function
The premotor cortex can be divided into two regions: (1) the lateral area responsible for selecting behaviors in response to environmental cues and (2) the supplementary area responsible for selecting behaviors on the basis of internalized knowledge. The prefrontal cortex can be divided into two general zones: (1) a dorsolateral zone responsible for selecting behavior with respect to temporal memory and (2) the inferior prefrontal region responsible for selecting behavior with respect to context. Context may be current or based on previous knowledge, including self-knowledge.

Symptoms of Frontal-Lobe Lesions
The wide range of symptoms that result from frontal-lobe lesions can be grouped, conceptually, into several categories: (1) disturbances of motor functions; (2) loss of divergent thinking; (3) impaired response inhibition and inflexible behavior; (4) poor temporal memory; and (5) impaired social and sexual behavior imaging. Left and right frontal lesions have a complementary effect in that left frontal lesions are more likely to affect language or movement-related behaviors, and right frontal lesions are more likely to alter nonlanguage functions, such as emotion.

Imaging Frontal-Lobe Function
The results of imaging studies show frontal participation in tasks with widely different cognitive demands, including attentional tasks, sensory discrimination tasks, motor tasks, spatial problem solving, and the semantic processing of words.

Diseases Affecting the Frontal Lobe
Dysfunction of the frontal lobe is implicated in many behavioral disorders, including, particularly, schizophrenia, Parkinson's disease, Korsakoff's syndrome, and drug addiction.

References

Amiez C., P. Kostopoulos, A. S. Champod, and M. Petrides. Local morphology predicts functional organization of the dorsal premotor region in the human brain. *Journal of Neuroscience* 26:2724–2731, 2006.

Bechara, A., D. Tranel, and H. Damasio. Characterization of the decision-making deficit of patients with ventromedial prefrontal cortex lesions. *Brain* 123:2189–2202, 2000.

Benton, A. L. Differential effects of frontal lobe disease. *Neuropsychologia* 6:53–60, 1968.

Bizzi, E., and P. H. Schiller. Single unit activity in the frontal eye fields of unanesthetized monkeys during head and eye movement. *Experimental Brain Research* 10:151–158, 1970.

Blumer, D., and D. F. Benson. Personality changes with frontal and temporal lobe lesions. In D. F. Benson and D. Blumer, Eds. *Psychiatric Aspects of Neurologic Disease.* New York: Grune & Stratton, 1975.

Brown, J. W. *Aphasia, Apraxia, and Agnosia: Clinical and Theoretical Aspects.* Springfield, Ill.: Charles C. Thomas, 1972.

Buckner, R. L., M. E. Raichle, and S. E. Petersen. Dissociation of human prefrontal cortical areas across different speech production tasks and gender groups. *Journal of Neurophysiology* 74:2163–2173, 1995.

Butter, C. M., and D. R. Snyder. Alterations in aversive and aggressive behaviors following orbital frontal lesions in rhesus monkeys. *Acta Neurobiologiae Experimentalis* 32:525–565, 1972.

de Renzi, E., and P. Faglioni. Normative data and screening power of a shortened version of the Token Test. *Cortex* 14:41–49, 1978.

Doyon J., R. Laforce, G. Bouchard, D. Gaudreau, J. Roy, M. Poirier, P. J. Bedard, F. Bedard, and J. P. Bouchard. Role of the striatum, cerebellum and frontal lobes in the automatization of a repeated visuomotor sequence of movements. *Neuropsychologia* 36:625–641, 1998.

Doyon, J., A. M. Owen, M. Petrides, V. Sziklas, and A. C. Evans. Functional anatomy of visuomotor skill learning in human subjects examined with positron emission tomography. *European Journal of Neuroscience* 8:637–648, 1996.

Drewe, E. A. Go–no-go learning after frontal lobe lesions in humans. *Cortex* 11:8–16, 1975.

Duncan, J., and A. M. Owen. Common origins of the human frontal lobe recruited by diverse cognitive demands. *Trends in Neuroscience* 23:475–483, 2000.

Freedman, M., and M. Oscar-Berman. Bilateral frontal lobe disease and selective delayed response deficits in humans. *Behavioral Neuroscience* 100:337–342, 1986a.

Freedman, M., and M. Oscar-Berman. Comparative neuropsychology of cortical and subcortical dementia. *Canadian Journal of Neurological Science* 13(Suppl 4):410–414, 1986b.

Frey, S., and M. Petrides. Orbitofrontal cortex: A key prefrontal region for encoding information. *Proceedings of the National Academy of Sciences of the United States of America* 97:8723–8727, 2000.

Frey, S., P. Kostopoulous, and M. Petrides. Orbitofrontal involvement in the processing of unpleasant auditory information. *European Journal of Neuroscience* 12:3709–3712, 2000.

Funahashi, S., C. J. Bruce, and P. S. Goldman-Rakic. Perimetry of spatial memory representation in primate prefrontal cortex. *Society for Neuroscience Abstracts* 12:554, 1986.

Fuster, J. M. The prefrontal cortex—an update: Time is of the essence. *Neuron* 30:319–333, 2001.

Fuster, J. M., M. Bodner, and J. K. Kroger. Cross-modal and cross-temporal association in neurons of frontal cortex. *Nature* 405:347–351, 2000.

Goel, V., and J. Grafman. Are the frontal lobes implicated in "planning" functions? Interpreting data from the Tower of Hanoi. *Neuropsychologia* 5:623–642, 1995.

Goldman-Rakic, P. S. Circuitry of the primate prefrontal cortex and regulation of behavior by representational memory. In F. Plum, Ed. *Handbook of Physiology; The Nervous System,* vol. 5, *Higher Functions of the Brain,* Part 1. Bethesda, Md.: American Physiological Society, 1987.

Gom, G., B. Sabbe, W. Hulstijn, and W. van den Brink. Substance use disorders and the orbitofrontal cortex. *British Journal of Psychiatry* 187:209–220, 2005.

Guilford, J. P. *The Nature of Human Intelligence.* New York: McGraw-Hill, 1967.

Guitton, D., H. A. Buchtel, and R. M. Douglas. Disturbances of voluntary saccadic eye-movement mechanisms following discrete unilateral frontal-lobe removals. In G. Lennerstrand, D. S. Lee, and E. L. Keller, Eds. *Functional Basis of Ocular Motility Disorders.* Oxford: Pergamon, 1982.

Hsu, M., M. Bhatt, R. Adolphs, D. Tranel, and C. F. Camerer. Neural systems responding to degrees of uncertainty in human-decision making. *Science* 310:1680–1684, 2005.

Iidaka, T., M. Omori, T. Murata, H. Kosaka, Y. Yonekura, T. Okada, and N. Sadato. Neural interaction of the amygdala with the prefrontal and temporal cortices in the processing of facial expressions as revealed by fMRI. *Journal of Cognitive Neuroscience* 15:1035–1047, 2001.

Jacobsen, C. F. Studies of cerebral function in primates. *Comparative Psychology Monographs* 13:1–68, 1936.

Jones-Gotman, M., and B. Milner. Design fluency: The invention of nonsense drawings after focal cortical lesions. *Neuropsychologia* 15:653–674, 1977.

Jones-Gotman, M., and R. J. Zatorre. Odor recognition memory in humans: Role of right temporal and orbitofrontal regions. *Brain and Cognition* 22:182–198, 1993.

Kolb, B., and B. Milner. Performance of complex arm and facial movements after focal brain lesions. *Neuropsychologia* 19:505–514, 1981a.

Kolb, B., and B. Milner. Observations on spontaneous facial expression after focal cerebral excisions and after intracarotid injection of sodium amytal. *Neuropsychologia* 19:514–515, 1981b.

Kolb, B., and L. Taylor. Affective behavior in patients with localized cortical excisions: An analysis of lesion site and side. *Science* 214:89–91, 1981.

Kuypers, H. G. J. M. Anatomy of the descending pathways. In V. B. Brooks, Ed. *Handbook of Physiology; The Nervous System,* vol. 2, *The Motor Systems.* Baltimore: Williams & Wilkins, 1981.

Lashley, K. S. The problem of serial order in behavior. In F. A. Beach, D. O. Hebb, C. T. Morgan, and H. W. Nissen, Eds. *The Neuropsychology of Lashley.* New York: McGraw-Hill, 1960.

Leonard, G., L. Jones, and B. Milner. Residual impairment in handgrip strength after unilateral frontal-lobe lesions. *Neuropsychologia* 26:555–564, 1988.

Lepage, M., O. Ghaffar, L. Nyberg, and E. Tulving. Prefrontal cortex and episodic memory retrieval mode. *Proceedings of the National Academy of Sciences of the United States of America* 97:506–511, 2000.

Levine, B., S. E. Black, R. Cabeza, M. Sinden, A. R. Mcintosh, J. P. Toth, E. Tulving, and D. T. Stuss. Episodic memory and the self in a case of isolated retrograde amnesia. *Brain* 121:1951–1973, 1998.

Luria, A. R. *The Working Brain.* New York: Penguin, 1973.

Luria, A. R., and E. D. Homskaya. Disturbance in the regulative role of speech with frontal lobe lesions. In J. M. Warren and K. Akert, Eds. *The Frontal Granular Cortex and Behavior.* New York: McGraw-Hill, 1964.

Miller, L. Cognitive risk taking after frontal or temporal lobectomy I: The synthesis of fragmented visual information. *Neuropsychologia* 23:359–369, 1985.

Miller, L., and B. Milner. Cognitive risk taking after frontal or temporal lobectomy II: The synthesis of phonemic and semantic information. *Neuropsychologia* 23:371–379, 1985.

Milner, B. Some effects of frontal lobectomy in man. In J. M. Warren and K. Akert, Eds. *The Frontal Granular Cortex and Behavior.* New York: McGraw-Hill, 1964.

Milner, B., P. Corsi, and G. Leonard. Frontal cortex contribution to recency judgements. *Neuropsychologia* 29:601–618, 1991.

Milner, B., and M. Petrides. Behavioural effects of frontal-lobe lesions in man. *Trends in Neurosciences* 7:403–407, 1984.

Mishkin, M., and F. J. Manning. Non-spatial memory after selective prefrontal lesions in monkeys. *Brain Research* 143:313–323, 1978.

Owen, A. M., J. J. Downes, B. J. Sahakian, C. E. Polkey, and T. W. Robbins. Planning and spatial working memory following frontal lobe lesions in man. *Neuropsychologia* 28:1021–1034, 1990.

Owen, A. M., B. Milner, M. Petrides, and A. C. Evans. Memory for object features versus memory for object location: A positron-emission tomography study of encoding and retrieval processes. *Proceedings of the National Academy of Sciences of the United States of America* 93:9212–9217, 1996.

Owen, A. M., B. J. Sahakian, J. R. Hodges, R. A. Summers, C. E. Polkey, and T. W. Robbins. Dopamine-dependent fronto-striatal planning deficits in early Parkinson's disease. *Neuropsychology* 9:126–140, 1995.

Passingham, R. E. Memory of monkeys *(Macaca mulatta)* with lesions in prefrontal cortex. *Behavioral Neuroscience* 99:3–21, 1985.

Passingham, R. E. *The Frontal Lobes and Voluntary Action.* Oxford: Oxford University Press, 1993.

Perret, E. The left frontal lobe of man and the suppression of habitual responses in verbal categorical behavior. *Neuropsychologia* 12:323–330, 1974.

Petrides, M. Motor conditional associative learning after selective prefrontal lesions in the monkey. *Behavioural Brain Research* 5:407–413, 1982.

Petrides, M. Functional specialization within the dorsolateral frontal cortex for serial order memory. *Proceedings of the Royal Society, London B* 246:299–306, 1991.

Petrides, M. Visuo-motor conditional associative learning after frontal and temporal lesions in the human brain. *Neuropsychologia* 35:989–997, 1997.

Petrides, M. Mapping prefrontal cortical systems for the control of cognition. In A. W. Toga and J. C. Mazziotta, Eds. *Brain Mapping: The Systems.* San Diego: Academic Press, 2000, pp. 159–176.

Petrides, M., B. Alivisatos, and A. C. Evans. Functional activation of the human ventrolateral frontal cortex during mnemonic retrieval of verbal information. *Proceedings of the National Academy of Sciences of the United States of America* 92:5803–5807, 1995.

Petrides, M., and B. Milner. Deficit on subject ordered tasks after frontal- and temporal-lobe lesions in man. *Neuropsychologia* 20:249–262, 1982.

Petrides, M., and D. N. Pandya. Dorsolateral prefrontal cortex: Comparative cytoarchitectonic analysis in the human and the macaque brain and corticocortical connection patterns. *European Journal of Neuroscience* 11:1011–1136, 1999.

Potter, H., and N. Butters. An assessment of olfactory deficits in patients with damage to prefrontal cortex. *Neuropsychologia* 18:621–628, 1980.

Pouchon, J.-B., R. Levy, J.-B Poline, S. Crozier, S. Lehericy, B. Pillon, B. Deweer, D. Le Bihan, and B. Dubois. The role of dorsolateral prefrontal cortex in the preparation of forthcoming actions: An f MRI study. *Cerebral Cortex* 11:260–266, 2001.

Ramier, A. M., and H. Hecaen. Role respectif des atteintes frontales et de la lateralisation lesionnelle dans les deficits de la "fluence verbale." *Revue de Neurologie* 123:17–22, 1970.

Reitan, R. M., and L. A. Davison. *Clinical Neuropsychology: Current Status and Application.* New York: Wiley, 1974.

Roberts, A. C., T. W. Robbins, and L. Weizkrantz, Eds. *The Prefrontal Cortex: Executive and Cognitive Functions.* Oxford: Oxford University Press, 1998.

Robinson, T. E., and B. Kolb. Structural plasticity associated with drugs of abuse. *Neuropharmacology* 47(Suppl 1):33–46, 2004.

Roland, P. E. Metabolic measurements of the working frontal cortex in man. *Trends in Neuroscience* 7:430–435, 1984.

Roland, P. E., and L. Friberg. Localization of cortical areas activated by thinking. *Journal of Neurophysiology* 3:1219–1243, 1985.

Roland, P. E., B. Larsen, N. A. Lassen, and E. Skinhoj. Supplementary motor area and other cortical areas in organization of voluntary movements in man. *Journal of Neurophysiology* 43:118–136, 1980.

Rolls, E. T. The orbitofrontal cortex. In A. C. Roberts, T. W. Robbins, and L. Weizkrantz, Eds. *The Prefrontal Cortex: Executive and Cognitive Functions.* Oxford: Oxford University Press, 1998, pp. 67–86.

Rolls, E. T. *The Brain and Emotion.* Oxford: Oxford University Press, 2000.

Rose, J. E., and C. N. Woolsey. The orbitofrontal cortex and its connections with the mediodorsal nucleus in rabbit, sheep and cat. *Research Publications of the Association of Nervous and Mental Disease* 27:210–232, 1948.

Schoenbaum G., M. R. Roesch, and T. A. Stalnaker. Orbitofrontal cortex, decision-making and drug addiction. *Trends in Neuroscience* 29:116–124, 2006.

Semmes, J., S. Weinstein, L. Ghent, and H.-L. Teuber. Impaired orientation in personal and extrapersonal space. *Brain* 6:747–772, 1963.

Shallice, T. *From Neuropsychology to Mental Structure.* Cambridge, U.K.: Cambridge University Press, 1988.

Shallice, T., and P. Burgess. Deficits in strategy application following frontal lobe damage in man. *Brain* 114:727–741, 1991.

Shallice, T., and M. E. Evans. The involvement of the frontal lobes in cognitive estimation. *Cortex* 14:294–303, 1978.

Smith, M. L., and B. Milner. Differential effects of frontal-lobe lesions on cognitive estimation and spatial memory. *Neuropsychologia* 22:697–705, 1984.

Stitt, C., and D. Huntington. Some relationships among articulation, auditory abilities, and certain other variables. *Journal of Speech and Learning Research* 12:576–593, 1969.

Svoboda, E., M. C. Mckinnon, and B. Levine. The functional neuroanatomy of autobiographical memory: A meta-analysis. *Neuropsychologia* 44:2189–2208, 2006.

Taylor, L. Psychological assessment of neurosurgical patients. In T. Rasmussen and R. Marino, Eds. *Functional Neurosurgery.* New York: Raven, 1979.

Teuber, H. L. The riddle of frontal lobe function in man. In J. M. Warren and K. Akert, Eds. *The Frontal Granular Cortex and Behavior.* New York: McGraw-Hill, 1964.

Teuber, H. L. Unity and diversity of frontal lobe function. *Acta Neurobiologiae Experimentalis* 32:615–656, 1972.

Tulving, E. Episodic memory: From mind to brain. *Annual Review of Psychology* 53:1–25, 2002.

Tulving E., S. Kapur, F. I. Craik, M. Moscovitch, and S. Houle. Hemispheric encoding/retrieval asymmetry in episodic memory: Positron emission tomography findings. *Proceedings of the National Academy of Sciences of the United States of America* 91:2016–2020, 1994.

Tyler, H. R. Disorders of visual scanning with frontal lobe lesions. In S. Locke, Ed. *Modern Neurology.* London: Churchill, 1969.

Walker, E. A., and D. Blumer. The localization of sex in the brain. In K. J. Zulch, O. Creutzfeldt, and G. C. Galbraith, Eds. *Cerebral Localization.* Berlin and New York: Springer-Verlag, 1975.

Zangwill, O. L. Psychological deficits associated with frontal lobe lesions. *International Journal of Neurology* 5:395–402, 1966.

Disconnection Syndromes

Portrait: At Cross Purposes

D.M. was the director of a large psychiatric hospital. He began to complain of headaches and memory problems, and a neurological examination found a cyst in the third ventricle.

The only available treatment was to drain the cyst and relieve the pressure that was causing D.M.'s symptoms. The surgical procedure was simple and required that the neurosurgeon insert a cannula from the top of the brain through the corpus callosum and a bit of brainstem to get to the ventricle.

The cyst was drained successfully and D.M. showed good recovery: his headaches disappeared, his memory improved, and he returned to work. A year later, D.M. still had some residual memory difficulties but, on the whole, he considered himself a lucky man. One new symptom bothered D.M., however.

Sabine Hofer and Jens Frahm, Max Planck Institut für biophysikalische Chemie, Göttingen, Germany

Throughout his life, he had found large-project jigsaw puzzles relaxing, but he was now having difficulty assembling them and was finding the whole experience frustrating.

On further examination, his neurologist discovered that, for certain types of tasks, such as puzzles, D.M.'s two hands did not seem to be working together. For example, the left hand would pick up one piece and the right

hand another, and, seemingly without realizing it, D.M. would try to put both pieces into the same place, one with each hand. No wonder D.M. was getting frustrated!

His surgeon had cut a part of the corpus callosum, and the connections linking the hands in the two hemispheres were severed. D.M.'s right hand literally did not know what his left hand was doing. The diffusion tensor image shown here represents the nerve fiber bundles projecting from the corpus callosum of a male subject into both hemispheres. Projections into the prefrontal cortex are in green, premotor and supplementary motor areas in light blue, M1 in dark blue, S1 in red, parietal lobes in orange, occipital lobes in yellow, and temporal lobes in purple.

I n the preceding chapters, we considered the connections among different cortical regions, the most obvious being the dorsal and ventral pathways of visual processing. But we have not yet considered what happens when the cortical pathways are disturbed. This chapter deals with the effects of cutting cerebral connections, beginning with a summary of cortical connectivity and the anatomy of cerebral connections.

In the remainder of the chapter, we revisit Roger Sperry's research on the split-brain patient as a model of disconnection syndromes. We then reconsider Norman Geschwind's reinterpretation of three classic symptoms of cortical damage (aphasia, apraxia, and agnosia) as disconnection syndromes and briefly study Mortimer Mishkin's animal model of disconnection in the visual system. Finally, we consider some unresolved questions on disconnection.

Disconnecting Cognitive Functions

To understand D.M.'s symptoms (described in the Portrait at the beginning of this chapter), we need to look back on the effects of cortical injuries on behavior. In Chapters 13 through 16, we associated particular behavioral deficits with different brain lesions and from these deficits tried to infer the function of the missing region. Similarly, we considered the results of imaging studies showing localized activity in the performance of different behavioral tasks. Two inescapable conclusions emerge from these discussions:

1. The different anatomically defined cortical lobes are each engaged in a wide range of cognitive activities. Thus, for example, the temporal lobe appears to play a significant role not in only vision and audition but also in more-complex cognitive functions such as memory, language, and emotion.

2. Although the various lobes are engaged in different cognitive activities, they overlap remarkably in function. Recall, for example, that the frontal lobe has cells that are responsive to visual, auditory, somatosensory, olfactory, and taste inputs. Furthermore, we identified a frontal role in functions such as memory, language, and emotion. Clearly, if we presume that the functions of the different anatomical regions differ in some manner, then the simplest explanation of how the cerebral regions function together is that they form some sort of neural network that combines their different contributions to virtually every function that we can describe.

By its very nature, a network implies connections. The cutting of cerebral connections is called **disconnection**, and the ensuing behavioral effects are called **disconnection syndromes**. Thus, we can see that D.M.'s disconnection syndrome was an accidental result of his surgical procedure to drain the third ventricle cyst.

The behavioral changes that result from disconnecting cerebral regions can be rather odd and are different from what could be expected if either area were damaged but remained connected. **Figure 17.1** presents an example in which

Figure 17.1

Downer's Experiment
(A) Anatomy of the normal monkey brain. (B) The commissures between the two hemispheres are severed, the amygdala on the left is removed, and an occluder covers the right eye. The monkey displays no species-typical responses to visual stimuli and is described as "tame." (C) The left eye is occluded; the monkey displays species-typical behavior in response to visual stimuli and is classified as "wild."

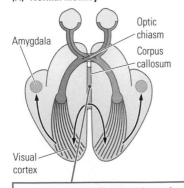

(A) Normal monkey

Amygdala
Optic chiasm
Corpus callosum
Visual cortex

In the anatomically normal monkey, the hemispheres are connected by commissures, including the optic chiasm and the corpus callosum.

(B) "Tame" monkey

Occluder
Optic chiasm severed
No motor response
Corpus callosum severed

With the commissures disconnected, the right eye covered, and the left amygdala removed, visual information is unavailable to the motor system.

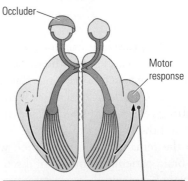

(C) "Wild" monkey

Occluder
Motor response

With the commissures disconnected, the right amygdala intact, and the left eye covered, the circuit in the right hemisphere for activating species-typical behavior is intact.

John Downer performed two different forms of disconnection on a monkey. In Downer's study, all commissures connecting the two halves of the brain were cut and the amygdala on the left side was removed.

Downer then covered one of the animal's eyes with an occluder and presented objects to the other eye. If the objects were presented to the eye ipsilateral to the hemisphere with the ablated amygdala, the animal appeared "tame," even if the objects were typically frightening to monkeys (see Figure 17.1B). If the objects were presented to the eye ipsilateral to the intact amygdala, the animal made its usual species-typical responses to threats and appeared "wild" (see Figure 17.1C). The results can be explained as follows.

For an animal to display species-typical responses to a visual stimulus, information must be projected from the eye to the visual cortex, through the temporal lobes to the amygdala, and from the amygdala to the brainstem and frontal cortex, where autonomic responses, movements, and facial expressions, respectively, are activated. When the commissures between the two halves of the brain are disconnected, visual information from one eye can project only to the ipsilateral hemisphere. If that hemisphere contains an intact amygdala, the circuit for activating species-typical behavior is complete and behavior will be normal. If the hemisphere does not have an intact amygdala, visual information will be disconnected from motor systems and cannot elicit species-typical behavior.

Had the commissures not been cut, the experiment would not have worked, because information from one hemisphere could have crossed to the other, and each eye would thus have had access to the intact amygdala. As the experiment was performed, however, the right hemisphere had access to an amygdala, whereas the left hemisphere did not.

Anatomy of Cerebral Connections

Three major types of neural fibers connect the neocortex—association, projection, and commissural fibers:

- Association fibers can be distinguished as (1) long fiber bundles that connect distant neocortical areas and (2) short subcortical U-shaped fibers that connect adjacent neocortical areas (review Figure 3.26).

- Projection fibers include ascending fibers from lower centers to the neocortex, such as projections from the thalamus, and descending fibers from the neocortex to the brainstem and spinal cord.

- Commissural fibers function primarily to connect the two hemispheres and include principally the corpus callosum, the anterior commissure, and the hippocampal commissures. The corpus callosum (from the Latin *callus*, meaning "hard body") provides the major connection of neocortical areas. In humans, it is made up of 200 million to 800 million fibers. About half of these fibers are unmyelinated and quite small. Most, but not all, areas of the two hemispheres are connected.

Figure 17.2 illustrates the patterns of connections between the hemispheres in a rhesus monkey. Most of the primary visual cortex (area V1) is devoid of

(A) Lateral view

Most of the two frontal lobes have corpus callosum connections,...

...whereas the occipital lobes have almost no connections.

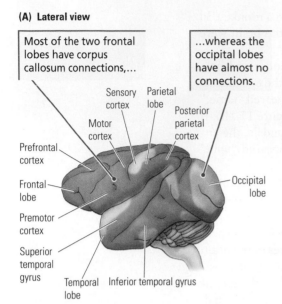

Sensory cortex

Parietal lobe

Motor cortex

Posterior parietal cortex

Prefrontal cortex

Frontal lobe

Premotor cortex

Superior temporal gyrus

Temporal lobe

Inferior temporal gyrus

Occipital lobe

(B) Medial view

Corpus callosum

Regions of the corpus callosum that connect specific regions of the cortex in each hemisphere

Motor cortex

Sensory cortex

Posterior parietal cortex

Superior temporal gyrus

Premotor cortex

Inferior temporal gyrus

Prefrontal cortex

Occipital visual cortex

Genu

Splenium

Fornix

Anterior commissure

Ventral hippocampal commissure

Dorsal hippocampal commissure

Figure 17.2

Patterns of Commissural Connections (A) The areas shaded red show regions of the cortex of a rhesus monkey that receive projections from the contralateral hemisphere through the corpus callosum. (B) Regions of the corpus callosum showing zones through which a radioactive label was transported after injections into specific locations in the monkey's cortex. (After Pandya and Seltzer, 1986.)

interhemispheric connections, except for that part representing the midline of the visual world, the *visual meridian*. The lack of such connections has been explained in functional terms: this cortex represents the visual world topographically, and there is no need for one half of the representation to be connected to the other.

The motor and sensory areas for distal parts of the limbs (mainly the hands and feet) also lack connections. It could be argued that, because their essential function is to work independently of one another, connections are not necessary.

Among the areas that do receive interhemispheric connections, the density of projections is not homogeneous (see Figure 17.2A). Areas of the cortex that represent the midline of the body—such as the central meridian of the visual fields, auditory fields, and trunk of the body on the somatosensory and motor cortex—have the densest connections.

The functional utility of this arrangement is that movements of the body or actions in central space require interhemispheric cooperation. A prominent working hypothesis concerning callosal function is the *zipper hypothesis*, which suggests that the corpus callosum knits together the representations of the midpoints of the body and space that are divided by the longitudinal fissure.

The connections of the corpus callosum appear to fall into three general classes:

1. Most of the projections are topographic; that is, they connect to identical points in the contralateral hemisphere. Presumably, these projections knit the two areas together functionally.

2. One group of projections goes to areas to which the homotopic area on the contralateral side projects. Thus, projection zones within a hemisphere also maintain close relations with parallel zones in the contralateral hemisphere. For example, recall that area V1 is connected to area V2. Not

only are these areas connected within a hemisphere, but they are also connected across hemispheres; so area V1 in one hemisphere also sends connections to area V2 in the opposite hemisphere.

3. Another group of projections has a diffuse terminal distribution. Possibly, these projections alert the appropriate zones of one hemisphere that the other is active.

The location of fiber projections within the corpus callosum is precise. The pattern in the rhesus monkey is illustrated in Figure 17.2B. The anterior part of the corpus callosum is called the genu (the knee), and it contains the fibers from the prefrontal cortex. Fibers through the body of the corpus callosum are, proceeding from front to back, from the premotor, motor, somatosensory, and posterior parietal cortices. Fibers in the posterior part, or splenium, are from the superior temporal, inferior temporal, and visual cortices. Note in the diffusion tensor image at the beginning of this chapter that the location of the fibers in the human brain and the organization of connections are generally similar to those in the monkey brain, except that the motor connections appear to be more extensive.

The anterior commissure is much smaller than the corpus callosum and connects parts of the anterior temporal lobe, the amygdala, and the paleocortex of the temporal lobe surrounding the amygdala. In humans born with no corpus callosum (**callosal agenesis**), the anterior commissure is greatly enlarged to connect far greater regions of the neocortex.

A variety of individual differences in callosal size and patterns are suggested to exist. For example, Sandra Witelson reported that the corpus callosum is larger in left-handers than in right-handers and in women than in men (see Chapter 12).

Behavioral Effects of Disconnection

Marc Colonnier recounted the conclusions of Monsieur de la Peyronie, who in 1741 reviewed all the literature concerning areas claimed to be the seat of the soul, and dismissed each claim in turn. François de la Peyronie then recounted some of his own patients' cases, from which he claimed that, "whereby it appears that the corpus callosum cannot be either compressed, sphacelated [affected with gangrene] or otherwise injured, but for both reason and all sensations are abolished" (Colonnier, p. 35), the corpus callosum must necessarily be the immediate seat of the soul. Colonnier then noted that, by 1941, W. S. McCulloch and H. W. Garol had reviewed the literature and concluded that few impairments could be found after callosum damage except perhaps in complicated symbolic activity.

The clinical effects of disconnection, however, were first seriously considered by Carl Wernicke in 1874 and were very much a part of early neurology. Wernicke predicted the existence of an aphasic syndrome (conduction aphasia) that would result from severing fiber connections between the anterior and the posterior speech zones. Later, in 1892, Joseph Dejerine was the first to demonstrate a distinctive behavioral deficit resulting from pathology of the corpus callosum.

In a series of papers published in about 1900, Hugo Liepmann most clearly demonstrated the importance of severed connections as an underlying factor in the effects of cerebral damage. Having carefully analyzed the behavior of a particular patient, Liepmann predicted a series of disconnections of the neocortex that could account for the behavior. In 1906, after the patient died, Liepmann published the postmortem findings, which supported his hypothesis. He wrote extensively on the principle of disconnection, particularly about the idea that some apraxias might result from disconnection.

Liepmann reasoned that, if a patient were given a verbal command to use the left hand in a particular way, only the verbal left hemisphere would understand the command. To move the left hand, a signal would then have to travel from the left hemisphere through the corpus callosum to the right hemispheric region that controls movements of the left hand, as illustrated in **Figure 17.3**A. Interrupting the part of the corpus callosum that carries the command from the left hemisphere to the right would disconnect the right hemisphere's motor region from the command.

Thus, although the subject would comprehend the command, the left hand would be unable to obey it (Figure 17.3B). This apraxia would occur in the absence of the weakness or incoordination of the left hand that would develop if there were a lesion in the motor cortex of the right hemisphere, which controls the actual movement of the left hand.

Liepmann's deduction, although brilliant, was ignored for a number of reasons. For one, it was published in German and so was not widely read by English-speaking neurologists. Additionally, except in the extremely unusual case of a patient with a natural lesion of only the corpus callosum, any observed behavioral deficits should be attributed to damage of gray matter itself without reference to connections. Finally, the results of a large number of animal studies consistently purported to demonstrate that no significant behavioral effects followed the cutting of the corpus callosum. Not until the late 1950s and 1960s did it become clear that the results from the animal studies could be attributed largely to crude behavioral testing.

An important series of papers by Ronald Myers and by Roger Sperry in the early 1950s revived interest in the effects of disconnecting neocortical regions. They examined the behavioral effects of severing the corpus callosum of the

Figure **17.3**

Liepmann's Theory of Apraxia
(A) Normal response to a verbal command to move the left hand. The command is processed through the posterior speech zone (areas 22, 39, and 40) from the motor cortex of the left hemisphere through the corpus callosum to the motor cortex (area 4) of the right hemisphere to move the left hand. (B) Apraxic response. The jagged line through the callosal area indicates sectioning of the callosum. The verbal command has no way of informing the right-hemisphere motor cortex to move the left hand. Liepmann proposed that bilateral apraxia could result from a lesion disconnecting the posterior speech zone from the motor cortex of the left hemisphere, because the verbal command cannot gain access to either the left or the right motor cortex.

(A) Normal response

Corpus callosum

4, 6   4, 6

22, 39, 40

Verbal command

(B) Apraxic response

No movement

4, 6   ✗   4, 6

22, 39, 40

Verbal command

cat. Their work confirmed others' earlier observations that the animals were virtually indistinguishable from their surgically intact counterparts and indeed appeared normal under most testing and training conditions.

Unlike those of earlier studies, however, the results of the Myers and Sperry studies revealed that, under special training procedures, the animals could be shown to have severe deficits. If the sensory information were allowed separate access to each hemisphere, each hemisphere could be shown to have its own independent perceptual, learning, and memory processes.

The corpus callosum does indeed serve an important function. This conclusion has been confirmed in subsequent studies by Sperry and his colleagues on the effects of surgical disconnection of the cerebral hemispheres of humans for the treatment of intractable epilepsy (see Chapter 11).

The success of the Myers and Sperry experiments stimulated interest in other connections within the brain. Geschwind began to reassess the clinical effects of naturally occurring neocortical lesions as possibly indicating disconnection of various regions of the cerebral hemispheres. In parallel work, Mishkin began to construct animal models of human disconnection syndromes by disconnecting related neocortical regions from one another. These researchers have demonstrated the critical interdependence of these normally connected regions.

In fact, the anatomical organization of the neocortex allows for fairly easy disconnection:

- The primary sensory areas have no direct connections among one another and so can be disconnected quite easily.

- Even in higher-order sensory zones, few if any direct connections exist among sensory systems, and so they can be disconnected easily.

- Because the hemispheres are in large part duplicate and are connected by only a few projection systems, they are easy to separate and, as noted earlier, are sometimes found separated congenitally.

Hemispheric Disconnection

The results of studies on surgical disconnection of the hemispheres indicate that many symptoms—aphasia, alexia, agnosia, agraphia, **acopia** (inability to copy a geometric design), and apraxia among them—can be demonstrated in the absence of any direct damage to particular cytoarchitectonic or functional neocortical regions. They can also be present for one side of the body and not the other.

The hemispheres may become completely separated under three conditions. First, in humans, the interhemispheric fibers are sometimes cut as a therapy for epilepsy. Second, people are born with congenitally reduced interhemispheric connections or callosal agenesis. Third, in animals, disconnections are performed to trace functional systems, to model human conditions, and to answer basic questions about interhemispheric development.

Epileptic seizures may begin in a restricted region of one hemisphere (most often the temporal lobes) and then spread through the fibers of the corpus callosum or anterior commissure to the homologous location in the opposite hemisphere. These seizures can usually be controlled by anticonvulsant medication but, in some cases, the medication is of little value and the seizures may actually become life threatening because they recur often, sometimes several times in an hour.

To relieve this seizure condition, the corpus callosum and anterior commissure can be surgically sectioned to prevent the spread of abnormal electrical activity from one hemisphere to the other. Patients who have received this treatment obtain substantial relief from their epilepsy and often show marked improvements in personal well being, competence, and intelligence.

The reason for collosal agenesis is not known. Interestingly, albinos of nearly all species and Siamese cats have peculiarities in fiber crossings, mostly a reduced number of uncrossed fibers in the visual system. A number of summaries of research on interhemispheric connections have been published, including one by Ian Steele-Russell and his colleagues in 1979 and another by Franco Lepore and his associates in 1986.

Commissurotomy

As described in Chapter 11, **commissurotomy** is the surgical cutting of the cerebral commissures as an elective treatment for epilepsy. Surgeons Philip Vogel and Joseph Bogen at the White Memorial Medical Center in Los Angeles reintroduced this technique, and the results obtained by Sperry and his coworkers with their split-brain patients are now well known. As a result of the surgery, each hemisphere retains fibers that allow it to see only the opposite side of the visual world. Likewise, each hemisphere predominantly receives information from the opposite side of the body and controls movements on the opposite side of the body.

The surgery also isolates speech in those persons with lateralized speech. Consequently, the dominant hemisphere (usually the left) is able to speak, and the nondominant hemisphere is not. About a year or so is required for recovery from the surgical trauma. Within 2 years, the typical commissurotomy patient is able to return to school or work. A standard medical examination would not reveal anything unusual in the behavior of these patients, and their scores on standardized tests are normal. The patients' everyday behavior appears similar to that of normal, "unified" people.

Specific tests, however, can show differences between the functioning of split-brain patients and that of people with normal cerebral connections. In the split brain, each hemisphere can be shown to have its own sensations, percepts, thoughts, and memories that are not accessible to the other hemisphere. The usual test procedures include the presentation of stimuli to one hemisphere and then the testing of each hemisphere for what transpired (see Figure 11.7). For example, a person who is asked to touch an out-of-view object with one hand and then find a similar object with the other hand is unable to match the objects correctly.

Odors presented to one nostril cannot be identified by the other, objects seen in one visual field cannot be recognized in the other, and so on. Although the hemispheres function independently, they both do so at a high level. High levels of function apply even to language skills. The nondominant hemisphere, although unable to speak, can understand instructions, read written words, match pictures to words, and match written to spoken words. Nondominant language ability is best for nouns and poorest for verbs.

The nondominant hemisphere performs in a superior fashion on a variety of spatial tasks, including copying designs, reading facial expressions, and fitting forms into molds. The nondominant hemisphere also has a concept of self and can recognize and identify social relations, pictures of the person in a social relation, pictures of family members, acquaintances, pets and belongings, and historical and social figures. Each hemisphere also has a general awareness of body states such as hunger and fatigue.

Callosal Agenesis and Early Transections

Exceptions to the pattern of results obtained with adult commissurotomy patients are found in persons who are born without a corpus callosum. These patients can perform interhemispheric comparisons of visual and tactile information. The interpretation of these results is that the patients have enhanced conduction in the remaining commissures (for example, for vision) and that they develop enhanced abilities to use their few uncrossed projections (for example, for tactile information).

These patients do have deficits in some features of the tasks, however. There are a number of reports of poor transfer of information if stimuli are complex. Furthermore, nonspecific deficits in task performance have been reported in these patients.

Maryse Lassonde presented pairs of stimuli to six patients with agenesis of the corpus callosum, asking them if the pairs were the same or different. Letters, numbers, colors, or forms were used. Either the pairs were presented one on top of the other in one visual field (intrahemispheric task) or one stimulus was presented in one visual field and the other stimulus in the other visual field (interhemispheric task).

The acallosal group was equally accurate in identifying same–different pairs under both conditions. Their reactions, however, were very slow for both forms of presentation. Lassonde suggested that the callosum participates in hemispheric activation as well as in the transfer of information. Thus, the acallosal group has alternative ways of obtaining the interhemispheric transfer of information but not of activation.

A particularly interesting question concerns the development of language laterality and other asymmetries in regard to agenesis patients (Jeeves, 1986). One explanation of why language is lateralized to one hemisphere is that it gets a start there and then that hemisphere actively inhibits its development in the other hemisphere. In people with callosal agenesis, the opportunity for such an inhibitory process to work is much reduced.

Yet the lateralization of language and other functions in most of these people is similar to that in the general population. They also tend to be right-handed, as is the general population. Thus, the corpus callosum and other commissures are not necessary for the development of asymmetries.

There are similarities in the effects of callosal agenesis and the effects of transections made early in life. Lassonde and coworkers compared the performances of five children aged 6 to 16 years on the interhemispheric transfer of tactile information and motor learning. The younger children were less affected by the callosal transections than the older children.

The researchers suggested that the younger children come to rely on ipsilateral pathways to obtain information and execute movements. That older children are more impaired suggests that, if transections are done early, ipsilateral pathways may make new connections, become functionally validated, or simply become more sensitive.

Disconnecting Sensorimotor Systems

Roger Sperry, Michael Gazzaniga, and others have extensively studied the effects of hemispheric disconnection on behaviors related to both sensory and motor systems. Their findings are summarized here, followed by a consideration of the effects of partial disconnection.

Olfaction

Unlike all the other senses, the olfactory system is not crossed. Input from the left nostril goes straight back to the left hemisphere, and input from the right nostril goes to the right hemisphere. Fibers traveling through the anterior commissure join the olfactory regions in each hemisphere, just as fibers traveling through the corpus callosum join the motor cortex of each hemisphere (see Figure 17.2).

A patient whose anterior commissure is severed cannot name odors presented to the right nostril, because the speaking left hemisphere is disconnected from the information. The right hemisphere has the information but has no control of speech. The olfactory function is still intact, however, because the patient can use the left hand to pick out an object, such as an orange, that corresponds to the odor smelled.

In this case, no connection with speech is necessary, because the right hemisphere both contains the olfactory information and controls the left hand. If requested to use the right hand, the patient would be unable to pick out the object, because the left hemisphere, which controls the right hand, is disconnected from the sensory information. Thus, the patient appears normal with one hand (**Figure 17.4**A) and **anosmic** (lacking the sense of smell) with the other (Figure 17.4B).

Vision

The visual system is crossed, and so information flashed to one visual field travels selectively to the contralateral hemisphere. Recall that, by using this fact, researchers have demonstrated left- and right-visual-field superiority for different types of input. For example, verbal material (such as words) is perceived more accurately when presented to the right visual field, presumably because the input travels to the left, speaking, hemisphere. On the other hand, visuospatial input (such as

Figure 17.4

Anosmia (A) In the normal condition, olfactory input to the right nostril travels directly back into the right hemisphere and crosses the anterior commissure, thus gaining access to the left (speech) hemisphere. (B) Anosmia results from section of the anterior commissure. (The jagged line indicates the lesion.) When the pathway is severed, the information is blocked, and the left hemisphere has no way of knowing what odor the right hemisphere perceived.

(A) Normal

(B) Anosmic

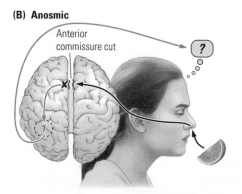

a map) produces a left-visual-field superiority, because the right hemisphere appears to have a more important role in analyzing spatial information.

Note, however, that the visual-field superiority observed in normal subjects is relative. That is, words presented to the left visual field, and hence right hemisphere, are sometimes perceived, although not as accurately or consistently as when they are presented to the right visual field. The relative effects occur because either hemisphere potentially has access to input to the opposite hemisphere through the corpus callosum, which connects the visual areas.

A commissurotomy patient no longer has such access, because the connection is severed. Given that speech is usually housed in the left hemisphere of right-handed patients, visual information presented to the left visual field will be disconnected from verbal associations because the input goes to the right, nonlinguistic, hemisphere. Similarly, complex visual material presented to the right visual field will be inadequately processed, because it will not have access to the visuospatial abilities of the right hemisphere. Thus, if material is appropriately presented, aphasia, agnosia, alexia, and acopia can be demonstrated in a patient who ordinarily exhibits none of these symptoms as follows.

If verbal material is presented to the left visual field, a commissurotomy patient will be unable to read it or to answer questions about it verbally, because the input is disconnected from the speech zones of the left hemisphere. Presentation of the same verbal material to the right visual field presents no difficulties, because the visual input projects to the verbal left hemisphere.

Similarly, if an object is presented to the left visual field, the patient will be unable to name it and thus will appear agnosic and aphasic. If presented to the right visual field, this same object will be correctly named, because the left visual cortex perceives the object and has access to the speech zones. Thus, we can see that the split-brain patient is aphasic, alexic, and agnosic if verbal material or an object requiring a verbal response is presented visually to the right hemisphere, but this person appears normal if material is presented to the left hemisphere.

A further deficit can be seen if the patient is asked to copy a complex visual figure. Because the right hemisphere controls the left hand, we might predict that the left hand will be able to copy the figure but the right hand, deprived of the expertise of the right hemisphere, will be severely impaired. This result is indeed the case: the left hand draws the figure well, whereas the right hand cannot and is thus acopic.

Somesthesis

Like the visual system, the somatosensory system is completely crossed. Sensations of touch in the left hand travel to the right hemisphere, and those in the right hand travel to the left hemisphere. An object placed in the left hand can be named because the tactile information projects to the right hemisphere, crosses to the left, and subsequently has access to the speech zones.

Similarly, if a subject is blindfolded and the right hand is molded to form a particular shape, the left hand is able to copy the shape. The tactile information goes from the right hand to the left hemisphere and then across the corpus callosum to the right hemisphere, and the left hand forms the same shape.

If, however, the two hemispheres are disconnected, the somatosensory functions of the left and right parts of the body become independent. For example, if some object is placed in the left hand of a blindfolded callosal patient, who is then asked to choose the presented object from an array of objects, the left hand can pick out the object, but the right hand cannot. If an object is placed in a blindfolded patient's right hand, the patient can name it but cannot do so if the object is placed in the left hand, because the sensory input is disconnected from the left (speech) hemisphere.

Disconnection effects can also be demonstrated without the use of objects. If the callosal patient is blindfolded and one hand is shaped in a particular way, for example, the opposite hand is unable to mimic the posture. One hand has no way of "knowing" what the other hand is doing in the absence of input coming from the opposite hemisphere through the corpus callosum. If the patient is not blindfolded, however, he or she can find out what the opposite hand is doing simply by looking at it.

Audition

The auditory system is more complex than the other sensory systems because it has both crossed and uncrossed connections. Although the left hemisphere appears to receive most of its input from the right ear, it also receives input from the left ear. Therefore, words played into the left ear can travel directly to the left hemisphere or can go to the right hemisphere and then to the left hemisphere through the corpus callosum.

In normal subjects, dichotic-listening tasks clearly show that the contralateral input is preferred: words presented to the right ear are selectively perceived over words presented to the left ear. Remember, however, that this difference is relative, because some words presented to the left ear also are reported (see Figure 11.11).

The bilateral anatomical arrangement just described appears to reduce the effects of disconnection, but nevertheless one effect has been demonstrated. In the dichotic-listening task, input from the left ear is totally suppressed; the patient reports only those words played to the right ear. That is, digits or words played to the right ear are reported, but no input to the left ear is reported.

This effect is a little surprising, because words played to the left ear, even under these conditions, would be expected to attain some direct access to the left hemisphere. This direct access does not appear to exist when the hemispheres are disconnected.

Movement

Because the motor system is largely crossed, we might predict that disconnection of the hemispheres will induce motor difficulties. Here, we consider responses to verbal commands and tasks requiring the cooperation of both hands.

On any task in which the left hand must either respond to a verbal command or write in response to verbal material, a form of apraxia and agraphia could be expected, because the left hand would not receive instructions from the left hemisphere. That is, the left hand would be unable to obey the command (apraxia) or to write (agraphia). These disabilities would not be seen in the right hand, because it has access to the speech hemisphere.

Similarly, if a patient were asked to use the right hand to copy a geometric design, it might be impaired (acopia) because it is disconnected from the right hemisphere, which ordinarily has a preferred role in rendering. These symptoms of disconnection are in fact observed in commissurotomy patients, although the severity of the deficit declines significantly with the passage of time after surgery, possibly because the left hemisphere's ipsilateral control of movement is being used.

A second situation that might produce severe motor deficits in commissurotomy patients is one in which the two arms must be used in cooperation. Ordinarily, one hand is informed of what the other is doing through the corpus callosum. Bruno Preilowski and, later, Dahlia Zaidel and Roger Sperry examined the effect of the disconnection of this type of bimanual cooperative movement.

Patients were severely impaired at alternating tapping movements of the index fingers. Likewise, in a task similar to using an Etch-a-Sketch, one requiring that a line inclined at an angle be traced, callosal patients did very poorly. This task requires the use of two cranks, one operated by each hand; one crank moves the tracing pen vertically, and the other moves it horizontally.

A high degree of manual cooperation is required to trace a diagonal line smoothly. If the hemispheres have been disconnected, this cooperation is severely retarded, because the left and right motor systems cannot gain information about what the opposite side is doing, except indirectly by a patient's watching them. Recall D.M.'s frustration with his jigsaw puzzles, described in the Portrait at the beginning of this chapter.

Dramatic illustrations of conflict between hands abound. In one case, a patient repeatedly picked up a newspaper with his right hand and laid it down with his left hand. He performed this sequence several times until, finally, the left hand threw the newspaper on the floor. Another patient was described by a physiotherapist: "He was buttoning his shirt with his right hand and the left hand was coming along just behind it undoing the buttons just as quickly as he could fasten them."

However, as in the praxic impairments described earlier, instances of intermanual conflict are generally confined to the first postoperative months and, again, seem related to the age of the patient and extent of extracallosal damage. It is of interest to note that the same patients, while inhibiting these episodes of intermanual conflict, were able to use their left hands in a purposeful and cooperative manner when "not thinking of what they were doing" (Preilowski, 1975, p. 119). For example, they could pour coffee from a pot held in the right hand into a cup held by its handle with the left hand. The aforementioned peculiarities in motor functions were observed only in complete-split-brain patients and not in patients with partial disconnections.

Effects of Partial Disconnection

Would a partial section of the corpus callosum have effects as severe as those of a complete disconnection? Surgeons have experimented with partial surgical disconnection of the hemispheres, hoping to attain the same clinical relief from seizures but with fewer neuropsychological side effects.

Although the results are still preliminary, partial disconnection, in which the posterior part of the corpus callosum is left intact, appears to combine markedly milder effects than those of complete commissurotomy with the same therapeutic benefits. For example, Sperry and his colleagues have found that patients

SNAPSHOT

An fMRI Study of Disconnection

Various imaging studies reveal that, if one hand is subjected to tactile stimulation, areas SI and SII in both the contralateral and the ipsilateral hemispheres become activated. To relieve drug-resistant epilepsy, M.C., age 41, underwent a partial callosotomy, which severed the anterior corpus cal-

(A) Before surgery

(B) After surgery

Activation in response to tactile stimulation. Before the second disconnection surgery (A), M.C. showed bilateral activation of somatosensory cortex, whereas, after surgery (B), he showed only unilateral activation. The second surgery prevented the transfer of information from one hemisphere to the other. (Fabri et al., 2001, p. 1071.)

losum. Because his seizures were unaffected by the surgery, M.C. later had the posterior callosum severed as well.

M.C. was placed in an MRI scanner a week before the second surgery, and his fMRI was recorded in response to the brushing of his palm and fingers of the right or left hand with a sponge at the rate of about 1 Hz (part A of the adjoining illustration). He was retested in the same manner 6 months after the second surgery. Part B shows that, whereas M.C. retained bilateral activation in response to tactile stimulation of either hand after the first surgery, he showed activation only in the contralateral hemisphere after the second surgery.

This result is due to the absence of callosal transfer of the tactile information after the posterior callosum was severed. This loss of activation was correlated with a functional loss as well: before the second surgery, M.C. was able to name objects placed into either hand, whereas, after the second surgery, he could no longer name objects placed into his left hand.

Fabri, M., G. Polonara, M. Del Pesce, A. Quatrinni, U. Salvolini, and T. Manzoni. Posterior corpus callosum and interhemispheric transfer of somatosensory information: An fMRI and neuropsychological study of a partially callosotomized patient. *Journal of Cognitive Neuroscience* 13:1071–1079, 2001.

with partial disconnection are significantly better at motor tasks such as those needed to use the Etch-a-Sketch.

The results of research on monkeys with partial commissurotomies suggest that the posterior part of the corpus callosum (splenium) subserves visual transfer (as does the anterior commissure), whereas the region just in front of the splenium affects somatosensory transfer (see Figure 17.2B). The functions of the more anterior parts of the corpus callosum are largely unknown, but the transfer of motor information is presumed to be one such function. The effect of the transection of the anterior versus the posterior part of the callosum is illustrated nicely in the Snapshot on this page.

Lesion Effects Reinterpreted As Disconnection Syndromes

In 1965, Geschwind wrote a theoretically significant paper titled "Disconnexion Syndromes in Animals and Man" that tied together a vast amount of literature and anticipated many of the effects of callosal surgery. Geschwind's thesis is that certain types of behavioral deficits result from disconnections between the hemispheres, within a hemisphere, or a combination of both. That is, symptoms such as aphasia and agnosia can be thought of as resulting from the *disconnection* of cortical regions rather than necessarily from *damage* to cortical regions.

The value of this paper is not its review of the data but rather its reintroduction of the concept first proposed by Dejerine and Liepmann nearly 70 years earlier: disconnection of neocortical regions can cause a variety of neurological symptoms. To demonstrate the utility of the model, we consider only the three classic symptoms of left hemisphere damage (apraxia, agnosia, and alexia) and one of right hemisphere damage (contralateral neglect).

Apraxia

As noted early in this chapter, if a lesion of the corpus callosum disconnects the left hand from the left hemisphere, that hand is unable to respond to verbal commands and is considered apraxic. Suppose, however, that the right hand is unable to respond to verbal commands. Geschwind speculated that this deficit results from a lesion in the left hemisphere that disconnects its motor cortex (which controls the right hand) from the speech zone (see Figure 17.3B). Thus, the right hand cannot respond to verbal commands and is considered apraxic.

Although Geschwind's model can explain bilateral apraxia in some patients, it must be emphasized that disconnection is not the only cause of apraxia. Because the posterior cortex has direct access to the subcortical neural mechanisms of arm and body movements (see Chapter 9), parietal input need not go through the motor cortex except for the control of finger movements. Further, as noted earlier, patients with sections of the corpus callosum are initially apraxic but show substantial recovery despite a disconnection of the motor cortex of the left and right hemispheres.

Agnosia and Alexia

Geschwind theorized that agnosia and alexia can result from a disconnection of the posterior speech area from the visual association cortex. Both symptoms can be produced by a lesion that disconnects the visual association region on the left from the speech zone or by a lesion that disconnects the right visual association cortex from the speech zone by damaging the corpus callosum, as illustrated in **Figure 17.5**. Thus, a patient who has such a lesion, although able to talk, is unable to identify words or objects, because the visual information is disconnected from the posterior speech zone in the left hemisphere.

Contralateral Neglect

Although Geschwind did not discuss contralateral neglect, it has become apparent that this syndrome also can be partly accounted for as a disconnection syndrome. Recall from Chapter 14 that

Figure **17.5**

Geschwind's Model of Disconnection Agnosia and alexia can result from disconnection of the visual cortex from the posterior speech zone. (A) Normally, the visual input of both hemispheres travels to the posterior speech zone and association cortex, where it is processed to allow speech describing the written word or the object. (B) In the absence of the connection, processing of the visual input is no longer possible, and agnosia and alexia result. The jagged lines indicate the lesion of the pathways.

(A) Normal

Posterior speech zone

Pencil!

Visual areas 17,18,19

(B) Agnosic and alexic

?

Pathways from visual areas to posterior speech zone cut

Figure **17.6**

**Anatomy of Contralateral
Neglect** The subregion of lesion
overlap most associated with
neglect in patients with right-
hemisphere stroke (left) lies within
the white matter just subcortical to
the anteroventral part of the angular
gyrus (right). (Mort et al., 2003,
p. 1990.)

damage to the right parietotemporal junction is most commonly associated with neglect. A recent MRI analysis confirms this location in a large group of patients and shows that white-matter damage is most closely associated with neglect, as illustrated in **Figure 17.6**. This result is consistent with our observation in Chapter 14 that patients with gray-matter excisions in the parietal lobe do not show contralateral neglect.

Experimental Verification of the Disconnection Effect

Disconnection can be used experimentally to demonstrate the function of various brain regions. This chapter began with a discussion of Downer's ingenious experiment to demonstrate the effects of disconnection. Mishkin and others have disconnected different brain areas in animals to demonstrate the functional connections in the hierarchical organization of the visual system and the somatosensory system. The results of this research clearly demonstrate the usefulness of the disconnection approach and have led to significant progress in understanding the sensory systems.

Disconnecting the Visual System

In the visual system, connections in each hemisphere run from area V1 to area V2 and to areas V3, V4, and V5 in the same hemisphere (**Figure 17.7**A). Connections from V3, V4, and V5 cross the corpus callosum to the analogous areas on the opposite side, as well as connecting with area TE on the same side. Area TE connects to the anterior temporal cortex and the amygdala on the same side and connects, through the anterior commissure, to these structures on the opposite side. What would happen to vision if the connections were cut?

This question has been addressed in experiments with the use of monkeys. Such experiments require that the monkeys first be tested to determine their visual capabilities. The easiest method is to teach the animals a visual discrimination, such as between a "+" and a "0." Food reinforcement is associated with one stimulus and not with the other.

A monkey's task is to identify the correct stimulus and respond to it. Control monkeys learn this problem in a maximum of 100 to 150 trials. If a monkey that has been lesioned fails to learn this problem in 1000 trials, the assumption is that it will not learn the task at all. The lesion can be inferred to have some important effect on the monkey's ability to discriminate between visual stimuli.

By using tasks of this sort, Mishkin and others have demonstrated that bilateral lesions in areas V1, V2, or TE result in an impaired or abolished ability to solve visual-discrimination problems. Because unilateral lesions do not have such an effect, what seems to be necessary is one intact trio of areas V1, V2, and TE. There is, however, one constraint: the remaining cortical regions must be connected.

(A) Intact visual system

Corpus callosum

Amygdala

TE

V3,V4, V5

V1

V2

This view of the monkey brain shows both hemispheres in lateral view, with an exaggerated corpus callosum connecting them.

In each hemisphere, connections run from V1 to V2 and to V3, V4, V5, TE, and the amygdala.

Connections from V3, V4, and V5 cross the corpus callosum.

(B) Lesions in left TE and right V1

TE

TE

V1

V1

V2

A lesion in V1 on the right and TE on the left does not disturb performance, because an intact triad of V1 on the left, V2, and TE on the right remains.

(C) Lesioned and disconnected

Corpus callosum cut

TE

TE

V1

V1

Sectioning the corpus callosum disconnects the remaining pathway, severely impairing vision.

Figure 17.7

Disconnection Effects (A) The monkey's visual system is intact. (B) After lesioning (dark gray areas), the left visual cortex still has access to the visual association cortex of the right hemisphere, and so vision is still possible. (C) The intact components of the visual system are disconnected (jagged line) after lesioning, producing major visual deficits. (After Mishkin, 1979.)

Thus, as illustrated in Figure 17.7B, a lesion in area V1 on the right and in area TE on the left does not disturb performance, because an intact system still functions. If the connection between the hemispheres is now severed, the neocortical areas are still intact but are not connected, and the result is failure on the visual-discrimination problem (Figure 17.7C). Clearly, the neocortical regions do not function properly if they are not connected to one another.

Disconnecting Nonvisual Regions from the Visual System

Mishkin first studied area TE, thinking it the final step in the neocortical visual system. He later studied the problem of how visual stimuli might gain what he called "motivational" or "emotional" significance. Monkeys with bilateral temporal lobectomies including the amygdalae attach no significance to visual stimuli. That is, they will repeatedly eat nasty-tasting objects or place inedible objects in their mouths.

In his 1965 paper, Geschwind proposed that this symptom represents a disconnection of the amygdala from the visual system. That is, although an animal's visuosensory system might be intact, the animal would behave as if it were not, because it is disconnected from another system that attaches meaning to visual information. **Figure 17.8**A illustrates the additional connections when the amygdala is included in an extended visual system. Area TE connects with

Figure 17.8

Disconnection of Affect from Visual Input (A) The connections of the intact visual system, including the callosal and anterior commissural connections. (B) Even if parts of the system are damaged (dark gray areas), it can still function. (C) If the anterior commissure is severed after lesioning, visual input is separated from affect, resulting in visual deficits. (After Mishkin, 1979.)

(A) Intact visual-system connections

Anterior commissure

Amygdala

TE

V2

Corpus callosum

V1

The amygdala attaches "motivational" or "emotional" significance to visual stimuli.

TE and the amygdala connect on the same side, and on opposite hemispheres through the anterior commissure.

(B) Lesions in left amygdala and right TE

Amygdala

TE

Even when the amygdala on the left and TE on the right are lesioned, one intact visual system remains and behavior is normal.

(C) Lesioned and disconnected

Anterior commissure

Severing the anterior commissure cuts the connections between contralateral TE and amygdala, resulting in visual performance deficits.

the amygdala on the same side and connects with the amygdala on the opposite side through the anterior commissure.

To test Geschwind's proposal, Mishkin devised an experiment. The amygdala was lesioned on the left and the inferior temporal cortex (area TE) on the right (Figure 17.8B). This arrangement left one complete system of areas V1, V2, TE, and the amygdala; using it, the monkey performed normally on visual problems, as would be expected.

The anterior commissure was then cut, leaving all the necessary pieces of the system intact but disconnecting the intact amygdala from the neocortical part of the system (Figure 17.8C). Performance on visual problems instantly deteriorated, indicating some interruption of the normal processing of visual material, as would be predicted from Geschwind's model.

In another application of the disconnection model to the study of the visual system, Richard Nakamura and Mishkin showed blindness in monkeys after disconnection of the intact visual system from nonvisual regions. Monkeys underwent unilateral decortications in which the visual areas (in addition to the motor and limbic cortices) were spared. Then the cerebral commissures and contralateral optic tract were severed.

Unexpectedly, the animals acted as though they were blind. None showed any detectable reaction to visually presented stimuli, whether food, fearful objects, threats, or sudden movements. When placed in an unfamiliar environment, they bumped into obstacles and found food objects only by touching them accidentally on tactile exploration.

Although some of the monkeys showed some recovery with the passage of time, others did not, remaining functionally blind even 2 years after surgery. Further experiments revealed that the visual cortex was still functioning electrophysiologically, yet the animals behaved as though it no longer functioned at all. The results point to an important role of the nonvisual cortex in visual perception and demonstrate the importance of studying the connections to a functional system as well as its anatomical areas. In the present case, if an animal cannot move in response to visual information, it appears to be essentially blind, even though the visual system may be processing the sensory input.

We can speculate at this point about what a person whose brain is placed in a bottle and kept alive might experience, which, in a real sense, is an extreme example of a disconnection syndrome, because the brain is disconnected from both its inputs and its outputs. It seems likely that, although the brain could still function, it would be unconscious in the absence of inputs or outputs.

Unresolved Questions

Here, we touch on questions related to cerebral disconnection, ranging from species differences to philosophical arguments.

Species Differences

Significant species differences exist in the anatomy and functions of interconnecting hemispheric commissures. Some primitive marsupials do not have a corpus callosum. Some birds, although having interhemispheric commissures, behave as might humans who have no corpus callosum. David Sherry reported that, if an occluder is placed over the eye of a food-caching bird, the information stored by the bird in its contralateral hemisphere about where its food is located is not accessible to the other eye. The animals apparently have separate memory stores for each eye.

Development

Disconnection hypotheses could be applicable to interpretations of various developmental stages of infants. The myelination of fibers is well known to be one of the last events in the maturation of neural systems. Recall from Chapter 12 that the corpus callosum does not become functional until about age 5. Therefore, if certain connections have not matured while others have, features of behavior may parallel symptoms observed in disconnection cases.

For example, young infants will extend their arms to reach for objects in the visual field of the limb. If an object moves across the visual midline, the hand will not follow it, but the other hand will be extended to grasp for it. A little later in development, the infant will follow the object with a hand even if the object crosses the midline. This behavior could be a result of hemispheric disconnection, attributable to immaturity or to a lack of myelination of the interhemispheric pathways.

Other behaviors displayed by infants could be interpreted in the same way. Human infants younger than about 1 year were found to be like split-brain patients in that they are unable to transfer information about objects obtained by touch (Mitchel, 1987). In the experiments, infants were conditioned to expect that someone would play "peek-a-boo" on one or the other side of their bodies. Shortly afterward, they were allowed to feel an object of a certain texture in one hand. Then, they were allowed to feel the object in the other hand. If information was transferred from one hand to the other in the infant's brain, the infants were expected to display the conditioned response, which they did not.

Rats trained on a spatial-navigation task learned the task with one hemisphere at 22 days of age but could not learn it with the other (Rudy and Stadler-Morris, 1987). By the time they were 25 days old, they did display interocular equivalence. The researchers suggest that the 22-day-old rat behaves like a split-brain animal.

Head Trauma

Disconnection may be especially relevant to symptoms that result from traumatic brain injury (TBI). People working with patients who have suffered head trauma (see Chapter 26) are often puzzled by the severe chronic impairments that these patients may display even with minimal direct brain injury. The impairments may be due to diffuse axonal injury (Gennarelli et al., 1986). Head trauma often causes twisting and shearing of the two hemispheres, which could result in a traumatic form of disconnection.

In contrast, TBI patients can also show surprisingly small and selective deficits. Bryan Fantie studied a group of university graduate students with mild closed-head injuries and no apparent deficits and found impairments in callosal transfer of tactile information. That these people were able to obtain graduate degrees in a variety of fields speaks to the specific nature of their brain pathology, which was likely largely restricted to the corpus callosum.

Philosophical Arguments

Many people have written about the implications of the split-brain cases to support theories of mind and concepts of individuality. Certainly for dualists, who hold that the brain has a separate corresponding mental representation (the mind), there are compelling reasons to consider that a split-brain person possesses two brains and two minds. For materialists, who hold that behavior is a function of the nervous system, without recourse to mind, the philosophical implications are not so weighty. But, for everyone, understanding how persons with separated hemispheres function in a seemingly integrated way is challenging.

Summary

Disconnecting Cognitive Functions

Historically enigmatic, the functions of the corpus callosum and associated forebrain commissures are now well understood. In general, the commissures function to allow the two hemispheres to engage in complementary functions and to do so in concert.

Anatomy of Cerebral Connections

There is more to connectivity than the interhemispheric connections; there are also intrahemispheric connections. These connections function to allow each hemisphere to work as a coordinated unit. The major interhemispheric connection is the corpus callosum, which joins most neocortical regions. The medial temporal regions, especially the amygdalae, are connected by the anterior commissure. The intrahemispheric connections include long fiber bundles that connect distant cortical areas as well as short fibers that connect adjacent neocortical areas.

Behavioral Effects of Disconnection

Disconnection of either inter- or intrahemispheric connections can produce a variety of neurological syndromes including apraxia, aphasia, agnosia, and acopia. Thus, such classic symptoms may result from damage to specific cortical regions or from damage to the connections between the cortical regions.

Hemispheric Disconnection

The cerebral hemispheres are sometimes surgically disconnected for the relief of intractable seizures. Such patients show a variety of symptoms that have been used to demonstrate functional asymmetry between the hemispheres.

Disconnecting Sensorimotor Systems

Researchers have taken advantage of disconnection syndromes to study the function of discrete cortical regions. This approach has proved especially useful in studies examining the hierarchical organization of the sensory systems.

Lesion Effects Reinterpreted As Disconnection Syndromes

Many neurological symptoms can be interpreted as a result of disconnection of cortical regions within a hemisphere. For example, neurological symptoms such as apraxia, agnosia, alexia, and contralateral neglect can all be associated with the disconnection of specific cortical regions within the left or right hemisphere.

Experimental Verification of the Disconnection Effect

Researchers have been able to use the disconnection effect to demonstrate functional connectivity within the visual and somatosensory systems as well as to show the role of the amygdala in emotional processing.

Unresolved Questions

Disconnection principles can be extended to understanding other observations, too, including interspecies differences in cognitive processing, developmental stages in infants, and various behavioral disorders resulting from conditions such as head trauma.

References

Colonnier, M. Notes on the early history of the corpus callosum with an introduction to the morphological papers published in this festschrift. In F. Lepore, M. Ptito, and H. H. Jasper, Eds. *Two Hemispheres—One Brain.* New York: Liss, 1986.

Downer, J. L. Changes in visual gnostic functions and emotional behavior following unilateral temporal pole damage in the "split-brain" monkey. *Nature* 191:50–51, 1961.

Fabri, M., G. Polonara, M. Del Pesce, A. Quatrinni, U. Salvolini, and T. Manzoni. Posterior corpus callosum and interhemispheric transfer of somatosensory information: An fMRI and neuropsychological study of a partially callosotomized patient. *Journal of Cognitive Neuroscience* 13:1071–1079, 2001.

Fantie, B., and B. Kolb. Tasks traditionally used to assess callosal function reveal performance deficits associated with mild head injury. *Neuroscience Abstracts* 15:132, 1989.

Gazzaniga, M. S. *The Bisected Brain.* New York: Appleton-Century-Crofts, 1970.

Gennarelli, T. A., J. H. Adams, and D. I. Graham. Diffuse axonal injury: A new conceptual approach to an old problem. In A. Baethmann, K. G. Go, and A. Unterberg, Eds. *Mechanisms of Secondary Brain Damage.* New York: Plenum, 1986.

Geschwind, N. Disconnexion syndromes in animals and man. *Brain* 88:237–294, 585–644, 1965.

Hofer, S., and J. Frahm. Topography of the human corpus callosum revisited: Comprehensive fiber tractography using diffusion tensor magnetic resonance imaging. *Neuroimage* 32:989–994, 2006.

Jeeves, M. A. Callosal agenesis: Neuronal and developmental adaptions. In F. Lepore, M. Ptito, and H. H. Jasper, Eds. *Two Hemispheres—One Brain.* New York: Liss, 1986.

Lassonde, M. The facilitatory influence of the corpus callosum on intrahemispheric processing. In F. Lepore, M. Ptito, and H. H. Jasper, Eds. *Two Hemispheres—One Brain.* New York: Liss, 1986.

Lassonde, M., H. Sauerwein, G. Geoffroy, and M. Decarie. Effects of early and late transection of the corpus callosum in children. *Brain* 109:953–967, 1986.

Lepore, F., M. Ptito, and H. H. Jasper, Eds. *Two Hemispheres—One Brain.* New York: Liss, 1986.

Mishkin, M. Analogous neural models for tactile and visual learning. *Neuropsychologia* 17:139–152, 1979.

Mitchel, G. F. Self-generated experience and the development of lateralized neurobehavioral organization in infants. *Advances in the Study of Behavior* 17:61–83, 1987.

Mort, D.J., P. Malhotra, S.K. Mannan, C. Rorden, A. Pambakian, C. Kennard, and M. Husain. The anatomy of visual neglect. *Brain* 126:1986–1997, 2003.

Myers, R. E. Functions of the corpus callosum in interocular transfer. *Brain* 57:358–363, 1956.

Nakamura, R. K., and M. Mishkin. Blindness in monkeys following non-visual cortical lesions. *Brain Research* 188:572–577, 1980.

Pandya, D. N., and B. Seltzer. The topography of commissural fibers. In F. Lepore, M. Ptito, and H. H. Jasper, Eds. *Two Hemispheres—One Brain*. New York: Liss, 1986.

Preilowski, B. Bilateral motor interaction: Perceptual-motor performance of partial and complete "split-brain" patients. In K. J. Zulch, O. Creutzfeldt, and G. C. Galbraith, Eds. *Cerebral Localization*. Berlin and New York: Springer, 1975.

Rudy, J. W., and S. Stadler-Morris. Development of interocular equivalence in rats trained on a distal-cue navigation task. *Behavioral Neuroscience* 101:141–143, 1987.

Schrift, M. J., H. Bandla, P. Shah, and M. A. Taylor. Interhemispheric transfer in major psychoses. *Journal of Nervous and Mental Disease* 174:203–207, 1986.

Sherry, D. F. Food storage by birds and mammals. *Advances in the Study of Behavior* 15:153–183, 1985.

Sperry, R. W. Lateral specialization in the surgically separated hemispheres. In F. O. Schmitt and F. G. Worden, Eds. *Neurosciences: Third Study Program*. Cambridge, Mass.: MIT Press, 1974.

Spiegler, B. J., and M. Mishkin. Evidence for the sequential participation of inferior temporal cortex and amygdala in the acquisition of stimulus–reward associations. *Behavioral Brain Research* 3:303–317, 1981.

Steele-Russell, I., M. W. Van Hof, and G. Berlucchi, Eds. *Structure and Function of Cerebral Commissures*. London: Macmillan, 1979.

Witelson, S. F. Wires of the mind: Anatomical variation in the corpus callosum in relation to hemispheric specialization and integration. In F. Lepore, M. Ptito, and H. H. Jasper, Eds. *Two Hemispheres—One Brain*. New York: Liss, 1986.

Zaidel, D., and R. W. Sperry. Some long term motor effects of cerebral commissurotomy in man. *Neuropsychologia* 15:193–204, 1977.

Learning and Memory

PORTRAIT: The Mystery of Memory

H.M. had experienced generalized epileptic seizures that had grown progressively worse in frequency and severity despite very high doses of medication. On 23 August 1953, William Scoville performed a bilateral medial-temporal-lobe resection in an attempt to stop the seizures. Afterward H.M. experienced a severe anterograde amnesia that has persisted with little improvement to this day: H.M.'s IQ is above average (118 on the Wechsler Adult Intelligence Scale), and he performed normally on perceptual tests. H.M.'s memory of events that took place before the surgery is good, as is his capacity to recall remote events such as incidents from his school days or jobs that he held in his late teens or early twenties. Socially, H.M. is quiet and well mannered. He dresses neatly but has to be reminded when to shave. He speaks in a monotone but articulates his words well and has a vocabulary in keeping with his above-average intelligence. His language comprehension is normal; he understands complex verbal material, including jokes; and he can engage in sophisticated conversations.

Left   Right

1992

2003

Salat et al., 2006

H.M. was given protected employment in a state rehabilitation center, where he spends weekdays participating in rather monotonous work, programmed for severely retarded patients. A typical task is the mounting of cigarette lighters on cardboard frames for display. He characteristically cannot give us any description of his place of work, the nature of his job, or the route along which he is driven each day, to and from the center.

In contrast with his inability to describe his job after 6 months of daily exposure (except for weekends), H.M. is able to draw an accurate floor plan of the bungalow in which he has lived for the past 8 years. He also seems to be familiar with the topography of the immediate neighborhood, at least within

two or three blocks of his home, but is lost beyond that. His limitations in this respect are illustrated by the manner in which he attempted to guide us to his house, in June 1966. After leaving the main highway, we asked him for help in locating his house. He promptly and courteously indicated to us several turns, until we arrived at a street that he said was quite familiar to him. At the same time, he admitted that we were not at the right address. A phone call to his mother revealed that we were on the street where he lived before his operation. With her directions, we made our way to the residential area where H.M. now lives. He did not get his bearings until we were within two short blocks of the house, which he could just glimpse through the trees. (Milner et al., 1968, pp. 216–217)

The MRIs reproduced here were made when H.M. was 40 years old and 50 years after H.M.'s surgery. Scoville originally believed that he had removed all of H.M.'s hippocampus, but the green arrows on each scan, pointing to the part of the hippocampus that survived the operation, reveal that the removal was only partial.

P atient H.M., described in the Portrait, received elective surgery for the relief of epilepsy when he was 27 years old. When William Scoville operated on H.M., he inadvertently opened one of the most widely studied cases of memory impairment in neuropsychological history. H.M.'s disorder has been documented in more than 100 scientific publications.

Long-term memory	Short-term memory
	Sensory, motor, cognitive

Explicit (conscious)		Implicit (unconscious)	Emotional (conscious and unconscious)
Episodic:	Semantic:	Skills	Attraction
Personal	Facts	Habits	Avoidance
Autobiographical	Knowledge	Priming	Fear
		Conditioning	

Figure 18.1

Multiple Memory Systems The broadest classification of memory distinguishes relatively permanent, long-term memory (knowledge of where you live, say) from short-term memory (where you left the coffee cup from which you are drinking). More-enduring memories are of three types. Explicit, or conscious, memory exists for events and facts that you can spontaneously recall, either of personal experiences, called episodic memories (your first day at school), or semantic memories, for facts (England is in Europe). Implicit, unconscious, memories consist of skills, conditioned responses, and events recalled on prompting. Emotional memory for the affective properties of stimuli or events (your first kiss) is vivid and appears to have characteristics of implicit and explicit memory. (After M.I. Posner and M. E. Raichle, *Images of Mind*, 1994.)

The discovery that **amnesia**, the partial or total loss of memory, can result from a localized brain lesion was surprising to everyone, given what had been learned about memory before H.M. arrived on the scene. H.M.'s case and other cases of temporal-lobe damage also reveal that different kinds of learning and memory, an idea expressed by the term "multiple memory systems" and charted in **Figure 18.1**, constitute completely independent neural processes.

The taxonomy of memory shown in Figure 18.1 distinguishes among the varieties of learning and memory revealed by studying subjects such as H.M. In the following sections, we describe these different systems, their neural substrates, and the insights that knowledge of the many kinds of memory brings to our understanding of our own memories. We begin by surveying the effects of amnesia on learning and remembering.

Learning and Amnesia

The first evidence that the temporal lobes might play a role in human memory preceded H.M. by 50 years. In 1900, when Vladimir Bekhterev autopsied the brain of a patient who had shown a severe memory impairment, he discovered a bilateral softening in the region of the medial temporal cortex. H.M. and additional patients with bilateral temporal cortex damage, described by Brenda Milner and her coworkers in the 1950s, not only confirmed the role of the temporal lobe in memory but also indicated the special contribution of different structures within the temporal lobes to different kinds of memory. (Recall from Chapter 15, for example, that damage to the inferotemporal cortex specifically interferes with conscious recall of information, the extent of the memory disturbance increasing in direct proportion to the amount of temporal-lobe damage.)

An 1885 monograph by Hermann Ebbinghaus stands as the first psychological study of memory, and its formal neuropsychological study is considered to have begun in 1915, when Karl Lashley embarked on a lifetime project to identify the neural locations of learned habits. Lashley either removed parts of the neocortex or severed different fiber pathways in experimental animals, hoping to prevent communication between regions of the cortex. He then studied the effects of these lesions on the animals' abilities to find their way in mazes, manipulate puzzles to open doors, and perform visual discriminations.

Lashley was unable to locate a neural center for memory. At the same time, he found that, as he damaged more and more tissue, the impairments in learning and memory became greater and greater. In 1950, 35 years after beginning this research, Lashley concluded that "it is not possible to demonstrate the isolated localization of a memory trace anywhere in the nervous system. Limited regions may be essential for learning or retention of a particular activity, but the engram [the memory] is represented throughout the region" (Lashley, 1950).

No one could have predicted from Lashley's work that the removal of any structure—let alone the small amount of tissue that Scoville removed from H.M. (**Figure 18.2**)—would result in a person's being capable of remembering things from the past but amnesic or incapable of acquiring new memories. Nevertheless, Lashely did anticipate what H.M. has taught us: that many different kinds of memory and memory systems exist.

Varieties of Amnesia

H.M.'s amnesia was caused by the surgical removal of structures within the medial temporal lobe, but amnesia can be produced in other ways. Other causes of amnesia, and presumably other ways of disrupting or damaging the medial temporal lobe and its pathways, also are sources of insight into the neural basis of learning and memory.

We have all experienced amnesia to some degree. The most dramatic example of forgetting common to all of us is **infantile amnesia**. Although the early years of life are generally regarded as critical in our development, we do not consciously remember these years. For example, we acquire many skills and much knowledge in those years but for the most part do not remember the experiences through which we acquired them. The likely reason for this failure to remember is that memory systems mature at different rates. Personal memories of infancy seem to be lost because the system that is central for adult personal memory is not yet mature in infants.

Adults also forget, as witnessed by occasional reports of people who turn up far from home with no knowledge of their former lives but with skills and language intact. This form of memory loss is referred to as a **fugue state**. The word *fugue* means "flight," and one interpretation of the condition is that the person has in effect fled a former life to form a new one. Perhaps the basis of the fugue state is the temporary suppression of medial-temporal-lobe memory systems.

Transient global amnesia is an acute form of amnesia with a sudden onset and, usually, a short course. It has been described as a loss of old memories and an inability to form new memories (Fisher and Adams, 1958). The condition has been linked to a number of possible causes, including concussion, migraine, hypoglycemia, and epilepsy, as well as to interruption of blood flow from either a transient ischemic stroke or an embolism (see Chapter 26 for details on many of these events).

Transient global amnesia can be a one-time event, but Hans Markowitsch suggests that, even so, some of the memory loss can be permanent. Indeed, a significant chronic memory loss is typical in transient global amnesia but is

(A)

Entorhinal cortex   Amygdala

(B)

Collateral   Entorhinal   Hippocampu
sulcus   cortex

(C)

Hippocampus

Figure **18.2**

Extent of H.M.'s Surgery H.M.'s brain viewed ventrally, with the right-hemisphere lesion highlighted. The right side of this brain diagram has been left intact to show the relative locations of the medial temporal structures. Because the lesion runs along the wall of the medial temporal lobe, it can be seen in several cross sections of the brain. Parts A, B, and C, based on MRI scans made in 1997, depict such sections of H.M.'s brain. (After Corkin et al., 1997.)

Area of lesion

usually overlooked because of the dramatic recovery and because careful memory testing after recovery is seldom done.

Electroconvulsive (shock) **therapy** (ECT), used to treat depression, produces a similar transient memory loss. In ECT, from 70 to 120 V of alternating current is passed briefly from one part of the brain to another through electrodes placed on the skull. In addition, the ingestion of alcohol or minor tranquilizers can result in periods of amnesia, usually for the period of intoxication.

Damage to restricted parts of the brain can cause amnesia that takes very curious forms; for example, there are clinical reports of people who become amnesic for the meaning of nouns but not verbs, and vice versa. Other reports describe people who become amnesic for recognizing animals but are not prosopagnosic (amnesic for human faces). Simona Siri and colleagues describe a patient with herpes simplex encephalitis who was severely amnesic for fruits, vegetables, and musical instruments but less so for animals and birds, suggesting a partial dichotomy in memory between living and nonliving things.

We all experience little everyday amnesias: we forget people's names or faces or where we put our keys, for instance. This kind of forgetting can increase with advancing age, in which case it is popularly known as "old timer's disease" or "senior moments." Its onset is typically characterized by amnesias for the names of people we do not often meet and for items of information that we encounter in news media and in conversation. For some people, memory disorders of aging can become incapacitating, as happens in Alzheimer's disease, which is characterized by the extensive loss of past memories and is accompanied by a loss of neurons that begins in the medial temporal lobe and then extends to other areas of the brain.

What can these kinds and causes of amnesia tell us about memory? Why should infants suffer amnesia for their experiences and yet retain the general skills and knowledge that they have acquired? Why should some people have selective memory loss for one class of objects, whereas memories for other objects are preserved? Why should we have a greater tendency to forget people's names than to forget certain other things as we age? H.M.'s amnesia and the symptoms of other patients with temporal-lobe surgery point to damage to a common neural substrate that includes the medial temporal lobe.

Anterograde and Retrograde Amnesia

The study of H.M., as well as other amnesiac patients, shows that his amnesia consists of two parts. H.M. is unable to acquire new memories, a condition called **anterograde amnesia**, and he has lost memories that must have been accessible to him before his surgery, a form of memory loss called **retrograde amnesia** (**Figure 18.3**).

The term *anterograde* refers to the future with respect to the time at which a person incurred damage to his or her brain. Because so many aspects of his ability to learn and remember appear to be affected, H.M.'s severe anterograde amnesia is referred to as *global anterograde amnesia*. He is impaired in spatial and topographic learning and in learning about all the events that take place around him, including the death of his loved ones. He shows little learning of new words and remembers only a few events or people who have made news since

Figure 18.3

Varieties of Amnesia Among the possible consequences of brain injury on old and new memories, note that retrograde amnesia may be incomplete, with older memories being more preserved than newer memories.

his injury. As H.M. himself has said, "Every day is alone in itself, whatever enjoyment I've had, and whatever sorrow I've had."

For H.M. and many other patients suffering from retrograde amnesia, some memories that were formed before the lesion or surgery are lost. The term retrograde signifies that memory loss extends back in time relative to the time of brain injury, as shown in Figure 18.3. H.M.'s retrograde amnesia is not as complete as his anterograde amnesia, because he remembers many things that he learned before his surgery. For example, he knows who he is; he can read, write, and speak; and he retains most of the skills that he acquired before his surgery. Typically, presurgical memory is much better for events that have taken place earlier in life than for events that have taken place more recently. Recall that H.M. was able to return to the house where he had lived before his surgery, for example.

Time-Dependent Retrograde Amnesia

Traumatic brain injury commonly produces **time-dependent retrograde amnesia**, with the severity of the injury determining how far back in time the amnesia extends. For example, after a head trauma, there is typically a transient loss of consciousness followed by a short period of confusion and retrograde amnesia. The retrograde extent of the amnesia (the period of personal history that it covers, extending from the present to the more-distant past), generally shrinks with the passage of time, often leaving a residual amnesia of only a few seconds to a minute for events immediately preceding the injury.

The duration of such posttraumatic amnesias can vary, however. In one series of patients with severe head injuries, 10% had durations of less than 1 week, 30% had durations of 2 to 3 weeks, and the remaining 60% had durations of more than 3 weeks (Whitty and Zangwill, 1966). Sometimes isolated events, such as the visit of a relative or some unusual occurrence, are retained as "islands of memory" during this amnesic period.

Theories of Retrograde Amnesia: Consolidation, Multiple Traces, and Reconsolidation

The peculiar patterns in retrograde memory ability that follow damage to the temporal lobe present a puzzle. Just how is it that old memories can be preserved and recent memories lost? We present three differing theoretical views that use the same evidence, both from case and group studies of patients who have sustained medial-temporal-lobe damage and from extensive testing of learning and memory in animals.

The **consolidation theory**, as articulated by Larry Squire and Peter Bayley, states that the role of the hippocampus is to *consolidate* new memories, a process that makes them permanent. When consolidation has been completed, the memories are stored somewhere else in the brain. According to this notion, memories are held in the hippocampus for a period of time and are then gradually consolidated in a new location in the neocortex.

Consolidation theory explains why older memories tend to be preserved in cases of hippocampal damage—they have been transferred elsewhere for storage—whereas more-recent memories are likely to be lost—they are still in the hippocampus. If damage is limited to the hippocampus, retrograde amnesia may extend back for only a few years because only recently acquired memories are still there. But, as more of the temporal lobe is affected, retrograde amnesia will extend back for one to two decades, depending on lesion size. In regard to animal studies, the durations of retrograde amnesia examined are much shorter than decades and usually consist of test durations of at most a few months. Nevertheless, the data presented are interpreted as being roughly similar to that obtained with human subjects.

Multiple-trace theory, as articulated by Lynn Nadel and Morris Moscovitch, postulates both multiple kinds of amnesia and changes in memory over time. Multiple-trace theory proposes three kinds of memory:

- Autobiographic memories or episodes for which a subject can describe his or her personal involvement at a particular time and place.

- Factual semantic memory, such as who the president of the country is, what actor starred in a movie, or which university was attended.

- General semantic memory for knowledge, such as language, that is unrelated to contextual constrains of time and place.

First, multiple-trace theory proposes that the three kinds of memory are differentially susceptible to medial-temporal-lobe injury. Autobiographic memory depends on the hippocampus, factual semantic memory depends on adjacent temporal-lobe structures, and general semantic memory depends on other areas of the cortex. Thus, variations in lesion size give the appearance of a temporally graded retrograde amnesia.

Second, the theory proposes that memories change with the passage of time as they are recalled, reevaluated, and restored throughout a person's life. In this way, for example, autobiographic events, through being recalled and discussed, can also be stored as factual memory and perhaps even as general memory. Older memories are subject to more of such changes than are recent memories and so will be stored in many forms and in different locations in the brain. Thus, the very process through which memories change as they are reused places them in different brain locations. As a result, some older memories will be more resistant to disruption.

Reconsolidation theory, as described by Natalie Tronson and Jane Taylor, proposes that memories will rarely consist of a single trace or neural substrate. They note that we frequently recall memories, think about them, and discuss them with others. In story telling or gossiping, a memory is not only recalled but shared and elaborated on by others. Thus, they suggest that each time a memory is used, it is **reconsolidated**; a process by which a memory reenters a labile phase when recalled and is then restored as a new memory. Thus, each use of memory is associated with a new phase of storage, resulting in many different traces for the "same" event. Reconsolidation complicates the study of amnesia, because spontaneous recall and even the investigation of a subject's memory change the memory that is the object of the investigation.

Thus, the three theories suggest that either storage, the type of memory, or the number of times a memory is used contributes to the temporal gradient of retrograde amnesia. A resolution to the debate will require advances in a number of research areas. First, further advances in MRI descriptions of lesions, which provide volumetric data of all areas of the brain affected by a lesion, will clarify the present, very general descriptions of various patients' brain injuries. Second, improved testing of memory impairments will clarify the relations between brain structure and kinds of amnesia. Third, a greater understanding of consolidation processes will clarify how memory changes with time.

Multiple Long-Term Memory Systems

Daniel Schacter described the 1980s as the beginning of the modern memory revolution, because investigators realized during that decade that memory comes in different forms. Again, studies of H.M. contributed to this discovery, as did the development of new approaches to investigating the neural basis of memory. These approaches include new theoretical models, an increasing interest in brain function on the part of cognitive psychologists (those who study how we "think"), and the use of brain-imaging techniques to investigate all these areas.

Long-term memories are of three types and are supported by three pathways in the brain (see Figure 18.1). We recall **implicit memories** of skills, conditioned reactions, and events unconsciously or on prompting, and we can spontaneously and consciously recall **explicit memories** for events and facts. **Emotional memory** for the affective properties of stimuli or events is vivid and has aspects of both conscious and unconscious long-term memory. All are distinguished by differences in the way in which the information is processed:

- *Explicit memory* is the conscious intentional remembering of fact-based *semantic memories* ($2 + 2 = 4$) and personal experiences, or *episodic memories* (what you did last night). Explicit memory depends on conceptually driven, or "top down," processing, in which a subject reorganizes the data to store it. The later recall of information is thus greatly influenced by the way in which the information was originally processed.

- *Implicit memory* is unconscious, nonintentional memory. Your abilities to use language and to perform motor skills such as riding a bicycle or playing a sport are implicit memories. Implicit information is encoded in very much the same way as it is received. This type of processing is data driven, or "bottom up." It depends simply on receiving the sensory information and does not require any manipulation by higher-level cortical processes.

- *Emotional memory* is arousing, vivid, and available on prompting. Thus, like implicit memory, it relies on bottom-up processing. Emotional memory likewise has the intentional, top-down element of explicit memory in that the internal cues that we use in processing emotional events can also be used to initiate their spontaneous recall.

Implicit Memory

The distinction between implicit and explicit memory is especially vivid in H.M. He exhibits severe explicit-memory defects on many kinds of tests, yet he is surprisingly competent at some kinds of implicit learning. Remember that

(A)

H.M.'s task is to trace between the two outlines of the star while looking only at his hand in a mirror.

Crossing a line constitutes an error.

(B)

H.M. shows normal improvement in this motor task, although he does not remember having performed it previously.

Figure 18.4

A Test of Motor Memory (A) The mirror-drawing task. (B) Patient H.M.'s performance over three training sessions.

he was put to work making cigarette-lighter displays and learned to do it. In one experiment, Milner trained H.M. on a mirror-drawing task that requires drawing a third outline between the double outline of a star while looking only at the reflection of the star and the pencil in a mirror (**Figure 18.4**A).

This task is difficult at first even for normal subjects, but they improve with practice. H.M., too, had a normal learning curve on this task. Although he did not remember having performed the task previously, his skill improved each time he performed it over a series of days (Figure 18.4B). Subsequently, Suzanne Corkin trained H.M. on a variety of manual tracking and coordination tasks. Although his initial performances tended to be inferior to those of control subjects, he showed nearly normal improvement from session to session. But, again, he had no explicit memory of ever having performed the tasks.

Sparing of Implicit Memory in Amnesia

For a time, motor learning was considered a curious exception to the deficits that result from temporal-lobe damage, but, in the 1980s, several lines of investigation indicated that other forms of implicit memory also survive in H.M. and other patients with amnesia. One phenomenon entails the technique of **priming**, in which a stimulus is used to sensitize the nervous system to a later presentation of the same or a similar stimulus.

Imagine a priming task in which a person is given a list of words to read. Then, the person is given a list containing the beginnings of words and is asked to complete each of them with the first word that comes to mind. If one of the incomplete words is TAB, the person might complete it as "table," "tablet," "tabby," "tabulation," or something similar. If one of the words on the first list is "table," however, a subject is more likely to complete TAB as "table" than as any other possibility, showing that he or she remembers the word from the first list. Researchers would say that the first list "primed" the subject to give a certain response later on.

The insight into the neural basis of memory is that amnesic subjects perform as well on priming as control subjects do, indicating through their performance that they, too, remember what was on the first study list even as they report no conscious recollection of ever having seen the list. That H.M., like many other amnesic patients, demonstrates the effects of priming in such tasks but has no conscious recall of having encountered the tasks before is evidence that implicit and explicit memory are different.

Priming can also be demonstrated in the following way. Subjects are shown an incomplete sketch and asked what it is. If they fail to identify the sketch, they are shown another sketch that is slightly more complete. This process continues until they eventually recognize the picture. When control subjects and amnesiacs are shown the same sketch at a later date, both groups will identify the sketch at an earlier stage than was possible for them the first time. Thus, control and amnesic subjects indicate through their performance that they remember the previous experience of seeing the lion in **Figure 18.5** completed, even though the amnesic subjects cannot consciously recall ever having seen the sketches before.

The independence of implicit and explicit memory can be demonstrated in other ways as well, especially in normal control subjects. If controls are asked to think about the meaning of a word or the shape of the word, their explicit recall of the word is greatly improved. Their scores on word completion, however, which taps implicit memory, are not affected by this manipulation. This phenomenon is known as the **depth-of-processing effect**. On the other hand, if subjects are shown a word in one modality (for example, if they hear the word) and are tested for recall in another modality (say, they must write the word or identify it by reading), their scores on a word-completion test are greatly reduced, but their explicit recall is little affected. This phenomenon is called a **study–test modality shift**.

Impairments in Implicit Memory

Just as implicit memory can be spared in people with impaired explicit memory, implicit memory can be impaired in people with preserved explicit memory. The case of J.K. is illustrative. J.K. was born on June 28, 1914. He was above average in intelligence and worked as a petroleum engineer for 45 years. In his mid-70s, he began to show symptoms of Parkinson's disease (in which the projections from the dopaminergic cells of the brainstem to the basal ganglia die), and, at about age 78, he started to have memory difficulties.

Curiously, J.K.'s memory disturbance seemed primarily to affect tasks that he had done all his life. On one occasion, he stood at the door of his bedroom frustrated by his inability to recall how to turn on the lights. He remarked, "I must be crazy. I've done this all my life, and now I can't remember how to do it!" On another occasion, he was seen trying to turn the radio off with the remote control for the television set. This time he explained, "I don't recall how to turn off the radio; so I thought I would try this thing!"

J.K. clearly had a deficit in implicit memory. In contrast, he was aware of current events and new experiences and could recall explicit details about them as well as most men his age. Once when we visited him, which is something that we seldom did together, one of us entered the room first and J.K. immediately asked where the other was, even though 2 weeks had elapsed since he had been told that both of us would be coming to visit.

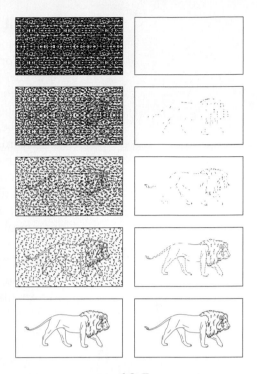

Figure **18.5**

The Gollin Incomplete-Figures Test Subjects are shown a series of drawings in sequence, from least to most clear, and asked to identify the object depicted. It is impossible to identify the object from the first sketch, and most people must see several panels before they can identify it correctly. On a retention test some time later, however, subjects identify the image sooner than they did on the first test, indicating some form of memory for the image. Amnesic subjects also show improvement on this test, even though they do not recall having taken it before.

Explicit Memory

Corkin and her colleagues, who recorded the MRIs of H.M.'s brain that appear in the Portrait at the beginning of this chapter, also studied his residual memory. They report that, if H.M. is asked to examine novel pictures for 20 seconds, he subsequently shows normal recognition of the pictures as long as 6 months later. Functional MRI analysis suggests that a remaining part of his medial temporal lobe, the parahippocampal gyrus, can acquire memory of pictures.

According to Corkin, this finding explains the answer to the most frequently asked question concerning H.M.'s amnesia: "What does he see when he looks in the mirror?" H.M.'s answer is, "Not a young man." Corkin explains that, because of the repeated exposure to his face year after year, H.M. is familiar with his face, and this familiarity may be supported through his intact parahippocampal gyrus.

Autobiographic Memory

Episodic, or **autobiographic**, **memory** consists of singular events that a person recalls. Episodic memory is uniquely different from other neurocognitive memory systems in that it enables human beings to remember past personal experiences. It is memory of life experiences centered on the person himself or herself.

The following excerpt illustrates a simple test for the presence of autobiographic memory. In reading through the example, note that the neuropsychologist is persistent in trying to determine whether the subject, G.O., can recall a single event or experience. Had he not been so persistent, G.O.'s impairment in episodic memory might well have been missed.

> *Do you have a memory of when you had to speak in public?*
>
> Well yes, I'm a call centre trainer with Modern Phone Systems; so I did a lot of speaking because I did a lot, a lot of training all across Canada. I also went to parts of the States.
>
> *Do you remember one time that you were speaking? Can you tell us about one incident?*
>
> Oh yes! Well I trained thousands and thousands of clients on a wide variety of topics including customer service, inbound and outbound telemarketing. Handling difficult customers.
>
> *Do you remember one training session that you gave? Something that may have happened, a specific incident?*
>
> Well for example I always recommended that people take customer-service first. And I always had people come up with four things about themselves, three that were true and one that was false. Not necessarily in that order.
>
> *But this was something ongoing, so every training session you would tell people this, right?*
>
> Yes.
>
> *So what we're looking for is one incident or one time that you gave a training session or any other speeches that you want to tell us about. A specific incident.*

Oh well I customized a lot of material for many, many companies. And I also did lots of training at the home office.

OK, so what we're asking is do you remember one time that you gave a talk?

Oh! yes I do.

One specific time not over a series of times, one time, can you tell us about that?

Oh sure yes, it was at the home office and yes, many many people were there.

One occasion. When did that take place?

When? Well I left Modern voluntarily in 1990.

But this one occasion when did it take place?

Ummm, well I started in the Modern home office.

I'm getting the impression that you have a really good memory for all the training that you've done but you don't seem to be able to come up with a specific talk that maybe stands out in your mind for any reason? Would you agree with that?

Oh yes well I always trained customer service.

So there was no talk that maybe something went wrong or something strange happened?

No, No I was a very good trainer. (Levine, 2000)

Autonoetic Awareness of Time

In Chapter 16, we described Endel Tulving's concept of **autonoetic awareness**, or self-knowledge, that makes it possible to bind together the awareness of oneself as a continuous entity through time—to travel in subjective time, either into the past or into the future. Patients with medial or ventral frontal injury often lose this self-knowledge and have real difficulty in daily living, because impairment in autonoetic awareness results in a deficit in self-regulating one's behavior. Tulving also proposes that "time travel" is a memory ability that characterizes humans but not nonhuman animals and depends on maturation and so will not be found in babies and young children. Tulving's patient K.C. further illustrates the effects of the loss of episodic, or autobiographic, memory.

K.C. was born in 1951. At the age of 30, as a result of a motorcycle accident, he suffered a serious traumatic brain injury, with extensive lesions in multiple cortical and subcortical brain regions, including the medial temporal lobes, and consequent severe amnesia. Nevertheless, most of K.C.'s cognitive capabilities are intact and indistinguishable from those of many healthy adults.

His intelligence and language are normal; he has no problems with reading or writing; his ability to concentrate and to maintain focused attention are normal; his thought processes are clear; he can play the organ, chess, and various card games; his ability to visualize things mentally is intact; and his performance on short-term-memory tasks is normal. K.C. knows many objective facts concerning his own life, such as his date of birth, the address of his home for the first 9 years of his life, the names of some of the schools that he attended, the make and color of the car that he once owned, and the fact that his parents owned and still own a summer cottage.

He knows the location of the cottage and can easily find it on a map. He knows the distance from his home to the cottage and how long it takes to drive there in weekend traffic. He also knows that he has spent a lot of time there. His knowledge of mathematics, history, geography, and other "school subjects," as well as his general knowledge of the world, is not greatly different from that of others at his educational level.

Along with all these normal abilities, however, K.C. has dense amnesia for personal experiences. Thus, he cannot recollect any autobiographic events, whether one-time happenings or repeating occurrences. This inability to remember any episodes or situations in which he was present covers his whole life, from birth to the present, although he does retain immediate experiences for a minute or two.

K.C. has no particular difficulty understanding and discussing either himself or physical time. He knows many facts about himself, and he knows what most other people know about physical time, its units, its structure, and its measurement by clocks and calendars. Nevertheless, he cannot "time travel," either to the past or future. He cannot say what he is going to be doing later today, tomorrow, or at any time in the rest of his life. In short, he cannot imagine his future any more than he can remember his past.

Because K.C. has diffuse damage, it is difficult to say which constellation of injuries accounts for his asymmetrical retrograde amnesia, in which episodic memory is lost but semantic memory is spared. Brian Levine and his coworkers describe similar symptoms for M.L., whose lesion is more localized, as shown by MRI.

Densely amnesic for episodic experiences predating his injury, M.L shows damage to the right ventral frontal cortex and underlying white matter, including the **uncinate fasciculus**, a band of fibers that connects the temporal lobe and ventral frontal cortex (**Figure 18.6**). Because H.M. also displays a complete loss of autobiographic memory both from before and from after his surgery, autobiographic memory must also depend on the medial temporal lobe, further suggesting that the medial temporal lobe and the ventral frontal cortex through the uncinate fasciculus together subserve autobiographic memory.

Figure **18.6**

Brain Regions of Episodic Memory The ventral frontal lobe and the temporal lobe are reciprocally connected by the uncinate fasciculus. The pathway is shown in blue in the adjacent diffusion tensor image. (Diffusion tensor image from A. S. Field, Diffusion tensor imaging of cerebral white matter. *American Journal of Neuroradiology* 25:356–369, 2004, Fig. 7B.)

Semantic Memory

Knowledge about the world—all knowledge that is not autobiographical—is categorized as **semantic memory** and includes knowledge of historical events and of historical and literary figures—for example, Who was Charles Darwin? It includes the ability to recognize family, friends, and acquaintances. It also includes information learned in school, such as specialized vocabularies and reading, writing, and mathematics.

Tulving's patient K.C. retains his semantic memory. He recalls the information that he learned in school, he remembers that his parents have a cabin, and he knows where it is. He also remembers the games that he learned before his injury, and he can still play them well. Similarly, H.M. retains semantic memory from before his surgery, and he has acquired some semantic memories after his surgery; for example, he knows that he has had brain surgery. Thus, semantic memory is not only different from episodic memory, it does not depend on the medial-temporal-lobe–ventral-frontal-lobe memory system that subserves episodic memory.

Neural Substrates of Explicit Memory

Evidence is growing that neural systems, each consisting of a number of structures, support different kinds of memory. On the basis of animal and human studies, including many of the studies that we have reviewed to this point, Herbert Petri and Mortimer Mishkin propose a largely temporal-frontal-lobe neural basis for explicit memory. **Figure 18.7**A illustrates the neural structures that they assign to explicit memory.

Most are in the temporal lobe or closely related to it, such as the hippocampus, the rhinal cortices in the temporal lobe, and the prefrontal cortex. Nuclei in the thalamus also are included, inasmuch as many connections between the prefrontal cortex and the temporal cortex are made through the thalamus. The regions that make up the explicit-memory circuit receive input from the

Figure 18.7

Neural Circuit Proposed for Explicit Memory (A) The general anatomical areas of explicit memory. (B) A circuit diagram showing the flow of information, which begins with inputs from the sensory and motor systems that are not considered part of the circuit.

(A)

Basal forebrain
Thalamus
Neocortex
Prefrontal cortex
Rhinal cortex Hippocampus

(B)

Prefrontal cortex
Temporal-lobe structures
Rest of neocortex
Medial thalamus
Sensory and motor information

From brainstem to cortex systems
Acetylcholine
Serotonin
Noradrenaline

neocortex and from the ascending systems in the brainstem, including the acetylcholine, serotonin, and noradrenaline systems Figure 18.7B).

Explicit-memory functions of different brain regions are described in the following sections. We begin with the structures of the medial temporal lobe, including the hippocampus and perirhinal cortex, the main regions damaged in H.M.'s brain (recall Figure 18.2) and then describe the contributions of other brain regions.

Anatomy of the Hippocampus

Because the hippocampus figures prominently in discussions of memory, we describe its anatomy in some detail, both in reference to its position as a way station between the posterior sensory cortex and the frontal cortex and in reference to its intrinsic complexity. In the 1960s, anatomist H. Chandler Elliott described the hippocampus as "quite archaic and vestigial, possibly concerned with primitive feeding reflexes no longer emergent in man." Quite to the contrary, this structure, small in comparison with the rest of the human forebrain, now plays a dominant role in the discussion of memory. (The term originated in the sixteenth century, when this structure was named after the half-horse half-fish called hippocampus that pulled the sea god Poseidon's chariot.)

The hippocampus is a limbic structure that extends in a curve from the lateral neocortex of the medial temporal lobe toward the midline of the brain and has a tubelike appearance (**Figure 18.8**A). It consists of two gyri, **Ammon's**

Figure 18.8

The Hippocampal Formation
(A) Lying within the temporal lobe, the hippocampus is connected to temporocortical structures by the perforant path and to the brainstem mammillary bodies, nucleus accumbens, and anterior thalamus by the fimbria-fornix. (B) Cross section through the hippocampus showing the location of Ammon's horn, with its pyramidal cells (CA1 through CA4), and the dentate gyrus. (C) Circuit diagram showing that neocortical structures project to the hippocampus through the entorhinal cortex, which receives feedback from the subiculum.

horn (a name for the horn of plenty, the mythological goat's horn from which fruits and vegetables flow endlessly) and the **dentate gyrus** (from the Latin *dentate*, meaning "tooth," because its main cell layer has a sharp bend like the edge of a tooth). If you imagine cutting a tube lengthwise and placing one half on top of the other so that their edges overlapped (like two interlocking Cs), the upper half would represent Ammon's horn and the lower one the dentate gyrus (which can be pictured as flowing out of Ammon's horn).

Each of these two gyri contains a distinctive type of cell. The cells of Ammon's horn are pyramidal cells, and the cells of the dentate gyrus are stellate (star-shaped) **granule cells**. The pyramidal cells of Ammon's horn are divided into four groups (Figure 18.8B): CA1, CA2, CA3, and CA4 (CA standing for *Cornu Ammonis*, the Latin name for Ammon's horn). For structural and functional reasons, the cells of Ammon's horn and the dentate gyrus are differentially sensitive to anoxia (lack of oxygen) and to many toxins. For example, with mild anoxia, CA1 cells are the most likely to die; and, with more-severe anoxia, other CA cells and, finally, the dentate gyrus cells will die.

The hippocampus is reciprocally connected to the rest of the brain through two major pathways. The **perforant pathway** (because it perforates the hippocampus) connects the hippocampus to the posterior neocortex as shown in Figure 18.7A. The other pathway, called the **fimbria-fornix** ("arch-fringe," because it arches along the edge of the hippocampus), connects the hippocampus to the thalamus and frontal cortex, the basal ganglia, and the hypothalamus.

Through its connection to these two pathways, the hippocampus can be envisioned as a way station between the posterior neocortex on one end of the journey and the frontal cortex, basal ganglia, and brainstem on the other. Within the hippocampus, input from the neocortex goes to the dentate gyrus, and the dentate gyrus projects to Ammon's horn. Thus, the granule cells are the "sensory" cells of the hippocampus, and the pyramidal cells are its "motor" cells. The CA1 cells project to another part of the temporal lobe called the subiculum, and the subicular cells project back to the temporal cortex and forward to the thalamus and brainstem (Figure 18.8C).

Case Histories of Hippocampal Function

H.M.'s neurosurgeon, William Scoville, estimated that the temporal-lobe resection removed 8 centimeters of medial-temporal-lobe tissue, including the temporal pole, amygdala, and a major part of the hippocampus. When Corkin and her colleagues reexamined the extent of H.M.'s temporal-lobe removal by using MRI to produce the images shown in the Portrait at the beginning of this chapter, they found that the resection was actually smaller than reported by Scoville. Specifically, it spared a part of the posterior hippocampus.

There is still debate about what contribution the hippocampus makes to memory. As our anatomical description shows, it is a complex structure, and each of the patients with damage to the hippocampus whose case histories are described herein have lesions that are somewhat different. In addition, it is very difficult to conclude that a lesion is selective and does not include injury to some other brain region. H.M.'s lesion spared a major part of the hippocampus but included other temporal-lobe structures. Described here are the findings of patients with the most-selective hippocampal lesions.

Squire and his colleagues describe two patients, R.B. and D.G., whose lesions are limited to the CA1 region of the hippocampus and have a limited retrograde amnesia covering perhaps 1 or 2 years. They also describe L.M. and W.H. who have more-extensive, but still incomplete, hippocampal damage, and their retrograde amnesia covers from 15 to 25 years. Patient E.P., with complete hippocampal damage plus some damage to surrounding structures, has retrograde amnesia covering from 40 to 50 years.

Thus, Squire and his colleagues conclude that the hippocampus itself is important in retaining memory for a relatively short period of time after learning and that adjacent cortices are responsible for memory that extends farther back in time. Additionally, they propose that the earliest memories can be accessed directly in the neocortex and so survive temporal-lobe lesions.

In contrast with the patients described by Squire for whom there is some limit on retrograde amnesia, Lisa Cipolottie and her colleagues report that V.C., a patient whose hippocampus was entirely removed, though surrounding structures were undamaged, has retrograde amnesia that covers his entire life before the lesion was incurred. In short, V.C.'s case suggests that the complete loss of the hippocampus results in complete retrograde and anterograde amnesia for explicit information for all age periods of life.

Early Hippocampal Damage

The symptoms seen in adult cases of hippocampal damage led some researchers to hypothesize that, if such damage occurred in infancy, the persons would be described not as amnesic but as severely retarded. That is, they would be unable to speak, being unable to learn new words; be unable to socialize, being unable to recognize other people; and be unable to develop problem-solving abilities, being unable to remember solutions to problems.

Faraneh Vargha-Khadem and her colleagues report on three cases in which hippocampal damage was incurred early in life: for one subject, just after birth; for another, at 4 years of age; and, for the third, at 9 years of age. None of these people can reliably find his or her way in familiar surroundings, remember where objects and belongings are usually located, or remember where the objects were last placed. None is well oriented in date and time, and all must be frequently reminded of regularly scheduled appointments and events, such as particular classes or extracurricular activities. None can provide a reliable account of the day's activities or reliably remember telephone conversations or messages, stories, television programs, visitors, holidays, and so on.

According to all three sets of parents, these everyday memory losses are so disabling that none of the affected persons can be left alone, much less lead lives commensurate with their ages or social environments. They are not retarded, however. All have fared very well in mainstream educational settings. They are competent in speech and language, have learned to read, and can write and spell. When tested for factual knowledge, they score in the average range. When tested on memory of faces and objects, they also score in the average range, although they are impaired on tasks requiring object–place associations and face–voice associations.

Neural Connections to the Hippocampus

Not only is it difficult to establish that a lesion is restricted to the hippocampus but, even if it is so restricted, the lesion nevertheless damages projections to and from other regions of the brain:

■ David Gaffan and Elizabeth Gaffan describe a series of patients who sustained damage to the fimbria-fornix pathway, sparing the hippocampus itself (see Figure 18.8A). These patients display retrograde and anterograde amnesia similar to that seen in patients with temporal-lobe damage, although perhaps not as extensive.

■ Damage to the temporal stem, a pathway that connects the temporal lobe to the frontal lobe, contributes to amnesia.

■ Severing of the reciprocal connections between the posterior neocortex and the temporal lobe may produce amnesia.

Nevertheless, even though the specific nature of the hippocampus's contribution to memory is debatable, the studies of hippocampal patients allow four conclusions to be drawn.

1. The neural mechanisms underlying anterograde and retrograde amnesias do appear to be at least partly different in that anterograde deficits in memory are more severe than retrograde deficits.

2. Episodic memories are more severely affected than semantic memories are.

3. Autobiographic memory is especially affected, given that patients, such as K.C. and H.M., who have hippocampal damage cannot recall personal experiences prior to their lesions.

4. Just as patients with hippocampal damage are unable to time travel to the past, they cannot imagine future events in which they play a personal role.

The Perirhinal Cortex

When Corkin and her colleagues used MRI to reexamine the extent of H.M.'s temporal-lobe removal, they found that the resection removed most of the entorhinal cortex. The rhinal cortex—the cortex surrounding the rhinal fissure, including the entorhinal cortex and the perirhinal cortex (**Figure 18.9**)—is often damaged in patients with medial-temporal-lobe lesions. These regions project to the hippocampus, and so conventional surgeries and many forms of brain injury that affect the hippocampus may also damage the rhinal cortex or the pathways from it to the hippocampus. In consequence, discriminating between deficits that stem from rhinal-cortex damage and deficits that result from

Figure **18.9**

Medial Temporal Structures That Play a Role in Memory
(A) A rhesus monkey brain viewed from below, visualizing subcortical medial temporal regions. On the left are the perirhinal cortex, the parahippocampal cortex, and the entorhinal cortex. On the right, the amygdala and hippocampus are not directly visible, because they lie beneath the medial temporocortical regions illustrated on the left. (B) Reciprocal connections among the medial temporal regions. Input from the sensory cortex flows to the parahippocampal and perirhinal regions, then to the entorhinal cortex, and finally to the hippocampus, which feeds information back to the medial temporocortical regions.

(A)

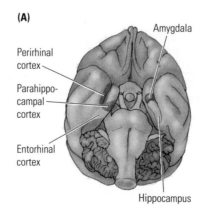

Perirhinal cortex
Parahippocampal cortex
Entorhinal cortex
Amygdala
Hippocampus

(B)

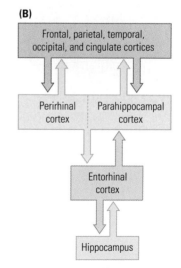

Frontal, parietal, temporal, occipital, and cingulate cortices

Perirhinal cortex

Parahippocampal cortex

Entorhinal cortex

Hippocampus

disconnection or damage to the hippocampus has not been possible in human subjects.

Elisabeth Murray and her colleagues have used neurotoxic lesion techniques to selectively damage the cells of either the hippocampus or the rhinal cortex in monkeys and then examined the specific contributions of each structure to amnesia. In Murray's studies, monkeys reach through the bars of their cage to displace objects under which a reward may be located (**Figure 18.10**A). To find the reward, the animals must make use of their abilities to (1) recognize objects or (2) recognize a given object in a given context.

Object recognition is tested with a matching-to-sample task. A monkey sees a sample object that it displaces to retrieve a food reward hidden underneath. After a brief interval, the monkey is allowed to choose between the sample and a different object and is rewarded for choosing the familiar object. In an alternate, non-matching-to-sample version of the task, the monkey must choose the novel object (Figure 18.10B). For both tasks, delays can be introduced between the sample part and the matching–nonmatching part of the test.

A contextual version of the task requires a monkey to choose an object by using cues based on the object's spatial location. The task may require choosing an object that remains in the same place, as shown in Figure 18.10C, or an object that appears in the same location in a visually presented scene in a picture.

In these studies of memory for objects and contexts, animals with selective hippocampal removal displayed no impairments on the object-recognition tests but were impaired when the test included context. In contrast, animals with rhinal-cortex lesions displayed severe anterograde and retrograde impairments on the object-recognition tests. Thus the conclusion from the results of these

Figure **18.10**

Two Memory Tasks for Monkeys

(A) Basic training

A monkey is shown an object,...

...which it then displaces to obtain a food reward.

(B) Recognition task

A monkey is trained to displace an object to obtain a food reward.

The monkey is then shown two objects, and the task is to displace the *new* object to obtain the reward.

(C) Context

The monkey is shown one object to displace for a food reward.

On the next trial, the monkey is shown two identical objects and must choose the one that is in the same location as in the initial presentation.

studies is that object recognition (factual, or semantic, knowledge) depends on the rhinal cortex, whereas contextual knowledge (autobiographic, or episodic, knowledge) depends on the hippocampus.

Hemispheric Specialization for Explicit Memory

A variety of investigations have revealed asymmetries in explicit memory that exist in all neocortical lobes.

Temporal Cortex

Because one treatment for epilepsy is the removal of the affected temporal lobe, including both neocortical and limbic systems, a large number of patients have undergone such surgery and have subsequently undergone neuropsychological study. The results of these studies suggest significant differences in the memory impairments stemming from damage to the left and right hemispheres (see Chapter 15). They also show that the temporal neocortex makes a significant contribution to these functional impairments.

After right-temporal-lobe removal, patients are impaired on face-recognition, spatial-position, and maze-learning tests (**Figure 18.11**). Impairments in memory for spatial position are also apparent in the Corsi Block-Tapping Test, in which a subject learns to tap out a sequence on a block board, illustrated in **Figure 18.12**A. Just as there is a memory span for digits (which is about seven digits), there is a similar memory span for locations in space.

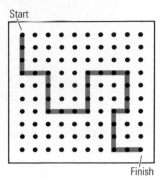

Figure **18.11**

Visually Guided Stylus Maze
The black circles represent metal bolt heads on a wooden base. The task is to discover and remember the correct route by trial and error, indicated here by the line. Deficits on this task are correlated with the amount of hippocampus damage in the left hemisphere.

(A) Corsi Block-Tapping Test

Examiner's view

(B) Hebb Recurring-Digits Test

```
1  4  3  9  2  8  6  7  5
3  6  4  5  7  2  1  9  8
5  9  1  3  4  8  6  2  7  (R)
8  5  2  1  6  9  3  7  4
7  1  4  8  3  2  5  9  6
5  9  1  3  4  8  6  2  7  (R)
2  9  3  5  6  1  8  7  4
8  4  6  9  5  3  7  1  2
5  9  1  3  4  8  6  2  7  (R)
```

(C) Learning-acquisition curve

(D) Performance

Figure **18.12**

Assessing the Temporal Lobes' Role in Memory (A) The Corsi Block-Tapping Test requires a subject to copy a sequence that the examiner taps out on the blocks. The blocks' numbers are visible on the examiner's side of the board but not on the subject's side, and one numerical sequence repeats. (B) In the Hebb Recurring-Digits Test, subjects are given multiple series of nine numbers, two digits longer than the usual digit-memory span. One series repeats (R) every third trial. (C) Performance on the repeated series of digits improves as the number of trials increases, but there is no improvement on the nonrepeating series. (D) Patients with medial temporal lesions of the left hemisphere are impaired on the Hebb Recurring-Digits Test; subjects with medial-temporal-lobe damage of the right hemisphere are impaired on the Corsi Block-Tapping Test.

In the Corsi test, patients and normal (control) subjects are tested on sequences of block locations that contain one item more than the number allowed by their memory spans. One sequence, however, is repeated every third trial. Normal subjects learn the repeated sequence in several trials, although they still have trouble with the novel sequences. Subjects with damage to the right temporal lobe either do not learn the repeated sequence or they learn it very slowly.

Left-temporal-lobe lesions are followed by functional impairments in the recall of word lists, the recall of consonant trigrams, and nonspatial associations. They may also cause impairments on the Hebb Recurring-Digits Test illustrated in Figure 18.12B. This test is similar to the block-tapping test in that subjects are given lists of digits to repeat that exceed their digit spans. Among the lists is one digit sequence that repeats. Patients with left-temporal-lobe lesions do not display the typical learning-acquisition curve, illustrated in Figure 18.12C, but instead fail to learn the repeated digit sequence.

Milner and her colleagues doubly dissociated the effects of damage to the neocortex of the temporal lobe of each hemisphere on several memory tasks. They conclude that lesions of the right temporal lobe result in impaired memory of nonverbal material. Lesions of the left temporal lobe, on the other hand, have little effect on the nonverbal tests but produce deficits on verbal tests such as the recall of previously presented stories and word pairs, as well as the recognition of words or numbers and recurring nonsense syllables. The results of these studies, graphed in Figure 18.12D, indicate that not only is the medial temporal lobe associated with severe memory deficits but the adjacent temporal neocortex also is associated with memory disturbance.

Parietal and Occipital Cortex

Cortical injuries in the parietal, posterior temporal, and, possibly, occipital cortices sometimes produce specific long-term memory difficulties. Examples include color amnesia, prosopagnosia, object anomia (inability to recall the names of objects), and topographic amnesia (inability to recall the location of an object in the environment). Many of these deficits appear to develop in the presence of bilateral lesions only.

Frontal Cortex

The frontal cortex also participates in memory. As described in Chapter 16, an interesting pattern of hemispheric asymmetry is seen in comparisons between the encoding of memory and its retrieval. The pattern is usually referred to as HERA, for hemispheric encoding and retrieval asymmetry. HERA makes three predictions:

1. The left prefrontal cortex is differentially more engaged in encoding semantic information than in retrieving it.

2. The left prefrontal cortex is differentially more engaged in encoding episodic information than in retrieving it.

3. The right prefrontal cortex is differentially more engaged in episodic memory retrieval than is the left prefrontal cortex.

For example, Tulving and coworkers show that the left ventrolateral frontal cortex is preferentially active during memory encoding of words or series of words, but these regions do not retrieve this information. Rather, the right dorsolateral frontal cortex and the posterior parietal cortex in both hemispheres are active during memory retrieval (**Figure 18.13**).

The asymmetry between encoding and retrieving may be related to hemispheric asymmetry in the use of language and spatial processes (see Chapter 12). Most information storage may include the use of language in some way, whereas retrieval may additionally include the use of spatial processes to locate stored information. Thus, Roberto Cabeza and Lars Nyberg, in a review of 275 PET and fMRI studies, note that brain activation during memory encoding and retrieval is likely due to general processes employed by the brain to handle information as well as to local processes related to the storage and retrieval of specific kinds of information.

Diffuse Damage and Explicit Memory

Memory impairments also result from diffuse damage, such as occurs in herpes simplex encephalitis infections, Alzheimer's disease, and Korsakoff's syndrome.

Herpes Simplex Encephalitis

Antonio Damasio and his coworkers describe a number of herpes simplex encephalitis cases in which damage to the temporal lobes is accompanied by severe memory impairments. One such patient, Boswell, is described in considerable detail. Boswell resembles many temporal-lobe-injury patients in having extensive anterograde amnesia while demonstrating normal intelligence and language abilities and performing normally on implicit-memory tests.

Boswell is different, however, in that he has retrograde amnesia that is much more severe than that displayed by most temporal-lobe-injury patients. He is described as being entirely unable to retrieve information from any part of his life history. The damage to the medial temporal cortex probably accounts for his anterograde amnesia, whereas additional damage in the lateral temporal cortex, the insula (diagrammed in Figure 18.6), and the medial frontal cortex probably contributes to his retrograde amnesia.

Damasio suggests that, in Boswell and other herpes simplex encephalitis patients, the insula may be especially implicated in retrograde amnesia. On the basis of the results of studies using a PET-imaging approach, Michael Posner

Figure 18.13

Hemispheric Encoding and Retrieval Asymmetry (HERA)
Areas of cortex that are active as revealed by PET during acquisition (red) or recall (yellow) of verbal information. During acquisition, there is activation in the left ventrolateral prefrontal cortex (areas 10, 46, 45, and 47). During recall of the same material, there is activation in the right dorsolateral cortex (areas 6, 8, 9, and 10) and in the parietal cortex bilaterally (areas 7 and 40). (After Tulving et al., 1994.)

Horizontal sections through the brains of two patients with selective retrograde amnesia for autobiographic information. The section on the left is from an amnesic patient who contracted herpes simplex encephalitis. The right frontal and temporal lobes are dark, corresponding to a metabolic reduction in the right temporal frontal region (arrow). The section on the right shows the brain of a patient with psychogenic amnesia. Again, a significant metabolic reduction is visible in the right temporal frontal area (arrow). (From H. J. Markowitsch, Functional neuroimaging correlates of functional amnesia. *Memory* 7, 561–583, Plate 2, 1999. Reprinted by permission of Psychology Press Ltd., Hove.)

and Marcus Raichle report that the insula is active when subjects perform a well-practiced verbal task but inactive when they perform a novel verbal task. This finding seems consistent with Damasio's suggestion that the insula accesses previously acquired memories.

Alzheimer's Disease

Alzheimer's disease exhibits a progressive loss of cells and the development of abnormalities in the cortex. It is characterized at first by anterograde amnesia and later by retrograde amnesia as well. Among the first areas of the brain to show histological change is the medial temporal cortex but, as the disease progresses, other cortical areas are affected.

Here, too, the pattern of brain change and the pattern of memory deficit suggest that damage to the medial temporal cortex is related to anterograde amnesia and that damage to other temporal association and frontal cortical areas is related to retrograde amnesia. As with the other amnesic patients described thus far, Alzheimer's-related amnesia is displayed mainly on tests of explicit memory, but, eventually, implicit memory also may suffer. (The anatomical correlates of Alzheimer's disease are detailed in Chapter 27.)

Korsakoff's Syndrome

Long-term alcoholism, especially when accompanied by malnutrition, has long been known to produce defects of memory. In the late 1800s, Russian physician Sergei Korsakoff called attention to a syndrome that he found to accompany chronic alcoholism, the most obvious symptom being a severe loss of memory. He wrote:

> The disorder of memory manifests itself in an extraordinarily peculiar amnesia, in which the memory of recent events, those that just happened, is chiefly disturbed, whereas the remote past is remembered fairly well. This reveals itself primarily in that the patient constantly asks the same questions and repeats the same stories. At first, during conversation with such a patient, it is difficult to note the presence of psychic disorder; the patient gives the impression of a person in complete possession of his faculties; he reasons about everything perfectly well, draws correct deductions from given premises, makes witty remarks, plays chess or a game of cards, in a word, comports himself as a mentally sound person. Only after a long conversation with the patient, one may note that at times he utterly confuses events and that he remembers absolutely nothing of what goes on around him: he does not remember whether he had his dinner, whether he was out of bed. On occasion the patient forgets what happened to him just an instant ago: you came in, conversed with him, and stepped out for one minute; then you come in again and the patient has absolutely no recollection that you had already been with him. . . . With all this, the remarkable fact is that, forgetting all events, which have just occurred, the patients usually remember quite accurately the past events, which occurred long before the illness. (Oscar-Berman, 1980, p. 410)

Korsakoff's syndrome has been studied intensively since a seminal article by Helen Sanders and Elizabeth Warrington was published in 1971, because

Korsakoff patients are far more readily available than are persons with other forms of global amnesia. Six major symptoms constitute the syndrome: (1) anterograde amnesia; (2) retrograde amnesia; (3) **confabulation**, in which patients glibly produce plausible stories about past events rather than admit memory loss (the stories are plausible because they tend to be based on past experiences; for example, a man once told us that he had been at the Legion with his pals, which, though untrue, had been his practice in the past); (4) meager content in conversation; (5) lack of insight; and (6) apathy (the patients lose interest in things quickly and generally appear indifferent to change).

The symptoms of Korsakoff's syndrome may appear suddenly, within the space of a few days. The cause is a thiamine (vitamin B₁) deficiency resulting from prolonged intake of large quantities of alcohol. The syndrome, which is usually progressive, can be arrested by massive doses of vitamin B₁ but cannot be reversed. Prognosis is poor, with only about 20% of patients showing much recovery in a year on a B₁-enriched diet. Many patients demonstrate no recovery even after 10 to 20 years.

Although the exact effect of the vitamin deficiency on the brain has been somewhat controversial, current thought is that damage occurs in the medial thalamus and, possibly, in the mammillary bodies of the hypothalamus, as well as there being generalized cerebral atrophy.

PET scans from a normal patient (larger image) and a Korsakoff patient (inset) reveal reduced activity in the frontal lobes of the diseased brain. (The frontal lobes lie at the bottom center of each scan.) Red and yellow represent areas of higher metabolic activity; activity is lower in the darker areas. (Courtesy Dr. Peter R. Martin from *Alcohol Health & Research World,* Spring 1985, 9, cover.)

Ascending Systems Critical for Explicit Memory

The brainstem is the source of at least three nonspecific systems ascending to the forebrain—cholinergic, serotinergic, and noradrenergic—each of which has been proposed at different times to be implicated in memory. For example, the loss of cholinergic cells has been proposed to be related to, even responsible for, the amnesia displayed by patients with Alzheimer's disease. Curiously, in animal experiments, selective lesioning of an ascending system has not produced amnesia, but conjoint damage to at least two systems has produced memory impairments.

Cholinergic cells of the basal forebrain project to the frontal lobes and the temporal lobes and help maintain a normal EEG. Selective damage to these cells are not associated with memory impairment. Serotonergic cells in the midbrain that project to the limbic system and cortex help to maintain a normal EEG. If only this cell group is removed in animals, no serious memory difficulty results. Profound amnesia can be produced, however, if the serotonergic cells and the cholinergic cells are damaged together. Cornelius Vanderwolf demonstrates that animals receiving such treatment behave as if the entire neocortex had been removed, in that they no longer display any intelligent behavior. Additionally, cortical EEG recordings from such animals show a pattern typical of sleep even though the animals can be behaviorally active.

Another example of the conjoint activity of the ascending systems is that between the acetylcholine and the noradrenaline systems. If either system is pharmacologically blocked, there is very little effect on learning. If both systems are blocked together, however, experimental rats are extremely impaired on learning tasks (Decker et al., 1990). Because a number of diseases of aging are associated with the loss of neurons of the ascending projections of the cholinergic, serotonergic, or noradrenergic systems, cell loss in more than one of these systems could be a cause of amnesia even when cortical or limbic structures are intact.

Neural Substrates of Implicit Memory

Petri and Mishkin suggest a brain circuit for implicit memory as well (Figure 18.14). The key structures in this proposed circuit are the neocortex and basal ganglia (the caudate nucleus and putamen). The basal ganglia receive projections from all regions of the neocortex and send projections through the globus pallidus and ventral thalamus to the premotor cortex. The basal ganglia also receive projections from cells in the substantia nigra. The motor cortex shares connections with the cerebellum, and it in turn also contributes to implicit memory.

The Basal Ganglia

Evidence from other clinical and experimental studies supports a formative role for the basal ganglia circuitry in implicit memory. In a study of patients with **Huntington's chorea**, a disorder characterized by the degeneration of cells in the basal ganglia, patients were impaired in the mirror-drawing task illustrated in Figure 18.4 on which patients with temporal-lobe lesions are unimpaired (Martone et al., 1984). Conversely, the patients with Huntington's chorea were unimpaired on a verbal-recognition task.

The Motor Cortex

Positron emission tomography was used to record regional cerebral blood flow as normal subjects learned to perform a motor task (Grafton et al., 1992). In this Pursuit-Rotor Task, a subject attempts to keep a stylus in a particular location on

Figure **18.14**

Neural Circuit Proposed for Implicit Memory (A) The general anatomical areas of implicit memory. (B) A circuit diagram showing the flow of information through the circuits. Information flow begins with inputs from the sensory and motor systems, which themselves are not considered part of the circuit.

a rotating turntable that is about the size of a vinyl record album. The task draws on skills that are very much like the skills needed in mirror drawing. The researchers found that performance of this motor task is associated with increases in regional cerebral blood flow in the motor cortex, basal ganglia, and cerebellum. Acquisition of the skill was associated with a subset of these structures, including the primary motor cortex, the supplementary motor cortex, and the pulvinar nucleus of the thalamus.

A more dramatic demonstration of the role of the motor cortex in implicit learning comes from a study by Alvaro Pascual-Leone and his colleagues. In this study, subjects were required to press one of four numbered buttons by using a correspondingly numbered finger in response to numbered cues provided on a television monitor; for example, when number 1 appears on the screen, push button 1 with finger 1. The measure of learning was the decrease in reaction time between the appearance of the cue and the pushing of the button on successive trials.

The subjects were tested with sequences of 12 cues. For the control group, there was no order to the sequences, but the sequence presented to the brain-damaged group was repeated so that, after they learned the pattern, they could anticipate the cue provided by the monitor and so respond very quickly. The implicit-memory component of this task was the improvement in reaction time with practice, whereas the explicit-memory component was the subjects' recognition of the sequence so that they could generate responses without needing the cues.

Transcranial magnetic stimulation was used to map the motor-cortex area representing the limb making the responses. In this technique, the motor cortex is stimulated through coils placed on the skull while muscle activity in the limb is recorded simultaneously. Thus, the researchers can discover which parts of the cortical area are sending commands to the muscles at various times in the course of learning.

Here, they found that the cortical maps of the muscles participating in the task became progressively larger as the task was mastered. That is, the area of the cortex controlling the limb appeared to increase in size as learning took place. When the subjects knew the sequence of the stimuli and thus had explicit knowledge of the task, however, the area of the motor cortex active during performance of the task returned to its baseline dimensions. In summary, the process of acquiring implicit knowledge requires a reorganization of the motor cortex that is not required for explicit-memory performance.

In the Pursuit-Rotor Task, a subject must keep the stylus in contact with a metal disc that is moving in a circular pattern on a turntable, which also is moving in a circular pattern.

The Cerebellum

The motor regions of the cortex also receive projections through the thalamus from the cerebellum. Kyu Lee and Richard Thompson present evidence that the cerebellum occupies an important position in the brain circuits taking part in motor learning (see Chapter 9). They suggest that the cerebellum plays an important role in a form of learning called **classical conditioning**.

In their model, a puff of air is administered to the eyelid of a rabbit, paired with a stimulus such as a tone. Eventually, the rabbit becomes "conditioned" to

"Eye-blink" conditioning is mediated
by circuits in the cerebellum.

1 Headgear is arranged for eye-blink conditioning.

Electrodes

2 Puff of air to eye causes eye to blink.

Air-jet tube

Audio speaker

3 After pairing of air puff with tone, tone alone elicits a blink.

blink in expectation of the air puff whenever the tone is sounded. Lesions to pathways from the cerebellum abolish this *conditioned response* but do not stop the rabbit from blinking in response to an actual air puff, the *unconditioned response*. The researchers further demonstrated the importance of the cerebellum in learning by showing that the neocortex is not necessary for the development of a conditioned response. This evidence suggests that the cerebellum takes part in learning discrete, adaptive, behavioral responses.

Neural Substrates of Emotional Memory

In **fear conditioning**, a noxious stimulus is used to elicit fear, an emotional response. A rat or other animal is placed in a box that has a grid floor through which a mild but noxious electrical current can be passed. (This shock is roughly equivalent to the static-electrical shock that we get when we rub our feet on a carpet and then touch a metal object or another person.) When the tone is later presented without the shock, the animal will act afraid. It may become motionless and may urinate in expectation of the shock. The presentation of a novel stimulus, such as a light, in the same environment has little effect on the animal. Thus, the animal tells us that it has learned the association between the tone and the shock.

Because the conditioned response is emotional, circuits of the amygdala, rather than the cerebellum, mediate fear conditioning. Although both eye-blink and fear conditioning are Pavlovian, different parts of the brain mediate the learning.

Whether emotional memories are implicit or explicit is not altogether clear; in fact, they could be both. Certainly, people can react with fear to specific stimuli that they can identify, and they can also fear situations for which they do not seem to have specific memories.

Indeed, a common pathology is a panic disorder in which people show marked anxiety but cannot identify a specific cause. For this reason, emotional memory can be seen as separate from explicit and implicit memory. Emotional memory also has a unique anatomical component—namely, the amygdala— which we discuss in detail in Chapter 20. The amygdala has connections to systems that control autonomic functions (for example, blood pressure and heart rate) as well as connections to the hypothalamus and its control of hormonal systems. Damage to the amygdala abolishes emotional memory but has little effect on implicit or explicit memory.

(A)

Hypothalamus
Amygdala

(B)

Frontal, parietal, temporal, occipital, and cingulate cortices

Hypothalamus and PAG

Basal ganglia — Amygdala — Medial temporal cortex

Figure **18.15**

Neural Circuit Proposed for Emotional Memory (A) The key structure in emotional memory is the amygdala. (B) Circuit showing the flow of information in emotional memory.

The amygdala has close connections with the medial temporocortical structures, as well as the rest of the cortex. It sends projections to structures taking part in the production of autonomic responses—namely, the hypothalamus and periaqueductal gray matter (PAG) of the brainstem (**Figure 18.15**). In addition, the amygdala is connected to the implicit-memory system through its connections with the basal ganglia.

Emotionally arousing experiences tend to be vividly remembered, a fact confirmed both by animal and by human studies. James McGaugh concludes that emotionally significant experiences, both pleasant and unpleasant, must activate hormonal and brain systems that act to "stamp in" these vivid memories. He notes that many neural systems likely take part, but the basolateral part of the amygdala is critical. The general idea is that emotionally driven hormonal and chemical systems (likely cholinergic and noradrenergic) stimulate the amygdala, which in turn modulates the laying down of memory circuits in the rest of the brain, especially in the medial temporal and prefrontal regions.

Thus, emotional memories can be both explicit and implicit. A study of severely demented patients by Bob Sainsbury and Marjorie Coristine illustrates a nonconscious aspect of remembering. The patients were believed to have severe cortical abnormalities but intact amygdala functioning. The researchers first established that the ability of these patients to recognize photographs of close relatives was severely impaired.

The patients were then shown four photographs, one of which depicted a relative (either a sibling or a child) who had visited in the preceding 2 weeks. The task was to identify the person whom they liked better than the others. Although the subjects were unaware that they knew anyone in the group of photographs, they consistently preferred the photographs of their relatives. This result suggests that, although the explicit, and probably implicit, memory of the relative was gone, each patient still had an implicit emotional memory that guided his or her preference.

Neural Substrates of Short-Term Memory

In 1890, William James drew a distinction between memories that endure for a very brief time and longer-term memories. Not until 1958, however, were separate short-term and long-term memories specifically postulated by Donald

Broadbent. **Short-term memory**, sometimes also called **working memory** or, as described in Chapter 16, *temporal memory* to refer to a neural record of recent events and their order, is the system that we use for holding sensory events, movements, and cognitive information such as digits, words, names, or other items for a brief period.

Because short-term information may be related to objects or to movements, these two different kinds of short-term memory may be related to the ventral (object-recognition) or dorsal (motor) streams of sensory processing. Recall that both streams project to the prefrontal cortex, although to different places (see Figure 16.3). Thus, short-term memory for both motor and object information is mediated by locations defined by the dorsal and ventral pathways to two different regions of the frontal cortex.

Short-Term Memory and the Temporal Lobes

Warrington and her colleagues describe patient K.F., who received a left posterior temporal lesion. The lesion resulted in an almost total inability to repeat verbal stimuli such as digits, letters, words, and sentences. In contrast, his long-term recall of paired-associates words or short stories was nearly normal. K.M. contrasts with H.M. and other medial-temporal-lobe subjects who retain functional short-term memory.

Warrington and her colleagues also found that some patients apparently have defects in short-term recall of visually presented digits or letters but have normal short-term recall of the same stimuli presented aurally. Russian neuropsychologist Alexander Luria describes patients with just the opposite difficulty: specific deficits for aurally presented but not visually presented verbal items. Short-term-memory deficits can also result from damage to the polymodal sensory areas of the posterior parietal cortex and the posterior temporal cortex. Warrington and Lawrence Weiskrantz present several cases of specific short-term-memory deficits in patients with lesions at the junction of the parietal, temporal, and occipital cortices.

Short-Term Memory and the Frontal Lobes

Damage to the frontal cortex is the recognized cause of many impairments of short-term memory for tasks in which subjects must remember the temporary location of stimuli (see Chapter 16). The tasks themselves may be rather simple: given this cue, make that response after a delay. But as one trial follows another, both animals and people with frontal-lobe lesions start to mix up the previously presented stimuli.

L. Prisko devised a "compound stimulus" task in which two stimuli in the same sensory modality are presented in succession, separated by a short interval. A subject's task is to report whether the second stimulus of the pair is identical with the first. In half the trials, the stimuli were the same; in the other trials, they were different. Thus, the task required the subject to remember the first stimulus of a pair in order to compare it with the second while suppressing the stimuli that had been presented in previous trials. The Snapshot on page 515 describes another compound-stimulus paradigm.

Similarly, two tasks, one verbal and one nonverbal, were used in another test (Corsi, 1972). Subjects were required to decide which of two stimuli had been

SNAPSHOT
Disrupting Memory Formation

Electroconvulsive therapy (ECT) was developed by Ladislas von Meduna in 1933 because he thought that people with epilepsy could not be schizophrenic and, therefore, that seizures could cure insanity. At first, the therapeutic seizures were induced with a drug called Metrazol, but, in 1937, Ugo Cerletti and Lucio Bini replaced Metrazol with electricity.

ECT does not in fact cure schizophrenia, but it can be effective for depression. A drawback in using ECT is that it causes memory impairment, and this observation led to the use of ECT to study memory.

According to consolidation theory, memory is not formed instantaneously but requires biochemical and structural changes that take some time. Neuroscientists reasoned that, if an animal was given a learning experience, the application of ECT at different times after the experience could be used to map the duration of the changes required for memory formation.

The results of many experiments with ECT suggest that not one but many memory-forming changes take place after a single experience, each with its own time course. Short-term processes are related to transitory, or short term, memory storage, whereas longer-term processes are related to the formation of permanent memories.

More-refined application of electrical stimulation makes use of transcranial magnetic stimulation (TMS), a noninvasive procedure of brain stimulation, in which an electrical current is applied to a restricted region of the brain. Justin Harris and his coworkers presented two vibratory stimuli to the fingertips of their subjects and required them to state whether the stimuli were the same or different. TSM delivered within 600 ms of the first stimulus disrupted choice accuracy, whereas TSM after 900 ms did not.

This experiment demonstrates that the primary sensory cortex is the site for short-term memory of somatosensory stimulation and that a memory can be formed within 900 ms. Thus, short-term memories are encoded at low hierarchical levels of the nervous system.

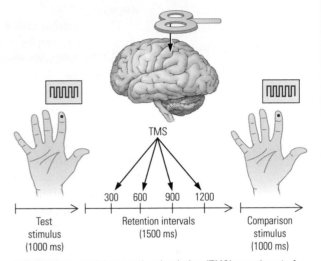

Design of transcranial magnetic stimulation (TMS) experiments for investigating short-term memory. TMS is applied to the finger region of the primary sensory cortex, contralaterally or ipsilaterally, at any one of a set of intervals between the application of two different tactile stimuli to the index fingertips. (After J. A. Harris et al. Transient storage of a tactile memory trace in primary somatosensory cortex. *Journal of Neuroscience* 22, p. 8721, 2002.)

Jacinta O'Shea and colleagues have used a "pop out" paradigm to study the specificity of short-term memory. (If the same stimulus is presented repeatedly in a number of pictures, subjects identify its shape and location more quickly.) They found that TMS applied to the frontal eye fields, a site of visual short-term memory, disrupted short-term memory for location but not for form. Thus, different features of a stimulus, such as form and location, are encoded by different short-term memories separately and in different neural locations.

Harris, J. A. Psychophysical investigations into cortical encoding of vibrotactile stimuli. *Novartis Foundation Symposium* 270:238–245, 2006.

O'Shea, J., N. G. Muggleton, A. Cowey, and V. Walsh. Human frontal eye fields and spatial priming of pop-out. *Journal of Cognitive Neuroscience* 19:1140–1151, 2007.

---

seen more recently. In the verbal task, they were asked to read pairs of words presented on a series of cards (for example, *cowboy–railroad*). From time to time, a card appeared bearing two words with a question mark between them. Subjects had to indicate which of the words they had read most recently.

Sometimes, both words had been seen before but, at other times, only one word had been seen. In the latter case, the task became a simple test of recognition, whereas, in the former case, it was a test of recency memory. Patients with left temporal removals showed a mild deficit in recognition, in keeping with their difficulty with verbal memory; the frontal-lobe patients performed normally. On the recency test, however, both frontal-lobe groups (left and right) were impaired, although the left-side group was significantly worse.

The nonverbal task was identical with the verbal task except that the stimuli were photographs of paintings rather than words. Patients with right-temporal-lobe removals showed mild deficits in recognition, consistent with their visual-memory deficit, whereas those with right-frontal-lobe lesions performed normally. On the recency test, the frontal-lobe groups were impaired, but now the right-side group was significantly worse.

Moscovitch devised a task in which patients were read five different lists of 12 words each and were instructed to recall as much as they could of each list immediately after presentation. In the first four lists, all the words were drawn from the same taxonomic category, such as sports; the words in the fifth list came from a different category, such as professions.

Normal subjects showed a decline from list 1 to list 4 in the number of words recalled correctly (that is, they exhibit proactive interference). But they also exhibit an additional phenomenon on list 5: they recall as many words as they did for list 1, thus demonstrating what is referred to as *release from proactive interference*. Frontal-lobe patients also showed strong proactive interference, as would be expected from the Prisko experiments, but they failed to show release from proactive interference on list 5.

Another memory deficit in patients with frontal-lobe lesions has been demonstrated in a test of movement copying (see Figure 14.10). When patients with cortical lesions were asked to copy complex arm and facial movements, in addition to making errors of sequence, frontal-lobe patients made many errors of intrusion and omission (Kolb and Milner, 1981). That is, when asked to copy a series of three discrete facial movements, frontal-lobe patients left one movement out (error of omission) or added a movement seen in a previous sequence (error of intrusion).

The results of experiments with monkeys confirm that different areas of the prefrontal cortex take part in different types of short-term memory. Joaquin Fuster demonstrated that, if monkeys are shown objects that they must remember for a short period before they are allowed to make a response, neurons in the frontal cortex will fire during the delay. This finding suggests that these neurons are active in bridging the stimulus–response gap. Patricia Goldman-Rakic and her colleagues examined this phenomenon further in two tasks, one of memory for the location of objects and the other of memory for the identity of objects.

For the first task, a monkey was required to fixate on a point in the center of a screen while a light was flashed in some part of its visual field. After a variable delay of a few seconds, the monkey was required to shift its eyes to look at the point where the light had been. In the second task, as the monkey fixated on the center of the screen, one of two objects appeared on the screen. The monkey was required to look to the left in response to one stimulus and to the right in response to the other (**Figure 18.16**). Cells that code spatial vision are located

Time 1	Time 2	Time 3
Cue	Delay	Response

1 The monkey fixes its gaze on the ×.

2 After the stimulus (S) disappears the monkey must maintain fixation for a few seconds.

3 Finally, it must look to the spatial location where the stimulus had been.

Figure 18.16

Testing Short-Term Memory
Single cells can code the spatial location of objects. During the delay in step 2, single cells in area 8 code the memory for the location of the second stimulus. (After Goldman-Rakic, 1992.)

in area 8 of the dorsolateral prefrontal cortex, whereas cells that code object recognition are located in areas 9 and 46 of the mid-dorsolateral frontal cortex (**Figure 18.17**A).

Michael Petrides and his coworkers used PET along with MRI to demonstrate similar function–anatomy relations in humans. In addition, they propose a model for two short-term-memory systems, spatial and object memory, respectively (Figure 18.17B). A spatial vision test required subjects to point to one of eight patterns on each of eight cards in response to a colored bar at the top of the card. That is, in response to a cue, a subject had to search for a specific pattern. Performance of this task was accompanied by increased activity in area 8 of the left hemisphere.

In contrast, an object task required subjects to point to a different pattern in an array of eight patterns repeated on eight successive cards, which meant that they had to keep track of the patterns that they had indicated already. During

Figure 18.17

Two Systems for Short-Term Memory in the Frontal Cortex
(A) The results of single-cell-recording experiments in monkeys show that area 8 participates in short-term memory for the spatial location of objects. It receives projections from the parietal cortex. Frontal-cortex areas 9 and 46 have roles in short-term memory for visual objects and receive information from the inferior temporal cortex. (B) The results of PET-recording experiments in human subjects show that area 8 searches for an object when a stimulus is presented and areas 9 and 46 remember objects that are identified sequentially. (Part A after Wilson et al., 1993; part B after Petrides et al., 1993.)

(A) Monkey
Spatial vision
Parietal cortex
Object-recognition vision
Inferior temporal cortex

(B) Human
Searching for an object
Remembering objects that are identified sequentially

this task, the researchers found increases in regional cerebral blood flow in the mid-dorsolateral frontal cortex (areas 9 and 46, mainly on the right).

Taken together, these different studies show that two different pathways—one from the parietal cortex and the other from the temporal lobes—project to two different regions of the prefrontal cortex and are implicated in different kinds of short-term memory. Note that, with respect to visual information, the two short-term-memory systems are represented in the dorsal stream for vision for action and in the ventral stream for vision for recognition, respectively.

Special Memory Abilities

People with intellectual disabilities may have special musical, artistic, mathematical, and memory abilities. Often, people with **Asperger's syndrome**, a form of autism in which intellectual function is high, have special abilities. Such people are often referred to as *savants*. An example is S.'s case, described by Luria.

S. was a newspaper reporter with an extraordinary ability to form explicit memories that he could not forget. The fact that, unlike other reporters, he never took notes at briefings brought him to the attention of his employer, who questioned him on the matter. S. responded by repeating verbatim the transcript of the briefing that they had just attended. At his employer's urging, S went to see a psychologist. In this way, S. met Luria, who began a study of this remarkable case of memory ability that continued for the following 30 years. Luria published an account of the investigation, and to this day *The Mind of a Mnemonist* is one of the most readable studies in the literature of memory.

For an example of S.'s abilities, consider **Table 18.1**. S. could look at this table for 2 or 3 minutes and then repeat it from memory: by columns, by rows, by diagonals, in reverse, or in sums. Tested unexpectedly 16 or more years later, S. could still reproduce the table, reciting the columns in any order or combination, without error.

For a good part of his life, S. supported himself as an mnemonist—an entertainer who specializes in feats of memory. In the course of his career, he memorized hundreds of such lists or lists of names, letters, nonsense syllables, and so on; after memorizing any of them, he was able to recall it at any later date.

S.'s ability to commit things to memory hinged on three processes. He could visualize stimuli mentally, recalling them simply by reading them from this internal image. He also made multisensory impressions of sensations. This ability, called **synesthesia**, usually entails perceiving a stimulus of one sense as the sensation of a different sense, such as when sound produces a sensation of color. But, for S., a word was recorded as a sound, as well as a splash of color, an odor, a taste, a texture, and a temperature. Finally, S. employed the "pegboard" technique used by many mnemonists; that is, he kept a collection of standard images in his mind and associated them with new material that he wanted to remember. This trick and others employed by mnemonists serve as sources of insight into how explicit memories are usually formed and how such an understanding can be exploited to improve memory in normal people, as well as in people with memory impairments.

Table **18.1** Example of tables memorized by S.

6	6	8	0
5	4	3	2
1	6	8	4
7	9	3	5
4	2	3	7
3	8	9	1
1	0	0	2
3	4	5	1
2	7	6	8
1	9	2	6
2	9	6	7
5	5	2	0
x	0	1	x

Note: With only 2 to 3 minutes' study of such a table, S. was able to reproduce it in reverse order, horizontally, or vertically and to reproduce the diagonals.

Here are some examples of how S. saw numbers:

> Even numbers remind me of images. Take the number 1. This is a proud, well-built man; 2 is a high-spirited woman; 3 a gloomy person (shy, I don't know); 6 a man with a swollen foot; 7 a man with a mustache; 8 a very stout woman—a sack within a sack. As for the number 87, what I see is a fat woman and a man twirling his mustache. (Luria, 1968)

Did S. pay a price for his memory abilities? Luria clearly has taken the position that he did. Luria characterizes S. as a person with little aim in life, seemingly dull and superficial. Luria suggests that S. was not able to reason, to categorize, and to see order in things, as ordinary people can. He also had little ability to use or understand metaphors (for example, the phrase "to weigh one's words"); he visualized and interpreted them literally and so was puzzled by what they meant. He often had difficulty understanding simple statements and had even more difficulty understanding the sense of poetry.

The idea of multiple memory systems might explain the extraordinary abilities of experts and savants. Memory systems likely compete with one another with the result that ordinary memory, although adaptive, is not excellent. Becoming an expert, however, likely entails the elaboration of a particular kind of memory. This expertise may come at the cost of the loss of other abilities.

With respect to savants, brain injury that affects one memory system but spares another frees the spared memory system from competition, thus allowing it to become expert. Allan Snyder and his coworkers report that applying transcranial magnetic stimulation to the left frontal lobe, which suppresses its normal effectiveness, improved drawing and proofreading in some subjects. They suggest that, released from competition of the left hemisphere, the right hemisphere is able to demonstrate savantlike qualities.

Remembering and Adapting

In his classic book *Remembering*, Fredric Bartlett made the point that remembering cannot be regarded as the mere revival of previous experience; rather remembering is an active process of reconstruction. "So long as the details which can be built up are such that they would give a "reasonable" setting," Bartlett stated, "most of us are fairly content, and are apt to think that what we build we have literally retained (Bartlett, 1932, p, 176)."

Daniel Schacter and Donna Addis, who use the term "gist" to describe the objective of the process of reconstructing a memory, make the point that the gist serves the adaptive purpose of allowing us to anticipate and respond to situations in the future in ways that benefit from our past experiences. Thus, memory does not just allow us to recreate the past, it is prospective in that it allows us to imagine or pre-experience episodes in the future. Because the gist is adaptive, details are often unimportant. As such, the very adaptive nature of the gist renders it prone to errors of commission as well as of omission, which Schacter describes as the seven "sins" of memory.

An adaptive sin that normal subjects commit far more often than amnesic subjects do illustrates the sacrifice in accuracy that formation of a gist incurs.

Participants are given a study list of words (tired, bed, awake, rest, dream, night, blanket, dose, slumber, snore, pillow, peace, yawn, and drowsy) that are related to an unpresented lure word (for example, sleep). On a subsequent old–new recognition test containing studied words (for example, tired and dream), new words that are unrelated to the study list (for example, butter) and new words that are related to the study-list items (for example, sleep) are presented.

Participants frequently claim that they previously studied the related lure words. Patients with damage to the hippocampus and related structures in the medial temporal lobe show significantly reduced false recognition of nonstudied words that are either semantically or perceptually related to previously studied words. The interpretation of this result is that healthy controls form and retain a well-organized representation of the semantic or perceptual gist of a list of related study items. This gist causes them to respond to lure words but allows them to reject unrelated words, whereas amnesic subjects may form and retain only a weak or degraded gist.

The notion that we have multiple memory systems allows for other errors caused by favoring one kind of memory over others. Thus, for example, if we witness an accident, we can usually give the gist of what we observed. We can note the temporal and spatial sequence of the action, we can identify the participants, and we can note the autobiographic framework of how we became observers.

When quizzed on the details, the fallibility of memory becomes apparent. Each observer may recall details not remembered by others. In addition, recollection can be distorted. We can be primed by the stories of others and by photographs or videos of the occasion to remark, "Oh yes, I remember that also," even when the stories, photographs, or videos are distorted.

A simple example of the relation between perceptual bias and memory reconstruction is illustrative. If subjects are asked to draw an upright glass half full of water as a tilted glass, some represent the glass with the water level in a horizontal position and others represent it with the water in a more vertical position (**Figure 18.18**). The former representation suggests encoding a spatial or action representation of the image, whereas the latter representation suggests encoding the representation as an icon. In Chapter 12, we reported a sex difference in the way in which this image is represented, with females more likely to report the icon and males the action. Note that both are accurate but obviously quite different.

We end this chapter by noting that, like all students, you may have your own problems with different kinds of memory when studying for examinations and taking them. A rule of thumb is that you will remember things in the way that you learned them. If you learn the gist, you will not do well when asked for details. If you just read over material or underline important passages or both, you will not do well when asked to write the material down. You can prevent the unpleasant experience of "I knew the information but had a mental block when I had to produce it" by performing the same operations during the study phase that will be required of you during the test phase. Therefore, effective studying should consist of practice in writing an exam as it will be administered. These operations usually require top-down rather than bottom-up processing.

Figure 18.18

Memory Bias Encoding a glass of water as an action image will render the water level horizontally, whereas encoding the glass of water as an icon will render the water level more vertically.

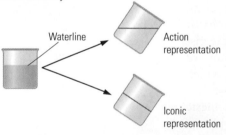

Waterline

Action representation

Iconic representation

Summary

Our multiple memory systems operate independently of one another (see Figure 18.1).

Learning and Amnesia

Research findings suggest differences in the processes of acquiring and storing memory. For example, anterograde amnesia, the inability to form new memories, is often more severe than retrograde amnesia, the inability to retrieve old memories.

The medial-temporal and inferior-frontal lobes and the circuits within and between them are associated with long-term learning and memory related to facts and to personal experiences. These sorts of memories are often lost after damage to medial temporal tissue. Long-term memory for motor skills and the ability to learn new memories are spared in amnesia.

Opposing theories of retrograde amnesia argue for a memory consolidation, for a multiple-trace memory, or for reconsolidated memory systems.

Multiple Long-Term Memory Systems

One long-term memory system, consisting of the prefrontal cortex and the medial temporal lobe and subcortical regions related to them, is the likely neural location of conscious, explicit memory. A second system, consisting of the basal ganglia and neocortex, forms the neural basis for unconscious, implicit memory. A third system, which includes the amygdala and its associated structures, forms the neural basis for emotional memory, a system that displays features of both explicit and implicit systems.

Explicit memory is further divided into episodic memory, or memory for personal or autobiographic experiences, and semantic memory, or memory for facts. Implicit memory is divided into motor memory, priming, and conditioning.

Neural Substrates of Explicit Memory

Explicit memory is associated with neural structures of the temporal lobe, including the hippocampus, perirhinal cortex, and connections with the ventral frontal cortex. Episodic, or autobiographic, memory is especially dependent on the hippocampus and ven-

tral frontal lobe, damage to which can be associated with the loss of all retrograde autobiographic memory as well as the ability to imagine a personal role in future events.

Neural Substrates of Implicit Memory

Implicit memory is associated with neural structures of the basal ganglia, motor cortex, and cerebellum. Damage to the basal ganglia can be associated with deficits in learned motor skills and habits, whereas damage to the cerebellum can be associated with the loss of conditioned responses.

Neural Substrates of Emotional Memory

Many experiences affect us emotionally, and neural systems centered in the amygdala of the temporal lobes encode our emotional recollections.

Neural Substrates of Short-Term Memory

Short-term memory has a structural basis different from that of long-term memory: sensory regions of the neocortex mediate short-term memory. In addition, the dorsal stream traversing the parietal and frontal cortex participates in short-term memory for locations, whereas the ventral stream from the sensory regions forward into the inferior temporal–dorsolateral frontal system mediates short-term memory for objects.

Special Memory Abilities

The extraordinary memory abilities in specific domains displayed by savants may be due a reduction of competition between memory systems, allowing one or another to become especially dominant. Thus, special abilities may coexist alongside islands of intellectual weakness.

Remembering and Adapting

The purpose of memory is to allow us to make future decisions on the basis of experience. Consequently, memory need not be exact but only adaptive. In extracting the gist from a situation, we may be selective in what we remember and make mistakes of omission and commission.

References

Baddely, A. *Working Memory*. London: Oxford University Press, 1986.

Bartlett, F. C. *Remembering*. Cambridge, U.K.: Cambridge University Press, 1932.

Bekhterev, V. M. Demonstration eines Gehirns mit Zerstörung der vorderen und inneren Theile der Hirnrinde beider Schlafenlappen. *Neurol. Zbl.* 19:990–991, 1900.

Broadbent, D. E. *Perception and Communication*. London: Pergamon, 1958.

Cabeza, R., and L. Nyberg. Imaging Cognition II: An empirical review of 275 PET and fMRI studies. *Journal of Cognitive Neuroscience* 12:1–47, 2000.

Cipolotti, L., T. Shallice, D. Chan, N. Fox, R. Scahill, G. Harrison, J. Stevens, and P. Rudge. Long-term retrograde amnesia: The crucial role of the hippocampus. *Neuropsychologia* 39:151–172, 2001.

Corkin, S. Tactually-guided maze-learning in man: Effects on unilateral cortical excisions and bilateral hippocampal lesions. *Neuropsychologia* 3:339–351, 1965.

Corkin, S. Acquisition of motor skill after bilateral medial temporal-lobe excision. *Neuropsychologia* 6:255–265, 1968.

Corkin, S. What's new with the amnesic patient H.M.? *Nature Reviews Neuroscience* 3:153–160, 2002.

Corkin, S., D. G. Amaral, R. G. Gonzalez, K. A. Johnson, and B. T. Hyman. H.M.'s medial temporal lobe lesion: Findings from magnetic resonance imaging. *Journal of Neuroscience* 17:3964–3979, 1997.

Corsi, P. M. Human Memory and the Medial Temporal Region of the Brain. Ph.D. dissertation. Montreal: McGill University, 1972.

Damasio, A. R., D. Tranel, and H. Damasio. Amnesia caused by herpes simplex encephalitis, infarctions in basal forebrain, Alzheimer's disease and anoxia/ischemia. In L. Squire and G. Gainotti, Eds. *Handbook of Neuropsychology*, vol 3. Amsterdam: Elsevier, 1991.

Decker, M. W., M. T. Gill, and J. L. McGaugh. Concurrent muscarenic and β-adrenergic blockade in rats impairs place learning in a water maze and retention of inhibitory avoidance. *Brain Research* 513:81–85, 1990.

Ebbinghaus, H. *Memory*. New York: Teachers College, 1913 (originally published in 1885). Reprinted by Dover, New York, 1964.

Elliott, H. C. *Textbook of Neuroanatomy*. Philadelphia: Lippincott, 1969.

Fisher, C. M., and R. D. Adams. Transient global amnesia. *Transactions of the American Neurological Association* 83:143, 1958.

Fuster, J. M. *The Prefrontal Cortex*. New York: Raven, 1989.

Gaffan, D., and E. Gaffan. Amnesia in man following transection of the fornix: A review. *Brain* 114:2611–2618, 1991.

Goldman-Rakic, P. S. Working memory and the mind. *Scientific American* 267(3):111–117, 1992.

Gollin, E. S. Developmental studies of visual recognition of incomplete objects. *Perceptual and Motor Skills* 11:289–298, 1960.

Grafton, S. T., J. C. Mazziotta, S. Presty, K. J. Friston, S. J. Frackowiak, and M. E. Phelps. Functional anatomy of human procedural learning determined with regional cerebral blood flow and PET. *Journal of Neuroscience* 12:2542–2548, 1992.

Hay, J. F., M. Moscovitch, and B. Levine. Dissociating habit and recollection: Evidence from Parkinson's disease, amnesia and focal lesion patients. *Neuropsychologia* 40:1324–1334. 2002.

James, W. *The Principles of Psychology*. New York: Holt, 1890.

Kolb, B., and B. Milner. Performance of complex arm and facial movements after focal brain lesions. *Neuropsychologia* 19:491–503, 1981.

Lashley, K. D. In search of the engram. *Symposia of the Society for Experimental Biology* 4:454–482, 1950.

Lee, K.H., R.F. Thompson Multiple memory mechanisms in the cerebellum? Neuron. 51:680–682, 2006.

Levine, B. Autonoetic consciousness and self-regulation in patients with brain injury. *International Journal of Psychology* 35:223, 2000.

Levine, B., S. E. Black, R. Cabeza, M. Sinden, A. R. Mcintosh, J. P. Toth, and E. Tulving. Episodic memory and the self in a case of isolated retrograde amnesia. *Brain* 121:1951–1973, 1998.

Luria, A. R. *The Mind of a Mnemonist*. New York: Basic Books, 1968.

Mair, W. G. P., E. K. Warrington, and L. Weiskrantz. Memory disorder in Korsakoff's psychosis. *Brain* 102:749–783, 1979.

Markowitsch, H. J. Transient global amnesia. *Neuroscience and Biobehavioral Reviews* 7:35–43, 1983.

Markowitsch, H. J., and M. Pritzel. The neuropathology of amnesia. *Progress in Neurobiology* 25:189–288, 1985.

Marsolek, C. J., S. M. Kosslyn, and L. R. Squire. Form-specific visual priming in the right cerebral hemisphere. *Journal of Experimental Psychology: Learning, Memory, and Cognition* 18:492–508, 1992.

Martone, M., N. Butlers, M. Payne, J. T. Baker, and D. S. Sax. Dissociations between skill learning and verbal recognition in amnesia and dementia. *Archives of Neurology* 41:965–970, 1984.

Mazzucchi, A., G. Moretti, P. Caffara, and M. Parma. Neuropsychological functions in the follow-up of transient global amnesia. *Brain* 103:161–178, 1980.

McGaugh, J. The amygdala modulates the consolidation of memories of emotionally arousing experiences. *Annual Review of Neuroscience* 27:1–28, 2004.

Milner, B. Visually-guided maze learning in man: Effects of bilateral hippocampal, bilateral frontal, and unilateral cerebral lesions. *Neuropsychologia* 3:317–338, 1965.

Milner, B. Memory and the medial temporal regions of the brain. In K. H. Pribram and D. E. Broadbent, Eds. *Biology of Memory*. New York: Academic Press, 1970.

Milner, B., S. Corkin, and H.-L. Teuber. Further analysis of the hippocampal amnesic syndrome: 14-year follow up study of H.M. *Neuropsychologia* 6:215–234, 1968.

Moscovitch, M. Multiple dissociations of function in amnesia. In L. S. Cermak, Ed. *Human Memory and Amnesia.* Hillsdale, N.J.: Lawrence Erlbaum, 1982.

Murray, E. Memory for objects in nonhuman primates. In M. S. Gazzaniga, Ed. *The New Cognitive Neurosciences*, 2nd ed. London: MIT Press, 2000, pp. 753–763.

Nadel, L., and M. Moscovitch. Memory consolidation, retrograde amnesia and the hippocampal complex. *Current Opinion in Neurobiology* 7:212–227, 1997.

Oscar-Berman, M. Neuropsychological consequences of long-term chronic alcoholism. *American Scientist* 68:410–419, 1980.

Pascual-Leone, A., J. Grafman, and M. Hallett. Modulation of cortical motor output maps during development of implicit and explicit knowledge. *Science* 263:1287–1289, 1994.

Penfield, W., and B. Milner. Memory deficit produced by bilateral lesions in the hippocampal zone. *Archives of Neurology and Psychiatry* 79:475–497, 1958.

Petri, H. L., and M. Mishkin. Behaviorism, cognitivism, and the neuropsychology of memory. *American Scientist* 82:30–37, 1994.

Petrides, M. Deficits on conditional associative-learning tasks after frontal- and temporal-lobe lesions in man. *Neuropsychologia* 23:601–614, 1985.

Petrides, M., B. Alivisatos, A. C. Evans, and E. Meyer. Dissociation of human mid-dorsolateral from posterior dorsolateral frontal cortex in memory processing. *Proceedings of the National Academy of Sciences of the United States of America* 90:873–877, 1993.

Posner, M. I., and M. E. Raichle. *Images of Mind.* New York: Scientific American Library, 1994.

Prisko, L. Short-Term Memory in Focal Cerebral Damage. Ph.D. dissertation. Montreal: McGill University, 1963.

Rosenbaum, R. S., S. Kohler, D. L. Schacter, M. Moscovitch, R. Westmacott, S. E. Black, F. Gao, and E. Tulving. The case of K.C.: Contributions of a memory-impaired person to memory theory. *Neuropsychologia* 43:989–1021, 2005.

Sainsbury, R., and M. Coristine. Affective discrimination in moderately to severely demented patients. *Canadian Journal on Aging* 5:99–104, 1986.

Salat, D. H., A. J. W. van der Kouwe, D. S. Tuch, B. T. Quinn, B. Fischl, A. M. Dale, and S. Corkin. Neuroimaging H.M.: A 10-year follow-up examination. *Hippocampus* 16:936–945, 2006.

Sanders, H. I., and E. K. Warrington. Memory for remote events in amnesic patients. *Brain* 94:661–668, 1971.

Sarter, M., and H. J. Markowitsch. The amygdala's role in human mnemonic processing. *Cortex* 21:7–24, 1985.

Schacter, D. L. Implicit knowledge: New perspectives on unconscious processes. *Proceedings of the National Academy of Sciences of the United States of America* 89:11113–11117, 1992.

Schacter, D. L., and D. L. Addis. The cognitive neuroscience of constructive memory: Remembering the past and imagining the future. *Philosophical Transactions of the Royal Society of London B* 362:773–786, 2007.

Scoville, W. B., and B. Milner. Loss of recent memory after bilateral hippocampal lesions. *Journal of Neurology, Neurosurgery and Psychiatry* 20:11–21, 1957.

Siri, S., E. A. Kensinger, S. F. Cappa, and S. Corkin. Questioning the living/nonliving dichotomy: Evidence from a patient with an unusual semantic dissociation. *Neuropsychology* 17:630–645, 2003.

Snyder, A. W., E. Mulcahy, J. L. Taylor, D. J. Mitchell, P. Sachdev, and S. C. Gandevia. Savant-like skills exposed in normal people by suppressing the left fronto-temporal lobe. *Journal of Integrative Neuroscience* 2:149–158, 2003.

Squire, L. R., and P. J. Bayley. The neuroscience of remote memory. *Current Opinion in Neurobiology* 17:185–196, 2007.

Taylor, J. R., R. Tompkins, R. Demers, and D. Anderson. Electroconvulsive therapy and memory dysfunction: Is there evidence for prolonged defects? *Biological Psychiatry* 17:1169–1193, 1982.

Tronson, N. C., and J. R. Taylor. Molecular mechanisms of memory reconsolidation. *Nature Reviews Neuroscience* 8:262–275, 2007.

Tulving, E. Episodic memory: From mind to brain. *Annual Review of Psychology* 53:1–25, 2002.

Tulving, E., S. Kapur, F. I. M. Craik, M. Moscovitch, and S. Houle. Hemispheric encoding/retrieval asymmetry in episodic memory: Positron emission tomography finding. *Proceedings of the National Academy of Sciences of the United States of America* 91:2016–2020, 1994.

Vanderwolf, C. H. Cerebral activity and behavior: Control by central cholinergic and serotonergic systems. *International Review of Neurobiology* 30:255–340, 1988.

Vargha-Khadem, F., D. G. Gadian, K. A. Watkins, W. Connelly, W. Van Paesschen, and M. Mishkin. Differential effects of early hippocampal pathology on episodic and semantic memory. *Science* 277:376–380, 1997.

von Cramen, D. Y., N. Hebel, and U. Schuri. A contribution of the anatomical basis of thalamic amnesia. *Brain* 108:993–1008, 1985.

Warrington, E. K., and L. Weiskrantz. Further analysis of the prior learning effect in amnesic patients. *Neuropsychologia* 16:169–177, 1978.

Weiskrantz, L. Neuroanatomy of memory and amnesia: A case for multiple memory systems. *Human Neurobiology* 6:93–105, 1987.

Whitty, C. W. M., and O. L. Zangwill. Traumatic amnesia. In C. W. M. Whitty and O. L. Zangwill, Eds. *Amnesia.* London: Butterworth, 1966.

Wilson, F. A. W., S. P. O. Scalaidhe, and P. S. Goldman-Rakic. Dissociation of object and spatial processing domains in primate prefrontal cortex. *Science* 260:1955–1958, 1993.

19 Language

K.H. was a Swiss-born architect working as a professor of architecture at a major U.S. university. Although German was his first language and he was fluent in French and Italian, his primary language had become English.

Because he had been an outstanding student, had excelled at writing, and was meticulous about his spelling and grammar, he was astonished when his mother complained that he was making spelling and grammatical errors in his letters to her, which, of course, were in German. He suspected that he must just be forgetting his German and resolved to prevent that from happening.

A few weeks later, K.H. asked a colleague to review a manuscript that he had just completed. His colleague read the manuscript and commented that K.H. must be working too hard because the manuscript was filled with errors of a kind that K.H. would

After Marco Catani

not have normally made. At about the same time, K.H. noticed that the right side of his face seemed to "feel funny." He went to a neurologist, who found a small tumor at the junction of the motor–face area and Broca's area in the left hemisphere. (The accompanying diffusion tensor image shows the various language pathways connecting Broca's area and Wernicke's area within the brain.)

The tumor was benign and was removed surgically. In the first few days after the surgery, K.H. was densely aphasic: he could not talk, and he

could not understand either oral or written language. Although he had been warned that aphasia was likely and that it would be temporary, he was visibly upset about his language difficulties. By the end of the first week, he could understand oral language, but his speech was still unintelligible and he could not read. By the end of the second week, he could speak German fluently but had difficulty with English, although his English was certainly understandable. He was still unable to read in any language, but he believed that he could read German and could be convinced otherwise only when he was informed that the book that he was reading was upside down. His reading and English slowly improved, but even now, years later, he has difficulty spelling in any language, and his reading is slower than would be expected for a person of his intelligence and education.

L anguage is one of our most precious abilities, yet most of us take it for granted, as did K.H. before his illness. We don't realize how much depends on our ability to talk, listen, and read. We even talk to ourselves. As children, we learn language long before we can catch a ball or ride a bicycle, using words to identify and learn about the things in our environment. We use language to entertain ourselves in poetry, song, and humor. Indeed, much humor is based on nuances of language and on double entendres. Because the use of language is our most complex skill, there are many ways to approach its study. One place to start is to consider what language is.

What Is Language?

There is no universally accepted definition of language. The word derives from *langue*, an Anglofrench word for "tongue," referring to the convention of describing language as the use of combinations of sounds for communication. But the term also includes the idea that this use of sounds is guided by rules, which, when translated into other sensory modalities, allows for equivalent communication through gestures, touches, and visual images. No other animal species uses language in the way that humans do, but many animal species have evolved forms of communication through sound, sight, touch, and olfaction.

Components of Language

Although most of us probably think of words as the meaningful units of language, linguists break language down differently (**Table 19.1**). They view words as consisting of fundamental language sounds called **phonemes**. An analysis of how phonemes are processed is called a phonological analysis.

Phonemes, in turn, are combined to form **morphemes**, the smallest meaningful units of words. A morpheme may be a base (*do* in un*do*), an affix (*un* in *un*do or *er* in do*er*), or an inflection (*ing* in do*ing* or *s* in girl*s*). Some morphemes are complete words by themselves; other morphemes must be combined to form words. A **lexicon** is the collection of all the words in a given language.

Words are strung together in patterns and conform to rules of grammar, also known as **syntax**. A key aspect of syntax is the appropriate choice of verb tenses. It is interesting that children develop syntactical skills independently of formal training, a characteristic that led the linguist Noam Chomsky to suggest that humans possess an innate brain organization for developing language.

The meaning connected to words and sentences is referred to, collectively, as **semantics**. Vocal intonations, the tone of voice that can modify the literal meaning of words and sentences, are collectively called **prosody**. Finally, stringing together sentences to form a meaningful narrative is called **discourse**. Although this discussion emphasizes the acoustical nature of these basic parts of

Table 19.1 Components of a sound-based language

Phonemes	Individual sound units whose concatenation, in particular order, produces morphemes
Morphemes	Smallest meaningful units of a word, whose combination creates a word
Syntax	Admissible combinations of words in phrases and sentences (called "grammar" in popular usage)
Lexicon	Collection of all words in a given language; each lexical entry includes all information with morphological or syntactical ramifications but does not include conceptual knowledge
Semantics	Meanings that correspond to all lexical items and all possible sentences
Prosody	Vocal intonation—the tone of voice—that can modify the literal meaning of words and sentences
Discourse	Linking sentences to constitute a narrative

language, there are analogues in visual language, such as American Sign Language (ASL, or Ameslan). A morpheme in ASL, for example, would be the smallest meaningful movement.

Although the presence of words and word components is the traditional criterion by which linguists recognize language, there are other ways to describe human language. One characteristic is its use of syllables that are made up of consonants and vowels. Nonhuman species do not produce syllables, primarily because they do not produce consonants. Thus, one special thing about human language is that our mouths are capable of producing consonants and combining them with vowels to produce syllables.

The Production of Sound

Speech and language are different. *Language* is any system for representing and communicating ideas, whereas *speech* refers to a particular audible manner of communicating language. Most of us have heard talking birds such as parrots or mynahs, and we may have even heard talking seals or dolphins. We have not heard talking apes, however, and not for lack of trying.

In the 1940s, Keith and Catherine Hayes raised Vicki, a chimpanzee, as a child and made a heroic effort to get her to produce words, but she produced only four sounds, including a poor rendition of "cup," after 6 years of training. Why do our nearest animal relatives lack vocal output capabilities comparable to ours?

The basic machinery that produces sound in apes and humans is similar (**Figure 19.1**A). It consists of two sets of parts, one set acting as the sound source and the other set as filters. First, air exhaled from the lungs provides power to drive oscillations of the **vocal folds** (commonly known as the *vocal cords*), which

Figure 19.1

The Source–Filter Theory of Vocal Production (A) Cross-sectional views of the larynx and the vocal tract in a chimpanzee and a human. (B) The formula for sound production, in which the larynx is the source of sound energy and the vocal tract filters the energy to produce the final sound output. (C) A model of how the formants of the vocal tract filter energy from the sound source to produce the final output. (After Fitch, 2000.)

are located in the **larynx**, or "voice box." The rate of vocal-fold oscillation (which varies from about 100 Hz in adult men to 500 Hz in small children) determines the pitch of the sound thus produced.

The acoustical energy generated then passes through the vocal tract (the pharyngeal, oral, and nasal cavities) and, finally, out through the nostrils and lips (Figure 19.1B). As this energy passes through the vocal tract, the structures there act as a series of "bandpass filters," which in the context of speech are called **formants** (Figure 19.1C). Formants modify the sound that is emitted, allowing specific frequencies to pass unhindered but blocking the transmission of others (review Figure 15.12). The filtering process plays a crucial role in speech. Formant characteristics are determined by the length and shape of the vocal tract and are modified rapidly during speech by the movements of the articulators (tongue, lips, soft palate, and so on).

Part of the difference between apes and ourselves lies in the part of the vocal apparatus that produces formants. The human oral cavity is longer than that of the ape, and the human larynx is situated much lower in the throat, as shown in Figure 19.1A. Starting at about 3 months of age, the human larynx begins a slow descent toward its adult position, which it reaches after 3 to 4 years. A second, shorter descent takes place in human males at puberty.

The descent of the larynx in humans was a key innovation in the evolution of speech, allowing humans to produce a much wider range of formant patterns than other mammals do. It allows the tongue to move both vertically and horizontally within the vocal tract, giving us the ability to vary the area of the oral and pharyngeal tubes independently, which adds to the variety of sounds that are easy for us to produce.

Origins of Language

The emphasis on the uniqueness of human language poses certain obstacles to understanding how language evolved. That no other species has language in the sense meant by linguists is puzzling and has led to a search for evolutionary antecedents. The search for such capacities is not a matter of idle curiosity. If we can determine which capacities were precursors of human language and why they were selected, we will have taken a giant step toward understanding how language came to be represented in our brains.

Precursors of Language

A hypothetical explanation for language is that it evolved slowly from various kinds of animal vocalizations. Perhaps it is a tribute to the imagination with which speculators approached the question of *which* vocalizations, in 1866, that the Linguistic Society of Paris banned future discussion of it. We will not let that ban deter us.

Gordon Hewes reviews many variants of the vocalization theory, including the *pooh-pooh* theory (language evolved from noises associated with strong emotion), the *bow-wow* theory (language evolved from noises first made to imitate natural sounds), the *yo-he-ho* theory (language evolved from sounds made to resonate with natural sounds), and the *sing-song* theory (language evolved from noises made

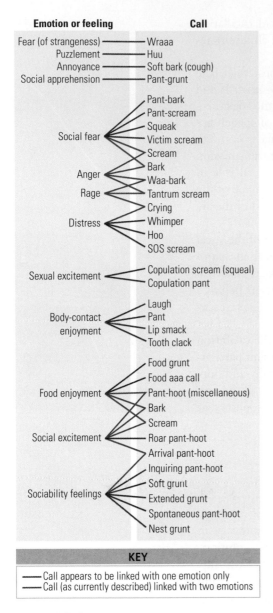

Emotion or feeling   **Call**

Fear (of strangeness) —— Wraaa
Puzzlement —— Huu
Annoyance —— Soft bark (cough)
Social apprehension —— Pant-grunt

Social fear
- Pant-bark
- Pant-scream
- Squeak
- Victim scream
- Scream

Anger
- Bark
- Waa-bark

Rage
- Tantrum scream

Distress
- Crying
- Whimper
- Hoo
- SOS scream

Sexual excitement
- Copulation scream (squeal)
- Copulation pant

Body-contact enjoyment
- Laugh
- Pant
- Lip smack
- Tooth clack

Food enjoyment
- Food grunt
- Food aaa call
- Pant-hoot (miscellaneous)
- Bark
- Scream

Social excitement
- Roar pant-hoot
- Arrival pant-hoot
- Inquiring pant-hoot

Sociability feelings
- Soft grunt
- Extended grunt
- Spontaneous pant-hoot
- Nest grunt

KEY

—— Call appears to be linked with one emotion only
—— Call (as currently described) linked with two emotions

Figure 19.2

Precursors of Language

Chimpanzee calls and the emotion or feeling with which they are most closely associated. (After Goodall, 1986. Reprinted with permission.)

while playing or dancing). These examples by no means exhaust the list of animal vocalization theories of language origin.

The best evidence for vocalization as a source of language origin comes from studying chimpanzees. The results of Jane Goodall's studies on the chimpanzees of Gombe in Tanzania indicate that our closest relatives have as many as 32 separate vocalizations. Goodall noted that the chimps seem to understand these calls much better than humans do, although her field assistants, the people most familiar with the chimps, can distinguish them well enough to claim that the actual number is higher than 32. **Figure 19.2** illustrates the wide range of vocalizations made by free-living chimpanzees.

Jared Taglialatela and his coworkers have recorded vocalizations made by the chimp Kanzi when the chimp eats food. Recall from the portrait of Kanzi on page 29 that these investigators found that the food peeps produced by Kanzi are structurally different in different contexts. This finding suggests that chimps use "chimpanzeeish," a primitive form of communication, as part of their feeding behavior.

Language As a Recently Evolved Ability

Let us consider the evidence that language (as used by modern humans) has a relatively recent origin. Morris Swadish developed a list of 100 basic lexical concepts that he expected to be found in every language. These concepts included such words as "I," "two," "woman," "sun," and "green." He then calculated the rate at which these words would have changed as new dialects of language were formed. His estimates suggest a rate of change of 14% every 1000 years. When he compared the lists of words spoken in different parts of the world today, he estimated that, between 10,000 and 100,000 years ago, everyone spoke the same language.

According to Swadish's logic, language would have had its origins at about the time when everyone spoke the same language, because diversification would have begun almost as soon as language developed. Hominids have been around for 4 million years; so how can the possibility that they were speaking much earlier than 100,000 years ago be ruled out?

Philip Lieberman studied the properties of the vocal tract that enable modern humans to make the sounds used for language. Recall that our low-placed larynx makes us unique among primates. Neither modern apes nor newborn humans have developed this characteristic and cannot produce all the sounds used in human speech.

On the basis of skull reconstructions, Lieberman suggested that Neanderthals also were unable to make the sounds necessary for modern speech. Specifically, they would not have been able to produce the vowels "a," "i," and "u." Because Neanderthals and modern humans are likely each other's closest relatives, having a common ancestor within the past 200,000 years, this inability is evidence that language developed in modern humans more recently. In opposition to this idea, X-rays of modern human skulls suggest no relation between skull morphology and larynx position.

Another argument for the recent development of language is that the ability to write and the ability to speak have a lot in common. Most notably, both require very fine movements and many movement transitions. Therefore, speech and writing could have appeared at about the same time. Alexander Marshack found that the first symbols made by humans date to about 30,000 years ago, which would be evidence that speech appeared before or at least at about this time.

What seems to link these three separate lines of evidence, making the recency hypothesis plausible, is that the first appearance of modern humans can be dated to within the past 200,000 years. The evolution of modern humans was quite sudden, and one of their adaptive strategies was language. Although the development of the vocal tract may have been crucial to human language, Peter MacNeilage argued that the critical feature of language is *articulation*. This characteristic can be described, basically, as what the mouth does: the mouth is usually opened once for each vocal episode, and the shape of the cavity between the lips and the vocal tract modulates the sound. Articulation is unique to humans. Furthermore, it is employed in virtually every utterance of every one of the world's languages (with the exception of a few words consisting of a single vowel).

In human speech, the mouth alternates more or less regularly between a relatively open and a relatively closed configuration, open for vowels and closed for consonants. To MacNeilage, the question raised by this observation is not how the vocal tract changed but how the brain changed to provide the motor control of the mouth necessary for making syllables.

Speech As a Gestural Language

Some researchers suggest that primitive gestures and other body movements slowly evolved into spoken language. This theory assumes that effective hunting and farming and the maintenance of social groups required some kind of communication system and provided the impetus for language to develop.

Two lines of evidence support the **gestural theory**. First, gestural language and vocal language depend on similar neural systems. The cortical regions that produce mouth and hand movements are adjacent in area 4. Second, nonhuman primates can use gestures or symbols for at least rudimentary communication (see Figure 12.14).

It has long been thought that an experiment showing that gestural language and vocal language depend on the same brain structure would support the idea that gestural language evolved into vocal language. As early as 1878, John Hughlings-Jackson suggested that a natural experiment, the loss of certain sign-language abilities by people who had previously depended on sign language (specifically, ASL), would provide the appropriate evidence, and he even observed a case that seemed to indicate that sign language was disrupted by a left-hemisphere lesion, as is vocal language.

Doreen Kimura confirmed that lesions disrupting vocal speech also disrupt signing. Of 11 patients with signing disorders subsequent to brain lesions, 9 right-handers had disorders subsequent to a left-hemisphere lesion. One left-handed patient had a signing disorder subsequent to a left-hemisphere lesion,

Native signers

Late signers

Figure 19.3

Signing Structures Functional MRI images comparing responses in native signers and late signers to American Sign Language sentences and to meaningless signlike gestures. Like spoken or written English, ASL activates extensive regions of the left hemisphere, as well as activating right-hemisphere superior temporal and inferior parietal regions. Right-hemisphere activation in native signers includes brain regions not active in later-learning signers. (From Newman et al., 2002.)

and another left-handed patient had a signing disorder subsequent to a right-hemisphere lesion. These proportions are identical with those found for vocal patients who become aphasic (see Chapter 12). Such results strongly support the idea that some of the language systems that control vocal speech also control signing.

The idea that verbal language and sign language depend on similar neural structures is supported by Aaron Newman and his colleagues in functional magnetic resonance imaging of areas of the brain active during speech and during signing by bilingual speakers. The Newman study also compared signers who acquired sign language early in life (native signers) with those who learned sign language later in life (late signers). As is illustrated in **Figure 19.3**, both native and late signers show activation in the frontal and temporal lobes of the left hemisphere. This finding confirms a left-hemisphere specialization for sign language, implicating the same left-hemisphere brain regions that are active during the use of vocal and written language. If vocal language evolved from gestures used by the ancestors of modern humans, those gestures were likely transmitted genetically rather than culturally. If so, the same gestures should still be transmitted genetically in humans and should still be found in all human groups. Our close relatives, the apes, also should use a subset of this group of gestures. The begging gesture, hand outstretched, of chimpanzees and humans could be an example of such a gesture.

A question that can be raised with respect to gestural theories is, Why was there a shift to vocalizing? There are at least two plausible explanations. First, the increasing use of tools meant that our ancestors' hands were more frequently occupied and often could not be used for gesturing. Second, gesturing requires visual contact, but individuals picking fruit in trees or gathering food in tall grass needed to communicate about both food and predators without being able to see one another.

Multimodal Language Theory

Some theories of language view speech as more than vocal utterances. David McNeill reported that gestures accompany more than 90% of verbal utterances. Gestures thus form an integral component of language communication, suggesting not that gestures preceded vocal communication but rather that vocal–hand communication is a composite. McNeill's view is that the neural basis of language is not simply a property of regions of the brain controlling the mouth but a property of the motor system more generally.

Other observations support this view. We may all be familiar with the *cocktail-party effect*. When listening to speech in a noisy environment we can "hear" what a speaker is saying much better if we can see the speakers lips. A phenomenon called the *McGurk effect* after its originator Harry McGurk gives another demonstration of seeing sounds. When viewers observe a speaker say one word or syllable while they hear a recording of a second word or syllable, they "hear" the articulated word or sound that they saw and not the word or sound that they actually heard. Or they hear a similar but different word entriely. For example, if the speaker is saying "ga" but the actual sound is "da," the listener hears "ga" or perhaps the related sound "ba". The McGurk phenomenon is robust, and knowledge about it or experience with it does not make the demonstration less compelling.

Additional evidence for the multimodal origins of langauge comes from a study by Amy Pollick and her colleagues on the use of vocalizations and gestures in chimpanzees. They find that chimpanzees use gestures meaningfully to communicate with others and that bonobos flexibly use gestures and vocalizations in combination to communicate. These various lines of evidence suggest that speech is not simply vocal but rather multimodal in its orgins and use.

Evidence for Languagelike Processes in Apes

A large number of studies have attempted to explore the multimodal hypothesis of language origins by examining gestural abilities in apes. Beatrice and Allen Gardner used a version of American Sign Language to train Washoe, a year-old chimp they brought into their home. They aimed to teach Washoe ASL hand signs for various objects or actions (called *exemplars*). These signing gestures, analogous to words in spoken language, consist of specific movements that begin and end in a prescribed manner in relation to the signer's body (**Figure 19.4**).

The Gardners molded Washoe's hands to form the desired shapes in the presence of exemplars of the signs, reinforcing her for correct movements. In addition, rather than using verbal language, the Gardners used ASL to communicate with each other in Washoe's presence. Thus, Washoe was raised in an environment filled with signs. Washoe did learn to understand and to use not only nouns but also pronouns and action verbs. For example, she could sign statements such as "You go me," meaning "Come with me." Attempts to teach ASL to other species of great apes (gorilla, orangutan) have had similar success.

The sign-language studies have been criticized. Herbert Terrace and his colleagues analyzed more than 19,000 multisign utterances of an infant chimpanzee (Nim Chimpsky), as well as reanalyzing films of Washoe and other chimps. They claimed to have found no evidence of grammatical construction: most of the chimps' utterances were prompted by their teachers' prior utterances and could thus be explained by nonlinguistic processes. Instead, Terrace and his coworkers were struck by the absence of creativity in the apes' utterances and by their dependence on the prior utterances of their teachers.

Thus, they concluded, chimp language is quite unlike the advanced multiword sequences produced by young children. In response, the Gardners have argued that Terrace used

Figure **19.4**

Exemplars from American Sign Language The Gardners and others taught such symbols to the chimpanzees in their studies. (After Gustason et al., 1975.)

Cat: Draw out two wiskers with thumb and index finger **Caterpillar:** Pull hand along arm

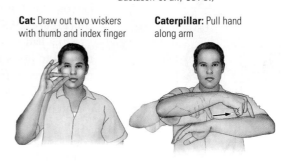

Fruit: Fingertip and thumbtip on cheek; twist **Orange:** Squeeze fist in front of chin

Me: Index finger points to and touches chest **Fond:** Cross arms over heart

(A)–Design elements

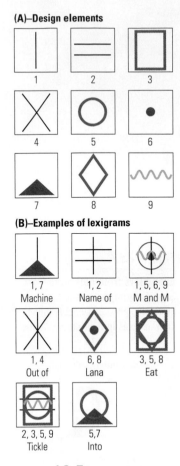

(B)–Examples of lexigrams

Figure **19.5**

Lana's Keyboard Yerkish consists of nine basic design elements (A) that are combined to form lexigrams (B). (After von Glaserfeld, 1977. © 1977. Reprinted with permission.)

training methods with Nim that were inappropriate for a highly social animal such as a chimp, producing stimulus-response actions in Nim rather than the social communication characterized by Washoe.

David Premack advanced the study of the language abilities of chimpanzees by teaching his chimpanzee, Sarah, to read and write with variously shaped and colored pieces of plastic, each representing a word. Premack first taught Sarah that different symbols represent different nouns, just as Washoe had been taught in sign language. Thus, for example, Sarah learned that a pink square was the symbol for banana. Sarah was then taught verbs so that she could write and read such combinations as "give apple" or "wash apple."

Her comprehension could be tested easily by "writing" messages to her (that is, by hanging up a series of symbols) and then observing her response. This procedure was followed by much more complicated tutoring in which Sarah mastered the interrogative ("Where is my banana?"), the negative, and finally the conditional (if, then). Sarah learned a fairly complicated communication system analogous in some ways to simple human language.

After studying the results of the Gardner and Premack projects, David Rumbaugh launched Project Lana, which called for teaching the chimp Lana to communicate by means of a keyboard programmed by a computer. The keyboard was composed of nine stimulus elements and nine primary colors, which could be combined in nearly 1800 lexigrams to form a language now known as Yerkish (**Figure 19.5**).

Lana had simply to type out her messages on the keyboard. First, she was trained to press keys for various single incentives. Then the requirements became increasingly complex, and she was taught to compose various types of statements, such as the indicative ("Tim move into room"), the interrogative ("Tim move into room?"), the imperative ("Please Tim move into room"), and the negative ("Don't Tim move into room"). Eventually, Lana was capable of composing strings of six lexigrams.

One of the weaknesses of Project Lana was its assumption that Lana was treating the lexigrams as symbols rather than as mere paired associates for certain stimuli. Indeed, some of the harshest criticisms have come from the Project Lana team itself. In their most recent project with Kanzi, they have altered the format.

As described in the Portrait at the beginning of Chapter 2, Sue Savage-Rumbaugh and coworkers attempted to teach Malatta, a pygmy chimpanzee caught in the wild, the Yerkish language used with Lana. Malatta did not do well. Serendipitously, Malatta's male offspring, Kanzi, accompanied her during her language training. Even though he was not specifically trained, Kanzi learned more Yerkish and English than his mother did. Remarkably, his knowledge of English words exceeded his knowledge of the lexigrams. To facilitate his learning, his keyboard was augmented with a speech synthesizer.

When he was 6 years old, Kanzi was tested on his comprehension of multi-symbol utterances. He responded correctly to 298 of 310 spoken sentences of two or more utterances. Joel Wallman concluded that Kanzi's use of lexigrams constitutes the best evidence available to date for the referential application of learned symbols by an ape.

In summary, from the study of both wild and captive apes, they clearly have a rudimentary capacity to use language. They also have a much greater predisposition to understand language than to produce it. Anyone watching films of their performance in response to human vocal commands cannot help but be impressed by their understanding. This body of research does suggest that the basic capacity for languagelike processes was there to be selected for in the common ancestor of humans and apes.

A Theory of Language

Moira Yip argues that, in the search for communication analogous to language in nonhuman animals, researchers have not yet begun to investigate language from the point of view of its core skills. Language can be viewed as a combination of four separate abilities, to (1) categorize, (2) label categories, (3) sequence behaviors, and (4) mimic. One or another core skill underlying human language may be present in other animal species, including other apes, songbirds, and even bees. Before we review evidence of core language skills in other animals, we will describe these core skills and consider their role in human language.

Categorization

We have stressed the idea that sensory information is processed by multiple, parallel hierarchical channels. Harry Jerison suggests that, as the cortex expands and the number of channels that process parallel sensory information increases, the integration, or binding, of the information into a single reality becomes more difficult. The brain must determine which of the many different kinds of sensory information reaching the cortex correspond to a given object in the external world. In other words, it becomes necessary to categorize information (for example, to designate some qualities as belonging to plants and others as belonging to animals).

Categorizing information makes it easier not only to perceive the information but also to retrieve it later when it is needed. Most animals are likely capable of categorizing objects to some extent, and all humans have sophisticated classification systems, including informal as well as formal systems for categorizing plants and animals.

Labeling Categories

Although words are the ultimate categorizers, the use of words to label categories must be based on a preexisting perception of categories. The development of human language may have entailed a selection for a novel means of categorization that not only allowed simple sensory stimuli to be combined and grouped but also provided a way of organizing events and relations.

This system can take a concept (that is, a category) and stimulate the production of word forms about that concept; conversely, it can take words and cause the brain to evoke the concepts. Thus, a man who was once a painter but is now color-blind can know and use the words (labels) for colors, even though he can no longer perceive or imagine what the labels mean. He has, in a sense, lost his concept of color, but words can still evoke it. In contrast, certain brain-lesion patients retain their perception of color, and thus the concept, but have lost the language with which to describe it. They experience colors but cannot attach labels to them.

Sequencing Behavior

We have already considered the fact that a unique property of human language is the employment of transitional lip, mouth, and hand movements to form syllables. Left-hemisphere structures associated with language are part of a system that has a fundamental role in the ordering of vocal and hand movements such as those used in speech and signing.

Mimicry

Mimicry plays a role in language development. Athena Vouloumanos and Janet Werker find that, from birth, babies have a preference for listening to speech over other sounds. When they begin to babble, they can make the sounds used in all languages. They also copy and subsequently prefer the sounds made by adults.

By some estimates, in the formative period of development, children may add as many as 60 new words each day to their vocabularies. In our description of the organization of the motor system, we described the "mirror neurons" in a monkey's frontal cortex that discharge both when the monkey makes a hand movement and when it observes a demonstrator make a similar hand movement (see Figure 9.11). Similar mirror neurons in the language regions of the frontal cortex are likely responsible for the mimicking of sounds and words by human children.

Core Language Skills Displayed by Nonhuman Animals

In our summary of the origins of langauge, we have ignored the many types of communication employed by different animal species, including birdsong, the elaborate songs and clicking of dolphins and whales, and the dances of honeybees. The preceding four-part description of some core skills underlying language allows us to see elements of some of the same skills in other animals. Languagelike abilities may also be present in many different brains, even brains extremely different from our own. Irene Pepperberg's African gray parrot Alex deserves mention. Alex could categorize, label, sequence, and mimic.

Pepperberg showed Alex a tray of four corks and asked, "How many?" Alex replied, "Four." He could correctly apply English labels to numerous colors, shapes, and materials and to various items made of metal, wood, plastic, or paper. He could use words to identify, request, and refuse items and to respond to questions about abstract ideas, such as the color, shape, material, relative size, and quantity of more than 100 different objects. Birds do not possess a neocortex, yet Alex was capable of forms of "thought," "speech," and "language."

Irene Pepperberg and Alex.
(Photograph by Wm. Munoz.)

Two views have been expressed on why other animals including parrots can engage in rudimentary language. The first view holds that, when the brain reaches a certain level of complexity, it has the ability to perform some of the core skills of language, even without the presence of a massive neocortex with dedicated neural structures. A different view is suggested by Simon Fisher and Gary Marcus, who propose that certain genes function in such a way that their expression in neural organization facilitates the development of core abilities that underlie language.

The Snapshot on page 535 describes how genetic research on a single family lends support to the idea that a "language" gene

Genetic Basis for an Inherited Speech and Language Disorder

Almost half the members of three generations of the KE family are affected by a severe disorder of speech and language that is inherited as an autosomal dominant trait. The impairment, displayed by 15 of 37 family members (part A of the adjoining illustration), is best characterized as a deficit in sequencing articulation patterns, rendering speech sometimes agrammatical and often unintelligible. The impairment is orofacial and affects the production of sound sequences; it thus resembles Broca's aphasia.

Genetic analysis of the KE family identified a genetic mutation that seems to be the basis for the abnormality. The mutation affects the ability of the gene, *foxhead P2*, or *FOXP2*, to regulate the transcription of other genes. Although *FOXP2* is highly conserved and plays a role in the development of many parts of the brain as well as other body organs, the gene has undergone two mutations since the human lineage separated from the ape lineage. This rapid evolution suggests that these mutations may have altered neuronal circuitry in motor regions of the brain to enable movements that contribute to human speech.

Affected and unaffected KE family members differ on neuropsychological tests. A score on a test of repetition of nonwords with complex articulation patterns successfully discriminated between the two groups. Moreover, the affected family members were impaired on verbal and performance IQ tests, including such nonverbal subtests as picture completion and picture arrangement. They were also impaired on most tests of language function. The affected members were impaired on tests of mouth movement (oral praxis), including simple movements of clicking the tongue and making sequences of movements (such as blowing up the cheeks, then licking the lips, and then smacking the lips).

When their brains were examined with MRI analysis, the affected family members were found to have significantly less gray matter in the caudate nuclei, sensorimotor cortex, inferotemporal cortex, cerebellum, and left inferofrontal cortex. These brain regions are associated with the production of facial movements necessary for language. The reduc-

(A)

(B)

(A) KE family pedigree, showing the extent of the inherited language impairment. (B) Graph (left) records the average volume of the caudate nucleus at various locations along its extent in affected and unaffected family members. Photograph (right) locates parts of the caudate nucleus near the ventricles. (After K. E. Watkins et al. *Brain* 125:453–464, 2002.)

tion in the volume of the caudate nucleus is particularly noteworthy, because difficulties in the use of expressive language subsequent to damage to the caudate nucleus have been reported in other studies.

Part B of the illustration charts the average volume of the caudate nucleus at different locations along its nostral–caudal extent in affected and unaffected family members. Only the head, not the tail, of the caudate nucleus was measured. The photograph shows its location. That a mutation found in the KE family mainly affects the frontal region of the brain is beginning to further understanding of how neural circuits for language develop.

Belton, E., C. H. Salmond, K. E. Watkins, F. Vargha-Khadem, and D. G. Gadian. Bilateral brain abnormalities associated with dominantly inherited verbal and orofacial dyspraxia. *Human Brain Mapping* 18:194–200, 2003.

Vargha-Khadem, F., D. G. Gadian, A. Copp, and M. Mishkin. *FOXP2* and the neuroanatomy of speech and language. *Nature Reviews Neuroscience* 32:131–138, 2005.

may exist. The *foxhead P2* gene, or *FOXP2*, plays a role in forming the speech regions in the human brain and the song areas in the songbird brain. These areas produce and sequence sounds in both species. The idea of a gene for language is analagous to that used to account for the evolution of the eye.

Because eyes in different species of animals are so different, the eye was once thought to have evolved a number of times. The discovery that Pax6, a highly conserved transcription factor, contributes to the development of all eyes across all species greatly simplified the understanding that a modification of a common substrate led to the development of different kinds of eyes.

The Localization of Language

Current ideas about the localization of language processes come from four basic lines of inquiry: (1) anatomical studies of language, (2) studies of lesions in human patients, (3) studies of brain stimulation in awake human patients, and (4) brain-imaging studies. We consider each in turn.

Anatomical Areas Associated with Language

The anatomical landmarks used by researchers for describing brain regions associated with language vary considerably. Some researchers refer to sulci, others to Brodmann's areas, and still others to areas associated with syndromes, such as Broca's area and Wernicke's area. **Figure 19.6** illustrates various ap-

(A) Fissures and gyri

(B) Brodmann's areas

(C) Insula and medial superior temporal gyrus

The temporal and frontal lobes have been pulled aside to reveal the insula.

Figure **19.6**

Core Language Regions of the Brain Areas associated with language functions are shown (A) in relation to fissures and gyri, (B) in relation to Brodmann's areas, and (C) with the lateral fissure retracted to expose the insula and the medial bank of the superior temporal gyrus. (Review the photograph of the insula on page 547.)

proaches to labeling the cortical regions most frequently described as playing a core role in language:

1. Figure 19.6A shows that these regions include the inferior frontal gyrus and the superior temporal gyrus, in which Broca's area (green) and Wernicke's area (yellow), respectively, are located. Parts of surrounding gyri, including the ventral parts of the precentral and postcentral gyrus, the supramarginal gyrus, the angular gyrus, and the medial temporal gyrus, also are within the core language regions.

2. Figure 19.6B depicts the language areas in accord with Brodmann's number system, in which Broca's area is equivalent to areas 45 and 44 and Wernicke's area is equivalent to area 22. Language regions also include parts of areas 9, 4, 3-1-2, 40, 39, and 21.

3. Figure 19.6C shows that, if the lateral fissure is opened up, a number of language-related areas can be found within it, including the insula, a large region of the neocortex lying within the dorsal bank of the lateral fissure; Heschl's gyrus (primary auditory cortex); and parts of the superior temporal gyrus referred to as the anterior and posterior superior temporal planes (aSTP and pSTP). Together, Heschl's gyrus, aSTP, and pSTP are sometimes referred to as the **planum temporale**.

This survey by no means covers all language areas. Other regions taking part in language include the dorsal part of area 6 of the motor cortex (also referred to as the supplementary motor area) that is responsible for rhythmic mouth movements to atriculate sounds; parts of the thalamus, the dorsolateral parts of the caudate nucleus, and the cerebellum; visual areas (required for reading), sensory pathways, and motor pathways; and pathways connecting all these various regions. Furthermore, many regions of the right hemisphere also have roles in language.

Lesion Studies in Humans

Most discussions of the neural basis of language have centered on Broca's area and Wernicke's area, the historical backgrounds of which are described in Chapter 1. The early neurological model of language by Carl Wernicke, as well as its later revival by Norman Geschwind, now called the **Wernicke–Geschwind model**, was based entirely on lesion data (**Figure 19.7**). This three-part model has played a formative role in directing research and organizing research results:

1. The meaning of words is represented in Wernicke's area. When a person listens to speech, word sounds are sent through the auditory pathways to the primary auditory cortex, Heschl's gyrus. From there, they are relayed to Wernicke's area, where the sense of the words is extracted.

2. To speak, word meanings must be sent over the arcuate fasciculus to Broca's area, where morphemes are assembled.

Figure **19.7**

Neurology of Language The Wernicke–Geschwind model, showing the regions of the cortex taking part. Sequences 1 through 3 illustrate how the model explains different language functions.

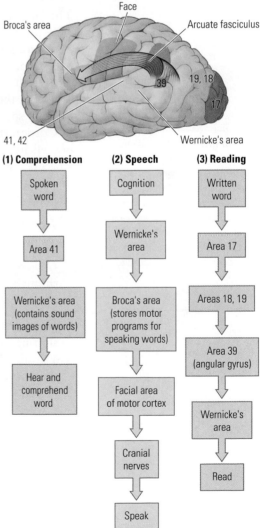

The model proposes that Broca's area holds a representation for articulating words. Instructions for speech are sent from Broca's area to the adjacent facial area of the motor cortex; and, from there, instructions are sent to facial motor neurons in the brainstem, which relay movement commands to facial muscles.

3. Reading requires that information concerning handwritten or printed words be sent from visual areas 17, 18, and 19 to the angular gyrus (area 39) and, from there, to Wernicke's area, which reads silently or, in conjunction with Broca's area, reads out loud.

Although useful conceptually, many aspects of the Wernicke–Geschwind model have been modified by improved lesion analysis, by mapping facilitated by transcranial magnetic stimulation (TMS), and by brain-imaging studies. In the sections that follow, we'll describe the ways in which newer findings are consistent or inconsistent with the model.

Speech Zones Mapped by Electrical Stimulation

The language zones of the neocortex, particularly those pertaining to speech, were identified by Wilder Penfield and others by using intracortical stimulation during surgery. Statistical analyses of results from hundreds of patients have made the construction of a map of these regions possible (**Figure 19.8**). They include the classical areas of Broca and Wernicke in the left hemisphere, as well as the sensory and motor representations of the face and the supplementary speech area in both hemispheres.

Cortical stimulation produces either positive effects, meaning that stimulation elicits vocalization that is not speech but rather a sustained or interrupted vowel cry, such as "Oh," or negative effects, meaning that stimulation inhibits the ability to vocalize or to use words properly, including a variety of aphasia-like errors:

- *Total arrest of speech, or an inability to vocalize spontaneously.* This error results from stimulation throughout the shaded zones in Figure 19.8.

- *Hesitation and slurring of speech.* Hesitation results from stimulation throughout the zones shaded in Figure 19.8, whereas slurring results primarily from stimulation of the facial motor area in either hemisphere.

- *Distortion and repetition of words and syllables.* Distortion differs from slurring in that the distorted sound is an unintelligible noise rather than a word. These effects result primarily from stimulation of the classical speech zones, although occasionally from stimulation of the face area as well.

- *Confusion of numbers while counting.* For example, a patient may jump from "6" to "19" to "4," and so on. Confusion in counting results from stimulation of Broca's or Wernicke's area.

- *Inability to name despite retained ability to speak.* An example is "That is a . . . I know. That is a. . . ." When the current was removed, the patient was able to name the object in the picture correctly. Another example is, "Oh, I know what it is. That is what you put in your shoes." After withdrawal of

Figure 19.8

Speech Interference Regions where stimulation or surgical lesions have been shown to affect speech. Damage to Broca's and Wernicke's areas produces chronic aphasia, damage to the sensory and motor areas produces transient aphasia, and damage outside these areas does not produce aphasia.

Broca's area
Transient aphasia
Motor
Sensory
Chronic aphasia
Wernicke's area

the stimulating electrodes, the patient immediately said "foot" (Penfield and Roberts, 1959, p. 123). Naming difficulties arise from stimulation throughout the anterior (Broca's) and posterior (Wernicke's) speech zones.

- *Misnaming and perseverating* Misnaming may occur when the subject uses words related in sound, such as "camel" for "comb," uses synonyms, such as "cutters" for "scissors," or perseverates by using the same word twice. For example, the subject may name a picture of a bird correctly but may also call the next picture, a table, a bird. Misnaming, like other naming difficulties, occurs during stimulation of both the anterior and the posterior speech zones.

George Ojemann and his colleagues reported that, during stimulation of Broca's area, patients are unable to make voluntary facial movements and that stimulation of these same points may also disrupt phonemic discrimination and gestures, such as hand movements, associated with speech. Most reports agree that the extent of the cortical language zones as marked by stimulation varies considerably among subjects.

Speech Zones Mapped by Transcranial Magnetic Stimulation

Intracortical microstimulation has a number of drawbacks as a method for studying the neural basis of language: the procedure is performed during surgery in which the skull is removed, and the patients who are to receive surgery often have preexisting brain conditions that may lead to anomolous language organization. Transcranial magnetic stimulation is a method of exploring the organization of language in healthy subjects without invading the brain directly. The procedure is relatively easy to use, can be used repeatedly, and, when combined with MRI, can allow predetermined regions of the brain to be examined under controlled experimental conditions. TMS has drawbacks in that the stimulator produces a sound that can cue a subject to the stimulation. In addition, the stimulation must pass through the scalp, skull, and meninges and can cause muscle contractions, discomfort, and pain.

TMS has served as a source of a number of insights into the organization of language (Devlin and Watkins, 2007). TMS can interfere with neural function, producing a "virtual lesion" lasting from tens of milliseconds to as long as an hour. TMS at appropriate frequencies and intensities can prime neurons such that reaction times for behaviors dependent on the region that is stimulated are enhanced.

TMS can also be used to evaluate connetions beween brain regions, such as brain regions used for selecting words and brain regions used for producing sounds. For example, a movement of the lips produced by TMS to the motor cortex might be enhanced if a subject thinks of a word such as "hammer," which produces a lip movement when said. Presumably, the part of the brain thinking "hammer" is connected to the part of the brain being stimulated to produce the lip movement.

Many studies show that TMS can duplicate most of the positive and negative effects produced by intracranial stimulation, thus confirming the findings concerning the localization of language produced by electrical stimulation. For example, stimulation is much more likely to interfere with speech if applied to the left hemisphere. It also interrupts speech without invoking facial movements when administered to Broca's area in the anterior region of the inferofrontal cortex, and it interrupts speech and invokes facial movements when administered to the the face region of the motor cortex in the posterior region of the inferofrontal cortex. In addition, muscle contractions of the hand induced by TMS delivered to the hand region of the motor cortex increase in size during speaking and reading aloud but not during silent speech and reading.

In other words, a functional connection exists between the brain's language areas and the hand region of the motor cortex during speech production. This connection may be responsible for the irrepressible use of hand gestures when a person is speaking and for the evolutionary link between vocalization and hand gestures. These results suggest that the human neural system is, indeed, similar to the mirror-neuron system identified by single-cell recording in monkeys. Hand movements produced by TMS are augmented when subjects think of or see similar hand movements, suggesting that the same brain regions that produce the movements also control the perception of the same movements by others.

TMS has been used to map specific regions of the brain, such as Broca's area. A number of brain-imaging studies suggest that the anterior region of Broca's area is implicated in semantic processing (processing the meaning of words) and the posterior region of Broca's area is implicated in phonological processing (the production of words). For example, subjects were presented word pairs on a computer screen and required to decide whether the words meant the same thing (say, "gift" and "present") or sounded the same (say, "key" and "quay"). Stimulation of the rostral region of Broca's area increased reaction times for the semantic condition but not for the phonological condition, whereas stimulation of the caudal region of Broca's area increased the reaction time for the phonological conditiion but not for the semantic condition.

TMS has also proved useful in studying the compensatory changes that take place after brain injury that produces aphasia. For example, in the debate concerning whether compensation is mediated by spared tissue surrounding a lesion or by the opposite intact hemisphere, several studies show that stimulation of the tissue surrounding the lesion is more disruptive to language production than is stimulation of the opposite hemisphere. This result suggests that the remaining tissue near a lesion has a much greater role in recovery than does the opposite hemisphere. In fact, TMS that suppresses the function of the opposite hemisphere has been found to improve fuctional recovery. Presumably, the homologous regions in the opposite hemisphere can interfere with functioning in the injured hemisphere and therefore retard recovery.

Phonological processing

Broca's area

Semantic processing

Stimulation of the rostral and caudal extent of Broca's area by TMS inhibits semantic and phonological processing, respectively. (After Devlin and Watkins, 2007.)

Speech Zones Mapped by Imaging

With the development of PET, fMRI, and ERP (event-related potential) procedures, cognitive psychologists have become more interested in the neural correlates of language processing.

After having used fMRI to measure brain areas implicated in language, Jeffery Binder and his colleagues reported that language-processing areas make up a remarkably large part of the brain. These researchers presented either tones or meaningful words to 30 right-handed subjects, half of whom were male and half female. Tone stimuli consisted of a number of 500- and 750-Hz pure tones presented in sequence. The subjects pressed a button if they heard two 750-Hz tones in a sequence. Word stimuli were spoken English nouns designating animals (for example, turtle). Subjects pushed a button if an animal was native to the United States and used by humans. A rest condition consisted of no stimulus presentations.

By subtracting the activation produced by tones from the activation seen during the rest condition, the researchers identified brain regions responding to tones. By subtracting the activation produced by words from the activation produced by tones, the researchers identified brain regions responding to words. The findings are that widespread regions of the brain are activated by words, including areas in the occipital, parietal, temporal, and frontal lobes; the thalamus; and the cerebellum (**Figure 19.9**).

With the use of PET and a wider range of stimuli, a number of research groups have identified more-specific functions for some of these language areas (**Figure 19.10**). Steven Petersen's group used a variety of different conditions to identify speech regions. In one task, they passively presented words (in some cases, pseudowords or pseudosounds) either visually or aurally to a passive subject. In the next task, the subject was to repeat the word (an output task). In the final task (an association task), the subject was to suggest a use for the object named by the target word (for example, if "cake" was presented, the subject might say "eat").

Figure 19.9

Aural Activation Left-hemisphere brain regions activated while subjects listened to speech, as measured by fMRI. Subjects listened to spoken English nouns designating animals and were required to decide, in each case, whether the word indicated an animal that was native to the United States and used by humans. (After Binder et al., 1997.)

(A) Word-processing areas

Each of the tasks in the word-generation experiment activates a distinct set of areas in the brain.

(B) Selecting words

Prefrontal cortex is active in a task requiring matching a noun to one of four target words.

(C) Tools

Premotor cortex and temporal cortex are active with nouns for tools.

(D) Tools, animals, or persons

These locations are active for different kinds of nouns.

Figure 19.10

Brain Areas Activated by Language Tasks Results obtained with the use of PET to monitor blood flow were analyzed by using subtraction methods. (Part A after Posner and Raichle, 1994; part B after Wagner et al., 2001; part C after Martin et al., 1996; part D after Damasio et al., 1996.)

The investigators monitored blood flow by using PET and analyzed their data by using a subtraction technique (see Chapter 6). Thus, in the sensory (reading or listening) tasks, they identified changes from baseline blood flow by taking the difference between the activities in the two states. In the output task, they subtracted the sensory activity, and, in the association task, they subtracted the output activity.

Their results (Figure 19.10A) illustrate the involvement of many brain regions in language and reveal some of the specific contributions of each region:

- There was no overlap in the visual and auditory activation during the passive task, implying that the processing of the word forms in the two modalities is completely independent.

- During the speaking tasks, there was bilateral activation of the motor and sensory facial areas, as well as bilateral activation of the supplementary speech area and activation of the right cerebellum.

- For the task that required generating verbs, there was activation of the frontal lobe, especially the left inferior region, including Broca's area. The verb-generation task also activated the posterior temporal cortex, the anterior cingulate cortex, and the cerebellum.

Other investigators have identified still other areas that are activated, depending on task demands. Anthony Wagner and colleagues presented subjects with a single cue word and four target words. A subject's task was to indicate which target word was most closely and globally related to the cue. Thus, the task measured the subject's ability to retrieve meaningful information. They found that an area in the left inferofrontal cortex just dorsal to Broca's area became active during this task (Figure 19.10B).

Alex Martin and his colleagues asked subjects to name tools or animals and subtracted activation produced by the animal brain response from the tool brain response. They found that naming tools activates a region of the premotor cortex that was also activated by imagined hand movements (Figure 19.10C). Finally, Antonio Damasio and his colleagues reported that naming persons, animals, and tools activates specific areas in the inferotemporal lobe (Figure 19.10D).

In summary, the results of imaging studies confirm the role of the classical anterior and posterior speech zones in language, but they also show that other regions are implicated. Furthermore, they suggest that the posterior speech zone may deal largely with the analysis of auditory input. They also indicate that Broca's area is not simply a cortical representation of the movements of speech, as has been traditionally believed. Finally, they provide evidence that "language" is mapped onto circuits that are ordinarily also engaged in more-primary functions such that visual attributes of words are represented in visual areas, auditory attributes are mapped onto auditory regions of the brain, motor attributes are mapped onto motor regions of the brain, and so on.

That so many different regions of the brain control language raises the question of its underlying organization. Riitta Salmelin and Jan Kujala suggest that the brain is organized in neural webs in which nodes, representing specific functions, are interconnected by pathways. Together, the nodes and pathways give language its more complex properties of discourse and narrative. Different nodes might represent verbs versus nouns, living versus nonliving things, animals with fur versus those without, and so on. Neural webs connect both sensory and motor representations of words. The webs are proposed to be flexible and to change as word use and meaning change, and information travels in both directions between nodes.

Some representative neural webs are illustrated in **Figure 19.11**. Note that, if a word contains visual content, the web includes visual areas of the brain, whereas, if it contains motor content, the web includes motor areas. Any given web will also include nodes within primary and secondary auditory areas as well as nodes within primary and secondary motor regions. We must point out that the objective of creating neural webs to represent language-related regions of the brain is not to eventually produce a wiring diagram of the brain's neurons and their connections but rather to develop classifications that will explain how the brain produces language.

(A) Word sounds

(C) Tool-related word

(B) Face-related word

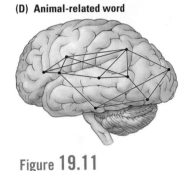

(D) Animal-related word

Figure **19.11**

Neural Webs for Language Tasks Nodes are symbolized by circles, and interconnecting axonal pathways are represented by lines. In this model, different word-related tasks are seen as using different neural webs.

Disorders of Language

In this section, we describe how neuropsychologists classify symptoms of language impairment. It is important to recognize that, whereas symptom classification was originally linked to brain regions (Broca's aphasia and Broca's area, for example), improved anatomical analysis suggests that such precise correlations do not exist.

Normal language depends on the complex interaction of sensory integration and symbolic association, motor skills, learned syntactical patterns, and verbal memory. *Aphasia* may refer to a disorder of language apparent in speech, in writing (in this case also called **agraphia**), or in reading (also called **alexia**) produced by injury to brain areas specialized for these functions. Thus, disturbances of language due to severe intellectual impairment, to loss of sensory input (especially vision and hearing), or to paralysis or incoordination of the musculature of the mouth (called **anarthria**) or hand (for writing) are not considered aphasic disturbances. These disorders may accompany aphasia, and they complicate its study.

Howard Goodglass and Edith Kaplan divide language disturbances into 10 basic types, which we have grouped into disorders of comprehension and disorders of production in **Table 19.2**. Most of these language

Table **19.2** **Summary of symptoms of language disorders**

Disorders of Comprehension
Poor auditory comprehension
Poor visual comprehension

Disorders of Production
Poor articulation
Word-finding deficit (anomia)
Unintended words or phrases (paraphasia)
Loss of grammar and syntax
Inability to repeat aurally presented material
Low verbal fluency
Inability to write (agraphia)
Loss of tone in voice (aprosidia)

disorders were described earlier, in our discussions of parietal-, temporal-, and frontal-lobe functions. The one exception is **paraphasia**, the production of unintended syllables, words, or phrases in an effort to speak. Paraphasia differs from difficulties in articulation in that sounds are correctly articulated, but they are the wrong sounds: people with paraphasia either distort the intended word (for example, "pike" instead of "pipe") or produce a completely unintended word (for example, "my mother" instead of "my wife").

Despite disagreement among experts concerning the number of types of aphasias, certain classification systems are widely used. The system presented in **Table 19.3** groups aphasias into three broadly defined categories:

- **Fluent aphasias**, in which there is fluent speech but difficulties either in auditory verbal comprehension or in the repetition of words, phrases, or sentences spoken by others.

- **Nonfluent aphasias**, in which there are difficulties in articulating but relatively good auditory verbal comprehension.

- **Pure aphasias**, in which there are selective impairments in reading, writing, or the recognition of words.

Within each category, Table 19.3 lists numerous subtypes that are often distinguished, including Wernicke's aphasia, transcortical aphasia, conduction aphasia, anomic aphasia, and Broca's aphasia.

Table **19.3** Definition of aphasic syndromes

Syndrome	Type of Speech Production	Type of Language Errors
Fluent Aphasias		
Wernicke (sensory)	Fluent speech, without articulatory disorders	Neologism or anomias, or paraphasias, poor comprehension; poor repetition
Transcortical (isolation syndrome)	Fluent speech, without articulatory disorders; good repetition	Verbal paraphasias and anomias; poor comprehension
Conduction	Fluent, sometimes halting speech, but without articulatory disorders	Phonemic paraphasias and neologisms; phonemic groping; poor repetition; fairly good comprehension
Anomic	Fluent speech, without articulatory disorders	Anomia and occasional paraphasias
Nonfluent Aphasias		
Broca (expressive), severe	Laborious articulation	Speechlessness with recurring utterances or syndrome of phonetic disintegration; poor repetition
Broca (expressive), mild	Slight but obvious articulatory disorders	Phonemic paraphasias with anomia; agrammatism; dysprosody
Transcortical motor	Marked tendency to reduction and inertia; without articulatory disorders; good repetition	Uncompleted sentences and anomias; naming better than spontaneous speech
Global	Laborious articulation	Speechlessness with recurring utterances; poor comprehension; poor repetition
"Pure" Asphasias		
Alexia without agraphia	Normal	Poor reading
Agraphia	Normal	Poor writing
Word deafness	Normal	Poor comprehension; poor repetition

Source: After Mazzocchi and Vignolo, 1979.

Fluent Aphasias

Fluent aphasias are impairments related mostly to the input or reception of language. A listener who did not speak the language of a fluent aphasic would receive the impression that the subject was speaking easily and correctly.

Wernicke's aphasia, or **sensory aphasia**, is the inability to comprehend words or to arrange sounds into coherent speech. Alexander Luria proposes that sensory aphasia has three characteristic deficits—in classifying sounds, in producing speech, and in writing.

First, to hear and make out the sounds of speech, one must be able to qualify sounds—that is, to recognize the different sounds in the system of phonemes that are the basic units of speech in a given language. For example, in the Japanese language, the sounds "l" and "r" are not distinguished; a Japanese-speaking person hearing English cannot distinguish these sounds, because the necessary template is not in the brain. Thus, although this distinction is perfectly clear to English-speaking persons, it is not clear to native Japanese. This problem is precisely what a person with Wernicke's aphasia has in his or her own language: the inability to isolate the significant phonemic characteristics and to classify sounds into known phonemic systems. Thus, we see in Wernicke's aphasia a deficit in the categorization of sounds.

The second characteristic of Wernicke's aphasia is a defect in speech. The affected person can speak and may speak a great deal, but he or she confuses phonetic characteristics, producing what is often called **word salad**. The third characteristic is impairment in writing. A person who cannot discern phonemic characteristics cannot be expected to write, because he or she does not know the graphemes (pictorial or written representations of a phoneme) that combine to form a word.

Transcortical aphasia, sometimes called **isolation syndrome**, is curious in that people can repeat and understand words and name objects but cannot speak spontaneously or they cannot comprehend words, although they can repeat them. Comprehension could be poor because words fail to arouse associations. The production of meaningful speech could be poor because, even though the production of words is normal, words are not associated with other cognitive activities in the brain.

Conduction aphasia is a paradoxical deficit: people with this disorder can speak easily, name objects, and understand speech, but they cannot repeat words. The simplest explanation for this problem is a disconnection between the "perceptual word image" and the motor systems producing the words.

People with *anomic aphasia* (sometimes called **amnesic aphasia**) comprehend speech, produce meaningful speech, and can repeat speech, but they have great difficulty in finding the names of objects. For example, we saw a patient who, when shown a picture of a ship anchor, simply could not think of the name and finally said, "I know what it does. . . . You use it to anchor a ship." Although he had actually used the word as a verb, he was unable to use it as a noun. Difficulties in finding nouns appear to result from damage throughout the temporal cortex (see Figure 19.10D). In contrast, verb-finding deficits are more likely to come from left frontal injuries (see Figure 19.10A).

Although the extent to which the brain differentiates between nouns and verbs may seem surprising, we can see that they have very different functions.

Nouns are categorizers. Verbs are action words that form the core of syntactical structure. It would make sense, therefore, to find that they are separated in such a way that nouns are a property of brain areas controlling recognition and classification, and verbs are a property of brain areas controlling movement.

Nonfluent Aphasias

In nonfluent aphasia (Broca's aphasia, or **expressive aphasia**), a person continues to understand speech but has to labor to produce it: the person speaks in short phrases interspersed with pauses, makes sound errors, makes repetitious errors in grammar, and frequently omits function words. Only the key words necessary for communication are used. Nevertheless, the deficit is not one of making sounds but rather of switching from one sound to another.

Nonfluent aphasia can be mild or severe. In one form, *transcortical motor aphasia*, repetition is good but spontaneous production of speech is labored. In *global aphasias*, speech is labored and comprehension is poor.

Pure Aphasias

The pure aphasias include alexia, an inability to read; agraphia, an inability to write; and word deafness, in which a person cannot hear or repeat words. These disorders may be quite selective. For example, a person is able to read but not write or is able to write but not read.

The Localization of Lesions in Aphasia

Beginning students of language are intrigued by the simplicity of the Wernicke–Geschwind model of language. In this model, Wernicke's area is associated with speech comprehension, Broca's area is associated with speech production, and the arcuate fibers that connect the two areas translate meaning into sound (see Figure 19.7). Seasoned researchers, on the other hand, are equally excited to learn that the neural organization of language is more complex than the model suggests and that, in fact, the key deficits of Wernicke's aphasia do not come from damage to Wernicke's area and the key deficits of Broca's aphasia do not come from damage to Broca's area.

Four points summarize why studying the neural basis of language is itself so complex:

1. As heretofore described, brain-imaging studies are now showing that most of the brain takes part in language in one way or another; and, indeed, it makes sense that a behavior as comprehensive and complex as language would not be the product of some small, circumscribed region of the brain.

2. Most of the patients who contribute information to the study of language have suffered strokes, usually of the middle cerebral artery (MCA). **Figure 19.12**A illustrates the location of this artery and its tributaries. Because stroke results from a blockage or bleeding of the artery, it is clear that all core language areas may be damaged or only smaller regions may be

Figure 19.12

Middle Cerebral Artery The amount of damage to the cortex by blockage of the middle cerebral artery (red) can vary widely in the neocortex (A) and the basal ganglia (B), depending on the location of the blockage.

(A)

(B)

damaged, depending on where a stroke occurs. Individual differences in the tributary pattern of the MCA add to the variation seen in stroke symptoms and outcomes. The artery supplies subcortical areas as well, including the basal ganglia, a region that includes the caudate nucleus and is important in language (Figure 19.12B).

3. Immediately following a stroke, symptoms are generally severe but, as time passes, there is considerable improvement. Thus, the symptoms cannot be easily ascribed to damage in a particular brain region.

4. Aphasias described as nonfluent (Broca's) or fluent (Wernicke's) are syndromes consisting of a number of different symptoms, each of which may have a different neural basis.

Keep these variables in mind as we consider some ideas concerning the neural basis of language.

Cortical Components of Language

In studying a series of stroke patients with language disorders, Nina Dronkers and her coworkers correlate different symptoms of nonfluent and fluent aphasia with specific cortical regions. Their analysis suggests that nonfluent aphasia consists of at least five kinds of symptoms: apraxia of speech (difficulty in producing sequences of speech sounds), impairment in sentence comprehension, recurring utterances, impairment in articulation of sounds, and impairment in working memory for sentences.

After using overlaying maps of brain injury to identify areas of common damage, the Dronkers team concludes that each of these impairments has a somewhat different neural basis (**Figure 19.13**). Their analysis also suggests that the core deficit, apraxia of speech, comes not from Broca's-area damage but from damage to the insula (see Figure 19.12B). Impairments in sentence comprehension seem to be associated with damage to the dorsal bank of the superior temporal gyrus, recurring utterances seem to stem from damage to the arcuate fasciculus, and impairments in working memory and articulation seem to be associated with damage to Broca's area.

Concerning fluent aphasia, Dronkers and her colleagues propose that most of the core difficulties, especially the lack of comprehension in speech, comes from damage to the medial temporal lobe and underlying white matter. Damage in this area not only destroys local language regions but also cuts off most of the occipital, temporal, and parietal regions from the core language region. The researchers also propose that damage to Wernicke's area does not result in the core deficits of fluent aphasia but contributes to deficits in holding sentences in memory until they can be repeated and in word rhyming. Thus, the patients appear to have impairment in the "iconic" memory for sounds but are not impaired in comprehension.

Figure **19.13**

Proposed Relations Between Brain Regions and Symptoms of Aphasia Note that these relations are different from those originally proposed by Wernicke and Geschwind, shown in Figure 19.7.

Broca's area: working memory, articulation

Heschl's gyrus

Arcuate fasciculus: recurring utterances

Superior temporal gyrus: sentence comprehension

Posterior middle temporal gyrus: fluent aphasia

Insula: apraxia of speech

Wernicke's area: holding sentences in memory, word rhyming

Subcortical Components of Language

At the same time that Broca was describing a cortical center for speech control, Hughlings-Jackson proposed that subcortical structures are critical to language. In 1866 he wrote: "I think it will be found that the nearer the disease is to the basal ganglia, the more likely is the defect of articulation to be the striking thing, and the farther off, the more likely it is to be one of mistakes of words."

The symptoms displayed by half of the members of the KE family described in the Snapshot on page 535 suggest that the basal ganglia may be important for the articulation of language. On the other hand, Alison Rowan and her colleagues used MRI and behavioral tests specifically to examine the language abilities of young patients who had suffered basal ganglia stroke. They conclude that the language deficits most likely derive from subtle damage to the neocortex.

Some of this evidence indicates that the thalamus has a role in language. Findings by George Ojemann's and Irving Cooper's research teams, in which the thalamus was electrically stimulated, indicate that the pulvinar nucleus and the lateral-posterior–lateral-central complex of the left thalamus have a role in language that is not common to other subcortical structures. Stimulation of the left ventrolateral and pulvinar nuclei of the thalamus produced speech arrest, difficulties in naming, perseveration, and reduced speed of talking. Stimulation of the thalamus has also been reported to have a positive effect on memory, because it improves later retrieval of words heard during the stimulation. As a result, some researchers have proposed that the thalamus influences language function by activating or arousing the cortex.

When the thalamus is damaged by electrical current applied for the treatment of abnormal movements, a variety of disturbances of speech and language have been found in association with lesions of the left ventrolateral thalamus or the pulvinar nucleus or both. Symptoms include postoperative dysphasia, which is usually transitory; increased verbal-response latency; decreases in voice volume; alterations in speaking rate and slurring or hesitation in speech; and impaired performance on tests of verbal IQ and memory.

Right-Hemisphere Contributions to Language

Although there is little doubt that the left hemisphere of right-handed people is dominant in language, the right hemisphere also has language abilities. The best evidence comes from studies of split-brain patients in whom the linguistic abilities of the right hemisphere have been studied systematically with the use of various techniques for lateralizing input to one hemisphere.

The results of these studies show that the right hemisphere has little or no speech but surprisingly good auditory comprehension of language, including both nouns and verbs. There is some reading ability but little writing ability in the right hemisphere. In addition, although the right hemisphere is able to recognize words (semantic processing), it has little understanding of grammatical rules and sentence structures (syntactical processing).

Complementary evidence of the right hemisphere's role in language comes from studies of people who have had the left hemisphere removed, a procedure known as **hemispherectomy**. If the left hemisphere is lost early in development, the right hemisphere can acquire considerable language abilities (see Chapter 10 for details), although people with left hemispherectomies are by no means normal. Left hemispherectomy in adulthood produces severe deficits in speech but leaves surprisingly good auditory comprehension. Reading ability is limited, however, and writing is usually absent. In general, left hemispherectomy appears to leave language abilities that are reminiscent of those achieved by the right hemisphere of commissurotomy patients.

The effects of right-hemisphere lesions on language functions provide further indication that the right hemisphere is capable of language comprehension, especially of auditory material, even though it cannot control speech. For example, aphasia is rare after right-hemisphere lesions, even after right hemispherectomy, but more-subtle linguistic impairments are noted, including changes in vocabulary selection, in responses to complex statements with unusual syntactical construction, and in the comprehension of metaphors. In addition, right orbitofrontal lesions reduce verbal fluency and lead to deficits in the comprehension of tone of voice and in the production of emotional tone (prosody).

The differences between the functioning of the right and left hemispheres in language have been summarized in the following way. The wife of a patient with Broca's aphasia comments that her husband understands everything, even though he cannot match spoken words with their pictured representations and cannot follow two-step commands. The wife of a patient with an equivalent right-hemisphere lesion comments that her husband has difficulty following a conversation, makes irrelevant remarks, and generally seems to miss the point of what people are saying, even though he performs quite well on the same tests failed by the patient with a left-hemisphere lesion.

In reviewing the role of the right hemisphere in language, both Frank Benson and Eran Zaidel conclude that the only strictly left-hemisphere function in language is syntax (**Table 19.4**). This function has many components, including the production, timing, and sequencing of the movements required for speaking, as well as an understanding of the rules of grammar. The relative roles of the two hemispheres in other aspects of language comprehension remain to be ascertained.

Table 19.4 Language activities of the two hemispheres

Function	Left Hemisphere	Right Hemisphere
Gestural Language	+	+
Prosodic Language		
Rhythm	++	
Inflection	+	+
Timbre	+	++
Melody		++
Semantic Language		
Word recognition	+	+
Verbal meaning	++	+
Concepts	+	+
Visual meaning	+	++
Syntactical Language		
Sequencing	++	
Relations	++	
Grammar	++	

Source: After Benson, 1986.

The Assessment of Aphasia

Since World War II, there has been widespread interest in establishing a standard systematic procedure for assessing aphasia, both to provide standardized clinical descriptions of patients and to facilitate comparison of patient populations in neuropsychological research. A number of manuals and their original references are summarized in **Table 19.5**.

Those in the first group are categorized as test batteries in that they contain a large number of subtests so as to systematically explore the language

Table **19.5** Summary of the major tests of aphasia

Test	Origin
Aphasia Test Batteries	
Boston Diagnostic Aphasia Test	Goodglass and Kaplan, 1972
Functional communicative profile	Sarno, 1969
Neurosensory center comprehensive examination for aphasia	Spreen and Benton, 1969
Porch Index of Communicative Ability	Porch, 1967
Minnesota Test for Differential Diagnosis of Aphasia	Schuell, 1965
Wepman–Jones Language Modalities Test for Aphasia	Wepman and Jones, 1961
Aphasia Screening Tests	
Conversation analysis	Beeke, Maxim, and Wilkinson, 2007
Halstead–Wepman Aphasia Screening Test	Halstead and Wepman, 1959
Token Test	de Renzi and Vignolo, 1962

capabilities of the subject. They typically include tests of (1) auditory and visual comprehension; (2) oral and written expression, including tests of repetition, reading, naming, and fluency; and (3) conversational speech.

Because test batteries have the disadvantages of being lengthy and requiring special training to administer, some brief aphasia screening tests also have been devised, including conversational analysis and some simpler formal tests. The Halstead–Wepman Aphasia Screening Test and the Token Test are often used as part of standard neuropsychological test batteries (see Chapter 28) because they are short and easy to administer and score. These tests do not take the place of the detailed aphasia test batteries, but they provide efficient means of discovering the presence of a language disorder. If a detailed description of the linguistic deficit is then desired, the more comprehensive aphasia batteries may be given.

Although theoretical models and test batteries may be useful for evaluating and classifying the status of a patient with aphasia, they are not a substitute for continued experimental analysis of language disorders. Whereas the test batteries attempt to classify patients into a number of groups, a psychobiological approach concentrates on individual differences and peculiarities and, from these differences, attempts to reconstruct the processes through which the brain produces language.

On the practical side, John Marshall notes that only about 60% of patients will fit into a classification scheme such as the one presented in Table 19.3. Similar inadequacies have been noted in the use of other classification methods. For example, most patients with a language impairment show a deficit in naming that can be elicited by having them look at pictures of objects and attempt to identify them.

Scores on standard tests often tell little about this naming impairment. A number of patients might be able to name a violin, but one patient might know only that it is a musical instrument, another that it is a stringed instrument, and still another that it is similar to a cello and not a trumpet. Some patients have highly selective naming deficits, such as being unable to name buildings or people or colors or objects found inside houses. Thus, it is inappropriate to simply classify all these different conditions as anomic and draw no further distinctions between them. The study of such differences can be a source of important insight into the neural organization of language.

Developmental Language Disorders

The assessment of reading disorders is becoming a special branch of the study of language for several reasons. First, it is possible to be more objective in the analysis of reading than in the analysis of writing and speaking. Additionally, there is a large pedagogical science of reading. Finally, in addition to the **acquired dyslexias** (impairments in reading subsequent to brain damage), cases of **developmental dyslexia** (failure to learn to read during development) are common and require diagnosis and remediation.

Max Coltheart argues that model building is the most objective approach to the study of reading. A model is much like an algorithm, a set of steps to follow to answer a question. Reading models are used to test reading-disabled people, both as a way of defining the impairment and as a way of testing the utility of the model.

The model-building approach views reading as being composed of a number of independent skills or subsystems, one or another of which may not be functioning in an impaired reader. The modeling approach thus differs from classical neurological approaches in two ways: (1) the latter define dyslexia according to whether it arises in conjunction with other disorders, such as dysgraphia or dysphasia, and (2) the primary intent is to correlate the impairment with the locus of brain damage.

Analyzing Acquired Dyslexia

The model-building approach can be traced to an analysis by James Hinshelwood, first published in 1900, in which he identified different types of reading disorders: (1) the inability to name letters (letter blindness), (2) the inability to read words (word blindness), and (3) the inability to read sentences (sentence blindness). Hinshelwood's taxonomy and its subsequent elaboration led to the current hypothesis that reading is composed of a number of independent abilities that may each have an independent anatomical basis.

Figure 19.14 shows a series of questions that an examiner might ask to identify the following impairments:

1. **Attentional dyslexia.** When one letter is present, letter naming is normal. When more than one letter is present, letter naming is difficult. Even if a letter is specially colored, underlined, has an arrow pointing to it, and is pointed to by the tester, it may be named incorrectly when it is not alone. The same phenomenon may occur for words when more than one word is present.

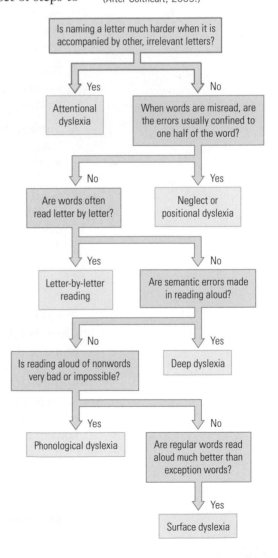

Figure **19.14**

Analyzing Acquired Dyslexia
(After Coltheart, 2005.)

2. **Neglect.** Persons displaying this impairment may misread the first half of a word (for example, reading "whether" as "smother") or they may misread the last part of a word (for example, reading "strong" as "stroke"). This positional syndrome has received little investigation.

3. **Letter-by-letter reading.** Affected persons read words only by spelling them out to themselves (aloud or silently). When the spelling is done silently, it can be detected by the additional time required for reading long words. Frequently, an affected person can write but then has difficulty reading what was written.

4. **Deep dyslexia.** The key symptoms of this disorder are semantic errors: persons with deep dyslexia read semantically related words in place of the word that they are trying to read (for instance, "tulip" as "crocus" and "merry" as "Christmas"). Nouns are easiest for them to read, followed by adjectives and then verbs. Function words present the greatest difficulty. Those who suffer from deep dyslexia also find it easier to read concrete words rather than abstract ones and are completely unable to read nonsense words. They are also generally impaired at writing and in short-term verbal memory (digit span).

5. **Phonological dyslexia.** The one symptom of phonological dyslexia is an inability to read nonwords aloud; otherwise reading may be nearly flawless.

6. **Surface dyslexia.** The surface dyslexic cannot recognize words directly but can understand them by using letter-to-sound relations; that is, the word can be understood if it is sounded out. This reading procedure works well as long as the words are regular ones ("home," "dome"), but not if the words are irregular ("come" will be read as "comb"). Spelling is also impaired but is phonetically correct. Surface dyslexia does not develop in languages that are totally phonetic (such as Italian). Surface dyslexia is a common symptom of children who have difficulty in learning to read.

Modeling Speech from Print

Central to the model-building idea of reading is the **dual-route theory**, which proposes that reading written language is accomplished by using two distinct but interactive procedures, the lexical and nonlexical routes. Reading by the lexical route relies on the activation of orthographic (picture) or phonological (sound) representations of a whole word. The lexical route can process all familiar words, both regular and irregular, but it fails with unfamiliar words or nonwords because it lacks a representation for them.

In contrast with the whole-word retrieval procedure used by the lexical route, the nonlexical route uses a subword procedure based on sound-spelling rules. The nonlexical route can succeed with nonwords (for example, klant) and regular words that obey letter-sound rules, but it cannot succeed with irregular words that do not obey these rules (for example, winding, choir).

The application of the dual-route theory is that normal readers compute sense and sound in parallel, whereas, in the dyslexic reader, one process or the other may be absent. In deep dyslexia, a subject is unable to process for sound and reads for sense. The subject may misread the word "bird" as "butterfly," both words referring to flying animals. In surface dyslexia, a subject is able to process for sound but not for sense. The subject might pronounce English words correctly and even read fluently but still not realize what he or she is saying. Stephen Rapcsak and his colleagues propose that the dual-route theory is effective in diagnosing both developmental and acquired dyslexia.

A model illustrating the dual-route theory is illustrated in **Figure 19.15**. Note that there are quite separate ways of obtaining speech from print and a still different way of producing letter names. The important feature of the dual-route approach is that it does not depend on function–anatomy relations, it can be applied to language disorders other than dyslexia, and it can lead to hypotheses concerning the anatomical organization of language.

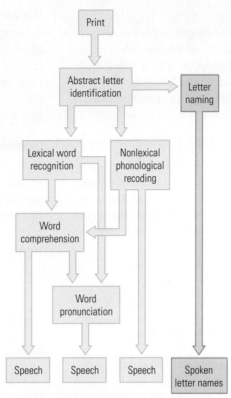

Figure 19.15

A Dual-Route Model
Note that speech from print can follow a number of different routes and can be independent of comprehension or pronunciation. (After Coltheart, 2005.)

Summary

What Is Language?
Language is a unique human ability that extends the development of multiple sensory channels. It gives us a way to organize sensory inputs by assigning tags to information, which allows us to categorize objects and, ultimately, concepts, and to speak to ourselves about our past and future. Language also includes the unique motor act of producing syllables, as well as the ability to impose grammatical rules, which dramatically increases the functional capacity of the system.

Origins of Language
The evolution of language does not represent the development of a single ability but rather the parallel development of multimodal processes. New investigations of language origins are directed toward understanding the component skills necessary for language and the genes that contribute to language-like processes in different animal species.

The Localization of Language
The various language functions take up a large part of the cortex. Some functions, such as the generation of verbs versus nouns or the understanding of visual versus auditory information, are found in precise locations. Like other cerebral functions, language seems to be organized in a series of parallel hierarchical channels that are best described as neural webs.

Disorders of Language

Traditional classifications of language disorders characterize fluent disorders, in which speech can be expressed, nonfluent disorders, in which speaking is impaired, and pure disorders, which may be quite selective. Various combinations of fluent and nonfluent types are identified, depending on the disorder.

The Localization of Lesions in Aphasia

The Wernicke–Geschwind model of left-hemisphere function still provides a simple approach to understanding deficits in speech production, but contributions of subcortical structures and the right hemisphere to language show that it is widely distributed in the brain.

The Assessment of Aphasia

A large number of assessment tools have been developed to describe language disorders. They include tests of perceptual disorders, disorders of comprehension, and disorders of speech production. The complexities of language are such that it remains difficult to group every disorder with any one assessment tool.

Developmental Langauge Disorders

Reading lends itself to analysis with the use of a model-building approach. The dual-route theory proposes that reading can be accomplished in two ways: by either (1) a lexical route in which words are recognized as wholes or (2) a nonlexical approach in which words are recognized by using letter-sound rules.

References

Beeke, S., J. Maxim, and R. Wilkinson. Using conversation analysis to assess and treat people with aphasia. *Seminars in Speech Language* 28(2):136–147, 2007.

Benson, D. F. Aphasia and lateralization of language. *Cortex* 22:71–86, 1986.

Benson, D. F. Aphasia. In K. M. Heilman and E. Valenstein, Eds. *Clinical Neuropsychology*, 3rd ed. New York: Oxford University Press, 1993.

Binder, J. R., J. A. Frost, T. A. Hammeke, R. W. Cox, S. M. Rao, and T. Prieto. Human brain language areas identified by functional magnetic resonance imaging. *Journal of Neuroscience* 17:353–362, 1997.

Caplan, D. *Language: Structure, Processing, and Disorders.* Cambridge, Mass.: MIT Press, 1992.

Caplan, D., and J. C. Marshall. Generative grammar and aphasic disorders: A theory of language representation in the human brain. *Foundations of Language* 12:583–596, 1976.

Chomsky, N. On the biological basis of language capabilities. In R. W. Rieber, Ed. *Neuropsychology of Language.* New York: Plenum, 1976.

Coltheart, M. Modelling reading: The dual-route approach. In M. J. Snowling and C. Hulme, Eds. *The Science of Reading: A Handbook.* Malden, Mass.: Blackwell, 2005, pp. 6–23.

Cooper, I. S., I. Amin, R. Chandra, and J. M. Waltz. A surgical investigation of the clinical physiology of the LP-pulvinar complex in man. *Journal of Neurological Science* 18:89–100, 1973.

Damasio, H., T. J. Grabowski, D. Tranel, R. D. Hichwa, and A. R. Damasio. A neural basis for lexical retrieval. *Nature* 380:499–505 1996.

Demonet, J. F., R. Wise, and R. S. J. Frackowiak. Language functions explored in normal subjects by positron emission tomography: A critical review. *Human Brain Mapping* 1:39–47, 1993.

de Renzi, E., and L. A. Vignolo. The Token Test: A sensitive test to detect disturbances in aphasics. *Brain* 85:665–678, 1962.

Devlin, J. T., and K. E. Watkins. Stimulating language: Insights from TMS. *Brain* 130:610–622, 2007.

Dronkers, N. F., B. B. Redfern, and R. T. Knight. The neural architecture of language disorders. In M. S. Gazzaniga, Ed. *The New Cognitive Neurosciences.* Cambridge, Mass.: MIT Press, 1999, pp. 949–958.

Fisher, S. E., and G. F. Marcus. The eloquent ape: Genes, brains and the evolution of language. *Nature Reviews Genetics* 7:9–20, 2006.

Fitch, W. T. The evolution of speech: A comparative review. *Trends in Cognitive Science* 4:258–267, 2000.

Gardner, R. A., and B. T. Gardner. Comparative psychology and language acquisition. *Annals of the New York Academy of Sciences* 309:37–76, 1978.

Geschwind, N. Language and the brain. *Scientific American* 226:76–83, 1972.

Goodall, J. *The Chimpanzees of Gombe.* Cambridge, Mass.: Harvard University Press, 1986.

Goodglass, H., and E. Kaplan. *The Assessment of Aphasia and Related Disorders.* Philadelphia: Lea & Febiger, 1972.

Green, E. Psycholinguistic approaches to aphasia. *Linguistics* 53:30–50, 1969.

Gustason, G., D. Pfetzing, and E. Zawoklow. *Signing Exact English.* Silver Spring, Md.: Modern Signs Press, 1975.

Halstead, W. C., and J. M. Wepman. The Halstead-Wepman aphasia screening test. *Journal of Speech and Hearing Disorders* 14:9–15, 1959.

Hewes, G. W. Language origin theories. In D. M. Rumbaugh, Ed. *Language Learning by a Chimpanzee*. New York: Academic Press, 1977.

Hinshelwood, J. *Congenital Word-Blindness*. London: H. K. Lewis, 1917.

Holloway, R. L. Human paleontological evidence relevant to language behavior. *Human Neurobiology* 2:105–114, 1983.

Jerison, H. J. *Brain Size and the Evolution of Mind*. New York: American Museum of Natural History, 1991.

Kellogg, W., and L. Kellogg. *The Ape and the Child*. New York: McGraw-Hill, 1933.

Kimura, D. Neural mechanisms in manual signing. *Sign Language Studies* 33:291–312, 1981.

Kimura, D. *Neuromotor Mechanisms in Human Communication*. Oxford: Oxford University Press, 1993.

Lieberman, P. *On the Origins of Language: An Introduction to the Evolution of Human Speech*. New York: Macmillan, 1975.

Luria, A. R., and J. T. Hutton. A modern assessment of basic forms of aphasia. *Brain and Language* 4:129–151, 1977.

MacNeilage, P. F. The frame/context theory of evolution of speech production. *Behavioral Brain Sciences* 21:499–511, 1998.

Marshack, A. *The Roots of Civilization: The Cognitive Beginnings of Man's First Art, Symbol, and Notation*. New York: McGraw-Hill, 1971.

Marshall, J. C. Biological constraints on orthographic representation. *Philosophical Transactions of the Royal Society of London* 298:165–172, 1982.

Marshall, J. C. The description and interpretation of aphasic language disorder. *Neuropsychologia* 24:5–24, 1986.

Martin, A., C. L. Wiggs, L. G. Ungerleider, and J. V. Haxby. Neural correlates of category-specific knowledge. *Nature* 379:649–652, 1996.

Mateer, C. Asymmetric effects of thalamic stimulation on rate of speech. *Neuropsychologia* 16:497–499, 1978.

Mazzocchi, R., and L. A. Vignolo. Localization of lesions in aphasia: Clinical–CT scan correlations in stroke patients. *Cortex* 15:627–654, 1979.

McNeill, D. *Gesture and Thought*. Chicago: University of Chicago Press, 2005.

Monrad-Krohn, H. The third element of speech: Prosody and its disorders. In L. Halpern, Ed. *Problems of Dynamic Neurology*. Jerusalem: Hebrew University Press, 1963.

Newman, A. J., D. Bavelier, D. Corina, P. Jezzard, and H. J. Neville. A critical period for right hemisphere recruitment in American Sign Language processing. *Nature Neuroscience* 5:76–80, 2002.

Ojemann, G. A. The neurobiology of language and verbal memory: Observations from awake neurosurgery. *International Journal of Psychophysiology* 48:141–146, 2003.

Penfield, W., and L. Roberts. *Speech and Brain Mechanisms*. Princeton, N.J.: Princeton University Press, 1959.

Petersen, S. E., P. T. Fox, M. I. Posner, M. Mintun, and M. E. Raichle. Positron emission tomographic studies of the processing of single words. *Journal of Cognitive Neuroscience* 1:153–170, 1988.

Pollick, A. S., and F. B. de Waal. Ape gestures and language evolution. *Proceedings of the National Academy of Sciences of the United States of America* 104:8184–8189, 2007.

Porch, B. E. *Index of Communicative Ability*. Palo Alto, Calif.: Consulting Psychologists Press, 1967.

Posner, M. I., and M. E. Raichle. Images of Mind. New York: Scientific American Library, 1994.

Premack, D. The codes of man and beasts. *Behavioral and Brain Sciences* 6:125–167, 1983.

Raichle, M. E., J. A. Fiez, T. O. Videen, A. K. Macleod, J. V. Pardo, P. T. Fox, and S. E. Petersen. Practice-related changes in human brain functional anatomy during non-motor learning. *Cerebral Cortex* 4:8–26, 1994.

Rapcsak, S. Z., M. L. Henry, S. L. Teague, S. D. Carnahan, and P. M. Beeson. Do dual-route models accurately predict reading and spelling performance in individuals with acquired alexia and agraphia? *Neuropsychologia* 45:2519–2524, 2007.

Ricklan, M., and I. S. Cooper. Psychometric studies of verbal functions following thalamic lesions in humans. *Brain and Language* 2:45–64, 1975.

Rowan, A., F. Vargha-Khadem, F. Calamante, J. D. Tournier, F. J. Kirkham, W. K. Chong, T. Baldeweg, A. Connelly, and D. G. Gadian. Cortical abnormalities and language function in young patients with basal ganglia stroke. *Neuroimage* 36:431–440, 2007.

Rumbaugh, D. M., and T. V. Gill. Lana's acquisition of language skills. In D. M. Rumbaugh, Ed. *Language Learning by a Chimpanzee*. New York: Academic Press, 1977.

Salmelin, R., and J. Kujala. Neural representation of language: Activation versus long-range connectivity. *Trends in Cognitive Sciences* 10:519–525, 2006.

Sarno, M. T. *The Functional Communication Profile: Manual of Directions*. New York: Institute of Rehabilitation Medicine, New York University Medical Center, 1969.

Savage-Rumbaugh, E. S., K. McDonald, R. A. Sevcik, W. D. Hopkins, and E. Rubert. Spontaneous symbol acquisition and communicative use by pygmy chimpanzees *(Pan paniscus)*. *Journal of Experimental Psychology: General* 115:211–235, 1986.

Schuell, H. *Differential Diagnosis of Aphasia with the Minnesota Test*. Minneapolis: University of Minnesota Press, 1965.

Spreen, O., and A. L. Benton. *Neurosensory Center Comprehensive Examination for Aphasia*. Victoria, Canada: University of Victoria, 1969.

Swadish, M. *The Origin and Diversification of Language*, J. Sherzer, Ed. Chicago: Aldine-Atherton, 1971.

Taglialatela, J. P., S. Savage-Rumbaugh, and L. A. Baker. Vocal production by a language-compentent *Pan paniscus*. *International Journal of Primatology* 24:1–17, 2003.

Terrace, H. S. *Nim.* New York: Knopf, 1979.

von Glaserfeld, E. The Yerkish language and its automatic parser. In D. M. Rumbaugh, Ed. *Language Learning by a Chimpanzee.* New York: Academic Press, 1977.

Vouloumanos, A., and J. F. Werker. Listening to language at birth: Evidence for a bias for speech in neonates. *Developmental Science* 10:159–164, 2007.

Wagner, A. D., E. J. Paré-Blagoev, J. Clark, and R. A. Poldrack. Recovering meaning: Left prefrontal cortex guides controlled semantic retrieval. *Neuron* 31:329–338, 2001.

Wallman, J. *Aping Language.* Cambridge, U.K.: Cambridge University Press, 1992.

Wepman, J. M., and L. V. Jones. *Studies in Aphasia: An Approach to Testing.* Chicago: University of Chicago Education-Industry Service, 1961.

Whitaker, H. A. *On the Representation of Language in the Human Brain.* Edmonton, Canada: Linguistic Research, 1971.

Yip, M. J. The search for phonology in other species. *Trends in Cognitive Sciences* 10:442–446, 2006.

Zaidel, E. Language in the right hemisphere. In D. F. Benson and E. Zaidel, Eds. *The Dual Brain.* New York: Guilford Press, 1985.

Zangwill, O. L. Excision of Broca's area without persistent aphasia. In K. J. Zulch, O. Creutzfeldt, and G. C. Galbraith, Eds. *Cerebral Localization.* Berlin and New York: Springer, 1975.

Emotion 20

P O R T R A I T : Agenesis of the Frontal Lobe

The year was 1912. After a difficult labor of 22 hours, a baby boy was born. J.P. weighed 11.5 pounds, but dropped to 5 pounds after postpartum complications. S. S. Ackerly reports that J.P. appeared to recover from his early trauma and, by age 1, was walking and talking with apparently normal intelligence. But he was a problem child. He was hyperactive and showed no emotion but anger, which he expressed in temper tantrums.

As J.P. grew to school age, he began to wander away. Police would find him miles from home but, evidently, he never showed any fear of being lost. Even severe whippings did not deter him. School was a real problem. Although he was extremely well mannered most of the time, J.P. unexpectedly engaged in inappropriate behaviors such as exposing himself and masturbating in the classroom.

Visuals Unlimited/Corbis

Growing up, he developed no close friendships and was generally disliked. The community blamed his parents for much of the boy's problems, but nothing they did was helpful. As an adolescent, J.P. pawned his mother's rings, stole his uncle's car, and drove to Chicago from Kentucky to spend the money. At 19, when his criminal record for theft began to mount, a psychiatrist began to investigate the nature of his behavioral problems, eventually

finding that J.P.'s right frontal lobe was missing and his left was only 50% of normal size. It was the 1930s, and few treatment options existed.

As an adult, J.P. could not hold down a job for more than a few weeks, largely because of his erratic behavior. At one moment, he was charming and, at the next, was reacting out of all proportion to some seemingly trivial matter. Even by age 50, J.P.'s behavior had not changed: he remained hyperactive and alone, largely detached from anything that gives meaning to life, such as love or friendship. He had virtually no social feelings at all and, evidently, was unable to understand what such feelings would be like or to react to emotions in others.

Absent frontal lobes, J.P. had no social skills and showed very little emotion, except in the form of temper tantrums.

E motion, like memory, entails cognitive processes that may either be conscious or lie outside our awareness. We begin this chapter by exploring the nature of emotion and how neuroscientists have studied emotion and developed theories over the past century. Then, we consider contemporary neuropsychological theories of emotion and reported asymmetries in how the brain produces, interprets, and reacts to emotion. Throughout the chapter, we describe how researchers are applying noninvasive imaging techniques to investigate how emotion contributes to social behavior. We end the chapter by detailing how emotion contributes to our sense of self.

The Nature of Emotion

J.P.'s behavior, described in the Portrait, was extreme and certainly not common. More typical is the observation that seemingly minor brain injury can change a person's personality. To neuropsychologists, impairments of movement, perception, language, or memory affect not only how a person expresses and reacts to emotion but also how others perceive that person's emotions. Not so evident to observers, however, is a subject's or patient's feeling of emotion.

Indeed, some view emotion as an inconvenient remnant of our evolutionary past, a nonconscious time when humans literally were driven by "instincts" such as emotion. They believe that humans are fundamentally rational creatures, but emotion is older than thought. People such as J.P., with blunted or lost emotions, may behave in a completely rational manner most of the time but, when making personal and social decisions, they act irrationally.

Antonio Damasio emphasizes that emotion is a cognitive process that actually contributes to logical thinking. He argues that the mechanisms of reasoning are influenced significantly by both unconscious and conscious signals that come from the neural machinery underlying emotion. Note the contrast between neuropsychologists' use of the word "unconscious" as a synonym for nonconscious brain activity and Freud's use as a hidden or repressed component of the mind. Neuropsychologists use unconscious as shorthand for Hermann von Helmholtz's notion of **unconscious inference**, processes outside of awareness and learned by experience, whereby observers use knowledge to perceive.

Feeling Emotion

What is the last strong emotion you felt? Perhaps you had a serious disagreement with a close friend or received some unexpected, wonderful news. An emotion cannot be described as a unitary event, because emotional processes differ in multiple ways from one another and from other cognitive processes.

An emotional experience may include all sorts of thoughts or plans about who said or did what or what will be done in the future. Your heart may pound, your throat tighten; you may sweat, tremble, or flush. Strong emotional feelings (rage or elation) are not always verbalized. Marked changes in facial expression, tone of voice, or body posture—even tears of sadness or joy—are sufficient to convey emotion to others.

These emotional signals are very powerful and little influenced by experience. Paul Ekman, for example, has documented that basic emotional expressions of anger, fear, disgust, surprise, happiness, and sadness are universally recognized by people throughout the world (**Figure 20.1**). In this context, that J.P. did not recognize such expressions is all the more curious.

Figure 20.1

Universality of Emotion Paul Ekman and his colleagues showed these photographs to people in societies throughout the world—ranging from hunting-and-gathering tribes to postindustrial enclaves—and found that humans of all cultures, regardless of experience, recognize facial expressions of basic emotions. (Courtesy of Dr. Paul Ekman, from P. Ekman and W. V. Friesen, 1984.)

What Is Emotion?

Neuropsychologists view emotion not as a thing but rather as an inferred behavioral state called **affect**, a conscious, subjective feeling about a stimulus independent of where or what it is. Affective behavior is internal and subjective. As observers, we can infer emotion in others only from their behavior (what they say and do) and by measuring physiological changes associated with emotional processes.

Emotion has many components, and each, in principle, can be quantified as well as observed. A contemporary theory of emotion must include at least four principal behavioral components:

1. **Physiology.** Physiological components include central and autonomic nervous system activity and the resulting changes in neurohormonal and visceral activity. Emotion produces changes in heart rate, blood pressure, the distribution of blood flow, perspiration, and the digestive system, among others, as well as the release of hormones that may affect the brain or the ANS. Although the topic of some debate, at least some emotional states (for example, happiness versus sadness) can likely be differentiated by their associated physiological changes.

2. **Distinctive motor behavior.** Facial expression, tone of voice, and posture express emotional states. These motor behaviors are especially important to observing emotions, because they convey overt action that can differ from observed verbal behavior. Our perception of a person who says that she is fine but is sobbing uncontrollably is different from our perception of the same person when smiling.

3. **Self-reported cognition.** Cognitive processes are inferred from self-reported rankings. Cognition operates in the realm of both subjective emotional feelings (feeling love or hate, feeling loved or hated) and other cognitive processes (plans, memories, or ideas).

4. **Unconscious behavior.** This component incorporates unconscious inference—cognitive processes that influence behavior of which we are not aware. We may make decisions on the basis of "intuition" or a hunch or on other apparently unfounded bases. Recall from Chapter 16, for example, the gambling task in which normal subjects gradually changed their behavior to optimize the outcome but seemed unconscious of why they had chosen to play certain decks of cards over others to win the game. (In contrast, frontal-lobe patients behaved irrationally: they failed to choose these decks, lost all their play money, and had to "borrow" more to continue the experiment.)

The theoretical distinction among physiology, movement, self-reports, and unconscious action as component behaviors of emotional experience is significant, because researchers detect little correlation among the physical states of emotion when all of them are measured in the same subjects. A brief review of a century's research on emotion will set the stage for exploring the anatomy of emotion and discussing contemporary theories in depth.

Historical Views

Interest in the biology of emotion dates to Darwin's book titled *The Expression of the Emotions in Man and Animals*, published in 1872. Darwin believed that, because emotional behavior is determined by evolution, human emotional expression could be understood only in the context of expression in other animals. Although Darwin's book was a bestseller in its time, its influence was short-lived and it was temporarily forgotten.

Investigating the Anatomy of Emotion

Psychologists began to speculate about emotions at the turn of the twentieth century, but they had little knowledge about the neural basis of emotional behavior. By the late 1920s, physiologists began to examine the relation between autonomic, endocrine, and neurohumoral factors and inferred emotional states, with particular emphasis on measuring indices such as heart rate, blood pressure, and skin temperature (see reviews by Dunbar and by Brady).

Philip Bard made one of the first major anatomical discoveries about emotion while working in Walter Cannon's laboratory in the late 1920s. Friedrich Goltz's studies in the 1890s had shown that decorticated dogs could show strong "rage" responses to seemingly trivial stimuli: the dogs behaved as though a seriously threatening stimulus confronted them (recall J.P.'s behavior). Working with cats, Bard showed that this response depended on the diencephalon, which includes the thalamus and hypothalamus. He found that, if the diencephalon was intact, animals showed strong "emotional" responses, but, if the animals were decerebrate (see Figure 10.2), leaving the diencephalon disconnected from the midbrain, they were unemotional.

The results of later studies by many investigators (especially Eckhard Hess in the 1940s and John Flynn in the 1960s) show that stimulating different regions of the hypothalamus elicits different "affective responses" in cats. Behaviors associated with attacking another cat (piloerection, hissing, baring of teeth) or attacking a prey animal (crouching, whiskers and ears forward, pouncing)—including eating the animal—can result.

The lesion and stimulation studies on the diencephalon were important, because they led to the idea that the thalamus and hypothalamus contain the neural circuits for the overt expression of emotion and for autonomic responses such as changes in blood pressure, heart rate, and respiration. The cortex was envisioned as inhibiting the thalamus and hypothalamus. Conversely, the thalamus was seen as activating the cortex during autonomic arousal, presumably to help direct the emotion to the appropriate stimulus.

The Emotional Brain

James Papez proposed the first major theory in the neurology of emotion in 1937. The structure of the "limbic lobe" (see Figure 3.20) forms the anatomical basis of emotion, Papez reasoned, and the limbic structures act on the hypothalamus to produce emotional states. Although, for Papez, the neocortex played no part in producing emotional behavior, he did believe the cortex to be necessary for transforming events produced by limbic structures into our experience of emotion.

The Papez theory had appeal: it combined behavioral phenomena having no known neurological substrates with anatomical structures having no known function. The idea of an emotional brain gained instant broad approval because Freudian thinking predominated in the 1930s. That an ancient, deep part of the central nervous system controls emotions and instincts in Freud's unconscious, with the neocortex producing consciousness, was a concept with natural appeal for the psychology of the time.

Cortical Connections of Emotion

Two contributions in the 1930s shed light on the nature of the cortical structures and connections implicated in emotion. In both cases, investigators were studying something other than emotion and made serendipitous findings that fundamentally changed our thinking about the emotional brain.

Klüver–Bucy Syndrome

A major finding came in 1939, when Heinrich Klüver and Paul Bucy announced the rediscovery of an extraordinary behavioral syndrome that had first been noted by Sanger Brown and Edward Schaefer in 1888. The *Klüver–Bucy syndrome* has been subsequently observed in people with a variety of neurological diseases. An obvious aspect of this extraordinary set of behaviors is lack of affect. For example, animals displaying Klüver–Bucy syndrome show no fear whatsoever to threatening stimuli such as snakes or to "threat" signals from humans or other animals, situations in which normal animals show strong aversion.

The behavioral syndrome, resulting experimentally from bilateral anterior temporal lobectomy in monkeys, includes

- tameness and a loss of fear;

- indiscriminate dietary behavior, the monkeys being willing to eat many types of previously rejected foods;

- greatly increased autoerotic, homosexual, and heterosexual activity, with inappropriate object choice (for example, sexual mounting of chairs);

- hypermetamorphosis, a tendency to attend and react to every visual stimulus;

- a tendency to examine all objects by mouth; and

- visual agnosia.

Wendy Marlowe and colleagues reported on a patient with Klüver–Bucy symptoms that resulted from meningoencephalitis (inflammation of the brain and the meninges):

> Behavioral patterns were distinctly abnormal. He exhibited a flat affect, and, although originally restless, ultimately became remarkably placid. He appeared indifferent to people or situations. He spent much time gazing at the television, but never learned to turn it on; when the set was off, he tended to watch reflections of others in the room on the glass screen. On occasion he became facetious, smiling inappropriately and mimicking the gestures and actions of others. Once initiating an

imitative series, he would perseverate copying all movements made by another for extended periods of time. In addition, he commonly generated a series of idiosyncratic, stereotyped gestures employing primarily his two little fingers which he would raise and touch end-to-end in repetitive fashion.

He engaged in oral exploration of all objects within his grasp, appearing unable to gain information via tactile or visual means alone. All objects that he could lift were placed in his mouth and sucked or chewed. He was commonly observed to place his fingers in his mouth and suck them. He did not attempt to pick up objects directly with his mouth, using his hands for that purpose, but was observed to engage in much olfactory behavior. When dining he would eat with his fingers until reprimanded and a fork placed in his hand; he was thereafter able to imitate use of a fork, but failed to remaster the task of eating with utensils spontaneously. He would eat one food item on his plate completely before turning to the next. Hyperbulimia [excessive, insatiable appetite] was prominent; he ingested virtually everything within reach, including the plastic wrapper from bread, cleaning pastes, ink, dog food, and feces. Although his tastes were clearly indiscriminate, he seemed to prefer liquids or soft solids.

The patient's sexual behavior was a particular source of concern while in hospital. Although vigorously heterosexual prior to his illness, he was observed in hospital to make advances toward other male patients by stroking their legs and inviting fellatio by gesture; at times he attempted to kiss them. Although on a sexually mixed floor during a portion of his recovery, he never made advances toward women, and, in fact, his apparent reversal of sexual polarity prompted his fiancee to sever their relationship. (Marlowe et. al., 1975, pp. 55–56)

The appearance of the Klüver–Bucy syndrome in humans and monkeys apparently requires that the amygdala and inferior temporal cortex be removed bilaterally. H.M., the amnesic patient featured in Chapter 18, does not exhibit the syndrome, despite bilateral removal of the medial temporal structures. Furthermore, monkeys with bilateral amygdalectomies do not show the Klüver–Bucy syndrome unless the temporal cortex also is removed. Finally, the single case of a man with a bilateral temporal lobectomy identical with the Klüver–Bucy removal showed all the Klüver–Bucy symptoms, with the exception of orality. Instead of placing novel objects in his mouth, he repeatedly inspected them visually.

Psychosurgery

At about the time of Klüver and Bucy's discovery, a less dramatic, but in many ways more important, discovery was made. Carlyle Jacobsen studied the behavior of chimpanzees in a variety of learning tasks subsequent to frontal-lobe removals. In 1935, he reported his findings on the effects of the lesions at the Second International Neurology Congress in London. He casually noted that one particularly neurotic

In this psychosurgical procedure, a transorbital leukotomy, the inferior frontal cortex is disconnected from the rest of the brain.

chimp appeared more relaxed after the surgery, leading a Portuguese neurologist, Egas Moniz, to propose that similar lesions in people might relieve various behavioral problems. Thus was born psychosurgery and the frontal lobotomy.

Unbelievably, frontal lobotomies were performed on humans without an empirical basis. Not until the late 1960s was any systematic research done on the effects of frontal-lobe lesions on the affective behavior of nonhuman animals. Experimental findings by several laboratories clearly confirm the results of frontal lobotomies on humans: frontal-lobe lesions in rats, cats, and monkeys have severe effects on social and affective behavior across the board.

Studies in Normal Subjects

Historically, studies in normal subjects have investigated laterality differences but, more recently, there has been an expansion to consider neural aspects of personality and related individual differences. This latter development has led to an emerging field of social cognitive neuroscience, which we shall return to at the end of the chapter.

Laterality studies look not only at the cognitive processes summarized in Chapter 11 but also at the lateralization of affective processes in normal subjects. The basic approach in these studies is to present stimuli to one hemisphere, by using dichotic (or tachistoscopic) techniques, to demonstrate a difference in the performance of the two hemispheres.

If one hemisphere were superior to the other at recognizing tone of voice or facial expression, for example, the superior hemisphere could be inferred to have a dominant role in emotion. We now survey laterality studies briefly, dividing them according to whether they investigate the production of affective behavior or its perception, and conclude by considering how personality differences might relate to brain structure.

The Production of Affective Behavior

The results of a series of studies by Ruth Campbell demonstrate that facial expressions are not always symmetrical but rather tend predominantly to the left side of the face. Asymmetries may range from the hardly noticeable—such as the flicker of a smile on the left side of Mona Lisa's face (on the right in the painting)—to the pronounced—such as a raised eyebrow, wink, or lopsided smile on the left side of the face. In one study, Morris Moscovitch and Janet Olds surreptitiously recorded the facial expressions of people in restaurants, finding a left-side preponderance. They confirmed this observation by carefully analyzing video recordings of people recounting sad and humorous stories, again finding a left-side bias in facial expressions.

Asymmetrical facial expressions show right-hemisphere specialization in producing emotion consistent with its presumed specialization in perceiving facial expressions (see Figure 11.8). It is tempting to speculate that right-hemisphere specialization in producing and interpreting nonverbal behavior is analogous to left-hemisphere specialization in producing and interpreting language, but it has yet to be proved. We caution that the apparent specialization of the right hemisphere in the perception of faces could easily be interpreted as a specialization for the perception of complex visual stimuli, of which faces are an example.

The Perception of Relevant Stimuli

To date, studies of the perception of emotionally loaded stimuli by normal subjects have examined only vision and audition. For both modalities, the stimulus is usually presented to one hemisphere selectively, either alone or in competition with information presented simultaneously to the opposite hemisphere.

Vision

Two procedures are used for the visual presentation. In one of them, faces with different expressions (for example, sad and happy) are presented tachistoscopically to the left or right visual field, and the subject is asked to identify the facial expression. The results show the left visual field to be superior at correct identification, which can be interpreted as demonstrating a right-hemisphere specialization for perceiving facial expression, an important aspect of nonverbal communication.

The second procedure employs an ingenious technique devised by Stuart Dimond (see also a more recent study by Wittling and Roschmann). By using special contact lenses, Dimond and his colleagues were able to project several types of films selectively to the left or right hemisphere. Subjects rated each film on a scale of 1 to 9 on four emotional dimensions—humorous, pleasant, horrific, or unpleasant.

Films presented to the right hemisphere were judged more unpleasant and horrific and produced greater ANS activation (as measured by heart rate) than did these same films presented to the left hemispheres of other subjects. Dimond and his colleagues concluded that the two hemispheres hold an essentially different emotional view of the world. Curiously, if the films were shown to both hemispheres simultaneously, the ratings closely resembled those of the right visual field (the left hemisphere), suggesting that left-hemisphere perception is dominant.

Audition

Studies of asymmetries in the auditory perception of emotions generally employ a dichotic-listening technique, which generally shows a left-ear superiority for emotion-laden sounds such as laughing or crying. A compelling experiment employed as stimuli a number of short sentences spoken in happy, sad, angry, and neutral voices (Ley and Bryden, 1982). These sentences were dichotically paired with neutral sentences of similar semantic content.

Subjects were instructed to attend to one ear and to report the emotional tone of the target sentence and indicate its content by checking off items on a multiple-choice recognition sheet. Virtually every subject showed a left-ear advantage for identifying the emotional tone of the voice and, at the same time, a right-ear advantage for identifying content. This result is analogous to that obtained by Dimond and his colleagues, who found that the two hemispheres deal with visual material in a similar manner: left eye for emotional tone and right eye for content.

Personality Differences and Brain Structure

Many personality traits or emotional behaviors characteristic of brain-damaged patients can be observed in people without known brain injury. This observation leads us to speculate that differences in cerebral organization, whether genetically or environmentally derived, form the basis of different human personalities. For example, one could hypothesize that people who are hypercritical may have relatively smaller or less-active temporal lobes than those who are not hypercritical. Or that people without much facial expression have smaller or less-active frontal lobes than normal.

Studies using noninvasive imaging have begun to show that individual differences in personality traits are correlated with individual differences in brain activation in specific brain regions. One of the best examples comes from a series of studies by Turhan Canli and his colleagues examining the neural basis of extraversion and neuroticism, two personality traits linked to both emotion and health. Personality tests can be used to identify the degree of extraversion versus introversion as well as the degree of neuroticism, a trait related to anxiety and mood.

In one study, subjects were shown emotionally positive or negative material. In response to positive stimuli, extroverts showed higher activity in the anterior cingulate cortex than did introverts. In a second study by Brian Haas, Canli, and their colleagues, the subjects were shown stimuli designed to elicit emotional conflict. When subjects viewed material containing high emotional conflict, those scoring higher in neuroticism showed higher activation in the amygdala and anterior cingulate cortex (**Figure 20.2**).

These types of data are sources of insight into the stable differences between extraverts and introverts and the manner in which mood can affect our perception of emotional stimuli. The results suggest that personality traits are indeed associated with activity in distinct cerebral regions. We return to this possibility at the end of the chapter.

Figure **20.2**

Neuroticism and Brain Activity
Changes in anterior cingulate activation in response to emotional conflict correlate positively with neuroticism. The investigators overlaid areas of significant activation, shown in red, on a template brain. EI = emotionally incongruent; EC = emotionally congruent. (Haas et al., 2007, p. 253.)

Candidate Structures in Emotional Behavior

A consistent principle of neural organization is that multiple systems control virtually every behavior. Sensory information enters the cortex through multiple, distinctly different sensory channels. When stimuli have been processed, information travels through multiple parallel systems subserving different functions.

Processing Emotional Stimuli

Visual information from the occipital lobe follows a ventral route through the temporal lobe to play a role in object recognition and a dorsal route through the parietal lobe to play a role in the control of movement. In keeping with this general principle of brain organization, we can speculate that multiple systems, both cortical and subcortical, contribute to the experience of an emotion.

Neural systems must process sensory stimuli as being significant to social behavior. Presumably, sensations are species specific for olfactory (pheromones), tactile (especially to sensitive body zones), visual (facial expressions), and auditory (phonemes, crying, screaming, and so forth) stimuli. Arguably, these socially significant stimuli are processed by the same systems that analyze other sensory inputs, but at least some sensory systems may be separate. Olfaction in cats provides a good example.

In many mammals, a receptor organ (Jacobson's organ) is specialized to analyze species-typical odors. When animals such as cats encounter certain odors (especially urine from other cats), they close their nostrils and appear to stare off into space with an odd look on their faces, a behavior known as *flehmen* (**Figure 20.3**). Actually, the cats are forcing the air through the roof of the mouth and into a special duct that is connected to the accessory olfactory system, allowing the air access to Jacobson's organ. (The accessory olfactory system functions to analyze species-specific odors and has direct connections to the hypothalamus and amygdala.)

Virtually the only odors that produce flehmen in cats are from other cats, including urine and ear wax but not feces. This neural system is thus specialized for species-typical odors. (Curiously, we have found that human urine also is often effective.) An interesting property is that the system shows habituation (repeated exposure to the same urine reduces the likelihood of flehmen), and cats appear able to remember the odors of familiar cats. Thus, they do not show flehmen to their own urine or to that of cats with which they live. Urine from novel cats will produce prolonged episodes of flehmen, and urine from familiar, but not co-resident, cats will produce shorter episodes.

Although little evidence points to such specialized systems for other senses, there is more evidence of specialized processing for emotionally relevant sensory information. Cells in the temporal lobes of monkeys are specially tuned for species-typical calls and are relatively insensitive to other sounds. Recall, too, the temporal cortical cells that are specialized for faces (see Chapter 15).

Higher-level systems possibly process other aspects of sensory information, including the internal generation of feelings. In addition to multiple systems that may encode specific species-typical information, a general cortical system may identify affective attributes of external stimuli. An interesting experiment by Michael Gazzaniga and Joseph LeDoux illustrates such a system. They presented split-brain subjects with visual information to one or the other visual field. A subject's task was to describe the stimulus verbally and to give it a rating on a five-point scale from "dislike very much" to "like very much."

The results are striking. As expected, only the items in the right visual field (and therefore sent to the left, speaking, hemisphere) were described accurately. In contrast, the five-point rating was identical for stimuli in each visual field. Clearly, the pathways that process the affective significance of the stimuli are distinct from the pathways that process their objective properties.

This distinction is reminiscent of the difference between knowing what a stimulus is and knowing where it is, as illustrated by blindsight (see Chapter 13). There may be a third system that processes affect. We have all recognized an odor, sound, or other physical stimulus, even though we cannot

Figure 20.3

Flehmen A cat sniffs a urine-soaked cotton ball (left), begins the gape response of the flehmen (middle), and follows with the full gape response (right). This behavior is mediated by the accessory olfactory system.

identify it at the moment. We may say that we have a "feeling" or "intuition" about the stimulus.

The effect is often true of sounds that may elicit a certain feeling because of the context in which we hear them normally. For example, music that is associated with being at some place or with some person may elicit emotional feelings when heard in another context, such as an elevator. We may not realize why we are suddenly melancholy or unusually happy. Recall from Chapter 18 that emotional memories are generally unconscious.

Brain Circuits for Emotion

Recall that, in the early 1930s, when the psychiatrist was beginning to study J.P., the limbic lobe (including the amygdala) and prefrontal cortex were identified as brain regions implicated in emotion. Although the original limbic structures identified by Papez in the late 1930s focused on the hippocampus and its connections with the hypothalamus, modern views of the limbic system include the amygdala and prefrontal cortex. **Figure 20.4** shows the amygdala lying adjacent to the hippocampus in the temporal lobe, with the prefrontal cortex lying just anterior.

Figure 20.5A diagrams the contemporary notion of the extent of the limbic system, and Figure 20.5B schematically illustrates the limbic circuit. The hippocampus, amygdala, and prefrontal cortex all connect with the hypothalamus. The mammillary nucleus of the hypothalamus connects to the anterior thalamus, which in turn connects to the cingulate cortex. Connections from the cingulate cortex complete the circuit by connecting to the hippocampus, amygdala, and prefrontal cortex.

Although the entire circuit is important for emotional behavior, the amygdala and prefrontal cortex hold the key to understanding the nature of emotional

Figure 20.4

Emotional Circuitry The limbic lobe, which encircles the brainstem, consists of the cingulate gyrus and hippocampal formation, the amygdala, the mammillothalamic tract, and the anterior thalamus.

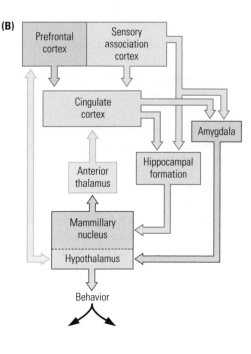

Figure 20.5

Contemporary View of the Limbic System (A) An interconnected network of structures including the cortex, thalamus, hypothalamus, hippocampal formation, and amygdala forms the basis of emotional experience. (B) In a schematic representation of the major connections in the limbic circuit, the prefrontal and sensory regions connect with the cingulate cortex, hippocampal formation, and amygdala. The last two structures connect with different regions in the hypothalamus, which in turn connects with the cingulate cortex through the thalamus.

experience. We considered the anatomy of the prefrontal cortex in detail in Chapter 16, and so we will briefly examine only the amygdala here.

From the Greek, meaning "almond," the amygdala is formed by three principal subdivisions—the corticomedial, basolateral, and central areas. Like the prefrontal cortex, the amygdala receives inputs from all sensory systems; to be excited, the cells of the amygdala, like those of the prefrontal cortex, require complex stimuli (such as faces). Many cells in the amygdala are multimodal; in fact, some respond to visual, auditory, somatic, gustatory, *and* olfactory stimuli, just as prefrontal cells do. The amygdala can therefore create a complex image of the sensory world, and we shall see later that this image is especially sensitive to stimuli that might be threatening or dangerous.

Frontal Lesions in Monkeys

Spouses or relatives often complain of personality changes in brain-damaged patients, but the parameters of these changes have been poorly specified in human subjects. Even the behavioral changes in people such as Phineas Gage (see Chapter 16) are described in general, subjective terms and seldom reported objectively. The results of research on animals, particularly nonhuman primates, make possible the identification of six behavioral changes associated with emotional processes after frontal lesions.

1. **Reduced social interaction.** Especially after orbitofrontal and anterior cingulate lesions, monkeys become socially withdrawn and even fail to reestablish close preoperative relations with family members. The animals sit alone; seldom if ever engage in social grooming or contact with other monkeys; and, in a free-ranging natural environment, become solitary, leaving the troop altogether.

2. **Loss of social dominance.** As reported in Chapter 16, after orbitofrontal lesions, monkeys that were formerly dominant in a group do not maintain their dominance, although the fall from power may take weeks to complete, depending on the aggressiveness of other monkeys in the group.

3. **Inappropriate social interaction.** Monkeys with orbitofrontal lesions fail to exhibit the appropriate gestures of submission to dominant animals and may approach any other animal without hesitation, irrespective of that animal's social dominance. This behavior often results in retaliatory aggression from the dominant, intact animals. Similarly, when approached by dominant animals, monkeys with frontal lesions may simply ignore them or run away rather than performing normal submissive gestures such as allowing mounting.

4. **Altered social preference.** When a normal monkey is released into a large enclosure that has conspecifics behind a glass barrier, it will generally sit against the glass next to an animal sitting on the opposite side. Although normal animals prefer to sit beside intact monkeys of the opposite sex, monkeys with large frontal lesions prefer to sit with other frontal-lesion monkeys of the same sex, presumably because they are less threatening.

5. **Reduced affect.** Monkeys with frontal lesions largely abandon facial expressions, posturings, and gesturings in social situations. (Lesions of the

cingulate or visual association cortex seem to have no effect.) Thus, monkeys with frontal lesions show a drastic drop in the frequency and variability of facial expressions and are described as "poker faced." This loss of facial expression is not a simple loss of muscle control of the face, because the animals do produce expressions, but not often.

6. **Reduced vocalization.** Lesions of the frontal cortex reduce spontaneous social vocalizations. Indeed, after anterior cingulate lesions, rhesus monkeys effectively make no normal vocalizations at all.

In general then, lesions of the monkey orbitofrontal cortex produce marked changes in social behavior. In particular, lesion monkeys become less socially responsive and fail to produce or respond to species-typical stimuli. Damage to the paralimbic cortex produces milder effects, the animals showing a reduction in social interaction. An important point is that, despite the significant changes in the sensory processing abilities of animals with visual association lesions, there appear to be very few obvious changes in their affective behavior.

The changes in emotional processes in monkeys with frontal lesions are especially intriguing, because they suggest that similar changes might be found in humans with frontal-lobe injuries. In particular, because monkeys fail to make appropriate vocal and gestural behaviors and fail to respond normally to those made by conspecifics, we can predict that humans with frontal-lobe injuries or abnormalities, such as those endured by J.P., will show similar changes in social behavior. Furthermore, disorders such as schizophrenia, which are characterized by significant changes in social interactions, also might be due to frontal dysfunction.

Premorbid Emotional Processes

The personality of a brain-injured patient at least partly depends on his or her premorbid (preinjury) state. A person who is depressive before the injury is likely to be depressive afterward; a person who is cheerful is likely to remain so. There has been no systematic study of this phenomenon, but, in our experience, there is far more intersubject variability in the emotional behavior of brain-damaged people than is revealed in most tests of their cognitive function.

A study on the social behavior of squirrel monkeys with frontal lesions is relevant here (Peters and Ploog, 1976). Although the researchers found many of the changes in social behavior previously observed by others, they also noted that some monkeys seemed less changed by their lesions. Two dominant monkeys received similar orbitofrontal lesions but, whereas one of them completely lost his dominant position, the other remained dominant but did not exert the dominance strongly. In a different social group, the second monkey might have been challenged and lost this position. Differences in the premorbid behavior of the lesioned monkeys, as well as in the group structure, appear to contribute to the change in social behavior after lesioning.

In contrast, when monkeys with frontal lesions are given neuropsychological learning tests, such as delayed-response tests, all animals typically show a much more similar behavioral change. This result is important because it is probably true of humans as well: the effects of brain damage on processes such as language and memory are more consistent than the effects on emotion. Stated differently, the premorbid personalities of human patients with cortical injuries are likely to influence the extent of postinjury changes in emotional processes. This possibility has been completely neglected in research to date and adds a major complication as we try to make generalizations about emotional processes.

The relation between premorbid behavior and the effects of cerebral injury leads to the logical idea that there must be some difference in the details of brain organization in response to social experience. A promising finding is that the density of serotonin receptors in the orbitofrontal cortex of a monkey correlates with the animal's social status. In fact, in one study, a pharmacological increase in serotonin receptors was shown to alter social behavior and increases social status (Raleigh et al., 1991). This result may offer some explanation for how drugs that selectively block serotonin reuptake (for example, Prozac; see Figure 7.10) can alter social behavior in humans (see review by Panksepp et al. for more on this idea).

Figure 20.6

Losing Emotion Spinal injury reduces the experience of emotion. The extent of emotional loss is greatest when the lesion is high on the spinal cord. (After *Principles of Behavioral Neuroscience*, by J. Beatty. Dubuque, Iowa: Brown & Benchmark, 1995, p. 339.)

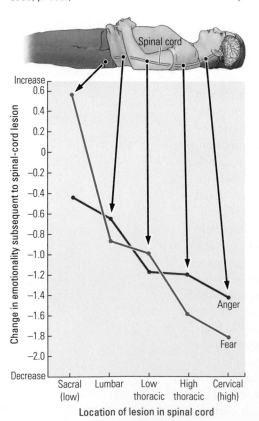

Neuropsychological Theories of Emotion

One theme runs through all modern theories of emotion: emotion and cognition are intimately related and likely entail overlapping neural systems. It therefore follows that changes in cognitive abilities will be related to changes in emotion and vice versa. (For a thorough review of theories of emotion, see Scherer.) Here, we outline three current theories that represent the major lines of thinking in cognitive neuroscience regarding emotion: Antonio Damasio's somatic marker hypothesis, Joseph LeDoux's cognitive–emotional interaction theory, and Guido Gainotti's lateralization theory. The reader is directed to books and reviews by these authors in the References at the end of this chapter.

Somatic Marker Hypothesis

The core of Damasio's somatic marker hypothesis—that when a person is confronted with a stimulus of biological importance, the brain and the body change as a result—comes from William James's ideas. In the late nineteenth century, James began to argue that an emotion consists of a change in body and brain states in response to the evaluation of a particular event. For example, if you encounter a poisonous snake as you walk along a path, your somatic markers, including heart rate, respiration, and sweating, increase. You interpret these physiological changes as fear.

A prediction that we could make here is that a reduction in the bodily reaction to a stimulus should reduce the intensity of emotions. **Figure 20.6** illustrates that people with spinal-cord injuries do indeed experience reduced emotionality, the loss being proportional to the level of injury.

Whereas James was really talking about intense emotions such as fear or anger, Damasio's theory encompasses a much broader range of bodily changes. For example, there may be a change in motor behavior, facial expression, autonomic arousal, or endocrine changes as well neuromodulatory changes in how the brain processes emotional information and other information. Hence, for Damasio, emotions engage those neural structures that represent body states and those structures that somehow link the perception of external stimuli to body states.

The somatic markers are thus linked to external events and influence cognitive processing. Damasio's theory uniquely specifies that the neural control of emotions includes both the brain structures that represent body states and the activity of neuromodulatory systems that link them and can produce global changes in neural processing, including, at the extremes, depression or mania.

A key aspect of Damasio's somatic marker hypothesis is that emotion is fundamental to the survival of the individual within a particular environment. The environment for mammals (certainly, for humans) includes not only the physical environment but also the social environment. Emotions therefore affect the survival of members of a social group.

The social aspect is of great importance in humans and includes the study of social development, social communication, and even culture. These topics have barely been addressed by neuroscientists, and virtually nothing is known about the neural underpinnings of social emotions such as jealousy, pride, and embarrassment. As the Snapshot on page 572 reveals, however, investigators are making strides in this area. Given that the frontal lobe has expanded so extensively in human evolution, social emotions probably require some form of frontal-lobe processing, but that they do so is conjecture at this point.

Finally, Damasio's theory emphasizes that emotion is not only a fundamental experience for all higher animals but also a necessary experience for us to make rationale decisions—especially in situations in which a person faces risk or conflict, as described in the Snapshot on page 572. People with reduced emotions, such as frontal-lobe patients, thus show impairments in personal or social matters, especially when they include the possibility of risk or conflict. The role of our emotions, especially subtle emotional states, is obviously not always conscious, and thus we may be unable to account for why we behave in certain ways.

Cognitive–Emotional Interactions

LeDoux's theory, like Damasio's, is evolutionary. The general idea is that emotions evolved to enhance the survival of animals and, as the brain evolved, cognitive and emotional processes grew more and more interrelated. In contrast with Damasio, LeDoux has not tried to account for all emotions but rather has chosen one emotion—namely, fear—as an exemplar of how to study brain–behavior relations in emotion.

In LeDoux's view, all animals inherently detect and respond to danger, and the related neural activities eventually evolve to produce a feeling—in this case, fear. When a mouse detects a cat, fear is obviously related to predation, and, in most situations, animals such as mice have fear related either to predation or to danger from other mice who may take exception to their presence in a particular place. For humans, however, fear is a much broader emotion that today is only rarely of predation but routinely includes stress—situations in which we must "defend" ourselves on short notice.

SNAPSHOT
Brain Activation in Social Cognition

Human decisions are strongly influenced by emotions. Take regret, for example, an emotion associated with a decision that turns out badly. Typically, regret embodies a feeling that some outcome would have been better if we had made a different decision. Regret is a common experience, and people try to anticipate and avoid it by making choices they believe have a higher probability of a positive outcome. Recent imaging and patient data point to a key role of the orbitofrontal cortex in mediating the experience of regret.

Nathalie Camille and her colleagues presented normal subjects and orbitofrontal patients with a gambling task in which subjects were asked to rate their emotional states after making a choice that led either to a $50 or 200 win or to a $50 or $200 loss. When normal subjects learned that the choice led to a $50 win but an alternative choice would have led to a $200 win, they experienced a strong negative emotion, whereas learning that the alternative would have led to a $200 loss produced a feeling of relief.

After several trials, the subjects began to make choices that optimized profitable outcomes, even if smaller than they might have been, largely to prevent the feeling of regret at losing. In contrast, orbitofrontal patients reported no regret and did not adjust their behavior to minimize losses. The absence of regret in the orbitofrontal patients suggests that they failed to grasp the concept of being responsible for one's own decisions—a concept that clearly biased the thinking of control subjects.

Georgio Coricelli and his colleagues used fMRI to investigate cerebral activity in control subjects when they participated in the gambling task. In the early stages of the task, the regret at choices was correlated with increased activity in the orbitorfrontal and anterior cingulate cortex and the medial temporal regions. As the subjects began to make choices that reduced the probability of regret, increased activity in the orbitofrontal cortex and amygdala preceded the choices, a result that suggests that the same neural system mediates both the experience and the anticipation of regret (see the adjoining figure).

IPL; DLPFC   DLPFC

Right OFC   Lateral OFC

Enhanced activity in the dorsolateral prefrontal cortex (DLPFC), parietal cortex (inferior parietal lobule, IPL), and right orbitofrontal cortex (OFC) was observed when subjects experienced regret. Activity in the lateral OFC (scan at lower right) was also found at the time of outcome evaluation during regret and disappointment, suggesting that the lateral orbitofrontal cortex might be responsible for the common process underlying the two emotions. (From G. Coricelli, R. J. Dolan, and A. Sirigu, 2007.)

These studies show that the orbitofrontal cortex contributes to optimizing our life choices. They also show that it is possible to begin to understand individual differences in traits such as regret because they may be related to individual differences in orbitofrontal activity.

Camille, N., G. Coricelli, J. Sallet, P. Pradat-Diehl, J. R. Duhamel, and A. Sirigu. The involvement of the orbitofrontal cortex in the experience of regret. *Science* 302:1167–1170, 2004.

Coricelli, G., R. J. Dolan, and A. Sirigu. Brain, emotion and decision making: The paradigmatic example of regret. *Trends in Cognitive Sciences* 11:258–265, 2007.

Modern humans face wide-ranging physical and psychological dangers, from sports injuries to terrorism, as well as more subtle dangers such those posed by chronic stress. An important implication of the LeDoux theory is that our fear system includes both unconscious fear responses, such as the mouse's response to the cat, and conscious awareness of subjective feelings of fear. He presumes, however, that the neural system underlying fear is similar in both cases and that the neural basis of fear can be studied by using a model system, which is fear conditioning.

Most behavioral studies of fear employ classical conditioning, the pairing of some initially neutral stimulus, such as a tone, with some biologically significant event, such as pain from a shock (see Chapter 18). Rats (and people) rapidly learn when a neutral stimulus is paired with a negative event (such as a shock). In this case, the auditory information (the tone) passes through the auditory pathways to the thalamus, which in turn sends the information to the cortex and to the amygdala, as illustrated in **Figure 20.7**.

The key brain structure in the development of conditioned fear is the amygdala, which sends outputs to stimulate hormone release and activate the ANS and thus generates emotion, which we interpret in this case as fear. Physiological measures of fear conditioning can rank autonomic functioning (for example, heart rate or respiration), and quantitative measures can rank behavior (for example, standing motionless) after the tone is heard.

Damage to the amygdala interferes with fear conditioning, regardless of how it is measured. People with damage to the temporal lobe that includes the amygdala are impaired at fear conditioning, yet imaging studies show activation of the amygdala during fear conditioning (see, for example, LaBar et al., 1998). How does the amygdala "know" that a stimulus is dangerous? LeDoux proposes two possibilities. Both implicate neural networks, one genetically evolved and one shaped by learning.

Genetically based neural networks in the amygdala evolve with the animal (for example, the scent or appearance of a predator). Rats born in the laboratory, for example, show fear responses to the sound of owls or the scent of predators even though they have never encountered them. Most primates show intense fear of snakes on their first encounter, which suggests that a "snake detector" has evolved to sensitize us to stimuli associated with danger. Recall that John Downer's split-brain monkey with one amygdala removed (see Chapter 17) had no fear of a snake from the side of brain lacking the amygdala but showed intense fear from the intact side.

Similarly, neurons in the amygdalae of primates evolved a sensitivity to negative facial expressions of others. This evolution makes sense because,

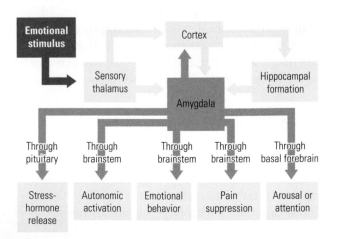

Figure 20.7

Processing an Emotional Stimulus Information about an emotion-laden stimulus travels from the sensory thalamus to the amygdala and cortex. The cortex feeds back to the amygdala, where several projections initiate stress-hormone release, activate the autonomic system, evoke emotion and suppress pain, and stimulate attention. The hippocampus provides information related to context. (After LeDoux, 2000.)

presumably, a cue to the presence of a threatening stimulus is the behavior of one's social group toward the stimulus.

Neural networks based in the amygdala likely also learn from experience about dangerous stimuli for which evolution could not prepare us. We may have learned, for instance, that a person wearing a certain type of insignia (such as one characteristic of a violent gang) is typically dangerous, whereas a person wearing another insignia (such as a police badge) is typically not dangerous.

LeDoux proposes that these circuits in the amygdala interact with cortical circuits to influence affective behavior. For example, if the amygdala functions to identify stimuli that signal danger, then the amygdala can act through the brainstem-activating systems to arouse the cortex and essentially to regulate cortical attention (awareness) to specific stimuli.

An important aspect of fear is context: a particular stimulus can be dangerous in one setting but not in another, and this distinction is clearly important to our behavior. A highly poisonous snake is extremely dangerous when suddenly encountered on a pathway but presents no danger behind a glass wall in a zoo. Furthermore, environmental contexts may acquire emotional properties through prior experiences (classical conditioning). If poisonous snakes are repeatedly encountered on a particular path in the woods, then the path itself becomes threatening.

Although the evidence is incomplete regarding exactly how context is associated with fear, the evidence is clear that hippocampal damage interferes with the development of contextual fear associations. How hippocampal activity normally acts to influence the association of context and fear remains to be understood.

How can the amygdala influence our thoughts about emotion-laden stimuli? People have all sorts of fears and worries that can interfere with everyday life, and, for some people, these fears become debilitating. People suffer from panic disorders, posttraumatic stress disorder, obsessive–compulsive disorders, anxiety disorders, and phobias. The extreme power of fear-related events to affect cognition suggests that evolution has crafted a powerful mechanism for forming such associations.

It is important in this context to recall that frontal-lobe patients show little anxiety or fear-related behavior. The orbital and medial prefrontal regions have significant reciprocal connections with the amygdala, suggesting that amygdalo-prefrontal circuits play a significant role in the formation of thoughts about fearful stimuli. The prefrontal cortex is possibly somehow modified in people with pathological fears and anxieties, making it difficult for them to extinguish learned fears or to suppress fears of evolutionarily significant events.

Cognitive Asymmetry and Emotion

We have seen in both Damasio's and LeDoux's theories that emotion entails cognitive appraisals. Because significant asymmetries exist in a variety of cognitive functions, it follows that related emotional systems also must be lateralized. This idea is not new and can be traced to at least the 1930s, when clinicians reported detailed observations of patients with large unilateral lesions, noting an apparent asymmetry in the effects of left- and right-hemisphere lesions on emotional behavior. (Through the decades in neuropsychology, many versions of asymmetry theories of emotional control have been compiled, and the reader is directed to the reviews by Gainotti and by Tucker et al. for details.)

The best-known early descriptions, contemporary with J.P.'s case presented in the Portrait at the beginning of the chapter, are those of Kurt Goldstein, who suggested that left-hemisphere lesions produce "catastrophic" reactions characterized by fearfulness and depression, whereas right-hemisphere lesions produce "indifference." The results of the first systematic study of these contrasting behavioral effects, by Gainotti in 1969, showed that catastrophic reactions were found in 62% of his left-hemisphere sample compared with only 10% of his right-hemisphere cases. In contrast, indifference was common in the right-hemisphere patients, found in 38% compared with only 11% of the left-hemisphere cases.

Significantly, however, Gainotti reported that catastrophic reactions were associated with aphasia and that indifference reactions were associated with contralateral neglect. A key point to remember in regard to Goldstein's and Gainotti's observations is that, if the left hemisphere is damaged extensively, then the behavior that we observe is in large part a function of what the right hemisphere can do. Thus, if we observe a catastrophic reaction after a left-hemisphere injury, one conclusion is that this behavior is coming from the right hemisphere. This conclusion leads directly to the idea that the right hemisphere normally plays a major role in the production of strong emotions, especially in emotions regarded as negative, such as fear and anger.

Gainotti concludes that the two sides of the brain play a complementary role in emotional behavior, the right hemisphere being more engaged in the automatic components of emotion and the left hemisphere in the overall cognitive control of emotion. The left hemisphere is presumed to have this general control because of language.

This idea is similar to one proposed by Gazzaniga, who suggests that a general control function of the speaking hemisphere characterizes the differences in thinking between humans and other animals. He calls the speaking hemisphere the "interpreter." What he means is illustrated in an experiment using split-brain patients as subjects. Each hemisphere is shown the same two pictures, such as a picture of a match followed by a picture of a piece of wood. A series of other pictures is then shown, and the task is to pick out a third picture that has an inferred relation with the other two. In our example, the pertinent third picture might be a bonfire.

The right hemisphere is incapable of making the inference that a match struck and held to a piece of wood could create a bonfire, whereas the left hemisphere can easily arrive at this interpretation. Evidently, the speaking left hemisphere can make logical inferences about sensory events that the nonspeaking right hemisphere cannot make. Gainotti applies this general idea to emotion and concludes that the right hemisphere generates emotional feelings, whereas the left hemisphere interprets these feelings, presumably through its language abilities, and produces a conceptual (cognitive) level of emotional processing (affective behavior).

Asymmetry in Emotional Processing

Emotional and cognitive behavior overlap in all three principal neuropsychological theories of emotional behavior. We now turn our attention to studies that focus on the nature of this overlap. Since the 1990s, interest has shifted toward the Damasio and LeDoux theories, which focus on "site" within the cerebral hemispheres. But, in the 1970s and 1980s, there was considerable interest in cerebral asymmetry, the possibility that the two hemispheres play complementary roles in controlling emotional behavior. We briefly consider the asymmetry literature, providing examples of research on the production and interpretation of emotional behavior as well as on changes in personality associated with temporal-lobe lesions.

The Production of Emotional Behavior

Mood is inferred largely from affect—facial expression, tone of voice, and frequency of talking—and so it is sensible to measure these behaviors first in an analysis of emotional behavior in brain-damaged people. **Table 20.1** summarizes a range of measures of emotional behavior. The general picture is that left-hemisphere lesions, especially left-frontal-lobe lesions, produce a flattening of mood and, in many people, an appearance of depression, especially after strokes that produce language difficulties.

Facial expression is one of the most obvious cues to emotion in humans, and overall studies of neurological patients find a reduction in the frequency and intensity of facial expressions in people with anterior lesions relative to those

Table 20.1 Summary of experiments on the production of emotional behavior in neurological patients

Behavior	Characteristics	Basic Reference
Clinical behavior of patients with natural lesions	Catastrophic reactions from left-hemisphere lesions; indifference from right-hemisphere lesions	Gainotti, 1969; Goldstein, 1939
Facial expression	Reduced by frontal lesions	Kolb and Milner, 1981
	Reduced by right-hemisphere lesions	Buck and Duffy, 1980; Borod et al., 1986
	Asymmetry altered	Bruyer, 1986
Spontaneous speech	Decreased by left-frontal-lobe lesions; increased by right-frontal-lobe lesions	Kolb and Taylor, 1981
Tone, or prosody, of speech	Right-hemisphere lesions impair mimicry of emotional states	Tucker et al., 1977; Kent and Rosenbek, 1982
Temporal-lobe traits	Temporal-lobe personality	Bear and Fedio, 1977; Waxman and Geshwind, 1974; Fedio and Martin, 1983
Sodium amytal	Catastrophic reactions to left injection; indifference reactions to right injection	Terzian, 1964; Rossi and Rosandini, 1974
	No evidence of asymmetric effects	Rovetta, 1960; Kolb and Milner, 1981

(A) Facial expressions

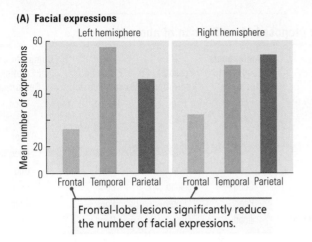

Frontal-lobe lesions significantly reduce the number of facial expressions.

(B) Talking

Spontaneous talking is significantly reduced for left frontal lesions...

...and increased for right frontal lesions.

Figure 20.8

Emotional Expression in Neurological Patients Relative frequencies of facial expressions (A) and spontaneous talking (B) during routine neuropsychological testing. (After Kolb and Milner, 1981, and Kolb and Taylor, 1981.)

with more-posterior lesions. For example, in a series of studies, one of us (Kolb) and colleagues found that whether facial expressions are measured in terms of frequency, quantitative scoring of facial-movement elements, or subjective rating by judges, both left- and right-frontal-lobe patients show a reduction in facial expression relative to temporal-lobe groups (**Figure 20.8**A). This result is obtained whether the expressions are spontaneous or posed.

In contrast with the reduction in facial expression from both left- and right-frontal-lobe lesions, the effects of side of the lesion on spontaneous talking in frontal-lobe patients differ. Right-frontal-lobe lesions appear to increase talking markedly, whereas left-frontal-lobe lesions decrease it (Figure 20.8B). Without doubt, loss of facial expression and changes in talkativeness would be perceived by friends and relatives of frontal-lobe patients as marked changes in personality.

Spoken language carries two types of information: content and prosody. Typically, content is a function of the left hemisphere, and there is reason to suspect that tone of voice is a function of the right. For example, when Don Tucker and his colleagues asked patients to express particular affective states such as anger, happiness, and sadness as they read emotionally neutral sentences, patients with right-hemisphere lesions produced the sentences with relatively flat affect compared with patients with left-hemisphere lesions. This absence of tone in speech has been termed **aprosodia**, and it can be measured on a wideband spectogram (see Kent and Rosenbek, 1982).

Abnormalities in tone of voice in right-hemisphere patients led Elliott Ross to propose a set of aprosodias analogous to aphasias in left-hemisphere speech (**Table 20.2**). For example, *motor aprosodia*, an inability to produce affective components of language, is proposed to result from damage to Broca's area in the right hemisphere. *Sensory aprosodia*, a deficit in the interpretation of the emotional components of language, is presumed to result from damage to the region in the right hemisphere analogous to Wernicke's area. Ross's proposal may have merit and deserves serious consideration, but, at present, it is without much scientific support. Furthermore, like aphasias, which are virtually never purely of one type, aprosodias may not be as pure as Ross has suggested.

Table **20.2** Ross's proposed classification of aprosodias

Type	Spontaneous Prosody and Gesturing	Prosodic Repetition	Prosodic Comprehension	Comprehension of Emotional Gesturing
Motor	Poor	Poor	Good	Good
Sensory	Good	Poor	Poor	Poor
Global	Poor	Poor	Poor	Poor
Conduction	Good	Poor	Good	Good
Transcortical motor	Poor	Good	Good	Good
Transcortical sensory	Good	Good	Poor	Poor
Mixed transcortical	Poor	Good	Poor	Poor
Anomic (alexia with agraphia)	Good	Good	Good	Poor

Interpretation of Emotional Behavior

Emotional behavior might appear to be abnormal not only because a person is unable to produce the appropriate behavior (expression, say) but also because he or she misinterprets the social or emotional signals coming from others. The importance of interpretation symptoms in understanding personality change after injury has led to the development of a variety of clinical tests of emotional perception, which are summarized by Joan Borod and her colleagues. As summarized in **Table 20.3**, right-hemisphere lesions produce deficits in a range of measures, especially including the comprehension of humor, as well as the judgment of mood, both in tone of voice and facial expression.

The ability to be humorous and to comprehend humor is one of humankind's most intriguing behaviors and certainly contributes to personality and is

Table **20.3** Summary of experiments on interpretation of emotional behavior in neurological patients

Experiment	Characteristics	Basic Reference
Judgment of mood in others	Right-hemisphere lesions impair comprehension	Heilman et al., 1993
	Right-temporal-lobe lesions impair perception of intonation	Tompkins and Mateer, 1985
Judgment of propositional affect	Left-hemisphere lesions impair comprehension	Kolb and Taylor, 1981
Comprehension of verbal humor	Right-hemisphere lesions alter appreciation	Gardner et al., 1975; Shammi and Stuss, 1999
Matching emotional expressions	Right-hemisphere lesions impair performance	DeKosky et al., 1980; Kolb and Taylor, 1981;
	Left-hemisphere lesions impair performance	Bowers et al., 1987; Young et al., 1993
Judgment of emotional expressions	Bilateral amygdala lesions impair perception of negative expressions	Adolphs et al., 1999

Figure **20.9**

Humor of a Frontal-Lobe Subject Depicted is the business card of a man who sold himself as an entrepreneur. Read carefully, the card says, "Holy cow, look at the ass on that tomato."

a basic ingredient in social life. In a study looking at humor in patients with focal injuries in various areas of the brain, those patients with right-frontal injuries were the most affected in that they reacted less than other patients, with diminished laughter and smiling, and failed to get the punch lines of jokes (Shammi and Stuss, 1999).

We should note here that not only do right-frontal-lobe patients fail to comprehend humor, in our experience, their efforts at humor exhibit a perverse aspect. **Figure 20.9** is the business card of a man who had a traumatic brain injury including damage to the right frontal lobe. This man was genuinely attempting to use humor to get business for his company.

Like humor, facial expression is a kind of social glue that bonds humans together: a lot of information is passed between and among us simply by the nuances of facial expression. Patients with lesions of the right temporal or right frontal lobe or both have difficulty recognizing facial expressions. To illustrate: subjects were asked to choose the appropriate facial expression for each of a set of cartoons in which one face was blank, as illustrated by social situations 1 and 2 in **Figure 20.10** (Kolb and Taylor, 1988). As summarized in **Figure 20.11**A, both frontal- and temporal-lobe patients were impaired at this test but, curiously, there was no asymmetry: lesions of either hemisphere were equally effective in disrupting performance, regardless of the appropriate emotion (Kolb and Taylor, 2000).

One explanation is that, although the right hemisphere may be dominant for processing faces and facial expressions, the left hemisphere may play a role in understanding context. We noted earlier that Gazzaniga's studies of split-brain patients led him to conclude that the left hemisphere acts as an "interpreter" of behavior. It may also be true of social situations.

Figure **20.10**

Testing Social Cognition Examples of cartoon situations in which patients were asked either to produce the appropriate expression for the blank face or to choose the appropriate expression from several choices. See Figure 20.1 for a representative range of choices. (After Kolb and Taylor, 1988.)

Situation 1

Situation 2

(A) Cartoon matching

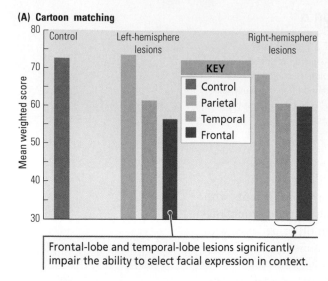

Frontal-lobe and temporal-lobe lesions significantly impair the ability to select facial expression in context.

(B) Matching photographs of negative emotions

Left-frontal-lobe and right-hemisphere lesions significantly impair the ability to match different faces when the expression is fear or disgust.

Figure 20.11

Matching Facial Expressions
(A) Performance of control subjects and surgical-excision patients on a test of matching facial expressions to cartoon situations such as those shown in Figure 20.10. (B) Performance of the same subjects tested on matching photographs of negative emotions to the appropriate Ekman face (see Figure 20.1). Lesions throughout the right hemisphere disturb this ability. (After Kolb and Taylor, 2000.)

Are different facial expressions (for example, frightened, happy) analyzed by different cerebral regions? Recall, for example, that the amygdala is believed to selectively perceive fear, and the results of studies by Ralph Adolphs and his colleagues show that subjects with bilateral amygdala lesions are impaired at recognizing negative expressions (such as fear) but not at recognizing happy faces. In a similar study, one of us (Kolb) and Laughlin Taylor showed that patients with unilateral frontal-lobe lesions were severely impaired at matching negative but not positive faces to the appropriate Ekman face. Patients with right, but not left, temporal or parietal lesions showed a similar pattern of deficits, as illustrated in Figure 20.11B.

Thus, facial expressions appear not to be a single stimulus category; rather, different expressions may be processed separately in the brain. An fMRI study addressed this idea by comparing the cerebral activation for fear and disgust (Phillips et al., 1997). Given that expressions of disgust are normally related to bad-tasting food, the researchers predicted that the perception of expressions of disgust might include the gustatory cortex, which is located in the insula within the temporal lobe. Indeed, that is exactly what they found: fearful expressions activate the amygdala, whereas disgust expressions activate the insula.

Temporal-Lobe Personality

The general clinical impression is that temporal-lobe patients have a clear personality change. For example, patients and their friends were asked to complete rating scales of behaviors such as "anger," "sadness," or religiosity, and the patients were found to display a distinctive set of traits (Bear and Fedio, 1977), summarized in **Table 20.4**, sometimes referred to as "temporal-lobe personality" (see also Chapter 15).

The epileptic patients self-reported a distinctive profile of humorless sobriety, dependence, and obsession. Raters differentiated the temporal-lobe patients on the basis of nearly every trait in Table 20.4 but rated them most strongly on the traits described as "circumstantiality," "philosophical interests,"

Table 20.4 Summary of characteristics attributed to temporal-lobe epileptics

Emotionality	Deepening of all emotions; sustained intense manic–depressive disease
Elation, euphoria	Grandiosity, exhilarated mood; diagnosis of manic–depressive disease
Sadness	Discouragement, fearfulness, self-depreciation; diagnosis of depression; suicide attempt
Anger	Increased temper, irritability
Aggression	Overt hostility, rape attacks, violent crimes, murder
Altered sexual interest	Loss of libido, hyposexualism; fetishism, transvestism, exhibitionism, hypersexual episodes
Guilt	Tendency to self-scrutiny and self-recrimination
Hypermoralism	Attention to rules with inability to distinguish significant from minor infractions, desire to punish offenders
Obsessionalism	Ritualism; orderliness; compulsive attention to detail
Circumstantiality	Loquaciousness; pedantry; being overly detailed or peripheral
Viscosity	Stickiness; tendency to repetition
Sense of personal destiny	Events given highly charged, personalized significance; divine guidance ascribed to many features of patient's life
Hypergraphia	Keeping extensive diaries, detailed notes; writing autobiography or novel
Religiosity	Holding deep religious beliefs; often idiosyncratic multiple conversions, mystical states
Philosophical interest	Nascent metaphysical or moral speculations, cosmological theories
Dependence, passivity	Cosmic helplessness, "at hands of fate"; protestations of helplessness
Humorlessness, sobriety	Overgeneralized ponderous concern; humor lacking or idiosyncratic
Paranoia	Suspicious, overinterpretative of motives and events; diagnosis of paranoid schizophrenia

Source: After Bear and Fedio, 1977.

and "anger." Furthermore, right- and left-temporal-lobe patients could be distinguished: the right-temporal-lobe patients were described as more obsessional, and the left-temporal-lobe patients as more concerned with "personal destiny."

Social Cognitive Neuroscience

Social psychology, the study of social behavior in humans, has traditionally been at arm's length from the study of brain function. Although the reasons for this estrangement are complex, a fundamental historical problem is that social psychology has focused on abstract constructs, such as moral dilemma, empathy, and cognitive dissonance, without any particular interest in how or what neural systems might underlie these inferred processes. The development of noninvasive imaging enabled social psychologists to look at brain activation while subjects engage in social cognitive tasks, as exemplified in the Snapshot on page 572 and elsewhere in this chapter, but it was necessary to develop models amenable to brain investigations.

We have seen in the preceding chapters that psychological constructs such as memory and language must be decomposed into chunks that can be related to brain processes. A similar process had to take place in social psychology to open a new door to research. Indeed, it has led to the emergence of a new field, **social cognitive neuroscience**, or **social neuroscience**, that encompasses all cognitive processes that take into account conspecifics either individually or at a group level.

Understanding Other's Actions

In Chapter 15, we considered biological motion—movements that have particular relevance to a species, which, for humans, includes movements of the eyes, face, mouth, hands, and body (see the review by Langton et al.). These movements can have social meanings and, presumably, contribute to our impressions of the mental states of others. Cells in the superior temporal sulcus (STS) code such movements; thus, we can infer that the STS must be a part of any neural network that controls social cognition.

However, cells beyond the STS also function to understand actions. Recall from Chapter 9 that neurophysiological research on monkeys identified mirror neurons in the premotor cortex that are activated when a monkey either executes limb movements or observes the same movements in another. The mirror neurons can distinguish between biological and nonbiological movements, responding, for example, to the manipulation of an object by a hand but not by a mechanical tool such as a pair of pliers.

Subsequent studies of humans with the use of noninvasive imaging have confirmed that similar processes take place in the human brain and that mirror neurons may play a role not only in understanding actions but perhaps even intentions (see review by Agnew et al.). Indeed, J.P.'s missing brain tissue included the region with the mirror neurons. Recall from the Portrait at the beginning of this chapter that he appeared unable to understand the intentions of others.

Understanding Other's Minds

We humans are social animals living in large groups. To thrive in such an environment requires a deft social intelligence that allows us to make sense of other people's actions and to discern their intentions. This ability plays a primary role in social cognition, or theory of mind, which we defined in Chapter 15 as the ability to attribute mental states to self and others and to predict and understand people's behavior on the basis of their mental states.

The attribution of intentions to others is so automatic in people that we humans seem compelled to attribute intentions and other psychological motives to nonhumans and even to abstract animations. Fulvia Castelli and colleagues showed subjects animations of triangles that were supposedly interacting (one triangle mocking another and so on) versus animations that were characterized as random. Functional magnetic resonance images showed that the attribution state increased activation in subjects' medial prefrontal regions, their basal temporal regions (fusiform gyrus and temporal poles adjacent to the amygdala), and their STS and occipital areas.

Subsequent studies consistently show that the medial frontal and orbitofrontal regions are activated when subjects try to outwit one another during games or are asked to identify traits such as trustworthiness in others. Joel Winston and his colleagues asked subjects either to judge whether a face was trustworthy or to indicate if it was that of a high-school or university student. **Figure 20.12** shows that the amygdala and insula were activated in both conditions, but the STS and orbitofrontal cortex were activated only when there was an instruction to make judgments about trustworthiness.

The results of a number of imaging studies provide corroborating evidence of the frontal lobe's judgmental role in social cognition. For example, subjects were asked to reflect on the thoughts and feelings of characters in comparison with control tasks in which thoughts and feelings were irrelevant, and specific medial frontal activation was found (Fletcher et al., 1995; see also Gallagher et al., 2000).

Damage to the orbitofrontal cortex consistently produces personality changes characterized by impaired social judgment. Donald Stuss and his colleagues devised a task to examine the ability to infer visual experience from others (see also a study by Rowe et al., 2001). In the Stuss task, a patient was presented with two Styrofoam cups, one of which had an object hidden under it. The patient was not permitted to watch the placement of the objects, but, in one test condition, the experimenter's assistant was able to watch the object (a 25-cent coin) placement. The patient kept the money for correct choices, and the assistant kept it for incorrect responses made by the subject.

The patient knew that the assistant was aware of the location of the object and that the assistant stood to gain by the patient's making an error. On each trial, the assistant pointed to the wrong cup, the one without the money, and the patient then made his or her choice. This condition continued for 14 trials or until the patient made five consecutive correct responses. Ventral medial frontal lesions, particularly on the right, were impaired at detecting the deception. Remarkably, the patients in this study did not appear to realize that the assistant was trying to deceive them.

Research on autism and related disorders (for example, Asperger's syndrome) has led to the conclusion that one consistent deficit is an inability to understand the intentions and inner mental states of other people. Autistic people consistently fail theory-of-mind tasks, and Simon Baron-Cohen theorized that the extreme abnormalities in social cognition in autism result from an abnormality in an amygdaloprefrontal circuit. John Allman and his colleagues have proposed that the social disabilities in autism-spectrum disorders are partly due to the abnormal development of the von Economo neurons.

Recall from Chapter 10 that one difference in human and ape brains compared with other brains is the emergence of von Economo neurons, which are found in the anterior cingulate cortex and frontal insular cortex. Allman and his colleagues do not propose that the von Economo neurons are responsible

Figure 20.12

Areas of the Brain Activated When Subjects Evaluated Faces
The amygdala and insula were activated regardless of whether there was an explicit instruction to evaluate trustworthiness, whereas the superior temporal sulcus and orbital frontal cortex was activated only when there was an instruction to make judgments about trustworthiness.

for theory of mind but rather that they are part of the frontal-lobe neural network that creates mental models of the thinking of others. This social-cognition network likely includes the amygdala, and evidence is accumulating that autistic people have consistent abnormalities in the cell density of the amygdala (for a review, see Courchesne et al; see also Chapter 24).

The Self and Social Cognition

We humans not only are aware of the actions and intentions of others but also develop a sense of our own: we are self-aware. Two distinct neural networks in frontal-lobe structures appear to be critical for generating the "self": (1) a right frontoparietal network and (2) a cortical midline network.

Humans and apes have a unique ability to recognize themselves—the *self-face*—in a mirror, and it has been known for more than 30 years that the right hemisphere of a split-brain patient can recognize the self-face and that the physiological reaction to the self-face is greater for the right than the left hemisphere (for a review see Uddin et al.). Both imaging and patient data provide evidence that recognition of the self-face is controlled by a right frontoparietal network.

Lucina Uddin and her colleagues showed, for example, that self-face recognition activates right frontal and parietal regions, as illustrated in **Figure 20.13**. Furthermore, the activated regions overlap with regions that contain mirror neurons, and the activated neurons have been proposed to provide a link between self-perception and associated mental states of the self and understanding the intentions of others. Uddin proposed that the frontoparietal mirror-neuron areas act as bridges between self and other, by co-opting a system for recognizing the actions of others to allow for recognition of the actions of self.

But the actions of self are only part of what we would call self-awareness. There is also a more abstract, mental, self. Matthew Lieberman has proposed that the processes that focus on one's own (or other's) mental states rely on medial frontal regions. In one study Jason Mitchell and colleagues asked subjects to perform one of two types of semantic judgement: "Does this description refer to a potential psychological state of the target (a person or a dog)?" or "Does this description refer to a physical part of the target?" fMRI shows that activation increased selectively in the medial frontal region in the psychological state condition regardless of whether the target was a person or dog. It is proposed that this medial frontal system acts to monitor psychological states in others as well as in the self.

Because the frontoparietal mirror neuron network and the medial frontal network seem to be involved in self–other representations, they likely interact to maintain self-other representations

(A)

Figure 20.13

The Neural Basis of Self-Recognition Humans are capable of self-recognition in a mirror or photograph. Brain activity during the presentation of self-faces or similar or different face morphs (A) provides a way to investigate selective brain activation for self-face. Self-faces typically activate the right frontoparietal network as shown in part B. Repetitive transcranial magnetic stimulation of those regions interferes with self-recognition. (From L. Q. Uddin et al. The self and social cognition: the role of cortical midline structures and mirror neurons. *Trends in Cognitive Sciences* 11:153–157, 2007.)

(B)

across multiple domains. The nature of this interaction and the details of how the self develops and changes is likely to be the source of considerable interest over the coming decade.

Cognitive Control of Emotion

Humans produce an amazing range of emotions, but we also have the cognitive capacity to control them. For example, we may have expectations about how a stimulus might feel (e.g., a syringe injection of penicillin) and our expectations can alter the actual feeling when we experience the event. Nobukatsu Sawamoto and colleagues found that nonpainful stimuli are perceived as painful when participants expect pain, and this is correlated with activation of the cingulate cortex, a region associated with pain perception.

The use of cognitive processes to change an existing emotional response has also recently been studied using noninvasive imaging. Kevin Ochsner and James Gross reviewed such studies and conclude that when subjects reappraise self-emotions there is concurrent activation of the prefrontal and cingulate cortex. In one study the authors showed subjects aversive photos and instructed them to think about the personal relevance of each image as it appeared.

In one condition the subjects were asked to increase their negative affect and to increase their sense of subjective closeness to pictured events, imagining themselves or a loved one as the central figure in a photo. In a second condition they were to decrease their negative affect by increasing their sense of objective distance, viewing pictured events from a detached, third-person perspective. The investigators observed that both up- and down-regulating negative emotion recruits prefrontal and anterior cingulate regions.

In summary, the emerging field of cognitive social neuroscience is radically changing our understanding of how the brain participates in the complex social behavior of humans. Historical lesion studies tended to focus on the perception and production of social behavior, but the new perspective is allowing insights into the very nature of how the brain allows humans to think about themselves and one another.

Summary

The Nature of Emotion

Emotions, or affective behaviors, are easily recognized but very difficult to quantify. Similarly, it is easy to identify brain structures in which injury can disrupt emotional behavior but difficult to determine what role different structures play in controlling emotional behavior.

Historical Views

Darwin first drew attention to the biology of emotion but not until the late 1920s did physiologists begin to look for neural and endocrine correlates of emotion, and they emphasized the role of thalamic and hypothalamic structures. Papez expanded the putative neural networks to include forebrain structures of the limbic system. The important role of the cerebral cortex emerged only in the past 30 years.

Studies in Normal Subjects

Neural correlates of emotion in normal subjects began with an exploration of hemispheric asymmetries in the control of emotion and a demonstration of a special role of the right hemisphere. More-recent investigations have demonstrated differential activity in the anterior cingulate cortex that is correlated with personality traits such as extroversion.

Candidate Structures in Emotional Behavior

As with other cognitive processes, multiple neural systems control different aspects of emotional behavior. The key candidate structures in emotional behavior include the frontal lobes, primarily the inferior frontal cortex, the amygdala and associated paralimbic cortex, and the hypothalamus. To the extent that changes in functions such as perception, movement, memory, and language affect our emotional behavior, we can see that the vast cortical regions taking part in cognitive processing also take part in producing emotion.

Neuropsychological Theories of Emotion

A theme that runs through all major theories of emotion, especially Damasio's somatic marker hypothesis, LeDoux's cognitive–social interaction theory, and Gainotti's asymmetry theory, is that emotion and cognition are intimately related and are likely controlled by overlapping neural systems.

Asymmetry in Emotional Processing

Studies of changes in emotional behavior after cerebral injury focus largely on changes in the production and perception of emotions. Overall, lesions of the left and right hemispheres have different effects on emotional behaviors, and damage to the right hemisphere appears to produce larger effects. Asymmetry in the effects of cerebral injury should not overshadow the importance of cortical site in understanding emotional behavior. Both the frontal lobes and the amygdala play special roles in emotional control, especially on behaviors related to producing and interpreting facial expression. The left amygdala appears to play a special role in generating one particular emotion—namely, fear.

Social Cognitive Neuroscience

This emerging field encompasses the neural correlates of all cognitive processes that take into account conspecifics, either individually or in groups. Such processes include understanding others' actions and intentions, the development of sense of "self," and the role of beliefs and expectations in emotional processing. The preliminary work has pointed to a fundamental role of the prefrontal and anterior cingulate regions in such processes.

References

Ackerly, S. S. A case of paranatal bilateral frontal lobe defect observed for thirty years. In J. M. Warren and K. Akert, Eds. *The Frontal Granular Cortex and Behavior.* New York: McGraw-Hill, 1964, pp. 192–218.

Adolphs, R. Social cognition and the human brain. *Trends in Cognitive Sciences* 3:469–479, 1999.

Adolphs, R., D. Tranel, S. Hamann, A. W. Young, A. J. Calder, E. A. Phelps, A. Anderson, G. P. Lee, and A. R. Damasio. Recognition of emotional expression in nine individuals with bilateral amygdala damage. *Neuropsychologia* 37:1111–1117, 1999.

Agnew, Z. K., K. K. Bhakoo, and B. K. Puri. The human mirror system: A motor resonance theory of mind-reading. *Brain Research Reviews* 54:286–293, 2007.

Allman, J. M., K. K. Watson, N. A. Tetreault, and A. Y. Hakeem. Intuition and autism: A possible role for von Economo neurons. *Trends in Cognitive Sciences* 8:367–373, 2005.

Baron-Cohen, S., M. K. Belmonte. Autism: a window onto the development of the social and the analytic brain. *Annual Reviews of Neuroscience* 28:109–126, 2005.

Bear, D. M., and P. Fedio. Quantitative analysis of interictal behavior in temporal lobe epilepsy. *Archives of Neurology* 34:454–467, 1977.

Bihrle, A. M., H. H. Brownell, J. A. Powelson, and H. Gardner. Comprehension of humorous and nonhumorous materials by left and right brain-damaged patients. *Brain and Cognition* 5:399–411, 1986.

Blakemore, S.-J., J. Winston, and U. Frith. Social cognitive neuroscience: Where are we heading? *Trends in Cognitive Sciences* 8:216–222, 2004.

Blonder, L. X., D. Bowers, and K. M. Heilman. The role of the right hemisphere on emotional communication. *Brain* 114:1115–1127, 1991.

Blumer, D. Temporal lobe epilepsy and its psychiatric significance. In D. F. Blumer and D. Benson, Eds. *Psychiatric Aspects of Neurological Disease.* New York: Grune & Stratton, 1975.

Borod, J. C., E. Koff, M. Perlman Lorch, and M. Nicholas. The expression and perception of facial emotion in brain-damaged patients. *Neuropsychologia* 24:169–180, 1986.

Borod, J. C., M. H. Tabert, C. Santschi, and E. H. Strauss. Neuropsychological assessment of emotional processing in brain-damaged patients. In J. C. Borod, Ed. *The Neuropsychology of Emotion.* New York: Oxford University Press, 2000, pp. 80–105.

Bowers, D., H. B. Coslett, R. M. Bauer, L. J. Speedie, and K. M. Heilman. Comprehension of emotional prosody following unilateral hemispheric lesions:Processing defect versus distraction defect. *Neuropsychologia* 25:317–328, 1987.

Brady, J. V. *Handbook of Physiology*, vol. 3, *Emotional Behavior.* Bethesda, Md.: American Physiological Society, 1960.

Brown, S., and E. A. Schaefer. An investigation into the functions of the occipital and temporal lobe of the monkey's brain. *Philosophical Transactions of the Royal Society Series B* 179:303–327, 1888.

Brownell, H. H., D. Michel, J. Powelson, and H. Gardner. Surprise but not coherence: Sensitivity to verbal humor in right-hemisphere patients. *Brain and Language* 18:20–27, 1983.

Bruyer, R., Ed. *The Neuropsychology of Face Perception and Facial Expression.* Hillsdale, N.J.: Lawrence Erlbaum, 1986.

Buck, R., and R. J. Duffy. Nonverbal communication of affect in brain-damaged patients. *Cortex* 16:351–362, 1980.

Butter, C. M., and D. R. Snyder. Alterations in aversive and aggressive behaviors following orbital frontal lesions in rhesus monkeys. *Acta Neurobiologiae Experimentalis* 32:525–565, 1972.

Campbell, R. The lateralisation of emotion: A critical review. *International Journal of Psychology* 17:211–229, 1982.

Canli, T., Z. Amin, B. Haas, K. Omura, and R. T. Constable. A double dissociation between mood states and personality traits in the anterior cingulate. *Behavioral Neuroscience* 118:897–904, 2004.

Castelli, F., F. Happe, U. Frith, and C. Frith. Movement and mind: A functional imaging study of perception and interpretation of complex intentional movement. *Neuroimage* 12:314–325, 2000.

Coricelli, G., R.J. Dolan, and A. Sirigu. Brain, emotion and decision making: the paradigmatic example of regret. Trends in Cognitive Science 11:258–265, 2007.

Courchesne, E., E. Redcay, J.T. Morgan, and D.P. Kennedy. Autism at the beginning: microstructural and growth abnormalities underlyhing the cognitive and behavioral phenotype of autism. Developmental Psychopathology 17:577–597, 2005.

Damasio, A. R. *Descartes' Error: Emotion, Reason, and the Human Brain.* New York: Putnam, 1994.

Damasio, A. R. A second chance for emotion. In R. D. Lane and L. Nadel, Eds. *Cognitive Neuroscience of Emotion.* New York: Oxford University Press, 2000, pp. 12–23.

DeKosky, S. T., K. M. Heilman, D. Bowers, and E. Valenstein. Recognition and discrimination of emotional faces and pictures. *Brain and Language* 9:206–214, 1980.

Dicks, D., R. E. Myers, and A. Kling. Uncus and amygdala lesions: Effects on social behavior in the free-ranging rhesus monkey. *Science* 165:69–71, 1968.

Dimond, S. J., and L. Farrington. Emotional response to films shown to the right or left hemisphere of the brain measured by heart rate. *Acta Psychologia* 41:255–260, 1977.

Dimond, S. J., L. Farrington, and P. Johnson. Differing emotional response from right and left hemispheres. *Nature* 261:690–692, 1976.

Dunbar, H. F. *Emotions and Bodily Changes*, 4th ed. New York: Columbia University Press, 1954.

Ekman, P., and W. V. Friesen. *Unmasking the Face.* Palo Alto, Calif.: Consulting Psychology Press, 1984.

Fedio, P., and A. Martin. Ideative–emotive behavioral characteristics of patients following left or right temporal lobectomy. *Epilepsia* 254:S117–S130, 1983.

Fletcher, P. C., F. Happe, U. Frith, S. C. Baker, R. J. Dolan, and R. S. Frakowiak. Other minds in the brain: A functional imaging study of "theory of mind" in story comprehension. *Cognition* 57:109–128, 1995.

Gainotti, G. Reactions "catastrophiques" et manifestations d'indifférence au cours des atteintes cerebrales. *Neuropsychologia* 7:195–204, 1969.

Gainotti, G. Emotional behavior and hemispheric side of the lesion. *Cortex* 8:41–55, 1972.

Gainotti, G. Neuropsychological theories of emotion. In J. C. Borod, Ed. *The Neuropsychology of Emotion.* New York: Oxford University Press, 2000, pp. 214–236.

Gallagher, H. L., F. Happe, N. Brunswick, P. C. Fletcher, U. Frith, and C. D. Frith. Reading the mind in cartoons and stories: An fMRI study of "theory of mind" in verbal and nonverbal tasks. *Neuropsychologia* 38:11–21, 2000.

Gardner, H., P. K. Ling, L. Flamm, and J. Silverman. Comprehension and appreciation of humorous material following brain damage. *Brain* 98:399–412, 1975.

Gazzaniga, M., and J. E. LeDoux. *The Integrated Mind.* New York: Plenum, 1978.

Goldstein, K. *The Organism: A Holistic Approach to Biology, Derived from Pathological Data in Man.* New York: American Book, 1939.

Haas, B. W., K. Omura, R. Constable, R. Todd, and T. Canli. Emotional conflict and neuroticism: Personality-dependent activation in the amygdala and subgenual anterior cingulate. *Behavioral Neuroscience* 121:249–256, 2007.

Haggard, M. P., and A. M. Parkinson. Stimulus and task factors as determinants of ear advantages. *Quarterly Journal of Experimental Psychology* 23:168–177, 1971.

Heilman, K. M., D. Bowers, and E. Valenstein. Emotional disorders associated with neurological diseases. In K. M. Heilman and E. Valenstein, Eds. *Clinical Neuropsychology*, 3rd ed. New York: Oxford University Press, 1993.

Iidaka, T., M. Omori, T. Murata, H. Kosaka, Y. Yonekura, T. Okada, and N. Sadato. Neural interaction of the amygdala with the prefrontal and temporal cortices in the processing of facial expressions as revealed by fMRI. *Journal of Cognitive Neuroscience* 13:1035–1047, 2001.

Kent, R. D., and J. C. Rosenbek. Prosodic disturbance and neurological lesion. *Brain and Language* 15:259–291, 1982.

Klüver, H., and P. C. Bucy. Preliminary analysis of the temporal lobes in monkeys. *Archives of Neurology and Psychiatry* 42:979–1000, 1939.

Kolb, B., and B. Milner. Observations on spontaneous facial expression after focal cerebral excisions and after intracarotid injection of sodium amytal. *Neuropsychologia* 19:505–514, 1981.

Kolb, B., and L. Taylor. Affective behavior in patients with localized cortical excisions: Role of lesion site and side. *Science* 214:89–91, 1981.

Kolb, B., and L. Taylor. Facial expression, emotion, and hemispheric organization. In R. D. Lane and L. Nadel, Eds. *Cognitive Neuroscience of Emotion.* New York: Oxford University Press, 2000, pp. 62–83.

LaBar, K. S., J. C. Gatenby, J. C. Gore, J. E. LeDoux, and E. A. Phelps. Human amygdala activation during conditioned fear acquisition and extinction: A mixed-trial fMRI study. *Neuron* 20:937–945, 1998.

Langton, S. R., R. J. Watt, and V. Bruce. Do the eyes have it? Cues to the direction of social attention. *Trends in Cognitive Sciences* 4:50–59, 2000.

LeDoux, J. E. Cognitive–emotional interactions. In R. D. Lane and L. Nadel, Eds. *Cognitive Neuroscience of Emotion.* New York: Oxford University Press, 2000, pp. 129–155.

Leiberman, M. D. Social cognitive neuroscience: A review of core processes. *Annual Review of Psychology* 58:259–289, 2007.

Ley, R. G., and M. P. Bryden. Hemispheric differences in processing emotions and faces. *Brain and Language* 7:127–138, 1979.

Ley, R. G., and M. P. Bryden. A dissociation of right and left hemispheric effects for recognizing emotional tone and verbal content. *Brain and Cognition* 1:3–9, 1982.

Marlowe, W. B., E. L. Mancall, and J. J. Thomas. Complete Klüver–Bucy syndrome in man. *Cortex* 11:53–59, 1975.

Milner, B. Brain mechanisms suggested by studies of the temporal lobes. In C. H. Millikan and F. L. Darley, Eds. *Brain Mechanisms Underlying Speech and Language.* New York: Grune & Stratton, 1967.

Mitchell, J. P., R. B. Mahzarin, and C. N. Macrae. General and specific contributions of the medial prefrontal cortex to knowledge about mental states. *Neuroimage* 28:757–762, 2005.

Moscovitch, M., and J. Olds. Asymmetries in spontaneous facial expressions and their possible relation to hemispheric specialization. *Neuropsychologia* 20:71–82, 1982.

Myers, R. E. Role of the prefrontal and anterior temporal cortex in social behavior and affect in monkeys. *Acta Neurobiologiae Experimentalis* 32:567–579, 1972.

Myers, R. E., C. Swett, and M. Miller. Loss of social group affinities following prefrontal lesions in free-ranging macaques. *Brain Research* 64:257–269, 1973.

Ochsner, K. N., and J. J. Gross. The cognitive control of emotion. *Trends in Cognitive Sciences* 9:242–249, 2005.

Ochsner, K. N., R. D. Ray, J. C. Cooper, E. R. Robertson, S. Chopra, J. D. E. Gabrieli, and J. J. Gross. For better or for worse: Neural systems supporting the cognitive down- and up-regulation of negative emotion. *Neuroimage* 23:483–499, 2004.

Panksepp, J., B. Knutson, and J. Burgdorf. The role of brain emotional systems in addictions: A neuro-evolutionary perspective and new "self-report" animal model. *Addiction* 97:459–69, 2002.

Papez, J. W. A proposed mechanism of emotion. *Archives of Neurology and Psychiatry* 38:725–744, 1937.

Peters, M., and D. Ploog. Frontal lobe lesions and social behavior in the squirrel monkey *(Saimiri):* A pilot study. *Acta Biologica Medica (Germany)* 35:1317–1326, 1976.

Phillips, M. L., A. W. Young, C. Senior, M. Brammer, C. Andrews, A. J. Calder, E. T. Bullmore, D. I. Perrett, D. Rowland, S. C. R. Williams, J. A. Gray, and A. S. David. A specific neural substrate for perceiving facial expressions of disgust. *Nature* 389:495–498, 1997.

Raleigh, M. J. Neural mechanisms supporting successful social decisions in simians. In Y. Christen, A. Damasio, and H. Damasio, Eds. *Neurobiology of Decision Making.* Berlin: Springer, 1996, pp. 63–82.

Raleigh, M. J., M. T. McGuire, G. L. Brammer, D. B. Pollack, and A. Yuwiler. Serotonergic mechanisms promote dominance acquisition in adult male vervet monkeys. *Brain Research* 559:181–190, 1991.

Raleigh, M. J., and H. D. Steklis. Effects of orbitofrontal and temporal neocortical lesions on the affiliative behavior of vervet monkeys *(Ceropithecus aethiops sabaeus). Experimental Neurology* 73:378–389, 1981.

Robinson, R. G., K. Kubos, L. B. Starr, K. Rao, and T. R. Price. Mood disorders in stroke patients. *Brain* 107:81–93, 1984.

Ross, E. D. The aprosodias: Functional–anatomical organization of the affective components of language in the right hemisphere. *Archives of Neurology* 38:561–569, 1981.

Ross, E. D., and M. Monnot. Neurology of affective prosody and its functional–anatomic organization in right hemisphere. *Brain and Language,* 2007, in press.

Ross, E. D., and A. J. Rush. Diagnosis and neuroanatomical correlates of depression in brain-damaged patients. *Archives of General Psychiatry* 38:1344–1354, 1981.

Rossi, G. F., and G. Rosadini. Experimental analysis of cerebral dominance in man. In C. J. Millikan and F. L. Darley, Eds. *Brain Mechanisms Underlying Speech and Language.* New York: Grune & Stratton, 1974, pp. 167–174.

Rovetta, P. Discussion of paper "Amytal intracaroitides per lo studio della dominanza emisferica." *Rivista di Neurologia* 30:460–470, 1960.

Rowe, A. D., P. R. Bullock, C. E. Polkey, and R. G. Morris. "Theory of mind" impairments and their relationship to executive functioning following frontal lobe excisions. *Brain* 124:600–616, 2001.

Sachdev, H. S., and S. G. Waxman. Frequency of hypergraphia in temporal lobe epilepsy: An index of interictal behaviour syndrome. *Journal of Neurology, Neurosurgery, and Psychiatry* 44:358–360, 1981.

Sawamoto, N., M. Honda, T. Okada, T. Hanakawa, M. Kanda, H. Fukuyama, H. Konishi, H. Shibasaki. Expectation of pain enhances responses to nonpainful somatosensory stimulaton in the anterior cingulate cortex and parietal operculum/posterior insula: an event-related functional magnetic resonance imaging study. *Journal of Neuroscience* 20:7438–7445, 2000.

Scherer, C. Psychological theories of emotion. In J. C. Borod, Ed. *The Neuropsychology of Emotion.* New York: Oxford University Press, 2000, pp. 137–162.

Shammi, P., and D. T. Stuss. Humour appreciation: A role of the right frontal lobe. *Brain* 122:657–666, 1999.

Stuss, D. T., G. G. Gallup, and M. P. Alexander. The frontal lobes are necessary for "theory of mind." *Brain* 124:279–286, 2001.

Suomi, S. J., H. F. Harlow, and J. K. Lewis. Effect of bilateral frontal lobectomy on social preferences of rhesus monkeys. *Journal of Comparative and Physiological Psychology* 70:448–453, 1970.

Terzian, H. Behavioral and EEG effects of intracarotid sodium amytal injection. *Acta Neurochirurgica* 12:230–239, 1964.

Thorne, B. M. Brain lesions and affective behavior in primates: A selected review. *Journal of General Psychology* 86:153–162, 1972.

Tompkins, C. A., and C. A. Mateer. Right hemisphere appreciation of intonational and linguistic indications of affect. *Brain and Language* 24:185–203, 1985.

Tucker, D. M., D. Derryberry, and P. Lau. Anatomy and physiology of human emotion: Vertical integration of brainstem, limbic, and cortical systems. In J. C. Borod, Ed. *The Neuropsychology of Emotion.* New York: Oxford University Press, 2000, pp. 56–79.

Tucker, D. M., R. T. Watson, and K. M. Heilman. Discrimination and evocation of affectively intoned speech in patients with right parietal disease. *Neurology* 27:947–950, 1977.

Uddin, L. Q., M. Iacoboni, C. Lange, and J. P. Keenan. The self and social cognition: The role of cortical midline structures and mirror neurons. *Trends in Cognitive Sciences* 11:153–157, 2007.

Waxman, S. G., and N. Geschwind. Hypergraphia in temporal lobe epilepsy. *Neurology* 24:629–636, 1974.

Winston, J. S., B. A. Strange, J. O'Doherty, and R. J. Dolan. Automatic and intentional brain responses during evaluation of trustworthiness of faces. *Nature Neuroscience* 5:277–283, 2002.

Wittling, W., and R. Roschmann. Emotion-related hemisphere asymmetry: Subjective emotional responses to laterally presented films. *Cortex* 29:431–438, 1993.

Young, A. W., F. Newcombe, E. H. de Haan, M. Small, and D. C. Hay. Face perception after brain injury: Selective impairments affecting identity and expression. *Brain* 116:941–959, 1993.

Spatial Behavior

PORTRAIT: Lost in Space

© Jason Henkes/Corbis

Whenever he left his room in the hospital, he had trouble in finding the way back, because at any chosen point of the route he did not know whether to go right, left, downstairs, or upstairs (on one occasion, he walked from the main floor down to the basement, instead of going up to the first floor, where his bed was located). When he eventually arrived in front of his own room, he did not recognize it unless he chanced to see some distinguishing feature, such as the black beard of his roommate or a particular object on the bedside table....

When taken to sections of the city he knew before his illness and required to lead the way, he tried hard to find familiar landmarks, such as a signboard, the name of a street, the tramcar numbers, etc., but this information, though effectively indicating to him he was near his home, failed to provide clues for choosing the right direction....

Required to provide verbal information concerning routes or places well known before the disease, he performed fairly well as long as he could rely on purely verbal knowledge. Thus he was able to give the names of the intermediate stations on the railway line he used daily or the location of the main building of the city. Yet, he met with considerable difficulty when the way had to be retraced from spatial memory; for instance, when required to tell how he would walk between two sites chosen at random in the city, he could only say the initial street and then he became confused....

He grossly mislocated cities and states on a map of his country as well as of Europe, a task with which he was familiar, since he had been a post office clerk. (Adolph Meyer's patient, summarized by de Renzi, 1982, p. 213)

The patient described in the Portrait was originally examined by Adolph Meyer in the early 1900s and is but one of many patients whose impairments can be sources of insight into one of our most complex behaviors—spatial behavior. Our bodies occupy space, move through space, and interact with other entities in space; our brains mentally rotate and manipulate representations of space. Other objects occupy space and maintain relations in space with one another and with us.

Philosophers have asked whether objects exist without space or, conversely, whether space exists without objects. They also ask whether space is a feature of the universe or merely a creation of our brains. And how do we acquire concepts of space? The spatial experiences of small animals, such as dogs and cats, or of children must be very different from those of airline pilots. Further complicating these questions is that many of the elements that we think of as aspects of "space" and spatial behavior—sensory perceptions, memory, attention processes, and motor behaviors, to name a few—fit equally well into other domains.

In this chapter, we present an overview of spatial behavior, along with a number of contemporary spatial theories and a survey of various models used to study spatial behavior. We also examine the roles of the temporal, parietal, and frontal lobes in spatial behavior and some of the factors that seem to affect individual performance on spatial tests.

Organization of Spatial Behavior

The term *spatial behavior* refers to all the behaviors with which we and other animals guide all or parts of our bodies through space. It also includes thought processes concerning space. The ability to move through space from one place to another is sometimes referred to as **topographic memory**, in recognition of the idea that the movements take place between or in relation to points or objects that are spatially distinct, such as the points on a map ("topography" refers to map making).

The mental representations that we have of space are frequently referred to as **cognitive maps**, on the assumption that we represent space with our brains in the same way that it is represented on a map. The mental representation allows us not only to solve spatial problems but also to remember that we have done so.

For the purpose of neurological study, space is sometimes broken down into subspaces of various kinds (**Figure 21.1**). One subspace is the surface of the body—the *body space*—on which things such as objects of clothing or contact with external objects can be localized. Another is the *grasping space* surrounding the body, and a third is *distal space* that the body moves into or out of. All these subspaces have their representations within the brain, which is able to assign locations to real or imagined objects on or within them. Space can also be thought of as having a time dimension of past and future, described as *time space*.

The challenge to scientists studying spatial behavior is to discover *how* the kinds and properties of space are represented. In this section of the chapter, after a brief historical overview of spatial function, we consider three theoretical approaches to understanding spatial behavior: spatial-navigation theories, cognitive-mapping theories, and the two-stream theory of spatial-information processing.

Historical Background

Modern accounts of cerebral organization describe spatial processing in humans as a special function of the right hemisphere. This view has had an irregular history. John Hughlings-Jackson was the first to propose that the right hemisphere might have some special perceptual function to complement the language functions of the left hemisphere. In his 1874 paper titled "On the

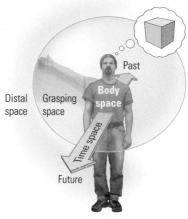

Figure 21.1

Conceptual Model of the Compartments of Space

Nature of the Duality of the Brain," he predicted that a person with damage restricted to the posterior part of the right hemisphere would have a distinctive syndrome:

> The patient would have difficulty in recognizing things; he would have difficulty in relating what had occurred, not from lack of words, but from a prior inability to revive images of persons, objects and places, of which the words are symbols. . . . He could not put before himself ideal images of places one after another; could not re-see where he had been, and could not therefore tell of it in words. (Jackson, 1915, p. 14)

Between 1876 and 1905, a number of investigators described various cases of spatial–perceptual difficulties, confirming Hughlings-Jackson's prediction that such disorders exist. But most of the patients described in these papers appeared to have bilateral damage rather than right-hemisphere damage. Experiences with brain injury in soldiers in World War I (1914–1918) led to advances in the understanding of spatial disturbances, but the possibility of a special association between spatial deficits and right-hemisphere damage was largely ignored. The more systematic work of Oliver Zangwill and of Henri Hécaen and their coworkers in the 1950s forced a reexamination of the role of the right hemisphere in spatial performance.

Little doubt remains that the right hemisphere has a special role in spatial behavior, although spatial impairments are sometimes also observed in people with damage to the left hemisphere. The lateralization of spatial behavior to the right hemisphere appears to be unique to humans. Nevertheless, we must emphasize that it is more difficult to study the human brain than the rat brain in tasks requiring free movement. Additionally, the neural structures mediating spatial behavior in humans cannot be regularly studied in detail with the use of the single-cell-recording methods that provide so much detail in rat studies. Finally, as we will describe, spatial behavior is complex, consisting of a number of abilities mediated by a number of different brain regions.

Topographic Disorientation

There are many clinical reports of patients suffering from **topographic disorientation**, a gross disability in finding their way about, even in environments with which they were familiar before the onset of their injuries. In 1890, Otfrid Foerster provided a description of a 44-year-old postal clerk who developed blindness on the right side of the visual field (a right hemianopia), followed a few days later by blindness on the left side of the visual field (a left hemianopia), a situation that left him with a small, central area of vision (recall Figure 13.10). This patient's most striking disability, however, was impairment in remembering where objects were located and in building up a picture of a route.

When blindfolded, he was unable to point toward furniture in his room or to remember the location of a toilet only a few steps away from his room. His amnesia was retrograde, extending back to things he knew before the onset of his disability. He could not describe or draw the spatial arrangement of his office or home or of well-known places in his city. He also could not draw general maps of the world or the city, although he could express some geographic ideas verbally.

In subsequent studies, a number of variations in the symptoms of topographic disorientation have been described. Some patients are unable to name buildings or landmarks that were formerly familiar to them. Others retain this ability. Some patients can describe routes and draw maps but become disoriented when they actually visit the locations, because they cannot identify familiar buildings or landmarks. Other patients can navigate routes but cannot describe or draw maps of them. Some patients can navigate in familiar places but become disoriented in new places, and others can eventually learn to navigate in new places by painstakingly memorizing buildings and landmarks and the routes from one to another.

Andrew Paterson and Oliver Zangwill attempted to sort out these complex clusters of symptoms by identifying subcomponents that may prove to have different anatomical loci. They suggested that topographic disorders be subdivided into two different impairments:

1. **Topographic agnosia** is defined as failing to identify individual landmarks, such as specific buildings, but retaining the ability to identify and recognize classes of objects, such as hills, office buildings, or churches. A person may recognize a building as a church but not recognize that it is the church of which he or she is a member.

2. **Topographic amnesia** refers to an inability to remember topographic relations between landmarks that can be identified individually. A person may recognize a church as his or her own but may not know where it is located.

In both conditions, it is necessary to distinguish between anterograde and retrograde impairments. People who lose the ability to navigate in environments that were familiar before their injuries have *retrograde spatial amnesia*. People who retain the ability to navigate in environments that were familiar before their injuries but who cannot navigate in novel environments have *anterograde spatial amnesia*. Patients may display both conditions, losing all topographic ability.

Brain Regions Compromised in Spatial Disorientation

Geoffrey Aguirre and Mark D'Esposito reviewed the literature on spatial disorientation for the purpose of relating deficits to brain regions. They propose the five different categories of deficits listed in **Figure 21.2**. Each impairment is traceable to a specific region of the posterior neocortex and limbic system.

Egocentric Disorientation

Patients described as having **egocentric disorientation** have difficulty perceiving the relative location of objects with respect to the self. They have either unilateral or bilateral injuries located in the posterior parietal cortex. Although they are able to gesture toward objects as long as their eyes are open, this ability is completely lost when their eyes are closed.

Their performance is impaired on a wide range of visuospatial tasks, including mental rotation (the ability to visualize the appearance of three-dimensional objects from different perspectives) and the ability to judge distances between objects. These patients are uniformly impaired in way-finding tasks both in

Figure 21.2

Relation Between Right-Hemisphere Brain Injuries and Spatial Deficits in Human Subjects Arrows show the dorsal stream and ventral stream in a lateral view of the right hemisphere. The subcortical structures linked to spatial impairments are shown in a medial view of the right hemisphere.

Impairment	Lesion	Description
Egocentric disorientation	Posterior parietal	Unable to represent the location of objects with respect to self
Heading disorientation	Posterior cingulate	Unable to represent direction of orientation with respect to environment
Landmark agnosia	Lingual gyrus	Unable to represent appearance of prominent landmarks
Anterograde disorientation	Parahippocampal gyrus	Unable to learn new representations of environmental information
Spatial-mapping or memory deficit	Hippocampus	Anterograde and retrograde amnesia, especially for rich spatial details

formerly familiar and in novel environments. A case reported by Levine exemplifies the condition:

> The most striking abnormalities were visual and spatial. . . . He could not reach accurately for visual objects, even those he identified, whether they were presented in central or peripheral visual fields. When shown two objects, he made frequent errors in stating which was nearer or farther, above or below, or to the right or left. . . . He could not find his way about. At four months after the hemorrhages, he frequently got lost in his own house and never went out without a companion. . . . Spatial imagery was severely impaired. He could not say how to get from his house to the corner grocery store, a trip he had made several times a week for more than 5 years. In contrast he could describe the store and its proprietor. (Levine et al., 1985)

Heading Disorientation

Patients said to have **heading disorientation** are unable to set a course to where they want to go, even though they are able to recognize landmarks, to recognize their own locations in relation to landmarks, and to describe where they want to go. In short, they have no "sense of direction." This condition is associated with injury in the right posterior cingulate cortex. The following description of a patient is representative:

> [A]s he was driving his taxi in the same city [in which he had worked for years], he suddenly lost his understanding of the route to his destination. As he could quickly recognize the buildings and landscapes

around him, he was able to determine his current location. However, he could not determine in which direction he should proceed. He stopped taking passengers and tried to return to the main office, but didn't know the appropriate direction in which to drive. Using the surrounding buildings, scenery, and road signs, he made several mistakes along the way. He remembered, during this time, passing the same places over and over again. (Takahashi et al., 1997)

Landmark Agnosia

Patients described as having **landmark agnosia** are unable to use prominent environmental features for the purposes of orientation. They can recognize churches, houses, and other landmarks—they do not have a deficit in the perception of environmental information—but they cannot use a particular church or house to guide their movement. They frequently use specific details as clues to help them recognize particular objects; for example, a patient may recognize his or her own house because of the car in the driveway or the tree in the yard.

The lesion sites reported to produce landmark agnosia are either bilateral or on the right side of the medial aspect of the occipital lobe, affecting the lingual and fusiform gyri and the parahippocampal gyrus. A patient identified as A.H. is an example:

> He complained a lot of his inability to recognize places. "In my mind's eye I know exactly where places are, what they look like. I can visualize R . . . Square without difficulty, and the streets that come into it. . . . I can draw you a plan of the roads from Cardiff to the Rhondda Valley. . . . It's when I'm out that the trouble starts. My reason tells me I must be in a certain place and yet I don't recognize it. It all has to be worked out each time." His topographic memory was good, as could be inferred from his accurate descriptions of paths, roads, the layout of the mineshafts [the patient was an engineer] and from his excellent performance in drawing maps of places familiar to him before his illness. (Pallis, 1955)

Anterograde Disorientation

In **anterograde disorientation**, patients have no problem navigating in formerly familiar environments but experience difficulty in novel environments because of an inability to learn about unfamiliar objects by looking at them. If shown a novel object, they are not likely to be able to select it from an array of objects a short while later. In contrast, they *are* able to recall auditory and tactile information that is novel. Damage in the parahippocampal gyrus of the inferior ventral cortex on the right side is associated with this condition. The following description exemplifies this kind of disorientation:

> The major problem he noted, besides a complete inability to recognize faces, was severe spatial disorientation. In order to find his way around the college campus or to walk to and from school, he was constantly forced to consult maps and written notes. . . . The patient had no difficulty in accurately reaching for objects in space. . . . He was never able to learn the spatial organization of the neurology wing during the entire month he spent in the hospital. . . . When asked to construct a map of the neurology wing, he was able to do this task if allowed to walk through the ward but was unable to do it from memory. . . . [T]he patient also

appeared spatially disoriented in the three-room apartment where he had been living for six months. In striking contrast, however, when he stayed at his parents' house, in which he grew up, there was no observable difficulty with spatial orientation. (Ross, 1980)

Spatial Learning

A very extensive literature implicates the hippocampus in **spatial learning**, but there is considerable controversy about the precise nature of the deficits caused by damage there. Spatial-learning theories vary from proposing that the hippocampus has a direct and specific role in spatial navigation to proposing that the hippocampus has a general role in memory and that anterograde spatial deficits arise as part of a general anterograde memory impairment.

The results of brain-imaging studies suggest that the right hippocampus has a special role in complex spatial abilities (see the Snapshot on page 597). E.P.'s case, reported by Edmond Teng and Larry Squire, illustrates the possible role of the hippocampus in spatial memory.

> E.P. was a 76-year-old former laboratory technician who became amnesic in 1992, after an episode of herpes simplex encephalitis. He had extensive bilateral damage to the hippocampus and surrounding areas, including the parahippocampal gyrus. The experimenters identified five individuals who had attended E.P.'s high school and who had since moved away, as had E.P. The subjects were asked to describe how they would navigate from their homes to different locations in the area served by the school, how they would navigate between different locations in the area, and how they would navigate if the most logical routes were blocked off. E.P. scored as well as the control subjects on these tests. In contrast, when E.P. was asked to describe how he would navigate in his present environs, a location to which he had moved after his brain injury, he was unable to provide any responses to any questions. (Teng and Squire, 1999)

Teng and Squire suggest that E.P.'s spatial impairments are part of general anterograde memory impairment. It is worth noting, however, that, because parahippocampal injury by itself is reported to produce anterograde disorientation, it is by no means certain that E.P.'s anterograde spatial-memory deficit is due principally to the damage to his hippocampus.

In their study of K.C., a patient with a similar hippocampal plus parahippocampal gyrus lesion, Shayna Rosenbaum and her colleagues report that, although the patient could produce what they called a "schematic cognitive map" of the environment in which he had lived before his injury, his memory of that environment's rich contextual details was impaired. For example, when shown a photograph of the neighborhood in which K.C. had lived before his brain injury, he had difficulty identifying the viewpoint from which the photograph was taken, and he was unable to describe the surrounding environment that was not visible in the photograph. Rosenbaum and colleagues agree with Teng and Squire that patients with hippocampal damage have some retrograde sparing of spatial abilities, but they also suggest that there is substantial retrograde amnesia for the richer contextual features of space.

In this respect it is noteworthy that H.M., who has extensive anterograde amnesia, can solve some simple spatial problems (see the Portrait in Chapter 18).

SNAPSHOT
Imaging the Hippocampi of London Taxi Drivers

To examine brain regions associated with topographic memory, Eleanor Maguire and her colleagues used licensed London taxi drivers as subjects. Official London taxi drivers must train for as long as 3 years and pass stringent examinations of spatial knowledge before receiving a license. The fact that these subjects had such an extensive knowledge of London meant that all of them could be tested with the same stimuli: the city's topography.

The taxi drivers were given a number of tasks, two of which required topographic knowledge:

1. They were given a starting and destination point in the greater London area and asked to describe overtly, while undergoing a PET scan, the shortest legal route between the two points.

2. They were required to recall and describe the appearance of individual world-renowned landmarks that were not in London and that they had never visited.

A control task for the driving-sequence test was the recall of the plot of a film. As a control for the renowned-building test, the subjects were asked to describe individual frames from a film.

PET-scan images were superimposed onto the MRI reconstructions of each subject's brain. The brain areas activated during the spatial test included the occipitotemporal areas, medial parietal cortex, posterior cingulate cortex, parahippocampal gyrus, and right hippocampus. The nonspatial tasks did not activate the right hippocampus (see the illustration below).

In a second study, Maguire and her colleagues used MRI to image the hippocampus. Increases in gray-matter volume (neurons) were found in the right and left hippocampi; no increases were seen in other parts of the brain. Analysis of hippocampal volume indicated that the control subjects had larger anterior hippocampal areas and the taxi drivers had larger posterior hippocampal areas. In addition, the measures indicated that the right posterior hippocampus increased in size as a function of years spent as a taxi driver.

To control for the influence of motion and the effects of stress in driving, the taxi drivers were compared with bus drivers. Bus drivers, who follow set routes, did not display hippocampal changes similar to those observed in taxi drivers.

As a result of these studies, Maguire and her coworkers suggest that the "mental map" of London used by the taxi drivers in delivering their passengers is located in the right posterior hippocampus. Furthermore, they propose that this region of the hippocampus expands to accommodate the map. This finding is confirmed in part by the study of a taxi driver, T.T., who had sustained bilateral hippocampal damage. In a virtual test of navigation, T.T. retained knowledge of the topography of London and its landmarks and could even navigate major routes. When he left the major routes, he became lost, however.

Findings from rodent studies have established that new cells migrate from the ventricular zone into the hippocampus and join the granular layer of the hippocampus. The survival of these new cells conjointly with the use of the mental map may underlie the expansion of the right hippocampus in humans. The expansion comes at a cost, however, indicated both by the decrease in size of the anterior hippocampus and by poorer performance on the part of taxi drivers compared with bus drivers on tests of new spatial information.

Maguire, E. A., R. S. J. Frackowiak, and C. D. Frith. Recalling routes around London: Activation of the right hippocampus in taxi drivers. *Journal of Neuroscience* 17:7103–7110, 1997.

Maguire, E. A., D. G. Gadian, I. S. Johnsrude, C. D. Good, J. Ashburner, R. S. J. Frackowiak, and C. D. Frith. Navigation-related structural change in the hippocampi of taxi drivers. *Proceedings of the National Academy of Sciences of the United States of America* 97:4398–4403, 2000.

Maguire, E. A., R. Nanner, and H. J. Spiers. Navigation around London by a taxi driver with bilateral hippocampal lesions. *Brain* 129:2894–907, 2006.

Maguire, E. A., K. Woollett, and H. J. Spiers. London taxi drivers and bus drivers: A structural MRI and neuropsychological analysis. *Hippocampus* 16:1091–101, 2006.

Horizontal sections

$z = -8$ mm $z = -6$ mm $z = -4$ mm

Right hippocampus

The location of activation seen in PET scans superimposed onto MRI brain images of taxi drivers as they recalled a complex route between two points in London. The peak activation is seen in the right hippocampus. (From Maguire et al., 2000.)

Verinoque Bohbot and Suzanne Corkin asked subjects, including H.M., to locate a sensor under a carpet by stepping on it (a human equivalent task to the Morris place task developed for rats). When the subjects stepped on the sensor, it activated a tone through a speaker some distance away.

H.M., who has an intact right parahippocampal gyrus, could learn the location of one sensor, but not two. Presumably, the right parahippocampal gyrus is sufficient for learning single locations, but additional temporal-lobe structures including the hippocampus are necessary for more complex spatial memory, including the memory of having previously performed and learned the task. The deficit displayed by H.M. is similar to that reported for rats in the Morris place task. The results of many studies show that they can learn one location of the hidden platform but fail when they are required to learn new locations.

Robert Astur and his coworkers, however, presented a virtual spatial-navigation problem to control subjects and to subjects with unilateral left- or right-hippocampal damage. The participants used a joystick to move about in a virtual three-dimensional swimming pool, trying to escape from the water by finding a platform hidden just beneath the surface as quickly as possible. The computer gave them both auditory and visual feedback when they had succeeded.

The view on the screen was a 60° first-person field of view, approximately the same visual field seen by the human eye. When participants pushed the joystick to the right, the view on the screen panned to the right, and so on. Each participant was given 20 trials, each of which might start from any of the four different starting locations around the edge of the pool. Then, each participant was each given a probe trial in which the escape platform was removed from the pool, and the time that the participant spent searching for the hidden platform at its former location was measured.

Astur and his colleagues report that both left- and right-hippocampal groups were severely impaired in solving the spatial-navigation task and in searching for the platform at a location where it had formerly been hidden. Although whether the deficit can be ascribed to the hippocampal damage alone is unclear, because the overlying cortex and amygdala also were damaged, the results not only confirm a role for the right hemisphere but also demonstrate that the left hemisphere is important.

The Dorsal and Ventral Streams

We have previously encountered David Milner and Melvyn Goodale's idea that at least two neural systems process the information used to represent objects in visual space: the posterior parietal cortex and the temporal cortex. Both systems receive information over pathways that begin in the visual cortex. The *dorsal stream* projects to the posterior parietal cortex, and the *ventral stream* projects to the inferior temporal cortex (see Figure 21.2). Both areas send projections to the frontal cortex to guide the movements of looking, reaching, and locomotion. In addition, we have encountered the idea that other sensory systems are similarly organized, with one component guiding movements in the dorsal stream and the other component guiding movements in the ventral stream.

Both neural processing systems likely contribute to spatial behavior but in different ways. The dorsal stream likely mediates actions toward or away from objects and is important for behaviors such as route following. The ventral stream likely guides actions that are more complex, including those in which objects are used as references to reach another location.

Thus, the dorsal stream mediates *egocentric* spatial behavior—that which moves the body toward objects or in relation to objects whose identity is unimportant except that they provide spatial guidance. Recall that patients with egocentric disorientation are impaired in way-finding in both familiar and novel environments, yet they have no difficulty in recognizing people or objects. The ventral stream mediates *allocentric* spatial behavior—that which moves the body in relation to objects or uses two or more objects to direct movement toward or away from a still different location.

In the following sections, we pursue the idea that at least two separate neural systems mediate spatial navigation. One system depends on the dorsal stream and on the parietal and frontal cortex; the other system depends on the ventral stream and temporal-lobe structures, including the hippocampal formation.

Types of Spatial Behavior

Experimental approaches to spatial behavior consider the spatial abilities of a remarkable range of animals, including ants, birds, rodents, and primates. Their spatial abilities are directed toward foraging for food, storing food, locating important objects in the environment, returning to a home base, and migration. Animals use a remarkable array of information to guide their spatial behavior, including visual, auditory, and olfactory information, sightings on the stars, geomagnetic fields, and gravitation force.

In keeping with the many applications of spatial skills to problem solving, animals have evolved a number of different spatial strategies that together form their spatial behavior. The distinctive nature of each of these spatial abilities suggests that they are mediated by partly different neural structures. In this section, we describe three forms of spatial navigation: route following, piloting, and dead reckoning.

Route Following

Perhaps the simplest spatial strategy is to follow a trail or move toward an object or cue, behaviors that can be referred to as *route following*. A salmon that swims for hundreds of miles through the ocean and then up a river to return to the site of its hatching is following an odor route. Similarly, ants that follow the trail left by other ants to a food source are following an odor route.

Some animals direct their movements toward the light, whereas other animals direct their movements toward the dark—examples of route following in which a light gradient forms the route. Our following a road or path or moving toward a landmark or even reaching for an object are still other examples of route following.

Piloting

Piloting is the ability to take a course to a place that is not directly marked by a cue or route. The pilot who guides a ship into a harbor may take a very irregular path by using a variety of landmarks that provide a spatial representation of the harbor and the obstacles that need to be avoided to enter safely.

Figure 21.3 illustrates a number of tasks used for studying route finding and piloting abilities in rats. Figure 21.3A shows a typical research room, containing a rich array of visual cues, such as cupboards, pictures, and windows. In the center of the room is a swimming pool used in the Morris water task (named after its inventor, Richard Morris). In this test of spatial abilities, a rat must escape from the water onto a platform, which can be visible or hidden.

If the platform is visible, it serves as a cue so that the rat can take a direct route toward it. If the platform is hidden, however, the rat must learn to use surrounding room cues to pilot to the platform. (Rats are well suited to this task. They are excellent swimmers, but their small size puts them at risk of losing normal body temperature if they stay in the water for long; so they are highly motivated to escape from the pool.)

The various mazes illustrated in Figure 21.3B through D are used in other laboratory tests of spatial navigation. For David Olton's radial-arm maze, an animal must learn that some arms contain food, whereas other arms do not. Because the arms appear similar, an animal must learn their location in relation

(A) Morris water task

Room cues

Submerged platform

Figure 21.3

Tasks Used to Study Spatial Behavior in Rodents (A) The swimming-pool task requires an animal to learn the location of a submerged, hidden platform. The only cue to the position of the platform is its spatial relation to cues about the room. (B) The radial-arm maze was designed as a test of foraging behavior in animals. A rat must learn which alleys contain food and which alleys have been visited on a given day. (C) In the T-maze, a rat has to differentiate right and left. (D) The Grice box also is a test of left–right differentiation. The food is placed in one alley until the animal has learned its location, and, then, the food is placed in the other alley instead. Usually, these various tasks are presented in open rooms, and the animals can use the many surrounding cues as aids to orientation.

(B) Olton radial-arm maze **(C) T-maze** **(D) Grice box**

to the room's topography and its cues. In the T-maze and Grice box, a correct response might consist of learning to go to only one location or learning to alternate locations on every trial.

Dead Reckoning

Dead reckoning—derived from the phrase "deduced reckoning"—is a form of navigation that depends on cues generated by an animal's own movement. It refers to the ability of an animal to know how far it has traveled and where in relation to a starting point, to monitor its speed and travel time, and to change direction as necessary.

Dead reckoning was an early form of navigation used by sailors and is believed to have been used by Columbus on his journeys between Europe and Central America (**Figure 21.4**A). Using a compass to monitor direction, the sailors calculated speed by throwing a piece of wood overboard at a certain point on the bow. As the ship moved past the piece of wood, a sailor chanted until the wood had passed a certain point on the stern. The chant was written in such a way that the last word spoken corresponded to a specific speed. If sailors could additionally tell time (for example, by using sun and star sightings), they could locate their position.

In other words, knowing direction, speed, and travel time allowed sailors to make an accurate record of a trip. This record could then be used to guide their return journey. Dead reckoning is still used today when fog interferes with the use of visual beacons; all that a sailor needs is a speedometer, watch, and compass.

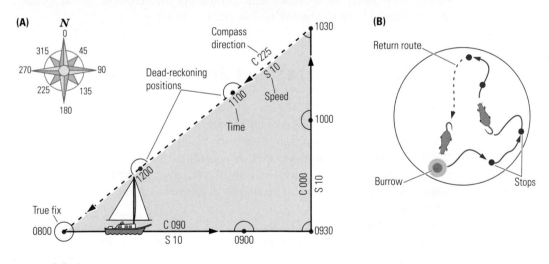

Figure 21.4

Dead Reckoning by Sailors and by Rats (A) A ship starts from a known location, arrives at a destination, and returns to the starting point without the use of external cues. The starting point is at 0800 hours; the direction (C stands for compass) is 90°; and the speed (S) is 10 knots. Time, direction, and speed are noted at each directional change, and dead-reckoning location is calculated and recorded each hour. Note that the return trip (dashed line) can be calculated from the plots made on the outward trip. (B) A rat foraging for a piece of food makes a number of turns, stops before finding the food and, on finding the food, returns directly home. The rat does not have a clock, compass, or speedometer and so must have internal processes for dead reckoning.

Nonhuman animals do not have mechanical means for measuring speed, time, and direction when they navigate by dead reckoning. Instead, they must derive cues from their own movement, which are collectively called **self-movement cues**. In principle, cues from a number of sensory systems, including proprioceptive and vestibular systems, can provide the necessary information. For example, sensory flow, including optical flow, gradients of sound and odors, and even of wind resistance, provide information about the speed and direction of movement.

In addition, an animal may monitor its movements by using the efferent copy of movement commands. That is, when an animal voluntarily decides to travel to a certain location, it can copy the instructions that it sends to its muscles. This efferent, or output, copy can be used to infer how far it has traveled and the direction that it has taken.

By using these cues to compute velocity and direction over time, an animal can keep track of its location in relation to a starting point. Then, by reversing these computations, the animal is able to return to that starting point (Figure 21.4B). Such behavior is useful when the starting point is a home to which the animal can carry food or to which it can escape from a predator. Dead reckoning is especially useful if an animal is traveling about in the dark, is in a new place where the environmental cues are unfamiliar, or is in a place where the visual cues often change.

Charles Darwin was the first to suggest that animals could use dead reckoning to navigate. Subsequently, many researchers have confirmed that they do so. When we speak of a person having a "sense of direction" or "sense of distance," most likely we are describing a conscious awareness of spatial location that is derived from the brain's skill at dead reckoning.

The Temporal Lobes and Spatial Behavior

Much research in the past 50 years on how the brain controls spatial behavior has been driven by John O'Keefe and Lynn Nadel's cognitive-mapping theory, which was initially proposed in their book titled *The Hippocampus As a Cognitive Map*. The theory proposes that, as an animal travels through its environment, it creates a brain representation of that environment in the form of a map, called a cognitive map. This map is then used to guide new trips through the same environment.

O'Keefe and Nadel located the cognitive map in the hippocampus, which, as you know, is in the temporal lobes and is thus part of the ventral stream. As will be described in the following sections, it is more correct to say that the hippocampal formation, which includes the hippocampus and many cortical and subcortical structures to which it connects, is the center of spatial mapping.

The Hippocampus As a Cognitive Map

The idea that animals use a cognitive map for spatial navigation has considerable appeal, because maps provide a very simple way of storing a large amount of data. The map of Napoleon's military campaign in Russia shown in **Figure 21.5**

Figure **21.5**

Efficient Data Storage Maps can represent vast amounts of information, as does this map drawn by Charles Joseph Minard portraying the losses suffered by Napoleon's army in the Russian campaign of 1812. Beginning at the left on the Polish–Russian border near the Niemen, the thick green band represents the size of the army (422,000 men) as it invaded Russia. The width of the band indicates the size of the army at each position. In September, the army reached Moscow, at the right side of the map, with 100,000 men. The path of Napoleon's retreat from Moscow in the bitterly cold winter is depicted by the dark blue band, which is tied to temperature and time scales. The remains of the Grande Armée struggled out of Russia with 10,000 men. This map may well be the best statistical graph ever drawn. (E. J. Marey, *La Methode Graphique*, Paris, 1885.)

vividly records the Grande Armee's losses on his disastrous trip to Moscow and back to France. To describe the losses in words would require substantially more space than is taken up by the map.

The theory that the hippocampus has a role in spatial behavior has also been supported by the results of many studies of the effect of damage to the hippocampus. In general, they show that damaging the hippocampus disrupts the ability of an animal to pilot or dead reckon through its environment.

The Hippocampus and the Food-Finding Behavior of Animals

The results of investigations with birds and rats point to the role of the hippocampus in spatial behavior.

Food Caching by Birds

Stimulated by O'Keefe and Nadel's theory that the hippocampus plays a central role in spatial behavior, other researchers, using other species and other testing methods, have produced a number of new lines of supporting evidence. One line of evidence, summarized by David Sherry and his coworkers, is based on the food-caching behavior of birds.

Many bird species will take pieces of food—sunflower seeds, for example—and hide them for later consumption. Some birds can hide many hundreds of items and find them later. A particularly large body of research concerns the abilities of birds in two major families, the chickadee and tit family (Paridae) and the jay and nutcracker family (Corvidae).

Chickadees store insect prey and seeds in scattered sites that typically include furrows in tree bark, conifer needle clusters, moss, and other natural hiding places. A small number of food items, often only one, are stored at each site, and cache sites are not reused. Cache sites may be scattered throughout a

Figure 21.6

Inferring Spatial Memory This graph relates hippocampal volume to forebrain volume in 3 food-storing (left) and 10 non-food-storing (right) families of songbirds. The hippocampi of birds that cache food, such as the black-capped chickadee, are about twice as large as the hippocampi of birds, such as the sparrow, that do not. (After D. F. Sherry, L. F. Jacobs, and S. J. C. Gaulin. *Trends in Neuroscience* 15, 1992, pp. 298–303.)

number of acres. Estimates of the number of items cached by a bird in a year total in the thousands. The items are left for periods ranging from hours to weeks before the bird returns to retrieve them.

The birds use distal spatial cues rather than local landmarks to recall the location of their caches. Distal spatial cues are objects that are at some distance away from a cache site, and landmarks are cues that are in close proximity to the cache site. If landmarks in the vicinity of a food item are disturbed, a bird's ability to find the food is not disturbed. Similarly, if an artificial cue, such as a colored object, is moved from a cache site, the bird is not prevented from retrieving the food at that location. If more-distal cues are displaced, however, the bird's search in a location is displaced to some degree.

If the caches on one side of an aviary are pilfered, the birds learn to avoid that side of the aviary. If cache sites marked by certain colored tapes are pilfered, but cache sites marked by different-colored tapes are not, the birds do not learn to differentiate between the colors, even though independent tests show that the birds can easily tell one color from another. The results of these experiments and many similar ones indicate that the birds are using distal spatial cues rather than local landmarks to mark the location of their cached food.

The results of studies comparing birds that cache food with birds that do not cache food indicate that the hippocampus is considerably larger in the birds that cache (**Figure 21.6**). If the hippocampus was damaged in birds that cached food, they continued to cache but were unable to retrieve the food. In a slightly different paradigm, female brown-headed cowbirds, which search for host nests in which to lay their eggs and must therefore retain a memory of many potential host nests, were found to have larger hippocampi than those of male cowbirds, which do not participate in searching for nests.

As summarized by David Sherry and his colleagues, changes in neurogenesis—in the number of cells added to the hippocampus—are related to food-storing behavior. Precursor cells migrate into the hippocampus and differentiate into new neurons during the season in which birds are storing food. Food storing in chickadees reaches its maximum in autumn, continues through the winter, and decreases in spring and summer. Both hippocampal neurogenesis and hippocampal size reach a maximum in autumn and decrease in spring. Food-storing experience also correlates with hippocampal size. If a food-storing marsh tit is prevented from storing food early in development, the relative size of its hippocampus lags behind that of age-matched controls.

Taken together, the findings in these studies, showing that food-storing birds can remember hundreds of locations at which food is stored, use distal spatial cues to locate food, and require the hippocampus to do so, suggest that the hippocampus plays an important role in spatial behavior.

Dead Reckoning in Rats

The results of a number of experiments suggest that the hippocampal formation also controls dead reckoning. In a testing situation in which rats emerge from a hidden burrow to forage on a circular table for large food pellets, when a rat finds a food pellet, it carries the pellet back to its refuge for eating (Whishaw et al., 2001).

The outward trip made by a rat as it is looking for food is circuitous, but the homeward trip is direct. When foraging in the light, a rat is able to use both room cues and self-movement cues for guidance. If the rat is tested in the dark and all olfactory and auditory cues are removed, the rat can return home only if it can access a record of the body movements made on the outward trip to calculate the homeward trip. It must dead reckon.

Normal rats are very accurate at returning home in both the light and the dark. If the hippocampal formation is damaged, however, the rats are accurate in the light but not in the dark. The finding that damage to the hippocampus disrupts dead reckoning as well as some forms of spatial mapping indicates that these two forms of navigation are related and that the hippocampus participates in both forms of spatial navigation.

Single-Cell Recording Within the Hippocampal Formation

The idea that cognitive mapping and the hippocampus play a role in spatial behavior is supported not only by findings that spatial behavior is disrupted by damage to the hippocampal formation but also by recordings of a remarkable number of cell types related to spatial behavior. These cells form three general classes:

1. **Place cells** discharge when an animal is in a specific location in its environment (**Figure 21.7**A and B).

2. **Head-direction cells** discharge when an animal faces a particular direction (Figure 21.7C).

3. **Grid cells** fire at regularly spaced nodes that appear to divide an environment into a grid (Figure 21.7D).

Many variations exist in the three classes of cells, cells can combine features of more than one cell class, and the different classes of cells are restricted to different areas within the hippocampal formation.

Figure 21.7

Classes of Spatially Related Cells in the Hippocampal Formation The X-Y coordinates at the right indicate the directional selectivity of the cell recorded at the left. (A and B) Place cells discharge when a rat is at a spatial location, irrespective of its orientation. (C) Head-direction cells discharge when the rat's head points in a given direction, irrespective of its location. (D) Grid cells discharge at many locations, forming a virtual grid that is invariant in the face of changes in the rat's direction, movement, or speed. (From P. Andersen, R. Morris, D. Amaral, T. Bliss, and J. O'Keefe. *The Hippocampus Book.* London: Oxford University Press, 2007, Fig. 11.21.)

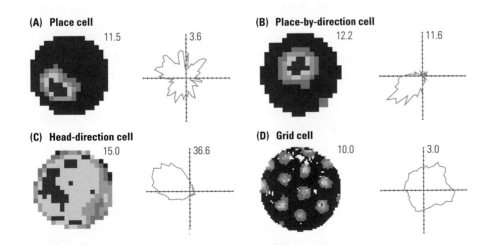

(A) Place cell 11.5 3.6

(B) Place-by-direction cell 12.2 11.6

(C) Head-direction cell 15.0 36.6

(D) Grid cell 10.0 3.0

Place Cells

Phillip Best and his coworkers give the following summary of the remarkable properties of place cells:

1. Within a short time of a rat's being placed in a novel environment, hippocampal formation place cells begin to discharge when the animal is in certain places in that environment. For some cells, whether the rat walks there itself or is carried there by the experimenter does not seem to matter. Other cells encode not only the rat's location but also the direction and speed of the rat's movement. (If the rat is walking on a straight path, the active cells are more likely to code direction as well as location.)

2. If the lights are turned off after the animals have explored the new environment, the place cells maintain their activity relative to the previously visualized location of cues. If a rat is removed temporarily and then returned after the cues in the environment have been changed, then the cells will modify their activity to represent the new environment. If the rat is present when a cue is removed, the cells are more likely to maintain their original firing relations.

3. Moving a few visual cues has little effect on the pattern of activity displayed by the cells, but, if all room cues are rotated, the cells will then discharge with respect to the new location of the cues.

4. If a rat is exploring a maze for food, some place cells will discharge when the rat is in a particular part of the maze. Moreover, these cells may discharge, say, only if the rat is intending to make a left turn but not if it is intending to make a right turn.

5. Place cells seem to prefer visual cues, although they can also be influenced by olfactory, vestibular, tactile, and auditory cues. For example, place cells in animals that are blind will respond to cues that the animals discover by touch.

6. If one of a number of cups in an apparatus contains water, some place cells will fire in relation to that cup. If the cup is moved, the preferred firing location for those place cells changes with the location of the cup.

7. If an animal is placed in an environment in which there is only one visual cue, then this single cue will determine where place cells discharge. If the single cue is removed, the cells continue to discharge, but the location at which they discharge begins to drift. If a visual cue that influences the firing of a place cell is moved about unpredictably relative to other cues, then the place cells eventually stop responding to that cue.

8. When numerous cells are recorded concurrently, many that are active in one environment will not be active when the rat is placed in another environment.

9. Place-cell activity is closely linked to an animal's ability to move; so, if a rat is restrained, the cells stop discharging.

Place cells can be recorded in structures other than the hippocampus, but only hippocampal cells appear to have the special versatility that allows them to change activity in response to changes in environmental cues. Nevertheless, some place cells in the hippocampus appear to have invariant properties. Longnian Lin and colleagues found cells in the hippocampus of mice that are activated only by a nest or bed. They argue that the hippocampus can represent higher-order "concepts" in addition to representing the location of objects.

Head-Direction Cells

Jeffrey Taube first summarized the extensive body of research suggesting the existence of head-direction cells in the hippocampal formation that indicate direction:

1. A head-direction cell discharges whenever a rat points its head in a particular direction. Different cells have different preferred directions. For example, one cell might discharge whenever the rat points its head to the west, whereas another cell will discharge whenever the rat points its head to the south.

2. The firing of head-direction cells is not related to the position of the animal's trunk and does not significantly depend on whether the rat is still or moving. Furthermore, head-direction cells do not adapt as time passes but maintain their rate of discharge as long as the rat's head is pointing in the preferred direction. A head-direction cell is not activated by the presence of a particular object in the environment. Rather, such a cell is responsive to direction itself and so is like the needle of a compass that continues to point north when the compass is moved.

3. Nevertheless, surrounding cues influence head-direction cells. If a rat is taken to a novel environment, its head-direction cells will quickly develop a preferred orientation there. If the rat is then removed from that environment while the cues are rotated and is subsequently returned, the head-direction cells' preferences will rotate with the cues. If the cues are rotated while the rat is in the environment, the preferred direction of head-direction cells is not as greatly influenced.

4. If the lights are turned off, head-direction cells maintain their tuning for many minutes.

5. When a rat is allowed to explore two environments connected by a tunnel, its head-direction cells will maintain the same preferred direction in both environments. But, if the cues in one environment are rotated while the rat is absent and then the rat is returned to that environment, the head-direction cells' preferences will again rotate with the cues. When the rat enters the tunnel and crosses to the second environment, the head-direction cells revert to their former orientation.

6. Head-direction cells are not limited to orienting the animal in a horizontal plane; they maintain their directional tuning when the animal climbs vertically up or down as well.

7. Head-direction cells continue to discharge when the rat is restrained, unlike place cells, which stop firing in such a situation.

8. Whereas place cells may fire in one environment but not in another and at different rates on different occasions, every head-direction cell is locked into a network that is constantly active, depending only on head direction.

Grid Cells

Grid cells were first described by Torkel Hafting and his colleagues. Each grid cell discharges at regular spatial intervals as if discharges marked nodes forming the points of equilateral triangles. The nodes represent points throughout the environment in which an animal is placed, forming a grid. The grid is invariant in the face of changes in the animal's direction, movement, or speed.

Different cells located at the same location have the same grid spacing and orientation relative to the environment. They differ, however, in the location of the nodes such that the firing peaks of one cell are slightly shifted from those of its neighbor. Cells located in different parts of the medial entorhinal cortex demark grids of different sizes. The orientation of the grids demarked by each cell can be oriented to different cues in the environment and can be influenced by the direction that an animal is facing.

Location of Spatial Cells

The regions of the hippocampal formation in which these three class of cells are found are largely different. **Figure 21.8** shows that place cells are recorded in the entorhinal cortex, subiculum, and hippocampus. Head-direction cells are recorded in the lateral mammillary nuclei, anterior thalamus, cingulate cortex, and postsubicular regions of the hippocampus. Grid cells are recorded in the medial entorhinal cortex.

This anatomical organization suggests that interactions among these three regions and their three classes of cells form the substrate of much of our spatial behavior. The place system allows an animal to navigate by using the relations between environmental cues, as proposed by the spatial-mapping theory. The head-direction system allows an animal to navigate in relation to its own spatial position. The grid cells provide a spatial framework that indicates the size of a space and the location in that space in which an animal finds itself.

Figure **21.8**

Locating Spatial Cells Locations in the brain where place cells, head-direction cells, and grid cells have been recorded in rats (sagittal section). Although the relations among the three systems is not well understood, the place-cell system mediates navigation by using environmental cues, the head-direction system mediates navigation in relation to the animal's own location, and the grid-cell system signals the size of a space and the animal's position within it.

They may provide a frame of reference similar to that provided by the latitude and longitude lines of a map.

Perhaps one way of thinking about the contribution of these three classes of cells is to say that the place-cell system tells us where things are in the world and the head-direction system and grid system tells us where we ourselves are.

As yet, few attempts have been made to record place, head-direction, or grid cells in primates or humans. Rats are small enough to move freely through complex environments while attached to electrodes; humans and monkeys are not. Edmund Rolls reports, however, that place cells are much less likely than head-direction cells to be recorded in monkeys, which, instead, seem to possess many "view cells"—cells that discharge when a monkey looks in particular directions. Therefore, place cells and head-direction cells may possibly be closely linked to eye movements in primates and to body movements in rats.

Similarly, although there have been many tests of piloting behavior in brain-damaged humans, there have been few tests of dead reckoning. However, in an examination of the performance of neurosurgical patients with left or right temporal lobectomies on tests of dead reckoning, the patients were walked away from their homes in one direction for a while and then turned and walked in another direction (Worsley et al., 2001). At this point, they were asked to return home. Patients with right-temporal lobectomies had difficulty finding their way home; they also had trouble when asked to walk in a given direction, make a turn of a certain size, and turn and walk for a certain distance again.

Spatial Activity and Episodic Memory

Despite the substantial body of evidence suggesting that the hippocampal formation plays some role in spatial behavior, other evidence suggests that this role is but one hippocampal function in memory. For example, Stuart Zola-Morgan and his coworkers favor the idea that the hippocampus has a role in memory and that spatial memory is but one kind of memory. They describe R.B., who displayed general anterograde amnesia.

R.B. was a male postal worker who, at 52 years of age, suffered a temporary shortage of arterial blood to the brain secondary to a coronary bypass operation. In the next 5 years, until his death, R.B. exhibited marked anterograde amnesia. A postmortem examination revealed a bilateral loss of all cells in CA1, a restricted part of the hippocampus (see Figure 18.8B). R.B.'s case seems to suggest that general anterograde amnesia can follow hippocampal damage, which would be inconsistent with the idea that the hippocampus is selectively engaged in spatial behavior.

Even the findings in studies on birds, although seemingly consistent with a special role of the hippocampus in spatial behavior, are amenable to a memory interpretation. Nicola Clayton and her colleagues report that, if birds are given especially tasty or perishable items to store, they are likely to retrieve those items before retrieving other ones. The food-storing bird also considers whether other birds are watching and takes preventative measures to protect cached food if they are. Thus spatial memories are also episodic, supporting the idea that the hippocampus plays a general role in memory.

Parietal and Frontal Lobes and Spatial Behavior

In our description of topographic dysfunction in human subjects, we mentioned the possibility that there are two systems for spatial behavior, one implicating the dorsal stream through the lateral parietal cortex and the other implicating the ventral stream through the temporal cortex. The former system may respond to cues and mediate route navigation, whereas the latter system may identify the location of places and tell us where we are in relation to those places. In keeping with this idea, we will describe the role of the parietal cortex and the frontal cortex in spatial navigation.

The Parietal Lobes

Not surprisingly, considering that it is a region that forms part of the dorsal stream, damage to the parietal cortex results in spatial impairments. Disorders of visuospatial exploration stemming from such damage were described by Rezsö Bálint and are referred to by Giuseppe Vallar as Bálint–Homes syndrome. Researchers now recognize about eight different defects of visual exploration that, in most known instances, have resulted from bilateral lesions of the parietal cortex but do not all coincide in every such case (**Table 21.1**). Perhaps the most dramatic symptoms are those first described by Bálint (see also Chapter 14).

Bálint's patient had bilateral damage to the occipital and parietal cortex that included parts of the dorsal temporal lobes. He also had a zone of unilateral damage to the dorsal parietal and motor cortex (**Figure 21.9**). He had come to Bálint's attention after suffering a stroke, and his condition remained unchanged for 6 years.

This man had complete visual fields, was reported to be capable of eye movements, and recognized and named colors, objects, and pictures. When presented with visual stimuli, he directed his gaze from 35° to 40° to the right of them and saw only what was in his direct line of sight. Only after prompting would he look to the left and notice that the stimuli were there. After his attention had been directed to an object, he noticed nothing else—a response that was true for objects of all sizes, from a pin to a human figure. The patient would not look over a picture or scene but fastened on the first item that he saw in it.

The impairment resulted in a reading defect, because he focused on a single letter and only with difficulty could he work backward through a word to decode it. The patient was also impaired in reaching. If asked to grasp an object or point to a target, he groped and hit the target only by chance. Misreaching extended to lighting a cigar, which he would attempt to light in the middle. The patient was also unable to estimate distance and could not tell which of two objects was closer.

Gordon Holmes described a group of patients who had suffered penetrating missile wounds to

Table 21.1 Deficits in visuospatial exploration

Displaced visual attention

Inability to perceive more than one stimulus

Defective visual control of movement (optic ataxia)

Inability to follow a moving target

Defective accommodation and convergence

Inability to maintain fixation

Inability to voluntarily direct gaze to targets (gaze apraxia)

Abnormal visual search

Figure 21.9

Bálint's Drawing of the Areas of Softening in His Patient's Brain
(After de Renzi, 1982.)

Left hemisphere

Right hemisphere

the brain. Their most notable symptoms were various impairments in eye movement. They had difficulty in looking at a stimulus, whether it was presented visually or aurally, in maintaining visual fixation, in following a moving target, in keeping the eyes focused on an approaching object, and in blinking in response to a visual threat.

These patients also failed to comprehend the spatial features of a stimulus that they were looking at and could recognize. That is, they had trouble judging the location of objects in space, estimating distance, discriminating length and size, and evaluating depth and thickness. As a result, they ran into objects when walking and had difficulty in reading and in counting scattered objects. The patients also sometimes failed to notice objects placed before them and, like Bálint's patient, did not notice anything else once their attention had been attracted by a stimulus.

Since these early reports, there have been many accounts of patients with similar problems, although the precise symptoms have varied, depending on how an injury was acquired, whether it was bilateral, and where it was located. **Figure 21.10** depicts misjudgment by a patient studied by Truett Allison and his colleagues who had bilateral posterior cortical lesions resulting in small lower-temporal-quadrant-field defects, accompanied by dramatic deficits in the visual control of reaching and other movements (optic ataxia) and by deficits in eye movements:

Figure 21.10

A Visuospatial Deficit A patient with Bálint's syndrome attempts to pour fluid into a glass. (After Allison et al., 1969.)

> A manifestation of visual disorientation noted by the nursing staff five months after operation was when he attempted to light a cigarette. He took it out of the packet and put it in his mouth, then clumsily took a match out of the matchbox and lit it, afterwards directing the flame towards his lower lip, missing the cigarette. . . . He could not pour fluid from a bottle into a glass but spilled it on the tablecloth. He was unable to shake hands without first groping for the proffered hand. It could be demonstrated that visual memory was intact and did not contribute to his errors. When an object (e.g., a matchbox) was held up either above his head, to the right, or to the left and he was asked to note its position, close his eyes for a moment, and then point in the general direction in which he had seen the object, he did this correctly. Therefore, it appeared that his ability to remember the position of an object in space was not impaired. (Allison et al., 1969, pp. 324–326)

To differentiate the many deficits that such patients suffer, investigators have focused on two aspects of visual function: visual localization and depth perception. For example, to demonstrate a disorder of spatial localization independent of a disorder of reaching or pointing, Julia Hannay and her co-workers projected one or two dots on a screen for 300 ms. Two seconds later, they projected an array of numbers, and the subjects were asked to pick the number (or numbers) located in the same position (or positions) as the dot (or dots).

Patients with right-hemisphere lesions were impaired at this task in comparison with control subjects and subjects with left-hemisphere lesions. This deficit is not simply a manifestation of neglect, because errors were distributed equally in the left and right visual fields. It is not surprising that a person who is unable to receive a sense impression of the location of points in space would have a hard time directing his or her movements, resulting in an apparent spatial deficit.

In a compelling example, researchers designed an experiment using random dot stereograms to study the cues necessary to perceive depth (Carmon and Bechtoldt, 1969). Looking into eyepieces, the subjects saw an apparently random array of dots. When viewed with one eye alone, the array had no contour or depth and looked rather like a complex crossword puzzle with black and white boxes. However, when the array was viewed as a stereogram—both eyes open and each looking independently at left-eye and right-eye views of the same image—a striking figure–background contour suddenly appeared (a figure appeared to float in front of a background), because of slight disparities between the images shown to the left and right eye.

Most normal subjects and patients with left-hemisphere damage easily perceived the contour, but most patients with right-hemisphere damage did very badly at this test, illustrating a defect in depth perception. The result supports the idea that at least some part of the mechanism for depth perception is more strongly represented in the right hemisphere.

Many deficits described in the preceding paragraphs appear related to parietal-cortex damage. In these cases, the dorsal stream, which projects through the parietal cortex, may be implicated. The function of the parietal cortex is to provide a coordinate system of visual space and to locate objects in this space. In the absence of this system, a patient will still see an object but will not be able to direct eye or hand movements toward it accurately.

Various investigators have identified neurons in the monkey posterior parietal cortex that respond to stimuli presented within a monkey's grasping space. These cells—or some of them—likely project to the motor system to guide the limbs in moving voluntarily toward targets in various spatial locations. The parietal cortex also contains neurons that appear to have a role in directing hand and eye movements toward stimuli presented in grasping space, providing further evidence that the parietal cortex has a special role in directing movements to visual targets.

The Frontal Lobes

The frontal cortex, too, is important for spatial discriminations. The most dramatic demonstration comes from experiments by Richard Nakamura and his coworkers. They spared all the visual areas of the posterior cortex while removing the entire cortex anterior to it in monkeys. The monkeys failed to show any signs of vision, but recordings of single-cell activity in the visual areas revealed that the cells were functioning normally. Thus, removal of the frontal cortex renders animals chronically blind and unable to navigate even though the visual system is functioning.

Findings in a number of studies have demonstrated that more-selective impairments follow more-restricted lesions in the visual cortex. For example, if the finger area of the motor cortex is disconnected from the visual centers, a monkey can no longer pick up food by using the pincer grasp (Haaxma and Kuypers, 1975).

It is difficult to distinguish impairments in the detection of objects from impairments in spatial behavior. Some features of object-detection impairments, however, do suggest that the underlying cause is a spatial impairment. Patricia Goldman-Rakic, using rhesus monkeys with small lesions in the frontal cortex along the principal sulcus, reported such an experiment.

The monkeys had been trained to fixate on a spot of light in the center of a television monitor. A second dot of light was flashed briefly in a monkey's visual field. The monkeys were reinforced with food for waiting until the fixation spot disappeared before directing their gaze to the new visual target. Monkeys with unilateral lesions failed to direct their gaze to the new target after even very short delays. If there was no delay, however, they performed normally. Varying the location of the lesion produced selective deficits associated with different parts of the visual field.

These findings demonstrate that the principal sulcus contains a mechanism for guiding responses on the basis of stored information in the absence of external cues. They also suggest that the memory for the location of objects may be mapped in visuospatial coordinates.

There is a parallel to these eye-movement results in experiments that require monkeys to reach toward a target. If a monkey with lesions in the principal sulcus is given a delayed-response task in which the object's location is the relevant variable, impairments are observed after short delays (see Figure 16.12A). Other discrimination tasks that do not require memory for spatial location are not impaired by these lesions.

Richard Passingham reports memory impairments in a less-artificial task in rhesus monkeys with principal sulcus lesions. In this experiment, the monkeys were trained to retrieve peanuts from behind 25 different doors in the shortest number of trials, without returning to a door a second time. This task tested each monkey's spatial memory for doors that it had already opened. The monkeys with lesions were severely impaired in their performance.

Michael Petrides and Brenda Milner report a somewhat analogous deficit in people with frontal-lobe damage. These patients were presented with a set of pages that each contained an array of the same visual stimuli but with the stimuli presented in a different order on each page. They were asked to point to one of the stimuli on each page but to do so without pointing to the same page location twice. Thus, the patients had to remember the locations of the selections that they had made previously. The frontal-lobe patients displayed impairments at this task.

Because the frontal cortex has important connections with the basal ganglia, researchers hypothesized that spatial-memory impairments of a similar kind would be found subsequent to basal ganglia lesions. David Ingle and Karin Hoff report the results of an interesting experiment with frogs, indicating that just such impairment can be obtained.

A visible barrier was placed beside a frog and then removed. After a delay, a large dark object was moved toward the frog, causing the frog to leap away. Normal frogs avoided leaping into the barrier's previous location or leaped in such a way that they landed behind its previous location, indicating that they remembered the location. Frogs with basal ganglia lesions behaved as if they failed to remember the barrier's previous location, although they avoided the barrier quite well when it was present.

Individual Differences in Spatial Abilities

Chapter 12 examined a range of biological and environmental factors that produce individual variations in cerebral asymmetry. In this section, we concentrate on differences attributed to sex and handedness that appear to influence individual spatial abilities.

Sex-Related Differences

Adult males tend to perform better than adult females on certain spatial tests. This male advantage in spatial ability is generally contrasted with a female advantage in language skills, fine motor movements, and perceptual speed. The female advantage in these areas is conceded to be quite small in statistical terms, about a 0.2 standard deviation, whereas the male advantage in spatial performance is large, about a 0.5 standard deviation.

In the tests of virtual water-maze learning described earlier, Astur and his coworkers reported one of the largest sex differences favoring males. Maguire and her colleagues, however, compiled evidence that females are more likely to navigate by using landmarks, whereas males are more likely to use spatial-mapping procedures (see Figure 12.2). In the Astur task, landmarks were not prominent.

Debora Saucier and her colleagues suggest that the sex differences in spatial ability apply not only to the task but also to the part of space in which a task is performed. They suggest that males excel in performing tasks in distant space, whereas the female advantage is most obvious in peripersonal space. Thus, the Astur task would provide an advantage to males.

The study of spatial abilities dates to the early part of the twentieth century, in association with studies designed to predict mechanical aptitude. As interest in spatial abilities developed, studies eventually began to include mixed age and sex groups, from which the generalization that adult males perform better than adult females gradually emerged.

When Eleanor Maccoby and Carol Jacklin reviewed this literature in 1974, the idea that this sex difference emerges in adolescence and is due to environmental influences became a dominant view. Subsequently, the results of many studies have demonstrated sex differences in much younger children. Part of the difficulty in ascertaining the validity of observed age and sex differences in spatial abilities stems from the large number of different kinds of tests that have been used and the diversity of the populations tested.

The research suggests that females and males differ in their abilities at such skills as chess, mathematics, music, and art. Mathematical aptitude has received the closest scrutiny. Findings in a large number of studies have shown that males outperform females on tests of quantitative ability. In the United States, scores on the Scholastic Aptitude Test and the Johns Hopkins University mathematical talent search indicate that these differences become apparent in adolescence and are more evident at the high end of the performance scale. Among top scorers on the College Board aptitude tests, males outnumber females by about 17 to 1.

The existence of sex differences, however small, is of great interest to students of spatial function. On the practical side, they must be considered when tests of brain function are developed, standardized, and administered. They must also be considered in interpreting the consequences of brain damage. More importantly, they provide a key to understanding brain organization and function.

Apart from environmental influences, the number of possible explanations for the differences between males and females is limited; therefore, the discovery of relevant factors through the use of the scientific method is a real possibility. The differences may be hormonally produced, emerging as a result of the action of hormones on neural organization and function. Alternatively, they may be genetic, in which case they are sex linked and are probably determined by a recessive gene on the X chromosome.

Genetic Contributions

The usual explanation for a genetic basis for male and female differences in spatial ability goes something like this. During the formative period of the evolution of modern humans, a differentiation of roles in food gathering was adaptive. A primary occupation of males was hunting, which requires an ability to find one's way about a large area. Hunting also requires the ability to throw spears and aim arrows, both of which are spatial skills. Males endowed with these abilities would be more successful than those who were not and consequently would be "selected" in the Darwinian sense. It is quite irrelevant that those skills are no longer vital today; if they are encoded in sex-linked genes, males will tend to inherit them anyway.

Mark McGee suggested that spatial skills are heritable through an X-linked, recessive gene. Females have two X chromosomes, and males have one. Thus, traits that are thought to be carried by a single gene on the X chromosome are said to be sex linked: if such a gene is recessive, more males than females will be affected. Under this arrangement, according to the usual estimates, 50% of males and 25% of females will carry the gene and have enhanced spatial abilities. In other words, about one-fourth of females will score above the male median on tests of spatial abilities, a finding obtained in most studies.

The recessive-gene hypothesis has been put to a number of tests, but it has not emerged unscathed. According to the hypothesis, certain correlations should emerge in the offspring of different families, but these correlations have not been obtained. Another problem concerns the tests used to obtain scores for correlations. Studies using different tests have obtained different correlations, raising the possibility that there may be different kinds of spatial abilities. The results suggest either that alternative inheritance models should be considered or that sex-related differences have other explanations.

Hormonal Influences

Three lines of evidence suggest that hormones influence sex differences in spatial abilities, including findings from: (1) developmental studies, (2) studies of persons with chromosomal–hormonal abnormalities, and (3) studies investigating the relation between androgenicity and spatial abilities.

As noted earlier, sex differences in spatial performance are found more reliably in adults than in prepubescent children, suggesting that such differences may be partly attributable to hormonal changes during puberty. Prenatal or early postnatal sex-related hormonal influences could account for differences obtained with prepubescent children. This hypothesis seems to be supported by the results of studies of patients with **Turner's syndrome**, a disorder found in females born with a single X chromosome rather than the normal XX pair. Their intelligence and verbal abilities are distributed throughout the normal range, but their spatial abilities are impaired. They get extremely low scores on tests of mental rotation, the block-design test of the Wechsler Adult Intelligence Scale, the spatial subtest of the Primary Mental Abilities Test, the Road-and-Map Test of Direction Sense, and tests of imaginary movements and direct rotation.

The results are counterintuitive and at variance with the recessive-gene hypothesis, which would predict that females with a single X chromosome ought to be similar to males, who also have one X chromosome. Because females with Turner's syndrome produce no gonadal hormones, the suggestion is that gonadal hormones influence spatial abilities. Current proposals from studies examining this hypothesis are that levels of androgens (masculinizing hormones) or the balance between estrogen and androgens might determine spatial abilities.

Some researchers have even argued that the more androgens females receive, the better their spatial abilities. For males, who are already receiving a high level of androgens, more might be too much, and spatial and other abilities might be impaired. Consequently, females receiving large amounts of androgen and males receiving moderate amounts would be expected to have enhanced spatial skills.

The mechanisms that hormones are thought to influence in modulating spatial abilities are in the brain. Presumably, they are the same neural systems that are responsible for spatial abilities in general. How these mechanisms might work is not known. Early in life, hormones may influence neural connections, neural growth, and cell death, thus sculpting a spatial neural system that is quite different in some persons (who therefore have enhanced spatial abilities) from that in others. On the other hand, hormones might selectively modulate neural function in these systems through still unknown mechanisms.

Handedness and Spatial Ability

Left-handedness is often proposed to confer a special spatial advantage. For example, Leonardo da Vinci and Michelangelo were left-handed, left-handedness is common in tennis players and baseball pitchers, and left-handers are reported to be disproportionately represented in engineering and architecture faculties.

Richard Harshman and his colleagues report results suggesting that the relations between cognitive functioning and handedness may be complex. Harshman's group administered an extensive battery of tests to three large samples representing three different populations, defined by the investigators as a "high-reasoning population," a "low-reasoning population," and a randomly selected control group. Overall, males performed better on spatial tests than females, as was expected.

In some of the populations, left-handedness in males was associated with lower spatial scores, but it was associated with higher spatial scores in females. In an attempt to find out why this effect existed only in certain populations, Harshman's group examined the effects of other variables and found that sex, handedness, and reasoning ability were all related to spatial scores. Among what he defined as a high-reasoning group, left-handed males had lower spatial scores and left-handed females had higher spatial scores than right-handed comparison groups. Among low-reasoning groups, the relation was reversed: left-handed males had high spatial scores and left-handed females had low spatial scores in relation to their comparison groups.

In a retrospective analysis of previous studies, Harshman suggests that differences in the groups sampled could account for the contradictory results obtained in previous work. That is, if a sample group was a university population, high spatial scores might be expected from left-handed females and low spatial scores from left-handed males. If a sample population was more heterogeneous, the opposite pattern of results might be obtained.

Neuropsychological Spatial Tests

A surprising number of tests have been devised for measuring spatial abilities. A noteworthy example is the test used in Mary-Lou Smith and Brenda Milner's studies of patients who had undergone elective surgery to remove the hippocampus as a treatment for epilepsy. These researchers employed 16 small toys as stimulus objects, spread out over a table. A subject was told that the purpose of the test was to measure the ability to estimate prices and that the task consisted of estimating the average price of a real object represented by the toy.

The subject was told to point to a toy, name it, and think of a price. After 10 seconds, the price was asked for and the subject was instructed to move on to another toy, and so on. Then the subject was moved away from the table and was asked to recall the objects that had been on it. After this test of object recall, a sheet of brown paper the same size as the original table was placed before the subject, and he or she was asked to place the toys on it in their original arrangement. The two recall tests were then repeated 24 hours later.

The object array is illustrated in **Figure 21.11**A. Scores were given for the recall of the objects' names; in addition, the researchers measured the distances between the objects' original locations and the patient's immediate recollection of where the objects had been, as well as between the original locations and the patient's delayed recollection of where the objects had been. On the measure of name recall, patients with right-hippocampus damage and patients with left-hippocampus damage were moderately impaired, with the left-hippocampal patients having lower scores than the right-hippocampal patients.

The results for the spatial component of the experiment are shown in Figure 21.11B, indicating a selective participation of the right hippocampus in spatial

Figure **21.11**

Test of Spatial Memory and Its Results (A) In this test of spatial memory for objects, showing a typical arrangement of 16 toys in 16 fixed locations, subjects are required to point to the objects and estimate their individual prices. The objects are then removed, and the subjects are asked to indicate where each object had been located within the array. (B) Graph of the performances of left-temporal and right-temporal patients and of controls on the recall of absolute location. (After Smith and Milner, 1981.)

(A) Test of spatial memory

(B) Results

(A)

Fold a paper...

...and punch a hole through the two sheets.

When the paper is unfolded, where will the holes be?

(B)

Examine this cube.

Which of these cubes is the same?

Figure **21.12**

Measuring Spatial Abilities

Sample test items for (A) a visualization test and (B) an orientation test. As you work on the orientation sample, note that no letter appears on more than one face of a given cube. (After Halpern, 1986.)

memory. Scores for the left-temporal group were comparable to scores for the control group, but scores for the right-temporal group were extremely low on both immediate and delayed recall tests.

Visualization tests evaluate the ability to manipulate, rotate, twist, or invert two- or three-dimensional stimulus objects mentally. The underlying ability seems to entail a process of recognition, retention, and recall of a configuration whose parts move and change place, as when an object is manipulated in three-dimensional space or a flat pattern is folded and unfolded (**Figure 21.12**A). McGee suggests that visualization is important to two aspects of mental functioning: imagery and mathematical ability, especially for the understanding of geometry and algebra.

Orientation tests evaluate comprehension of the arrangement of elements within a visual stimulus pattern and the aptitude to remain unconfused by the changing orientation in which a spatial configuration may be presented (Figure 21.12B). McGee suggests that orientation ability is related to field independence—the ability to orient an object accurately while ignoring the background against which it is viewed.

There is a growing consensus among researchers that two-dimensional paper-and-pencil tests may not tap the same spatial abilities that are exercised in the real-life process of way-finding. Just as it is difficult to subject brain-injured patients to real-life tests of navigating through novel and familiar environments, it is not possible to perform brain scans on subjects as they perform real-life tasks. Consequently, the use of computer-based virtual spatial tasks has increased in the hope that these tasks can enable investigators to evaluate the same abilities as those used in a real spatial world.

Summary

Organization of Spatial Behavior

Evidence obtained from brain-injured people suggests that the right hemisphere plays a special role in spatial behavior. Damage to the right hemisphere produces a number of different kinds of impairment in spatial abilities, depending on the location of the damage. Damage to the dorsal parietal cortex and cingulate cortex impairs egocentric spatial behavior in which body position plays a central role. Damage to the lingual gyrus and parahippocampal gyrus impairs the use of external cues in spatial behavior.

Types of Spatial Behavior

There are many kinds of spatial behavior. Route following includes (1) moving toward or away from landmarks or cues or (2) following a sensory gradient such as an odor trail. Piloting includes the use of landmarks or cues to plot routes or locate places in relation to those cues. Dead reckoning entails the use of self-movement cues to locate a present position and to return to a starting location.

The Temporal Lobes and Spatial Behavior

The results of lesion studies in rodents, correlative studies of food caching in birds, and imaging studies suggest that the right temporal lobe including the hippocampal formation plays a central role in complex navigation, such as that used by taxi drivers in traveling between two locations.

Single-Cell Recording Within the Hippocampal Formation

Single-cell-recording studies show that that at least three general classes of cells code spatial behavior.

Place cells are active when an animal is at a particular spatial location or views a particular scene. Head-direction cells are active when an animal's head points in a specific direction. Grid cells are active at nodes that appear to subdivide a spatial region into a grid. Although each class of cell can include properties of other cells, the regions of the brain in which the classes are found are distinct.

Parietal and Frontal Lobes and Spatial Behavior
Damage to the parietal cortex results in a number of impairments affecting the accuracy with which eye movements or hand movements are directed toward objects. Damage to the frontal cortex impairs the memory process employed in directing the eyes to a target.

Individual Differences in Spatial Abilities
Several lines of evidence suggest that sex and handedness influence human spatial abilities. Thus, sex hormones and cortical organization can influence spatial behavior. Tests of spatial abilities are useful in indicating both the site and the side of damage in humans.

References

Aguirre, G. K., and M. D'Esposito. Topographical disorientation: A synthesis and taxonomy. *Brain* 122:1613–1628, 1999.

Allison, R. S., L. J. Hurwitz, J. G. White, and T. J. Wilmot. A follow-up study of a patient with Bálint's syndrome. *Neuropsychologia* 7:319–333, 1969.

Astur, R. S., M. L. Ortiz, and R. J. Sutherland. A characterization of performance by men and women in a virtual Morris water task: A large and reliable sex difference. *Behavioural Brain Research* 93:185–190, 1998.

Astur, R. S., L. B. Taylor, A. N. Mamelak, L. Philpott, and R. J. Sutherland. Humans with hippocampus damage display severe spatial memory impairments in a virtual Morris water task. *Behavioural Brain Research* 132:77–84, 2002.

Bálint, R. Seelenlahmung des "Schauens," optische Ataxie, raumlielie Störung der Aufmerksamkeit. *Monatsschrift fuer Psychiatrie und Neurologie* 25:51–81, 1909.

Benton, A. L. *Right–Left Discrimination and Finger Localization*. New York: Hoeber-Harper, 1959.

Benton, A. L. Visuoperceptive, visuospatial, and visuoconstructive disorders. In K. M. Heilman and E. Valenstein, Eds. *Clinical Neuropsychology*. New York: Oxford University Press, 1979.

Benton, A. L., N. R. Varney, and K. deS. Hamsher. Visuospatial judgment: A clinical test. *Archives of Neurology* 35:364–367, 1978.

Best, P. J., A. M. White, and A. Minai. Spatial processing in the brain: The activity of hippocampal place cells. *Annual Review of Neuroscience* 24:459–486, 2001.

Bohbot, V. D., and S. Corkin. Posterior parahippocampal place learning in H.M. *Hippocampus* 17:863–872, 2007.

Brain, W. R. Visual disorientation with special reference to lesions of the right cerebral hemisphere. *Brain* 64:244–272, 1941.

Carmon, A., and H. P. Bechtoldt. Dominance of the right cerebral hemisphere for stereopsis. *Neuropsychologia* 7:29–39, 1969.

Corballis, M. C. Mental rotation: Anatomy of a paradigm. In M. Potegal, Ed. *Spatial Abilities: Development and Physiological Foundations*. New York: Academic Press, 1982.

Corkin, S. Tactually-guided maze-learning in man: Effects of unilateral cortical excisions and bilateral hippocampal lesions. *Neuropsychologia* 3:339–351, 1965.

Corkin, S. The role of different cerebral structures in somaesthetic perception. In E. C. Carterette and M. P. Friedman, Eds. *Handbook of Perception*, vol. 6. New York: Academic Press, 1978.

Clayton, N. S., J. M. Dally, and N. J. Emery. Social cognition by food-caching corvids: The western scrub-jay as a natural psychologist. *Philosophical Transaction of the Royal Society of London: Biological Sciences* 362:507–522, 2007.

Darwin, C. On the origin of certain instincts. *Nature* 7:417–418, 1873.

de Renzi, E. *Disorders of Space Exploration and Cognition*. New York: Wiley, 1982.

Goldman-Rakic, P. S. Circuitry of primate prefrontal cortex and regulation of behavior by representational memory. In V. B. Mountcastle, F. Plum, and S. R. Geiger, Eds. *Handbook of Physiology*, vol. 5, *Higher Functions of the Brain*. Bethesda, Md.: American Physiological Society, 1987.

Grusser, O. J. The multimodal structure of the extrapersonal space. In A. Hein and M. Jeannerod, Eds. *Spatially Oriented Behavior*. New York: Springer, 1987.

Haaxma, R., and H. G. J. M. Kuypers. Intrahemispheric cortical connections and visual guidance of hand and finger movements in the rhesus monkey. *Brain* 98:239–260, 1975.

Hafting, T., M. Fyhn, S. Molden, M. B. Moser, and E. I. Moser. Microstructure of a spatial map in the entorhinal cortex. *Nature* 436:801–806, 2005.

Halpern, D. F. *Sex Differences in Cognitive Abilities*. Hillsdale, N.J.: Lawrence Erlbaum, 1986.

Hannay, H. J., N. R. Varney, and A. L. Benton. Visual localization in patients with unilateral brain disease. *Journal of Neurology, Neurosurgery and Psychiatry* 39:307–313, 1976.

Harshman, R. A., E. Hampson, and S. A. Berenbaum. Individual differences in cognitive abilities and brain organization I: Sex and handedness differences in ability. *Canadian Journal of Psychology* 37:144–192, 1983.

Head, H. *Studies in Neurology.* London: Oxford University Press, 1920.

Hécaen, H., J. de Ajuriaguerra, and J. Massonet. Les troubles visuoconstructifs par lesions parieto-occipitales droites: Role des perturbations vestibulaires. *Encephale* 1:122–179, 1951.

Hécaen, H., C. Tzortzis, and P. Rondot. Loss of topographical memory with learning deficits. *Cortex* 16:525–542, 1980.

Holmes, G., and G. Horax. Disturbances of spatial orientation and visual attention, with loss of stereoscopic vision. *Archives of Neurology and Psychiatry* 1:385–407, 1919.

Hoshooley, J. S., and D. F. Sherry. Greater hippocampal neuronal recruitment in food-storing than in non-food-storing birds. *Developmental Neurobiology* 67:406–414, 2007.

Ingle, D., and K. S. Hoff. Neural mechanisms of short-term memory in frogs. *Society for Neuroscience Abstracts* 14:692, 1988.

Jackson, J. H. On the nature of duality of the brain. *Brain* 38:80–103, 1915.

Levine, D. N., J. Warach, and M. J. Farah. Two visual systems in mental imagery: Dissociation of "what" and "where" in imagery disorders due to bilateral posterior cerebral lesions. *Neurology* 35:1010–1015, 1985.

Lin, L., G. Chen, H. Kuang, D. Wang, and J. Z. Tsien. Neural encoding of the concept of nest in the mouse brain. *Proceedings of the National Academy of Sciences of the United States of America* 104:6066–6071, 2007.

Maccoby, E. E., and C. N. Jacklin. *The Psychology of Sex Differences.* Stanford, Calif.: Stanford University Press, 1974.

Maguire, E. A., N. Burgess, and J. O'Keefe. Human spatial navigation: Cognitive maps, sexual dimorphism, and neural substrates. *Current Opinion in Neurobiology* 9:171–177, 1999.

McFie, J., and O. L. Zangwill. Visual-constructive disabilities associated with lesions of the left hemisphere. *Brain* 83:243–260, 1960.

McGee, M. G. Human spatial abilities: Psychometric studies and environmental, genetic, hormonal, and neurological influences. *Psychological Bulletin* 86:889–918, 1979.

Milner, A. D., and M. A. Goodale. *The Visual Brain in Action.* Oxford: Oxford University Press, 1995.

Milner, B. Visually-guided maze learning in man: Effects of bilateral hippocampal, bilateral frontal, and unilateral cerebral lesions. *Neuropsychologia* 3:317–338, 1965.

Milner, B. Interhemispheric differences in the localization of psychological processes in man. *British Medical Bulletin* 27:272–277, 1971.

Milner, B., S. Corkin, and H.-L. Teuber. Further analysis of the hippocampal amnesic syndrome: 14-year follow-up study of H.M. *Neuropsychologia* 6:215–234, 1968.

Morris, R. G. M., P. Garrud, J. Rawlings, and J. O'Keefe. Place navigation impaired in rats with hippocampal lesions. *Nature* 297:681–683, 1982.

Nakamura, R. K., S. J. Schein, and R. Desimone. Visual responses from cells in striate cortex of monkeys rendered chronically "blind" by lesions of nonvisual cortex. *Experimental Brain Research* 63:185–190, 1986.

O'Keefe, J., and J. Dostrovsky. The hippocampus as a spatial map: Preliminary evidence from unit activity in the freely-moving rat. *Brain Research* 34:171–175, 1971.

O'Keefe, J., and L. Nadel. *The Hippocampus As a Cognitive Map.* New York: Clarendon Press, 1978.

Oxbury, J. M., D. C. Campbell, and S. M. Oxbury. Unilateral spatial neglect and impairments of spatial analysis and visual perception. *Brain* 97:551–564, 1974.

Pallis, C. A. Impaired identification of faces and places with agnosia for colors. *Journal of Neurology, Neurosurgery and Psychiatry* 18:218–224, 1955.

Parkinson, J. K., E. A. Murray, and M. Mishkin. A selective mnemonic role for the hippocampus in monkeys: Memory for the location of objects. *Journal of Neuroscience* 8:4159–4167, 1988.

Passingham, R. E. Memory of monkeys *(Maccaca mulatta)* with lesions in prefrontal cortex. *Behavioral Neuroscience* 99:3–21, 1985.

Paterson, A., and O. L. Zangwill. Disorders of visual space perception associated with lesions of the right cerebral hemisphere. *Brain* 67:331–358, 1944.

Petrides, M., and S. K. Iversen. Restricted posterior parietal lesions in the rhesus monkey and performance on visuospatial tasks. *Brain Research* 161:63–77, 1979.

Petrides, M., and B. Milner. Deficits on subject-ordered tasks after frontal- and temporal-lobe lesions in man. *Neuropsychologia* 20:249–292, 1982.

Posner, M. I., and M. E. Raichle. *Images of Mind.* New York: Scientific American Library, 1994.

Rolls, E. T., and J. Z. Xiang. Spatial view cells in the primate hippocampus and memory recall. *Reviews of Neuroscience* 17:175–200, 2006.

Rosenbaum, R. S., S. Kohler, D. L. Schacter, M. Moscovitch, R. Westmacott, S. E. Black, F. Gao, and E. Tulving. The case of K.C.: Contributions of a memory-impaired person to memory theory. *Neuropsychologia* 43:989–1021, 2005.

Ross, E. D. Sensory-specific and fractional disorders of recent memory in man I: Isolated loss of visual recent memory. *Archives of Neurology* 37:193–200, 1980.

Saucier, D., A. Lisoway, S. Green, and L. Elias. Female advantage for object location memory in peripersonal but not extrapersonal space. *Journal of the International Neuropsychological Society* 13:683–686, 2007.

Semmes, J. A non-tactual factor in astereognosis. *Neuropsychologia* 3:295–315, 1965.

Shankweiler, D. Performance of brain damaged patients on two tests of sound localization. *Journal of Comparative and Physiological Psychology* 54:375–381, 1951.

Sherry, D. F., and J. S. Hoshooley. The neurobiology of spatial ability. In: K. Otter, Ed. *Parid Evolution and Behavior.* New York: Oxford University Press, forthcoming.

Smith, M. L., and B. Milner. The role of the right hippocampus in the recall of spatial location. *Neuropsychologia* 19:781–793, 1981.

Takahashi, N., M. Kawamura, J. Shiota, N. Kasahata, and K. Hirayama. Pure topographic disorientation due to a right retrosplenial lesion. *Neurology* 49:464–469, 1997.

Taube, J. S. The head direction signal: Origins and sensory-motor integration. *Annual Review of Neuroscience* 30:181–207, 2007.

Teng, E., and L. R. Squire. Memory for places learned long ago is intact after hippocampal damage. *Science* 400:675–677, 1999.

Tyler, H. R. Abnormalities of perception and defective eye movements (Bálint's syndrome). *Cortex* 4:15–171, 1968.

Vallar, G. Spatial neglect, Bálint-Homes' and Gerstmann's syndrome, and other spatial disorders. *CNS Spectrums* 12:527–36, 2007.

Whishaw, I. Q., D. J. Hines, and D. G. Wallace. Dead reckoning (path integration) requires the hippocampal formation: Evidence from spontaneous exploration and spatial learning tasks in light (allothetic) and dark (idiothetic) tests. *Behavioural Brain Research* 127, 49–70, 2001.

Worsley, C. L., M. Recce, H. J. Spiers, J. Marley, C. E. Polkey, and R. G. Morris. Path integration following temporal lobectomy in humans. *Neuropsychologia* 39:452–464, 2001.

Zangwill, O. L. *Cerebral Dominance and Its Relation to Psychological Function.* Edinburgh: Oliver & Boyd, 1960.

Zola-Morgan, S., L. Squire, and D. G. Amaral. Human amnesia and the medial temporal region: Enduring memory impairment following a bilateral lesion limited to field CA1 of the hippocampus. *Journal of Neuroscience* 6:2950–2967, 1986.

22 Attention, Mental Images, and Consciousness

PORTRAIT: A Curious Case of Neglect

After returning from a trip abroad at age 28, R.P. developed a terrible headache and flulike aches and fever. The flu symptoms disappeared after a few days, but the headache remained for several weeks. During this time, R.P. noticed that she was unusually clumsy and started having difficulty recognizing people's faces.

We first met R.P. 2 years later. Among a variety of visuoperceptual problems, she presented especially severe deficits in facial recognition, a mental neglect of the left side of space, and constructional apraxia.

- The face-recognition deficit was so severe that R.P. was unable to recognize her identical twin sister except by movement and voice.

- The mental neglect was particularly intriguing. Before her illness, R.P. had earned a master's degree in library science. She was

Dennis O'Brien

also an excellent cook, and one of her joys in life was having friends over for supper. She now found it impossible to entertain in the same way, however, because she could not remember where items were located in the kitchen, especially items on her left side. (The adjoining photograph shows such neglect in a dog that has a right-hemisphere brain tumor and eats only the food in the right side of its dish.)

- R.P.'s apraxia was not severe, but she had become unable to assemble things such as a bookshelf unit that she had bought. In fact, R.P. noted that she could not even imagine how the shelf could be put together.

Imaging studies found abnormally low blood flow in the superior parietal regions in both hemispheres and throughout the right temporal lobe, but the causes of R.P.'s symptoms were never really understood. It seems likely that a viral infection caused her symptoms and the abnormal blood flow.

R.P. had one other persisting symptom: her social cognition was impaired. She had been duped on two occasions by con artists who tricked her into giving them money for bogus projects. She complained that she did not seem to be able to tell when people were not trustworthy.

A ttention, images, and consciousness are properties of the nervous system that direct complex actions of body and brain. They are not epiphenomena—properties that emerge simply because the brain is complex. R.P., whose case is described in the Portrait, showed deficits in attention and visual guidance of movements, in imaging movements, in recognizing faces, and in identifying the intentions of others. These deficits are among the topics of this chapter. At its end, we address questions about the neural basis of consciousness and why we are conscious.

Defining Attention and Consciousness

Donald Hebb and others have argued that the central question in neuropsychology is the relation between the mind and the brain. The question is easy to ask, yet it is not so easy to grasp what it is that we need to explain. One needed explanation is how we select information on which to act. Another is how we select behaviors.

Simple animals, such as worms, have a limited sensory capacity and an equally limited repertoire of behaviors. Animals such as dogs have a much more sophisticated sensory capacity and a corresponding increase in behavioral options. Primates, including humans, have even further developed sensory capacity and behavioral complexity.

Thus, as sensory and motor capacities increase, so does the problem of selection, both of information and of behavior. Furthermore, as the brain expands, memory increases, providing an internal variable in both stimulus interpretation and response selection. Finally, as the number of sensory channels increases, the need to correlate the different inputs to produce a single "reality" arises. We first encountered this problem in Chapter 10 when we examined the binding problem.

One way to consider these evolutionary changes is to posit that, as the brain expands to increase sensorimotor capacity, so does some other process (or processes) having a role in sensory and motor selection. One proposed process for selective awareness and response to stimuli is **attention**, which allows either a selective awareness of a part or aspect of the sensory environment or a selective responsiveness to one class of stimuli.

The concept of attention implies that we somehow focus a "mental spotlight" on certain sensory inputs, motor programs, memories, or internal representations. This spotlight might be unconscious, in that we are not aware of the process, or it might be conscious, such as when we scan our memories for someone's name. The development of language should increase the likelihood of conscious attention, but it is unlikely that all conscious processing is verbal. One can speculate, for example, that the "Eureka" insight of Archimedes entailed conscious processing that was more than just verbal.

The point is that, as sensorimotor capacities expand, so do the processes of attention and consciousness. In broad terms, consciousness is synonymous, at a primary level, with awareness and, at a secondary level, with awareness of awareness. The clear implication is that consciousness is not a dichotomous phenomenon; rather, a gradual evolutionary increase in consciousness is correlated with the ability to organize sensory and motor capacities. The most-evolved organizer is language, which implies an increased capacity for the processes of attention.

You encountered problems of attention and conscious awareness earlier. Recall, for example, the concepts of blindsight and blind touch discussed in Chapters 13 and 14, respectively. Patients can describe the location of sensory information for which they have no conscious awareness. Similarly, amnesic patients can show evidence of procedural memory even when they have no conscious recollection of having been in a room before, let alone having learned a task (recall H.M.'s case in the Portrait in Chapter 18).

People such as R.P. who have right posterior parietotemporal lesions show hemispatial neglect: they behave as though the left side of the world were not present. That this problem is not one of input was illustrated beautifully in experiments showing that patients have a cognitive hemispatial neglect, too. For example, when asked to imagine a familiar scene from a particular perspective, patients neglected the left side; but, when asked to imagine the same scene from a perspective 180° removed, they described the previously neglected regions and this time neglected the previously described regions.

The close relation between consciousness and attention has led to the question whether these processes are different manifestations of the same process or are distinct brain processes. Christof Koch and Naotsugu Tsuchiya have argued that consciousness and attention are fundamentally different and require two distinct brain processes. For them, the key difference is that attention is primarily a top-down process that selects information from a specific part of the sensory world, such as point in space or an object, and that doing so takes time. In contrast, consciousness acts to summarize all information that pertains to the individual and its environment and is not so selective.

Thus, whereas attention is focused on specific features of the world, consciousness gives us the gist of the world. Keep this distinction in mind as we look more closely at the nature of attention and consciousness.

Attention

The concept of attention has an uneven history in psychology. Periods when attentional processes were simply assumed to be present contrast with periods when the need for specific attentional systems was rejected. For example, the behaviorist view held that a full account of behavior is possible in strictly physiological terms, with no reference to cognitive concepts such as attention or even consciousness. The emergence of cognitive science led to a reevaluation of this perspective. Investigators in both cognitive science and neuroscience have returned to the position first espoused by William James in the late 1800s: "Everyone knows what attention is. It is the taking possession by the mind, in clear and vivid form, of one out of what seems several simultaneously possible objects or trains of thought."

Renewed interest in such concepts as attention has led to the establishment of distinct subcultures among students of attention. Perhaps the biggest division is between investigators interested in the automatic processes taking part in attention and those interested in the conscious selection of sensory information. There has been less interest in the question of motor attention, which could be defined as the process of selecting behaviors. In addition, some researchers are interested in imagination (imagery) and the role that it plays in behavioral selection.

Automatic and Conscious Processing Compared

An area of agreement in cognitive psychology is that certain behaviors can be performed with little, if any, focused attention, whereas others are highly sensitive to the allocation of attention. Automatic processes direct behavior that occurs without intention, involuntarily, without conscious awareness, and without producing interference with ongoing activities. Automatic processing may be an innate property of the way in which sensory information is processed or it can be produced by extended training. (For more details, see reviews by Logan and by Bargh and Ferguson.)

Operations that are not automatic have been referred to by various terms, including controlled, effortful, attentive, and conscious. Conscious operations differ fundamentally from automatic processing in that they require focused attention. One way to look at the difference is to regard the automatic processes as bottom-up processing and the conscious processes as top-down processing. A person stopping at a red light is an example of bottom-up processing, whereas a person actively searching for a street at which to turn is an example of top-down processing.

Remember from the discussion of memory in Chapter 18 that bottom-up processing is data driven; that is, it relies almost exclusively on the stimulus information being presented in the environment. In contrast, top-down processing is conceptually driven. It relies on information already in memory, including whatever expectation might exist regarding the task at hand. Viewed in this way, automatic and conscious processing can be reasonably presumed to require at least some different cortical circuits. One hypothesis is that whatever unique cortical circuits are recruited in attentive processing must include processes of consciousness.

Another way to examine the difference between automatic and conscious processing is to try it yourself. Consider the following experiment. Anne Treisman and her colleagues presented subjects with boxed arrays of stimuli such as the four shown in **Figure 22.1**. The task in each case is to identify the target that is different from all the others. Try it now.

Did you find some targets easier to find than others? Treisman's subjects did as well. Response time differs dramatically, depending on the nature of the stimulus. When the task requires the identification of a target with an *extra* line, as at the upper left in Figure 22.1, search time is independent of the number of detractors. Apparently, the target visually "pops out" of the display. But, when the task requires the subject to find a target distinguished by the *lack* of a feature present in the other items, as on the upper right, the time taken to find the target varies directly with the number of detractors. Evidently, we must subject the items in the display to a serial search.

The result of Treisman's experiment is not intuitive. After all, each case requires the same discrimination between the same two stimuli. Thus, we can infer that

- certain aspects of visual processing are automatic. We need not focus attention on any particular aspect of the visual field. Analysis requires only a specific visual feature, such as a vertical line (the popouts in Figure 22.1), to locate the target.

- other aspects of visual processing depend on focused attention to locate the conjunction—the combinations of features, such as circles and lines—that leads to the target. **Conjunction search** is a serial process, as if a mental spotlight were scanning from one location to another, searching for particular combinations of sensory information. In the lower panels of Figure 22.1, for example, the conjunction of shading and form identifies the target.

In principle, it should be possible to develop feature processing with practice. Treisman and her colleagues have studied this possibility intensively, but

Figure 22.1

Visual Processing Tasks (Left) Feature search. Here, the ⵕ and the **T** "pop out" of the display automatically. (Right) Serial search. You must scan from symbol to symbol to locate the ○ and the **T** in each display. (Bottom) Conjunction search. With focused attention, the combination of line weight and form identifies the target. (After Treisman and Gormican, 1988.)

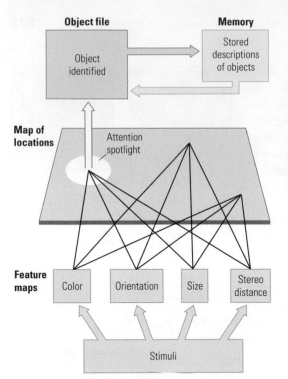

Treisman's Model of Feature Search Beginning at the bottom of the illustration, early vision encodes some simple and useful properties of a scene in a number of feature maps, which may preserve the spatial relations of the visual world but do not themselves make spatial information available to subsequent processing stages. Instead, focused attention selects and integrates the features present at particular locations. At later stages, the integrated information serves to create and update recognition "files" on perceptual objects. In turn, the file contents are compared with descriptions stored in a recognition network (memory). (After Treisman, 1986.)

they conclude that, although practice can speed up feature processing, it remains dependent on specific automatic neural associations between features as well as on serial-processing pathways. Feature processing appears to be innate to the visual system.

Treisman has explained her results with a perceptual model of **feature search**, the cognitive strategy for scanning for specific features of stimuli. As illustrated in **Figure 22.2**, a stimulus registered in area V1 is broken down into separate feature maps (see Chapter 13 for more details). This information is then serially processed in parallel pathways (for example, to area V3, V4, or V5). A characteristic of the later processing is that, at some point, different features of the object are integrated or conjoined. Because no single visual area specifically does this job, bits of the visual world must be processed serially, presumably by using some sort of reentry process (see Chapter 10).

Thus, the idea is that attention is directed to each location in turn and that features present in the same "fixation" of attention are combined to form a single object. Michael Posner and Marcus Raichle suggested that, in a sense, the attentional process provides the "glue" that integrates features into a unitary object. When the features have been put together, the object can be perceived and held in memory as a unit.

A clear prediction from Treisman's theory is that neurons in the visual areas outside area V1 and probably outside area V2 should respond differentially, depending on whether attention is focused on the corresponding receptive field. In the next section, we consider evidence that these neurons do indeed respond differentially.

A question that arises from the results of the feature-detector research is, What constitutes a feature? Treisman presumes that features are the properties that cells in the visual system are coded to detect. But features may perhaps be biologically significant stimuli, as illustrated in an experiment by John Eastwood and his colleagues. The researchers presented subjects with displays of schematic faces similar to those shown in **Figure 22.3**. The task was to identify the odd face, which could be a happy face in a sea of sad ones or visa versa. Before you try this one, turn your book upside down.

Subjects were faster at detecting sad faces, whether they were upside down or right side up. Furthermore, when Eastwood and his colleagues redid the ex-

Feature-Search Demonstration Visual displays in which subjects must detect happy or sad faces. Subjects detect sad faces faster, even if presented upside down. (After Eastwood et al., 2001.)

periment with abstract targets that signified either a happy or a sad state, subjects still found the sad-related feature faster.

Given that the features should be equally conspicuous in the happy and sad conditions, it follows that, biologically, something is more important about detecting sad (negative) than happy (positive) stimuli. As mentioned in Chapter 20, certain cells in the amygdala are especially tuned to fear-related stimuli, and so negative stimuli (potentially dangerous or threatening features as well as sad ones) appear to be attended to very efficiently and demand attention more than do targets for more-positive features.

From an evolutionary perspective, favoring the nervous system attentive to stimuli that can make a difference to an animal's survival makes sense. The evolution of biological targets is likely more important to survival than are the simpler targets detected by cells in area V1.

Neurophysiological Evidence of Attention

Any experiment purporting to demonstrate that the focus of attention determines the responses of neurons must meet one important criterion. The *same stimulus* must activate a neuron at one time and not at another. This condition rules out the possibility that the changes in neural activity are somehow related to the actual features of the stimulus target. Consider the following experiment.

Jeffrey Moran and Robert Desimone trained a monkey to hold a bar while it gazed at a fixation point on a screen. A sample stimulus (for instance, a vertical red bar) appeared briefly at one location in the receptive field, followed about 500 ms later by two stimuli: one at the same location and another in a separate one, as illustrated in **Figure 22.4**. The key point is that both targets were in the cell's receptive field, but only one target was in the correct location.

Figure **22.4**

Demonstrating Selective Attention A monkey performing an attentional task demonstrating that, even though a given neuron normally responds to a stimulus in many locations, the neuron can adapt to attend selectively to information in a specific region of its receptive field. (After Moran and Desimone, 1985.)

Experimental procedure

Monkeys were trained to release a bar when a certain stimulus was presented in a certain location. The monkeys learned to ignore stimuli in all other locations.

Fixation point   Stimulus

Results

During performance of this task, researchers recorded the firing of neurons in visual area V4, which are sensitive to color and form. Stimuli were presented in either rewarded or unrewarded locations.

Pretraining recordings:

Rewarded location

Strong response

Unrewarded location

Strong response

Before training, neurons responded to stimuli in all locations.

Posttraining recordings:

Rewarded location

Strong response

Unrewarded location

Baseline response

After training, neurons responded only when the visual stimuli were in the rewarded location.

Conclusion

A neuron can learn to respond selectively to information in its receptive field.

When the test stimulus was identical with the sample and in the same location, the animal was rewarded if it released the bar immediately. In this way, the same visual stimulus could be presented to different regions of the neurons' receptive fields, but the importance of the information varied with its location.

As the animals performed the task, the researchers recorded the firing of cells in area V4. Cells in area V4 are sensitive to color and form; so different neurons responded to different conjunctions of features. Thus, a given cell might respond to one stimulus (for example, a horizontal green bar) but not to another (for example, a vertical red bar). These stimuli were presented either in the correct location or in an incorrect location for predicting reward, as illustrated in Figure 22.4.

The critical result is the behavior of the neuron in response to the effective target stimulus. When the effective stimulus was presented in the correct location, the cell was highly active. When the *same stimulus* was presented in an incorrect location, however, the cell was not responsive. When attention is focused on a place in the visual world, the cell appears to respond only to stimuli appropriate to that place.

Ineffective stimuli remained so regardless of where they were in the visual field. Moran and Desimone considered the possibility that visual areas activated earlier (V1) or later (TE) in visual processing also might show attentional effects. Cells in area V1 did not show attentional effects, whereas cells in area TE did. Presumably, the features detected in area V1 were too simple to direct attention, whereas those in area TE could do so.

Moran and Desimone's results are also theoretically important to the general matter of space. The cells showing constraints in spatial attention were in areas V4 and TE, both parts of the object-recognition stream. Thus, neurons in this system are coding spatial location. This spatial coding in the ventral stream is consistent with David Milner and Melvyn Goodale's idea that both the dorsal and the ventral streams of visual processing play a role in perceiving space, but their roles are different (see Chapters 13, 18, and 21).

Note that Moran and Desimone's monkey did not actually have to move. If it did, we would predict that cells in the posterior parietal cortex would be sensitive to attentional demands. In fact, Vernon Mountcastle and his colleagues report just such results. They found that posterior parietal cells are active when animals reach to obtain an object, such as food, but are not active when the same movements are made for other reasons. Notice that these cells are responding not to the features of the stimuli but rather to the movements needed to get to them. Thus, there appear to be two types of visual attention, one related to the selection of stimuli and the other to the selection and direction of movements.

Divided Attention

Attention can affect neurons in other ways as well. Daniel Kahneman noted that perceptual systems do not always work at peak efficiency. One explanation for their failure to do so is that we can process only so much information at once, and, if we are overloaded, there is a "bottleneck" in processing. Kahneman proposed that the capacity to perform mental activity is limited and that this limited capacity must be allocated among concurrent activities.

Thus, for Kahneman, one aspect of attention is the amount of effort directed toward a particular task. If a task is routine (such as driving on a road without much traffic), little attentional focus is used, and the driver can carry on a conversation. When the driver is turning across traffic at a busy intersection, however, attention must be focused on the task and the conversation briefly interrupted. Some process must be active to shift and focus attention in response to changes in task demands.

In fact, in many jurisdictions, it is illegal for a driver to use a cell phone in a moving vehicle, because the evidence is clear that attention is divided when we perform the two tasks concurrently. You may have noticed that, when you attempt a difficult maneuver with a car, such as parking in a tight spot, you turn down your car radio. We see this problem whenever we multitask—reading and watching television at the same time, for instance. We can pay attention to only one task at any particular instant. If we try to divide our attention among several tasks, performance on each task suffers.

Selective Attention

Hedva Spitzer, working with Moran and Desimone, wondered if cells in area V4 might vary their firing characteristics in accord with the amount of effort needed to solve a particular visual problem. She and her colleagues trained monkeys much as was done in the Moran and Desimone experiment, except that they varied the difficulty of the task by taking advantage of the fact that cells respond to a range of stimuli (**Figure 22.5**A). Thus, a given cell responds optimally to a given orientation and color. This tuning is not precise, however, and the cell will respond to orientations and colors that approximate the preferred range.

Spitzer and her colleagues reasoned that it should be easy for a cell to discriminate between a stimulus within its preferred orientation or color and a stimulus outside this orientation or color. For example, an easy discrimination would be one in which the test stimulus is orthogonal (oriented at 90°) to the sample (Figure 22.5B). In contrast, a difficult discrimination would be one in which both stimuli are within the range of a cell's preferred orientations—say, if the difference in orientation were only 22.5°, which is within the acceptable range for most cells (Figure 22.5C). They trained animals to make this discrimination, and the animals' performance confirmed that the finer discrimination was more difficult: 93% of their responses were correct under the easy conditions compared with 73% under the difficult conditions.

The change in response characteristics of the area V4 cells is intriguing. First, under the difficult condition, the cells increased their firing rate by an average of about 20%. Second, the tuning characteristics of the cells changed. Thus, whereas the cells tolerated an orientation difference of about 81° under the easy condition, the same cells became more selective about the stimuli to which they would respond under the difficult condition, the orientation range having been reduced to 53°.

The more difficult task appears to have required increased attention to the differences between the stimuli, as manifested in a change in the stimulus selectivity of neurons in area V4. Stated differently, both the behavioral and the electrophysiological results indicate that increasing the amount of effort needed to perform a perceptual task can affect how information is processed in the visual system.

How this attentional effect can alter the cell's activity is now known. One possibility is that a signal from the thalamus plays some role. The results of

Figure **22.5**

Effort and Attention (A) Range of line orientations to which a given cell will respond. (B) Easy condition. The left line is within the orientation preference of the cell, but the right line is outside this range. (C) Difficult condition. Both line orientations fall within the cell's preferred range of response. (Spitzer et al., 1988.)

(A) Preferred range

(B) Easy discrimination

(C) Difficult discrimination

studies on monkeys have led to the idea that the critical region may be the pulvinar, which is a thalamic nucleus that projects to secondary visual areas in the tectopulvinar system (see Figure 8.8). Thus, cells in the pulvinar also respond to visual stimuli in a way that implies some type of selection process.

Steven Petersen and his colleagues found that neurons in the pulvinar respond more vigorously to stimuli that are targets of behavior than they do to the same stimuli when they are not targets of behavior. That is, when a visual stimulus is present but has no meaning for the animal, the cells have a low firing rate. When the same stimulus now signifies a reward, the cells become more active.

Because the pulvinar complex projects to the posterior parietal cortex, temporal cortex, and prefrontal cortex, it may play some role in directing Treisman's "spotlight" to different parts of space. Petersen and his colleagues tested this predication by finding that disrupting the pulvinar does disrupt spatial attention. The pulvinar receives visual input from the colliculus, which is known to play a role in orienting to visual information; so it may be a collicular-pulvinar spotlight that is at work.

We are still left with the problem of how the collicular-pulvinar spotlight is turned on. At present, we must be satisfied with the observation that knowledge of the task demands can somehow alter the activity of neurons in the visual system—the essence of a top-down process.

Parallel Processing of Sensory Input

Even when a spotlight has been directed to a part of the sensory world, the brain still has an attentional problem. If a single object falls in the spotlight, the visual system can bind together all its visual elements to form the single object. But if multiple objects, such as on a cluttered desk, capture the attentional spotlight, the visual system has a binding problem insofar as the different objects must be retained as separate items (see reviews by Awh et al. and Rousselet et al.).

Recent electrophysiological studies in monkeys show that the neurons in TE appear able to process items from cluttered scenes in parallel. One way in which the brain could do so is to have cells that are sensitive to complex configurations such that a neuron could respond to a square above a circle but not to a circle above a square, for example. But we could not possibly have enough complex neurons to decipher a really cluttered scene. Another solution is to serially select items. In this way, a scene would be processed in very brief cycles that allow us to process items in parallel (for example, see Woodman and Luck).

Another form of parallel processing is cross-modal. We typically have competing visual, auditory, and somatosensory inputs and must allocate attention both within and between modalities. A consistently reported sensory interaction is the demonstrated decreases in auditory activation to specific auditory inputs when subjects must also attend to a visual stimulus.

Jennifer Johnson and Robert Zatorre presented subjects with visual (geometric shapes) and auditory (melodies) stimuli either separately or together, and the subjects were to perform a task requiring that they attend to the stimuli. Functional magnetic resonance imaging recorded greater brain activation

Figure 22.6

Divided Attention Recruits Prefrontal Cortex Prefrontal cortices activated during the bimodal divided-attention condition compared with the bimodal passive condition. When subjects attend only to auditory or visual stimuli, there is no activation of the frontal lobe. But to attend to both modalities simultaneously requires a recruitment of the frontal lobe. Color bar indicates level of significant activity (*t* values) at each voxel. Abbreviations: DLPFC, dorsolateral prefrontal cortex; BA, Brodmann's area; BOLD, blood-oxygenation-level-dependent MRI. (Johnson and Zatorre, 2006)

in the secondary auditory cortex when attention was directed to the auditory stimulus and the opposite effect when attention was directed to the visual stimulus. Thus, selective attention led to increased activation in relevant sensory cortices and decreases in irrelevant regions.

More interesting, however, was the response to dividing attention between the two modalities. Here, fMRI recorded no change in sensory cortical activation relative to a passive baseline condition of exposure to the competing stimuli, and in fact the sensory activation was less than the sum of the acitivties seen in the unimodal conditions. The major change in activation was actually in the left dorsolateral prefrontal cortex (DLPFC; **Figure 22.6**). The contrasting results of the selective and bimodal conditions suggest that distinct neural processes control the two forms of attentional processing.

Although we know of no direct studies, when we multitask, such as by using the cell phone while driving, we likely must recruit additional prefrontal cortex. If the prefrontal cortex is already engaged—say, in planning a driving route—attention to one or more of the concurrent tasks will likely be lost.

Functional Imaging and Attention

One place to start our search for neural correlates of attention in normal humans is to look at attentional processes in the visual system that parallel those already studied in monkeys. Maurizio Corbetta and his colleagues designed the experiment illustrated in **Figure 22.7**A. A row of boxes streamed across a screen viewed by subjects who fixated on another box located just above the row. The task required subjects to maintain fixation on the upper box and to do one of two things: (1) to shift attention as a light moved from box to box across the row or (2) to maintain fixation on the central box and to ignore the movement of the

(A) Experimental condition

Shifting attention

The subject fixates on the crosshair...

...and covertly shifts attention to follow the streaming light.

The subject fixates on the central light ...

Fixed attention

...and ignores the streaming light.

(B) Brain activation in shifting attention

In the shifting-attention condition, the left parietal lobe is activated when the stimulus is in the right visual field,...

...whereas the right parietal lobe is activated when the stimulus is in either visual field.

Figure 22.7

Shifting Attention Compared with Fixed Attention

(A) Experimental setups for the shifting and fixed conditions.
(B) A summary of PET scans for the shifting-attention task reveals that activation of the parietal cortex increases compared with the fixed-attention task and is more extensive in the right parietal lobe. (After Corbetta et al., 1993.)

light. Thus, as in the Moran and Desimone study of monkeys, the stimuli presented were identical, but the attentional requirements were different.

The results were clear. Relative to the fixed-attention task, attending to the moving light increased activation in the posterior parietal cortex (Figure 22.7B). Furthermore, if the moving light was presented to the left visual field, only the right parietal cortex was activated; whereas, if the moving light was presented to the right visual field, both the left and the right parietal cortices were activated. In other words, the right parietal cortex was active when the stimulus was either in the left or in the right visual field, but the left parietal cortex was active only when the stimulus was in the contralateral (right) visual field.

In addition, two distinct foci of activation appeared in the right parietal lobe, one corresponding to the left visual field and the other corresponding to the right visual field. These findings may explain why patients with right posterior parietotemporal lesions show more-pronounced contralateral neglect than do patients with left-hemisphere lesions. In the absence of the left parietal cortex, there is still a representation of the right visual field, which is in the right parietal cortex. In the absence of the right parietal cortex, there is no representation of the left visual field in the parietal cortex, and the region is neglected, as we saw in R.P.'s case in the Portrait at the beginning of this chapter.

An intriguing aspect of this study is that there was no activation in area V4, such as might be predicted from the results of electrophysiological studies of monkeys. An explanation is that the task did not require an integration of different stimulus properties; rather, it simply required a record of where something was. This possibility was confirmed in a parallel study by the same researchers.

In this case, Corbetta and his colleagues presented the subjects with a screen with a small white spot in the center (**Figure 22.8**). Each target stimulus (frame 1, for example) was a spatially random distribution of 30 elements, all of identical shape and color and moving horizontally as a coherent sheet to the left or right. The shape, color, or speed of movement or all three might be changed in the second stimulus (frame 2). A stimulus was presented for 400 ms, followed by a second stimulus 200 ms later.

A subject had two different tasks. In the "selective attention" task, the subject was to report whether the two sets of stimuli differed for a specific stimulus feature (for example, color). In the "divided attention" task, the subject was to indicate if there had been a change in *any* feature. The fundamental difference between the two tasks is that the selective task requires the adoption of a specific mental set for a specific feature, whereas the divided task does not.

The researchers posited that the selective task would require more focused attention and the divided task would require more memory. Therefore, they predicted a different pattern of cortical activation in the two tasks.

PET measurements showed that the selective-attention task activated specific visual regions, the region varying with the feature detected. Thus, attention to color activated a region probably corresponding to area V4, whereas attention to shape activated regions corresponding to areas V3 and TE. The selective task also activated the insula, the posterior thalamus (probably pulvinar), the superior colliculus, and the orbital frontal cortex.

In contrast, the divided-attention task activated a mutually exclusive set of areas. Thus, although there was no activation of visual areas beyond the activation on passive presentation of the stimuli, there was activation of the anterior cingulate and dorsolateral prefrontal cortex. The important point is that the stimuli were identical in the two conditions, even though the tasks were different. The selective-attention task led to increased activation of visual areas that presumably were recruited to solve the task.

Taken together, the results of the Corbetta studies show that different cortical areas are activated in different attentional tasks:

- The parietal cortex is activated for attention to location; the occipitotemporal cortex is activated for attention to features such as color and form.

- The anterior cingulate and prefrontal areas show activation during both visual tasks. Thus, attention appears to generally require the activation of the anterior cingulate and some prefrontal areas in addition to the activation of specific sensory areas related to a particular sensory modality, such as vision or touch.

Do these activations outside the visual areas indicate the existence of some general attentional system or are they specific to visual attention? And what about other sensory systems? One way to answer these questions is to examine attentional processes in other sensory systems. For example, the somatosensory system also must select stimuli for processing; so we can reasonably ask whether it has an attentional organization that parallels that of the visual system.

A PET study was undertaken in which subjects had to direct their attention either to the roughness or the length of tactile stimuli (Burton et al., 1999). The same stimulus was used, but the feature attended to varied. In control conditions, the subjects were stimulated but did not attend to any particular feature. As would be predicted, tactile stimulation activated areas S1 and S2, but, during the

Selective-attention task: Were objects moving at different speeds in the two frames?

Divided-attention task: Was any feature of the two frames different?

Stimulus displays

Frame 1   Frame 2

Subjects were shown frame 1...   ...and, one-fifth second later, frame 2.

Frame 1   Frame 2

Response time

0   400   600   1000   2500

Time (ms)

Figure **22.8**

Selective-Attention Compared with Divided-Attention Tasks

Frames 1 and 2 model stimulus displays in the study by Corbetta and colleagues. The selective-attention task is to determine if there is a change from frame 1 to frame 2 in a particular feature (color, shape, speed of movement). In the divided-attention task, subjects report a change in any of the features. The bottom panel shows the timing of the frame presentations. (After Corbetta et al., 1991.)

attentional task, there also was activation in the posterior parietal cortex, likely in Brodmann's area 7. This activation did not overlap foci seen in studies of visual attention. Thus, distinct regions in the posterior parietal cortex appear to have roles in attention to different types of sensory inputs.

Networks of Attention

Let us recap what we have learned so that we can put our observations together. Our goal is to build a framework for a unifying theory of an attentional network in the brain.

- The electrophysiological evidence from monkeys shows four different attentional mechanisms: (1) a mechanism in the parietal cortex enhances spatial attention, (2) one in the visual and posterior temporal cortex selects object features, (3) one in the inferior temporal region selects objects themselves, and (4) one in the frontal eye fields selects movements.

- PET studies show parallel results in human subjects.

- The results of many studies show that regions of the frontal lobe also are activated during response selection. In particular, there is activation of the anterior cingulate cortex in divided-attention tasks (see the preceding section), as well as in tasks requiring response selection (see Chapter 16) or verb generation (see Chapter 19).

- There is activation of the premotor and prefrontal regions in specific tasks. Recall that Corbetta's divided-attention task activated the dorsolateral prefrontal cortex, as did Johnson and Zatorre's auditory–visual task.

- In PET studies performed during verb-generation tasks (see Chapter 19), investigators found that verb generation activates the inferior frontal cortex.

Posner and Raichle suggested a model featuring two attentional spotlights. The first highlights a place in the world to analyze, and the second selects specific features for analysis. Posner proposed that, when we search for objects in the world, our focus of attention shifts from one location to another. To do so, attention must disengage from the current object of interest, move to a new object, and engage it. In an environment that is visually cluttered, another system that inhibits or filters out irrelevant information may be required.

The posterior parietal system may function to disengage, move, or engage attention. Indeed, damage to the posterior parietal cortex impairs performance on any task that requires this ability (see Chapter 14). In contrast, the focusing of attention on features of the object engaged may be a function of the posterior temporal regions. Damage to these regions produces agnosias, which must indicate, in part, a deficit in attending to specific features of stimuli.

Posner and Petersen proposed a second type of attentional system in addition to the posterior spotlights. This system is based in the frontal lobe and is closely related to the short-term-memory functions of the frontal lobe. Posner and Petersen cited four lines of evidence for an anterior attentional system:

1. Various frontal-lobe sites, especially the anterior cingulate, are active in a variety of tasks, both those entailing perceptual demands and those entailing response selection. Consider the divided-attention task described in Figure 22.8. A subject must detect a feature and then respond. This task

requires a working memory of what the features are and a recognition that one of the features has been detected. Posner and Raichle emphasized the importance of feature detection in response selection. Frontal-lobe patients are notorious for doing one thing and saying another, as though they do not detect the incongruity.

2. The involvement of frontal-lobe structures is proportional to the attentional effort. Thus, as the number of targets in a target-monitoring task increases, the involvement of frontal-lobe regions increases.

3. The frontal-lobe involvement in response selection is inversely related to practice. For example, in Chapter 19, we considered a verb-generation task in which subjects had to generate an action word in response to a noun (for instance, "cake–eat"). If subjects had practiced on specific nouns before the test, the insular cortex was active but the frontal areas were not.

4. Evidence from studies on both human patients and laboratory animals confirm that the frontal lobe has an important role in working (temporal) memory for both sensory events and movements.

Posner and Petersen call their frontal-lobe attentional system an "executive attentional system" and make the bold proposal that the contents of consciousness at any moment consist of the information being operated on by this executive system. In their view, the frontal lobe has charge of programming mental operations. Thus, it must play a major role in the activation of the selective-attention systems of the posterior cortex.

The direct evidence in favor of the Posner and Petersen model is not overwhelming, but their proposal does provide an interesting way to think about the brain systems engaged in consciousness. A feature of cortical evolution is that, as each new sensory channel was added, there was a corresponding development of the frontal lobe. This increase may very well be necessary for the brain to operate on the sensory world and make sense of it. In the absence of frontal-lobe structures or in the event of dysfunction (such as schizophrenia), behavior would become muddled, because conscious awareness of what the overwhelming sensory inputs mean and how they relate one to another would be lacking.

Mechanisms of Attention

The Posner and Petersen model does not specify how the executive attentional system might influence neuronal activity in sensory areas. That is, how does the spotlight choose important events from among all the ongoing sensory information? Although several mechanisms are possible, one that is generating increasing interest is that the attentional system induces synchrony across a population of neurons that assess some sensory signal.

Figure 22.9 illustrates how a change in synchrony across a population of neurons can be affected by shifting the temporal positions of action potentials slightly so that two inputs to a given neuron arrive together. When this event

Figure **22.9**

Inducing Neural Synchrony
Ernst Niebur and his colleagues suggest how synchrony may modify the representation of attended stimuli. In the unattended condition, outputs arrive asynchronously on neuron 3 and are unlikely to lead to action potentials. In the attended condition, neural outputs that are in synchrony and thus summate on neuron 3 are more likely to lead to action potentials. Abbreviation : EPSPs, excitatory postsynaptic potentials. (After Niebur et al., 2002.)

Unattended condition

Asynchronous outputs from neurons 1 and 2 arrive on neuron 3,...

...resulting in small EPSPs that do not lead to action potentials.

Asynchronous outputs

Attended condition

Synchronous outputs from the same neurons summate on neuron 3,...

...resulting in larger EPSPs, which lead to action potentials.

Synchronous outputs

happens, the excitatory postsynaptic potentials (EPSPs) are summed and thus more likely to initiate an action potential in the postsynaptic neuron.

Francis Crick and Christof Koch proposed that the neural basis of attention is the change in synchrony of neural activity in cells that are within the focus of attention. Ernst Nieber and his colleagues proposed that this synchrony can be induced by sending simultaneous action potentials to all neurons in a given population. Each neuron that receives the simultaneous input is nudged toward a threshold to fire, which would enhance the synchrony of firing of all neurons receiving the synchronous input.

Although what the optimal signal for inducing synchrony might be is not entirely clear, many researchers believe it to be a signal of about 40 Hz. We will return to the idea of synchrony in cognitive processing in a discussion of consciousness and the binding problem at the end of this chapter.

Inattention

Each year more than 40,000 people are killed and more than 3 million are injured in automobile accidents in the United States. Most traffic accidents are due to human error, with inattention being one of the biggest villains. It is commonplace to hear of accidents in which one driver seemed not to see another and made a left-hand turn directly into the path of the oncoming vehicle. Sometimes, the cause is obvious (the driver was changing a CD or using a cell phone) but, many times, there is no obvious cause.

On the surface, such errors without apparent cause seem incomprehensible. Understanding failures of attention is obviously important and is complementary to the study of how attention facilitates perception. Most studies of inattention are based either on demonstrations of inattention in cognitive-science laboratories or on observations of sensory neglect in patients. We consider each separately.

Absence of Visual Attention

Three of the most popular tasks for demonstrating what Marvin Chun and René Marois refer to as the "dark side of attention" are inattentional blindness, change blindness, and attentional blink.

In *inattentional blindness*, a subject fails to notice an event that occurs during the performance of another task. A simple example is a failure to notice a dot flashed on a computer screen while performing a visual task. Perhaps the most stunning example of inattentional blindness was exhibited in an experiment by Daniel Simons and Christopher Chabris.

Subjects were shown a film clip in which people were passing a basketball back and forth. The task was to count the number of passes. After about 45 seconds, a person wearing a gorilla suit walked across the display and exited the other side 5 seconds later. Remarkably, on average, more than 70% of the subjects did not see the gorilla. (Shortened versions of the displays can be downloaded from www.wjh.harvard.edu/~viscog/lab/demos.html.)

Subjects are often shocked when shown the clip again and asked to look for the gorilla, sometimes even exclaiming, "I missed *that?*" Importantly, when subjects have been alerted to expect unusual events, they readily detect them.

In many ways, the failure to see the gorilla is like the failure to see an oncoming car. If a person is focused on something else, such as reading a street sign, fiddling with the radio, or talking on a cell phone, the perception of other visual events that would normally be obvious is suppressed.

Change blindness refers to a failure to detect changes in the presence, identity, or location of objects in scenes. Like inattention blindness, change blindness is most likely to occur when people do not expect changes. Simons conducted an experiment in which about 50% of real-world observers failed to note a change in the identity of a person with whom they were conversing when the change consisted of a brief occlusion as a worker carried a door between the conversants.

This type of inattention seems as preposterous as that in the gorilla experiment, but similar results can be shown in laboratory experiments, too. For example, subjects may take seconds to notice that an item is appearing and disappearing from a scene on a video screen. Again, when subjects have been told to expect change, they notice it more quickly.

Finally, *attentional blink* refers to a phenomenon in which subjects fail to detect a second visual target if it is presented within 500 ms of the first one. Attention to the first target prevents awareness of the second one, even if it is extremely conspicuous. Subjects have no difficulty in detecting the second target if they are told to ignore the first one. Presumably, the visual system is taxed to the limit by requiring subjects to process so much information in such a short time.

These three paradigms of inattention are similar in that each shows a failure to attend to stimuli that are quite detectable. The visual system must be filtering the information out, but when? That is, is the information filtered out during an early stage of processing or is it kept at an unconscious level?

The latter appears to be correct. Clever imaging experiments have shown, for example, that, in change-blindness experiments, the changing stimulus activates ventral-stream regions; in attentional-blink experiments, there is ERP evidence that the second stimulus was processed. But why do the unattended stimuli remain outside conscious awareness? One reason would be that the executive attentional system, in conjunction with the posterior parietal engagement system, functions to selectively activate areas in the ventral stream.

Note that this reason implies not that the conscious perception takes place in the frontoparietal network but that the activity in the network acts to filter information. A prediction from this conclusion is that people with damage to this network should have deficits in conscious perception, an example of which is **sensory neglect**, a condition in which a person does not respond to sensory stimulation.

Sensory Neglect

We first encountered the problem of neglect in a discussion of the effects of parietal-cortex lesions in Chapter 14, and it turned up again in R.P.'s case in the Portrait at the beginning of this chapter. Patients with lesions at the junction of the parietotemporal cortex (see Figure 14.8) behave as if the left side of the surrounding space had ceased to exist.

As noted earlier, the results of imaging studies have shown that the right parietal region is engaged when attended stimuli are in the right or left visual fields, whereas the left parietal region is engaged only for stimuli in the right visual field. When the right parietal region is damaged, there is no backup system for the left side of space, and it is not brought into conscious awareness. Recall, too, that, when patients are presented with two stimuli simultaneously, they show extinction and ignore the stimulus on the left side (see Figure 14.7).

Yves Rossetti and his colleagues wondered whether it is possible to modify the attentional system to attend to left-side information. In the 1960s, Richard Held and others performed experiments by fitting prisms to the eyes of laboratory animals and humans. Whatever the subject saw was displaced to one side or another. Such manipulations were initially disrupting, but, after the prisms had been worn for a few hours, the distortions diminished and subjects performed acts, such as reaching for objects, normally.

Rossetti placed prisms that induced a 10° shift of the visual field to the right on patients with contralateral neglect. In contrast with the Held experiments, however, the subjects wore the prisms only for about 5 minutes each day. In the course of the prism adaptation, the subjects made 50 pointing movements to stimuli presented 10° to the left or right of the midline.

The results were stunning. The neglect patients showed an immediate reduction in the field defect, as illustrated in **Figure 22.10**. This improvement was surprisingly long lived, lasting for at least 2 hours after prism removal, and, in F.D.'s case, performance was even better after 2 hours.

There are two likely explanations for the prism effect. One explanation is that the activity in either the normal left or the remaining right parietal region was recruited to deal with the distorted visual inputs. The other explanation is that a cerebellar or frontal region was recruited. Recall from Chapter 9 that cerebellar lesions impair the adaptation to prisms; so the activity in the cerebellum is likely important for motor aspects of the adaptation. The frontal lobe may have a complementary role that is related to attention more than to direct motor control.

Frontal, but not parietal or temporal, lesions in monkeys disrupt prism adaptation (Bossom, 1965). The frontal lobe's role in prism adaptation in the Rosetti study may have been through the executive attentional system, which became activated as the subjects adapted to the sensory distortion. The role of the frontal lobe need not be strictly attentional, however. As noted in Chapter 16, the frontal lobe plays a central role in controlling movements through corollary

Figure **22.10**

The Prism Effect Two patients with contralateral neglect were asked to copy the same drawing. Both displayed complete neglect of the left side. Patient F.D. then wore prisms for 5 minutes. Control patient M.Y.R. wore neutral goggles. In both the immediate postprism test and 2 hours later, F.D.'s drawings (A) show attention to items in the left visual field, whereas M.Y.R.'s drawings (B) show no change. (After Rossetti et al., 1998.)

(A) With prisms (patient F.D.)

Without prisms, F.D.'s copy of the drawing showed complete neglect of the left side.

F.D. then examined the drawing for 5 minutes while wearing prisms.

Copies made as much as 2 hours later showed attention to items in the left visual field.

Model drawing to copy

Copy without prisms

Copy after removing prisms

Copy 2 hours later

(B) Control patient (patient M.Y.R.)

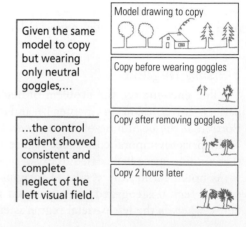

Given the same model to copy but wearing only neutral goggles,…

…the control patient showed consistent and complete neglect of the left visual field.

Model drawing to copy

Copy before wearing goggles

Copy after removing goggles

Copy 2 hours later

discharge, which is the signal from the motor system to the sensory system indicating what movement has been produced.

The role of the frontal lobe in directing attention leads us to wonder whether frontal-lobe lesions would also produce a neglect syndrome. Although not as common as neglect in patients who have parietal-lobe injuries, neglect in both humans and laboratory animals with frontal-lobe injuries—especially injuries in area 6, the premotor cortex—has been reported on numerous occasions. The neglect in frontal-lobe patients is quite unlike that seen in parietal-lobe patients, however, because it tends to be directed only to the region related to the perception of grasping space, leaving the perception of distant space intact.

Anna Berti and Francesca Frassinetti described a patient who, after a right frontal stroke, exhibited a selective neglect of peripersonal space. The neglect was apparent in a line-bisection task in which the patient used a light pen to bisect near or distant lines: bisecting the near lines showed neglect, but bisecting the distant lines did not. Curiously, when the patient acted on far lines by using a stick to touch the lines, the impairment appeared in distant space. The use of the stick apparently extended personal space to include all the space between the body and the stimulus. Evidently, the frontal attentional system can influence the way in which space is perceived.

Mental Images

When freestyle ski jumpers stand at the starting position, they spend time going through contortions, moving their feet and their arms. They seem to be rehearsing the upcoming jump. Divers, in contrast, stand very still and then jump, as described in the Snapshot in Chapter 9. Because they are going to make similar movements and their style is evaluated from the time they arrive on the diving board, they presumably must rehearse without making movements.

What is going on in the brains of these athletes? They describe their activities as preparing, focusing, and rehearsing. Are they examining the layout of the jump or dive visually? Are they practicing the movements? Are they comparing the movements that they are going to make with the conditions of the moment? An early theory of what takes place during this preparation is that people, in their heads, adjust sensory and motor events so that the right outcome will occur. Although people may report that making this adjustment is exactly what they are doing, psychologists invariably argue that there is no little person in their heads to do such adjusting.

To escape the problem of the "little person in the head," various proposals have been advanced and abandoned in the past 200 years. The theory of afference suggested that sensations, presumably arising from the environment and the act of moving, guide behavior. The source of this theory was the idea that the brain is a passive recipient of impulses and is not capable of generating spontaneous activity. The theory of efference, which replaced the afference theory, suggested that the sensations of movement arise from the perception of the nervous system's activity in generating a movement.

The problem with both theories is the difficulty that they had in explaining how errors of movement are corrected. The problem can be seen more clearly in the strength of the theory that replaced them, the theory of reafference, referred to earlier as corollary discharge. According to reafference theory, when a movement is initiated, it leaves a trace or record of what the intended movement should be. As the movement is performed, it generates a second record that can be compared with the first. If the movement is not performed correctly, the error can be detected by comparing the two records and then making an adjustment on the next attempt.

The theory of reafference was generated separately by Roger Sperry and Erich von Holst. Sperry rotated the eyes of frogs so that the perceived location of an object was in a direction opposite that of its true location. The rotation caused the frogs to move in a direction opposite that of the real location of the object. Von Holst asked how an animal could disentangle its own movement from the movements of objects around it; that is, how does one distinguish self-movement from object movement? Both Sperry's experiments and von Holst's questions led to the conclusion that, to move successfully, an animal must generate a record of its movement and use this record as a reference to locate or plot the movements of other objects.

The idea that an animal generates a record of its movements, separate from the activity that generates the movement or the sensory information generated by the movement, suggests a central mental process or representation that contains schemas of movements. The function of sensations produced by movements is to update and correct the central representation, much as in the prism-adaptation studies described earlier. People can correct for massive distortions produced by prisms, including left–right reversals and dorsal–ventral reversals. The important point is that, even though sensory information is grossly misleading, the system that represents and instructs movements is very good at compensating for the sensory distortions.

There have been a number of attempts to characterize the properties of central representations or images. What do they look like? Experiments designed to answer this question examine whether the formation and topography of representations, as well as changes in them, match similar features of the real world. For example, a person who is asked to take one die of a pair of dice and rotate it so that the numbers that are visible match those of its mate will manipulate it several times until the two are matched. The manipulation consists of a number of movements and takes a certain amount of time.

When asked to perform the same task mentally, the person appears to require the same number of mental movements and to take about the same amount of time. Similarly, if people are asked to imagine walking a certain distance, they take about the same amount of time and make the same number of steps as they would to walk the same distance in reality. Such experiments suggest that mental images have very much the same features as real movements.

A criticism of equating the real dimensions of movements with those of mental representations on the basis of these experiments is that subjects have some knowledge of the tasks and so can generate appropriate mental parallels. This criticism does not seem entirely valid, because, when subjects are given tasks that contain answers unknown to them in advance, similar results are obtained. For example, when people reach for an object that is close by or for one that is farther away, they take the same length of time. When they write their names in small script and in large script, the times are again equivalent.

A priori, most subjects do not know that the times are equal and, if asked, will say that they are different. Nevertheless, when people are asked to imagine reaching different distances or writing their names in letters of different sizes, the times that they report for the tasks are similar to the times actually required to perform those tasks. This result strengthens the idea that such features as the time and topography of movement images parallel those of actual movements.

The Neural Basis of Images

Where in the brain are mental images located? There are three possibilities:

1. The very same structures that produce movements could produce images.

2. Only a part of the structures that produce movements could produce images.

3. Movements and images are produced by completely independent areas.

Surprisingly, whereas it once might have been thought that the third possibility was most likely, at present most of the debate concerning these three possibilities considers only the first two as serious options.

Per Roland performed one of the first experiments in which imagined movements and real movements were compared while regional cerebral blood flow (rCBF) was monitored (see Figure 9.3). When subjects imagined a series of finger movements, the premotor cortex was active. When they performed the movements, both the premotor cortex and the motor cortex were active.

The results of this experiment demonstrate that imagined and real movements are represented in the premotor cortex. They also favor the second possibility: that only a part of an area engaged in making a movement is engaged in forming images of that movement. Similar results favoring this position are obtained from case studies of patients with visual-system lesions, including one study of a patient who could recognize visual patterns but could not form visual images of them. Other favorable results, as described by Marlene Behrmann and her coworkers, are of patients who have severe trouble identifying real objects but have preserved visual imagery. These case studies suggest that earlier cortical visual levels (for example, areas V1 through V5) are engaged in perception, whereas only later visual levels (for example, area TE) form images.

Per Roland and Balázs Gulyas presented further evidence that the higher-level cortices take part in both memory and images. They presented auditory, motor, and a variety of visual tasks to subjects and measured rCBF. In all their experiments, the areas activated were in the association cortices of the temporal, parietal, and frontal lobes. Neither lower-level sensory areas nor primary motor areas were activated.

Roland and Gulyas favor the idea that the higher-level areas form a distributed system whose function is also to represent memory. The memories do not contain the dimensions of time and space, but the simultaneous activation of a number of regions could generate these properties. For Roland and Gulyas, mental images are activated memories.

There is also evidence against this view. Three lines of evidence from studies of the visual system favor the idea that the same structures participating in perception take part in forming images in the absence of visual stimulation. This position does not disagree that higher visual areas are engaged in imagery but argues that lower areas of the visual system also take part. Thus, in normal viewing, visual stimulation successively excites lower visual areas and then higher visual areas; whereas, in imagining, higher visual areas activate lower visual areas through reentrant fibers and so the same sets of neurons are activated in both perception and imaging. Here is the evidence:

1. Martha Farah described patient M.G.S., before and after the occipital cortex was unilaterally removed as a treatment for epilepsy. M.G.S. was asked to imagine walking toward an object, such as a mouse or a dog, or to imagine an approaching car. She was to indicate when the object completely filled the visual field (which would occur when M.G.S. was closer to the mouse than to the dog). Before surgery, her response was similar to that of control subjects. After surgery, the visual angle was reduced significantly relative both to that of the normal subjects and to her preoperative results (the objects now filled her visual field when she was farther away from them, presumably because her visual field was smaller). This finding is consistent with the idea that images have a topographic organization in the visual areas and that the area available to contain an image is reduced after the loss of the primary visual cortex.

2. A number of rCBF studies find activation in primary visual areas during imagining (see the Snapshot in Chapter 13).

3. Evidence that could be taken to support the commonality of structures engaged in perception and imagining comes from studies of eye movements. In viewing, the eyes make saccades in a typical way to catch key elements of the stimulus. The same kinds of eye movements are made when looking at an object and in later imagining of the same object (Norton and Stark, 1972).

At present, research cannot distinguish between the position that only higher-level structures take part in imagining and the position that the same set of structures controlling viewing also control imagining. The disagreement between studies using rCBF may be related to differences in the kinds of tasks presented to the subjects, differences in the methods used to subtract baseline blood-flow activity in control conditions and test conditions, or even differences in subject populations.

With respect to the last point, we were surprised to learn from a colleague, who is internationally known for his work in visual perception, that he has no idea what visual imagery is, because he is unable to experience it. We both asserted, to his surprise, that we had no difficulty forming visual images.

An additional problem with studies comparing perception and imaging relates to quantifying what it is that is seen. When two viewers look at a scene, they can come to reasonable agreement about what they are seeing. When they compare their mental images of the same scene, they have no reliable way to confirm that they are imagining the same thing.

Kinds of Images

Is there more than one type of mental image? If we return to our ski jumpers, we can see that they can imagine their jump in at least two different ways. They can use a process referred to as internal imagery—a first-person process in which they imagine that they themselves are making the movement. Alternatively, they can use what is called external imagery, in which they see some person, perhaps themselves or perhaps someone else, making the jump.

In the first case, the imagery is of the movements that they themselves will make; the anticipatory movements that they make in the imagery presumably correspond to the movements that they will make when they jump. This process is somewhat like practicing a golf swing before hitting the ball, without actually making the swing. In the second case, they are imagining themselves or some other person. They see that person, they see the jump, and they see the surrounding area. Furthermore, the view can change at will. It is as though they are actually watching some other person jump or are watching a jump on television.

The properties of internal and external images are quite different, although both are images of movement and both can represent the upcoming jump. Marc Jeannerod refers to internal imagery as motor imagery; it is the self in action. External imagery is really the imagery of objects: a jumper, a jump, the surrounding area.

To gain an idea of how the two differ, consider the following example. A coach demonstrates a basketball shot to a player. The player watches and forms an image of the movements that the coach has made. The player then tries the shot. As the player does so, the coach (mentally, perhaps with a little muscle tensing and grimacing) makes the same shot along with the player. If the player succeeds, the coach gives a little cheer, and, if the player misses, the coach groans and they begin again.

The two kinds of imagery differ in another way. When the player imagines the coach's movements, the image is created without muscle tension, effort, or exertion. When the coach imagines the player's shot, the image includes tension, effort, and exertion, as if the coach were actually taking the shot.

Images of the movements used in sports are relatively simple. They are movements that the participant has practiced and viewed hundreds of times. People form other images as well, images that are more complex and that can be unique in some way. Consider the following example.

You need a book on bats. You look up the catalogue number on your computer and then set off to the library to get the book. On the way to the library, you meet a friend who wants to know where you are going. You explain. You both talk about bats, and then you continue on your way. When you get to the library, you find that you have forgotten the catalogue number. You look it up. When you get to the stacks, the book is not there. The librarian tells you that the book is checked out, and it is impossible to get it back.

In this example, you have an image of a goal but no image of the movements that you must make or the terrain that you must traverse to reach the goal and, certainly, no image of where the book might be located. A goal image is very flexible in that it allows the incorporation of a variety of actions and subgoals. Other images that we have include thoughts, which are usually verbal images. That is, we talk to ourselves and hear the sounds of words, but we do not make sounds or movements. We also hum tunes and sing little songs to ourselves.

If we consider all the different kinds of images that we can form, it becomes clear that they closely parallel the things that we do. If we postulate that the images are formed by the same brain areas that produce actions, then each kind of image maps onto its own brain area. Thus, verbal images or thinking to oneself use language phonemic circuitry in the left hemisphere, whereas images of music or spatial events use right-hemisphere structures that normally subserve those events.

A dramatic example of the interplay between image and movement comes from the studies of mirror neurons (see Figure 9.11). In humans, the mirror neurons are found not only in area 6 but may also be in area 44, which is Broca's area. Giacomo Rizzolatti and his colleagues reviewed the literature on this subject and make the unexpected conclusion that the results of brain-imaging studies have shown that activity in area 44 is related to the imaging of hand movements or mental rotation of objects by hand. Thus, area 44 participates not only in the generation of verbs that describe movements (see Chapter 19), which presumably entails a form of imagery, but also in imagining the movements represented by the verbs.

The parts of the brain engaged in internal versus external imagery are not known, but it seems unlikely that the same brain regions produce both kinds of images. The internal imagery of movements may use the object-location system (the parietofrontal cortex system, or dorsal stream), and the external imagery of movements in relation to objects may use the object-recognition system (inferior temporofrontal cortex system, or ventral stream). Images are probably also closely related to memories, as Roland suggests, in that they are in some ways active memories. Thus, each brain system is responsible for a triumvirate of functions: action, memory, and imagining.

A disruption in the ability to imagine movements may be partly responsible for the symptoms of apraxia (see Chapters 14 and 17). For example, if the same neural structures represent perception and images, then damage to those structures will have equivalent effects on perception and images. If the same structures represent movements and their images, then brain damage will have equivalent effects on actions and their images. If, on the other hand, images are formed in only a part of the circuitry or in some other location, then the effects of damage to the structures that control images will differ from those of damage to structures that control perception or action.

Because movements can be conceived as consisting of a goal, a series of subgoals, and a series of movements, different kinds of apraxia should be related to impairments in subcomponents of the actions. Consider the following patient:

> A woman with a biparietal lesion had worked for years as a fish-filleter. With the development of her symptoms, she began to experience difficulty in carrying on with her job. She did not seem to know what to do with her knife. She would stick the point in the head of a fish, start the first stroke, and then come to a stop. In her own mind she knew how to fillet fish, but yet she could not execute the maneuver. The foreman accused her of being drunk and sent her home for mutilating fish.
>
> This same patient also showed another unusual phenomenon which might possibly be apraxic in nature. She could never finish an undertaking. She would begin a job, drop it, start another, abandon that one, and within a short while would have four or five uncompleted tasks on her hands. This would cause her to do such inappropriate actions as putting the sugar bowl in the refrigerator, and the coffee pot inside the oven. (Critchley, 1953, pp. 158–159)

If the fish filleter could not conceive of the goal of filleting fish, she would perform the actions of filleting, but they would be haphazard (as was the case). She would be classified as having **ideational apraxia**. (In the example of going to the library for a book on bats, ideational apraxia would prevent the formation of this goal.)

On the other hand, the fish filleter might be able to form the goal of filleting a fish but not be able to form the subgoals of making the appropriate steps of filleting. In this case, she would be classified as having **ideomotor apraxia**. (In the library example, one might set off for the library but never arrive there, because of an inability to make appropriate course adjustments along the way.)

Finally, if the fish filleter could form the goal and know the movement sequence but not execute the movement, she would be classified as having **motor apraxia**. (In the library example, one could not get the catalogue number of the book, because the fingers would not produce the movements to operate the keys of the computer, and possibly one would not be able to execute the walking movements.)

The classification of apraxia in this way is both a strength and a weakness. The classification appears to allow some obvious distinctions between knowing what to do and being able to do it, which is diagnostically useful. But this distinction is difficult to make. For example, which kind of apraxia does the fish filleter really have? When she stabs at the fish, is her problem not knowing what she wants to do or not knowing how to do it?

The several standard clinical tests often used to assess apraxia have similar weaknesses. For example, a patient might be asked to demonstrate the use of a particular object in its absence—to comb the hair or to hammer a nail. An apraxic person's response might be to do nothing or to use a part of the body as if it were the implement—to stroke a finger through the hair as if it were a comb or to hit the table with a fist as though it were a hammer. A normal person would pretend to hold the comb or hammer. Another test of apraxia might be to ask a person to perform such symbolic movements as saluting or waving goodbye; the person might remain still or respond by making an unrecognizable movement.

A final aspect of movement images relates to the conscious experience of intention to move. The subjective experience of intention to act is a central component of human mental life, but it is elusive. Patrick Haggard argues that intention for action provides a strong sense of controlling events in the external world.

The supplementary motor cortex is an important site for intention to move. Findings from studies using transcranial magnetic stimulation have shown that low-frequency stimulation leads to an urge to move a specific body part and, if the stimulation is increased, an actual movement of that part. The frontal and parietal mirror neurons also must be part of the intentional circuit, but the details of the neural networks underlying intentions remain unknown.

Consciousness

Conscious experience is probably the most familiar mental process that we know, yet its workings remain mysterious. Everyone has a vague idea of what is meant by being conscious, but consciousness is easier to identify than to define.

Definitions of **consciousness**, which we define as the level of responsiveness of the mind to impressions made by the senses, range from the view that it merely refers to complex thought processes to the more slippery implication that it is the subjective experience of awareness or of "inner self." Nonetheless, there is general agreement that, whatever conscious experience is, it is a process.

Recall from Chapter 1 that Descartes proposed one of the first modern theories of consciousness. He proposed that being able to remember past events and being able to speak were the primary abilities that enable consciousness. In preceding chapters, we have encountered people who have lost the ability to remember and have lost the ability to speak. Those who knew these patients would not have described them as no longer being conscious. In fact, consciousness is probably not a single process but a collection of many processes, such as those associated with seeing, talking, thinking, emotion, and so on.

Consciousness is also not always the same. A person at different ages of life is not thought to be equally conscious at each age; young children and demented adults are usually not considered to experience the same type of consciousness as healthy adults do. Indeed, part of the process of maturation is becoming fully conscious. And consciousness varies across the span of a day as we pass through various states of sleep and waking.

Most definitions of consciousness exclude the conditions of simply being responsive to sensory stimulation or simply being able to produce movement. Thus, animals whose behavior is simply reflexive are not conscious. Similarly, the isolated spinal cord, although a repository for many reflexes, is not conscious. Machines that are responsive to sensory events and are capable of complex movements are not conscious. Many of the physiological functions of normal humans, such as the beating of the heart, are not conscious processes. Similarly, many processes of the nervous system, including simple sensory processes and motor actions, are not conscious. Consciousness requires processes that differ from all the aforementioned.

Some people have argued that certain processes are much more important for consciousness than others. Language is often argued to be essential to consciousness, because language makes a fundamental change in the nature of human consciousness. Recall that Michael Gazzaniga (see Chapter 20) suggested that language acts as an interpreter, which he believes led to an important difference between the functions of the hemispheres.

People who are aphasic are not considered to have lost conscious awareness, however; nor are people who have their right hemispheres removed. Patient H.M., whom we met in in the Portrait in Chapter 18, had a dense amnesia, yet he was quite conscious and could engage in intelligent conversations. In sum, although language may alter the nature of our conscious experience, any one brain structure seems unlikely to be equated with consciousness. Rather, to view consciousness as a product of all cortical areas, their connections, and their cognitive operations makes more sense.

The simplest explanation of why we are conscious is that consciousness provides adaptive advantage. In other words, either our creation of the sensory world or our selection of behavior is enhanced by being conscious. Consider visual consciousness as an example. Crick and Koch noted that an animal such as a frog acts a bit like a zombie when it responds to visual input. Frogs respond to small, preylike objects by snapping; they respond to large, looming objects by jumping. These responses are controlled by different visual systems and are best thought of as being reflexive rather than conscious. But these visual systems work well for the frog; so why do we need to add consciousness?

Crick and Koch suggested that reflexive systems are fine when the number of such systems are few but, as the number grows, such a reflexive arrangement becomes inefficient, especially if systems are in conflict. When the amount of information about some event increases, it is better to produce a single but complex representation and make it available for a sufficient amount of time to the parts of the brain (such as the frontal lobe) that make a choice among many different but possible plans for action.

We still need the ability to respond quickly and, presumably, unconsciously. In the human brain, the ventral stream is conscious, but the dorsal stream, which acts more rapidly, is not. The action of the unconscious, on-line dorsal stream can be seen anecdotally in many athletes. To hit a baseball or a tennis ball traveling at more than 90 or even 100 miles per hour is believed to require athletes to swing before they are consciously aware of actually seeing the ball. The conscious awareness of the ball comes just after an athlete hits it.

The results of a series of experiments by Jeannerod's group have shown a similar dissociation between behavior and awareness in normal volunteers making grasping movements. **Figure 22.11** illustrates the results of a representative experiment. Subjects were required to move one hand and grasp one of three rods as quickly as possible. The correct target on any given trial was determined by the illumination of a light on the target.

On some trials, unbeknown to the subjects, the light jumped from one target to another. Subjects were asked to indicate if such a jump had taken place. As shown in Figure 22.11, subjects were able to make the trajectory correction on-line but, to the surprise of many of them, on some trials, they were actually grasping the target before they were aware that it had moved. As with ballplayers, the conscious awareness of the stimulus event occurred after the movement had taken place. Clearly, no thought was required to make the movement, just as frogs appear to catch flies without thinking about the task.

Such movements contrast, however, with movements that must be directed toward a specific object. If we are reaching toward a bowl to grasp a jellybean of a specific color, we must be aware of the difference between red, green, and yellow jellybeans, and we must direct our reach toward the desired color. Thus, the action of the conscious ventral stream is needed when we must discriminate and respond differentially to particular stimuli. Consciousness allows us to select behaviors that correspond to an understanding of the nuances of sensory inputs.

The Neural Basis of Consciousness

As stated earlier, consciousness must be a function of numerous interacting systems, presumably including sensory areas, memory structures, and perhaps structures underlying other processes such as emotion and executive functions.

Experimental procedure

Subjects were required to move their hands and grasp the illuminated rod as quickly as possible.

In this trial, the subject reaches for illuminated rod 3.

Results

On some trials, the light jumps from one target to another,…

… causing the subject to correct his trajectory. Most subjects found that they were actually grasping the new target before they were aware that it had moved.

Conclusion

It is possible to dissociate behavior and conscious awareness.

Figure 22.11

Dissociating Behavior and Conscious Awareness Paths that the hand follows to grasp the illuminated rod are indicated by the arrows. On some trials, the light switched unexpectedly from one target to another. The switch elicited a smooth and rapid movement correction. Subjects were asked to give a vocal response to indicate that they were aware of the target switch. On some trials, there was a dissociation between motor and vocal responses such that, to their surprise, subjects had already grasped the target some 300 ms before they emitted the vocal response. (After Frith et al., 1999.)

The problem for a theory of the neural basis of consciousness is to explain how all these systems can be integrated.

We have returned to the binding problem that we first encountered in Chapter 10. Recall that Harry Jerison suggested that one solution to the binding problem within the sensory domain is temporal integration. Crick and Koch went further and proposed that binding is the solution to consciousness.

Before examining this idea more closely, we need to examine processes that are believed to be prerequisites of consciousness. Most investigators agree that at least four processes must take part:

1. **Arousal,** the waking up of the brain by nonspecific modulatory systems

2. **Perception,** the detection and binding of sensory features

3. **Attention,** the selection of a restricted sample of all available information

4. **Working memory,** the short-term storage of ongoing events

Andreas Engel and Wolf Singer proposed that all these processes either require or modify the operation of an overall binding process and that binding is implemented by the transient and precise synchronization of neural discharges in diffuse neural networks. The general idea is that neurons that represent the same object or event fire their action potentials in a temporal synchrony with a precision of milliseconds.

No such synchronization should take place among cells that are part of different neural networks. Recall that the idea of synchrony was proposed earlier as a mechanism of attention (see Figure 22.9). Taken further, without attention to an input, there is no awareness of it (see Taylor for more on this point).

But what produces the synchrony? Neuronal groups exhibit a wide range of synchronous oscillations (6–80 Hz) and can shift from a desynchronized state to a rhythmic state in milliseconds. Thus, we can predict that, when we become consciously aware of some event, there should be evidence of synchronous activity among widely separated brain regions.

Figure 22.12 illustrates this process in regard to synchronous activity in the gamma range (roughly 40 Hz) recorded when subjects viewed Mooney faces (see Chapter 14) either right side up or upside down. When viewed upright, faces can be found but, when viewed inverted, finding the face is impossible. A subject's task was to find the face and push one of two buttons to signify the presence or absence of a face.

Figure 22.12 shows a marked difference in neural activity in the two conditions. About 200 ms after the stimulus presentation (Figure 22.12A), there was synchrony in the left hemisphere in the upright-face condition inasmuch as electrodes in all lobes showed synchronous activity (Figure 22.12B) followed

Face perceived   **Face not perceived**

(A) Image presented (0–180 ms)

Image perception is followed by...

(B) Recognition (180–360 ms)

... synchronous activity over the left hemisphere.

(C) Synchrony scatter (360–540 ms)

Brief asynchrony in both hemispheres...

(D) Motor response (540-720 ms)

...is followed by synchrony when the subject presses the button.

Figure 22.12

The Shadow of a Perception Average scalp distribution of phase synchrony in EEG recorded from electrodes on the scalp marked by dots. The blue lines indicate synchrony, and the red lines indicate asynchrony. (A) When subjects were shown an upright Mooney figure, they were able to perceive a face; whereas, when shown the figure inverted, they did not perceive a face. Synchrony is correlated with recognition of the face (B) and the motor response (D). Motor activity is preceded by a period of asynchrony (C). (After Rodriguez et al., 1999.)

by a period of asynchrony in most of both hemispheres (Figure 22.12C). Such desynchronization is postulated to be necessary, because there is a shift between synchrony in different neural assemblies. Finally, a return of synchrony coincided with the subject's button pressing (Figure 22.12D). Notice that, in the inverted condition, there was no synchrony during the analysis of the stimulus, as shown in Figure 22.12A and B, but there was during the motor response shown in Figure 22.12D.

A review of the evidence on synchrony and consciousness concludes that phase synchrony acts not only to bind the sensory attributes but also to bind all dimensions of the cognitive act, including associative memory, emotional tone, and motor planning (Thompson and Varella, 2001). The problem, however, is that all studies to date are correlative. There is no direct evidence that changes in synchrony lead to changes in either behavior or consciousness. A search for such evidence is the likely direction of studies on consciousness in both laboratory animals and human subjects in the coming decade.

Cerebral Substrates of Consciousness

Little is known about the essential cerebral regions for consciousness. One way to investigate this matter is to identify which structures in the brain are inactive when we are unconscious and active when we are conscious. **Figure 22.13**A summarizes the regions of cortex that are compromised when people are in a coma, a persistent vegetative state, sleep, or under general anesthesia. Notice that, in all cases, there is inactivation of the dorsolateral prefrontal cortex, the medial frontal cortex, the posterior parietal cortex and the posterior cingulate cortex. Figure 22.13B illustrates brain activation in a quiet resting state and identifies two distinct neural networks of structures that are either correlated or anticorrelated; again, there is evidence of a general frontoparietal network. We return to this network shortly when we consider emotion and consciousness.

A second way to look for cerebral substrates is to look for structures that might synchronize activity. Crick and Koch introduced the novel idea that a little-studied brain region may play a central role in the processes that bind diverse sensory attributes. The **claustrum**, meaning "hidden away," is a thin sheet of gray matter that, in the human brain, lies below the general region of the insula. Its connectivity is unique in that it receives input from virtually all regions of the cortex and projects back to almost all regions of the cortex.

Virtually nothing is known about the functions of the claustrum in any mammalian species, in large part because it is almost impossible to damage selectively. Crick and Koch proposed that this unique anatomy is compatible with a global role in integrating information to provide the gist of sensory input on a fast time

Figure **22.13**

Neural Substrates Necessary for Consciousness (A) Data from functional imaging show that a frontoparietal network (areas in black) is compromised in coma, vegetative state, sleep, and general anesthesia. These regions appear to be necessary for consciousness. Abbreviations: F, prefrontal; MF, medial frontal; P, posterior parietal; Pr, posterior cingulate. (B) In a quiet but awake resting state, two distinct networks of structures are either correlated (color coded red to orange) or anticorrelated (blue to green) with the parietal cortex, indicated by the arrow. (Tsuchiya and Adolphs, 2007, p. 161.)

(A)

(B)

−10.0　　0.0　　10.0

Figure 22.14

Linking Emotion and Consciousness Note the overlap in brain regions critical to emotional state (blue), emotional feeling (red), and level of consciousness (green). (Tsuchiya and Adolphs, 2007, p. 160.)

scale. They provocatively state: "This should be further experimentally investigated, in particular if this structure plays a key role in consciousness. What could be more important? So why wait?" (Crick and Koch, 2005, p.1277).

Emotion and Consciousness

Naotsugu Tsuchiya and Ralph Adolphs recently raised the question of whether a relation exists between emotion and consciousness. They began with the observation that there is considerable overlap in the brain regions underlying these quite different experiences and the experience of self, as summarized in **Figure 22.14**. The principal overlap is seen in the medial frontal cortex and posterior cingulate cortex, regions that we have identified as central to the concept of self-awareness (see Chapter 20).

SNAPSHOT
Stimulating Nonconscious Emotion

Faces convey considerable information about the mood of others, an ability that R.P., whose case is described in this chapter's Portrait, apparently had lost when it came to gauging people's trustworthiness. Yi Jiang and Sheng He used fMRI to examine hemodynamic (blood flow) changes as measured by blood-oxygenation-level-dependent (BOLD) MRI when subjects viewed neutral, fearful, and scrambled faces that were either visible or rendered invisible through a process called intraocular suppression. The suppression is produced by showing the face image to the nondominant eye and a scrambled face to the dominant eye as shown in part A of the adjoining illustration.

The face can be completely suppressed from awareness by using this procedure. The fusiform face area (FFA), superior temporal sulcus (STS), and the amygdala responded strongly to the visible faces as would be expected (see Chapters 13 and 20). When the faces were made invisible, however, activity in the FFA was much reduced and the STS was active only when fearful faces were shown (part B of the illustration).

The amygdala still responded strongly to the visible faces but was much more active when the faces showed fear (part C of the illustration). For the invisible-face condition, activity in the amygdala was correlated with that in the STS but not in the FFA. Thus, even though the subjects were not consciously aware of having seen the faces, the STS and amygdala responded strongly to the fearful face and less so or not at all to the neutral face. The study thus shows that nonconscious stimuli can evoke emotional states.

(A) Invisible condition

Dominant eye — Nondominant eye — Percept

Neutral face

Fearful face

Scrambled face

Time

How did the suppressed image manage to activate the FFA and STS? Jiang and He hypothesize that the face information may travel through subcortical pathways to eventually reach the STS, FFA, and amygdala. Findings from studies on blindsight patients support the idea that unperceived fearful stimuli can activate fear-related activity in the amygdala.

Jiang, Y., and S. He. Cortical responses to invisible faces: Dissociating subsystems for facial-information processing. *Current Biology*, 16:2023–2029, 2006.

Tsuchiya and Adolphs further asked whether consciousness is essential to experience emotion. Although it seems unlikely that we experience emotion when we are not conscious, such as being in a coma or vegetative state, there is considerable evidence that we can have unconscious emotions. An example is fear conditioning to subliminal stimuli in which a person develops emotional responses without awareness of their triggering stimuli. The pathway for this learning includes the amygdala and related subcortical structures (see Chapter 18).

Neuroimaging studies, such as the one described in the Snapshot below, also show amygdala activation to emotional stimuli of which subjects are not consciously aware. Whether emotional processing is necessary for consciousness, however, is less clear. If it is, the implication is that a severe impairment in emotional experience would lead to compromised consciousness, an idea that is novel and currently wide open for future study.

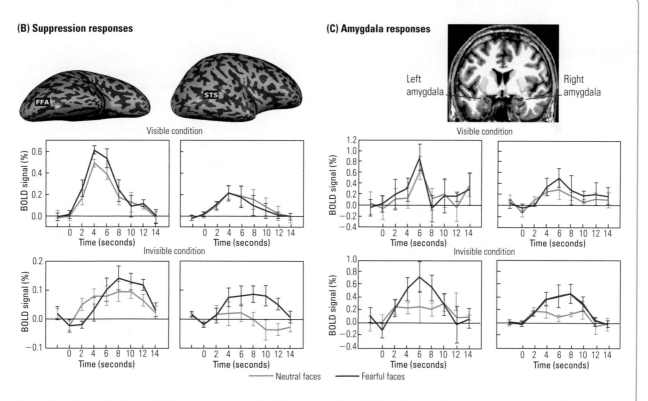

(B) Suppression responses

(C) Amygdala responses

Responding to invisible faces. (A) Faces are rendered invisible to the subjects by presenting the scrambled patterns to the dominant eye and the face to nondominant eye. The dominant eye suppresses the perception. (B and C) Functional MRI responses of the fusiform face area (FFA), superior temporal sulcus (STS), and amygdala to the invisible and visible faces. All areas had strong responses to the visible face images, but the STS did not respond to the invisible neutral faces. (Jiang and He, 2006, pp. 2024–2026. ©2006 Elsevier Ltd. All rights reserved.)

Summary

Defining Attention and Consciousness

Attention, mental images, and consciousness are not epiphenomena resulting from the complexities of the brain. They are properties of the nervous system that direct complex actions of the body and the brain. Neuropsychologists have not quantified attention, imagery, or consciousness. Still, it is possible to theorize that they are functions of one or another brain region. It is also possible to create theories of how brain processes produce these phenomena.

Attention and Inattention

Attention allows the nervous system to focus on aspects of the world and on aspects of the brain itself. The processes of attention can be demonstrated by using behavioral, neurophysiological, and imaging techniques. The neural mechanisms underlying attention are extensive and are best thought of as a network of structures including sensory regions as well as the parietal, prefrontal, and anterior cingulate cortex. Inattention ("the dark side of attention") is a necessary fallout from the focusing of attention on specific information.

Mental Images

The process of imagining allows the nervous system to represent places and objects so that a person can reach those places and obtain those objects.

Consciousness and the Neural Basis of Consciousness

Consciousness, a property of complex brains, binds diverse aspects of sensory information into a single event that we experience as reality. Consciousness is hypothesized to be a property of synchronized brain activity that may implicate the claustrum or cingulate regions.

References

Awh, E., K. M. Armstrong, and T. Moore. Visual and occulomotor selection: Links, causes and implications for spatial attention. *Trends in Cognitive Sciences* 10:124–130, 2006.

Bargh, J. A., and M. J. Ferguson. Beyond behaviorism: On the automaticity of higher mental processes. *Psychological Bulletin* 126:925–945, 2000.

Behrmann, M., M. Moscovitch, and G. Winocur. Intact visual imagery and impaired visual perception in a patient with visual agnosia. *Journal of Experimental Psychology: Human Perception and Performance* 20:1068–1087, 1994.

Berti, A., and F. Frassinetti. When far becomes near: Re-mapping of space by tool use. *Journal of Cognitive Neuroscience* 12:415–420, 2000.

Bossom, J. The effect of brain lesions on adaptation in monkeys. *Psychonomic Science* 2:45–46, 1965.

Burton, H., N. S. Abend, A.-M. K. MacLeod, R. J. Sinclair, A. Z. Snyder, and M. E. Raichle. Tactile attention tasks enhance activation in somatosensory regions of parietal cortex: A positron emission tomography study. *Cerebral Cortex* 9:662–674, 1999.

Chelazzi, L., E. K. Miller, J. Duncan, and R. Desimone. A neural basis for visual search in inferior temporal cortex. *Nature* 363:345–347, 1993.

Chun, M. M., and R. Marois. The dark side of visual attention. *Current Opinion in Neurobiology* 12:184–189, 2002.

Corbetta, M., F. M. Miezin, S. Dobmeyer, G. L. Shulman, and S. E. Petersen. Selective and divided attention during visual discrimination of shape, color, and speed: Functional anatomy by positron emission tomography. *Journal of Neuroscience* 11:2383–2402, 1991.

Corbetta, M., F. M. Miezin, G. L. Shulman, and S. E. Petersen. A PET study of visuospatial attention. *Journal of Neuroscience* 13:1202–1226, 1993.

Courchesne, E. Brainstem, cerebellar and limbic neuroanatomical abnormalities in autism. *Current Opinion in Neurobiology* 7:269–278, 1997.

Crick, F., and C. Koch. The problem of consciousness. *Scientific American* 267:152–159, 1992.

Crick, F., and C. Koch. Consciousness and neuroscience. *Cerebral Cortex* 8:97–107, 1998.

Crick, F., and C. Koch. What is the function of the claustrum? *Philosophical Transactions of the Royal Society: Biological Sciences* 360:1271–1279, 2005.

Critchley, M. *The Parietal Lobes.* London: Arnold, 1953.

Eastwood, J. D., D. Smilek, and P. M. Merikle. Differential attentional guidance by unattended faces expressing positive and negative emotion. *Perception and Psychophysics* 63:1004–1013, 2001.

Engel, A. K., and W. Singer. Temporal binding and the neural correlates of sensory awareness. *Trends in Cognitive Sciences* 5:16–25, 2001.

Farah, M. J. *Visual Agnosia.* Cambridge, Mass.: MIT Press, 1990.

Fine, C., J. Lumsden, and R. J. R. Blair. Dissociation between "theory of mind" and executive functions in a patient with early left amygdala damage. *Brain* 124:287–298, 2001.

Fletcher, P. C., F. Happe, U. Frith, S. C. Baker, R. J. Dolan, and R. S. Frakowiak. Other minds in the brain: A functional imaging study of "theory of mind" in story comprehension. *Cognition* 57:109–128, 1995.

Frith, C., R. Perry, and E. Lumer. The neural correlates of conscious experience. *Trends in Cognitive Sciences* 3:105–114, 1999.

Gallagher, H. L., F. Happe, N. Brunswick, P. C. Fletcher, U. Frith, and C. D. Frith. Reading the mind in cartoons and stories: An fMRI study of "theory of mind" in verbal and nonverbal tasks. *Neuropsychologia* 38:11–21, 2000.

Geschwind, N. The apraxias: Neural mechanisms of disorders of learned movement. *American Scientist* 63:188–195, 1975.

Haggard, P. Conscious intention and motor cognition. *Trends in Cognitive Sceinces* 9:290–295, 2005.

Hebb, D. O. *Essay on Mind.* Hillsdale, N.J.: Lawrence Earlbaum, 1980.

Jeannerod, M. The representing brain: Neural correlates of motor intention and imagery. *Behavioral and Brain Sciences* 17:187–245, 1994.

Jenkins, I. H., D. J. Brooks, P. D. Nixon, R. S. J. Frackowiak, and R. E. Passingham. Motor sequence learning: A study with positron emission tomography. *Journal of Neuroscience* 14:3775–3790, 1994.

Johnson, J. A., and R. J. Zatorre. Neural substrates for dividing and focusing attention between simultaneous auditory and visual events. *Neuroimage* 31:1673–1681, 2006.

Kahneman, D. *Attention and Effort.* Englewood Cliffs, N.J.: Prentice-Hall, 1973.

Karnath, H.-O., S. Ferber, and M. Himmelbach. Spatial awareness is a function of the temporal not the posterior parietal lobe. *Nature* 411:950–953, 2001.

Kastner, S., P. De Weerd, R. Desimone, and L. G. Ungerleider. Mechanisms of directed attention in the human extrastriate cortex as revealed by functional MRI. *Science* 282:108–112, 2001.

Kimura, D. Left-hemisphere control of oral and brachial movements and their relation to communication. *Philosophical Transactions of the Royal Society of London: Biological Sciences* 298:135–149, 1982.

Kimura, D. *Neuromotor Mechanisms in the Evolution of Human Communication.* New York: Oxford University Press, 1993.

Koch, C., and N. Tsuchiya. Attention and consciousness: Two distinct brain processes. *Trends in Cognitive Sciences* 11:16–22, 2007.

Langton, S. R., R. J. Watt, and V. Bruce. Do the eyes have it? Cues to the direction of social attention. *Trends in Cognitive Sciences* 4:50–59, 2000.

Liepmann, H. *Die linke Hemisphare und das Handeln: Drei Aufsatze aus dem Apraxiegebiet.* Berlin: Springer, 1908.

Logan, G. D. Attention and preattention in theories of automaticity. *American Journal of Psychology* 105:317–340, 1992.

Milner, B. Hemispheric asymmetry in the control of gesture sequences. *Proceedings of the XXI International Congress of Psychology.* Paris, 1976, p. 149.

Moran, J., and R. Desimone. Selective attention gates visual processing in the extrastriate cortex. *Science* 229:782–784, 1985.

Mountcastle, V. B. The parietal system and some higher brain functions. *Cerebral Cortex* 5:377–390, 1995.

Naatanen, T. *Attention and Brain Function.* Hillsdale, N.J.: Lawrence Erlbaum, 1992.

Niebur, E., S. S. Hsiao, and K. O. Johnson. Synchrony: A neuron mechanism for attentional selection? *Current Opinion in Neurobiology* 12:190–194, 2002.

Norton, D., and L. Stark. Eye movements and visual perception. In R. Held and W. Richards, Eds. *Perception: Mechanisms and Models.* Readings from *Scientific American.* San Francisco: W. H. Freeman and Company, 1972.

Petersen, S. E., D. L. Robinson, and J. D. Morris. Contributions of the pulvinar to visual spatial orientation. *Neuropsychologia* 25:97–106, 1987.

Posner, M. I., and S. E. Petersen. The attention system of the brain. *Annual Review of Neuroscience* 13:25–42, 1990.

Posner, M. I., and M. E. Raichle. *Images of Mind.* New York: Scientific American Library, 1993.

Rizzolatti, G., L. Fogassi, and V. Gallese. Motor and cognitive functions of the ventral premotor cortex. *Current Opinion in Neurobiology* 12:149–154, 2002.

Rodriguez, E., N. George, J. P. Lachaux, J. Martinerie, B. Renault, and F. J. Varela. Perception's shadow: Long-distance synchronization of human brain activity. *Nature* 397:430–433, 1999.

Roland, P. E. *Brain Activation.* New York: Wiley, 1993.

Roland, P. E., and B. Gulyas. Visual imagery and visual representation. *Trends in Neuroscience* 17:281–287, 1994.

Rossetti, Y., G. Rode, L. Pisella, A. Farne, L. Li, D. Boisson, and M.-T. Perenin. Prism adaptation to a rightward optical deviation rehabilitates left hemispatial neglect. *Nature* 395:166–169, 1998.

Rousselet, G. A., S. J. Thorpe, and M. Fabre-Thorpe. How parallel is visual processing in the ventral pathway? *Trends in Cognitive Sciences* 8:363–370, 2004.

Rowe, A. D., P. R. Bullock, C. E. Polkey, and R. G. Morris. "Theory of mind" impairments and their relationship to executive functioning following frontal lobe excisions. *Brain* 124:600–616, 2001.

Schall, J. D., and D. P. Hanes. Neural basis of saccade target selection in frontal eye field during visual search. *Nature* 366:467–469, 1993.

Simons, D. J. Attentional capture and inattentional blindness. *Trends in Cognitive Sciences* 4:147–155, 2000.

Simons, D. J., and C. F. Chabris. Gorillas in our midst: Sustained inattentional blindness for dynamic events. *Perception* 28:1059–1074, 1999.

Spitzer, H., R. Desimone, and J. Moran. Increased attention enhances both behavioral and neuronal performance. *Science* 240:338–340, 1988.

Stuss, D. T., G. G. Gallup, and M. P. Alexander. The frontal lobes are necessary for "theory of mind." *Brain* 124:279–286, 2001.

Taylor, J. G. Paying attention to consciousness. *Trends in Cognitive Sciences* 6:206–210, 2002.

Thompson, E., and F. J. Varela. Radical embodiment: Neural dynamics and consciousness. *Trends in Cognitive Sciences* 5:418–425, 2001.

Treisman, A. Features and objects in visual processing. *Scientific American* 254(11):114–124, 1986.

Treisman, A., and S. Gormican. Feature analysis in early vision. *Psychological Review* 95:15–30, 1988.

Tsuchiya, N., and R. Adolphs. Emotion and consciousness. *Trends in Cognitive Sciences* 11:158–167, 2007.

Woodman, G. F., and S. J. Luck. Serial deployment of attention during visual search. *Journal of Experimental Psychology: Human Perception and Performance* 29:121–138, 2003.

Zatorre, R. There's more to auditory cortex than meets the ear. *Hearing Research* 229:24–30, 2007.

Brain Development and Plasticity

Alex had a congenital condition known as Sturge–Weber syndrome affecting his left hemisphere. Faraneh Vargha-Khadem and colleagues reported that, by age 8, he had failed to develop speech, and his comprehension of single words and simple commands was equivalent to an average 3-year-old's.

At 8½ years of age, his left hemisphere was removed to alleviate his poorly controlled seizure condition, allowing discontinuation of anticonvulsant medication by the time he was 9 years old. At that time, Alex unexpectedly began to acquire speech and language. By age 15, he had the expressive and receptive language capacities of a 10-year-old, which is remarkable given that he had

(A) (B)

V. Holloway et al., 2000, p. 2438

no expressive language at all when he was 9.

Although Alex still has severe cognitive difficulties compared with average children his age, he appears to have suffered little disadvantage from his protracted period of mutism and limited language comprehension. This outcome contrasts with the widely held view that early childhood is a particu-

larly critical period for the acquisition of speech and language, including phonology, grammar, prosody, and semantics.

Alex's case suggests that it is possible to develop clearly articulated, well structured, and appropriate language for the first time as late as age 9 and with the right hemisphere alone. Alex thus provides an unusually good example of brain plasticity during development. The fMRI images shown here record similar sensorimotor plasticity in a child with congenital left-hemisphere damage: the right hemisphere shows activation during movement of the normal left hand (A) and similar activation during passive movement by the hemiplegic right hand (B).

Why does the brain in early life appear to be flexible in compensating for injury? A parallel question is whether one kind of environment is more likely than others are to stimulate plastic changes in the damaged or, indeed, even the normal brain. To answer such questions, we need first to examine the normal development of the brain and how it influences behavior.

Approaches to Studying Development

Behavioral changes resulting from neural function can be examined in three ways. The first approach is to look at nervous system maturation and correlate it with the development of specific behaviors. For example, we can link the development of certain brain structures to the development of, say, grasping or crawling in infants.

As the brain structures develop, their functions emerge and are manifested in behaviors that we can observe. Thus, structures that develop quickly exhibit their functions sooner than structures, such as the frontal lobes, that develop more slowly. And, because the human brain continues to develop well past adolescence, it is not surprising that some behavioral abilities do not emerge until that time.

The second approach, the converse of the first, is to look at a growing child's behavior and then make inferences about neural maturation. For example, as language emerges in the young child, we expect to find corresponding changes in the neural structures that control language. In fact, such changes are what we do find.

At birth, children do not speak, and even extensive speech training would not enable them to do so. The neural structures that enable people to speak are not yet mature enough. As language emerges, we can conclude that the speech-related structures in the brain are undergoing the necessary maturation.

The same reasoning can be applied to frontal-lobe development. As frontal-lobe structures mature in adolescence, we look for related changes in behavior, but we can also do the reverse: because we observe new abilities emerging in the teenage years, we infer that they must be controlled by late-maturing neural structures.

The third approach to studying the relation between brain and behavioral development is to identify and study factors that influence both. From this perspective, the mere emergence of a certain brain structure is not enough; we must also know the experiences that shape how the structure functions and that therefore lead to the production of certain kinds of behaviors. Some of the experiences that influence brain function are related to the effects of hormones, injuries, and abnormal genes.

Logically, if behavior is influenced by one of these experiences, then structures in the brain that are changed by that experience are responsible for the behavioral outcomes. For example, we might study how an abnormal secretion of a hormone affects both a certain brain structure and a certain behavior. We can then infer that, because the observed behavioral abnormality results from the abnormal functioning of the brain structure, that structure must normally play some role in controlling the behavior. In the following sections, we will consider some of the findings obtained by using these different approaches to studying brain development and plasticity.

The Development of the Human Brain

At the time that an egg is fertilized by a sperm, a human embryo consists of just a single cell. But this cell soon begins to divide; and, by the 14th day, the embryo consists of several sheets of cells with a raised area in the middle and looks something like a fried egg. The raised area is the primitive body. By 3 weeks after conception, it possesses a primitive brain, which is essentially a

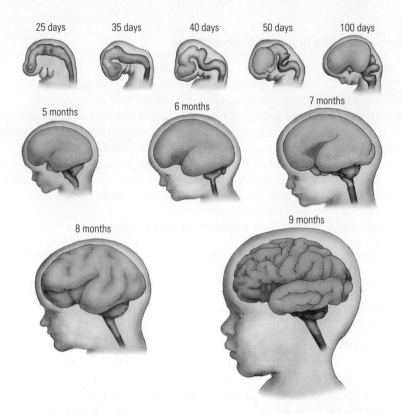

Figure 23.1

Prenatal Brain Development In these diagrams of embryonic and fetal stages of development of the human brain, forebrain areas are represented in yellow, the midbrain in teal, and the hindbrain in purple. (After W. M. Cowan. Copyright © 1979 by Scientific American, Inc. All rights reserved.)

sheet of cells at one end of the embryo. This sheet of cells rolls up to form a structure called the **neural tube**, much as a flat sheet of paper can be curled to make a cylinder.

The body and the nervous system change rapidly in the next 3 weeks of development. By 7 weeks (49 days), the embryo begins to resemble a miniature person, and, as **Figure 23.1** shows, by about 100 days after conception, the brain looks distinctly human; however, it does not begin to form gyri and sulci until about 7 months. By the end of the 9th month, the brain has the gross appearance of the adult human organ, even though its cellular structure is different.

The results of research into the development of the child's brain have identified a series of changes that take place in a fixed sequence, as summarized in **Table 23.1**. This program of development has two extraordinary features. First, subcomponents of the nervous system are formed from cells whose destination and function are largely predetermined before they migrate from the ventricular wall where they originate. Second, development is marked by an initial abundance of cells, branches, and connections, with an important part of subsequent maturation consisting of cell death or pruning back of the initial surfeit.

Deficits in the genetic program, intrauterine trauma, the influence of toxic agents, or other factors may lead to peculiarities or errors in development that contribute to obvious and severe deformities, such as those listed in **Table 23.2**. Less-pronounced deficits may lead to such problems as learning disabilities or may appear only as subtle changes in behavior.

Table 23.1 Stages of brain development

1. Cell birth (neurogenesis; gliogenesis)
2. Cell migration
3. Cell differentiation
4. Cell maturation (dendrite and axon growth)
5. Synaptogenesis (formation of synapses)
6. Cell death and synaptic pruning
7. Myelogenesis (formation of myelin)

Table **23.2** Types of abnormal development

Type	Symptom
Anencephaly	Cerebral hemispheres, diencephalon, and midbrain are absent.
Holoprosencephaly	Cortex forms as a single undifferentiated hemisphere.
Lissencephaly	Brain fails to form sulci and gyri and corresponds to a 12-week embryo.
Micropolygyria	Gyri are more numerous, smaller, and more poorly developed than normal.
Macrogyria	Gyri are broader and less numerous than normal.
Microencephaly	Development of the brain is rudimentary and the person has low-grade intelligence.
Porencephaly	Cortex has symmetrical cavities where cortex and white matter should be.
Heterotopia	Displaced islands of gray matter appear in the ventricular walls or white matter, caused by aborted cell migration.
Agenesis of the corpus callosum	Entire corpus callosum or a part of it is absent.
Cerebellar agenesis	Parts of the cerebellum, basal ganglia, or spinal cord are absent or malformed.

Neuron Generation

The neural tube is the brain's nursery. The cells lining it are known as **neural stem cells**, a stem cell being a cell with an extensive capacity for self-renewal. When a stem cell divides, it produces two stem cells; one dies and the other lives to divide again. This process repeats again and again throughout a person's lifetime. In an adult, the neural stem cells line the ventricles, forming the **ventricular zone**.

If lining the ventricles were all that stem cells did throughout a human life span, they would seem like an odd kind of cell to possess. But stem cells have another function: they give rise to **progenitor** (precursor) **cells**. These progenitor cells also can divide, but they eventually produce nondividing cells known as **neuroblasts** and **glioblasts**, which mature into specialized neurons and glial cells (review Figure 3.5).

Neural stem cells, then, are the cells that give rise to all the many specialized cells of the brain and spinal cord. Stem cells continue to produce neurons and glia not just into early adulthood, but even in an aging brain, at least in the olfactory bulb and hippocampus. The fact that neurogenesis can continue into adulthood and even into senescence is important because it means that, when injury or disease causes neurons to die in an adult, perhaps the brain can be induced to replace those neurons. Unfortunately, we do not yet know how to instruct stem cells to carry out this replacement process. Consequently, injury to central nervous system tissue usually remains permanent.

A contentious question concerns what the new neurons might be doing in adult brains (see Gould et al.). The production of new neurons continuously throughout the life span suggests that perhaps old neurons are dying. They are. In fact, given the balance of cell generation and death in the olfactory bulb and hippocampus, we might speculate that the addition of new neurons and consequently their novel contribution to neural circuits could play a role in the formation of new memories, whereas the death of neurons and the subsequent loss of neural circuits could be related to the loss of old memories. The survival of new neurons in the hippocampus does appear to be related to experience: animals that learn tasks requiring activation of the hippocampus retain more of the newly formed neurons than do animals trained on tasks that do not require hippocampal circuitry. This question is far from settled, however, and is bound to remain controversial for some time (see Rakic for a provocative review).

Cell Migration and Differentiation

The production of neuroblasts destined to form the cerebral cortex is largely complete by the middle of gestation (4½ months), whereas the migration of cells to various regions continues for a number of months, even postnatally, with some regions not completing migration until about 8 months after birth. During the last 4½ months of gestation, the brain is especially delicate and is extremely vulnerable to injury or trauma, including asphyxia.

Apparently, the brain can more easily cope with injury during neuron generation than it can during cell migration and differentiation. One reason may be that, after general neurogenesis has stopped, it does not naturally start again. If neurogenesis is still progressing, however, the brain may be able to replace its own injured cells or perhaps allocate existing healthy cells differently.

Cell migration begins shortly after the first neurons are generated, but it continues for weeks after neurogenesis is complete. At the completion of general neurogenesis, cell differentiation begins, the process in which neuroblasts become specific types of neurons (see Figure 3.5). Cell differentiation is essentially complete at birth, although neuron maturation, which includes the growth of dendrites, axons, and synapses, continues for years and, in some parts of the brain, may continue into adulthood.

As seen throughout this book, the cortex is organized into various areas that differ from one another in their cellular makeup. How are different areas created in the course of development? Pasko Rakic and his colleagues argue that the ventricular zone contains a primitive map of the cortex that predisposes cells born in a certain ventricular region to migrate to a certain cortical location. For example, one region of the ventricular zone may produce cells destined to migrate to the visual cortex, whereas another region produces cells destined to migrate to the frontal lobes.

But how do the cells know where these different parts of the cortex are located? The answer is that they travel along "roads" made of **radial glial cells**, each of which has a fiber extending from the ventricular zone to the surface of the cortex, as illustrated in **Figure 23.2**. The cells from a given region of the ventricular zone need only follow the glial road and they will end up in the right location.

The advantage of this system is that, as the brain grows, the glial fibers stretch, but they still go to the same place. Figure 23.2B shows a cell that is migrating perpendicularly to the radial glial fibers. Although most cortical neurons follow the radial glial fibers, a small number appear to migrate by following some type of chemical signal. We do not yet know why some neurons function in this different way.

A curious feature of neuronal migration in the cerebral cortex is that the layers develop from the inside out, much as layers are added to a ball. The neurons of layer VI, the innermost layer, migrate to their locations first, followed by those destined for layer V, and so on.

Figure 23.2

Development of Cortical Maps
(A) The map for the cortex is hypothesized to be represented in the ventricular zone. (B) Radial glial fibers extend from the ventricular zone to the cortical surface. (C) Neurons migrate along the radial glial fibers, which take them from the protomap in the ventricular zone to the corresponding region in the cortex. (After P. Rakic, *Science* 183:425, 1974.)

(A) Brain surface

Ventricle
Ventricular zone
Radial glia

(B) Brain surface
Primitive cortex
Nonradially migrating neuron
Radial glial process
Radial glia
Migrating neuron
Radial glial cell body
Ventricular zone

(C) Direction of movement
Migrating neuron
Radial glial processes

In this way, successive waves of neurons pass earlier-arriving neurons to assume progressively more exterior positions in the cortex. The formation of the cortex is a bit like building the ground floor of a house first, then the second floor, and so on, until the roof is reached. The materials needed to build higher floors must pass through lower floors to get to their destinations.

Migration can stop prematurely, leaving a group of cells that belong in an outer layer scattered, instead, among inner layers of cells. Verne Caviness and Richard Sidman made a major study of disturbed cell migration in the cerebellar cortex of a genetically mutant mouse called the reeler mouse. In this animal, the first cells to be generated lie near the surface and those generated last lie deepest, creating a cortical organization that is inverted compared with that of a normal mouse. Despite their aberrant position, the cells receive and send out appropriate connections, but the mice exhibit an abnormal, reeling movement. Failed or incomplete cell migration in humans also has been described, although the consequences differ from those in the reeler mouse, the most common effect in humans being disorders such as dyslexia or epilepsy.

Neural Maturation

After neurons have migrated to their final destinations and differentiated into specific neuron types, they must begin the process of growing dendrites to provide the surface area for synapses with other cells. They must also extend their axons to appropriate targets to initiate the formation of other synapses. These processes are part of neural maturation.

Two events take place in the development of a dendrite: (1) dendritic *arborization*, or branching, and (2) the growth of dendritic spines. As illustrated in **Figure 23.3**, dendrites begin as simple, individual processes protruding from the cell body. Later, they develop increasingly complex extensions that look much like the branches of trees visible in winter. This event is arborization. The dendritic branches then begin to form spines, on which most dendritic synapses take place.

Although dendritic development begins prenatally in humans, it continues for a long time after birth. In contrast with the development of axons, which grow at the rate of a millimeter per day, dendritic growth proceeds at a relatively slow rate, measurable in micrometers per day. The disparity between the developmental rates of axons and dendrites is important, allowing the faster-growing axon to contact its target cell before the dendrites of that cell are completely formed and enabling the axon to play a role in dendritic differentiation.

A major enigma in developmental neurobiology is the mechanism that initiates and guides axonal growth. Axons have specific targets that they must reach if the neuron is to survive and become functional. Some axons seem to grow by being pulled from their cell bodies by a structure that is growing away from the region, such as a muscle growing away from the spinal cord early in development. Other axons traverse enormous distances and cope with such obstacles as being moved to another location, having their cell bodies rotated, or having

Figure **23.3**

Neural Maturation In postnatal differentiation of the human cerebral cortex around Broca's area, the neurons first display simple dendritic fields. These fields become progressively more complex until a child reaches about 2 years of age, paralleling the development of language. (After E. Lenneberg, *Biological Foundations of Language.* New York: Wiley, 1967, pp. 160–161.)

Newborn   1   3   6   15   24
Age (months)

their targets moved. Some axons follow an electrical or chemical gradient or a particular physical substrate. Some send out many branches or shoots and, when one of them reaches an appropriate target, the others follow. Several such mechanisms possibly operate simultaneously or sequentially.

The formation of appropriate neural pathways can be disrupted in a number of ways. An axon may fail to reach its target if its way is blocked, as can happen after scarring from head trauma in the early months of life. The development of axons can also be disrupted by anoxia, the ingestion of toxic materials, malnutrition, or some other disturbance.

Several reports of anomalous fiber systems in mutant strains of mice suggest that abnormalities can also have a genetic basis. There have been mouse strains in which the corpus callosum is of abnormal size or is absent and mouse strains in which the fiber pathways in the hippocampal system are abnormal. In a number of albino animal species and possibly also in human albinos, the ipsilateral optic pathway is reduced in size and area of distribution.

Axonal development can also be disrupted if the axonal system's target is damaged, in which case the system may degenerate or may connect with an inappropriate target. Should the latter occur, the behavior supported by the invaded area may be affected, too. In a well-documented study of abnormal fiber growth, Gerald Schneider showed that, if the optic tectum in a hamster is removed on one side at birth, the fibers that should normally project to it project instead to the opposite side. This aberrant pathway is functional, but in a curious way.

If a visual stimulus is presented to the eye contralateral to the damaged tectum, the hamster turns in the direction opposite that of the stimulus. The message has traveled from the eye to the tectum that would ordinarily receive input from the opposite side of the world. The abnormalities of posture and movement seen in children with certain kinds of **athetosis** (slow involuntary movement) and **dystonia** (imbalances in muscle tone) may arise because fiber systems meant to support posture and movement have connected to the wrong target.

To some extent, axons appear to be capable of overcoming obstacles to reach their targets. For example, if the spinal cord is partly sectioned, pyramidal-tract axons that should pass through the damaged part of the cord may cross over to the undamaged side of the cord and then complete their journey to the appropriate target by recrossing the cord. Axons may also substitute for other axons. If the pyramidal cells of one hemisphere of the cortex are destroyed early in life, the axons of pyramidal cells from the other hemisphere will occupy the targets of the missing cells. There are many ways in which a developing brain can adjust its growth to achieve functional connections if its normal development is hindered.

Synapse Formation and Pruning

The number of synapses in the human cerebral cortex is staggering, on the order of 10^{14}. Our genetic program could not possibly produce this huge number of connections by assigning each synapse a specific location. It is more likely that only the general outlines of neural connections in the brain are predetermined. The vast array of specific synaptic contacts are then guided into place by a variety of cues and signals.

Five distinct phases of synapse formation in the cerebral cortex of primates are shown in **Figure 23.4**A for the macaque (see Bourgeois). The first two phases take place in early embryonic life and are characterized by the generation of low-density synapses represented by the areas of shading in the vertical bars below the graph. The synapses formed in phases 1 and 2 differ in their origin, but both groups are thought to be generated independently of experience.

In phase 3, the number of synapses grows rapidly. The rate in the macaque peaks at about 40,000 synapses per second. This phase begins before birth and continues until nearly 2 years of age in humans. Phase 4 is characterized by an initial plateau in synapse number followed by a rapid elimination of synapses that continues through puberty. The rate of loss may be maximal during puberty, although it is not shown in Figure 23.4.

The reduction in synapses is dramatic; they may fall to 50% of the number present at age 2. And, just as synapses can be formed very rapidly during development, they may be lost at a rate of as many as 100,000 per second in adolescence. It should not surprise us that teenagers are so moody when their brains are undergoing such rapid changes in organization.

In phases 3 and 4, synapses are formed both by experience-expectant and by experience-dependent mechanisms (Figure 23.4A). *Experience expectant* means that the synaptic development depends on the presence of certain sensory experiences for the organization of cortical circuits. For example, in the visual cortex, the synapses depend on exposure to features such as line orientation, color, and movement. The general pattern of these synapses is presumed to be common to all members of a species—provided that the individual members

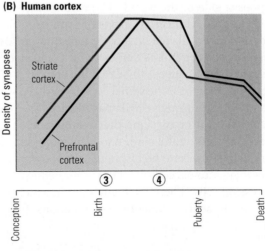

Figure 23.4

Phases of Synapse Formation and Pruning (A) Five different phases of synaptogenesis are identified between conception and death in the primate visual cortex. The shading in the vertical bars indicates the areas of synapse formation during each phase. (B) Changes in the relative density of synapses in the human visual cortex and prefrontal cortex as a function of days after conception. (After Bourgeois, 2001.)

receive the appropriate experience. *Experience dependent* refers to the generation of synapses that are unique to an individual organism, because they are produced in response to experiences that are unique and personal. For example, in the visual system, these synapses can correspond to the learning of specific visual information such as the features of a particular face.

Phase 5 is characterized by a plateau in synapse number through middle age, followed by a slow, steady decline in the density of synapses with advancing age and a final rapid drop during senescence before death. All phase 5 synapses are experience dependent.

As Figure 23.4B illustrates, synapse loss is not the same all over the cortex, and synapse loss in primary sensory areas such as area V1 likely precedes synapse loss in the prefrontal cortex. One perplexing puzzle concerns the static, even slightly declining number of synapses in adulthood. After all, we continue to learn throughout adulthood, and presumably the formation of memories requires the formation of new synapses; so why don't we see an increase in synapse number corresponding to the formation of neural circuits underlying new memories? The only simple conclusion is that experience modifies existing circuits, and the generation of new synapses is somehow balanced by the loss of old ones. But we are still left with the problem of how we maintain so many memories for so long.

Glial Development

The birth of glial cells (both astrocytes and oligodendrocytes) begins after most neurons are born and continues throughout life. Although axons can function before they are encased by myelin, normal adult function is attained only after myelination is complete. Consequently, myelination is useful as a rough index of cerebral maturation.

In the early 1920s, Paul Flechsig noticed that myelination of the human cortex begins just after birth and continues until nearly 18 years of age. He also noticed that some cortical regions are myelinated by 3 to 4 years of age, whereas others show virtually no myelination at that time. **Figure 23.5** shows one of Flechsig's maps of the brain, with areas shaded according to the age at which myelination takes place. Flechsig hypothesized that the areas maturing earliest control relatively simple movements or sensory analyses, whereas the late-myelinating areas control the highest mental functions. Investigators currently use MRI analyses to look at myelin development.

Figure **23.5**

Progress of Myelination in the Human Cortex The fact that the light-colored zones are very late to myelinate led Flechsig to propose that they are qualitatively different in function from those that mature earlier.

Light-colored zones myelinate last.

Imaging Studies of Brain Development

MRI and fMRI techniques are revolutionizing the study of human brain development. Early studies of gray-matter volumes showed that, whereas a decline in gray-matter volume beginning at 6 to 7 years of age continues through adolescence, white-matter volumes increase in the same time frame. A more recent study by Nitin Gogtay and colleagues at the National Institute of Mental Health (NIMH) quantified the changes in gray-matter density at specific cortical points by using serial MRI scans of children followed for a 10-year period.

5 yrs

Age

20 yrs

>0.5
0.4
0.3
0.2
0.1
0.0
Gray-
matter
volume

Figure 23.6

Progressive Changes in Cortical Thickness Trajectory of cortical gray-matter density in children scanned longitudinally every 2 years for 8 years. The reduction in gray-matter density begins in primary areas and spreads to secondary and teritiary regions. (Courtesy of Paul Thompson, Kiralee Hayashi, and Arthur Toga, UCLA; and Nitin Gogtay, Jay Gledd, and Judy Rappoport, NIMH.)

This study reveals a shifting pattern of gray-matter loss, which is presumably due to neuron and synaptic pruning, beginning in the dorsal parietal and sensorimotor regions and spreading laterally, caudally, and rostrally as shown in **Figure 23.6**. The first regions to mature are primary cortical regions controlling basic sensory and motor functions. Parietal regions controlling space and language mature at puberty (age 11–13 years). Tertiary cortical areas such as the prefrontal cortex begin to mature last in late adolescence and continue well beyond.

The trajectory of cortical maturation appears to continue until at least age 30. A large-scale study by Elizabeth Sowell and her colleagues raises the intriguing possibility that cortical sculpting may continue even longer. These investigators collected MRIs from a large sample of normal people from 7 to 87 years of age. Significant decline in gray-matter density continued until age 60, with no decline after that. The question that remains unanswered is when maturational changes shift to degenerative changes of aging.

Few studies have considered the cognitive correlates of cortical thinning, but we would predict a negative correlation between cognitive performance and cortical thickness. Another study by Sowell and her colleagues confirms this prediction by correlating performance on the vocabulary subtest of the Wechsler Intelligence Scales with cortical thickness, as shown in **Figure 23.7**.

In the course of studying "normal" changes in gray matter, it has also been possible to assess group differences between healthy children and those displaying developmental disorders. Such comparisons now routinely find disorder-

Figure 23.7

Brain–Behavior Correlations for Vocabulary and Cortical Thickness The probability of significant negative correlation, indicated by the color regions, corresponds to brain areas where greater cortical thinning is negatively correlated with greater vocabulary improvement. (From Toga et al., 2006, p. 151, with permission.)

$P = .1–.05$
$P = .05–.01$
$P < .01$

specific patterns of brain development. The images in **Figure 23.8**, for example, show percentage differences in gray-matter density between normally developing controls and children with genetic disorders of brain development (for example, Williams syndrome, a mental-retardation disorder), those with neuropsychiatric disorders (for example, schizophrenia, attention-deficit-hyperactivity disorder), and those exposed to teratogens such as drugs in the course of development (for example, fetal alcohol syndrome).

Another way to image brain development is with fMRI, although there are few published studies to date. In one of them, cortical activity was recorded while children and adults performed a task of response inhibition that is presumed to entail the prefrontal cortex (Casey et al., 2001). The area of prefrontal activation was nearly four times as large in the children as it was in the adults, suggesting that, with age, cortical areas may become more specific in their participation in particular tasks. Another interpretation could be that the task was more difficult for the children, and thus to perform it required more activation in a child's brain than in an adult's brain.

Attention-deficit-hyperactivity disorder (ADHD) is characterized by a slightly smaller-than-normal (by 4%) total brain volume (both white and gray matter), abnormalities of the basal ganglia, and a striking (15%) decrease in the volume of a restricted region of the posterior cerebellum. These structural abnormalities do not progress with age, however. In contrast, patients with childhood-onset schizophrenia have smaller brain volume because of a 10% decrease in cortical gray volume. Moreover, they exhibit a progressive loss of regional gray volume, particularly in frontal and temporal regions, in adolescence. This loss of gray matter correlates with the emergence of more-severe psychiatric symptoms. In sum, although research has just begun to use functional imaging in developmental studies, MRI and fMRI promise to transform our current understanding of both normal and abnormal brain development.

Figure 23.8

Brain Development in Neurobehavioral Disorders

Differences in gray-matter density relative to control (arbitrarily set at 0) are color coded in Williams syndrome (WS), attention-deficit-hyperactivity disorder (ADHD), and fetal alcohol syndrome (FAS). Each disorder has a unique pattern of brain development. (From Toga et al., 2006, p. 155, with permission.)

The Development of Problem-Solving Ability

It seems reasonable to assume that, as a particular brain area matures, a person will exhibit behaviors corresponding to the maturation of that brain structure. The strongest advocate of this view has been Eric Lenneberg, who, in 1967, published a seminal book titled *Biological Foundations of Language*. A principal theme is that children's acquisition of language is tied to the development of critical language areas in the cerebral cortex.

This idea immediately stimulated debate about the merits of correlating brain and behavioral development. Today, this relation is widely accepted, although the influence of experience and learning on behavior is still considered critical. Psychologists believe that behaviors cannot emerge until the neural machinery for them has developed; however, when the machinery is in place, related behaviors develop quickly and are shaped significantly by experience. We use the development of problem solving as an example.

The first person to try to identify stages of cognitive development was Swiss psychologist Jean Piaget. He realized that the behavior of children could be used to make inferences about their understanding of the world. For example, a baby who lifts a cloth to retrieve a hidden toy is showing an understanding that objects continue to exist even when out of sight, a behavior said to correspond to the concept of *object permanence*.

An absence of understanding also can be seen in children's behavior, as illustrated by a very young child's difficulty in grasping the principle of *conservation of liquid volume*, which is not displayed until about age 7. In a typical example, a child might watch a colored fluid being poured from a short fat beaker into a tall cylindrical one. Because the second beaker is taller, young children do not understand that the amount of liquid remains constant despite the difference in appearance.

By studying children's performances on such tasks, Piaget concluded that cognitive development is a continuous process. Children's strategies for exploring the world and their understanding of it are constantly changing. These changes are not simply the result of acquiring specific pieces of knowledge. Rather, at certain points in development, fundamental changes take place in the organization of a child's apparatus for learning about the world, and with these changes come new understandings.

Piaget identified four major stages of cognitive development, which are summarized in **Table 23.3**. Stage 1 is the sensorimotor period, from birth to about 18 to 24 months of age. In this period, babies learn to distinguish between themselves and the external world, they come to realize that objects exist

Table **23.3** Piaget's stages of cognitive development

Typical age range	Description of the stage	Developmental phenomena
Birth to 18–24 months	*Stage 1: Sensorimotor* Experiences the world through senses and actions (looking, touching, mouthing)	Object permanence Stranger anxiety
About 2–6 years	*Stage 2: Preoperational* Represents things with words and images but lacks logical reasoning	Pretend play Egocentrism Language development
About 7–11 years	*Stage 3: Concrete operational* Thinks logically about concrete events; grasps concrete analogies and performs arithmetical operations	Conservation Mathematical transformations
About 12+ years	*Stage 4: Formal operational* Reasons abstractly	Abstract logic Potential for mature moral reasoning

Source: After D. G. Myers, *Psychology*, 5th ed. (New York: Worth Publishers, 1998), p. 89.

even when out of sight, and they gain some understanding of cause-and-effect relations. In stage 2, the preoperational period, roughly from ages 2 to 6 years, children acquire the ability to form mental representations of things in their world and to represent those things in words and drawings. Stage 3 is the period of concrete operations, from about 7 to 11 years of age. Now children are able to mentally manipulate concrete ideas such as volumes of liquid and dimensions of objects. Finally, stage 4 is the period of formal operations, which is usually reached after age 11. Children are now able to reason in the abstract, not just in concrete terms.

If we take Piaget's stages as rough approximations of qualitative changes that take place in children's thinking as they grow older, we can ask what changes in the brain might produce them. One place to look for brain changes is in the relative rate of brain growth. After birth, the brain does not grow uniformly but instead tends to increase in mass during irregularly occurring periods commonly called **growth spurts**.

In an analysis of brain-to-body weight ratios, Epstein found consistent spurts in brain growth from 3 to 10 months (accounting for an increase of 30% in brain weight by the age of 1½ years) as well as between ages 2 and 4, 6 and 8, 10 and 12, and 14 and 16+ years. Brain weight increased by about 5% to 10% in each of these 2-year periods. The brain growth takes place without a concurrent increase in the number of neurons; so it is most likely due to the growth of glial cells and synapses. Although synapses themselves would be unlikely to add much weight to the brain, the growth of synapses is accompanied by increased metabolic demands, which causes neurons to become larger, new blood vessels to form, and new astrocytes to be produced.

We would expect such an increase in the complexity of the cortex to generate more-complex behaviors; so we might predict significant, perhaps qualitative, changes in cognitive function during each of the growth spurts. The first four brain-growth spurts coincide nicely with the four main stages of cognitive development described by Piaget. This correspondence suggests that significant alterations in neural functioning accompany the onset of each of Piaget's stages. At the same time, differences in the rate of brain development or perhaps in the rate at which specific groups of neurons mature may account for individual differences in the age at which the various cognitive advances identified by Piaget emerge. Although Piaget did not identify a fifth stage of cognitive development in later adolescence, the presence of a growth spurt during that time implies that one may in fact occur.

A difficulty in linking brain-growth spurts to cognitive development is that growth spurts are superficial measures of changes taking place in the brain. We need to know what neural events are contributing to brain growth and just where they are taking place. A way to find out is to observe children's attempts to solve specific problems that are diagnostic of damage to discrete brain regions in adults. If children perform a particular task poorly, then whatever brain region is engaged in that task in adults must not yet be mature in children. Similarly, if children can perform one task but not another, the tasks apparently require different brain structures, and these structures must mature at different rates.

William Overman and Jocelyne Bachevalier used this logic to study the development of forebrain structures participating in learning and memory in young children and monkeys. **Figure 23.9** shows the test situations that

Procedure

I. Displacement task

II. Nonmatching-to-sample learning task

Subject is shown object that can be displaced for a food reward (+).

15 seconds

Preceding object and new object are presented.

Displacement of new object is rewarded with food.

III. Concurrent-discrimination learning task

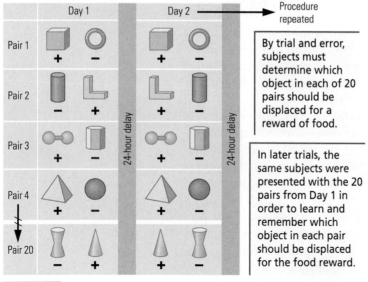

Procedure repeated

By trial and error, subjects must determine which object in each of 20 pairs should be displaced for a reward of food.

In later trials, the same subjects were presented with the 20 pairs from Day 1 in order to learn and remember which object in each pair should be displaced for the food reward.

Conclusion

Both human and monkey infants learn the concurrent-discrimination task at a younger age than the nonmatching-to-sample task, implying that the neural structures underlying the former task mature sooner than those underlying the latter.

Figure 23.9

Demonstrating Cognitive Development This experiment is designed to show the order in which forebrain structures participating in learning and memory mature. In these versions of the Wisconsin General Test Apparatus, the subject's task is to displace an object to reveal a food reward. The nonmatching-to-sample task requires maturation of the temporal lobe, and the concurrent-discrimination task requires maturation of the basal ganglia. (After W. H. Overman, J. Bachevalier, F. Sewell, and J. Drew, 1993.)

they presented to their subjects. The first task was simply to learn to displace an object to obtain a food reward. After the subjects learned this task, they were trained on two more tasks that are believed to measure the functioning of the temporal lobes and the basal ganglia, respectively.

In the first of these two additional tasks, the subjects were shown an object that they could displace to receive a food reward. After a brief (15-s) delay, two objects were presented: the original object and a novel object. The subjects now had to displace the novel object to obtain the food reward. This *nonmatching-to-sample* task is thought to measure object recognition, which is a function of the temporal lobes. The subject can find the food only by recognizing the original object and *not* displacing it.

In the second of the two additional tasks, subjects were presented with a pair of objects and had to learn that one object in that pair was always associated with a food reward, whereas the other object was never rewarded. The researchers made the task more difficult by sequentially giving the subjects 20 different object pairs. Each day the subjects were given one trial per pair. This task, called *concurrent discrimination*, is thought to measure trial-and-error learning of specific object information, which is a function of the basal ganglia.

Adults easily perform both tasks but describe the concurrent task as the more difficult of the two, because it requires remembering far more information than does the nonmatching-to-sample task. The key question developmentally is whether there is a difference in the age at which children (or monkeys) can solve these two tasks. It turns out that children can solve the concurrent task by about 12 months of age, but not until about 18 months of age can they solve what most adults believe to be the easier task. These results imply that the basal ganglia, the critical site for the concurrent task, mature more quickly than does the temporal lobe, the critical region for the nonmatching-to-sample task.

Environmental Effects on Brain Development

The results of studies regarding the fate of the wave of Romanian orphans adopted into families after the fall of its communist regime in the 1980s provide clear evidence that (1) early experience has profound effects on brain development and (2) age at adoption is critical (see papers by by Ames, by Gunnar, and by Rutter). In general, infants adopted before 6 months of age have average IQs, whereas those adopted at 18 months or older have an IQ drop of 15 or more points.

Brain-imaging studies have found the latter group to have smaller-than-normal brains. Thus, the brain appears to be able to recover from a brief period of deprivation, but periods of deprivation longer than 6 months appear to produce significant abnormalities in brain development that cannot be completely repaired. Recall Genie, whom we met in Chapter 12. Genie experienced severe social and experiential deprivation as well as chronic malnutrition and showed severe retardation in cognitive development, especially language.

There is a tendency to think of environmental effects as beginning after birth, but growing evidence reveals that prenatal experiences also can influence brain development. For example, in an extensive series of studies, prenatal tactile experience or stress has been shown to fundamentally change the dendritic organization and, later, the behavior in rats (see Gibb et al.; Kolb, Comeau, and Gibb; Kolb, Halliwell, and Gibb). Tactile stimulation of a pregnant mother improves motor and cognitive outcome; stress has the opposite effect. Furthermore, there is emerging evidence that prenatal exposure to therapeutic drugs such as antidepressants (SSRIs, for example) also may interfere with normal brain development in both rats and human children (see Oberlander for a human study).

How do the conditions of a person's early environment affect nervous system development? The brain is pliable, like plastic, as suggested by the term **brain plasticity**, which neuroscientists use to describe the constantly accruing changes in the structure of the brain that accompany experience: at least at the microscopic level, the structure can be molded into different forms. Brains exposed to different environmental experiences—not only external ones but also events taking place within a person's body—are molded in different ways.

Internal events include the effects of hormones, injury, and abnormal genes. Early in life, the developing brain is especially responsive to these internal factors, which, in turn, alter the way that the brain reacts to external experiences. In this section, we explore a range of environmental influences—both external and internal—on brain development. We start with the question of exactly how experience alters brain structure.

Environmental Influences on Brain Organization

The simplest way of measuring the effects of environment on the nervous system is by documenting differences in brain size. The results of studies of animal brain size have shown that certain cortical areas are as much as 10% to 20% smaller in domestic animals than in animals of the same species and strain raised in the wild. These differences are apparently related to factors encountered

(A) Dendritic length

(B) Spine density

Figure **23.10**

Effects of Complex Housing on Rats A comparison of the effects of 3 months of complex housing, beginning at different ages, on (A) dendritic length and (B) spine density. Although all three age groups show similar increases in dendritic length, a qualitative difference in spine density emerges: juveniles show a drop in spine density, whereas adults show an increase in density. (After Kolb et al., 2003.)

early in life, because animals born in the wild and later domesticated have brains the same size as those of animals raised in the wild. The part of the brain that seems to be most affected by a domestic upbringing is the occipital cortex, which is reduced in size by as much as 35% in some animals. This reduction may be related to smaller eye and retina size.

Exposure to a complex rather than impoverished environment increases brain size, most noticeably of the neocortex, with the greatest increase being in the occipital neocortex. Related to increased size are increases in the density of glial cells, the length of dendrites, the density of spines (the location of most excitatory synapses), and the size of synapses. Curiously, although many have assumed that the young brain will show greater changes in response to experience than an older brain will, the young and adult brain may actually respond differently to the same experience.

For example, housing animals in complex environments with changing objects to play with increases the length of pyramidal-cell dendrites in the cortices of both younger and older animals. However, spine density *decreases* in young animals and *increases* in the older animals (**Figure 23.10**). Both young and old animals show similar functional benefits, performing better than their impoverished counterparts on a number of tests of skilled motor behavior as well as on tests of learning and memory.

We can speculate that the qualitative differences in experience-dependent synaptic changes at these different times in life must have some functional implications. One possibility is that an animal whose brain is stimulated in development may more easily change its brain in response to experience later in life. An example might be children who are exposed to different languages in development and who then learn additional languages later in life more quickly than do peers whose early experience was unilingual.

The fact that very early experience can alter brain structure and behavior in adulthood leads to the question whether prenatal experiences—those taking place in phase 1, 2, or early phase 3 synaptogenesis—also might alter brain development. The results of several studies show that newborns can identify the maternal voice that they heard in utero; so it seems possible that prenatal experience *can* influence brain development.

Robbin Gibb and her colleagues manipulated prenatal experience in rats either by placing the pregnant dams in complex environments or by giving them daily tactile stimulation. This experience resulted in larger brains in the offspring, a result that could be due either to increased numbers of neurons or glia or both or to increased numbers of synapses. The larger-brained offspring then showed superior performance on both cognitive and motor tasks, just like animals raised in complex environments postnatally.

Experience and Neural Connectivity

Disturbances of the optics of the eye early in life (for example, cataracts and astigmatism) cause long-lasting impairments of vision even after the optical defects are corrected. Adults who have had lifelong cataracts removed to allow light to finally reach the retina have difficulty learning the identity of objects by looking at them. These visual impairments, called **amblyopia**—deficits of vision without obvious impairment of the eye—are thought to be caused by changes in the central nervous system. The results of behavioral studies have shown that amblyopia can be produced in animals; the process has been analyzed extensively in studies of cats and monkeys.

David Hubel and Torsten Wiesel approached the problem by asking how the functional organization of the visual system of kittens might be altered by elimination of the visual input to one eye. The researchers were aware that inputs from each eye go to adjacent, alternating columns, called *ocular dominance columns*, in area V1. (In each column, the alternate eye is dominant, as shown in **Figure 23.11**). This alternating arrangement of inputs from the two eyes presumably plays an important role in merging the images from each eye.

The specific question asked by Hubel and Wiesel was whether restricting visual experience to one eye might alter the structure of the ocular dominance columns. They discovered that, if one eye is sewn shut for a time in early life, the eye appears to be essentially blind for a period of weeks after opening, although its function does improve somewhat with time. The results of cell-recording studies show that either stimulation in the deprived eye cannot activate cells in the cortex or, in those few cases in which it can, the cells are highly abnormal. The results also show that, the earlier the deprivation takes place, the shorter the length of deprivation required to produce effects and the more severe the effects.

These results confirm that environmental deprivation can retard development and that early deprivation is the most damaging. Findings from later studies by other researchers have shown that one reason for the abnormal functioning of the deprived eye is that the connections from that eye have been weakened by the lack of visual experience, as illustrated in Figure 23.11. Apparently, visual experience is necessary to validate (that is, to reinforce) functional connections in the brain. In the absence of activity, the synapses are lost. This principle of "use it or lose it" can be applied to the nervous system in general, although the effect of experience is not always as severe as that seen in the example of the deprived eye.

Can the visual system be changed by manipulation less drastic than complete sensory deprivation? Kittens were fitted with lenses that brought a set of horizontal stripes into focus on one retina and a set of vertical stripes into focus on the other (see Hirsch and Spinelli). After later removal of the lenses, the eye that had seen horizontal stripes during the exposure period responded only to a stimulus oriented close to the horizontal, and the eye that had seen vertical stripes responded only to a stimulus oriented close to the vertical. These findings have been confirmed for kittens raised in an environment of stripes only or spots only or in an environment organized to be devoid of movement. In fact, work by Colin Blakemore and Donald Mitchell indicates that 1 hour of exposure on day 28 after birth is sufficient to bias a cortical unit to respond to a particular pattern.

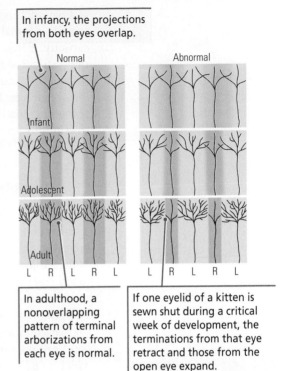

In infancy, the projections from both eyes overlap.

Normal　　　Abnormal

Infant

Adolescent

Adult

L R L R L　　L R L R L

In adulthood, a nonoverlapping pattern of terminal arborizations from each eye is normal.

If one eyelid of a kitten is sewn shut during a critical week of development, the terminations from that eye retract and those from the open eye expand.

Figure 23.11

Critical Period in Development

In the postnatal development of ocular dominance columns in the cat, axons enter the cortex, where they grow large terminal arborizations. Abbreviations: L, left eye; R, right eye.

Overall, this work suggests that the visual system is genetically programmed to make normal connections and normal responses, but it can lose much of this capacity if it is not exercised during the early months of life. When part of the system is deprived, some degree of capacity is lost. Moreover, the deprived part of the system is inhibited by the remaining functional areas, reinforcing the defect. Even so, removal of the inhibition can permit some degree of recovery. Finally, if the environment is so arranged that the system is exposed to stimuli of one type, the cells in the system develop a preference for those stimuli.

The Plasticity of Representational Zones in the Developing Brain

The tendency for cortical organization to be influenced by experience can be seen not only in the brain subjected to restricted experience but also in the brain subjected to enriched experience. Consider, for example, the effect of practicing some skill, such as playing a musical instrument, for hours a day for many years in childhood. Thomas Elbert and his colleagues studied stringed-instrument players as a model for how experience can alter the organization of the sensorimotor maps of the hand. The second through fifth digits of the left hand are continuously engaged in fingering the strings, whereas the thumb, which grasps the neck of the instrument, is less active. The right hand moves the bow, which also requires much less finger movement.

Neuroimaging showed that representation of the fingers of the left hand not only occupied more space than did the thumb or the fingers of the right hand but also that the amount of change was proportional to the age at which musical training began, as illustrated in **Figure 23.12**. The representational zone of the left-hand fingers was largest in subjects who had begun regular practice before age 13—that is, before puberty. But, even if training began later in life, the representation of the relevant digits still exceeded the representation seen in subjects without musical training. A later study found similar effects on the representation of piano-music frequencies in the auditory cortexes of piano players (see also the study represented in Figure 15.14).

A characteristic of human speech perception is that adults are skilled at distinguishing speech sounds in their native language but often have difficulties making sound distinctions in other languages. For example, the difficulty that Japanese or Korean speakers have in making the distinction between "r" and "l" in English is well known. Janet Werker and Richard Tees compared the ability of infants to discriminate speech sounds taken from widely disparate languages, such as English, Hindi (from India), and Salish (a Native American language). Their results showed that young

Figure 23.12

Effects of Enrichment This graph plots the age at which subjects began practicing on stringed instruments against the amount of neural activation that they showed in response to tactile stimulation of the fifth digit of the left hand. (After Elbert et al., 2001.)

Musicians with early training show the greatest neural activation.

Even those who began late show more activation...

...than non-musician controls.

infants can discriminate between the speech sounds of different languages without previous experience, but their ability to do so declines over the first year of life.

In studies by others, event-related potentials (ERPs) have been used to examine this phenomenon, with the use of what is known as mismatch negativity (MMN). If a repeated speech sound, such as "l, l, l, . . . ," is played to an infant and a different sound, such as "r," is embedded in the middle, the ERP will show a negative deflection—a mismatch negativity—if the difference in the sound is detected by the baby's auditory system (**Figure 23.13**). In studies by various groups (see reviews by Elbert et al. and by Kuhl), MMNs were detected for language-specific speech sounds in infants at 6 months of age, but 12-month-old infants no longer made many of the distinctions. These results imply that the auditory representation of sounds is altered by each infant's linguistically biased environment.

Knowledge of how experience reorganizes the cortex can be used to treat cognitive deficits in children. For example, some preschool children with no apparent psychiatric or neurological impairment have great difficulty learning language, in which case their condition is referred to as a *specific language impairment*. One theory suggests that such impairments may be caused by an abnormal representation of speech sounds in the auditory system. If so, then specific training ought to produce improvement. It does. (See Chapter 24 for more details.)

Figure 23.13

An Infant in an ERP Recording Cap On the left is an example of the mismatch negativity signal. One wave comes from a standard signal from one sound, and the other comes from a deviant signal. The MMN is the difference between the waves. If the brain detects that two signals are different, there will be a mismatch, but, if the brain does not discriminate between the signals, there will be no difference. (After Kuhl, 1999.)

Brain Injury and Plasticity

By 1868, Jules Cotard—who knew that damage to the left frontal cortex could abolish speech—had observed children with left frontal lesions who nevertheless developed normal adult language functions. This observation was the origin of the idea that brain injury has milder and more short-lived effects if it is sustained in childhood. (Recall Alex' case in the Portrait at the beginning of the chapter.) Then, in the 1930s, Margaret Kennard compared the effects of unilateral motor-cortex lesions on infant and adult monkeys and found that the impairments in the infant monkeys seemed milder than those in the adults.

The generalization that sparing of function follows infant lesions became known as the *Kennard principle*. For a time, the idea received wide acceptance, but neuroscientists began to realize that earlier may not always be better and can sometimes be worse. Donald Hebb, for example, showed that children who incur prefrontal injuries in infancy or early childhood have very poor outcomes. The ultimate effect of a brain injury depends on the behavior affected, the extent and location of the damage, and the precise age at which the injury occurs. With respect to cognitive function in humans, it is clear that speech survives early brain damage, but some elements of syntax and some nonlanguage functions may not survive, and general intellectual ability may decline.

The Effects of Age

Age is an important determinant of the effects of early lesions. Three critical age divisions have been identified: before 1 year of age, between 1 and 5 years, and older than 5 years. Lesions incurred before the age of 1 tend to produce disproportionately greater impairments than do those incurred later. Lesions incurred between 1 and 5 years of age are followed by some reorganization of brain function, including the rescue of language functions. Lesions incurred later than age 5 permit little or no sparing of function.

For example, in a comparison of the effects of lesions incurred before and after age 1, earlier lesions reduced IQ more than did later lesions (see Riva and Cazzaniga). An implication of the age-related effects of injury on language development is that the brain's manner of acquiring languages differs at different times in development. Further evidence for this hypothesis is described in the Snapshot on page 675.

The Effect of Brain Damage on Language

Language deficits resulting from cerebral injury in young children are usually short-lived, and an injured child usually seems to nearly fully recover. This is the case even though language disorders subsequent to right-hemisphere damage are more frequent in children than in adults, the incidence being about 8% in children and 2% in adults (**Table 23.4**).

Théophile Alajouanine and F. Lhermitte studied 32 cases of childhood aphasia, finding writing deficits in all and reading deficits in about half the children, in addition to their difficulty in speaking. Six months after injury, the researchers observed total recovery of spontaneous language in about a third of these subjects, and significant improvement was noted in all the others. When

Table 23.4 Summary of studies of aphasia resulting from unilateral lesions

Study	Age range of subjects	Number of cases	Percentage with right-hemisphere lesions
Childhood Lesions			
Guttman, 1942	2–14	15	7
Alajouanine and Lhermitte, 1965	6–15	32	0
McCarthy, 1963	After language acquisition	114	4
Basser, 1962*	Before 5	20	35
Hécaen, 1976	3½–15	17	11
Total	2–15	198	8
Adult Lesions			
Russell and Espir, 1961	—	205	3
Hécaen, 1976	—	232	0.43
Total	—	437	1.6

*The Basser study, which describes 35% of young children with right-hemisphere lesions as suffering from aphasia, is thought to be inaccurate, because many of the subjects may have had bilateral lesions.
Source: After Krashen, 1973, and Hécaen, 1976.

SNAPSHOT
Distinct Cortical Areas for Second Languages

Children generally find it easier than adults to acquire more than one language and to speak each one with a native accent. Karl Kim and his colleagues, asking whether the age at language acquisition might influence the way in which the language is represented in the brain, used fMRI to determine the spatial relation between native and second languages in the cortex.

Bilingual subjects were instructed to describe in their minds, without speaking aloud, the events that had taken place during a certain period of the preceding day (for example, in the morning). On different scans, they used different languages. Some subjects had learned a second language as children, whereas others learned a second language as adults.

As would be expected in a sentence-generation task, both Broca's and Wernicke's areas were activated. There was a difference between childhood and adult acquisition of the second language in the activation in Broca's area but not in Wernicke's area.

As shown in the illustration, activation in Broca's area overlapped virtually completely for the childhood-acquisition subjects, but there was an anatomical separation of the two languages in the adulthood-acquisition group. This spatial separation of the two languages in Broca's area suggests that language acquisition may alter the functional organization of Broca's area.

Thus, as human infants learn languages, Broca's area undergoes modification according to the nature of the languages being learned. When modified, the region appears to resist subsequent modification, which necessitates utilizing adjacent cortical areas for the second language learned as an adult.

Kim, K. H. S., N. R. Relkin, K. Young-Min Lee, and J. Hirsch. Distinct cortical areas associated with native and second languages. *Nature* 388: 171–174, 1997.

KEY
- Native language
- Second language

When two languages are learned in childhood, they share the same parts of Broca's area,...

...but, when a second language is learned in adulthood, it is anatomically separated from the first.

Cortical representations of second-language acquisition. (After Kim et al., 1997.)

reexamined 1 year or more after injury, 24 of the 32 children had normal or almost normal language, although 14 still had some degree of dysgraphia, and 22 of the children were eventually able to return to school.

Similarly, Henri Hécaen followed postinjury recovery from aphasia and related symptoms in 15 children with left-hemisphere unilateral lesions, as summarized in **Table 23.5**. Besides disorders of speech, nearly all the children had disorders of writing and calculation. Of these 15 children, 5 showed complete recovery within 6 weeks to 2 years. Most of the remaining children showed considerable improvement; in many cases, the only remaining deficit was a mild difficulty in writing, a finding similar to that of Alajouanine and Lhermitte.

Table **23.5** Frequency of different symptoms in 15 cases caused by left-hemisphere lesions in childhood

Symptom	Number of cases	Percentage	Evolution of symptoms
Mutism	9	60	From 5 days to 30 months
Articulatory disorders	12	80	Persistent in 4 cases
Auditory verbal comprehension disorders	6	40	Persistent in 1 case
Naming disorders	7	46	Persistent in 3 cases
Paraphasia	1	7	Disappearance
Reading disorders	9	60	Persistent in 3 cases
Writing disorders	13	86	Persistent in 7 cases
Facial apraxia	2	—	Transient
Acalculia	11	—	(Not reported)

Source: After Hécaen, 1976.

Figure **23.14**

IQ Scores on Subtests of the Wechsler Adult Intelligence Scale The adults being tested suffered a lesion of the left or the right hemisphere in infancy, as determined by the occurrence of hemiparesis. Note that both verbal and performance scores are depressed by left-hemisphere lesions, whereas only performance scores are depressed by right-hemisphere lesions (average IQ is 100). The results suggest that, if language moves to the right hemisphere, its usual functions are sacrificed to accommodate the shift. The results also suggest that right-hemisphere functions do not shift sufficiently to interfere with language. (After Teuber, 1975.)

Bryan Woods and Hans-Leukas Teuber studied about 50 patients with prenatal or early postnatal brain damage to either the left or the right hemisphere. Using normal siblings as controls, they came to the following conclusions:

1. Language survives after early left-hemisphere injury.

2. Much of this survival seems attributable to appropriation of a potential language zone in the right hemisphere.

3. This shift of language location has a price: specifically, some kinds of visuospatial orientation are impaired.

4. Early lesions of the right hemisphere produce deficits similar to those produced by such lesions in adulthood.

In other words, if a child sustains a lesion of the left hemisphere that produces right hemiplegia, language functions are recovered to a remarkably greater degree than after a comparable lesion in an adult, presumably because some or all of the language abilities move to the right hemisphere. Presumably, language crowds into the right hemisphere at the expense of visuospatial functions. On the other hand, a lesion of the right hemisphere, which produces left hemiplegia, does not impair language ability.

A summary of this pattern of results, obtained from verbal and performance scores of the Wechsler Adult Intelligence Scale, is shown in **Figure 23.14**. Left-hemisphere lesions depress both verbal and performance scores. Right-hemisphere lesions depress only performance scores. In a subsequent study, Woods examined the effects of lesions incurred earlier than age 1. The main finding was that right-hemisphere lesions impaired both verbal and performance IQ. Daria Riva and L. Cazzaniga confirmed these results and noted that lesions incurred before 1 year of age produce more-severe overall impairments than do those incurred after age 1.

Not all aspects of language function are spared after lesions incurred between the ages of 1 and 5. Woods found that, on a speech-shadowing task, which requires a person to repeat passages of speech as they are read, adult right- and left-hemisphere lesions produce equal impairments. Virtually identical impairments are observed subsequent to early-childhood lesions, even though speech is significantly spared in the early left-hemisphere lesions.

The Reorganization of Language

The evidence that language is spared after early brain damage because the control of language is transferred to the opposite hemisphere raises three questions. What actual language functions are transferred? What type of brain damage causes them to be transferred? What is the age range during which transfer can take place? The first two questions have been addressed experimentally by Ted Rasmussen and Brenda Milner, but the third has not yet been answered completely.

Using carotid sodium amobarbital injection and dichotic-listening tests (see Chapter 11), Rasmussen and Milner localized language in a large number of patients who had suffered left-hemisphere injury early in life and returned to the hospital years later because of complications. They found that the patients assorted into three groups, as shown in **Table 23.6**. In the first group, speech was in the left hemisphere; in the second group, it was represented bilaterally; and, in the third group, it was in the right hemisphere. The patients who had speech in the left hemisphere were found to have damage that did not invade the anterior speech zone (Broca's area) or the posterior speech zone (Wernicke's area).

Examples of brain damage that did not produce a shift in language lateralization are shown in **Figure 23.15**A. Both exemplar lesions are large, yet the dichotic-listening test showed a right-ear advantage (a sign that a person's speech is localized in the left hemisphere). In the sodium amobarbital tests following left-hemisphere injection, the patients were mute both on naming tasks (for example, identifying objects as an experimenter holds each up and asks "What is this?") and on repetition tasks (for example, "Name the days of the week in

Table 23.6 Changes in hemispheric speech representation after early brain damage

| | | PERCENTAGE WITH SPEECH REPRESENTATION | | |
	Handedness	Left	Bilateral	Right
No early damage	Right	96	0	4
	Left or mixed	70	15	15
Early damage	Right	81	7	12
	Left or mixed	28	19	53

Source: After Rasmussen and Milner, 1975, pp. 248–249.

(B) Complete shift of language

(A) No shift in language
Early brain damage

Anterior language area (Broca's area)   Posterior language area (Wernicke's area)

(C) Shift of anterior speech functions

(D) Shift of posterior speech function

Figure 23.15

Reorganization of Language Relations between early brain damage and hemisphere changes in language organization: (A) anterior and posterior lesions (red) after which language remained in the left hemisphere; (B) an anterior–posterior lesion causes all language to move to the right hemisphere; (C) an anterior lesion causes bilateral representation, with the anterior speech zone shifting to the right hemisphere; (D) a posterior lesion also causes bilateral representation, with the posterior speech zone shifting to the right hemisphere. (After Rasmussen and Milner, 1977.)

order."). The locations of the anterior and posterior speech zones are shown in green and yellow, respectively, in Figure 23.15A.

An example of a lesion that produced a complete shift of language to the right hemisphere is illustrated in Figure 23.15B. This patient showed a left-ear advantage on the dichotic-listening test and was mute for naming and repetition after right-hemisphere sodium amobarbital injection. Note that the lesion invaded both the anterior and the posterior speech zones, which was typical for patients who developed right-hemisphere speech after early left-hemisphere lesions.

Examples of the lesions in patients who had bilateral speech are shown in Figure 23.15C and D. The patient whose lesion is shown in Figure 23.15C incurred a large left-frontal-lobe lesion at 6 years of age that included the anterior language zone. At age 18, the patient was right-handed and had a right-ear advantage for digits and a left-ear advantage for melodies. On the sodium amobarbital tests, a left-hemisphere injection produced a disturbance in series repetition (counting, reciting the days of the week forward or backward, or oral spelling), but naming was less disturbed. A right-hemisphere injection produced a disturbance in both series repetition and naming.

With the assumptions that the right-ear advantage for digits is an indication of left-hemisphere speech and that the absence of series repetition after left-hemisphere sodium amobarbital injection is an indication of intact speech in the left posterior speech zone, we can conclude that the lesion did not cause a complete shift of speech from the posterior left speech zone. Because naming was disturbed after a right-hemisphere injection of sodium amobarbital, the left-hemisphere speech functions of the anterior zone are assumed to have shifted to the right hemisphere.

The patient whose lesion is shown in Figure 23.15D had a large posterior lesion that was incurred at $2\frac{1}{2}$ years of age. Testing at age 16 showed that she was left-handed and had a left-ear advantage for both digits and melodies. Sodium amobarbital tests showed that naming was disturbed by both left- and right-hemisphere injections, whereas series repetition was performed competently after the left but not the right hemisphere was injected. In this case, the large posterior lesion incurred early in life seems to have caused speech functions of the posterior zone to shift to the right, whereas the anterior speech zone still retained some speech function.

The results described so far, particularly those of Rasmussen and Milner, show that speech has a strong affinity for the left hemisphere and will not abandon it unless an entire center is destroyed; even then, it might shift only partly to the other hemisphere. This affinity is thought to be based on the special innate anatomical organization of the left hemisphere. In examining their patients with early left-hemisphere lesions, Rasmussen and Milner also noted that childhood injuries to the left hemisphere after 5 years of age rarely caused a change in speech patterns.

They thus inferred that recovery after about age 6 is not due to transfer to the other hemisphere but to intrahemispheric reorganization, possibly with intact surrounding zones acquiring some control over speech. Further evidence comes from Woods and Teuber's study. Recall from Figure 23.14 that left- but not right-hemisphere lesions cause a decline in both verbal and performance IQ scores, a result that argues against the idea that the right hemisphere has equal potential for language.

Although the evidence supports the left-for-speech hypothesis, there is reason to believe that functional validation is still required; that is, practice with language is necessary to establish left-hemisphere preeminence. Woods reported that, if left-hemisphere lesions occur before the first birthday, both verbal and performance IQ are severely depressed. If left-hemisphere lesions occur after 1 year of age, neither verbal nor performance IQ is affected. Right-hemisphere lesions at any age lower only performance IQ. The effects of lesions before age 1 might be due to a disruption of verbal functions that had not yet been sufficiently validated or that perhaps were disrupted by the invasion of performance functions. We must note, however, that this suggestion is speculative, that IQ score is at best an imprecise measure of language, and that a more systematic study of these patients—one using linguistic tests—is called for.

The Absence of Language after Bilateral Lesions

Bilateral cortical lesions in children are rare. Nevertheless, a number of reports suggest that, when bilateral lesions do occur, the plasticity required for the acquisition or reacquisition of language subsequent to injury is absent. Vargha-Khadem and coworkers report such a case.

A.C. was born after a normal pregnancy, but the delivery was difficult and required forceps. The next day, A.C. began to have epileptic seizures. He was given anticonvulsants and, after a couple weeks of treatment, was seizure free. When he began to walk, he had left hemiparesis that affected the left limbs. His language development was very delayed and did not advance beyond primitive speech consisting of a few two-word utterances. His rare attempts to make sentences could not be understood. Although he could follow instructions, suggesting a somewhat preserved capacity for comprehension, he did poorly on the token test, which evaluates the ability to follow a number of sequentially presented instructions, and very poorly on most other tests of language ability. At the same time, his performance on the nonverbal parts of IQ tests suggested that he had at least normal intelligence.

A CT scan performed at age 6½ indicated that he had a lesion largely restricted to Broca's area in the left hemisphere and another lesion restricted to the middle part of the sensorimotor cortex on the right side. Thus, even though A.C. had a spared Broca's area on the right and spared posterior speech zones on both the left and the right, he failed to acquire language as he might be expected to have done had he received only a unilateral left-hemisphere lesion. The reason that A.C. failed to show sufficient plasticity to develop more-normal language is not known, but this case history strongly suggests that, for some reason, plasticity depends on at least one intact hemisphere.

Experimental Approaches to Studying Plasticity after Early Brain Injury

The mechanisms mediating the recovery of function after injury sustained in infancy can be studied experimentally by systematically varying the age at injury and the location of injury in laboratory animals. We first consider the behavioral effects of injury and then look at what the anatomical correlates might be.

The Effects of Early Brain Lesions on Behaviors Later in Life

We have already considered the relation between age at injury and functional outcome in human infants. We might expect to see a similar phenomenon in laboratory animals, and, in fact, as mentioned earlier, Kennard showed that motor-cortex lesions in infant monkeys allow better functional outcome than do similar lesions in adulthood. This view was presumed to be correct until the 1970s, when contradictory findings began to emerge from laboratory studies. As in all fields of science, reality has proved much more complex than our original descriptions of it, and we now know that many factors influence the general dependability of the Kennard principle. These factors include the brain region injured, the precise developmental stage at injury, the age at assessment, the type of behavior measured, and exposure to gonadal hormones (for a review, see Kolb).

In the past 20 years, we (the authors) have removed virtually every region of the rat cortical mantle at varying ages, ranging from embryonic day 18 to adolescence (see Kolb and Gibb for a review). Our general finding is that recovery varies with the precise embryological age at which the removal took place (**Table 23.7**). If the cortex is injured bilaterally during neurogenesis, there is virtually complete functional recovery.

The ability of the brain to compensate for injury incurred at the time of neurogenesis is remarkable. Sam Hicks demonstrated as much 40 years ago when he found that, if the developing brain was treated with X-radiation at the early stages of cortical neurogenesis (which effectively killed the entire cerebrum), the brain compensated by regenerating a substantial proportion of the lost cells. In short, the cerebrum was destroyed by the treatment, and the stem cells responded by overproducing new cortical neurons that rebuilt about 50% of what was lost. In contrast, however, if a rat's cortex is injured in the first few days after birth, which is a time of neural migration and cell differentiation, the effect is functionally devastating: the animal shows much more severe effects of injury than would be expected even if it had been aged at the time of injury.

This poor outcome is not a function of lesion size or of damage to particular cortical areas. Rather, something about the cortex during this developmental time makes it especially vulnerable. For example, damage at this time may disturb the process of synaptogenesis or may even alter stem-cell activity in

Table 23.7 Summary of the effects of frontal cortical injury at different ages in the rat

Age at Injury	Behavioral Result	Anatomical Result
E18	Functional recovery	Gross anomalies in structure Brain size close to normal
P1–P5	Dismal functional outcome	Small brain, dendritic atrophy Abnormal connectivity
P7–P12	Functional recovery	Neurogenesis; astrogenesis Increased synapse number
P120	Partial return of function	Dendritic atrophy, then regrowth

Abbreviations: E18, embryonic day 18; P followed by number, postnatal day.
Source: After Kolb and Gibb (2007).

some way. When this phase of development has ended, however, the brain is especially able to compensate for injury.

Rats incurring cortical injuries at 7 to 12 days of age show behavioral capacities in adulthood that exceed those of animals receiving similar lesions at any other time. In fact, on some behavioral tests, these animals show recovery that is virtually complete. Importantly, far more extensive recovery is seen in the ability to perform cognitive tasks, such as learning how to solve various spatial-navigation problems, than is seen in the performance of tests of species-typical behaviors such as nest building.

This difference is likely due to the relative ease of reorganizing cortical circuitry compared with connections in other parts of the brain. We must emphasize, too, that the extent of functional recovery also depends on the specific locations of cortical lesions. The most-extensive recovery is associated with lesions of the frontal areas, and the least-extensive recovery is associated with damage to the primary sensory areas. For example, rats with occipital lesions show no recovery of visually guided behaviors. In contrast, they do show an enhanced somatosensory capacity that is not observed in rats receiving similar lesions on day 4. This finding is consistent with the general idea that something is special about recovery from injuries received at about 10 days of age.

These findings are further complicated when we increase the lesion size to remove all of the cortex (decortication) or all of the cortex of one hemisphere (hemidecortication). Totally decorticated rats show no functional recovery regardless of the age at injury, suggesting that the plastic changes underlying recovery from focal cortical lesions are likely taking place in the remaining cortex and not in subcortical structures. Hemidecortication produces a quite different outcome: the earlier the removal, the greater the extent of functional recovery, although there are no data on the effects of prenatal hemidecortications.

Thus, rats with hemidecortication on the day of birth have a far better functional outcome than do animals with later hemidecortications. One explanation for this result is that the lesion does not interfere with migration and differentiation in the intact hemisphere, which is presumably where the recovery is being mediated. We have tested this hypothesis by making very small lesions in the intact hemispheres of hemidecorticated neonates and have seen that recovery is substantially compromised. This connection between unilateral injury and increased likelihood of recovery is reminiscent of the effects of cortical injuries on language in human infants. Recall the studies in which infants with bilateral injuries were shown to be at risk for permanent aphasia.

The only other laboratory species normally used for studies of early brain injury are cats and rhesus monkeys. In comparing these species with rats, one must take care to remember that rats, cats, and monkeys are not born at the same developmental age. Rats are born in a more immature state than are cats, and cats at birth are much more immature than monkeys.

Both rats and kittens are helpless at birth, and some time elapses before their eyes are mature enough even to open, let alone to process visual information. In contrast, monkeys are relatively mature at birth; they are developmentally older than human newborns as well. **Figure 23.16** compares the

Figure **23.16**

Developmental Age This diagram compares the developmental ages of the brains of the rat and human at various times after conception. Note that the day of birth is not related to the stage of neural development.

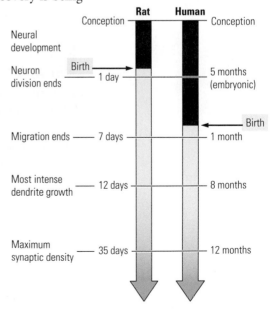

approximate relative ages at birth of the different species. Jaime Villablanca emphasizes the age-at-birth confound and concludes that, like newborn rats, kittens with prenatal injuries are functionally better off than kittens receiving lesions slightly later, during the time of synaptogenesis, as would be predicted from Figure 23.16.

The importance of the site of injury in the developing brain is shown nicely in studies by Jocelyne Bachevalier and Mort Mishkin, who varied the size and location of temporal-lobe injury in infant monkeys. In their first studies, they and their colleagues examined the effects of neonatal visual-system lesions on the performance of the delayed nonmatching-to-sample task illustrated in Figure 23.9. In adult monkeys, lesions of the medial temporal cortex and of more laterally placed neocortex (area TE) severely impair performance on the task, especially when the intervals between presentations of the objects are increased. The researchers removed these areas in monkeys that were from 1 to 2 weeks old and then tested them on the nonmatching task, beginning at 10 months of age. The monkeys with medial temporal lesions were nearly as impaired as monkeys that received lesions as adults, whereas the monkeys that received TE lesions in infancy performed much better than monkeys that received lesions as adults.

These results suggest that functional recovery may be better after some brain injuries than others. In further studies, Bachevalier and Mishkin examined the social behavior of monkeys that received lesions of the medial temporal area as infants. As they develop, these monkeys shun social contact with other monkeys and display stereotypical behavior, excessive self-directed behavior, and a lack of facial expression. In short, these animals appear autistic.

If the temporal-lobe lesions are restricted to the amygdala and entorhinal cortex, the autistic behavior is present but is not as severe. If the lesion is restricted to the parahippocampal gyrus and hippocampus, the autistic behavior emerges only in adulthood. Monkeys that receive damage to TE neonatally are not autistic but are hyperactive. Their behavior is annoying to adult monkeys, who do not like to interact with them.

The Effects of Early Brain Lesions on Brain Structure Later in Life

In principle, the brain could show plastic changes that might support recovery after early injury in three ways:

1. **Changes in the organization of the remaining, intact circuits in the brain.** The general idea is that the brain could reorganize in some way "to do more with less." It is unlikely that a complexly integrated structure such as the cerebral cortex could undergo a wholesale reorganization of cortical connectivity. Instead, recovery from cortical injury would be most likely to result from a change in the intrinsic organization of local cortical circuits in regions directly or indirectly disrupted by the injury. Although significant reorganization of cortical connectivity in the young brain might be possible, the overwhelming evidence in experimental animals is that such reorganization is rare and, as we shall see, just as likely to be associated with abnormal functioning as with recovery.

2. **Generation of new circuitry.** We have already seen that cerebral reorganization can be stimulated by experience in the normal brain, and it seems reasonable to expect that experience or some other treatment, such as a drug, could influence reparative processes in the remaining brain or could enhance the production of new circuitry. Once again, the induced neuronal changes would most likely take place in the intrinsic organization of the cortex rather than throughout the brain as a whole.

3. **Generation of neurons and glia to replace at least some lost neurons.** As stated earlier, the stem cells that give rise to the neurons and glia of the brain remain active in the subventricular zone throughout life. Thus, perhaps neurogenesis could be stimulated after injury, especially in development, and these new neurons could replace those lost to injury or disease (see, for example, Weiss et al.).

Evidence exists that supports all three of these possible explanations for cerebral plasticity after early injury. We begin with the most-obvious changes in the early-injured brain and then consider more-subtle changes.

Brain Size

A dramatic consequence of brain damage in infancy is that it causes the brain to be smaller than average in adulthood. Furthermore, the earlier the lesion occurs, the smaller the brain's ultimate size. For example, as shown in **Figure 23.17**, the brains of rats with neonatal lesions were reduced in size by as much as 25%, whereas the brains of rats that were operated on as adults shrank by less than 12%.

This size reduction, which in humans would be the equivalent of about 200 g, was due not to a proportionately larger lesion in the young brain but to shrinkage of the entire neocortex. No systematic analysis of this phenomenon has been made in monkeys or humans, but the same result is likely produced in humans. **Figure 23.18** shows the results from a CT scan of a 16-year-old girl who had suffered an injury to the right parietal cortex at birth. It is clear from the scan that her entire right hemisphere is smaller than the left.

Neuronal Morphology

To examine why lesions might cause the brain to shrink, we examined the structure of cells in the neocortex (see review by Kolb and Gibb). With very early lesions, given to rats on their day of birth, the cells showed reduced complexity compared with adult cells. If the lesions were produced at 10 days of age, the cells had more-extensive dendritic fields than seen in controls; whereas, if the

Area of frontal lesion

(A)

(B)

Control   10 days (frontal)   1 day (frontal)

Figure 23.17

Effects of Neonatal Lesions on Brain Weight and Cell Structure (A) Brain weights of control rats and rats that received frontal lesions (top) as adults or at 1, 5, or 10 days of age. (B) Drawings of cortical pyramidal cells from the parietal cortex. Note the very low brain weights (A) and the poorly developed dendritic arbor on the cells (B) subsequent to the day-1 lesions. (After Kolb and Whishaw, 1989.)

Most dorsal section

1   2   3   4   5   6   7
      Lesion   Most ventral section

Figure 23.18

Effects of Injury Summary of the CT-scan results from a subject who had a birth-related injury in the right posterior cortex. The right hemisphere is smaller at every horizontal section plane. (After Kolb and Whishaw, 1989.)

lesions were produced at 1 day of age, the cells had less-extensive dendritic fields (see Figure 23.17). The difference in dendritic fields leads to differences in the number of synapses: the more space for synapses, the more synapses there are.

In addition to differences in synapse number, there is a parallel difference in the number of astrocytes. Rats given lesions on day 10 have a markedly higher number of astrocytes than do controls, whereas rats given lesions on day 1 are no different from controls in that respect. The astrocyte difference may explain the increased synapse number, because one function of astrocytes is to produce **neurotrophic factors**, compounds that support growth and differentiation in developing neurons and may act to keep neurons alive in adulthood. One neurotrophic factor, basic fibroblast growth factor (bFGF), has been shown to be elevated after day-10 lesions but not after day-1 lesions. Furthermore, the administration of bFGF can attenuate the effects of day-1 lesions.

Cortical Connectivity

Contrary to what might be expected, the best functional outcome does not appear to be correlated with the most-extensive rewiring of the cerebrum. In one series of studies, cortical–cortical, cortical–striatal, and certain subcortical–cortical connections were compared after the production of frontal or parietal lesions on postnatal days 1 or 10 (see Kolb, Comeau, and Gibb). The general finding was that adult rats with day-1 lesions had abnormalities in all types of connections examined. For example, there were aberrant thalamic–cortical connections, such as projections from the medial geniculate (which should project to auditory cortex) to the visual cortex in the frontal-lesion animals.

These abnormal connections were probably not formed after the lesions, however, because results of the studies also showed that newborn animals had the same connections. Instead, these connections appear to be pruned off by day 7 or so in normal animals but not in the brain-injured rats. In contrast, rats with day-10 lesions had no obvious abnormalities in these connections.

Hence, the day-1 animals had the worst functional outcomes, which were associated with the most-extensive abnormalities in connectivity, whereas the day-10 animals had the best functional outcomes, which were associated with no obvious abnormalities. A reasonable hypothesis is that the abnormal connections were interfering with the normal functioning of the remaining brain, presumably owing to the fact that these connections are pathological and are normally eliminated in the course of development. After early cortical injury, the pruning of these connections appears to decrease or perhaps even stop.

Not all abnormal connections are harmful. Investigators have known for some time that both rats and cats with unilateral lesions of the motor cortex or complete hemidecortications show an expansion of corticospinal projections from the normal hemisphere to the ipsilateral side and that this expansion is correlated with improved function (see the Snapshot in Chapter 11 on page 301). These connections are particularly extensive in hemidecorticates and include anomalous projections from the intact hemisphere to the striatum on the injured side. Thus, abnormal connections are perhaps not always detrimental and may in fact be beneficial. In contrast with the abnormal connections seen in animals with early frontal lesions, the abnormalities in the corticospinal projections are not present in normal infants and must therefore indicate the growth of de novo connections.

Neurogenesis after Early Cortical Injury

The results of studies in adult animals have shown a small number of new neurons to be generated after cortical injury, but, because of the small number, they are unlikely to provide any functional benefit. Given that Hicks showed that impressive neurogenesis could be stimulated after prenatal cerebral injury, we can reasonably wonder if there is a way to restart neurogenesis after cerebral injury at other times in development.

Damage to the anterior midline telencephalon (olfactory bulb or anterior midline cortex) of a rat at about 10 days of age leads to the generation of significant numbers of new neurons, enough to fill the lesion cavities. The results of our studies have shown that these cells are functional and that they establish appropriate connections with the intact regions of the brain (although the tissue is not completely normal and the neurogenesis replaces only about 65% of the lost tissue). However, lesions earlier or later in life or lesions in other cortical areas do not stimulate neurogenesis; so there appears to be something special about the midline tissue at about 10 days of age. Nonetheless, the results do show that neurogenesis is possible after cortical injury at a time when cortical neurogenesis is normally complete. (For a review of this work, see Kolb, Comeau, and Gibb).

Although there are no reports of neurogenesis after early lesions in other species, it may take place in kittens with early frontal lesions. Villablanca and his group found that a kitten's striatum is unusually large after an early cortical lesion. These researchers suggest no explanation for this result, but one possibility is that the lesion stimulates the genesis of new striatal neurons.

Factors Influencing Plasticity after Early Cortical Injury

As already mentioned, the normal brain is affected by a wide variety of factors, ranging from general sensory experience to gonadal hormones and neurotrophic factors (for a review, see Kolb and Whishaw, 1998). It is reasonable to suppose that these factors will also influence the damaged brain. Although virtually all research to date has been done in rats, the evidence is compelling that a wide range of factors can facilitate functional recovery (**Table 23.8**).

Table **23.8** Summary of the effects of factors on plasticity after early cortical lesions

Treatment	Behavioral Result	Anatomical Result
Tactile stimulation	Recovery after P4 frontal, motor, or parietal lesions	Dendritic growth, bFGF increased, acetylcholine increased
Handling	No effect	Synaptic pruning
Prenatal tactile stimulation of dam	Recovery after P4 frontal lesions	Dendritic growth
Complex rearing from weaning	Recovery after P4 frontal or parietal lesions	Dendritic growth
Nicotine	Recovery after P3 frontal lesions	Acetylcholine increased dendritic change?
Choline supplement	Enhanced recovery after P4 lesions	Increased dendritic growth
Hormone depletion	Blocks recovery after P7 frontal lesions	Blocks dendritic changes
Noradrenaline depletion	Blocks recovery after P7 frontal lesions	Blocks dendritic hypertrophy

Abbreviation: P followed by number, postnatal day.
Source: After Kolb, Comeau, and Gibb; and Kolb, Halliwell, and Gibb.

Perhaps one of the most potent treatments is tactile stimulation. A series of studies by Gibb and her colleagues have shown that stroking infant rats with a soft brush for 15 minutes, three times a day, for 10 days after a perinatal lesion of the frontal, parietal, or motor cortex can stimulate significant functional recovery in adulthood. The tactile stimulation promotes synaptogenesis in the remaining cortex, possibly because the treatment increases bFGF and acetylcholine levels in the cortex.

Even more interesting is Gibb's finding that tactile stimulation of pregnant dams with a child's hairbrush for 15 minutes, three times a day, throughout the pregnancy can not only alter the synaptic organization of the as yet unborn progeny's brain in adulthood, but also facilitate recovery from cortical injury incurred in infancy. The mechanism of this behavioral effect is not yet known, although we can speculate that it may be related to the increased production of one or more neurotrophic factors.

Summary

Approaches to Studying Development

Brain development can be studied by correlating it with specific behaviors, by studying cognitive development and making inferences about which brain structures must be maturing, and by studying factors that influence brain and behavioral development. The merging of all three types of evidence has led to our current understanding of brain development.

The Development of the Human Brain

The process of brain maturation in humans is long, lasting beyond adolescence. Neurons, the elementary components of the brain, are born, migrate, and, as their processes elaborate, establish connections with other neurons. Because the brain contains such a large number of cells and an even larger number of connections, the newborn brain possesses more neurons and connections than it needs and prunes them back to a stable adult level.

Imaging Studies of Brain Development

The increased use of MRI techniques across the lifespan has led to a new understanding of the processes of brain maturation. The human cortex is sculpted by a reduction in cortical thickness beginning before age 4 and continuing until at least 30 years of age. These changes take place first in primary regions and later in secondary and tertiary regions and are inversely correlated with measures of cognitive development.

The Development of Problem-Solving Ability

Behavioral and cognitive capacities follow parallel sequences of development, from the rudimentary to the complex. Stages of cognitive development identified by Piaget correlate with growth spurts in the brain. Similarly, neuropsychological measures of cognitive development correlate with changes in brain structure in the basal ganglia and cerebral cortex. Development does not take place without sensory input, however; experience has major effects on normal brain development. These effects can be seen not only in the morphology of the cerebral cortex and patterns of cortical connectivity but also in the representational maps.

Environmental Effects on Brain Development

Just as "normal" experiences shape brain development, abnormal experiences alter brain structure and behavior. Furthermore, perturbations of the brain in the course of development can significantly alter brain development and result in severe behavioral abnormalities.

Brain Injury and Plasticity

The sensitivity of the brain to experience or injury varies with time, because there are periods in the course of development during which different brain regions are particularly sensitive to different events. Functional recovery after early injury may result from the modification of remaining circuits, the generation of new (abnormal) circuits, or the generation of neurons and glia.

Experimental Approaches to Studying Plasticity after Early Brain Injury

Various factors can influence recovery from early cortical injury, including experience, hormones, stress, drugs, and neurotrophic factors. These factors act to stimulate neurogenesis, gliogenesis, and synaptic remodeling.

References

Alajouanine, T., and F. Lhermitte. Acquired aphasia in children. *Brain* 88:653–662, 1965.

Ames, E. *The Development of Romanian Orphanage Children Adopted to Canada.* (Final report to the National Welfare Grants Program: Human Resources Development Canada). Burnaby, British Columbia: Simon Fraser University, 1997.

Bachevalier, J. Neural bases of memory development: Insights from neuropsychological studies in primates. In C. A. Nelson and M. Luciana, Eds. *Handbook of Developmental Cognitive Neuroscience.* Cambridge, MA: MIT Press, 2001, pp. 365–380.

Bachevalier J., L. Malkova, and M. Mishkin. Effects of selective neonatal temporal lobe lesions on socioemotional behavior in infant rhesus monkeys *(Macaca mulatta).* *Behavioral Neuroscience* 115:545–559, 2001.

Bachevalier, J., and M. Mishkin. Effects of selective neonatal temporal lobe lesions on visual recognition memory in rhesus monkeys. *Journal of Neuroscience* 14:2128–2139, 1994.

Basser, L. Hemiplegia of early onset and the faculty of speech with special reference to the effects of hemispherectomy. *Brain* 85:427–460, 1962.

Blakemore, C., and D. E. Mitchell. Environmental modification of the visual cortex and the neural basis of learning and memory. *Nature* 241:467–468, 1973.

Bourgeois, J.-P. Synaptogenesis in the neocortex of the newborn: The ultimate frontier for individuation? In C. A. Nelson and M. Luciana, Eds. *Handbook of Developmental Cognitive Neuroscience.* Cambridge, Mass.: MIT Press, 2001.

Casey, B. J., K. M. Thomas, and B. McCandliss. Applications of magnetic resonance imaging to the study of development. In C. A. Nelson and M. Luciana, Eds. *Handbook of Developmental Cognitive Neuroscience.* Cambridge, Mass.: MIT Press, 2001, pp. 137–147.

Caviness, V. S., Jr., and R. L. Sidman. Time of origin of corresponding cell classes in the cerebral cortex of normal and reeler mutant mice: An autoradiographic analysis. *Journal of Comparative Neurology* 148:141–152, 1973.

Crowley, J. C., and L. C. Katz. Ocular dominance development revisited. *Current Opinion in Neurobiology* 12:104–114, 2002.

Elbert, T., S. Heim, and B. Rockstroh. Neural plasticity and development. In C. A. Nelson and M. Luciana, Eds. *Handbook of Developmental Cognitive Neuroscience.* Cambridge, Mass.: MIT Press, 2001, pp. 191–204.

Epstein, H. T. Growth spurts during brain development: Implications for educational policy and practice. In J. S. Chard and A. F. Mirsky, Eds. *Education and the Brain.* Chicago: University of Chicago Press, 1978.

Flechsig, P. *Anatomie des menschlichen Gehirns und Ruckenmarks.* Leipzig: Georg Thieme, 1920.

Fuchs, E., and E. Gould. Mini-review—In vivo neurogenesis in the adult brain: Regulation and functional implications. *European Journal of Neuroscience* 12:2211–2214, 2000.

Gibb, R., C. R. Gonzalez, and B. Kolb. Prenatal enrichment leads to improved functional recovery following perinatal frontal cortex injury: Effects of maternal complex housing. *Society for Neuroscience Abstracts* 27:476.4, 2001.

Gogtay, N., J. N. Gledd, L. Lusk, K. M. Hayashi, D. Greenstein, A. C. Valtuzis, T. F. Nugent III, D. H. Herman, L. S. Clasen, A. W. Toga, J. L. Rapoport, and P. M. Thompson. Dynamic mapping of human cortical development during childhood and adolescence. *Proceedings of the National Academy of Sciences of the United States of America* 101:8174–8179, 2004.

Goldman, P. S. Functional development of the prefrontal cortex in early life and the problem of neuronal plasticity. *Experimental Neurology* 32:366–387, 1971.

Goldman, P. S., and T. W. Galkin. Prenatal removal of frontal association cortex in the fetal rhesus monkey: Anatomical and functional consequences in postnatal life. *Brain Research* 152:451–485, 1978.

Gould E., P. Tanapat, N. B. Hastings, and T. J. Shors. Neurogenesis in adulthood: A possible role in learning. *Trends in Cognitive Science* 3:186–192, 1999.

Gunnar, M. E. Effects of early deprivation: Findings from orphanage-reared infants and children. In C. A. Nelson and M. Luciana, Eds. *Developmental Cognitive Neuroscience.* Cambridge, Mass.: MIT Press, 2001, pp. 617–629.

Guttman, E. Aphasia in children. *Brain* 65:205–219, 1942.

Hebb, D. O. *The Organization of Behavior.* New York: McGraw-Hill, 1949.

Hécaen, H. Acquired aphasia in children and the ontogenesis of hemispheric functional specialization. *Brain and Language* 3:114–134, 1976.

Hicks, S. P., and C. J. D'Amato. Effects of ionizing radiation on developing brain and behavior. In *Studies on the Development of Behavior and the Nervous System.* New York: Academic Press, 1973, pp. 35–72.

Hirsch, H. V. B., and D. N. Spinelli. Modification of the distribution of receptive field orientation in cats by selective visual exposure during development. *Experimental Brain Research* 13:509–527, 1971.

Holloway, V., D. G. Gadian, F. Vargha-Khadem, D. A. Porter, S. G. Boyd, and A. Connelly. The reorganization of sensorimotor function in children after hemispherectomy. *Brain* 123:2432–2444, 2000.

Hubel, D. H., and T. N. Wiesel. Receptive fields of cells in striate cortex of very young, visually inexperienced kittens. *Journal of Neurophysiology* 26:994–1002, 1963.

Jacobsen, M. *Developmental Neurobiology*, 3rd ed. New York, Plenum, 1991.

Kolb, B. *Brain Plasticity and Behavior.* Mahwah, N.J.: Lawrence Erlbaum, 1995.

Kolb, B., W. Comeau, and R. Gibb. Early brain injury, plasticity, and behavior. In C. A. Nelson and M. Luciana, Eds. *Handbook of Developmental Cognitive Neuroscience*, 2nd ed. MIT Press: Cambridge, Mass., forthcoming.

Kolb, B., and R. Gibb. Brain plasticity and recovery from early cortical injury. *Developmental Psychobiology* 49(2):107–118, 2007.

Kolb, B., R. Gibb, and G. Gorn. Experience-dependent changes in dendritic arbor and spine density in neocortex vary with age and sex. *Neurobiology of Learning and Memory* 79:1–10, 2003.

Kolb, B., C. Halliwell, and R. Gibb. Factors influencing neocortical development in the normal and injured brain. In M. S. Blumberg, J. H. Freeman, and S. R. Robinson, Eds. *Developmental and Comparative Neuroscience: Epigenetics, Evolution, and Behavior.* New York: Oxford University Press, forthcoming.

Kolb, B., and I. Q. Whishaw. Plasticity in the neocortex: Mechanisms underlying recovery from early brain damage. *Progress in Neurobiology* 32:235–276, 1989.

Kolb, B., and I. Q. Whishaw. Brain plasticity and behavior. *Annual Review of Psychology* 49:43–64, 1998.

Kornhuber, H. H., D. Bechinger, H. Jung, and E. Sauer. A quantitative relationship between the extent of localized cerebral lesions and the intellectual and behavioural deficiency in children. *European Archives of Psychiatry and Neurological Sciences* 235:129–133, 1985.

Krashen, S. D. Lateralization, language learning, and the critical period: Some new evidence. *Language Learning* 23:63–74, 1973.

Kuhl, P. K. The role of early experience in early language development: Linguistic experience alters the perception and production of speech. In N. A. Fox, L. A. Leavitt, and J. G. Warhol, Eds. *The Role of Early Experience in Infant Development.* Johnson & Johnson Consumer Companies, 1999, p. 120.

Kuhl, P. K., F. M. Tsao, H. M. Liu, Y. Zhang, and B. De Boer. Language/culture/mind/brain: Progress at the margins between disciplines. *Annals of the New York Academy of Sciences* 935:136–174, 2001.

McCarthy, G., 1963. Quoted in Krashen, S. D. Lateralization, language learning, and the critical period: Some new evidence. *Language Learning* 23: 63–74, 1973.

Milner, B. Psychological aspects of focal epilepsy and its neurological management. *Advances in Neurology* 8:299–321, 1975.

Oberlander, T. F., R. J. Bonaguro, S. Misri, M. Papsdorf, C. J. Ross, and E. M. Simpson. Infant serotonin transporter (SLC6A4) promoter genotype is associated with adverse neonatal outcomes after prenatal exposure to serotonin reuptake inhibitor medications. *Molecular Psychiatry* 2007, epub.

Overman, W. H., and J. Bachevalier. Inferences about functional development of neural systems in children via the application of animal tests of cognition. In C. A. Nelson and M. Luciana, Eds. *Developmental Cognitive Neuroscience.* Cambridge, Mass.: MIT Press, 2001, pp. 109–124.

Overman, W. H., J. Bachevalier, T. Sewell, and J. Drew. A comparison of children's performance on two recognition memory tasks: delayed nonmatch-to-sample versus visual paired-comparison. *Developmental Psychobiology* 26:345–357, 1993.

Piaget, J. *Biology and Knowledge.* Chicago: University of Chicago Press, 1971.

Price, B. H., K. R. Daffner, R. M. Stowe, and M. M. Mesulam. The compartmental learning disabilities of early frontal lobe damage. *Brain* 113:1383–1393, 1990.

Rakic, P. Neurogenesis in adult primate neocortex: An evaluation of the evidence. *Nature Reviews Neuroscience* 3:65–71, 2002.

Rapoport J. L., F. X. Castellanos, N. Gogate, K. Janson, S. Kohler, and P. Nelson. Imaging normal and abnormal brain development: New perspectives for child psychiatry. *Australia and New Zealand Journal of Psychiatry* 35:272–281, 2001.

Rasmussen, T., and B. Milner. Clinical and surgical studies of the cerebral speech areas in man. In K. J. Zulch, O. Creutzfeldt, and G. C. Galbraith, Eds. *Cerebral Localization.* Berlin and New York: Springer, 1975.

Rasmussen, T., and B. Milner. The role of early left-brain injury in determining lateralization of cerebral speech functions. *Annals of the New York Academy of Sciences* 299:355–369, 1977.

Riva, D., and L. Cazzaniga. Late effects of unilateral brain lesions sustained before and after age one. *Neuropsychologia* 24:423–428, 1986.

Russell, R., and M. Espir. *Traumatic Aphasia.* Oxford: Oxford University Press, 1961.

Rutter, M., T. G. O'Connor, and the English and Romanian Adoptees (ERA) Study Team. Are there biological programming effects for psychological development? Findings from a study of Romanian adoptees. *Developmental Psychology* 40:81–94, 2004.

Schneider, G. E. Is it really better to have your brain injury early? A revision of the "Kennard Principle." *Neuropsychologia* 17:557–583, 1979.

Sowell, E. R., B. S. Peterson, P. M. Thompson, S. E. Welcome, A. L. Henkenius, and A. W. Toga. Mapping cortical change across the human life span. *Nature Neuroscience* 6:309–315, 2003.

Sowell, E. R., P. M.Thompson, C. M. Leonard, S. E. Welcome, E. Kan, and A. W. Toga. Longitudinal mapping of cortical thickness and brain gowth in normal children. *Journal of Neuroscience* 24:8223–8231, 2004.

Teuber, H. L. Recovery of function after brain injury in man. In *Outcomes of Severe Damage to the Nervous System*, Ciba Foundation Symposium 34. Amsterdam: Elsevier-North Holland, 1975.

Toga, A. W., P. M. Thompson, and E. R. Sowell. Mapping brain maturation. *Trends in Neuroscience* 29:148–159, 2006.

Vargha-Khadem, F., L. J. Carr, E. Brett, C. Adams, and M. Mishkin. Onset of speech after left hemispherectomy in a nine-year-old boy. *Brain* 120:159–182, 1997.

Vargha-Khadem, F., and G. V. Watters. Development of speech and language following bilateral frontal lesions. *Brain and Language* 25:167–183, 1985.

Villablanca, J. R., D. A. Hovda, G. F. Jackson, and C. Infante. Neurological and behavioral effects of a unilateral frontal cortical lesion in fetal kittens II: Visual system tests, and proposing a "critical period" for lesion effects. *Behavioral Brain Research* 57:79–92, 1993.

Weiss, S., B. A. Reynolds, A. L. Vescovi, C. Morshead, C. G. Craig, and D. van der Kooy. Is there a neural stem cell in the mammalian forebrain? *Trends in Neuroscience* 19:387–393, 1996.

Werker, J. F., and R. C. Tees. Developmental changes across childhood in the perception of non-native speech sounds. *Canadian Journal of Psychology* 37:278–286, 1983.

Werker, J. F., and A. Vouloumanos. Speech and language processing in infancy: A neurocognitive approach. In C. A. Nelson and M. Luciana, Eds. *Developmental Cognitive Neuroscience*. Cambridge, Mass.: MIT Press, 2001, pp. 269–280.

Woods, B. T. The restricted effects of right-hemisphere lesions after age one: Wechsler test data. *Neuropsychologia* 18:65–70, 1980.

Woods, B. T. Impaired speech shadowing after early lesions of either hemisphere. *Neuropsychologia* 25:519–525, 1987.

Woods, B. T., and H.-L. Teuber. Early onset of complementary specialization of cerebral hemispheres in man. *Transactions of the American Neurological Association* 98:113–117, 1973.

24 Developmental Disorders

PORTRAIT: Life Without Reading

Ms. P., 19 years old, was referred to us by a friend. She was working as a nurse's aide and had found her work so enjoyable that she was considering entering a nursing program. Because she had not completed high school and generally had a poor academic record, she came to us for guidance in deciding whether she could handle such a program.

Ms. P. had particular difficulty with language skills, and her reading was so bad that she was unable to pass the written examination for a driver's license. In view of Ms. P.'s interest in furthering her nursing education, we decided to test her reading abilities and to administer a complete neuropsychological battery. The results showed an overall IQ of 85 on the Wechsler Adult Intelligence Scale, but there was a 32-point difference between her verbal IQ of 74 and her performance (nonverbal) IQ of 106.

Specific tests of left-hemisphere function confirmed this discrepancy: although her verbal memory, verbal fluency, spelling, reading, and arithmetic scores were extremely low, her spatial skills were good, as were her nonverbal memory and her perform-

© The Kobal Collection

ance on tests such as the Wisconsin Card-Sorting Test and the Semmes Body-Placing Test. In short, her language skills were those of a 6-year-old, although she had attended school for 11 years, but her other abilities were normal for a person of her age.

In view of her deficient language skills, we concluded that Ms. P. was currently not capable of handling a nursing program. We also felt that she was unlikely to be able to develop the necessary language skills, especially because—as we inadvertently discovered—none of her five brothers and sisters could read either.

We explained to Ms. P. that she was by no means retarded but that, just as some people had poor musical ability,

she had poor verbal ability. (We were able to arrange an aural administration of the driver's test, which she passed.)

Finally, we explained Ms. P.'s problem to her husband, a well-educated man with a master's degree. In the short time that they had been married, he had become totally frustrated with her inability to balance the bank account, read recipes, and so forth, and he was beginning to believe that his wife was either "crazy or retarded." They now had an understanding of the problem, which we hoped would help them work out domestic routines to minimize its effect.

Countless people with learning disabilities make adequate adjustments in their lives, but those with severe developmental disabilities need various degrees of lifelong assistance or care. Savants, such as Luria's patient S., whom we profiled in Chapter 18, are characterized by mental handicaps combined with a talent that may far exceed the abilities of the general population. You may have seen the movie *Rain Man,* in which real-life savant, Kim Peek, is portrayed by Dustin Hoffman, shown here in the role.

The Portrait illustrates one type of a *developmental disorder,* a disorder that seems to have its origin in some abnormality in the way in which the brain develops. Ms. P.'s restricted difficulty with language skills must have made school an arduous and frustrating experience and was clearly continuing to cause problems for her as an adult. In this chapter, we survey a number of developmental disorders, including disorders of learning, attention, social behavior, and general intellectual functioning. We conclude the chapter with a survey of research on adult outcomes of learning disabilities.

Learning Disabilities

Most children enter schools in which they are required to master a core curriculum. Some are completely unable to meet any demands of the school system that they enter; others learn, but only with great difficulty. Some have to repeat one or more grades; some graduate but fail to master certain subject areas; and some even graduate without mastering basic knowledge in any area. For those who fail, the educational experience often leaves emotional and attitudinal scars that are carried throughout life.

The difficulties that children encounter in school can have any of a number of causes. A child may be disturbed by an unhappy home life, have endured abuse, be bored by school, dislike school, dislike a teacher, have no aptitude for school, have low "intelligence," or have a physical handicap or a brain dysfunction or brain damage. Some school systems may be equipped to assess and deal with these kinds of problems, but most have no resources for either assessment or remediation. Even when a school is not equipped to deal with learning problems, neuropsychology now receives enough publicity that, if a child is not learning effectively, the question whether the cause is brain damage or dysfunction or something else will arise.

Historical Background

Learning disability is an umbrella term used for a wide variety of school-related problems. Formal definitions of learning disabilities describe these diagnoses as applying to people who have adequate intelligence, opportunity to learn, instruction, and home environment, yet still do not succeed in acquiring certain scholastic abilities. Because reading is central to success in school, the study of the inability to read—**dyslexia** (from the Greek *dys*, for "impaired," and *lexia*, for "word")—has been central in the study of learning disabilities. Dyslexia is defined by the World Health Organization as a "disorder manifested by difficulty in learning to read despite conventional instruction, adequate intelligence, and sociocultural opportunity. It is dependent upon fundamental cognitive disabilities which are frequently of constitutional origin."

This definition, and other similar definitions, pose some difficulties in understanding the condition. For example, why should a learning disability be called a disorder? What is meant by conventional instruction? What is meant by adequate intelligence? And so on. To comprehend the difficulty of arriving at satisfactory definitions, knowing some of the history of ideas about learning disabilities can be helpful.

The identification of dyslexia emerged within the context of **aphasia**, a condition in which brain injury leads to the loss of language ability. In the late 1890s, James Hinshelwood, a Glasgow eye surgeon, and Pringle Morgan, a Seaford general practitioner, proposed that students who could not learn to read

Table **24.1** "Do-it-yourself terminology generator"

Secondary	Nervous	Deficit
Minimal	Brain	Dysfunction
Mild	Cerebral	Damage
Minor	Neurological	Disorder
Chronic	Neurologic	Desynchronization
Diffuse	CNS	Handicap
Specific	Language	Disability
Primary	Reading	Retardation
Developmental	Perceptual	Deficiency
Disorganized	Impulsive	Impairment
Organic	Visual-motor	Pathology
Clumsy	Behavior	Syndrome
Functional	Psychoneurologic	Complex

Directions: Select any word from first column, add any word from second and third columns. If you don't like the result, try again. It will mean about the same thing. Source: Fry, 1968, Reprinted with the permission of Edward Fry and the International Reading Association.

had prerequisite brain areas that were absent or abnormal. It seemed logical to conclude that **developmental dyslexia**, which is acquired before birth or during early postbirth years, is similar in nature to **acquired dyslexia**, which is due to brain damage after learning to read. Developmental deficits in other spheres, such as mathematics, also would be due to some underlying brain problem.

In the 1920s and 1930s, Samuel T. Orton proposed that dyslexia is due to delayed function, not anatomical absence. Orton, the director of a medical clinic in Iowa, noted that dyslexia was correlated with left-handedness and with tendencies to reverse or invert letters and words when learning to read or write. He termed such dyslexia **strephosymbolia** (from the Greek, meaning "twisted symbols"). Orton thought that the nondominant hemisphere, usually the right hemisphere, which he postulated had a reversed image of things, was excessively dominant or not sufficiently controlled. He suggested that, if an instructor was clever or persevering, education could establish normal dominance of reading in the left hemisphere, and the problem would be resolved.

When sociologists and educational psychologists became interested in learning disabilities, they supposed that environmental explanations, rather than neurological ones, accounted for learning impairments. This stance may perhaps have been motivated by the belief, or hope, that environmental causes could be reversed more easily than neurological ones.

The term "learning disability" had its origins in an address given by Samuel A. Kirk in 1963. Kirk argued for better descriptions of children's school problems, but he excluded children with sensory handicaps and mental retardation from the group that he called learning-disabled. The members of his audience, who later joined together to form the Association for Children with Learning Disabilities, were influenced both by his address and by his definition and further popularized the expression that he had coined.

The search for causes of learning disabilities has resulted in a proliferation of terms whose purpose seems to be to dissociate the learning-disabled from the retarded and brain damaged. Edward Fry published a tongue-in-cheek "Do-It-Yourself Terminology Generator," shown in **Table 24.1** (from which about 2000 terms can be constructed), to emphasize their overabundance and consequent confusion and inaccuracy. Frequently, terms that are widely used take on a pejorative connotation and are then dropped in favor of a new term. As reviewed by Angela Fawcett and Roderick Nicolson, the promise of improved methods of brain imaging in neuroscience is better diagnosis of learning abilities and the identification of brain regions implicated in learning difficulties.

Incidence of Learning Disabilities

Most estimates of the number of students needing special training to overcome learning disabilities range from 10% to 15% of the school-age population. A problem that complicates the calculation of prevalence estimates is that a learning disability is an emerging condition. When children enter the first grade, few of them qualify as being learning-disabled, largely because a popular method of defining a learning disability is to estimate how far a person is behind an expected norm: for example, if a person is 2 years behind in academic progress as determined by a standard test, then that person is learning-disabled.

When this criterion is used, fewer than 1% of 6-year-olds are disabled, 2% of 7-year-olds are disabled, and so on, until, at age 19, 25% qualify as being disabled. This pattern of emerging incidence develops because the learning-disabled are falling behind at a rate that is proportional to their degree of impairment.

Further complicating the process of calculating and utilizing prevalence rates is the variation in scholastic achievement from one school system to another. Achievement tests are often used to determine grade-equivalent performance, but even nondisabled school populations do not all display equivalent performance. Prevalence rates might be obtained by asking teachers to report the number of children in their classes who are receiving special help, but many schools cannot provide such information, because they have no resources for special education. Nevertheless, in the United States, the National Assessment of Educational Progress found, as of 2005, that as many as one-third of children lacked fundamental reading skills.

Types of Learning Disabilities

The American Psychiatric Association's *Diagnostic and Statistical Manual of Mental Disorders* (DSM-IV-R) recognizes several categories of disorders arising in childhood, including mental retardation and mental disorders; disorders in reading, arithmetic, and motor activity; and certain mixed classifications. **Table 24.2** lists a range of characteristics related to learning disabilities. Not all learning-disabled children exhibit all these symptoms. For example, for every learning-disabled child with coordination problems, there is a learning-disabled child whose coordination is better than normal.

The classification and incidence of learning disabilities correspond to the emphasis placed on self-control and on certain academic specialties in most public school systems. Good behavior, reading, arithmetic, and spelling are emphasized, and learning-disability classifications correspond to this focus. Although art, music, and physical education are taught in many schools, referrals for failure in these areas are uncommon. If art, rather than reading, were the core subject in the early years of school, we suspect that current catalogues of types of disabilities would be different. Nevertheless, disabilities can interfere with the acquisition of reading, spatial orientation, mathematics, and social skills.

Table **24.2** Symptoms associated with learning disabilities
1. Hyperactivity
2. Perceptual–motor impairments
3. Emotional lability
4. General coordination deficits
5. Disorders of attention (short attention span, distractibility, perseveration)
6. Impulsivity
7. Disorders of memory and thinking
8. Specific learning disabilities, including, especially, those of reading (dyslexia) arithmetic, writing, and spelling
9. Disorders of speech and hearing
10. Neurological signs and irregular EEG

Reading Disabilities

Reading requires letter-identification skills, phonological skills (converting letters into sounds by using certain rules), grapheme-association skills (using the visual gestalt of a word to access a previously learned sound), sequencing skills (in which a number of sounds are analyzed and combined in sequence), and short-term-memory skills (to retain pieces of information as they are sequentially extracted from written material). Acquired information also is important, including knowledge of words in the form of a **lexicon**, a dictionary-like store of words in the brain containing their meanings, knowledge of the way in which they can be combined, and information about the ideas with which they can be associated. Thus, reading is a multiprocess and multistage behavior. As such, one would expect that it could be disrupted in many different ways. In the following sections, we describe (1) types of reading, (2) causes of reading disabilities, and (3) the role of neuropsychological evaluation in reading.

Types of Reading

Reading can be accomplished in either of two ways, (1) phonetically, by decoding the sounds of words, or (2) graphemically, by using the image of the word to access its sound. In phonetic reading, you simply convert a letter or group of letters into sounds (phonemes) that clue the meaning of the words. Stated differently, the sounds that you get by analyzing letter groups will lead you to a pronunciation, and you will be able to access your memory, or lexicon, for the meaning and connection of the word. This type of reading is known as **phonological reading**. In **graphemic reading** (also called *lexical* or *whole-word reading*) the word is memorized.

Most English words can be decoded phonetically, by sounding them out. But many are irregular and must be memorized. Such graphemic reading is also how Arabic numerals (such as 4) and international symbolic road and direction signs must be read and learned. Fluent reading thus requires both strategies. In addition, after readers learn to read phonetically and become fluent readers, they become more dependent on grapheme reading. Thus, reading initially relies on phonological skills and later becomes dependent on grapheme skills.

This progression may explain why many fluent readers have difficulty finding typographic errors when they proofread. Rather than reading phonologically, they read graphemically and, practiced at graphemic reading, they need to read only part of a word before recognizing its meaning and shifting attention to the next word. If the spelling error is not within the part of the word actually read, it will not be noticed.

Given the differences between these two reading processes, different kinds of reading impairments arise at different ages. A child who is incompetent in the phonological procedure has difficulty in the early stages of reading. A child who is competent in the phonological procedure but incompetent in the grapheme procedure will have difficulty later on. Moreover, a child who is impaired at the first type will be hampered in making the transition to the second type.

We should note here that these types of impairments would not by any means exhaust the classifications of poor readers. People with a poor short-term auditory memory may not make proper sense of written material, because they quickly forget the words and phrases as they proceed. This type of disability may be particularly obvious at older ages, when reading material becomes more complex.

People with poor long-term memory may not understand the sense of words despite good decoding skills, simply because they do not have much information about the meaning of the words. This situation is similar to that faced by a person who speaks only English trying to read Italian. The person can sound out the words by using general phonetic rules but, not knowing what the words mean, cannot understand what he or she is reading. In fact, people who are demented often behave in this way. They can read, but they understand nothing.

Further compounding the difficulty in understanding the causes of learning disabilities is the lack of uniformity in the way that reading is taught. The disagreement between advocates of initiating reading instruction with phonological versus gaphemic, or "whole word," reading has been referred to as a "war." Carol Connor and coworkers suggest that more-scientific approaches to reading, such as algorithm-guided individual instruction, can maximize the benefits of both systems.

Causes of Reading Disabilities

It would be helpful if reading deficits displayed themselves in a straightforward manner, but, unfortunately, they do not. People with dyslexia exhibit a wide range of different symptom clusters, as well as individual variations. These symptoms include deficits in attention, eye movement, development, memory, coordination, spatial abilities, movement sequencing, map reading, and visuospatial processing. The reason that language disorders are associated with so many kinds of symptoms is that language has a high-level role in managing our mental processes and thus is affected by and affects many different kinds of behavior. Despite the variability and complexity of symptoms associated with reading disabilities, a number of theories, including the phonological, attention, sensory, and motor theories, posit primary causes.

Phonological Deficiency

Impairments in language and reading may stem from difficulties that children have in consciously decomposing words into their constituent speech sounds—an ability called *phonemic awareness*. An early investigation describes the sound-categorization ability of children who have not yet started to read (see Bradley and Bryant). Children were given three or four words and asked to pick out the word that does not have a sound (phoneme) in common with the others. For example, in the series "hill, pig, pin," "hill" would be the correct choice; in the series "cot, pot, hat," "hat" would be the correct choice, and in the series "pin, bun, gun," "pin" would be the correct choice.

When the same children were older and had started to learn to read, those initially weak at sound categorization later fell behind in reading and spelling. This outcome argues that the initial insensitivity to rhyme and alliteration causes subsequent reading impairment, because, if a child who was initially impaired was given special training in rhyme and alliteration, his or her reading was far less impaired after training in reading began. In short, at least one cause of reading deficiency is a basic deficiency in phonological, or sound, awareness. Olivier Dufor and coworkers associate such impairments in phoneme use and recognition with language regions of the left hemisphere. According to this view, reading impairments stem from impairments within language-processing systems of the brain.

Attentional Deficiency

Other theorists propose that reading impairments can stem from problems not directly related to language use. Impairments in separating stimuli have been found in all sensory modalities in dyslexic people, as have impairments in producing movements. Thus, language-impaired persons may require longer intervals between stimuli before they can detect two separate lights or two separate touches, and they may be impaired in producing rapid movements. They may also be impaired in sound-frequency discriminations and in detecting a target sound obscured by background noise.

Riitta Hari and Hanna Renvall, in reviewing the many sensory and motor deficits associated with dyslexia, suggest that the central problem could be "sluggish attention shifting." In other words, when the attention of these dyslexic subjects is engaged, it cannot be easily disengaged, and vice versa. They suggest that the problem arises in the associational areas of the parietal lobe, which receive input from all sensory systems and then initiate movements. A problem there, they believe, could lead to an inability to switch attention that would affect many sensory domains as well as the production of movements.

Sensory Deficiency

Because reading depends on the detection of words both visually and aurally, sensory impairments have been examined in association with reading disabilities. Paula Tallal and her coworkers examined the sensory detection abilities of children with learning disabilities and found them impaired in detecting sound events that take place in rapid succession. If two tones are presented in succession very quickly, they will be heard as one tone. If the interval between the tones is gradually increased, a point will be reached at which they are heard as two tones. For most people, a separation of tens of milliseconds, from about 10 to 40 ms, is required before the two tones are discriminated. For some people with reading disabilities, a much greater separation is needed (**Figure 24.1**).

The relevance of this finding to language impairments is that stop consonants ("ba," "da," "ga," "pa," and "ta") contain a transition period in which the sounds (called *formants*) change very rapidly, usually within 40 ms. When stop consonants are used as stimuli, reading-impaired people have difficulty differentiating one such consonant from another, whereas they have no difficulty in detecting vowels. They also have no difficulty in detecting stop consonants if the transition period is lengthened. When this difficulty is detected in infants, it is predictive of later language impairment.

This idea points to possible strategies for remediation. Tallal and her coworkers suggest that remediation of language-related disorders should focus on training in sound discrimination. For example, they reason that, if a child has difficulty in discriminating "da" from "de" when the sounds are presented at a normal rate, then slowing the presentation down so that the duration of the sounds is dragged out would make discrimination easier.

They constructed computer games in which the subjects, rewarded each time that they made a correct discrimination (either between verbal or between nonverbal stimuli), gradually worked their way from simple to more-complex discrimination problems. They also designed computerized listening exercises that teach phonological discrimination through the use of acoustically modified speech. The computer-based exercises measured each subject's initial performance

Figure 24.1

Sound-Detection Ability

Percentage of trials in which controls and language-impaired subjects discriminate two tones separated by different interstimulus intervals. (After Tallal et al., 1993.)

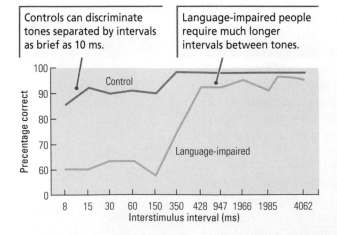

Controls can discriminate tones separated by intervals as brief as 10 ms.

Language-impaired people require much longer intervals between tones.

level and then led the subject through extensive daily training for a number of weeks, after which the subject's performance level was found to be closer to normal. Training in sound-processing rates resulted in improvement in temporal integration on the discrimination tasks (see the Snapshot below).

SNAPSHOT
Imaging Sound Perception in Normal and Dyslexic Subjects

Developmental dyslexia—inherent difficulty in learning to read—affects between 5% and 20% of the population, yet its neural basis is not known. Bart Boets and his coworkers find that some dyslexics have a deficit in phonemic awareness.

Other dyslexics have a more fundamental deficit in processing rapidly changing acoustical signals, an ability necessary for language comprehension. This idea, known as the *rapid-processing hypothesis*, suggests that subjects given training in discriminating rapidly changing acoustical signals would improve in their ability to discriminate between the signals and in their comprehension of auditory language.

Elise Temple and her colleagues tested a group of adult subjects with a history of developmental dyslexia and a matched group of control subjects on their discrimination of rapid acoustical signals while obtaining fMRI images of the subjects' brain activity. The images revealed a specific disruption of the neural responses to transient, rapidly changing acoustical stimuli in the adults with developmental dyslexia. The largest activation in the control subjects was in the left prefrontal region, between the middle and superior frontal gyri in Brodmann's areas 46-10-9.

Analysis of the dyslexic readers revealed no increase in left frontal response to the rapid relative to the slow stimuli. The illustration shows examples of rapid and slowed nonspeech acoustical signals (part A) and examples of normal and dyslexic subjects' fMRI responses to rapid auditory stimuli (part B). Note the greater activation of the left prefrontal cortex in normal readers.

Dyslexic subjects then underwent a training program designed to improve rapid processing, after which they were again examined with the use of fMRI. After training, some subjects improved on tests of rapid auditory processing and auditory language comprehension, and their fMRIs showed significantly increased activity in the left prefrontal cortex.

Taken together, these results suggest that a subset of dyslexics is impaired in their sensitivity to rapidly changing acoustical stimuli and that fMRI can assist in the diagnosis and treatment of the impairment.

Analyzing sound perception in normal and dyslexic readers. (A) Rapid and slowed nonspeech acoustic signals used as test stimuli and in training. (B) fMRI responses to rapid auditory stimuli in normal readers and dyslexic subjects. (From E. Temple et al. Disruption of the neural response to rapid acoustic stimuli in dyslexia: Evidence from functional MRI. *Proceedings of the National Academy of Sciences of the United States of America* 97:13907–13912, 2000.)

Boets, B., J. Wouters, A. van Wieringen, and P. Ghesquiere. Auditory processing, speech perception and phonological ability in pre-school children at high-risk for dyslexia: A longitudinal study of the auditory temporal processing theory. *Neuropsychologia* 45(8):1608–1620, 2007.

Temple, E. Brain mechanisms in normal and dyslexic readers. *Current Opinion in Neurobiology* 12:178–183, 2002.

Temple, E., G. K. Deutsch, R. A. Poldrack, S. L. Miller, P. Tallal, M. M. Merzenich, and J. D. Gabrieli. Neural deficits in children with dyslexia ameliorated by behavioral remediation: Evidence from functional MRI. *Proceedings of the National Academy of Sciences of the United States of America* 100:2860–2865, 2003.

The magnocellular visual theory is similar to the auditory sensory theory except that it postulates the deficit to be in the magnocellular part of the visual system, which processes black–white vision and movement. If a child's detection of visual motion is disturbed, the child may have difficulty reading because the words on the page appear to jump around. Magnocellular theory also suggests that, if reading is done through a color filter or with only one eye, the perception of word movement can be reduced and reading can be improved. Bernt Skottun and John Skoyles have questioned the magnocellular theory, the utility of using color filters, and the support for the theory.

Motor Deficiency

The most prominent motor theory of reading disabilities is the cerebellar theory. As is summarized by Filippos Vlachos and his coworkers, the cerebellum controls many acts of movement, including timing and coordination—skills relevant to reading. Because rapid sensory processing and attentional shifts also likely depend on the cerebellum, the cerebellar theory easily incorporates deficits that are suggested to be causal by other theories.

Evaluating the Theories

Each causative theory of reading disabilities presented here is supported by substantial experimentation, tests sensitive to the relevant deficits, as well and brain imaging and autopsy studies. A parsimonious interpretation of this range of evidence is the likelihood that subpopulations of disabled readers display different deficits. Franck Ramus and his coworkers attempted to evaluate all the theories in a single study by giving a small population of 17 disabled readers an extensive series of cognitive, sensory, motor, and reading tests.

They found that all their subjects had language impairments in the use of sounds. They also found that a subset of their subjects had sensory deficits in both the visual and the auditory domains; a second group had motor deficits, and, of these subjects, most also had auditory deficts; and a third group had language deficits with neither sensory nor motor symptoms. They suggest that the major cause of reading disability lies in language processes stemming from language-related areas of the brain, but other areas related to attentional, sensory, or motor function may additionally be impaired and contribute to the disability.

Neuropsychological Evaluation

Neuropsychological approaches to assessing dyslexia generally rest on the following assumptions: (1) the disability may affect only one or a few spheres of endeavor; (2) a specific skill or lack of that skill can be detected through a neuropsychological testing procedure; (3) if one method or strategy of instruction is unsuccessful, another might be more successful; and (4) the neuropsychological test results should suggest a possible strategy for remediation of the learning disability. As summarized by Ara Schmitt and David Wodrich, although none of these assumptions has yet received anything like adequate scientific support, the neuropsychological testing strategy does provide a comprehensive evaluation of a person that is useful for counseling, as Ms. P.'s case in the Portrait at the beginning of this chapter demonstrates.

Neuropsychological testing assesses performance on a wide range of tasks, providing feedback on all areas of brain function (see Chapter 28). Most learning-disabled children are not dyslexic or dyscalculic (can't do math) alone but rather have a number of associated symptoms that teachers and parents are usually unaware exist. The discovery of these associated deficits often helps the adults in a learning-disabled child's life to understand the difficulties with which the child is struggling. Neuropsychological tests can also help distinguish between children who have central reading impairments and those whose problems have emotional or social causes.

Many studies have focused on the IQ test results of learning-disabled children. These analyses attempt to correlate learning impairments with performance on the subtests of the Wechsler Intelligence Scale for Children (WISC). A compilation of the results from studies in which, collectively, a total of 1521 reading-disabled children and 554 control children were tested and compared is presented in **Figure 24.2** (see Rugel).

The dyslexic group displays low scores on four subtests: arithmetic, coding, information, and digit span. This profile, typical of many such studies, is referred to as the ACID profile. Dyslexic children characteristically have an overall IQ score that averages about 7 points lower than the same score attained by control children, but their mean IQ is roughly 100. Children above the age of 8 show the ACID profile, whereas those younger than 8 may not show a deficit in the information or arithmetic subscales (see Whishaw and Kolb). Although the deficits in digit span and coding are commonly seen with dyslexia, there is no agreement that they are necessarily related to a disability in reading.

Many researchers have commented on the large differences between verbal IQ and performance IQ in dyslexic persons (recall Ms P.'s results). Some experts believe that two types of dyslexics can be identified on the basis of these scores. Generally speaking, however, a dyslexic child's subscores will vary greatly (the child will score in the high range on some subtests, in the low range on others, and in the average range on still others). Nevertheless, for an experienced counselor, the pattern displayed by any child may be meaningful.

In comparing the performance of a dyslexic group with that of the control group on other sections of our composite test battery, we found that the tests

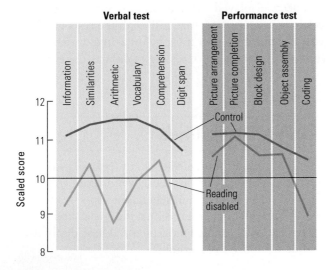

Figure **24.2**

The ACID Profile Intelligence test profiles of developmentally dyslexic subjects and controls. Note the low scores on arithmetic, coding, information, and digit span (ACID) typical of children with reading disabilities. (From Rugel, 1974; after Whishaw and Kolb, 1984.)

	Reading-disabled	Control
Verbal IQ	98	108
Performance IQ	102	106
Full-scale IQ	100	107
Number of subjects	1521	554

Test stimuli

Hands   Lapel   Knee

Figure 24.3

Performance Comparison The scores of control subjects and dyslexic subjects on a left–right discrimination test show significant group differences among adolescent and adult groups but not among children under the age of 8. (After Whishaw and Kolb, 1984.)

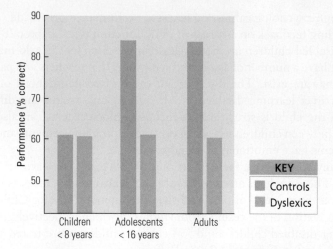

did discriminate between the two groups but that their doing so depended in part on the person's age. This age dependence was particularly evident in three tests:

- In a test of left–right differentiation (**Figure 24.3**), neither dyslexic children nor age-matched controls could score above chance if they were younger than 8 years old. After the age of 8, the control children performed well, whereas the dyslexic children continued to perform at chance.

- A different kind of emerging difference was found on tests of word fluency (for example, "Give as many words beginning with the letter 'S' as you can"). Dyslexic and control scores were similar in children younger than 8 years but diverged increasingly in older age groups, suggesting that the fluency performance in the control group improved with age, whereas the dyslexic group remained almost static.

- A third pattern was obtained on the Semmes Body-Placing Test (another test of left–right discrimination). Here, significant group differences emerged only in adults, and these differences seemed to depend on the fact that adult control subjects displayed virtually perfect performance on the tests. These observations suggest to us that, although the tests can be applied with some success to children, they must be interpreted with caution in regard to younger children, and retesting at different ages is worthwhile.

Nonlanguage Learning Disabilities

In the six nonlanguage learning disabilities described in this section—hyperactivity, cerebral palsy, hydrocephalus, autism, fragile-X syndrome, and fetal alcohol syndrome—children have difficulty comprehending aspects of their environment, pretending and anticipating, interpreting the facial and emotional gestures of others, and performing skilled movements. These disabilities can seriously compromise independence in adulthood.

Hyperactive-Child Syndrome

Hyperactive-child syndrome is distinguished from other types of learning disabilities in that an affected child is a behavioral problem in school, and all aspects of school performance are usually disrupted. This syndrome is sometimes called attention-deficit disorder (ADD) or attention-deficit-hyperactivity disorder (ADHD). Hyperactive children may have specific learning disabilities in addition to the hyperactivity, and these disabilities possibly contribute to it.

A number of diagnostic labels have been given to this disorder, including *minimal brain dysfunction*, *hyperkinetic-child syndrome*, and *hyperkinetic impulsive disorder*. The DSM-IV-R lists the following diagnostic criteria:

1. *Excessive general hyperactivity or motor restlessness for the child's age* In preschool and early school years, there may be incessant, haphazard, impulsive running, climbing, or crawling. During middle childhood or adolescence, marked inability to sit still, up-and-down activity, and fidgeting are characteristic. The level of activity differs from the norms for the age both in quality and in quantity.

2. *Difficulty in sustaining attention, such as inability to complete tasks initiated or a disorganized approach to tasks* The child frequently "forgets" demands made or tasks assigned and shows poor attention in unstructured situations or when demands are made for independent, unsupervised performance.

3. *Impulsive behavior*

4. *Duration of at least 1 year*

In infancy, hyperactive children are thought to exhibit poor and irregular sleep, colic, and feeding problems and to not like being cuddled or held still for long. Later, they are described as learning to run rather than to walk and as being driven to handle and play with everything. By the time they reach kindergarten, they are demanding, do not listen, and do not play well with other children. People outside the home may begin to reject a hyperactive child because of his or her behavior.

By the time the child enters school, his or her high level of activity, low tolerance for frustration, poor concentration, and poor self-esteem lead to a referral for assessment. By adolescence, many of these children are failing in school, and from 25% to 50% of them have begun to encounter problems with the law. Their behavior remains restless, they withdraw from school, and they fail to develop social relations and maintain steady employment.

The hyperactive syndrome is the most common behavioral disturbance among children. Estimates of its incidence vary because of different definitions and cultural differences in tolerance of hyperactive behavior. The American Psychiatric Association suggests a prevelance rate of between 3% and 5%, with a higher incidence in boys than in girls.

The suggested causes of hyperactivity include brain damage, encephalitis, genetics, food allergies, high lead concentrations, and various home and school environments. A single cause is unlikely to be responsible for all cases. Andrea Berger and her coworkers propose that circuits in frontal regions of the brain, including the frontal lobe and basal ganglia, evaluate situational contexts from moment to moment to select appropriate motivational, emotional, and cognitive behavior. They suggest that what may be common to all cases of hyperactive syndrome are functional impairments in these self-regulation circuits. Impaired self-regulation leads not only to disruption in ongoing actions but also to failure to learn from experience.

Therapy includes counseling for the child and parents and careful structuring of the home and school environments. Beginning in the 1960s and continuing to the present, treatment with amphetamine-like stimulant drugs such as Ritalin has been popular, although the effectiveness of drug treatment as a long-term solution is controversial. When Ritalin is effective, it may be because, as a stimulant, it allows the person to concentrate on the task at hand. The drug may also have a general sedating effect on prepubescent children.

Cerebral Palsy

Cerebral palsy is a disorder primarily of motor function caused by brain trauma in the course of fetal development or birth. Any simple definition is difficult, however, because (1) the motor symptoms take many forms, (2) there can be various kinds of accompanying cognitive impairments, and (3) the causes are diverse. In consequence, cerebral palsy cannot be accurately called a disease, a syndrome, or even a condition; it will take a different form in each person, depending on the nature of the brain damage. The term "cerebral palsy" is therefore most useful in an administrative sense, as a category of persons who are handicapped in many different ways by motor disorders due to nonprogressive brain abnormalities. Because brain damage is the underlying cause, cerebral palsy is not curable, but it is often amenable to therapy and training.

Cerebral palsy was first described in the medical literature in 1853 by London physician William Little. He recognized that the motor abnormalities of some babies are a result of abnormal parturition, difficult labor, premature birth, or asphyxia. He also recognized the permanence of the disabilities and their associated intellectual impairments; effects on personality (such as irritability and temper tantrums); and epilepsy. More important, he pointed out that these problems could be severely aggravated by subsequent improper training and education.

The incidence of cerebral palsy is estimated at about 6 per 1000 births. The numbers of males and females afflicted are about equal. Estimates of the degree of impairment suggest that about 10% of afflicted persons require no special services, 65% need services on an occasional basis, and about 25% need special schooling or custodial care. When cases of cerebral palsy are categorized by motor symptoms, about 50% of persons with the disorder are spastic (their limbs resist being moved), about 25% are athetoid (they make slow involuntary movements), about 10% are afflicted with rigidity (muscles around joints are stiff), and about 10% are ataxic (have difficulty making voluntary movements).

As noted earlier, cerebral palsy has many causes; the most frequent are listed in **Table 24.3**. Nearly 50% of all cases are due to birth injury or injury suffered during development, 9% are secondary to convulsions, and 8% are due to prematurity. Smaller numbers result from other diverse causes. Incidence is also related to the mother's ability to carry a baby to term and to factors such as her body size, health habits, and weight gain during pregnancy.

Lesions of the corticospinal tracts, basal ganglia, brainstem, and cerebellum are presumed to be responsible for the disorders, but it has been difficult to es-

Table **24.3** Potential causes of cerebral palsy

Hereditary

Static—familial athetosis, familial paraplegia, familial tremor

Progressive—demyelinating diseases of viral or undetermined origin (chromosomal breakages are rare in cerebral palsy, as are disorders of metabolism)

Congenital (acquired in utero)

Infectious rubella, toxoplasmosis, cytomegalic inclusions, herpes simplex, and other viral or infectious agents

Maternal anoxia, carbon monoxide poisoning, strangulation, anemia, hypotension associated with spinal anesthesia, placental infarcts, placenta abruptio

Prenatal cerebral hemorrhage, maternal toxemia, direct trauma, maternal bleeding, diathesis

Prenatal anoxia, twisting or kinking of the cord

Miscellaneous toxins, drugs

Perinatal (obstetrical)

Mechanical anoxia—respiratory obstruction, narcotism due to oversedation with drugs, placenta previa or abruptio, hypotension associated with spinal anesthesia, breech delivery with delay of the after-coming head

Trauma—hemorrhage associated with dystocia, disproportions and malpositions of labor, sudden pressure changes, precipitate delivery, caesarean delivery

Complications of birth—"small for date" babies, prematurity, immaturity, dysmaturity, postmaturity, hyperbilirubinemia and isoimmunization factors (kernicterus due to Rh factor, ABO incompatibility), hemolytic disorders, "respiratory distress" disorders, syphilis, meningitis, and other infections, drug-addiction reactions, hypoglycemic reactions, hypocalcemic reactions

Postnatal–Infancy

Trauma—subdural hematoma, skull fracture, cerebral contusion

Infections—meningitis, encephalitis, brain abscess

Vascular accidents—congenital cerebral aneurism, thrombosis, embolism, hypertensive encephalopathy, sudden pressure changes

Toxins—lead, arsenic, coal-tar derivatives

Anoxia—carbon monoxide poisoning, strangulation, high-altitude and deep-pressure anoxia, hypoglycemia

Neoplastic and late neurodevelopmental defects—tumor, cyst, progressive hydrocephalus

Source: E. Denhoff, Medical aspects. In W. M. Cruickshank, Ed. *Cerebral Palsy.* Syracuse, N.Y.: Syracuse University Press, 1976, p. 3. Reprinted with permission.

tablish clear-cut relations between lesions and clinical findings. There are no specific treatments for cerebral palsy, but physical therapy, small lesions to the spinal cord, and the injection of Botox to immobilize muscles have been used to relieve muscle cramps and to promote movement in immobilized limbs.

Hydrocephalus

Characterized by an increase in the volume of the cerebrospinal fluid (CSF), **hydrocephalus** can be caused in two ways. In one, more likely to develop in adults, enlarged ventricles can be a secondary result of shrinkage or atrophy of surrounding brain tissue. In the other, more typical cause of hydrocephalus— especially in infants—obstruction of the flow of CSF results in a buildup of pressure in one or more ventricles that eventually causes their expansion.

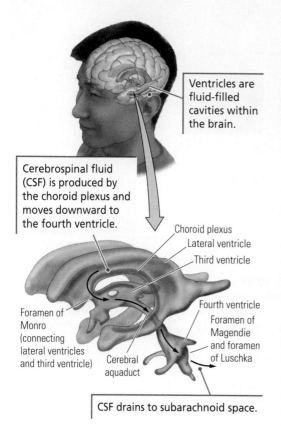

Ventricles are fluid-filled cavities within the brain.

Cerebrospinal fluid (CSF) is produced by the choroid plexus and moves downward to the fourth ventricle.

Choroid plexus
Lateral ventricle
Third ventricle

Foramen of Monro (connecting lateral ventricles and third ventricle)

Cerebral aquaduct

Fourth ventricle
Foramen of Magendie and foramen of Luschka

CSF drains to subarachnoid space.

Figure 24.4

Cerebral Ventricles (Top) Drawing of a cast of the brain's ventricular system viewed laterally. (Bottom) Arrows indicate the direction of flow of cerebrospinal fluid. A blockage of CSF flow in the narrower parts of the ventricles (for example, the cerebral aqueduct) can cause the symptoms of hydrocephalus.

Whether a simple overproduction of CSF is ever a cause of hydrocephalus is uncertain.

Figure 24.4 is a drawing made from a cast of the ventricular system in a normal brain. In a living brain, the ventricles are filled with CSF. The usual amount in an adult is only about 130 cm³, of which about one-third is in the spinal cord's great lumbar cistern. The CSF is made by the choroid plexus in the ventricles, most of it in the lateral ventricles. From there, it flows through the interventricular foramina (windows) of Monro into the third ventricle, through the cerebral aqueduct, and then into the fourth ventricle. It finally escapes through three little holes in the roof of the fourth ventricle. These holes are the two laterally located foramina of Luschka and the medial foramen of Magendie. (The mnemonic is: lateral, Luschka; medial, Magendie.) The fluid then enters the subarachnoid space—the space beneath the arachnoid covering of the brain and spinal cord. It is absorbed into the veins and carried away by the bloodstream.

Circulation in the ventricles can be blocked at either of the interventricular foramina, causing an increase in pressure followed by the expansion of either lateral ventricle. CSF can also be blocked at the level of the cerebral aqueduct (causing hydrocephalus of the first three ventricles) or by closure of the foramina in the roof of the fourth ventricle (producing hydrocephalus of the entire ventricular system). Any sudden obstruction of CSF flow causes a rapid rise in intracranial pressure, ventricular dilation, and finally coma. A gradual obstruction, such as by a tumor, causes a less-rapid increase in pressure and consequent dilation, and the symptoms may include the gradual appearance of visual disturbances, palsies, dementia, and so on.

Infant hydrocephalus, characterized by a conspicuous enlargement of the head, usually develops during the first few months of life. As many as 27 of 100,000 newborn babies may suffer from it. In about 14% of these cases, a malformation impedes CSF circulation; most other cases are produced by inflammation or trauma, although about 4% are due to tumors. As the ventricles distend, they push the cerebral hemispheres into a balloon shape. Because the skull bones of an infant are not yet fused, continued pressure causes the head to expand in all directions. If expansion damages the cortex, intelligence may be impaired and dementia may result; but, if the cortex is not damaged, intelligence may be unimpaired even after the cortex has been stretched into a sheet of tissue less than a centimeter thick.

Hydrocephalus can be treated with some success by the insertion into one lateral ventricle of a valve and a tube that passes into a jugular vein to drain into the cardiac atrium. Untreated, it often causes death or severe mental or motor disabilities.

Autism Spectrum Disorders

The term **autism** was first used by Leo Kanner and Hans Asperger in the 1940s to describe individual children without obvious signs of focal cerebral disease who display such symptoms as severely impaired social interaction, a bizarre and narrow range of interests, language and communication abnormalities, and, in some cases, preserved intellect. Some autistic people are severely impaired, others can function on their own, and still others have exceptional abilities in some areas, such as music, art, or mathematics. The disorder is now referred to as **autism spectrum disorder** to include children with either mild or severe symptoms. Other rare, very severe disorders that are included in the autism spectrum are Rett syndrome, which affects mainly females, and childhood disintegrative disorder, which affects mainly males. If a child's symptoms do not meet the specific criteria for autism, their diagnosis is **pervasive developmental disorder not otherwise specified** (PDD-NOS).

Autism is estimated to affect as many as 1 to 3.5 of every 1,000 children, is four times as prevalent in boys as in girls, and has no known racial, ethnic, or social boundaries. The incidence of autism is reported to have increased dramatically in the past 20 years, but Ashley Wazana and her colleagues calculate that the apparent increase is due to methodological factors such as better reporting and earlier diagnosis.

Many autistic infants behave oddly from birth, avoiding physical contact with caregivers by arching their backs or going limp when held. Approximately one-third of autistic children develop normally until between 1 and 3 years of age, when caregivers begin to notice the autistic symptoms. Common among them are a failure to interact socially and an insistence on sameness. One possible reason for the latter may be an inability to understand and cope with novel situations. Autistic persons may exhibit repeated body movements (hand flapping, rocking), unusual facial movements and features, unusual responses to people or unusual attachments to objects, and resistance to any changes in routine. In some cases, aggressive or self-injurious behavior or both behaviors are seen as well.

Autism is proposed to be under strong genetic influence. It is more likely to develop in two identical twins than in two fraternal twins. The mechanisms of genetic inheritance are not known, and a number of genes and mutations are likely implicated. In some families, autism is highly heritable and, in others, heritability is lower.

There is also evidence that a virus can cause autism: women have an increased risk of having an autistic child after exposure to rubella in the first trimester of pregnancy. Although some voice suspicion that autism can be caused by industrial toxins and other environmental pollutants, the evidence for these causes is uncertain. There has been concern as well that mercury used as a preservative in vaccines can cause autism. Mercury is no longer found in childhood vaccines in the United States, and many well-done, large-scale studies fail to show a link between vaccines and autism.

Extensive research now shows that brain abnormalities of various types correlate with the degree of impairment displayed by an autistic person. For example, impairments in explicit memories (memories for daily events) might be related to temporal-lobe abnormalities, and impairments in implicit memory (skills and conditioned responses) might be related to cerebellar abnormalities.

Evidence that the cerebellum controls conditioned responses suggests that the desire for sameness and the avoidance of novelty also may be related to cerebellar abnormality. One feature of conditioned learning is **habituation**, learning to ignore irrelevant or repeated stimuli. In the absence of an ability to habituate to ongoing events, a person may find such stimuli especially noxious and so avoid them in favor of maintaining sameness. This theory could explain, for example, why autistic people report that the sound of traffic, to which most people quickly habituate, remains for them frighteningly loud.

Although retrospective studies show that head size prebirth in autistic children is normal, by 1 year of age, head size and brain size are larger than normal. This finding suggests that plastic processes related to development, including cell loss and synaptic pruning, are not normal. Such changes in developmental processes would lead to widespread brain abnormalities.

Additionally, more-specific changes in brain structure are hypothesized. John Allman and his colleagues propose that large frontal cortex cells called von Economo neurons fail to develop normally, resulting in abnormal social development in affected persons (see Figure 10.21). Patricia Rodier suggests that one cause of autism may be an abnormality in the expression of genes that play a central role in the development of the brainstem. She finds that an area in the caudal part of the pons is small in autistic subjects and that several nuclei in this area, including the facial nucleus, which controls facial musculature, are small or missing (**Figure 24.5**). Many autistic children have subtle facial abnormalities that may be due to abnormalities of the facial nerve. Perhaps mutation of the *HOSA1* gene, which plays a role in the development of the brainstem, or interference in the expression of this gene is responsible for many cases of autism.

A less-severe condition of withdrawal in children is referred to as **Asperger's syndrome**. These children, although withdrawn, exhibit early speech and good grammar, but they also exhibit narrow repetitive play, poor peer relations, and a need for routine and sameness. They, too, may excel in some aspect of behavior, such as reading, calculations, music, or art. **Hyperlexia** is a term describing unusual reading ability in otherwise cognitively impaired persons, such as children with Asperger's syndrome. It is marked by a precocious

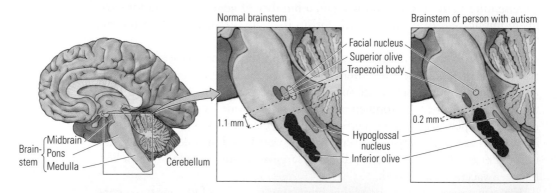

Figure 24.5

Effects of Autism (Top) Autism's effects include changes to the brainstem in which the posterior part of the pons is reduced in size. Several nuclei in this region, including the facial nucleus, superior olive, and trapezoid body, are either smaller than normal or missing. (Bottom) A child with autism is normal in appearance but may have some physical anomalies characteristic of the disorder. The corners of the mouth may be unusually low in relation to the upper lip, the tops of the ears may flop over (left), and the ears may be a bit lower than normal and have an almost square shape (right). (Drawings after Rodier, © 2000 by Scientific American, Inc., all rights reserved; photographs courtesy of Susan L. Hyman.)

development of reading abilities between the ages of 3 and 5 years. Very often the children teach themselves to read.

Related to Asperger's syndrome is **savant syndrome**, or *idiot savant syndrome*, first described by John Langdon Down in 1887. Since then, several hundred cases have been reported in the literature. Affected persons are remarkably similar in that they have a narrow range of special abilities and a common symptomatic triad of retardation, blindness, and musical genius.

In Asperger's and the savant syndromes, exceptional memory abilities can develop, such as an unusual ability to remember words, television shows, names of streets, the weather, birthdays, and so forth. Reading may not be completely fluid, because many of those affected have articulatory defects and prosodic abnormalities of intonation and rate of speech. Generally, comprehension of reading is impaired, and these children show emotional withdrawal, occasional echolalia (repeating words that they hear), and autistic symptoms. Recall Luria's description of S. in Chapter 18 and Dustin Hoffman's portrayal of *Rain Man* pictured in the Portrait at the beginning of this chapter.

The oxymoronic "idiot savant" was coined by combining the word *idiot*, at one time an accepted label for a subcategory of mental retardation, with *savant*, which means a knowledgeable person. The term has endured despite its now pejorative connotation. Savants are characterized by mental handicaps, resulting from a developmental disability or mental illness, combined with a talent that far exceeds their other abilities (talented savants) or the abilities of the general population (prodigious savants). The syndrome affects males about six times as frequently as females. The special skill can appear quite suddenly and disappear equally quickly.

Skills commonly displayed by savants include calendar calculations (some can tell the day of a person's birthday in any year of a 1000-year period); mathematical ability; musical ability, including the ability to play new pieces of music after hearing them once; sculpting; drawing; and peculiar feats of memory, such as memory of what the weather was like on every day of the savant's life, retention of the names of all visitors ever received by the savant and the dates of their visits, and the date of every burial in a parish in a 35-year time span as well as the names of all the attendees.

The causes of precocious abilities displayed by cognitively impaired children are not known. Some suggestions are that these children have islands capable of normal function in an otherwise impaired brain, that through some developmental abnormality they are overdeveloped in some brain areas and underdeveloped in others, or that they are using otherwise adequate brains in a functionally unusual manner.

Fragile-X Syndrome

Fragile-X syndrome is the most common inherited cause of mental impairment. It affects about 1 in 2000 males and 1 in 4000 females. About 1 in 259 women and 1 in 800 men carry the fragile-X gene and could pass it on to their children. Fragile-X syndrome is characterized by facial abnormalities and by mental handicaps ranging from subtle learning disabilities to severe mental retardation and is associated with attention deficits, hyperactivity, anxiety and unstable mood, and autistic-like behaviors. The physical abnormalities include a long face, large ears, flat feet, and hyperextensible joints, especially fingers. Boys are typically more severely affected than girls in that most boys with fragile-X syndrome are typically retarded, whereas only about one-third of affected girls are retarded.

Fragile-X syndrome is caused by an abnormality of the *FMR1* gene, which is located on the long arm of the X chromosome. When functional, this gene encodes a protein (fragile-X protein) that plays a role in the translation of mRNA into protein in neurons and that plays a role in synapse formation and elimination. The mutation occurs in a stretch of CGG repeats in the DNA. This sequence of repeats is prone to increase in length as it is passed from generation to generation.

When the number of repeats exceeds a critical level of about 100, the gene no longer makes a functional protein. Examination of neurons in affected persons at autopsy shows that dendritic spines are poorly formed and more numerous. Thus, the protein encoded by the *FMR1* gene may be required for the normal development and elimination of synapses. MRI scans of children with fragile-X syndrome show thinning of the cortex, an unusually small caudate, and an increase in ventricular size. The increase in ventricular size suggests a general loss of brain cells.

The symptoms of females are generally less severe than those of males because females have two X chromosomes; if one chromosome is abnormal, the other is usually able to manufacture the necessary protein. This difference suggests that—in theory at least—if a normal copy of the *FMR1* gene could be inserted into brain cells, neuronal abnormalities could be reduced. Gene insertion has been achieved in neurons cultured in a dish and in a mouse that had previously lacked the fragile-X gene. Another investigational approach to developing a treatment is based on the fact that the gene is capable of producing the protein but is turned off by the excessive number of CGG repeats. Researchers are exploring the possibility of restoring the gene's function without introducing any new genetic material.

Fetal Alcohol Syndrome

The term **fetal alcohol syndrome** (FAS) was coined by Kenneth Jones and David Smith in 1973 to describe a pattern of physical malformation and mental retardation observed in children born of alcoholic mothers. As illustrated in **Figure 24.6**A, children with FAS may have abnormal facial features including a smooth philtrum (the fissure below the nose), a thin upper lip, and short palpebral fissures (the distance across the eyelids). They also have a range of brain abnormalities, from small brains with abnormal gyri (Figure 24.6B) to

Figure 24.6

Fetal Alcoholism Syndrome

(A) Diagram of the characteristics of FAS in the face of a young child. Discriminating features, which indicate that the child has fetal alcohol syndrome, can be accompanied by associated features. (B) The convolutions characteristic of a normal child's brain (left) are grossly underdeveloped in the brain of a child striken with FAS. (Part A, after Streissguth and Connor, 2001. Part B, University of Washington, School of Medicine.)

(A)

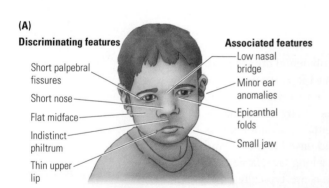

Discriminating features

- Short palpebral fissures
- Short nose
- Flat midface
- Indistinct philtrum
- Thin upper lip

Associated features

- Low nasal bridge
- Minor ear anomalies
- Epicanthal folds
- Small jaw

(B)

brains of normal size with abnormal clusters of cells and misaligned cells in the cortex.

Related to these anatomical abnormalities are certain behavioral symptoms common to FAS children. They have varying degrees of learning disability and lowered intelligence scores, as well as hyperactivity and other social problems. They have other physical symptoms, too, including small size and a tendency to be thin.

The recognition of FAS stimulated widespread interest in the effects of alcohol consumption by pregnant women. Pronounced FAS is found in the offspring of approximately 6% of alcoholic mothers. Its incidence in different geographic regions varies widely, depending largely on the pattern and degree of alcohol abuse in those locations. Ann Streissguth and Paul Connor suggest that from about 1 in 700 to 1 in 100 newborns in the United States have FAS.

Fetal alcohol syndrome is not an "all or none" diagnosis. Alcohol-induced abnormalities can range from hardly noticeable physical and psychological effects to the full-blown FAS syndrome. The severity is thought to be related to when, how much, and how frequently alcohol is consumed in a pregnancy. Apparently, the effects are the worst if drinking takes place in the first 3 months, which, unfortunately, may be a time when many women do not realize that they are pregnant. Severe FAS is also more likely to be caused by binge drinking, which produces high blood-alcohol levels. Other factors related to a more severe outcome are poor nutritional health of the mother and the mother's use of other drugs, including cigarettes.

A major question raised by FAS is how much alcohol is too much to drink during pregnancy. The matter is complex because the effects of alcohol on a fetus depend on so many factors. To be completely safe, it is best not to drink at all in the months preceding pregnancy and during it. This conclusion is supported by findings that as little as one drink of alcohol per day during pregnancy can lead to a decrease in intelligence test scores of children.

Fetal alcohol syndrome in both its full-blown and milder forms has important lessons to teach us. Alcohol is a widely used drug. It poses risks when used inappropriately but, when taken in moderation, is thought to have some health benefits. Even so, it should be avoided completely by women who are pregnant. A major problem is that women who are most at risk for bearing FAS babies are poor and not well educated, with alcohol-consumption problems that predate pregnancy and little access to prenatal care. Often they are unaware of the dangers that alcohol poses to a fetus and do not understand the need to abstain from drinking while they are pregnant.

Developmental Influences on Learning Disabilities

In the early half of the twentieth century, learning disabilities were widely accepted to be inherited. Since then, it has become clear that many factors, including (1) structural damage and toxic effects, (2) hormonal effects, (3) abnormal cerebral lateralization, (4) maturational lag, and (5) environmental deprivation, in addition to (6) genetic influences, influence the incidence of learning disabilities.

Structural Damage and Toxic Effects

When a childhood learning disability—dyslexia is an example—resembles a symptom seen in brain-damaged adults, it is only natural to wonder whether the learning disability was caused by structural damage of a similar nature, perhaps resulting from birth trauma, encephalitis, anoxia, or an early-childhood accident. It is no doubt the case for a small minority of children, but many of the neurological symptoms associated with brain damage in adults are not typically observed in children, suggesting that structural damage is not the likely cause of most childhood learning disorders. For example, children with developmental dyslexia do not have hemianopia (blindness in half of the visual field) or scotomas (blind spots in the visual field), symptoms present in a large percentage of brain-damaged adults with dyslexia. Furthermore, the results of EEG and CT-scan studies do not support a structural-damage hypothesis: abnormal EEGs similar to those correlated with known brain damage are not consistently correlated with learning disabilities.

Other possible causal factors include poor nutrition, drug use, and exposure to environmental contaminants. Clearly, exposure to environmental toxins such as mercury and some other metals can lead to learning disabilities, and exposure to alcohol in utero can cause brain damage and learning disabilities. As is reviewed by Dirk Pallapies, forming one-to-one causal relations between learning disabilities and environmental toxins is difficult. It is hard to identify both the presence and the extent of toxins retrospectively and equally difficult to identify a toxin as a causative agent in a learning disability.

Hormonal Effects: The Geschwind–Galaburda Theory

The Geschwind–Galaburda hypothesis proposes that hormones may affect brain development and learning. The seed of this hypothesis lies in Norman Geschwind's observation that the planum temporale (an area thought to represent speech in the left hemisphere) is asymmetrical, being larger on the left and smaller on the right in most right-handers. This asymmetry is thought to be the basis of the underlying neural asymmetry that gives rise to the left hemisphere's dominant role in language. Because males are thought to show greater deviance from this asymmetrical pattern, the possibility that testosterone plays a role is suggested.

During embryonic development, the male fetal gonads produce high levels of testosterone, comparable to the levels in adult males. The Geschwind–Galaburda hypothesis proposes that the embryonic surges of testosterone delay the development of the left hemisphere, allowing the right hemisphere both space and time for greater development. Thus, males in general have some comparatively better developed areas in the right hemisphere, which would presumably endow them with excellent spatial skills.

If the testosterone-induced asymmetry produces some particularly large right-hemisphere areas, perhaps special abilities, such as precocious mathematical reasoning ability, may result. On the other hand, perhaps testosterone also produces some casualties, characterized by brain abnormalities and learning disabilities. An additional aspect of the hypothesis is that it explains the high incidence of autoimmune disorders (migraines, allergies, asthma, thyroid disorders, ulcerative colitis, and so forth) both among males in general and among males with exceptional abilities. The hypothesis proposes that testosterone also affects the development of the immune system, with a consequent increase in susceptibility to autoimmune disorders.

The appeal of the Geschwind–Galaburda hypothesis is that it can account for the general observation that females tend to do better than males at language-related tasks and males tend to do better than females at spatial tasks. It also accounts for the high incidence both of precocity and of learning disabilities among males. The proposed shift in cerebral dominance further suggests an explanation for the high incidence of left-handedness among the precocious and among the learning-disabled.

And, because the effects of testosterone on the brain will in some ways parallel its effects on the immune system, the hypothesis accounts for the high incidence of autoimmune disease in the precocious and learning-disabled male populations. Additionally, the theory allows for deviations in hormonal functions to produce increased incidences of learning disabilities, precociousness, left-handedness, and autoimmune disorders in females. Another appealing aspect is that the hypothesis is testable and can be explored by using animal models.

The first dissection of the brain of a person with a reading disability was performed on the brain of a 12-year-old boy who died of cerebral hemorrhage (see Drake). The boy's intelligence had been normal, but, in school, he had been impaired in arithmetic, writing, and reading. The autopsy revealed atypical gyral patterns in the parietal lobes, an atrophied corpus callosum, and neurons in the underlying white matter that should have migrated to the cortex.

Later, Albert Galaburda's group examined the brain of a 20-year-old man who had had a reading disability despite average intelligence. Visual inspection showed nothing abnormal, but microscopic examination revealed several abnormalities. Polymicrogyria (numerous small convolutions) and other architectonic abnormalities were found in the left frontal and parietal cortex. The locations of the abnormal brain regions are shown in **Figure 24.7**. Subcortical abnormalities in the medial geniculate nucleus and the lateral posterior nucleus of the thalamus were discovered as well. Since the original study, this group has reported similar findings in other cases.

Abnormal Cerebral Lateralization

A variety of theories rest on Orton's premise that learning disabilities result from slowed cerebral lateralization. This premise is based on the assumption that, because language is lateralized in the left hemisphere of most adults, such lateralization must be advantageous and acquired with language acquisition, and its slowed development would be deleterious to the acquisition of language skills. In the past 50 years, dozens of studies have examined dichotic and visual-field asymmetries, but the data are far from unequivocal. Paul Satz concludes:

> One might ask what light laterality studies shed, if any, on the problem of cerebral dominance and reading disability. The answer should be—not much. The reason for this somewhat discouraging view lies in the numerous methodological and conceptual problems that continue to plague research efforts in this area. (Satz, 1976, p. 288)

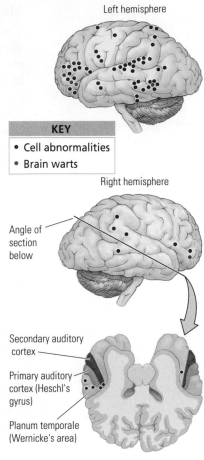

Figure 24.7

Proposed Hormonal Effects

Locations of cell abnormalities found on autopsy in the brain of a person diagnosed as being reading-disabled. The horizontal section illustrates the asymmetrical pattern of the planum temporale in which the dots show areas of cortical anomalies. (After Geschwind and Galaburda, 1985.)

Maturational Lag

The maturational-lag hypothesis postulates that the cognitive functions producing language, reading, and other complex behaviors are organized hierarchically and that the levels of the hierarchy develop sequentially in the course of ontogeny. Should one level of the hierarchy be slow to develop, the development of all subsequent levels will be delayed, inasmuch as higher functions depend on the integrity of lower ones. The original delay in maturation could result from a variety of factors. Two possibilities are delayed myelinization of a particular region and slow development of cortical connections.

Although the results of some studies do suggest that various functions in learning-disabled children are slow in maturing, the type of study needed for a definitive test of this hypothesis is a careful longitudinal analysis of children tested on a large number of perceptual, motor, and cognitive skills for a period of 10 to 15 years. When learning-disabled children have been reexamined in adulthood, they have been found to retain their characteristic impairments even though maturation should have been complete. Nevertheless, there are changes that might support the maturation lag. Gunnel Ingesson reports that, with aging, verbal IQ declines and performance IQ increases. The increase in performance IQ is suggested to correspond to compensatory changes that could overcome some consequences of a learning disability.

Environmental Deprivation

Environmental deprivation can have long-lasting consequences for physical and intellectual function (see Chapters 12 and 23), as is well known. Children raised in orphanages with adequate physical care but without adequate social stimulation fail to thrive. They fall below age norms in both physical and intellectual development. A recent example is that of Romanian orphans. In the 1970s, the Communist regime then governing Romania outlawed all forms of birth control and abortion. The result was hundreds of thousands of unwanted pregnancies, with children placed in orphanages, where the conditions were appalling.

After the Communist government fell and the outside world was able to intervene, hundreds of these children were placed in adoptive homes throughout the world. There have been several studies of the fate of these children. Initially malnourished and small in size, they improved spectacularly in their adoptive homes. Their average height and weight became almost normal, and most achieved normal motor and cognitive development. A significant number were retarded, however, and many had psychosocial problems—difficulty in developing relations with peers and in developing secure attachments with adults. Children who were adopted before 6 months of age had significantly better outcomes than did those adopted at older ages.

People in developed countries continue to adopt children from developing countries—children who have been subjected to various degrees of deprivation. In addition, many children in even the most economically advanced countries suffer varying degrees of deprivation and abuse. Accordingly, environmental deprivation continues to be a leading cause of learning disabilities.

The Birthday Effect

A subtle variant of the deprivation hypothesis is called the **birthday effect**. One perspective on this hypothesis comes from studies undertaken by Roger Barnsley and his colleagues of birthdays of North American hockey players. In senior hockey leagues, there is a negative correlation between birth month and number of players. More than 30% of players have birth dates in the first quarter of the year (16% in January), whereas fewer than 15% have birth dates in the last quarter of the year (5% in December). Furthermore, a disproportionate number of the superstars have first-quarter birthdays.

This birth discrepancy is not present in beginning leagues but emerges progressively as players are promoted through the leagues. The explanation appears to be straightforward. Players enter the most junior league according to age—children must be 8 years old between January 1 and December 31 of the year in which they enter Mite hockey. Equal numbers of children born in each month enter. But children born in December enter hockey almost a year earlier than children born in January, who in effect have had to wait a year. The younger, smaller children are at a developmental disadvantage from the outset. They receive less playing time and reinforcement and are more likely to drop out.

Research on the effects of relative age on educational achievement produce similar results. Lars Lien and his coworkers find that children entering school at a younger age perform at a significantly lower level than do their older classmates and have more emotional problems. Thus, maturational age, although not a primary factor in learning disabilities, could aggravate performance of learning-disabled children.

Genetic Bases of Learning Disabilities

Any consideration of the possibility that learning disorders have a genetic basis must recognize some of the obstacles to demonstrating such a hypothesis:

- The environment can affect development in many ways. Consequently, it is extremely difficult to separate environmental influences from genetic effects in any kind of research.

- Learning disabilities take many forms. At present, criteria for categorizing types of learning disabilities are poorly developed, which makes it difficult for researchers to correlate specific types of disabilities with specific causes.

- The incidence of learning disabilities is related to the quality of schooling. The average length of schooling and the demands made by schools on students have changed greatly in the past two generations; so it is difficult to compare the reading abilities of children with those of their parents.

- Learning-disabled children are typically of average intelligence, as are their parents (that is, their overall IQs are about 100), and people with strictly average IQs generally find school difficult, even when no specific disability exists.

- The ability to read is itself probably inherited, making it difficult to sort out the contribution made by inherited reading skill from that made by a supposedly inherited causal factor underlying a disability.

Despite the difficulties of obtaining meaningful research results, the possibility of genetic causes has been raised repeatedly, as evidenced in the preceding sections on the hyperactive syndrome and autistic spectrum disorders, and in Ms. P.'s case in the Portrait at the beginning of the chapter. Since the early twentieth century, many authors have referred to the high incidence of learning disabilities within certain families, and studies of twins have found a higher incidence of dyslexia in identical compared with fraternal twins. Many genes are likely implicated in learning disorders (see Asherson and Curran). The results of different studies of families with a high incidence of reading disabilities suggest that genes on chromosomes 1, 2, 6, and 15 may be related to the disorder. As our understanding of genes and their influence advances, it is quite possible that hundreds rather than just a few genetic abnormalities will prove to be associated with learning disabilities.

Adult Outcome of Learning Disabilities

There are a variety of views about the outcome of children with learning disabilities. In the most optimistic outcome study, reported by MacDonald Critchley, 20 dyslexic boys attended a private school and received special instruction using training methods. As adults, two of the boys became medical doctors, two college professors, one a lawyer, two research scientists, six owners or managers of businesses, one a school principal, three teachers, one an actor, one a factory foreman, and one a skilled laborer. The popular press periodically reports similar, though perhaps not so absolute, successes at various private schools for learning-disabled children.

Most studies do not report such optimistic outcomes, however, and the most thorough of them reaches frankly pessimistic conclusions concerning academic outcome. Otfried Spreen examined the progress of 203 learning-disabled people over a long period, deriving the following findings from assessments, personal interviews, parental interviews, and other observations and data:

1. Persons in all but the control group suffered through a miserable and usually short school career and then experienced a miserable social life full of disappointments and failures. They also had a relatively poor chance of obtaining advanced training and skilled employment. They did not, however, have a higher incidence of juvenile delinquency or psychiatric problems.

2. Interviewed separately, subjects and their parents were largely in agreement concerning factual information, but parents tended to regard the learning disabilities as having had more serious effects on the well-being, happiness, and social interaction of their children than were reported by the children themselves. The affected children also had less-detailed memories of their childhood than the control children did. As the subjects aged, they developed firmer plans for their future and made better occupational adjustments, but they also gave increasingly negative descriptions of their school experiences. The eventual social adjustments of the females were worse than those of the males.

3. Although the learning-disabled eventually managed to make personal adjustments and find jobs, their dislike of school and dissatisfaction with it persisted.

We end this section by emphasizing the importance of careful assessment in evaluating the particular cognitive deficits of each learning-disabled child. After problem areas are identified, specialized teaching programs can be devised to circumvent handicaps. There may be little point in trying to teach a given child a particular skill that he or she is clearly not capable of learning. Perhaps the educational program for that child should instead be directed toward the acquisition of skills that can be used to gain employment. Counseling is an important part of the educational process both for the learning-disabled child and for the parents. It should focus not only on overcoming negative attitudes toward the educational system but also on understanding the child's unique handicaps and on devising strategies for circumventing some of them.

Summary

Learning Disabilities

A variety of disorders appear in childhood and interfere with progress in school and in social adjustments. The acquisition of reading is central in school, and so disorders that result in reading impairments are understandably an obstacle to satisfactory academic progress.

Reading Disabilities

Reading is a complex activity that can be disrupted in many different ways. Research focuses on causes that include deficits in phonological awareness, deficits in attention shifting, impairments in rapid sensory discrimination, and impairments in fine motor skills.

Nonlanguage Learning Disabilities

A number of common nonverbal disabilities lead to academic and social difficulties. Many of these conditions are associated with general diffuse damage that varies from case to case. Causes include gene-

tically based abnormalities in brain development, brain injury in utero, and deleterious environmental influences including the use of alcohol during pregnancy.

Developmental Influences on Learning Disabilities

A variety of environmental conditions can influence brain function and developmental success, including brain injury, toxins, drugs, and environmental deprivation. Even somewhat more subtle influences such as the age at which a child begins school can have a surprisingly large effect on school success.

Adult Outcome of Learning Disabilities

Although people with learning disabilities that are not severe do make adequate adjustments in later life, their disability and negative experiences in learning have a lasting effect. People with severe learning disabilities need various degrees of life-long assistance or care.

References

Allman, J. M., K. K. Watson, N. A. Tetreault, and A. Y. Hakeem. Intuition and autism: A possible role for von Economo neurons. *Trends in Cognitive Sciences* 9:367–373, 2005.

Asherson, P. J., and S. Curran. Approaches to gene mapping in complex disorders and their application in child psychiatry and psychology. *British Journal of Psychiatry* 179:122–128, 2001.

Barnsley, R. H., A. H. Thompson, and P. E. Barnsley. Hockey success and birth date: The relative age effect. *Canadian Association of Health, Physical Education, and Recreation*, November–December, 1985, pp. 23–27.

Bauman, M. L., and T. L. Kempor. *The Neurobiology of Autism.* Baltimore: Johns Hopkins University Press, 1994.

Benton, A. *Right–Left Discrimination and Finger Localization.* New York: Hoeber-Harper, 1959.

Berger, A., O. Kofman, U. Livneh, and A. Henik. Multidisciplinary perspectives on attenton and the development of self-regulation. *Progress in Neurobiology* 82:256–286, 2007.

Bradley, L., and P. E. Bryant. Categorizing sounds and learning to read: A causal connection. *Nature* 301:419–421, 1983.

Cobrinik, L. Unusual reading ability in severely disturbed children. *Journal of Autism and Childhood Schizophrenia* 4:163–175, 1974.

Connor, C. M., F. J. Morrison, B. J. C. Fishman, C. Schatschneider, and P. Underwood. Algorithm-guided individualized reading instruction. *Science* 315:464–465, 2007.

Critchley, M. *Developmental Dyslexia.* Springfield, Ill. Charles C Thomas, 1964.

Cruickshank, W. M., Ed. *Cerebral Palsy.* Syracuse, NY: Syracuse University Press, 1976.

Drake, W. Clinical and pathological findings in a child with a developmental learning disability. *Journal of Learning Disabilities* 1:468–475, 1968.

Dufor, O., W. Serniclaes, L. Sprenger-Charolles, and J.-F. Démonet. Top-down processes during auditory phoneme categorization in dyslexia: A PET study. *Neuroimage* 34:1692–1707, 2007.

Fawcett, A. J., and R. I. Nicolson. Dyslexia, learning, and pedagogical neuroscience. *Developmental Medicine and Child Neurology* 49:306–311, 2007.

Frith U. What framework should we use for understanding developmental disorders? *Developmental Neuropsychology* 20:555–563, 2001.

Fry, E. A do-it-yourself terminology generator. *Journal of Reading* 11:428–430, 1968.

Gaddes, W. H. *Learning Disabilities and Brain Function.* New York: Springer, 1980.

Galaburda, A. M., J. LoTurco, F. Ramus, R. H. Fitch, and G. D. Rosen. From genes to behavior in developmental dyslexia. *Nature Neuroscience* 9:1213–1217, 2006.

Geschwind, N., and A. M. Galaburda. *Cerebral Lateralization.* Cambridge, Mass.: MIT Press, 1985.

Gould, S. J. *The Mismeasure of Man.* New York: Norton, 1981.

Hari, R., and H. Renvall. Impaired processing of rapid stimulus sequences in dyslexia. *Trends in Cognitive Sciences* 15:525–532, 2001.

Huelsman, C. B. The WISC syndrome for disabled readers. *Perceptual and Motor Skills* 30:535–550, 1970.

Ingesson, S. G. Stability of IQ measures in teenagers and young adults with developmental dyslexia. *Dyslexia* 12:81–95, 2006.

Langmore, S. E., and G. J. Canter. Written spelling deficit of Broca's aphasics. *Brain and Language* 18:293–314, 1983.

Leonard, C. M., K. K. Voeller, L. J. Lombardino, et al. Anomalous cerebral structure in dyslexia revealed with magnetic resonance imaging. *Archives of Neurology* 50:461–469, 1993.

Lien, L., K. Tambs, B. Oppedal, S. Heyerdahl, and E. Bjertness. Is relatively young age within a school year a risk factor for mental health problems and poor school performance? A population-based cross-sectional study of adolescents in Oslo, Norway. *BMC Public Health* 5:102, 2005.

Little, W. J. *Deformities of the Human Frame.* London: Longmans, 1853.

Lorber, J. The results of early treatment of extreme hydrocephalus. *Developmental Medicine and Child Neurology Supplement* 16:21–29, 1968.

Lyle, J. G., and J. D. Goyen. Performance of retarded readers on the WISC and educational tests. *Journal of Abnormal Psychology* 74:105–112, 1969.

National Assessment of Educational Progress, The Nation's Report Card (National Center for Education Statistics, Washington, D.C., 2005).

Orton, S. T. *Reading, Writing, and Speech Problems in Children.* New York: Norton, 1937.

Pallapies D. Trends in childhood disease. *Mutation Research* 28:100–111, 2006.

Ramus, F., S. Rosen, S. C. Dakin, B. L. Day, J. M. Castellote, S. White, and U. Frith. Theories of developmental dyslexia: Insights from a multiple case study of dyslexic adults. *Brain* 126:841–865, 2003.

Rodier, P. M. The early origins of autism. *Scientific American* 282(2):56–63, 2000.

Rosensweig, M. R., D. Krech, E. L. Bennett, and M. C. Diamond. Effects of environmental complexity and training on brain chemistry and anatomy: A replication and extension. *Journal of Comparative and Physiological Psychology* 55:427–429, 1962.

Rugel, R. P. WISC subtest scores of disabled readers: A review with respect to Bannatyne's categorization. *Journal of Learning Disability* 17:48–55, 1974.

Rutter, M., and W. Yule. The concept of specific reading retardation. *Journal of Child Psychology and Psychiatry* 16:181–197, 1975.

Satz, P. Cerebral dominance and reading disability: An old problem revisited. In R. M. Knights and D. J. Bakker, Eds. *The Neuropsychology of Learning Disorders.* Baltimore: University Park Press, 1976.

Schmitt, A. J., and D. L. Wodrich. Validation of a developmental neuropsychological assessment (NEPSY) through comparison of neurological, scholastic concerns, and control groups. *Archives of Clinical Neuropsychology* 19(8):1077–1093, 2004.

Semrud-Clikeman, M., and G. W. Hynd. Right hemispheric dysfunction in nonverbal learning disabilities: Social, academic, and adaptive functioning in adults and children. *Psychological Bulletin* 107:196–209, 1990.

Skottun, B. C., and J. Skoyles. Yellow filters, magnocellular responses, and reading. *International Journal of Neuroscience* 117:287–293, 2007.

Spreen, O. *Learning Disabled Children Growing Up.* New York: Oxford University Press, 1988.

Streissguth, A. P., and P. D. Connor. Fetal alcohol syndrome and other effects of prenatal alcohol: Developmental cognitive neuroscience implications. In C. A. Nelson and M. Luciana, Eds. *Handbook of Developmental Cognitive Neuroscience.* Cambridge, Mass.: MIT Press, 2001, pp. 505–518.

Tallal, P., and N. Gaab. Dynamic auditory processing, musical experience and language development. *Trends in Neuroscience* 29:382–390, 2006.

Tallal, P., S. Miller, and R. H. Fitch. Neurobiological basis of speech: A case for the preeminence of temporal processing. In P. Tallal, A. M. Galaburda, R. R. Llinas, and C. von Euler, Eds. *Temporal Information Processing in the Nervous System.* New York: New York Academy of Sciences, 1993.

Treffert, D. A. The idiot savant: A review of the syndrome. *American Journal of Psychiatry* 145:563–572, 1988.

Vlachos, F., I. Papathanasiou, and G. Andreou. Cerebellum and reading. *Folia Phoniatrica et Logopaedica* 59:177–183, 2007.

Wazana, A., M. Bresnahan, and J. Kline. The autism epidemic: Fact or artifact? *Journal of the American Academy of Child Adolescent Psychiatry* 46:721–730, 2007.

Whishaw, I. Q., and B. Kolb. Neuropsychological assessment of children and adults with developmental dyslexia. In R. N. Malatesha and H. A. Whitaker, Eds. *Dyslexia: A Global Issue.* The Hague: Martinus Nijhoff, 1984.

Zaidel, E. The split and half brains as models of congenital language disability. In C. L. Ludlow and M. E. Doran-Quine, Eds. *The Neuropsychological Basis of Language Disorders in Children.* Bethesda, Md.: National Institute of Neurological and Communicative Disorders and Stroke, 1978.

Zangwill, O. L., and C. Blakemore. Dyslexia: Reversal of eye-movements during reading. *Neuropsychologia* 10:371–373, 1972.

25 Plasticity, Recovery, and Rehabilitation of the Adult Brain

PORTRAIT: A Casualty of War

In the World War II battle of Smolensk in 1943, a bullet fractured the skull of soldier Lyova Saletsky, injuring the brain within. The damage was centered in the posterior left-hemisphere intersections of the occipital, temporal, and parietal cortex. Alexander Luria first examined Saletsky 3 months after the injury and then at 3-week intervals for the next 26 years, after which Luria wrote a wonderful little book, *The Man with a Shattered World.*

In these 26 years, Saletsky painfully and slowly recovered the ability to read and write—in the process, compiling a diary that gives a moving account of his initial deficits, slow recovery, and residual problems. The following excerpt exemplifies what Saletsky had to say about his condition:

I remember nothing, absolutely nothing! Just separate bits of information that I sense have to do with one field or another. But that's all! I have

© ISM/Phototake

no real knowledge of any subject. My past has just been wiped out! Before my injury I understood everything people said and had no trouble learning any of the sciences. Afterwards I forgot everything I learned about science. All my education was gone.

I know that I went to elementary school, graduated with honors from the middle school, completed three years of courses at the Tula Polytechnic Institute, did advanced work in chemistry, and before the war, finished all these requirements ahead of

time. I remember that I was on the western front, was wounded in the head in 1943 when we tried to break through the Germans' defense in Smolensk, and that I've never been able to put my life together again. But I can't remember what I did or studied, the sciences I learned, subjects I took. I've forgotten everything. Words like *trigonometry, solid geometry, chemistry, algebra,* etc., come to mind, but I have no idea what they mean. (Luria, 1972, pp. 140–142)

Saletsky improved considerably in the 26 years of Luria's study, but he could never return to his original level of functioning. Luria summed up Saletsky's problems when he wrote, "The damaged areas of the cerebral cortex could not be restored. Hence when he tried to think, his mind had to detour around these scorched areas and employ other faculties with which to learn and try to recover some lost skills" (Luria, 1972, p. 158).

Saletsky's case, described in the Portrait, vividly illustrates the difficulty of stimulating functional recovery after brain injury. After a healthy brain has been injured, it will always be coping with damaged circuits. Nonetheless, there is often some restitution of function, in part because of the plastic properties of the brain and in part because brain-injured people learn to compensate, or, as Luria put it, "detour around these scorched areas."

In this chapter, we begin by considering the nature of plasticity in the normal adult brain. We then examine how the brain responds to injury and, finally, how various forms of rehabilitation may be used to stimulate change in the brain.

Cortical Plasticity in the Intact Adult Brain

The nervous system is not static but rather changes with time. This capacity to change, one of the system's most basic characteristics, can be seen in even the simplest of organisms, such as the tiny worm *Caenorhabditis elegans*, which has only 302 neurons (for a comprehensive survey of plasticity, see Shaw and McEachern). For example, *C. elegans* can learn to make associations between sensory events, such as smells, and consequences, such as mild shocks (Morrison and van der Kooy, 2001).

For the animal to learn such associations, the nervous system must undergo some type of change that can code them. Thus, as a general rule, we can say that behavioral changes, described (depending on the circumstances) as learning, memory, addiction, maturation, recovery, and so on, are accompanied by corresponding changes in the nervous system. To understand processes such as memory and addiction, it is therefore necessary to understand the nature of the brain's plasticity.

Neural plasticity can be studied at many levels, from observable behavioral changes to cerebral maps, synaptic organization, physiological organization, molecular structure, and mitosis. We consider each level in turn.

Caenorhabditis elegans, a small roundworm about 1 millimeter long that lives in soil, was the first species to have all its neurons, synapses, and genome described. (© Carolina Biological/Visuals Unlimited.)

Inferring Plasticity from Changes in Behavior

Learning and remembering new information must entail some kind of change in the cells of the nervous system. Such changes are presumed to constitute the neural record of the learned information. A comprehensive survey of what the study of behavioral change has contributed to the research on nervous system plasticity is beyond the scope of this discussion, but an example will serve to illustrate how such research is done.

Humans show a remarkable ability to adapt to a visually rearranged world. For example, Wolfgang Köhler fitted subjects with special glasses made of prisms that inverted the visual field and reversed left and right so that the subjects saw the world upside down and backward. For the first few days of constantly wearing these glasses, a subject's struggle to navigate an upside-down, backward world was confusing and debilitating, but, within a few days, the world seemed to right itself. The subject was once again able to dress, eat, walk about, and perform other daily activities with ease. Eventually, subjects could even perform complex activities such as skiing and riding a bicycle. When the glasses were finally removed, the subjects again needed time to adjust, because the world again appeared distorted to them, just as when they had first been fitted with the prisms.

The adaptation of Köhler's subjects to the transformed visual world included several behavioral changes, each associated with changes in certain regions of the brain (Sugita, 2001). One of these regions is the premotor cortex. If normal monkeys are fitted with adapting prisms, the monkeys adapt to the change just as the human subjects did; but, if a monkey's premotor cortex has been inactivated, the animal has great difficulty adapting. Another locus of change is the posterior parietal cortex. Dottie Clower and her colleagues used PET to locate changes in regional blood flow in subjects adapting to prisms and found that, when the subjects used their eyes to guide them in reaching for objects, activation in the posterior parietal cortex greatly increased.

The properties of cells in the visual cortex were found to change as monkeys adapt to prisms (Sugita, 2001). Normally, cells in area V1 would respond only to cells in the contralateral visual field, but, with adaptation, the cells began to respond to stimuli in the ipsilateral field as well. These changes disappeared soon after the prisms were removed. Parallel changes were also seen in other ventral-stream pathways, such as area V4.

Whatever the plastic changes are that support prism adaptation, they presumably correspond to changes in synaptic organization, although the consistency and dependability of adaptation in both humans and monkeys suggest that the connections necessary for the adaptation are already in place. If so, adaptation would be a matter of enhancing the efficiency of these connections relative to the connections used for seeing the "normal" visual world.

Much remains to be learned about the nature of the plastic changes in the visually adapting brain; but, clearly, by studying novel situations in which behavior changes in dramatic ways, researchers are able to make inferences about the plastic properties of the nervous system. An understanding of such processes not only is of general interest with respect to how the normal brain functions but can also be a source of insight into ways of stimulating functional recovery after injury. Recall, for example, that Yves Rossetti used prism adaptation as a way of stimulating recovery from contralateral neglect in stroke patients (see Chapter 22).

Plasticity in Cortical Maps

As described in Chapters 8 and 10, each sensory system has multiple maps providing topographic representations of the external world. The homunculi in the motor and somatosensory cortices serve as excellent examples of these representations (see Chapter 8). The size and organization of motor maps can be determined by stimulating the cortex either directly, with microelectrodes, or transcranially, by using magnetic stimulation to induce movements or by using functional imaging to map the areas activated when subjects are engaged in different behaviors.

The results of studies in rats, monkeys, and humans demonstrate that specific motor training can increase the size of different components of the motor maps. Recall from Chapter 23 that the motor maps of violinists have a larger representation of the digits of the left hand than do the motor maps of nonmusicians. Randy Nudo and his colleagues used a direct method to examine motor-map changes in squirrel monkeys that they trained to retrieve food objects from either small or large wells. To obtain food from the small wells, the animals had to use a pincer grasp of the digits; to obtain food from the large wells, they used gross movements of the whole hand and wrist. As illustrated in **Figure 25.1**, when the researchers mapped the motor cortex with microelectrodes, they found that the area representing the digits was increased in the animals making digit movements, whereas no similar change took place in animals making larger movements.

Like motor maps, sensory maps are modified by experience. For example, Christo Pantev and his colleagues used MEG to show a 25% increase in the

(A)

Difficult task

One group of monkeys was trained to retrieve food from a small well.

Simple task

Another group of monkeys was trained to retrieve food from a large well.

(B)

The motor representation of digit, wrist, and arm was mapped.

KEY

■ Digit   ■ Wrist/forearm   ▨ Digit, wrist, and forearm

The digit representation in the brain of the animal with the more difficult task is larger, corresponding to the neuronal changes necessary for the acquired skill.

cortical representation for the musical scale in musicians compared with nonmusicians. This enlargement correlated with the age at which the musicians began to practice music. Josef Rauschecker, who notes that early blindness results in an expansion of the auditory-responsive areas in the parietal and occipital lobes (areas that would not have auditory functions in sighted people), goes as far as to claim that this finding lends credibility to the generalization that blind people have greater musical abilities.

Plasticity in somatosensory representations has been extensively studied by Michael Merzenich and his colleagues, who showed that the organization of the maps can be changed by the manipulation of afferent inputs to the cortex. For example, if the afferent nerve from one or more digits is cut, the representation of the remaining digits expands, presumably allowing greater sensitivity in those digits. Furthermore, if two digits are sewn together, a single digit area replaces the two formerly separate digit areas on the map.

A similar fusion of digit representation has been found in humans born with webbed fingers. If the digits are then separated surgically, the map reorganizes to produce a separate field for each (Moligner et al., 1993). In the same vein, Annette Sterr and her colleagues, studying Braille readers, found that extensive stimulation of one or more digits can increase the relative representation of those digits.

Such changes are not always adaptive. Focal hand dystonia, the loss of motor control of one or more digits, can result from repetitive synchronous movements of the digits, such as those made by musicians in a lifetime of playing. Thomas Elbert and his colleagues studied the somatosensory maps of musicians with focal hand dystonia and found that they contained smaller-than-normal distances between the representations of the digits, much as in people with webbed fingers. Presumably, the musical training inadvertently caused the mapped representations of the digits to fuse. A logical extrapolation of this finding is that dystonia should be treatable by training affected persons to make independent asynchronous finger movements. Indeed, Victor Candia and his colleagues found it to be the case.

Figure 25.1

Effects of Motor Training
(A) To test the differential effects of motor-skill acquisition and motor use on the functional organization of the squirrel monkey motor cortex, the training procedures consisted of practice retrieving small food pellets from either a small or a large well. The monkey is able to insert the entire hand into the large well but only one or two fingers into the small well. (B) Maps of brain activity during forelimb movements, produced by microelectrode stimulation of the cortex, show systematic neural changes in the animals trained with the small well but not with the large one. (After Nudo et al., 1997.)

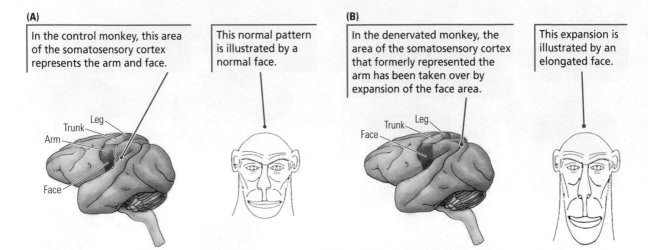

(A)

In the control monkey, this area of the somatosensory cortex represents the arm and face.

This normal pattern is illustrated by a normal face.

Leg
Trunk
Arm
Face

(B)

In the denervated monkey, the area of the somatosensory cortex that formerly represented the arm has been taken over by expansion of the face area.

This expansion is illustrated by an elongated face.

Trunk
Leg
Face

Figure 25.2

Somatosensory Plasticity The neural face representations, mapped by electrical recordings in a normal (A) and a denervated (B) monkey, are shown right side up for simplicity. Note in part B that only the lower part of the face area has expanded. (After Pons et al., 1991, p. 1858.)

One of the best-known examples of somatosensory plasticity is described repeatedly in the extensive literature concerning studies of people and monkeys with amputations. In a classic study, Tim Pons and his colleagues mapped the somatosensory representation of monkeys that had been deprived of somatosensory input to one limb by a nerve transection 12 years earlier. The researchers found that the denervated hand and arm area responded to tactile stimulation of the face on the affected side of the body. What was most surprising, however, was that the changes in the map were very large—covering more than 1 cm—as shown in **Figure 25.2**. The major change was an expansion of the face area to invade the denervated limb area.

Parallel studies have been done with people and have yielded similar results (see review by Elbert et al.). But what happens to the original map? Vilayanur Ramachandran and William Hirstein demonstrated that the original maps are still present and can be detected by lightly stimulating the face (**Figure 25.3**). Studies by others document similar rearrangements of sensory maps subse-

Figure 25.3

Mapping an Amputated Hand (A) When an amputee is stroked lightly on the face with a cotton swab, he or she experiences the sensation of the missing hand being lightly touched. (B) Touching different parts of the face and noting what part of the hand each touch evokes allow a representation of the hand to be mapped on the face. As in the normal somatosensory cortex map, the area representing the thumb is disproportionately large. (After Ramachandran and Hirstein, 1998, p. 1603.)

(A)

Cotton swab

(B)

Thumb
Ball of thumb
Index finger
Pinkie finger

quent to the amputation of other body parts. Salvatore Aglioti found that, in women who have undergone bilateral mastectomies, the nipples, interestingly enough, seem to relocate to the ear lobes.

Plasticity in Synaptic Organization

Synaptic organization has been studied by using Golgi-type stains to reveal dendritic arborization and by using electron-microscope technology to inspect synapse number and size. Inasmuch as both these approaches require postmortem tissue, the number of studies of synaptic changes in human brains has necessarily been limited.

In one series of human synapse studies, Bob Jacobs and Arnold Scheibel examined the dendritic structure of neurons in different cortical regions taking part in different computational tasks. They were looking for a relation between the complexity of dendritic arborization in a given area and the nature of the computational task performed there. For example, when they compared the structure of neurons from the somatosensory representation of the trunk with the structure of neurons from the somatosensory representation of the fingers, they found greater complexity in the latter group of cells. They reasoned that the computational challenge to cortical neurons by somatosensory inputs from receptive fields on the chest wall must be less than that from the inputs from the fingers, and so the neurons representing the chest are less complex (**Figure 25.4**). Similarly, when they compared the cells in the finger area with those in the supramarginal gyrus, a region of the parietal lobe associated with higher cognitive processes (that is, with thinking), they found the neurons in the supramarginal gyrus to be more complex.

A second hypothesis was that dendritic trees in all regions are subject to experience-dependent change. As a result, Jacobs and his colleagues predicted, predominant life experiences, such as a person's occupation, should alter the structure of dendritic trees. Although they did not test this hypothesis directly, they did make an interesting observation. In comparing cells in the trunk area, finger area, and supramarginal gyrus, they found curious individual differences. For example, especially large differences in trunk and finger neurons were found in the brains of people who had achieved a high level of finger dexterity and maintained it for long periods (as would a typist). In contrast, no trunk–finger difference was found in the brain of a person whose career as a sales representative did not require a high degree of specialized finger use and thus made less-complex demands on the finger neurons.

The results of Golgi-type studies of the brain tissue of laboratory animals support

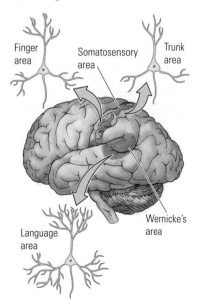

Figure 25.4

Experience and Neuronal Complexity Evidence of Jacobs and Scheibel's hypothesis that cell complexity is related to the computational demands on the cell. Cells that represent the trunk area of the body perform less-demanding computations than are performed by cells representing the finger region and are therefore less complex in structure. In contrast, cells engaged in higher-level cognitive functions (such as language, in Wernicke's area) perform more-demanding computations than are performed by cells engaged in finger functions and are even more complex in structure.

these conclusions. Experience-dependent changes have been seen in every species of animal tested, from fruit flies and bees to rats, cats, and monkeys (for a review, see Kolb and Whishaw).

Plasticity in Physiological Organization

The general hypothesis tested in physiological studies of brain plasticity is that the nervous system can be changed by electrical stimulation. Two primary examples of such change are long-term potentiation and kindling.

A brief, high-frequency, electrical stimulation applied to the hippocampus resulted in a long-term change in the efficiency of the synapses that were activated by the stimulation (Bliss and Lømo, 1973), a phenomenon called **long-term potentiation** (LTP). Brief pulses of current were delivered to a neuron for a period of a few seconds, and the magnitude of the response was recorded from neurons known to receive projections from the stimulated neuron (**Figure 25.5**A). After a stable baseline of response (the excitatory postsynaptic potential, or EPSP) to the stimulation was established, the stimulation was changed to a burst of high frequency, driving the system very hard. (The high-frequency stimulation can be thought of as a "training stimulus.") After a brief rest period, the original test pulse was presented again, and this time the magnitude of the response (that is, the EPSP) was greater than before.

Under optimal experimental conditions, this enhanced response can persist indefinitely and can be shown to correlate with changes in dendritic length and spine density in the postsynaptic neuron (see Figure 25.5B). This synaptic change has been adopted by many as a general model of how simple learning (if not more-complex forms of learning) might take place, although it has been viewed with skepticism by many others. In any case, LTP remains an important example of synaptic plasticity, is now known to be a characteristic of cells in the cerebral neocortex and hippocampus, and has been shown to correlate with various molecular changes as well as changes in dendritic morphology (see reviews by Cain and by Teyler).

Kindling refers to the development of persistent seizure activity after repeated exposure to an initially subconvulsant stimulus. This phenomenon was first

(A) Enhanced response
Procedure

1 A stimulation electrode is placed in one set of neurons...

2 ...and a recording electrode is placed in another set known to receive projections from the first.

Stimulating electrode

Recording electrode

Presynaptic cell

Postsynaptic cell

Results

3 A weak test stimulation produces an excitatory postsynaptic potential (EPSP).

4 After a strong burst of stimulation, the original test stimulation was repeated and the EPSP from the postsynaptic cell was recorded. Long-term potentiation (LTP) had resulted.

(B) Enhanced synaptic formation
Dendrite before stimulation

Dendrite 30 minutes after stimulation

About 30 minutes after stimulation,...

...two new spines appeared on the postsynaptic dendrite.

Figure **25.5**

Demonstrating Long-Term Potentiation (A) Each dot on the graph represents the size of an EPSP in response to a single test stimulus. (B) New dendritic spines can grow in conjunction with LTP.

described by Graham Goddard, who inadvertently discovered that repeated stimulation of the amygdala, though initially having little behavioral effect, would eventually produce epileptic seizures. Goddard chose the name *kindling* as an analogy to starting a fire with an initially ineffective bit of fuel.

Like LTP, kindling is presumed to activate mechanisms similar to those activated for at least some kinds of learning. It can be demonstrated in most forebrain structures and, like LTP, is associated with a change in synaptic organization and with a variety of molecular-level events, such as the production of growth factors (for a review, see Teskey). Both LTP and kindling have been studied for more than three decades, leading to a substantial body of literature on both. Their connection with behavior, however, is still a matter of some conjecture, although both techniques have begun to be used to study functional plasticity after cerebral injury.

Plasticity in Molecular Structure

The studies using maps, Golgi stains, or physiological techniques to show that the brain changes in response to experience are phenomenological: they describe and classify but do not explain. If we wish to know why the brain changes or understand how, we need to look at the mechanisms that actually produce synaptic change. In the final analysis, we must look at how different proteins are produced, which ultimately means looking at the effects of experience on genes.

The development of new techniques of genetic screening—for example, *gene-chip arrays*—has allowed researchers to take bits of brain tissue and use them to analyze which genes have been affected by a particular experience. In these techniques, a miniature grid (on a chip about 1 cm in diameter) that can identify as many as 10,000 genes, each in a different location on the grid, is exposed to a homogenate of tissue. If certain genes are present in the tissue, they will react with a substance at one of the locations on the chip. Such techniques are undoubtedly powerful, providing a lot of information about which genes change when, for example, an animal is housed in a complex rather than a deprived environment; but, as yet, what the changes actually tell us about brain function is far from clear. For example, rats placed in complex environments for different lengths of time significantly increased the activity of more than 100 genes (of 11,000 genes screened in a study by Rampon et al.) in response to the experience.

In short, knowing that genes change is only the start. The real question is what the changes mean. Nonetheless, the effort to understand how genes are altered by experience is an important step in understanding how to enhance (or reduce) plastic changes in the brain, especially the changes that take place after injury.

Mitotic Activity

A real surprise of the late 1990s was the discovery that not only is the adult brain capable of manufacturing new neurons and glia but the generation of new cells is affected by experience. Both the olfactory bulbs and the hippocampus of mammals, including humans, incorporate new neurons into their existing circuitry. The olfactory-bulb cells are generated by mitosis of stem cells along

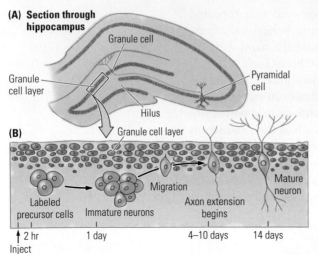

(A) Section through hippocampus

Granule cell

Granule cell layer

Pyramidal cell

Hilus

(B)

Granule cell layer

Labeled precursor cells

Immature neurons

Migration

Axon extension begins

Mature neuron

2 hr — Inject tracer

1 day

4–10 days

14 days

Figure 25.6

Neurogenesis in the Hippocampus (A) Section through the hippocampus illustrates the dentate gyrus, with a granule cell extending its dendrites upward and sending an axon to a pyramidal cell. (B) Displayed over the time course of cell division and maturation, precursor cells differentiate into immature neurons, migrate to the appropriate location, and grow mature connections. (After Ormerod and Galea, 2001.)

the wall of the lateral ventricles, in the subventricular zone. The olfactory precursor cells migrate from the anterior part of the subventricular zone along a pathway known as the rostral migratory stream until they reach the olfactory bulb, where they differentiate into neurons. In contrast, the precursor cells in the hippocampus are located between the granule-cell layer and the hilus, as illustrated in **Figure 25.6**.

The debate about whether new neurons are produced in the cerebral cortex of the normal, noninjured brain has been vigorous, but there is little doubt that new neurons *are* produced in small numbers in the injured cortex. Their presence has led to the idea that a treatment for cortical injury might be to increase the number of cortical cells produced. If neurons are produced in the intact cerebral cortex, however, they are clearly produced in rather small numbers.

Pasko Rakic notes that evolution appears to have gone to great lengths to prevent the production of new neurons in most of the adult brain. He observes that, although tumors made up of astrocytes (astrocytomas), for example, are common in the adult brain, there are virtually no neuron tumors (neuromas) in the adult brain, a fact that indicates the rarity of the production of new neurons in adults. Indeed, Rakic even suggests that, if we could understand why neurons are not produced more often, we might know how to stop tumorous growths of other types of body cells, including astrocytes.

The newly generated neurons in the olfactory bulb and hippocampus are assumed to have some function, but the nature of that function is not yet known. Certain possibilities are suggested by the principle that, if new neurons are being produced, room must be made for them or the brain cavity will fill up. Therefore, either the new neurons are being generated to replace lost ones or they somehow stimulate the death of old neurons or the new neurons themselves may be destined to be short-lived.

New neurons likely do replace old ones; however, the survival of new neurons is not certain and can be affected by many types of experience. **Table 25.1** summarizes some of the factors that influence neuron generation and neuron survival in the hippocampus. Note especially that, when animals engage the hippocampus to solve some type of neuropsychological problem, the survival of new granule cells is enhanced.

We can speculate that the cell survival is related to the successful acquisition of the task. If so, the implication is that learning could be compromised if cell proliferation or survival or both were compromised. Note, too, that stress is correlated with decreases in hippocampal-cell proliferation

Table 25.1 **Effects of various factors on cell proliferation and hippocampal granule-neuron survival**

Factor	Effect on Proliferation	Effect on Survival
Adrenal steroids	Down	No change
Aging (rats)	Down	Down?
Adrenalectomy	Up	Up
Dentate gyrus lesions	Up	Up
Running-wheel activity	Up	Unknown
High levels of estradiol	Up	Up
Serotonin agonists (e.g., Prozac)	Up	Unknown
Hippocampal-dependent learning	No change	Up
Season (reduced daylight)	Up	Up
Kindling	Up	No change
Exposure to stress	Down	Down?

Source: After Ormerod and Galea, 2001.

and survival, which is interesting in light of the evidence that stress reduces mental efficiency and may especially impair some forms of memory.

Perhaps even more interesting is that chronic stress is related to depression, and antidepressants that stimulate serotonin production (that is, the SSRIs such as fluoxitine) also increase neuron generation in the hippocampus. These observations suggest that the therapeutic activity of antidepressants may be related to their ability to stimulate neurogenesis, which in turn may alter mental activity (for a further discussion, see Chapter 27). Just how this sequence of events might happen is still unknown.

In sum, neurogenesis is a selective form of plasticity that may be important for both olfactory- and hippocampal-related behaviors, although the precise role of cell generation and survival is largely a matter of speculation at this point. No doubt the study of neurogenesis in the adult brain will remain a rich broth of controversy for some time to come.

The Downside of Brain Plasticity

We have emphasized the positive side of plastic changes in the brain. But plastic changes can have a dark side, too. For example, exposure to mind-altering drugs such as amphetamine, cocaine, nicotine, and morphine produce alterations in dendritic length and spine density, the details of the changes varying with the particular drug (see a review by Robinson and Kolb).

Some of the maladaptive behavior of drug addicts has been proposed to result from drug-related changes in prefrontal morphology. After all, drug addicts have many behavioral symptoms reminiscent of frontal-lobe-injured people. Other examples of plasticity gone awry include the development of pathological pain, pathological response to sickness, epilepsy, and dementia (see the Shaw and McEachern for extensive discussions). One goal is to find ways to block or reverse pathological plasticity, although finding them is likely to prove difficult.

Experience-Dependent Changes Interact

As we travel through life, we encounter an almost infinite number of experiences that could alter brain organization. Until recently, virtually no experimental studies have attempted to determine how a lifetime's experiences interact. Terry Robinson and one of us (Kolb) and our colleagues attempted to address this question in a series of studies in which animals received stimulant drugs (amphetamine, cocaine, methylphenidate, or nicotine) before placement in complex environments.

Complex environments normally produce extensive increases in dendritic arborization and spine density, but these increases are completely blocked by the earlier exposure to the stimulants. An obvious question is whether the complex housing would alter the drug effects. It does. Animals given several months of complex-housing experience before they receive repeated doses of nicotine show a much reduced response to the drug. One reason for individual differences in susceptibility to drug addiction may likely be related to predrug experiences.

One of the most common experiences of everyday life is stress. It is known to produce striking changes in dendritic morphology and neurogenesis (see a review by McEwen), and so it would not be surprising to find that stress interacts with other experience-dependent changes related to drugs, brain injury, complex housing, and so on. Preliminary studies by Robbin Gibb and colleagues suggest that such is the case. For example, prenatal stress can block recovery from perinatal cortical injury in rats.

Can Plasticity Support Functional Recovery after Injury?

Clinical neurologists have long known that some recovery of function is possible after injury to the nervous system, but the nature and mechanisms of the mediating processes are still poorly understood. A significant problem is the lack of a generally accepted definition of what constitutes "recovery." The word could mean a complete return of function, a marked improvement in function, or indeed any degree of improvement. Another problem is a lack of knowledge concerning what plastic changes might take place in the nervous system after injury. The nature of these changes will influence how we conceptualize the processes related to recovery. Let us explore these problems briefly before considering the topic of brain plasticity and behavior after injury.

Compensation Compared with Recovery

We like to call the question of compensation "the problem of the three-legged cat." When cats are struck by automobiles, they commonly suffer severe injury to one of the back legs. The usual veterinary treatment is to remove the affected leg. Initially, the cats have a great deal of difficulty getting around, leading their owners to wonder, in despair, whether the cats wouldn't be better off dead. Fortunately, cats are resilient; in a few weeks, they seem as agile as before the amputation. This restoration of mobility is often so complete that an observer may not even realize that a leg is missing. In short, the cat has regained lost functions but has not recovered its lost leg. Rather, the cat has compensated for its difficulties and developed new behavioral strategies for locomoting through the world.

Many would argue that it is exactly what happens after brain injury. People do not actually recover lost behaviors or capacities; instead, they develop a new way of functioning to compensate. Consider two cases that we have already encountered. Lyova Saletsky, who was introduced in the Portrait at the beginning of this chapter, had severe cognitive deficits with which he eventually learned to cope, but he clearly did not recover his lost abilities. Similarly, in Chapter 13, we encountered B.K., who had suffered a stroke that left him with a left-upper-field defect in which one-quarter of the fovea was devoid of pattern vision.

B.K. was initially unable to read and was seriously impaired at recognizing faces. With the passage of time, he regained both these abilities, but not because his lost visual functions were somehow magically restored. Instead, B.K. learned to direct his vision so that parts of words that once disappeared into the scotoma are now captured in the lower visual fields. Similarly, when looking at a face, he directs his gaze to the person's right eye, a shift that places most of the face in the functioning part of his visual field and allows him to recognize who the person is. It is important to note that B.K. did not set out consciously to learn these strategies. They developed spontaneously. Thus, although he had "recovered" the ability to read and recognize faces, the original behaviors did not return.

Is all post-brain-injury improvement compensation or do some improvements actually constitute functional restitution? As stated in Chapter 23, some functional recovery is clearly possible in the infant brain, the best example being the partial return of language functions after left hemispherectomy. But even this "recovery" is not complete and includes compensation in the sense that the right hemisphere now controls talking, a function that develops at the expense of some of the usual right-hemisphere functions. The extreme view is that actual restitution of function is possible only if the injured brain can be replaced and stimulated to function like the original brain—a tall order that seems unlikely to be an option for the adult brain in the near future.

A goal for those studying rehabilitation, therefore, is to find ways of stimulating plastic responses in the brain to provide the best possible compensation. We have seen, for example, that cortical maps can change in response to experience, including amputation. Is it not reasonable, then, to suppose that, if the brain itself is injured, there may be a way to encourage its maps to reorganize? However, we might find that plastic changes after cerebral injury could actually make functional outcome worse.

Consider a hypothetical example in which, instead of a limb being amputated, the cortical representation of a limb was damaged by stroke (which could be thought of as "amputation" of the arm representation in the brain). If the arm representation were to reappear in the face area, the person's arm movements might improve, but his or her facial movements could be compromised. If such a change interfered with speech, the problem would not be trivial. Fortunately, deleterious effects of plastic changes are not common.

What Happens When a Brain Is Injured?

Although we may be able to point to a specific immediate cause of brain injury (stroke is such a cause), the damage that is then wrought on the brain is not the result of a single causative event. Rather, the initial event is followed by a cascade of cellular events that can seriously compromise not only the injured part of the brain but other brain regions as well. Consider what happens after a stroke, in which there is an interruption of the blood supply to one of the cerebral arteries.

The lack of blood, called *ischemia*, results in a sequence of events that progresses even if the blood flow is restored. In the first seconds to minutes, as illustrated in **Figure 25.7**, there are changes in the ionic balance of the affected regions, including changes in pH and properties of the cell membrane. These ionic changes result in a variety of pathological events, such as the release of massive amounts of glutamate and the prolonged opening of calcium channels. The open calcium channels in turn allow toxic levels of calcium to enter the cell, not only producing direct toxic effects but also instigating various second-messenger pathways that can prove harmful to the neurons.

Figure 25.7

Results of Ischemia The cascade of changes taking place after a stroke. In the first seconds to minutes, ionic changes are followed by changes in second messengers and RNA production. These changes are followed by changes in protein production and inflammation, which slowly resolves in hours to days. Recovery follows and takes from weeks to months or years.

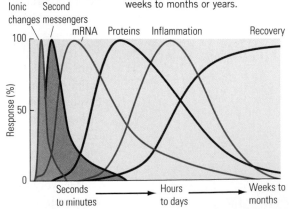

In the ensuing minutes to hours, mRNA is stimulated, altering the production of proteins in the neurons and possibly proving toxic to the cells. Next, the tissues become inflamed and swollen, threatening the integrity of cells that may be far removed from the site of injury. Finally, a form of neural shock—Constantin von Monakow called it **diaschisis**—occurs. As von Monakow noted, after the brain is injured, not only are localized neural tissue and its function lost, but areas related to the damaged region suffer a sudden withdrawal of excitation or inhibition. Such sudden changes in input can lead to a temporary loss of function, both in areas adjacent to an injury and in regions that may be quite distant.

A stroke may also be followed by changes in the metabolism or in the glucose utilization of the injured hemisphere or in both—changes that may persist for days. Like diaschisis, these metabolic changes can have severe effects on the functioning of otherwise normal tissue. After a cortical stroke, for example, metabolic rate throughout the rest of the hemisphere has been shown to decrease by about 25%.

Treatments for cerebral injury are directed at various targets in the postinjury cascade. For example, as detailed in Chapter 26, drugs called *neuroprotectants* can be used to block calcium channels or prevent ionic imbalance, in the hope that they will protect neurons from the cascade of toxic events that follow an ischemic episode. Other drugs can be used to reduce swelling or to enhance metabolic activity. The effects of neuroprotectants and anti-inflammatory drugs are quite different from the effect of treatments aimed at stimulating plasticity and functional compensation.

Examples of Functional Restitution

The return of function is seldom sudden. An examination of the stages of functional restitution and their associated behaviors often reveals a slow reemergence of restored functions that resembles the sequence of developmental stages in infants. We consider two common examples of functional restoration after cortical stroke: recovery of movement and recovery of language. We then examine some of the characteristics of functional improvement in two particular populations: soldiers with head injuries and neurosurgical cases. Finally, we look at patients' prospects of returning to work and having a "normal" life after cerebral injury.

Recovery from Motor-Cortex Damage

Tom Twitchell described recovery from hemiplegia (inability to move the contralateral limbs) produced by thrombosis, embolism, or stroke of the middle cerebral artery in humans. The recovery sequence closely parallels the development of reaching and of the grasp response described by Twitchell in infants. The hemiplegia, which appeared immediately after the damage occurred, was marked by complete flaccidity of the muscles and loss of all reflexes and voluntary movements.

Recovery took place over a period of days or weeks and followed an orderly sequence: (1) return of reflexes; (2) development of rigidity; (3) grasping that was facilitated by or occurred as part of other movements; and (4) development of voluntary grasping (which entailed recovery of movement sequentially in the shoulder, elbow, wrist, and hand—first in the flexor musculature and then in the extensor musculature; review Figure 9.19). Voluntary grasping continued to improve until independent movements of the fingers were well developed. Complete recovery of use of the arms, when it occurred, appeared between 23 and 40 days after the lesion. About 30% of patients reached the last stage of recovery; the others showed arrested recovery at one of the preceding stages.

Recovery from Aphasia

Andrew Kertesz reviewed the prospects of recovery from aphasia and used the case histories of his own patients as examples. **Figure 25.8** graphs the recovery of a typical patient from each of his subgroups. (The "aphasia quotients" were derived from the patients' scores on the Western Aphasia Battery, which tests spontaneous speech content, fluency, comprehension, repetition, and so forth). Kertesz made the following generalizations:

1. Posttrauma (head-injury) patients showed the most rapid and often almost complete recovery, whereas recovery in stroke patients was less pronounced and in some groups was almost absent.

2. Initial deficits were the least severe in anomic patients (that is, people who are unable to generate the names for common objects) and the most severe in global aphasics, with intermediate severity seen in other groups. The actual rate of recovery, given initial impairments, was often quite similar in all groups.

3. When recovery occurred, patients tended to progress to one of the other stages, but recovery usually stopped with anomic aphasia.

4. Most recovery took place in the first 3 months (illustrated only for the posttrauma patient in Figure 25.8), with some recovery taking place in the next 6 months and less recovery taking place in the following 6 months. Thereafter, there was little or no recovery.

5. There was some evidence that younger patients showed better recovery; the effects of intelligence, occupation, and sex in those patients were slight if present.

6. The language components that were most resistant to brain damage were naming, oral imitation, comprehension of nouns, and yes–no responses, functions that may be partly mediated by the right hemisphere.

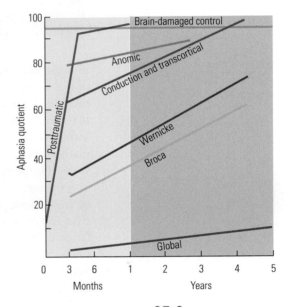

Figure **25.8**

Recovery from Aphasia Initial deficits and recovery in stroke patients with different language disorders and in a posttrauma patient. Each line is a representative patient. (After Kertesz, 1979.)

Recovery from Traumatic Lesions

More than a generation ago, Hans-Leukas Teuber described the deficits of war veterans as assessed in tests given 1 week after each suffered an open-head injury and, again, 20 years later. These patients are excellent candidates for study for a number of reasons: they underwent standardized testing after induction

Figure 25.9

Recovery from Brain Trauma
Estimated improvement, based on initial examination (no later than 1 week after injury) and follow-up examination (20 years later), for some body regions (extremities, sides of face) for which symptoms were recorded (reflex changes, paralysis, weakness) in the motor system; for noted sensory losses in the somatosensory system; for the visual field (diminution in number of quadrants known to be affected); and for symptoms interpreted as dysphasia. Note the advantage of younger age at the time of wounding. (After Teuber, 1975.)

into the army, they were young at the time of injury, the immediate aftermath of the injury is documented, and the kind and extent of recovery can be documented through prolonged follow-up examinations by veterans' services. Teuber's results, summarized in **Figure 25.9**, reveal that 4% of the veterans showed some recovery from motor defects, 36% showed some recovery from somatosensory defects, 43% showed some recovery from visual defects, and 24% showed some recovery from initial dysphasia.

Two comments must be made about Teuber's analysis. First, more than 50% of the patient population showed no recovery at all, and the failure of more than 75% of patients to show recovery from dysphasia is not encouraging. The latter percentage is in line with Luria's report that 66% of his dysphasic patients showed no recovery. Second, the usefulness of Teuber's analysis is limited because the assessments are not quantitative: there is no estimate of the *degree* of recovery.

A study of a larger population of veterans, of the Vietnam War, was undertaken by Jay Mohr and his coworkers. In general, their results are consistent with those of Teuber in that a great deal of recovery of function is seen subsequent to penetrating brain injury. In fact, Mohr reports more-extensive recovery from aphasia (34%) than does Teuber and reports that the recovery continued for years after injury.

More recently, Josef Zihl and Yves Cramon reported that practice in locating lights led to an increase in the visual field of partly blind patients, an improvement that would not have taken place without the practice. What effect specific therapy might have had on the patients reported in the veteran studies is not known.

Recovery from Surgical Lesions

Surgery to remove brain tumors or relieve epilepsy often damages parts of the brain that were intact and functional before the operation. Assessment tests have been administered to patients within days of tumor surgery and as long as 20 years after surgery to evaluate such damage and gauge recovery. Unfortunately, recovery seems to have been so infrequent that the breakdown of data at different test–retest intervals is not reported. **Table 25.2** summarizes the results from some studies in which tests were given a few days before surgery,

Table 25.2 Presurgical, postsurgical, and follow-up performance on neuropsychological tests taken by patients with cortical lesions

Test	Lesion	Preop	Postop	Follow-up	Control	Reference
Card-sorting categories	Frontal	3.3	1.4	1.3	4.6	Milner, 1963
Card-sorting errors	Frontal	54.9	73.2	78.2	37.7	Milner, 1963
Rey-figure copy score	Right temporal	31.2	30.6	29.8	34.9	Taylor, 1969
Rey-figure recall score	Right temporal	15.4	15.3	13.8	24.2	Taylor, 1969
Finger-position sense	Central					
Incidence of deficit (%)						
Ipsilateral		24	14	6	—	Taylor, 1969
Contralateral		36	43	65	—	
Arm-movement copying	Left parietal		73	75.8	90.2	Kolb and Milner, 1981

within 20 days after surgery, and from 1 to 20 years after surgery. These results show, after dorsolateral frontal lesions, no recovery in card sorting; after right temporal lesions, no recovery in recall of the Rey figure (see Figure 15.15C); and, after parietal lesions, no recovery in finger-position sense or arm-movement copying.

The finding of no recovery is also reported in some other studies. Marilyn Jones-Gotman and Brenda Milner tested patient groups within 2 weeks of surgery and 1 or more years later on spontaneous drawing tasks. The subjects were told to draw as many unnamable objects as they could within 5 minutes. Although all patient groups showed some reduction in performance level relative to control groups, patients with right frontal lesions were the most impaired, and there were no differences in performance between patients tested shortly after surgery and those tested more than a year after it.

There also seems to be little or no recovery in memory after bilateral medial-temporal-lobe removal. In a 14-year follow-up, Milner and her colleagues reported that the amnesic patient H.M., profiled in Chapter 18, had a presurgical IQ of 104, a 2-year-follow-up IQ of 112, and a 9-year-follow-up IQ of 118. Yet, despite this improvement in intelligence score, his anterograde amnesia remained essentially unchanged.

In some studies of patients with long-standing lesions, a degree of recovery has been noted on some tests. Milner reported in 1975 that patients with left temporal lesions had preoperative memory scores of 12, early postoperative scores of 4.4, and 5- to 20-year-follow-up scores of 8. This improvement is significant. There are three possible explanations for the improvements observed on this test. First, the score is a composite of logical memory (recall of stories) and paired-associates learning (learning pairs of words, such as "frog" and "flower," and remembering one when given the other). Which component of the test showed recovery is not clear.

Colin Blakemore and Murray Falconer studied paired-associates learning in 86 temporal-lobectomy patients for as long as 10 years after surgery. They found that the deficit lasted for 2 to 3 years, after which they saw progressive recovery, provided the patients were young. Thus, the recovery observed by Milner could have been due to improvement in one facet of the task.

As a second possible explanation for improvement following surgery, Jones-Gotman showed that, if left-temporal-lobe patients are taught to use imagery (for example, they imagine an elephant with a bouquet of flowers in its trunk for the associate word pair "bouquet–elephant"), they show substantial improvement in memory. Hence, recovery may have been due to the development of alternative memory strategies. The third possibility is that the temporal cortex must have rather special properties to allow rapid memory storage. Those properties probably also make it especially prone to epilepsy. If any of the temporal cortex remains intact, it possibly retains a special capacity for plasticity that is not characteristic of other brain areas.

In summary, we think that the results from some of the studies reported here are sources of important insight into the question of recovery of function. The results imply that, if the test is specific for certain brain areas and if the lesions destroy or disable the entire area, there will be no recovery. What makes this position particularly persuasive is that the surgical patients had tumors or epilepsy at the site of the lesions, which could have encouraged the function to move elsewhere. Nevertheless, there is little or no evidence in the test results to suggest that any such transfer took place.

Return to Daily Life

A person's capacity to work and earn a living clearly depends on many behavioral abilities and configurations of abilities. Brain damage may affect some of them more than others, but people can compensate for brain damage in many ways. For example, when gainful employment is used as a measure of recovery, as was done for veterans injured in the Korean War, the resulting rates of recovery are quite high: approximately 80% (Dresser et al., 1973). This measure gives the highest rate of recovery of any that we have found in the literature and strongly suggests that some factor, such as behavioral compensation, is operating.

This high rate of recovery does not minimize the difficulties of the 20% who were not employed. Furthermore, it does not take into consideration the quality of employment. In fact, work may not be a sensitive index of recovery. For example, of 54 patients with closed-head injuries, 48 were back at work within 2 years, but many were restricted in their work activity and reported that they had not regained their full working capacity (see Oddy and Humprey).

Other aspects of their lives also suffered, because these patients had not fully resumed their leisure activities and social contacts. Interestingly, of all aspects of social relations, those with siblings suffered most. The researchers emphasized that therapy should be directed not only toward returning to work but also toward pursuing leisure activities and social relations.

One way to examine the chronic effects of brain damage and how those affected cope is to study the self-reports of people who have been brain damaged. Generally, very little attention is given to these reports, but they can be sources of valuable insight into questions of recovery. Fredrick Linge, a clinical psychologist, described the changes that he underwent after suffering brain damage in an automobile accident.

He was in a coma for the first week after the accident and was not expected to recover significantly. Nevertheless, he did manage to return to a demanding clinical practice about a year after his accident; but, even so, he was changed by the brain damage and had to make adjustments in life style and work routine to cope. He describes his adjustments in the following way:

> In learning to live with my brain damage, I have found through trial and error that certain things help greatly and others hinder my coping. In order to learn and retain information best, I try to eliminate as many distractions as possible and concentrate all my mental energy on the task at hand. . . . In the past I enjoyed a rather chaotic life style, but I now find that I want "a place for everything and everything in its place." When remembering is difficult, order and habit make the minutiae of daily living much easier.
>
> I cannot cope with anger as well as I was able to do before my accident. . . . [O]nce I become angry, I find it impossible to "put the brakes on" and I attribute this directly to my brain damage. It is extremely frightening to me to find myself in this state, and I still have not worked out a truly satisfactory solution, except insofar as I try to avoid anger-provoking situations or try to deal with them before they become too provoking.
>
> My one-track mind seems to help me to take each day as it comes without excessive worry and to enjoy the simple things of life in a way that I never did before. As well, I seem to be a more effective therapist, since I stick to the basic issues at hand and have more empathy with others than I did previously. (Linge, 1980, pp. 6–7)

This self-report by Linge shows that assessments of recovery cannot be limited to measures such as reemployment or even levels of renewed social contacts. Such measures may fail to indicate the ways in which a person has changed and the coping mechanisms that he or she has learned to employ. Note that Linge was a professional psychologist who lived in a social milieu in which people were willing to help him reestablish himself. Many people who do not have similar support systems and resources will have a much more difficult time in recovering. Linge's comments also demonstrate that the brain-damaged person must change not only the external environment but the internal environment as well.

Plasticity in the Injured Brain

Just as plasticity in the normal brain can be investigated at different levels, so too can plasticity in the injured brain. To date, most work has focused on changes in maps, determined either by functional imaging or by brain stimulation. We consider each method in turn.

Functional Imaging after Cerebral Injury

The functional changes observed after stroke provide an excellent window into cerebral plasticity. If patients can recover from stroke, despite having lost significant areas of cerebral cortex, then we can conclude that some type of change has taken place in the remaining parts of the brain. Functional-imaging techniques, especially PET, fMRI, and TMS, can be used repeatedly in the weeks and months after stroke to document changes in cerebral activation that might correlate with functional improvement. Several recent reviews of such studies have led us to the following conclusions (see, especially, reviews by Cramer and Bastings and by Rijntjes and Weiller):

1. If the primary sensorimotor cortex survives a stroke, some functional improvement is likely to take place with the passage of time, even if hemiparesis immediately follows the stroke. Although the efferent fiber tracts may be damaged, thus causing the hemiparesis, the remaining cortex may yet become activated. Functional improvement is correlated with the appearance of this activation.

2. Activation of the motor areas during limb movements recruits cortical areas along the rim of cortical injury. In addition, larger areas of the motor cortex are often activated by particular movements. For example, hand or limb movements often activate regions of the face area, possibly because of intact pyramidal-tract fibers leaving the face area (see Figure 25.3).

3. The motions of stroke patients activate much larger areas of cortex, especially parietal and premotor areas, than do similar movements by control subjects. These regions of activation are extended both for language and for motor functions. The relation between recovery and activation is not always straightforward, however, as shown in the Snapshot on page 737.

4. Reorganization is not restricted to one hemisphere; instead, similar changes take place bilaterally. Thus, although the performance of a unilateral motor task largely activates only the contralateral cortex, the brains of stroke victims show a marked increase in bilateral activation. The increased activation in the contralateral hemisphere is especially notable in patients with disturbances of language in which regions opposite the language areas (so-called homologous areas) show activation.

5. The capacity for reorganization declines with increasing size of stroke and increasing age. The relation to stroke size is likely due to the fact that the presence of incompletely damaged regions, such as Wernicke's area, is a good predictor of functional improvement. Recall that the severity of the initial deficit in aphasia correlates with later outcome (see Figure 25.8). Presumably, the extent of the initial deficit is related to the extent of injury.

6. Variability among stroke victims is considerable. This variability is probably related to differences in the degree of prestroke activations and is particularly true of language. People who show the greatest bilateral activation for language functions after stroke are probably those who already had some bilateral activation before the stroke, as with left-handers. Michel Rijntjes and Cornelius Weiller note that the extent of activation of the right hemisphere during language tasks is highly variable and that the pattern of activation in people who have exhibited recovery from Wernicke's aphasia is remarkably similar to the maximal areas of right-hemisphere activation seen in normal brains.

In conclusion, functional improvement after stroke corresponds to a change in functional organization of the remaining brain, as shown in functional-imaging studies. We hasten to point out, however, that such studies are usually

SNAPSHOT
Using Imaging to Study Recovery

Nick Ward and Richard Frackiowiak used fMRI to study a large group of stroke patients and control subjects as they performed an isometric hand-grip task. The advantage of using such a task is that all subjects were capable of doing it, although they varied considerably in their abilities. The aim of the experiments was to answer two questions:

1. Does the task-related activation pattern differ in control subjects and stroke patients?

2. Do the degree of task-related brain activation and the outcome correlate?

On the basis of the existing literature, the obvious expectation was that patients with better recovery would show greater recruitment of perilesional regions that would be presumed to assist in the recovery. The results were surprisingly different.

The 20 stroke patients all had cortical infarcts, but none extended into M1. Hand grip activated a motor network of cortical and subcortical regions including motor cortex, premotor cortex, supplementary motor cortex, anterior cingulate cortex, and parietal cortex. About half of the patients showed overactivations of cortex relative to the control group. These novel activations were found not only in the expected motor regions but also in the prefrontal and insular cortex in the lesion hemisphere as well as in M1 and S1 in the contralateral hemisphere.

Curiously, when Ward and Frackowiak correlated fMRI activation and recovery, they found an inverse correlation in several brain regions, as shown in part A of the adjoining illustration. Especially apparent is that the subjects with a poorer outcome had extensive activation in *both* hemispheres.

One explanation for this finding is that the patients with poorer recovery may have had infarcts that made direct access to M1 difficult, requiring the activation of parallel pathways that are less efficient. In attempting to reconcile the results with previous studies by others who found a positive correlation between activation and recovery, Ward and Frackowiak suggested that the measures of recovery may be the critical difference and emphasize the importance of *detailed* outcome measurements.

They then asked how brain activation might be related to recovery longitudinally. They performed repeated fMRIs over time in individual patients and correlated the performance

(A) CL IL

(B) IL CL

decreases increases

(A) Brain regions in which a linear inverse correlation is observed between recovery and task-related fMRI brain activation across 20 patients. (Frontal lobes are at the top in the central image. CL, contralesional; IL, ipsilesional.) (B) Results of single-subject longitudinal analysis (done in multiple sessions) examining for linear changes in task-related brain activations as a function of recovery. The patient suffered a left-side pontine infarct resulting in right hemiparesis. The results are rendered onto a canonical brain. Red areas represent recovery-related decreases in task-related activation, and green areas represent the equivalent recovery-related areas. (Courtesy of Nick Ward. From Ward and Frackowiak, 2006.)

with outcome. As expected, there was a bilateral overactivation in motor regions immediately after stroke, but, as time passed, these activations lessened and other regions began to show activation, as shown in part B of the illustration.

Ward and Frackowiak suggest that different mechanisms may facilitate recovery at different time points after the stroke. Early on after stroke, any voluntary movement is associated with the massive recruitment of motor areas, but, with the passage of time, new learning of motor control will be related to the precise amount and site of the anatomical damage. This conclusion is supported by one of us (Whishaw) and his colleagues, whose work with rat models suggests that recovery after M1 damage is related to the animals' relearning the lost movements.

Ward, N. S., and R. S. J. Frackowiak. The functional anatomy of cerebral reorganization after focal brain injury. *Journal of Physiology, Paris* 99:425–436, 2006.

reported only for patients who show good recovery; even so, the studies typically provide little information about the details of treatments that the patients might have received.

Physiological Mapping after Cerebral Injury

Nudo and his coworkers mapped the hand and digit areas of the motor cortex of the squirrel monkey. When they subsequently removed a part of the digit area, they found that use of the contralateral hand was reduced. When they then remapped the motor cortex, they found that the monkeys were unable to produce movements of the lower part of the arm, wrist, and digits, as illustrated in **Figure 25.10**. In other words, the hand area had disappeared from the cortical map, and only a representation of the stump of the upper arm remained.

They subjected additional animals to the same procedure, except that, after surgery, they provided therapy for the affected limb. The therapy consisted of substantial forced use in which the good limb was bound so that the monkey was forced to use the affected limb. When the researchers examined the motor maps of these monkeys again, the hand and digit area was present, except for the area that had originally been removed. Nevertheless, the therapy brought about some recovery of the use of the digits represented by the missing area. Presumably, the movements made by the digits that had lost their cortical representation were mediated by the representations of the remaining digits.

The importance of therapy is the significant feature of the Nudo experiments. Therapy is necessary to maintain the functions of the undamaged cortex and the movements that it represents. Therapy can also promote compensation for the affected body parts.

The form of plasticity described by Nudo and his coworkers may explain the recovery in the following case reported by Paul Bucy and his coworkers. They studied a man with a pyramidal tract sectioned in the lower brainstem as a treatment for involuntary movements. During the first 24 hours after surgery, he had complete flaccid hemiplegia, followed by a slight return of voluntary movement in his extremities. By the 10th day, he could stand alone and walk with assistance. By the 24th day, he could walk unaided. Within 7 months, maximum recovery seemed to have been reached, and he could move his feet, hands, fingers, and toes with only slight impairment.

At autopsy, 2½ years later, about 17% of his pyramidal tract fibers were found to be intact. The recovery of his ability to move his toes and fingers seems attributable to that remaining 17%, which did the job formerly done by the entire tract. We venture to observe that, if the man had been discouraged from using the afflicted limbs, his recovery would have been lessened.

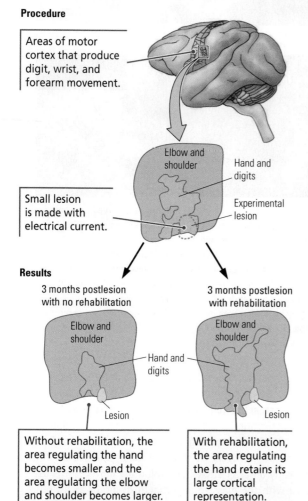

Procedure

Areas of motor cortex that produce digit, wrist, and forearm movement.

Small lesion is made with electrical current.

Elbow and shoulder

Hand and digits

Experimental lesion

Results

3 months postlesion with no rehabilitation

Elbow and shoulder

Hand and digits

Lesion

Without rehabilitation, the area regulating the hand becomes smaller and the area regulating the elbow and shoulder becomes larger.

3 months postlesion with rehabilitation

Elbow and shoulder

Lesion

With rehabilitation, the area regulating the hand retains its large cortical representation.

Conclusion

Rehabilitation prevents both a loss of movement in the hand and a decrease in the hand's cortical representation.

Figure 25.10

Use It or Lose It (After Nudo et al., 1996.)

Variables Affecting Recovery

Several variables in addition to lesion size affect the rate of recovery from brain damage. These variables are not fully discussed in many papers for the following reasons: measurements are difficult to make; many of the patient groups are small, which lessens the validity of any statistics derived from them; or a particular researcher simply may not consider them important. These variables include age, sex, handedness, intelligence, and personality. Overall, recovery from brain damage seems likely to be best if the patient is a young, intelligent, optimistic, left-handed female.

Youth is one of the easier variables to measure. Teuber and his coworkers found that, on a number of tests, recovery by soldiers from head injuries is greater in the 17-to-20 age group than in the 21-to-25 age group, which in turn is greater than in the age group 26+ (see Figure 25.9). Milner reported that patients older than 40 who have removals near the posterior temporal speech zone in the left hemisphere show less recovery than do younger patients. Note that age does not always appear as a significant factor in studies of recovery, as reported by Kertesz.

An analysis of age effects is complicated by the fact that age is a contributing factor to the onset of many kinds of brain damage. Strokes and other kinds of brain abnormality are common in older people, who are more likely in any case to be declining in motor and cognitive function owing to the normal processes of aging. Thus, recovery may tend to be obscured by aging.

Handedness and sex, both for much the same reason, may influence the outcome of brain damage. Recall from Chapter 12 that a number of theories argue that female and male brains differ in both anatomy and functional organization, with imaging studies revealing less functional lateralization in the female. Considering the imaging evidence in brain-injured patients discussed earlier, if females have more bilateral functional activation, then they should show more functional recovery. Likewise, familial left-handers appear to be less lateralized in function than right-handers, again providing an advantage for recruiting undamaged regions after brain injury.

People with superior intelligence are generally believed to have better recovery than are those with lower intelligence. There is no clear reason for this difference, although whatever neural properties allow for higher intelligence may also provide an advantage after injury. For example, people of higher intelligence may have more-plastic brains and thus respond better to injury, although this possibility is not easy to prove. Alternatively, people of higher intelligence may be able to generate more strategies to solve problems than less-intelligent people can.

A complication is that, although the ultimate recovery of a very intelligent person may be excellent in relation to the recovery of others, the actual residual deficit may be equal simply because the very intelligent person would normally function at a higher level. Thus, in our experience, highly intelligent people generally complain more about the negative effects of residual deficits on quality of life.

The role of personality in recovery is difficult to evaluate, but optimistic, extroverted, and easygoing people are widely thought to have a better prognosis after brain injury. One reason could be that people who are more optimistic about recovering are more likely to comply with rehabilitation programs.

Unfortunately, brain damage may have a negative influence on personality. For example, patients may develop postinjury depression and, as a result, would be expected to show poor or at least slow recovery until the depression is treated. Indeed, stroke patients are now commonly placed on antidepressants such as SSRIs because they are believed to aid in recovery.

Therapeutic Approaches to Brain Damage

We conclude this chapter by reviewing four major experimental therapeutic approaches to brain damage:

1. Rehabilitation procedures consist of a variety of behavioral and psychological therapies.

2. Pharmacological therapies are intended to promote recovery in the immediate postsurgery period.

3. Brain stimulation increases brain activity.

4. Brain-tissue transplants and stem-cell-induction techniques are being developed in the hope of restoring normal brain function.

Rehabilitation procedures are used widely, with mixed results; pharmacological, stimulation, and implantation techniques are moving past the animal-experimentation stage with preliminary clinical trials.

Rehabilitation

It would seem logical that people with brain injuries should be placed in a rehabilitation program of some sort. Surprisingly, however, neuroscientists as yet have little information concerning the value of different kinds of rehabilitation programs, the optimal timing for initiating a rehabilitation program, or even the optimal duration of rehabilitative therapy. Although both speech and physical therapies are often assumed to be effective, the role of any specific therapy—the kinds of changes that it brings about and how or why it takes place—is a matter of debate (see reviews by Teasel et al. and by Muñoz-Céspedes et al.).

Consider, for example, that patients undergoing speech therapy not only receive speech training but also have daily contact with a therapist. Much of this interaction is social and not strictly related to language. The importance of this type of stimulation cannot be overstated. For example, there is growing evidence that patients who are placed in a dedicated stroke unit, rather than treated as an outpatient, are likely to have a better outcome. Such a unit has a variety of professional rehabilitation therapists working together and providing stimulation for much of the waking day.

The results of studies of laboratory animals consistently show that the single most successful treatment strategy for optimizing functional recovery is placing animals in complex, stimulating environments (see Johansson and Belichenko). But far from suggesting that rehabilitation therapies are not useful, the results of laboratory studies reinforce that specific types of training can alter motor maps. Consider two more examples: movement therapy and cognitive rehabilitation.

Movement Therapy

Edward Taub and his colleagues developed a therapy referred to as *constraint-induced movement therapy*. They based it on the observation that, after stroke, many patients have initial hemiparesis; develop strategies to use the unimpaired, opposite limb; and, in so doing, fail to attempt to use the impaired limb. The goal of constraint-induced therapy is to induce patients to use the affected limb for several hours a day for a period of weeks. This induced use is accomplished by placing the unaffected limb in a sling and forcing the patient to perform daily activities with the impaired limb.

Additionally, patients are given various tasks to practice with the affected limb—tasks such as picking up objects or turning the pages of magazines. This therapy is effective in stimulating sometimes dramatic improvement in the affected limb. An explanation for the improvement is that the motor training stimulates plastic changes in the brain, leading to an enlargement of the motor representation of the affected arm and hand.

Joachim Leipert and colleagues measured this increase by using TMS both before and after 12 days of constraint-induced therapy. They found that the training stimulated a dramatic increase in the area of the cortex representing the paretic hand (a 50% increase in map size after 12 days of training and still present 6 months later). The location of the map expansion varied from patient to patient, presumably because the precise area of injury varied from person to person. As already mentioned, parallel studies on monkeys by Nudo yielded similar results (see Figure 25.10).

Cognitive Rehabilitation

The most critical problems faced by many brain-injured people are not strictly sensory or motor; rather, they are more-complex cognitive problems, such as the problems of patients with different forms of memory disturbances or spatial disorientation. For these patients, some form of cognitive rehabilitation is needed, and several cognitive programs are now available (see books by Sohlberg and Mateer and by Prigatano). Treating patients in hospitals is expensive, and, recently, there has been a push for outpatient programs, often referred to as community neurorehabilitation (see review by Chard).

A broader matter, however, is the difficulty of coping with residual cognitive deficits outside the clinic. For example, a person with spatial disorientations might benefit somewhat from practicing various paper-and-pencil tasks but, in the end, the patient may continue to struggle with the real-world problem of finding his or her way home. Thus, therapy for brain damage often requires creativity and initiative on the part of the therapist trying to develop techniques that are relevant to an individual patient.

We were once asked to recommend a therapy for a depressed motorcycle racer who had suffered extensive brain damage after crashing a hang glider. We half seriously suggested a tricycle, which his caregivers then had constructed for him. His attitude improved dramatically, and he was soon racing the tricycle around the hospital grounds and taking trips to town. The exercise and attitude change helped him tackle other tasks that furthered his recovery.

Substitution systems may be useful for some patients. For example, visual information can be recorded with a video camera and transformed by computer into a tactile message presented on the skin as a partial substitute for vision. Various machines, especially computers, can be used to perform specific tasks.

Pharmacological Therapies

Interest in the use of pharmacological therapies for ameliorating the effects of brain damage is longstanding. The general idea is to use compounds that will facilitate plastic changes in the brain. For example, psychomotor stimulants such as amphetamine or nicotine are known to stimulate changes in cortical and subcortical circuits in the normal brain.

The hope is that the use of such compounds in the injured brain can stimulate synaptic changes that might facilitate functional recovery (see review by Feeney). Research results suggest that the rate of recovery can be increased if pharmacological treatments and experience are combined shortly after brain damage. The success of such treatments in the laboratory has led to the initiation of clinical trials using amphetamine with stroke patients, with promising results.

Psychomotor stimulants not only increase transmitter levels but also stimulate the production of various growth factors. For instance, Cecilia Flores and Jane Stewart showed that amphetamine stimulates an increase in the production of basic fibroblast growth factor (bFGF). This factor acts to enhance synaptogenesis in the brain and, presumably, could stimulate functional improvement after injury. Because the production of growth factors is stimulated not only by drugs but also by behavioral treatments, such as placing animals in complex environments, we may find that combinations of growth factors and behavioral therapies are more beneficial than the use of either modality alone.

It has recently been recognized that the brain is subject to inflammatory processes related both to acute brain injury and to more progressive diseases such as dementia. The first group of compounds shown to influence inflammation in the brain comprises the cytokines, which are induced rapidly by injury, disease, or infection, and are believed to have many negative effects (for a review see Lucas et al.). One cytokine, interluekin-1, has complex actions: acutely, it appears to be neurotoxic, whereas, chronically, it appears to initiate a range of beneficial processes.

The idea is that acute reduction in inflammatory processes, partly by blocking cytokines from inducing inflammation or by reducing inflammation with drugs such as COX-2 inhibitors (for example, Celebrex) or with statins. Statins (examples are Lipitor and Crestor) are commonly used to lower cholesterol but appear to have the unexpected side effects of reducing inflammation in the vascular system and reducing the incidence of stroke as well as improving recovery after stroke.

Brain Stimulation

One effect of brain injury is a reduction in brain activity in perilesional regions. Several strategies pioneered in the past decade include increasing blood pressure (see Hillis), low-level electrical stimulation (see Teskey et al.), and transcranial magnetic stimulation (see Pape et al.). Although all these techniques would seem to have risk of complication, the preliminary clinical trials have proved very promising and without complication.

Brain-Tissue Transplants and Stem-Cell Induction

The idea of transplanting neural tissue in mammals and the techniques for doing so date back a century. Yet, until recently, the possibility that neural transplantation could have a practical application was viewed as rather remote. In the 1980s, researchers discovered that, if fetal tissue containing immature cells was extracted from particular brain regions and then inserted into the appropriate region of a recipient animal, the fetal tissue would grow and integrate into the host brain. Such a procedure would be impractical for repairing damage to a complex circuit such as the neocortex, but perhaps transplantation of specific cell types, such as dopaminergic cells from the brainstem, could benefit patients missing those cells—Parkinson patients, for example.

More than 100 Parkinson patients have now received fetal stem-cell transplants. Improvements have been reported in some cases, but a large study by Curt Freed and his colleagues is not encouraging. By and large, the relief from symptoms has been minor or only short-lived. Perhaps the transplants do not grow sufficiently in the large human brain, are not adequately incorporated into brain circuitry, or are affected by the same disease process that is causing the original loss of dopamine cells.

Another approach to transplanting fetal tissue is to stimulate stem cells within the host brain by using growth factors. Knowing that the brain is capable of making new neurons even in adulthood, researchers hypothesize that it ought to be possible to potentiate the production of new neurons after injury. If these new neurons can then be induced to migrate to the site of injury and integrate into that part of the brain, they may be able restore some level of functioning there. One of us (Kolb) and his colleagues have recently shown in laboratory animals that this approach has considerable potential.

An alternate approach is to take stem cells from a patient's brain or perhaps even from some other part of a patient's body (such as bone marrow), culture the cells to form thousands or millions of neurons of a particular type (such as dopaminergic cells), and then place these cells into the injured part of the brain, where they will differentiate and become integrated into the circuitry. Findings from preliminary studies suggest that both procedures are workable, at least in principle.

Summary

Cortical Plasticity in the Intact Adult Brain

The brain is not a static organ but is constantly changing throughout life. Brain plasticity in adults can be studied at several levels: by analyzing behavioral change; by measuring cortical maps with the use of imaging or physiological techniques, synaptic change with the use of Golgi or electron-microscopic techniques, and molecular changes (including genetic changes); and by demonstrating the generation of new neurons or glia or both.

Can Plasticity Support Functional Recovery after Injury?

Brain damage is a major cause of loss of function. A cascade of damaging molecular events unfolds within the first 48 hours after a brain injury, followed by an extended period of repair that may last years. The brain can compensate for injury, but true recovery of function is probably impossible without regenerating lost brain tissues and restoring the original connections. The practical definition of restitution of function must be based on the extent to which a patient regains an acceptable daily life.

Examples of Functional Restitution

Functional restitution after brain injury is slow, often revealing a gradual reemergence of functions that resembles the sequence of developmental stages in infants.

Plasticity in the Injured Brain

Most studies of plasticity in the injured human brain have used noninvasive neuroimaging to show altered patterns of brain activation in both sensory and motor maps. There appear to be dynamic changes in brain activation in the course of recovery, representing different recovery processes at work as time passes.

Variables Affecting Recovery

Recovery shows considerable variance from person to person. Functional improvement is affected by a variety of factors, including age, handedness, sex, intelligence, personality, and treatment.

Therapeutic Approaches to Brain Damage

Therapy for brain injury currently includes (1) rehabilitation emphasizing the repeated use of affected limbs or cognitive processes, (2) pharmacological treatments designed to stimulate brain plasticity and to reduce inflammation, (3) brain stimulation intended to increase brain activity, and (4) stem-cell treatments consisting of either the endogenous induction of neurogenesis or the transplantation of stem cells to replace neurons lost to disease or injury.

References

Aglioti, S. "Anomalous" representations and perceptions. In J. Grafman and Y. Christen, Eds. *Neuronal Plasticity: Building a Bridge from the Laboratory to the Clinic.* New York: Springer, 1999, pp.79–91.

Bach-y-Rita, P., Ed. *Recovery of Function: Theoretical Considerations for Brain Injury Rehabilitation.* Bern, Switzerland: Hyuber, 1980.

Blakemore, C. B., and M. A. Falconer. Long-term effects of anterior temporal lobectomy on certain cognitive functions. *Journal of Neurology, Neurosurgery, and Psychiatry* 30:364–367, 1967.

Bliss, T. V. P., and T. Lømo. Long lasting potentiation of synaptic transmission in the dentate area of the anesthetized rabbit following stimulation of the perforant path. *Journal of Physiology* 232:331–356, 1973.

Brown, J. A. Recovery of motor function after stroke. *Progress in Brain Research* 157:223–238, 2006.

Buckner, R. L., M. Corbetta, J. Schatz, M. E. Raichele, and S. E. Petersen. Preserved speech abilities and compensation following prefrontal damage. *Proceedings of the National Academy of Sciences of the United States of America* 93:1249–1253, 1996.

Bucy, P. C., J. E. Keplinger, and E. B. Siqueira. Destruction of the "pyramidal tract" in man. *Journal of Neurosurgery* 21:385–398, 1964.

Cain, D. P. Synaptic models of neuroplasticity: What is LTP? In C. A. Shaw and J. C. McEachern, Eds. *Toward a Theory of Neuroplasticity.* Lillington, N.C.: Taylor & Francis, 2001, pp. 118–129.

Candia, V., T. Elbert, E. Altenmuller, H. Rau, T. Schafer, and E. Taub. Constraint-induced movement therapy for focal hand dystonia in musicians. *Lancet* 353:42, 1999.

Chard, S. E. Community neurorehabilitation: A synthesis of current evidence and future research directions. *NeuroRx: Journal for American Society for Experimental NeuroTherapeutics* 3:525–534, 2006.

Clower, D. M., J. M. Hoffman, J. R. Voraw, T. L. Faber, R. P. Woods, and G. E. Alexander. Role of posterior parietal cortex in the recalibration of visually-guided reaching. *Nature* 383:618–621, 1996.

Cramer, S. C., and E. P. Bastings. Mapping clinically relevant plasticity after stroke. *Neuropharmacology* 39:842–851, 2000.

Dresser, A. C., A. M. Meirowsky, G. H. Weiss, M. L. McNeel, A. G. Simon, and W. F. Caveness. Gainful employment following head injury. *Archives of Neurology* 29:111–116, 1973.

Elbert, T., S. Heim, and B. Rockstroh. Neural plasticity and development. In C. A. Nelson and M. Luciana, Eds. *Handbook of Developmental Cognitive Neuroscience.* Cambridge, Mass.: MIT Press, 2001, pp. 191–204.

Feeney, D. M. From laboratory to clinic: Noradrenergic enhancement of physical therapy for stroke or trauma patients. *Advances in Neurology* 73:383–394, 1997.

Flores, C., and J. Stewart. Basic fibroblast growth factor as a mediator of the effects of glutamate in the development of long-lasting sensitization to stimulant drugs: Studies in the rat. *Psychopharmacology (Berlin)* 151:152–165, 2000.

Freed, C. R., P. E. Greene, R. E. Breeze, W. Y. Tsai, W. DuMouchel, R. Kao, S. Dillon, H. Winfield, S. Culver, J. Q. Trojanowski, D. Eidelberg, and S. Fahn. Transplantation of embryonic dopamine neurons for severe Parkinson's disease. *New England Journal of Medicine* 344:710–719, 2001.

Goddard, G. V. Development of epileptic seizures through brain stimulation at low intensity. *Nature* 214 (5092): 1020–1021, 1967.

Hillis, A. E. Pharmacological, surgical, and neurovascular interventions to augment acute aphasia recovery. *American Journal of Physical Medicine and Rehabilitation* 86:426–634, 2007.

Jacobs, B., M. Schall, and A. B. Scheibel. A quantitative dendritic analysis of Wernicke's area in humans II: Gender, hemispheric, and environmental factors. *Journal of Comparative Neurology* 327:97–111, 1993.

Jacobs, B., and A. B. Scheibel. A quantitative dendritic analysis of Wernicke's area in humans I: Lifespan changes. *Journal of Comparative Neurology* 327:83–96, 1993.

Jenkins, W. M., M. M. Merzenich, M. T. Ochs, T. Allard, and E. Guic-Robles. Functional reorganization of primary somatosensory cortex in adult owl monkeys after behaviorally controlled tactile stimulation. *Journal of Neurophysiology* 63:82–104, 1990.

Johansson, B. B., and P. V. Belichenko. Neuronal plasticity and dendritic spines: Effect of environmental enrichment on intact and postischemic rat brain. *Journal of Cerebral Blood Flow and Metabolism* 22:89–96, 2002.

Jones, M. K. Imagery as a mnemonic aid after left temporal lobectomy: Contrast between material-specific and generalized memory disorders. *Neuropsychologia* 12:21–30, 1974.

Jones-Gotman, M., and B. Milner. Design fluency: The invention of nonsense drawings after focal cortical lesions. *Neuropsychologia* 15:653–674, 1977.

Kertesz, A. *Aphasia and Associated Disorders.* New York: Grune & Stratton, 1979.

Kohler, I. The formation and transformation of the perceptual world. *Psychological Issues* 3:1–173, 1964.

Kolb, B., and B. Milner. Performance of complex arm and facial movements after focal brain lesions. *Neuropsychologia* 19:491–503, 1981.

Kolb, B., C. Morshead, C. Gonzalez, N. Kim, T. Shingo, C. Gregg, and S. Weiss. Growth factor-stimulated generation of new cortical tissue and functional recovery after stroke damage to the motor cortex of rats. *Journal of Cerebral Blood Flow and Metabolism* 27:983–997, 2007.

Kolb, B., and I. Q. Whishaw. Brain plasticity and behavior. *Annual Review of Psychology* 49:43–64, 1998.

Leipert, J. Transcranial magnetic stimulation in neurorehabilitation. *Acta Neurochirurgica Supplement* 93:71–74, 2005.

Linge, F. What does it feel like to be brain-damaged? *Canada's Mental Health* 28:4–7, 1980.

Lucas, S. M., N. J. Rothwell, and R. M. Gibson. The role of inflammation in CNS injury and disease. *British Journal of Pharmacology* 147:S232–S240, 2006.

Luria, A. R. *The Man with a Shattered World.* New York: Basic Books, Jonathan Cape, 1972.

McEwen, B. S. Physiology and neurobiology of stress and adaptation: Central role of the brain. *Physiological Reviews* 87:873–904, 2007.

Merzenich, M. M., and W. M. Jenkins. Reorganization of cortical representations of the hand following alterations of skin inputs induced by nerve injury, skin island transfers, and experience. *Journal of Hand Therapy* 6:89–104, 1993.

Milner, B. Effect of different brain lesions on card sorting. *Archives of Neurology* 9:90–100, 1963.

Milner, B. Psychological aspects of focal epilepsy and its neurosurgical management. *Advances in Neurology* 8:299–321, 1975.

Milner, B., S. Corkin, and H.-L. Teuber. Further analysis of the hippocampal amnesic syndrome: 14-year follow-up study of H.M. *Neuropsychologia* 6:215–234, 1968.

Mohr, J. P., G. H. Weiss, W. F. Caveness, J. D. Dillon, J. P. Kistler, A. M. Meirowsky, and B. L. Rish. Language and motor disorders after penetrating head injury in Viet Nam. *Neurology* 30:1273–1279, 1980.

Moligner, A. J., A. I. Grossman, U. Ribary, M. Joliot, J. Volkmann, D. Rapaport, R. W. Beasley, and R. R. Llinas. Somatosensory cortical plasticity in adult humans revealed by magnetoencephalography. *Proceedings of the National Academy of Sciences of the United States of America* 90:3593–3597, 1993.

Morrison, G. E., and D. van der Kooy. A mutation in the AMPA-type glutamate receptor, glr-1, blocks olfactory associative and nonassociative learning in *Caenorhabditis elegans*. *Behavioral Neuroscience* 115:640–649, 2001.

Muñoz-Céspedes, J., M. Rios-Lago, N. Paul, and F. Maestú. Functional neuroimaging studies of cognitive recovery after acquired brain damage in adults. *Neuropsychology Review* 15:169–183, 2005.

Nudo, R. J., E. J. Plautz, and S. B. Frost. Role of adaptive plasticity in recovery of function after damage to motor cortex. *Muscle and Nerve* 24:1000–1019, 2001.

Nudo, R. J., E. J. Plautz, and G. W. Millikan. Adaptive plasticity in primate motor cortex as a consequence of behavioral experience and neuronal injury. *Seminars in Neuroscience* 9:13–23, 1997.

Nudo, R. J., B. M. Wise, F. SiFuentes, and G. W. Milliken. Neural substrates for the effects of rehabilitative training on motor recovery after ischemic infarct. *Science* 272:1793, 1996.

Oddy, M., and M. Humphrey. Social recovery during the year following severe head injury. *Journal of Neurology, Neurosurgery, and Psychiatry* 43:798–802, 1980.

Ormerod, B. K., and L. A. M. Galea. Mechanism and function of adult neurogenesis. In C. A. Shaw and J. C. McEachern, Eds. *Toward a Theory of Neuroplasticity.* Lillington, N.C.: Taylor & Francis, 2001, pp. 85–100.

Pantev, C., R. Oostenveld, A. Engelien, B. Ross, L. E. Roberts, and M. Hoke. Increased auditory cortical representation in musicians. *Nature* 392:811–814, 1998.

Pape, T. L., J. Rosenow, and G. Lewis. Transcranial magnetic stimulation: A possible treatment for TBI. *Journal of Head Trauma Rehabilitation* 21:437–451, 2006.

Pons, T. P., P. E. Garraghty, A. K. Ommaya, J. H. Kaas, E. Taum, and M. Mishkin. Massive cortical reorganization after sensory deafferentation in adult macaques. *Science* 272:1857–1860, 1991.

Prigatano, G. P. *Principles of Neuropsychological Rehabilitation.* New York: Oxford University Press, 2001.

Rakic, P. Adult neurogenesis in mammals: An identity crisis. *Journal of Neuroscience* 22:614–618, 2002.

Ramachandran, V. S., and W. Hirstein. The perception of phantom limbs: The D. O. Hebb lecture. *Brain* 121:1603–1630, 1998.

Rampon C., C. H. Jiang, H. Dong, Y. P. Tang, D. J. Lockhart, P. G. Schultz, J. Z. Tsien, and Y. Hu. Effects of environmental enrichment on gene expression in the brain. *Proceedings of the National Academy of Sciences of the United States of America* 97:12880–12884, 2000.

Rauschecker, J. P. Cortical plasticity and music. *Annals of the New York Academy of Sciences* 930:330–336, 2001.

Reynolds, B. A., and S. Weiss. Generation of neurons and astrocytes from isolated cells of the adult mammalian central nervous system. *Science* 255:1613–1808, 1992.

Rijntjes, M., and C. Weiller. Recovery of motor and language abilities after stroke: The contribution of functional imaging. *Progress in Neurobiology* 66:109–122, 2002.

Robinson, T. E., and B. Kolb. Structural plasticity associated with drugs of abuse. *Neuropharmacology* 47(Suppl 1):33–46, 2004.

Shaw, C. A., and J. C. McEachern, Eds. *Toward a Theory of Neuroplasticity.* Philadelphia: Taylor & Francis, 2001.

Sohlberg, M. M., and C. A. Mateer. *Introduction to Cognitive Rehabilitation.* New York: Guilford Press, 1989.

Sterr, A., M. Muller, T. Elbert, B. Rockstroh, and E. Taub. Development of cortical reorganization in the somatosensory cortex of adult Braille students.

Electroencephalography and Clinical Neurophysiology Supplement 49:292–298, 1999.

Sugita, Y. Global plasticity of adult visual system. In C. A. Shaw and J. C. McEachern, Eds. *Toward a Theory of Neuroplasticity.* Philadelphia: Taylor & Francis, 2001, pp. 44–50.

Taub, E., and D. M. Morris. Constraint-induced movement therapy to enhance recovery after stroke. *Current Atherosclerosis Reports* 3:279–286, 2001.

Taylor, L. B. Localization of cerebral lesions by psychological testing. *Clinical Neurosurgery* 16:269–287, 1969.

Teasell, R., N. Foley, K. Salter, S. Bhogal, N. Bayona, J. Jutai, and M. Speechley. *Evidence-Based Review of Stroke Rehabilitation,* 6th ed. Heart & Stroke Foundation of Ontario and the Canadian Stroke Network, Ottawa, Canada.

Teskey, G. C. Using kindling to model the neuroplastic changes associated with learning and memory, neuropsychiatric disorders, and epilepsy. In C. A. Shaw and J. C. McEachern, Eds. *Toward a Theory of Neuroplasticity.* Lillington, N.C.: Taylor & Francis, 2001, pp. 347–358.

Teskey, G. C., C. Flynn, C. D. Goertzen, M. H. Monfils, and N. A. Young. Cortical stimulation improves skilled forelimb use following a focal ischemic infarct in the rat. *Neurological Research* 25:794–800, 2003.

Teuber, H.-L. Recovery of function after brain injury in man. In *Outcome of Severe Damage to the Nervous System: Ciba Foundation Symposium 34.* Amsterdam: Elsevier North-Holland, 1975.

Teyler, T. J. LTP and the superfamily of synaptic plasticities. In C. A. Shaw and J. C. McEachern, Eds. *Toward a Theory of Neuroplasticity.* Lillington, N.C.: Taylor & Francis, 2001, pp. 101–117.

Twitchell, T. E. The restoration of motor function following hemiplegia in man. *Brain* 74:443–480, 1951.

Twitchell, T. E. The automatic grasping response of infants. *Neuropsychologia* 3:247–259, 1965.

von Monakow, C. Lokalization der Hirnfunktionen. *Journal fur Psychologie and Neurologie* 17:185–200, 1911. Reprinted in G. von Bonin. *The Cerebral Cortex.* Springfield, Ill.: Charles C Thomas, 1960.

Ward, N. S., and S. J. Frackowiak. The functional anatomy of cerebral reorganization after focal brain injury. *Journal of Physiology, Paris* 99:425–436, 2006.

Zihl, J., and D. von Cramon. Visual field rehabilitation in the cortically blind? *Journal of Neurology, Neurosurgery, and Psychiatry* 49:965–967, 1986.

Neurological Disorders 26

PORTRAIT: Dr. Johnson's Transitory Aphasia

On the afternoon of June 16, 1783, Dr. Samuel Johnson, the famed English lexicographer, sat for his portrait (shown here) by Sir Joshua Reynolds. Despite his 73 years and marked obesity, Johnson afterwards walked the considerable distance from the studio to his home. He went to sleep at his usual hour in the evening and awoke according to his account around 3 a.m. on June 17. To his surprise and horror, he found that he could not speak. He immediately tested his mental faculties by successfully composing a prayer in Latin verse. Next he tried to loosen his powers of speech by drinking some wine, violating his recently acquired habits of temperance. The wine only put him back to sleep. Upon reawakening after sunrise, Johnson still could not speak. He found, however, that he could understand others and that he could write. His penmanship and composition were somewhat defective. Johnson proceeded to summon his physicians, Drs. Brocklesby and Heberden, who came and examined him. They prescribed blisters on each side of the throat up to the ear, one on the head, and one on the back, along with salts of hartshorn [ammonium carbonate]. Heberden, who was one of London's leading doctors,

© Private collection/The Bridgeman Art Library

predicted a speedy recovery. His confidence proved quite justified: the therapeutic regimen was so efficacious that Johnson's speech began returning within a day or two. Recovery proceeded smoothly over the next month, and even the mild disorders in writing lessened. Johnson finally was left with a slight but stable dysarthria [difficulty articulating words] until he succumbed to other causes later in the next year. (Rosner, 1974, p. 1)

Dr. Johnson's case has been described and discussed many times because he was an interesting and celebrated person—the author of the first English dictionary—and because his transitory illness was never fully explained. His aphasia provides an example of almost complete loss of a specific function (speech) and seemingly rapid and almost complete recovery. The story also contains a testimony to the knowledge and insight of his doctors, because their prediction of the outcome was correct.

There are, however, many questions that the critical reader may wish to ask. How much weight should self-testimony be accorded? Did Johnson in fact experience a stroke or some other brain disorder? His claiming to have discovered, when alone in the middle of the night, that he could not speak is not unreasonable, because he was known to have the habit of talking to himself. But, because he was an eccentric, we might also wonder if the speechlessness was faked for some purpose or if its cause was psychological.

If his disorder was real, what was it and where was it? Some neurologists have thought that the lesion must have been very small or was only a transitory blood clot. Others have speculated that, because he could not speak for a time but could still think, compose Latin verse, and write, he might normally have had the functions of speech in both hemispheres. Obviously, Dr. Johnson's case provides substance for much speculation.

I n this chapter, we first describe the examination given to a patient by a neurologist. Then we survey a number of common neurological disorders and their treatment, from vascular insults and head trauma to epilepsy, tumors, headaches, and infections, to disorders of the spinal cord and of sleep.

The Neurological Examination

People suspected of sustaining a disorder of the nervous system are usually examined by a **neurologist**, a physician specializing in the treatment of such disorders. The neurologist takes a history from the patient, makes a general assessment of the patient's condition, and perhaps recommends additional tests (for example, an EEG or a brain scan) that seem to be indicated by the history or the initial examination. At the end of this initial assessment, the neurologist writes a case summary.

The Patient's History

The neurologist's first step is to ask the patient about the problem. Information is also collected about the patient's background, with particular attention paid to any history of disease, accidents, and the occurrence of symptoms such as headache, loss of consciousness, and sleep disturbances. Family background is reviewed as well, because many diseases, such as epilepsy, have a high familial incidence.

While the history is being taken, the neurologist observes the patient's behavior, assessing mental status, watching facial features for abnormalities or asymmetries, listening for speech abnormalities, and observing posture. The patient's state of awareness is described with adjectives such as *alert, drowsy, stuporous, confused*, and so forth. Any evidence of delusions and hallucinations is reported. Facial expression and behavior reveal whether the patient is agitated, anxious, depressed, apathetic, or restless.

The neurologist may test some simple aspects of memory by reciting a series of digits and asking the patient to repeat it. In addition, the neurologist may look to see whether the patient is left- or right-handed and ask about the history of handedness in the family, because handedness can be a clue to which hemisphere controls speech. A number of simple tests for speech may be given, such as asking the meaning of words, having rhymes or words repeated (for example, "la-la," "ta-ta"), having objects named, and having the patient read and write.

The Physical Examination

The neurologist uses a number of tools in the course of the physical examination. They include (1) a measuring tape to measure head and body size, the size of skin lesions, and so on; (2) a stethoscope to listen to the sounds of the heart and blood vessels and an otoscope to examine the auditory canal and eardrum; (3) a flashlight to elicit pupillary reflexes; (4) tongue blades to elicit the gag reflex and abdominal and plantar reflexes; (5) a vial of coffee to assess smell and vials of salt and sugar to assess taste; (6) a 256-Hz tuning fork to test vibratory sensation and hearing; (7) a cotton wisp to elicit the corneal reflex and to test sensitivity to light touch, plastic tubes to test temperature sensations, and pins to test pain sensation; (8) a hammer to elicit muscle stretch reflexes, such as the knee-jerk reflex; (9) some coins and keys to test the recognition of objects through touch; and (10) a blood-pressure cuff to measure blood pressure.

One of the most important parts of the neurological examination is the study of the head. Its general features such as size and shape are assessed, and a detailed examination is made of the sensory and motor functioning of its 12 sets of cranial nerves. Cranial-nerve malfunctions discovered in this part of the examination can be important clues to the location and nature of nervous system damage.

The motor system in other parts of the body is examined to assess muscle bulk, tone, and power; to test for the occurrence of involuntary muscle movements, such as shaking and tremors; and to assess the status of reflexes. In addition, coordination is examined by having a patient perform such tasks as walking heel to toe in a straight line, touching the neurologist's finger and his or her own nose repeatedly, making rapid alternating movements of the fingers, tapping the foot as rapidly as possible, and so on. Generally, all the muscles of the body are tested in head-to-foot order, and the status of each is recorded on a standard chart.

A sensory examination includes an investigation of sensitivity to painful stimulation, to touch, and to temperature, as well as an analysis of vibration sense, joint-position sense, two-point discrimination, tactile localization, identification of objects, and the ability to identify numbers or letters traced on the skin with a blunt object. These sensory tests allow assessment of the functions of individual sensory systems and provide information about the location of possible dysfunctions.

Vascular Disorders

Normal central nervous system functioning can be affected by a number of vascular problems, because blood-vessel disease or damage can greatly—even totally—reduce the flow of oxygen and glucose to a brain region. If such interference lasts longer than 10 minutes, all cells in the affected region die. Most disease of the cerebral vascular system develops in the arterial system (review Figure 3.4); disease of venous drainage is uncommon in the CNS. Cerebral vascular diseases are among the most common causes of death and chronic disability in the Western world.

A common term used in a discussion of cerebral vascular disorder is *stroke*, also known as **cerebral vascular accident**. A **stroke** is the sudden appearance of neurological symptoms as a result of the interruption of blood flow. Stroke can result from a wide variety of vascular disorders, but not all vascular disorders produce stroke. The onset of dysfunction can be insidious, spanning months or even years. Stroke often produces an **infarct**, an area of dead or dying tissue resulting from an obstruction of the blood vessels normally supplying the area. Stroke is the most common cause of death worldwide. As you read this paragraph, someone in the United States will suffer a vascular accident.

If the flow through small blood vessels, such as capillaries, is interrupted, the effects are more limited than the often-devastating consequences of damage to large vessels. If a stroke or other cerebral vascular disorder is in one restricted part of a vessel (and other parts of the system are relatively healthy), the prognosis can be rather good, because vessels in the surrounding areas can often supply blood to at least some of the deprived area. On the other hand, if a stroke affects a region supplied largely by weak or diseased vessels, the effects can be much more serious, because there is no possibility of compensation. In addition, the surrounding weak zones themselves may be at increased risk of stroke.

In the long run, a small vascular lesion in a healthy brain will have a good prognosis for substantial recovery of function. In the event of preexisting vascular lesions, the effects of the new lesions may be extremely variable. The lesions can be cumulative and obliterate a functional zone of brain tissue, producing serious consequences. As with other lesions, the behavioral symptoms subsequent to vascular lesions depend on the location of damage.

Of the numerous vascular disorders that affect the central nervous system, the most common are ischemia, migraine stroke, cerebral hemorrhage, angiomas, and arteriovenous aneurysms.

Cerebral Ischemia

Ischemia refers to any of a group of disorders in which the symptoms are caused by vessel blockage preventing a sufficient supply of blood to the brain. In **thrombosis**, for example, some of the blood in a vessel has coagulated to form a plug or clot that has remained at the place of its formation. An **embolism** is a clot or other plug brought through the blood from a larger vessel and forced into a smaller one, where it obstructs circulation. An embolism can be a blood clot, a bubble of air, a deposit of oil or fat, or a small mass of cells detached from a tumor. Curiously, embolisms most often affect the middle cerebral artery of the left side of the brain.

Reduction in blood flow can also result from other factors that narrow the vessel. The most common example of such narrowing is a condition marked by thickening and hardening of the arteries, called **cerebral arteriosclerosis**. When ischemia is temporary, it may be termed **cerebral vascular insufficiency** or **transient ischemia**, indicating the variable nature of the disorder with the passage of time. The onset of transient attacks is often abrupt; in many cases, they are experienced as fleeting sensations of giddiness or impaired consciousness.

Migraine Stroke

Since the late 1800s, physicians have recognized that **migraine attacks** may lead to infarcts and permanent neurological deficits. Such migraine strokes are relatively rare compared with other types, but they are believed to account for a significant proportion of strokes in young people (under 40 years of age), especially women. The immediate cause of these strokes is probably some form of vasospasm—constriction of blood vessels—but the underlying cause of the vasospasm remains a mystery.

The classic migraine stroke is experienced as a transient ischemic attack with a variety of neurological symptoms, including impaired sensory function (especially vision), numbness of the skin (especially in the arms), difficulties in moving, and aphasia. The precise symptoms depend on the vessels affected; however, the posterior cerebral artery is most commonly affected.

Cerebral Hemorrhage

Cerebral hemorrhage is a massive bleeding into the substance of the brain. The most frequent cause is high blood pressure, or *hypertension*. Other causes include congenital defects in cerebral arteries, blood disorders such as leukemia, and toxic chemicals. The onset of cerebral hemorrhage is abrupt, and the bleeding may quickly prove fatal. It usually occurs when a person is awake, presumably because the person is more active and thus has higher blood pressure. Prognosis is poor in cerebral hemorrhage, especially if the patient is unconscious for more than 48 hours.

Angiomas and Aneurysms

Angiomas are congenital collections of abnormal vessels that divert the normal flow of blood. These capillary, venous, or **arteriovenous** (A–V) **malformations** are masses of enlarged and tortuous cortical vessels that are supplied by one or more large arteries and are drained by one or more large veins, most often in the field of the middle cerebral artery. Because they create abnormalities in the amount and pattern of blood flow and are inherently weak, angiomas may lead to stroke or to an inadequate distribution of blood in the regions surrounding the vessels. In some cases, they cause arterial blood to flow directly into veins only briefly, or sometimes not at all, after servicing the surrounding brain tissue.

MRI angiogram looking down on the surface of the brain of an 18-year-old girl with an angioma. The abnormal cerebral blood vessels (white) formed a balloonlike structure (blue area at lower right) that caused the death of brain tissue around it in the right occipital cortex. (Simon Frasier, Royal Victoria Infirmary, Newcastle Upon Tyne, Science Photo Library/Photo Researchers.)

    Aneurysms are vascular dilations resulting from localized defects in the elasticity of a vessel. They can be visualized as balloonlike expansions of vessels that are usually weak and prone to rupture. Although aneurysms are usually due to congenital defects, they may also develop from hypertension, arteriosclerosis, embolisms, or infections. A characteristic symptom of an aneurysm is severe headache, which may be present for years, because the aneurysm is exerting pressure on the dura mater, which is richly endowed with pain receptors.

The Treatment of Vascular Disorders

Most vascular disorders have no specific treatment, although the most common remedies include drug therapy and surgery. Supportive therapies are useful only if they are delivered within 3 hours after a vascular emergency. They include such drugs as anticoagulants to dissolve clots or prevent clotting, vasodilators to dilate the vessels, drugs to reduce blood pressure, and salty solutions or steroids to reduce cerebral **edema** (the accumulation of fluid in and around damaged tissue).

    Surgical techniques have improved greatly in recent years but are not always practical. For example, the only certain cure for an aneurysm is total removal, which is usually not feasible. Aneurysms are sometimes painted with various plastic substances to prevent them from rupturing. In regard to cerebral hemorrhage, it may be necessary to perform surgery to relieve the pressure of the blood from the ruptured vessel on the rest of the brain.

Figure **26.1**

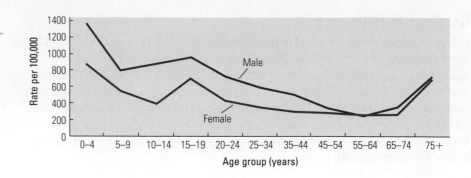

Traumatic Brain Injury in the United States by Sex, 1995–2001 Based on combined reports of emergency-room visits, hospitalizations, and deaths, this chart graphs the average annual rates of TBI per 100,000 people. (After the Centers for Disease Control report *TBI in the United States: Emergency Department Visits, Hospitalizations, and Deaths,* 2004.)

Traumatic Brain Injuries

Brain injury is a common result of automobile and industrial accidents and of war injuries. According to the Joint Theater Trauma Registry, compiled by the U.S. Army Institute of Surgical Research, 22% of U.S. soldiers wounded in the aftermath of the Iraq war have traumatic brain injury. Back at home, cerebral trauma or injury from a blow to the head is the most common form of brain damage in people under the age of 40. TBI is about eight times as frequent as breast cancer, AIDS, spinal-cord injury, and multiple sclerosis combined.

The two most important factors in the incidence of head injury are age and sex. Sport activities account for about 20% of TBI, with injuries occurring most commonly in contact sports such as American football, hockey, rugby, and lacrosse. Heading in soccer can also cause TBI, but the incidence and severity of such injury is unknown. The difficulty in evaluating TBI in sports relates to the underreporting of mild TBI and the problem of tracking repeated injuries. Children and elderly people are more likely to suffer head injuries from falls than are others, and males between 15 and 30 years of age are very likely to incur brain injuries, especially from automobile and motorcycle accidents (**Figure 26.1**).

Head injury can affect brain function by causing direct damage to the brain; by disrupting blood supply; by inducing bleeding, leading to increased intracranial pressure; by causing swelling, leading to increased intracranial pressure; by opening the brain to infection; and by producing the scarring of brain tissue (the scarred tissue becomes a focus for later epileptic seizures). There are two main types of brain trauma: open-head injury and closed-head injury.

Open-Head Injuries

Open-head injuries are TBIs in which the skull is penetrated, as in gunshot or missile wounds, or in which fragments of bone penetrate the brain substance. In many cases, the injury does not cause the victim to lose consciousness.

Open-head injuries tend to produce distinctive symptoms that may undergo rapid and spontaneous recovery. The neurological signs may be highly specific, and many of the effects of the injuries closely resemble those of the surgical excision of a small area of cortex. The specificity of neurological symptoms subsequent to open-head injuries makes such patients especially good research subjects. Three thorough investigations of World War II (1939–1945) veterans with open-head injuries have been published—by Freda Newcombe, by Alexander Luria, and by Hans-Leukas Teuber and his coworkers.

Closed-Head Injuries

Closed-head injuries result from a blow to the head, which can subject the brain to a variety of mechanical forces:

- Damage at the site of the blow, a bruise (contusion) called a **coup**, is incurred where the brain has been compacted by the bone's pushing inward, even when the skull is not fractured (**Figure 26.2**).

- The pressure that produces the coup may push the brain against the opposite side or end of the skull, producing an additional bruise, known as a **countercoup** (see Figure 26.2).

- The movement of the brain may cause a twisting or shearing of nerve fibers, producing microscopic lesions. These lesions may be throughout the brain but are most common in the frontal and temporal lobes. In addition, twisting and shearing may damage the major fiber tracts of the brain, especially those crossing the midline, such as the corpus callosum and anterior commissure. As a result, connection between the two sides of the brain may be disrupted, leading to a disconnection syndrome (see Chapter 17).

- Bruises and strains caused by the impact may produce bleeding (hemorrhage). Because the blood is trapped within the skull, it acts as a growing mass (hematoma), exerting pressure on surrounding structures.

- As with blows to other parts of the body, blows to the brain produce edema, another source of pressure on the brain tissue.

Closed-head injuries resulting from traffic accidents are particularly severe because the head is moving when the blow is struck, thereby increasing the velocity of the impact and multiplying the number and severity of small lesions

A variety of mechanical forces cause traumatic brain injuries as a result of a blow to the head.

Damage at the site of impact is called a coup (shown in pink).

← **Direction of blow**   **Direction of blow** →

Pressure resulting from a coup produces a countercoup on the opposite end or side of the brain (shown in blue).

Movement of the brain may shear nerve fibers, causing microscopic lesions, especially in frontal and temporal lobes. Blood trapped in the skull (hematoma) and swelling (edema) cause pressure on the brain.

Figure **26.2**

Results of TBI Brain regions most frequently damaged in closed-head injury are indicated by pink and blue shading. A blow can produce a contusion both at the site of impact and at the opposite side of the brain, owing to compression of the brain against the front or the back of the skull.

throughout the brain. Computerized tomographic scans of accident victims suffering prolonged **coma** (loss of consciousness) show diffuse brain injury and enlarged ventricles, signs associated with poor outcomes.

Closed-head injuries are commonly accompanied by coma. According to Muriel Lezak, the duration of unconsciousness can serve as a measure of the severity of damage, because it correlates directly with mortality, intellectual impairment, and deficits in social skills. The longer a coma lasts, the greater the possibility of serious impairment and death.

Two kinds of behavioral effects result from closed-head injuries: (1) discrete impairment of the specific functions mediated by the cortex at the site of the coup or countercoup lesion and (2) more generalized impairments from widespread trauma throughout the brain. Discrete impairment is most commonly associated with damage to the frontal and temporal lobes, the areas most susceptible to closed-head injuries. More general impairment, resulting from minute lesions and lacerations scattered throughout the brain and from tears due to movement of the hemispheres in relation to each other, is characterized by a loss of complex cognitive functions, including reductions in mental speed, concentration, and overall cognitive efficiency.

Patients generally complain of an inability to concentrate or to do things as well as they could before the accident, even though their intelligence rating may still be well above average. In fact, in our experience, it seems that bright people are the most affected by closed-head injuries because they are acutely aware of any loss of cognitive skill that prevents them from returning to their former competence level.

Closed-head injuries that damage the frontal and temporal lobes also tend to have significant effects on personality and social behavior. According to Lezak, relatively few victims of traffic accidents who have sustained severe head injuries ever resume their studies or return to gainful employment; if they do reenter the work force, they do so at a level lower than that before their accidents.

Often, the chronic effects of closed-head injuries are not accompanied by any obvious neurological signs, and the patients may therefore be referred for psychiatric evaluation. Thorough psychological assessments are especially useful in these cases for uncovering seriously handicapping cognitive deficits that have not yet become apparent. The pathological effects of closed-head injury are summarized in **Table 26.1**.

People who once sustain head injuries are more likely to sustain subsequent head injuries, both because they are likely to become more careless and because they may continue with the activity that resulted in the injury. There is a strong suggestion in the literature that the effects of even very mild head injuries may be cumulative. For example, it is well established that a boxer will sustain a significant level of brain injury—culminating in a condition called *traumatic encephalopathy* (known more commonly as the "punch-drunk syndrome")—even though the periods of unconsciousness experienced by the boxer may have been few and of short duration.

Table 26.1 Primary and secondary brain injury after closed-head trauma

Primary (Immediate on Impact) Brain Injuries
Macroscopic lesions
  Contusions underlying the site of impact (coup)
  Countercoup contusion, frequently in the undersurfaces of the frontal lobes and the tips of the temporal lobes
  Laceration of the brain from depressed skull fracture
Microscopic lesions
  Widespread shearing or stretching of fibers

Secondary Consequences of Brain Injury
Intracranial hemorrhage
Edema in white matter adjacent to focal mass lesions
Diffuse brain swelling—hyperemia
Ischemic brain damage
Raised intracranial pressure
Brain shift and herniation

Secondary Insult from Extracerebral Events
Effects of multiple or systemic injury or both
  Hypoxia
  Fat embolism

Delayed Effects
Degeneration of white matter
Disturbed flow of cerebrospinal fluid—hydrocephalus

Source: After Levin et al., 1987.

Repetitive head injury is likely to occur in many other contact sports but, because each incidence may be relatively mild, such effects are likely underreported and so are difficult to track. For example, 30% of bouts of extreme fighting are stopped owing to a head blow, but the number of blows to the head that cause TBI is not known. Surprisingly, fewer brain injuries may be incurred in extreme fighting than in boxing because fighters can tap out when injured and fights are stopped quickly when one fighter has an advantage.

Behavioral Assessment in Head Injury

Although neuroradiological measures can provide objective indicators of neural status after head injury, behavior is the most important measure of the integrity of the nervous system. In the immediate postinjury period, the two most obvious behavioral symptoms are coma and amnesia. Clinical judgment of the depth of coma was largely subjective and unreliable until the Glasgow Coma Scale (**Table 26.2**) was designed to provide an objective indicator of the degree of unconsciousness and of recovery from unconsciousness.

Table **26.2** The Glasgow Coma Scale

Response	Points	Index of Wakefulness
		Eye Opening (E)
None	1	Not attributable to ocular swelling
To pain	2	Pain stimulus is applied to chest or limbs
To speech	3	Nonspecific response to speech or shout; does not imply that the patient obeys command to open eyes
Spontaneous	4	Eyes are open; does not imply intact awareness
		Motor Response (M)
No response	1	Flaccid
Extension	2	"Decerebrate," adduction, internal rotation of shoulder, and pronation of the forearm
Abnormal flexion	3	"Decorticate," abnormal flexion, adduction of the shoulder
Withdrawal	4	Normal flexor response; withdraws from pain stimulus with abduction of the shoulder
Localizes pain	5	Pain stimulus applied to supraocular region or fingertip causes limb to move to attempt to avoid it
Obeys commands	6	Follows simple commands
		Verbal Response (V)
No response	1	(Self-explanatory)
Incomprehensible	2	Moaning and groaning, but no recognizable words
Inappropriate	3	Intelligible speech (e.g., shouting or swearing), but no sustained or coherent conversation
Confused	4	Patient responds to questions in a conversational manner, but the responses indicate varying degrees of disorientation and confusion
Oriented	5	Normal orientation to time, place, and person

Note: The summed Glasgow Coma Scale is equal to E + M + V (3–15 points).
Source: After B. Teasdale and B. Jennett, 1974.

(A)

(B)

Figure 26.3

Acute Alterations in Memory after Closed-Head Injury (A) A diagram showing the sequence of alterations. The period of coma and anterograde amnesia are often called the period of posttraumatic amnesia (PTA), although by some definitions PTA is limited to the anterograde amnesia. (B) Histograms showing the distribution of individual scores of story recall by patients in three groups distinguished by the period of PTA. Scores represent recall of the second of two stories. (Part A after Levin et al., 1987; part B after Newcombe, 1969.)

In this scale, three indices of wakefulness are evaluated: eye opening, motor response, and verbal response. A score of 8 or less is often used as a criterion for severe closed-head injury, with a score ranging from 9 to 12 being a criterion for moderate injury. A shortcoming of the scale as a measure of the severity of brain injury is that as many as 50% of brain-injury victims admitted to hospitals have scores ranging from 13 to 15, indicating an absence of coma, and yet, later, such patients may suffer many of the consequences of head injury.

The length of posttraumatic amnesia (PTA) is an alternative measure of the severity of injury. Even though definitions of PTA vary (some include the period of coma, whereas others are restricted to the period of anterograde amnesia), there is good evidence that the duration of amnesia is correlated (imperfectly) with later memory disturbance, as illustrated in **Figure 26.3**. A commonly used scale is as follows: amnesia lasting less than 10 minutes corresponds to very mild injury; amnesia lasting 10 to 60 minutes corresponds to mild injury; amnesia lasting 1 to 24 hours corresponds to moderate injury; amnesia lasting 1 to 7 days corresponds to severe injury; amnesia lasting more than 7 days corresponds to very severe injury.

A problem with using amnesia as a measure is that there is no consistent method of measuring it. Researchers evaluate it, variously, by retrospective questioning, by measures of disorientation, or by neuropsychological assessment, and each method yields a different estimate of the severity of amnesia and, hence, of the extent of injury.

Recovery from Head Injury

Although it is often stated that recovery from head trauma may continue for 2 to 3 years, there is little doubt that the bulk of the cognitive recovery takes place in the first 6 to 9 months. Recovery of memory functions appears to be somewhat slower than recovery of general intelligence, and the final level of memory performance is lower than that of other cognitive functions. People with brainstem damage, as inferred from oculomotor disturbance, have a poorer cognitive outcome, and it is probably true of people with initial dysphasias or hemipareses as well.

Although the prognosis for significant recovery of cognitive functions is good, there is less optimism about the recovery of social skills or normal personality, areas that often change significantly. The results of numerous studies support the conclusion that the quality of life—in regard to social interactions, perceived stress levels, and enjoyment of leisure activities—is significantly reduced after closed-head injury and that this reduction is chronic. There have been few attempts to develop tools to measure changes in psychosocial adjustment in brain-injured people; so we must rely largely on subjective descriptions and self-reports, which provide little information about the specific causes of these problems.

Epilepsy

In epilepsy, a person suffers recurrent seizures of various types that register on an electroencephalogram and are associated with disturbances of consciousness (see Figure 6.5). Epileptic episodes have been called *convulsions, seizures, fits,* and *attacks,* but none of these terms on its own is entirely satisfactory, because the character of the episodes can vary greatly. Epileptic seizures are common; 1 person in 20 will experience at least one seizure in his or her lifetime. The prevalence of multiple seizures is much lower, however—about 1 in 200.

Epileptic seizures are classified as **symptomatic seizures** if they can be identified with a specific cause, such as infection, trauma, tumor, vascular malformation, toxic chemicals, very high fever, or other neurological disorders. They are called **idiopathic seizures** if they appear to arise spontaneously and in the absence of other diseases of the central nervous system. **Table 26.3** summarizes the great variety of circumstances that appear to be able to precipitate seizures. Although the range of these circumstances is striking, a consistent feature is that the brain is most epileptogenic when it is relatively inactive and the patient is sitting still.

Although epilepsy has long been known to run in families, its incidence is lower than a one-gene genetic model would predict. What is more likely is that certain genotypes have a predisposition to seizure problems given certain environmental circumstances. The most remarkable clinical feature of epileptic disorders is the widely varying length of intervals between attacks—from minutes to hours to weeks or even years. In fact, it is almost impossible to describe a basic set of symptoms to be expected in all or even most people with the disorder. At the same time, three particular symptoms are found in many types of epilepsy:

1. **An aura, or warning, of impending seizure.** This aura may take the form of a sensation—an odor or a noise—or it may simply be a "feeling" that the seizure is going to take place.

2. **Loss of consciousness.** Ranging from complete collapse in some people to simply staring off into space in others, loss of consciousness is often accompanied by amnesia in which the victim forgets the seizure itself and the period of lost consciousness.

3. **Movement.** Seizures commonly have a motor component, although the characteristics vary considerably. Some people shake during an attack; others exhibit automatic movements, such as rubbing the hands or chewing.

A diagnosis of epilepsy is usually confirmed by an EEG. In some epileptics, however, seizures are difficult to demonstrate in this way except under special circumstances (for example, in an EEG recorded during sleep). Moreover, not all persons with an EEG suggestive of epilepsy actually have seizures. In fact, some estimates suggest that 1 person in 5 has an abnormal EEG pattern, which is many more than the number of people thought to suffer from epilepsy. Several schemes for classifying epilepsy have been published through the years. Four commonly recognized types of seizures are: focal seizures, generalized seizures, and akinetic and myoclonic seizures.

Table 26.3 Factors that may precipitate seizures in susceptible persons

Hyperventilation
Sleep
Sleep deprivation
Sensory stimuli
    Flashing lights
    Reading, speaking, coughing
    Laughing
    Sounds: music, bells
Trauma
Hormonal changes
    Menses
    Puberty
    Adrenal steroids
    Adrenocorticotrophic hormone (ACTH)
Fever
Emotional stress
Drugs
    Phenothiazines
    Analeptics
    Tricyclic antidepressants
    Alcohol
    Excessive anticonvulsants

Source: After Pincus and Tucker, 2003.

Focal Seizures

A **focal seizure** begins in one place and then spreads. In a **Jacksonian focal seizure**, for example, the attack begins with jerking movements in one part of the body (for example, a finger, a toe, or the mouth) and then spreads to adjacent parts. If the attack begins with a finger, the jerks might spread to other fingers, then the hand, the arm, and so on, producing the so-called Jacksonian march. John Hughlings-Jackson hypothesized in 1870 that such seizures probably originate from the point (focus) in the neocortex representing the region of the body where the movement is first seen. He was later proved correct.

Complex partial seizures, another type of focal seizure, originate most commonly in the temporal lobe and somewhat less frequently in the frontal lobe. Complex partial seizures are characterized by three common manifestations: (1) subjective experiences that presage the attack such as forced, repetitive thoughts, sudden alterations in mood, feelings of déjà vu, or hallucinations; (2) **automatisms**, which are repetitive stereotyped movements such as lip smacking or chewing or activities such as undoing buttons; and (3) postural changes, such as when the person assumes a catatonic, or frozen, posture.

Generalized Seizures

Generalized seizures are bilaterally symmetrical without focal onset. One subtype, the grand mal attack, is characterized by loss of consciousness and by stereotyped motor activity. This kind of seizure typically comprises three stages: (1) a tonic stage, in which the body stiffens and breathing stops; (2) a clonic stage, in which there is rhythmic shaking; and (3) a postseizure, also called **postictal**, depression, during which the patient is confused. About 50% of these seizures are preceded by an aura.

The **petit mal attack** is a loss of awareness during which there is no motor activity except for blinking, turning the head, or rolling the eyes. These attacks are of brief duration, seldom exceeding about 10 seconds. The EEG recording of a petit mal seizure has a typical pattern known as the three-per-second spike and wave.

Akinetic and Myoclonic Seizures

Akinetic seizures are ordinarily seen only in children. Usually, an affected child collapses suddenly and without warning. These seizures are often of very short duration, and the child may get up after only a few seconds. The fall can be dangerous, however, and a common recommendation is to have the children wear football helmets until the seizures can be controlled by medication. **Myoclonic spasms** are massive seizures that basically consist of a sudden flexion or extension of the body and often begin with a cry.

The Treatment of Epilepsy

The treatment of choice for epilepsy is an anticonvulsant drug such as diphenylhydantoin (DPH, Dilantin), phenobarbital, or one of several others. These drugs inhibit the discharge of abnormal neurons by stabilizing the neuronal membrane. If medication fails to alleviate the seizure problem satisfactorily, surgery can be performed to remove the focus of abnormal functioning in patients with focal seizures.

Tumors

A **tumor**, or *neoplasm*, is a mass of new tissue that persists and grows independently of its surrounding structures and has no physiological use. Brain tumors grow from glia or other support cells rather than from neurons. The rate at which tumors grow varies widely, depending on the type of cell that gave rise to them. Tumors account for a relatively high proportion of neurological disease compared with other causes; after the uterus, the brain is the most common site for them.

Tumors that are not likely to recur after removal are called *benign*, and tumors that are likely to recur after removal—often progressing and becoming a threat to life—are called *malignant*. Although there are good reasons for distinguishing between benign and malignant tumors, the benign tumor may be as serious as the malignant one, because benign tumors in the brain are often inaccessible to the surgeon. The brain is affected by many types of tumors, and no region of the brain is immune to tumor formation.

Tumors can affect behavior in a number of ways. A tumor may develop as a distinct entity in the brain, a so-called encapsulated tumor, and put pressure on the other parts of the brain (**Figure 26.4**). Some encapsulated tumors are also cystic, which means that they produce a fluid-filled cavity in the brain, usually lined with the tumor cells. Because the skull is of fixed size, any increase in its contents compresses the brain, resulting in dysfunctions.

In contrast with encapsulating tumors, so-called infiltrating tumors are not clearly marked off from the surrounding tissue; they may either destroy normal cells and occupy their place or surround existing cells (both neurons and glia) and interfere with their normal functioning (**Figure 26.5**). The general symptoms of brain tumors, which result from increased intracranial pressure, include headache, vomiting, swelling of the optic disc (papilledema), slowing of the heart rate (bradycardia), mental dullness, double vision (diplopia), and, finally, convulsions, as well as functional impairments due to damage to the brain where the tumor is located.

Brain tumors are distinguished on the basis of where they originate: they can be gliomas, meningiomas, or metastatic tumors. **Glioma** is a general term for the roughly 45% of brain tumors that arise from glial cells and infiltrate the brain substance. Gliomas, ranging from the relatively benign to the highly malignant, vary considerably in their response to treatment.

Meningiomas are growths attached to the meninges, the protective outer layer of the brain. They grow entirely outside the brain, are well encapsulated, and are the most benign of all brain tumors (see Figure 26.4). But, even though meningiomas do not invade the brain, they are often multiple and disturb brain function by putting pressure on the brain, often producing seizures as a symptom. Although most meningiomas lie over the hemispheres, some develop between them and are therefore more difficult to remove. If meningiomas are

Figure 26.4

Encapsulated Tumor Frontal section showing a meningioma arising in the dura mater and compressing the right cerebral hemisphere. Notice that the tumor has not infiltrated the brain. (From Zacks, © 1971; reprinted with permission.)

Meningioma

Figure 26.5

Infiltrating Tumor Frontal section showing a glioblastoma (a malignant type of glia-derived tumor) in the right cerebral hemisphere. Note the displacement of the ventricular system and the invasion of brain tissue (dark area). (From Bannister, © 1978; reprinted with permission.)

Ventricles   Glioblastoma

removed completely, they tend not to recur. When they are present, however, it is not uncommon for these tumors to erode the overlying bone of the skull.

Metastasis is the transfer of disease from one organ or part to another not directly connected with it. Thus, a **metastatic tumor** in the brain is one that has become established by a transfer of tumor cells from some other region of the body, most often a lung or a breast. Indeed, it is not uncommon for the first indication of lung cancer to be evidence of a brain tumor. Metastases to the brain are usually multiple, making treatment complicated, and prognosis poor.

The most straightforward treatment of brain tumors is surgery, which is also the only way to make a definite histological diagnosis. If feasible, tumors are removed, but, as with tumors elsewhere in the body, success depends on early diagnosis. Radiation therapy is useful for treating certain types of tumors. Chemotherapy has not yet been very successful in the treatment of brain tumors, partly because of the difficulty of getting drugs to pass the blood–brain barrier and enter the tumor.

Headaches

Headache is so common among the general population that rare indeed is the person who has never suffered one. Headache may constitute a neurological disorder in itself, as in migraine; it may be secondary to neurological disease such as tumor or infection; or it may result from psychological factors, especially stress, as in tension headaches. The pain-sensitive structures within the skull that can produce the headache include the dura mater; the large arteries of the brain; the venous sinuses; and the branches of the 5th, 9th, and 10th cranial nerves and the 1st and 3rd cervical nerves. Pain can be elicited in these structures by pressure, displacement, or inflammation. There are a number of different kinds of headache, including migraine, headache associated with neurological disease, muscle-contraction headaches, and nonmigrainous vascular headaches.

Migraine

Perhaps the most common neurological disorder, **migraine** (derived from the Greek *hemi* and *kranion*, meaning "half of skull") afflicts some 5% to 20% of the population at some time in their lives. The World Federation of Neurology defines migraine as a "familial disorder characterized by recurrent attacks of headache widely variable in intensity, frequency, and duration. Attacks are commonly unilateral and are usually associated with anorexia, nausea, and vomiting. In some cases they are preceded by, or associated with, neurological and mood disturbances."

There are several types of migraine, including classic migraine, common migraine, cluster headache, and hemiplegic and ophthalmologic migraine. **Classic migraine** is probably the most interesting form, occurring in about 12% of migraine sufferers, because it begins with an aura, which usually lasts for 20 to 40 minutes. Karl Lashley, arguably the first neuropsychologist, suffered from classic migraine and carefully described his visual aura, which turned out to be common to many migraine sufferers (**Figure 26.6**).

X = Fixation point

Figure **26.6**

Development of a Migraine Scotoma As described by Karl Lashley, the person first sees a small patch of stripes in the center of the visual field, as shown near the small "x" in the center of the left-hand photograph. Information from the world is no longer visible in that part of the visual field. The striped area spreads progressively outward, leaving a white area where the stripes had been before. Within 15 to 20 minutes, the visual field is almost completely blocked by the scotoma (photograph at far right). Normal vision returns shortly thereafter. (Novastock/Stock Connection/Picture Quest.)

The aura is thought to occur because constriction of one or more cerebral arteries has produced ischemia of the occipital cortex. The results of PET studies have shown that, during the aura, there is a reduction in blood flow in the posterior cortex, and this reduction spreads at the rate of about 2 millimeters per minute, without regard to its location with respect to major blood vessels. Why the reduction in blood flow should spread independently of the major vessels is not known, but its doing so suggests that the vascular changes are secondary to changes in neural function.

The actual headache begins as the vasoconstriction reverses (ending the neurological disturbance) and vasodilation takes place. The headache is experienced as an intense pain localized in one side of the head, although it often spreads on that side and sometimes extends to the opposite side as well. A severe headache can be accompanied by nausea and vomiting, and it may last for hours or even days. A significant number of people considered to have classic migraine never suffer the headache but experience the aura.

Common migraine is the most frequent type, occurring in more than 80% of migraine sufferers. There is no clear aura as there is in classic migraine, but there may be a gastrointestinal or other "signal" that an attack is pending. **Cluster headache** is a unilateral pain in the head or face that rarely lasts longer than 2 hours but recurs repeatedly for a period of weeks or even months before disappearing. Sometimes long periods pass between one series of cluster headaches and the next. The remaining two types of migraine, **hemiplegic migraine** and **ophthalmologic migraine**, are relatively rare and include loss of movement of the limbs and eyes, respectively.

The frequency of migraine attacks varies from as often as once a week to as seldom as once in a lifetime. In cases in which migraine is frequent, the occurrence generally decreases with age and usually ceases in middle age. Migraine was generally believed to be rare before adolescence, but, in recent years, it has been recognized to afflict children as well, although the actual incidence in this population is uncertain.

Headache Associated with Neurological Disease

Headache is a symptom of many nervous system disorders, usually resulting from the distortion of pain-sensitive structures. Common disorders producing headache include tumor, head trauma, infection, vascular malformations, and severe hypertension (high blood pressure). The characteristics and locations of these headaches vary according to the underlying cause. For example, headache from a brain tumor is almost always located on the same side of the head as the tumor, particularly in the early stages of tumor growth. Headaches induced by brain tumors have no characteristic severity; they may vary from mild to excruciating. Likewise, hypertension headache, although it is nearly always located in the occipital region, is highly variable in severity.

Muscle-Contraction Headache

The most common headaches are **muscle-contraction headaches**, also known as tension or nervous headaches. They result from sustained contraction of the muscles of the scalp and neck caused by constant stress and tension, especially if poor posture is maintained for any time. Patients describe their pain as steady, nonpulsing, tight, squeezing, or pressing or as the feeling of having the head in a vise. Some patients complain of a crawling sensation. The headaches may be accompanied by anxiety, dizziness, and bright spots in front of the eyes. In some people, caffeine may exacerbate the headaches, presumably because it exacerbates anxiety.

Nonmigrainous Vascular Headaches

Headache associated with dilation of the cranial arteries can be induced by a wide variety of diseases and conditions. The most common causes are fever, anoxia (lack of oxygen), anemia, high altitude, physical effort, hypoglycemia (low blood sugar), foods, and chemical agents. In addition, headache may result from congestion and edema of the nasal membranes, often termed vasomotor rhinitis, which is assumed to be a localized vascular reaction to stress.

The Treatment of Headaches

Migraine is treated by specific drugs at the time of an attack and by preventive measures between attacks. In an acute attack, **ergotamine** compounds, often given in conjunction with caffeine, are useful in alleviating the headache, probably because they produce constriction of the cerebral arteries, thus reducing dilation, which is the source of the pain. In addition, most migraine sufferers find that the headache is reduced in a totally dark room.

The most obvious treatment for headache arising from neurological disease is to treat the disease itself. Tension headaches can be relieved by muscle-relaxant drugs, minor tranquilizers, the application of heat to the affected muscles, and improvement of posture. They can also be prevented by avoiding the life situations that give rise to stress.

Infections

Infection is the invasion of the body by disease-producing (pathogenic) microorganisms and the reaction of the tissues to their presence and to the toxins generated by them. Because the central nervous system can be invaded by a wide variety of infectious agents—including viruses, bacteria, fungi, and metazoan parasites—the diagnosis and treatment of infection are important components of clinical neurology. Although infections of the nervous system usually spread from infection elsewhere in the body—especially the ears, nose, and throat—they also may be introduced directly into the brain as a result of head trauma, skull fractures, or surgery. Infections of the nervous system are particularly serious because the affected neurons and glia usually die, leaving permanent lesions.

There are a number of processes by which infections kill neural cells:

- Infections may interfere with the blood supply to neurons, thus producing thrombosis, hemorrhaging of capillaries, or even the complete choking of larger blood vessels.

- An infection may disturb glucose or oxygen metabolism in brain cells severely enough to kill them.

- An infection may alter the characteristics of neural-cell membranes, thus changing the electrical properties of the neurons, or it may interfere with the basic enzymatic processes of neurons, producing any number of abnormal conditions.

- Infection leads to the formation of *pus*, a by-product of the body's defense against infection. Pus is a fluid composed basically of white blood cells, their by-products, by-products of the infectious microorganisms, and a thin fluid called liquor puris. Pus impairs neuronal functioning in at least two ways: it changes the composition of the extracellular fluids surrounding a neuron, thus altering neuronal function; and its presence increases pressure on the brain, disturbing normal functioning.

- Infection often causes edema, which leads to compression of the brain tissues, again resulting in dysfunction.

Many infections of the nervous system are secondary to infections elsewhere in the body and are accompanied by symptoms of those other infections, including lowered blood pressure and other changes in blood circulation, fever, general malaise, headache, and delirium. In addition, symptoms of cerebral infections include both generalized symptoms of increased intracranial pressure—such as headache, vertigo, nausea, convulsions, and mental confusion—and symptoms specifically associated with the disturbance of particular brain functions.

Diagnostic tests for infection include studies of the cerebral spinal fluid in addition to conventional methods of infection identification, such as smear and culture studies. Additionally, CT and other brain scans may be used to diagnose and locate some infectious disorders. Four types of infection can affect the central nervous system: viral infections, bacterial infections, mycotic (fungal) infections, and parasitic infestations.

Viral Infections

A **virus** is an encapsulated aggregate of nucleic acid that may be made of either DNA or RNA. Some viruses, such as those causing poliomyelitis and rabies, are called **neurotropic viruses**, because they have a special affinity for cells of the central nervous system. In contrast, **pantropic viruses** (such as those that cause mumps and herpes simplex) attack other body tissues in addition to the

CNS. Most viral infections of the nervous system produce nonspecific lesions affecting widespread regions of the brain, such as lesions due to St. Louis encephalitis, rabies, and poliomyelitis.

Bacterial Infections

Bacterium is a loose generic name for any microorganism (typically one-celled) that has no chlorophyll and multiplies by simple division. Bacterial infections of the central nervous system result from an infestation of these organisms, usually through the bloodstream. The most common neurological disorders resulting from bacterial infection are meningitis and brain abscess.

In **meningitis**, the meninges are infected by any of a variety of bacteria. **Brain abscesses** also are produced by a variety of bacteria, secondary to infection elsewhere in the body. An abscess begins as a small focus of purulent (pus-producing) bacteria that cause necrosis (death) of cells in the affected region. As the bacteria multiply and destroy more brain cells, the abscess behaves like an expanding mass (one that is often hollow in the center), producing increasing intracranial pressure.

Pus is visible over the anterior surface of this brain infected with meningitis. (Biophoto Associates/ Science Source/Photo Researchers.)

Mycotic Infections

Invasion of the nervous system by a fungus is known as a **mycotic infection**. A fungus is any member of a large group of lower plants (in some taxonomic schemes) that lack chlorophyll and subsist on living or dead organic matter; the fungi include yeasts, molds, and mushrooms. Ordinarily, the central nervous system is highly resistant to mycotic infections, but fungi may invade a brain whose resistance has been reduced by diseases such as cancer or tuberculosis.

Parasitic Infestations

A **parasite** is an organism that lives on or within another living organism—the host—at the host's expense. Several kinds of parasites invade the CNS and produce diseases, the most important of which are amebiasis and malaria. **Amebiasis** (also known as amebic dysentery), caused by an infestation of the protozoan ameba *Entamoeba histolytica* (protozoa are one-celled animals), results in encephalitis and brain abscesses. **Malaria** is caused by protozoa of the genus *Plasmodium*, which are transmitted by the bites of infected mosquitoes. Cerebral malaria arises when the plasmodia infect the capillaries of the brain, producing local hemorrhages and the subsequent degeneration of neurons.

The Treatment of Infections

Treatment varies with the type of infection. Viral infections are extremely difficult to treat because there are no specific antidotes, and the only option is to let the disease run its course. Sedatives are sometimes administered to make the patient more comfortable. The important exception to this general rule is the treatment of rabies. When a person has had contact with a rabid animal, antirabies vaccine is administered over a period of 2 to 4 weeks to produce immunity before the disease actually develops. When the disease does develop, rabies is fatal.

Bacterial cerebral infections have become less common with the introduction of antibiotic drugs, the usual treatment for these infections. In some cases, it may be necessary to drain abscesses to relieve intracranial pressure or to do spinal taps to remove cerebral spinal fluid and thus reduce the pressure of edema or a buildup of pus. Neither mycotic nor parasitic infections can be treated satisfactorily, although antibiotics are often used to treat associated disorders.

Disorders of Motor Neurons and the Spinal Cord

A number of movement disorders are produced by damage either to the spinal cord or to cortical projections to the spinal cord. These disorders include myasthenia gravis, a disorder of the muscle receptors; poliomyelitis, a disorder of the motor-neuron cell bodies; multiple sclerosis, a disorder of myelinated motor fibers; paraplegia and Brown-Séquard syndrome, caused by complete transection or hemitransection of the spinal cord, respectively; and hemiplegia, caused by cortical damage. **Table 26.4** lists some of the medical terms used in describing movement disorders.

Table **26.4** Commonly used terms for movement disorders

Apraxia. Inability to carry out purposeful movements or movements on command in the absence of paralysis or other motor or sensory impairments. Usually follows damage to the neocortex.

Ataxia. Failure of muscular coordination or an irregularity of muscular action. Commonly follows cerebellar damage.

Athetosis. A condition in which ceaseless slow, sinuous writhing movements occur, especially in the hands. Due to abnormal function of the extrapyramidal system.

Catalepsy. A condition marked by muscular rigidity in which voluntary movements are reduced or absent but posture is maintained. A feature of Parkinson's disease due to dopamine loss.

Cataplexy. Complete loss of movement and posture during which muscle tone is absent but consciousness is spared.

Chorea. Literally means dance but refers to the ceaseless occurrence of a wide variety of jerky movements that appear to be well coordinated but are performed involuntarily.

Hemiplegia. Complete or partial paralysis to one half of the body. Usually follows damage to the contralateral motor cortex.

Palsy. A paralysis of movement that usually refers to persisting movement disorders due to brain damage acquired perinatally.

Paralysis. Complete loss of movement or sensation (but more commonly movement) in a part of the body. Usually permanent after damage to motor neurons; temporary after damage to motor cortex (area 4).

Paraplegia. Paralysis or paresis of the lower torso and legs. Follows spinal-cord damage.

Spasticity. Increase in the tone of certain muscle groups that maintain posture against the force of gravity. If the limb is moved against the rigidity, resistance will initially increase, but then tone will suddenly melt (clasp-knife reflex). Thought to be produced by damage to the extrapyramidal motor fibers.

Tardive dyskinesia. Slow, persistent movements, particularly of the mouth and tongue. Usually follows long-term treatment with antipsychotic drugs.

Asked to look up (1) a myasthenia gravis patient's eyelids quickly become fatigued and droop (2 and 3). Her eyelids open normally after a few minutes rest (4). (Courtesy of Y. Harati, M.D., Baylor College of Medicine, Houston, Texas.)

Myasthenia Gravis

Myasthenia gravis (severe muscle weakness) is characterized by muscular fatigue in the wake of very little exercise. It may be apparent after a short period of exercise or work, toward the end of a long conversation, or sometimes even after a few repetitions of a movement. Rest brings a feeling of recovery.

The rapid onset of weakness after exercise has begun distinguishes myasthenia gravis from other disorders such as depression or general fatigue. There are no visible signs of muscle pathology. Although myasthenia can affect people of any age, it is most likely to begin in the third decade of life and is more common in women than in men.

All the muscles of the body may be affected, but those supplied by the cranial nerves are usually affected first. In this case, the initial symptoms are diplopia (double vision), ptosis (drooping of the eyelid), weakness of voice, and difficulty in chewing and swallowing or holding up the head. In some people, only the limbs are affected. Usually the symptoms are most apparent at the end of the day and are relieved after sleep. The severity of the disease varies from a mild unilateral ptosis in some people to an incapacitating generalized weakness, threatening death by respiratory paralysis, in others.

The muscular weakness is caused by a failure of normal neuromuscular transmission due to a paucity of muscle receptors for acetylcholine. These receptors may have been attacked by antibodies from the patient's own immune system. Treatment for myasthenia gravis has two objectives. First, acetylcholine therapy is used to relieve the symptoms. Second, thymectomy (surgical removal of the thymus to reduce antibody formation) and immunosuppressive drug treatment are used in the hope of arresting the disease's further progress. With these recent advances in treatment, mortality is currently very low.

Poliomyelitis

Poliomyelitis is an acute infectious disease caused by a virus that has a special affinity for the motor neurons of the spinal cord and sometimes for the motor neurons of the cranial nerves. The loss of these motor neurons causes paralysis and wasting of the muscles. If the motor neurons of the respiratory centers are attacked, death can result from asphyxia. The occurrence of the disease was sporadic and sometimes epidemic in North America until the Salk and Sabin vaccines were developed in the 1950s and 1960s. Since then, poliomyelitis has been well controlled. Why the virus has a special affinity for motor neurons remains an interesting scientific question.

Multiple Sclerosis

Multiple sclerosis (MS; *sclerosis*, from Greek, meaning "hardness") is a disease characterized by the loss of myelin, largely in motor tracts but also in sensory tracts. The loss of myelin is not uniform; rather, it is lost in patches—small, hard, circumscribed scars, called **sclerotic plaques** in which the myelin sheath and sometimes the axons are destroyed.

Multiple sclerosis produces strange symptoms that usually appear first in adulthood. The initial symptoms may be loss of sensation in the face, limbs, or body; blurring of vision; or loss of sensation and control in one or more limbs.

Often, these early symptoms go into remission, after which they may not appear again for years. In some forms, however, the disease may progress rapidly in just a few years until an affected person is limited to bed care.

The cause of MS is still not known. Proposed causes include bacterial infection, a virus, environmental factors, and an immune response of the central nervous system. Often, a number of cases will be seen in a single family, suggesting that MS is related to a genetic predisposition. Multiple sclerosis is most prevalent in northern Europe, somewhat less prevalent in North America, and rare in Japan and in more southerly or tropical countries. Where MS is prevalent, its incidence of 50 per 100,000 makes it one of the most common structural diseases of the nervous system. Only Parkinson's disease is equally common.

Multiple sclerosis has a female-to-male ratio of about 3 to 2, and its progress is often more rapid in females than in males. The prevalence of MS in the northern hemisphere has raised the question of its possible relation to vitamin D deficency. Vitamin D is obtained from sunlight and oily fish, and access to both sources are reduced in the northern hemisphere. According to Abhijit Chaudhuri, vitimin D may be important for the development of myelin in childhood and for the maintenance of myelin in adulthood.

Paraplegia

Paraplegia (from the Greek *para*, "alongside of," and *plegia*, "stroke") is a condition in which both lower limbs are paralyzed (**quadriplegia** is the paralysis of all four extremities). Paraplegia is a direct consequence of complete transection of the spinal cord. Immediately after the cord has been severed, all activity ceases in the part distal to the cut, and all movement, sensation, and reflexes distal to the cut disappear. Owing to the loss of reflex activity, thermoregulatory control is absent (ending perspiration and leaving the skin cool and dry), as is bladder control (necessitating drainage of the bladder to prevent urinary retention). This condition, called *spinal shock*, lasts from 4 days to about 6 weeks.

Gradually, some spinal reflexes return until, after a year or so, a stabilized condition is reached. A pinprick, for example, may again elicit a withdrawal reflex such as the triple response, which consists of flexion of the hip, knee, and ankle. No sensations, voluntary movements, or thermoregulatory control ever reappears below the lesion. Eventually, extensor activity may become sufficiently strong that weight can be supported briefly, but spinal circuits are too dependent on brain facilitation to permit prolonged standing in its absence.

Brown-Séquard Syndrome

Brown-Séquard syndrome refers to the consequences of a unilateral section through the spinal cord (**Figure 26.7**). Because some of the ascending and descending pathways cross the spinal cord and others do not, different symptoms appear on the two sides of the body below the cut. Contralateral to the side of the section, there is a loss of pain and temperature sensation because these pathways cross at the point at which they enter the cord. Sensations of fine touch and pressure are preserved there, however, because their pathways do not cross until they reach the caudal medulla. Fine touch and pressure

Figure **26.7**

Spinal Hemitransection The differing effects of unilateral damage to the spinal cord on fine touch and pressure and on pain and temperature sensations.

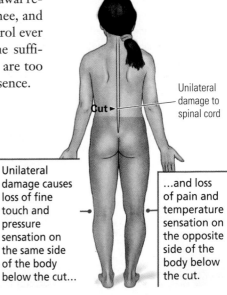

Unilateral damage to spinal cord

Cut ▶

Unilateral damage causes loss of fine touch and pressure sensation on the same side of the body below the cut...

...and loss of pain and temperature sensation on the opposite side of the body below the cut.

sensation, but not pain and temperature sensation, is lost ipsilateral to the section, as are sensation and voluntary movements of distal musculature. Walking ability is recovered within 2 to 3 days, because control of this activity is bilateral.

Hemiplegia

The characteristics of **hemiplegia** (again, *hemi* means "half") are loss of voluntary movements on one side of the body, changes in postural tone, and changes in the status of various reflexes. Hemiplegia results from damage to the neocortex and basal ganglia contralateral to the motor symptoms. In infancy, such damage may result from birth injury, epilepsy, or fever. (Infant hemiplegia is usually discussed under the umbrella of cerebral palsy.) In young adults, hemiplegia is usually caused by rupture of a congenital aneurysm or by an embolism, a tumor, or a head injury. Most cases of hemiplegia, however, are found in middle-aged to elderly people and are usually due to hemorrhaging as a consequence of high blood pressure and degeneration of the blood vessels.

The damage that produces hemiplegia also affects a number of diagnostically important reflexes. In normal subjects, scratching the sole of the foot with a dull object produces a downward flexion of all toes. A person with hemiplegia, in contrast, responds with an upward flexion, especially of the big toe, and an outward fanning of the toes (**Figure 26.8**).

This response, called the **Babinski sign** or **extensor plantar response**, is caused by the activation of flexor muscles and is often accompanied by flexion of the leg at the knee and hip. It is one of a family of flexion responses subsequent to motor-cortex or pyramidal-tract damage. Two reflexes are absent in hemiplegia: the **abdominal reflex**, which in normal people causes the abdominal muscles to retract when stroked, and the **cremasteric reflex**, which in normal males causes retraction of the testicles when the inner thigh is stroked.

The extent of recovery after hemiplegia varies a great deal, and treatment may have one or a combination of objectives. A patient may be trained to use the unaffected side, to use the affected side as much as spasticity and residual abilities allow, or to make movements that lessen spasticity and maximize voluntary control. The last strategy, described in detail by Berta Bobath, is based on the fact that the strength of spasticity is related to posture. Bending over lessens spasticity and, if the arm is extended and the head is turned toward the arm, flexion spasticity is lessened. Such knowledge may enable some patients to make considerable use of their affected limbs.

(A)

Normal adult response

(B)

Normal infant response, abnormal adult response

Figure **26.8**

Hemiplegia Effect (A) The normal adult response to stimulation of the lateral plantar surface of the left foot. (B) The normal infant and abnormal adult response, known as the Babinski sign.

Disorders of Sleep

The need for sleep varies considerably from one person to another, as well as in the same person at different stages of life. We have all been told that we need 8 hours of sleep each night for good health. In fact, there are both long and short sleepers. Some people can stay healthy on as little as an hour of sleep per day, whereas others may need to sleep as much as 10 to 12 hours. The definition of what constitutes adequate sleep must be decided within the context of a person's sleep history. Not surprisingly, because sleep may take up one-third of a person's life, it is also associated with a number of disorders.

(A) Electroencephalogram (EEG)

(B) Electromyogram (EMG)

(C) Electrooculogram (EOG)

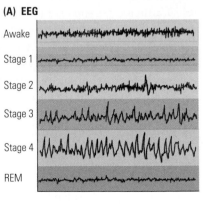

Figure 26.9

Sleep-Laboratory Protocol Readouts from electrodes attached to a sleeping subject record (A) brain-wave activity, (B) muscle activity, and (C) eye movements. (Photograph from Hank Morgan/Rainbow.)

People who suffer from disorders related to sleep are usually examined in a sleep laboratory for 1 to 2 days (**Figure 26.9**). A **polygraph** (*poly*, meaning "many") records their brain waves, or EEG (see Figure 26.9A); an electromyogram, or EMG, records muscle activity (see Figure 26.9B); an **electrooculogram,** or EOG, records eye movements (see Figure 26.9C); and a thermometer measures body temperature during sleep. Together, these recordings provide a comprehensive and reliable description of sleep–waking behavior.

The EEG recording traces distinct patterns of brain-wave activity and is the primary measure of sleep states. Sleep consists of at least two states that alternate periodically in the course of a complete sleep session. One state is a characterized by vivid dreaming, during which the subjects display rapid eye movements, or REMs. This state is called **REM sleep**, and the other is called **non-REM** (NREM) **sleep**.

A summary of the brain activity recorded from one subject during a typical night's sleep is illustrated in **Figure 26.10**. Part A of the illustration displays

Figure 26.10

Sleep Cycles
(A) Electroencephalograph patterns associated with waking, with the four NREM sleep stages, and with REM sleep. (B) The duration of each sleep stage in the course of a typical night's sleep cycles through periods roughly 90 minutes in length. NREM sleep dominates the early periods, and REM sleep dominates later sleep cycles. The lengths of these cycles are indicated by the thickness of each bar, which is color coded to the corresponding stage in part A. The depth of each stage is graphed as the relative length of the bar. (After "Sleep and Dreaming," by D. D. Kelley, in E. R. Kandel, H. H. Schwartz, and T. M. Jessell, Eds., *Principles of Neuroscience,* 2000, New York: Elsevier, p. 794.)

(A) EEG

Awake
Stage 1
Stage 2
Stage 3
Stage 4
REM

(B) Sleep

NREM dominant
REM dominant

Time (hr)

REM
REM
REM
REM
REM

Depth of sleep →

the EEG patterns associated with waking and with the four stages of sleep. Notice that the main change characterizing a sleeper's progression from stage 1 through stage 4 sleep is that that EEG waves become larger and slower. The numbering of these stages assumes that the sleeper moves from relatively shallow sleep in stage 1 to deeper sleep in stage 4. Notice that the EEG of REM sleep resembles that of waking.

Figure 26.10B shows the subject cycling from one stage of sleep to another as the night progresses. Depth of sleep is shown by steps indicating when the subject descends and ascends through the four sleep stages and how long each stage lasts. REM sleep is periodical. Notice that earlier sleep cycles are dominated by stage 4 sleep and later cycles are dominated by REM sleep.

Typically, centers in the brainstem produce a condition of muscular paralysis during REM sleep, and so, apart from REMs and short bursts of twitches in the fingers, toes, and other body parts, the body remains largely motionless. Even so, EEGs taken during dreams resemble the patterns seen when subjects are awake. NREM sleep is characterized by large movements, such as tossing and turning, and by a slow-wave EEG of various amplitudes.

Sleep disorders are generally divided into two major groups: (1) **narcolepsy**, which is characterized by excessive sleep or brief inappropriate episodes of sleep, often associated with other symptoms; and (2) **insomnia**, which is characterized by an inadequate amount of sleep, an inability to fall asleep, or frequent inconvenient arousals from sleep. In addition to these two groups of disorders, other behaviors during sleep are disturbing to the afflicted person. These behaviors include night terrors, sleepwalking, grinding of the teeth, and myoclonic jerks (sudden vigorous movements). They are usually too transitory, too infrequent, or not sufficiently disruptive to be called sleep disorders.

Narcolepsy

In narcolepsy, an inappropriate attack of sleep, the affected person has an overwhelming impulse to fall asleep or simply collapses into sleep at inconvenient times. Attacks may be infrequent or may occur many times a day. Narcolepsy disorders are surprisingly common; estimates suggest that as much as 0.02% of the population may suffer from them. Males and females seem equally affected.

The incidence of narcolepsy in the families of afflicted persons is high. In both mouse and dog, genetic mutations related to some types of narcolepsy have been identified, but the extent to which human narcolepsy has a genetic basis is unclear. Symptoms usually appear when people are between the ages of 10 and 20, and, once sleep attacks develop, they continue throughout life. Amphetamine-like stimulants and tricyclic antidepressants have been found to be useful in treatment.

The narcolepsies include (1) sleep attacks, (2) cataplexy, (3) sleep paralysis, and (4) hypnagogic hallucinations. Although all these disorders do not generally exist at the same time or in the same person, they are present together often enough to be considered interrelated.

Sleep attacks are brief, often irresistible, episodes of sleep—probably slow-wave, NREM, naplike sleep—that last about 15 minutes and can occur at any time. Their approach is sometimes recognizable, but they can also occur without warning. Episodes are most apt to occur in times of boredom or after meals, but they can also occur during such activities as sexual intercourse, scuba diving, or baseball games. After a brief sleep attack, the affected person may awaken completely alert and remain attack free for a number of hours.

Cataplexy (Greek *cata*, meaning "down," and *plexy*, meaning "strike") is a complete loss of muscle tone or a sudden paralysis that results in "buckling" of the knees or complete collapse. The attack may be so sudden that the fall results in injury, particularly because the loss of muscle tone and reflexes prevents an affected person from making any motion that would break the fall. During the attack, the person remains conscious and, if the eyelids stay open or are opened, can recall seeing events that took place during the attack. In contrast with sleep attacks, cataplexic attacks usually occur at times of emotional excitement, such as when a person is laughing or angry. If emotions are held under tight control, the attacks can be prevented. Cataplexy is probably an attack of REM, or dream, sleep.

Sleep paralysis is an episode of paralysis in the transition between wakefulness and sleep. The period of paralysis is usually brief but can last as long as 20 minutes. Sleep paralysis has been experienced by half of all people, if classroom surveys are a true indication of its frequency. In contrast with cataplexy, the paralyzed person can be easily aroused by being touched or called by name and, if experienced with the attacks, can terminate them by grunting or using some other strategy that shakes off the sleep. What appears to happen in sleep paralysis is that the person wakes up but is still in the state of paralysis associated with dream sleep.

Hypnagogic hallucinations (Greek *hypnos*, meaning "sleep," and *gogic*, meaning "enter into") are episodes of auditory, visual, or tactile hallucination during sleep paralysis as an affected person is falling asleep or waking up. The hallucinations are generally frightening; the person may feel that a monster or something equally terrifying is lurking nearby. The same kinds of hallucinations can occur during episodes of cataplexy. A curious feature of the hallucinations is that the person is conscious and often aware of things that are actually happening, and so the hallucinations are even more bizarre because they can become intermixed with real events. These hallucinations may actually be dreams that a person is having while still conscious.

Insomnia

The results from studies of people who claim that they do not sleep, do not sleep well, or wake up frequently from sleep show that their insomnia can have many causes. Nevertheless, systematic recordings of EEGs from poor sleepers before and during sleep show that the sleepers exaggerated the length of time that it took them to get to sleep. But poor sleepers do have decreased dream sleep, move more during sleep, and go through more transitions between sleep stages than normal people do. Moreover, when awakened from slow-wave sleep, they claim that they have not been sleeping.

Even though poor sleepers do sleep by EEG criteria, they do not seem to benefit completely from the restorative properties of sleep. Surveys suggest that as many as 14% of people claim to suffer from insomnia, but the causes are diverse and include general factors such as anxiety, depression, fear of sleeping, environmental disturbances, and travel into new time zones (jet lag). Insomnia may be associated with nightmares and night terrors, sleep apnea (arrested breathing during sleep), restless legs syndrome (RLS, described in the Snapshot below), myoclonus (involuntary muscle contraction), the use of certain kinds of drugs, and certain kinds of brain damage.

Nightmares are intense, frightening dreams that lead to waking. Less common are *night terrors*, attempts to fight or flee accompanied by panic and screams or similar utterances. Nightmares occur during dream sleep, but night terrors occur during NREM sleep. Night terrors are usually brief (1 or 2 min-

SNAPSHOT
Restless Legs Syndrome

Restless legs syndrome (RLS) is a sleep disorder in which a person experiences unpleasant sensations in the legs described as creeping, crawling, tingling, pulling, or pain. The sensations are usually in the calf area but may be felt anywhere from the thigh to the ankle. One or both legs may be affected; for some people, the sensations are also felt in the arms.

Restless legs syndrome can affect as many as 10 of every 100 people, and the propensity for RLS may be inherited. Other causes include iron deficiency and Parkinson's disease, anemia, kidney failure, diabetes, disease, and peripheral neuropathy. Some pregnant women experience RLS, especially in their last trimester. For most of these women, symptoms usually disappear within 4 weeks after giving birth. Certain medications, including antinausea drugs (prochlorperazine or metoclopramide), antiseizure drugs (phenytoin or droperidol), antipsychotic drugs (haloperidol or phenothiazine derivatives), and some cold and allergy medications, may aggravate symptoms. Although RLS is common, the number of people requiring medication for the condition uncertain.

People with RLS describe an irresistible urge to move the legs when the sensations occur. Many have a related sleep disorder called periodic limb movement in sleep (PLMS), characterized by involuntary jerking or bending leg movements that typically occur every 10 to 60 seconds. Some people experience hundreds of such movements per night, which can wake them, disturb their sleep, and annoy bed partners. People who have these disorders get less sleep at night and may feel sleepy during the day.

Restless legs syndrome affects both sexes, and symptoms can begin at any age but are more severe among older people. Young people who experience symptoms are sometimes thought to have "growing pains" or may be comsidered hyperactive because they cannot easily sit still in school.

Red areas indicate fMRI regions positively associated with leg movements; blue areas indicate negative correlations. (Courtesy Kai Spiegehalder.)

There is no laboratory test for RLS, and a doctor cannot detect anything abnormal in a physical examination. The disorder is likely of central nervous system origin, because the syndrome has been reported in a patient who had no legs. A direct cause of the symptoms may be due to low levels of dopamine in the nigrostriatal pathway, but there are widespread changes in the brain accompanying leg movements, as shown in the illustration.

Because iron takes part in the synthesis and the use of dopamine, some people find improvement with iron supplements. For those who are not responsive to iron, L-dopa, a drug that is also used to increase dopamine and thus treat Parkinson's disease, has proved useful, as have dopamine-receptor agonists such as pramipexole (trade names Mirapex and Sifrol). Symptomatic treatment for RLS includes massage, exercise, stretching, and hot baths. Patients can also restrict their intake of caffeine or take benzodiazepines or both to help them get to sleep.

Allen, R. P., and D. J. Earley. The role of iron in restless legs syndrome. *Movement Disorders,* in press.

Cerimagic, D., J. Glavic, and I. Cupkovic. Restless legs syndrome (Wittmaack-Ekbom) "a most common disorder that you never heard of." *Lijec Vjesn* 129:84–86, 2007.

utes) and are usually forgotten on waking. Both phenomena are more common in children than in adults, perhaps because adults have had more experience with disturbing dreams and so are less easily awakened by them. Both can be sufficiently disturbing to disrupt sleep and lead to insomnia.

Sleep apnea (from the Greek for "not breathing"), a periodic cessation of respiration in sleep that ranges in length from about 10 seconds to 3 minutes, is of two types. **Obstructive sleep apnea** occurs mainly in the course of dream sleep and seems to be caused by a collapse of the oropharynx during the paralysis of dream sleep. Patients with this problem invariably have a history of loud snoring—sounds produced as a consequence of the difficulty of breathing through the constricted air passage. The obstruction can be reduced through surgical intervention. **Central sleep apnea** stems from a central nervous system disorder. It primarily affects males and is characterized by a failure of the diaphragm and accessory muscles to move. (For more information on sleep apnea and its possible relation to sudden infant death syndrome (SIDS), see the Snapshot on page 130.)

Sleep apnea can be caused or aggravated by obesity, which contributes to narrowing of the air passage. All-night recording sessions are needed to detect and diagnose both types of sleep apnea. Both interrupt sleep, because an affected person is awakened partly or fully by the oxygen deprivation. According to Caterina Tonon, oxygen deprivation incurred in sleep apnea can lead to neuronal loss in the brain. Accordingly, sleep apnea should be a suspected cause of daytime sleepiness, is easily diagnosed, and can be treated both by weight loss and negative pressure treatment in sleep.

Most psychoactive drugs, whether stimulants or sedatives, eventually lead to insomnia. Hypnotics and sedatives may promote sleep at first, but only until habituation sets in. Furthermore, when drugs do induce sleep, it is not dream sleep, and so the user continues to feel sleep-deprived. Stimulants directly reduce sleep, but they may have their greatest effect on slow-wave sleep. Withdrawal from the drug usually puts an end to drug-induced insomnia.

Summary

The Neurological Examination
A neurologist is a physician specializing in nervous system disorders who gives patients a nervous system examination, takes their personal histories, and recommends treatment.

Vascular Disorders
Vascular disorders entailing the constriction of blood vessels in the brain or bleeding are the most common cause of disability and death.

Traumatic Brain Injuries
Brain traumas include open-head injuries, in which the skull and brain are penetrated, and closed-head injuries, in which the brain is bruised by a blow. Traumatic brain injuries are most common in the very young and very old; they can also occur with very mild insults, such as blows to the head encountered in sports.

Epilepsy
Epilepsy includes several varieties of abnormal discharges of brain neurons that occur spontaneoously, as a result of scarring from injury, infections, or tumors.

Tumors, Headaches, and Infections
A variety of tumors, including tumors of glial cells, and infections—viral, bacterial, mycotic, and parasitic—may affect the brain. Headaches include migraine, muscle contraction, and those associed with neurological diseases such as stroke and tumors.

Disorders of Motor Neurons and the Spinal Cord

Disorders of motor neurons and the spinal cord include myasthenia gravis, poliomyelitis, multiple sclerosis, and injuries that transect the spinal cord partly or completely.

Disorders of Sleep

Sleep disorders include insomnia, an inability to sleep, and narcolepsy, excessive sleep. They can have a central origin but also include sleep apnea, failure to breathe while asleep, and disorders related to drug use.

References

Bannister, R. *Brain and Bannister's Clinical Neurology*. Oxford: Oxford Univerty Press, 1978.

Bigal, M. E., J. N. Liberman, and R. B. Lipton. Age-dependent prevalence and clinical features of migraine. *Neurology* 67:246–251, 2006.

Bobath, B. *Adult Hemiplegia: Evaluation and Treatment*. London: Heinemann Medical Books, 1970.

Bond, M. R. Neurobehavioral sequelae of closed head injury. In I. Grant and K. M. Adams, Eds. *Neuropsychological Assessment of Neuropsychiatric Disorders*. New York: Oxford University Press, 1986.

Brooks, N., L. Campsie, C. Symington, A. Beattie, and W. McKinlay. The five year outcome of severe blunt head injury: A relative's view. *Journal of Neurology, Neurosurgery, and Psychiatry* 49:764–770, 1986.

Catroppa, C., and V. Anderson. Recovery in memory function, and its relationship to academic success, at 24 months following pediatric TBI. *Child Neuropsychology* 13:240–261, 2007.

Chaudhuri, A. Why we should offer routine vitamin D supplementation in pregnancy and childhood to prevent multiple sclerosis. *Medical Hypotheses* 64:608–618, 2005.

Dement, W., and N. Kleitman. Cyclic variations in EEG during sleep and their relation to eye movements, body motility and dreaming. *Electroencephalography and Clinical Neurophysiology* 9:673–690, 1957.

Echemendia, R. J., and L. J. Julian. Mild traumatic brain injury in sports: Neuropsychology's contribution to a developing field. *Neuropsychology Review* 11(2):69–88, 2001.

Hardy, J. A hundred years of Alzheimer's disease research. *Neuron* 52:3–13, 2006.

Kryger, M. H., T. Roth, and W. C. Dement. *Principles and Practice of Sleep Medicine*, 4th ed. New York: Saunders, 2005.

Lashley, K. S. Patterns of cerebral integration indicated by the scotomas of migraine. *Archives of Neurology and Psychiatry* 46:331–339, 1941.

Levin, H. S., H. E. Gary, W. M. High, S. Mattis, R. M Ruff, H. M. Eisenberg, L. F. Marshall, and K. Tabaddor. Minor head injury and the postconcussion syndrome: Methodological issues in outcome studies. In H. S. Levin, J. Grafman, and H. M.Eisenberg, Eds. *Neurobehavioural Recovery from Head Injury*. New York: Oxford University Press, 1987.

Lezak, M. D. *Neuropsychological Assessment*, 4th ed. New York: Oxford University Press, 2004.

Lovell, M. R., R. J. Echemendia, and M. W. Collins. *Traumatic Brain Injury in Sports*. New York: Swets & Zeitlinger, 2005.

Luria, A. R. *The Working Brain*. New York: Penguin, 1973.

Marinkovic, S. V., M. M. Milisavljevic, V. Lolic-Draganic, and M. S. Kovacevic. Distribution of the occipital branches of the posterior cerebral artery: Correlation with occipital lobe infarcts. *Stroke* 18:728–732, 1987.

McNeil, E. B. *The Psychoses*. Englewood Cliffs, N.J.: Prentice-Hall, 1970.

Nathan, P., and M. Smith. Effects of two unilateral cordotomies on the mobility of the lower limbs. *Brain* 96:471–494, 1973.

Newcombe, F. *Missile Wounds of the Brain*. London: Oxford University Press, 1969.

Oppenheimer, D. R. Microscopic lesions in the brain following head injury. *Journal of Neurology, Neurosurgery, and Psychiatry* 31:299–306, 1968.

Pincus, J. H., and G. J. Tucker. *Behavioral Neurology*. New York: Oxford University Press, 2003.

Rasmussen, T. Cortical resection in the treatment of focal epilepsy. *Advances in Neurology* 8:139–154, 1975.

Rosner, B. B. Recovery of function and localization of function in a historical perspective. In D. G. Stein, J. J. Rosen, and N. Butters, Eds. *Plasticity and Recovery of Function in the Central Nervous System*. New York: Academic Press, 1974.

Simon, R. R., D. A. Greenberg, and M. J. Aminoff. *Clinical Neurology*. New York: McGraw-Hill, 2005.

Stalnacke, B. M., E. Elgh, and P. Sojka. One-year follow-up of mild traumatic brain injury: Cognition, disability and life satisfaction of patients seeking consultation. *Journal of Rehabilitative Medicine* 39:405–411, 2007.

Teasdale, G., and B. Jennett. The Glasgow Coma Scale. *Lancet* 2:81–84, 1974.

Teuber, H.-L., W. S. Battersby, and M. B. Bender. *Visual Field Defects after Penetrating Wounds of the Brain*. Cambridge, Mass.: Harvard University Press, 1960.

Tonon, C., R. Vetrugno, R. Lodi, R. Gallassi, F. Provini, S. Iotti, G. Plazzi P. Montagna, E. Lugaresi, and B. Barbiroli. Proton magnetic resonance spectroscopy study of brain metabolism in obstructive sleep apnea syndrome before and after continuous positive airway pressure treatment. *Sleep* 30:305–311, 2007.

Zacks, S. I. *Atlas of Neuropathology*. New York: Harper & Row, 1971.

Psychiatric and Related Disorders

PORTRAIT: Losing Touch with Reality

When Mrs. T. was 16 years old, she began to experience her first symptom of schizophrenia: a profound feeling that people were staring at her. These bouts of self-consciousness soon forced her to end her public piano performances. Her self-consciousness led to withdrawal, then to fearful delusions that others were speaking of her, and finally to suspicions that they were plotting to harm her. At first Mrs. T.'s illness was intermittent, and the return of her intelligence, warmth, and ambition between episodes allowed her to complete several years of college, to marry, and to rear three children. She had to enter a hospital for the first time at 28, after the birth of her third child, when she began to hallucinate.

Hank Morgan/Photo Researchers

Now, at 45, Mrs. T. is never entirely well. She has seen dinosaurs on the street and live animals in her refrigerator. While hallucinating, she speaks and writes in an incoherent, but almost poetic, way. At other times, she is more lucid, but even then her voices sometimes lead her to do dangerous things, such as driving very fast down the highway in the middle of the night, dressed only in a

nightgown. . . . At other times and without any apparent stimulus, Mrs. T. has bizarre visual hallucinations. For example, she saw cherubs in the grocery store. These experiences leave her preoccupied, confused and frightened, unable to perform such everyday tasks as cooking or playing the piano. (Gershon and Rieder, 1992, p. 127)

The accompanying PET scans reveal the metabolic changes that accompany schizophrenia, shown on the left, and are characterized by abnormally low blood flow in the prefrontal cortex (top of scan). The scan on the right shows the brain of a person who does not have schizophrenia.

This chapter focuses on behavioral disorders—those characterized by dramatic abnormalities in cognitive functioning absent obvious lesions to the brain. We begin with the disorders commonly regarded as mental illness (schizophrenia and affective disorders) and then consider psychiatric symptoms that can result from vascular disease. A brief review of the history of psychosurgery precedes a survey of the physical and mental aspects of motor disorders (for example, Parkinson's disease), and a discussion of dementias related to aging concludes the chapter.

The Brain and Behavior

Throughout the centuries since René Descartes first posed the mind–body problem, the contrast between psychological and biological views of mental disorders has mirrored the debate between dualists and monists. Like these polar philosophical views, the mind–body problem is with us still.

Religion and poetry have viewed madness as an affliction of the spirit. Madness is central to classic as well as to contemporary fiction. Think of Shakespeare's *Macbeth* and *Othello* or *The Idiot* by Dostoyesky. In contrast, medicine has explained madness as a disorder of various bodily humors and organs, although, in most cases, without much evidence or success.

In the past three decades, it has become clear that psychiatric, or behavioral, disorders have biochemical, anatomical, and genetic bases. It has also become clear that the distinction between behavioral disorders often referred to as mental illness, such as schizophrenia, and those described as motor disorders, such as Parkinson's disease, is not as clear-cut as it once seemed.

Schizophrenia

Schizophrenia is an extraordinary disorder. It has always been easier to identify schizophrenic behavior than to define what schizophrenia is. Perhaps the one universally accepted criterion for diagnosing schizophrenia is by eliminating the presence of other neurological disturbances or affective disorders—a definition by default.

The revised fourth edition of the *Diagnostic and Statistical Manual of the American Psychiatric Association* (DSM-IV-R) lists five symptoms of schizophrenia:

1. Delusions, or beliefs that distort reality, such as Mrs. T.'s suspicions that people were plotting against her (described in the Portrait)

2. Hallucinations, or altered perceptions, such as hearing voices

3. Disorganized speech, such as incoherent statements or senseless rhyming

4. Disorganized, or excessively agitated, behavior

5. Various "negative" symptoms, such as blunted emotions, or loss of interest and drive, all are characterized by the absence of some normal response

Not all patients will exhibit all symptoms; rather, the symptoms observed in different patients are heterogeneous, which suggests that the biological correlates also will be heterogeneous.

Although schizophrenia was once believed to be characterized by a progressively deteriorating course with a dismal final outcome, this view is probably incorrect. Most patients appear to stay at a fairly stable level after the first few years of the disease, with little evidence of a decline in neuropsychological functioning. The symptoms come and go, much as in Mrs. T.'s case, but the severity is relatively constant after the first few years.

Structural Abnormalities in Schizophrenic Brains

Numerous studies have looked at the gross morphology of the brains of schizophrenics, both in tissue obtained at autopsy and in MRI and CT scans. Although the results are variable, most researchers agree that schizophrenic brains weigh less than normal brains and that the ventricles are enlarged. Schizophrenics have also been suggested to have smaller frontal lobes or at least a reduction in the number of neurons in the prefrontal cortex, as well as thinner parahippocampal gyri. The results of studies of cellular structure have shown abnormalities in both the prefrontal cortex and the hippocampus. The dorsolateral prefrontal cells have a simple dendritic organization, indicating fewer synapses than normal, whereas the pyramidal neurons in the hippocampus have a haphazard orientation, as illustrated in **Figure 27.1**.

The disorientation of the hippocampal neurons seems unlikely to develop at any time other than embryogenesis, which suggests some developmental abnormality in the hippocampus. Barbara Lipska, Daniel Weinberger, and their colleagues proposed that the early hippocampal abnormality may be at least partly responsible for the abnormalities in the structure and function of the prefrontal cortex. They developed an intriguing animal model in which rats with perinatal hippocampal injuries develop abnormal dopaminergic organization in the prefrontal cortex. Not only do the animals have symptoms of prefrontal dysfunction but, like schizophrenia patients, the rats also have reduced synaptic space in the dorsolateral prefrontal pyramidal cells. Surprisingly, however, the rats have increased synaptic space in oribtofrontal neurons.

Another intriguing cellular abnormality is found in a subpopulation of GABA neurons in the dorsolateral prefrontal cortex of people with schizophrenia. (GABA is the main inhibitory transmitter in the forebrain.) These neurons have a reduced GABA synthesis that is associated with poor working memory (see review by Lewis et al.).

Investigators are using neuroimaging to study brain activation in schizophrenics while they perform tasks such as the Wisconsin Card-Sorting Test (see Figure 16.8). For example, the results of experiments by Weinberger and his colleagues show that normal control subjects exhibit significant activation of the prefrontal cortex during card-sorting performance. Patients with schizophrenia do not. In one intriguing report, Karen Berman and Daniel Weinberger studied identical twins who were discordant for schizophrenia (that is, only one was schizophrenic). PET scans showed differences between the twins during resting or control conditions, but, during card sorting, every schizophrenic twin's brain was hypofrontal compared with that of the well twin. This result is consistent with the hypothesis that the prefrontal cortex of schizophrenia patients is abnormal in both structure and function.

Organized (normal) pyramidal neurons

Disorganized (schizophrenic) pyramidal neurons

Figure 27.1

Suspect Brain Structure
Examples of pyramidal-cell orientation from the hippocampus of (A) a normal (organized) brain and (B) a schizophrenic (disorganized) brain. Note the haphazard orientations of these cells. (After Kovelman and Scheibel, 1984.)

Biochemical Abnormalities in Schizophrenic Brains

An important pathway in the prefrontal cortex is its dopaminergic input from the tegmental area. Interference with dopaminergic function disturbs the performance of cognitive tasks in laboratory animals, and so a reasonable inference is that an abnormality in dopamine activity in the frontal lobe could be responsible for at least some symptoms of schizophrenia.

Perhaps the strongest evidence favoring a role for dopamine in schizophrenia comes from studies of the action of **antipsychotic drugs** (also called **neuroleptic drugs**) that principally affect psychomotor activity, generally without hypnotic effects. These drugs act on the dopamine synapse, and dopamine agonists (such as cocaine, amphetamine, and L-dopa) that enhance the

---

Table 27.1 Biochemical changes in schizophrenia

Decreased dopamine metabolites in cerebrospinal fluid

Increased striatal D_2 receptors

Decreased expression of D_3 and D_4 mRNA in specific cortical regions

Decreased cortical glutamate

Increased cortical glutamate receptors

Decreased glutamate uptake sites in cingulate cortex

Decreased mRNA for the synthesis of GABA in prefrontal cortex

Increased $GABA_A$-binding sites in cingulate cortex

Abbreviations: D, dopamine; GABA, gamma-aminobutyric acid.
Source: Byne et al., 1999, p. 242.

---

action of dopamine can induce psychotic symptoms that are almost indistinguishable from those of classic paranoid schizophrenia. Moreover, if a schizophrenic takes amphetamine, the schizophrenic symptoms are heightened.

Although dopamine abnormalities are most commonly emphasized in schizophrenia, other chemical abnormalities have been found. **Table 27.1** summarizes some major neurochemical changes associated with schizophrenia. In particular, added to the abnormalities in dopamine and dopamine receptors are abnormalities in glutamate and glutamate receptors and in GABA and GABA-binding sites. There appears to be considerable variation in the degree of the different abnormalities in individual patients, and how the neurochemical variations might be related to specific symptoms is not yet known.

Types of Schizophrenia?

The variability in both brain abnormalities and behavioral symptomatology led Timothy Crow to propose two distinct pathological syndromes in schizophrenia:

- **Type I**, equivalent to acute schizophrenia, is characterized by positive symptoms, those that consist of behavioral excess, such as the delusions and hallucinations described for Mrs. T. in the Portrait at the beginning of this chapter. Type I is hypothesized to result from a dopaminergic dysfunction, and Type I schizophrenics are expected to be more responsive to neuroleptic drugs.

- **Type II**, equivalent to chronic schizophrenia, is characterized by negative symptoms including flattened affect and poverty of speech. Type II is characterized by structural abnormalities in the brain and poor response to antipsychotic drugs.

Crow's analysis had a major effect on clinical thinking about schizophrenia, although a major difficulty is that as many as 30% of schizophrenia patients show a pattern of mixed type I and type II symptoms. The type I and type II groupings may actually represent opposite end points on a continuum of biological and behavioral manifestations.

Schizophrenia As a Disorder of Development

Schizophrenia symptoms typically develop in late adolescence, and schizophrenia has long been seen as a developmental disorder. David Lewis and Pat Levitt conclude that people who develop schizophrenia are much more likely to have experienced a combination of potentially adverse events in pre- or perinatal life, including poor maternal nutrition, maternal infection, and obstetrical complications. Analyses of home movies of people who later developed schizophrenia have shown subtle, but reliable, disturbances in a variety of behavioral types (motor, cognitive, social) many years before there are clinical symptoms of schizophrenia. In addition, there is evidence of a slow emergence of brain abnormalities, especially in the frontal lobe, during adolescence.

The general idea emerging is that some combination of genetic predisposition and environmental insults establish a developmental trajectory that eventually leads to the clinical syndrome. No single gene is implicated, and the extent to which early environmental insults trigger changes in gene expression that contribute to the disorder is unknown.

Neuropsychological Assessment

Schizophrenics do poorly on neuropsychological tests, although the nature of the neuropsychological impairment in schizophrenia is controversial. Overall, schizophrenics perform poorly on tests of long-term verbal and nonverbal memory as well as on tests sensitive to frontal-lobe function. Performance on tests of visual discrimination, spatial orientation, and short-term verbal and nonverbal memory appears to be less affected. These results are concordant with the view that schizophrenia primarily affects frontal- and temporal-lobe structures. (We must caution, however, that people who have been chronically institutionalized for schizophrenia may not perform normally on *any* test, rendering their test assessments futile.)

Mood Disorders

Although the DSM-IV-R identifies many types of mood disorders, those of principal interest here are depression and mania, disorders that represent the extremes on a continuum of affect. The main symptoms of **clinical depression** are prolonged feelings of worthlessness and guilt, disruption of normal eating habits, sleep disturbances, a general slowing of behavior, and frequent thoughts of suicide. **Mania**, in contrast, is characterized by excessive euphoria, in which an affected person often formulates grandiose plans and behaves with uncontrollable hyperactivity. Periods of mania often switch, sometimes abruptly, into states of depression and back again; hence the condition is called **bipolar disorder**.

Neurochemical Aspects of Depression

A source of insight into the neurobiological basis of depression was the observation that patients given reserpine for high blood pressure often became severely depressed. Reserpine depletes monoamines, which include norepinephrine, dopamine, and serotonin. This observation led to the idea that monoamines might be reduced in depression, and postmortem studies of suicide victims supported this hypothesis.

Research in the past decade has complicated the picture, because it is now clear that many different receptors exist for each monoamine and that specific monoamine receptors may be disrupted in depression. An added complication is that no clear unifying theory accounts for the action of antidepressant medications to treat depression. For example, neurotrophic (that is, growth-supporting) factors may play a role in the action of antidepressants. Brain-derived neurotrophic factor (BDNF) is upregulated by antidepressant medication and is downregulated by stress. Given that BDNF acts to enhance the growth and survival of neurons and synapses, BDNF dysfunction may adversely affect monoamine systems through the loss of either neurons or synapses.

The possible role of stress in altering the production of BDNF is important because, as has become increasingly clear, monoamines modulate the secretion of hormones by the hypothalamic–adrenal system, as illustrated in **Figure 27.2**. The best-established abnormality in the hypothalamic–adrenal system (known as the **HPA axis**) is an oversecretion of the hormone hydrocortisone (cortisol). Cortisol, secreted by the adrenal glands, is associated with stress reactions.

As explained in Chapter 7, when you are stressed, the hypothalamus secretes corticotropin-releasing hormone, which stimulates the pituitary to produce adrenocorticotropin (ACTH). The ACTH circulates through the blood and stimulates the adrenal gland to produce cortisol. The hypothalamic neurons that begin this cascade are regulated by norepinephrine neurons in the locus coeruleus. The possibility that the body's stress reaction is abnormal in depression has important implications, because stress-related hormones and transmitters have a widespread influence on cerebral functioning.

The development of fluoxetine (that is, Prozac) as a major drug for treating depression has an interesting story related to neurotrophic factors. Fluoxetine is a selective serotonin reuptake blocker (see Chapter 7) that effectively increases the amount of serotonin in the cortex. But fluoxetine may also have ac-

Figure 27.2

The HPA Axis (A) Medial view of the right hemisphere illustrating the brain-stress system. Neurons containing norepinephrine have their cell bodies in the locus coeruleus, neurons containing corticotrophin-releasing hormone are in the hypothalamus, and neurons containing dopamine have their cell bodies in the ventral tegmentum. (B) Medial view illustrating the serotonin cell bodies in the Raphé nuclei and their projections to the rest of the brain. (C) When activated, this system affects mood, thought, and, indirectly, the secretion of cortisol by the adrenal glands. Deactivation normally begins when cortisol binds to hypothalamic receptors.

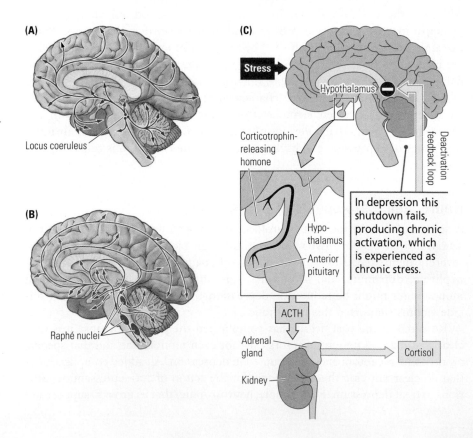

tions that are important to the hippocampus independent of serotonin. The sustained elevation of stress-related hormones, the glucocorticoids, results in the death of granule cells in the hippocampus. This cell death could be a result of the lowered BDNF production. Fluoxetine stimulates both BDNF production and neurogenesis in the hippocampus, resulting in a net increase in the number of granule cells (see Chapter 18). The effects of fluoxetine on depression may therefore tell us a great deal about the relation between the HPA axis and behavior.

Blood Flow and Metabolic Abnormalities in Depression

The general symptoms of depression might lead us to predict a diffuse reduction in cerebral activity, which was the general finding in the early PET studies looking at depressives. Striking regional differences have become clear, however, especially within the frontal lobe.

In their review of the literature, Wayne Drevets and his coworkers concluded that, whereas dorsolateral and medial prefrontal areas show decreased blood flow and metabolism, the orbital regions actually show an abnormal increase in these measures (see the Snapshot on page 782). Similarly, metabolism increases in the amygdala and medial thalamus, two structures intimately related to the prefrontal cortex in the control of emotional behavior (see Chapter 20). When depressives are imaged both before and in the course of effective antidepressant treatment, the activity in the orbital cortex and amygdala decreases. If antidepressant medication is unsuccessful, PET studies fail to find a decrease in activity.

What do the observed changes in blood flow and metabolism mean for our understanding of depression? The increased activity in the amygdala may hold the key. An abnormal increase in resting activity in the amygdala is specific to mood disorders and is the only structure in which the severity of the symptoms positively correlates with the increase in glucose metabolism. Recall from Chapter 20 that the amygdala assigns emotional significance to stimuli. In addition, the amygdala activity stimulates cortisol release, suggesting that amygdala activity may increase HPA-axis activity in depression. The increased activity in the orbital cortex could correspond to an attempt to modulate or inhibit amygdala activity.

Drevets and his colleagues reported that, in contrast with a positive relation between amygdala activity and depression, there is actually a negative relation for the orbital cortex. That is, higher activity appears to reduce depressive symptoms. Thus, the high activity in the orbital cortex may correspond to an attempt to break perseverative patterns of negative thought and emotion, which in turn result from overactivity in the amygdala.

Although speculative, the Drevets hypothesis is intriguing and worth watching in future studies. A question not addressed in the hypothesis, however, is why drugs, such as fluoxetine, that increase serotonin would reduce the overactivity in the amygdala. The answer is not entirely clear, although Drevets points out that reducing serotonin levels by diet actually increases amygdala activity, suggesting that serotonin may act to decrease amygdala activity.

But what is the significance of the decreased activity in the dorsolateral prefrontal cortex? Raymond Dolan and his colleagues suggest that the lowered

ꝒƧΛΛPƧHOT

Cortical Metabolic and Anatomical Abnormalities in Mood Disorders

Disorders of mood may follow either a "unipolar" course consisting only of depression or a "bipolar" course in which normal affect alternates with episodes of both depression and mania.

Wayne Drevets and his colleagues collected PET images of cerebral blood flow from unmedicated unipolar and bipolar subjects (both groups were in a depressive phase and had a familial history of mood disorder) and from control subjects. The brain area exhibiting the largest difference between control and depressive groups was the medial frontal region

Medial section   **Cross section**

Location of
section at right

Corpus callosum

c.c.

Subgenual prefrontal cortex

Reduced PET activation in depression, specifically an area of reduced metabolism and blood flow in a region just below the corpus callosum (subgenual prefrontal cortex). (From Drevets, Gadde, and Krishman, 1999. © Nature Publishing Group, 1997.)

lying immediately below the most anterior region of the corpus callosum (a region referred to as subgenual prefrontal cortex; see the adjoining illustration), which showed about a 12% decrease in blood flow.

In a follow-up series, the researchers compared control subjects with bipolar subjects who were in a manic phase and found a significant increase in activity in the same subgenual area. One bipolar patient, had decreased blood flow in the depressive phase and increased blood flow in the manic phase.

Because the decreased blood flow in depressives could be due to changes either in synaptic activity or in tissue volume, the investigators collected MRI images in mood-disordered and control subjects in a parallel set of studies. The gray-matter volume of the left subgenual prefrontal cortex was reduced by about 39% in both the unipolar and the bipolar groups. This reduced volume was present regardless of the mood state.

The Drevets group concludes that the reduction in gray-matter volume in mood disorders could correspond either to an abnormality of brain development related to the tendency to develop mood episodes or to a degenerative change resulting from the illness.

Drevets, W. C., J. L. Price, J. R. Simpson, R. D. Todd, T. Relch, M. Vannier, and M. E. Raichle. Subgenual prefrontal cortex abnormalities in mood disorders. *Nature* 386:824–827, 1997.

activity relates to the reduced memory and attentional processing in depression. The cause of the lowered activity is not clear but may result from the increased activation related to emotional processing or depressive ruminations.

Because serotonin is thought to play a key role in the sleep–wake cycle, electroencephalographic studies might be expected to reveal cortical abnormalities in this cycle. In one such study, the researchers found that slow-wave sleep is abnormal and that the onset of paradoxical sleep (REM sleep, or dreaming) is more rapid in depressed people (see Kupfer and Thase). The researchers believe this measure to be a sensitive clinical test for depression. Further, they believe that the prognosis for the effectiveness of any particular antidepressant agent is likely to appear in the EEG before it does so clinically.

Finally, some depressed people might be predicted to exhibit only regional reduction in cortical activity because of some local disruption of neurotransmitter levels, and thus there might be different types of depressions characterized by different patterns of cerebral dysfunction. One possibility is that decreased thyroid-hormone production (hypothyroidism) may influence mood. The addition of thyroid hormone to antidepressant drug regimes, for example, is known to potentiate and hasten the effectiveness of the drugs. To our knowledge, there have not yet been imaging studies of people with hypothyroid conditions, however.

Neurobiological Aspects of Bipolar Disorder

Consistent changes have been much harder to find in the brains of bipolar patients than in the brains of depressives. When positive results have been found, the effects are typically similar to those observed in depression, although there appears to be less consistency across patients. Robert Post and Susan Weiss hypothesized that many mood-disorder episodes are initially precipitated by psychosocial stressors but the episodes begin to recur spontaneously and unrelated to external stressors in predisposed people.

These episodes can become very rapid, with cycling occurring daily. Bipolar episodes may also be triggered by pharmacological agents such as antidepressants or in postpartum manic and depressive episodes and then develop an autonomous course. When bipolar disorders have begun an autonomous course, unrelated to external events, medication appears to become increasingly less effective.

William Moorhead and his colleagues performed MRI scans at each end of a 4-year period, in the course of which each patient had at least one bipolar episode and some as many as six. All patients showed a decrease in gray matter in the temporal lobe (fusiform gyrus and hippocampus) and cerebellum relative to the controls (**Figure 27.3**). Importantly, there was a positive relation between the number of episodes and the amount of gray-matter and cognitive loss. These findings suggest that bipolar disorder has a progressive neurodegenerative aspect.

What causes the autonomous recurrence of bipolar episodes? One possibility is that the brain of the bipolar patient is especially sensitive to the effects of stressors or drugs and that episodes of mood disorder actually change the brain. One model of such change is drug- or stress-induced sensitization, which we shall consider briefly. (For a more extensive discussion, see Post and Weiss.)

If animals are subjected to stress or are given psychomotor stimulants repeatedly, behavioral responsivity progressively increases. This increased responsivity is correlated with changes both in neurochemistry and in the morphology of neurons in dopamine-recipient regions—especially the prefrontal cortex. Terry Robinson and one of us (Kolb) discovered that drugs of abuse have different effects on the medial and orbital prefrontal regions, a finding reminiscent of the differences in blood flow and metabolism found in the homologous areas in human depressives. Thus, in predisposed people, an episode of some kind may sensitize the brain and produce changes in brain morphology.

Three factors make this **sensitization model** intriguing for understanding bipolar disorder:

1. There are large individual differences in the degree of sensitization and drug effects in laboratory animals and people. Genetically predisposed individuals may be especially sensitive and produce faster and likely larger neuronal changes in response to stressors.

Left   **Right**

Figure **27.3**

Brain Atrophy in Bipolar Disorder This series of MRI scans shows regions of gray matter loss in bipolar subjects. (From Moorhead et al., 2007, p. 897.)

2. The abuse of psychomotor stimulants such as cocaine is associated with full-blown manic episodes, suggesting a link between psychomotor-stimulant-induced neuronal change and mania.

3. Bipolars are at high risk for substance abuse, suggesting that they are especially sensitive to drug effects.

The sensitization model of bipolar disorder is still largely hypothetical, but it does explain a disorder that has proved so difficult to understand and to treat. A challenge for researchers is to find a treatment that can effectively reverse the effects of sensitization.

Vitamins, Minerals, and Mood

As long ago as the 1920s, scattered sources suggested that mood disorders might be linked to dietary vitamins and minerals. Although the idea that poor nutrition can be related to behavioral disorders seems sensible on the surface, there has been considerable skepticism, because no one has offered a reasonable conceptual explanation for how micronutrients could influence mood.

Bonnie Kaplan and her colleagues have been collecting evidence of a clear link between mood and micronutrients. In a thoughtful review, they propose that mood symptoms may be expressions of (1) inborn errors in metabolism, (2) alterations in gene expression, (3) **epigenetic** alterations in genes—changes in gene regulation that take place without a change in the DNA sequence—by environmental interactions related to abnormal gene methylation, or (4) long-latency effects of nutritional abnormalities, much as cardiovascular disease is a slow-developing disorder. This topic will likely lead to vigorous research and debate in the coming decade.

Psychiatric Symptoms of Cerebral Vascular Disease

Vascular disease such as stroke has long been associated with depression. Estimates of the incidence of poststroke depression range from 25% to 50%, and treatment of stroke patients with antidepressants has become commonplace in the United States. What is less studied, however, is the prevalence of other forms of psychiatric disorder after stroke.

In view of the relation between depression and mania, we might expect some patients to show poststroke mania, but the incidence is very low (about 0.5% or less). In view of the involvement of medial temporal regions in mania noted earlier, a stroke would likely have to include this region to lead to mania.

Generalized anxiety disorder, defined by the DSM-IV-R as a sustained worrying state, is associated with at least three anxiety symptoms, including restlessness, decreased energy, concentration difficulties, irritability, muscle tension, and sleep disturbance. About 25% of stroke patients have poststroke anxiety, with left-hemisphere-stroke patients often having depression as well (see review by Chemerinski and Levine). The preferred treatment appears to be SSRIs, because elderly patients do not tolerate anxiolytics well.

Two other disorders associated with stroke are the catastrophic reaction discussed in Chapter 20 and a condition often referred to as *pathological affect,* which refers to conditions of uncontrollable laughing or crying. There are few studies of poststroke pathological affect, but estimates of incidence range from 11% to 50%.

Psychosurgery

Before the development of drugs for treating schizophrenia and affective disorders, few treatments were available. One treatment that emerged in the 1930s was surgical. Although no longer commonly used, it is worth reviewing here in the context of schizophrenia and depression. For an excellent discussion of psychosurgery and its history, we recommend two books by Eliot Valenstein: *The Psychosurgery Debate* and *Great and Desperate Cures*.

Psychosurgery is the destruction of some region in the brain to alleviate severe and otherwise intractable psychiatric disorders. To distinguish current psychosurgical techniques from earlier, cruder lobotomy operations, the term *psychiatric surgery* has been suggested as a substitute, although the term refers to the same procedures. **Neurosurgery**, brain surgery intended to repair damage to alleviate symptoms resulting from known neurological disease, is not considered psychosurgery, even if the patient has severe behavioral and emotional symptoms. Brain surgery to alleviate intractable pain is normally considered psychosurgery, because the operations are performed on normal brain tissue and because serious emotional disturbances often accompany chronic pain.

The belief that mental aberrations are related to disturbances of brain function dates to primitive times. The practice of opening the skull (trephining) for magical–medical purposes was apparently performed extensively dating to at least about 2000 B.C. (see Figure 1.12, left). Modern psychosurgery is usually traced to Portuguese neurologist Egas Moniz, who started the prefrontal procedures in 1935 (see Chapter 20).

Later modifications in the procedure were made in the United States by Walter Freeman and James Watts, including the Freeman–Watts procedure of drilling holes in the temples and Freeman's lateral transorbital procedure (**Figure 27.4**A). An accurate estimate of how many psychosurgical procedures were performed worldwide is impossible, although Valenstein thinks that the best estimate for the United States between 1936 and 1978 is 35,000.

The introduction of antipsychotic drugs in the mid-1950s led to a sharp reduction in the number of psychosurgical operations, but still a significant

Figure **27.4**

Targets for Psychosurgery (A) In the procedure for a transorbital leukotomy, a special surgical knife (leukotome) is inserted through the bone of the eye socket above the eyeball, disconnecting the inferior frontal cortex from the rest of the brain. (B) Approximate targets of psychosurgical operations currently in use. *Frontal-lobe procedures:* (1) bimedial leukotomy; (2) yttrium lesions in subcortical white matter; (3) orbital undercutting; (4) bifrontal stereotaxic subcaudate tractotomy; (5) anterior capsulotomy (destruction of fibers of internal capsule); (6) mesoloviotomy (similar to rostral cingulotomy, but lesion invades the genu, or "knee," of the corpus callosum). *Cingulotomies:* (7) anterior cingulotomy; (8) midcingulotomy; (9) posterior cingulotomy. *Amygdalectomy:* (10) amygdalectomy or amygdalotomy. *Thalamotomies:* (11) thalamotomy of the dorsomedial, centromedian, or parafascicular nuclei; (12) anterior thalamotomy. *Hypothalamotomy:* (13) section of the posterior, ventromedial, or lateral hypothalamus. (Part B after Valenstein, 1980.)

(A)

(B)

Cingulate gyrus
Corpus callosum
Orbital cortex
Olfactory bulb
Amygdala
Hippocampal gyrus
Hippocampus
Thalamus
Hypothalamus

number of psychiatric patients were not helped by the drugs. Thus, interest in surgical intervention to change behavior has continued, but, since the 1960s, the psychosurgical procedures employed have changed, in part because of advances in the neurosciences. There are currently about 13 different targets of psychosurgical operations, which are summarized in Figure 27.4B.

These procedures generally produce smaller lesions than did the original lobotomy-type procedures and, today, even the smaller lesions are rarely performed. The development of new generations of psychiatric drugs has meant that virtually everybody is responsive to some form of psychoactive medication. We note, parenthetically, that the most common form of psychosurgery—namely, frontal leukotomy—disconnected regions of the prefrontal cortex from the rest of the brain, and we have seen that abnormalities in the prefrontal cortex are associated with both schizophrenia and depression. The difficulty with psychosurgery, however, is that, although the abnormal activity of the prefrontal regions was removed, it was not replaced by normalized activity. The goal of drug treatment is to do just that.

Motor Disorders

The group of diseases comprising motor disorders has clinical symptoms marked by abnormalities in movement and posture that are referable to dysfunctions of the basal ganglia. Although the most obvious symptom is the motor affliction, all produce cognitive changes as well, changes that become especially marked as the diseases progress. Indeed, many patients with motor disorders develop symptoms similar to those of schizophrenia. Clinically, two groups of symptoms are distinguished: (1) a loss of movement, which is referred to as a hypokinetic-rigid syndrome (for example, Parkinson's disease); and (2) an increase in motor activity, which is known as a hyperkinetic-dystonic syndrome (for example Tourette's syndrome).

Hyperkinetic Disorders

The earliest descriptions of women afflicted with either Huntington's chorea or Tourette's syndrome dwelt on increased motor activity as a symptom of hysteria.

Huntington's Chorea

George Huntington was 8 years old when he first saw people with "that disorder," as it was then called. He was riding with his father in his native New York when they came upon two women who were tall and thin and were twisting and grimacing. No doubt the disorder was familiar to his father and grandfather, both of whom were physicians.

Nevertheless, the sight of these women left such a profound impression on young George that he studied the disease when he, too, became a physician. In 1872, when he was 22 years old, he wrote the first complete description of the disease. Its history in the United States can be traced to the village of Bures in England in 1630. At that time, whole families in Bures and its vicinity were branded and tried as witches. Some family members, who had or carried the disease, sailed to America among the 700 passengers of the John Winthrop fleet in

1630. In 1653, Ellin Wilkie (name fictitious), who had arrived with Winthrop, apparently had the disorder, because she was tried and hanged for witchcraft. Her granddaughter was later tried and pardoned in 1692.

Part of the early history of establishing the genetic basis for the disease entailed tracing the family backgrounds of afflicted persons whose ancestors were among the Winthrop passengers and settled in various parts of the United States. In other countries colonized by Europeans, similar family histories have been constructed that trace the disease to one or a few immigrants. Huntington's chorea is quite rare, with death rates of 1.6 per million people worldwide per year. It is most common among white Europeans and their descendants; it is rare among Asian and African racial groups. The number of people who will develop the disease is likely on the decline because of advances in genetic counseling.

Woody Guthrie, a founder of American folk music whose songs inspired farm workers during the Great Depression of the 1930s, struggled with the symptoms of Huntington's chorea in the years before he died in 1967. Two of Guthrie's five children developed the disease, and his mother had died of similar symptoms, although her illness was never diagnosed. (Photofest.)

Huntington's chorea (from the Greek *choreia*, meaning "dance") is a genetic disorder that results in intellectual deterioration and abnormal movements as an afflicted person reaches certain ages. Also called *hereditary chorea*, the first symptom of this progressive degenerative disease is usually a reduction of activity and restriction of interest. The first restless and involuntary movements may be attributed to an anxiety disorder (for example, to hysteria in earlier times).

The first involuntary movements usually appear within a year of the onset of the behavioral symptoms. The movements are initially slight and consist of little more than continual fidgeting, but they slowly increase until they are almost incessant. The movements never entail single muscles but include whole limbs or parts of a limb. They are also irregular and follow no set pattern.

A reliable marker is that a sustained muscular contraction is not possible: when an object is held, the grip fluctuates; in addition, the tongue cannot be held protruded. Eventually, the movements become uncontrollable and affect the head, face, trunk, and limbs—impeding speech, swallowing, walking, writing, and other voluntary movements. Sometimes an afflicted person attempts to mask the abnormal movements with purposeful ones.

Behavioral symptoms include personality changes and cognitive impairments—of recent memory, defective ability to manipulate acquired knowledge, and slowing of information processing. Apraxia, aphasia, and agnosias, which result from certain cortical diseases such as Alzheimer's disease, do not develop, however. Emotional changes include anxiety, depression, mania, and schizophrenia-like psychoses. Suicide is not uncommon in younger patients.

The first symptoms usually appear in people from 30 to 50 years of age. About 5% of cases begin before age 20 and are sometimes called "juvenile chorea." In contrast with adults, juveniles may exhibit muscle rigidity and slow movements, somewhat similar to those in Parkinson's disease, and they may endure muscle spasms, tremor, disturbances of eye movement, and epilepsy. Adult patients live an average of 12 years after disease onset, but the progress of the disease is far more rapid in the juvenile cases.

Huntington's chorea is transmitted genetically as an autosomal dominant allele with complete penetrance, meaning that half the offspring of an affected

(A) Normal transmitter system

(B) Huntington's chorea

Figure 27.5

Neurochemical Progress of Huntington's Chorea

Acetylcholine (ACh) and gamma-aminobutyric acid (GABA) neurons in the basal ganglia are thought to die, and, as a result, dopamine cells are released from GABA inhibition and become hyperactive, thus producing abnormal movements. The death of GABA cells may be caused by excessive activity of the glutamate pathway.

person will develop the disease. The approximate location of the gene is now known, and a marker can be used before symptoms appear to determine whether a family member (even in utero) will develop the disease. Applying recombinant DNA procedures on a population in Venezuela, James Gusella and his colleagues narrowed the locus of the gene to a part of the short arm of chromosome 4 and detected a marker linked with this gene.

At autopsy, the brains of people with Huntington's chorea show shrinkage and thinning of the cerebral cortex. The basal ganglia are grossly atrophied and show a marked loss of intrinsic neurons. A dominant explanation of the disease is an imbalance among the various neurotransmitter systems of the basal ganglia. A simplified model of these transmitter systems is shown in **Figure 27.5**A. They include

1. a glutamate projection from the cortex to the basal ganglia,

2. a gamma-aminobutyric acid (GABA) projection from the basal ganglia to the substantia nigra,

3. a dopamine (DA) projection from the substantia nigra to the basal ganglia, and

4. acetylcholine (ACh) neurons in the basal ganglia.

As shown in Figure 27.5B, researchers postulate that the intrinsic neurons of the basal ganglia (GABA and ACh neurons) die in the course of the disease, leaving a largely intact nigrostriatal DA pathway. As a result of the decrease in inhibition of the DA cells by the GABA pathway, DA release in the basal ganglia increases. The hyperactivity of the dopamine system is believed to produce the characteristic abnormal movements, although exactly how is not clear.

The results of extensive neuropsychological studies show that Huntington patients are impaired in a broad range of memory tests, as well as in visual, auditory, and tactile perceptual tests (see Fedio et al. and Wexler). In addition, patients are especially poor at performing various frontal-lobe tests (for example, the Chicago Word-Fluency Test and the stylus–maze test). People who have at least one parent with the disease and can thus be considered at risk appear to perform poorly only on the frontal-lobe tests, suggesting that these tests might be useful predictors of the disease. The effectiveness of these tests will be seen in the coming years as the subjects in these studies either begin to display other symptoms or do not do so.

Tourette's Syndrome

Georges Gilles de la Tourette described **Tourette's syndrome** in 1885, and, in most important ways, his description is still remarkably good. Until his review, this syndrome was seen either as an undifferentiated chorea or as a symptom of hysteria, and it had a variety of names, depending on where it had been observed.

The symptoms tend to evolve and to become more elaborate with age. Gilles de la Tourette described three stages of the syndrome. In the first stage, the only symptoms are multiple tics (twitches of the face, limbs, or the whole body). In the second stage, inarticulate cries are added to the multiple tics. In the third stage, the emission of articulate words with **echolalia** (repeating what others have said, as well as repeating actions) and **coprolalia** (from the Greek *copro*, meaning "dung," but its current meaning is "obscene" or "lewd," and *lalia*, meaning "speech") are added to the multiple tics and inarticulate cries.

The following case history, reported by Gilles de la Tourette, illustrates most of the major features of the syndrome:

> Miss X., 15 years old, spent several months at the Longchamps hydrotherapy institution at Bordeaux in the winter of 1883, where she was treated for convulsive attacks of chorea and ejaculations of loud vulgar and obscene words. Miss X. was very intelligent, she learned the lessons given her by her teacher with the greatest ease, and she played the piano well. She was tall and largely built. She was not well disciplined.
>
> When 9, Miss X. began having violent and irregular choreiform tics of the face, arms, and legs. At the same time she occasionally uttered a few vulgar words. After a few months the attacks disappeared. A year later they came back again. The tics first reappeared in the shoulders, then in the arms, and then in the face, where they were accompanied by loud guttural sounds. These indistinct sounds became very clearly articulated when she was 13. At that time her most frequent words were "get away, go away, imbecile." A little later her words became more frequent and much clearer, and were rough and lewd. She remained that way until the present.
>
> Miss X. belonged to an upper-class family. Her education was excellent. She never left her mother, who surrounded her in continuous, tender loving care. One had to wonder how and where she picked up the words she continually uttered: for example, "In God's name, fuck, shit, et cetera." When she is in her calm, normal state such words never pass her lips. (Gilles de la Tourette, 1885, pp. 41–42; translated by Lorna Whishaw)

Gilles de la Tourette recognized that people with the syndrome could be intelligent and productive and were not neurotic or psychotic. He also noted that the syndrome, or parts of it, ran in families and thus seemed hereditary. He pointed out that there was no treatment (although the symptoms lessened or disappeared during fevers), and so the symptoms were likely to be with the person for life.

Recent renewed interest in Tourette's syndrome is largely through the work of the Tourette Society in North America. Many patients with Tourette's syndrome have been misdiagnosed as troublemakers, hysterics, schizophrenics, and more—no doubt because they seem intelligent yet display bizarre behavior. Such diagnoses are now changing, and there is great interest in trying to understand the cause of the disorder in relation to brain function.

The incidence of Tourette's syndrome is less than 1 in 100,000, but the incidence can vary with the degree of professional knowledge about the disorder. In southwestern Alberta, Canada, which has a population base of about 100,000, a child psychiatrist interested in the disorder diagnosed more than 10 cases in 10 years. Thus, the actual incidence may be somewhat higher than the estimated incidence.

The average age of onset ranges between 2 and 15 years, with a median of 7 years; by 11 years of age, symptoms have appeared in 97% of cases. The most frequent symptoms are tics of the eye, head, or face (97%), upper limbs (81%), and lower limbs and body (55%). Complex movements including touching, hitting, and jumping appear in 30% to 40% of cases.

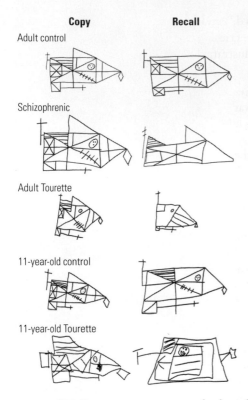

Copy   Recall

Adult control

Schizophrenic

Adult Tourette

11-year-old control

11-year-old Tourette

Figure 27.6

Viewing the World Differently

Representative performance by a normal adult control, a schizophrenic patient, an adult Tourette patient, a normal child, and a child Tourette patient on the Rey Complex-Figure Test: copying and recall. The Tourette patients are impaired at both the copying and the recall; the schizophrenic patient is impaired only at recall. (After Sutherland et al., 1982.)

Coprolalia may develop in as many as 60% of cases and then disappear in a third of them. As already noted, Tourette's syndrome is not associated with neuroses, psychoses, or other disorders. Electroencephalographic activity is often normal, although some patients may display abnormalities. The results of evoked-potential studies show that the premovement potentials associated with willed, voluntary movements do not occur with the tics in Tourette-syndrome patients, which confirms that these movements are involuntary.

Tourette's syndrome is presumed to have a subcortical origin, likely in the basal ganglia. There have been very few autopsy examinations of the brains of Tourette-syndrome patients, and, of those that have been done, only one reports an excessive number of small cells in the basal ganglia; others report that the cells there are normal. To date, the most consistent improvements are obtained with antidopaminergic agents such as haloperidol; thus, there may be some abnormality in the dopamine system in the basal ganglia. Clonidine, a norepinephrine-receptor agonist, also is reported to be effective in some cases.

In general, the results of neuropsychological studies suggest abnormalities in some cognitive functions usually supported by the right hemisphere. For example, Robert Sutherland and his colleagues gave a composite test battery to a large sample of children and adults with Tourette's syndrome and found that the patients were especially bad at drawing and remembering complex geometric figures. The poor performance of these patients on the Rey Complex-Figure Test was particularly striking, because even patients with superior verbal IQ scores performed very poorly compared with control children or schizophrenic patients (**Figure 27.6**). The visuospatial difficulties observed in the Rey figure may have a real-world analogue as well: many Tourette-syndrome patients complain of having difficulty in remembering the locations of things in their daily lives.

Hypokinetic Disorders

In 1817, James Parkinson, a London physician, published an essay in which he argued that several different motor symptoms could be considered together as a group forming a distinctive condition that he referred to as the shaking palsy. His observations are interesting not only because his conclusion was correct but also because he made his observations in part at a distance, by watching the movements of victims in the streets of London. French neurologist Jean-Martin Charcot suggested that the disease be renamed to honor James Parkinson's recognition of its essential nature.

Parkinson's disease is fairly common; estimates of its incidence vary from 0.1% to 1.0% of the population worldwide, and the incidence rises sharply in old age. In view of the increasingly aging population in Western Europe and North America, the incidence of Parkinson's disease is certain to rise in the coming decades. It is also of interest for a number of other reasons:

- Parkinson's disease seems to be related to the degeneration of the **substantia nigra** and to the loss of the neurotransmitter dopamine, which is produced by cells of this nucleus. The disease, therefore, is an important source of insight into the role of this brainstem nucleus and its neurotransmitter in the control of movement.

■ Because a variety of pharmacological treatments for Parkinson's disease relieve different features of its symptoms to some extent, the disease provides a model for understanding pharmacological treatments of motor disorders more generally.

■ Although Parkinson's is described as a disease entity, the symptoms vary enormously among people, thus illustrating the complexity with which the components of movement are organized to produce fluid motion.

■ Many symptoms of Parkinson's disease strikingly resemble changes in motor activity that take place as a consequence of aging. Thus, the disease is an indirect source of insight into the more general problems of neural changes in aging.

The four major symptoms of Parkinson's disease are tremor, rigidity, akinesia, and disturbances of posture; each symptom may be manifested in different body parts in different combinations. Because some of the symptoms are the acquisition of abnormal behaviors (positive symptoms) and others the loss of normal behaviors (negative symptoms), we will consider the symptoms in these two major categories. Positive symptoms are behaviors not seen in normal people or seen only so rarely, and then in such special circumstances, that they can be considered abnormal. Negative symptoms are marked not by any particular behavior but rather by the absence of a behavior or by the inability to engage in an activity.

Positive Symptoms

Because positive symptoms are common in Parkinson's disease, they are thought to be held in check, or inhibited, in normal people but released from inhibition in the process of the disease. The most common positive symptoms are:

1. **Tremor at rest.** Tremor consists of alternating movements of the limbs when they are at rest; these movements stop during voluntary movements or during sleep. The tremors of the hands often have a "pill rolling" quality, as if a pill were being rolled between the thumb and forefinger.

2. **Muscular rigidity.** Muscular rigidity consists of simultaneously increased muscle tone in both extensor and flexor muscles. It is particularly evident when the limbs are moved passively at a joint; movement is resisted, but, with sufficient force, the muscles yield for a short distance and then resist movement again. Thus, complete passive flexion or extension of a joint is in a series of steps, giving rise to the term *cogwheel rigidity*. Muscular rigidity may be severe enough to make all movements difficult. One man less severely afflicted by rigidity was moved to comment to us, "The slowness of movement is conscious but not willed. That is, I form a plan in my mind; for instance, I wish to uncork that bottle. Then I deliberately invoke the effort that sets the muscles in motion. I'm aware of the slowness of the process; I'm unable to increase [its speed], but I always get the bottle open."

3. **Involuntary movements.** These movements may consist of continual changes in posture, sometimes to relieve tremor and sometimes to relieve stiffness, but often for no apparent reason. These small movements or changes in posture, sometimes referred to as **akathesia** or *cruel restlessness*, may be concurrent with general inactivity. Other involuntary movements are distortions of posture, such as those during *oculogyric crisis* (involuntary turns of the head and eyes to one side), which last for periods of minutes to hours.

Because the positive symptoms are actions, they are caused by the activity of some brain area. Before drug therapy became common, one treatment used to stop the positive symptoms was to localize the source of the symptom in the brain and make a lesion there. Tremor was treated by lesions made in the ventral lateral thalamus, for example. This treatment was abandoned because improvement was only temporary. Recently, improvements in how the lesions are made and in their accurate placement has led to a resurgence of this therapy. Additionally, the best results have been obtained with lesions to the internal part of the globus pallidus, a part of the basal ganglia that eventually projects to the ventral lateral thalamus.

Negative Symptoms

After detailed analysis of negative symptoms, James Purdon Martin divided patients severely affected with Parkinson's disease into five groups:

1. **Disorders of posture.** These disorders include disorders of fixation and of equilibrium. A *disorder of fixation* consists of an inability to maintain or difficulty in maintaining a part of the body (head, limbs, and so forth) in its normal position in relation to other parts. Thus, a person's head may droop forward or a standing person may gradually bend forward until he or she ends up on the knees. *Disorders of equilibrium* consist of difficulties in standing or even sitting unsupported. In less-severe cases, patients may have difficulty standing on one leg or, if pushed lightly on the shoulders, they may fall passively without taking corrective steps or attempting to catch themselves.

2. **Disorders of righting.** These disorders consist of difficulty in achieving a standing position from a supine position. Many advanced patients have difficulty even in rolling over.

3. **Disorders of locomotion.** Normal locomotion requires support of the body against gravity, stepping, balancing while the weight of the body is transferred from one limb to another, and pushing forward. Parkinson patients have difficulty initiating stepping, and, when they do walk, they shuffle with short footsteps on a fairly wide base of support, because they have trouble maintaining equilibrium when shifting weight from one limb to the other. Often, Parkinson patients who have begun to walk demonstrate **festination**: they take faster and faster steps and end up running forward.

4. **Disturbances of speech.** One of the symptoms most noticeable to relatives is the almost complete absence of tone (prosody) in the speaker's voice.

5. Akinesia. A poverty or slowness of movement may also manifest itself in a blankness of facial expression or a lack of blinking, swinging of the arms when walking, spontaneous speech, or normal movements of fidgeting. It is also manifested in difficulty in making repetitive movements, such as tapping, even in the absence of rigidity. People who sit motionless for hours show akinesia in its most striking manifestation.

Progression of Parkinsonism

Positive and negative symptoms of Parkinson's disease begin insidiously, often with a tremor in one hand and with slight stiffness in the distal parts of the limbs. Movements may then slow, the face becoming masklike with loss of eye blinking and poverty of emotional expression. Thereafter, the body may become stooped, and gait becomes a shuffle with the arms hanging motionless at the sides. Speech may become slow and monotonous, and difficulty in swallowing saliva may result in drooling.

Although the disease is progressive, the rate at which the symptoms worsen is variable, and only rarely is progression so rapid that a person becomes disabled within 5 years; usually from 10 to 20 years elapse before symptoms cause incapacity. A most curious aspect of Parkinson's disease is its on-again–off-again quality: symptoms may appear suddenly and disappear just as suddenly. Partial remission may also occur in response to interesting or stimulating situations. Oliver Sacks recounted an incident in which a Parkinson patient leaped from his wheelchair at the seaside and rushed into the breakers to save a drowning man, only to fall back into his chair immediately afterward and become inactive again. Although remission of some symptoms in activating situations is common, remission is not usually as dramatic as in this case.

Causes of Parkinsonism

The three major types of Parkinson's disease are idiopathic, postencephalitic, and drug induced. Parkinson's disease may also result from arteriosclerosis, syphilis, the development of tumors, poisoning by carbon monoxide, or manganese intoxication.

As suggested by its name, the cause of *idiopathic* Parkinson's disease is not known. Its origin may be familial or it may be part of the aging process, but it is also widely thought to have a viral origin. This type most often develops in people older than 50 years of age.

The *postencephalitic* form originated in the sleeping sickness (*encephalitis lethargica*) that appeared in the winter of 1916–1917 and vanished by 1927. Although the array of symptoms was bewilderingly varied, such that hardly any two patients seemed alike, Constantin von Economo demonstrated a unique pattern of brain damage—namely, the death of cells in the substantia nigra. Although many people seemed to recover completely from the encephalitis, most subsequently developed neurological or psychiatric disorders and parkinsonism. The latency between the initial occurrence and subsequent occurrences of the disease has never been adequately explained. Specific searches for viral particles or virus-specific products in Parkinson patients without encephalitis have revealed no evidence of viral cause, although it is still believed to be likely.

Drug-induced Parkinson's disease developed most recently and is associated with the ingestion of various drugs, particularly major tranquilizers that include reserpine and several phenothiazine and butyrophenone derivatives. The symptoms are usually reversible, but they are difficult to distinguish from those of the genuine disorder.

External agents can cause Parkinson's symptoms quite rapidly. J. William Langston and his coworkers reported that a contaminant, MPTP, of synthetic heroin is converted into MPP+, which is extremely toxic to dopamine cells. A number of young drug users were found to display a complete parkinsonian syndrome shortly after using contaminated drugs. This finding suggests that other substances might cause similar effects. The results of demographic studies of patient admission in the cities of Vancouver and Helsinki show an increase in the incidence of patients getting the disease at ages younger than 40. This finding suggests that water and air might contain environmental toxins that work in a fashion similar to MPTP.

The cells of the substantia nigra are the point of origin of fibers that go to the frontal cortex and basal ganglia and to the spinal cord. The neurotransmitter at the synapses of these projections is dopamine. Bioassay of the brains of deceased Parkinson patients and analysis of the major metabolite of dopamine—homovanallic acid, which is excreted in the urine—demonstrate that the amount of dopamine in the brain is reduced by more than 90% and is often reduced to undetectable amounts. Thus, the cause of Parkinson's disease has been identified with some certainty as a lack of dopamine or, in drug-induced cases, as a lack of dopamine action. Dopamine depletion may not account for the whole problem in some people, however, because decreases in norepinephrine have been recorded, and a number of results show that cells in some of the nuclei in the basal ganglia may degenerate as well.

The Treatment of Parkinson's Disease

No known cure for Parkinson's disease exists, and none will be in sight until the factors that produce the progressive deterioration of the substantia nigra are known. Thus, treatment is symptomatic and directed toward support and comfort. The major symptoms of parkinsonism are influenced by psychological factors, a person's outcome being affected by how well he or she copes with the disability. As a result, patients should be counseled early regarding the meaning of symptoms, the nature of the disease, and the potential for most of them to lead long and productive lives. Physical therapy should consist of simple measures such as heat and massage to alleviate painful muscle cramps and training and exercise to cope with the debilitating changes in movement.

Pharmacological treatment has two main objectives: first, increase the activity in whatever dopamine synapses remain and, second, suppress the activity in structures that show heightened activity in the absence of adequate dopamine action. Drugs such as L-dopa, which is converted into dopamine in the brain, amantadine, amphetamine, monoamine oxidase inhibitors, and tricyclic antidepressants are used to enhance effective dopamine transmission. Naturally occurring anticholinergic drugs, such as atropine and scopolamine, and synthetic anticholinergics, such as benztropine (Cogentin), and trihexyphenidyl (Artane), are used to block the cholinergic systems of the brain that seem to show heightened activity in the absence of adequate dopamine activity.

One promising treatment is to try to increase the number of dopamine-producing cells. The simplest way to do so is to transplant embryonic dopamine cells into the basal ganglia; in the 1980s and 1990s, this treatment was used with varying degrees of success. A newer course of treatment proposes to increase the number of dopamine cells either by transplanting fetal stem cells, which could then be induced to adopt a dopaminergic phenotype, or by stimulating endogenous stem cells to be produced and migrate to the basal ganglia. Both treatments are still highly experimental, and, unfortunately, recent results are not as encouraging as the initial studies were.

Finally, the development of deep brain stimulation (DBS) for Parkinson's is detailed in Chapter 6. Electrodes applied to several brainstem regions can lessen both tremor and akinesia but not without risk. Nevertheless, the combination of drug and DBS therapies may prove to be the most effective treatment.

These PET scans contrast the brain of a Parkinson patient before the implantation of fetal dopamine neurons (left) and 12 months after the operation (right). The increased areas of red and gold show that the transplanted neurons are producing DA. (From Dr. Hakan Widner, M.D., Ph.D., Lund University, Sweden.)

Psychological Aspects of Parkinson's Disease

Psychological symptoms in Parkinson patients are as variable as the motor symptoms. Nonetheless, a significant percentage of patients have cognitive symptoms that mirror their motor symptoms. Sacks, for example, reported the negative effects of the disease on cognitive function. There is an impoverishment of feeling, libido, motive, and attention; people may sit for hours, apparently lacking the will to enter or continue any course of activity. In our experience, thinking seems generally to be slowed and is easily confused with dementia because patients do not appear to be processing the content of conversations. In fact, they are simply processing very slowly.

The results of neuropsychological studies confirm that Parkinson patients often show cognitive symptoms similar to those shown by people with frontal-lobe or basal-ganglia lesions, such as deficits on the Wisconsin Card-Sorting Test. This association is not surprising, because of the close relations between the functions of the basal ganglia and the frontal cortex and because dopamine projections into the frontal cortex might be expected to degenerate in the same way as those of the basal ganglia degenerate. Test performance is not noticeably improved by drug therapy.

The cognitive slowing in Parkinson patients has some parallels to changes of Alzheimer's disease, and findings in postmortem studies show clear evidence of Alzheimer-like abnormalities in most patients, even if they did not have obvious signs of dementia. Neuropsychological investigations of other populations confirm the possibility of a general cognitive deterioration in Parkinson patients. For example, in their extensive study, Francis Pirozzolo and his coworkers found Parkinson patients significantly impaired—relative to age-matched controls—on several subtests of the Wechsler Adult Intelligence Scale, including information, digit span, digit symbol, and block design, and on measures of verbal memory (logical stories and paired associates). Finally, François Boller and his colleagues found Parkinson patients impaired on a wide array of visuospatial tests, independent of intellectual impairment.

Dementia

Demographic structures such as those now developing in North America and Europe have never been experienced before. Since 1900, when about 4% of the population had attained 65 years of age, the percentage of older people has been steadily increasing. By 2030, about 20% of the population will be older than 65 years of age—about 50 million people in the United States alone. Dementia affects between 1% and 6% of the population older than 65 years of age and between 10% and 20% older than 80 years of age. Furthermore, for every demented person, several others suffer cognitive impairments that affect the quality of their lives (see Larrabee and Crook).

In the next 30 years, projections estimate that between 10 million and 20 million elderly people in the United States will have mild to severe cognitive impairments. When this projection is extended to the rest of the developed world, the social and economic costs are truly staggering. Not every person who becomes old also becomes depressed, forgetful, or demented. Some people live to very old age and enjoy active, healthy, productive lives. The question for most of us is how to ensure that we are in this group but, at present, there are depressingly few answers.

Dementia refers to an acquired and persistent syndrome of intellectual impairment. The DSM-IV-R defines the two essential diagnostic features of dementia as (1) memory and other cognitive deficits and (2) impairment in social and occupational functioning. Daniel Kaufer and Steven DeKosky divide dementias into two broad categories: degenerative and nondegenerative (**Table 27.2**).

Degenerative dementias are pathological processes that are primarily intrinsic to the nervous system and tend to affect certain neural systems selectively. Many degenerative dementias are presumed to have a degree of genetic transmission. *Nondegenerative dementias* are a heterogeneous group of disorders with

Table **27.2** **Degenerative and nondegenerative dementias**

Degenerative	Nondegenerative
Alzheimer's disease,	Vascular dementias, e.g., multi-infarct dementia
Extrapyramidal syndromes: e.g., progressive supernuclear palsy	Infectious dementia, e.g., AIDS dementia
Wilson's disease	Neurosyphilis
Huntington's chorea	Posttraumatic dementia
Parkinson's disease	Demyelinating dementia, e.g., multiple sclerosis
Frontotemporal dementia corticobasal degeneration	Toxic or metabolic disorders, e.g., vitamin deficiencies (B_{12}, niacin)
Leukodystrophies, e.g., adrenoleukodystrophy	Chronic alcohol or drug abuse e.g., Korsakoff's syndrome
Prion-related dementias, e.g., Creutzfeld–Jakob disease	

Source: After Kaufer and DeKosky, 1999.

diverse etiologies, including vascular, endocrine, inflammatory, nutritional deficiency, and toxic conditions.

The most prevalent form of dementia is **Alzheimer's disease**, which accounts for about 65% of all dementias and is named for German physician Alois Alzheimer, who published a case study in 1906. The patient was a 51-year-old woman for whom Alzheimer described a set of clinical and neuropathological findings.

Anatomical Correlates of Alzheimer's Disease

Until the 1990s, the only way to identify and to study Alzheimer's disease was to study postmortem pathology. This approach was less than ideal, however, because it was impossible to determine which changes came early in the disease and which followed as a result of the early changes. Nonetheless, it became clear that there are widespread changes in the neocortex and limbic cortex and associated changes in a number of neurotransmitter systems, none of which alone can be correlated simply with the clinical symptoms. Interestingly, most of the brainstem, cerebellum, and spinal cord are spared the major ravages.

Neuritic (Amyloid) Plaques

Neuritic plaques, also known as senile plaques, are found chiefly in the cerebral cortex. Their increased concentration in the cortex has been correlated with the magnitude of cognitive deterioration. The plaques consist of a central core of homogeneous protein material known as *amyloid*, surrounded by degenerative cellular fragments (**Figure 27.7**). These fragments include axonal and dendritic processes and other components of neural cells. Neuritic plaques are generally considered nonspecific phenomena in that they can be found in non-Alzheimer patients and in dementias caused by other known events.

Figure **27.7**

Neuritic Plaque Often found in the cerebral cortices of Alzheimer patients, the amyloid core of the plaque (dark spot in the center) is surrounded by the residue of degenerate cells. (Cecil Fox/Science Source/Photo Researchers.)

Paired Helical Filaments

Also known as neurofibrillary tangles, paired helical filaments are found in both the cerebral cortex and the hippocampus. The posterior half of the hippocampus is affected more severely than the anterior half. Light-microscopic examination has shown that the filaments have a double-helical configuration. They have been described mainly in human tissue and have been observed not only in Alzheimer patients but also in patients with Down syndrome, patients with Parkinson's disease, and patients with other dementias.

Figure **27.8**

Cortical Atrophy Distribution and severity of degeneration on (A) lateral and (B) medial aspects of the brain in an average Alzheimer case. The darker the area, the more pronounced the degeneration. White areas are spared, with only basic change discernible. (After Brun, 1983.)

Neocortical Changes

The neocortical changes are not uniform. Although the cortex shrinks, or atrophies, losing as much as one-third of its volume as the disease progresses, some areas are relatively spared. **Figure 27.8** shows lateral and medial views of the human brain;

(A) Posterior parietal cortex

Inferior temporal cortex

(B) Limbic cortex

shading indicates the areas of degeneration. The darker the red, the more severe the degeneration.

As is clearly shown in Figure 27.8, the primary sensory and motor areas of the cortex, especially the visual cortex and the sensorimotor cortex, are spared. The frontal lobes are less affected than the posterior cortex, but the areas of most extensive change are the posterior parietal areas, inferior temporal cortex, and limbic cortex.

Paralimbic Cortex Changes

The limbic system undergoes the most severe degenerative changes in Alzheimer's disease and, of the limbic structures, the entorhinal cortex is affected earliest and most severely (see Figure 27.8). A number of investigators agree that the entorhinal cortex shows the clearest evidence of cell loss, which has important implications for understanding some of the disease symptoms. The entorhinal cortex is the major relay through which information from the neocortex gets to the hippocampus and related structures and is then sent back to the neocortex. Damage to the entorhinal cortex is associated with memory loss, and, given that memory loss is an early and enduring symptom of the disease, it is most likely caused by the degenerative changes that take place in this area of the limbic cortex.

Cell Changes

Many studies describe loss of cells in the cortices of Alzheimer patients, but this loss is disputed. There seems to be a substantial reduction in large neurons, but these cells may shrink rather than disappear. The more widespread cause of cortical atrophy, however, appears to be a loss of dendritic arborization, as illustrated in **Figure 27.9**A.

The cause of these changes is not known. Note, however, that the degradation is not simply typical of aging. Normal people actually show increases in dendritic length and branching between their 50s and 70s (see Coleman and Flood). Only in very old age does the pattern of degeneration begin to look like the neural cells typical of Alzheimer's disease (Figure 27.9B).

Neurotransmitter Changes

In the 1970s, it was believed that a treatment for Alzheimer's could be found to parallel L-dopa treatment of Parkinson's disease, and the prime candidate neurotransmitter was acetylcholine. Unfortunately, the disease has proved to be far more complex, because other transmitters are clearly changed as well. Noradrenaline, dopamine, and serotonin are reduced, as are the NMDA (N-methyl-D-aspartate)and AMPA (α-amino-3-hydroxy-5-methylisoazole-4-proprionic acid) receptors for glutamate.

The most interesting feature of the neurotransmitter changes is not the absolute decreases in any individual patient but the pattern of decreases. Although age-matched controls also show reductions in transmitter levels, when the pattern of reductions

Figure 27.9

Neuronal Pathology in Alzheimer's Disease (A) Early stages of disease are marked in cortical pyramidal cells by patchy spine loss and thinning out of the dendritic tree, especially horizontally oriented branches, advanced stages with almost complete loss of basilar dendrites, continuing into the terminal stage. (B) The average length of dendrites in healthy adults increases from middle age into old age, decreasing only in late old age. Dendrites in brains with Alzheimer's disease do not show the age-related growth. (Part A drawn from Golgi-stained sections of human prefrontal cortex; after Scheibel, 1983. Part B after Selkoe, 1992.)

(A) Cortical pyramidal cells

| Normal adult pattern | Early Alzheimer's disease | Advanced Alzheimer's disease | Terminal Alzheimer's disease |

(B) Hippocampal neurons

| Middle age (50s) | Older (70s) | Very old (90s) | Alzheimer's disease |

in all transmitter substances is plotted, the Alzheimer patients distinguish themselves from the control groups by showing greater reductions in two or more neurotransmitters.

Putative Causes of Alzheimer's Disease

At present, the cause of Alzheimer's disease is unknown. Given the increasing population of elderly people and thus of those with Alzheimer's disease, a good deal of research is being directed toward several potential causes, summarized in the following sections.

Genetics

The frequency of Alzheimer's disease increases in families that have had a member with Alzheimer's disease. The risk increases to 3.8% if a sibling has had the disease and to 10% if a parent has had the disease.

The application of molecular genetic methods has led to the discovery of three Alzheimer-disease-susceptibility genes; they encode β-amyloid precursor protein (B-APP), presenilin 1, and presenilin 2. These susceptibilities were discovered by examining families with an unusually high incidence of Alzheimer's disease. The B-APP gene maps on chromosome 21, the chromosome found to be abnormal in Down syndrome. People with Down syndrome almost invariably develop dementia by age 40.

How an abnormality in the gene for B-APP produces dementia is not known, but the abnormality is believed to cause the formation of amyloid plaques and neurofibrillary tangles. The genes for presenilins 1 and 2 were found only in the past decade, and they, too, appear to contribute to the production of amyloid, although the mechanism is not yet known (for a review, see Sherrington et al.).

Trace Metals

Early studies with animals identified neurofibrillary degeneration, similar to that in Alzheimer's disease, after the animals were given aluminum salts. Research that followed up this hint found increases ranging from 10 to 30 times the normal concentration of aluminum in Alzheimer patients' brains. At present, the reason for the accumulation of aluminum is not known; whether taking action to reduce the accumulation would be helpful also is not known.

Immune Reactions

Some researchers think that, in old age, the immune system loses its ability to recognize a person's own body. As a result, it develops antibrain antibodies that then cause neuronal degeneration. In other words, the body actually begins to kill its own neurons, which in turn leads to dementia.

Blood Flow

Historically, Alzheimer's disease was attributed to poor circulation. The results of PET studies confirm an extreme reduction in the amount of blood delivered to the brain and the amount of glucose extracted from the blood by neural tissue.

In normal people, blood flow to the brain declines by more than 20% between the ages of 30 and 60, but the brain compensates by more-efficient oxygen

Normal pyramidal neuron

Damaged neuron

Deteriorating Neurons in Dementia Pathological changes in neurons are associated with Alzheimers disease. (Part A courtesy of Bryan Kolb. Part B, © SPL/Photo Researchers.)

uptake. In Alzheimer's disease, the decline is enhanced, but there are no compensatory mechanisms. The greatest decreases in blood flow are found in those areas of the brain in which the most degenerative change is seen (see Figure 27.8). What is not known is whether the declines in blood flow and glucose metabolism are causal or secondary to degenerative brain changes. At least one pharmacological attempt to treat Alzheimer's disease stimulates brain blood flow.

Abnormal Proteins

The three main pathological changes associated with Alzheimer's disease—plaques, neurofibrillary tangles, and granulovacuolar bodies (small vacuoles about 3 μm in diameter, each containing a small granule)—consist of an accumulation of protein that is not seen in normal brains. This abnormal accumulation has led to the suggestion that unusual proteins are being produced and are accumulating, thus disrupting normal protein production and use. The increased protein accumulation in the brain of an Alzheimer patient may be the brain's attempt to repair itself, but for some reason the reparative processes go awry.

Clinical Symptoms and the Progression of Alzheimer's Disease

The most insidious feature of Alzheimer's disease is its slow onset and steady progress, which gradually rob a person, first, of recent memory, then, of more remote memory, and, finally, of the abilities to recognize family members and to function independently. An adaptation of Barry Reisberg's detailed description of the stages of the disease and clinical symptoms appears in **Table 27.3**. As Reisberg pointed out, the disease progress is gradual, and patients spend from several months to several years in each stage. Reisberg also described levels of impairment in five measures of cognitive function (concentration, recent and past memory, orientation, social functioning, and self-care) that are descriptive parallels of the stages shown in Table 27.3.

In view of the distinctive pattern of anatomical changes in the disease, one might expect a distinctive pattern of cognitive changes. Finding such a pattern would be important, because the symptoms displayed by Alzheimer patients are often confused with those seen in other disorders, such as depression or a series of small strokes. In view of the distinctly different approaches to managing depressed patients and Alzheimer patients, differential diagnosis would be very useful.

IQ subtest scales from the Wechsler Adult Intelligence Scale can be used to distinguish the impairment patterns of Alzheimer's disease from those produced by cerebrovascular disease (see Fuld). Alzheimer patients are marked by the striking deficits that they show on digit symbol and block design, with successively milder impairments on object assembly, similarities and digit span, and information and vocabulary. Other Alzheimer-sensitive tests include backward digits, telling the time on clocks without numbers, and object naming. Additionally, Alzheimer patients typically show deficits on tests of both left- and right-hemisphere function, and the impairments are not marked by sudden onset.

Perhaps the most striking impairment in Alzheimer patients is related to memory performance. Virtually every neuropsychological test of memory re-

Table **27.3** Scale of behavioral change in Alzheimer's disease

Degree of Cognitive Decline	Symptoms
None	No subjective complaints of memory deficit. No memory deficit evident on clinical interview.
Very mild	Complaints of memory deficit, most often in (1) forgetting where one has placed familiar objects and (2) forgetting names that one formerly knew well. No objective evidence of memory deficit on clinical interview. No objective deficits in employment or social situations. Appropriate concern with respect to symptomatology.
Mild	Earliest clear-cut deficits. Manifestations in more than one of the following areas: (1) patient may get lost when traveling to an unfamiliar location; (2) coworkers become aware of patient's relatively poor performance; (3) patient may read a passage or a book and retain little material; (4) patient may demonstrate decreased facility in remembering names when introduced to new people; (5) patient may have lost or misplaced an object of value; (6) concentration deficit may be evident on clinical testing. Objective evidence of memory deficit obtained only with formal tests. Decreased performance in demanding employment and social settings. Denial begins to set in, and mild to moderate anxiety is displayed.
Moderate	Clear-cut deficit in clinical interview in (1) decreased knowledge of current and recent events; (2) memory of personal history; (3) concentration deficit in serial subtractions; (4) decreased ability to travel, handle finances, etc. Inability to perform complex tasks. Denial is dominant defense mechanism. Flattening of affect and withdrawal from challenging situations.
Moderately severe	Cannot function without some assistance. Unable to recall a major relevant aspect of current life, such as address or telephone number, names of close family members, name of schools attended. Frequent disorientation to date, day, season, and place. An educated person may have difficulty counting backward by fours from 40 and by twos from 20.
Severe	May occasionally forget name of spouse. Largely unaware of all recent events and experiences. Retains some knowledge of past life though sketchy. May have difficulty counting backward or forward from 10. Requires some assistance with activities of daily living (e.g., may become incontinent, requires travel assistance but occasionally displays ability to travel to familiar locations). Diurnal rhythm often disturbed. Can recall own name and distinguish familiar from unfamiliar persons in the environment. Changes in personality and emotional aspects, including delusional behavior, obsessive symptoms, anxiety, or loss of purposeful behavior.
Very severe	All verbal abilities are lost. Often, there is no speech at all—only grunting; incontinent of urine; requires assistance in toileting and feeding. Loses basic psychomotor skill (e.g., ability to walk). The brain appears no longer to be able to tell the body what to do.

Source: After Reisburg, 1983.

veals impairments relative to age-matched controls. Alzheimer patients are particularly prone to difficulties in producing the names of objects and in distinguishing among objects within a category.

F. Jacob Huff and his colleagues concluded that the anomia deficit is characterized by a loss of information about specific objects and their names, rather than by a simple difficulty in retrieving information. The difficulties in naming are unlikely to be simply due to difficulties with memory, because

Alzheimer patients have a variety of language impairments that are most obvious as the complexity of the cognitive processing required increases. Thus, when engaging in simple conversations about the weather and so on, the patients appear to have normal language functioning but, if they are required to engage in more-complex discussions, their difficulty with language becomes more apparent.

Although Alzheimer's disease is usually seen as a single disorder, emerging evidence suggests that the age-at-onset may predict different cognitive and anatomical changes. Giovani Frisoni and colleagues compared the MRI scans of Alzheimer patients with early-onset (before age 65) and late-onset (age 65 and older) disease and found that the early-onset cases had more diffuse atrophy across the cerebral hemispheres but less atrophy in the hippocampus than did the late-onset cases. There thus appear to be different patterns of brain atrophy, depending on age at onset, suggesting different predisposing or etiological factors.

Summary

The Brain and Behavior

Historically, psychiatry and neurology were the same field, and only recently have two separate specialties emerged. For many patients, however, the distinction is arbitrary. Diseases of the brain can produce severe psychological disturbances, and the causes are only beginning to be understood.

Schizophrenia

Schizophrenia is a disease that emerges in the course of development, usually in late adolescence, and is associated especially with abnormalities in the structure and function of the dorsolateral prefrontal cortex and medial temporal region. Schizophrenia is likely not a single disorder but rather a continuum of disorders varying in the degree of positive and negative symptoms.

Mood Disorders

The primary disorders of mood are depression and bipolar disorder. Both are related to abnormalities in the brain's response to stress through the HPA axis. Depression is associated with abnormally high activity in the orbitofrontal cortex and amygdala. The action of antidepressants is to reduce amygdala activity, likely by increasing monoamine levels. Bipolar disorder may be a result of the brain's oversensitive response to stressors, including drugs, which in turn alters the chemistry and morphology of cells, especially in the orbital cortex or the amygdala or both. Repeated bipolar episodes are associated with atrophy of the hippocampus and fusiform gyrus.

Psychiatric Symptoms of Cerebral Vascular Disease

The most common poststroke psychiatric symptoms include depression, generalized anxiety, catastrophic reactions, and pathological affect.

Psychosurgery

Surgical treatments for schizophrenia and depression, rare today, were developed in the 1930s and became known as psychosurgery. The best-known form, frontal lobotomy, was commonly used to treat schizophrenia until the late 1950s when drug treatments became widely used.

Motor Disorders

Traditionally, motor disorders, both hyper- and hypokinetic, have been considered neurological disorders, but they can produce significant psychological abnormalities, likely owing to an imbalance of neurotransmitter systems, especially the catecholamines and acetylcholine. These chemical changes appear to have significant effects on frontal- and temporal-lobe function, leading to a variety of behavioral disturbances prominent in disorders such as Tourette's syndrome and Parkinson's disease.

Dementia

Dementias are an increasing problem for society, owing to changing demographics. By far the most common dementia is Alzheimer's disease, which is associated with a variety of pathological changes in the forebrain. The cause or causes are not known, although research in molecular genetics has identified at least three genes that predispose people to the disease.

References

Becker, J. T., F. Boller, J. Saxton, and K. L. McGonigle-Gibson. Normal rates of forgetting of verbal and non-verbal material in Alzheimer's disease. *Cortex* 23:59–72, 1987.

Benes, F. M., J. Davidson, and E. D. Bird. Quantitative cytoarchitectural studies of the cerebral cortex of schizophrenics. *Archives of General Psychiatry* 43:31–35, 1986.

Berman, K. F., and D. R. Weinberger. Regional cerebral blood flow in monozygotic twins concordant and discordant for schizophrenia. *Archives of General Psychiatry* 49:927–934, 1992.

Boller, F., D. Passafiume, M. C. Keefe, K. Rogers, L. Morrow, and Y. Kim. Visuospatial impairment in Parkinson's disease: Role of perceptual and motor factors. *Archives of Neurology* 41:485–490, 1984.

Bowen, F. P. Behavioral alterations in patients with Parkinson's disease. In M. D. Yahr, Ed. *The Basal Ganglia*. New York: Raven Press, 1976.

Bowles, N. L., L. K. Obler, and M. L. Albert. Naming errors in healthy aging and dementia of the Alzheimer type. *Cortex* 23:519–524, 1987.

Brown, R., N. Colter, J. A. Corsellis, T. J. Crow, C. D. Frith, R. Jagoe, and E. C. Johnstone. Postmortem evidence of structural brain changes in schizophrenia. *Archives of General Psychiatry* 43:35–42, 1986.

Brun, A. An overview of light and electron microscopic changes. In B. Reisberg, Ed. *Alzheimer's Disease*. New York: The Free Press, 1983.

Byne, W., E. Kemegther, L. Jones, V. Harouthunian, and K. L. Davis. The neurochemistry of schizophrenia. In D. S. Charney, E. J. Nestler, and B. S. Bunney, Eds. *The Neurobiology of Mental Illness*. New York: Oxford University Press, 1999, pp. 236–245.

Carlsson, M., and A. Carlsson. Interactions between glutamatergic and monoaminergic systems within the basal ganglia: Implications for schizophrenia and Parkinson's disease. *Trends in Neurosciences* 13:272–276, 1990.

Charney, D. S., E. J. Nestler, B. S. Bunney, Eds. *The Neurobiology of Mental Illness*. New York: Oxford University Press, 1999.

Chase, T. N., N. S. Wexler, and A. Barbeau, Eds. *Advances in Neurology*, vol. 23, *Huntington's Disease*. New York: Raven Press, 1979.

Chemerinski, E., and S. R. Levine. Neuropsychiatric disorders following vascular brain injury. *The Mount Sinai Journal of Medicine* 76:1006–1014, 2006.

Coleman, P. D., and D. G. Flood. Neuron numbers and dendritic extent in normal aging and Alzheimer's disease. *Neurobiology of Aging* 8:521–545, 1987.

Crow, T. J., and E. C. Johnstone. Schizophrenia: Nature of the disease process and its biological correlates. In F. Plum, Ed. *Handbook of Physiology*, vol. 5. Bethesda, Md.: American Physiological Society, 1987.

Dolan, R. J., C. J. Bench, R. G. Brown, L. C. Scott, and R. S. J. Frackowiak. Neuropsychological dysfunction in depression: The relationship to regional cerebral blood flow. *Psychological Medicine* 24:849–857, 1994.

Drevets, W. C., K. M. Gadde, and R. R. Krishman. Neuroimaging studies of mood disorders. In D. S. Charney, E. J. Nestler, and B. S. Bunney, Eds. *The Neurobiology of Mental Illness*. New York: Oxford University Press, 1999, pp. 394–418.

Fedio, P., C. S. Cox, A. Neophytides, G. Canal Frederick, and T. N. Chase. Neuropsychological profile of Huntington's disease: Patients and those at risk. *Advances in Neurology* 23:239–256, 1979.

Friedhoff, A. J., and T. N. Chase, Eds. *Advances in Neurology*, vol. 35, *Gilles de la Tourette Syndrome*. New York: Raven Press, 1982.

Frisoni, G. B., M. Pievai, C. Testa, F. Sabattoli, L. Bresciani, M. Bonetti, A. Beltramello, K. M. Hayashi, A. W. Toga, and P. M. Thompson. The topography of grey matter involvement in early and late onset Alzheimer's disease. *Brain* 130:720–730, 2007.

Fuld, P. A. Psychometric differentiation of the dementias: An overview. In B. Reisberg, Ed. *Alzheimer's Disease*. New York: The Free Press, 1983.

Gershon, E. S., and R.O. Rieder. Major disorders of mind and brain. *Scientific American* 267(3):126–133, 1992.

Gilles de la Tourette, G. Étude sur un affection, nerveuse characterisee par l'incoordination motrice accompanagnee d'echolalie et de copralalie (jumping, latah, myriachit). *Archives of Neurology* 9:19–42, 158–200, 1885.

Grady, C. L., J. B. Haxby, B. Horowitz, G. Berg, and S. I. Rapoport. Neuropsychological and cerebral metabolic function in early vs. late onset dementia of the Alzheimer type. *Neuropsychologia* 25:807–815, 1987.

Grant, I., and K. M. Adams, Eds. *Neuropsychological Assessment of Neuropsychiatric Disorders*. New York: Oxford University Press, 1986.

Gusella, J. F., M. E. MacDonald, C. M. Ambrose, and M. P. Duyao. Molecular genetics of Huntington's disease (Review). *Archives of Neurology* 50:1157–1163, 1993.

Healy, D. Rhythm and blues: Neurochemical, neuropharmacological and neuropsychological implications of a hypothesis of circadian rhythm dysfunction in the affective disorders. *Psychopharmacology* 93:271–285, 1987.

Heaton, R. K., L. E. Badde, and K. L. Johnson. Neuropsychological test results associated with psychiatric disorders in adults. *Psychological Bulletin* 85:141–162, 1978.

Heaton, R. K., and T. J. Crowley. Effects of psychiatric disorders and their somatic treatments on neuropsychological test results. In S. B. Gilskov and G. J. Boll, Eds. *Handbook of Clinical Neuropsychology.* New York: Wiley, 1981.

Huff, F. J., S. Corkin, and J. H. Growdon. Semantic impairment and anomia in Alzheimer's disease. *Brain and Language* 28:235–249, 1986.

Kaplan, B. J., S. G. Crawford, C. J. Field, and J. S. A. Simpson. Vitamins, minerals, and mood. *Psychological Bulletin* 133:747–760, 2007.

Kaufer, D. I., and S. T. DeKosky. Diagnostic classifications: Relationship to the neurobiology of dementia. In D. S. Charney, E. J. Nestler, and B. S. Bunney, Eds. *The Neurobiology of Mental Illness.* New York: Oxford University Press, 1999, pp. 641–649.

Kovelman, J. A., and A. B. Scheibel. A neurohistologic correlate of schizophrenia. *Biological Psychiatry* 19:1601–1621, 1984.

Kupfer, D. J., and M. E. Thase. The use of the sleep laboratory in the diagnosis of affective disorders. *Psychiatric Clinics of North America* 6:3–25, 1983.

Langston, J. W., P. Ballard, J. W. Tegrud, and I. Irwin. Chronic parkinsonism in humans due to a product of meperidine-analog synthesis. *Science* 219:979–980, 1983.

Larrabee, G. J., and T. H. Crook. Estimated prevalence of age-associated memory impairment derived from standardized tests of memory function. *International Psychogeriatrics* 6:945–1004, 1994.

Lewis, D. A., T. Hashimoto, and D. W. Volk. Cortical inhibitory neurons and schizophrenia. *Nature Reviews Neuroscience* 6:312–324, 2005.

Lewis, D. A., and P. Levitt. Schizophrenia as a disorder of development. *Annual Review of Neuroscience* 25:409–432, 2002.

Lipska, B. K., Z. Z. Khaing, C. S. Weickert, and D. R. Weinberger. BDNF mRNA expression in rat hippocampus and prefrontal cortex: Effects of neonatal ventral hippocampal damage and antipsychotic drugs. *European Journal of Neuroscience* 14:135–144, 2001.

Loring, D. W., and J. W. Largen. Neuropsychological patterns of presenile and senile dementia of the Alzheimer type. *Neuropsychologia* 23:351–357, 1985.

Martin, A., C. Cox, P. Brouwers, and P. Fedio. A note on different patterns of impaired and preserved cognitive abilities and their relation to episodic memory deficits in Alzheimer's patients. *Brain and Language* 25:181–198, 1985.

Martin, J. P. *The Basal Ganglia and Posture.* London: Ritman Medical Publishing, 1967.

Moorhead, T. W., J. McKirdy, J. E. Sussmann, J. Hall, S. M. Lawrie, E. C. Johnstone, and A. M. McIntosh. Progressive gray matter loss in patients with bipolar disorder. *Biological Psychiatry* 62:894–900, 2007.

Murdoch, B. E., H. J. Chenery, V. Wilks, and R. S. Boyle. Language disorders in dementia of the Alzheimer type. *Brain and Language* 31:122–137, 1987.

Parkinson, J. Essay on the shaking palsy. Reprinted in M. Critchley, Ed. *James Parkinson.* London: Macmillan, 1955.

Pirozzolo, F. J., E. C. Hansch, J. A. Mortimer, D. D. Webster, and M. A. Kuskowski. Dementia in Parkinson's disease: A neuropsychological analysis. *Brain and Cognition* 1:71–83, 1982.

Post, R. M., and S. R. B. Weiss. Neurobiological models of recurrence in mood disorder. In D. S. Charney, E. J. Nestler, and B. S. Bunney, Eds. *The Neurobiology of Mental Illness.* New York: Oxford University Press, 1999, pp. 365–384.

Randolph, C., T. E. Goldberg, and D. Weinberger. The neuropsychology of schizophrenia. In K. M. Heilman and E. Valenstein, Eds. *Clinical Neuropsychology,* 3rd ed. New York: Oxford University Press, 1993.

Reisberg, B. Clinical presentation, diagnosis, and symptomatology of age-associated cognitive decline and Alzheimer's disease. In B. Reisberg, Ed. *Alzheimer's Disease.* New York: The Free Press, 1983.

Robinson, T. E., and B. Kolb. Structural plasticity associated with drugs of abuse. *Neuropharmacology,* 47(Suppl 1):33–46, 2004.

Sacks, O. *Awakenings.* New York: Doubleday, 1973.

Scheibel, A. B. Dendritic changes. In B. Reisberg, Ed. *Alzheimer's Disease.* New York: The Free Press, 1983.

Selkoe, D. J. Aging brain, aging mind. *Scientific American* 267(3):135–142, 1992.

Sherrington, R., P. St. George Hyslop, M. Hutton, J. Perez-Tur, and J. Hardy. The molecular biology of Alzheimer's disease. In D. S. Charney, E. J. Nestler, and B. S. Bunney. Eds. *The Neurobiology of Mental Illness.* New York: Oxford University Press, 1999, pp. 650–658.

Spinnler, H., and S. Della Sala. The role of clinical neuropsychology in the neurological diagnosis of Alzheimer's disease. *Journal of Neurology* 235:258–271, 1988.

Sutherland, R. J., B. Kolb, W. M. Schoel, I. Q. Whishaw, and D. Davies. Neuropsychological assessment of children and adults with Tourette's syndrome: A comparison with learning disabilities and schizophrenia. *Advances in Neurology* 35:311–322, 1982.

Valenstein, E. S., Ed. *The Psychosurgery Debate.* San Francisco: W. H. Freeman and Company, 1980.

Valenstein, E. S. *Great and Desperate Cures.* New York: Basic Books, 1986.

Von Economo, C. *Encephalitis Lethargica:Iits Sequelae and Treatment.* London: Oxford University Press, 1931.

Weinberger, D. R., K. F. Berman, R. L. Suddath, and E. F. Torrey. Evidence for dysfunction of a prefrontal-limbic network in schizophrenia: An MRI and regional cerebral blood flow study of discordant monozygotic twins. *American Journal of Psychiatry* 149:890–897, 1992.

Wexler, N. S. Perceptual-motor, cognitive, and emotional characteristics of persons at risk for Huntington's disease. *Advances in Neurology* 23:257–272, 1979.

Neuropsychological Assessment

CHAPTER 28

PORTRAIT: Lingering Effects of Brain Trauma

R.L. was a 32-year-old nurse and mother of four. Driving home from work one afternoon, she stopped at a red light and was rear-ended by another vehicle.

R.L.'s head snapped back and struck the headrest and then the side window as she bounced forward. She blacked out for a few minutes, but, when the emergency vehicles arrived, she was conscious, although disoriented and dysphasic, and was experiencing severe pain in her back and neck from the whiplash as well.

R.L. spent about a week in the hospital, where neither CT nor MRI scans identified any cerebral injury, although several vertebrae were damaged. An accomplished musician, she could still play the piano well from memory, but she could no longer read music. In addition, her oral language skills remained impaired and she was completely unable to read.

R.L.'s difficulties did not abate, and she had spells of apraxia. For example, she often found herself unable to

figure out how to put on her makeup; she would stare at her lipstick and have no idea how to use it. When R.L. came to us, she was depressed because, although the neurologists could find no reason for her impairments, she continued to have significant difficulties.

As described in Chapter 16, perhaps the most commonly observed trait of frontal-lobe patients is difficulty in using environmental feedback to regulate or change their behavior. One manifestation is response inhibition: patients with frontal-lobe lesions consistently perseverate on responses in a variety of test situations, particularly those such as the Wisconsin Card-Sorting Test, in which the solution demands change.

In the test setup diagrammed here, a subject's task is to place each card from the bottom pile under the appropriate card in the row above, sorting by one of three possible categories: color, number of elements, or shape. Subjects are never told the correct sorting category but only whether their responses are correct or incorrect.

When the subject selects the correct category ten times in a row, the correct solution changes unexpectedly. Shifting response strategies is particularly difficult for people with frontal damage. Although R.L. eventually performed the task, she had great difficulty.

Our neuropsychological evaluation revealed a woman of above-average intelligence who had a significant loss of verbal fluency and verbal memory, as well as severe dyslexia even a year after the accident. Now nearly 10 years later, she is still unable to read music and reads text only with great difficulty.

People with closed-head traumatic brain injuries often have little or no sign of cerebral injury visible on neuroimaging but still have significant cognitive deficits, often so severe that they cannot resume their preinjury life styles. For many, the extent of neurological disorder becomes clear from neuropsychological tests.

The 1980s were the heyday of neuropsychological assessment. Clinically trained neuropsychologists were in demand and neuropsychological evaluation was regarded as an essential tool in neurological assessment. The role of neuropsychological assessment has changed radically, however, and it has begun to develop a new face that is likely to continue changing for some time. In this chapter, we describe this changing role for neuropsychological assessment, consider the rationale behind assessment, and present summaries of three actual case assessments.

The Changing Face of Neuropsychological Assessment

The roots of neuropsychological assessment lie in neurology and psychiatry. Clinician Kurt Goldstein, for example, was expert in neurology, psychology, and psychiatry. The psychological basis of assessment began to diverge from medicine in the 1940s. The first neuropsychological tests were designed to identify people suffering from cerebral dysfunction attributable to organic disease processes (brain pathology), rather than to "functional disorders" linked to behavior.

Although test designers originally believed that a single test for brain damage could be constructed, with a cutoff point that separated the brain-damaged from the non-brain-damaged patient, the task proved impossible. Gradually, more-sophisticated testing procedures were developed, largely in a few locations in Europe and North America, including Cambridge (Oliver Zangwill), Oxford (Freda Newcombe), Moscow (Alexander Luria), Montreal (Brenda Milner and Laughlin Taylor), Boston (Edith Kaplan and Hans-Leukas Teuber), and Iowa City (Arthur Benton).

By the early 1980s, neuropsychology was no longer confined to a few elite laboratories, and the new field of clinical neuropsychology blossomed in clinics and hospitals. Since that time, three factors have enhanced the rate of change in neuropsychological assessment: functional imaging, cognitive neuroscience, and managed health care. We consider each briefly.

Functional Imaging

Perhaps the biggest change in both neurology and neuropsychology in the past three decades has been the development of functional imaging. Indeed, we have emphasized the importance of functional imaging in the Snapshots in each of the preceding chapters. Whereas, in earlier eras, the effects of cerebral injury or disease often had to be inferred from behavioral symptoms, neuroimaging has allowed investigators to identify changes in cerebral functioning in a wide variety of disorders, including most of the neurological, developmental, and behavioral disorders discussed in Chapters 23 through 27.

The main role of the clinical neuropsychologist has therefore changed from that of diagnostician to that of participant in rehabilitation, especially in cases of chronic disease such as stroke and head trauma. As charted in **Figure 28.1** about 3 in 10 patients are seen for rehabilitation and another 4 in 10 are seen as medical referrals, with the most common question being related to general cognitive functioning.

An important point to bear in mind, however, is that even the most sophisticated functional-imaging techniques often do not predict the extent

Figure **28.1**

Presenting Problems More than two-thirds of all patients undergoing neuropsychological assessment are referred either for rehabilitation or in connection with medical problems. (After Zillmer and Spiers, 2001.)

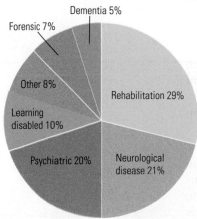

Dementia 5%
Forensic 7%
Other 8%
Learning disabled 10%
Psychiatric 20%
Rehabilitation 29%
Neurological disease 21%

of behavioral disturbance observed in people with certain types of brain injury, especially in head trauma, as R.L.'s case, described in the Portrait, illustrates. For people with closed-head injury, often the only way to document the nature and extent of disability is a thorough neuropsychological assessment (see Christensen and Uzzell).

Cognitive Neuroscience

One effect of the growth of clinical neuropsychology is the diversification of methods used by individual neuropsychologists, the choice of tests varying with the disorder being investigated and the question being asked. From the early 1950s through the early 1980s, batteries of tests were developed, each with a different focus (**Table 28.1**). Many, such as the Halstead–Reitan Battery, retain the concept of cutoff scores, although this assumption presents difficulties, because performance below a particular level cannot always be taken as indicative of brain damage.

One difficulty with cutoff scores is that cerebral organization varies with such factors as sex, handedness, age, education, and experience. Furthermore, test problems can be solved by using different strategies and can thus entail different cortical regions. Symptoms of cortical injury can be highly specific (recall the color-blind painter's case described in Chapter 13). Finally, because many tests require problem solving of various kinds, we might expect task performance to vary with intelligence. All these factors make the use of cutoff scores difficult to justify.

A serious handicap in the development of test batteries was the absence of neurological theory in test construction or use. Knowledge of brain function was based largely on clinical observation, and few clinicians other than Alexander Luria had tried to formulate a general theory of how the brain functions to produce cognition.

The emergence of cognitive neuroscience in the 1990s produced a dramatic change in the theoretical understanding of brain and cognition. Case studies once again became popular, each directed by sophisticated cognitive theory and assisted by structural- and functional-imaging technologies (see Shallice). These

Table 28.1 Overview of neuropsychological test batteries

Test Battery	Type	Basic Reference
Benton's neuropsychological investigation	Composite	Benton et al., 1983
Boston Process Approach	Composite	Kaplan, 1988
Oxford neuropsychological procedures	Composite	Newcombe, 1969
Montreal Neurological Institute approach	Composite	Taylor, 1979
Frontal-lobe assessment	Composite	Stuss and Levine, 2002
Western Ontario procedures	Composite	Kimura and McGlone, 1983
Halstead–Reitan Battery	Standardized	Reitan and Davison, 1974
Luria's neuropsychological investigation	Standardized	Christensen, 1975
Luria–Nebraska Battery	Standardized	Golden, 1981
CANTAB	Computerized	Robbins et al., 1998

more-cognitive approaches also use multivariate statistical methods such as structural equation modeling to attempt to understand the way in which neural networks are disrupted in both individual cases and in groups. Test design has begun to incorporate this knowledge, but the emerging field of cognitive neuroscience will certainly change the way in which neuropsychological assessment is conducted in the future.

Perhaps the area most influenced to date is in understanding the functions of the right frontal lobe (see a review by Stuss and Levine). Historically, the right frontal lobe proved remarkably unresponsive to neuropsychological assessment. The combination of functional imaging and neuropsychological test development has now led to an understanding of the role of the right frontal lobe in formerly inaccessible functions such as social cognition (see Chapter 20).

Managed Care

Perhaps economics is the greatest challenge faced by practicing psychologists in the past decade. In the era of managed health care, clinicians are pressured to reduce the time and money spent on neuropsychological services. In particular, there is sometimes unreasonable pressure to reduce the number of tests given to individual patients, especially in view of the perception that medical imaging can provide faster and more accurate assessments of cerebral dysfunction.

As already noted, imaging has changed the way in which neuropsychological assessment will be used, but, in head-trauma cases, as R.L.'s case and the many examples of traumatic brain injury given throughout this book demonstrate, neuropsychological assessment is often the only way to document cognitive disturbances. Gary Groth-Marnat suggests that psychologists must develop and promote assessment procedures that

- focus on diagnostic matters that are most clearly linked to treatment choice and outcomes;

- identify conditions that are likely to result in cost savings;

- are time efficient; and

- integrate treatment planning, progress monitoring, and outcome evaluation.

Clearly, clinical assessment will have to change if it is to survive the challenge of managed health care.

Rationale Behind Neuropsychological Assessment

By the 1990s, neuropsychologists had an impressive array of tests from which to choose, as summarized in Table 28.1. At one end of the spectrum are standardized test batteries with fixed criteria for organicity. These tests have in common the advantage of straightforward administration, scoring, and interpretation. There is little need to understand the theoretical bases of the tests or the nuances of cerebral organization to administer the tests, although such understanding is necessary for interpretation. Examples include the Halstead–Reitan Battery and the Luria–Nebraska Battery. More recently, Trevor Robbins and his colleagues at the University of Cambridge devised a computerized version of a standardized battery (CANTAB) that has the advantage of being administered in a highly structured manner.

At the other end of the spectrum are individualized test batteries that require particular theoretical knowledge to administer and interpret. These assessments are more qualitative than quantitative. The testing of each patient is tailored to that person's etiology and by the qualitative nature of the performance on each test. An example is Luria's neurological approach, which is not really so much a test battery as a strategy for examining patients. (The Luria–Nebraska Battery was an attempt to make Luria's procedure more structured and quantitative but, in doing so, the Luria–Nebraska Battery became a completely different analysis.)

There is a middle ground, too, represented by composite batteries in which each test is given in a formalized way and may have comparison norms, but the qualitative performance on tests and the pattern of test results are considered. An example is the Boston Process Approach (**Table 28.2**). Other examples are described by Arthur Benton and his colleagues, by Muriel Lezak, by Pat McKenna and Elizabeth Warrington, by William Milberg and his colleagues, by Freda Newcombe, by Aaron Smith, and by Laughlin Taylor.

Across this spectrum, each battery is constantly changing in response to test revisions and developments, as well as to the clinical population being evaluated. One constraint on the choice of any test, however, is the training of clinical neuropsychologists. The use of tests based on theory requires an understanding of the theory of cerebral organization.

Factors Affecting Test Choice

Throughout this book, we have seen that circumscribed lesions in different cortical regions can produce discrete behavioral changes. Thus, working backward from this knowledge to localize unknown brain damage would seem reasonable. That is, given a particular behavioral change, we should be able to predict the site or sites of the disturbance most likely to be causing the change.

There are problems in working backward in such a manner, however. Research patients are often chosen for specific reasons. For example, whereas patients with rapidly expanding tumors would not be chosen for research, because their results are so difficult to interpret, neurosurgical patients are ideal research subjects, because the extent of their damage is known. Therefore, differences in the etiology of the neurological disorder might be expected to make assessment difficult. Indeed, people with diffuse dysfunction, as in head trauma, would seem likely to perform very differently from people with surgical removals.

Even after the practitioner has chosen tests that are appropriate for the etiology in question, significant questions must be resolved. First, how sensitive are the tests? If a large region of the brain is dysfunctioning, the assessment test need not be particularly sensitive to demonstrate the dysfunction. If the lesion is small, on the other hand, the behavioral effect may be rather specific. As we have seen, for example, a lesion in the right somatosensory representation of the face may produce very subtle sensory changes, and, unless specific tests of

Table 28.2 Representative sample of the tests used in the Boston Process Approach to neuropsychological assessment

Intellectual and Conceptual Functions
Wechsler Adult Intelligence Scale III
Raven's Standard Progressive Matrices
Shipley Institute of Living Scale
Wisconsin Card-Sorting Test
Proverbs test

Memory Functions
Wechsler Memory Scale III
Rey Auditory Verbal Learning Test
Rey Complex-Figure Test
Benton Visual-Recognition Test
Consonant trigrams test
Cowboy Story-Reading Memory Test

Language Functions
Narrative writing sample
Tests of verbal fluency
Visual-perceptual functions
Cow-and-circle experimental test
Automobile puzzle
Parietal-lobe battery
Hooper Visual Organization Test

Academic Skills
Wide Range Achievement Test

Self-Control and Motor Functions
Proteus Maze Test
Stroop Color-Word Interference Test
Luria Three-Step Motor Program
Finger tapping

nonverbal fluency are used (see Chapter 16), the cognitive changes may go unnoticed, even with dozens of tests.

A related problem is that various factors may interact with brain pathology to make the interpretation of test results difficult. Both age and ethnic or cultural background can influence test performance. Therefore, as noted earlier, test scores cannot be interpreted with strict cutoff criteria.

Furthermore, intelligence alters an investigator's expectations of performance on tests: someone with an IQ score of 130 may be relatively impaired on a test of verbal memory but may appear normal compared with someone with a score of 90. Thus, unlike standard, quantitative psychometric assessment, neuropsychological assessment must be flexible. This flexibility makes interpretation difficult and requires extensive training in fundamental neuropsychology and neurology as well as in neuropsychological assessment.

Finally, we have seen in several earlier discussions that significant differences in test performance are related to factors such as sex and handedness. In addition, test performance is often biased by demographics. For example, in one three-city study of the effects of head trauma, investigators found that normal subjects in one city performed as poorly as brain-damaged subjects in another. Significant demographic differences influenced the test performance and thus had to be considered in interpreting the results.

Goals of Neuropsychological Assessment

The goal of assessment in general clinical psychology is the diagnosis of a disorder for the purpose of changing behavior. For example, intelligence and achievement tests may be given to school children to try to identify particular problem areas (poor short-term memory, for example, or slow reading) as an aid in teaching. Similarly, personality tests are used with an eye toward defining and curing a behavioral disorder, such as generalized anxiety. The goals of clinical neuropsychology are different in some respects:

- Assessment aims to determine a person's general level of cerebral functioning and to identify cerebral dysfunction and localize it where possible. In doing so, there is an attempt to provide an accurate and unbiased estimate of a person's cognitive capacity.

- Assessment is used to facilitate patient care and rehabilitation. Serial assessments can provide information about the rate of recovery and the potential for resuming a former life style.

- Neuropsychological assessment can identify the presence of mild disturbances in cases in which other diagnostic studies have produced equivocal results. Examples are the effects of head trauma or the early symptoms of a degenerative disease.

- A related goal is to identify unusual brain organization that may exist in left-handers or in people who have suffered childhood brain injury. This information is particularly valuable to surgeons, who would not want, for example, to inadvertently remove primary speech zones while performing surgery. Such information is likely to be obtained only from behavioral measures.

- In disorders such as focal epilepsy, the primary evidence corroborating an abnormal EEG may emerge from behavioral assessment, because radiological procedures, including noninvasive imaging, can fail to specifically identify the abnormal brain tissue giving rise to the seizures.

- Because some recovery of function may be expected after brain injury, this recovery must be documented not only with rehabilitation in mind but also to determine the effectiveness of any medical treatment, particularly for neoplasms (tumors) or vascular abnormalities.

- Assessment assists a patient and the patient's family in understanding the patient's possible residual deficits so that realistic life goals and rehabilitation programs can be planned.

Intelligence Testing in Neuropsychological Assessment

Most neuropsychological assessments begin with a measure of general intelligence, most often one of the Wechsler scales, the most recent version being the Wechsler Adult Intelligence Scale—Third Edition (WAIS-III). The Wechsler scales have proved to be invaluable in determining a base level of cognitive functioning. These scales provide the distinct advantage of producing separate scores for verbal and performance subtests, as well as an overall IQ score.

The WAIS-III has seven subtests for evaluating verbal and performance scales. The verbal score is a measure of acquired knowledge, verbal reasoning, and comprehension of verbal information. The performance score provides an indication of a person's nonverbal reasoning, spatial-processing skills, attentiveness to detail, and visuomotor integration.

Although the verbal and performance subtests were not designed to measure left- and right-hemisphere functions, respectively, the subtests have proved useful as a rough measure of left- and right-hemisphere function, respectively. The IQ scores obtained on both the verbal and the performance sections have a mean of 100 and a standard deviation of 15. A difference of more than 10 points between the verbal and the performance scores is usually taken as a clinically significant difference, although, statistically, this interpretation is liberal.

The results of a number of studies have demonstrated that well-defined left-hemisphere lesions produce a relatively low verbal IQ score compared with performance score, whereas well-defined right-hemisphere lesions produce a relatively low performance score. Diffuse damage, on the other hand, tends to produce a low performance score, leading to the erroneous belief that the verbal–performance IQ difference is not diagnostically useful. Although a reduced performance score is not definitive, it is rare to obtain a relatively low verbal IQ, and its appearance should not be ignored.

Warrington and her colleagues evaluated the WAIS subscales and IQ values in a retrospective study of 656 unselected patients with unilateral brain damage. Overall, their results showed that lesions of the left hemisphere depress verbal IQs, whereas lesions of the right hemisphere depress performance IQs, the exception in both cases being that of occipital lesions. However, the verbal–performance discrepancy score was less than 10 points in 53% of left-hemisphere cases and in 43% of right-hemisphere cases. A small number of cases had discrepancy scores greater than 10 points in the opposite direction:

6% with left-hemisphere lesions and 3% with right-hemisphere lesions. (It is curious that the patients with left parietal or temporoparietal lesions did not show a large drop in IQ, considering that they would be expected to be dysphasic. Because language skills were not mentioned in the Warrington study, her analysis could have excluded aphasic subjects. In our experience, dysphasic patients have very depressed verbal IQs, as would be expected.)

Warrington also analyzed a subset of WAIS subtests, including four verbal instruments (arithmetic, similarities, digit span, and vocabulary) and three nonverbal (picture completion, block design, and picture arrangement). Overall, the performance of left-hemisphere frontal, temporal, and parietal patients was significantly poorer on the four verbal tests. There were no differences between these left-hemisphere groups on the tests, however. The performance tests were less predictive of lesion side, because only the right parietal patients were significantly poorer on block design and picture arrangement.

One difficulty with postinjury intelligence testing is that a premorbid estimate of intellectual level must exist. A relatively low IQ score cannot be ascribed to a brain injury unless there is some idea of what the IQ was before the injury. This estimate is usually informal and based on a patient's education, occupation, and socioeconomic background. Robert Wilson and his colleagues describe a statistical procedure for estimating premorbid IQ scores.

Categories of Neuropsychological Assessment

Eric Zillmer and Mary Spiers reviewed a survey of 2000 neuropsychologists and identified the most frequently used categories of neuropsychological assessment tests, summarized in **Table 28.3**. Several volumes catalogue the range of neuropsychological tests available, the two most extensive being those by Muriel Lezack and her colleagues and by Otfried Spreen and Esther Strauss.

Deborah Waber and her colleagues recently published a landmark longitudinal study of neuropsychological performance in children aged 6 to 18 years in which normative data are presented for a wide range of measures. For many measures, raw scores improved steeply from 6 to 10 years of age before decelerating during adolescence. Household income predicted IQ and achievement scores but not other test performance. The neuropsychological scores are linked to an MRI developmental database. This study will likely be an invaluable resource for researchers over the next decade.

A growing area of neuropsychological assessment is sports medicine. In particular, there is interest in tracking athletes with concussions. Alison Cernich and colleagues describe a test battery (the Automated Neuropsychological Assessment Metrics sports medicine battery, ASMB) specifically designed for use in concussion surveillance and management. The ASMB

Table **28.3** Common areas of neuropsychological assessment

Abstract reasoning/Compensation (e.g., problem solving, executive functions)

Activities of daily living (e.g., toileting, dressing, feeding)

Attention (e.g, selective, sustained, or shifting, neglect)

Emotional/Psychological distress (e.g., depression, impulsivity)

Language skills (e.g., receptive or expressive speech)

Memory (e.g., verbal, visual, working)

Motor (e.g., dexterity, speed, strength)

Orientation (e.g., awareness of place, time)

Sensation/Perception (e.g., visual acuity, taste/smell, tactile)

Visuospatial (e.g., construction, route finding, facial recognition)

Source: After Zillmer and Spiers, 2001.

is currently being refined with the development of appropriate norms and with the goal of pretesting athletes in sports with high incidence of concussion (for example, U.S. football and ice hockey).

Neuropsychological Tests and Brain Activity

Neuropsychological tests have been developed to identify cerebral dysfunction, and the presumption is that tests are actually measuring the activity of specific cerebral regions. An obvious problem, however, is that cognitive processes correspond to the activity of distributed neural networks (see Chapter 19 for an example in language processing). One way to examine the question of what brain regions are active in the performance of specific tests is by noninvasive imaging in normal subjects during the performance of one or more tests.

The most common studies focus on frontal-lobe tests such as the Wisconsin Card-Sorting Task. Julie Alvarez and Eugene Emory's meta-analysis of such studies reveals clearly reliable activation of frontal regions when subjects perform tasks such as the Wisconsin Card-Sorting Test, the Stroop Test, and the Chicago Word-Fluency Test (see Chapter 16 for test details). But there is always activation in other cerebral regions, too, even when studies use subtraction methods (see Chapter 6) to reduce general activity related to functions such as sensory processing.

Such results suggest that the interpretation of neuropsychological test performance should move away from the historical anatomical localization approach, in which anatomy and function are inseparable, to an approach that is more consistent with the developing view of extended neural networks. Indeed, we have seen dozens of cases in which patients with verified localized brain injuries fail to show symptoms that we would expect on the basis of our experience and that may actually show some symptoms that we would not predict.

We need to remain cognizant of the facts: considerable intersubject variation exists in brain organization; there are large effects of education and specific experiences (for example, playing video games or not); and large individual differences emerge in how cognitively engaged aging people remain. All these factors will influence both test performance and the specificity of brain activation.

The Problem of Effort

A major challenge for neuropsychologists is a determination of whether subjects are performing tests as requested. The DSM IV-R defines malingering as "the intentional production of false or grossly exaggerated physical or psychological symptoms, motivated by external incentives such as avoiding work, obtaining financial compensation, evading criminal prosecution, or obtaining drugs." In neuropsychological practice, this malingering usually means exaggerating cognitive deficits.

Paul Green and his colleagues gave 904 consecutive patients a battery of neuropsychological tests, including a test of effort. Suboptimal effort suppressed the overall test-battery performance 4.5 times as much as moderate-to-severe brain injury did. Their conclusion is that effort has a greater effect on test performance than brain damage. In a follow-up study, Green also found that poor performance on tests of effort not only affects memory performance but actually influences performance across the entire test battery.

Although we would like to hope that expert clinicians would be able to detect malingering, the general consensus is that clinical judgment is not impressive. The only valid method of assessing a lack of effort appears to be the use of specific tests of effort. A variety of tests have been published in the past 20 years, but the most sensitive is consistently found to be the Forced Choice Digit Memory Test devised by Merille Hiscock (see, for example, Guilmette et al.).

The test is extremely simple: subjects are shown a number (for example, 56093) and are then immediately shown two numbers, including the first one and a novel one (for example, 56093 and 82104) and asked which of the two they have already seen. Jeanette McGlone, at Dalhousie University, has shown that even severely amnesic patients usually score nearly perfectly on a series of 32 trials, provided that they are not distracted (McGlone, personal communication, August 2007). People faking memory problems may score as low as chance, indicating a lack of effort and invalidating the entire assessment. A cutoff of no lower than 90% correct is generally used in scoring the Forced Choice Digit Memory Test.

Although the actual incidence of malingering is not known, at least 20% of people with head traumas or alleged exposure to toxic substances likely exert low effort. Such estimates emphasize the need to employ such testing measures in any assessment in which an advantage accrues to the people malingering, such as in cases in which there is potential financial compensation.

The question of motivation in test performance is perhaps most clearly shown in a comparison of neuropsychological test performance between people with mild head injury seeking compensation from the Workers' Compensation Board and people ordered by a court to undergo a parenting assessment. The former group gains financially by doing poorly and the latter group by doing well: they retain custody of their children. Lloyd Flaro and his colleagues found that the group seeking compensation was 23 times as likely to fail a test of effort as those in the parenting group. In fact, the mild TBI group was twice as likely to fail the test as the more severe TBI group. Such effects cannot be explained by differences in cognitive skills, but they are explainable by differences in external incentives.

Case Histories

Having surveyed the basic principles of neuropsychological theory and assessment, we now apply the tests and theory to a sample of clinical problems. In this section, we consider the test results and case histories of three patients. These case histories illustrate the use of neuropsychological tests in neuropsychological assessment.

Because of our affiliation with the Montreal Neurological Institute, our composite assessment battery is based on the tests derived from the study of neurosurgical patients by Brenda Milner, Laughlin Taylor, and their colleagues. Most

Case 1 Left-frontal-lobe lesion

	Preop	Postop
Full-scale IQ	115	102
Verbal IQ	111	103
Performance IQ	117	99
Memory quotient	118	108
Verbal recall	20	14
Nonverbal recall	10.5	10
Card sorting	1 category*	1 category*
Finger-position sense	Left Right 60/60 60/60	Left Right 60/60 60/60
Drawings: Copy	36/36	35/36
Recall	21/36	24/36

* Significantly low score.

Case 2 Right-face-area lesion extending into frontal lobe

	Preop	Postop
Full-scale IQ	97	97
Verbal IQ	100	106
Performance IQ	94	88*
Memory quotient	94	92
Verbal recall	13.5	14.0
Nonverbal recall	3.5*	7.0
Card sorting	0 category*	1 category*
Finger-position sense	Left Right 55/60* 59/60	Left Right 54/60* 60/60
Drawings: Copy	28/36*	26.5/36*
Recall	4/36*	9.5/36*

* Significantly low score.

Figure 28.2

Neuropsychological Test Results Before and After Surgery in Two Cases

of the tests have been discussed elsewhere in the text, especially in Chapters 14 through 16 in relation to neuropsychological assessment of parietal-, temporal, and frontal-lobe function.

Case 1

This 33-year-old man had a history of seizures beginning 4 years before his admission to the hospital. His neurological examination on admission was negative, but he was having increasingly frequent seizures, characterized by his head and eyes turning to the right, a pattern that suggests supplementary motor cortex involvement.

The results of radiological and electroencephalographic studies suggested a left-frontal-lobe lesion (**Figure 28.2**), which was confirmed at surgery when a poorly differentiated astrocytoma was removed. The only difficulty that the patient experienced before surgery was in doing the Wisconsin Card-Sorting Test, where he made numerous perseverative errors and sorted only one category correctly. Two weeks after surgery, all the intelligence ratings, memory quotients, and delayed verbal-recall scores decreased, but these scores remained in essentially the same ratio to one another. Other tests were unchanged, the only significantly low score again being on the card-sorting test.

If this patient were like other patients with similar lesions, on follow-up a year after surgery, his intelligence ratings and memory scores would likely have returned to the preoperative level. However, his card sorting would be unlikely to show any improvement.

Case 2

This 26-year-old man had an 8-year history of seizures dating to an episode of meningitis in which he was thought to have an intracerebral abscess. Subsequently, he developed seizures beginning in the left side of his face and left hand, and he was referred as a candidate for surgery because his seizures were uncontrolled by medication.

Before surgery, the patient scored within normal limits on tests of intelligence and general memory, although he did have difficulty with delayed recall of verbal material. He had slight defects of finger-position sense on the left hand, which, together with some weakness in the left arm and leg, pointed to damage in the right central area of the cortex. In addition, he had difficulty copying and recalling the Rey Complex Figure and was unable to perform the Wisconsin Card-Sorting Test, suggesting that his lesion might extend into the frontal and temporal areas as well.

The right facial area and a region extending into the right frontal lobe were removed at surgery (see Figure 28.2). Afterward, some residual epileptiform abnormality in both the frontal lobe and the superior temporal gyrus remained. Postoperative testing showed improvement in both verbal IQ and long-term verbal memory, but the patient had persistent difficulties on the card-sorting test, with finger-position sense on the left hand, and on the copy and recall of the Rey Complex Figure. His performance IQ score also declined.

The difficulty with finger position would be expected in such a case, but the continuing difficulties with card sorting and the Rey Complex Figure imply that areas in his right hemisphere are still dysfunctioning. This dysfunction is seen in residual abnormalities in the EEG recordings from the frontal and temporal regions.

Case 3

This 37-year-old man had been in a traffic accident some 15 years earlier. He was in a coma for 6 weeks and suffered secondary injury from brain infection. At the time of his accident, he was a student in a graduate program in journalism, having previously obtained a bachelor's degree with honors in English literature.

When we first met him, he had severe motor problems, used canes to walk, and was both apraxic and ataxic. He had great difficulty in pronouncing words, especially when hurried or stressed, but careful language testing on the token test revealed no aphasic symptoms; his language problems were entirely due to a difficulty in coordinating the muscles of the mouth (that is, anarthria).

Since the time of his accident, this man had lived at home with his parents and had not learned the social skills necessary to cope with his handicap. In short, he was being treated as though he were retarded and was being completely looked after by his family. Indeed, the patient himself believed he was retarded and was very reluctant to attempt rehabilitation.

At the urging of his family, we gave him a thorough assessment to evaluate his potential. His results were surprising, even to us. His intellect was superior (WAIS verbal IQ score of 127) and, although he had deficits on some tests, especially those requiring motor skills, his performance on most tests was average or above average. Despite his obvious motor handicaps, this man was clearly not retarded.

One significant cognitive loss, however, was his nonverbal memory, which was very poor. Armed with our test results, we were able to show him—and his family—that he could look after himself and should seek occupational therapy. He is now a chartered accountant.

Summary

The Changing Face of Neuropsychological Assessment

Neurology and clinical neuropsychology have changed radically in the span of a generation. Significant developments in functional and structural imaging have had a significant effect on both fields. Whereas neuropsychological assessment had promised a way to localize focal cerebral injury, it has now largely been replaced in this function by medical imaging techniques. But not all neurological disease can be detected by imaging. The most sensitive measure of cerebral integrity is behavior, and behavioral analysis can identify dysfunction that is not seen in MRI, especially in cases of traumatic brain injury and epilepsy.

The tests used in neuropsychological assessment have changed in recent decades, owing in part to the dramatic development of cognitive neuroscience. And the use of test results has changed. Rather than being largely diagnostic, test results are becoming an integral part of rehabilitation. This changing role has economic implications as managed health care challenges the use of extensive neuropsychological evaluations, especially when adequate imaging data are available, regardless of its effectiveness.

Rationale Behind Neuropsychological Assessment

A wide range of clinical neuropsychological assessment tools are now available, the choice varying with the particular clinical question being asked. Analysis of the test results must consider a range of variables including age, sex, cultural background, and IQ score.

Neuropsychological Tests and Brain Activity

One way to validate neuropsychological tests is to measure brain activity while subjects are performing them. Although activity in the expected regions is usually enhanced, activity elsewhere in the brain increases as well, corresponding to the diffuse neural networks that underlie cognition. Such results remind us that test performance does not necessarily equal neural anatomy.

The Problem of Effort

A serious problem for the assessment of people who might benefit from doing poorly on neuropsychological tests, such as in cases in which the subjects are seeking compensation of some sort, is a lack of effort that invalidates the entire assessment. A number of tests have been devised that detect a lack of effort and are simple to administer.

Case Histories

Case histories demonstrate that, despite technological advances, neuropsychological assessment is still an important tool for demonstrating functional localization after discrete functional injury and for assisting in planning for rehabilitation.

References

Alvarez, J. A., and E. Emory. Executive function and the frontal lobes: A meta-analytic review. *Neuropsychology Review* 16:17–42, 2006.

Benton, A. L. Neuropsychological assessment. *Annual Review of Psychology* 45:1–23, 1994.

Benton, A. L., D. de S. Hamsher, N. R. Varney, and O. Spreen. *Contributions to Neuropsychological Assessment: A Clinical Manual.* New York: Oxford University Press, 1983.

Cernich, A., D. Reeves, W. Sun, and J. Bleiberg. Automated neuropsychological assessment metrics sports medicine battery. *Archives of Clinical Neuropsychology* 22:S101–S114, 2007.

Christensen, A.-L. *Luria's Neuropsychological Investigation.* New York: Spectrum, 1975.

Christensen, A.-L., and B. P. Uzzell. *International Handbook of Neuropsychological Rehabilitation.* New York: Plenum, 2000.

Damasio, H., and A. R. Damasio. *Lesion Analysis in Neuropsychology.* New York: Oxford University Press, 1989.

Flaro, L., P. Green, and E. Robertson. Word memory test failure 23 times higher in mild brain injury than in parents seeking custody: The power of external incentives. *Brain Injury* 21:373–383, 2007.

Golden, C. J. A standardized version of Luria's neuropsychological tests. In S. Filskov and T. J. Boll, Eds. *Handbook of Clinical Neuropsychology.* New York: Wiley-Interscience, 1981.

Green, P. The pervasive effect of effort on neuropsychological tests. *Archives of Clincial Neuropsychology* 18:43–68, 2007.

Green, P., M. L. Rohling, P. R. Lees-Haley, and L. M. Allen. Effort has a greater effect on test scores than severe brain injury in compensation claimants. *Brain Injury* 15:1045–1060, 2001.

Greve, K. W., S. Springer, K. J. Bianchini, F. W. Black, M. T. Heinly, J. M. Love, D. A. Swift, and M. A. Ciota. Malingering in toxic exposure: Classification accuracy of reliable digit span and WAIS-III Digit Span scaled scores. *Assessment* 14:12–21, 2007.

Groth-Marnat, G. Financial efficacy of clinical assessment: Rationale guidelines and issues for future research. *Journal of Clinical Psychology* 55:813–824, 1999.

Guilmette, T. J., W. Whelihan, F. R. Sparadeo, and G. Buongiorno. Validity of neuropsychological test results in disability evaluations. *Perceptual Motor Skills* 78: 1179–1186, 1994.

Inman, T. H., and D. T. Berry. Cross-validation of indicators of malingering: A comparison of nine neuropsychological tests, four tests of malingering, and behavioral observations. *Archives of Clinical Neuropsychology* 17:1–23, 2002.

Kaplan, E. A process approach to neuropsychological assessment. In T. Boll and B. K. Bryant, Eds. *Clinical Neuropsychology and Brain Function: Research, Development, and Practice*. Washington, D.C.: American Psychological Association, 1988, pp. 129–167.

Kimura, D., and J. McGlone. *Neuropsychology Test Procedures*. Manual used at the University Hospital, London, Ontario, Canada, 1983.

Levin, H. S., and A. L. Benton. Neuropsychologic assessment. In A. B. Baker and R. J. Joynt, Eds. *Clinical Neurology*, vol. 1. New York: Harper & Row, 1986.

Lezak, M. D., D. B. Howieson, D. W. Loring, H. J. Hannay, and J. S. Fischer. *Neuropsychological Assessment*, 4th ed. New York: Oxford University Press, 2004.

McFie, J. *Assessment of Organic Intellectual Impairment*. New York: Wiley, 1975.

McKenna, P., and E. K. Warrington. The analytical approach to neuropsychological assessment. In I. Grant and K. M. Adams, Eds. *Assessment of Neuropsychiatric Disorders*. New York: Oxford University Press, 1986.

Milberg, W. P., N. Hebben, and E. Kaplan. The Boston Process Approach to neuropsychological assessment. In I. Grant and K. M. Adams, Eds. *Assessment of Neuropsychiatric Disorders*. New York: Oxford University Press, 1986.

Newcombe, F. *Missile Wounds of the Brain*. London: Oxford University Press, 1969.

Owen, A. M., A. C. Roberts, C. E. Polkey, B. J. Sahakian, and T. W. Robbins. Extradimensional versus intradimensional set shifting performance following frontal lobe excisions, temporal lobe excisions or amygdalo-hippocampectomy in man. *Neuropsychologia* 29:993–1006, 1991.

Reitan, R. M., and L. A. Davison. *Clinical Neuropsychology: Current Status and Application*. New York: Wiley, 1974.

Robbins, T. W., M. James, A. M. Owen, B. J. Sahakian, A. D. Lawrence, L. McInnes, and P. M. Rabbitt. A study of performance on tests from the CANTAB battery sensitive to frontal lobe dysfunction in a large sample of normal volunteers: Implications for theories of executive functioning and cognitive aging. Cambridge Neuropsychological Test Automated Battery. *Journal of the International Neuropsychology Society* 4:474–490, 1998.

Shallice, T. *From Neuropsychology to Mental Structure*. Cambridge, U.K.: Cambridge University Press, 1988.

Smith, A. Principles underlying human brain functions in neuropsychological sequelae of different neuropathological processes. In S. B. Filskov and T. J. Boll, Eds. *Handbook of Clinical Neuropsychology*. New York: Wiley-Interscience, 1981.

Spreen, O., and E. Strauss. *A Compendium of Neuropsychological Tests*. New York: Oxford University Press, 1991.

Stuss, D. T., and B. Levine. Adult clinical neuropsychology: Lessons from studies of the frontal lobes. *Annual Review of Psychology* 53:401–433, 2002.

Taylor, L. B. Psychological assessment of neurosurgical patients. In T. Rasmussen and R. Marino, Eds. *Functional Neurosurgery*. New York: Raven Press, 1979.

Waber, D. P., C. De Moor, P. W. Forbes, R. Almli, K. N. Botteron, G. Leonard, D. Milovan, T. Paus, and J. Rumsey. The NIH MRI study of normal brain development: Performance of a population based sample of healthy children aged 6 to 18 years. *Journal of the International Neuropsychological Society* 13:1–18, 2007.

Walsh, K. W. *Understanding Brain Damage*, 2nd ed. London: Churchill Livingstone, 1991.

Warrington, E. K., M. James, and C. Maciejewski. The WAIS as a lateralizing and localizing diagnostic instrument: A study of 656 patients with unilateral cerebral excisions. *Neuropsychologia* 24:223–239, 1986.

Wilson, R. S., G. Rosenbaum, and G. Brown. The problem of premorbid intelligence in neuropsychological assessment. *Journal of Clinical Neuropsychology* 1:49–56, 1979.

Wood, J. M., H. N. Garb, S. O. Lilienfeld, and M. T. Nezworski. Clinical assessment. *Annual Review of Psychology* 53:519–543, 2002.

Zillmer, E. A., and M. V. Spiers. *Principles of Neuropsychology*. Wadsworth: Belmont, Calif., 2001.

ablation. Intentional destruction or removal of parts of the brain or spinal cord; brain lesion.

abdominal reflex. Contraction of the abdominal muscles in response to stroking the abdomen.

absence attack. Temporary loss of consciousness in some forms of epilepsy.

absolutely refractory. Refers to the period in an action potential during which a new action potential cannot be elicited, because of the closing of gate 2 of voltage-sensitive sodium channels.

acalculia. Inability to perform mathematical operations.

accessory cells. Cells that originate from germinal cells (spongioblasts) and contribute to the support, nourishment, conduction, and repair of neurons; occasionally the origins of tumors. Accessory cells are the astrocytes; the oligodendrocytes; and the ependymal, microglial, and Schwann cells.

acetylcholine (ACh). A chemical neurotransmitter.

achromatopsia. Inability to distinguish different hues despite the presence of normally pigmented cells in the retina. Sometimes called *cortical color blindness*.

acopia. Inability to copy a geometric design.

acquired dyslexia. Inability to read caused by brain damage in a person who could read formerly; distinguished from developmental dyslexia, which is a failure to learn to read.

action potential. Brief electrical impulse by which information is conducted along an axon; results from brief changes in the membrane's permeability to potassium and sodium ions.

activating system. Neural system that coordinates wide areas of the brain to act in concert. Each small-molecule neurotransmitter has its own activating system, with the cell bodies of each system's neurons—cholinergic, dopaminergic, noradrenergic, and serotonergic—located in a restricted region of the brainstem and their axons distributed widely throughout the brain.

active-transport system. Protein pump specialized for the transport of a particular substance across a membrane.

addiction. Physiological or psychological dependence on an agent (for example, alcohol, drug), with a tendency to increase its use.

adenosine triphosphate (ATP). Molecule important to cellular energy metabolism. The conversion of ATP into ADP (adenosine diphosphate) liberates energy. ATP can also be converted into cyclic AMP (adenosine monophosphate), which serves as an intermediate messenger in the production of postsynaptic potentials by some neurotransmitters and in the mediation of the effects of polypeptide hormones.

affect. Freudian term for the feeling of pleasantness or unpleasantness evoked by a stimulus; also the emotional complex associated with a mental state; the feeling experienced in connection with an emotion.

afference theory. States that all behavior is driven by sensory events. Compare **efference theory**.

afferent. Conducting toward the central nervous system or toward its higher centers.

afferent paresis. Loss of kinesthetic feedback that results from lesions to the postcentral gyrus (areas 1, 2, 3) and produces clumsy movements.

afterdischarge. Abnormal discharges from neurons subsequent to an epileptic seizure or brain stimulation.

agenesis of the corpus callosum. Condition in which the corpus callosum fails to develop.

agnosia. Partial or complete inability to recognize sensory stimuli, unexplainable by a defect in elementary sensation or by a reduced level of alertness.

agonist. A muscle that, in contracting to move a part, is opposed by another muscle (its antagonist).

agrammatitism. Impairment in the ability to use verbs and to produce appropriate grammar.

agraphia. Decline in the ability to write or its loss.

akathesia. Condition of motor restlessness, ranging from a feeling of inner disquiet to an inability to sit or lie quietly.

akinesia. Absence or poverty of movement.

akinetic seizure. Seizure producing temporary paralysis of muscles, characterized by a sudden collapse without warning; most common in children.

alcohol. Any organic compound containing a hydroxyl group.

alcohol myopia. Behavior displayed after the consumption of alcohol in which local and immediate cues become the focus of attention.

alexia. Inability to read.

allesthesia. Sensation of touch experienced at a point remote from the place touched.

allocentric space. Space made up of the relations of objects, independent of the perspective of the observer and usually at a distance.

alpha rhythm. Regular (approximately 10 Hz) wave pattern in an electroencephalogram; found in most people when they are relaxed with eyes closed.

Alzheimer's disease. Degenerative brain disorder related to aging that first appears as a progressive memory loss and later develops into a generalized dementia. The origin of the disease is unknown, but cholinergic cells in the basal forebrain and cells in the entorhinal cortex appear to degenerate first.

amativeness. Inclination to love; localized by the phrenologists in the nape of the neck.

amblyopia. Dimness of vision without obvious impairment of the eye itself.

amebiasis. Infection due to amebas, especially *Entamoeba histolytica*, the causative agent of amebic dysentery.

amino acids. Class of biologically active compounds containing an NH_2 chemical group.

Ammon's horn. Part of the hippocampus.

amnesia. Partial or total loss of memory.

amnesic aphasia. Aphasic syndrome characterized by the inability to name objects and by the production of unintended syllables, words, or phrases while speaking.

amphetamine. Synthetic powerful central nervous system stimulant; abuse may lead to dependence.

amusia. Inability to produce (motor) or to comprehend (sensory) musical sounds.

amygdala. Set of nuclei in the base of the temporal lobe; part of the limbic system.

anandamide. A chemical neurotransmitter.

anarthria. Incoordination of the musculature of the mouth, resulting in speechlessness.

anastomosis. Connection between parallel blood vessels that allows them to communicate their blood flows.

aneurysm. Vascular dilation resulting from a localized defect in vascular elasticity. A sac is formed by the dilation of the walls of an artery or a vein and is filled with blood.

angiography. Radiographic imaging of blood vessels filled with a contrast medium.

angioma. Collections of abnormal blood vessels, including capillary, venous, and arteriovenous malformations, resulting in abnormal blood flow.

angular gyrus. Gyrus in the parietal lobe corresponding roughly to Brodmann's area 39; important in language functions.

anion. Negatively charged ion.

anomia. Difficulty in finding words, especially those naming objects.

anomic aphasia. Inability to name objects.

anopia. Loss of vision.

anosmia. Absence of the sense of smell.

anosodiaphoria. Indifference to illness.

anosognosia. Loss of ability to recognize or to acknowledge an illness or bodily defect; usually associated with right parietal lesions.

antagonist. A muscle that counteracts the action of another muscle, its agonist; also a drug that blocks or reduces the effect of a neurotransmitter.

anterior cerebral artery (ACA). Originates from the carotid artery and services the orbitofrontal and dorsolateral frontal regions, the anterior cingulate cortex, the corpus callosum, and the striatum.

anterior commissure. Fiber tract that connects the temporal lobes.

anterograde amnesia. Inability to remember events subsequent to a disturbance of the brain such as head injury, electroconvulsive shock, or certain degenerative diseases.

anterograde degeneration. Degeneration of the parts of a nerve cell that lie distal to damage to the cell, with the cell body used as reference. For example, when an axon is cut, anterograde degeneration occurs in the section from the cut to the synaptic terminals. Also called *Wallerian degeneration*.

anterograde disorientation. Impairment in spatial orientation that persists after a brain injury.

anterograde transport. Transport by a neuron, usually along axons, of substances in a direction that is away from the cell body.

antianxiety agent. A drug that reduces anxiety; benzodiazepines and sedative-hypnotic agents are of this type.

antianxiety site. Accepts benzodiazepines and enhances the binding of gamma-aminobutryic acid (GABA) to its receptors, which means that the availability of GABA determines the potency of an antianxiety drug.

antipsychotic drug. A drug that acts on the dopamine synapse and affects psychomotor activity, generally without hyponotic effects.

anvil. The middle of the three ossicles of the ear. In turn with the stapes and malleus, the anvil conducts vibrations from the tymponic membrane to the inner ear. Also called the *incus*.

aphagia. Inability to eat or chew.

aphasia. Defect or loss of the power of expression by speech, writing, or signs or of comprehending spoken or written language due to injury or disease of the brain.

apoptosis. Cell death that is genetically programmed.

apperceptive agnosia. Broad category of visual agnosia in which elementary sensory functions appear to be intact but a perceptual deficit that prevents recognition of an object is present.

apraxia. Inability to make voluntary movements in the absence of paralysis or other motor or sensory impairment; especially an inability to make proper use of an object.

aprosodia. Condition in which there is a loss of production or comprehension of the meaning of different tones of voice.

arachnoid. Thin sheet of delicate collagenous connective tissue that follows the contours of the brain.

archicortex. Part of the cerebral cortex that develops in association with the olfactory cortex and is phylogenetically older than the neopallium and lacks its layered structure. Also called archipallium, allocortex, or olfactory cortex. Corresponds to the dentate gyrus and hippocampal gyrus in mature mammals.

area postrema. Nucleus in the brainstem that is sensitive to blood-borne toxins and causes vomiting.

arcuate fasciculus. Long bundle of fibers connecting Wernicke's and Broca's areas.

Argyll-Robertson pupil. Constriction of the pupil of the eye to accommodation but not to light; used to diagnose damage to the midbrain relays of the third cranial (oculomotor) nerve.

arteriovenous (A–V) malformation. Abnormality of both the arterial and the venous blood flow, which often appears as a mass of vessels that are intertwined and lie on the surface of the cortex.

asomatognosia. Loss of knowledge or sensory awareness of one's own body and bodily condition; may be on one or both sides of the body; most commonly results from damage to the right parietal lobe.

Asperger's syndrome. Disorder in which a person has relatively good verbal communication but has unusual difficulty with social communication. Sometimes called high-functioning autism.

aspiny neurons. Class of inhibitory neurons that do not have dendritic spines.

association cell layers. Layers II and III of the cerebral cortex.

association cortex. All cortex that is not specialized motor or sensory cortex (the term survives from an earlier belief that inputs from the different senses meet and become associated). *See also* **prefrontal cortex** and **tertiary area**.

associative agnosia. Form of agnosia in which there is an object-identification deficit in the context of a preserved ability to copy or match stimuli presented in the affected modality.

associative learning. Form of learning in which two or more unrelated stimuli become associated with one another so that any one of them can elicit the same behavioral response.

astereognosis. Inability, with no defect in elementary tactile sensation, to recognize familiar objects by touch.

astrocyte. Type of glial cell. *See also* **accessory cells**.

astrocytoma. Slow-growing brain tumor resulting from the growth of astrocytes.

asymbolia. Inability to employ a conventional sign to stand for another object or event.

asymbolia for pain. Inability to understand the meaning of pain.

ataxia. Failure of muscular coordination; any of various irregularities of muscular action.

athetosis. Motor disorder marked by involuntary movements or slow writhing movements, especially in the hands.

attention. Hypothetical process that either allows a selective awareness of a part or aspect of the sensory environment or allows selective responsiveness to one class of stimuli.

attentional dyslexia. Disorder in which naming a letter is more difficult when it is accompanied by a second letter.

auditory agnosia. Impaired capacity to identify nonverbal acoustical stimuli.

auditory flow. Change in sound heard as a person moves past a sound source or as a sound source moves past a person.

aura. Subjective sensation, perceptual experience, or motor phenomenon that precedes and marks the onset of an epileptic seizure or migraine.

autism. Condition in which a person is dominated by self-centered thoughts or behaviors that are not subject to change by external stimulation. In children, the condition is often called infantile autism and is characterized by a failure to relate normally to people or external stimulation. Such children generally have severe language disorders and exhibit repetitive behaviors such as rocking.

autism spectrum disorder. Refers to a range of symptoms—from mild to severe—of autism.

autobiographic (episodic) memory. Recall of singular events; enables human beings to remember past personal experiences.

autoimmune disease. Immune reaction directed against one's own body.

automatic behaviors. Stereotyped units of behavior linked in a fixed sequence—for example, grooming and chewing. Also called reflexive, consummatory, or respondent behaviors. *See also* **automatism**.

automatic movement. Spontaneous or involuntary movement.

automatism. Performance of nonreflex acts without conscious volition. Also called *automatic behaviors*.

autonoetic awareness. Awareness of one's self, or self-knowledge.

autonomic nervous system (ANS). The part of the nervous system that controls the functions of all the parts of the body, with the exception of the skeletal muscles, so that the body and its organs are prepared for rest or for vigorous activity.

autopagnosia. Inability to localize and name the parts of one's own body—for example, finger agnosia.

autoradiography. Process by which radiolabeled substances are injected into the bloodstream, incorporated into cells, and transported along the cells' processes. When the tissue is exposed to a photographic film, it "takes its own picture" and reveals the route taken by the radiolabeled substance.

autoreceptor. Receptor in the membrane of a neuron that responds to the transmitter released by that neuron.

axoaxonic synapse. Synapse between two axons.

axodendritic synapse. Synapse between an axon and a dendrite.

axoextrascellular synapse. Synapse that releases its neurotransmitter chemical into the extracellular space.

axomuscular synapse. Synapse between an axon and a muscle.

axon. Thin neuronal process that transmits action potentials away from the cell body to other neurons (or to muscles or glands).

axon collateral. A major branch of an axon.

axon hillock. Site of origin of a nerve impulse.

axosecretory synapse. Synapse between an axon and a blood vessel in which the transmitter substance is passed into the bloodstream as a hormone.

axosomatic synapse. Synapse between an axon and the cell body of a neuron.

axosynaptic synapse. Synapse between an axon and another synapse.

Babinski sign. Abnormal response to stimulation on the sole of the foot in which there is an upward, extensor movement of the big toe; indicative of a corticospinal-tract lesion. Also called *extensor plantar response*.

bacterium. Any prokaryotic organism.

Balint's syndrome. Agnosic syndrome that results from large bilateral parietal lesions and is composed of three deficits: (1) paralysis of eye fixation with inability to look voluntarily into the peripheral visual field, (2) optic ataxia, and (3) disturbance of visual attention such that the peripheral field is neglected.

balloonist theories. State that muscles move as they are filled with a substance such as a fluid from nerves.

barbiturates. Drugs used for their hypnotic and sedative effects.

basal ganglia. Group of large nuclei in the forebrain, including the caudate nucleus, putamen, globus pallidus, claustrum, and amygdala.

basilar membrane. In the cochlea, the receptor surface that transduces sound waves into neural activity.

behavioral compensation. Mechanism of recovery from brain injury in which behavior is modified to compensate for lost functions. Neither the recovered behavior nor the area that mediates recovery are the same as those that are lost.

Bell–Magendie law. Law, named after its cofounders, stating that the dorsal roots of the spinal cord are sensory and the ventral roots of the spinal cord are motor.

benzodiazepine. Any of a group of minor tranquilizers, having a common molecular structure and similar pharmacological activities, such as antianxiety, muscle relaxing, and sedative and hypnotic effects.

beta-endorphin. Endogenous peptide that has actions similar to those of ingested opium.

beta rhythm. Irregular electroencephalographic activity ranging from 13 to 30 Hz and generally associated with an alert state.

bilateral. Applying to both sides of the body.

binding problem. Theoretical problem with the integration of sensory information. Because a single sensory event is analyzed by multiple parallel channels that do not converge on a single region, there is said to be a problem in binding together the segregated analyses into a single sensory experience.

binocular deprivation. Removal of visual stimulation from both eyes by raising an animal in the dark, bandaging the eyes, or a similar technique.

biochemical techniques. Techniques that measure biologically relevant chemicals in tissue, including various types of assay procedures for determining the presence or concentration of different compounds.

biogenic amines. Group of neurotransmitters that includes *norepinephrine, dopamine,* and *serotonin.*

bipolar cells. Neurons having processes at both poles; characteristic especially of retinal cells.

bipolar disorder. Affective disorder in which a person alternates from periods of depression to periods of mania.

birthday effect. Effect of date of birth on subsequent success at sports or school (some entrants are older and others are younger than average, producing differential advantages due to age).

bitemporal hemianopia. Loss of vision in both temporal fields due to damage to the medial region of the optic chiasm.

black widow spider venom. Poison, produced by the black widow spider, that promotes the release of acetylcholine from the synapse.

blast. Immature neuron or glial cell.

blindsight. Ability to make better-than-chance decisions about the nature of visual stimuli that are not consciously perceived by patients with visual-field defects.

blood–brain barrier. Functional barrier, produced by the glial cells and by cells in the walls of the capillaries in the brain, that prevents the passage of many substances into the brain.

botulinum toxin. Toxin, associated with food poisoning, that blocks the release of acetylcholine from the synapse; used clinically to block unwanted activity in muscles.

brain. Encephalon; the part of the central nervous system contained within the cranium, comprising the forebrain, midbrain, and hindbrain, and developed from the anterior part of the embryonic neural tube.

brain abscess. Localized collection of pus in the brain; formed from tissues that have disintegrated as a result of infection.

brain hypothesis. Idea that the brain, rather than some other body organ such as the heart, produces behavior.

brain plasticity. Ability of the brain to change its structure in response to experience, drugs, hormones, or injury.

brain scan. Any procedure of imaging the structure and function of the living brain. *See also* **radioisotope scan.**

brainstem. Hypothalamus, midbrain, and hindbrain. (Some authorities also include the thalamus and basal ganglia.)

brain stimulation. Method that induces changes in the electrical activity of the brain.

Broca's aphasia. Expressive, or nonfluent, aphasia that is chiefly a defect of speech; results from a lesion to Broca's area.

Broca's area. Region of the left frontal lobe (frontal operculum) believed to take part in the production of language. Damage to this area results in Broca's aphasia.

Brodmann's map. Map of the cerebral cortex devised by Korbinian Brodmann. It is based on cytoarchitectonic structure, and anatomical areas are identified by number. (It conforms remarkably closely to functional areas identified by the results of lesion and recording studies.)

Brown-Séquard syndrome. Condition of unilateral paralysis and loss of joint sensation and contralateral loss of pain and temperature sensation caused by damage to one half of the spinal cord.

butyrophenones. One class of drugs that block dopamine receptors.

caffeine. Central nervous system stimulant. Coffee and tea contain caffeine.

calcification. Accumulation of calcium in various brain regions after brain damage.

callosal agenesis. Lack of a corpus callosum as a result of a developmental abnormality.

calmodulin. Protein that, on stimulation by Ca^{2+}, plays a role in undocking vesicles containing a neurotransmitter so that the neurotransmitter can be released into the synaptic cleft.

carbon monoxide (CO). Gas that acts as a chemical neurotransmitter.

cataplexy. Condition in which a person collapses owing to the loss of all muscle activity or tone; often triggered by an emotional stimulus such as mirth, anger, or fear, among others, and often associated with narcolepsy.

catecholamines. Class of neurotransmitters that includes *epinephrine*, *norepinephrine*, and *dopamine*.

cation. Positively charged ion.

caudate nucleus. Nucleus of the basal ganglia. Sometimes referred to as the *caudate putamen*.

caudate putamen. *See* **caudate nucleus.**

cell assembly. Hypothetical collection of neurons that become functionally connected; proposed by Donald Hebb to be the basis of ideation, perception, and memory.

cell body. The part of the cell containing the nucleus and other organelles for making proteins.

cellular tolerance. Adjustments in the activities of brain cells so as to minimize the effects of alcohol in the blood; explains why the behavioral signs of intoxication may be very low despite a high blood-alcohol level.

central nervous system (CNS). The part of the nervous system that is encased in the bones and includes the brain and spinal cord.

central sleep apnea. Sleep disturbance in which breathing stops when a person falls into deep sleep; may be associated with muscle relaxation during dream sleep.

central sulcus. Fissure running from the dorsal border of the hemisphere near its midpoint and obliquely downward and forward until it nearly meets the lateral fissure, dividing the frontal and parietal lobes. Also called fissure of Rolando.

cerebellum. Major structure of the hindbrain specialized for motor coordination.

cerebral arteriosclerosis. Condition marked by loss of elasticity and by thickening and hardening of the arteries; eventually results in dementia.

cerebral compression. Contraction of the brain substance due to an injury that has caused hemorrhage and the development of a hematoma.

cerebral contusion. Vascular injury resulting in bruising and edema and in hemorrhaging of capillaries.

cerebral cortex. Layer of gray matter on the surface of the cerebral hemispheres and composed of neurons and their synaptic connections, which form from four to six sublayers.

cerebral hemorrhage. Bleeding into the brain.

cerebral hypoxia. Deficiency in the amount of oxygen getting into the brain through the bloodstream.

cerebral ischemia. Deficiency in the amount of blood getting to the brain; may be restricted to limited regions and may be caused by an obstruction or constriction of cerebral arteries.

cerebral laceration. Contusion severe enough to breach the brain substance.

cerebral palsy. Group of disorders that result from brain damage acquired prenatally.

cerebral trauma. Injury to the brain, usually resulting from a blow to the head.

cerebral vascular accident. *See* **stroke.**

cerebral vascular insufficiency. Deficiency in the amount of blood getting to the brain.

cerebrospinal fluid (CSF). Clear solution of sodium chloride and other salts that fills the ventricles inside the brain and circulates around the brain beneath the arachnoid layer in the subarachnoid space.

channel. Any passageway across the neuron membrane that allows the passage of different ions, which subsequently influence the membrane potential; different channels are opened by different ions or by voltage changes in the membrane.

chemical neurotransmitter. Chemical that binds to a receptor site of a membrane protein.

colinergic neuron. Neuron that releases acetylcholine.

choroid plexus. Tissue that lines the cerebral ventricles and produces cerebrospinal fluid.

chromatolysis. Loss of protein in a damaged cell, resulting in the loss of the cell's ability to absorb stain; literally, the breakdown of its ability to be colored.

chromosome. Consists of protein and DNA in the nucleus of each cell. DNA contains the genes that determine the traits and function of each individual organism.

cingulate cortex. Strip of limbic cortex lying just above the corpus callosum along the medial walls of the cerebral hemispheres.

cingulate sulcus. Cortical sulcus located on the medial wall of the cerebral hemisphere just above the corpus callosum.

cladogram. Phylogenetic tree that branches repeatedly, suggesting a classification of organisms based on the time sequence in which evoluntionary branches arise.

class-common behaviors. Behaviors and behavioral capacities common to all members of a phylogenetic class.

classical (Pavlovian) conditioning. Form of unconscious learning in which a neutral stimulus is paired with a stimulus that evokes behavior.

classic migraine. Symptom complex of periodic headaches, usually temporal and unilateral. *See also* **common migraine**.

claustrum. Thin sheet of gray matter that, in the human brain, lies below the general region of the insula. Its connectivity is unique in that it receives input from virtually all regions of the cortex and projects back to almost all regions of the cortex.

clinical depression. Serious mood disorder characterized by persistent periods of depression that normally require some type of clinical treatment for remission.

cluster headache. Migrainelike disorder marked by attacks of unilateral intense pain over the eye and forehead, with flushing and watering of the eyes and nose. Attacks last about an hour and occur in clusters.

cocaine. Alkaloid obtained from the leaves of various species of *Erytroxylon* (coca plants) or produced synthetically; used as a local anesthetic.

cochlea. Spiral tube forming part of the inner ear, which is the essential organ of hearing.

codeine. Alkaloid obtained from opium or prepared from morphine by methylation; used as a narcotic analgesic and as an antitussive agent.

cognition. General term for the processes of thinking.

cognitive map. Hypothetical map of some cognitive process such as spatial localization.

cognitive set. Tendency to approach a problem with a particular bias in thought; for example, when searching for a mailbox, a person will have a cognitive set for mailboxes but not for, say, cats.

cognitive space. Space or time about which a person has knowledge.

collaterals. Side branches of axons or blood vessels.

color agnosia. Inability to associate particular colors with objects or objects with colors.

color amnesia. Inability to remember the colors of common objects.

color anomia. Inability to name colors; generally associated with other aphasic symptoms. Also called color aphasia.

column. Hypothetical unit of cortical organization; believed to represent a vertically organized intracortical connectivity that is assumed to be a single functional unit. Sometimes used as a synonym for a *module*.

coma. State of deep unconsciousness due to brain injury or disease.

commissure. Bundle of fibers connecting corresponding points on the two sides of the central nervous system.

commissurotomy. Surgical disconnection of the two hemispheres by cutting the corpus callosum.

common descent. Refers to the evolutionary theory that all animals descend from the same ancestor.

common migraine. Symptom complex of periodic headaches, usually temporal and unilateral, often accompanied by irritability, nausea, vomiting, constipation or diarrhea, and photo-phobia; preceded by constriction of the cranial arteries, usually with resultant prodromal sensory symptoms and commencing symptoms, and commencing with the vasodilation that follows.

comparative approach. Method of study in which similarities and differences in morphology or behavior across different species are emphasized as a means to understanding the organization of the brain and behavior.

complex partial seizure. Focal seizure that most commonly originates in the temporal lobe; characterized by subjective feelings, automatisms, and motor symptoms. Sometimes referred to as a temporal-lobe seizure.

computerized tomography (CT) scan. X-ray procedure in which a computer draws a map from the measured densities of the brain; superior to a conventional X-ray because it provides a three-dimensional representation of the brain. Also called EMI-Scan, a trade name.

computerized transaxial tomography. Technique by which a series of brain X-rays are used to construct a three-dimensional representation of the brain.

concentration gradient. Difference in the concentrations of an ion on the two sides of a membrane.

concussion. Condition of widespread paralysis of the functions of the brain that arises immediately after a blow to the head.

conduction aphasia. Type of *fluent aphasia* in which, despite alleged normal comprehension of spoken language, words are repeated incorrectly.

cones. Highly specialized conical or flask-shaped cells in the retina that are maximally sensitive to light of particular wavelengths; are the basis of color vision.

confabulation. The recitation of imaginary experiences to fill gaps in memory.

conjunction search. Concept in attentional theory that assumes the existence of a mechanism with which the sensory system searches for particular combinations of sensory information.

consciousness. The state of being conscious; responsiveness of the mind to impressions made by the senses.

consolidation of memories. Process through which short-term memories are converted into long-term memories.

consolidation theory. States that the role of the hippocampus is to consolidate new memories, a process that makes them permanent.

constructional apraxia. Inability to perform well-rehearsed and familiar sequences of movements when making or preparing something. The deficit is not attributable to an inability to move or to perform the individual acts required for the task.

contralateral. Residing in the side of the body opposite the reference points.

contralateral neglect. Neglect of part of the body or space contralateral to a lesion.

contrast X-ray. Radiographic procedure using the injection of radiopaque dye or air into the ventricles or of dye into the arteries for purposes of diagnosis.

conventional radiography. X-ray.

convergent thinking. Form of thinking in which there is a search for a single answer to a question (for example, 2 + 2 = ?), in contrast with divergent thinking, in which multiple solutions are sought.

conversion reaction. Formerly called hysteria in reference to paralysis, changes in sensory ability such as loss of vision, and a variety of other illnesses that seemingly could not be explained as physical ailments.

coprolalia. The utterance of obscene words, especially words relating to feces.

corollary discharge. Transmission by one area of the brain to another, informing the latter area of the former's actions; commonly used more specifically for a signal from the motor system to the sensory system that a particular movement is being produced.

corollary-discharge theory. States that, when an individual initiates a movement, the nervous system keeps a record of the intended movement with which it compares the actual movement. The intended movement is the *corollary discharge*. Also known as *reafference theory*.

corpus callosum. Fiber system connecting the homotopic areas of the two hemispheres. A split-brain patient is one whose corpus callosum has been severed.

cortex. External layer of the brain; in this book, synonymous with neocortex. *See also* **neocortex**.

cortical quotient (CQ). Measure of the relative size of the cortex; analogous to *encephalization quotient* but applied only to the cortex.

corticobulbar fibers. Traditionally, refers to connections between the cerebral cortex and the medulla oblongata; in more common usage, refers to connections between the cerebral cortex and the lower brainstem.

corticobulbar tracts. Descending tracts from the neocortex that innervate facial motor neurons; are initially part of the corticospinal tracts.

corticospinal fibers. Connect the cerebral cortex and the spinal cord.

corticospinal pathway. Motor pathway originating in layer V of the cerebral cortex and ending in the spinal cord.

corticospinal tract. Bundle of fibers directly connecting the cerebral cortex to the spinal cord.

countercoup. Brain injury suffered by tissue at the end of the skull opposite the region striking an object.

coup. Brain injury suffered by tissue underlying the region of the skull striking an object.

cranial nerves. Set of 12 pairs of nerves conveying sensory and motor signals to and from the head.

cranioscopy. Technique of measuring the skull to determine the location of bumps and depressions for phrenological analysis.

cremasteric reflex. Retraction of testicles in response to stroking the inner thigh.

Creutzfeldt-Jakob disease. Prion-related dementia in which there is generalized cortical atrophy.

crossed aphasia. Aphasia that results from damage to the right hemisphere.

cross-modal matching. Ability to match sensory characteristics of objects across sensory modalities—for example, the ability to visually recognize an object that was previously perceived by touch.

cross-tolerance. Form of tolerance in which the response to a novel drug is reduced because of tolerance developed in response to a related drug.

CT scan. *See* **computerized tomography (CT) scan**.

cue response. Navigational behavior in which an animal locomotes to a position on the basis of its location relative to a single cue. Distinguished from *place response* or *position response*.

curare. A drug, obtained from a South American plant, that blocks acetylcholine receptors.

cytoarchitectonic analysis. An analysis of *cytoarchitectonic maps*.

cytoarchitectonic map. Map of the cortex based on the organization, structure, and distribution of the cells.

cytochrome oxidase. Enzyme made in mitochondria. Increased enzyme activity is thought to correspond to heightened neural activity; tissue can be stained for this enzyme to estimate which areas of the brain display high levels of activity.

dead reckoning. Ability to monitor one's movement by using cues generated by the movement.

deafferentation. Process of removing the afferent input to a structure or region of the nervous system.

decerebrate. Refers to the elimination of cerebral function by transecting the brainstem just above the superior colliculi; an animal so prepared is said to be decerebrate.

decerebrate rigidity. Excessive tone in all muscles, producing extension of the limbs and dorsoflexion of the head because antigravity musculature overpowers other muscles; caused by brainstem or cerebellar lesions.

decerebration. Disconnection of the cerebral hemispheres from the brainstem, resulting in the deprivation of sensory input and the ability to affect behavior.

declarative memory. Type of memory illustrated by the ability to recount the details of events, including time, place, and circumstances, compared with the ability to perform some act or behavior. Literally, it refers to the ability to recount what one knows, which is lost in many types of amnesia.

decortication. Removal of the cortex of the brain.

decussation. Crossing of pathways from one side of the brain to the other.

deep brain stimulation (DBS). Neurosurgery in which electrodes are implanted in the brain; used in the treatment of Parkinson patients to facilitate normal movement.

deep dyslexia. Reading impairment characterized by a peculiar constellation of errors, suggesting that the reading is being performed by the nondominant hemisphere.

degeneration. Death of neurons or neuronal processes in response to injury in the degenerating neuron or, in some cases, in other neurons.

delayed non-matching-to-sample task. Behavioral task in which a subject is presented with a sample stimulus and then, after some delay, is presented with the same stimulus and another, novel stimulus. The subject's task is to choose the novel stimulus to obtain reward.

delta (δ) wave. Rhythmic electroencephalographic waveform with a frequency ranging from 0 to 3 Hz that can be recorded from the scalp of a subject who is sleeping.

delusion. Belief opposed to reality but firmly held despite evidence of its falsity; characteristic of some types of psychotic disorders.

dementia. Organic loss of intellectual function.

dendrite. Treelike process at the receiving end of the neuron.

dendritic spine. Protuberence on the dendrites of excitatory neurons; the location of most synapses on such neurons.

dendrodendritic synapse. Synapse between two dendrites.

denervation supersensitivity. Condition of increased susceptibility to drugs, resulting from the proliferation of receptors after denervation (removal of terminations) of an area.

dentate gyrus. A region of the hippocampal formation.

2-deoxyglucose. Sugar that interferes with the metabolism of glucose. It is used to measure metabolic activity in the brain: a radioactive marker (such as ^{14}C) can be attached to 2-deoxyglucose; when this compound is taken up by the blood, it is transported to the brain and will stay in the brain regions that have been most active.

deoxyribonucleic acid (DNA). Long, complex macromolecule consisting of two interconnected helical strands. Double-helical DNA, which contains an organism's genetic information, and its associated proteins constitute the chromosomes.

dependence. State in which doses of a drug are required to prevent the onset of abstinence (that is, withdrawal) symptoms.

dependence hypothesis. Drug-addiction hypothesis that postulates that drug use is maintained to prevent withdrawal symptoms.

depolarization. Inward transfer of positive ions, erasing a difference of potential between the inside and the outside of a neuron.

depression. A rather enduring change in mood in which a person feels unhappy.

depth-of-processing effect. Improvement in subsequent recall of an object about which a person has given thought to its meaning or shape.

depth perception. Ability to perceive three-dimensionality in visual stimuli.

dermatome. Area of skin supplied with afferent nerve fibers by a single spinal dorsal root.

desynchronization. Change in electroencephalographic activity from a high-amplitude slow pattern to a low-amplitude fast pattern.

developmental approach. Method of study in which changes in the brain and behavior across different ages are used as a way to understand relations between the brain and behavior.

developmental dyslexia. Inability to learn adequate reading skills even when opportunity and appropriate instruction are given.

diaschisis. Special kind of shock subsequent to brain damage in which areas connected to the damaged area show a transitory arrest of function.

dichaptic test. Procedure for simultaneously presenting different objects to each hand to determine which hand is most effective at identifying the objects.

dichotic listening. Procedure for simultaneously presenting a different auditory input to each ear through stereophonic earphones.

diencephalic animal. Animal in which the diencephalon is the highest functioning region.

diencephalon. Region of the brain that includes the hypothalamus, thalamus, and epithalamus.

diffusion. Process of becoming diffused, or widely spread.

diffusion tensor imaging (DTI). Magnetic resonance imaging method that, by detecting the directional movements of water molecules, can image fiber pathways in the brain. (Diffusion refers to the movement of water molecules, tensor is a linear quality, and imaging detects the direction of diffusion.)

diplopia. Perception of two images of a single object; double vision.

disconnection. Severing, by damage or by surgery, of the fibers that connect two areas of the brain such that the two areas can no longer communicate; the condition that results.

disconnection syndrome. Behavioral syndrome resulting from the disconnection of two or more brain regions rather than from damage to a specific brain region.

discourse. Highest level of language processing. In discourse, sentences are strung together to form a meaningful narrative.

disengagement. Process by which attention is shifted from one stimulus to another.

disinhibition. Removal of inhibition from a system.

disinhibition theory. Explains the effects of alcohol in which intoxication is associated with the loss of moral and social values in favor of instinctual behaviors.

disorientation. Loss of proper bearings, or a state of mental confusion concerning time, place, or identity.

dissolution. A conceptual notion in which disease or damage in the highest levels of the brain would produce a repertory of simpler behaviors seen in animals that have not evolved that particular brain structure.

dissociative anesthetic. Anesthetic agent belonging to a group of sedative-hyphotics that produce altered states of consciousness and hallucinations; group includes gamma-hydroxybutyric acid, flunitrazepam, and ketamine. Also known as "date rape" or "drug-assisted sexual assault" drugs, dissociative anesthetics are soluble in alcohol, act quickly, and impair memory for recent events.

distal. Being away from, or distant to, some point.

distributed hierarchy. Theory stating that widespread networks of neurons represent behavior, with some networks responsible for more complex behaviors than others.

distributed systems. Mediation of behavior by neurons and connections between neurons that are located in different areas of the brain.

divergent thinking. Form of thinking in which there is a search for multiple solutions to a problem (for example, how many ways in which to use a pen?), in contrast with *convergent thinking*, in which a single solution is sought.

dopamine (DA). Monoamine formed in the body by the decarboxylation of L-dopa. An intermediate product in the synthesis of norepinephrine, dopamine acts as a neurotrasmitter in the central nervous system.

dopamine hypothesis of schizophrenia. Proposes that schizophrenic symptoms are due to excess activity of the neurotransmitter dopamine.

dorsal column. Cells in the dorsal spinal cord, which, in upright humans, can be thought of as forming a column from the bottom to the top of the spinal cord, in contrast with ventral column.

dorsal root. Nerve, composed of fibers carrying sensory information, that enters each segment of the dorsal (posterior in humans) part of the spinal cord.

dorsal-root ganglion. Protuberance produced by the aggregation of cell bodies of the sensory fibers, which are located adjacent to the part of the spinal cord into which their axons enter.

dorsal stream. Visual processing pathway that orginates in the visual cortex; controls the visual guidance of movement.

dorsomedial thalamus. Thalamic nucleus providing a major afferent input to the prefrontal cortex; degenerates in Korsakoff's syndrome, leading to a severe amnesic syndrome.

double dissociation. Experimental technique by which two areas of neocortex are functionally dissociated by two behavioral tests, each test being affected by a lesion in one zone and not the other.

dream sleep. Stage of sleep in which muscles are paralyzed, sensory input to the brain is blocked, and the brain shows a waking state of activity, during which vivid dreaming takes place. *See also* **REM (rapid eye movement) sleep.**

D$_2$ receptor. Receptor for the neurotransmitter dopamine; target for major tranquilizers.

drug. Any medicinal substance.

dualism. Theory that there are two distinct entities that underlie human consciousness: one is mind (or soul), the other is the body.

dual-route theory. States that reading written language is accomplished by using two distinct but interactive procedures: the lexical and the nonlexical routes.

dura mater. Tough double layer of collagenous fiber enclosing the brain in a kind of loose sac.

dynamic imaging. Method for recording and manipulating ongoing changes in brain activity, including the electrical activity of cells, biochemical events, differences in glucose consumption, and the flow of blood to various regions.

dysarthria. Difficulty in speech production caused by incoordination of the speech apparatus.

dyscalculia. Difficulty in performing arithmetical operations.

dyseidetic. Refers to difficulty in recognizing words by their visual configurations.

dyskinesia. Any disturbance of movement.

dyslexia. Difficulty in reading.

dysphasia. Impairment of speech caused by damage to the central nervous system.

dysphonetic. Refers to the inability to decode words or to recognize them by using phonic or sound principles.

dystonia. Abnormality of muscle tone; usually excessive muscle tone.

echolalia. Condition in which a person repeats words or noises that he or she hears.

edema. An abnormal accumulation of fluid in intercellular spaces of the body.

efference theory. States that the sensations produced by an act provide the conscious perception of the act.

efferent. Conducting away from higher centers in the central nervous system and toward muscle or gland.

egocentric disorientation. Difficulty in determining one's location in space.

egocentric space. Space that is relative to a person's perspective. Compare **allocentric space.**

electrical recording. Detects changes in the electrical activity of neurons.

electroconvulsive therapy (ECT). Application of a massive electrical shock across the brain as a treatment for affective disorders.

electroencephalogram (EEG). Recording of electrical potentials that is made by placing electrodes on the scalp or in the brain.

electromyogram (EM). Recording of electrical activity of the muscles as well as the electrical response of the peripheral nerves.

electron microscope. Microscope that creates images of very small objects by bouncing electrons off an object and creating a picture through the object's resistance to the electrons.

electrooculogram (EOG). Electroencephalographic tracings made while a subject moves his or her eyes a constant distance between two fixation points.

electrostatic gradient. Gradient between an area of low electrical charge and an area of high electrical charge; develops across the membrane of a cell or between two parts of the same cell.

embolism. Sudden blocking of an artery or a vein by a blood clot, bubble of air, deposit of fat, or small mass of cells deposited by the blood current.

emotion. State of mental excitement characterized by alteration of feeling tone and by physiological and behavorial changes.

emotional memory. Memory that is arousing, vivid, and available on prompting.

encephalitis. Inflammation of the central nervous system as a result of infection.

encephalization. Process by which higher structures, such as the cerebral cortex, take over the functions of lower centers; may imply either a phylogenetic or an ontogenetic shift of function. Also called *encorticalization*.

encephalization quotient (EQ). Ratio of actual brain size to expected brain size for a typical mammal of a particular body size.

encephalomalacia. Softening of the brain, resulting from vascular disorders caused by inadequate blood flow.

encephalon. *See* **brain**.

encephalopathy. Chemical, physical, allergic, or toxic inflammation of the central nervous system.

encorticalization. *See* **encephalization**.

end foot. Terminal part of an axon; conveys information to other neurons. Also called a *terminal button*.

endoplasmic reticulum (ER). Extensive internal membrane system in the cytoplasm. Ribosomes attach to part of the ER to form what is known as the rough ER.

endorphins. Any of a group of endogenous polypeptide brain substances that bind to opiate receptors in various areas of the brain and thereby raise the pain threshold.

endothelial cells. Cells that form blood vessels.

enhancement. *See* **long-term enhancement (LTE)**.

entorhinal cortex. Cortex found on the medial surface of the temporal lobe; provides a major route for neocortical input to the hippocampal formation; often shows degeneration in Alzheimer's disease.

ependymal cells. Glial cells forming the lining of the ventricles; some produce cerebrospinal fluid.

epigenetic. Refers to changes in gene regulation that take place without a change in the DNA sequence.

epilepsy. Condition characterized by recurrent seizures of various types associated with a disturbance of consciousness.

epinephrine (EP). Neurotransmitter found in the sympathetic nervous system; mobilizes the body for fight or flight.

episodic (autobiographic) memory. Memory containing autobiographic events that took place in specifiable temporal and spatial contexts.

epithalamus. Collection of nuclei forming the phylogenetically most primitive region of the thalamus; includes the habenulae, pineal body, and stria medullaris.

equipotentiality. Hypothesis that each part of a given area of the brain is able to encode or produce the behavior normally controlled by the entire area.

ergotamine. Drug used in the treatment of migraine and tension headaches that acts by constricting cerebral arteries.

ethology. Study of the natural behavior of animals.

Euclidean space. Real space, with three dimensions, according to the laws of Euclid.

event-related potential (ERP). Complex electroencephalographic waveform that is related in time to a specific sensory event; composed of a series of specific subunits that are related to specific aspects of cerebral processing (for example, P_3).

evoked potential. Short train of large, slow waves recorded from the scalp and corresponding to dendritic activity.

excitatory neurotransmitter. Transmitter substance that decreases a cell's membrane potential and increases the likelihood that the cell will fire.

excitatory postsynaptic potential (EPSP). Small change in the membrane potential of a cell that leads to depolarization and increased likelihood that the cell will fire.

exocytosis. Discharge from a cell of particles that are too large to diffuse through the wall.

explicit memory. Memory in which a subject can retrieve an item and indicate that he or she knows the item (that is, conscious memory). Compare **implicit memory**.

expressive aphasia. Disturbance of language in which there is a severe deficit in producing language.

extension. Movement by which a limb is straightened.

extensor muscle. Muscle that acts to straighten a limb.

extensor plantar response. Extensor movement of the foot toward a surface that the foot touches.

extensor reflex. Advancement of a limb to contact a stimulus in response to tactile stimuli that activate fine touch and pressure receptors. The response is mediated by a multisynaptic spinal reflex circuit.

external imagery. Third-person imagery in which a person engaging in an act imagines that it is another person doing so.

exteroceptive. Charles Scott Sherrington's term in reference to the external surface field of distribution of receptor organs—for example, the skin and mucous membranes.

exteroceptive receptor. Receptor that functions to identify events that take place outside the body. Compare **interoceptive receptor**.

extinction. Term used in learning theory for the decreased probability that a behavior will occur if reinforcement is withheld.

extracellular fluid. Fluid and its contents that surround a neuron or glial cell.

face amnesia. Inability to remember faces.

factor analysis. Statistical procedure designed to determine if the variability in scores can be related to one or more factors that are reliably influencing performance.

fasciculation. Small local contraction of muscles, visible through the skin, representing a spontaneous discharge of a number of fibers innervated by a single motor-nerve filament.

fear conditioning. Form of learning in which a noxious stimulus is used to elicit fear, an emotional response.

feature search. Cognitive strategy in which sensory stimuli are scanned for a specific feature, such as color.

festination. Tendency to engage in behavior at faster and faster speeds; usually refers to walking but can include other behaviors such as talking and thinking.

fetal alcohol syndrome (FAS). Disorder characterized by mental retardation as well as stunted growth and congenital defects of the face and head; caused by excessive alcohol intake by the mother during pregnancy.

fimbria-fornix. Anatomical pathway running from the septal region to the hippocampus.

finger agnosia. Inability to distinguish fingers.

fissure. Cleft, produced by folds of the neocortex, that extends to the ventricles.

flexion. Movement by which a limb is bent at the joint, bringing the limb toward the body.

flexor muscle. Muscle that acts to bend a limb at a joint.

flocculus. Small mass on the lower side of each cerebral hemisphere and continuous with the nodule of the vermis.

fluent aphasia. Speech disorder in which a person articulates words in a languagelike fashion, but what is said actually makes little sense; usually results from damage to the left posterior cortex. *See also* **Wernicke's aphasia**.

fMRI. *See* **functional magnetic resonance imaging**.

focal seizure. Seizure that begins locally and then spreads—for example, from one finger to the whole body.

folia. Narrow folds of the cerebellum.

forebrain. Cerebral hemispheres, basal ganglia, thalamus, amygdala, hippocampus, and septum.

formant. Group of sound waves specific to each vowel sound.

fovea. Region at the center of the retina that is specialized for high acuity. Its receptive fields are at the center of the eye's visual field.

fragile-X syndrome. Form of mental retardation caused by an abnormality in a gene, *FMR1 (fragile-X mental retardation 1)*, of the X chromosome.

frontal lobes. All the neocortex forward of the central sulcus.

frontal operculum. Upper region of the inferior frontal gyrus.

fugue state. Transient disturbance of consciousness in which a person performs purposeful acts but has no conscious recollection of those actions.

functional analysis. Analysis of brain organization based on studying the effects of brain damage, stimulating areas of the brain chemically or electrically, or recording the activity of cells in relation to behavior.

functional magnetic resonance imaging (fMRI). Magnetic resonance imaging in which changes in elements such as iron or oxygen are measured during the performance of a specific behavior; used to measure brain activity during rest or behavior. *See also* **magnetic resonance imaging (MRI)**.

functional map. Map of the cortex constructed by stimulating areas of the brain electrically and noting elicited behavior or by recording electrical activity during certain behaviors; relates specific behaviors to brain areas.

functional validation. According to theory, a neural system requires sensory stimulation to become fully functional.

GABA$_A$ receptor. Gamma-aminobutyric acid receptor on which sedative hypnotics and antianxiety drugs act.

gamma-aminobutyric acid (GABA). Amino acid neurotransmitter that inhibits neurons.

ganglion cells. Cells of the retina that give rise to the optic nerve.

gated channel. Membrane channel that allows the passage of specific ions when the gate is open and prevents such passage when the gate is closed.

gating. Inhibition of sensory information that can be produced by descending signals from the cortex. For example, descending messages from the brain can gate the transmission of a pain stimulus from the spinal cord to the brain.

generalized anxiety disorder. Sustained worrying state associated with at least three anxiety symptoms, among which are restlessness, decreased energy, concentration difficulties, irritability, muscle tension, and sleep disturbance.

generalized seizure. Seizure that spreads from a starting point to encompass large regions of the brain; usually results in gross motor movements.

general mover theory. Theory of evolutionary change that argues that genetic movement is driven simultaneously by multiple factors rather than by a specific factor.

generator. Something that produces or causes to exist.

genes. Functional units controlling the transmission and expression of traits from one generation to the next.

geniculostriate pathway. Visual pathway from the eye to the lateral geniculate nucleus of the thalamus to the primary visual cortex (striate cortex).

geniculostriate system. Consists of projections from the retina of the eye to the lateral geniculate nucleus of the thalamus, then to areas 17, 18, and 19, and then to areas 20 and 21; controls the perception of form, color, and pattern.

genu. Bulbous part of the anterior part of the corpus callosum.

germinal cells. Cells from which particular tissues are formed in the course of development.

Gerstmann syndrome. Collection of symptoms due to left parietal lesion; alleged to include finger agnosia, right–left confusion, acalculia, and agraphia (a source of some controversy).

gestalt. Unified and coherent whole.

gestural theory. Theory of language evolution stating that language developed from gestures used for communication.

glia. One of two classes of cells in the nervous system, the other one being neurons; provide insulation, nutrients, and support for neurons.

glial cells. Supportive cells of the central nervous system. *See also* **glia**.

glial sheath. Glial cells, such as oligodendrocytes and Schwann cells, that wrap themselves around the axons of neurons, thus forming a sheath.

glioblast. Progenitor cell that gives rise to different types of glial cells.

glioblastoma. Highly malignant, rapidly growing brain tumor; most common in adults older than 35 years of age; results from the sudden growth of spongioblasts.

glioma. Any brain tumor that arises from glial cells.

gliosis. Migration and proliferation of glial cells in areas of neural tissue that have undergone damage. Their presence serves as a sign of tissue damage.

globus pallidus. Part of the basal ganglia that receives projections from the caudate nucleus and sends projections to the ventral lateral nucleus of the thalamus; literally, pale globe or sphere.

glucocorticoids. Group of steroid hormones secreted in times of stress and important in protein and carbohydrate metabolism, controlling blood-sugar levels and the absorption of sugars by cells. Examples are cortisol and corticosterone.

glutamate. An excitatory amino acid transmitter.

glycine. Amino acid that serves as an inhibitory neurotransmitter in the brainstem and spinal cord, where it acts within the Renshaw loop, for example.

glycoprotein. A protein with an attached carbohydrate group.

Golgi apparatus. Complex of parallel membranes in the cytoplasm that wraps the product of a secretory cell or a protein manufactured by a nerve cell.

Golgi body. Membrane in neurons that covers proteins made in neurons.

gonadal (sex) hormones. Control reproductive functions; instruct the body to develop as male (testerone) or female (estrogen), influence sexual behavior and conception, control the menstrual cycle in women (estrogen, progesterone), the birthing of babies, and the release of breast milk (prolactin, oxytocin).

graded potential. Electrical potential in a neuron or receptor cell that changes with the intensity of the stimulus. Also known as a generator potential.

grand mal attack. Seizure characterized by loss of consciousness and stereotyped, generalized convulsions.

grand mal epilepsy. Often preceded by an aura, in which a sudden loss of conciousness is immediately followed by generalized convulsions.

granule cells. Neurons that are round in appearance, in contrast with *pyramidal cells*, which have pyramidal-shaped cell bodies.

granulovacuolar bodies. Abnormal structures in the brain characterized by granules (small beadlike masses of tissue) and vacuoles (small cavities in the protoplasm of cells).

grapheme. Refers to the pictorial qualities of a written word that permit it to be understood without being sounded out; a group of letters that conveys a meaning.

graphemic reading. Reading in which the meaning of a word is derived from the picture that it makes as a whole rather than by sounding out the syllables.

graphesthesia. Ability to identify numbers or letters traced on the skin with a blunt object.

gray matter. Any brain area composed predominantly of cell bodies.

grid cell. Type of neuron in the limbic system (entorhinal cortex) that fires at regularly spaced nodes that seem to divide an environment into a grid.

growth spurt. Sudden growth in development that lasts for a finite time.

guanyl nucleotide-binding protein (G protein). Protein that carries a message from a metabotropic receptor to other receptors or to second messengers.

gyrus (pl. gyri). Convolution of the cortex of the cerebral hemispheres.

habituation. Gradual quantitative decrease in a response after repeated exposure to a stimulus.

hair cells. Auditory sensory receptors in the cochlea, which lies in the inner ear.

hallucination. Perception for which there is no appropriate external stimulus; characteristic of some types of psychotic disorders.

hammer. Ossicle in the middle ear.

hapsis. Perception of objects with the use of fine-touch and pressure receptors.

head-direction cell. Neuron in the hippocampus that discharges when an animal faces in a particular direction.

heading disorientation. Inability to move or guide one's movements in a direction appropriate to the perceived cues.

Hebb synapse. Hypothetical synapse formed when two neurons are concurrently in the same state of activity; named after Donald Hebb, who postulated such a mechanism in 1949.

hebephrenic schizophrenia. Form of schizophrenia characterized by silly behavior and mannerisms, giggling, and shallow affect.

hedonic hypothesis. Proposes that people abuse drugs because the drugs make them feel good.

hematoma. Local swelling or tumor filled with effused blood.

heme group. Nonprotein, insoluble, iron protoporphyrin constituent of hemoglobin, a constituent of blood.

hemianopia. Loss of pattern vision in either the left or the right visual field.

hemiballism. Motor disorder characterized by sudden involuntary movements of a single limb.

hemiparesis. Muscular weakness affecting one side of the body.

hemiplegia. Paralysis of one side of the body.

hemiplegic migraine. Migraine that leads to paralysis of one side of the body.

hemisphere. In the brain, either of the pair of structures constituting the telencephalon; sometimes also used to refer to either side of the cerebellum.

hemispherectomy. Removal of a cerebral hemisphere.

heroin. Diacetylmorphinc, a highly addictive morphine derivative.

Heschl's gyrus. Gyrus of the human temporal lobe that is roughly equivalent to auditory area I. Also known as the transverse temporal gyrus.

hierarchical organization. Principle of cerebral organization in which information is processed serially, with each level of processing assumed to represent the elaboration of some hypothetical process.

high decerebrate. Refers to a preparation in which an animal has an intact midbrain, hindbrain, and spinal cord. *See also* **decerebrate** and **decerebration**.

high decerebration. Injury to the brainstem in which the highest intact functioning structure is the midbrain.

higher-order area. Brain area that is of more recent evolutionary origin and receives its inputs from older (lower) areas.

hindbrain. Region of the brain that consists primarily of the cerebellum, medulla oblongata, pons, and fourth ventricle.

hippocampus. Primitive cortical structure lying in the anterior medial region of the temporal lobe.

histamine. Amino acid neurotransmitter whose functions include the control of arousal and of waking; can cause the constriction of smooth muscles and so, when activated in allergic reactions, contributes to asthma, a constriction of the airways.

histochemical techniques. Various techniques that rely on chemical reactions in cells to mark features of a cell for microscopic visualization.

histofluorescent technique. Literally, cell fluorescence, a technique in which a fluorescent compound is used to label cells.

homeostasis. Maintenance of a chemically and physically constant internal environment.

hominid. General term referring to primates that walk upright, including all forms of humans, living and extinct.

homonymous hemianopia. Total loss of vision due to complete cuts of the optic tract, lateral geniculate body, or area 17.

homotopic. At the same place on the body.

homotopic areas. Corresponding points in the two hemispheres of the brain that are related to the midline of the body.

homunculus. Representation of the human body in the sensory or motor cortex; any topographic representation of the body by a neural area.

horseradish peroxidase (HRP). Compound that, when introduced into a cell, is then distributed to all its parts, allowing the cell to be visualized.

HPA (hypothalamic–adrenal) axis. The hypothalamic–pituitary–adrenal circuit controlling hormone production.

Huntington's chorea. Hereditary disease characterized by chorea (ceaseless, involuntary, jerky movements) and progressive dementia, ending in death.

hydrocephalus. Condition characterized by abnormal accumulation of fluid in the cranium, accompanied by enlargement of the head, prominence of the forehead, atrophy of the brain, mental deterioration, and convulsions.

6-hydroxydopamine (6-OHDA). Chemical selectively taken up by axons and terminals of norepinephrinergic or dopaminergic neurons that acts as a poison, damaging or killing the neurons.

hyperactive-child syndrome. Characterized by low attention span and poor impulse control, which results in disruptive behavior.

hyperactivity. More activity than normally expected, usually applied to children.

hyperkinesia. Condition in which movements of a part or all of the body increase.

hyperkinetic symptom. Symptom of brain damage; consists of involuntary excessive movements. Compare **hypokinetic symptom**.

hyperlexia. Condition in which a person is given to excessive reading or is a precocious reader, often without understanding the meaning of what is read.

hypermetamorphosis. Tendency to attend and react to every visual stimulus, leading to mental distraction and confusion.

hyperpolarization. Process by which a nerve membrane becomes more resistant to the passage of sodium ions and consequently more difficult to excite with adequate stimulation; during hyperpolarization, the electrical charge on the inside of the membrane relative to that on the outside becomes more negative.

hypnogogic hallucination. Dreamlike event at the beginning of sleep.

hypokinetic symptom. Symptom of brain damage resulting in difficulty in making movements. Compare **hyperkinetic symptom**.

hypothalamus. Collection of nuclei located below the thalamus; controls behavior including movement, feeding, sexual activity, sleeping, emotional expression, temperature regulation, and endocrine regulation.

ideational apraxia. Vague term used to describe a disorder of gestural behavior in which the overall conception of how a movement is carried out is lost; emerges when a person is required to manipulate objects.

ideomotor apraxia. Inability to use and understand nonverbal communication such as gesture and pantomime.

idiopathic seizure. Seizure disorder that appears to arise spontaneously and in the absence of other diseases of the central nervous system.

idiothetic cue. Derives from the self; a cue generated by one's own movement.

illusion. False or misinterpreted sensory impression of a real sensory image.

immunohistochemical staining. Antibody-based label that, when applied to tissue postmortem, reveals the presence of a specific molecule or close relatives of that molecule.

implicit memory. Memory in which a subject can demonstrate knowledge but cannot explicitly retrieve the information (for example, a motor skill). Compare **explicit memory**.

incentive salience. Refers to cues that, after having been associated with drug use, become sought.

incentive-sensitization theory. Holds that, when a drug has been used in association with certain cues, the cues themselves will elicit desire for the drug.

infantile amnesia. Inability to remember events from early infancy or early childhood.

infarct. Area of dead or dying tissue resulting from an obstruction of the blood vessels normally supplying the area.

infection. Invasion and multiplication of microorganisms in body tissues.

inferior colliculus. Nucleus of the tectum of the midbrain that receives auditory projections and takes part in whole-body orientation to auditory stimuli.

inferotemporal cortex. Visual regions of the temporal cortex. Also known by von Economo's designation, TE.

inhibitory neurotransmitter. Increases the membrane polarity of a cell, making an action potential less likely.

inhibitory postsynaptic potential (IPSP). Small localized change that increases a membrane's potential, making an action potential less likely.

input cell layers. Layers of tissue that receive inputs, such as layer 4 in the cerebral cortex.

insomnia. Inability to sleep.

insula. Formed from tissue in the lateral (Sylvian) fissure; includes the gustatory and the auditory association cortices.

intelligence quotient (IQ). Defined originally as the ratio of mental age to chronological age multiplied by 100. On contemporary intelligence tests, the average performance for a given age is assigned a value of 100 and a person's intelligence quotient is expressed relative to 100.

intermediate zone. Layer of cells in the spinal cord that lies immediately above the motor neurons of the ventral horn.

internal carotid artery. Branch of the carotid artery that is a major source of blood to the brain.

internal imagery. First-person imagery in which a person imagines that it is himself or herself who engages in an act.

interneuron. Any neuron lying between a sensory neuron and a motor neuron.

interoceptive. Charles Scott Sherrington's term referring to the internal sensory receptors, such as those in the viscera.

interoceptive receptor. Receptor that responds to information originating inside the body. Compare **exteroceptive receptor**.

intracellular fluid. Fluid and its contents found within neurons and glial cells.

invariance hypothesis. Suggests that the structure of each cerebral hemisphere ensures that the hemisphere will develop a set of specialized functions; for example, the left hemisphere is specialized at birth for language.

ion. Positively or negatively charged particle.

ionotropic receptor. Receptor that has two parts: a binding site for a neurotransmitter and a pore that regulates ion flow.

ipsilateral. Residing in the same side of the body as the point of reference.

ischemia. Deficiency of blood due to functional constriction or actual obstruction of a blood vessel.

isolation syndrome. *See* **transcortical aphasia**.

Jacksonian focal seizure. Seizure that has consistent sensory or motor symptoms such as a twitching in the face or hand.

Kennard principle. Idea that early brain damage produces less-severe behavioral effects than does brain damage incurred later in life; coined after Margaret Kennard reported this phenomenon in a series of papers on the study of neonatally brain-damaged monkeys.

kindling. Development of persistent seizure activity after repeated exposure to an initially subconvulsant stimulus.

kinesthesis. Perception of movement or position of the limbs and body; commonly used to refer to the perception of changes in the angles of joints.

Klüver–Bucy syndrome. Group of symptoms resulting from bilateral damage to the temporal lobes; characterized especially by hypersexuality, excessive oral behavior, and visual agnosia.

Korsakoff's syndrome. Group of symptoms resulting from degeneration of thalamic nuclei and produced by chronic alcoholism; metabolic disorder of the central nervous system due to a lack of vitamin B_1 (thiamine) and often associated with chronic alcoholism. Also called *Korsakoff–Wernicke disease.*

landmark agnosia. Loss of the ability to know one's location or guide one's movement in relation to a building or landmark that had once been familiar.

landmark test. Behavioral test in which the subject must learn the association between a specific cue (the landmark) and the location of reward.

larynx. Organ of voice; the air passage between the lower pharynx and trachea, containing the vocal cords and formed by nine cartilages: the thyroid, cricoid, and epiglottis and the paired arytenoid, corniculate, and cuneiform cartilages.

lateral corticospinal tract. In the lateral spinal cord, a pathway that carries information instructing movement.

lateral fissure. Deep cleft on the basal surface of the brain that extends laterally, posteriorly, and upward, thus separating the temporal and parietal lobes. Also called *Sylvian fissure.*

laterality. Refers to the side of the brain that controls a given function. Hence, studies of laterality are undertaken to determine which side of the brain controls various functions.

lateralization. Process by which functions become located primarily on one side of the brain.

learned-behavior theory. States that behavior under the influence of alcohol changes from one context to another because of learning; contradicts the idea that alcohol lowers inhibitions.

learned tolerance. Experience in performing a behavior under the influence of a drug results in improved performance of the behavior when subsequently under the influence of the drug.

learning disability. Generally defined by work performance in a specific school subject that falls significantly below average; for example, a reading disability is sometimes defined as reading 2 years below the class average.

lesion. Any damage to the nervous system.

letter-by-letter reading. Reading in which the meaning of a text is determined by extracting information from each letter, one letter at a time.

leu-enkephalin. Peptide neurotransmitter that produces some of the effects of opioid drugs.

lexicon. Dictionary (that is, memory store) in the brain that contains words and their meanings.

light microscope. Microscope that relies on shining light through tissue to visualize that tissue through an eyepiece.

limbic lobe. Term coined by Paul Broca to refer to the structures between the brainstem and the telencephalon; in modern usage, equivalent to the *limbic system,* which includes the hippocampus, septum, cingulate cortex, hypothalamus, and amygdala.

limbic system. Elaboration of the structures of the limbic lobe to form a hypothetical functional system originally believed to be important in controlling affective behavior; neural systems that line the inside wall of the neocortex.

limb-kinetic apraxia. Form of apraxia in which a person is unable to make voluntary movements of the limbs in response to verbal commands; presumed to result from a disconnection of the motor program from language.

lipofuscin granule. Dark-pigmented substance that accumulates in brain cells as they age.

localization of function. Hypothetically, the control of each kind of behavior by a different specific brain area.

longitudinal fissure. Divides the two hemispheres. Also known as the sagittal fissure.

long-term enhancement (LTE). Long-lasting change in the postsynaptic response of a cell that results from previous experience with a high-frequency stimulation. Also known as *enhancement* or *long-term potentiation (LTP).*

long-term memory. Form of memory postulated by Donald Broadbent in which information is assumed to be stored for longer than about 15 minutes.

long-term potentiation (LTP). *See* **long-term enhancement (LTE).**

low decerebrate. Refers to a preparation in which both the hindbrain and spinal cord of an animal remain intact. *See also* **decerebrate** and **decerebration.**

lysergic acid diethylamide (LSD). Drug that produces visual hallucinations, presumably by influencing the serotonin system.

lysosome. Small body containing digestive enzymes seen with the use of an electron microscope in many types of cells.

macular sparing. Condition in which the central region of the visual field is not lost, even though temporal or nasal visual fields are lost.

magnetic resonance imaging (MRI). Imaging procedure in which a computer draws a map from the measured changes in the magnetic resonance of atoms in the brain; allows the production of a structural map of the brain without opening the skull. Also known as magnetic resonance spectroscopy and nuclear magnetic resonance (NMR). *See also* **functional magnetic resonance imaging (fMRI).**

magnetic resonance spectroscopy (MRS). Technique used to image the brain material, including all macromolecules (DNA, RNA, most proteins, and phospholipids), cell membranes, organelles (such as mitochondria), and glial cells, not imaged by *magnetic resonance imaging.*

magnetoencephalogram (MEG). Magnetic potentials recorded from detectors placed outside the skull.

magnocellular layer. Layer of neurons composed of large cells.

major depression. Mood disorder characterized by prolonged feelings of worthlessness and guilt, disruption of normal eating habits, sleep disturbances, a general slowing of behavior, and frequent thoughts of suicide.

major tranquilizer. Drug that blocks the dopamine 2 (D_2) receptor; used mainly for treating schizophrenia. Also called a *neuroleptic drug.*

malaria. Infectious febrile disease caused by protozoa of the genus *Plasmodium*, which are parasitc in red blood cells; transmitted by *Anopheles* mosquitoes and marked by attacks of chills, fever, and sweating occurring at intervals that depend on the time required for the devlopment of a new generation of parasites in the body.

mania. Disordered mental state of extreme excitment; specifically, the manic type of manic–depressive psychosis.

mass-action hypothesis. Proposes that the entire neocortex participates in every behavior.

massa intermedia. An area of gray matter (cells) that connects the left and right sides of the thalamus across the midline.

materialism. Philosophical position that holds that behavior can be explained as a function of the nervous system without explanatory recourse to the mind.

maturation hypothesis. Argues that both hemispheres initially have roles in language but the left hemisphere gradually becomes more specialized for language control.

maturational-lag hypothesis. Explains a disability by suggesting that a system is not yet mature or is maturing slowly.

MDMA (3,4-methylenedioxymethamphetamine). Synthetic, psychoactive drug chemically similar to the stimulant methamphetamine and the hallucinogen mescaline.

medial longitudinal fissure. Fissure that separates the two hemispheres.

median eminence. Pathway connecting the two sides of the thalamus.

medulla oblongata. Part of the hindbrain immediately rostral to the spinal cord.

medulloblastoma. Highly malignant brain tumor found almost exclusively in the cerebellums of children; results from the growth of germinal cells that infiltrate the cerebellum.

meninges. Three layers of protective tissue—the dura mater, arachnoid, and pia mater—that encase the brain and spinal cord.

meningioma. Encapsulated brain tumor growing from the meninges.

meningitis. Inflammation of the meninges.

mental level. Measure of intelligence in which ability is expressed as a level of performance that is average for a given age.

mental rotation. Ability to make a mental image of an object and imagine it in a new location relative to its background.

mescaline. Poisonous alkaloid from the flowering heads of a Mexican cactus; produces an intoxication with delusions of color and sound.

mesencephalon. Middle brain; term for the middle one of the three primary embryonic vesicles, which subsequently comprises the tectum and tegmentum.

mesolimbic dopamine system. Dopamine neurons in the midbrain that project to the nucleus accumbens and to medial parts of the basal ganglia, limbic system, and neocortex.

messenger RNA (mRNA). Type of ribonucleic acid synthesized from DNA (deoxyribonucleic acid); attaches to ribosomes to specify the sequences of amino acids that form proteins.

metabolic tolerance. Reduced sensitivity to a substance that results from the increased ability of cells to metabolize the substance.

metabotropic receptor. Receptor linked to a G protein (guanyl nuleotide-binding protein); can affect other receptors or act with second messengers to affect other cellular processes.

metastasis. Transfer of a disease from one part of the body to another; common characteristic of *malignant tumors*.

metastatic tumor. Tumor that arises through the transfer of tumor cells from elsewhere in the body.

metencephalon. Anterior part of the rhombencephalon; composed of the cerebellum and pons.

met-enkephalin. Peptide neurotransmitter that produces some of the effects of opioid drugs.

mGluR4. Receptor on the tongue; sensitive to glutamate.

microfilaments. Small tubelike processes in cells. Their function is uncertain, but it may be to control the shape, movement, or fluidity of the cytoplasm or substances within the cell.

micrometer. One-millionth of a meter or one-thousandth of a millimeter. The neurons of most animals, including humans, are very tiny, on the order of 1 to 20 micrometers.

microtubules. Fiberlike substances in the soma and processes of nerve cells; transport substances from the soma to the distal elements of the cell or from distal parts of the cell to the soma.

midbrain. Short segment between the forebrain and hindbrain, including the tectum and tegmentum.

middle cerebral artery (MCA). Runs along the length of the lateral (Sylvian) fissure and sends blood to the ventral part of the frontal lobe, most of the parietal lobe, and the temporal lobe.

migraine attack. Type of headache that is severe and may last for hours. *See also* **migraine stroke**.

migraine. From the Greek word meaning "one half of the head"; a headache characterized by an aching, throbbing pain, often unilateral; may be preceded by a visual aura presumed to result from ischemia of the occipital cortex induced by vasoconstriction of cerebral arteries.

migraine stroke. Condition in which a cerebral vessel constricts, cutting off the blood supply to a cortical region. If the constriction is severe enough and lasts more than a few minutes, neuronal death may occur, leading to an infarct.

millisecond. One-thousandth of a second.

millivolt. One-thousandth of a volt.

mind. The psyche; the faculty, or brain function, by which one is aware of one's surroundings and by which one experiences feeling, emotions, and desires and is able to attend, reason, and make decisions.

mind–body problem. Problem of how to explain how a nonmaterial mind can command a material body.

miniature postsynaptic potential (MPP). Small excitatory or inhibitory graded potential, the amplitude of which is related to the number of quanta of neurotransmitter released at the synapse.

minor tranquilizers. Class of drugs used to treat anxiety. *See also* **benzodiazepines**.

mirror neurons. Neurons that represent actions, whether one's own or those of others. The representations can be used both for imitating and for understanding the meaning of others' actions, thus permitting the selection of appropriate responses.

mitochondrion. Complex cellular organelle that produces most of a cell's energy through a number of processes.

module. Hypothetical unit of cortical organization, believed to represent a vertically organized intracortical connectivity that is assumed to correspond to a single functional unit. Sometimes used as a synonym for *column*.

monist. Person who believes that the mind and body are one.

monoamine oxidase (MAO) inhibitor. Chemical that blocks MAO from degrading neurotransmitters such as dopamine, noradrenaline, and serotonin.

monoamines. Group of neurotransmitters, including norepinephrine and dopamine, that have an amine (NH_2) group.

monoclonal antibody. Antibody that is cloned or derived from a single cell.

monocular blindness. Blindness in one eye caused by the destruction of its retina or optic nerve.

monocular deprivation. Removal of visual stimulation to one eye by closure or bandaging.

mood stabilizer. Drug used to treat bipolar disorder; examples are lithium and valproate. Typically, mood stabilizers mute the intensity of one pole of the disorder, thus making the other pole less likely to reoccur.

morpheme. Smallest meaningful unit of speech.

morphine. Principal and most active alkaloid of opium. Its hydrochloride and sulfate salts are used as narcotic analgesics.

morphological reconstruction. Reconstruction of the body of an animal, often from only skeletal remains.

motoneuron. Charles Scott Sherrington's term for the unit formed by motor neurons and the muscle fiber to which their axon terminations are connected.

motor aphasia. Disorder in which an affected person is unable to make the correct movements of the mouth and tongue to form words, in contrast with *Wernicke's aphasia (sensory aphasia)*, in which speech is fluent but without content; a form of *nonfluent aphasia*.

motor apraxia. Inability, in the absence of paralysis, to execute the voluntary movements needed to perform a goal-oriented action.

motor cortex. Region of the cerebral cortex that, when stimulated electrically, produces muscle movements.

motor neuron. Neuron that has its cell body in the spinal cord and projects to muscles.

motor pathway. Anatomical pathway from the brain to the spinal cord and muscles.

motor program. Hypothetical neural circuit so arranged that it produces a certain type of movement—for example, walking.

movement. Act of moving; motion.

multimodal (polymodal) cortex. Receives sensory inputs from more than one sensory modality—for example, vision and audition.

multiple sclerosis (MS). Disease of unknown cause in which there are patches of demyelination in the central nervous system; may lead to motor weakness or incoordination, speech disturbance, and sometimes to other cognitive symptoms.

multiple-trace theory. Postulates both multiple kinds of amnesia and changes in memory with the passage of time.

muscarine receptor. An acetylcholine receptor acted on by acetylcholine psychedelic drugs. Muscarine is a chemical obtained from *Amanita muscaria*, a mushroom that affects the parasympathetic system but does not cross the blood–brain barrier.

muscle-contraction headache. Caused by prolonged contraction of the muscles on the skull.

mutation. Permanent transmissible change in the genetic material.

myasthenia gravis. Condition of fatigue and weakness of the muscular system without sensory disturbance or atrophy; results from a reduction in acetylcholine available at the synapse.

mycotic infection. Invasion of the nervous system by a fungus.

myelencephalon. Posterior part of the rhombencephalon, including the medulla oblongata and fourth ventricle.

myelin. Lipid substance forming an insulating sheath around certain nerve fibers; formed by oligodendroglia in the central nervous system and by Schwann cells in the peripheral nervous system.

myelination. Formation of myelin on axons; sometimes used as an index of maturation.

myelin sheath. *See* **myelin**.

myelin stains. Dyes that stain glial cells, particularly those that wrap themselves around axons.

myoclonic spasm. Massive seizure consisting of sudden flexions or extensions of the body and often beginning with a cry.

nalorphine. Semisynthetic congener of morphine; used as an antagonist to morphine and related narcotics and in the diagnosis of narcotic addiction.

naloxone. Narcotic antagonist structurally related to oxymorphone; used as an antidote to narcotic overdosage.

narcolepsy. Condition in which a person is overcome by uncontrollable, recurrent, brief episodes of sleep.

narcotic analgesic. Drug that has sedative and pain-relieving properties.

nasal hemianopia. Loss of vision of one nasal visual field due to damage to the lateral region of the optic chiasm.

natural selection. Proposition in the theory of evolution that animals with certain adaptive characteristics will survive in certain environments and pass their genetic characteristics to their offspring, whereas animals lacking those characteristics die off.

necrosis. Tissue death, usually as individual cells, groups of cells, or in small localized areas.

negative symptoms. The absence of behaviors; contrasts with *positive symptoms*, which indicate the presence of abnormal behaviors.

neglect dyslexia. Misreading errors usually confined to a single half of a word.

neocortex. Newest layer of the brain, forming the outer layer, or "new bark"; has from four to six layers of cells; in this book, synonymous with *cortex*.

neotony. Fact that newly evolved species often resemble the young of their ancestors.

nerve. Macroscopic, cordlike structure comprising a collection of nerve fibers that convey impulses between a part of the central nervous system and some other body region.

nerve fiber. As part of a neuron, a long process that carries information from the neuron to other neurons; also a collection of nerve fibers.

nerve growth factor (NGF). Protein that plays a role in maintaining the growth of a cell.

nerve impulse. Movement or propagation of an action potential along the length of an axon; begins at a point close to the cell body and travels away from it.

nerve-net hypothesis. Idea that the brain is composed of a continuous network of interconnected fibers.

neural stem cells. Cells that gives rise to all neurons in the nervous system.

neural tube. Structure in the early stage of brain development from which the brain and spinal cord develop.

neuritic plaques. Areas of incomplete necrosis that are often seen in the cortices of people with senile dementias such as Alzheimer's disease.

neuroblast. Any embryonic cell that develops into a neuron.

neuroendocrine. Refers to the interaction of the neural and endocrine (hormonal) systems.

neurofibril. Any of numerous fibrils making up part of the internal structure of a neuron; may be active in transporting precursor chemicals for the synthesis of neurotransmitters.

neurohumoral. Refers in general to the action of hormones on the brain.

neuroleptic. Drug used to treat psychosis. Also called *major tranquilizer. See also* **neuroleptic drug**.

neuroleptic drug. Drug that has an antipsychotic action principally affecting psychomotor activity and that is generally without hypnotic effects.

neurologist. Physician specializing in the treatment of disorders of the nervous system.

neurology. Branch of medical science dealing with the nervous system, both normal and diseased.

neuron. Basic unit of the nervous system; the nerve cell; includes the cell body (soma), many processes called dendrites, and an axon. Its function is to transmit and store information.

neuron hypothesis. Idea that the functional units of the brain are neurons.

neuropeptides. Multifunctional chains of amino acids that act as neurotransmitters.

neuropsychology. Study of the relations between brain function and behavior.

neuroscience. Embryology, anatomy, physiology, biochemistry, and pharmacology of the nervous system.

neurosurgery. Brain surgery intended to repair damage to alleviate symptoms resulting from known neurological disease.

neurotoxin. Any substance that is poisonous or destructive to nerve tissue; for example, 6-hydroxydopamine, placed in the ventricles of the brain, will selectively destroy the norepinephrine and dopamine systems.

neurotransmitter. Chemical that is released from a synapse in response to an action potential and acts on postsynaptic receptors to change the *resting potential* of the receiving cell; transmits information chemically from one neuron to another.

neurotrophic factors. Class of compounds that act to support growth and differentiation in developing neurons and may act to keep certain neurons alive in adulthood.

neurotropic viruses. Viruses having a strong affinity for cells of the central nervous system. *See also* **pantropic viruses**.

nicotine. Poisonous alkaloid, obtained from tobacco or produced synthetically; used as an agricultural insecticide and, in veterinary medicine, as an external parasiticide.

nicotinic receptor. Cholinergic receptor at the neuro-muscular junction. Nicotine's structure is enough like that of acetylcholine to fit into the acetylcholine receptors' binding sites.

nightmares. Terrifying dreams.

Nissl stain. Used to stain neurons for microscopic examination.

Nissl substance. Large granular body that stains with basic dyes; collectively forms the substance of the reticulum of the cytoplasm of a nerve cell.

nitric oxide (NO). Gas that acts as a chemical neurotransmitter in many cells.

nocioception. Perception of unpleasant stimuli, touch, temperature, and pressure; a major somatosensory submodality.

node of Ranvier. Space separating the Schwann cells that form the covering (or myelin) on a nerve axon; richly endowed with voltage-sensitive ion channels. Nodes of Ranvier accelerate the propagation of nerve impulses.

nonfluent aphasia. Impairment of speech subsequent to brain damage, particularly to the frontal part of the hemisphere dominant for speech; characterized by difficulty in articulating words.

non-REM (NREM) sleep. All segments of sleep excluding REM sleep.

nonspecific afferents. Presumably serve general functions, such as maintaining a level of activity or arousal so that the cortex can process information; terminate diffusely over large regions of the cortex. Compare **specific afferents**.

noradrenergic neuron. Neuron that uses norepinephrine, closely related to epinephrine, as its neurotransmitter.

norepinephrine (NE). Chemical neurotransmitter in the brain; found in one of the nonspecific ascending systems.

norepinephrinergic neuron. Neuron that contains norepinephrine in its synapses or uses norepinephrine as its neurotransmitter.

nuclear magnetic resonance (NMR). *See* **magnetic resonance imaging (MRI)**.

nuclear membrane. Surrounds the nucleus of a cell.

nucleolus. Organelle within the nucleus of a cell; produces ribosomes.

nucleus. Spherical structure in the soma of a cell; contains DNA and is essential to cell function; also, a group of cells forming a cluster that can be identified histologically.

nystagmus. Constant, tiny involuntary eye movements that have a variety of causes.

object constancy. Perceptual experience in which objects are identified as being the same regardless of the angle of view.

object recognition. Ability to identify the characteristics of objects, including their names and functions.

obsessive–compulsive disorder (OCD). Condition in which the affected person compulsively repeats acts (such as hand washing) and has repetitive and often unpleasant thoughts (obsessions).

obstructive sleep apnea. Constriction of the breathing apparatus that results in loss of breath during sleep; thought to be a major cause of snoring.

occipital horns. Most-posterior projections of the lateral ventricles that protrude into the occipital lobe.

occipital lobe. General area of the cortex lying in the back part of the head.

olfaction. Sense of smell or the act of smelling.

oligodendrocytes. Specialized support, or glial, cells in the brain that form a covering of myelin on nerve cells to speed the nerve impulse. Also called oligodendroglia.

ophthalmologic migraine. Migraine affecting vision.

opium. Crude resinous extract from the opium poppy.

optic ataxia. Deficit in the visual control of reaching and other movements and in eye movements.

optic chiasm. Point at which the optic nerve from one eye partly crosses to join the other, forming a junction at the base of the brain.

optic flow. Apparent motion of visual information when an animal is in motion.

orbitofrontal cortex. Lies adjacent to the cavity containing the eye but, anatomically defined, receives projections from the dorsomedial nucleus of the thalamus.

organic brain syndrome. General term for behavioral disorders that result from brain malfunction attributable to known or unknown causes.

organicity. General term (of limited value in neuropsychology) used to refer to abnormal behavior that is assumed to have a biological (organic) basis.

organizational hypothesis. Proposes that actions of hormones in the course of development alter tissue differentiation.

organ of Corti. Organ lying against the basilar membrane in the cochlear duct; contains special sensory receptors for hearing and consists of neuroepithelial hair cells and several types of supporting cells.

organophosphate. Organic ester of phosphoric or thiophosphoric acid.

orientation. Direction.

orienting reaction. Process by which an animal's attention is engaged by a novel stimulus.

oscilloscope. Instrument that displays a visual representation of electrical variations on the fluorescent screen of a cathode-ray tube.

otolith organs. Bodies in the inner ear that provide vestibular information.

output cell. Cell that conveys information away from a circuit; motor neuron that conveys information to a muscle.

output cell layers. Cell layers that send efferent connections to other parts of the nervous system; layers 5 and 6 in the cerebral cortex.

oval window. Region in the inner ear where the ossicles amplify and convey vibrations that subsequently stimulate the basilar membrane.

paired helical filaments. Two spiral filaments made of chains of amino acids.

paleocortex. Part of the cerebral cortex forming the pyriform cortex and parahippocampal gyrus. Also called the paleopallium.

pantropic viruses. Viruses that attack any body tissue. *See also* **neurotropic viruses**.

papilledema. Swelling of the optic disc caused by increased pressure from cerebrospinal fluid; used as a diagnostic indicator of tumors or other swellings in the brain.

paragraphia. Writing of incorrect words or perseveration in writing the same word.

paralimbic cortex. Area of three-layered cortex that is adjacent to the classically defined limbic cortex and has a direct connection with the limbic cortex—for example, the *cingulate cortex*.

parallel-development hypothesis. Proposes that both hemispheres, by virtue of their anatomy, play special roles, one for language and one for space.

paraphasia. Production of unintended syllables, words, or phrases during speech.

paraplegia. Paralysis of the legs due to spinal-cord damage.

paraplegic. Refers to persons whose spinal cords have been cut, making them unable to have control over their legs.

parasite. Plant or animal that lives on or within another living organism at whose expense it obtains some advantage.

parasympathetic nerves. Calming nerves that enable the body to "rest and digest." Compare **sympathetic nerves**.

paresis. General term for loss of physical and mental ability due to brain disease, particularly from syphilitic infection; a term for slight or incomplete paralysis.

parietal lobe. General region of the brain lying beneath the parietal bone.

parietal occipital sulcus. Sulcus in the occipital cortex.

Parkinson's disease. Disease of the motor system that is correlated with a loss of dopamine in the brain and is characterized by tremors, rigidity, and reduction in voluntary movement.

pars opercularis. Part of the inferior frontal lobe adjacent to the parietal lobe and overhanging the insula.

parvocellular layer. Layer of neurons containing small cells.

Pavlovian (classical) conditioning. Form of *associative learning*.

peptide. Any member of a class of compounds of low molecular weight that yield two or more amino acids on hydrolysis. Peptides form the consistent parts of proteins.

peptide hormone. Hormone that influences its target cell's activity by binding to metabotropic receptors on the cell membrane, generating a second messenger that affects the cell's physiology.

perception. Cognition resulting from the activity of cells in the various sensory regions of the neocortex beyond the primary sensory cortex.

perforant pathway. Large anatomical pathway connecting the entorhinal cortex and subiculum with the hippocampal formation.

periaqueductal gray matter (PAG). Surrounds the cerebral aqueduct; responsible for a number of complex responses to pain stimuli, including behavioral activation and emotional responses.

peripheral nerves. Nerves that lie outside the spinal cord and the brain.

peripheral nervous system (PNS). Collective name for all of the neurons in the body that are located outside the brain and spinal cord.

perseveration. Tendency to emit repeatedly the same verbal or motor response to varied stimuli.

persistent vegetative state (PVS). Condition in which a person is alive but unable to communicate or to function independently at even the most basic level.

pervasive developmental disorder not otherwise specified (PDD-NOS). A form of autism that does not meet the specific criteria for autism.

petit mal attack. Seizure characterized by a loss of awareness during which there is no motor activity except blinking of the eyes or turning of the head and rolling of the eyes; of brief duration (typically, 10 seconds).

petit mal epilepsy. Epilepsy, seen especially in children, in which there is sudden momentary unconsciousness with only minor myoclonic jerks.

phagocytes. Cells that engulf microorganisms, other cells, and foreign particles as part of the lymphatic system's defenses.

phenothiazines. Group of major tranquilizers (for example, chlorpromazine) that are similar in molecular structure to the compound phenothiazine.

pheromone. Substance produced by one individual that is perceived (as an odor) by a second individual of the same species and that leads to a specific behavioral reaction in the second individual; acts as a chemical signal between animals of the same species.

phoneme. Unit of sound that forms a word or part of a word.

phonological. Refers to sound, as in theories of reading that emphasize the role of sound in decoding the meaning of words.

phonological reading. Reading that relies on sounding out the parts of words.

phospholipid. Molecule having a "head" that contains phosphorus and two tails that are lipid, or fat. Phospholipids constitute the membrane bilayer, a double-layered cell membrane.

phrenology. Long-discredited study of the relation between mental faculties and the skull's surface features.

physical dependence. Indicated by the display of withdrawal symptoms on cessation of drug use.

physostigmine. Drug that inhibits acetylcholinesterase, the enzyme that breaks down acetylcholine, therefore acting as an agonist to increase the amount of acetylcholine available in the synapse. Large doses can be toxic because they produce excessive excitation of the neuromuscular synapse and so disrupt movement and breathing.

pia mater. Moderately tough connective tissue that clings to the surface of the brain.

piloerection. Erection of the hair.

pineal body. Symmetrical structure in the epithalamus, thought by Descartes to be the seat of the soul, but now thought to take part in circadian rhythms and known as the *pineal gland*.

pineal gland. *See* **pineal body**.

pinna. The part of the ear outside the head.

pituitary gland. Collection of neurons at the base of the hypothalamus.

place cells. Cells that are maximally responsive to specific locations in the world.

place response. Navigational behavior in which an animal locomotes to a position on the basis of its location relative to two or more cues. Compare **cue response** and **position response**.

place task. Task in which an animal must find a place that it cannot see by using the relation between two or more cues in its surroundings.

planum temporale. Cortical area just posterior to the auditory cortex (Heschl's gyrus) within the lateral (Sylvian) fissure.

Plasmodium. Genus of a sporozoan parasite in the red blood cells of animals and humans; causative agent of malaria.

plasticity. The ability of neurons to form new connections; the ability of the brain to change in various ways to compensate for loss of function due to damage.

pneumoencephalography. X-ray technique in which the cerebrospinal fluid is replaced by air introduced through a lumbar puncture.

poliomyelitis. Acute viral disease characterized by involvement of the nervous system and possibly by paralysis. There may be atrophy of the affected muscles, leading to a permanent deformity.

polygraph. Apparatus for simultaneously recording blood pressure, pulse, and respiration, as well as variations in electrical resistance of the skin; popularly known as a lie detector.

polymodal cortex. Cortex that receives sensory inputs from more than one sensory modality—for example, vision and audition.

polypeptide chain. Peptide containing more than two amino acids linked by peptide bonds.

polyribosome. Structure formed by the combination of mRNA and ribosomes that serves as the site for protein synthesis.

polysensory neuron. Neuron that responds to information from more than one sensory modality.

pons. Part of the hindbrain; composed mostly of motor-fiber tracts going to such areas as the cerebellum and spinal tract.

position response. Navigational behavior in which an animal uses its previous movements as a cue—that is, movements (for example, left or right) previously made to arrive at the same location. Compare **cue response** and **place response**.

positive symptoms. Occurrence of abnormal behaviors. Compare **negative symptoms**.

positron-emission tomography (PET). Imaging technique in which a subject is given a radioactively labeled compound such as glucose, which is metabolized by the brain, and the radioactivity is later recorded by a special detector.

postconcussional syndrome. Constellation of somatic and psychological symptoms including headache, dizziness, fatigue, diminished concentration, memory deficit, irritability, anxiety, insomnia, hypochondriacal concern, and hypersensitivity to noise and light, all of which are typical after suffering a brief period of disturbed consciousness, usually after a blow to the head.

posterior cerebral artery (PCA). Cerebral artery that supplies blood to the posterior part of the cerebral hemispheres, including the occipital lobe and hippocampal formation.

posterior cortex. General term applied to the cortex posterior to the central fissure.

posterior parietal cortex. Expression referring to parietal-cortex tissue beyond the primary somatosensory areas; usually includes areas PE, PF, and PG.

postictal. Subsequent to a seizure.

postictal depression. State of reduced affect subsequent to a seizure.

postsynaptic membrane. Membrane lying adjacent to a synaptic connection across the synaptic space from the terminal.

posttraumatic psychosis. Psychotic reaction after head trauma.

posttraumatic stress disorder (PTSD). Disorder characterized by physiological arousal symptoms related to recurring memories and dreams concerning a traumatic event—for months or years after the event.

praxis. Action, movement, or series of movements.

preadaption. Behavior that evolves for one purpose but then becomes useful for another purpose.

precentral gyrus. Gyrus lying in front of the central sulcus.

precession. Act of preceding.

preferred cognitive mode. Use of one type of thought process in preference to another—for example, visuospatial instead of verbal; sometimes attributed to the assumed superior function of one hemisphere over the other.

prefrontal cortex. Cortex lying in front of the primary and secondary motor cortex and thus the association, or tertiary, cortex in the frontal lobe.

premotor cortex. Cerebral cortex lying immediately anterior to the motor cortex; includes several functional areas, especially the supplementary motor area and Broca's area.

presynaptic membrane. Terminal membrane adjacent to the subsynaptic space.

primary areas. Areas of the neocortex that receive projections from the major sensory systems or send projections to the muscles.

primary motor cortex. Neocortical area corresponding to Brodmann's area 4; forms a major source of the corticospinal tract.

primary projection area. *See* **primary areas**.

primary sensory cortex. Neocortical areas that receive the projections of the principal thalamic regions for each sensory modality; corresponds to Brodmann's areas 17 (vision), 41 (audition), and 3-1-2 (somatosensation).

primary zones. *See* **primary areas**.

prime-mover theories. Explain brain size in regard to a single factor.

priming. Experimental technique by which a stimulus is used to sensitize the nervous system to a later presentation of the same or a similar stimulus.

priming task. Task in which subjects are presented with information that will subsequently influence their behavior but that they may not subsequently consciously recall; for example, given a list of words, a subject may be more likely to subsequently use a word on the list than some other word that also would be appropriate.

proactive interference. Interference of something already experienced with the learning of new information.

procedural memory. Memory for certain ways of doing things or for certain movements; this memory system is thought to be independent of declarative memory (that is, memory used to "tell about" some event).

progenitor cell. Cell that is derived from a stem cell and acts as a precursor cell that migrates and produces a neuron or glial cell.

projection map. Map of the cortex made by tracing axons from the sensory systems into the brain and from the neocortex to the motor systems of the brainstem and spinal cord.

proprioception. Perception of the position and movement of the body, limbs, and head.

proprioceptive. Refers to sensory stimuli coming from the muscles and tendons.

prosencephalon. Front brain; term for the most anterior part of the embryonic brain, which subsequently evolves into the telencephalon and diencephalon.

prosody. Variation in stress, pitch, and rhythm of speech by which different shades of meaning are conveyed.

prosopagnosia. Inability, not explained by defective visual acuity or reduced consciousness or alertness, to recognize familiar faces; rare in pure form and thought to be secondary to right parietal lesions or bilateral lesions.

protein. Any of a group of complex organic compounds containing carbon, hydrogen, oxygen, nitrogen, and, in some cases, sulfur. Proteins, the principal constituents of the protoplasm of all cells, are of high molecular weight and consist of α-amino acids connected by peptide linkages.

proximal. Being close to something.

pseudodepression. Condition of personality subsequent to frontal-lobe lesion in which apathy, indifference, and loss of initiative are apparent symptoms but are not accompanied by a patient's sense of depression.

pseudopsychopathy. Condition of personality subsequent to frontal-lobe lesion in which immature behavior, lack of tact and restraint, and other behaviors symptomatic of psychopathology are apparent but are not accompanied by the equivalent mental or emotional components of psychopathology.

psilocybin. Psychedelic drug obtained from the mushroom *Psilocybe mexicana*.

psychedelic drug. Any drug that induces behavior characterized by visual hallucinations, intensified perception, and, sometimes, behavior similar to that observed in psychosis.

psychoactive drug. Any chemical substance that alters mood or behavior by altering the functions of the brain.

psychology. Science dealing with the mind and mental processes, especially in relation to human and animal behavior.

psychometrics. Science of measuring human abilities.

psychomotor activation. Increase in cognitive or motor behavior often seen in response to a stimulant drug.

psychopharmacology. Study of how drugs affect the nervous system and behavior.

psychosis. Major mental disorder of organic or emotional origin in which a person's ability to think, respond emotionally, remember, communicate, interpret reality, and behave appropriately is sufficiently impaired that the ordinary demands of life cannot be met; applicable to conditions having a wide range of severity and duration—for example, schizophrenia or depression.

psychosurgery. Surgical intervention to sever fibers connecting one part of the brain to another or to remove or destroy brain tissue with the intent of modifying or altering disturbances of behavior, thought content, or mood for which no organic pathological cause can be demonstrated by established tests and techniques (for example, lobotomy).

ptosis. Drooping of the upper eyelid from paralysis of the third nerve (oculomotor).

pulvinar. Thalamic nucleus that receives projections from the visual cortex and superior colliculus and sends connections to the secondary and tertiary temporal and parietal cortex.

pump. Protein in the cell membrane that actively transports a substance across the membrane. Also called a *transporter*.

punctate evolution. Evolution that appears to occur suddenly, rather than in gradual steps; sometimes referred to as *punctuated evolution*.

punctuated evolution. *See* **punctate evolution**.

pure aphasia. Aphasia in the absence of other language disorders such as *alexia* or *agraphia*.

putamen. Nucleus of the basal ganglia complex.

putative transmitters. Chemicals strongly suspected of being neurotransmitters but not conclusively proved to be so.

pyramid. Pointed or cone-shaped structure or part; refers to protrusion of corticospinal tract on the ventral surface of the brainstem.

pyramidal cells. Cells that have pyramid-shaped cell bodies. Pyramidal cells usually send information from one region of the cortex to some other brain area.

pyramidalis area. Brodmann's area 4.

pyramidal tract. Corticospinal tract; pathway from the neocortex to the spinal cord that crosses after the pyramids in the brainstem

pyriform cortex. Old cortex; subserves olfactory functions.

quadrantanopia. Defective vision or blindness in one-fourth of the visual field.

quadriplegia. Paralysis of the legs and arms due to spinal cord damage.

quadriplegic. Refers to persons whose spinal cords have been cut high enough on the cord that they are unable to use their arms and legs.

quantum. Unit of measure in quantum theory.

quasi-evolutionary sequence. Hypothetical ancestral lineage of a contemporary species; comprises the currently living species that most closely resemble the ancestors—for example, the ancestral lineage for humans would include hedgehogs, tree shrews, bush babies, rhesus monkeys, and chimpanzees.

radial glial cells. Cells that form miniature "highways" that provide pathways for migrating neurons to follow to their appropriate destinations.

radioisotope scan. Scanning of the cranial surface with a Geiger counter, after an intravenous injection of a radioisotope has been given, to detect tumors, vascular disturbances, atrophy, and so forth.

rapidly adapting receptor. Body sensory receptor that responds briefly to the onset of a stimulus on the body.

rate-limiting factor. Any enzyme that is in limited supply and so limits the rate at which a chemical can be produced.

readiness potential. Evoked potential that occurs just before a movement.

reading disabled. Refers to the inability to read, irrespective of the cause.

reafference. Confirmation by one part of the nervous system of the activity in another. *See also* **corollary discharge**.

reafference theory. *See* **corollary-discharge theory**.

real space. Space that one sees around oneself; three-dimensional space.

receptive field. Area from which a stimulus can activate a sensory receptor.

receptor. On a cell membrane, protein to which another molecule can attach.

reciprocal inhibition. Activation of one muscle group with inhibition of its antagonists.

reconsolidated memory. Memory that reenters a labile phase when recalled and is then restored as a new memory.

reconsolidation theory. Proposes that memories rarely consist of a single trace or neural substrate.

red nucleus. Nucleus in the anterior part of the tegmentum that is the source of a major motor projection.

reentry. Process by which cortical regions send projections back to regions from which they receive afferents; proposed as a mechanism for solving the *binding problem*.

referred pain. Pain that is felt in a body part other than that in which the cause that produced it is situated.

reflex. Specific movement that is dependent only on a simple spinal-cord circuit and is elicited by specific forms of sensory stimulation.

regeneration. Process by which neurons damaged by trauma regrow connections to the area that they innervated before the trauma.

relatively refractory. Refers to the later phase of an action potential during which increased electrical current is required to produce another action potential; a phase during which potassium channels are still open.

REM (rapid eye movement) sleep. Part of sleep during which rapid eye movements occur; associated with loss of muscle tone and vivid dreams.

Renshaw loop. Circular set of connections in which the axon collateral of motor-neuron axon leaving the spinal cord synapses on a nearby CNS interneuron, which, in turn, synapses back on the motor neuron's cell body.

resting potential. Normal voltage across a nerve-cell membrane; varies between 60 and 90 mV in the cells of various animals.

reticular activating system. *See* **reticular formation**.

reticular formation. Mixture of nerve cells and fibers in the lower and ventral part of the brainstem, extending from the spinal cord to the thalamus and giving rise to important ascending and descending systems to produce waking. Also known as the *reticular activating system.*

reticular matter. Area of the nervous system composed of intermixed cell bodies and axons; has a mottled gray and white, or netlike, appearance.

retrograde amnesia. Inability to remember events that took place before the onset of amnesia.

retrograde degeneration. Degeneration of a nerve cell between the site of damage and the cell body, including the cell body and all its remaining processes.

retrograde transport. Transport of material by a neuron from its axon back to the cell body. Labels or dyes can be placed at the termination of an axon, picked up by the axonal arborization, and transported to the cell body, which makes it possible to trace pathways.

reuptake. Deactivation of a neurotransmitter by its being brought back up into the axon terminal.

rhinencephalon. Alternative term for the limbic system; literally, smell brain.

rhombencephalon. Hindmost posterior embryonic part of the brain, which divides into the *metencephalon* and *myelencephalon.*

ribonucleic acid (RNA). Complex macromolecule composed of a sequence of nucleotide bases attached to a sugar–phosphate backbone. Messenger RNA delivers genetic information from DNA to a ribosome (containing ribosomal RNA), where the appropriate molecules of transfer RNA assemble the appropriate amino acids to produce the polypeptide encoded by the DNA.

ribosome. Large complex of enzymes and ribosomal RNA molecules that catalyzes reactions in the formation of proteins.

righting reflex. Behavior by which an animal placed in an inverted posture returns to upright; survives low decerebration.

rods. Light-sensitive retinal receptor cells that contain rhodopsin. Together with cones, rods form the receptor layer of the retina.

roentgenography. Photography in which X-rays are used.

rubrospinal tract. Pathway from the red nucleus to the spinal cord; has a role in the control of the limbs.

saccade. Series of involuntary, abrupt, and rapid small movements or jerks of both eyes simultaneously in changing the point of fixation.

saccule. One of two vestibular receptors of the middle ear; stimulated when the head is oriented normally; maintains head and body in an upright position.

saltatory conduction. Propagation of a nerve impulse on a myelinated axon; characterized by its leaping from one node of Ranvier to another.

savant syndrome. Characterized by various degrees of retardation, along with some special, sometimes supranormal, skill.

scanning electron microscope. Electron microscope that can produce three-dimensional images of an object.

schizophrenia. Type of psychosis characterized by disordered cognitive functioning and poor social adjustment; literally, splitting of thought and emotive processes; probably due to brain malfunction.

Schwann cells. Glial cells that form myelin in the peripheral nervous system.

sclera. Tough white outer coat of the eyeball.

sclerotic plaque. Hardened or inflamed connective tissue or blood vessels. Sclerotic plaques are often seen in the brains of people with Alzheimer's disease.

scotoma. Small blind spot in the visual field caused by small lesions, an epileptic focus, or migraines of the occipital lobe.

secondary area. Cortical region that receives inputs from the primary areas and is thought to participate in more-complex sensory and perceptual or motor functions.

secondary cortex. Cortex that Paul Fleshig found to develop after the primary motor and sensory regions. Alexander Luria proposed that these regions have roles in perception (secondary sensory) and in the organization of movements (secondary motor).

secondary projection area. Area of the cortex that receives projections from a *primary projection area* or sends projections to it.

second-generation antidepressant. Antidepressant thought to be more selective than a first-generation antidepressant in its action on serotonin reuptake transporters.

second messengers. Carry messages from neurotransmitters, the first messengers; molecules (usually a G protein) that influence a variety of cellular constituents, including ion channels.

sedative-hypnotic. Any drug that acts to depress neural activity (and behavior) by either decreasing noradrenergic activity or increasing GABAergic activity.

selective serotonin reuptake inhibitor (SSRI). Drug that acts to selectively prevent the reuptake of serotonin at the synapse, resulting in a relative increase in the action of serotonin on the postsynaptic membrane.

self-movement cues. Cues derived from an animal's own movement.

semantic memory. Memory of world knowledge that is stored independently of the time and place at which it was acquired.

semantics. Study of meaning in language.

semicircular canals. Structures in the middle ear that are open on one side and act as part of the receptor unit for balance.

sensation. Result of activity of receptors and their associated afferent pathways to the corresponding primary sensory neocortical areas.

sensitization. Condition in which subsequent exposures to a drug (or other agent) induce a stronger behavioral response than did the original exposure.

sensitization model. Model of bipolar illness that proposes that the brain of the bipolar patient is especially sensitive to the effects of stressors or drugs and that episodes of mood disorder actually change the brain.

sensorimotor transformation. Neural calculations that integrate the movements of different body parts (eyes, body, arm, and so forth) with the sensory feedback of what movements are actually being made and the plans to make the movements. Sensorimotor transformation depends on both movement-related and sensory-related signals produced by cells in the posterior parietal cortex.

sensory aphasia. *See* **Wernicke's aphasia.**

sensory neglect. Condition in which an organism does not respond to sensory stimulation.

sensory pathway. Conveys sensory information to the brain.

sensory receptor. Cell that transduces sensory information into nervous activity.

septum. Nucleus in the limbic system that, when lesioned in rats, produces sham rage and abolishes the theta EEG waveform.

serial lesion effect. Effect in which slowly acquired lesions or lesions acquired in stages tend to have less-severe symptoms than those of lesions of equivalent size that are acquired at one time.

serotonin. An amine neurotransmitter.

serotonin reuptake inhibitor. Drug that selectively blocks the reuptake of serotonin into the terminal.

sex-related differences. Behavioral differences between males and females that are related to experience, genes, or hormones, or some combination of them.

sexual selection. Mechanism of evolution in which the processes of determining who mates with whom also determine the characteristics of the offspring that will be produced.

short-term (working) memory. Form of memory postulated by Donald Broadbent in which information is assumed to be stored for no more than about 15 minutes.

silent synapses. Synapses that do not appear to be functional until other, dominant synapses are removed.

simultagnosia. Symptom in which a person is unable to perceive more than one object at a time.

simultaneous extinction. Second stage of recovery from contralateral neglect; characterized by response to stimuli on the neglected side as if there were a simultaneous stimulation on the contralateral side.

single-photon emission computerized tomography (SPECT). Imaging technique in which a subject is given a radioactively labeled compound such as glucose, which is metabolized by the brain. The radioactivity is later recorded by a special detector.

skull. The cranium; the bony framework of the head, composed of the cranial and facial bones.

sleep apnea. Condition in which breathing stops when a person falls into deep sleep.

sleep attack. Sudden loss of consciousness.

sleep paralysis. Inability to move on awakening from sleep.

slowly adapting receptor. Body sensory receptor that responds as long as a sensory stimulus is on the body.

slow-wave sleep. Stage of sleep characterized by an electroencephalogram dominated by large-amplitude slow waves.

small-molecule transmitters. Class of neurotransmitters made in the synapse from products derived from the diet.

social cognition. Enables a person to develop hypotheses about other people's intentions. Also referred to as *theory of mind.*

social cognitive neuroscience (social neuroscience). Field of neuroscience that encompasses all cognitive processes that take into account conspecifics either individually or at a group level.

sodium–potassium (Na⁺–K⁺) pump. Pumplike mechanism that shunts sodium out of the cell and potassium into it.

soma. Cell body, including the cell membrane, nucleus, and cytoplasm.

somatic muscles. Muscles of the body that are attached to the skeleton.

somatic nervous system. Subdivision of the *peripheral nervous system*.

somatosensory neurons. Neurons that project from the body's sensory receptors into the spinal cord; modified so that the dendrite and axon are connected, which speeds information conduction because messages do not have to pass through the cell body.

somatosensory system. Neural system pertaining to the tactile senses, including touch, kinesthesia, pain, and proprioception.

somatosensory threshold. Threshold for detecting different tactile sensations.

somatosensory zone. Any region of the brain responsible for analyzing sensations of fine touch and pressure and possibly of pain and temperature.

somnolence. Sleepiness; excessive drowsiness.

sparing. Phenomenon by which some brain functions are saved from disruption after the occurrence of a lesion early in life, usually before the particular function has developed.

spatial learning. Learning spatial information such as the location of a goal object.

spatial summation. Tendency of two adjacent events to add. Hence, two adjacent postsynaptic potentials add or subtract.

specific afferents. Bring information (sensory information, for example) to an area of the cortex and terminate in relatively discrete cortical regions, usually in only one or two layers. Compare **nonspecific afferents**.

specifically reading retarded. Refers to people who have adequate intelligence to be able to read but cannot read.

spinal cord. Part of the nervous system enclosed in the vertebral column.

spinal reflex. Response obtained when only the spinal cord is functioning.

spiny neurons. Class of neurons that have dendritic spines; most are excitatory.

splenium. Generally, a bandlike structure; used in reference to the posterior rounded end of the corpus callosum.

split brain. Brain in which the two hemispheres are separated.

spongioblasts. Immature cells that develop into glial cells.

spreading depression. Condition in which a wave of depolarization spreads across the cortical surface, leading to a period in which the tissue is functionally blocked.

sprouting. Phenomenon subsequent to partial damage in which the remaining neurons or parts of a neuron sprout terminations to connect to the previously innervated area.

SQUID (superconducting quantum interferance device). Machine used to measure small magnetic fields produced by neurons in the brain.

stellate cell. Nerve cell characterized by having a star-shaped cell body. Such cells serve largely as association cells whose processes remain within the region of the brain in which the cell body is located.

stem cell. Cell capable of producing daughter cells that then differentiate into other more specialized cells.

stereognosis. Recognition of objects through the sense of touch.

steroid hormone. Lipid-soluble hormone synthesized from cholesterol.

stimulation. Act of applying a stimulus or an irritant to something.

stimulus. Irritant or event that causes a change in action of some brain area.

stimulus gradient. Gradient along which the intensity of a cue increases or decreases—for example, an odor becomes stronger as its source is approached.

storage granules. Vesicles in the terminal that are presumed to store neurotransmitters.

stirrup. One of the ossicle bones of the middle ear. Also known as the stapes.

storage granules. Hold several synaptic vesicles in some axon terminals.

strephosymbolia. Disorder of perception in which objects seem reversed, as in a mirror; disability in which there is confusion between similar but oppositely oriented letters (for example, "b" and "d") or words and a tendency to reverse direction in reading or writing.

stretch reflex. Contraction of a muscle to resist stretching; mediated through a muscle spindle, a special sensory-receptor system in the muscle.

striate cortex. Primary visual cortex in the occipital lobe; has a striped appearance when stained, which gives it its name.

stroke. Sudden appearance of neurological symptoms as a result of severe interruption of blood flow.

study–test modality shift. Process by which subjects, when presented with information in one modality (reading) and tested in another modality (aurally), display poorer performance than when they are instructed and tested in the same modality.

subarachnoid space. Space between the arachnoid layer and the pia mater of the meninges.

subcortical loop. Anatomical pathway in which information goes from a subcortical structure, such as the amygdala, to the cortex and then back to the originating structure.

substance abuse. Use of a drug for the psychological and behavioral changes that it produces aside from its possible therapeutic effects.

substance dependence. Desire for a drug manifested by frequent use of the drug.

substantia gelatinosa. Gelatinous-appearing cap forming the dorsal part of the posterior horn of the spinal cord.

substantia nigra. Nucleus area in the midbrain containing the cell bodies of axons containing dopamine. In freshly prepared human tissue, the region appears black; hence the name (Latin for "black substance").

sudden infant death syndrome (SIDS). Sudden unexplained death of an infant less than 1 year of age.

sulcus (pl. sulci). Small cleft produced by folding of the cortex.

superior colliculus. Nucleus of the tectum in the midbrain that receives visual projections and controls whole-body reflexes to visual stimuli.

superior temporal sulcus (STS). Separates the superior and middle temporal gyri and contains a significant amount of neocortex.

supplementary motor cortex. Small region of the cortex that lies outside the primary motor cortex but produces movements when stimulated.

surface dyslexia. Inability to read words on the basis of their pictographic or graphemic representations, although the ability to read by using phonological, or sounding-out, procedures is retained.

Sylvian fissure. *See* **lateral fissure**.

sympathetic nerves. Arousing nerves that enable the body to "fight and flee" or engage in vigorous activity. Compare **parasympathetic nerves**.

symptomatic seizures. Seizures that have specific symptoms that may aid in localizing the seizure origin.

synapse. Junction between an axonal terminal and another cell, but there are other types of contacts as well.

synaptic cleft. Space between the end foot of a neuron and the cell to which it connects.

synaptic knob. Also called terminal button, end foot, synapsis, synapse, or terminal knob. *See also* **synapse**.

synaptic vesicles. Small vesicles visible in electron micrographs of terminals; believed to contain neurotransmitters.

synesthesia. Ability to perceive a stimulus of one sense as a sensation of a different sense, as when sound produces a sensation of color.

syntax. Way in which words are put together, following the rules of grammar, to form phrases, clauses, or sentences; proposed as a unique characteristic of human language.

tachistoscope. Mechanical apparatus consisting of projector, viewer, and screen by which visual stimuli can be presented to selective parts of the visual field.

tactile. Refers to the sense of touch.

tactile form recognition. Recognition of the shape of an object by touch.

tardive dyskinesia. Slow, abnormal limb or body-part movements.

tectopulvinar pathway. Visual pathway from the eye to the tectum to the pulvinar (thalamus) to the secondary visual areas.

tectopulvinar system. Part of the visual system that functions to locate visual stimuli; includes the superior colliculus, posterior thalamus, and areas 20 and 21.

tectum. Area of the midbrain above the cerebral aqueduct (the roof); consists of the superior and inferior colliculi, which mediate whole-body response to visual and auditory stimuli, respectively.

tegmentum. Area of the midbrain below the cerebral aqueduct (the floor); contains sensory and motor tracts and a number of nuclei.

telencephalon. Endbrain; includes the cortex, basal ganglia, limbic system, and olfactory bulbs.

teleodendria. Fine terminal branches of an axon.

temporal lobe. Area of the cortex found laterally on the head, below the lateral sulci adjacent to the temporal bones.

temporal memory. Memory for the order of events in time.

temporal summation. Tendency of two events related in time to add. Hence, two temporally related postsynaptic potentials add or subtract.

terminal button. *See* **end foot**.

terminal degeneration. Degeneration of the terminals of neurons; can be detected by selective tissue staining.

tertiary area. Area of the cortex that receives projections from a secondary projection area or sends projections to it. *See also* **association cortex**.

tetrahydrocannabinol (THC). The active ingredient in marijuana and obtained from the female hemp plant *Cannabis sativa*.

thalamus. Group of nuclei of the diencephalon.

theory of mind. Ability to predict what others are thinking or planning to do.

thermoregulation. Ability to regulate body temperature.

theta rhythm. Brain rhythm with a frequency of 4 to 7 Hz.

threshold. Point at which a stimulus produces a response.

threshold potential. Voltage level of a neural membrane at which an action potential is triggered by the opening of sodium and potassium voltage-sensitive channels; about -50 millivolts.

thrombosis. Plug or clot in a blood vessel; formed by the coagulation of blood.

tight junction. Connection between cells when their membranes are fused. Normally, cells are separated by a small space.

time-dependent amnesia. Amnesia that lasts for a brief period.

time-dependent retrograde amnesia. Amnesia for which the severity of the injury determines how far back in time the amnesia extends. The period of personal history that retrograde amnesia covers, extending from the present to the more-distant past, generally shrinks with the passage of time, often leaving a residual amnesia of only a few seconds to a minute for events immediately preceding the injury.

tissue plasminogen activator (t-PA). Drug for treating ischemic stroke; breaks up clots and allows the return of normal blood flow to the affected region.

tolerance. Ability to endure unusually large doses of a drug without ill effect as a result of continuing use of the drug.

tonotopic theory. Pertains to the organization of the auditory cortex in which different frequencies of sound are represented in different cortical regions.

topographic agnosia. Loss of knowledge about the organization of a space; inability to recognize one's location in space, such as a failure to recognize one's own neighborhood.

topographic amnesia. Inability to remember the location of things or places; difficulty in remembering one's way in one's environment.

topograhic disorientation. Confusion regarding one's location in space; likely due to topographic agnosia or amnesia.

topographic map. Map of the neocortex showing various features, projections, cell distributions, and so on.

topographic memory. Memory for the organization of the world.

topographic organization. A neural-spatial representation of the body or areas of the sensory world perceived by a sensory organ.

topographic representation. Representation of the auditory world in which sounds are located in a systematic fashion in a progression from lower to higher frequencies.

Tourette's syndrome. Disease characterized by involuntary movements of body parts and involuntary utterance of words and sounds.

tract. Large collection of axons coursing together within the central nervous system.

transcortical aphasia. Aphasia in which a person can repeat and understand words and name objects but cannot speak spontaneously or can repeat words but cannot comprehend them. Also called *isolation syndrome*.

transcranial magnetic stimulation (TMS). Procedure in which a magnetic coil is placed over the skull to stimulate the underlying brain; can be used either to induce behavior or to disrupt ongoing behavior.

transcranially. Across the skull.

transcription. Synthesis of RNA from a DNA template, catalyzed by RNA polymerase. The base sequences of the RNA and DNA are complementary.

transient global amnesia. Short-lived neurological disturbance characterized by memory loss; may result from transient episodes of ischemia.

transient ischemia. Short-lived condition of inadequate supply of blood to a brain area.

translation. Synthesis of a polypeptide with the use of messenger RNA as a template.

transmitter-activated receptor. In the membrane of a cell, a receptor that has a binding site for a neurotransmitter.

transmitter substance. Allows neurons to communicate with one another and with glands, muscles, and other body organs.

transneuronal degeneration. Degeneration of a cell that synapses with a damaged cell or a cell onto which a damaged cell synapses; for example, sectioning of optic tracts results in the degeneration of lateral geniculate body cells.

transporter. Protein molecule that pumps a substance across a membrane.

traumatic brain injury (TBI). A wound to the brain that results from a blow to the head.

traumatic encephalopathy. Degenerative disease of the brain brought on by a head trauma.

trephining. Removing a circular disc of bone, chiefly from the skull.

tricyclic antidepressant. Antidepressant that blocks the serotonin reuptake transporter.

tubules. Variety of kinds of thin rods of material in cells that provide structure, aid in movement, and serve as pathways for the transport of material within a cell.

tumor. Mass of new tissue that persists and grows independently; a neoplasm; surrounds tissue and has no physiological use.

Turner's syndrome. Genetic condition in which a female has only a single X chromosome. Women with Turner's syndrome have severe spatial deficits.

two-point discrimination. Ability to discriminate two individual points on the skin. The two-point threshold is the minimum distance apart that two points must be placed to be perceived as two points rather than one point.

two-point sensitivity. *See* **two-point discrimination**.

uncinate fasciculus. Fiber tract connecting the temporal and frontal cortex; a hooked or curved tract.

unconscious inference. Decision or judgment made without knowing the source of the information leading to the judgment.

unilateral visual neglect. Neglect of all sensory events of one or more modalities of stimulation when the stimulation is restricted to one half of the world as defined by the central axis of the body.

unit activity. Electrical potential of a single cell.

utricle. Largest of the subdivisions of the labyrinth of the middle ear; major organ of the vestibular system, which provides information about the position of the head.

ventral corticospinal tract. Pathway from the cortex to the spinal cord carrying instructions for the movement of the trunk. This pathway does not cross over to the opposite side of the brainstem at the pyramidal protrusion.

ventral root. Tract of fibers leaving the spinal cord; on the ventral part of an animal's spinal cord and on the anterior part of a human's spinal cord.

ventral stream. Visual pathway from the primary visual cortex to the temporal cortex; primarily responsible for the conscious identification of visual stimuli.

ventricle. Cavity of the brain that contains cerebral spinal fluid.

ventricular zone. Zone in which stem cells reside that surrounds the ventricles.

ventriculography. X-ray technique by which the contours of the ventricles are highlighted with the use of an opaque medium introduced into the ventricle through a cannula inserted through the skull.

ventromedial system. One of the two major groups of tracts in the motor system; made up of the vestibulospinal tract, reticulospinal tract, and tectospinal tract, which originate in the brainstem, and the ventral corticospinal tract, which originates in the neocortex.

vertebral artery. Major artery supplying blood to the hindbrain and spinal cord.

vesicle. Small bladder or sac containing liquid.

vestibular system. Sensory system with receptors in the middle ear that respond to body position and movement.

virus. One of a group of minute infectious agents characterized by a lack of independent metabolism and by the ability to replicate only within living host cells.

visual agnosia. Inability to combine visual impressions into complete patterns and therefore an inability to recognize objects; inability to perceive objects and to draw or copy them.

visual form agnosia. Inability to see the shapes of objects and to recognize objects visually by their shape.

visualization. Ability to form a mental image of an object.

visual localization. Identification of a place in visual space.

vocal cords. Folds of mucous membrane in the larynx that are attached to the vocal muscles.

vocal folds. *See* **vocal cords.**

voltage. Strength of a charged electrical current.

voltage gradient. Difference in voltage between two regions that allows a flow of current if the two regions are connected.

voltage-sensitive channel. Narrow passageway across the neuron membrane that is opened and closed in response to changes in the voltage across the membrane.

voltage-sensitive potassium channel. Voltage-sensitive channel that allows the passage of potassium ions.

voltage-sensitive sodium channel. Voltage-sensitive channel that allows the passage of sodium ions.

volume conducted. Refers to electrical potential recorded in tissue at some distance away from its source.

volume-conducted wave. Wave recorded through the brain and through the skull—conducted in the manner in which waves travel through water.

voluntary movement. Any movement that takes an animal from one place to another to accomplish some adaptive purpose. Also called appetitive, instrumental, purposive, or operant movement.

voxel. Area from which a measurement is taken, thus defining the resolution of an MRI measurement.

Wallerian degeneration. *See* **anterograde degeneration.**

wanting-and-liking theory. Defines "wanting" as equivalent to craving a drug, which increases in addiction, whereas "liking" is defined as the pleasure produced by drug taking, which decreases in addiction. Also called *incentive-sensitization theory.*

Wernicke–Geschwind model. Theoretical model of the neurological organization of language in which there is a serial passage of information from the auditory cortex to the posterior speech zone to the anterior speech zone.

Wernicke's aphasia. Inability to comprehend speech or to produce meaningful speech; subsequent to lesions to the posterior cortex. Also called *sensory aphasia. See also* **fluent aphasia.**

Wernicke's area. Posterior part of the superior temporal gyrus, roughly equivalent to area 22.

white matter. Areas of the nervous system rich in axons covered with glial cells.

Wilson's disease. Genetic disease characterized by the failure to metabolize copper, which is concentrated in the brain.

withdrawal reflex. Withdrawal of a limb in response to applied stimuli that activate pain and temperature fibers. The reflex is mediated by a multisynaptic pathway in the spinal cord.

withdrawal symptom. A behavior displayed by a user when drug use ends.

word salad. Refers to fluent aphasia in which a person produces intelligible words that appear to be strung together randomly.

working memory. Short-term memory; memory for information just received and necessary for the "on line" performance of a task.

X-ray imaging. Imaging methods sensitive to the density of different parts of the brain, the ventricles, nuclei, and pathways.

Note: Page numbers followed by t indicate tables.